# SYNERGETICS
### DICTIONARY

# IN FOUR VOLUMES

# SYNERGETICS DICTIONARY

## The Mind of Buckminster Fuller

Compiled and Edited by E. J. Applewhite
With an Introduction and Appendices

Volume 3: N–Sp

Garland Publishing, Inc.
New York and London
1986

Material quoted from *Synergetics*
(copyright © 1975 by Macmillan Publishing
Company) and *Synergetics 2* (copyright
© 1979 by Macmillan Publishing Company)
is used here by permission of Macmillan
Publishing Company.


**Library of Congress
Cataloging-in-Publication Data**

Main entry under title:

Synergetics dictionary.

Includes bibliographies.
1. Fuller, R. Buckminster (Richard
Buckminster), 1895–1983.
Synergetics.   2. Fuller, R. Buckminster
(Richard Buckminster), 1895–1983—
Dictionaries, indexes, etc.   I. Applewhite,
E. J.   II. Title.
Q295.S954   1986      003      85-27450
ISBN 0-8240-8729-1 (set : alk. paper)

*Design by Jonathan Billing*

This volume has been printed on acid-free,
250-year-life paper.

Printed in the United States of America

N

VI

RBF DEFINITIONS

N:

"NP = Prime Number

"A capital N is a precessed Z.

"Z = Vector."

- Cite RBF to EJA
  Beverly Hotel, New York
  7 March 1971

---

RBF DEFINITIONS

Naga to Eden:

"I work on different books at the same time-- like a painter.
Naga to Eden goes from a speculative prehistory to the stage
of humanity gradually coming out of the Pacific onto the land.
I've been exploring that side of history since I was in the
Navy in World War I. This book will reconstruct history from
the sailor's and shipbuilder's viewpoint."

- Cite RBF to Australian journalist Jane Ram; Hongkong, 17 Oct'74

---

RBF DEFINITIONS

Naga:                                                        (1)

"Goldy then introduces Naga, the sea serpent: god of the
oceanic world of the ancients. Naga is the wave. Naga is
a live tetrahelix. At sea the wavilinear profile of Naga's
back always rims the horizon.

"Influenced by the language of previous milleniums of long
distance ocean-traveling sailors coming originally from the
atolls of the South Pacific and Indian Oceans into the
Arabian Sea to reach Mesopotamia, and by the subsequent
tracing of those world-encircling, deep sea routes by the
Phoenicians, the ancient Hebraic language of the earliest
Biblical scripture came to contain the word nachash, which
means 'serpent,' or 'whisper,' or 'divine,' (the ch being a
guttural or 'g' sound); i.e., naga and nachashol (or nagashol)
means the sea, and the root verb Nacha (=naga) means to lead,
conduct, guide, and Nacha (pronounced naga) is also the name
of the ancient seafarer N (O) (A) (CH-- Noah.

"'Nachan' (pronounced nagan) is the word for copper or bronze
alloy, the latter being the high-strength form of the nonrustable
metal with which all ship fastenings, fittings and instruments
have of necessity been fashioned since copper's first discovery,"

- Cite GOLDYLOCKS, pp. I1,I2, 30 May'75

---

Naga:  Naga Theme:  Naga to Eden:                            (1)

See Rafts: Early World Drifting on Rafts
           Secrecy of Mathematical Knowledge

---

RBF DEFINITIONS

Naga:                                                        (2)

"and its alloyed production as bronze by humans 5,000 years
ago at Ban Chiang in Thailand, where the bronze age first took
over from the stone age, in what was once a Venice-like
complex of canals leading from the sea into all of the Southeast Asian lowlands on the Indochina coast nearest to all the
seafaring activities of the Southwest Pacific in the region
where the Naga nation long ago came off the sea and out upon
the mainland, and as yet lives, where Hanoi now exists.

"Two thousand years ago there existed a place called NGanna.

"This bronze age birth occurs at the final peak of the Austro-
nesian civilization, of which there are evidences going back
16,000 years or more. These ancient water peoples' world
embraced the Central and South Pacific, South Indian Ocean all
the way westward to include Madagascar, and all the way eastward
to include Easter Island, and all the way northward to include
both Japan and the Hawaiian Islands, and southward to include
New Zealand. This is the world of Naga, the 'na' prefix' being
the 'na' of na-vy; na-tivity; na-vi-ga-tion; na-tion. 180 million of these Austronesians as yet are alive and many are as yet
living with the same maritime and insular artifacts as those of"

- Cite GOLDYLOCKS, p.I2, 30 May'75

---

Naga:  Naga Theme:  Naga to Eden:                            (2)

See Discovery, 11 Jul'62

---

RBF DEFINITIONS

Naga:                                                        (3)

"their possibly millions-of-years-ago forbears.

"When the god of the sea, Naga, tidally enters the river
mouths of the land, as seen from the high mountain, his snake
shape is clearly revealed by the river's shape. The Japanese
word for river, 'Nagala,' indicates that the ancient water
people looked upon the river's banks and bed as constituting
the female organ of the land being sexually intruded by Naga,
the god of the sea, as the oceanic tides pulsed inwardly and
outwardly for great distances at the lower extremities of the
rivers. The early humans sensed and revered the greater pattern
events of Universe as manifesting an ever and everywhere
presence of a knowing, life-giving, supporting and terminating
competence vastly greater than that of humans. They saw themselves and all that they could see, including the Sun, Moon,
and stars, as having only minuscule local parts in an organic
whole whose shape and size transcended both the ranges of
their vision and the scope of their imagining."

- Cite GOLDYLOCKS, p.J1, 30 May'75

---

Nail:

See Wind Stress & Housing, (1)

RBF DEFINITIONS

**Naivete:**

"Naivete means not knowing it all, not being a sucker about everything, not pretending to know about the safety razor in the pyramid. Too many people miss things because they dismiss them when they think they know all about them. Be as a child and a child is naive. Adults say young people must get over that sensibility but I say we must open it up again. I feel very much about life as I did as a child. Once I was blasé about flowers as something for funerals but now I try to look at a flower as a child seeing it for the first time."

- Cite RBF in videotaping session, Philadelphia. PA., 1 Feb'75

---

**Naive: Naiveté:** (2)

See Tomorrow, Feb'67
  Children as Only Pure Scientists, 28 Apr'77

---

RBF DEFINITIONS

**Naive:**

"I often think that the motto on the shield of Milton Academy-- "Dare to be True"-- ought really to have been "Dare to be Naive." In 1927 I tried to recapture what it was to be young, to recapture naiveté . . . which is innate; I wanted to recapture the innate.

"Man cannot invent naiveté; it is innate.

"Like Chris Morley's poem:

        In your unstained, transparent eyes
        There is no conscience, no surprise
        Life's queer conundrums you accept
        Your strange divinity still kept.

So I think that divinity and naiveté must be akin."

- Cite RBF to EJA, 3200 Idaho, Washington DC, 23 Jan '72;

---

**Naked Girl on the Bed:**

See Ecology, 15 Feb'73
  Anger, (1)(2)

---

RBF DEFINITIONS

**Naiveté:**

"Much of the most exciting and important part about

tomorrow is not the technology or the automation at all,

but that man is going to come into entirely new relationships

with his fellow men. He will retain much more in his

everyday relations of what we term the naiveté and idealism

of the child. This will be completely justified and not

exploited or exploitable in any way. I think then that the

way to see what tomorrow is going to look like is just to

look at our children."

- Cite THE YEAR 2000, San Jose State College
  Mar'66

---

RBF DEFINITIONS

▬▬▬▬ **Naked Universe:**

"Pure science events represent openings of windows through the wall of ignorance and fiction to reveal the only reality-- the behavior of the naked Universe that always was, is, and will be. True it is that the first glimpse may be hazy and imperfect, but the behavior itself is absolute and progressively clarified. Therefore, this comprehensive curve of the chronological rate of acquisition of knowledge concerning the pure science absolutes, separated out from all other events of history, may be inspected as the basic means of prediction of inherent technical and social events-- immediate or somewhat distant."

- Cite Earth, Inc., Part II, Fuller Research Foundation, p.13, 1947
  (Also cited at Science, 1947)
- Citation & context at Science, 1947

---

**Naive: Naiveté:** (1)

See Creativity of Children
  Dare to Be Naive
  How Little I Know
  Invisible: Nothing so Invisible as the Obvious
  Spontaneous Truth of Childhood
  Unknowable

---

**Naked Universe:**

See Reality, 1947

Naked: (1)

See Helpless: Humans Born Helpless
    Naked Girl on the Bed
    Naked Universe
    Stark

Names: "Named" Phenomena: Name-words: (1)

See Angular Name for Tetrahedron
    Local Identifications
    Number: Names for Numbers
    Remembering Names
    Sound Name
    Untitled
    Sound Word
    Interrelatedness vs. Names

Naked: (2)

See Homosexuality, 1972

Names: "Named" Phenomena: Name-words: (2)

See Environment, 22 Sep'73
    Etymology, Aug'71
    Human, 22 Sep'73
    Memory, 2 Jul'62
    Noun, 1938
    Rationalization Sequence (6)
    Television, Feb'73
    Trinity: Equation of Trinity, 1938
    Thinking, 12 Mar'71*; 6 Nov'73
    Iceland, 7 Oct'75
    Democritus, 1970
    Teleology, 1938
    Subconscious, 20 Feb'77

RBF DEFINITIONS

Names:

"The brain has a limited number of memory cubbyholes for names,
like a stack of magazines. When the Smith smithed and the
Miller milled it was clear and easy to remember, but once
'Miller' becomes a sound word it has to be filed in the limited
place for names."

Nameless: (1)

See Ineffable
    Pattern Integrity = Phenomenon Without Name
    Untitled
    Nonverbal
    Wordless

- Cite RBF videotaping Session Philadelphia, Pa., 20 Jan'75

RBF DEFINITIONS

Names:

"Names don't have meaning. Therefore they are harder for
our mental retrieval system to remember."

Nameless: (2)

See Conversation Sequence, (1)(2)
    Self-communicate, 8 Apr'75

- Cite RBF to BJA
  Beverly Hotel, New York
  13 March 1971

- Citation & context at Thinking, 12 Mar'71

TEXT CITATIONS

Narcotics as a Political Strategy:

DSI Press Conference, NYC, p. 17, 28 Jun'72

Playboy Interview (Barry Farrell), p. 200 - Feb'72

Nation: Nationality: (1)

See Countries
 International Affairs
 Invented National Hates
 Local Identifications
 Overspecialization of Biological Species & Nations
 Sovereignty
 Transnationalism
 Transnationalism vs. Colonialism
 United States is Not a Nation
 United States
 Ethnic
 Race
 Homogenizing of Nations
 Settlements

Narcotics as a Political Strategy:

See China (A)

Nation: Nationality: (2)

See Invention, 9 Feb'64
 Revolution by Inadvertence, 10 Oct'63
 World Man, 10 Jun'71
 World Pattern vs. Local Pattern, 29 Jan'75
 Naga, (2)
 Building Business, (2)
 Spaceship Earth, 21 Jan'77
 Enough to Go Around, (2)

RBF DEFINITIONS

Nation:

"All the customs, all the languages, all laws, all accounting systems, viewpoints, cliches, and axioms are of th old, divided, ignorant days. The corollary of 'divide and conquer' is 'to be divided is to be conquered.' To be specialized is to be divided. The specialization which humanity perseveres in was invented by yesterday's armed conqueror illiterates. The separation of humans into more countries made them easy to manage. Nations may unite, as at present, without success. Strife is proliferating. Not until specialization and nations are dispensed with will all humanity have a chance of survival. It is to be all or none."

- Cite RBF Intro. to Gene Youngblood's EXPANDED CINEMA, P. 32. Oct'70

RBF DEFINITIONS

Natural:

"The child's book of ducks and pigs was as unfamiliar as a polio virus to our child Alexandra as an infant.

"When people say something is 'natural' it means that's the way they found it when they checked in. Our parents' traditions are just no longer appropriate. What's natural for them is not natural for their children.

"If you were a lily you might think you'd grow up as a seed and not be at all prepared to become a flower.

"Unfamiliarity ≠ unnatural."

- Cite RBF videotaping session, Philadelphia, Pa., 20 Jan'75

Nations As Inventions:

See Inventions, 9 Feb'64

RBF DEFINITIONS

Natural:

"And people talk about artificial and we point out that if nature permits it, it's natural; if nature doesn't permit it, you can't do it."

- Cite RBF to World Game at NY Studio School, 12 Jun-31 Jul'69, Saturn Film Transcript, Sound 1, Reel 1, pp.83-84.

RBF DEFINITIONS

Natural:

"If nature permits a formulation
It is natural.
If nature's laws of behavior
Do not permit the formulation
The latter does not occur.
Whatever can be done
Is natural,
No matter how grotesque, boring,
Unfamiliar, or unprecedented.
In the same way
Nature never 'fails.'
Nature complies with her own laws.
Nature is the law.

When man lacks understanding
Of nature's laws
And a man-contrived structure
Buckles unexpectedly,
It does not fail.
It only demonstrates that man  ⟨Man's knowledge or estimating
Did not understand              ⟨Was inadequate.
Nature's laws and behaviors.
Nothing failed.
                    – Cite HOW LITTLE I KNOW, Oct. '66, P. 55.

Natural Law:                                                    (2)

          See Generalization:  Second Degree, 1959

Natural Education:

          See Periodic Experience, (8)

Natural Time Increment:

          See Heartbeat
               Time Increment

RBF DEFINITIONS

Natural Law:

"... Those generalized principles consituting natural law."

          – For citation and context see China, May '65

RBF DEFINITIONS

Nature:

"Nature doesn't have goods and bads.  We must get away from
this idea of good and bad people."

          – Cite RBF to EJA, Pagano's Rest., Phila., PA., 22 Jun'75

Natural Law:                                                    (1)

          See Relativity:  Marriage of Social & Natural Law

RBF DEFINITIONS

Nature:

"Nature is never at a loss about what to do about anything."

          – Cite RBF rewrite of SYNERGETICS galley at Sec. 504.03,
            6 Nov'73

RBF DEFINITIONS

Nature:

"N = Nature: The totality of both all that is known, U (Universe), and all that is unknown, O. N is the integral of all the integrities always manifest in the progressively discovered generalized eternal principles."

- Cite SYNERGETICS text at Sec. 1056.13, 13 May'73

RBF DEFINITIONS

Nature:

"Nature has a very basic pattern governing frequencies and energy event magnitudes."

- Citation and context at Universal Requirements of a Dwelling Advantage (1), Dec'72

RBF DEFINITIONS

Nature:

"Nature is all that we think that we do know plus all that we don't know whether or not we know that we don't know. Whatever nature permits is natural. If nature does not permit it, it cannot and does not occur."

- Cite SYNERGETICS draft at Sec. 1056.02, 13 May'73

RBF DEFINITIONS

Nature:

"How do you get nature to keep you going? You don't know why the little thing grows into the big things, but it does. And you've just got to take advantage of that fact."

- Citation and context at Fire (B), 20 Apr '72

RBF DEFINITIONS

Nature:

"Nature is all that we think we do know plus all that we obviously don't know."

- Citation and context at Unknowable, 8 Mar'73

RBF DEFINITIONS

Nature:

"Little man is not running this Universe. If nature permits it, it's natural. If it's unnatural, nature doesn't permit it."

- Cite RBF to EJA recapitulation of a common theme, 3200 Idaho, DC, 13 Feb. '72

RBF DEFINITIONS

Nature:

"Man does not recognize technology other than his own so he speaks of the rest as something he ignorantly calls nature."

- Context and citation at Technology, 13 Mar'73

RBF DEFINITIONS

Nature:

"Man has invented the word 'failure.' Nature never fails; nature never goes backward."

- RBF quoted by Lee Dembart, New York Post, 26 April 1971

RBF DEFINITIONS

Nature:

"Nature has mathematic behaviors."

- RBF taping GHANA Message
  17 March 1971

- Citation at Mathematics, 14 Mar'71

---

RBF DEFINITIONS

Nature:

"Nature always employs the most energy-economical
tactics."

- Cite Carbondale Draft
  Return to Modelability, p. V.7

- Cite NASA Speech, p. 72, Jun'66

---

RBF DEFINITIONS

Nature:

"I am very eager to have humanists participate with me
in my feelings about the phenomenon of technology-- a
word that is bandied about constantly and often thought
of as the cause of our troubles and pain. I do not see
technology as something that is foreign to man. I hear
the word 'natural' and I hear the word 'artificial' and
I am convinced that those words are words of ignorance.

"I am convinced that whatever nature permits is natural,
and that which nature does not permit, you cannot do.
And if nature has this as a generalized principle, it has
in it the option that man can employ to alter the
environment to the advantage of his fellow man. There are
ways in which you can alter the environment to decrease
the freedoms of your fellow man. But you can also go
very far in increasing his degrees of freedom and
accelerating the rate at which he can comprehend,
communicate, and be effective. That is what we are doing."

- Cite COMMITMENT TO HUMANITY, p. 32, May'70

---

RBF DEFINITIONS

Nature:

"Nature, which is ever pulsive and impulsive,
refuses to get caught unrecoverably at the zero phase
of energy. Therefore there will always be positive and
negative sets which are ever interchangeably intertransformative with uniquely differentiable characteristics."

- Cite Carbondale Draft
  Return to Modelability, p. V.16

- Cite NASA Speech, p. 83, Jun'66

---

RBF DEFINITIONS

Nature:

"Nature never pauses her cycling at the equilibrium
phase. She always closes her transformative cycles at
the maximum positive or negative ████ asymmetry stages.
See the delicate crystal asymmetry in nature."

- Cite NEHRU SPEECH, p. 27
  13 Nov'69

---

RBF DEFINITIONS

Nature:

"We have vector equilibriums mildly distorted as
nature goes positive and negative in respect to the
equilibrium and everything that we know as reality has to
be either a positive or negative condition."

- Cite Carbondale Draft
  Return to Modelability, p. V.16

- Cite NASA Speech, p.83, Jun'66

---

RBF DEFINITIONS

Nature:

"There is nothing in nature but structure."

- Citation and context at Trees (I), 7 Nov'67

---

RBF DEFINITIONS

Nature:

"Nature does not use rectilinear coordination in
its continual intertransformings."

- Cite NASA Speech, p. 23, Jun '66

RBF DEFINITIONS

## Nature:

"Nature always insists on being most economical.
Nature 'triangles.' Nature accounts all of her
structuring entirely <u>rationally</u> when measuring with
triangles."

- Cite KEPES, Caption
  Fig. 8a, p.85
  1965

---

## Nature Comes Back on Itself: (1)

See Patterns of Experience Return Upon Themselves
Returning Upon Itself: Systems Return Upon
Themselves

---

## Nature Comes Back on Itself: (2)

See Congruence, 25 Jan'72

---

RBF DEFINITIONS

## Nature in a Corner:

"Getting nature in a corner is a way of making a somethingness out of a nothingness."

- Cite RBF to World Game Worshop'77; Phila., PA; 20 Jun'77

---

RBF DEFINITIONS

## Nature in a Corner:

"Getting nature into a corner--the windows of nothingness
and the nuclear sphere--it all comes from getting away from
the up-and-down language and bringing in all the in-out-and-
aroundness in the language of frequency."

- Cite RBF to EJA by telephone from Beverly Hotel, NYC; 17 Nov'75

---

RBF DEFINITIONS

## Nature in a Corner:

"Getting nature into a corner is the essence of synergetics.
It is the coordination of thought and physical action, the
genesis of geometry, system and structure. Physics and
metaphysics are resonantly integral: the integrity of their
intertransformative mathematics into all the special case,
variably enduring associabilities cognized by humans as
structural design. The frequency rates are the separate
static frame rates of inspection and are recognized by
humans' brains as mechanics when the frequency of inspection
by humans synchronizes with the cinema frames' running. The
difference between structures and machinery is the same as the
difference between "moving" and "static" pictures as both
relate to human information comprehending. This is the
grand strategy."

- Cite SYNERGETICS, 2nd. Ed. at Sec. 261.01; 13 Nov'75

---

RBF DEFINITIONS

## Nature in a Corner:

"The synergetic coordinate of nature and its hierarchy of
ascending or descending components provides human mind with
a means of resolving problems by bringing nature into a
corner--a four dimensional corner of the four-dimensional
planes of the tetrahedron. Only with the four-dimensional
convergence and divergence of synergetics can the human mind
resolve comprehension by minimum limit corners. The
minimum polygon is a triangle; the minimum polyhedron is a
tetrahedron: both of their structural behaviors are unique.
Because humans think only in terms of parallel and rectilinear
coordination, they tend to hold to the parallel conditions of
their lives, seek to maintain the status quo, and fail despite
birth and death and organic and biological manifests, to be
able to take advantage of the cornerability and the positional
fix provided by the four-dimensional synergetic convergent-
divergent coordination."

Cite SYNERGETICS, 2nd. Ed., at Sec. 260.42; 12 Nov'75

---

RBF DEFINITIONS

## Nature in a Corner:

"You can never figure out what nature is up to if you are
working in parallels and perpendiculars. You have to deal
in convergence and divergence. That's the only way you can
get nature into a corner. And when you have nature in a
corner, then you don't need anybody to mark your paper."

- Cite RBF to EJA, enroute Union Station, Wash. DC; 6 Nov'75

Nature in a Corner:                                    (1)

   See Conceptual Genesis
      Omnidirectional Terminal Case Corner
      Minimum Limit Case
      Terminal Condition
      Starting Point
      Event Embryo

Nature is Neither Good Nor Bad:

   See Aesthetics of Uniformity, (1)
      Belief, 6 Jul'75

Nature in a Corner:                                    (2)

   See Polyhedra, 18 Jul'76
      Tetrahedron, 22 Mar'76
      Tetrahedron as Microsystem, 12 May'77
      Convergence & Divergence, 1 May'77

Nature Modulates Probability:

   See Reality, 26 Sep'73

Nature Always Knows What To Do:                        (1)

   See Coin Toss into the Air

Nature:  What Nature Needs to be Done:                 (1)

   See Doing What Needs to be Done
      Making the World Work

RBF DEFINITIONS

Nature Always Knows What To Do:                        (2)

   See Surf Poundings, Spring'66

Nature:  What Nature Needs to be Done:                 (2)

   See Individual Economic Initiative, 13 Jul'74
      Rearrange the Scenery (1)
      Teleology, 15 Jun'74

RBF DEFINITIONS

Nature Has No Separate Departments:

"And wherever they came from
Thethoughts arranged in this book
Are discoveries of its author
Since he first came in 1913
To think that nature did not have
Separate departments of
Mathematics, Physics,
Chemistry, biology,
History and languages,
Which would require
Department head meetings
To decide what to do
Whenever a boy threw
A stone in the water,
With the complex of consequences
Crossing all departmental lines.
Ergo, I came to think that nature
Has only one department--
And I set to discover its
Obviously
Omnirational
Comprehensively co-ordinate system."

- Cite BRAIN & MIND, p.171 May '72

---

Nature Has No Separate Departments:                    (2)

See Mathematics, 18 Apr'63

---

RBF DEFINITIONS

Nature Has No Separate Departments:

"When I grew older I was intrigued with the geometry of
mathematics and I kept thinking a lot about the alleged
ineffability of the so-called fourth dimension. When I left
Harvard and went into the Navy I remember saying to myself,
"If nature has a department of physics, a department of
chemistry, a department of biology, and a department of
mathematics it would have to have meetings of all department
heads in order to decide what to do when I throw an apple
core into the water. The omni-departmentalization seems too
awkward a system. I think nature has only one department
and I think she has one comprehensive coordinate system
to interaccommodate any and all events, and that system is
probably rational as nature's chemical associating and
disassociating is all done with whole, low order numbers."

- Cite RBF marginalia in old Chap. 2, "Synergy," I.11, 18 Mar'69

---

Nature's Logistics:

See Tensegrity: Unlimited Frequency of Geodesic
    Tensegrities, (8)
    Trees, (2)

---

RBF DEFINITIONS

Nature Has No Separate Departments:

"Now, in order to understand universal structure one must
consider the fundamental coordinating system employed by
nature. It occurred to me half a century ago that nature might
have a coordinating system of her own-- which might not be the
same system as that which man has arbitrarily invented,
adopted, and applied to his measuring of nature. It also
occurred to me that nature probably did not have separate
departments of physics, chemistry, biology, mathematics, and
sociology, etc. In formulating the quadrillions of bubbles
per second in the waters of Niagara Falls, nature has no time
in which to refer her structural formulation decisions to
bureaucratic conventions of department heads of academic
categorical states."

- Cite Conceptuality of Fundamental Structures (Kepes) p.68, 1965

---

RBF DEFINITIONS

Nature Has So Many Options:

"I say: if nature permits it, it's natural. If nature

doesn't permit it, you can't do it. And you can see that

nature has so many options. And we're used to using only

a few of the options and we think that the not-frequently-

used options are unnatural. But they're just as natural."

Soleri: "So the typewriter is a natural phenomenon?"

RBF: "Absolutely."

- Cite WATTS TAPE, 19 Oct '70, p.23

---

Nature Has No Separate Departments:                    (1)

See Bubbles in the Wake of a Ship
    Orderliness Operative in Nature

---

RBF DEFINITIONS

Nature's Subvisible Order:                             (1)

"Man talks carelessly and ignorantly of such words as 'chaos'
... 'turbulence'... 'turmoil'.. and (the popular, modern)
'pollution'... where nothing but absolute order is subvisibly
maintained by nature and her transformation arrangements
unfamiliar to man. Universe does not have any pollution. All
the chemistries of Universe are always essential to the
integrity of eternal intertransformation and eternal self-
regeneration.
          Physicists invent nothing
              Chemists invent nothing.
... They find out what nature does from time to time and learn
something of what her laws of rearrangement may be, and fortunate
humans employ those rules to cooperate consciously with nature's
evolution.

"All humans, endowed at birth with a billion capabilities beyond
the knowledge of the parents, evolve in ways that are utter
mystery to them. The exquisite, myriadly endowed child employs
that mysterious endowment and intuitionally apprehends itself
as inventor of ways of using the orderly laws of Universe to
produce tools, substances, and service integrities, to communicate
and allow humans to participate in Universe's ever-transforming"

- Cite SYNERGETICS text at Secs. 1024.22 &.23; rewrite of 27 Dec'73

RBF DEFINITIONS

### Nature's Subvisible Order: (2)

"evolutionary events in an as yet preposterously meager degree, which has given rise to a nature-permitted variety of little humans on tiny planet Earth each becoming Mr. Big, with a suddenly mistaken sense of power over environmental transformations-- participation in which permitted him to feel himself as a manager of inventories of logistical multiplicity which, at the most ignorant level, manifests itself as politically assured mandates and political-world gambling ▪ gambling▪ ideological warfare ▪ national sovereignties ▪ morally rationalizing public ▪ body politic ▪ individual nations as United Nations."

- Cite SYNERGETICS text at Secs. 1024.22 & .23; galley rewrite of 27 Dec'73

### Nature Permits It:

See Nature, 13 May'73
Industrialization, (A)
Reduction to Practice, 29 Jan'75

---

RBF DEFINITIONS

### Nature Permits It Sequence: (1)

"Stress-producing metaphysical gas stretches and strains nature to yield into social-evolution conformations such as the gas-filled plastic tube of Universe. There is an a priori universal law in the controlled complexity that tolerates man's pressurized nonsense, as nature permits each day's seemingly new Universe of semifamiliarities, semiwonders and semimystery, what humans might think of as history unfolding on this little planet. There is the Game of Cosmic History, in which Universe goes on approximately unaware of human nonsense while accommodating its omnilocal game-playing. Flies have their game. Mosquitoes have their game. Microbes have their game. Lion cubs have their game. Whatever games they may be playing, positive or negative, realistic or make-believe, all the games are fail-safe, alternate circuits, omniconsequential to eternally regenerative Universe integrity. It's all permitted. It all belongs.

"Only humans play 'Deceive yourself and you can fool the world'; or 'I know what it's all about'; or 'Life is just chemistry'; and 'We humans invented and are running the world.' Dogs play 'Fetch it' to please their masters, not to deceive themselves. The most affectionate of dogs do not play 'Burial of our dead'--"

- Cite SYNERGETICS text at Secs. 1024.24 & .25; rewrite of 27 Dec'73

### Nature ▪ Scenario Universe:

See Cosmic Accounting, 20 Sep'76

---

RBF DEFINITIONS

### Nature Permits It Sequence: (2)

"'Chemistry is for real.' Only humans play the game of masks and monuments. Fictional history. Historical architecture. Crabs walk sideways; but only human society keeps its eyes on the past as it backs into its future. Madison avenue aesthetics and ethics. Comic strips and cartoons... truth emergent, laughing at self-deception... momentary, fleeting glimpses of the glory, inadvertently revealed through faithful accuracy of observation-- lucid conceptioning-- spoken of as the music of the stars, inadequate to the mystery of integrity...
          All the poetry,
          all the chemistry,
          all the stars
... are permitted transformations of all the eternal integrity.
          All the constants,
          gravitational constant,
          radiational constant,
          Planck's constant,
... above all, mathematics, geometry, physics, are only manifests of the eternal mysteries, love, harmonic integrity beyond further words."

- Cite SYNERGETICS text at Sec. 1024.25, rewrite of 27 Dec'73

### Nature Trying to Make Man a Success: (1)▪

See Man as a Function of Universe

---

RBF DEFINITIONS

### Nature Permits It Sequence: (3)

"The isotropic vector matrix yields to palm trees and jellyfish as a complex of mathematical integrities. As one will always be to one other. But no other: no one. Other is four-- but whereas one has no relations; two have only one interrelationship; three have three interrelationships; but four have a minimum of relationships synergetics. No insideness without four. Without four, no womb; no birth: no life... the dawning awareness of the integrity of Universe. For humanity the only permitted infallibly predictable is the eternal cosmic integrity."

- Cite SYNERGETICS text at Sec. 1024.25, rewrite of 27 Dec'73

### Nature Trying to Make Man a Success: (2)

See Desovereignization Sequence, (3) (4)
Doing What Needs to be Done, (B)

Nature's Technology vs. Humans' Technology:

    See Load Distribution, 17 Oct'77

---

Nature: Natural:              (1A)

    See Animate & Inanimate
        Artificial
        Automation of Metabolic & Regenerative Processes
        Charting Alternate Experiences of Man & Nature
        Clams
        Coin Toss in the Air
        Control Line of Nature
        Coordinate System of Nature
        Crocodile
        Environment
        Geodesic Design in Nature: Confirmation Of
        Intimacy with Nature's every Phase
        Radiolaria
        Tetrahedral Coordination of Nature
        Trees
        Wilderness Resource
        Worms
        Unnatural
        Society Does Not Understand Nature
        Congruent with Nature
        No Right Angles in Nature

---

RBF DEFINITIONS

Nature Ships Tension:

"This is a whole new generation, where you ship tension.
Nature ships tension patterns and uses locally available
compression."

- Cite RBF to Ron Goodfellow, Philadelphia, PA; 29 Jul'76

---

Nature: Natural:              (1B)

    See Impounding Sun Energy: Nature's Most Important Trick
        Intimacy with Nature

---

Nature's Basic Designing Tools:       (1)

    See Angle & Frequency Modulation

---

Nature: Natural:              (2)

        Attic Window, 20 Jan'75
    See Anticipatory, 3 Nov'64; 6 Jul'62
        Fire (B)*
        Mathematics, 14 Mar'71*
        Reality, 26 Sep'73
        Trees (1)*
        Universal Requirements of a Dwelling Advantage (1)*
        Unknowable, 8 Mar'73*
        Why: The Unanswerable Why, 8 Mar'73
        Symbolism in Buildings, 1 Feb'75
        Science Opened the Wrong Door, 30 Dec'73
        Technology, 21 Jan'75
        Success, 29 Jan'75
        Gestation Rates, 1 Mar'77
        Tetrahedron, 26 Apr'77
        Experiment: We Are Not the Only Experiment, 30 Apr'78

---

Nature's Basic Designing Tools:       (2)

    See Angle & Frequency Modulation, Jun'66
        Angle & Frequency Design Control, Jul'71

---

Nature: Natural:              (3)

    See Natural Law
        Natural Time Increment
        Nature Always Comes Back on Itself
        Nature Always Knows What To Do
        Nature: What Nature Needs to be Done
        Nature Has No Separate Departments
        Nature's Logistical Strategy
        Nature Has So Many Options
        Nature's Subvisible Order
        Nature Permits It Sequence
        Nature's Basic Designing Tools
        Nature Modulates Probability
        Natural Education
        Nature Trying to Make Man a Success
        Nature is Neither Good Nor Bad
        Nature Ships Tension
        Nature = Scenario Universe
        Nature's Technology vs. Humans' Technology

Naught:

See How Little I Know, 13 May'73

Navel:

See Nose-to-navel
Umbilical

RBF DEFINITIONS

Navigation:

"Probability could not get you to a given port.  Navigation
can do so.  Navigation is discrete and is a powerful tool."

- Citation and context at Probability, Sep'73

Navigation to Faraway Places to Bring Back Miracle Objects:

See Wizard, 18 Jul'72

Navigation vs. Probability:

See Navigation, Sep'73

TEXT CITATIONS

Navigational Science:

Intuition, p.55 May '72

Navigation:                                                (1)

See Sea Technology
Naga Theme
Rafts:  Early World Drifting on Rafts

Navigation:                                                (2)

See Cartography:  Conventional Projections, (2)
Probability, Sep'73*
Pretending, 8 Apr'75
Navy:  Theory Of, 22 Dec'74
Navy Phonetic Sequence, 23 Jan'75
Halo, 1938
Naga, (2)
Dymaxion Airocean World Map. (a)

Navigators: Early Navigators: (1)

See Rafts: Early World Drifting on Rafts
Secrecy of Mathematical Knowledge
Naga Theme

---

RBF DEFINITIONS

Navy Sequence: (1)

"... I look in various directions because I'm interested in big patterns is one reason why my intuition solves some big patterns... And my Navy experience brought me into celestial navigation. Goodness gracious! My navy experience brought me into...logistics, ballistics, controlling the trajectory of missiles. This brought me into the realization of variables where I realized I had never heard anybody say this, they didn't say this in the Naval Academy, the flight-- shooting from a fixed position to another fixed position is not in the same category as flying from a moving ship on a heaving sea against another moving ship on a heaving sea. And not on a planar base either but on a spherical base. It turns out that all the variables in the Universe in a spherical planet are in the latter base and not a fixed one. I find that really so much of man's thinking is on the fixed-position-to-fixed-position.

"So I then got into the concept of what I call the Theory of the Navy, the theory of ships, of designing the ship itself, what its particular function was, then designing the blast furnace to make the steel... all of this just to get that platform out there and taking you 25 years before you get all the things done... and then the forward supply bases;"
15 Jun'74

- Cite Tape transcript #5, p.9; RBF to W. Wolf, Phila. Pa.,

---

Navigators: Early Navigators: (2)

See Death, 1970
Discovery, 11 Jul'62
Raft, 3 Apr'75

---

RBF DEFINITIONS

Navy Sequence: (2)

"the industrial [ ] fallout rebuild bases; ships of the train and ships of the line... finally the line then was in contact and we did all these things against possible contact and when contact came after 50 years then you had an obsolete battleship...

"You have to have all this general industrial comprehensive anticipatory design science. Not a single thing in the Navy was there at the university until the principles discovered by man were actually reduced to practice and this extraordinary package could float all these things... Could float a fantastic power plant, to drive anything you wanted. So I realized that I'd really been trained in an extrordinary field where at that time there was nothing comparable to what was on land. We've put a lot on the land since that time. And I was really not just a passenger but was trained to know where everything was on that ship and how it worked. I got to know navigation dealing with the stars and the Universe. I got to understand the laws of storms. I learned to understand the social behaviors of peoples as well as the storms of humans and the ways they behave. These are great responsibilities and the line officer was a line officer because back then you were in line of command"

- Tape transcript #5, p.10; RBF to W.Wolf, Phila., Pa., 15 Jun'74

---

Navigator: (1)

See Astrogator
Fog-shrouded Navigator

---

RBF DEFINITIONS

Navy Sequence: (3)

"immediately if your seniors were killed, you had to take over the ship. If the other seniors were killed you had to take over the fleet. You had to be trained this way. You might be young, but that's the kind of training given you to be a comprehensivist. ... Then came finally contact. And it was said that in the first and second world wars we would know who was going to run the world for the next 25 years. You knew what the other man's tonnage was but you wouldn't really know what he could do with the same, or more with less, until you came into contact: And the other one went to the bottom. So he didn't know either. And these were kept secrets. This was what was meant by classified information. Anyway, I was privy to all this...

"And of all things, here I was in the Navy at an extraordinary moment of history where the masses of the waterocean world were running the world, the British Empire at that time; and they suddenly were about to lose if they couldn't get America in because the submarines had not been anticipated and they were sinking their great line of supply. If they couldn't keep up their line of supply the war would come from Europe on to the British Isles and whoever controlled the British Isles was"

- Tape transcript #5, p.10; RBF to W. Wolf, Phila., PA, 15 Jun'74

---

Navigator: (2)

See Mark Your Own Paper, late'70

---

RBF DEFINITIONS

Navy Sequence: (4)

"going to run the world. That was considered the unsinkable flagship that commanded all the harbors of the customers of Europe... where you cashed in everything you stole from the Orient.

"The Navy at that time was very secondhand... This was before World War I. Our chief battleship was Admiral Dewey's flagship. Because of their enormous sinkings they had to be refurbished from America; enormous production, and they wanted all these ships, and many men brought across the ocean to fight; and above everything they needed to build up their naval strength. Therefore, they had to allow the American Navy to come to parity with the British Navy... And I was at the Naval Academy and they had to have the men that ran ships: That was the big show.

"I want you to realize, then, how very different this whole complex of events is... And I'd become so familiar with my filing problem. In those days we didn't have a computer. The only thing we had was something called the Ford Range Keeper. And that became the property of the Sperry Corporation. We had it on the bridge of obly the very biggest ships.. and we had to do everything lomghand. And they had, down in the plotting room down in the bowels of the ship; it was really the command"

- Tape transcript #5, p.11; RBF to W.Wolf, Phila., Pa., 15 Jun'74

RBF DEFINITIONS

Navy Sequence:                                                    (5)

"position of the ship.  It was the most armored of all and in
that plotting room we had enormous charts with all the variables
that went into the firing problem.  And anything you could put
in there... the logistics were broken down into two things: the
internal and external ballistics.  And the internal ballistics
were all the things that happened before you fired the gun.  And
the external were all the things that happened to the missile
after the gun was fired.  You could get all the previous...
temperature, what the wind was blowing, direction, speed of your
ship, keeping track of the speed of another ship, all those
things were in there.  Suddenly then, we had to get this... and
there was a spotting problem.  You're only firing still at
visible range in those days.  Five thousand yards; you're talking
about three miles, five miles, ten miles.  Ten miles was a very
long one.

"Anyway, having learned what I just learned... immediately after
World War I a series of things happened.  We learned to scramble
all the radio.  We had never dared send messages by radio.  But
then we radioed information coded and ciphered , but you really
didn't send any strategic ones.  But the messages couldn't go
any faster than the coding.  For this reason the authority in"

- Tape transcript #5, p.11; RBF to W. Wolf, Phila. Pa., 15 Jun'74

---

RBF DEFINITIONS

Navy Sequence:                                                    (6)

"the Navy remained in the Navy and the commander in the Navy had
to make decisions way away from home.  After Abraham Lincoln
decisions were made by telegram: all the land controls went into
central position.  Only in the Navy were decisions made way
out there.  After the war we then learned to scramble messages and
from this time on they no longer needed to have comprehensivists.
... They wanted specialists.  Men became Naval aviators, or
submarine, and so forth.  I was the last of the breed of
comprehensivists being trained in that way.  This is very
relative to the problem you're up against now.

"I was fascinated with the things that some people improved on
the firing data.  They introduced theis and they introduced that
and I said I wonder if some of these things aren't redundant.
We put them all in to calculate.  So I tried firing where you
dropped this out; and if the answer was so badly altered that
you could fire anywhere in the sky with equal success, then I
put that one back in.  When I found it really hardly varied at
all, I said which one of these should be dropped out.  And I
could weed out.  I feel that's what brought me down to Earth,
(hmm - eja), down to what I called min-max-fam-fax-- the
minimum-maximum family of facts."

- Tape transcript #5, p.12; RBF to W. Wol, Phila. Pa., 15 Jun'74

---

RBF DEFINITIONS

Navy Sequence:                                                    (7)

"Now I did that in 1927 when I was out of the Navy and was
trying to think how it could all be reestablished.  But I had
to start with the Universe.  The Navy started with Universe.
We're dealing in the celestial.  It's important to realize
that this long, long training had been in really a very diff-
erant category.  The Navy automatically looked on the whole
Earth.  You assume there's only one Navy.  And the other ones
go on the bottom so you have any resources of Earth.  You didn't
have to think in terms of the barriers the Army had.  That was
when the great war games were the world games.  That's when I
turned those into positives."

- Tape transcript #5, p.12; RBF to W.Wolf, Phila. Pa., 15 Jun'74

---

RBF DEFINITIONS

Navy Phonetic Sequence:

"Navy -- Na-tive -- Nativity -- Navigate..."

- Cite RBF videotaping Penn Bell Studios, Phila., PA, 23 Jan'75

---

RBF DEFINITIONS

Navy:  Theory of the Navy:

"In the Navy I became exposed to the really big patterns.
It was unlike the maps of early man where you would go from
flat empire → wilderness → off the map → infinity.

"All the law belonged to the land.  Three-quarters of the
Earth is covered with water and when you're out there on the
water you soon learn that physical law is the only law!

"The British Isles were simply the western terminal of
the East India Company.

"That's what the Theory of the Navy is: a generalized theory
of all the variables as in general systems theory.  This is
how you develop those great forecasting capabilities in both
ballistics and in navigation."

- Cite RBF to State Dept. Senior Seminar, Rosslyn, Va., 22 Dec'74

---

Navy:  Theory of the Navy:

See Navy Sequence (1)

---

Navy:                                                            (1)

See Sea Power
    Battle Ship
    Sea Technology

---

Navy:                                                            (2)

See Secondhand, 1946
    Naga, (2)
    General Systems Theory, (1)
    Psychiatry, (3)
    Halfway-round-the-worlding, 12 May'77

Near-miss:

See Vectorial Near-miss

Necessity:

See Need : Necessity

RBF DEFINITIONS

Nebula:

EJA: Is nebula a complementary of nucleus?

RBF: "No. A nebula is a random aggregate of nuclei."

Neck:

See Stick the Neck Out

- Cite RBF to EJA, 3200 Idaho, 29 Oct'72

Nebula:                                                    (1)

See Nuclear & Nebular Zonal Waves

RBF DEFINITIONS

Necklace:                                                  (A)

"A necklace is unstable. The beads of a necklace may be
superficially dissimilar, but they all have similar tubes running
through them with the closed tension string leading through all
the tubes. The simplest necklace would be one made only of
externally undecorated tubes and of tubes all of the same
length. As the overall shape of the necklace changes to any
and all polygonal shapes and wavy drapings, we discover that
the lengths of the beads in a necklace do not change. Only
the angles between the tubes change. Therefore, stable refers
only to angular invariability.

"A six-edged polygon is unstable; it forms a drapable necklace.
If we make a five-sided polygon, i.e., a pentagonal necklace,
it is unstable. It, too, is a drapable necklace and is structurally unstable. Why? A necklace of three rigid tubes also has
three flexible angle-accommodating tension joints. Here are
six separate parts, each with its unique behavior characteristics
which self-interfere to produce a stable pattern. How and why?
We are familiar with the principle of lever advantage gained
per length of lever arm from the fulcrum. We are familiar
with the principle of the shears in which two levers share a
common fulcrum, and the stronger and longer the shear arms,"

- Cite SYNERGETICS text at Secs. 608.01-.02; galley rewrite
  9 Nov'73

Nebula:                                                    (2)

See Gravity, (B)
Mass, 29 Dec'58

RBF DEFINITIONS

Necklace:                                                  (B)

"the more powerfully do they cut. Steel-bolt cutters have
long lever arms."

"In every triangle each corner angle tension connector serves
as the common interfulcrum of the two push-pull, rigid lever
arms comprising two of the three sides of the triangle adjacent
to their respectively common angular corners; each pair of the
triangle's tubular necklace sides, in respect to a given corner
of the triangle, represent levers whose maximum-advantage ends
are seized by the two ends of the third, rigid, push-pull,
tubular side of the triangle, whose rigidity is imposed by its
command of the two lever arm ends upon the otherwise flexible
opposite angle. Thus we find that each of the necklace's
triangular rigid tube sides stabilizes its opposite angke with
minimum effort by controlling the ends of the two levers
fulcrumed by that opposite tension fastening of the triangle.
Thus we find the triangle to be not only the unique pattern-
self-stabilizing, multienergied complex, but also accomplishing pattern stabilization at minimum effort, which behavior
coincides with science's discovery of the omni-minimum-effort
behavior of all physical Universe."

- Cite SYNERGETICS text at Sec. 608.03; galley rewrite 9 Nov'73

RBF DEFINITIONS

## Necklace: (C)

"The six independent energy units of the triangle that interact to produce pattern stability are the only plural polygon-surrounding, energy-event complexes to produce stabilized patterns. (The necklace corners can be fastened together with three separate tension-connectors, instead of by the string running all the way through the tubes, wherefore the three rigid tubes and the three flexible tension connectors are six unique, independent, energy events.)

"We may say that structure is a self-stabilizing, pattern-integrity complex. Only the triangle produces structure and structure means only triangle, and vice versa.

"Since tension and compression always and only coexist with first one at high tide and the other at low tide, and then vice versa, the necklace tubes are rigid with compression at visible high tide and tension at invisible low tide; and each of the tension-connectord has compression at invisible low tide and tension at visible high tide; ergo, each triangle has both a positive and a negative triangle congruently coexistent and each visible triangle is two triangles: one visible and one invisible."

- Cite SYNERGETICS text at Secss 608.05-.06; rewrite of 9 Nov''73

---

RBF DEFINITIONS

## Necklace: (1)

"Necklace flexibility is a function of angular tensions and not of the compressional islands or beads. Relative flexibility decreases as beads are progressively removed. When the numbers of beads are odd the waves in the necklace are blocked; when the number is even the waves are continuous.

"When the number of beads is reduced to six, continuous wave flexibility is permitted. When the number of beads is reduced to five the waves are blocked so the necklace is flexible. When reduced to four beads the necklace can be draped over human shoulders; one "V" in front and one "V" in back. When the beads of the necklace are reduced to three all flexibility ceases. Each angle is stabilized by the opposite side, exercizing its push-pull effectiveness upon the two lever-ends of the angle's adjacent sides, as would a pair of scissors be held in fixed opening by a pencil with the pencil's two ends tied respectively to the two finger circle terminals of the scissors. (Drawing.)

"If we take out one more bead the scissors become closed; There is no opening or area between them. The openaing

- Cite RBF dictation to Alexandra Snyder, New Delhi, Nov. '71

---

RBF DEFINITIONS

## Necklace:

"A necklace has no pattern stability."

- Cite RBF to H.U.D. Engineers, Washington, 26 Jan '72

---

RBF DEFINITIONS

## Necklace: (2)

"or area is always bound by push-pull energy actions and mass attraction interlinkages identical with the necklace in principle. The triangle is the only self-stabilizing polygon. By structural we mean energy patterns whose polygonal patterns are self-stabilizing; that is exhibiting inherent properties of the mass attractions and mass repulsions of the radiational and gravitational laws. We discover that the triangle is the only self-stabilizing polygonal pattern integrity."

- Cite RBF dication to Alexandra Snyder, New Delhi, Nov. '71

---

RBF DEFINITIONS

## Necklace:

"In a necklace the angles between the pieces are transformable until you reduce them to a triangle. The triangle is then not transformable."

- Cite RBF to EJA, 3200 Idaho, DC, 23 Jan '72

---

RBF DEFINITIONS

## Necklace:

"A necklace is unstable. The lengths of the beads in the necklace do not change. Only the angles between them change. Stable refers only to angular invariability. By structure we mean self-stabilizing. The triangle is the only self-stabilizing polygon."

- Cite NEHRU SPEECH, p. 14. 13 Nov'69

TRIANGULATION - SEC 611.04

---

RBF DEFINITIONS

## Necklace:

"Chain-linkage necklace structures take advantage of the triangulation of geodesic lines and permit us to encompass relatively large volumes with relatively low logistic investment. Slackened necklace geodesic spheres can be made as compactable as hairnets and self-motor-opened after being shot into orbit."

- Cite SYNERGETICS text at Sec. 608.07; Nov'71

---

RBF DEFINITIONS

## Necklace:

"I have a very crude necklace. What is unique about the necklace is its flexibility, so it can be draped over the shoulders. . . . Looking closely to see how and why it can flex, we find that the individual pieces of wood here are not changing their length at all. . . . What is changing are the angles. All the flexing is in the terms of the angular change and not linear. . . In other words an angle is an angle independently of the length of its edges. So these are angular behaviors. I'm going to take several pieces out of the necklace. IT's still very flexible so we take another one out. Still very flexible. Take out another piece. Still very flexible. Now I'll take out one more piece-- we're down to four pieces and it's still very flexible. This we'll drape over my shoulders with a triangle in front and a triangle in back. Man calls this a square, but we see this square as completely unstable. I became extremely interested in this when I was young, the fact that the square does not have any structural integrity of its own. It only behaves the way it did because the teacher put it on a rigid blackboard, and it couldn't ~~change~~ change there. Now I'm going to take out one more piece. . and for the first time it will no longer flex."

- Cite RBF at SIMS Seminar U.Mass, Amherst 22 July '71, p. 17

# Synergetics Dictionary

RBF DEFINITIONS

Necklace Structure:

". . .Tube-and-cable 'necklace' structure . .
takes advantage of triangulation of geodesic lines
/and/ entitles us to the encompassment of relatively
large volumes with relatively low logistic investment. . .
Slackened necklace geodesic spheres, compactible as
tight as hairnets, may be shot to the moon and
tensibly self-motor ▬ opened."

-Cite PREVIEW, I&I., Pp. 222,223
1 Apr'49

TRIANGULATION ~ SEC. 608.07

---

TEXT CITATIONS

Necklace:

Synergetics text was rearranged at galley stage, 9 Nov'73:
New citation for Necklace is Sec. 608.00 ff.

---

Necklace: Necklace Structure: (1)

See Chain Linkage
String-connected Polyhedra

---

Necklace: Necklace Structure: (2)

See Transformable, 23 Jan'72
Stable & Unstable Structures, 7 Jun'72
Cube & VE as Wave Propagation Model, 23 Feb'72

---

RBF DEFINITIONS

Need: Necessity:

"Anything man needs to do he can afford to do."

- RBF quoted by Lee Dembart, New York Post, 26 April 1971

- Citation at Afford, 26 Apr'71

---

Need: Necessity: (1)

See Doing What Needs to be Done
Nature: What Nature Needs to be Done
Determinism
Spherical Necessity

---

Need: Necessity: (2) ▬

See Fuller, R.B: Crisis of 1927, 26 Sep'68

---

Needham, Joseph:

See Synergetic Hierarchy, 5 May'74

RBF DEFINITIONS

20

RBF DEFINITIONS

Needle:

"... The point of a needle is a pile of oranges."

- Cite SYNERGETICS draft at Sec. 1009.41, 10 Feb'73

---

Needle Floating on Water:

See Fourth Dimension, 6 May'48

---

Needle: (1)

See Rowing Needles
Knitting Needles

---

Needle: (2)

See Crystallography, 17 Aug'70

---

RBF DEFINITIONS

Negative:

"Each vector is reversible having its negative alternate."

* Cite SYNERGETICS Corollaries, Sec. 240. 1971

---

RBF DEFINITIONS

Negative:

"Science is remiss and unnecessarily prejudicial in calling one of a pair of complementary behaviors negative. There are always much better descriptive terms."

- Citation and context at Complementarity, 2 Mar'68

---

RBF DEFINITIONS

Negative:

"The negative is never the mirror-image of the positive."

- Citation and context at Complementarity, Spring'66

---

Negative Accounting:

See Wealth, (E)(F)

Negative Entropy:

      See Antientropy
         Syntropy

---

RBF DEFINITIONS

Negative Tetrahedron:

"Entropy is not random;

It is always one negative tetrahedron."

* Cite OMNIDIRECTIONAL HALO, p. 157, 1960

---

RBF DEFINITIONS

Negative Matter:

"Negative Matter is coequal with positive matter."

- Cite NO MORE SECONDHAND GOD, p. 36, 9 Apr'40

---

Negative Tetrahedron:   (1)

      See Antitetrahedron
         Invisible Tetrahedron
         Inside-outing Tetrahedron

---

Negative Matter:   (1)

      See Antimatter
         Matter & Antimatter
         Matterlessness

---

Negative Tetrahedron:   (2)

      See Tetrahedron: One Tetrahedron, 1960
         Black Holes & Synergetics, 1 Mar'77

---

Negative Matter:   (2)

      See Antientropy, 10 Oct'63

---

RBF DEFINITIONS

Negative Universe:

"The star tetrahedron may explain a whole new phase of

energetic Universe such, for instance, as the Negative

Universe."

- Cite SYNERGETICS draft "Antitetrahedron," 8 Oct. '71, p. 10.

SYNERGETICS- UNIVERSE- SEC.353

RBF DEFINITIONS

Negative Universe:

"Negative Universe is the complementary but invisible
Universe."

- Cite RBF to EJA, Bear Island, 25 August 1971.

SYNERGETICS UNIVERSE SEC. 351

---

Negative Universe: (2)

See Discontinuity, 22 Apr'71
Ninety-two Elements, 10 Dec'64
Thinkability, 6 Nov'73
Wave, 22 Apr'71*
Transuranium Elements, 23 Feb'72

---

RBF DEFINITIONS

██████ Negative Universe:

"Physics finds only waves. Some are of exquisitely
high frequency, but inherently discontinuous because
consisting of separate event packages. They are
oscillating to and from negative universe, that is to
say, in pulsation."

- (Cite RBF to EJA, Somerset Club, Boston, 22 April 1971

- Citation & context at Wave, 22 Apr'71

---

Negative Vectors:

See Twelve Universal Degrees of Freedom, Feb'72

---

RBF DEFINITIONS

Negative Universe:

"Those subsequently isolated elements beyond the 92
prime chemical elements constitute super atomics; they
are the non-selfregenerative chemical elements of
negative Universe."

(Rearranged and amplified.)

▲ Cite MUSIC, p. 45.   10 Dec'64

SYNERGETICS - UNIVERSE - SEC 352

---

RBF DEFINITIONS

██████████ Negative Vector Equilibrium:

"The non-mirror imaged complementary ⌐Star Tetrahedron⌐
is not a negative vector equilibrium.  The vector
equilibrium has its own integral negative."

(Sec. 636.01, footnote)

- Cite SYNERGETICS draft "Antitetrahedron," 8 Oct. '71,
Footnote, p.6.

---

Negative Universe: (1)

See Black Hole
Superatomics
Mite:  Positive & Negtaive Functions
Stars:  Implosive Forces Of
Star Tetrahedron
Inside-out Universe
Invisible Universe

---

Negative Vector Equilibrium:

See Star Tetrahedron & VE

Negative Weight:

See Zero Weight

Neighbor:  Neighborhood:                    (1)

See Proximity ≠ Neighborliness

Negative:                                    (1)

See Degenerative Negative Limits
    Integral Negative
    Positive & Negative
    Positive ≠ Negative
    Againstness
    De-structures = Inside-out
    Trap of Dismay, Fear & Negativism
    Anti-
    Prohibition
    Invisible ≠ Negative

Neighbor:  Neighborhood:                    (2)

See Community, (1)-(2)

Negative:                                    (2)

See Complementarity, Spring'66*
    Electron, 18 Aug'70
    Radiation, 1959
    Entropy, (p.157) 1960
    Optimism:  I Am Not an Optimist, 26 Apr'77

Neo-Platonism:

See Fuller, R.B:  His Neo-Platonism

Negentropy:

See Antientropy
    Syntropy

Nerve Circuit:

See Sensings & Eventings, 28 Apr'77

RBF DEFINITIONS

<u>Nestable</u>: <u>Nestability</u>:

"There are in closest packing, we find, always alternate
spaces that are not being used so that triangular groups
can be rotated into one position or 60 degrees to an
alternate <u>nestable</u> place. . . In other words you take the
vector equilibrium , rotate it 60 degrees to the next
<u>nestable</u> position and suddenly it is polarized."

- ~~Gite Oregon Lecture #7, pp. 234-235~~.    11 Jul'62
  Citation at <u>Sixty Degreeness</u>

---

<u>Nestable</u>: <u>Nestability</u>:                                      (1)

　　　　See Closest Packing
　　　　　　Innestible
　　　　　　Internestability
　　　　　　Basic Nestable Configurations:  Hierarchy Of

---

<u>Nestable</u>: <u>Nestability</u>:                                      (2)

　　　　See Octahedron, 16 Dec'73
　　　　　　Sixty-degreeness, 11 Jul'62*
　　　　　　Vector Equilibrium:  Polarization, (1)(2)

---

<u>Nest is Part of the Bird</u>:

　　　　See Industrialization, (A)

---

<u>Nest</u>:

　　　　See Bird'sNest as a Tool

---

<u>Net Bet</u>:

　　　　See Corporation, (2)

---

<u>Net Set</u>:

　　　　See Radome Sequence, (4)

---

<u>Net</u>:

　　　　See Balloon

25

Network: (1)

See Absolute Network
    Dwelling: World-around Network Dwelling Service
    Electrical Network
    Industrial Network
    Tool Networks
    Wave Network

---

Neuron-transistored:

See Brain's TV Studio, 22 Nov'73

---

Network: (2)

See Boats at Anchor Retard the River's Flow, 1960
    Satellite: World Satellite Sensing, 25 Jan'73

---

Neuron:

See Brain Bank: Brain's Neuron Bank

---

Neumann, John von: (1903-1957)

See World Game, (1)

---

RBF DEFINITIONS

Neutral:

"Everything should be neutral until muted. A piano, like
a house, or like fog, should be neutral. I found in building
that the grays of aluminum were not neutral enough. Brown
Earth is what the human eye is most accustomed to; it is
the best color for floors and walls. Seek first for the
neutral tones, but arrange them so that the human occupant
can change things."

- Citation & context at Harmonics, (1), 1 Feb'75

---

RBF DEFINITIONS

Neuron:

N.Y. Times, 15 May'72, H.M. Schmeck, Jr., "Immunology: A Code
Spelling Life or Death": "And some scientists see links
between the brain and the immunologic system as possibly highly
rewarding to study."

R.B.F. Marginalia: "Neurons are tetra structures."

- Cite RBF marbinalia presumably 15 May'72

---

RBF DEFINITIONS

Neutral Angle:

"... The spherical excess of 6° (one quantum) may be apportioned
totally to the biggest and littlest corners of the triangle,
leaving the 60-degree, vector equilibrium, neutral corner
undisturbed. As we have discovered in the isotropic vector
matrix nature coordinates crystallographically in 60° and not
in 90°. Sixty degress is the vector equilibrium neutral angle
relative to which life-in-time aberrates."

- Cite SYNERGETICS text at Sec. 905.64, 16 Dec'73

RBF DEFINITIONS

Neutral Axis:

"Every system has a neutral axis with two polar points
(vertexes - fixes).  In synergetics topology these two polar
points of every system become the constants of topological
inventorying.  Every system has two polar ▮▮▮▮▮ vertexes
which function as the spin axis of the system.  In synergetics
the two polar vertexes terminating the axis identify conceptually the abstract-- supposedly nonconceptual-- function of
nuclear physics' 'spin' in quantum Theory."

- Cite SYNERGETICS, 2nd. Ed. at Sec. 1007.29, 1 Jan'75

Neutral Axis:                                            (1)

See Additive Twoness
      Plus Two

Neutral Axis:                                            (2)

See Axis of Spin, (2)
      Brouwer's Theorem, 1960; 1 Jan'75
      Centers of Equilibrious Symmetry, May'72
      Euler, 11 Jul'62
      Sphere, 1971; 2 Mar'68; 15 Oct'64
      Two, (1)

Neutral Center:

See Interrelationship Twoness, 27 Dec'74

Neutral Corner:

See Neutral Angle, 16 Dec'73

Neutral Phase:

See Invisible Quantum as Tetrahelix Gap Closer,
      23 May'75
      Octahedron as Conservation & Annihilation Model, (4)

Neutral:                                                 (1)

See Cosmic Neutral
      Nine: Nineness
      Sixty Degreeness
      Zone of Neutral Resonance
      Medio: Macro-medio-micro
      Middle: Middleness: Midway

Neutral:                                                 (2)

See Precession & Degrees of Freedom, (1)
      Sixty Degreeness, 8 Dec'72
      Vector Equilibrium, 18 Sep'69
      Hole in the Victrola Disc, 24 Jan'75
      Information Transmitting & Nontransmitting Model,
      27 May'75

Neutron: (1)

See Electron & Neutron
    Nucleon
    Proton & Neutron

New Forms vs. Reforms:

WDSD Doc. #1, p.54, 1963

Neutron: (2)

See Modules:  A & B Quanta Modules, Apr'72

New Forms vs. Reforms:

See Robin Hood Sequence (2)

Never-never Land:

See Perfect, 1938

New Life: (1)

See Continuous Man
    Old Life
    Young World
    Young & Elders

RBF DEFINITIONS

New:

"Society only takes on the new when nothing else will work."

- Cite RBF at Penn Bell videotaping, Philadelphia, 28 Jan'75

New Life: (2)

See Environment Events Hierarchy, (2)
    Evolution:  Man as Evolution Modifier, May'49
    Poets, 1970

New:

See Adoption of the New Only as Last Resort
Emergence
Future

---

RBF DEFINITIONS

News:

"Today's news consists of aggregates of fragments. Anyone who has taken part in any event that has subsequently appeared in the news is aware of the gross disparity between the actual and reported events. The insistence of reporters upon having advance 'releases' of what, for instance, convocation speakers are supposedly going to say, but in fact have not yet said, automatically discredits the value of the largely prefabricated news. We also learn frequently of prefabricated and prevaricated events of a complex nature purportedly undertaken for purposes either of suppressing or rigging the news, which in turn perverts humanity's tactical information resources. All history becomes suspect. Probably our most polluted resource is that of the tactical information to which humanity spontaneously reflexes."

- Cite SYNERGETICS text at Sec. 'Introduction,' p.12, 25 Jul'72

---

RBF DEFINITIONS

News & Evolution: (1)

"Daily news is a major ingredient of human evolution. Advertising alone provides the economic sustenance of the western world's news media. The magnitude of paid-for advertising received by each news media is directly proportional to the number of ▆▆▆ its buying readers. News media management searches for the type of news that sells the best. Year after year the publishers find that 'bad' news attracts the most paying readers--possibly because the readers can congratulate themselves on not being the unfortunate ones. Whether or not this is the right explanation, it is a demonstrable fact that powerful economic sustenance for negative voices exists. Though the majority of humans are born positivists, popular acknowledgement of the effectiveness of their expressions is difficult to come by, and has little or no economic support. Positivist poets are proverbially poor.

"While there are many positively committed institutions-- religious, academic, and political--we are considering here only the few independently thoughtful, positive individuals alive today whose work has come to be generally recognized in this era of billions of humans integrating into a common world culture, in contradistinction to the few millions of"

- Cite RBF Ltr. Yasuji Fujita re Ruth Asawa; 15 Mar'77

---

RBF DEFINITIONS

News & Evolution: (2)

"individuals of yesteryears who were physically deployed in a myriad of small local cultures.

"One needs to know nothing in order to be negative. One need only be clever with words or cartoon to become famous as an amusingly consistent sceptic or a dramatically devastating cynic. To be creditably positive, not just optimistic, one needs to know a great deal as learned only by direct experience. To be productively positive, one must also have great vision and the confidence of proven technical accomplishments manifest as physical products that work. To be effectively positive and also to inspire others to envision and realize humanity's constructive options is to be a great artist.

"In the 20th century's unprecedented and utterly unforeseen transformation from a local to a universal culture, Ruth Asawa Lanier's ever earthily pure, exquisitely ephemeral sculptures, sculptural murals, paintings, drawings, and her innumerable other exploratory formulations are probably the most embracing and exciting arts and artifacts of an emerging, world-around, classless democracy."

- Cite RBF Ltr. to Yasuji Fujita re Ruth Asawa; 15 Mar'77

---

RBF DEFINITIONS

News & Evolution: (3)

"This historically unpredicted, swiftly emergent, world embracing classless democracy is both evolutionary and revolutionary. Unlike all past revolutions which were accomplished by destroying the successful few, this total emancipation of humanity and the integrity of its sustainability is being realized instead only by increasing the physical and metaphysical advantages of all humanity. This greatest of history's evolutions inadvertently makes obsolete the technical effectiveness and relevance of the older cultures' artifacts and value structures, and thus painlessly and spontaneously abandons the privileges enjoyed exclusively by the few in yesterday's class-stratified and selfishness-rationalizing society....

"As of 1977, human evolution on planet Earth has attained enough know-how to operate this planet to the enduring high physical advantage of all; but nature's checks and balances of human fear, ignorance, and ill-conditioned reflexes have the scales of human fate in dynamic balance. They may readily tip in the negative to terminate human occupation of the planet. Preponderant hope for tipping the scales to the lasting living advantage of humans lies in the world of"

- Cite RBF Ltr. to Yasuji Fujita re Ruth Asawa; 15 Mar'77

---

RBF DEFINITIONS

News & Evolution: (4)

"children. Each child is born in the presence of less misinformation than were their predecessors. Each is born in the presence of a vastly greater amount of reliable information. Each child is born free of the mis- and ill-conditioned reflexes of the older humans. Each child is born with the innate artistry and imagination capable of realizing new and increased advantage for the many. Evolution seems intent upon giving humanity every opportunity to win successful continuance. Clearly, all of our hope lies in the hands and minds of the young."

- Cite RBF Ltr. to Japanese Deputy Consul General in San Francisco, Yasuji Fujita in support of nomination of Ruth Asawa Lanier for Japan's Medal of Honor; 15 Mar'77

---

News & Evolution: (1)

See Communications & Culture
Invisible News
World-around Communication Transcends Politics

---

News & Evolution: (2)

See Impossible: Only the Impossib... ﹍ppens, (A)-(B)

News Ignores Invisible Reality:

See Generalization & Special Case, 12 May'75

Newspaper: Newsprint:

See Rolls, 14 Mar'72; 20 Apr'72
   Individuality & Degrees of Freedom, (3)
   Wood Technology, (1)

News:                                          (1)

See Common Sense:  Official News
   Tactical Information
   Invisible News

Newton's Cosmic Norm of "At Rest":              (1)

See Instant Universe
   Norm of Einstein as Absolute Speed
   Instant Universe vs. All-motion Universe
   Immobility:  Immobilized

News:                                          (2)

See Metabilical Cord, (1)
   Myopia:  Incasting vs. Broadcasting, 22 Jan'75
   Television, Feb'73
   Telegraph, 8 Jun'75
   Transnational Capitalism & Export of Know-how, (2)(3)
   Propaganda, 29 Mar'77

Newton's Cosmic Norm of "At Rest":              (2)

See Invisible Architecture, (1)
   Omnimotions, May'72
   Dictionary, (1)

RBF DEFINITIONS

Newspaper:

"It isn't really very important what we read in the newspaper
because all the very extraordinarily rapid evolution is going
on in the invisible spectrum and the press and TV are really
missing the big show.  What I'm saying is that right now all
of humanity is really breaking through to a completely different way of looking at Universe."

Newton vs. Einstein:

"Isaac Newton discovered the celestial gravitation interrelationship and expressed it in terms of the second power of the
relative distance between the different masses as determined by
reference to the radius of one of the interattracted masses.
The gravitational relationship is also synergetically statable
in terms of the second power of relative frequency of volumetric
quanta concentrations of the respectively interattracted
masses.  Newton's gravitational constant is a radially
(frequency) measured rate of spherical surface contraction,
while Einstein's radiational constant is a radial (frequency)
rate of spherical expansion."

- Citation and context at Cosmic Fish Sequence (1), 16 Oct'72

- Cite RBF rewrite of SYNERGETICS galley at Sec. 1052.21,
   9 Jan'74

RBF DEFINITIONS

### Newton vs. Einstein: (1)

"Beginning in 1917 I determined to make myself a guinea pig in
a life-long research project, documenting the life of an
individual born in the gay '90's... having his boyhood during
the turn of the century and maturing during humanity's
epochal graduation from the inert materialistic 19th into the
dynamic, abstract 20th century.

"Had I the perceptivity at the time equal in magnitude to the
scale of my intuitive prospecting of forward events this case-
history era might have been more accurately identified as that
which terminated Sir Isaac Newton's normal at rest and myriadly
isolated hybrid world cultures to which change was anathema
on the one hand, and on the other, opened Einstein's normally
dynamic, omniintegrating world culture to which change has
come to seem essential and popularly acceptable....

"The experience pattern of my generation was not to be just one
more duplicate generation in a succession of millions of
generations of humanity within an approximately imperceptible
degree of environmental change as compared to the immediately
previous generation.  I was convinced that unannounced by any
authority a much greater environmental and ecological change"

- Tape transcript #6, Side A, pp.12-13; RBF to Barry Farrell;
   Bear Island, 16 Aug'70

RBF DEFINITIONS

### Newton vs. Einstein: (2)

"was beginning to take place in my generation's unfolding
experience than had occurred between my father's and grandfather's
and my great grandfather's and great great grandfather's successive
generations.  It was clearly an environment that was changing;
and though the environment changes might not alter man's genes,
changes in his external conditions might permit man to realize
many more of his innate capabilities. Dwellings are environment
modifying machines; so are automobiles.  Automobiles are little
part-time dwellings on wheels.  Both autos and dwellings are
complex tools within the far vaster tool complex of world-
embracing industrialization.  Life continually alters the
environment and the altered environment in turn alters the
potentials and realities of life.  The environment is basically
a complex of nonsimultaneously occurring but omniintegrating
or interstimulating, and therefore interregenerating, mutations
of man's integral, internal metabolic regeneration organism,
on the one hand; on the other is his external, invention-
realized, metabolic regeneration organism, which we think of and
speak of as industrialization."

- Tape transcript #6, Side A, pp.13-14; RBF to Barry Farrell;
   Bear Island, 16 Aug'70

### Newton Vs. Einstein: (1)

See Pendulum Model vs. Scenario Model
    Instant Universe vs. All-motion Universe
    Universal Integrity:  Principle Of

### Newton vs. Einstein:

See Immobility, 4 May'57
    New York, 1970; (2)(3)(12)
    Radiation-gravitation:  Harmonics, 3 Jan'75
    Time, 2 Jul'62

### Newton Was a Noun:

See Quick & the Dead:  Song Of, Oct'66

RBF DEFINITIONS

### Newton's First Law of Motion:  RBF Restatement Of:

"Ask Newton what gravity is and he will answer, 'It is
a covarying interrelationship of two or more bodies
inherently nondisclosable by any one of the bodies
considered separately."

- Cite RBF Tribute to Josef Albers; Dec'77

RBF DEFINITIONS

### Newton's First Law of Motion:  RBF Restatement Of:

"I have attempted a new generalized statement of a 'First
Law of Acceleration,' which goes as follows:

    All local event systems (Newton's 'bodies') are
    in relevant continuity of frequency accelerations
    with a plurality of local and comprehensive
    patterning consequences, and all other local
    systems of macro and micro degrees affect all
    other local systems of Universe in varying degrees
    of angle and frequency modulation; and the effect
    of all the local systems of events upon any
    and all other systems of local events is pre-
    cessional."

- Citation and context at Tetrahedral Dynamics (1), 4 May'57

### Newton's First Law of Motion:  RBF Restatement Of:

See Intereffects, 23 Sep'73
    Interference (2)
    Precession (1); 6 Jul'62
    Otherness Restraints & Elliptical Orbits, (2)(3)
    New York City, (2)

31

RBF DEFINITIONS

Newton's Second Law of Motion:  RBF Restatement Of:

"The astrophysical chain of events altogether compounded to
permit Newton's discovery of the only-metaphysically-statable
gravitational law which showed that the intensity of the
interattraction of any two celestial bodies is initially
proportional to the product of their masses and varies at
a rate of the second power of the arithmetical distances
progressively intervening--double the distance and reduce
the interattraction to one-quarter of its previous
intensity."

- Cite RBF tribute to Josef Albers, Dec'77

---

RBF DEFINITIONS

Newton's Second Law of Motion:  RBF Restatement Of:

"Gravity... is the variable interattractiveness of nonmagnetic
bodies, which interattractiveness varies at a second-power rate
inversely proportional to the relative distances intervening
the masses, as those distances vary only at an arithmetical
rate of change."

- Citation at Gravity, 31 May'74

---

RBF DEFINITIONS

Newton's Second Law of Motion:  RBF Restatement Of:

"Synergy... is a part of the great mystery
Which always remains unexplained
By such discoveries as Newton's
Of the first-power arithmetical
Vs. the second-power augmentation
Rates of constantly intercovarying
Gravitational interattractiveness
Of separate bodies in Universe..."

- Cite WHAT I AM TRYING TO DO, p.2 revised, 10 Sep'74

---

RBF DEFINITIONS

Newton's Second Law of Motion:  RBF Restatement Of:

"The relative interattraction increases as the second power
of the rate at which the interdistances diminish."

- Citation & context at Hammering Sheet Metal, (2), 30 Dec'73

---

RBF DEFINITIONS

Newton's Second Law of Motion:  RBF Restatement Of:

"Isaac Newton discovers
The rational geometrical rate of change
Characterizing the interattractiveness
Of any two celestial bodies
While their relative distances apart
Vary only at an arithmetical rate
Which attractiveness itself
Let alone its inverse
Second power rate of gain
Is not manifest
In any of the physical characteristics
Of either of the celestial bodies
When either is considered only separately
And only in terms of its
Integral dimensions, mass, chemistry
And independent electromagnetic properties..."

- Cite WHAT I AM TRYING TO DO, p.1., 4 Aug'74

---

RBF DEFINITIONS

Newton's Second Law of Motion:  RBF Restatement Of:

"Gravity is omnidirectional mass interattraction which, as
Newton discovered, is directly interproportional relative to
the respective mass involved, and varies as the second power
relative to the interproximities of the respective bodies
considered: Halving the distance between any two will fourfold
their interaction."

- Citation & context at Radiation-gravitation Sequence, (1),
5 Jun'73

---

RBF DEFINITIONS

Newton's Second Law of Motion:  RBF Restatement Of:

"Acceleration is second power, multiplying the number times
itself.  As a hypothetical arrangement, when you doubled the
distance apart you decrease the interattraction fourfold.
You have this increase in fourfold, which is second power."

- Cite tape transcript RBF to W. Wolf, Gloucester, Mass., p.12,
2 Jun'74

---

RBF DEFINITIONS

Newton's Second Law of Motion:  RBF Restatement Of:

"...As one energy event comes into critical proximity with
any two, the mass attraction fourfolds every time the
distance between them is halved."

- Citation & context at Critical Proximity, 10 Feb'73

RBF DEFINITIONS

Newton's Second Law of Motion:    RBF Restatement Of:

"Newton's intermass attraction increases at the second power
as the time-distance between is halved."

- Citation & context at Mass, 16 Nov'72
- Cite SYNERGETICS draft at Sec. 960.12, 16 Nov'72

TEXT CITATIONS

Newton:

Intuition, pp.25-31, May '72

Synergetics draft Sec. 1052.20, et. seq., 7 Mar'73

Synergetics draft at Sec. 1009.80 et. seq., 8 Mar'73

| | |
|---|---|
| 529.03 | |
| 529.23 | s201.22 |
| 530.02 | s935.13 |
| 645.01 | s1052.88 |
| 960.10 | |
| 960.12 | |
| 982.81 | |
| 1051.54 | |
| 1210 (pp.728 & 738) | |

TEXT CITATIONS

Newton's Second Law of Motion:    RBF Restatement Of:

Synergetics text at Sec. 1052.21
                           1052.44

Rbf Address to YPO, transcript p.33, 11 Mar'73

Synergetics text at Sec. 960.12

| | | | |
|---|---|---|---|
| | | | s621.30 |
| 103 | 646.03 | 1009.93 | s1052.81 |
| 111 | 710.01 | 1024.14 | s1052.88 |
| 112 | 723.06 | 1051.53-1051.55 | |
| 120.01 | 960.12 | 1052.21 | |
| 251.25 | 981.09 | 1052.44 | |
| 518.02 | 1009.33 | | |
| 645.01 | 1009.80 | | |
| 645.03 | 1009.82 | | |

Newton:                                                    (1)

See Instant Universe

Newton's Second Law of Motion:    RBF Restatement Of:

See Critical Proximity, 10 Feb'73*
    Gravity, (1)(2); 31 May'74*; (b)-(d); 11 Feb'76
    Hammering Sheet Metal, (2)*
    Inverse, 11 Jul'62
    Mass, 16 Nov'72*
    Mystery, 13 Dec'73
    Newton vs. Einstein, 9 Jan'74
    Universal Integrity:  Second-power Congruence Of
       Gravitational & Radiational Constants, (1)-(3)
    VE & Icosa, 9 Jan'74
    Radiation-gravitation Sequence, (1)*
    Gravity:  Circumferential Leverage, (4)
    Radiation-gravitation:  Harmonics, 3 Jan'75
    Co-orbiting of Earth & Moon around Sun, Apr'71
    Human Beings & Complex Universe, (2)

Newton:                                                    (2)

See Acceleration, 1 Apr'67
    Axis of Spin (2)(3)
    Blind Man's Buff, 1 Oct'71
    Energetic Words, 1 Jul'62
    Gravity, 5 Jun'73; 5 Feb'71
    Intereffects, 23 Sep'73
    Isotropic Vector Matrix, 16 Nov'72
    Mass, 16 Nov'72
    Motion, 27 May'72
    Omnimotions, 27 May'72
    Whole System:  Synergetics Principle Of (1)
    Tetrahedral Dynamics (1)
    Time, 2 Jul'62
    Universal Integrity:  Second-power Congruence of
       Gravitational & Radiational Constants (1)
    Conceptual Physics, (2)

Newton:  As Newton Might Have Said It But Did Not:

See Newton's First Law of Motion:  RBF Restatement of
    Newton's Second Law of Motion:  RBF Restatement Of

Newton:                                                    (3)

See Newton's Cosmic Norm of "At Rest"
    Newton vs. Einstein
    Newton Was a Noun
    Newton's First Law of Motion:  RBF Restatement Of
    Newton's Second Law of Motion:  RBF Restatement Of
    Newton:  As Newton Might Have Said It (But Did Not)

RBF DEFINITIONS

New Universe: Disclosure of Entirely New Universe in Next Decade:

"Since Earthians' astronomical measurements have only been
conducted for a few thousand years, and nine-tenths of the
information has been accumulated in the last five centuries,
to be conservative, we can say that 11,000 years exploration
has brought in data covering 11 billion years.

"The ratio $\frac{11,000}{11 \text{ billion}} = \frac{1}{1 \text{ million}}$ clearly manifests a
high-order experiential acceleration in the rate of information
gaining. Thus we take note of how ▮▮▮▮ really little we know
and alert ourselves to the probability that the next decade
will disclose what in effect must seem an entirely new Universe--
so much more of the cosmically eternal a priori mystery will
have been vouchsafed to us."

- Cite HEARTBEATS AND ILLION, World Mag. p.23, 27 Mar'73

---

RBF DEFINITIONS

New York:

"New York is a continual evolutionary process of evacuations,
demolitions, removals, temporarily vacant lots, new installations and repeat. This process is identical in principle to
the annual rotation of crops in farm acreage-- plowing,
planting the new seed, harvesting, plowing under, and putting
in another type of crop....

"Most people think of the building operations blocking New
York's streets as temporary annoyances, soon to disappear in
a static peace. They still think of permanence as normal,
a hangover from the Newtonian view of the Universe. But those
who have lived in and with New York since the beginning of the
century have literally experienced living with Einsteinian
relativity."

(Original citation & context at New York City,
(1)(2), 1964)

- RBF quoted by Alvin Toffler in FUTURE SHOCK, p.51, 1970

---

RBF DEFINITIONS

New York City:

"The appropriate metaphor for New York City is that of a
ship. All of the equipment and the data are there. The ship
is not sunk. The pumps all work.

"The people of New York could take one of several routes:

-- U.S. Army; they could turn it over to the Army to run it,
   but this would be fascist.

-- Communist; to go communist would be equally unthinkable.

-- Unions; they could accept the leadership of the unions.

"The union heads with all their talent and leadership could
decide to operate the city. The confrontation of the unions
has not been so much with the city itself as it has been with
the banks, the bankers, and their paper money game. The union
leaders should issue their own paper money scrip and enlist the
support of all the other union leaders in the country. It is
a game of paper money; they might as well play their own."

- Cite RBF via telephone from Djakarta to EJA; revised statement for N.Y. Times, 31 Jul'75

---

RBF DEFINITIONS

New York City:                                                    (1)

"Viewed from a ship entering New York harbor or from a
plane coming in over the city, New York appears as an enormous
complex of hard, permanent towers--crystalline asparagus.
But these 'permanents' are as impermanent as women's hairdo's.
New York City's permanent-wave architecture is in fact a
progressively rippling dynamic wave system. The last half-
century has seen three successive replacements of would-be-
permanent New York City buildings.

"New York is a continual evolutionary process of evacuations,
demolitions, removals, temporarily vacant lots, new installations, and repeat. This process is identical in principle
to the annual rotation of crops in farm acreage--plowing,
planting the new seed, harvesting, plowing under, and putting
in another type of crop.

"New York's dynamic pattern of continually accelerating
transformation was entirely unpremeditated by its static-
minded, permanence-intending designers and their patrons.
Up to the time when its earliest skyscrapers were built (the
first was the Tower Building at 50 Broadway, completed in
1889 and demolished in 1914), its stone buildings, fine"

- Cite WAVE TRANSFORMATIONS OF THE CITY, N.Y. Guidebook, 1964

---

RBF DEFINITIONS

New York City:

"The city physically will stay there, but New York is
obsolete. Factories, harbor, warehouses-- all these have
gone elsewhere. They only way to make New York work would
be if the people decided to make it work. If everybody
said, 'My life is involved, my family is involved,' and
started to work cooperatively, it could be made to work.
I don't know any other way."

*Cite RBF in reply to query from Israel Shenker about the
economic crisis of New York: N.Y. Times, p.31, 30 Jul'75

---

RBF DEFINITIONS

New York City:                                                    (2)

"residences, banks, and commercial structures were thought
of by architects, owners, and the public as 'permanent'
monuments of their conceivers' era. And the building arts
being the most laggard of all men's activities, this conception of buildings as 'permanent' still persists in most
men's minds. Most people look upon the building operations
blocking New York's streets--the piles of sand and brick, the
huge cranes fishing steel girders from curb-parked trucks--
as temporary annoyances, soon to disappear in a static
peace. They still think of permanence as normal, a hangover
from the Newtonian view of the Universe. But those who have
lived in and with New York since the beginning of this
century have literally experienced living with Einsteinian
relativity.

"Said Newton, in the first phase of his first law of motion,
'A body persists in a state of rest' (and then as an after-
thought, 'or in a line of motion') except as it is affected
by another body. This Newtonian norm of 'at rest' which
means without change, has long been the base line of all our
economic charts. From this point of view all events and"

- Cite WAVE TRANSFORMATION OF THE CITY, N.Y. Guidebook, 1964

---

RBF DEFINITIONS

New York City:

"When I was young the architects and their patrons assumed,
and in fact hoped, that their great buildings would be permanent
contributions to the world scene. Though the architects...
thought of their buildings in this way, I have seen three
separate sets of permanent buildings in New York City pulled
down to be replaced by another set of assumedly permanent
buildings, with the whole unexpected evolutionary displacement pheneomenon repeating itself again. I have, in effect,
seen three permanent waves of architecture forsaken and
replaced by other permanent waves as the waves flowed northward on Manhattan Island. In the last 15 years I have seen
two- and three-story-high cities of the world transformed
into identical-building type skyscraper cities."

- Cite RBF Foreword to "Great Architecture of the World,"
  13 Mar'75

---

RBF DEFINITIONS

New York City:                                                    (3)

"their growth curves are abnormal. On such charts the curves
of industrial and economic performance rise abnormally above,
or more normally fall back to, or parallel with, the base-line
norm of 'no change.' The would-be conservators of peace and
of economic health have throughout history sought to 'iron
out' the abnormal humps, to 'return to normal,' to no change.

"Einstein's relativity theory, evolved early in the century,
made the static verities of Newtonian mechanics untenable.
But it took almost a half-century for the dynamics of Einstein's
relativity to emerge in the daily papers as the atomic bomb,
followed by a pattern of dynamic events clearly demonstrating
that accelerating change is normal--just as normal as the
human appetite for news of the accelerating accomplishment of
breakthroughs that swiftly expand man's domain in the Universe.

"To the Newtonian conservative, the deliberately accelerated
obsolescence of structures and equipment, such as we see
everywhere about us in contemporary New York, constitues
waste. To the Einsteinian conservative, obsolete structures
and equipment are a new mine of selectively concentrated
chemical elements--a fundamental resource of the industrial"

- Cite WAVE TRANSFORMATION OF THE CITY, N.Y. Guidebook, 1964

RBF DEFINITIONS

New York City:                                                          (4)

"commonwealth. The materials from this mine are the means
of realizing ever more advanced design out of our improving
scientific potentials. As a consequence, metal scrap and
plastic scrap now recirculate increasingly.

"New inventions increase our productive capacity per man-
hour and per pound of resource--our 'performance capability',
as it is called. Every time we mine obsolete structures or
equipment for metal or plastic to use in improved designs,
we get increased performance out of the same tonnage of fundamental chemical resources. Which suggests, for instance,
that we should take all the obsolete two-ton automobiles off
the road, melt them up, and produce from the resulting scrap
twice as many one-ton automobiles, each of higher capability
than the former cars in terms of performance per passenger
and of fuel gallons per safely accomplished higher-velocity
mile.

"All the world's great cities that grew up prior to New York
were products of the Newtonian 'no change' norms. Their
romance lies in their preoccupation with man's historical-
bastioned past. What makes New York City 'the most important
something' in all history is that long before the atomic"

- Cite WAVE TRANSFORMATION OF THE CITY, N.Y. GUIDEBOOK, 1964

---

RBF DEFINITIONS

New York City:                                                          (5)

"bomb hit the front page, this city had become the first
Einsteinian reality. Its romance is its living manifestation
of history continually in the making. Its streets and
districts gradually grow, swell, transform, and disappear
altogether. In the 'gay '90s' New York's great exposition and
sports building on Madison Square was known as Madison Square
Garden. In 1924, the owners of that building built a new
modern Madison Square Garden 1½ miles north of Madison Square
on Eighth Avenue. New York's Bowery, now the deadbeat's
lingering threshold to death, was once the most splendid of
growing New York's districts and boasted its Bowery Savings
Bank. The Bowery Savings Bank now has its main office five
miles north of the Bowery on East 42nd Street. The Madison
Avenue of the 'gay '90s' meant the area between Madison
Square and 42nd Street, dominated by the J.P. Morgan residence
at 38th and Madison. Madison Avenue of the first half of the
20th century referred to shopping section from 42nd Street to
72nd Street, dominated at its base by Brooks Brothers, the
Biltmore Hotel, and the Roosevelt Hotel. So attractive did
the Madison Avenue vantage appear to so many corporate
newcomers that they, in effect, have pulled down all the old"

- Cite WAVE TRANSFORMATION OF THE CITY, N.Y. Guidebook, 1964

---

RBF DEFINITIONS

New York City:                                                          (6)

"buildings and thus terminated all the old enterprises that
constituted Madison Avenue. They have built a new canyon in
the Universe, whose preoccupation with the abstract function
of shaping men's conditionable reflexes, through advertising,
has caused the words 'Madison Avenue' to hold an entirely new
meaning--having nothing to do with a physical avenue itself,
but with their 'corporate image'--the collective archpropagan-
dist, proselytizer, inducer, and seducer.

"Propaganda, like most of New York's manufactured products, has
little weight or physical substance. Pittsburgh produces
steel; Chicago warehouses wheat, steel, and cattle. New York
manufactures pattern abstractions. London's stock market,
the Paris Bourse, and other world exchanges long predate New
york in the exchange of abstract enterprise equities, but
New York today centralizes all the world's anticipatory dis-
counting of forwardly reckonable values.

"The United Nations' world headquarters came naturally to New
York as the most concentrated pattern-processing and exchanging center. New York is today the world's chief publishing"

- Cite WAVE TRANSFORMATION OF THE CITY, N.Y. Guidebook, 1964

---

RBF DEFINITIONS

New York City:                                                          (7)

"headquarters, its leading drama and art market. One
Oklahoma stockyard, last year, collected and sent forward to
the slaughter house a nose-to-tail chain of cattle 550 miles
long. New York's two million typewriters and calculating
machines last years produced rows of letters and figures
long enough to run 20 ribbons between the planets Earth and
Venus when these two are in closest proximity.

"The ideas in which New York traffics emanate from all
around the Earth. It is the world's greatest import-export
idea exchange. New York is not an idea factory, nor an idea
mine, nor an idea garden, but it is the world's point of
highest velocity in idea exchanging. As such, New York is
the world's greatest traffic center in hopes and fears, valid
or invalid.

"There are but relatively few native New Yorkers. Its
population is transient. The average residence is three
years. Visitors to New York from around the world frequently assert antipathy to New York's coldness and bigness. They
have not seen the New York we have been describing. They
have seen one frame of a moving picture. It looks static."

- Cite WAVE TRANSFORMATION OF THE CITY, N.Y. Guidebook, 1964

---

RBF DEFINITIONS

New York City:                                                          (8)

"Only the old-time New Yorkers can know the great transforming dynamics and, more importantly, the city's myriad of
rich abstract resources. Because pure abstractions such as
love, hate, happiness, and inspiration are as invisible as
they are nonmerchandisable, all the real meaning of New York
is both invisible and nonmarketed. The lucky few millions
who are old-time New Yorkers usually love New York passionate-
ly for they know not why specifically.

"While the statistical voices warn us that the world population threatens to crowd itself off the Earth, it is comforting
to discover that New York City's buildings could contain the
whole population of the Earth with no more crowding than that
experienced at a cocktail party--not room for anyone to lie
down but all under cover. New York is so knit together with
underground wires, tubes, cables, and pipes--that in effect
Manhattan Island could be lifted in one piece and stood upon
end, with its roadways and tunnels acting as its supporting
columns with Battery Park on top and Harlem as its base. In
such a position its subways would become elevators and its
elevators subway shuttles."

- Cite WAVE TRANSFORMATION OF THE CITY, N.Y. Guidebook, 1964

---

RBF DEFINITIONS

New York City:                                                          (9)

"Its street level is not the bottom level of New York. Legal
statutes adopted by early Knickerbocker burgers required that
when the utility companies dug up its streets and inserted
pipes, cables, and subways, they should thereafter put all
the same earth back where they found it and the city would
then resurface it. This the public utilities have done to
the letter. The earth tucked back into the street is no more
the Earth's natural top crust than is the earth tucked into
the flower pots high above in Manhattan's skyscraper apartments. The concrete and steel intrusions, below the streets
and buildings, have become so multitudinous and penetrate at
so many levels that they reach hundreds of feet below the
theoretical surface. Like an iceberg, structural and mechanical Manhattan is now chiefly below the surface.

"Old-time New Yorkers remember the unique commercial districts--
the leather district around Gold Street; the tea and spice
districts along Water, Front, and Pearl Streets; the cotton
and linen district on White Street; the machinery exchanges
of Lafayette Street; and the great Gansevoort, Washington, and
Manhattan market districts. These districts have been almost
wholly diffused into uptown invisible districts. The real"

- Cite WAVE TRANSFORMATION OF THE CITY; N.Y. Guidebook, 1964

---

RBF DEFINITIONS

New York City:                                                          (10)

"The real long-time New Yorker knows, however, that nothing
has gone from New York and that its interests have multiplied
a thousandfold. The unique vortexes continually transform
and interchange.

"Old-world church and cathedral spires were originally conceived and built to reach high above the surrounding houses
and stores. In New York one can look down from on high into
a deep valley wherein minuscule spires reach up from the
bottom like fine jewelry spicules,for, unlike business enterprises, the churches have usually been unable to move and have
been swallowed by the commercial avalanche, being no longer
the centers of their parish dwellings. But their spires as
yet inspire when, in our thoughts, our eyes wander down into
those New York deeps wherein approximately all that is
physically left of yesterday is wedded with the physical of
today, and we remember that we are as yet 'quick' and not
dead, and that yesterday only the dead were normal, and that
New York City is now being synchronized with the dynamism of
the quick whose norm is Einstein's c², that is 186,000 times
186,000 miles per second, the normal rate at which we see."

- Cite WAVE TRANSFORMATION OF THE CITY, N.Y. Guidebook, 1964

---

RBF DEFINITIONS

New York City:                                                          (11)

"'I lift up mine eyes unto the hills from whence cometh my
help'--possibly because of all our faculties, it is only our
eyes that can apprehend the distant presence of the high hills--
a presence of which we are informed by radiation from the Sun,
reflected from the hills to our eyes at 186,000 miles per
second, all of which seems so instantaneous that we mistakenly
say that we 'lift our eyes.' And we know that no man--no
mere human being--invented that velocity, nor its reliable
regularity throughout the full spectrum range of all electromagnetic wave phenomena, nor the regularity of its ultra-
high-frequency inter-trafficking.

"Men of yesterday looked outwardly self-helplessly to the
macrocosm, praying for miraculous salvation; today they look
inwardly self-disciplinedly to the nuclear microcosm for vast
sources of reliable physical power. What men thought they
understood yesterday of their local experiences seemed regular,
orderly, and logical; what they did not comprehend, extending outward to the macrocosm and inward to the microcosm, they
thought of as turbulent, random, and chaotic."

- Cite WAVE TRANSFORMATION OF THE CITY, N.Y. Guidebook, 1964

RBF DEFINITIONS

New York City:          (12)

"Men of the Einstein Age are discovering the universal orderliness of constant, comprehensive transformation, utterly
transcendental in the exquisite and magnificent orderliness
of its wavelength and frequency when compared to the crude,
disorderly, conscious thinking and articulation of mere humans.

"And as the bees intent upon their honey-commerce are utterly
unaware of the pollination-function of their bumbling tails,
which inadvertently and unbeknownst to the bees service the
organization of tomorrow's flowers and honey sources, so are
the little, local real-estate manipulators and separate venture
builders who redot the New York City map utterly unaware of
their part in the--only retrospectively scannable-- comprehensive orderlines of New York City's transformative growth.
That growth is an invisible function of all men's experience
of all history, translated now into the world-surrounding,
dynamically functioning industrial network-system in which New
York City is, for the moment, the most radiant communication-
relaying center on Planet Earth."

- Cite WAVE TRANSFORMATION OF THE CITY, N.Y. Guidebook, 1964

RBF DEFINITIONS

New York City:

"New York City! A one-piece dormitory, work, and play shop
300 square miles in the horizontal plane and 30 to 1,000
feet in thickness."

- Cite NINE CHAINS TO THE MOON, p.2, 1938

New York City:          (1)

See Population Density: Manhattan Cocktail Party
Population Density: Manhattan Jet Dispersal
University: New York City as a Vast University
Dome Over Manhattan

New York City:          (2)

See City, (B); (3)
City as Center of Abstract Intercourse (1)(2)
Everybody's Business, (1)
North-south Mobility of World Man, (1)
Fortress Mentality, 12 May'77

Niagara Falls:

See Nature Has No Separate Departments, 1965

RBF DEFINITIONS

Nice:

"Nice means comprehensively adequate and of incisive fit."

- Cite RBF to Ron Goodfellow; Philadelphia, PA: 29 Jul'76

Night:

See Nothingness of Night
Rotation of Night as a Shadow
Undimensional Night

RBF DEFINITIONS

Nine:

"Each prime structural system in Universe has nine separate
and unique states of existence-- four positive, four negative,
plus one schematic unfolded nothiness state... the same
schematic 'game' set-up as that of physics' quantum mechanics
with four positive and four negative quanta as we go from a
central nothingness equilibrium to first one, then two, then
three, then four, high-frequency, regenerated, alternate,
equi-integrity, tetrahedral quanta."

- Citation & context at Geometrical Functions of Nine, (3)(4),
16 May'75

Nine Chains to the Moon:

"Remember the original subtitle of 'Nine Chains to the Moon'
was 'an Adventure Story of Thought.' Not very different from
the subtitle of 'Synergetics.'"

- Cite RBF to EJA, 28 May'75

RBF DEFINITIONS

Nine: None: Zero:

"There is an octave pattern in every system and every time
we come to nine-- whether it be 3 + 6, 2 + 7, or 8 + 1--
it is zero. Waves are octave and one reason they do not
interfere with each other is because of the zero....."

- Cite SYNERGETICS, "Numerology," pp. 11-12. Oct. '71.

RBF DEFINITIONS

Nine Chains to the Moon:

"The title Nine Chains to the Moon was chosen to encourage
and stimulate the broadest attitude toward thought. Simultaneously, it emphasizes the littleness of our Universe from
the mind viewpoint. A statistical cartoon would show that
if, in imagination, all the people of the world were to stand
upon one another's shoulders, they would make nine complete
chains between the Earth and the Moon. If it is not so far
to the Moon, then it is not so far to the limits-- whatever,
whenever, and wherever they may be."

"Limits are what we have feared. So much has been done to make
us conscious of our infinite physical smallness that the time
has come to dare to include the complete Universe in our
rationalizing."

- Citation and context at Rationalization Sequence (5), 1938

RBF DEFINITIONS

Nine = None = Zero:

"Nine is zero
Nine is none
None (Lat.) is none
N-one = not one = none."

- Cite RBF holograph at Table of Indigs, 2 Mar'73

Nine Chains to the Moon:                                    (1)

            See Continuous Man

RBF DEFINITIONS

Nine = None = Zero:

"Indigs can be played only with one through nine.
Nine is zero = nein = none = nothing. Zero effect.

"'Casting out nines,' means working only with the energy
left over after the nines have been taken out."

- Cite RBF to EJA, Chez H. Wolf, Fairfield, Conn., 18 Jun'71

Nine Chains to the Moon:                                    (2)

            See Local vs. Comprehensive (1)

Nine: Nineness:                                            (1)

            See Eightness: 'Begeted' Eightness
                Interwave Behavior of Number
                Nucleus = Nine = Nothing
                Octantation
                Zero-niness
                Geometrical Function of Nine

Nine: Nineness:                                                        (2)


See Cube: Volume-3 Cube, 16 Dec'73
        Indig, 3 Mar'73
        Synergetic Constant, Jul'57

        Zero Wave, 9 Mar'73

RBF DEFINITIONS

Ninety Degreeness:

"Gradually humanity as a whole is beginning to realize that
it is not just a matter of idealistic 'unselfishness' but a
synergetic effect of all the great generalized principles
governing the Universe that the Universe and its evoluting
transformations are cooperative only in 90 degrees, or orbitally
interlinking, directions; that is, circumferentially. 'I go
for my honey' is linear, specialized, disintegrative. Ideologies,
sovereign states, corporations, bureaucracies, bureacrats-- all
are linearly programmed, biased, and competitive."


- Citation and context at Ecology Sequence (E)(F), 5 Jun'73

---

Nineteen Twenty-seven: 1927:


See Fuller, R.B: Crisis of 1927

Ninety Degreeness vs. 180-degreeness:


See Critical Proximity, May'71

---

Nineteen Seventy-two: 1972: History's Most Critical Year:


See Economic Accounting System: Human Life-hour
        Production, (1)

    Gross World Product Sequence, (2)(3)

Ninety Degreeness:                                                     (1)


See Charts: We Need Only Rotate Our Charts 90 Degrees
        Normal to Universe
        Rectilinear
        Right Angle
        Trigonometric Limit
        XYZ Coordinate System
        Precession & Degrees of Freedom
        Precession of Side Effects & Primary Effects
        Primary vs. Side Effects
        Sixty Degreeness vs. Ninety Degreeness

---

Nineteen:


See Closest Packing of Spheres, 29 May'72
        Tetrahedroning, (2)(3)
        Twenty, (1)

Ninety Degreeness:                                                     (2)


See Distaff, 22 Jul'71
        Ecology Sequence (H)(I); (E)(F)*
        Octahedron: One-eighth Octahedron (2)
        Spherical Octahedron, Aug'72; 29 Nov'72
        Precession (a)(b)
        Compression, 19 Jun'71
        Triacontrahedron, 31 Jul'77

RBF DEFINITIONS

Ninety-two Elements:

"....The chemical elements are not things, they are
behaviors...."

- Citation & context at Communication, 21 Jun'77

RBF DEFINITIONS

Ninety-Two Elements:

"Each of the chemical elements are pattern integrities
formed by their self-knotting, inwardly precessing,
periodically synchronized self-interferences."

- Citation at Pattern Integrity, 25 Aug'71
- Cite RBF Insert Synergetics Draft Sec. 416.4. Bear Island
25 August 1971.

RBF DEFINITIONS

Ninety-two Elements:

"Nature does not have any pollutants.  She has only chemical
elements.  The eternally regenerative Universe depends very
heavily on the very valuable total inventory of those chemical
elements.  They are not things; they are behaviors, all the
reciprocal behaviors of the regenerative Universe having their
innate frequencies."

- Tape #2, transcipt p.5; RBF to W. Wolf, 15 Jun'74

RBF DEFINITIONS

Ninety-Two Elements:

"Unique pattern evolvement constitutes elementality.
What is unique about each of the 92 self-regenerative
chemical elements is their nonrepetitive pattern
evolvement which terminates with the third layer of 92."

- Citation at Elementality, 25 Aug'71
- Cite RBF Insert Synergetics Text, Sec 416.4, Bear Island,
25 August 1971.

RBF DEFINITIONS

Ninety-Two Elements:

"All the fundamental nuclear simplexes of the 92 inherently
self-regenerative physical Universe elements are a priori to
human mind formulation and invention and are only discoverable
by mind."

- Citation and context at Design:  Apriori Design vs. Deliberate
Design, 13 Mar'73

RBF DEFINITIONS

Ninety-Two Elements:

"... Planets, stars, galaxies, and their contained behaviors
such as the periodic regularities of the chemical elements
are all design-accomplishments."

- Citation and context at Design (1), 9 Apr'71

RBF DEFINITIONS

Ninety-Two Elements:

"The 92 regenerative chemical elements themselves are
only non-dissipatable and are only re-circulatable."

- Cite World Game, 29 Jun'72

RBF DEFINITIONS

Ninety-Two Elements:

"...The 92 regenerative chemical elements of associative
energy or of the various radiations of energy in its
disassociative phase."

- Citation and context at Optical Motion Spectrum (1)(2),
4 Mar'69

RBF DEFINITIONS

Ninety-Two Elements:

"What is unique about each of the 92 regenerative chemical elements is their unique <u>behavioral</u>-- or <u>energetical</u>-- characteristics."

* - Cite HOW TO MAINTAIN MAN AS A SUCCESS
Utopia or Oblivion, p. 216, 18 Mar'65

---

RBF DEFINITIONS

Ninety-Two Elements:

"The original chaotic disposition of (the) ninety-two regenerative chemical elements is gradually being converted by the industrial principle to orderly separation and systematic distribution over the face of earth in structural or mechanical arrangements of active or potential leverage-augmentation."

". . . the aspect of energy as <u>mass</u>, inventoried as the ninety-two regenerative chemical elements which constitute earth and its enclosing film of alternating liquid-gaseous sequence."

- Cite COMPREHENSIVE DESIGNING (I&I), P. 177, 1 Jun'49
~~Date undetermined~~

---

RBF DEFINITIONS

Ninety-Two Elements:

"Each of the chemical elements are pattern integrities

in the form of local self-interferences."

- Cite OREGON Lecture #5 - p. 164, 9 Jul '62

---

RBF DEFINITIONS

Ninety-Two Elements:

"Unique behavior constitutes elementality."

~~- Cite I&I, p. 189~~
~~"Design For Survival - Plus"~~
~~Date undetermined~~
- Citation & context at <u>Science</u> (2), Jan'49

---

RBF DEFINITIONS

Ninety-Two Elements:

"No longer do I want to talk about the chemical elements as things, but as pattern integrities. Each one is a unique pattern integrity and each one of them is in a sense a form of knots. So we get where there are chemical compounds and the knots tend to be interlinkable and they will catch on one another. This one is holding together all right, but this ball of twine and this ball of twine, suddenly one weaves into the other every so often and associates."

- Cite Oregon Lecture #5 - pp. 164-165. 9 Jul '62

---

RBF DEFINITIONS

Ninety-Two Elements:

"All the first ninety-two chemical 'elements'

are the finitely comprehensive set

of purely abstract 'physical' principles

governing all the fundamental cases

of dynamically symmetrical vectorial geometries

and their systematically self-knotting

precessionally regenerative in-shunting events."

- Cite Comprehensive Anticpatory Design Science (Ltr. to Jonas Salk.)
- Cite NO MORE SECOND HAND GOD, p. 103
9 Apr'40

---

RBF DEFINITIONS

Ninety-Two Elements:

"The 92 regenerative chemical elements are the basic inventory of Cosmic Absolutes.
[OF PRIME ELEMENTS]
"The family consists of 92 unique sets from 1 to 92 electron-proton counts inclusive, and none other.

"Those subsequently isolated elements beyond 92 /constitute $per atomics/; they are the nonselfregenerative chemical elements of negative universe."

- Cite MUSIC Pp 45-50, 10 Dec'64

---

<u>Ninety-two Elements as Cargoes of Energy</u>:

See Wealth, 1947

RBF DEFINITIONS

Ninety-Two Elements: Chart of Rate of Acquisition: (1)

"I have sought fundamental information on the experiences of man on Earth which might govern the shape of all developments men are experiencing. Charts of inventions, for example, are not satiffactory as the list is open-ended and is difficult to assess in terms of the relative importance of specific inventions. The significant area of information is the rate at which scientists have successively isolated the chemical elements.

"This is the most important pattern of discovery with which man deals, embracing, as it does, all physical phenomena. The rate at which man found chemical elements seems to be the key controlling the development of the application of science to technology, and following from this, the application and effect of that technology on economics and, ultimately, the effect of the new technology on society itself."

"The chart... 'Profile of the Industrial Revolution,' begins"

- Cite THE YEAR 2000, San Jose State
College, Mar'66
- Cite The YEAR 2000, reprinted in AD, Feb'67

RBF DEFINITIONS

Ninety Two Elements: Chart of Rate of Acquisition: (2)

"begihs with the year A.D. 1200 going up to A.D. 2000. We begin with a list of nine elements: carbon, lead, tin, mercury, silver, copper, sulphur, gold, and iron, which were known to man at the opening of our history. We do not know when they were first isolated or knowingly used. The first known isolation of a chemical element is arsenic, in 1200. Following this, there is a 200-year gap and we come to antimony; another 200-year gap and we come to phosphorus. Then the gap narrows to 75 years and we have cobalt. From here on we average an isolation of an element every two years. It is an extrordinary period in history that the rate begins to accelerate.

"If you check the date 1730, not long before the American Revolution, you will notice that there are some separate shoulders or plateaus, appearing on the chart. Those shoulders are slowdowns when we have major wars-- the American Revolution, various civil wars, and World War I. They show that pure science does not prosper at the time of war-- which is contrary to all popular notions. Scientists are made to apply science in wartime, rather than look for fundamental information.

"We can also see that in 1932, which was thought to be the"

- Cite THE YEAR 2000, reprinted in AD, Feb'67

RBF DEFINITIONS

Ninety-Two Elements: Chart of Rate of Acquisition: (3)

"depth of the depression, man made his 92nd isolation of a chemical element. This completed the element table representing the full family now mastered by man-- in the sense of his ability to repeat element isolation and to rearrange elements, as fundamental ingredients of physical environment, in preferred patterns of use. From this point on we may notice something strange. Previous to completion of the table, element isolation occurred irregularly-- for example, element number 19 would be the 43rd element isolated; the 45th isolation would number 30, etc. With the post-uraniums the isolations show an absolute regularity of increase-- they come in by number. Man begins to control consciously the rate of development of his capability.

"We must note this in reviewing the contiguous developments in environment control (as shown at the top of the chart). Just as man is able to go into cold climates by putting on fur skins, or into hot by taking off clothes, he enters more hostile environments by having more control devices. The development of these devices is a fundamental measure of man's degree of advantage over his environment. The first time, to our knowledge, that he goes around the world in an invention was, as"

- Cite THE YEAR 2000 reprinted in AD, Feb'67

RBF DEFINITIONS

Ninety-Two Elements: Chart of Rate of Acquisition: (4)

"shown on the chart, in a wooden sailing ship. It comes after the second isolation. Then there is a gap of 350 years and he now goes around the world in a steel steamship. This is an entirely new magnitude of control, no longer dependent on the wind. Upon this, there swiftly follows the world journey in an aluminum airplane, then in an exotic metals rocket. There is a very great contraction in time between these developments. The wooden ship takes two years to circumnavigate the Earth; the steamship, two months, the airplane two days, and the orbiting satellite just over an hour. We have at least three accelerations of accelerating accelerations involved here.

"The consequence of what we have considered then, in relation to our charting is that the next point for a significant new chapter would be around 1975, nine years from now. What that will be we can only guess at-- sending ourselves around the world by radio?

"The key realization is the degree of acceleration of change, and that better than 99 percent of all important technologies affecting such change are invisible. Man cannot see what is going on. He cannot 'see' the chemistries; he cannot see the"

- Cite THE YEAR 2000 reprinted in AD, Feb'67

RBF DEFINITIONS

Ninety-Two Elements: Chart of Rate of Acquisition: (5)

"alloys. Most of the important rates and patterns of change cannot be apprehended by him directly in a sensorial manner. Not only does man have a very narrow range of tunability in the electromagnetic spectrum where he can actually see, but he also has a very narrow spectrum of motion apprehension. He cannot see the hands of the clock moving, or the stars, or any of the atoms in motion."

- Cite THE YEAR 2000 reprinted in AD, Feb'67

RBF DEFINITIONS

Ninety-two Elements: Chart of Rate of Aøcquisition:

"This comprehensive curve of the chronological rate of acquisition of knowledge concerning the pure science absolutes separated out from all other events of history may be inspected as the basic means of prediction of inherent technical and social events-- immediate or somewhat distant."

- Citation and context at Science, 1947

Ninety-two Elements: Chart of Rate of Acquisition: (1)

See Industrialization: Curve Of
Industrial Revolution: Profile Of

Ninety-two Elements: Chart of Rate of Acquisition: (2)

See Science, 1947
Science: Pure & Applied, 8 Sep'75

41

RBF DEFINITIONS

### Ninety-Two Elements: Periodic Regularities of:

"The omni-interorderliness, per se, characterizing the
chemical elements' component periodicities, as well as the
electromagnetic wavelength and frequency regularities of
the 92 regenerative chemical elements, which hold true--
and exploratorily reliable-- throughout the macro and microcosmic behaviors of energy-- as radiation or matter-- is
consistent throughout the thus-far explored multibillion
light-year ranges of the astrophysical, symphonic scenario
Universe."

- Cite RBF Ltr. to Prime Minister Indira Gandhi, 4 Jan '70, p.1.

---

RBF DEFINITIONS

### Ninety-Two Elements: Periodic Regularities Of:                    (1)

(The generalized laws first disclosed by Avogadro, compounded
with Boyle's chemical law, to informedly inspire Mendeleyev...)

"To differentiate out and predict
The existence of a closed family
Of ninety-two
Regenerative chemical elements.
These elements, when found,
They said would display
Such-and-such
Unique and orderly characteristics,
And they mathematically identified in advance
The respective constituent quantities
Of the as yet undiscovered discrete characteristics
Of the as yet undiscovered elements.
All the members of this interregenerative
Information relay team
Did not know one another personally.
Their accumulatingly inspired prediction occurred
At the historical moment
When, a century ago--
Only fifty-two

- Cite INTUITION, p.18, May '72

---

RBF DEFINITIONS

### Ninety-Two Elements: Periodic Regularities Of:                    (2)

"Of the ninety-two
Of those heretofore unexpected chemical elements
Had as yet been discovered
And physically isolated
By humans on Earth-- . . .

Mendeleyev, attempting scientifically
To find an order
In which to set
The first fifty-two chemical elements
Inadvertently uncovered
A previously unknown
System of regularities
Common to all fifty-two,
Which, if their implied generalization
Proved in due course
To hold true,
Would require the presence in Universe
Of the additional unknown forty
To fill in the membership vacancies
Occurring in the revealed periodic behaviors
Of the already discovered chemical elements.

- Cite INTUITION, pp.18-19, May '72

---

RBF DEFINITIONS

### Ninety-Two Elements: Periodic Regularities Of:                    (3)

"Since Mendeleyev's prediction,
Every few years--
One by one--
All ninety-two have been identified
As being present in various abundances
In all the known stars of the heavens,
While ninety-one of them
Have been isolated by scientists
Somewhere on planet Earth,
And all of them have the exact characteristics
Predicted by Mendeleyev and his colleagues.

"And all the foregoing ▮▮▮▮▮▮▮▮▮▮▮▮▮
Subjective harvesting--
Accomplished by individuals
Bound together
By naught other than intellectual integrity--
Has enabled still other
Remotely exploring
Educatively inspired individuals
First to discover
Then inventively to employ

- Cite INTUITION, pp.19-20, May '72

---

RBF DEFINITIONS

### Ninety-Two Elements: Periodic Regularities Of:                    (4)

"The originally unknown
Uniquely recombining
Synergetic behaviors--
In structural groupings--
Of those ninety-two regenerative elements,
Thereby attaining utterly surprising
Structural, mechanical,
Chemical and electromagnetic characteristics,
Which have enormously increased
The relative advantage
Of ever-increasing numbers of humans
To cope with the challenges of life
By accomplishing ever more difficult tasks,
Previously considered impossible to do;
With ever less
Time, weight and energy investments,
Augmented exponentially
By ever-greater investment of unweighables
Of the metaphysical resources--
Of hours of thoughtful reconsiderations,
Anticipations, conceptualizing,
Searchings and researchings
Calculations and experiments."
- Cite INTUITION, p.20, May '72

---

### Ninety-two Elements: Periodic Regularities Of:                    (1)

See Periodicity

---

### Ninety-two Elements: Periodic Regularities Of:                    (2)

See Resonance, 18 Jun '71
        Individuality & Degrees of Freedom, (2)

---

RBF DEFINITIONS

### Ninety-Two Tendencies to Self-Impoundment of Energy:

"... As we come to explore for the fundamental principles
of interpotentials and iteractions called atoms, we find
that, despite the stronomical number of aspects and events,
only a few principles of behavior pervade the whole of
Universe as, for instance, 92 tendencies to self-impoundment
▮▮▮▮▮ of energy;..."

- Citation and context at Reciprocity (1), May'49

RBF DEFINITIONS

▇▇▇▇▇▇▇ Ninety-two Elements: Four Unique Frequencies:

"This is just what Einstein was working on in his $E = Mc^2$ trying to explain a given mass and the way it interfered with itself to give itself this local uniqueness of relative concentration, because these precessions can give you angular changes and it gets tighter and tighter, which will give you unique frequencies and every one of our chemical elements has these unique frequencies and you can actually pick them out of the electromagnetic spectrum by a plurality of usually four unique frequencies characterizing each of the elements."

- Citation & context at Matter, 9 Jul'62

- Cite Oregon Lecture #3, pp.164-165, 9 Jul'62

▇▇▇▇▇ ▇ ▇▇▇▇▇▇ ▇▇▇▇▇▇▇▇▇▇▇▇▇▇ ▇▇▇▇▇▇▇▇▇▇▇▇▇▇▇ '74

---

Ninety-two Elements: Four Unique Frequencies: (1)

See Number: Cosmically Absolute Numbers
Family of Unique Frequencies

---

Ninety-two Elements: Unique Frequencies: (2)

See Integer, 15 Oct'72
Physics: Difference Between Physics and Chemistry, 22 Jun'72
Railroad Tracks: Great-circle Energy Tracks on the Surface of a Sphere (A)(B)
Reality, 14 Oct'69
Matter, 9 Jul'62*
Meshing & Nonmeshing, 1970; 19 Oct'70
Domains of Actions, 21 Dec'71
Sweepout: Spherical Sweepout (1)(2)
Chess: Game of Universe, 7 Oct'71
Orbital Escape from Critical Proximity, (3)
Alloys, 30 May'75
Geometrical Function of Nine, (7)
Cube & VE as Wave Propagating Model, 23 Feb'72
▇▇▇▇▇▇▇▇▇▇▇▇▇▇▇▇▇
Electromagnetic Spectrum, 26 Jan'76
Heard & Unheard Resonances, 17 Jan'75
Quantum Mechanics: Minimum Geometrical Fourness, (1)

---

Ninety-two Elements: (1)

See Atom
Chemical Phenomenon
Cosmic Absolutes
Elementality
Man: Relative Abundance of Chemical Elements in Man and Universe
Minimum Set of Patterns
Periodic Atomics
Periodic Table and Closest Packing
Relative Abundance
Superatomics
Energy Involvement of 92 Elements
Family of Chemical Elements
Isotopes

---

Ninety-two Elements: (2A)

See A Priori, 19 Oct'70
Complex & Simplex, May'72
Cosmic, 3 Oct'72
Design Science, 29 Jun'72
Design (1)*
Design: A Priori vs. Deliberate, 13 Mar'73*
Economic Accounting System (A)(D)
Elementality, 25 Aug'71*
Eternal Designing Capability (3)
Frequency, 1970
Industrialization (2)
Industrial Principle, 1 Jun'49*
Intereffects, 25 Sep'73
Integer, 15 Oct'72
Invisible Colors, 4 Mar'69
Meshing & Nonmeshing, 1970
Octahedron: Nuclear Asymmetric, 1 Apr'73
Optical Motion Spectrum (1)(2)*

---

Ninety-two Elements: (2B)

Human Beings & Complex Universe, (6)
See Pattern Integrity (A); 25 Aug'71*
Pollution, 24 Feb'72
Pollution Control (2)
Railroad Tracks: Great Circle Energy Tracks (B)
Relative Abundance, 9 Jul'62
Reciprocity (2)
Science (2)*
Universe, 4 Jan'70; 9 Jul'62; 15 Dec'71
Wealth, 1947
World Game, 29 Jun'72*
Scrap Sorting & Mongering (1)
Individual Universes, (1)
Single Integer Differentials, (1)
Coupler, 27 Jan'75
Orbital Escape from Critical Proximity, (4)
Geometrical Function of Nine, (7)
Darwin: Evolution May be Going the Other Way, 5 Jun'75
Closed System, 10 Nov'75
Building Industry, (11)
Mite as Model for Quark, 3 May'77
Communication, 21 Jun'77*

---

Ninety-eight Point Six:

See Degrees: 98.6

---

Niwrad:

See Darwin: Evolution May be Going the Other Way

Nixon:  Richard M:

See The One:  Waterhate, 13 May'73
United States:  Most Difficult Sovereignty to
    Break Up, (2)
Building Industry, (6)

---

RBF DEFINITIONS

No Absolute Division Into Parts:

"There may be no absolute division of energetic Universe into isolated or noncommunicable parts..."

- Citation & context at Sphere Integrity:  There Is No, 1962

---

No Absolute Debt:

See Debt, 1944
Deficit Accounting, Feb'67

---

RBF DEFINITIONS

No Absolute Enclosed Surface or Volume:

"As there may be no absolute division of energetic universe into isolated or non-communicable parts, there is no absolute enclosed surface or absolutely enclosed volume; therefore, no true or absolutely defined surface sphere integrity."

- Cite ECHALE, Plate 16, caption, 1962

- Citation & context at Sphere Integrity:  There Is No, 1962

UNIVERSE  SEC. 307.3

---

No Absolute Disorder:

See Chaos, 1971
Entropy, (p.90) May'72
Primordial, (p.156) May'72

---

No Absolute Enclosed Surface or Volume:

See Realms vs. Surface

---

No Absolute Identity:

See Noun, 1938

---

No Absolute Enclosed Surface or Volume:                    (2)

See Frequency, Jun'71

No Absolute Time:

See Eternity vs Energy, 2 May'78

TITLE OF RBF PAPER

Noah's Ark:

"Project Noah's Ark

Discovering New Man Advantage

Summer, 1950"

- Cite RBF Paper, 24 pp., Summer '50

No Absolute Understanding:

See Invisible Reality, May'72

No Altitudeless Triangle:

See Systematic Realization, 20 Dec'74

No Absolute Void:

See Halo Concept; 25 Apr'71; Jun'71

Nobel Prize:

See Fuller, R.B: Nobel Prize

No Absolutes:

See No Absolute Division into Parts
No Absolute Identity
No Absolute Enclosed Surface or Volume
No Sphere Integrity
No Absolute Understanding
No Absolute Disorder
No Absolute Debt
No Absolute Void
No Absolute Time

Nobility: Nobles:                    (1)

See Kings and Nobles

TITLE OF RBF PAPER

Nobility: <u>Nobles</u>:                                                (2)

    See Design Revolution: Pulling the Bottom Up, (3)-(5)
       Race, (2)(3)

---

RBF DEFINITIONS

<u>No Building Block</u>:

    "Man has an innate proclivity for wanting to monopolize,
or to be monological. He wants to fibd the <u>key</u>, <u>the
building block</u>. Every news reporter tries to talk in terms
of 'finding the building blocks of universe.' But the
physicists keep tryingt to tell society that it takes
fundamental 'complementarity.' That is to say two
different and complementšy '<u>building blocks</u>.' They are
the proton and the neutron. The two are intertransformable.
But if one transforms to the other, the other does likewbse.
But they are always unique in themselves. You cannot build
universe with just the rightness or leftness '<u>blocks</u>'
exclusively of one another."

    - Cite NASA SPEECH, Pp. 67,68, Jun'66

---

<u>Nobody to Mark Your Paper</u>:

    See Mark Your Own Paper: Nobody to Mark Your Paper

---

RBF DEFINITIONS

<u>No Building Blocks</u>:                                              (1)

    "Starting with the elementary viewpoint: you get a few things
and put them together... The Darwinian idea. At his time the
smallest thing you knew much about, you could look at it with
a microscope, was a cell. We had again, Dalton, and his
atoms, but not much was known about them in physics and basic
chemistry. It came as a pretty nice idea from Darwin that he
could seem to find the same cells occurring in all the things.
You could say he started with the simplest cells and built up
to the more complex cells. <u>Cells were the building blocks</u>.

    "We have to note that man loves the idea of a building block.
Man has a tremendous propensity for one thing. He wants the
key. He loves to talk about the building block or the key.

    "What the modern physicist has found, and what Oppenheimer was
giving us in his farewell address on TV (although it was not
his discovery) was the idea of fundamental complementarity.
We discover that we are dealing in a Universe of functions and
there is a plurality of unique patterns. They are not the
same patterns and fundamental complementarity means that you"

    - Cite Oregon Lecture #5, pp.168-169, 9 Jul'62

---

<u>No Breadth</u>:

    See Systematic Realization, 20 Dec'74

---

RBF DEFINITIONS

<u>No</u> Building Blocks:                                              (2)

    "cannot talk about the Universe in terms of any one of them.
There is no way you can talk about it in one. The oneness,
or key, or building-block idea, has been found completely
irrelevant by the physicists. It has no meaning at all."

    - Cite Oregon Lecture #5, p. 169, 9 Jul'62

---

RBF DEFINITIONS

<u>No Building Block</u>:

    "All monological explanations of Universe
Are inherently inadequate
And axiomatically fallacious.
There can be no <u>single key</u>
Nor <u>unit building block</u> of Universe."

    - Cite INTUITION, p.13, May '72

---

RBF DEFINITIONS

<u>No Building Blocks</u>:

    "... All present economic criteria ... generated generated
from the limited facets of generalization which seek 'keys'
or '<u>basic building parts</u>' from which to predict wholes is
fallacious and obsolete."

    - Citation and context at ▮▮▮▮ <u>Hierarchy of Patterns</u>, 1954
      to Ltr. to Jim Fitzgibbons, ▮▮▮▮

No Building Blocks: (1)

See Amoeba as Building Block
Darwin: Evolution May Be Going the Other Way
Key-keyhole Sequence
Monological

No Change: (2)

See Charts, 3 Oct'73
Now, 14 Feb'72
Truth as Progressive Diminution of Residual Error,
1 Feb'75

No Building Blocks: (2)

See A Priori Four-dimensional Reality, (2)
Cosmic Accounting, 20 Dec'73
Democritus, May'72
Dictionary, (1)
Education, 6 Mar'60
Four-dimensional Reality, 30 Apr'77
Hierarchy of Patterns, 1954*
Intertransformable, Jun'66
Mutual Survival Principles, (3)
Particle, 6 Jul'62
Quantum Sequence, (3)
Tetrahedron, 26 Apr'77
Twenty Questions, (1)(2)
You & I as Pattern Integrities, 22 Jan'75
Human Beings & Complex Universe, (2)(3)(6)

No Chaos:

See Integrity, 24 Jan'72

No Center of Gravity:

See Gravitational System Zone, 14 Jan'55

(Sec. 1030.20)

No Chemistry of Life:

See Life is Not Physical, (2)
Life, 5 Jun'75

No Change: (1)

See Changeless
Rest: At Rest

No Physical Entity Cold:

See Cold & Vacuum, 1946

RBF DEFINITIONS

No Conceptual Totality:

"Conceptual totality
Is inherently prohibited.
But exactitude can be bettered
And measurement refined
By progressively reducing
Residual errors,
Thereby disclosing
The directions of truths
Ever progressing
Toward the eternally exact
Utter perfection,
Complete understanding
Absolute wisdom,
Unattainable by humans
But affirming God
Omnipermeative,
Omniregenerative,
All incorruptible
As infinitely inclusive
Exquisite love."

- Cite LOVE, p.176 May '72
CONCEPTUALITY - SEC. 501.02

---

No Conceptual Totality:

See Structure, Nov'71

---

No Considerability:

See System, 26 Dec'74

---

RBF DEFINITIONS

No Continuums:

"There are no impervious surface continuums:"

- Cite SYNERGETICS text at Sec. 240.61; draft 1971

---

No Continuums:                                      (2)

See Discontinuity, Jun'66
    Event, 26 Jan'72
    Radiation:  Speed Of,(C)
    Frequency, Jun'71
    Subvisible Discontinuity, 19 Oct'72
    Experiential Mathematics, 15 Oct'76
    O Module, 29 Sep'76
    Fourth-dimensional Synergetics Mathematics, 14 Dec'76

---

No Country Doctor on Mars:

See Rationalization Sequence, (6)

---

Node:  Nodal:

See Topology:  Synergetic & Eulerian (1)

---

No Domain of a Face:

See Domain, 29 Jan'75; 11 Feb'73; 31 May'71; 11 Jul'62
    Domain of an Area, Dec'71

RBF DEFINITIONS

No End in Itself:

"... There are no 'absolutes'
-- No 'ends' in themselves-- no 'things'--
Only transitionally transformative verbing."

- Citation at Absolute, (p.52) Oct'66

---

No End in Itself:                                              (1)

    See Teleology

---

No End in Itself:                                              (2)

    See Pencil, 1938

---

RBF DEFINITIONS

No Energy Crisis:                                              (A)

"The Universe is nothing but energy. There is no energy
crisis at all. It's a crisis of ignorance, fear, wrong
thinking, an overblown bureaucracy, and conditioned reflexes.

"The poor President [Carter] has a cabinet without an
inventor on it.... to switch to coal is just deferring the
crisis to another time, leaving it to another generation.
You can't do it by politics. Carter is a politician. He is
at the tail of the dragon where things are really snapping....

"Money-makers say they don't know how to put a meter between
the people and the wind. This amount of energy is not being
employed because people don't make money off it....We continue
live on the cream and not on the milk. We go after high-grade
oil, making money on high-grade power, but what you're actually
doing is using up nature's own savings account. The Universe
has accumulated that energy over billions of years by impounding photosynthesized energy. With people making billions
of dollars it's difficult to stop that kind of thing....

"When the German oil wells were bombed, they got by on
alcohols, converting trees into fuel, and they also were the"

- Cite RBF to Susan Watters in W (Women's Wear Daily); 13 May'77

---

RBF DEFINITIONS

No Energy Crisis:                                              (B)

first to make synthetic rubber from alcohol.... But America
in World War II didn't have enough high-octane energy to
satisfy both our aviation and our synthetic rubber needs, so
the U.S. furtively made enormous amounts of synthetic rubber
from alcohol. Then, when Eisenhower came in, the oil companies
and the administration were careful not to let the public
realize they were ever able to do it.

"Nature doesn't have pollution. Pollution is valuable
chemicals in the wrong place....

"I don't get any gold medals from the oil companies, but I
do know David Rockefeller was impressed by the book [Medard
Gabel's 'Energy, Earth & Everyone']. He knows that it's so.
I've been asked to speak at a luncheon given by the chairman
of the board of Atlantic Richfield. They also know it's so.
They don't say 'I hate you' or anything like that. They just
don't know how to let go of a hot poker. It's not that
they're bad human beings, but some are hooked on a bad game....

"Settling the energy crisis on the basis of how to make
money may accelerate the coming of something we might not like--"

* Cite RBF to Susan Watters in W (Women's Wear Daily); 13 May'77

---

RBF DEFINITIONS

No Energy Crisis:                                              (C)

"socialism or communism....

"The whole thing started with Yankee ingenuity. The Yankee
inventor was well-thought-of. He gave people a service and
people admired him because of his product. Then the conglom-
erates came along and reduced that human pride. The power
of money was equated with progress. For the moment, we are
losing something tremendously valuable. If the energy crisis
isn't properly handled, it could bring on another political
system which promises to divide more equally an energy supply
which people have incorrectly been led to perceive as limited.
We could end up losing a very great battle."

- Cite RBF to Susan Watters in W (Women's Wear Daily); 13 May'77

---

RBF DEFINITIONS

No Energy Crisis:                                              (1)

"We are on a tiny little planet. Our nervous system still
sees the sun set, even though the sun doesn't set... we're
just rotating out of its sight. We talk about things being
'up' and 'down' even though there are no such directions.
We say the wind is blowing from the northwest when it is
really being sucked from the southeast.

"The depth of ocean is really only ▮▮▮▮▮ 18,000th of the
diameter of our Earth and yet we think of it as huge.

"They talk about the drought as if there had been no way to
prepare for it... but we've known how to desalinate since
the steamship. Instead of putting some pipes up through the
hills, which takes enormous amounts of energy, we should
have taken some of the billions we're going to lose now and
desalinate some of the vast Pacific Ocean.

"When we go to the bathroom we waste four gallons of water
to get rid of one pint of liquid. We should try dry toilets
that don't splash. There's no energy problem, its ignorance--
not recognizing that the solutions have always been available
until the crisis is upon us.

- Cite RBF to Karen Winner, Copley News Service; 9 Apr'77

---

RBF DEFINITIONS

No Energy Crisis:                                              (2)

"We have this philosophy that there's not enough to go
around, therefore we're obsessed with 'survival.'

"There's ample to go around, we just need to understand how
to use and dispose of it properly. People don't want to
listen--they just want to forge blindly ahead with their
drives and curiosities.

"This is a totally regenerative Universe. There is energy
all around us. Take windmills--one windmill would provide
the needed energy per household instead of diminishing coal,
natural gas, or oil ▮▮▮▮▮▮ resources. There is the
problem of converting wind from direct to alternating current.
So you take the wind and put it in the main public utility
lines where you can store it."

- Cite RBF inerview with Karen Winner, Copley News Service
    as clipped from Baton Rouge, LA "Advocate," ; 9 Apr'77

RBF DEFINITIONS

No Energy Crisis:

"There is no energy shortage. There is no energy crisis.
There is a crisis of ignorance."

- Cite RBF quoted in Medard Gabel's "Energy, Earth, and
  Everyone," front matter, Jan'75

---

RBF DEFINITIONS

No Energy Crisis:

"There is no energy problem. The physical Universe is
naught but energy. It is a matter of educating all humanity
regarding these matters, thus nullifying the fears which
paralyze human competence and adequately comprehensive
thinking and acting. The crisis is not an energy crisis.
It is a crisis of fearfully sustained self-deceit and lack
of faith in the cosmic integrity."

- Cite RBF Ltr. to James Coley, Sep'73

---

RBF DEFINITION

No Energy Crisis:

"There is not even a mild energy crisis because energy is
eternally regenerative.

"The so-called energy crisis is a myth. We will have a
curtailment of ███ activities due to our conditioned reflexes,
the way we expect energy to come through a pipe or out of a
barrel.

"But there is no energy crisis in our Universe. The Universe
is getting on great. It is eternally regenerative.

"Man is using only a tiny fraction of the energy available
through all sources, including wind power.

"We are simply in the crisis of conditioned reflexes, inertia,
fear, and ineptitude of how to cope.

"This is really fundamental to the alarm and intuition of the
younger world about the older world being preoccupied with
carrying on in a conditioned reflex way."

- Cite RBF quoted by Marian Bruce in Vancouver SUN, 14 Jun'73

---

No Exemption:

See Exempt: We are Not Exempt from Universe

---

RBF DEFINITIONS

No Favorites:

"I don't have favorite people, or favorite days. I like
███ the rain and the Sun both."

* Cite RBF to Kay Elliot, Washington Star, Jour et Nuit
  Restaurant, Wash., DC, 10 Sep'75

---

No Favorites:

See Humanity, 1 Feb'75

---

No Finality of Human Comprehension:                    (1)

See Heisenberg-Eliot-Pound Sequence
    Truth as Progressive Dimunution of Residual
    Error

---

No Finality of Human Comprehension:                    (2)

See Generalized Principle, 28 Feb'71

No Frequency:

See Frequencyless

---

RBF DEFINITIONS

No Generalized Boat:                                            (B)

"You can design
Only special case boats,
Ferries, or aircraft carriers,
Or canoes, or sloops,
Submarines or gondolas.
And within those general categories
You can only design special case boats
Each having its unique dimensions
And performance limitations,
And very special
Displacement characteristics."

- Cite GENERALIZED PRINCIPLES, p.4, 28 Jan '69

---

RBF DEFINITIONS

No Generalized Boat:

"There is no generalized boat.  There is no physically
realized generalization in our lifetime."

- Cite RBF at Penn Bell videotaping session, Philadelphia,
  22 Jan'75

---

No Generalized Boat:

See Invention Sequence, (I)(II)
    Ship, 1954
    Generalized Principles, 22 Jun'75
    Physical, 12 Nov'75

---

RBF DEFINITIONS

No Generalized Boat:

"While Archimedes discovered
The generalized principle
Governing displacement,
    .   .   .
We cannot design
A generalized boat.
It must be a specific canoe,
A ferryboat, or sloop--
And each of unique size and capability and durability
For all special-case embodiments
Are entropically fated
To disintegrate in time
Whether the experience episodes
Are passive or active--
I.e., involuntary or voluntary,
Subjective or objective--..."

- Cite INTUITION, p.21, May '72

---

RBF DEFINITIONS

No Geometry of Space:

"There is no geometry of space-- only of local aggregates
of principles, of special cases."

- Cite RBF to Brendan O'Regan, in re: Cleveland, 23 May'72
- Citation & context at Rubber Glove, 23 May'72

---

RBF DEFINITIONS

No Generalized Boat:                                            (A)

"You can abstract
From many experiences
With floating objects
The principle of displacement
As did Archimedes,
But you cannot design
A generalized displacement
Nor a generalized boat."

- Citation & Context at Generalized Principle (6), 28 Jan'69
- Cite GENERALIZED PRINCIPLES, p.4, 28 Jan'69

---

No Half-profile:

                              H
See Profile:  Tere is No Half-profile
                            ∧

No Innocence of Otherness:

See No Linear Acceleration, 20 May'75

Noise:                                          (1)

See No Noise

No Instant Cognition:

See Time & Cognition, 11 Sep'75

Noise:                                          (2)

See Pronouns: I = We = Us, (1)

No Insulation:  We Can't Really Insulate Anything:

See Trespassing, (1)

No Largest Case:

See Time, (p.102) Jun'66

RBF DEFINITIONS

Noise:

"Noise is only one of many important human behavior-conditioning mechanical factors known to exist, with the knowledge of that existence recorded and measured, which are as yet popularly unconsidered (beyond the area of the unscientifically phrased 'very annoying.')"

No Leaders:

See Enough to Go Around, (2)
     Fuller, R.B: On Drinking Liquor, 22 Jun'77

- Cite NINE CHAINS TO THE MOON, p.6, 1938

No License to Be of Service:

    See Rationalization Sequence, (4)

---

RBF DEFINITIONS

No Local Change:

"All parts of Universe act theoretically upon all other parts."

- Citation & context at Epigenetic Landscape, May'49

---

RBF DEFINITIONS

No Linear Acceleration:

"Linear acceleration never occurs because there is never innocence of otherness."

- Citation & context at Acceleration: Angular & Linear, 20 May'75

---

No Local Change:            (1)

    See Rest of Universe
        Intereffects
        Local Events
        Tennis Ball Hits the Big Earth
        Cosmic & Local
        Newton's First Law of Motion: RBF Restatement Of

---

RBF DEFINITIONS

No Local Change:

"All bodies of Universe are affecting the other bodies in varying degrees..."

- Citation & context at Gravity, Oct'66

---

No Local Change:            (2)

    See Allspace Filling: Octahedron & VE, 22 Jun'72
        Co-orbiting of Earth & Moon around Sun, Apr'71
        Epigenetic Landscape, May'49*
        Gravity, Oct'66*
        Platonic Solids, 12 Jul'62*
        Responsibility, 13 Nov'69
        Restraints, Dec'71
        Step, Nov'71; 22 Jul'71
        Tetrahedron: Coordinate Symmetry, 15 Oct'64
        Tidal, May'72
        Transformation, 12 Jul'62
        Universe as a Kaleidoscope, May'49

---

RBF DEFINITIONS

No Local Change:

"Nothing can change locally without changing everything else."

- Citation and context at Platonic Solids, 12 Jul'62

---

RBF DEFINITIONS

No Local Identifications:

"All of humanity will be enjoying not only all of Earth but a great deal of local Universe. 'Where do you live?' 'I live on the Moon,' or 'I live on Mothership Earth,' will be the kinds of answers."

- Cite RBF transcipt of "2000, If...," for Philadelphia journalist given to Stewart Brand for Co-Evolution Qtrly., San Francisco, 9 Jan'75

RBF DEFINITIONS

No Local Identifications:

"This is the new world coming up when local town, county, state, and national identifications are absurd other than as APO foci for communications between a world-around circulating and integrating humanity."

- Citation and context at World Corporations, 9 May'57

No Magic:

See Invisible Tetrahedron, (1)

No Local Identifications:                              (1)

See Address
    Backyard:  My Backyard is Getting Bigger
    Names:  "Named" Phenomena

No Maximum Limits:

See Minimum Limit Case, 9 Jun'75

No Local Identifications:                              (2)

See Building Business, (2)

No Measurement:

See System, 26 Dec'74

RBF DEFINITIONS

No Magic Universe:

"I try to keep an open mind about extrasensory perception and the things the parapsychology people are doing but it seems to me that these people are inclined to ride the gullibility of humanity. They seem to act as if there were two kinds of Universe: a magic Universe and a metaphysical Universe. And of course there is no magic Universe."

- Cite RBF to EJA, 3200 Idaho, Wash., DC, 8 Apr'75

RBF DEFINITIONS

No Mechanical Mind:

"We hear quite frequently of someone proposing the idea of a mechanical mind-- a mechanical mind that's going to do all the whole thinking for man. I will point out to you that this is completely impossible because the fact is that what the mind finds is not of the parts; it is not in the data that you can put in the machine. You cannot program in what is not of the parts. You can program in any of the parts, but you cannot program in a discovery of what's between and not. This is of the mind and mind alone; it will always be of the mind; always only of the mind. It will never be manifest by any calculating machines."

- Cite RBF at Students International Meditation Seminar, U. Mass., Amherst, 22 July '71, p. 11

No Mechanical Mind:               (1)

      See Feedback Comprehensivity:  Computers vs. Humans
          Artificial Intelligence
          Intelligence Machines

Non-aurally Tunable:

      See Rigidity, 9 Jul'62

No Mechanical Mind:               (2)

      See Teleology, (2)(3)
          Life is Not Physical, 12 Dec'75

Nonbeing:

      See Model of Nonbeing

Nonanthropomorphic God:

      See Intellectual Integrity, Aug'64
          Technology: Enchantment vs. Disenchantment, (2)

Nonbiologicals:

      See Biologicals vs. Nonbiologicals

Nonarea:

      See Area, 11 Feb'73

Noncircuit:

      See Circuit & Noncircuit

Noncoexisting:

See Universe, 26 May'72

Nonconceptuality: (1)

See Conceptuality & Nonconceptuality
Imaginary Universe
Inconceivability
Invisible ≠ Nonconceptual
Mathematical Symbols
Nonunitarily Conceptual
Out
Vacuum of Universe
Stark Nonconceptual Irrelevancy

Noncompressible:

See Water, 12 Nov'75

Nonconceptuality: Nonconceivable: (2)

See Halo Concept, 1960; 22 Feb'72; Nov'71
Invisible Hole, 16 Jun'72
Joyce, James, 1965
Key-keyhole Sequence (2)
Space, 17 Feb'73
Vacuum, 19 Feb'72*
Powering: Fourth & Fifth Dimensions, 18 Nov'72

RBF DEFINITIONS

Nonconceptuality:

"At the indispensable center of the sphere Universe turns
itself inside-out. The invisible, a priori, multiplicative
twoness, differentially disclosed in the synergetics'
topological systems' hierarchy, is manifest of the integrity
of the sizeless, timeless nonconceptuality always complementing
the conceptual system take-out from nonconceptual scenario
Universe's eternal self-regenerating."

- For full context see Vacuum, 19 Feb re-write. 19 Feb'72

Nonconformity:

See Child Sequence, (4)

RBF DEFINITIONS

Nonconceptuality:

". . . Humanity is frustrated by the fact that
scientific evolution . . . is almost entirely invisible
and its integrated significances are too difficult for
total and effective comprehension by society. One reason
for the latter frustration is that the language of
science has been up to now almost exclusively mathematical,
-- i.e., nonconceptual."

- Cite DOXIADIS (UorO), p. 304
20 Jun'66

Noncongruence:

See Mite: Positive & Negative Functions, (1)(2)

56

Nonconsiderable:

See Mystery, 24 Jan'76

Noncrossing: (2)

See Vertexes, Faces & Lines, 1 Jan'75

Noncontiguous: Noncontiguity:

See Critical Proximity, Jun'71

RBF DEFINITIONS

Nondefinable:

"The limits of an allspace-filling array are nondefinable. Nondefinable is not the same as infinite."

- Cite SYNERGETICS text at Sec.780.14, 22 Oct'72

Nonconvergence:

See Convergence & Nonconvergence

RBF DEFINITIONS

Nondefinable:

"Not being simultaneous
Universe cannot consist of one function.
Functions only coexist.
Universe while finite is not definable.
I can define many of its parts
But I cannot define
The nonsimultaneously occurring
Aggregate of experiences
Whose total set of relationships
Constitutes the whole Universe
The the latter as an aggregate of finites
is finite."

- Cite HOW LITTLE I KNOW, p.60, Oct'66

Noncrossing: (1)

See Opening

Nondefinable ≠ Infinite:

See Nondefinable, 22 Oct'72

Nondefinable: Undefinable: (1)

    See Definite: De-finite

---

RBF DEFINITIONS

Nondimensionality:

"Tension is shown experientially to be nondimensional, omnipresent, finitely accountable, continuous, comprehensive, ergo timeless, ergo eternal."

- Cite RBF SYNERGETICS draft 'Tension and Compression,' revision of Orgaon Lecture #5, pp. 157-158. 9 Jul'62
- Citation at Tension, 9 Jul'62

---

Nondefinable: Undefinable: (2)

    See Bias on One Side of the Line, 4 May'67
    De-finite, (pp.133-134) 1960

---

Nondimensional: (1)

    See Undimensional

---

Nondifferentiable: (1)

    See Differentiable and Nondifferentiable
    Undifferentiated

---

Nondimensional: (2)

    See Tension, 9 Jul'62*
    Points, 1 Apr'72*
    Point-to-able Something, 30 Apr'77

---

Nondifferentiable: (2)

    See Integral, 16 Feb'73
    Resolution, 19 Jun'71

---

RBF DEFINITIONS

Nondemonstrability:

"Points are inherently nondemonstrable."

- For citation and context see Points 19 Feb '72,
  as rewritten 1 Apr '72.

---

Nondefinable: Undefinable: (1)

Nondisciplining:

See Dream, 2 Jul'62

---

**NONEQUALS: CHECKLIST** (C)

See Conceptuality ≠ Thinkability
Compression ≠ Tension*
Cause ≠ Reason*
Conceptual ≠ Visible

* Indexed under other formulation

---

Nondivisive:

See Gravity, 11 Feb'76

---

Nonequals: ( ≠ ) : Checklist: (D)

See Differentiation ≠ Integration

---

None: Non: Noneness:

See Nothing: None

---

Nonequals: ( ≠ ) : Checklist: (E)

See Endless ≠ Infinite
Entropy ≠ Randomness

---

Non-empirically-discoverable:

See Vector Equilibrium as Starting Point, (1)

---

Nonequals: ( ≠ ) : Checklist: (F)

See Frequency ≠ One
Fourth Dimension ≠ Time*

Nonequals: ( ≠ ) : Checklist:                                         (G)

See Gravity ≠ Implosion
    Gravitational ≠ Radiational*
    Geometry: Space ≠ Unoccupied Geometry

* Indexed under other formulation

Nonequals: ( ≠ ) Checklist:                                           (M)

See Macro→micro ≠ Micro→macro
    Metabolic Flow ≠ Man
    Money-making ≠ Industrialization*
    Minimum ≠ Integer

* Indexed under other formulation

Nonequals: ( ≠ ) : Checklist:                                         (H)

See Holism ≠ Synergy

Nonequals: ( ≠ ) : Checklist:                                         (N)

See Negative ≠ Positive*
    Nonconceptual ≠ Invisible*
    Normal ≠ Permanence*
    Nondefinable ≠ Infinite
    Neighborliness ≠ Proximity*
    Negative ≠ Invisible*

* Indexed under other formulation

Nonequals: ( ≠ ) : Checklist:                                         (I)

See Interattraction ≠ Pressure
    Invisible ≠ Nonconceptual
    Inconceivable ≠ Infinite
    Inconceivable ≠ Invisible
    Implosion ≠ Gravity*
    Integration ≠ Differentiation
    Infinite ≠ Endless*
    Infinity ≠ Universally Extensive*
    Industrialization ≠ Money-making
    Infinite ≠ Nondefinable*
    Integer ≠ Minimum*
    Invisible ≠ Negative

* Indexed under other formulation

Nonequals: ( ≠ ) : Checklist:                                         (O)

See Organism ≠ Life
    One ≠ Frequency*
    Options ≠ Optimism

* Indexed under other formulation

Nonequals: ( ≠ ) : Checklist:                                         (L)

See Life ≠ Organism*
    Layer ≠ Surface*

Nonequals: ( ≠ ) : Checklist:                                         (P)

See Positive ≠ Negative
    Pressure ≠ Interattraction*
    Permanence ≠ Normal
    Proximity ≠ Neighborliness

* Indexed under other formulation

* Indexed under other formulation

Nonequals: ( ≠ ) : Checklist:                                    (R)

      See Reason ≠ Cause
         Radiational ≠ Gravitational
         Randomness ≠ Entropy*
         Restraints ≠ Vectors*

* Indexed under other formulation

---

Nonequals: ( ≠ ) : Checklist:                                    (V)

      See Visible ≠ Conceptual*
         Vectors ≠ Restraints

* Indexed under other formulation

---

Nonequals: ( ≠ ) : Checklist:                                    (S)

      See Surface ≠ Layer
         System ≠ World*
         Space ≠ Unoccupied Geometry
         Synergy ≠ Holism*

* Indexed under other formulation

---

Nonequals: ( ≠ ) : Checklist:                                    (W)

      See World ≠ System
         World ≠ Universe

---

Nonequals: ( ≠ ) : Checklist:                                    (T)

      See Tension ≠ Compression
         Time ≠ Fourth Dimension
         Thinkability ≠ Conceptuality*

* Indexed under other formulation

---

Nonequals: ( ≠ ) : Checklist:                                    (2)

      See Complementarities: Always & Only Coexisting
         Equals: Checklist
         Paired Concepts: Checklist
         Versus: Checklist

---

Nonequals: ( ≠ ) : Checklist:                                    (U)

      See Universally Extensive ≠ Infinity
         Unfamiliarity ≠ Unnatural
         Universe ≠ World*

* Indexed under other formulation

---

Nonequals: Nonequality:

      See Teleology: Bow-tie Symbol

Nonevent:

    See Novent

---

Nonexistent:                                          (2)

    See Systematic Realization, 20 Dec'74
        Zerophase, (1)

---

Nonexperience:  Nonexperienceability:          (1)

    See Experienceable & Nonexperienceable
        Novent

---

Nonform:

    See Formless
        Liquid = Nonform

---

Nonexperience:  Nonexperienceable:         (2)

    See Absurd, Jun'66
        Systematic Realization, 20 Dec'74

---

Nonhappening:

    See Vector Equilibrium, 11 Dec'75

---

Nonexistent:                                          (1)

    See Unremembered = Nonexistent

---

Nonidentically Repetitive:

    See Heisenberg-Eliot-Pound Sequence, 28 Jan'69
        Irreversible, 6 Nov'73
        Irreversibility, 22 Apr'68
        Kaleidoscopes, ▬▬▬▬ Dec'69
        Scenario Universe, May'72; Dec'69

Nonidentical:

See Phantom Captain, 1938
Universe, Spring'71; (p.62) 1969

RBF DEFINITIONS

Noninterfering Zero Points:

"Thus we discover the modus operandi by which radio waves and other waves pass uninterferingly through seeming solids, which are themselves only wave complexes. The lack of interference is explained by the crossing of the high-frequency waves through the much lower frequency waves at the noninterfering zero points, or indeed by the vari-frequenced waves through both one another's internal or external zero intervals."

[15]

- Cite SYNERGETICS draft at Sec. 1223.16, 9 Mar'73

---

Nonintercontradictory:                                    (1)

See Interaccommodation: Interaccommodative

Noninterference: Noninterfering:                          (1)

See Uninterferable
   Interference-noninterference Relaying
   Interference & Noninterference
   Frequencyless

---

Nonintercontradictory:                                    (2)

See Motion, 27 May'72
Truth, 30 Jun'75

Noninterference: Noninterfering:                          (2)

See Carrier Wave, 9 Mar'73
Resonance Field, 13 May'73

---

Noninterference Relaying:

See Valvability, 30 Nov'72

Nonintersecting Lines:

See Individual: Theory Of, May'65

Nonintersubstitutability:

See General Systems Theory, ■ (A)

Nonline:

See Line & Nonline

RBF DEFINITIONS

Nonlimit:

"... In synergetics the energy as Mass is constant and nonlimit frequency is variable."

- Citation and context at Einstein, 16 Nov'72

Nonlocal:                                                          (1)

See Cosmic

RBF DEFINITIONS

Nonlimit:                                                          (1)

See Limit-Limitless
    Unlimited

Nonlocal:                                                          (2)

See Invisible Hole, 16 Jun'72

Nonlimit:                                                          (2)

See Hydraulics, 20 Apr'72

Nonmeaning:

See Meaningless

Nonmerchandisable:

See Abstractions, 1964

---

RBF DEFINITIONS

Non-mirror Image:

"The complementary of parity is disparity and not a reflective image."

- ~~Cite RBF rewrite of SYNERGETICS galley at Sec. 507.06, 7 Nov'73~~
- Citation at Disparity, 7 Nov'73

---

Nonmeshing:

See Meshing & Nonmeshing
Unsynchronized

---

RBF DEFINITIONS

Non-Mirror Image:

"'Non-mirror image,' i.e., dissimilar complementarity, is the conservation-producing principle."

- Citation and context at Ecology Sequence (A), 22 May'73

---

RBF DEFINITIONS

Nonmirror Image:

"Concave is not a mirror image of convex. Ruth Asawa makes them and they don't look like you at all-- it's all the rest of the Universe and that doesn't have a shape, ever. What you see in the mirror is strictly a planar pattern-- a reverse series in a plane."

- Cite RBF to EJA, 200 Locust, Phila, PA, 13 Jun'74

---

RBF DEFINITIONS

Non-mirror Image:

"Mite's can fill allspace. They are either positive or negative affording a beautiful confirmation of negative Universe.... They are true rights and lefts and are not mirror images; they are inside-out and asymmetrical."

- Citation & context at Mite: Positive & Negative Functions (1) 27 May'72

---

R BF DEFINITIONS

Non-mirror Image:

"Order is obviously the complementary, but not mirror image, of disorder."

- Citation & Context at Syntropy & Entropy, 5 May'74

---

RBF DEFINITIONS

Non-mirror Image:

"The antientropic metaphysical is not a mirror-imaged reversal of the entropic physical world's disorderly expansiveness."

- Citation & context at Irreversibility: Principle Of, Apr'71

RBF DEFINITIONS

### Non-mirror Image:

"Negative is never the mirror image of the positive."

- Citation & context at Complementarity, Spring'66

### Nonmoment: (1)

See Zero Moment

### Nonmirror Image: (1)

See Complementarity:  Principle Of
   Disparity
   Irreversibility:  Principle Of
   Left & Right
   Mirror Image
   Nonreflective Complementarity
   Rubber Glove
   Tetrahedron:  Inside-outing Of

### Nonmoment: (2)

See Vector Equilibrium as Starting Point, 8 Apr'75
   Model of Nonbeing, 11 Sep'75

### Nonmirror Image: (2A)

See Complementarity, 2 Mar'68; spring'66*; 1971
   Complementarity:  Principle Of, Mar'71
   Complementary, May'72
   Coupler, (2)
   Disparity, 7 Nov'73*
   Ecology Sequence, (A); 22 May'73*
   In & Out, 13 Nov'69
   Irreversibility:  Principle Of, Apr'71*
   Multiplicative Twoness, 14 Feb'66
   Mite:  Positive & Negative Functions, (1)*
   Now, May'72
   Negative, spring '66
   Negative Vector Equilibrium, 8 Oct'71
   Order & Disorder, 5 May'71
   Proton & Neutron, 13 Nov'69; (1)
   Relative Asymmetry Sequence, (1)
   Scenario, May'72
   Sphere, 2 Mar'68
   Human Beings & Complex Universe, (2)

### Nonnuclear: (1)

See  Dodecahedron   (all frequencies)
   Icosahedron    (all frequencies)
   Octahedron     (odd-numbered frequencies)
   Tetrahedron    (odd-numbered frequencies)
   Cube           (odd-numbered frequencies)
   Nuclear & Nonnuclear
   Nuclear & Nonnuclear Polyhedra
   Prime Volumes
   Prime Structural Systems
   Domains of Tetra, Octa & Icosa
   Denucleated Phase
   Tetrahedron as Prime Nonnucleated Structural
     System
   Subnuclear

### Nonmirror Image: (2B)

See Syntropy & Entropy, 5 May'74*
   Zero, 13 Nov'69
   Complementarity of Growth & Aging, 22 Jan'75
   Geometrical Function of Nine, (2)
   Cube & VE as Wave Propagation Model, 23 Feb'72

### Nonnuclear: (2)

See Omnitopology, 17 Feb'73
   Prime Structural Systems (1)
   Carbon, 8 Jun'72
   Nucleus vs. Boundaries, 28 Jan'75
   Domain & Quantum, (1)
   Powering:  Fifth & Eighth Powering, 11 Dec'75
   Cube:  Volume-3 Cube, 16 Dec'73
   Powering:  Fifth & Eighth Powering, 11 Dec'75;
     25 Jan'76
   Basic Nestable Configurations:  Hierarchy Of,
     29 May'72

Nonobvious:

      See Obvious & Nonobvious

---

Nonparallel:             (1)

      See Antiparallel
         Tetrahedron:, Four Unique Planes

---

RBF DEFINITIONS

▋   No Noise:

"There is no true 'noise' or 'static.' There are only
as yet undifferentiated and uncomprehended orders."

▬▬▬▬▬▬▬▬▬▬▬▬▬

- ~~Cite Synergetics draft, "Symmetry," Sec533.04, July 1971.~~

- ~~Cite NASA Speech, p.90, Jun'66~~

- Citation & context at Chaos, Jun'66

---

Nonparallel:             (2) ▬

      See Fourth Dimension, 14 Sep'71
         Sphere, 22 Jul'71
         Three: Number Function of Three in a Four-axial
            System, 24 Jan'76

---

No Noise:

      See Order, 7 Nov'73

---

Nonperpendicular:

      See Three: Number Function of Three in a Four-axial
         System, 24 Jan'76

---

RBF DEFINITIONS

No Nouns:

    "Physics having found no things,
    There are no nouns."

- Cite A DEFINITION OF EVOLUTION, 15 Sep'71

---

RBF DEFINITIONS

Nonpolarized:

"All systems have poles, ergo spin axes, ergo they are
polarizably identifiable. Nonpolarized simply means that
the spin axis is unrecognized under the conditions considered.
There is no such thing as a nonpolarized point because if
you tuned-in the subvisible system--appearing only as a
directionally-positioned micro-something--to visible comprehension, you would find that, as a system, it has poles and
that it has seven potential alternately employable poles.

"So we may call a point a focal center, i.e., a 'noise' with
a direction, but it is an as-yet undistinguished system, with
all the latter's characteristics.

"There is inherent polarity in all observation which always
introduces an additive twoness:

      Nonpolarized = unrecognized

      Focal event = infratunable system"

- Cite SYNERGETICS, 2nd. Ed. at Secs. 527.25 & .26; RBF rewrite
    11 Dec'75

RBF DEFINITIONS

Nonpolarized:

"All systems are polarized. Nonpolarized simply means
unrecognized. There is no such thing as a nonpolarized
point because if you tuned it in you would find that it had
■ poles. So we may call it a focal center, i.e., a noise
with a direction but with nondistinguished system characteristics.

"There is inherent polarity in all observation: that is the
additive twoness.

"Nonpolarized = unrecognized."
"Focal event = Infratunable system."

- Cite RBF to EJA, 3200 Idaho, Wash. DC; 12 Nov'75

Nonpolarized = Unrecognized:

See Nonpolarized, 12 Nov'75

---

RBF DEFINITIONS

■■■■ Nonpolar Points:

"Nonpolar points, or localities, are four-dimensional-- there
is the inside-out (i.e., concave and convex) dimension and
three symmetrically interacting, great-circle-ways-around--
producing spherical octation, with eight tetrahedra having
three internal (central) angles and three external spherical
surface triangles' angles, each.

- Cite RBF rewrite of SYNERGETICS galley at Sec. 527.22,
  7 Nov'73

Nonpolar Points: Nonpolar Vertexes:

See Constant Relative Abundance, 29 Nov'72; 26 Sep'73
Fourth Dimension, 29 Nov'72
Magic Numbers, 1967
Twelve Universal Degrees of Freedom, Feb'72; 7 Nov'73
In, Out & Around Experiences, (1)

---

RBF DEFINITIONS

■■■■ Nonpolar Points:

"Nonpolar points, or localities, are four-dimensional:
inside-out and three symmetrically interacting great-circle-
ways-around; producing spherical octation with eight tetrahedra
having three internal (central) angles and three external
(spherical surface) angles each."

- Citation at Fourth Dimension, 29 Nov'72
- ~~Cite SYNERGETICS draft at Sec.527.22, 29 Nov'72~~

Nonpolar: Nonpolarized:                          (1)

See Focal Event

---

RBF DEFINITIONS

■■■■ Nonpolar Points:

"The nonpolar point is not fixable or structurally
stabilized until it is three-way great circled."

- Cite SYNERGETICS draft at Sec. 527.24, 29 Nov'72

Nonpolar: Nonpolarized:                          (2)

See Convergence & Divergence, 9 Apr'75

Nonpolitical:

See Surprise: The Nonpolitical Surprise Has Already
Occurred

RBF DEFINITIONS

Nonproduction:

"The kind of strategies that have been calling for paying
for nonproduction have been done in the terms of man's
assuming there's nowhere nearly enough to go around anyway,
and it has to be you or me, and those who are looking out for
me then find that their particular price advantage is greatly
enhanced by the nonproduction. These are always very egocentric viewpoints that bring about that kind of strategy."

- Cite RBF to World Game at NY Studio School, 12 Jun        '69,
  Satrun Film transcript, Sound 2, Part 3, pp.80-81.

Nonponderable:                                              (1)

See Weightless

Nonradial Line:

See Cube Edge
    Radial Line
    Starting with Parts: The Nonradial Line

Nonponderable:                                              (2)

See Finite, 14 Feb'66

Nonreality:

See Status Quo, 15 Sep'71
    Vector Equilibrium: Zero Condition, 11 Jul'62

Nonpredictable:

See Unpredictable: Unpredicted

Nonredundance: Nonredundant:                                (1)

See Stable = Nonredundant

Nonredundance: Nonredundant: (2)

See Cork: Triangular Corks in Spherical Barrels,
   15 Feb'66
   Description, 25 Aug'71
   Differentiation, 27 May'72; 22 Jun'72
   Geodesics & Tensegrities, 9 Sep'74
   Geometry of Vectors, 15 Jun'74
   Insinuatability, 6 Nov'72
   Probability, (1)
   Spherical Barrel, 15 Feb'66
   Spin Twoness & Duality Twoness, 27 Dec'74
   Prime Nuclear Structural Systems, 27 Dec'74
   Stable & Unstable Structures, 7 Jun'72
   Cube & VE as Wave Propagation Model, 23 Feb'72
   Universal Vertex Center Model, 29 Apr'43

Nonrelationship: (2)

See In & Out, 7 Nov'72

Nonreflective Complementarity: (1)

See Non-mirror Image

Nonrepresentational:

See James Joyce, 1965

Nonreflective Complementarity: (2)

See Boltzmann Sequence, (5)

Non-self-interfering:

See Radiation, 1959
   Spiral, 7 Nov'73

Nonrelationship: (1)

See Arelational

Nonselfregenerative: (1)

See Negative Universe
   Superatomics
   Transuranium Elements
   Isotope

Nonselfregenerative:                                        (2)

       See Geometrical Function of Nine, (7)
           Nuclear Domain & Elementality, (1)(2)

---

Nonsensoriality:                                            (2)

       See Ephemeralization, 1938
           Geometry of Reality, May'49
           Pattern Generalization (2)
           Gravitational Continuum, Nov'71

---

Non-self-requested:

     See Birth:  Non-self requested

---

Nonsense:

       See History, 27 Dec'73

---

Nonself:

       See Self & Nonself

---

RBF DEFINITIONS

    Nonsimultaneity:

    "Any point can tune in any other point in Universe.  Between
any two pints in Universe there is a tetrahedral connection.
Thus systematic connection of two points results in the
interconnecting of four points.  But none of the four event
points of the tetrahedron are simultaneous.  They are all
overlappingly co-occurrent, each with diffrent beginnings and
endings.  All of the atoms are independently introduced and
terminaled; many are in gear, but many are also way out of
gear."

     - Cite SYNERGETICS, 2nd. Ed., Sec. 530.11, 30 May'75

---

Nonsensoriality:                                            (1)

     See Cipher
         Extrasensoriality
         Invisibility
         Invisible Reality
         Mathematical Symbols
         Infratunable
         Tunability:  Infra & Ultra

---

RBF DEFINITIONS

    Nonsimultaneity:

    "Because of our overspecialization and our narrow electromagnet-
ic spectrum range of our vision, we have very limited integrated
comprehension of the significance of total information.  For
this reason, we see and comprehend very few motions among the
vast inventory of unique motions and transformation developments
of Universe.  Universe is a nonsimultaneous complex of unique
motions and transformations.  Of course, we do not 'see' and
our eyes cannot 'stop' the 186,000-miles-per-second kind of
motion.  We do not see the atomic motion.  We do not even see
the stars in motion, though they move at speeds of over a
million miles per day.  We do not see the tree's or child's
moment-to-moment growth.  We do not even see the hands of
a clock in motion.  We remember where the hands of a clock
were when we last looked and thus we accredit that motion has
occurred.  In fact, experiment shows that we see and comprehend very little of the totality of motions."

     - Cite SYNERGETICS text at Sec. 537.32; galley rewrite 7 Nov'73

RBF DEFINITIONS

## Nonsimultaneity:

"Thought discovers that we divide Universe into an 'outwardness and inwardness,' so thinking is the first subdivision of
Universe, because Universe, we discovered, was finite.
Thinking is a nonsimultaneously recallable aggregate of
inherently finite experiences and finite experience furniture--
such as photons of light. One of the most important observations about our thought is the discovery that experiences are
nonsimultaneous. Nonsimultaneity is a fundamental characteristic, and if experiences are nonsimultaneous, you cannot
have simultaneous reconsideration."

- Cite SYNERGETICS text at Sec. 530.01; RBF galley rerwite 7 Nov'8
73

---

RBF DEFINITIONS

## Nonsimultaneous:

"Different shapes, ergo different abstractions, are
nonsimultaneous; but all shapes are de-finite components of
integral though nonsimultaneous, ergo shapess, Universe."

- Cite SYNERGETICS, "Corolllaries," Sec. 240.60. 1971

- Citation & context at Abstraction, 1971

---

RBF DEFINITIONS

## Nonsimultaneous:

"Until the present age, people thought that all of their
faculties were simultaneously and instantly coordinate and
operating at equal velocities. Einstein showed that neither
'simultaneous' nor 'instant' are valid, i.e., experimentally
demonstrable. Observe that when we send up four rockets
one-half second apart, their afterimages are approximately
simultaneous. So we say that we see four rocket bursts 'at
the same time.' The illusion of simultaneity is one of the
most important illusions for us to consider. Musicians may be
able to comprehend nonsimultaneity better than others do.
Einstein emphasized the importance of attempted spontaneous
comprehension of the nonsimultaneity of all events of Universe--
a concept akin to our discovery that in our Universe, none
of the lines can ever go simultaneously through the same
points (See Sec. 517.). What Einstein is telling us is that
there is no conceptual validity to the notion that everything
in Universe is actually in simultaneous static array."

- Cite SYNERGETICS text at Sec. 510.09, May'71

---

RBF DEFINITIONS

## Non-Simultaneous:

We "do not have to be simultaneous to be inter-

connected. We can telephone across the international

date line from Sunday back to Saturday."

- Cite NASA Speech, p. 92, Jun'66

NONSIMULTANEITY - SEC 530.04

---

RBF DEFINITIONS

## Nonsimultaneous:

"Minimal consciousness evokes a nonsimultaneous

sequence, ergo time."

- Citation at Time, 7 Feb'71
- Cite SYNERGETICS, Sec. 529.06 (Dec. '71).
- Cite RBF to EdA, Sarasota, Florida, 7 Feb. '71.

---

RBF DEFINITIONS

## Non-simultaneous:                                    (1)

"Engineering holds that the prime difference
between the point of view of laymen and engineers is that
the layman does not recognize, anticipate, and pay
heed, as do engineers, to the experimentally demonstrable
fact that every action always has an equal and opposite
reaction. But the engineers have not modernized their
concept to accommodate and adjust refiningly to two of
the scientists' recent          physical discoveries
and measurements:-- first, of light's speed, as well as
the speed of all electromagnetically propagated
radiation, and secondly, the phenomenon known as
precession. The approximately one billion kilometers-
per-hour, speed of all radiation being too fast for
human sense apprehendability, the engineers have not yet
been constrained to recognize as must the physicist,
that there is no instant universe as was mis-assumed
by all pre-Twentieth Century scientific cosmologies and
cosmogonies-- before the knowledge that light had indeed
a speed.. Engineering must now acknowledge realistically
and accommodate analytically, the experimentally"

- Citation at Engineering, 13 Nov'69

---

RBF DEFINITIONS

## Non-simultaneous:

"Non-simultaneous means not occuring at the same time."

- Cite RBF marginalis
  Beverly Hotel ,N.Y.
  28 February 1971

- Cite also SYNERGETICS, "Universe," Sec. 302. Oct. 1971.

---

RBF DEFINITIONS

## Nonsimultaneous:                                    (2)

"demonstrable fact that every action has not only a reaction
but also a nonsimultaneous but immediately subsequent resultant."

- Citation at Engineering, 13 Nov'69

RBF DEFINITIONS

Non-simultaneity:

"The majority of academic people are still thinking
in terms of Newtonian (classical) science's 'instant
universe.' While light's speed of 700 million miles an
hour is <u>very fast</u> in relation to automobiles it is <u>very
slow</u> in relation to the 'no time at all' of society's
(obsolete) instant universe thinking.

"It was part of the classical scientists' concept of
instant universe that universe is a system in which all
parts affect one another simultaneously, in varying degrees."

- Citation at <u>Time</u>, Jun'66

—Cite NASA Speech, pp. 25,26, Jun'66

(CONCEPTUALITY- TIME)

RBF DEFINITIONS

Non-Simultaneous:

"It takes entirely different lengths of time to
remember of 'look up' different names or past event facts.
Universe, like the dictionary, though integral is ipso
facto nonsimultaneously recollectable and, therefore, as
with the set of all the words of the dictionary, is
nonsimultaneously considerable and therefore is also nonsimultaneously reviewable, ergo is synergetically incomprehen-
sible, yet progressively revealing."

- Citation & Context at Dictionary, 1960

- Cite OMNIDIRECTIONAL HALO, p. 132, 1960

(UNIVERSE)

RBF DEFINITIONS

Non-simultaneous:

"Before the speed of light was measured, sight
seemed, to all humanity, to be instantaneous. Newton's
universe was instantaneous. . . Neither light nor any
other phenomenon is instantaneous."

- Cite NASA Speech, p. 52, Jun'66

[SYNERGETICS - ENERGY EVENT]

RBF DEFINITIONS

Non-simultaneous:

"Neither the set of all experiences nor the set of
all the words which describe them nor the set of all the
generalized conceptual principles harvested from the
total of experiences are either instantly or <u>simultaneously</u>
reviewable."

(Hyphens deleted.)

- Cite OMNIDIRECTIONAL HALO, pp. 131,132, 1960

CONSIDERABLE SET - SEC. 569.05)

RBF DEFINITIONS

Non-simultaneous:

"The speed of light measurements plus Planck's
quantum mechanics and Einstein's relativity showed that
the universe is an aggregate of <u>non-simultaneous</u> events
and their experiments showed that as each of the non-simultaneous events lost their energy they lost it to newly
occuring events. Thus energy always became 100 percent
accounted for."

- Cite NASA Speech, p. 26, Jun'66

[NONSIMULTANEITY - SEC. 530.06]

RBF DEFINITIONS

Non-simultaneous:

"As Einstein clearly demonstrated, 
the data coming in from all the scientists makes it clear
that the whole Universe is in continual transformation.
The geology of our Spaceship Earth makes it very clear
how severe have been the great transformations of history.
The moment of top soils and burdens around the surface
of the Earth is very new geologically speaking. As Einstein
interpreted the speed of light information and the observation
of the brownian movement of the constant motion in water,
etc., he then posited a Universe in which we now knew that
light took eight minutes to get to us from the Sun and
two-and-a-half years to get to us from the nearest star,
and astronomical information which shows that some of the
stars we are looking at having been there for a million
years--- with that kind of information Einstein had to
say physical Universe is quite obviously an aggregate of
<u>non-simultaneous</u> and only partially overlapping trans-
formation events."

have live shows coming in from 100 years ago, others from 1,000
years ago, and some of the stars we are looking at

- Cite "The Artists and the Scientists", p.1
Undated

NONSIMULTANEITY - SEC. 530.07]

RBF DEFINITIONS

Nonsimultaneous:

"We discovered that experiences were nonsimultaneous and
therefore we had a finite but nonsimultaneous universe.
Therefore, being nonsimultaneous it was nonsimultaneously
conceptual. It was not a unit picture that could be
given to us. We have had a tendency in our general
thinking to say that which is finite is that which is
statically conceptual as one unit glimpse so we have been
seemingly, frustrated in trying to understand a universe
which was more or less infinite and yet it was an
omnidirectional experience and you felt there ought to be
an outwardness of this sphere. That is a static concept and
we begin to discover that we are not dealing with such a
sphere because we have all these nonsimultaneous reports
and all we have is interconnectedness of the nonsimultaneity.
One of Einstein's most intellectual discoveries was this
nonsimultaneity which he said apparently he could have
come upon by virtue of his experience in examining the
thoughts and patent claims regarding time-keeping devices,
watches and clocks."

- Cite OREGON Lecture #3 - pp. 76-77, 5 Jul'62

NONSIMULTANEITY - SEC. 530.65]

Nonsimultaneous Set:

See Comprehensive, 9 Jul'62

Nonsimultaneity:  Nonsimultaneous:                    (1)

    See Children's Pictures of the Sun and the Moon
        Four Nonsimultaneous Rocket Bursts
        Instantaneity
        Juggler
        Lag
        Overlapping
        Partially Overlapping
        Perception
        Scenario
        Scenario Principle
        Time
        Instant Universe vs. All-motion Universe
        Recall Lags
        Nonunitarily Conceptual
        Star Events
        Live Shows Reaching Us Took Place Billions of
            Years Ago
        Big Dipper

---

RBF DEFINITIONS

Nonstate:

"The vector equilibrium is such a physically abhorred nonstate
as to be the eternal self-starter, ergo the eternal re-self-
starter ever regenerating the off-zero perturbations, oscillations, and all the wave propagation of all humanly experienceable physical and metaphysical phenomena."

- Citation & context at Vector Equilibrium as  Starting Point, (2)
    11 Sep'75

---

Nonsimultaneity:  Nonsimultaneous:                    (2)

    See Abstraction, 1971*
        All-motion Universe, 1965
        Complementary, May'72
        Congruence, 25 Jan'72
        Consideration, 1965
        De-finite, 1960
        Dictionary, Oct'66; Jun'66*
        Engineering, 13 Nov'69*
        Interaccommodative, 13 Mar'73
        Relationships, 5 Jul'62
        Resultant, 22 Jul'71
        Time, 7 Feb'71*; Jun'66* ; Dec'71
        Vector Equilibrium, 1971
        Now, May'72
        Physical is Always the Imperfect, 26 May'72
        Synergetic Integral, 1960
        Individual Universes, (2)
        Parity, Nov'71
        Conceptuality, 6 Nov'73
        Tetratuning, 30 May'75
        Structure, 1965

---

Nonstraight:

    See Deliberately Nonstraight Lines
        Wavilinear

---

Nonsolid:

    See Vectors & Tensors, 19 Oct'72

---

Nonstructural Coincidence:

    See Tensegrity:  Vertexial Connections:  Locked Kiss,
        10 Oct'63

---

Nonstable:

    See Instability
        Stability:  Stable & Nonstable Systems
        Unstable

---

Nonsynchronous:  Nonsynchronization:                    (1)

    See Dissynchronous
        Nonmeshing

Nonsynchronization:   Nonsynchronous:                    (2)


See Universe, 26 May'72

---

Non-Thinking:

"Design logic requires . . . a bit of the eternal design
capability . . . operating through human organisms . . .
to offset the gamut of non-thinking conditioned reflexes
of all biological systems."

- Cite Museums Keynote Address Denver, pp. 13-14. 2 Jun'71
- Citation at Eternal Designing Capability, 2 Jun'71

---

Nonsystem Parts:


See Synergetic vs. Model (D)

---

Nonthinking:                                           (1)


See Antithinking
    Ignorance ▮▮▮▮▮▮
    Reflexes
    Expensive = Nonthinking

---

Nonsystem:


See Systems & Nonsystems
    Subsystem ≠ Nonsystem

---

Nonthinking:                                           (2)


See Eternal Designing Capability, 2 Jun'71*
    Order & Disorder, Jun'66
    Reflexes, 2 Jun'71
    Thinkable You, (1)
    Mistake, 7 Nov'75
    Crowd-reflexing, 7 Nov'75

---

Nonthing:

"As specialists scientists seek only for somethings....
Specializing science seeking only somethings inherently
overlooked the nonthing vector equilibrium."

- Citation & context at Vector Equilibrium as Starting Point, (1)
  11 Sep'75

---

Nontransformable:

"The absolute would be nontransformable... experimentally
meaningless."

- Citation and context at Absolute, Oct'66

Nontransmitting:

See Information Transmitting & Nontransmitting Model

RBF DEFINITIONS

Nonunitarily Conceptual:

"Aggregate means sumtotally but nonunitarily conceptual as of any one moment."

- Citation at Aggregate, 28 Feb'71

501.67

---

Nontuned:

See Space as Nontuned Angle & Frequency Information
Untunable: Untuned
Space = Nontunability

Nonunitarily Conceptual:     (1)

See Finite Event Scenario
Nonsimultaneity
Overlapping
Unitary Conceptuality
Scenario Universe

---

Nontruth:

Truth & Nontruth

Nonunitarily Conceptual:     (2)

See Aggregate, 28 Feb'71*
Conceptualize, 17 Feb'73
Definable, 1960
Earth, 1965
Spherical Triangle Sequence (iii)*
Universe, 1965; (p.134)1960; 2 Jun'74
Tunability: Intra & Ultra, 1954
Two Kinds of Twoness, (B)
Conceptual Systems, 27 May'75
Structural Sequence, (B)
Finite Event Scenario, (2)

---

RBF DEFINITIONS

Nonunitarily Conceptual:

"...Invisible or nonunitarily conceptual minimum inventorying..."

- Citation and cotext at Spherical Triangle Sequence (iii),
26 Jan'73

Nonuse:

See Use vs. Nonuse

Nonverbal: (1)

See Nameless
    Wordless
    Gestured Communication
    Gross Communication
    Mute Communication
    Unspoken Communication
    Unarticulated

---

RBF DEFINITIONS

No Open Endings:

"There are no open endings in Universe."

- Citation and context at Acceleration, 14 Feb'73

---

Nonverbal: (2)

See Self-communicate, 8 Apr'75

---

RBF DEFINITIONS

No Opposites:

"The 'opposite' of the engineers' equal-and-opposite action and reaction is strictly linear and planar. But macro is not opposite to micro: these are opposed, inward-and-outward, explosive-contractive, intertransformative accommodations, such as that displayed by the eight-triangular-cammed, perimeter-tangent, contact-driven, involuting-evoluting, rubber doughnut jitterbug.

"Macro and micro are not opposed: they are the poles of inward-outward considerations of experience."

(Sec. 465.02; 2nd. Ed.)

- Cite RBF to EJA, 3200 Idaho Ave., Wash. DC; 12 Nov'75

---

Nonvertex:

See Vertexes & Nonvertexes

---

No Organization:

See Impossible: Only the Impossible Happens, (A)

---

RBF DEFINITIONS

No One:

"Unity does not mean the number one... One does not and cannot exist by itself."

- Citation & context at Subjective & Objective, 16 May'75

---

No Otherness; No awareness:

See Geometry of Thinking, 16 Dec'73
    Thirty Minimum Aspects of a System, (B)
    Somethingness & Otherness, 7 Oct'75
    Human Beings & Complex Universe, (3)

No Other:  No Me:

See Other, 5 Jun'73

No Politics:

See Apolitical

No Planes:

See Spiralinearity, Nov'71
Six Motion Freedoms & Degrees of Freedom, (1)

No Promotion:

See Promote:  I Don't Promote

RBF DEFINITIONS

No-point:

"All the no-points are always embracing all the points."

- Citation and context at Integrity of Universe, 23 Sep'73

TEXT CITATION

No Race:  No Class:

World Game Document #1: pp. 157-164, 1971

No-point:

See Integrity of Universe, 23 Sep'73*
Novent, 23 Sep'73
Omniembracing, 23 Sep'73
Tetrahedron, 23 Sep'73

RBF DEFINITION

No Right Angles in Nature:

"There are no right angles in nature.  Look at all those
trees.  Look at the angles of all those branches.  Just let
me know if you ever see branches coming out at 90 degrees."

* Cite RBF to JZA on porch deck, 3200 Idaho, Wash, DC., 1972

No Right Angles in Nature:

      See No Straight Lines

---

RBF DEFINITIONS

Normal:

The average of all plus (+) and minus (-) weights of
universe is Zero weight.  The normal is eternal."

- Cite SYNERGETICS Draft - "Conceptuality: Life" - RBF
      marginalia, Somerset Club, Boston, 25 April 1971

---

RBF DEFINITIONS

Normal:

"Ninety-nine point nine-nine percent of the bodies in motion
in physical Universe are operating orbitally; therefore
normally; i,e., at 90° to the direction of the applied force.

"The special case of critical proximity where bodies converge
due to the extreme disparity of relative mass magnitude is
the rare special case at which special exceptional case point
in Universe humans happen to exist, being thereby conditioned
to think of the special-case exceptional as 'normal,' thus
to misapprehend the normal general behavior.  The misapprehension regards the normal as strangely perverse.  There is
much within the critical proximity environment which
demonstrates the normal-- where the disparate mass relativities
are not operating, as, for instance, when a rope is tensed and
reacting at 90° to the direction of the tensing and thus
becomes tauter.  Compression members precess to bend."

- Cite SYNERGETICS draft at Secs. 1054.61+62, 6 Mar'73

---

RBF DEFINITIONS

Normal:

"Normal for Universe is 'in orbit'."

- Cite RBF to EJA, 200 Locust, Phila., 22 Jan'73

---

Normalizer:

      See Sleep, 11 Feb'73

---

RBF DEFINITIONS

    Norm of Einstein as Absolute Speed:

"We have a new norm. . . The norm of Einstein is absolute
speed instead of 'at rest.'"

- Citation and context at Eternal Instantaneity (1) 22 Jun'72

---

RBF DEFINITIONS

Normal:

"I use 60 degrees as normal instead of 90 degrees."

- Citation & context at Pulse Pattern, 2 May'71

---

RBF DEFINITIONS
    Norm of Einstein as Absolute Speed:

"Einstein's adoption as normal speed, the adoption of
electromagnetic radiation expansion-- omnidirectionally
in vacuo-- because the speeds of all the known different
phases of measured radiation are apparently identical,
despite vast differences in wavelength and frequencies,
suggests a top speed of omnidirectional entropic disorder
increase accommodation at which radiant speed reaches
highest velocity when the last of the eternally
regenerative Universe cyclic frequencies of multi-
billions of years have been accommodated, all of which
complex of nonsimultaneous transforming multivarieted
frequency synchronizations is complementarily balanced
to equate as zero by the sum-totality of locally
converging orderly and synchronously concentrating
energy phases of scenario universe's eternally pulsative,
and only sum-totally synchronous, disintegrative,
divergent, omnidirectionally exporting and only sum-totally
synchronous integrative, convergent and discretely
directional individual importings."

- Cite RBF to EJA in response to request to repeat his
   'brief sentence' on sphere as a meeting of convergences.
   See SYNERGETICS draft 'Tension and Compression,' Sec. 641.08-
   See Sec. 325, Oct'71 Citation at Radiation: Speed Of

RBF DEFINITIONS

Norm of Einstein as Absolute Speed:

"Einstein's relativity, born at 20th century's opening, and its security in comprehended dynamic equilibrium becomes the newly acquired norm of the Airocean World, replacing the no longer tenable static norm of 'at rest' and 'death' and its invalidated securities of mass and inertia."

- Citation and context at Dymaxion Airocean World (11), Jun'50

---

Normal Speed:                                                    (2)

See All-acceleration Universe, 20 Jun'66

---

Norm of Einstein as Absolute Speed:                              (1)

See Absolute Velocity
    All-acceleration Universe
    Instant Universe vs. All-motion Universe
    Newton's Cosmic Norm of "At rest"
    Cosmic Norm
    Top Speed

---

RBF DEFINITIONS

Norm: Tetrahedron As Norm:

N.Y. Times, 15 May'72, H.M. Schmeck, Jr, "Immunology: A Code Spelling Life or Death": "The basic antibody structure is known to consist of four chains of chemical subunits-- two light chains and two heavy chains. On these are large 'constant regions' that are the same from antibody to antibody... Variable regions... confer specificity... the factor that allows antibodies to be formed to fit. (Underlining by R.B.F.)

R.B.F. Marginalia: "Purely structural law. Purely triangle and tetra forming. 1 Tet = Norm. 6 = Norm.

"6 = 2 x 3; 6 = 2 triangles; 2 triangles = 4 triangles; 4 triangles = Tet; 3 = ½ Norm.

        1 = Redundant Excess

        2 = Deficient

        3 = ■■■ ½ Norm

        6 = ■ Norm"

- Cite RBF marginalia presumably 15 May'72

---

Norm of Einstein as Absolute Speed:                              (2)

See Omnimotions, May'72
    Eternal Instantaneity (1)*
    Radiation: Speed Of, Oct'71*
    Dymaxion Airocean World (II)*
    Intuition, 1 Feb'75
    T Module, 31 Jul'77

---

RBF DEFINITIONS

Normal to Universe:

Q:      "In the metaphor of the child pushing the spoon off the table, 90 degrees is normal to Universe; Precession. In what respect can 60 degrees be considered as normal?"

RBF:    "The interference energies of three-great-circle orbits automatically intertriangulate and automatically interequalize the interference energies to produce omniequilateral spherical triangles which always project flat-out as 60-degree triangles."

- Cite RBF holograph answer to query by EJA, 3200 Idaho Ave., Wash, DC, 10 Sep'74

---

Normal Speed:                                                    (1)

See Norm of Einstein as Absolute Speed
    Top Speed

---

Normal to Universe:                                              (1)

See Sixty Degrees as Normal

Normal to Universe:

See Child Pushes Spoon Off Edge of Table, 16 Jun'72

---

RBF DEFINITIONS

North-south Mobility of World Man: (1)

"All humanity is now prone to become world beings, so we're going to have to accommodate the comings and going in very new places.

"When the United Nations was formed New York City was chosen as the headquarters because it could be reached by ships. At that time the chief way of getting around the world was by water, by vessel and ship. In 1961, long after the forming of the United Nations, three jet airplanes in one year outperformed the Queen Mary and the steamship United States at very much less cost; and suddenly the sea became obsolete as a way in which human beings would get from here to there.

"We have been in an east-west orientation. New York City and San Francisco have been ports of embarkation and debarkation for freight and traffic. You fly over New York City today and look at the thousands of docks and you'll find about a dozen of them in use. And look at the great Jersey City railroad yards: absolutely empty. New York City has become completely obsolete from what it was.

"That farm machinery I talked to you about /See Building Business, (2)_7 that brought about the farming in an entirely"

- Cite RBF to "Town Meeting of the Air," Wash, DC; 10 Sep'75

---

Norm: Normal: (1)

See Cosmic Norm
    Failure as Norm
    Success as Norm
    Static Norm
    Newton's Cosmic Norm of "At Rest"
    Norm of Einstein as Absolute Speed
    Sixty Degrees as Normal
    Change is Normal
    Permanence ≠ Normal
    Zero = Normal

---

RBF DEFINITIONS

North-south Mobility of World Man: (2)

"different way, and mechanical implements created enormous agricultural industrial operations. Ninety percent of humanity yesterday were on the farms and they now have no other place to go but into the cities, occupying housing completely obsolete in the way it was built. I say that not only the building industry is obsolete but the whole of the cities are obsolete. And it is all at great cost to the human beings that are there... and we're going to have to do everything we can to make them as livable as we can. But we're in really for a completely new pattern, a new pattern of mobility for all of world man. Instead of the east-west world of the sea they're going to be flying over the pole."

- Cite RBF to "Town Meeting of the Air," Wash, DC; 10 Sep'75

---

Norm: Normal: (2)

See Charts, 3 Oct'73
    Eternal Instantaneity, (1)
    Problems, 9 Dec'73
    Pulse Pattern, 2 May'71*
    Quick & the Dead: Song Of, Oct'66
    New York City (10)
    Human Beings & Complex Universe, (15)

---

North-south Mobility of World Man:

See World-around Communication Transcends Politics

---

RBF DEFINITIONS

North Face Domes:

"At our Vancouver site, in addition to the four MFG 'Molded Fiberglass' Company's Turtle Domes, there were two smaller North Face Domes. The name 'North Face' derives from the north face of Mt. Everest. These two North Face domes were developed by successful Everest climbers for their ▮▮▮▮▮ high altitude, advanced base, dwelling devices--designed for environmental conditions far more formidable than those with which humans anywhere had ever before swiftly and effectively coped. The North Face domes are oval in plan. They are geodesic. They are made with the highest tensile strength aircraft aluminum struts and have inner and outer dome skins of nylon with a double skin floor. They disassemble and roll into a pack two feet long by eight inches in diameter and weigh only eight pounds. An eight-pound home compounded with a sleeping bag permits human beings to be very intimate with nature under most hostile conditions."

- Cite Accommodating Human Unsettlement, p.20; 20 Sep'76

---

No Secondhand Battleships:

See Secondhand, 1946

No Secondhand God:

    See Religion, (1)
      Iceland, 7 Oct'75
      Young World, 9 Jul'62

---

No Sinking:  Man Cannot Sink:

    See Down, May'49

---

Nose-to-navel Axis:

    See Axis of Reference:  Nose-to-navel

---

RBF DEFINITIONS

No-Size Conceptual Model:

"Because I don't talk space, I don't have to have a
vacuum.  I don't start with space.  I start with nothing.
Things are always special-case temporary realizations of
a specifically detailed dimension and behavior complex
of generalized laws applied to a local inventory of
physical resources.  I start thinking with a no-size
conceptual model of a whole system."

    - Cite 19 Feb re-write of Vacuum, 17 Feb '72

---

No Shape:

    See Shapeless:  Universe Does Not Have a Shape

---

No-size Conceptual Model:

    See Conceptuality Independent of Size
      Zerosize

---

No Short Cuts:

    See Short Cuts

---

RBF DEFINITIONS

No Solids:

    "Such objects, however,
    On closer inspection
    Are theselves mass-attractively integrated
    Energy event aggregates,
    Each of which is so closely amassed
    As to be superficially deceptive
    And therefore misidentified
    By humanity's optically limited discernment,
    As bodies--
    Separate 'solid' bodies--
    Despite that physics has never found
    And 'solid' phenomena."

    - Cite INTUITION, p.22, May '72

RBF DEFINITIONS

No Solids:

"If lines cannot go through the same point at the same
time, there can be no continuous perfectly level planes.
Planes are not experimentally demonstrable. Solids are
not experimentally demonstrable. Physical experiment has
never discovered any phenomena other than discontinuous
discrete energy events, each uniquely identifiable
amongst the gamut of frequencies of cyclic disconinuity
of all the physical phenomena as comprehensively and
overlappingly arrayed as the vast frequency ranges of
the electromagnetic spectrum. The electromagnetic
spectrum 'reality' has been found experimentally to
embrace all known physical phenomena: visible, subvisible
or ultravisible thus far detected as present in universe.
There are no solids. The synergetic behaviors of
structures satisfactorily explains as discontinuous that
which we have in the past superficially misidentified
as 'solid.'"

- Cite SYNERGETIC Draft, "Conceptuality: Solid" - RBF
       Marginalia, Somerset Club, Boston, 25 April 1971

SOLIDS: MATTER - SEC. 525.01)

---

No Solids:                                                    (2)

See Subvisible Discontinuity, 19 Oct'72
    Experiential Mathematics, 15 Oct'76
    Fourth-dimensional Synergetics Mathematics, 14 Dec'76
    Conceptual Physics, (1)(2)
    Four-dimensional Reality, 30 Apr'77
    Tuning-in & Tuning-out, 17 May'77

---

RBF DEFINITIONS

No Solids:

"For a microcosmic example of our spontaneous and
superficial misapprehending and miscomprehending the
environmental events we must concede that both theoretically
and experimentally we have now learned and 'know' that
there are no 'solids,' no continuous surfaces, only
'milky-way-like' aggregations of remotely interdistanced
atomic events. Thre are no 'things'-- no particles--
only energetic events. Nonetheless society keeps right
on 'seeing,' dealing and superficially cerebrating in
respect to 'things' called 'solids.'"

- Cite WHAT QUALITY ENVIRONMENT, 24 Apr'67

SOLIDS: MATTER - SEC. 525.02)

---

RBF DEFINITIONS

No Speed:

"The top speed of radiation is simply the minimum operational
lag before making the cosmic leap to the eternal No-speed,
where the instantaneity spontaneous to a child's conceptioning
is normal and eternal."

- Citation and context at Intellect, 27 May'72

---

RBF DEFINITIONS

No Solids:

"If lines can't go through the same point at the
same time, we Can't even have 'planes'. So planes are
'out.' Solids are also gone because physical experiment
has never disclosed any phenomena other than discontin-
uities identified as the gamut of frequencies of cyclic
discontinuity of all the physical phenomena as arrayed
within the vast frequency ranges of the electromagnetic
spectrum which embraces all physical phenomena visible,
sub-visible, or ultra-visible thus far detected in
universe. Solids are 'out.'"

- Cite NASA SPEECH, p. 52. Jun'66   -Cite CARBONDALE TEXT IV.29, IV.30-

SOLIDS: MATTER - SEC 525.01)

---

No Spherical Continuum:

See O Module, 29 Sep'76

---

No Solids:                                                    (1)

See Static Invalidity of Solid Things vs. Empty Space

---

RBF DEFINITIONS

No Sphere Integrity:

"As there may be no absolute division of energetic Universe
into isolated or noncommunicable parts, there is no absolute
enclosed surface or absolutely enclosed volume; therefore, no
true or absolutely defined simultaneous surface sphere integrity.
Therefore, a sphere is a polyhedron of invisible plurality of
trussed facets..."

- Cite RBF caption in McHale's "RBFuller,", Plate 36, 1962

UNIVERSE - SEC. 307.3)

No Square Stability:

See Triclinic, 31 Aug'76

RBF DEFINITIONS

No Static:

"There is no true 'noise' or 'static.'  There are ▮▮▮▮
only as yet undifferentiated and uncomprehended orders."

(From NASA Speech, p. 90.)

- Cite Synergetics draft, "Symmetry," Sec. 532.04, July 1971.

- Citation & context at Chaos, Jun'66

---

Nostalgia:

See Spherical Nostalgia
Yesterdays

No Straight Lines:                              (1)

See Deliberately Nonstraight Line
Nonstraight
No Right Angles in Nature
Zigzag

---

RBF DEFINITIONS

No Start:

"You don't have to find where Universe starts.  It doesn't
start.  It's eternal."

- Cite RBF at Penn Bell videotaping session, Philadelphia,
22 Jan'75

No Straight Lines:                              (2)

See Line, 28 Oct'73; Mar'71
Servomechanism, 15 May'75
Social Sciences:  Analogue to Physical Sciences, (1)
Left & Right, 7 Nov'75

---

No Static Frame of Reference:

See Eternity, (1)

RBF DEFINITIONS

Not A Priori:

"The octet truss is not a priori."

- Citation & context at Octet Truss, 24 Sep'73

Not A Priori:                                    (1)

    See Self is not A Priori

---

Not-everywhere:

    See Distributive, 23 Sep'73

---

Not A Priori:                                    (2)

    See Octet Truss, 24 Sep'73*

---

No Thickness:

    See Systematic Realization, 20 Dec'74

---

Note:  Notes:

    See Basic Notes
        Chords & Notes

---

RBF DEFINITIONS

    Nothing:

    "I don't start with space.  I start with nothing."

    - For citation and context see Vacuum, 17/19 Feb '72

---

Not Enough to Go Round:

    See Scarcity

---

RBF DEFINTIONS

    Nothing:

    "Lags are intervals-- nothing."

    - Cite SYNERGETICS Draft - "Conceptuality: Life" - RBF
      Marginalia, Somerset Club, Boston, 25 April 1971.

    - Citation & context at Eternal & Temporal, 25 Apr'71

RBF DEFINITIONS

No-thing:

"There are no solids, nor particles-- no-things."

- Cite SYNERGETICS corollaries, Sec. 240. 1971

RBF DEFINITIONS

Nothingness:

"When the vector equilibrium assembly of eight triangles and six squares is opened up it may be hand held in the omnisymmetry conformation of the 'idealized nothingness of absolute middleness.'"

- Cite SYNERGETICS draft at Sec. 460.02, 5 Oct'72

RBF DEFINITIONS

Nothingness:

"The nothingness is just where you are not tuning. Nothingness = untuned somethingness."

- Cite RBF to EJA, Pagano's Rest., Phila., PA., 22 Jun'75

No Thing:  No Thing-in-itself:                                   (1)

See Connections & Relatedness
    Starting Point
    System vs. Thing-in-itself
    Verbs: No 'Where's, No 'What's, Only 'When's
    Zero Model vs. Thing-in-itself
    Static Invalidity of Solid Things vs. Empty Space

RBF DEFINITIONS

Nothingness:

"The nothingness area is one unbounded by any visible closed line. Nothingness is the part of the system unencompassed by the observer."

- Citation & Context at Minimum Awareness Model, (1)(2), 9 Jun'75

No Thing-in-itself:  No Thing:                                   (2)

See Vector Equilibrium as Starting Point, 8 Apr'75
    Ninety-two Elements, 21 Jun'77

RBF DEFINITIONS

Nothingness:

"The total nothingness involved is accounted by 20 $F^3$. The third power accounts both the untuned nothingness and the finitely tuned somethingness. The 20 is both Einstein's M and all the other untuned non-M of Universe. The 20 $F^3$ is the total Universe momentarily all at one ~~time~~ center."

(time or timeless)

PER RBF CORRECTION -26 NOV'72

- Cite SYNERGETICS draft at Sec. 960.09, 16 Nov'72

Nothingness Local:

See Zero-niness, 11 Sep'75

# Synergetics Dictionary

RBF DEFINITIONS

Nothingness:  Mold of Nothingness:

"-- We suddely see the mold of nothingness.  That's all
it is!"

- Fpr citation and context see Black Hole (2) , 27 Jan'72

RBF DEFINITIONS

Nothingness of Areal and Volumetric Spaces:

"The function of the chords is to relate. . . And the
resultant is the inadvertent definition of the nothingness
of the areal and volumetric spaces. . . Areas do not
create themselves.  They are incidental to the lines
between the events.  The faces are the bounding of nothingness.
Areas and volumes are incidental resultants to finding the
connections between the events of experience."

- Citation and context at Connections and Relatedness, 20 Feb'73

Nothingness of Night:

See Fireworks, May'72

Nothingness of Areal & Volumetric Spaces:

See Domain & Quantum, (1)(2)

Nothingness Phase:

See Vacuum, 11 Sep'75

RBF DEFINITIONS

Nothingness of Universe:

"What the blowtorch does is to let infinity-- or the
nothingness of Universe-- into the system."

- For citation and context see Barrel (2) , Dec'70

Nothingness = Silence:

See Silence, 30 Sep'76

Nothingness = Untuned Somethingness:

See Nothingness, 22 Jun'75

Nothing: Nothingness: None:         (1)

    See Background Nothingness
        Central Nothingness Equilibrium
        Field of Omnidirectional Nothingness
        Infinite = Nothingness
        Mold of Nothingness
        Nonstate
        Nonthing
        Nothingness = Untuned Somethingness
        Novent
        Nucleus = Nine = Nothing
        One = None
        Something-nothing-something-nothing
        Space Nothingness
        Straight-nothingness
        Unfolded Nothingness
        Untuned
        Windows of Nothingness

No Time: No-time-at-all:         (1)

    See Absolute Velocity
        Cosmic Synergy
        Eternal Instantaneity
        Eternity: Equatuon of Eternity
        Instantaneity
        Timeless
        Top Speed: Top Velocity

---

Nothing: Nothingness:         (2)

    Domes, 12 May'77
    See A Priori Environment, May'72
        A Priori Four-dimensional Reality, (2)
        Black Hole, (2)*
        Bow Ties, 6 Oct'72
        Eternal & Temporal, 25 Apr'71*
        In & Out, 13 Nov'69
        Intervals, 25 Apr'71
        Lavoisier, 1 Oct'71
        Tetrahedron, 20 Feb'73
        Triangle, 16 Dec'73
        Vacuum, 19 Feb'72*
        Vector Equilibrium: Zerophase. 1 May'71
        Whole, 17 Feb'72
        In & Out: Go In To Go Out, 16 Dec'73
        Zerophase, (1)
        Star Events & Degrees of Freedom, 12 May'75
        Thirty Minimum Topological Characteristics, (1)
        Self & Otherness: Four Minimal Aspects, 22 Jun'75
        Minimum Awareness Model, (1)(2)*
        Dynamic Equilibrium, 24 Apr'76
        Space, 2 Jul'76

No Time: No Time at All:         (2)

    See Intellect, 27 May'72
        Motion, 27 May'72
        Time & Space, 7 Feb'71
        Pole Vaulter, 2 Jul'75

---

Nothing: Nothingness:         (3)

    See No-thing
        No Thing-in-itself
        Nothingness of Areal & Volumetric Spaces
        Nothingness: Mold of Nothingness
        Nothingness of Night
        Nothingness Phase
        Nothingness of Universe
        Nothingness = Untuned Somethingness
        Nothingness = Silence

Not Of:

    See Between and Not Of

---

RBF DEFINITIONS

No-time-and-away-ago:

"'No-time-and-away-ago' is my new phrase in the Goldilocks
piece for a theme like Dante's. The otherness is broken down
into past otherness, present otherness, and future otherness."

No Totality:

    See No Conceptual Totality

- Cite RBF to EJA, 28 May'75

# Synergetics Dictionary

Not Out of This World: (1)

See Imaginary Universe vs. This Universe
Outside: What's Outside Outside?

---

No Two-dimensionality:

See Fourth-dimensional Synergetics Mathematics, 14 Dec'76

---

Not Out of This World: (2)

See Omnigeometric, 27 May'72
Public Relations, 28 Jan'75

---

RBF DEFINITIONS

No Twogon:

"There is no twogon."

- Cite SYNERGETICS, 2nd. Ed. at Sec. 608.24, 11 Apr'75

---

Not Touching: Never-quite-touching:

See Rules of Never-quite-touching
Vertexial Connections
Vertexial Connections: Rules of Never-quite-touching

---

RBF DEFINITIONS

Noun:

"In architecture 'form' is a noun; in industry, 'form' is a verb. Industry is concerned with doing, whereas architecture has been engrossed with making replicas of end results of what people have industrially demonstrated in the past. Noun, in our phonetic etymology, means 'now-one,' i.e., the most recent chaos of thought reduced to an answer. The 'now-one' or noun must, in due course through selection by the intellect, become two or more observed characteristics of the one, there being no absolute identity. Nouns, from a language viewpoint, are tenable only as 'names' for facts recently determined. The noun is, therefore, more subject to constant revision than is any other part of speech. No longer is it 'stone.' No longer is it 'steel.' Industry is dealing in hundreds of different steels, physically more dissimilar than the Chinese and the Swiss."

- Cite NINE CHAINS TO THE MOON, p.41, 1938

---

Not Trespassing:

See Trespassing: Not Trespassing

---

Noun: (1)

See Name
"Named" Phenomena: Name Words
Newton was a Noun
Thing: Thingness
Verb vs. Noun
No Nouns

Noun:                                                     (2)

See Event, 26 Jan'72
    Meaningless, Oct'66

---

RBF DEFINITIONS

Novent:

"Alan Watts:   But I mean there is a common assumption--
               it is ordinary common sense-- that space is
               nothing at all.

Fuller:        That's novent.  I call it no-event.
               I don't like the word space anymore because
               it implies something.  We have only frequencies.
               We have events and no-events.  We have the
               unique energy packages.

Watts:         But any sort of solid energy package seems to
               me inconceivable without a special ground.

Fuller:        It doesn't bother me at all about the no-event.

Watts:         Well, how can you talk of curved space, the
               properties of space?

Fuller:        But you can't talk of straight space.  There
               are no straight lines.  Physics has found
               nothing but waves."

- Cite WATTS TAPE, p .52, 19 Oct'70
- Citation at Space, 19 Oct'70

---

No Up & Down:

See Death, 29 Mar'77
    Dynamic Frame of Reference, (3)(4)
    In, Out & Around, 17 Mar'77; 10 Dec'73
    Nature in a Corner, 17 Nov'75
    Spaceship, (1)
    Spaceship Earth, 22 Jun'74
    Synergetic Hierarchy, 5 May'74
    No Energy Crisis, (1)
    Conceptual Limits, 22 Jun'77

---

RBF DEFINITIONS

Novent:                                                   (1)

   "There are no specific directions or localities in
Universe which may be opposingly designated as UP or DOWN.
In their place we must use the words OUT and IN.  We move
in towards various individual masses or we move out
from them.  But the words IN and OUT are not mirror image
opposites.  IN is in respect to individual experience
foci-- OUT is common to all.  IN is discrete.  OUT is
general.  The IN's are discontinuous.  The OUT's are
continuous.  OUT is nothingness, i.e. non-experience.
Only the non-experience nothingness infers a continuum.
The non-event continuum is the Novent.  Inferentially,
the Novent continuum permeates the finitely populated
withinness and comprises the finit Novent withoutness.
The rubber glove stripped inside-outingly from off the
left hand now fits only the right hand.  First the left
hand was conceptual and the right hand was non-conceptual--
and then the process of stripping off inside-outingly
seemingly annihilated the left hand and created the
right hand-- then vice versa as the next strip-off
occurred.  When physics finds experimentally that a
unique energy patterning,-- erroneously referred to in
archaic terms as a particle,-- is annihilated, that

CONCEPTUALITY   SEC.524  N/OVENT)   - Cite NEHRUS SPEECH, p.12, 13 Nov'69

---

Novel:  Novels:

See Fuller, R.B: The Thinking Me, a8 Dec'76

---

RBF DEFINITIONS

Novent:                                                   (2)

   "Annihilation is only of the rubber glove kind.  The positive
becomes the negative and the positive only seems to have been
annihilated.  We begin to realize conceptually the finite,
yet non-sensorial, outness which can be converted into
sensorial inness by the inside-outing process.  Ergo, novent
is the finite but non-sensorial continuum.  Sensoriality is a
corporeally external pheneomenon-- reportingly relayed inwardly
to the brain and therein imaginatively scanned by the mind
which conceptualized independently in generalized formulations
such as the conception of a nuclear grouping around a nucleus,
quite independent of size..."

- Cite NEHRU SPEECH, p.12, 13 Nov'69

---

RBF DEFINITIONS

Novent:

"The limit case of prime otherness is that of the point and
the no-points: the events and the novents.  Numerically,
one vs. zero.  Because it is the limit case it is prime.
Zero is prime otherness."

- Citation and context at Prime Otherness, 23 Sep'73

---

RBF DEFINITIONS

Novent:

"There is no static geometry.  There are momentarily existant
geometrical relationships.  There are events and lack-of-events.
The electromagnetic spectrum is a manifest of the gamut of
unique frequencies of recurrence.  There are no 'solids,' no
'surfaces,' no continuums,' no straight lines or planes.  We
have only events and no-events-- the events being finite and
their energies limited. . . .

"We are talking about no event, so let us contract those two
words into one word, novent, meaning nothing occurs."

- Citation and context at Space, 1968

---

90

RBF DEFINITIONS

Novent Continuum:

"The non-event continuum is the Novent. . . The Novent
continuum permeates the finitely populated withinness and
comprises the finite Novent withoutness. . . Only the
non-experience nothingness constitutes continuum."

- Cite Synergetics draft, Secs. 524.04 + 524.05. 1971

---

RBF DEFINITIONS

Now:

"The future is not linear. Time is wavilinear. Experience
is expansive, omnidirectionally including and refining the
future. It probably consists of omnidirectional wave
propagations. We seem to be talking about a greater range
of known cycling. It is both a subjective 'now' and an
objective 'now'; a forward-looking now and a backward-looking
now which combine synergetically as one complete "now."
Because every action has both a reaction and a resultant,
every now must have both a fading past and a dawning future."

- Cite RBF rewrite of SYNERGETICS galley at Sec. 529.11
  7 Nov'73

---

Novent Continuum:

        See Gravitational Continuum

---

RBF DEFINITIONS

Now:

"I cannot think simultaneously

About all the special-case events which I have experienced,

But I can think about one special set

Of closely associated events

At any one now."

- Cite BRAIN & MIND, p.132 May '72

---

Novent:                                          (1)

        See Epistemological Stepping Stones
            Events & Nonevents
            Invisible
            No-point
            Nothing
            No-thing
            Nothingness: Mold of Nothingness
            Novent Continuum
            Vacuum
            Vacuum = Novent = Invisible
            Events, Novents & Event Interrelatabilities
            Space Nothingness

---

RBF DEFINITIONS

Now:

"Universe is the aggregate

.    .    .    .    .

Which aggregate
Of only partially overlapping events
Is sum-totally a lot of yesterdays
Plus an awareness of now."

- Cite BRAIN AND MIND, p. 125, galley p.131 May '72

---

Novent:                                          (2)

        See Connections & Relatedness, 20 Feb'73
            Prime Otherness, 23 Sep'73*
            Space, 19 Oct'70; May'71
            Star Event & Degrees of Freedom, 12 May'75

---

RBF DEFINITIONS

Now:

"Yesterday and now
Are neither simultaneous
Nor mirror-imaged;
But through them run themes
As overlappingly woven threads,
Which though multipliedly individualized
Sum-totally comprise a scenario."

- Cite BRAIN & MIND, p.131 May '72

RBF DEFINITIONS

Now:

"Now is where man has kidded himself into thinking that
there's no change at all.

"Take the gestation rates from the elephant to the half-
life radioactivity of atoms which approach cosmic speeds
and get back into eternity. What we call now is just a
slow-down. In the Gay 90's most people thought that there
was no change at all. Even Newton could say 'at rest.'

"I ramified the idealistic-- which is essential to all the
palpitations. It goes back to angle, and triangle, and
conceptuality independent of size and starting with the
fundamental idea that there must be a nucleus. There is
no straight line; only the wave coincides with reality."

- Cite RBF to EJA, at breakfast 3200, Idaho, DC, after
  RBF had read first three chapters of Eccles 'Facing
  Reality,' until 3:00 a.m. the night before, 14 Feb '72.

---

RBF DEFINITIONS

Now:

"We cannot view the great confluences of separately and
remotely significant events forwardly resultant to now."

- Citation & context at Surprise, May'49

---

RBF DEFINITIONS

Now:

"Life is the now event with its reaction past and resultant
future."

- Citation & context at Life, 1 Jun'71

---

No Wave:

    See Waveless

---

RBF DEFINITIONS

Now:

"Because every action has both a reaction and a resultant
every now must have a past and a dawning future."

- Cite SYNERGETICS draft, 'Conceptuality: Time,' - RBF
  marginalia added at Somerset Club Boston, 25 Apr'71

---

RBF DEFINITIONS

Now Hourglass:   Cross Section of Teleological Bow Tie:        (1)

"The macrocosm of minimum frequency of omnidirectional self-
interference restraints whose greatest degrees of outward expansions occur when the last of the least-frequent self-interfering
cycles is completed, and cycles, being geodesic great circles,
must always interfere with one another twice in each wave and
   frequency cycle, which 'twiceness' imposes eternally regen-
     erative cosmic resonance, and all the latter's inher-
       ent quanta- wave- frequency- time- interference-
         mass- and effort- aspects in exquisite speed-
           of-light 700-million miles per hour,
             self-interfering radiation patterns'
               energetic self-tying into con-
                 centric knots of relative
                   mass in a mathematically
                     idealized variety of symmet-
                       rical-asymmetrical atomic
                         assemblages whose local
                           subvisibly resolvable
                             micro-orbiting induces
                               the superficially decep-
                                 tive motionless thing-
                                   ness of mini-micro-
TIME - 2ND.ED,                       microcosm of
SEC. 529.40 - Cite RBF rewrite, 25 Sep'73    NOW

---

RBF DEFINITIONS

Now:

"The future is not something linear. So we seem to be

talking about a greater range of known cycling. . . We're

talking a complete 'now.' It really is a subjective 'now'

and an objective 'now' and so forth, but it really is

all 'now.'"

- Cite WATTS TAPE, p.39, 19 Oct'70
  - Citation at ████████ Time, Oct'70
                          19

---

RBF DEFINITIONS

Now Hourglass:   Cross Section of Teleological Bow Tie:        (2)

                        "NOW
                    which pro-
                  gressive exper-
                ience-won knowledge
              multiplies by progress-
            ive intellectually contrived,
          instrumentally implemented explora-
        tmory subdividing into microscopically
      ever greater speeds of transformation
    through insectine phase magnitudes dividing
  into the micro-organisms phase, and then
    dividing progressively into molecular and atomic
      phases; then phasing into radioactivity at 700-million
    miles per hour, expanding once more into the macrocosm and
repeat: ad infinitum.

TIME - 2ND. ED
SEC. 529.40 - Cite RBF rewrite, 25 Sep'73

TEXT CITATIONS

Now Hourglass:  Cross Section of Teleological Bow Tie:

See Shelter, Vol. 2., No. 4, p.43, May'32

Synergetics, 2nd. Ed. : Sec. 529.40

---

Now Hourglass:  Cross Section of Teleological Bow Tie:

See Self-now, Mar'72

---

RBF DEFINITIONS

Now House:                                                         (1)

"What was present and physically demonstrated at Vancouver's
/UN Habitat Conference/ Jericho Beach site was a mushroom
group of swiftly foldable and movable geodesic domes and
modernized Indian tepees produced, developed, and installed
by a young world inspired to do something about its own
future.

"Our World Game staff... put on an exhibit of four geodesic
domes, which are now in manufacture by the Molded Fiberglass
Company (MFG) of Ashtabula, Ohio... Their 14-foot, 5/8-sphere
polyester fiberglass geodesic domes have alternate translucent or opaque fiberglass hexagon or pentagon panels. Their
domes retail for $750.

"The World Game staff called their Exhibit the 'Now House.'
This name derived from the fact that everything they had on
display could be purchased right now from industrial mass
production sources. All labor of their production occurred
under the controlled environment-conditioning of factories:
no rain, cold, heat, snow, ice, or wind. The MFG domes had
no more need for old building technology than has the
opening of an umbrella--a mobile, environment-controlling"

- Cite ACCOMMODATING HUMAN UNSETTLEMENT, p.10; 20 Sep'76

---

RBF DEFINITIONS

Now House:                                                         (2)

"artifact. The World Gamers brought their exhibit from
Philadelphia to Vancouver in one camper truck pulling one
trailer.

"The World Gamers first dug circular trenches slightly
larger in diameter than the domes' circular bases. As they
trenched they threw their shovelfuls of Earth into the
enclosed circle and leveled it to form an elevated base for
each dome. On the top of the Earth they laid edge-overlap-
ping corrugated aluminum panels which were surmounted first
by aluminized foamboard to reradiate heat, and next by
plywood, and again by indoor-outdoor carpeting. This made a
very comfortable, springy and dry floor.

"They anchored the domes so that they could not blow away,
for the domes weighed only 225 pounds each.

"Three of the domes were positioned in a triangular pattern
with ten feet between them. A high pole was mounted at the
center of the triangular area, which in turn supported a
watertight translucent canopy. The large between-domes
triangular area below the canopy was covered with the"

- Cite ACCOMMODATING HUMAN UNSETTLEMENT, p.11; 20 Sep'76

---

RBF DEFINITIONS

Now House:                                                         (3)

"indoor-outdoor carpeting. The fourth dome stood mildly
apart and could have been connected by a canopy but was not.

"One of the World Gamers' domes contained a complete
workshop with all manner of handtools, benches, metal- and
wood-working equipment and general electronics servicing
gear. Another dome was used for the kitchen, bathroom,
toilet, office, and clothes hanging. The third dome was
used as a video theater and dormitory. The fourth dome was
used for storage and laundry drying....

"Ten of the World Gamers lived in the Now House installation.
They lived very comfortably and happily (as do a crew of
10 sailors living together on an ocean yacht, many of which
are later equipped with hundreds of thousands of dollars
worth of low-input, high-output, invisible performance
instruments.)

"The Now House had been voluntarily equipped by many major
corporations. Largest single supplier of all was the J.C.
Penney Company. SONY let them have its most advanced multi-
color videotape production and viewing system. Minnesota"

- Cite ACCOMMODATING HUMAN UNSETTLEMENT, p.12; 20 Sep'76

---

RBF DEFINITIONS

Now House:                                                         (4)

"Mining had given them their best duplicating equipment.
They had silk-screening equipment, printing equipment, and
typewriters, and were able to broadcastingly communicate to
society from their headquarters and received their feedback
from a thousand visitors a day.

"In the kitchen-bathing dome Herman Miller had provided most
compact, economic but adequate, shelving on which to mount
their kitchen equipment. They had a toilet which converted
human waste into high-grade fertilizer. The heat necessary
for this odorless process was provided alternatingly by
electricity from the windmill hookup or by heat from the
solar panel water-heating device. The toilet system produced
fertilizer as a rich, dry, manured, loam-like substance
which needed to be taken out of the system only once a year....

"The domes were equipped with a remote control telephone.
Arrayed between two of the three domes under a translucent
canopy were banks of tomatoes and other ████████ food
vegetation in hydroponic tanks, with noticeable growth
accomplished during only the short two-week period of the
installation."

- Cite ACCOMMODATING HUMAN UNSETTLEMENT, p.13; 20 Sep'76

---

RBF DEFINITIONS

Now House:                                                         (5)

"While the domes, as already noted, were priced at $750
each, the total package with all its $17,000-worth of
equipment amounted to $20,000. This ratio of $3,000 for
the environmental dwelling shells and skin to $20,000 for
the totally and luxuriously equipped living facility--
approximately 1 : 7--is very close to the international
ocean racing yachts' bareboat to sailaway equipped cost
ratio. A modern 37-foot-overall length one-tonner
at $30,000 for the bare boat with full transoceanic racing
equipment, sails, instruments, et al., costs approximately
$200,000. The reason the bareboat yacht hulls cost so much
more than the bare Now House domes is due to all the stresses,
strains, and other formidable conditions which must be coped
with by the boat and their lightweight, high-strength
equipment while operating at the interface of the airocean
and the waterocean. The conditions are not present in the
land installations....

"The #2 Now House will be ready for exhibit by August 28,
1977, and will soon therafter become publicly available as
the air-deliverable, only rentable, world-around dwelling
machine service right on its scheduled 50th birthday."....

- Cite ACCOMMODATING HUMAN UNSETTLEMENT; pp.13-14; 20 Sep'76

---

RBF DEFINITIONS

Now House:                                                         (6)

"One of the most impressive facts at Vancouver was that
disclosed by nature. During the first four days of the
installation there were torrential rains. Mud was everywhere
around the Jericho Beach forum grounds.... The World Gamers
had placed large heavy planks on the ground leading to
their installations so that by the time the visitors came
over mats into the complex their feet were reasonably dry.
With the large numbers coming daily it was amazing that the
flooring of the complex remained comfortably dry throughout
the rains.

"The domes consisted of half opaque panels and half
translucent panels and could be rotatingly rearranged with
the translucent side south to impound enormous amounts of Sun
radiation. With the translucent panels north, they remained
cool and let in only the north light so desirable to
artists."

- Cite ACCOMMODATING HUMAN UNSETTLEMENT; p.15; 20 Sep'76

RBF DEFINITIONS

Now Necessity:

The mathematicians by their pseudo-escape to abstraction
from a now necessity often get to kidding themselves.  They
do not understand an hierarchy of events."

- Cite Moebius Strip, 10 Jan'50

---

Now: (1)

See Eternal Slowdown
    Instantaneity
    Future:  Man Backs into his Future
    Here & Now
    Reality is Eternally Now
    Self-now
    Status Quo
    Present
    Time is Only Now

---

RBF DEFINITIONS

Now Set:

"...the olfactoral and aural (what you are smelling, eating,
saying, and hearing) are the now set."

- Citation and context at Senses (1), 22 Nov'73

---

Now: (2)

See Apprehending, 22 Nov'73
    Dynamic Frame of Reference, (5)
    Life, 1 Jun'71*
    Prime Enclosure, 17 Feb'73
    Scenario, May'72
    Sensorial Identification of Reality, (2)
    Surprise, May'49*
    Time, Oct'70*
    Time, Oct'70*
    Tuning-in & Tuning-out, 17 May'77

---

Now-you-see-it-now-you-don't: (1)

See Binary
    Conceptuality & Nonconceptuality
    Pulse Pattern
    Visible & Invisible
    Something-nothing-something-nothing

---

Nowhere & Nowhen: (1)

See No Time

---

Now-you-see-it-now-you-don't: (2)

See Fourth Quantum, 9 Jun'75
    Nuclear Sphere, 16 Dec'73
    Resolvability Limits, 30 Apr'77

---

Nowhere & Nowhen: (2)

See Cosmic Synergy, Jan'72

Nozzle: Harvesting Pollution at the Nozzle:

    See Pollution, 1970
       Pollution Control, (1)(2)

Nuclear Assemblage Components:

    See Mites Make All Regular Polyhedra, 27 May'72

Nuances of Angles:

    See Angle: Pumping Fraction Factors, 15 Mar'48

Nuclear Computer Design:

    See Atomic Computer Complex
       Omnidirectional Typewriter

Nuance:

    See Dictionary, 23 Feb'72; 24 Feb'72; 19 Jul'76
       Truth, 1967
       Words, 2 Jun'74
       Scheherazade Numbers: Declining Powers Of,
         17 Mar'75
       Words & Coping, 7 Nov'75

Nuclear Cube:
    See Nucleated Cube

RBF DEFINITIONS

Nuclear:

"Synergetics is primarily the geometry of the nucleus rather
than of the ▇▇▇▇▇ geometry of chemistry. It's mostly the
fundamental behaviors, the central behaviors. It is inherently
nuclear in its own right."

    - Citation & context at Synergetics, 23 Mar'74

RBF DEFINITIONS

Nuclear Domain:

"Vector equilibrium is the maximum domain of a nucleus."

    - Cite RBF at Penn Bell videotaping session, Philadelphia,
      22 Jan'75

RBF DEFINITIONS

Nuclear Domain & Elementality:                                    (1)

"The closest-packed sphere shell growth rate is governed by
the formula 10 F² + 2. The formula is reliably predictable
in the identification of chemical elements, but that
identification is limited to the unique nuclear domain
pattern involvement.

"When a new nucleus becomes completely surrounded by two
layers then the exclusively unique pattern surroundment of
the first nucleus is terminated. It is no longer the
unique nucleus. The word elemental relates to the original
unique patterning around any one nucleus of closest-packed
spheres. When we get beyond the original unique patterning
and find the patternings repeating themselves, we get into
the molecular world.

"Uranium 92 is the limit case of what we call inherently
self-regenerative chemical elements. Beyond these, we get
into split-second life demonstrations of the elements.
These demonstrations are similar to having a rubber ball
with a hole and stretching that hole's rubber outwardly
around the hole until we can see the markings on the inner"

- Cite RBF Ltr. to Paul Baclaski; 6 May'77

---

Nuclear Geometrical Limit of Rational Differentiation:

See Mites as Prime Minimum System, 15 Nov'72

---

RBF DEFINITIONS

Nuclear Domain & Elementality:                                    (2)

"skin corresponding to markings on the outer skin, but
when we release the ball the momentarily-outwardly-displayed
markings of the inside will quickly resume their internal
positions.

"As we see in (Sec. 624), the inside-outing of Universe
occurs only at the tetrahedral level. In the nucleated
tetrahedral, closest-packked-sphere-shell growth rates, the
outward layer sphere count increases as frequency to the
second power times two plus two--with the outer layer also
always doubled in value."

--Incorporated in SYNERGETICS 2 at Sec. 419.10-419.13

- Cite RBF Ltr. to Paul Baclaski; 6 May'77

---

Nuclear Gyro:

See Hen, 6 May'48

---

Nuclear Domain:                                                   (1)

See Spheric Domain vs. Nuclear Domain
    Domain of a Nucleus

---

RBF DEFINITIONS

Nuclear and Nebular Zonal Waves:

"Discontinuous compression, continuous-tension structures
are finite islands of microcosmic, inwardly precessing,
zonal wave sequence displacements of radial-to-circumferan-
tial-to-radial energy knotting regeneratins as nuclear
phenomena-- and the whole, enclosed in infinitely macro-
cosmically trending precessional unravelings, regenerates
precessionally as radial-to-circumferential-to-radial
nebular phenomena-- circumferential micro- or macro- being
finite, and radial being infinite. Compression is micro
and tension is macro."

- Cite Synergetics Notes, p.9, et. seq., 1955. Incorporated
  in SYNERGETICS at Sec647.04, 3 Aug-1 Oct'72

---

Nuclear Domain:                                                   (2)

See Nuclear Cube, 11 Dec'75; 23 Feb'76

---

Nuclear & Nebular Zonal Waves:

See Oscillation & Pulsation
    Tidal

Nuclear & Nebular:  Nucleus & Galaxies

See Astro & Nucleic
Cosmic & Local
Orbiting Magnitudes
Relative Acticity Diameters of Stars & Electrons

---

RBF DEFINITIONS

Nuclear and Non-nuclear Polyhedra:

"The closest packed" nucleated "octahedron requires 18
spheres; the tetrahedron 34; the rhombic dodecahedron 92; and
the cube 364███.  The other two symmetric Platonic solids,
the icosahedron and the dodecahedron, are inherently devoid
of equiradius nuclear spheres, having insufficient radius
space within the triangular void.  This suggests both
electron and neutron behavior relationships for the icosahedron and the dodecahedron.  The nucleation of the ███
octahedron, tetrahedron, rhombic dodecahedron, and cube very
probably play important parts in the atomic structuring as
well as in the chemical compounding and in crystallography."

- Cite SYNERGETICS draft at Sec. 415.13, 19 May'72

---

RBF DEFINITIONS

███  Nucleus = Nine = Nothing:

"Nucleus as nine; i.e., non (Latin); i.e.,
none (English); i.e., nothing; i.e. interval integrity;
i.e., the integrity of absolute generalized discontinuity
accommodating all special-case 'space' of space-time
reality."

- Cite SYNERGETICS draft at Sec. 1012.01, 18 Feb'73

---

Nuclear & Nonnuclear:                                    (1)

See Denucleated Phase
Organics & the Nucleus
Subnuclear

---

Nuclear:  Outward Limit of Nuclear Phenomena:

See Vector Equilibrium:  Three-frequency VE

---

Nuclear & Nonnuclear:                                    (2)

See Potential vs. Primitive, 12 May'77
S Quanta Module, 4 Jun'77

---

RBF DEFINITIONS

████████████  Nuclear & Nonnuclear:

"It could be that organics do not require a nucleus.
Whatever the mysterious weightless phenomenon life may
be, also may be the nucleus of all biological species,
including you and me."

- Citation and context at Organics and the Nucleus (2nd draft)
- Cite SYNERGETICS draft at Sec. 415.20, 8 Jun'72    28 May'72

---

RBF DEFINITIONS

Nuclear Power Generation:

Q:      "How do you feel about the protesters who were
        arrested at the Seabrook Nuclear Power site in New
        Hampshire?"

RBF:    "Make it obsolete... That's how you become
effective."

- Cite RBF to World Game Workshop'77; Phila., PA; 22 Jun'77

Nuclear Power Generation:

    See Fail-safe, 13 Sep'77

RBF DEFINITIONS

Nuclear Set:

". . . At the third layer of enclosure some of the angular
interrelationship patternings begin to repeat themselves.
Thus we are able to inventory what we are going to call a
nuclear set of unique interrelationship patterns."

- Citation and context at Atomic Computer Complex (3), 13 May'73

Nuclear Propagation Rate:

    See Powering: Fourth Powering, 15 Oct'72; 9 Sep'75

Nuclear Simplex:

    See Compound, 13 Mar'73
        Ninety-two Elements, 13 Mar'73

Nuclear = Regenerative:          (1)

    See Infinite = Eternally Regenerative

Nuclear-smallest:

    See Man as Halfway in Range of Size of All Creatures,
      22 Jun'75

Nuclear = Regenerative:          (2)

    See Prime Volumes, 17 Feb'73

RBF DEFINITIONS

Nuclear Sphere:

This half-in-the-physical, half-in-the-metaphysical; i.e.,
half-conceptual, half-nonconceptual; i.e., now you see it,
now you don't-- and repeat, behavior is characteristic of
synergetics ▓▓ with its nuclear sphere being both concave
and convex simultaneously, which elucidates the microcosmic,
turn-around limit of Universe as does the c² the spherical-
wave-terminal-limit velocity of outwardness elucidate the
turn-around-and-return limit of the macrocosm."

- Cite RBF rewrite of SYNERGETICS galley at Sec. 1053.16,
  16 Dec'73

Nuclear Sphere:                                              (1)

See Ball at the Center
    Initial Sphere
    Sphere Center
    Central Ball:  Central Sphere

RBF DEFINITIONS

Nuclear Uniqueness:

"...So the vector equilibrium is a nuclear uniqueness
for the first layer of 12 and the next layer of 42, with
no other potential nucleus as yet appearing in its system--
in its exterior shell's structural triangular facets-- to
challenge its nuclear pristinity."

- Cite SYNERGETICS draft at Sec. 1011.59, 18 Feb'73

Nuclear Sphere:                                              (2)

See Nature in a Corner, 17 Nov'75
    Omnidirectional Terminal Case Corner, 13 Nov'75
    Vector Equilibrium:  Potential & Primitive
        Tetravolumes, 12 May'77

RBF DEFINITIONS

Nuclear Uniqueness:

"And we have the concept of the limits of asymmetry in
respect to the vector equilibrium as the limit of coming to
the molecules.  That's what we have: nuclear uniqueness and
all of its variables within the domain of the three-frequency
vector equilibrium. . . .

". . . Dealing with our original concept that the vector
equilibriums are nuclear structures embracing all the variables
of Universe."

- Citation and context at Vector Equilibrium, 16 Oct'73

Nuclear vs. Superficial:

See Push-pull Members, 28 Oct'72

Nuclear Uniqueness:

See Vector Equilibrium:  Three-frequency VE

Nuclear Symmetry:

See Limit, 29 May'72
    Rhombic Dodecahedron, 24 Feb'72

Nuclear Vertex:

See Vector Equilibrium as Empty Set Tetrahedron,
    2 Nov'73

RBF DEFINITIONS

██████████ Nucleated Cube:

"The minimum allspace-filling nuclear cube is formed by
adding eight Eighth-octahedra to the eight triangular facets
of the vector equilibrium of tetravolume 5; i.e., 5 x 24 =
120 quanta modules. This produces a cubical nuclear
involvement domain (see Sec. 1006.30) of tetravolume 6;
i.e., 6 x 24 = 144 quanta modules.

"The nuclear cube is the maximum sizeless, timeless,
subfrequency generalized nuclear domain of synergetic-
energetic geometry.

"The construction of the first nuclear cube in effect
restores the vector equilibrium truncations. The minimum
has 142 balls in the vector equilibrium. The first
nucleated cube has 2181 balls in the total aggregation."

(Secs. 415.17; 415.171; 415.172, 2nd. Ed.)

- Cite SYNERGETICS, 2nd. Ed. at above Secs; 23 Feb'76

---

██████████ Nucleated Cube: (2)

See Vector Equilibrium Involvement Domain, 11 Dec'75;
10 Dec'75; 12 Dec'75
Allspace Filling, 11 Jul'62
Quantum Jump, 26 Aug'76

---

RBF DEFINITIONS

██████████ Nucleated Cube:

"The minimum allspace-filling nuclear cube is formed by
adding eight eighth-octahedra to the eight triangular facets
of the vector equilibrium of tetravolume 5; i.e. 5 x 24 = 120
quanta modules. This produces a cubical nuclear involvement
domain of tetravolume 6; i.e., 6 x 24 = 144 quanta modules.

"This nuclear cube is the maximum sizeless, timeless, subfrequency generalized nuclear domain of synergetic-energetic
geometry."

.17
(Sec. 415.06, 2nd. Ed.)

- Cit RBF to EJA, 3200 Idaho, Wash., DC. + RBF holograph; 11 Dec'75

---

RBF DEFINITIONS

Nucleus & Embracement:

"You can't have a nucleus without an embracement."

- Cite RBF to EJA, 3200 Idaho, Wash., DC.; 24 Jan'76

---

RBF DEFINITIONS

███ Nucleated Cube:

"To find the first nucleated cube, you just untruncate
(restore) the vector equilibrium truncations. The
minimum has 142 balls in the vector equilibrium part.
The first nucleated cube has 2181 balls."

(Sec. 415.062, 2nd. Ed.)

- Cite RBF to EJA, Wash DC. 7 Oct. '71.

---

RBF DEFINITIONS

Nuclear Pattern of Growth & Decay:

"There is no way in parallel thinking that man can come to
any important conclusions. We tend to think in parallels
and perpendiculars when our Universe is not operating in
parallels. Our Universe operates from a nucleus; it radiates
and converges--it's a gravitational pulling together and
entropy trying to come apart. Everything is either growing
or decaying. There is nothing in parallel at all; there is
no nucleus in parallels. In nuclear growth a two goes into
a three and a three goes back to two as electromagnetic waves
go out and then converge. Waves are not drawn on a piece of
paper in a plane; they are convergent and divergent expressing
the great pulsations in our Universe. I find this is a very
important part of fundamental thinking."

- Cite RBF National Geographic Land Use Seminar; transcript
pp. 17-18 Side II & p.1 Side III; 8 Dec'75

---

██████████ Nucleated Cube: (1)

See Vector Equilibrium Involvement Domain

---

RBF DEFINITIONS

Nucleated Systems: Idealistic Vectorial Geometry Of:

"It is experientially demonstrable that the structural
interpatterning principles governing all the atomic behaviors
are characterized by triangular and tetrahedral-based associations governed by the 12 degrees of freedom.

"These structural, pattern-governing, conceptualizable principles,
in turn govern all eternally regenerative design evolution
including the complex patternings of potential, symmetrically-
and asymmetrically-limited, pulsative regeneration, only in
respect to all of which are ideals conceivable, as is experientially manifest in synergetics and in my closed-system,
topological hierarchy discovered only through a half century
of persistent exploration of the ramifications of the
idealistic vectorial geometry characteristics of inherently
nucleated systems and their experientially demonstrable
properties."

(See Principle, 14 Feb'72 for first draft.)

- Cite RBF marginalis in Eccles ' "Facing Reality," as
rewriteen by RBF, 15 Feb'72

421.20)
(- Incorporated in SYNERGETICS, 2nd. Ed. at Sec. 537.06.)

Nucleated System:  Nuclear Systems:                    (1)

    See VE as Prime Nucleated System

---

RBF DEFINITIONS

Nucleus:

"The coordinate system of nature as revealed in synergetics
is one in which nature operates in convergent-divergent,
associative-disassociative agglomerating, a system in which
the inherent symmetry is maintained only by the equilateral
triangles.  Nature is syhergetically both expansively radiant
and convergently gravitational: radiant as radiation or as an
expansive, disintegrative, coming apart, or nature as
gravitationally convergent with increasing symmetry and order.
Nature resolves her problems by convergence to an inherent
nucleus."

- Cite SYNERGETICS, 2nd. Ed., at Sec. 260.41; 13 Nov'75

---

Nucleated Systems:  Nuclear Systems:                   (2)

    See Vector Equilibrium, Oct'75
        Vector Equilibrium Involvement Domain, 10 Dec'75

---

RBF DEFINITIONS

Nucleus:

"Two spheres in Universe --- mass attraction --- vector
equilibrium --- nuclear assembly.  Nuclear assembly starts
with an inherent volume of 20, which is the minimum model
of nucleation."

- Citation & context at Quantum Sequence, (4), 23 Jun'75

---

Nucleon:

    See Octahedron:  Nuclear Asymmetric Octahedra, 1 Apr'73

---

RBF DEFINITIONS

Nucleus:

"The divergent characteristics of the tetrahedra at the
center of the vector equilibrium demonstrate the nucleus.
This is because the tetrahedron is a system and not anything
in its own right.

"A nucleus is a complex of systems.  A nucleus could not
possibly be a simplex.  Spherically and symmetrically there
are 12-around-1.  Volumetrically and asymmetrically there are
20 tetrahedra around a nucleus: that is what nucleates it."

- Cite RBF to EJA, Pagano Rest., Phila., PA., 22  Jun'75

---

RBF DEFINITIONS

Nucleus:

"...the XYZ coordinates have nothing to do with the way
Universe works.....That's why you couldn't have a nucleus
in a perpendicular or a parallel system.  You can only have
nuclei when you have convergence."

- Citation & context at Convergence & Divergence, 1 May'77

---

RBF DEFINITIONS

Nucleus:

"The nucleus can accommodate wave passage without disrupting
the fundamental resonance of the octaves.  The tetrahedron
is the minimum, ergo, prime nonnucleated structural system
of Universe.  The vector equilibrium is the minimum, ergo
prime, nucleated structural system of Universe."

- Cite SYNERGETICS text at Sec. 421.05; galley rewrite, 2 Nov'73

RBF DEFINITIONS

Nucleus:

"...The common center ball, being two-in-one, can be used
for a pulse or a space; for an integer or a zero. The one
active nucleus is the key to the binary Yes-No of the
invisible transistor circuitry."

- Cite SYNERGETICS draft at Sec. 1012.12, 18 Feb'73

RBF DEFINITIONS

Nucleus:

"A nucleus, by definition,
Must be surrounded in all directions.
This means that there must be a ball
In every possible angular relationship to the nucleus.
This does not happen with one layer of twelve balls,
Nor with a second layer of forty-two balls.
Not until a third layer of ninety-two balls is added
Are all the angular relationships to the nucleus filled.
We now have a true nucleus."

- Cite RBF Draft, Numerology, 4.21
1971

RBF DEFINITIONS

Nucleus:                                                    (1)

"Operationally speaking the word omnidirectional involves
a speaker who is observing from some viewing point. He says,
'People and things are going every which way around me.' It
sounds chaotic. We cannot and do not live and experience in
a two-dimensional infinitely extended planar world. We live
in an omnidirectionally viewable world. Omnidirectional
means that a center of a sphere of observation that resolves
all that can be observed to either passing by tangentially
which is always perpendicular to the radii of the observer,
which means that the multiplicity of his real events does
not produce chaos but instead produces orderly relationships
to the very orderly radii of the observer, all of which events
are subject to orderly recording and interrelating in
relationship to the observer's inherently orderly sphere of
reference. The expression 'frame' of reference is not only
'square', but its two-dimensional 3-D axes of reference such
as XYZ coordinates requires inept rectilinear defining
quite uncharacteristic of omniwavilinear orbiting Universe
events; whereas the infinite dimensioning of tangential
radii referencing can always be 'right on ' the actual event
tracery. Omnidirectional implies a nucleus. Because of
omni-closest-packing of 12 spheres triangularly surrounding

- Cite RBF to EJA, 3200 Idaho, DC, 14 Feb '72. Rewritten 17 Feb.

RBF DEFINITIONS

Nucleus:

The definition of a nucleus as defined for the symmetrical
and tangential closest packing of equiradius spheres does
"not apply to an asymmetrical or single-axis system, e.g.
Hydrogen, where a nucleus may be encircled by action within
a single plane and where the surround is generated by a
single orbit."

- Cite RBF to EJA as footnote to Sec 415.1 of Synergetics draft.
Bear Island, 25 August 1971

RBF DEFINITIONS

Nucleus:                                                    (2)

"one. Energy cannot be distributed inwardly, therefore
it has to be distributed outwardly. With 12 omnidirectional
alternate moves with each event, complex distribution
swiftly ensues. Because there are spaces between closest
packed sphere energy can be imported which can only be
articulated outwardly-- ergo entropy."

- Cite RBF to EJA, 3200 Idaho, DC, 14 Feb '72. Rewritten 17 Feb.
rewritten as SYNERGETICS draft Secs, 1001 + 1002, 27 Feb '72

RBF DEFINITIONS

Nucleus:
"Omnitopology differs from Euler's superficial
topology, omnitopology being nuclear."

- Cite RBF to EJA, Fairfield, Conn., Chez Wolf.
18 June 1971.
- Citation at Omnitopology, 18 Jun'71

RBF DEFINITIONS

Nucleus:

"Omnidirectional implies a nucleus. Because of
closest packing energy cannot be distributed inwardly,
therefore it has to be distributed outwardly.
With 12 omnidirectional alternate moves with each
event, complex distribution swiftly ensues."

- Cite RBF to EJA, 3200 Idaho, DC, 14 Feb '72

RBF DEFINITIONS

Nucleus:

"Each ball can always have a neutral function among these
aggregates. It is a nuclear ball whether it's an planar
array or in an omnidirectional array. It has a function in
each of the two adjacent systems which performs like
bonding."

- Cite tape transcript RBF to EJA, Chez Wolf, 18 June 1971

NUCLEUS IN ISO. VEC. MATRIX- SEC 421.63

RBF DEFINITIONS

Nucleus:

"The nucleus can accommodate waves without breaking

up the fundamental resonance of the octaves."

- Cite RBF to EJA, Fairfield, Conn. Chez Wolf.
  18 June 1971.

NUCLEUS IN ISO. VEC. MATRIX — SEC 421.04)

---

RBF DEFINITIONS

Nucleus:

In closest packing of spheres "the third layer of 92 spheres
contains eight new potential nuclei which, however, do not
become active nuclei until each has three more layers
surrounding it-- three layers being unique to each nucleus.
This tells us that the nuclear group with 92 spheres in its
outer or third layer is the limit of unique, closest-
packed assemblages of unit-wavelength and frequency, nuclear
symmetry systems."

- Cite NEHRU SPEECH, p, 25, 13 Nov'69

---

RBF DEFINITIONS

Nucleus:

"Systems can have nuclei and prime volumes cannot.
There are only three prime volumes."

- Citation at Prime Volumes, 18 Jun'71
- Cite RBF to EJA, Fairfield, Conn., Chez Wolf.
  18 June 1971.

---

RBF DEFINITIONS

Nucleus:

"In this dynamically opposed system... every nuclear component
has its positive or negative opposite with each reversing
every characteristic of the other."

- Citation & context at Energy, 16 Sep'67

---

RB F DEFINITIONS

Nucleus:

"A nucleus, by definition,

Must be surrounded in all directions."

- Cite NUMEROLOGY Draft, p. 34 - April 1971

---

RBF DEFINITIONS

Nucleus:

The vector equilibrium is the "most compact spherical

agglomeration;" it "expands to infinity" with " a new

nucleus every four orbits."

(Adapted.)

- Cite Geometrical Chart of 35 Synergetic Figures:
  - Fig. 22. 1967

---

RBF DEFINITIONS

Nucleus:

"A formula for the nucleus: a ball with a ball inside

it-- concave and convex."

- Cite RBF to EJA by telephone
  from Los Angeles, January 1971

---

RBF DEFINITIONS

Nucleus:

"All the internal or nuclear affairs of the atom

occur internally to the vector equilibrium and all the

external or chemical associations occur externally to the

vector equilibrium."

- Citation at Physics: Difference Between Physics and
  Chemistry, Jun'66
    - Cite Carbondale Draft
      Return to Modelability, p. V.16
- Cite NASA Speech, p.83, Jun'66

RBF DEFINITIONS

Nucleus:

"It is characteristic of a nucleus that it has at least
two layers in which there is no new nucleus showing up,
no potential. In the third layer, however, a potential
new nucleus shows up, but it does not have its own two
unique layers to protect it-- so you would not say it
is as yet a realized nucleus, only a potential nucleus."

- Cite Oregon Lecture #8, p. 304. 12 Jul'62

---

Nucleus: Nucleation: Nuclear: (2A)

See Closest Packing of Spheres, 29 May'72; 13 Mar'71
    Coupler (2)
    Domain, 11 Feb'73
    Energy, 16 Sep'67*
    Environment, 22 Sep'73
    Growthability, 6 Mar'73
    Human, 22 Sep'73
    In & Out, 4 May'57
    Invisible Circuitry (1)(2)
    Isotropic Vector Matrix, 4 Mar'73
    Limit, 29 May'72
    Now, 14 Feb'72
    Omnitopology, 18 Jun'71*
    Experience, 28 Apr'74
    Crystallography, 17 Aug'70
    Hydrogen, 29 May'72

---

RBF DEFINITIONS

Nucleus vs. Boundaries:

"The Greeks had the myopic bias of a game of boundaries;
there was no nucleus at all in the Greek geometry."

- Cite RBF at videotaping session, Penn Bell Labs., Philadelphia,
  28 Jan'75

---

Nucleus: Nucleation: Nuclear: (2B)

See Particle, 6 Jul'62
    Physics: Difference Between Physics & Chemistry,
        Jun'66*
    Prime Volumes, 18 Jun'71*
    Regenerative Design: Law Of, (2)
    Spherical Nostalgia, 12 Jun'74
    Universe, 4 May'57
    Vector Equilibrium, 17 Aug'70; 19 Nov'74
    Vertex, 11 Oct'73
    Self & Otherness, 19 Nov'74
    Quantum Sequence, (4)*
    Cloud Chamber, Nov'71
    Vector Equilibrium Growth, 13 Nov'75
    Zero Volume Tetrahedron, 10 Dec'75
    Gravity: Speed of, 21 Oct'72
    Parallel, 28 Mar'77
    Potential vs. Primitive, 12 May'77
    Convergence & Divergence, 1 May'77*
    Mites & Quarks as Basic Notes, (1)

---

Nucleus: Nucleation: Nuclear: (1A)

See Astro & Nucleic Interpositioning
    Atomics
    Ball at the Center
    Convex & Concave
    Cube: Nucleated Cube
    Initial Sphere
    Internuclear Vector Modulus
    Nebula
    Nine: Nucleus = Nine = Nothing
    Nonnuclear
    Nuclear & Nebular Zonal Waves
    Nuclear & Nonnuclear
    Biological Cell Nucleus
    Octahedron: Nuclear Asymmetric Octahedra
    Omnitopology
    Organics & the Nucleus
    Orbiting Magnitudes
    Outward Limit of Nuclear Phenomena

---

Nucleus: Nucleation: Nuclear: (3A)

See Nuclear Computer Design
    Nuclear Domain
    Nuclear Gyro
    Nuclear & Nebular Zonal Waves
    Nucleus = Nine = Nothing
    Nuclear: Outward Limit
    Nuclear & Nonnuclear
    Nuclear Propagation Rate
    Nuclear Set
    Nuclear Simplex
    Nuclear Sphere
    Nuclear Symmetry
    Nuclear Uniqueness
    Nuclear Vertex
    Nucleated Cube
    Nucleated Systems: Idealistic Vectorial Geometry Of
    Nucleon
    Nucleus vs. Boundaries
    Nuclear Assemblage Components

---

Nucleus: Nucleation: Nuclear: (1B)

See Prime Nucleus
    Prime Nucleated System
    Terminal Condition
    Topological Aspects: Inventory Of
    Topology: Synergetic & Eulerian
    Zero Frequency
    Prime Nuclear Structural Systems
    Coupler: Nuclear Asymmetric Octahedron
    Central Symmetry
    Domain of a Nucleus
    Zero Nineness
    Internuclear Voids
    Subnuclear

---

Nucleus: Nucleation: Nuclear: (3B)

See Nuclear Geometrical Limit of Rational Differentiation
    Nucleus & Embracement
    Nuclear = Regenerative
    Nuclear vs. Superficial
    Nuclear Pattern of Growth & Decay
    Nuclear & Nebular: Nucleus & Galaxies
    Nuclear Limit
    Nuclear Poer Generation

RBF DEFINITIONS

Number:

"All number awareness is discovered through experiences, which are all special cases. Every time you write a number-- every time you say, write, or read a number-- you see resolvable clusters of light differentiation. And clusters are an experience. Conscious thoughts of numbers, either subjective or objective are always special case."

- Cite SYNERGETICS text at Sec. 508.04, galley rewrite, 7 Nov'73

---

RBF DEFINITIONS

Number:

"Numbers are experiences. You have one experience and another experience, which, when reviewed, are composited. Numbers have unique experiential meaning. Even the development of sets derives from experience because mathematics is generalization-- but generalization itself is sequitur to experience-- where intuition and mind discover the synergetic inter-behavior that is not implicit in any of the data of the past.

"The mathematician talks of "pure imaginary numbers" on the false assumption that mathematics could be a priori to experience. All number awareness is discovered through experiences, which are all special cases. Every time you write a number-- every time you say, or write, or read a number-- you see clusters and clusters are an experience. Conscious thinking of number, subjective and objective, are always special case."

- Cite RBF to EJA
  Beverly Hotel, New York
  13 March 1971

CONCEPTUALITY- NUMBER- Secs. 508.01-508.04)

---

RBF DEFINITIONS

Number:

"... Numbers are both abstract (empty sets) or special case (filled sets)."

- Citation and context at Vector, 26 May'72

---

RBF DEFINITIONS

Number:

Synergetics provides for "the identification of energy with number."

- Citation at Synergetics, 19 Jan'71

- Cite RBF to EJA by telephone from Los Angeles, 19 Jan'71 pursuant to Coxeter's letter offering mathematical proof of 'Planetary Planning' in Am. Scholar, Winter 70-71

---

RBF DEFINITIONS

Number:

"Only number can self-communicate as structural or destructural associabilities."

- Citation at Self-communicate, 15 May'72

---

RBF DEFINITIONS

Number:

"Mathematicians theretofore /i.e., before topology_7 had erroneously thought that they had attained utter abstraction, or utter non-conceptuality-- ergo 'pure' non-sensoriality, by employing a series of algebraic symbols ▬▬▬ substituted for calculus symbols and substituted for again by 'empty set' symbols.

"They overlooked that even their symbols themselves were conceptual patterns and only recognizable that way, for instance numbers or phonetic letters, consist of physical ingredients and physical experience recalls. The physical ingredients consist inherently of event-paired quanta and the latter's six-vectored, positive and negative actions, reactions, and resultants else they would not have become employable by the deluding, experience-immersed 'purists.'

CONCEPTUALITY NUMBER SEC. 508.10 PATTERN - SEC. 505.12 - Cite CARBONDALE DRAFT IV.41 / - Cite NASA Speech, p. 58. Jun'66

---

RBF DEFINITIONS

Number:

"The number itself has its own integrity And therefore ought to be integrated."

- Cite Numerology draft August 1971, p. 30.
- Citation at Integrity, Aug'71

---

RBF DEFINITIONS

Number:

"Tetrahedra have a fundamental prime number: oneness. The octahedron has a fundamental twoness, its volume of four being made up of the prime number two; even the topological accountings of vertexes and faces disclose their respective fundamental oneness, twoness, and threeness."

- Cite Carbondale Draft Return to Modelability, p. V.7
- Cite NASA Speech, p. 72, Jun'66

RBF DEFINITIONS

Number:

"Numbers are meaningless independent of pattern."

- Citation and context at Synergy, 1954

---

RBF DEFINITIONS

Number:    Even Number:

"Because of a hemisphere's polar symmetry to its opposite
polar hemisphere the total inventory of great circle grid
triangles in the comprehensive world grid is always even
in number."

- Cite Undated Sheet: THE DYMAXION AIROCEAN WORLD FULLER
  PROJECTIVE-TRANSFORMATION.

---

RBF DEFINITIONS

Number:

"The number itself has its own integrity
And therefore ought to be integrated."

. . .

"Nature does all her associating and disassociating in
Whole rational numbers."

- Cite RBF Draft, NUMEROLOGY 4.11, 4.18

---

RBF DEFINITIONS

Number:  Even Number:

"...It is mathematically discovered that the total number of
points, or areas, or lines, of a system are always even numbers;
and that this divisibility by two accommodates polar-and-hemispherical positive-negativeness of all systems."

- Citation and context at Probability Model of Three Cars on a
  Highway (1), 26 Sep'73

---

RBF DEFINITIONS

Number:  Cosmically Absolute Numbers:

"There are apparently no cosmically absolute numbers other
than 1, 2, 3, and 4.  This primitive fourness identifies
exactly with one quantum of energy and with the fourness of
the tetrahedron's  primitive structuring as constituting the
'prime structural system of Universe,' i.e., as the
minimum omnitriangulated differentiator of Universe into
insideness and outsideness, which alone, of all macrO-micro
Universe differentiators pulsates inside-outingly and vice
versa as instigated by only one force vector impinging
upon it."

- Cite SYNERGETICS draft at Sec. 1222.21, 5 Mar'73

---

Number:  Cosmically Absolute Numbers:

        See Cosmic Absolutes
            Ninety-two Elements:  Four Unique Frequencies

---

Number:  Even Numbers:

        See Geodesic Diamonds, 31 Jan'75
            Polarity, undated sheet
            Vertexial Spheres, 8 Apr'75

---

Number:  Even & Odd Numbers:                                    (1)

        See Locking & Blocking
            Vector Equilibrium:  Odd or Even Shell Growth

Number:  Even & Odd Numbers:                                    (2)


See Gear Train:  Locking & Blocking, 25 Feb'69
    Necklace, (1)(2)

---

Number:  Tetrahedral Number:

"$\frac{N^2 - N}{2}$ is always a triangular number as, for instance, the number of balls in the rack on a pool table.  A telephone connection is a circuit; a circuit is a circle; two people need one circuit and three people need three circles, which make a triangle.  Four people need six circuits, and six circuits cluster most economically and symmetrically in a triangle.  Five people need 10 private circuits, six people need 15, and seven people need 21, and so on: all are triangular numbers.

"Successive stackings of the number of relationships of our experiences are a stacking of triangles.  The number of balls in the longest row of any triangular cluster will always be the same number as the number of rows of balls in the triangle, each row always having one more than the preceding row.  The number of balls in any triangle will always be

$$\frac{(R + 1)^2 - (R + 1)}{2}$$ where $\underline{R}$ = the number of rows

(or the number of balls in the longest row)."

- Cite SYNERGETICS text at Sec.s 508.20, .30, May'71

---

Number:  Names for Numbers:


See Etymology, Aug'71
    Old Words, 22 Jul'71

---

Number:  Tetrahedral Number:  $\frac{N^2 - N}{2}$ :

"$\frac{N^2 - N}{2}$ is also the number of balls in a triangular grouping such as that of pool balls grouped for the 'break.'"

- Cite PLANETARY PLANNING, p. 18 , 13 Nov'69
(Am. Scholar, p. 48

---

Number System is Inherently Octave:

"Number system is inherently octave and corresponds to the four positive and four negative facets of the octahedron which polyhedrally represents the eight 45° angle constituents of 360° unity in the trigonometric function calculations."

- Citation and context at Indig, 3 Mar'73

---

Number:  Tetrahedral Number:  $\frac{N^2 - N}{2}$ :

"Comprehension means identifying all the most uniquely economical interrelationships of the focal point entities involved.  We may say that:  Comprehension = $\frac{N^2 - N}{2}$.

Cite OPERATING MANUAL, P. 70 , 1969

---

Number Pattern:

"Number behavior phenomena is pattern.  Number treatment or function treatment without pattern is unthinkable.  Formulations and equations are pattern.  Numbers are therefore nonexistent without pattern.  There are no empty sets of number independent of pattern.  There are empty sets but the word 'sets' is inherently a subclass of 'pattern.'"

"There are no number 'abstractions.'  There are pattern abstractions.  What is abstracted is the residual generalized pattern.  Pattern phenomena is synergetic-- which means behavior of whole systems unpredicted by behavior of respective subsystems-- which is to say that numbers are meaningless independent of pattern."

- Cite Ltr. to Jim Fitzgibbon (?), Raleigh, NC, undated. (1954-59)

---

Number:  Tetrahedral Number:  $\frac{N^2 - N}{2}$ :

"The number of relationships between items

Is always  $\frac{N^2 - N}{2}$ .

The relationships between four or more items

Are always greater in number

Than the number of items.

- Cite HOW LITTLE, p. 56 , Oct'66

RBF DEFINITIONS

■■■ Number: Tetrahedral Number: $\frac{N^2 - N}{2}$ :

"We look at the stars and they look very random scattered throughout the sky. I will tell you then that the numbers of relationships between all the stars is always $\frac{N^2 - N}{2}$ and . . . that I am mathematically justified in so doing. This will give you a personal sense of the power of the infinitely tiny human's mind in the presence of that vast array of star's whose distances and occurrences can only be identified in terms of millions and billions and higher number of years and miles away."

- Cite NASA Speech, p. 94, Jun'66
- Citation & context at Relationship Analysis (1), Jun'66

---

RBF DEFINITIONS

Number: Tetrahedral Number: $\frac{N^2 - N}{2}$ :

". . . The numbers of relationships between all the stars is always $\frac{n^2 - n}{2}$ . . . "

". . . When we add up all the accumulated relationships between all the successive experiences in our lives . . . they will always combine cumulatively to comprise a tetrahedron."

- Cite NASA Speech p. 94, Jun'66

---

RBF DEFINITIONS

Number: Tetrahedral Number: $\frac{N^2 - N}{2}$ :

"$\frac{N^2 - N}{2}$ = the number of connections necessary to understanding.

"When we understand we have all the fundamental connections between the star events of our consideration."

- Cite ▓▓▓▓▓▓▓▓▓▓▓▓▓▓▓▓
- Citation and context at Understanding, 23 Oct'65

---

RBF DEFINTIONS

Number: Tetrahedral Number: $\frac{N^2 - N}{2}$ :

"The connecting trail 'line' was the basis of the establishment of communication. Today it is the essence of communication theory. Understanding involves the discovery of all the linears or interconnecting lines, the $\frac{N^2 - N}{2}$ connections."

- Cite AAUW JOURNAL, May 1965, Pp. 176, 177
- Citation and context at Communication, May'65

---

RBF DEFINITIONS

Number: Tetrahedral Number; $\frac{N^2 - N}{2}$ :

"The orderliness of the universe and all the potential $\frac{N^2 - N}{2}$ relationships are by experience a priori to man's exploration and discovery of them."

- CITE AAUW JOURNAL, May 1965, P. 173
- Citation and context at Discovery, May'65

---

Number: Tetrahedral Number: $\frac{N^2 - N}{2}$ :                    (1)

See Connections & Relatedness
Order Underlying Randomness
Relationship Analysis

---

Number: Tetrahedral Number: $\frac{N^2 - N}{2}$ :                    (2)

See Communication, May'65
Compression, 1969
God, May'65
Line, 13 Nov'72
Logistics, 10 Dec'73
Relationship Analysis, (1)*
Relativity, 7 Nov'72
Understanding, 23 Oct'65; May'67
Geometrical Function of Nine, (7)
Multidimensionality, (2)

---

RBF DEFINITIONS

■■■■■■■■■■■■■■ Number Theory:

"The concept of being alive may be inherent only in the eternal principle of differentiability, and of a theoretical number system, and of complexes of different numbers. Seeming consciousness and life may well be inherent only in mind conceivable theories of differentiations."

- Cite RBF Marginalia 20 Dec. '71 at SYNERGETICS Draft, Sec. 529.07
* Citation at Consciousness, 20 Dec'71

RBF DEFINITIONS

Number:  Triangular Numbers:

$\frac{{}^nN^2 - N}{2}$ is always a triangular number, as for instance, the number of balls in the rack on a pool table. A telephone connection is a circuit, a circuit is a circle; two people need one circuit; three people need three circles; these make a triangle. Four people need four circuiys. Successive stackings of the number of relationships of our experiences are a stacking of triangles where the sum-total of balls in the succesive rows will always be $\frac{(R + 1)^2 - (R + 1)}{2}$.

- Cite RBF to EJA
  Beverly Hotel, New York
  13 March 1971

CONCEPTUALITY- NUMBER- SECS. 508.2 + 508.30

---

Number:                                    (1B)

See Powering
    Rate:  Fundamental Rates of Change of Number
    Scheherazade Number
    Six-wave (Sexave) Phenomenon of Number
    SSRCD
    Volume-number Ratios
    ██████████
    Rational Whole Numbers
    Figures & Words
    Generalized Topological Definability
    Energy & Number
    Complementary & Reciprocal Numbers
    Zero-nineness
    Geometry & Number

---

Number-value Accounting:                    (1)

See Intertransformative Number-value Accounting

---

Number:                                    (2)

See Integrity, Aug'71*
    Line, 7 Nov'72
    Self-communicate, 15 May'72
    Sensorial Reflex, 13 Mar'73
    Synergetics, 19 Jan'71*
    Synergy, 1954*
    Vector, 26 May'72*
    Vector Equilibrium, 10 Nov'74
    Human Beings & Complex Universe, (7)

---

Number-value Accounting:                    (2)

See Models, 9 Jan'74
    Synergetics, 19 Jan'71

---

Number:                                    (3)

See Number:  Cosmically Absolute Numbers
    Number:  Even Numbers
    Number:  Even & Odd Numbers
    Number:  Names for Numbers
    Number System is Inherently Octave
    Number Pattern
    Number:  Tetrahedral Number: $\frac{N^2 - N}{2}$
    Number Theory
    Number:  Triangular Numbers
    Number-value Accounting

---

Number:                                    (1A)

            Beginning Number
See Cipher
    Constants
    Decimal & Duodecimal
    Empty Set
    Even Number
    Imaginary Number
    Indig
    Interwave Behavior of Number
    Illions
    Irrational Number
    Intertransformative Number-value Accounting
    Limit Number
    Low-order Prime Numbers
    Old Words
    Pi
    Prime Number
    ████████████
    Rememberable Number

---

**NUMBERS IN THIS FILE**                    (1)

See Degrees in This File
    SSRCD Numbers

RBF DEFINITIONS

Numbers in This File:                                              (2)

        See One
            Two:  Twoness
            Three:  Threefoldness
            Four:  Fourness
            Six:  Sixness
            Eight:  Eightness
            Nine:  Nineness:  Nine as Zero
            Ten:  Ten-ness
            Twelve
            Thirteen
            Fourteen:  Fourteeness
            Fifteen:  Fifteeness
            Eighteen
            Twentyness

    (N.B.  For numbers over Twenty see Arabic listings after Number)

---

RBF DEFINITIONS

    Number:  3.702 :

            See Vector Equilibrium:  Ratio of Volume to Quantum,
                    23 Jan'72
                Immaculate Conception, 25 Jan'72
                Environment Control, 3 Oct'72

---

RBF DEFINITIONS

    Number:  2½ :                                                 (1)

            See Askewness
                Frequency:  Half Frequency

---

RBF DEFINITIONS

    Number:  6.28 :

            See Universal Integrity:  Principle Of, 5 Jan'72,
                    21 Dec'71
                Gravity, 21 Dec'71

---

    Number:  2½ :                                                 (2)

            See Basic Triangle:  Basic Disequilibrium 120 LCD
                    Triangle, 20 Dec'73
                Basic Triangle:  Basic Equilibrium 48 LCD Triangle,
                    17 Dec'73
                Constant Relative Abundance, 29 Nov'72
                Fiveness, 7 Mar'73
                Rhombic Dodecahedron, 12 May'77
                Split Personality, 15 Jan'74
                Vector Equilibrium:  Potential & Primitive Tetra-
                    volumes, 12 May'77
                T Module, 21 Jun'77

---

RBF DEFINITIONS

    Number:  6.6666+ :

            See Universal Integrity:  Principle Of, 8 May'72
                    13 Nov'69

---

    Number:  3.7 :

            See Structural Quanta, 9 Nov'73
                Units of Environment Control, 9 Nov'73

---

RBF DEFINITIONS

    Number:  18.36 :

            See Icosahedron as Electron Model, 7 Mar'73

# Synergetics Dictionary

RBF DEFINITIONS

Number: 18.51 :

See Twentyness in Mass Ratio of Electron & Proton
Universal Integrity:  Vector Equilibrium &
    Icosahedron (1)
Vector Equilibrium:  Ratio of Volume to Quantum,
    23 Jan'72
Icosahedron and Vector-edged Cube, 11 Mar'69
Icosahedron as Electron Model, 15 Oct'64
Electron & Neutron, 2 Oct'72
Gravitational Constant (2)
Structural Quanta, 9 Nov'73; 3 Oct'72

FILE INDICATORS

Number: 24 :                                      (a)

See Basic Triangle:  Basic Equilibrium 48 LCD Triangle,
    16 Dec'73
Control Quantum, 19 Apr'73
Coupler, 27 Jan'75
Gravitational Constant, (1)
Module:  A Quanta Module:  Introduction Of,
    22 Feb'77
Nuclear Cube, 23 Feb'76
Octahedron:  Eight-octahedra, 16 Dec'73
Powering:  Fifth & Eighth Powering, 11 Dec'75
Sphere:  Volume-surface Ratios, 11 Dec'75
Stabilized Vector Equilibrium, 23 Feb'72
Tetrahedroning, (3)
Twelve Universal Degrees of Freedom, (1)
Tetrahedron:  Twenty-fourth Tetrahedron
Vectors, 25 Aug'71
Vector Equilibrium, 19 Nov'74
Wire Wheel, 4 May'57
Quanta Loss by Congruence, (1)
Rhombic Dodecahedron, 12 May'77
Vector Equilibrium:  Potential & Primitive
    Tetravolumes, 12 May'77

Number: 18.63 :

See Icosahedron as Electron Model, 11 Jul'62

Number: 24 :                                      (b)

See Mites & Quarks as Basic Notes, (3)

FILE INDICATORS

Number: 23 :

See Trigonometric Limit:  First 14 Primes

Number: 25 :

See Gravitational Constant, (1)
Octahedron, 7 Mar'73
Railroad Tracks:  Great Circle Energy Tracks On
    The Surface of a Sphere
Symmetry:  Seven Axes of Symmetry
Vector Equilibrium:  Great Circles Of

TEXT CITATIONS

Number: 24 :

Sec. 015.06          954.10
    223.16*          954.21-954.22      537.131 (2nd.Ed.)
    982.62           954.46             1012.11
    982.70           954.49             450.11
    943.00 (Table)   954.51             1053.12
    453.01           955.02             1053.36 (2nd.Ed.)
    905.51           955.40 (Table)     961.44
    905.55           974.01
    910.11           974.03-974.04
    905.44*          1011.40
                     1052.30

TEXT CITATIONS

Number: 26 :

John McHale's R. BUCKMINSTER FULLER (George Braziller),
    p.44, 1962

Number: 26 :

    See Thirty Minimum Topological Characteristics, (1)
       Geometrical Function of Nine, (6)

Number: 30 :

    See Gravitational Constant (1)(2)
       Thirty Minimum Topological Characteristics
       Thirty Minimum Aspects of a System
       Unity as Thirty
       Hex-pent Sphere, 15 Sep'76

RBF DEFINITIONS

Number: 27 :

    See Icosahedron and Vector-edged Cube, 11 Mar'69
       Tetrahedroning (3)

FILE INDICATORS

Number: 31 :
(1)

    See Trigonometric Limit: First 14 Primes

RBF DEFINITIONS

Number: 28 :

    See Vector Equilibrium: Eight-pointed Star System,
       16 Dec'73
       Humans as Machines, (1)

RBF DEFINITIONS

Number: 31 :
(2)

    See Icosahedron
       Symmetry: Seven Axes of Symmetry
       Octahedron, 7 Mar'73
       Railroad Tracks: Great-circle Energy Tracks
       On the Surface of a Sphere
       Prime Number, Oct'71
       Spherical Barrel: Kumasi Dome, (1)(2)

FILE INDICATORS

Number: 29 :

    See Trigonometric Limit: First 14 Primes

RBF DEFINITIONS

Number: 32 :

    See Dodecahedron, 22 Feb'72
       Mite as Prime Minimum System, 15 Nov'72

BBF DEFINITIONS

Number: 34 :

See Nuclear and Non-nuclear Polyhedra, 19 May'72

Number: 35 :

See Closest Packing of Spheres, 29 May'72
Vectorial & Vertexial Geometry, (3)

Number: 36 :

See Closest Packing of Spheres, 29 May'72
Periodic Table: Harmonics of 18, 22 May'75

FILE INDICATORS

Number: 37 :                                                (1)

See Trigonometric Limit: First 14 Primes

FILE INDICATORS

Number: 37 :                                                (2)

See Tetrahedroning (3)

FILE INDICATORS

Number: 41 :

See Trigonometric Limit: First 14 Primes

Number: 42 :

See Axis of Spin, (5)
Closest Packing of Spheres, (2)
Energetic Frequency, 18 Feb'73
Mite as Model for Quark, 3 May'77
Nuclear Uniqueness, 18 Feb'73
Periodic Table & Closest Packing, 13 Nov'69
Tetrakaidecahedron, 25 Feb'72
Vector Equilibrium:  Eight New Nuclei At
    Fifth Frequency, 18 Jun'71; 7 Oct'71

FILE INDICATORS

Number: 43 :

See Trigonometric Limit: First 14 Primes

RBF DEFINITIONS

Number: 45 :

See Information Transaction and Valving Models
   Tetrahedron: Dissimilar Rate of Change Accommodation
   Trigonometric Limit

---

Number: 60:

See Dodecahedron, 22 Feb'72
   Hex-pent Sphere, 15 Sep'76

---

Number: 48 :

See Basic Triangle: Basic Equilibrium 48 LCD Triangle
   Quanta Loss by Congruence, (2)
   Twelve Universal Degrees of Freedom, (1)
   Rhombic Dodecahedron, 12 May'77

---

RBF DEFINITIONS

Number: 64 :

"The sixty-fourness is the octave system to the fourth power.
It shows up in quite a few ways, for instance in the periodic
table."

- Cite RBF to EJA, 200 Locust, Phila., 22 Jan'73

---

RBF DEFINITIONS

Number: 50 :

See Magic Numbers:  Isotopal Magic Numbers

---

RBF DEFINITIONS

Number: 64 :

See Spherical Triangle Sequence (iv)
   Rope, Dec'71
   Tetrahedroning, Jun'66; (3)

---

FILE INDICATORS

Number: 56 :

See Foldability of Great Circles, 2 May'71
   Great Circle Subdivisions of Spherical Unity, May'72
   Seven Axes of Symmetry, 25 Aug'71; 13 May'73
   Tetrakaidecahedron, 25 Feb'72
   Precession & Degrees of Freedom, (2)

---

RBF DEFINITIONS

Number: 68 :

See Tetrakaidecahedron, 25 Feb'72

RBF DEFINITIONS

Number: 82 :

See Magic Numbers:  Isotopal Magic Numbers

RBF DEFINITIONS

Number:  98.6 :

See Temperature of the Human Body
    Degrees: 98.6

Number:  90:

See Dodecahedron, 22 Feb'72
    Hex-pent Sphere, 15 Sep'76

Number:  104  :

See Geometrical Function of Nine, (6)

Number:  92:

See Axis of Spin, (5)(6)
    Closest Packing of Spheres Sequence, (2)
    Coupler, 27 Jan'75
    Hex-pent Sphere, 15 Sep'76
    Limit, 29 May'72
    Nuclear & Nonnuclear Polyhedra, 19 May'72
    Nucleus, 13 Nov'69
    Ten, 22 Jun'75
    Twelve Universal Degrees of Freedom, (2)
    Vector Equilibrium:  Eight New Nuclei at Fifth
        Frequency, 18 Jun'71; 7 Oct'71
    Modules:  A & B Quanta Modules:  Subtetrahedra,
        14 May'73

Number:  120  :

See Basic Triangle:  Basic ▮ Disequilibrium 120
        LCD Triangle
    Decimal & Duodecimal
    Precession of Two Sets of 60 Closest-packed
        Spheres

    Equilateral, 11 Oct'71
    Fourth Dimension, Mar'72
    Powering:  Fifth & Eighth Powering, 11 Dec'75
    Sphere:  Volume-surface Ratios, 11 Dec'75
    Triacontrahedron, 3 May'77
    T Quanta Module, (1)

RBF DEFINITIONS

Number:  96 :

See Modules:  A & B Quanta Modules (ii)
    Bubbles (1)
    Twelve Universal Degrees of Freedom (2)

Number:  126 :

See Magic Numbers:  Isotopal Magic Numbers

RBF DEFINITIONS

Number: 142 :

See Nucleated Cube, 7 Oct'71
Nuclear Cube, 23 Feb'76

RBF DEFINITIONS

Number: 162 :

See Vector Equilibrium: Eight New Nuclei at Fifth
Frequency, 18 Jun'71, 7 Oct'71
Closest Packing of Spheres Sequence (2)
Ten, 22 Jun'75

RBF DEFINITIONS

Number: 144 :

See Valvability, 30 Nov'72
Nuclear Cube, 23 Feb'76

Number: 180:

See Hex-pent Sphere, 15 Sep'76
Hex-pent Sphere: Transformation into Geodesic
Spiral Tube, (1)
Information Transaction and Valving Models, 9 Nov'73

RBF DEFINITIONS

Number: 146 :

See Periodic Table and Closest Packing, 13 Nov'69
Super-Atomics Sequence (3)(A)(B)

RBF DEFINITIONS

Number: 184 :

See Super-Atomics Sequence (1)

RBF DEFINITIONS

Number: 160 :

See Fourth Dimension, 10 Jul'62
Frequency, 2 Nov'73
Powering: Fourth and Fifth Dimensions, Jun'66
Mite as Prime Minimum System, 15 Nov'72
Multidimensionality, (1)(2)
Powering: Fifth & Eighth Powering, 11 Dec'75

SEC 431.03

Number: 192 :

See Multidimensionality, (2)

RBF DEFINITIONS

Number: 234 :


See Super-Atomics Sequence (4) (B)
Chain Reaction, Aug'71

---

RBF DEFINITIONS

Number: 236 :


See Periodic Table and Closest Packing, 13 Nov'73

---

RBF DEFINITIONS

Number: 238 :


See Periodic Table and Closest Packing, 13 Nov'69
Super-Atomics Sequence (3)(B)

---

Number: 240:

See Tensegrity:  Twelve Pentagons, Aug'72

---

RBF DEFINITIONS

Number: 252 :


See Vector Equilibrium:  Eight New Nuclei at Fifth
Frequency, 18 Jun'71, 7 Oct'71
Closest Packing of Spheres Sequence (2)
Ten, 22 Jun'75

---

RBF DEFINITIONS

Number: 360 :


See Information Transaction and Valving Models, 9 Nov'73

---

RBF DEFINITIONS

Number: 362 :


See Vector Equilibrium:  Eight New Nuclei at Fifth
Frequency, 18 Jun'71, 7 Oct'71
Ten, 22 Jun'75

---

RBF DEFINITIONS

Number: 364 :


See Nuclear and Non-nuclear Polyhedra, 10 May'72

---

NUMBER 242

FIG. 986.471

Number: 459 :

See S Quanta Module, 4 Jun'77

Number: 768 :

See Rope, Dec'71

RBF DEFINITIONS

Number: 480 :

See Subfrequency (1)(2)
Modules: A & B Quanta Modules (ii), 12 Jul'62
Modules: A & B Quanta Modules: Unity as 480
Vector Equilibrium, 12 Jul'62

FIG 986.471

RBF DEFINITIONS

Number: 1001 :

See Scheherazade Number

RBF DEFINITIONS

Number: 552 :

See Complexocta, 20 Dec'73

Number: 1280 :

See Mites as Prime Minimum System, 15 Nov'72

Number: 644 :

See Modules: A & B Quanta Modules: Subtetrahedra,
14 May'73

Number: 1836 :

See S Quanta Module, 4 Jun'77

# Synergetics Dictionary

RBF DEFINITIONS

Number: 2181 :

See Nucleated Cube, 7 Oct'71
Nuclear Cube, 23 Feb'76

---

RBF DEFINITIONS

Numerology:

"It is probable
That many of the experiences which humanity has been unable
                                                    to explain,
And therefore has treated with superstition,
Often embrace phenomena
Which turn out, in due course,
To be of importance.

"For this reason
I have paid a lot of attention to numerology,
Thinking that it might contain
Very important bases
For understanding
New properties of mathematics."

- Cite RBF draft NUMEROLOGY, 4.1, 1971

---

Number: 2520 :

See Vectorial & Vertexial Geometry, (3)

---

Numerology:                                              (1)

See Astrology

---

Number: 2880 :

See Powering: Fifth & Eighth Powering, 11 Dec'75

---

Numerology:                                              (2)

See Modelability, (3)

---

RBF DEFINITIONS

Numerology:

"What the numerologists does
Is to add numbers horizontally (120 = 1+2+0 = 3)
Until they are left with one digit.
They have also assigned
To the letters of the alphabet
Corresponding numbers: A is one, B is two, C is three, etc.
Numerologists wishfully assume thatthey can identify
Characteristics of people
By the residual digit
Derived from integrating
Of all the digits
Corresponding to all the letters
In the individual's complete set of names.
Numerologists do not pretend to be scientific.
They are just fascinated with
Correspondence of their key digits
With various happenstances of existence.

- Cite Numerology draft August 1971, p. 31

---

Nut, Bolt & Screw Standards:

See World-around Language, (2)

Nutcrackers:

See Earth Model as Bundle of Nutcrackers

**Nutriment:**

See Bird's Nest as a Tool, (A)

**Nuts:**

See Gonads
Vessel

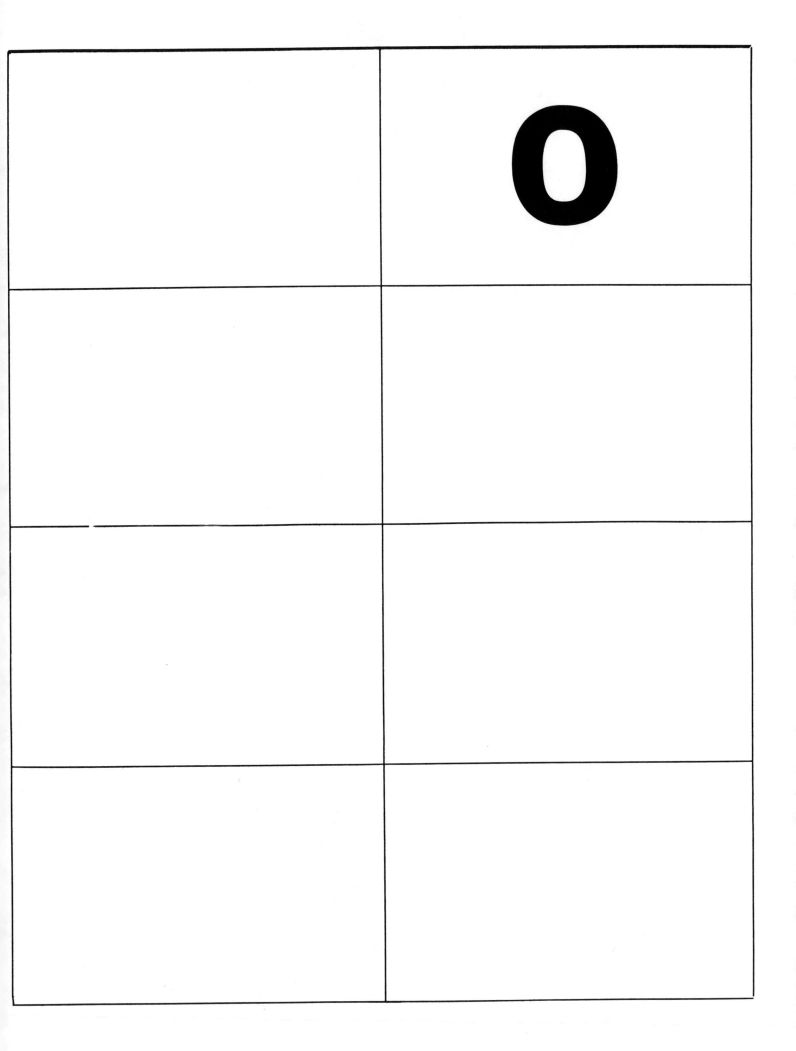

o

"O" - Circle:

See Geometry, 1 Oct'71

---

Oar: (2)

See Lever (b)
Precession (b) ; (II)

---

RBF DEFINITIONS

O Module:

"The O Module is a tetrahedron with its apex at the
center of the sphere and its base described by the 15
great circles of the Basic Disequilibrium 120 LCD triangle
of the 31-great-circle spherical icosahedron system.
See Fig. 901.03.

"The icosahedron is a "double" as a result of the 30 whole
great circles from which it may be folded.  This results
in 120 transformable O Modules.

"O Module = A Quanta Module = 1/24th of a tetravolume.

"There is no spherical continuum.  120/24 = 5.  The
icosahedron is the sphere.  When tetra is 1, the sphere
is 5."

- Cite EJA composite of RBF holograph rewrite and statements
   to EJA, 3200 Idaho, 29 Sep'76.

---

Oath Giving in Courts:

See Measurement, (1)

---

O Module:

See T Quanta Module:

---

Oath:

See Cussing

---

Oar: (1)

See Vacuum-fulcrumed Oars

---

RBF DEFINITIONS

Object:

"To be referred to as a remememberable entity, an object must
be membered with structural integrity, whether maple leaf or
crystal complex.  To have structural integrity, it must
consist entirely of triangles, which are the only complex of
energy events that are self-interference-regenerating
systems resulting in polygonal pattern stabilization."

- Cite SYNERGETICS text at Sec. 615.01; galley rewrite 9 Nov'73

RBF DEFINITIONS

Object;

What we call an object or an entity is always an aggregate; it is never a solid."

- Cite RBF to EJA, Beverly Hotel, NY, 28 Feb '71

Objective Employment of Principles:                (1)

See Invention

Object: Objects:

See Group Design, 1 Feb'75
General Systems Theory, (1)

Objective Employment of Principles:                (2)

See Design Science & World Game (A)
Orbital Escape from Critical Proximity, (1)
Loss: Discovery Through Loss, 2 Nov'73
Dymaxion Airocean World Map, (1)

Objective Coping:

See Generalized Principle (1)

RBF DEFINITIONS

Objective Integrity:

"Realization is objective integrity."

- Citation at Realization, May'60
- Cite I&I, PRIME DESIGN, p. 245. May'60

Objective Design:

See Design, (1); 9 Apr'71

RBF DEFINITIONS

Objective Intellect:

"The more you discover scientifically, the more you are overwhelmed by what we don't know. We're dealing in a fantastic mystery, and yet that mystery does have all this extraordinary orderliness, so that you can't help but realize that it can only be found by intellect. Apparently we learn it subjectively, so apparently there must be an objective intellect. There seems to be an a priori greater intellect than that of man operative."

- Citation and context at Generalization Sequence (4), Jun-Jul'69

Objective Intellect: (1)

See God as a Verb
        Intellect in Physical Universe
        Verb:  I Seem to be a Verb

Objective: (2)

See Size-zelective, 30 Nov'72
        Work, Dec'72

Objective Intellect: (2)

See Generalization Sequence, (4)*
        Laissez-faire Process, 10 Oct'63

Objective: (3)

See Objective Coping
        Objective Design
        Objective Employment of Principles
        Objective Integrity
        Objective Intellect
        Objective:  Making Thought Objective

Objective:  Making Thought Objective:

See Pencil, 1938
        Teleology, (2) (3)

RBF DEFINITIONS

Objets d'art:

"I have shunned daily the recurrent opportunities to exploit
the energetic-synergetic geometry either as toys or as
objets d'art . . ."

- Citation and context at Tensegrity:  Depolarized Orientation
        Of Tensegrity-Octahedron Universal Joint (2), Dec'61

Objective: (1)

See Medical Man is Objective
        Subjective & Objective
        Teleologic Objective

Objets d'Art:

See Energy Quanta Values, (1)

Oblique = Sideways:

    See Trial & Error, 5 Jun'73

---

Obnoxica:

"...For purchasable accoutrements, architecture, equipment, and gadgets of distinction; and for the plethora of behavioral obnoxica imposed or induced by the supposed■ inexorability of the Malthus-Darwin theorem of survival only for the slickest fittest."

- Citation and context at Meek Have Inherited the Earth (1)
- Cite PROSPECT FOR HUMANITY, Sat. Review, 29 Aug'64

---

Oblique:

    See Trial & Error, 5 Jun'73

---

Obnoxico:

RBF award for "the obnoxious, e.g. bronzed training pants."

- Cite Wm. Marlin. 1971

---

Oblivion:

    See Utopia or Oblivion
    Forget the Universe

---

Obnoxica:  Obnoxico:             (1)

    See A-bomb: Souvenir A-bomb
        Objets d'Art
        Plastic Call-girl Angels
        Plastic Replica of a Cotswold Cottage
        Plastic Flowers

---

Obnoxico:

"When I was living in Manhattan in the 30s and seeing a lot of architects and artists I invented the word 'obnoxico' to describe the most dreadful objects we could imagine that exploited peoples' ignorance and sentimentality... almost anything that could be gilded or bronzed and hung in a car's back window. We thought we would have a lot of fun with a contest, seeing if we could actually sell them. But we had to stop because it wasn't funny; no matter how awful the thing was you couldn't avoid making money on it. It was too mean a game to play."

- Cite RBF to Lee Nordness at Martin's Carriage House, Wash, DC; 24 Apr'76

---

Obnoxica:  Obnoxico:             (2)

    See Meek Have Inherited the Earth, (1)
    Reproducible, 30 May'72

Obscenity:

    See Cussing

---

Observation Alters the Phenomenon Observed:

    See Heisenberg-Eliot-Pound Sequence, autumn'68

---

RBF DEFINITIONS

    Observation:

    "Conception is metaphysical;
    Observation is physical.

    And the observed is physical."

    - ~~Cite RBF Draft BRAIN & MIND, pencil, 1971.~~

- Citation & context at Considerable, 1971

---

RBF DEFINITIONS

    Observer & Observed:

    "Starting with whole Universe as observer and observed, we
    can subdivide the unity of Universe...."

    - Citation & context at Starting With Universe, 24 Sep'73

---

RBF DEFINITIONS

    Observation:

    "At the end of a piece of rope we make a metaphysical
    disconnect and a new set of observations are inaugurated,
    each consisting of finite quanta integral ingredients
    such as the time quality of all finite-energy quanta."

    - ~~Cite RBF marginalia of Infinity entry from HOW LITTLE, made
    on 13 Mar '71 Beverly Hotel, N.Y. Confirmed and expanded,
    Beverly Hotel, N.Y., 19 June '71.~~

    - Citation at Metaphysical Disconnect, 19 Jun'71

---

RBF DEFINITIONS

    ■■■■■ Observer & Observed:

    "To be experiential we must have an observer and the
    observed."

    - ~~Cite RBF editing SYNERGETICS Mar '71~~

    - Citation & context at Happening, Apr'71

---

RBF DEFINITIONS

    Observation:

    "Heisenberg said that observation alters the phenomenon
    observed."

    - Compare this with Truth entry cited to TOTAL THINKING, I&I, p.226

    - Cite High Kenner, "The Rope and the Knot," Kentucky
    Review, Autumn 1968, who attributes this quote to
    an RBF conversation with Calvin Tomkins ~~reported in
    the "New Yorker" for 8 Jan 1966 where RBF does
    not find it.~~

---

Observer & Observed:        (1)

    See Axis of Conceptual Observation
        Line of Interrelationshp
        Observer & Otherness
        Self & Otherness
        Integral Otherness
        Universe Considers Itself
        World Looks at Itself

Observer & Observed: (2)

See Experiment, Nov'71
Starting With Universe, 24 Sep'73*
Time, 16 Dec'73
Happening, Apr'71*
Self & Otherness: Four Minimal Aspects, 9 Jun'75
Experiential, 25 Mar'71
Subjective & Objective, 16 May'75
Pronouns: I = We = Us, (1)(2)
Height, Length & Width, 19 Jul'76
Polyhedra, 18 Jul'76
Awareness, 28 Apr'77

Observer & Otherness: Tetrahedral Relationship Between: (2)

See Geometry of Thinking, 16 Dec'73
Pronouns: I = We = Us, (2)

RBF DEFINITIONS

Observer & Otherness: Tetrahedral Relationship Between:

"The relationship between the observer and otherness is tetrahedral."

(See Sketch, RBF at Beverly Hotel, NYC, 10 Jan'74

- Cite RBF to EJA, 10 Jan'74

RBF DEFINITIONS

Observing & Articulating:

"The articulations are ever reenacted to reduce the magnitude tolerance of residual inaccuracy of either observation or articulation."

- Cite SYNERGETICS, 2nd. Ed., at Sec. 513.08; inadvertently omitted from Ms. at 513.07 of Mar'71), 4 Aug'75

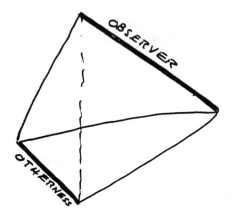

RBF DEFINITIONS

Observing vs. Articulating:

"My life is the progressive harvestings of trying to be accurate-- the harvesting of ever more accurate observational citations. Life consists of observing and articulating. Resonantly propagated evolution oscillates between observation and articulation ever reenacted hopefully to reduce the magnitude tolerance of residual innacuracy of observation or articulation."

(See Life, 25 Mar'71 for later citation.)

- Cite RBF SYNERGETICS Draft Mar '71

VECTORIAL ORIENTATION - SEC. 513.06

Observer & Otherness: Tetrahedral Relationship Between: (1)

See Metaphysical & Physical Tetrahedral Quanta

TEXT CITATIONS

Observing & Articulating:

Sec. 420.041

Observing vs. Articulating:   Observing & Articulating:

See Life, 25 Mar'71*
    Metaphysical & Physical Tetrahedral Quanta,
        25 Mar'71
    Environment, 29 Mar'77

Observation:   Observer:   Observing:                    (3)

See Observation Alters the Phenomenon Observed
    Observer & Observed
    Observer & Otherness:   Tetrahedral Relationship
        Between
    Observing vs. Articulating

Observer:                                              (2)

        See Environment (1)
            Locality, May'71
            Twelve Universal Degrees of Freedom (2)
            Self & Otherness, 19 Nov'74
            Experiment, 25 Mar'71

RBF DEFINITIONS

Obsolescence:

"To go by obsolescence:   Sovereignties

                          Property

                          Geographically Based Politics

                          Geographically Based Identity

                          Money

                          Jobs

                          You or Me

                          Selling Anything."


- Cite RBF holograph, on yellow scratch pad, undated,
    with papers left behind, April 1972.

Observation:   Observer:   Observing:                    (1)

        See Axis of Conceptual Observation
            Me the Observer
            Omnidirectional Observation
            Spherical Observation
            System Center of Observation
            Teleology
            Axis of Observation
            Orientability

Obsolete:   Inventory of Obsolete Concepts:            (1)

        See Disapproved Words:   Inventory Of
            Meaningless:   Inventory of Meaningless Concepts

Observation:   Observing:                              (2)

        See Considerable, 1971*
            Omnidirectional, 1960
            Metaphysical Disconnect, 19 Jun'71*
            Relativity, May'49
            Stature, 20 Feb'73
            Wow, (2)
            XYZ Coordinate System, (A)
            Fix, 25 Mar'71
            Life, 25 Mar'71
            Polarity, 12 Nov'75
            Pronouns:  I = We = Us, (1)
            Environment, (B)

Obsolete:   Inventory of Obsolete Concepts:           (1A) ▬

        See Axiom
            Credo, Oct'71
            Creeds
            Cliches
            Customs
            Dogma, Oct'71
            Exclusivity, 25 Sep'72
            Failure, 26 Apr'71
            Laws
            Language
            Lying, 3 Oct'73
            Ownership
            Private Property
            Spending, 1968
            Viewpoints
            Umbilical Cord, 4 Mar'73; 5 Jun'73
            ▬▬▬▬▬▬
            Assumptions

Obsolete:  Inventory of Obsolete Concepts:                    (1B) ▬▬

See Nation, Oct'70
    Ninety Degreeness, 5 Jun'73
    Obsolescence, Apr'72
    Polyhedron, 20 Feb'73
    Possession, 1969
    Scarcity, 23 Feb'72
    Selling Anything, Apr'72
    Capitalism, 1962
    Sovereignty, Jun'66
    Square, 8 Jan'66
    Superstition, circa 1955
    Propaganda, circa 1955
    Tradition:  In Tradition Lies Fallacy
    Daddy, 2 Jun'74
    Educational Theories
    Romances
    Mores
    Geographical Identity
    Immobility, 4 May'57

Obtuse:  Obtuseness:

See Quantum Wave Phenomenon Sequence, (1)
    Tetrahedron:  Regular, 29 Nov'72

Obsolete:  Inventory of Obsolete Concepts:                    (1C)

See Atlantic Ocean ( Dymaxion Airocean World,
    Pacific Ocean (        20 Jan'75
    Indian Ocean  (
    Textbooks
    New York City, 30 Jul'75
    Sea, 10 Sep'75
    Energy Environment-harvesting Machines, 27 Jan'77
    Belief, 20 Feb'77
    Holistic
    Good & Bad, 22 Jun'77

Obverse & Reverse:

See Axis of Spin, (2)
    Octantation, 14 May'73
    Brouwer's Theorem, 1 Jan'75
    Pauli's Exclusion Principle, 1960
    Triangle, Jun'71
    Geometrical Function of Nine, (1)
    Two-dimensional Polarity, 11 Sep'75
    Structural System, 9 Nov'73

Obsolescence:  Obsolete:                                      (1)

See Sailing Ship Effect
    Weapons Technology
    Yesterday's Certainties

Obverse:

See Re-exterior

Obsolescence:  Obsolete:                                      (2)

See Automation, 1970
    Artifact (A)
    Capitalism, 1962
    City (A)
    Ecology Sequence (H)(I)
    Hunting, 19 Dec'71
    Inventions, 1947
    Pollution, Feb'73
    New York City, 30 Jul'75
    Everybody's Business, (1)
    East-west Mobility of World Man, (2)
    Transnational Capitalism & Export of Know-how, (1)-(3)
    Building Industry, (1)(6) (12)
    Detente, 20 Sep'76
    Nuclear Power Generation, 22 Jun'77
    Technology & Culture, 25 Oct'77

RBF DEFINITIONS

Obvious:

"Due to the myopia of popularized selfishness
Naught is so invisible
As the obvious
Whose immediate relevancy
Can be seen
Only through deep focussed wide angled lenses."

- Cite EVOLUTIONARY 1972-1975 ABOARD SPACE VEHICLE EARTH,
  Jan '72, pp. 6-7.

RBF DEFINITIONS

Obvious:

"Complementarity requires that where there is conceptuality
there must be nonconceptuality.  The explicable requires
the inexplicable.  Experience requires the nonexperienciable.
The obvious requires the mystical. . . "

- Citation at Complementarity █████████, 12 Sep'71
- Cite RBF to EJA, Beverly Hotel, New York, 12 Sept. 1971.

---

Obvious: (1)

See Obvious & Nonobvious
   Invisibility: Naught so Invisible as the Obvious
   Obvious = Axiomatic

---

RBF DEFINITIONS

Obvious:

"...Apparently ample tolerance for their many errors.. was
included in the design of the ship and the celestial support
system.  Though often obvious for millions of years, most
of these vital advantage-giving principles long have remained
unrecognized for what they are and can do; it would seem to be
a part of the ████████████████ designed scheme of
Universe that-- for the nonce, anyway-- nothing is quite so
invisible to Spaceship Earth's passengers as the obvious."

- Citation and context at Spaceship Earth (c), 1968

---

Obvious: (2)

See Axiom, 13 Nov'69
   Complementary, 12 Sep'71*
   Improvement, 1954
   Octahedron, 16 Dec'73
   Spaceship Earth, (c)*
   Periodic Experience, (3)
   Concave & Convex, 7 Nov'73

---

Obvious = Axiomatic:

See Infinity, 1971

---

Occulting Membranes:

See Privacy, 22 Apr'71

---

Obvious & Nonobvious:

See Conceptuality & Nonconceptuality, 12 Sep'71
   Symmetry & Asymmetry, Jul'71
   Repetition, 2 Jul'75

---

Occulting:

See Opaque: Opacity

Occupancy:

See Air Space, May'65
    Empty, May'70
    Office Building, 28 Jan'72

Ocean: (1)

See Gulf Stream
    Surf Poundings
    Hole in the Ocean
    Airocean
    Waterocean
    Landocean
    Water

RBF DEFINITIONS

Occur:

"Events Occur. Occur is a time word."

- Citation & context at Overlapping, 30 May'75

Ocean: (2)

See Island, Sep'72
    Dymaxion Airocean World, 20 Jan'75
    Rain, 11 Feb'76
    Airspace Technology, 20 Sep'76
    No Energy Crisis, (1)

Occurrence:

See Events & Novents, Nov'71

Octa Edge:

See Precession of Octa Edge-vector

Ocean Liner:

See Queen Mary
    Ships

RBF DEFINITIONS

Octahedron:

"The octahedron--both numerically and geometrically--should always be considered as quadrivalent: ie., congruent with self; i.e., doubly present.

"In the volumetric hierarchy of prime number identities we identify the octahedron's prime number twoness and the inherent volume fourness (in tetra terms) as volume $2^2$, which produces the experiential volume four."

- Cite RBF to EJA, 3200 Idaho, Wash., DC; incorporated in SYNERGETICS, 2nd. Ed. at Sec. 1053.601; 10 Dec'75

RBF DEFINITIONS

Octahedron:

"Octahedron: So we have the octahedron in the middle. (Between the tetra and icosa.) It is also the second power of the only even prime number: $2^2 = 4$. The octahedron is the most common form of energy associated as matter."

- Citation & context at Quantum Sequence, (5), 23 Jun'75

---

RBF DEFINITIONS

Octahedron:

"The octahedron, mostly outside but partly inside the nuclear sphere, is four."

- Citation and context at Constant Relative Abundance, 29 Nov'72

---

RBF DEFINITIONS

Octahedron:

"The octahedron... restrainingly vector-blocked... can only infold itself pulsatingly to a condition of hemispherical congruence like a deflated basketball. Thus the octahedron's concave-convex, unity-twoness state remains plurally obvious. You can see the concave infolded hemisphere nested into the as yet outfolded convex hemisphere.

"Verifying the octahedron's fourness as being an evolutionary transformation of the tetrahedron's unity-twoness, we may take the four triangles of the tetrahedron which were edge-hinged together (bivalently) and reassemble them univalently (that is, corner-to-corner) and produce the octahedron, four of whose faces are triangular (ergo structurally stable) voids. This, incidentally, intoduces the structural stability of the triangle as a visualizable yet physical nothingness."

- Citation & context at Octahedron as Model of Doubleness of Unity, (2)(3), 16 Dec'73

[45]

- Cite SYNERGETICS draft at Sec. 905.15, 16 Dec'73

---

RBF DEFINITIONS

Octahedron:

"I see the octahedron as a complex of two tetrahdra always. . . . They are half way to the condition of four planes going through the same point.

- Cite RBF tape, Blackstone Hotel, Chicago, 31 May 1971. p.33.

SYSTEM - SEC 470.03

---

RBF DEFINITIONS

Octahedron:

"The octahedron ... polyhedrally represents the eight $45^\circ$ angle constituents of $360^\circ$ unity in the trigonometric function ████████ calculations."

- Citation and context at Indig, 3 Mar'73

---

RBF DEFINITIONS

Octahedron:

"The octahedron has very many strange effects because closest packed spheres then have the spaces and the spaces are concave octahedra and concave vector equilibria. The octahedron is part of the exchange between being spheres and spaces."

- Cite RBF tape, Blackstone Hotel, Chicago, 31 May 1971, p. 35.

SYSTEM - SEC. 470.03

---

RBF DEFINITIONS

Octahedron:

"The tetrahedron. . . is structured with three triangles around each vertex while the octahedron has four, and the icosahedron has five triangles around each vertex. We find the octahedron in between, doubling its prime number twoness into volumetric fourness as is manifest in the great-circle foldability of the octahedron, which always requires two sets of great circles, whereas all the other icosahedron and vector equilibrium 31 and 25 great circles are foldable from single sets of great circles."

[60]

- Cite SYNERGETICS draft at Sec. 1053.61, 7 Mar'73

---

RBF DEFINITIONS

Octahedron:

"The tetrahedron, octahedron and icosahedron relate to physics, the internal affairs of the atom."

- Cite RBF to EJA, Blackstone Hotel, Chicago, 31 May 1971.

- Citation & context at Physics: Difference Between Physics and Chemistry, 31 May'71

RBF DEFINITIONS

Octahedron:

"The octahedron is infoldable, or innestible-- hemi-hedrally."

- Cite RBF holographs and sketches on "Annihilation."
Somerset Club, Boston, 22 April 1971

- Citation & context at Insideoutable, 22 Apr'71

---

RBF DEFINITIONS

Octahedron:

"A polyhedron having eight equal equilateral triangular plane faces or sides; may be skeletal, as when made of interconnected struts; or continuous, as when made of interlocking or interconnected sheets or plates; or partly skeletal and partly continuous."

- Cite Patent No. 2,986,241, May 30, 1961
SYNERGETIC BUILDING CONSTRUCTION

---

RBF DEFINITIONS

Octahedron:

"The octahedron provides an example of ▓▓▓▓▓ volumetric annihilation when you remove one vector and reduce the figure to three tetrahedra triple-bonded. This also reduces from the volumetric value of four to the volumetric value of three. The process is, of course, reversible."

- Cite Sketch #1, 28 Feb '71
and RBF marginalis on p. 3 - SYNERGETICS DRAFT.

- Citation at ▓▓▓▓▓▓ Volumetric Annihilation, 28 Feb'71

---

RBF DEFINITIONS

Octahedron as Annihilation Model:

"Just reorienting one vector of the octahedron shows how it goes into the tetrahelix as a model of how energy goes from matter to radiation and vice versa. This shows how you can have annihilation and no energy is lost."

- Cite RBF to EJA by telephone from 200 Locust, Philadelphia, 8 Mar'75

---

RBF DEFINITIONS

Octahedron:

"The octahedron has a fundamental twoness, its volume of four being made up of the prime number two . . . "

- Cite Carbondale Draft
Return to Modelability, p. V.7

- Cite Nasa Speech, p. 73, Jun'66

---

RBF DEFINITIONS

Octahedron as Annihilation Model:

"This an illustration of the symmetry of matter and how it precesses to radiation... It is that moment of Universe that Einstein was preoccupied with. Just as three triangles edge-to-edge become four... topologically... they have made a tetrahedron... when you turn the triangle inside-out it makes a new vertex and the four have become five.

"We used to think that two is company and three is a crowd but now we see that four is company and five is a crowd... it's only the fifth ball that has to find a place to go. This is very exciting...."

- Cite RBF to EJA from Hope Watts, DelRay, FL., 23 Feb'75

---

RBF DEFINITIONS

Octahedron:

"The tetrahedron will not fill all space. . . But we can fill all space with tetrahedra and octahedra."

- Cite Carbondale Draft
Nature's Coordination, p. VI.13

- Cite Oregon Lecture #6, p.216, 10 Jul'62

---

RBF DEFINITIONS

Octahedron as Annihilation Model:

"The one-quantum 'leap' is also manifest when one vector edge of the volume 4 octahedron is rotated 90 degrees by disconnecting two of its ends and reconnecting them with the next set of vertexes occurring at 90 degrees from the previously interconnected-with vertexes, transforming the same unit-length, 12-vector structuring from the octahedron to the first three-triple-bonded-together (face-to-face) tetrahedra of the tetrahelix of the DNA-RNA formulation.

"One 90-degree vector reorientation in the complex alters the volume from exactly 4 to exactly 3. This relationship of one quantum disappearance coincident to the transformation of the nuclear symmetrical octahedron into the asymmetrical initiation of the DNA-RNA helix is a reminder of the disappearing-quanta behavior of the always integrally end-cohered jitterbugging transformational stages from the 20 tetrahedral volumes of the vector equilibrium to the octahedron's 4 and thence to the tetrahedron's 1 volume. All of these stages are rationally concentric in our unified operational field of 12-around-one closest-packed spheres that is only conceptual as equilibrious. We note also that per each sphere space between closest packed spheres is a volume of exactly one tetrahedron: 6 - 5 = 1."

- Cite SYNERGETICS text at Sec. 982.73, RBF galley rewrite 30 Dec'73

RBF DEFINITIONS

Octahedron as Conservation & Annihilation Model:

"We may consider the octahedron as a water-filled tube, pulling on a water-filled tube. The pulling will make it bulge in the middle. As we pull, the gravitational embracement causes a precessional rearrangement of the vector edge whereby one tetrahedron drops out. One quantum has dropped out, but, topologically it is still an octahedron:

6V + 8F = 12 + 2 (three face-bonded tetra), or
6V + 8F = 12 + 2 (octahedron)

Topologically there is no difference.

"This is the quantum leap, the quantum jump. With interference it precesses from matter to radiation; and then back into matter again. This is the lever that will bring science into further consideration of synergetics."

- Citation & context at Quantum Sequence, (5), 23 Jun'75

---

RBF DEFINITIONS

Octahedron as Conservation and Annihilation Model:

"The octahedron goes from a volume of four to a volume of three as one tensor is precessed at 90 degrees. This is a demonstration in terms of tension and compression of how energy can disappear and reappear. The process is reversible like Boltzmann's law and like the operation of syntropy and entropy. The lost tetrahedron ■can reappear and become symmetrical in its optimum form as a ball-bearing-sphere octahedron. There are six great circles doubled up in the octahedron. Compression is radiational: it reappears. Out of the fundamental fourness of all systems we have a model of how four can become three in the octahedron conservation and annihilation model.

"See the Iceland spar crystals for the octahedron's double vector-edge image."

- Cite SYNERGETICS, 2nd. Ed., at Sec. 936.15-.16, 23 May'75

---

RBF DEFINITIONS

Octahedron as Conservation & Annihilation Model:          (1)

"Suddenly Goldy realizes that all these discoveries she has been making combine to explain how it can be that the stars of the billions of now-discovered galaxies are giving off energies at incredible rates in such a manner that, as discrete quanta of energy, they become discontinued and apparently annihilated, yet the same quanta of energies reappear elsewhere, as for instance in the terrestrial vegetation's photosynthetic reduction and proliferation of hydrocarbon molecules in biologic organisms and in crystallographic growths.

"Since the pattern of two most dominant critical proximity, mass-interattraction (gravity) forces pulling diametrically on any one body produces the same model as that of Goldy's water-filled, rubber tube, the precessional squeezing of a symmetrical body, such as that of an octahedron, by two diametric gravitational forces, pulling embracingly upon it as it passes between two neighboring cosmic bodies, will cause some part of the octahedron's integral vectorial structure to yield precessionally in a plane oriented at right angles to the line between the two pulling forces, thus to transform the octahedron from its symmetrical form into an asymmetrical form."

- Cite GOLDYLOCKS, pp. G11, G12, 16 May'75

---

RBF DEFINITIONS

Octahedron as Conservation & Annihilation Model:          (2)

"This is most economically accomplished by one of the octahedron's equatorial vector-edges disconnecting at both of its equatorially engaged, end vertexes and rotating precessionally 90 degrees to rejoin its two ends with the octahedron's two polar vertexes. This local rotation results in the disappearance of the symmetrical octahedron and leaves in its stead the asymmetrical, face-bonded, three tetrahedra assembly in the form of an arc which is the neutral electromagnetic-wave-initiating state.

"The asymmetrical arc-wave consists of the same 12 vector edges and the same eight equiangled triangles and the same six vertexes as those of the original octahedron. Topologically described, it is the same polyhedron. However, it is clearly observable that the transformation not only converted omni-directional symmetry into two-directional asymmetry, but it also reduced the octahedron's exact volume of four quanta to a volume of exactly three quanta in the form of the three face-interbonded tetrahedra. What has happened here is that matter (as the synergetic octahedron) is precessionally transformed into a directionally oriented electromagnetic wave which, upon interference with other radiation or matter, will"

- Cite GOLDYLOCKS, p. G12, 16 May'75

---

RBF DEFINITIONS

Octahedron as Conservation & Annihilation Model:          (3)

"again be precessionally transformed back into the crystallographic form of the octahedron, thus syntropically regaining not only its symmetry but the one tetrahedron quantum of energy which it had entropically lost.

"Goldy realizes that the scientist Boltzmann had long ago hypothesized that the physical Universe of energy as matter was able to export energies from all the stars only because those energies were being importingly reassembled in vast numbers of elsewheres. Einstein, too, assumed the foregoing to be true. However, many scientists remained skeptical, saying that entropy was universal and increasingly disorderly and expansive, wherefore Universe is spending itself inexorably and irrevocably.

"Since photons show that energy occurs only in discrete packages and is discontinuous, and since the stars lose energy quanta entropically, how can the lost quanta reappear elsewhere? Goldy says to the bears, 'Vectorial geometry conceptually demonstrates the exact way in which energy quanta are lost and regained in the course of the entropic-syntropic turnaround events of astrophysics. The topological integrity of"

- Cite GOLDYLOCKS, p. G13, 16 May'75

---

RBF DEFINITIONS

Octahedron as Conservation & Annihilation Model:          (4)

"vectorial geometry elucidates both the one-quantum loss and the one-quantum of energy recovery incidental to the entropic transforming from matter to radiation and the syntropic transforming from radiation to matter, as clearly manifest in the octahedron to tetra-arc transformation and its reversal to the octahedron. This topological transformation, but not its energy-quantum relationship, was originally discovered in 1951 by the geodesic engineer-scientist, D.L. Richter.

"This elucidation of the way in which Universe can temporarily drop out or regain its energy quanta, elucidates much more, says Goldy. 'It explains what happens in the photosynthetic process as planet Earth's vegetation converts Sun radiation receipts into beautiful hydrocarbon molecules. Energy quanta are regained on Earth. It explains even more. It shows how the weightless metaphysical tetrahedron is lost and regained in Universe as life dies out here and is reborn there. It shows how the tripli-bonded addition of the recoverable one tetrahedron, when added to the neutral phase, W-profiled, tetra-arc, triple-bonded assembly of three tetrahedra, must always produce either a male or a female twisting helix, which, when extended, becomes the DNA-RNA tetrahelix which is the structural system programmer of all living species and individuals of those species."

- Cite GOLDYLOCKS, pp.G13,G14, 16 May'75

---

TEXT CITATIONS

Octahedron as Conservation & Annihilation Model:

Synergetics, Sec. 982.73

RBF Videotaping Marathon: Penn Bell Studios, Philadelphia,
  Session #3 : 22 Jan'75 : 2044 studio time    (See EJA Log)
  Session #4 : 23 Jan'75 : 1925 studio time
  Session #6 : 25 Jan'75 : 1430 studio time

RBF marginalia at SYNERGETICS draft (undated):"Synergy",
  p.3 - Sec. 108
Synergetics, 2nd. Ed. : Secs. 935-938

Synergetics, Sec. 985.08

---

Octahedron as Annihilation Model:

See Volumetric Annihilation
  Tensegrity Model of Self-interference of Energy
  Octahedron as Conservation & Annihilation Model

Octahedron as Conservation & Annihilation Model: (1)

See Discontinuity Accommodation Model
 Invisible Quantum as Tetrahelix Gap Closer
 Octahedron as Annihilation Model
 Quantum Jump: Quantum Leap
 Fourth Quantum
 Radiation vs. Crystal Model
 Information Transmitting & Nontransmitting Model
 Richter Transformation
 Octahedron as Photosynthesis Model
 Precession of Octa Edge-vector

---

Octahedron as Conservation & Annihilation Model: (2)

See Geometrical Function of Nine, (5)(6)
 Six - Five = One, 8 Jan'74
 Vector Equilibrium Involvement Domain, 24 Apr'76

---

RBF DEFINITIONS

Octahedron: Eighth-octahedra: (1)

"....Though I have twice visited the Great Pyramid at Gizeh,
I have never carried a sextant and tape with me so I do not
have the angular data I need. I know there are others who
have made measurements, but my experience teaches me not to
be too confident of the published statements of others when
I do not know those personalities nor the degree of exactitude
at which they operate.

"At the present moment I can give you some very interesting
information regarding not only octahedra, but in particular
eighth-octahedra. In the spherical octahedron each of the
eight spherical surface corners are 90°. Each of the spherical
octahedron's eight triangular edges are 90° of arc, which
means that they subtend central angles of 90° each.

"Here is a very extraordinary asymmetrical tetrahedron with
three 90-degree central angles and three 90-degree surface
angles--as well as having six 90-degree internal corners where
the three radii of the octahedron impinge perpendicularly
upon the three great-circle arcs. All of the spherical
octahedron's one-eighth symmetrical self-divisions have eight
corners each of 90°.

           '76
- Cite RBF Ltr. to Stephen A. Barba, North Miami Beach, FL; 4 May

---

RBF DEFINITIONS

Octahedron: Eighth-octahedra: (2)

"The spherical octahedron's triangle is the only triangle
in which the center of area of the triangle occurs at
mid-altitude of the triangle's three perpendicular bisectors
of its three corner angles:

"In modern ocean cruising sailing craft in the high seas
routes often cross the main ocean highway of steam and diesel
ship channels. These great new high speed ships often operate
by automatic navigational equipment with a watch officer
idly standing by. They rush forward through night and fog at
speeds in the 20-knot range. Little sailing craft up to
72 feet in length with their minuscule red, green, and white
navigational lights are not visible from any great distance--
and often in high waves they are approximately invisible.
Such sailing ships have relatively little metal in them. The
radar scopes of the big ships show readily recognizable pips"

- Cite RBF Ltr. to Stephen Barba, N. Miami Beach, Fl.; 4 May'76

---

RBF DEFINITIONS

Octahedron: Eighth-octahedra: (3)

"for big steel ships and the radar scopes clearly outline
land masses and other sizable objects. Because they do not
show the little sailing ships, those little ships are in
incredible danger as they cross--as they must--those big
sailing ship lanes. As a consequence of this hazard, there
has been evolved a device which can be mounted on the topmast
or the yard-arm of sailing ships which does register as a
clearly-defined pip on the radar scopes. This device consists
of a spherical octahedron with three great circles made of
aluminum-foil-covered cardboard surface. The three great
circles cross each other at 90 degrees. The spherical surface
is uncovered.

"As you look at the device--a radar reflector--you look into
whatever number of the spherical octahedron's central-angular
tetrahedra as may be within the line of view. It has been
discovered that the ship's radar signals, when impinging on
any one of those eighth-octahedra's concave tetrahedra, produce
a reflection pattern which returns directly back to the
radar-sending ship to register on the radar scope.

"What the radar's invisible-to-the-human-eye electromagnetic"

- Cite RBF Ltr. to Stephen Barba, N. Miami Beach, FL; 4 May'76

---

RBF DEFINITIONS

Octahedron: Eighth-octahedra: (4)

radiation wave does is to make it optically clear--as when
a searchlight is aimed at such a ▆▆▆ sailing ship, at which
time a very bright reflection beam returns to the viewer who
is manipulating the searchlight aimed at the sailing ship.
This is just one of the eight eighth-octahedra's concave
tetrahedron's three faces, glowing vividly, beaming the light
back to the source of the searchlight. You can diagram this
yourself to see what happens....

"As you know, when light strikes a surface it bounces away at
an angle which is exactly the same as the angle at which it
impinges on its surface. Any beam entering the eighth-octahedra
will bounce off at the same angle to a second side of the
concave octahedron and then bounce off again at the same
angle. This means that the two bouncings add up to 180°,
which means sending the radiation directly back to its source.

"These angular bouncings of electromagnetics... may relate
very importantly to all the phenomena seeming to be mystically
produced by the pyramid mystery cults."

- Cite RBF Ltr. to Stephen Barba, N. Miami Beach, FL; 4 May'76

---

RBF DEFINITIONS

Octahedron: Eighth-Octahedra:

"By internally interconnecting its six vertexes with three
polar axes: X, Y, and Z, and rotating the octahedron succesively
upon those three axes, three planes are internally generated
that symmetrically subdivide the octahedron into eight uniformly
equal, equiangle-triangle-based, asymmetrical tetrahedra, with
three convergent, 90-degree-angle-surrounded apexes, each of
whose volume is one-eighth of the volume of one octahedron: this
is called the Eighth-Octahedron. (See also Sec. 912.) The
octahedron having a volume of four tetrahedra, allows each
Eighth-Octahedra to have a volume of one-half of one tetrahedron. If we apply the equiangled-triangular base of one each
of these eight Eighth-Octahedra to each of the vector equilibrium's eight equiangle-triangle facets, with the Eighth-Octahedra's three-90-degree-angle-surrounded vertexes pointing
outwardly, they will exactly and symmetrically produce the
24-volume, nucleus-embracing cube symmetrically surrounding the
20-volume vector equilibrium; thus with 8 x ½ = 4 being added
to the 20-volume vector equilibrium producing a 24-volume total."

          44
- Cite SYNERGETICS text at Sec. 905.43, 16 Dec'73

---

Octahedron: Eighth-octahedra:

See Allspace Filling, 11 Jul'62
 Cube: Volume-3 Cube, 16 Dec'73
 Modules: A & B Quanta Modules, 27 Jan'75
 Quantum Sequence, (4)
 Nuclear Cube, 11 Dec'75; 23 Feb'76
 Basic Nestable Configurations: Hierarchy Of, 29 May'72
 Rhombic Dodecahedron, 12 May'77

Octahedron:  Energy Holding Pattern:

See Holding Patterns of Energy, Apr'72

Octahedron:  Half-octahedron:                                    (2)

See Allspace Filling, 11 Jul'62
    Cube, 14 Sep'71
    Equilibrious, 23 Jan'72

---

RBF DEFINITIONS

Octahedron:  Half Octahedron:

"A half-octahedron, to be stable, has to have its other
half.  The vector equilibrium has only the half-octahedra,
so the circumferential instability of its six square
faces invites structural instability: it is, ergo,
equilibrious."

- Cite RBF marginalia at 3200 Idahon, D8, 23 Jan '72.
  at SYNERGETICS Draft Sec. 884.10 of 9 Feb '72.
SYSTEM - SEC 470.03

RBF DEFINITIONS

Octahedron Model of Doubleness of Unity:                         (1)

"The prime number twoness of the octahedron always occurs in
structuring doubled together as four-- i.e., 2²-- a fourness
which is also doubleness of unity.  Unity is plural and, at
minimum, is two.  The unity volume 1 of the tetrahedron is,
in structural verity, two, being both the outwardly displayed
convex tetrahedron and the inwardly contained concave tetrahedron.

"The three-great-circle model of the spherical octahedron only
'seems' to be three; it is in fact 'double'; it is only foldably
produceable in unbroken (whole) great-circle sheets by edge-
combining six hemicircularly folded whole great circles.  Thus
it is seen that the octahedron-- as in Iceland spar crystals--
occurs only doubly, i.e., omnicongruent with itself, which is
'quadrivalent.'

"Among the three possible omnisymmetrical prime structural
systems-- the tetrahedron, octahedron, and icosahedron-- only
the tetrahedron has each of its vertexes diametrically opposite
a triangular opening.  In the octahedron and icosahedron, each
vertex is opposite another vertex; and each of their vertexes
is diametrically blocked against articulating a self-inside-"

- Cite SYNERGETICS text at Secs. 905.11-.13, 16 Dec'73

---

RBF DEFINITIONS

Octahedron  Half Octahedron:  Lending: Model

"Half octahedra can be pulled out of the square faces of
the vector equilibria.  This goes on in atoms joining one
another and they are able to lend something to one
another sometimes, they are able to lend electrons.  We
can lend out of the square faces without in any way
jeopardizing the structural system which was dependent upon
the triangulation of the tetrahedronal parts."

"We can lend up to four without bothering it."

- Cite Oregon Lecture #7, pp. 255.  11 Jun'62

RBF DEFINITIONS

Octahedron Model of Doubleness of Unity:                         (2)

"-outing transformation.  In both the octahedron and the icosahedron, each of the vertexes is tense-vector-restrained from
escaping outwardly by the convergent vectorial strength of the
system's other immediately surrounding-- at minimum three--
vertexial event neighbors.  But contrariwise, each of the octahedron's and icosahedron's vertex events are constrainingly
impulsed inwardly in an exact central-system direction and
thence impelled toward diametric exit and inside-outing transformation; and their vertex events would do so were it not for
their diametrically opposed vertexes, which are surroundingly
tense-vector-restrained from permitting such outward egress.

"As a consequence of its uniquely unopposed diametric vertexing--
ergo permitted-- diametric exit, only the tetrahedron among all
the symmetric polyhedra can turn itself pulsatingly inside-out,
and can do so in eight different ways (see Sec. 624); and in
each instance, as it does so, one-half of its combined concave-
convex unity 'twoness' is always inherently invisible.

"The octahedron, however, restrainingly vector-blocked as
described, can only infold itself pulsatingly to a condition
of hemispherical congruence like a deflated basketball."

- Cite SYNERGETICS text at Secs 905.13-.15, 16 Dec'73

---

Octahedron:  Half-octahedron:                                    (1)

See Mite
    Pyramid = Half-octahedron
    Vector Equilibrium:  Lending & Borrowing Model

RBF DEFINITIONS

Octahedron as Model of Doubleness of Unity:                      (3)

"Thus the octahedron's concave-convex, unity-twoness state
remains plurally obvious.  You can see the concave infolded
hemisphere nested into the as-yet outfolded convex hemisphere.

"Verifying the octahedron's fourness as being an evolutionary
transformation of the tetrahedron's unity-twoness, we may
take the four triangles of the tetrahedron which were edge-
hinged together (bivalently) and reassemble them univalently
(that is, corner-to-corner) and produce the octahedron, four
of whose faces are triangular (ergo structurally stable)
voids.  This, incidentally, introduces the structural stability
of the triangle as a visualizable yet physical nothingness."

- Cite SYNERGETICS text at Sec. 905.15, 16 Dec'73

RBF DEFINITIONS

## Octahedron: Nuclear Asymmetric Octahedra:

"There are eight asymmetric octahedra which surround each face of the 'coupler.' It is probable that these eight asymmetric nuclear octahedra account all the varieties of intercomplex complexity required for the permutations of the 92 regenerative chemical elements. These eight variables alone provide for a fantastic number of rearrangements and reorientations of the A and B Quanta Modules within exactly the same volume.

"I now believe it is possible that there are no other fundamental complex varieties. So we have a limit of variation. With our friend octave coming in as before. This is how we now find out what we have been looking for when we have been talking about 'number one.' It is one nucleon, which can be either neutron or proton, depending on how you rearrange the modules in the same space."

- Cite RBF to EJA, by telephone from Phila., 1 Apr'73
Incorporated in SYNERGETICS text at Sec. 954.30

RBF DEFINITIONS

## Octahedron: Nuclear Asymmetric Octahedron:

See Coupler

RBF DEFINITIONS

## Octahedron as Photosynthesis Model:

The vector-precessed, three-quanta octahedron manifests interference and demonstrates radiation; when the vector-edge precesses again, the fourth quantum reappears, the inter-ference disappears, and gravity is demonstrated. This is the way photosynthesis functions-- the conversion of radiation in the leaf, or on your skin.

- Cite RBF to EJA, 3200 Idaho, Wash., DC., 11 Dec'75

RBF DEFINITIONS

## Octahedron as Photosynthesis Model:                     (A)

"Gravity must always be thought of as embracing. For instance, it would be like the hoops of a barrel. The staves are wedges. Unless you have truncated the wedges they could all go right to the center of the sphere; and they would like to get out of the system, but the bands hold them together. They cannot get any closer together because their outer parts are larger than their inner parts. They can't fall in. But the point is that the bands are finite: they come back upon themselves and they embrace. You have to return on to yourself to embrace. Gravity operates then by embracement. The larger the phenomenon that it embraces, the more leverage effect it has because you simply tighten the screws and the bands at the ends of the lever. This is why the pressures increase as you go into the Earth; they continually increase the further in you go due to the leverage effect of the embracement.

"Gravity does not operate perpendicularly. It operates not as a radius but at 90 degrees to the radius. All the radiation goes outward radiantly; the gravity is always circumferential and therefore finite and enclosing. I give you, for instance, the hexagon, where the six radii are trying to come apart explosively. They disintegrate; the radii do not help each other. But if you have the same number of sticks arranged"
- Cite RBF to Hugh Kenner, Phila., PA, Transcript p.7; 8 Jun'75

RBF DEFINITIONS

## Octahedron as Photosynthesis Model:                     (B)

"end-to-end, where mass interattraction works, they close back upon themselves and are always more effective. So the tendency of Universe to come apart is always well offset by the finite closure of the same six vectors.

"We must consider the effect of gravity on the octahedron in terms of embracement. Of the three structural systems in Universe--tetra, octa, and icosa--the octahedron is in the middle and always is inherently doubled-up, the vectors double up. ▬▬▬▬▬▬▬▬▬▬ The most plentiful of all the crystals are octahedral crystals. The embracement of the octahedron is typical of matter, but the embracement is precessed causing a reaction at 90 degrees. Our pulling makes for greater pressure for it to try to come apart.

"The 12 vectors of the octahedron are embraced by gravity. The two polar pyramids join in a quadrangular equator. This crystal gets between two other celestial masses and is pulled by them. They are pulling linke the Chinese finger puzzle device that pulls your finger in and squeezes it. Precessionally, you pull it one way and it squeezes the other way. So this octahedron is a sort of rubber tube; if you pull on it it makes the tube contract. Compression operates on it."
- Cite RBF to Hugh Kenner, Phila.,PA, Transcript p.7; 8 Jun'75

RBF DEFINITIONS

## Octahedron as Photosynthesis Model:                     (C)

"The precessional effect operates on the octahedron's 12 vectors, and one of them precesses. I want you to think of the six vertexes. You've got four ▬▬▬ ▬'▬ the top like a pyramid--a regular Egyptian pyramid--and a reflecting pyramid at the bottom. So there are four vectors at the north pole; four at the south; and four around the equator. The embracing effect is to make one of the four equatorial vectors precess; it lets go from the two adjacent points in the equator and rotates 90 degrees to join the north pole to the south pole.

"We still have exactly the same six vertexes; we simply connected the poles instead of the adjacent equator points. You will find that what this does is to turn this form into an arc where you have three tetrahedra face-bonded. We go from an octahedron of volume four to three tetrahedra face-bonded: six vertexes, eight faces, 12 edges. There is no way topologically that you can tell that anything has happened. But you have dropped out one tetrahedron, or one unit of quantum.

"This explains why Boltzmann saw the Universe with all the stars giving off energy entropically. He said the energy must be being collected elsewhere. Einstein went along with it."

- Cite RBF to Hugh Kenner, Phila. PA., transcript p.7; 8 Jun'75

RBF DEFINITIONS

## Octahedron as Photosynthesis Model:                     (D)

"But the scientists said that entropy means that energy gets lost: How could it possibly be picked up again over here? So we suddenly see how it does in this form of the three-tetra-arc. One minute you add a tetrahedron to it and the next you have lost one and it disappears... It comes out on th end and becomes the tetrahelix. The tetrahelix is always this wave, an electromagnetic wave. This wave is the way gravitation becomes radiation. The quantum is separated out when the radiation has an interference with anything, then it immediately precesses again and becomes matter-- and it goes from the three-tetra back to the four. And we suddenly have one unit of quantum seemingly disappear in the Universe and it's picked up again over there.

"This is how the quantum gets picked up by photosynthesis. Photosynthesis had not been understood before: it is simply the picking up of that one unit of quantum.

"The transformation from the octahedron to the three tetrahedra was discovered by Don Richter, but he did not know the signif-icance of it as he had not been thinking about it that way. He was not thinking about it as an accounting of energetic phenomena; but it completely explains how the gravitational effect will"
- Cite RBF to Hugh Kenner, Phila. PA., transcript p.8; 8 Jun'75

RBF DEFINITIONS

## Octahedron as Photosynthesis Model:                     (E)

"convert matter into radiation... and how the energy is only apparently lost. All the topological accounting is there. But nobody would ever know it because it is topologically the same. A unit of quantum absolutely disappears from the described Universe. It explains how syntropy could occur. The entropy was there but no one could understand the syntropy. But there it is."

- Cite RBF to Hugh Kenner, Phila. PA, transcript p.8; 8 Jun'75

Octahedron as Photosynthesis Model:

See Radiation-gravitation Model

Octahedron-tetrahedron System:

See Octet Truss

Octahedral Tensegrity:

See Tensegrity: Depolarized Orientation of Tensegrity-
Octahedron Universal Joint

RBF DEFINITIONS

Octahedron: Volume of Cube as Three: (3)

"I am going to take these four one-eighth octahedra, and
because each has an equilateral triangular face, I can
superimpose it on the equilateral triangular faces of a
regular tetrahedron. There are four faces, so the four
faces of the tetrahedra will accommodate four one-eighth
octahedra superimposed so that the equilateral triangle
faces are becoming congruent. This leaves a 90-degree
angle sticking outwardly, and it makes the cube. So the
cube then is one regular tetrahedron, with four one-eighth
octahedra superimposed on its surface. The volume of a
one-eighth octahedron is one-half, and four times one-half
on the faces ( 4 x ½ = 2 ) and so the volume of the
tetrahedron which I superimposed is one, so ( 2 + 1 = 3 ),
so the volume of a cube in the system is three. That gets
to ■ be very interesting. Here is another nice whole
number. You have the tetrahedron as one, octahedron is
four, and cube is three. A cube as three is not what
people have been thinking. They have been thinking that
a cube was one, but I am using unity where a tetrahedron is one."

- Cite Oregon Lecture #6, pp. 215-216. 10 Jul'62

RBF DEFINITIONS

Octahedron-tetrahedron System:

"You cannot make big tetrahedra or octahedra out of littler
tetrahedra or octahedra respectively. Octahedron and
tetrahedron may not be realized independently of one another.

"Tetrahedron is inherently positive or negative. It is not
multidimensionally modulatable except in frequency greater
than two, which is unity. Tetrahedron cannot be realized out
of tetra alone; ergo, has an octahedron."

- Citation & context at Multidimensionality, (1), 11 Sep'63

RBF DEFINITIONS

Octahedron: XYZ Coordinates: (1)

"Here we take an octahedron which has a volume of four.
An octahedron has six vertexes and it is symmetrical because
they are all equilateral triangles and all the edges are
the same. Therefore we know by it being symmetrical that if
we interconnect its opposite vertexes, being six of them,
there will be three axes between the six opposite vertexes.
Those three axes would be the well-known XYZ coordinate
system and the XYZ coordinates then do exist inside the
octahedron. If I cut the octahedron through one of the
four planes, one of the planes of its equator, it makes me
two half-octahedra. If the volume of an octahedron in
respect to a tetrahedron is four, then a half-octahedron
has a volume of two, and 2 + 2 = 4."

- Cite Oregon Lecture #6, p.214. 10 Jul'62

RBF DEFINITIONS

Octahedron-Tetrahedron System:

"An assemblage of octahedrons and tetrahedrons in

face to face relationship. Thus when four tetrahedrons are

grouped to define a larger tetrahedron, the resulting

central space is an octahedron; together, these figures are

comprised in a single, or 'common,' octahedron-tetrahedron

system."

- Cite Patent No. 2,986,241, May 30, 1961
SYNERGETIC BUILDING CONSTRUCTION

RBF DEFINITIONS

Octahedron: ▨▨▨▨▨▨▨ XYZ Coordinates: (2)

"There is a center of gravity of the octahedron and it has
eight equilateral triangular faces and there is a little
pyramid, or irregular tetrahedron which can be formed on
one of the faces of the octahedron whose interior apex is
at the center of gravity of the octahedron. . . Because
there are eight such faces and it is at the center of volume,
there are eight of these that make up one octahedron so
this is a one-eighth octahedron. If the volume of an
octahedron is four, the one-eighth of an octahedron has
the volume of one-half of one tetrahedron."

"Each of the one-eighth octahedra has interiorly 90-degree
angles because they are the XYZ coordinates and when the
XYZ coordinates cross, it is 90 degrees. They have a
central angle of 90 degrees and the external angles are
60 degrees each. . . "

- Cite Oregon Lecture #6, p. 215. 10 Jul'62

Octahedron:  XYZ Coordinates:                                           (1)


                 See XYZ Quadrant at Center of Octahedron

---

Octahedron:                                                             (3)


                 See Octahedron as Annihilation Model
                     Octahedron as Conservation & Annihilation Model
                     Octahedron:  Eighth-octahedra
                     Octahedron:  Energy Holding Pattern
                     Octahedron:  Half Octahedron
                     Octahedron:  Half Octahedron: Lening Model
                     Octahedron Model of Doubleness of Unity
                     Octahedron:  Nuclear Asymmetric Octahedron
                     Octahedron:  Super Octahedron
                     Octahedral Tensegrity
                     Octahedron-tetrahedron System
                     Octahedron:  Volume of Cube as Three
                     Octahedron:  XYZ Coordinates
                     Octahedron as Photosynthesis Model
                     Octa Edge

---

Octahedron:  XYZ Coordinates:                                           (2)


                 See Planck's Constant, 16 Aug'70
                     Spherical Octahedron, 29 Nov'72

---

**RBF DEFINITIONS**

**Octant:**

"3 x $10^{41}$ : 300 thirteen-illion SSRCD : 312,858,158,319,499,
960,973,208,642,615,613,036,800,000, i.e., all of the prime
numbers in 45°, which is one 'octant' of trigonometry, which
covers all general systems relationships."


- Cite SYNERGETICS draft at Sec. 1238.80, 20 Jul'73
  (From RBF holograph revision of WORLD pieceof
  27 Mar'73)

---

Octahedron:                                                             (1)


                 See Allspace Filling:  Octahedron & Tetrahedron
                     Allspace Filling:  Octahedron & Vector Equilibrium
                     Complexocta
                     Domain of Octahedron
                     Prime Structural Systems
                     Spherical Octahedron
                     XYZ Quadrant at the Center of Octahedron
                     Hedra
                     Coupler:  Nuclear Asymmetric Octahedron
                     Tetra, Octa & Icosa
                     Dihedral Angles of Tetra & Octa
                     Superoctahedron
                     Precession of Octa Edge-vector
                     ▬▬▬▬▬▬
                     Tetra, Octa & VE
                     Universal Fabric Joint = Octahedron

---

**RBF DEFINITIONS**

▬▬▬▬     **Octantation:**

"Indig congruences demonstrate that nine is zero and that
number system is inherently octave and corresponds to the four
positive and four negative octants of the two polar domains
(obverse and reverse) of the octahedron-- and of all systems--
which systematic polyhedral octantation limits also govern
the eight 45° angle constituent limits of 360° unity in the
trigonometric function calculations.

"The inherent +4, -4, 0, +4, -4, 0 --- of number also corresponds to the octantation of "The Coupler" (see section 954.20)
by its eight allspace-filling MItes (AAB Modules) which, being
inherently plus-or-minus biased, though superficially invariant,
i,e., are conformationally identical, altogether provides
lucidly synergetic integration (at a kindergarten comprehendable
level) of cosmically basic number behavior, quantum mechanics,
synergetics, nuclear physics, wave phenomena in general, and
topologically rational accountability of experience in general."


                                                              ,12
- Cite RBF holograph in SYNERGETICS draft at Secs. 1221,8+13,
  14 May'73

---

Octahedron:                                                             (2)


                 See Allspace Filling, 10 Jul'62
                     Constant Relative Abundance, 29 Nov'72*
                     Holding Patterns of Energy, Apr'72
                     Indig, 3 Mar'73*
                     Insideoutable, 22 Apr'71*
                     Physics as Internal Affairs of the Atom, 31 May'71
                     Physics:  Difference Between Physics and Chemistry,
                         31 May'71*
                     Sphere, 25 Feb'74
                     Tetrahedron (2)
                     Volumetric Annihilation, 28 Feb'71*
                     Prism, 31 May'71
                     Quantum Sequence, (5)*

---

**RBF DEFINITIONS**

**Octant Zone:**

"Three disparately conformed, nonequitriangular, polarized
half-octahedra, each consisting of the same four equivolumetric
octant zones occur around the three half-octants' common
volumetric center.  These eight octant zones are all occupied,
in three possible different system arrangements, by identical
asymmetrical tetrahedra, which are MItes, each consisting of
the three AAB Modules."


- Cite RBF partial rewrite of SYNERGETICS galley at Sec.954.01,
  20 Dec'73; deleted by him, and restored to text by EJA

RBF DEFINITIONS

Octant Zone:

"Three disparately conformed, nonequitriangular, polarized
octahedra each consist of the same eight equivolumetric octant
zones occurring around the three octants' common volumetric
center. These eight octant zones are all occupied, in three
possible different system arrangements, by identical asymmetrical tetrahedra, which are Mites, each consisting of the
three AAB Modules."

- Cite SYNERGETICS draft at Sec. 954.01, 27 May'72

---

Octant: Octantation:                                    (1)

See Degrees: 45°
    Trigonometric Limit
    XYZ Quadrant at Center of Octahedron

---

Octant: Octation: Octantation:                          (2)

See Coupler, 27 Jan'75
    Fourth Dimension, 29 Nov'72

---

Octa-sphere:

See Spherical Octahedron, Aug'72

---

Octavalent:

See Tetrahedron: Hierarchy of Pulsating Tetrahedral
    Arrays, 16 Dec'73

---

RBF DEFINITIONS

Octave:

"Compression is locally expressive in discrete tones and

frequencies internal to the octave.

"Tension is both internal and external to the octave and is

harmonic with either the unit octave or octave pluralities.

- Cite Synergetics Draft at Sec. 640.70, Dec. '71.

---

RBF DEFINITIONS

Octave:

"The nucleus can accommodate waves without breaking

up the fundamental resonance of the octaves."

- Cite RBF to EJA, Fairfield, Conn., Chez Wolf.
  18 June 1971.

- Citation at Nucleus, 18 Jun'71

---

RBF DEFINITIONS

Octave:

"Waves are octave."

- Cite NUMEROLOGY Draft, April 1971

RBF DEFINITIONS

### Octave:

"Relative to the symmetry of equilibrium it gets to be relatively asymmetrical, and I find that it goes to a maximum asymmetry and then it comes back to symmetry again.

"I think this is why we might have something we call octaves in music. There are sort of octaves in our thinking. We think octavely. . . "

- Citation and context at Relative Asymmetry Sequence (1), Jun'69

---

RBF DEFINITIONS

### Octave Wave:

"The interaction of all numbers other than nine creates the wave phenomenon described, i.e., the self-invertable, self-inside-outable octave increasing and decreasing pulsatively, fourfoldedly, and tetrahedrally. No matter how complex a number aggregating sequence of events may be, this phenomenon is all that ever happens. There is thus a primitively comprehensive, isotropically distributive, carrier-wave order omni-accommodatively permeating and embracing all phenomena."

- Cite SYNERGETICS draft at Sec. 1223.11, 5 Mar'73

---

RBF DEFINITIONS

### Octave

"Doubling or halving dimension

Increases or decreases respectively

The magnitude of volume or force

By expansive or contractive

Increments of eight,

That is, by octave values."

- Cite SYNERGETICS Corollaries
Sec. 240.49.

- Citation at Dimension, Oct'59

---

RBF DEFINITIONS

### Octave Wave Model:

"The eight hedra triangles of the inside-out tetrahedron which are the same deployed eight triangles of the vector equilibrium provide a model for the octave wave limit at the number eight where the wave turns back again before the zero-nineness."

- Cite RBF to EJA enroute Union Station, Wash., DC., 9 Apr'75

---

### Octave Limit of Variation:

See Octahedron: Nuclear Asymmetric Octahedra, 1 Apr'73
Octave Wave Model, 9 Apr'75

---

TEXT CITATIONS

| Octave Wave: | Octantation: | Octation: |
|---|---|---|
| 415.40-415.41 | 1221.18 | s1006.36 |
| 421.05 | Table 1221.20 | s1013.41 |
| 527.22 | 1222: 1222.10-1222.32 | |
| 527.31 | 1223: 1223.10-1223.15 | |
| 905.45 | Fig. 1223.12 | |
| 954.46 (footnote) | 1236.02 | |
| Table 962.10 note | 1239.10 | |
| 1011.61 | 1239.31 | |
| 1012.01 | | |
| 1012.10-1012.16 | | |
| Fig.1012.15 | | |

---

### Octavely Ventilated:

See Carrier Wave, 9 Mar'73

---

### Octave Wave:                                              (1)

See Interwave Behavior of Number
Number System is Inherently Octave
Octantation
Tetrahedral Octave Phase Model
Zero Wave

Octave Wave: (2)

See Cube: Volume-3 Cube, 16 Dec'73
Pythagoras, 18 Jun'71
Scheherazade Numbers: Declining Powers Of, 1 Feb'75
Synchronization, Oct'71
Tension, 1944
Zero Wave, 9 Mar'73
Ball at the Center, 9 Mar'73
Scheherazade Numbers: Declining Powers Of, 22 May'75
**Teleology: Bow Tie Symbol, 19 Jul'76**

RBF DEFINITIONS

Octet Truss:

"The octet truss is not a priori. The octet truss is simply
the most economical way of behaving relative to unity and to
self. The octet truss is the evolutionary patterning,
intervectory-ing, and intertrajectory-ing of the ever-recurrent
12 alternative options of action, all 12 of which are
equally the most economical ways of self-and-otherness
interbehaving-- all of which interbehavings we speak of as
Universe."

- Cite SYNERGETICS draft at Sec. 540.02, 24 Sep'73

Octation: Spherical Octation:

See Nonpolar Points, 29 Nov'72; 7 Nov'73

RBF DEFINITIONS

Octet Truss:

"The icosahedron and the octet truss display

circumferential closest packing."

(N.B. Above is not accurate. See Synergetics text at Sec.
422.03, Apr '72, and Sec. 222.52 Jan '72.)

- Cite RBF to EJA, Fairfield, Conn. Chez Wolf, 18 June 1971.

Octave: (1)

See Number System is Inherently Octave
Harmonic: Harmony

RBF DEFINITIONS

Octet Truss:

"In 60° coordination the angles are congruent and logically

integratable with the radii."

- Cite tape transcript RBF to EJA, Chez Wolf, 18 June 1971, p. 35.

60-DEGREE COORDINATION - SEC. 423.01

Octave: (2)

See Dimension, Oct'59*
Geometry of Vectors, Aug'71
Mites & Quarks as Basic Notes, (2)(3)
Nucleus, 18 Jun'71*
Relative Asymmetry Sequence, (1)*
Tension & Compression, 1944

RBF DEFINITIONS

Octet Truss:

". . . The octet truss-- whose omnidirectional growth fills

all space with all the lines or vectors being of identical

length, and all the triangles being equilateral, and all

the vertexes being omnidirectionally evenly spaced from

one another. This is the pattern of closest packing of

spheres."

- Cite MEXICO '63, (Illus. #0-2-30), p. 20, 10 Oct '63

TETRAHELIX SEC. 940.02

143

RBF DEFINITIONS

Octet Truss:

"In the octet truss system all the vectors are of identical
length and all the angles around any convergence are the
same. The patterns repeat themselves consistently. At every
convergence there are always 12 vectors coming together and
they are always 60° in respect to the next adjacent one.
(There are other angles in the system. By embracing additional
angles we can find 90° relationships.) The prime relationship
is with the 60° angle." ▆

- Cite Oregon Lecture #8, p. 299. 12 Jul'62

ISOTROPIC VECTOR MATRIX - SEC. 423.01)

---

RBF DEFINITIONS

Octet Truss:

"The octet truss-- a name componded from octahedron and
tetrahedron-- can be produced from complexes of tetrahedra
or complexes of octahedra, whichever is economically
preferable."

- Cite DYMAXION WORLD OF RBF, Caption L2. 1960

---

RBF DEFINITIONS

Octet Truss:

"The octet truss can be fashioned from flat ribbons by
spot welding or other high-speed cohering processes.

"The octet truss can be fashioned from hubs employing the
12 faces of the rhombic dodecahedron. . .

"The octet truss can be woven together with continuous rods
and wires, seized together by male and female turbining hubs.

"The octet truss can be assembled of tubes and rhombic dodecahedron hubs having face-mounted studs to slip into and
fasten to tubes.

"The octet truss can be woven continuously from wire-like
fencing structures."

- Cite DYMAXION WORLD OF RBF, Captions L3 - L11. (1959)

---

RBF DEFINITIONS

Octet Truss:

"The octet truss consist entirely of struts. No hubs
are required. The x-shaped terminals of the struts unite
in such a manner as to weave around the hub nuclei,
forming the four planes of the vector equilibrium. The
truss has phenomenal three-way 'finite' strength.

"In conventional beam structure systems, the supporting
units are parallel to one another. Their ends are infinite
(in that they do not curve back into the system) and
therefore they do not help one another. In the three-way
grid octet truss system loads applied to any one point are
distributed radially outward in six directions and are
immediately frustrated by the finite hexagonal circles
entirely enclosing the six-way-distributed load. Each
circle distributes the load 18 ways to the next circle,
which 'finitely' inhibits the radially distributed load.
Thus the system joins together synergetically to distribute
and inhibit the loads. The total loads are finally
distributed three ways to the three point support."

(Slightly r-written)

IN PART - Cite DYMAXION WORLD OF RBF, Caption L1A, by RBF, 1959.
OCTET TRUSS - SEC. 422.10)

---

RBF DEFINITIONS

Octet Truss:

"The equilibriously regenerative octet truss is regenerated
as fast and as extensively as man explores and experiences
it. As I define Universe as the sum-total aggregate of men's
experiences, then we may say that the octet truss-vector
equilibrium is universally extensive. 'Universally extensive'
is a term quite other than 'to infinity'-- a term which
synergetic geometry may not permit. The open end of an
angle is infinite, but so is its convergent end, in that
the actions cannot pass instantaneously or either simultaneously through the same point. As with the vector
equilibrium, infinite is only increasing degrees of
experience-- meaning: more or less tunable."

- Cite Synergetics Notes, p.9, et. seq., 1955. Incorporated at
SYNERGETICS Sec. 647.20, 1 Oct'72

---

RBF DEFINITIONS

Octet Truss:

"Octet Truss (Octahedron Plus Tetrahedron: octetruss)

"Truss" - "Tres" - "Threes"

Three Phase - Triangular."

- Cite Caption of RBF Ltr to D.W. Robertson, 8 Jan '55.

---

RBF DEFINITIONS

Octet Truss:

"Considered solely as geometry of structure, the final
identification of the octet truss by the chemists and
physicists as 'closest packing', puts it into the
universal domain as pure principle."

- Cite RBF Ltr. to Donald W. Robertson, 8 Jan '55, p. 2.
OCTET TRUSS - SEC. 422.11)

---

RBF DEFINITIONS

Octet Truss as an Invention:

"...Down to the minutest atomic components, the octet truss is
therefore proved to be synergetic, and its discovery as a structure-
in contradistinction to its aesthetic or superficial appearance--
is synergetic in performance; that is, its behavior as a whole
is unpredicted by its parts. This makes its discovery as a
structure a true surprise, and therefore it is a true invention."

- Cite SYNERGETICS text at Sec. 650.11, Jan'72

RBF DEFINITIONS

Octet Truss in Yale Art Gallery:

"When a Yale Professor of architecture, Louis Kahn, employed
my octet truss in a design for the floor structuring throughout
the new Art Gallery at Yale University, that truss, in economic
compliance with the building code, had to be fabricated in
reinforced concrete. But the Yale Engineering Department and
its consulting engineers refused to credit my three-way beam
for the task on the grounds of the invalidity of two cross
crisscross beams, 'because,' they said, 'three were even more
redundant.' Yale, therefore, built the floors on the basis
that only one axis of the truss could carry the load. They
called it a 'slanting beam construction.' Result: the octet
truss was reduced to a role of aesthetic nonsense-- a fantas-
tically expensive set of lampshades.

"Fallacy here was that the architect should not have employed
a system which he could not defend structurally before the
ignorance of the engineers. Result: relegation of an important new development to submergence in ignorance."

- Cite RBF Ltr. to Donald W. Robertson, Pp.3-4, 8 Jan'55

---

Octet Truss:                                                    (1)

        See Isotropic Vector Matrix
            Octahedron-tetrahedron System
            Truss
            Vector Equilibrium
            Model of Toothpicks & Semi-dried Peas

---

Octet Truss:                                                    (2)

        See Einstein: RBF Draft Letter To, (5)
            Invention Sequence, (A)-(D)
            Rhombic Dodecahedron, 19 Apr'66
            Tetrahedral Coordination of Nature, 1965
            Icosahedron: Subtriangulation, (1)
            Bubble Bursting, 20 Jan'78

---

RBF DEFINITIONS

Odd Ball:

"There is a phenomenon that we might describe as the eternal
disquietude of the Odd Ball promulgating eternal reprderings,
realignments, and inexorable transformings to accommodate the
eternal regeneration integrity of intellectually-differentiable
Universe, which suggests philosophically that the individual
metaphysical human viewpoint-- the individual ego of the human--
is indeed an essential function of the eternally regenerative
integrity of complex law-governed Universe.

"Possibly this mathematical Odd-Ball-oneness inherently
regenerates the ever-reborn ego. Just when you think you are
negative you find that you are positively so. This is the
eternal wellspring of positive-negative regeneration of
accelerating heating entropy and cooling off syntropy, which
is synergetically interoperative between the inherently terminal
physical differentiating and the inherently eternal metaphysical integration."

- Cite SYNERGETICS, 2nd. Ed. at Secs. 310.13 + .14, 10 Nov'74

---

RBF DEFINITIONS

Odd Ball:

"What we might describe as the eternal disquietude of the
Odd Ball promulgating eternal reorderings and realignments
to accommodate, in a sense, philosophically suggesting the
individual viewpoint, the individual ego of the human.

"Possibly this mathematical Odd Ball oneness inherently
regenerates the ever-reborn ego. Just when you think you're
negative, you find you're positive. This is the eternal
wellspring of positive-negative regeneration, entropy, and
everything."

- Cite RBF in "metaphysical precession" while dictating Sec.
  1051.32, 3200 Idaho, 27 Sep'72

---

Odd Ball:

        See Single Integer Differentials

---

Odd Number:

        See Number: Even & Odd

---

Odor: Odors:                                                   (1)

        See Perfume
            Smellable

Odor: Odors:                                              (2)

See Communications Hierarchy, (1)

---

Off-zero:

See Nonstate, 11 Sep'75

---

Of:

See Between and Not Of

---

RBF DEFINITIONS

Office Buildings:  Conversion to Apartments:

"Before 1985 we will have abandoned the concept of having
to earn a living.  We will have given life-long scholarships
to everyone.  We will have converted all the big city
buildings to apartments and will have eliminated 70 percent
of local commuting while vastly increasing long-distance
travel."

- Citation & context at Building Industry, (10); 20 Sep'76

---

Off-Center:                                               (1)

See Eccentricity
Off-zero

---

RBF DEFINITIONS

Office Buildings:  Conversion to Apartments:

"We have a great deal of nonsense such as occupancy.  We have
a law that you can't work and sleep in the same place.  But
we have all the typewriters sleeping with all the plumbing
and all the people sleeping in the slums.  All these office
buildings are waiting to be converted.  The answer is actually
right here. . . Unless you have the technical solution,
politics can't do anything."

- Cite RBF at DSI Press Conference, NYC, p.19, 28 Jun'72

---

Off Center:  Off-center Effects:                          (2)

See Aberration, 22 Nov'73
Apprehension Lags, 11 Sep'75

---

Office Buildings:                                         (1)

See Buildings:  Multiple Occupancy

Office Buildings: (2)

See Air Space, May'65
Empty, May'70
Invented Jobs, 20 Sep'76

RBF DEFINITIONS

Official Reality:

"There is an official reality which is sometimes unnatural."

- Cite ENVIRONMENT AND CHANGE, Ed. W.R. Ewald, P. 350, Omitted from OPERATING MANUAL FOR SPACESHIP EARTH.

- Citation and context at Realm, 1968

Office:

See Carbondale Office

Official War:

See War: Official & Unofficial

Official News:

See Common Sense: Official News

RBF DEFINITIONS

Ohm: Georg Simon, (1787-1854) German Physicist

Official Panic:

See War as Official Panic

Ohm: Ohm's Law:

See Whole System: Synergetics Principle Of (1)

RBF DEFINITIONS

Official Reality:

RBF DEFINITIONS

Oil:

"We pour 95 out of every 100 barrels of oil right down the
drain-- all as a result of inefficient design decisions, all
of which are avoidable."

- Cite RBF at Penn Bell Videotaping session, Philadelphia,
22 Jan'75

Oil: (1)

See Petroleum

Oil: (2)

See Wood Technology, (2)

Older Generation: Old Life: Older World: (1)

See Continuous Man
Elders: That Doesn't Mean Young Don't Like Their
Elders
Grownup
New Life
Young World
Young & Elders

Older Generation: Old Life: Older World: (2)

see Child as Laboratory (1)
Evolution: Man as Evolution Modifier, May'49
Poets, 1970
Design Revolution: Pulling the Bottom Up (1)(9)
Depression: Great Depression of 1930's, (1)

RBF DEFINITIONS

Old Man River Project:

"With the general disarmament and the release to life-
promoting account of the fabulous production capacity of
the world's industrial complexes, will come one-day air-
delivery of whole cities similar to the Old Man River
Project wherein the operating energy efficiencies will be
significantly multiplied and the social conditions provided
by the omnivisible central community and the completely
private deployed dwelling areas, or the air-delivery of
single-family dwelling machines to the remotest sites, or
of whole clusters of single-family dwelling machines to
near or far sites."

- Citation & context at Building Industry, (10); 20 Sep'76

RBF DEFINITIONS

Old Man River Project:

". . . Moon-crater conformed, domed-over cities on Earth
(such as the Old Man River Project)."

- Citation and context at Inventability Sequence (1)

Old Man River Project:

See Building Industry, (10)*
Inventability Sequence, (1)*

RBF DEFINITIONS

<u>Old Questions</u>:

"Once asked . . . original questions become an additional
brain-inventory item to be passed on to the next generation
in the chromosomic inventory.  All old questions were once
original questions. . . "

- Citation and context at <u>Computer</u> (D), 10 Dec'64

RBF DEFINITIONS

<u>Old Words</u>:

"If you take the names for numbers, there are amongst old
words-- etymologically-- there are a few words that go back
of any knowledge of their derivation by any of the scholars,
and these are spoken of as <u>old words</u>.  And the names for
numbers are all in the old words, that is, they transcend any
possible discovery by man today-- of anything we know so far
about how they were evolved.  None of them have any identity
with experience other than just the abstract number itself,
except for the name for five, which very often has the same
root as that for hand... which is very logical."

- Cite RBF at SIMS, U. Mass., Amherst, Talk 12, p.23, 22 Jul'71

RBF DEFINITIONS

<u>Old Words</u>:

"There are metaphysical yet cogent early words emerging from
the limbo of prehistory's quasi-logical accounting
continuities.... For instance, divine, the concept of a
DEvining deity."

- Citation and context at <u>Division</u>, 1960

<u>Old World</u>:

See Early Man

RBF DEFINITIONS

<u>Olfactoral</u>:

"Olfactoral: preponderantly sensing the liquid and double-
bonded atom and molecule state, including all of the
humanly tunable ranges of the harmonic resonances of the
complex, chemical, liquid substances."

- Cite SYNERGETICS 2 draft at Sec. ~~100.03~~; 100.020, 22 Feb'77

RBF DEFINITIONS

<u>Olfactoral Sense</u>:

"After birth, first the <u>olfactoral sense</u> comes into play,
as the child breathes in its own oxygen and sucks in its
own nutriment."

- Citation and context at <u>Brain's TV Studio</u> (1) + (2), 6 Jun'69

<u>Olfactoral</u>:  <u>Olfactory</u>:                                    (1)

    See Human Sense Ranging & Information Gathering
        Smell: Smellable

<u>Olfactoral</u>:  <u>Olfactory</u>:                                    (2)

        See Fail-safe, 17 Oct'72
            Privacy, 22 Apr'71
            Senses, 9 Apr'40; (1)(2)

Omission vs. Admission:

    See Sin, 7 Nov'75

Omniangular:

    See Triangle, Aug'72

RBF DEFINITIONS

Omni-accelerating:

"By antientropy I refers to the omniaccelerating-

acceleration of the clarifyingly differentiated and
intercommunicated, experience-derived pattern

cognitions of the human mind. . . "

    - Cite Doxiadis, p. 310. 20 Jun'66

RBF DEFINITIONS

Omni-Aroundness:

"A system is a patterning of enclosure consisting of a
conceptual aggregate of recalled experience items, or
events, having inherent insideness, outsideness, and
omni-aroundness."

    - Cite SYNERGETICS draft at Sec. 40Q25, 26 May'72

Omniaccommodation:

    See Isotropic Vector Matrix, 9 Nov'72

RBF DEFINITIONS

Omniasymmetry:

"Synergetics both equates and accommodates Heisenberg's
indeterminism of mensuration inherent in the omniasymmetry
of wavilinear physical pulsations in respect to the only
metaphysical (ergo, physically unattainable) waveless
exactitude of absolute equilibrium."

    - Cite SYNERGETICS text at Sec. 211.00; as rewritten by RBF
      on galley, 11 Oct'73

Omniadjacent:

    See Rhombic Dodecahedron, 22 Mar'73

RBF DEFINITIONS

Omni-automation:

"All the money-making drives toward omni-automation and
complete unemployment. Politics keeps inventing the jobs
by law."

    - Citation & context at Invented Jobs, 20 Sep'76

<u>Omniautomated</u>:  <u>Omni-automation</u>:

    See Industrial Complex, 13 Mar'73
        Invented Jobs, 20 Sep'76*

---

RBF DEFINITIONS

<u>Omni-coexisting</u>:

"Because the tetrahedron is inherently the minimum structural system of universe, it provides the minimum <u>omni-coexisting</u> convexity and concavity condition in universe."

- Cite RBF on Synergetics draft, U. Mass., Amherst, 22 July 1971. "Omnitopology," Sec. 810. et. seq.

- Citation & context at <u>Convex & Concave Tetrahedron</u>, Aug'71

---

<u>Omnibalanced</u>:

    See Dynamic Symmetry, 31 May'71

---

<u>Omnicoexisting</u>:

    See Convex & Concave Tetrahedron, Aug'71*

---

<u>Omnicircumferential</u>:

    See Big System, 5 Jun'73

---

<u>Omnicohering</u>:  <u>Omnicoherent</u>:

    See Truth & Love, 16 Feb'73
        Tunability, 19 Oct'72

---

<u>Omni-closest Packing</u>:

    See Nucleus, (1)
        Model of Toothpicks & Semi-dried Peas, (1)(2)

---

<u>Omnicollective</u>:

    See Gravity, 23 Sep'73

Omniconcurrent:


See Design, 8 Sep'75

---

RBF DEFINITIONS

Omnicongruence:

"When two or more systems are joined vertex to vertex, edge to edge, or in omnicongruence-- in single, double, triple, or quadruple bonding, then the topological accounting must take cognizance of the congruent vectorial build in growth."


- Cite SYNERGETICS text at Sec. 931.10, galley rewrite, 19 Dec'73

---

RBF DEFINITIONS

Omnicondition:

"The universally infrequent meshing of wavelengths and frequencies

Produces an omnicondition

In which the new omnidirectional system's center must, as each

is created,

Continually occupy omnidirectionally greater domains of disorder."


- Cite BRAIN & MIND, p.89 May '72

---

Omnicongruence:   Omnicongruent;                    (1)


See Bonding
    Congruence
    Geometry of Vectors
    Omniadjacent
    Self-congruence Packing
    Quadrivalent
    Chemical Bonds: Quadruple Bond

---

Omnicondition:


See System, 1971

---

Omnicongruence:   Omnicongruent:                    (2)


See Synergetics Constant, (A)
    Overlapping, 30 May'75
    Vector Equilibrium, 23 Oct'72

---

RBF DEFINITIONS

Omnicongruence:

"When two or more structural systems are joined vertex to vertex, edge to edge, or face to face or to omni-congruence-- in a single, double, triple or quadruple bonding, then the topological accounting must take cognizance of the congruent components.'


- Cite NASA Speech, pp. 61-62, Jun '66

TETRAHELIX- CHEMICAL BONDS - SEC. 941.01

---

Omniconsiderate:   Omniconsideration:                (1)


See Consideration for Others
    Not Trespassing

Omniconsiderate:  Omniconsideration:                                    (2)

        See A Priori Intellect, (1)
           Boltzmann Sequence, (20
           Rearranging the Environment, 9 Apr'71
           Universal Requirements of a Dwelling Advantage,
             31 May'74
           World Game, Feb'73
           Mind vs. Energy, 19 May'75

---

RBF DEFINITIONS

Omniconvertex:

"Nuclear structural systems consist internally entirely of
tetrahedra which have only one common interior vertex:
omniconvertex."

    - Citation & context at Prime Nuclear Structural Systems, 27 Dec'74

---

Omnicontinuous:

    See Frequency Islands of Perception, 13 Nov'75

---

Omni-co-Occurring:

    See Jitterbug, 4 Oct'72

---

RBF DEFINITIONS

Omniconvergent:

"Omniconvergent

Is the opposite of radius."

    - Cite RBF to EJA
      Sarasota, Florida
      7 February 1971

---

Omnicoordinate:

    See Graphable, 27 May'72
       Pole Vaulter, 2 Jul'75

---

Omniconvergent:

    See Gravity, (2)
       Three:  Number Function of Three in a Four-axial
         System, 24 Jan'76

---

RBF DEFINITIONS

Omnicurvilinear:

"Experience is omnicurvilinear."

    - Citation at Experience, 27 May'72
    - Cite RBF marginalia at SYNERGETICS draft Sec. 410.03, 27 May'72

RBF DEFINITIONS

Omnicurvilinear:

"Calculus treats discretely and predictively with
frequency rates and discrete direction of angles of
change of the <u>omnicurvilinear</u> event quanta's
successively recurring positionings: fixes."

~~- Cite The Synergetics draft, Mar '71~~

- Citation at <u>Fix</u>, Mar'71

---

TEXT CITATIONS

Omnideployed Patterns:

Synergetics, Sec. 931.02 - Apr'72

---

RBF DEFINITIONS

Omnidiametric:

"Omnidiametric can be either inwardly or outwardly diametric,
but it does not allow for wavilinear operation. It cannot
wander; it will always be regenerative from the center.
It is a special case of omnidirectional. If the outwardly
omnidiametric source were in motion-- and all phenomena is
in motion-- then there is a lag in the rate its output
could reach a distant point. Ergo, to itself, nonwandering
omnidiametric radiation would appear to be bent as the
whiskers of a cat would appear to be bent backwardly of
its trajectory."

- Cite RBF to EJA, 3200 Idaho NW, 23 Sep'73

---

Omnidiametric:                                    (1)

See Multidiametric
Omniradial

---

Omnidiametric:                                    (2)

See Distributive, 23 Sep'73
Package, 23 Sep'73
Radiation, 23 Sep'73

---

Omnidifferential Lag Rates:

See Prime Dichotomy, (2)

---

Omnidifferentiated Rates:

See Perceptual Peephole as Fraction of Reality, Dec'69

---

Omnidimensional Light Matrix:

See Atomic Computer Complex, (8)

Omnidimensional:

> See Force Lines: Omnidimensional, (2)
>     Size, 22 Jun'72
>     Triangle, (a)
>     Fourth-dimensional Synergetics Mathematics, 14 Dec'76

RBF DEFINITIONS

Omnidirectional:

"It is a surprising thing that all closest packing begins with two balls rather than omnidirectionally. Two balls coming together is where thought begins . . . it is a wedding thing. . . and it is very beautiful the way the two balls reoccur at each wave outwardly."

- Citation at Two Balls Coming Together, 19 Jun'71
- Cite RBF to EJA, Beverly Hotel, New York, 19 June 1971.

RBF DEFINITIONS

Omnidirectional:

"Omnidirectional can be chaos. It can mean everywhere, including returning upon itself. It is indiscrete. It is general case."

- Cite RBF to EJA, 3200 Idaho, 23 Sep'73

RBF DEFINITIONS

Omnidirectional:

"In book /Synergetics/ I must eliminate the words 'three-dimensional' as meaningful /sic/, and always use omnidirectional observation of multi-dimensional characteristics, with angle and frequency of cyclic reference as the only requirements."

- Citation and context at Size (2), circa 1970

RBF DEFINITIONS

Omnidirectional

"Operationally speaking the word omnidirectional involves a speaker who is observing from some viewing point. He says, 'People and things are going every which way around me.' It seems chaotic to him at first but on further consideration he finds the opposite to be true and that only inherent order is being manifest. First we observe that we cannot and do not live and experience either in a one-dimensional linear world, nor in a two-dimensional ████ infinitely extended planar world."

- Cite SYNERGETICS draft at Sec. 1001.01, 27 Feb '72
- Citation & context at Nucleus (1), 17 Feb'72

RBF DEFINITIONS

Omnidirectional:

". . . Energy goes in all directions, expanding as a bubble-- a spheroidal wave. A spheroidal wave is omnidirectional-- like light going in all directions from a candle. So our energy is going in all directions as a bubble, and the surface of any spherical system always increases as the second power of the linear. The rate at which the surface will grow will be 186,000 miles a second to the second power, that is, $c^2$."

Cite MERGERS & ACQUISITIONS Vol. 1, No. 1, p. 46, 1965

RBF DEFINITIONS

Omnidirectional:

"Instead of omnidirectional, say timeless."

- Citation at Timeless, 19 Jun'71
- Cite RBF to EJA, Beverly Hotel, New York, 19 June 1971.

RBF DEFINITIONS

Omnidirectional:

"Our experiences are inherently omnidirectional. We ourselves are walking around like this and before we were born in the womb we were moving in all directions. Our Earth is continually rotating and our milky way is continually rotating in the heavens, and so forth."

- Cite OREGON Lecture #2 - p. 65, 2 Jul'62

RBF DEFINITIONS

Omnidirectional:

"Because of the incessant wheeling about of humans first in the womb, then in the baby carriage, then on foot, in the auto and ship and plane roundabout a spinning earth in a spinning solar system within an involuting-evoluting, spirally spinning galaxy, totally inventoried experiences are inherently omnidirectional when considered as the sum of observational orientations."

- Cite OMNIDIRECTIONAL HALO, p. 138, 1960

---

RBF DEFINITIONS

Omnidirectional:

"This very initiation itself of first division of Universe into an omnidirectional, radially defined zone, between maxima and minima within-ness and without-ness sense and experience tunability, affects not only the local tuned-in system, but also the balance of Universe, within and without, even as does the little and big spherical triangle subdivide the system's 'surface' zoneness, circumferentially, so also here do the basic maxima and minima, radial and circumferential dichotomies, which are the basically differentiated acceleration functions and inherent reciprocal self-precessors."

(Above text closely parallels Ltr. to Donald W. Robertson, p.4, 8 Jan'55 at Zoneness: System Zoneness.)

- Cite RBF draft Ltr. to Jim (Fitzgibbon?), Raleigh, NC, 1954-59

---

RBF DEFINITIONS

Omnidirectional:

"...Omnidirectional relationships are only angularly configured and are independent of size or dimension."

- Citation and context at Brain's TV Studio, 1960

---

RBF DEFINITIONS

Omnidirectional:

"Electromagnetic wave phenomena are . . . omnidirectional and omnipermeative."

- Citation at Omnipermeative, 9 Apr'40

- Cite NO MORE SECON - HAND CON. p. 89, 9 Apr'4(

---

RBF DEFINITIONS

Omnidirectional:

"Universe, as all experience, is inherently omnidirectional in its observational orientations."

- Cite OMNIDIRECTIONAL HALO, p. 138, 1960

---

Omnidirectional Clock:

See Fourth Dimensional Modelability, 24 Feb'75

---

RBF DEFINITIONS

Omnidirectional:

"'In' is unique to individual systems. One 'out' is common to all systems and is omnidirectional in respect to any one system..."

- Citation and context at In and Out, 4 May'57

---

RBF DEFINITIONS

Omnidirectional Closest Packing of Spheres. Synergetics Principle of:

". . . Frequency to the second power times ten plus two: is the number of balls in any given layer. This simple formula governing the rate at which balls are agglomerated around other balls or shells in closest packing is an elegant manifest of the reliably incisive transactions, formings and transformings of universe. I made that discovery and published it in 1944. This is the mathematics which the molecular biologists have confirmed and developed by virtue of which wem can predict the number of nodes in the external ▬▬▬ protein shells of all the viruses, within which shells are housed the DNA-RNA programmed design controls of all the biological species and individuals within those species. Although the polio virus is quite different from the common cold virus, and both are different from other viruses, all of them employ frequency to the second power times ten plus two in producing those most powerful structural enclosures of all the biological regeneration of life. It is the power of these geodesic-sphere shells that make so lethal those viruses unfriendly to man. They are almost indestructible."

- Cite RBF marginalia, New York, 19 June 1971, to Synergetics draft, Section. 222.32.

RBF DEFINITIONS

Omnidirectional Closest Packing of Spheres. Synergetics Principle of:

"Omnidirectional concentric closest packing of equal spheres about a nuclear sphere forms a series of vector equilibria of progressively higher frequencies. The number of vertexes or spheres in any given shell or layer is always edge frequency (F) to the second power times ten plus two.

Equation: $10\ F^2 + 2$ = number of vertexes or spheres in any layer.

"The equation for the total number of vertexes, or sphere centers, in all symmetrically concentric shells =

$$10\ (F_1^2 + F_2^2 + F_3^2 + \ldots \ F_n^2) + 2F_n + 1."$$

- Cite SYNERGETICS DRAFT, "Synergetics Principles," March 1971

---

Omnidirectional Closest Packing of Spheres:                    (1)

See Closest Packing of Spheres
    Equation: Omnidirectional Closest Packing Of
        Spheres
    Prime Number Inherency & Constant Relative
        Abundance of the Topology of Symmetrical
        Structural Systems
    Concentric Layering
    Shell Growth Rate
    Vector Equilibrium

---

RBF DEFINITIONS

Omnidirectional Closest Packing of Spheres: Synergetics Principle Of:                    (1)

"Now I am going to take an inventory of those balls in the different layers. There are 12 balls in this layer and if we count these up we find that there are 42 balls in the next layer. In this top layer there are 92 balls. If I put on another layer you will find that there are 162-- and another layer will be 252. The number of layers always comes out with the number two as a suffix. We know that this system is a decimal system of notation. Therefore we are counting in what the mathematician calls congruence in modulo ten-- a modulus of 10 units-- and there is a constant excess of two.

"We find in algebraic work if you use a constant suffix (where you always have, say, 33 and 53, you could treat it as 50 and come out with the same algebraic conditions.) Therefore if all these come out with the number two, I can drop off the number two and not affect the algebraic relationships.

"If I drop off the number two in that column they will all be zeros; so this would read, 10, 40, 90, 160, 250, and if I had another one it would be 360. I see each one of these are 10's,"

- Cite Oregon Lecture #7, pp.238-239, 11 Jul'62

---

Omnidirectional Closest Packing of Spheres:                    (2)

See Powering, 11 Jul'62
    Powering: Fifth Dimension, 29 Nov'72
    Synergetics, 29 Nov'72
    Mite as Model for Quark, 3 May'77

---

RBF DEFINITIONS

Omnidirectional Closest Packing of Spheres: Synergetics Principle Of:                    (2)

"so I divide each one by 10 and then I have 1, 4, 9, 16, 25 and you recognize that it is a progression of second powering. The next one would be 36, then 49. Each one of these are two to the second power, three to the second power, and so forth.

"We then discover that the number of balls in any one layer-- we could call it frequency, or radius, because we have found that they are the same words. In the vector equilibrium the number of units coming from the center outwardly are exactly the same as the edge units; so I can say frequency to the second power times ten plus two: that is how many balls there will always be in a given layer. It is a very simple kind of formula-- frequency to the second power, times 10, plus 2. That is the formula I have discovered regarding the rate at which balls are agglomerated around other balls or shells. I made that discovery and published it in 1944.

"An d that was the mathematics that the molecular biologists discovered that I had developed by virtue of which I was able to predict the number of external shell members they found were following this form in the virus, and that is when they really"

- Cite Oregon Lecture #7, pp.238-239, 11 Jul'62

---

Omnidirectional Frame of Reference:

See Vector Equilibrium, 19 Nov'74

---

RBF DEFINITIONS

Omnidirectional Closest Packing of Spheres: Synergetics Principle Of:                    (3)

"began to get their clues. All the different viruses had different kinds of protein shells and so the polio virus was quite different from the other-- as was the common cold virus, but all of them were some kind of frequency brought out in this system, and the mathematics of it was cleanly predictable."

- Cite Oregon Lecture #7, pp.238-239, 11 Jul'62

---

Omnidirectional Games:

See Heaven, 23 May'72
    How Little I Know, 1 Feb'75

RBF DEFINITIONS

Omnidirectional Growth:

"A cone is simply a tetrahedron being rotated. Omnidirectional growth-- which means all life-- can only be accommodated by tetrahedron."

- Cite RBF to EJA, Bear Island, 25 August 1971.

- Citation at Tetrahedron, 25 Aug'71

Omnidirectional Growth:

See Fireworks, (2)

RBF DEFINITIONS

Omnidirectional Halo:

"Any conceptual thought is a system and is structured tetra-hedrally. This is because all conceptuality is polyhedral. The sums of all the angles around all the vertexes-- even crocodile, or a 10,000 frequency geodesic (which is what the Earth really is)-- will always be 720° less then the number of vertexes times 360°."

- Cite RBF answer to Hugh Kenner query, 2 Mar'72
- Incorporated in SYNERGETICS draft at Sec. 501.10, 14 Mar'72

Omnidirectional Halo:                                (1)

See Halo: Halo Concept
          Omnihalo

Omnidirectional Halo:                                (2)

See Epistemology, 9 May'62

Omnidirectional Infoscope:

See Infoscope, 13 Nov'75

RBF DEFINITIONS

Omnidirectionality:

"The connection between the six degrees of freedom and omnidirectionality is, of course, the vector equilibrium, which combines the threeness of the cube in relation to 20 as unity = VE." . . .
"Experience is inherently omnidirectional."

- Cite RBF to EJA, Bear Island, 25 August 1971.
- Citation & context at Experience, 25 Aug'71

RBF DEFINITIONS

Omnidirectionality:

"Empirically we have only omnidirectionality without any fixed universal reference points."

- Cite RBF holograph with old Synergetics Manuscript, circa 1970

Omnidirectional Observation:

See Center, 21 Jan '75

---

RBF DEFINITIONS

Omnidirectional: Physical Existence Environment Surrounds: (2)

"The observer's unfamiliarity with the phenomena which he is observing, and the multiplicity of items of interaction and their velocity of transformations and their omni-engulfing occurences tend to dismay the observer's hope of reasonable or immediate comprehension. Therefore observer's are often induced to surrender their attempts at technical comprehension of their experience-- which surrender of the drive to comprehend fills the observer with a sense of chaos, which sensation he then subconsciously converts into an understanding by saying to himself that the environment is inherently chaotic, ergo inherently incomprehendible. Thus he satisfies himself that he is super-reasonable, and that the Universe is just annoyingly disorderly; ergo frequently dismissible, which seemingly warrants his invention of whatever kind of Universe seems momentarily most satisfying to him.

"The more humanity probes and verifies experimentally by reducing its theories to demonstrable practice in order to learn whether their theories are valid or not, the more clearly does Universe reveal itself as being generated and regenerated only upon a complex of entirely orderly relationships. The inherent spherical center viewpoint

RBF CORRECTIONS
9 FEB '73  - Cite SYNERGETICS draftat Secs. 1001.03+04, 27 Feb '72

---

RBF DEFINITIONS

Omnidirectional Pattern:

"The Department of Mathematics at M.I.T states categorically the following:

        Mathematics is the science of structure
        and pattern.

"I will state our case in the terms of an omnidirectional pattern- an isotropic vector matrix-- rather then in the more usually employed linear or planar patterns, and thus satisfy M.I.T.'s primary mathematical premise of structural patterning, which structure is inherently an omnidirectional plural wavelength and frequency event system."

- Cite Ltr. to Jim Fitzgibbon (?), Raleigh NC, pp.j3-j4, undated

---

RBF DEFINITIONS

Omnidirectional: Physical Existence Environment Surrounds: (3)

"with which each individual is endowed generates its own orderly radii of observation in a closed finite system of event observations which are subject to orderly angular subdividing, recording, and interrelating in spherically trigonometric computational relationships to the observer's inherently orderly sphere of reference."

- Cite SYNERGETICS draft At Sec. 1001.04, 27 Feb '72

---

Omnidirectional Pattern:

See Angle & Frequency Design Control, Jul'71

---

Omnidirectionality vs. Polarization:

See Cornucopia, 24 Feb'72

---

RBF DEFINITIONS

Omnidirectional: Physical Existence Environment Surrounds: (1)

"Omnidirectional means that a center of a movable sphere of observation has been established a priori by Universe for each individual's life's inescapably mobile viewpoint which, like humans' shadows, move everywhere silently with them. These physical existence environment surrounds of life events spontaneously resolve into two classes:

        (1) those events which are passing tangentially by
            the observer, and

        (2) those events in entities other than self which
            are moving radially either towards or away
            from the observer.

"The tangentially passing energy events are always and only moving in lines perpendicular to the radii of the observer, which means that the multiplicity of his real events does not produce chaos: it produces discretely apprehendable experience increments all of which can be chartingly identified by angle and frequency data."

- Cite SYNEREGTICS draft at Sec. 1001.02, 27 Feb '72

* RBF DELETION 9 FEB '73

---

RBF DEFINITIONS

Omnidirectional Precession:

"Omnidirectional precession is generalized."

- Citation and context at General Case, 16 Feb'73

RBF DEFINITIONS

### Omnidirectional Shutterable Sieve:

"We need an omnidirectional shutterable sieve
where we can increase or reduce the magnitudes of our omnidirectional valve openings.

"Since we wish to be able to see in any direction
and likewise be able to obscure in any direction,
we recognize that it is difficult to make an opaque wall transparent
but it is very easy to opaque a transparent wall
by curtaining and shuttering."

- Citation & context at Environmental Controls (2), 31 May'74

---

### Omnidirectional Shutterable Sieve:

See Membrane
    Occulting Membranes

---

RBF DEFINITIONS

### Omnidirectional Terminal Case Corner:

"Since the central or nuclear sphere has no outer layer and is
only the nucleus, its frequency of layer enclosures iz zero.
Following our symmetrically and convergently diminishing
uniform rate of contraction to its inherent minimum and terminal
frequency case of zero, and applying our generalized formula
$10 F^2 + 2$, we have $6^2 = 0$, $0 \cdot 10 = 0$, $0 + 2 = 2$, we discover
that unity is two. This single nuclear sphere consists of both
its concave inside and its exterior convex sphere, its
inbounding turnaround to become outboundness consequently
co-occurring. Unity is plural and at minimum two. That the
nuclear ball is inherently two has been incontrovertibly
discovered by getting nature into her omnidirectional terminal
case corner."

- Cite SYNERGETICS, 2nd. Ed. at Sec. 261.04; 13 Nov'75

---

RBF DEFINITIONS

### Omnidirectional Typewriter:                                    (1)

"All model studies are mainly probability studies and nearly
always deal with linear probability. But my problems are not
linear; they are omnidirectional. I am dealing with total
system. That's what the world is not paying any attention to
and that's why we're in trouble: Synergy shows that you cannot
solve comprehensive problems by exclusively local linear models.

"We must begin with the general coordinating system used by
nature in the closest packing of atoms such as the coordinates
of the Dymaxion airocean world map. Another example is the omnitriangulated strip whose width ■ exactly equals the altitude of
the tetrahedron. You can completely spool-wrap all four faces
of the tetrahedron; and the tetrahedron so wrapped has an axis
running through it and out through the two unwrapped edges of the
tetrahedron spool. Being a tetrahedron, this spool may be end-
lessly wrapped as an omnidirectionally closed system. Ergo, we
have a device for recording all of the omnidirectionally
occurring and observed data into a minimum system which is
unwrappable into a flat ribbon printout with four-dimensional
coordination."

"In this way of doing things everything remains in perpendicu-"

- Tape transcript, phila. Pa. pp.4-8; SYNERGETICS draft new
   Sec. 1130, 10 Sep'74

---

RBF DEFINITIONS

### Omnidirectional Typewriter:                                    (2)

"larity, as in the Dymaxion map where any star remains in exact
perpendicularity over the point on the map of the world. The
same triangles are going to come out flat and the same stars
are in exact zenith over that point, as the radii remain
perpendicular to the system independent of whether the triangular
area edges are arcs or chords. This is an extraordinary mathematical transformation in which you can have omnidirectionality
phenomena of all systems-- all gravitation, radiation, stars,
fishes, everything-- all coming into coordinate printout in
one flat ribbon map.

"What we have is an actual literal model of an omnidirectional
typewriter providing a complete convergent-divergent modelability
for the data. When you put the data on such a strip it is
identified specifically in the transformation wherever it is
at all times.

"This can really identify the largest of all the computers on the
Earth due to the fact that it reflects the pattern of the great-
circle railroad tracks of energy. In other words, if you want
to go from here to there in Universe, you've got to go through"

- Tape transcript, Phila. Pa., pp. 4-8, 15 Jun'74: SYNERGETICS
   draft new Sec. 1130, 10 Sep'74

---

RBF DEFINITIONS

### Omnidirectional Typewriter:                                    ■(3)

"the points of intertangency of the 25 great circles of fundamental symmetry which apply to all the atoms and their association
as crystals in all the seven of the fundamental symmetry subsets.
The 31 great circles of the icosahedron always shunt energies
into local holding great-circle orbits, while the vector
equilibrium opens the switching to omniuniverse energy travel.
The icosahedron is red light, holding, No-Go; whereas vector
equilibrium is a green light Go. The six great circles of the
icosahedron act as holding patterns for energies. The 25 great
circles of the vector equilibrium all go through the 12 tangential contact points of the 12 atomic spheres always closest
packed around any one spherical atom domain. The 25 great circles
of the vector equilibrium are the only railroad tracks of energy
in the Universe, and as they get opened up some of them go
through the 12 points just twice per circuit; whereas some of
them go through the 12 points six times per circuit. That is,
each of the four sets of great circles of the vector equilibrium's
total of 25 (3, 4, 6, 12 = 25) have different numbers of local
switch-off points per great-circle circuiting. With all these
beautiful switches and stop-go controls, we comprehend the"

- Tape transcript, Phil., Pa. pp.4-8, 15 Jun'74; SYNERGETICS
   draft new Sec. 1130, 10 Sep'74

---

RBF DEFINITIONS

### Omnidirectional Typewriter:                                    (4)

"method by which nature can shunt, valve, hold, and transmit
all information in Universe. This is the information control
system of the Universe. This is the way spheres transmit
through closest packing patterns. This is why transistors
work; that's how somebody suddenly discovered this little piece
of metal valving energy with reliable regularities. Science
stupidly called it 'solid State' physics because they couldn't
see those beautiful little atoms and electrons' railroad tracks
and their great-circle energy holding patterns.

"So we have here the design for an omnidirectional info-storing-
and-retrieving and printout typewriter for communicating all
acquirable info. Synergetics mathematics has the ability to take
the spherical and pull it out in the flat. The least distorted
transformational projection of the Dymaxion airocean world map
is an icosahedron, but the simplest frame of reference is the
spherical tetrahedron which provides the omnitriangulated grid,
strip-wrapped tetrahedron.

"This is how you bring the omnidirectional into a flat projection.
This is how the tetrahedron, the basic structural system of"

- Tape transcript, Phila. Pa., pp.4-8, 15 Jun'74; SYNERGETICS
   draft new Sec. 1130, 10 Sep'74

---

RBF DEFINITIONS

### Omnidirectional Typewriter:                                    (5)

"Universe, unwraps linearly to an infinity of varying frequencies
of angle and frequency modulation. Here we have a conceptual ■
model that you can program: that is exactly what all the
theoretical computer model specialists have been missing, ergo
the chasm between their projective strategies and mine; they
are running blindly into catastrophe but they need not do so."

- Tape transcript, Phila. Pa. pp.4-8, 15 Jun'74; SYNERGETICS
   draft new Sec. 1130, 10 Sep'74

Omnidirectional Typewriter:

          Atomic Computer Complex
       See Tetrahelix: Continuous Pattern Strip

Omnidirectional:                          (2A)

    See Bird's Nest as A Tool, (A)(B)
        Brain's TV Studio, 1960*
        Child, 1970
        Cyclic Bundling of Experiences, May'49
        Directionless, 19 Jun'71
        Ecology, 16 Feb'73
        Experience, 25 Aug'71*; 20 Dec'71
        Fuller, R.B.: His Writing Style, 22 Jan'75
        In & Out, 4 May'57*
        Inhibit, 29 Oct'72
        Linear & Curvilinear, Jun'66
        Min-Max Limits, 22 Jun'75
        Nucleus, (1)* (2)
        Omnipermeative, 9 Apr'40*
        Radial Depth, 20 Dec'74
        Resolution, 12 May'75
        Size, (2)*
        Individuality & Degrees of Freedom, (1)

Omnidirectional Wave:

    See Wave Pattern of a Stone Dropped in Liquid, (1)

Omnidirectional:                          (2B)

    See Tetrahedron, 25 Aug'71*
        Timeless, 19 Jun'71*
        Two Balls Coming Together, 19 Jun'71*
        Vector Equilibrium, 30 Oct'73; 25 Aug'71
        Twilight Zone, 22 Jun'75
        Four Intergeared Mobility Freedoms, 2 Nov'73
        Human Beings at the Center, (1)
        Human Beings & Complex Universe, (14)(15)

Omnidirectional Wheel:

    See Stone as Omnidirectional Wheel

Omnidirectional:                          (3)

    See Omnidirectional Clock
        Omnidirectional Closest Packing of Spheres
        Omnidirectional Frame of Reference
        Omnidirectional Games
        Omnidirectional Growth
        Omnidirectional Halo
        Omnidirectionality
        Omnidirectional Observation
        Omnidirectional Pattern
        Omnidirectional: Physical Existence Environment
          Surrounds
        Omnidirectionality vs. Polarization
        Omnidirectional Precession
        Omnidirectional Shutterable Sieve
        Omnidirectional Typewriter
        Omnidirectional Wheel
        Omnidirectional Wave

Omnidirectional:                          (1)

    See Closest Packing of Spheres
        Force Lines: Omnidirectional Lines Of
        Halo Concept
        Inhibit = Omnidirectional Indrinking
        Inwardness vs. Omnidirectional
        Omnidirectionality & Polarization
        Radial-circumferential Coordination
        Radiation
        Shell Growth Rate
        Spherical Wave
        Supradirectional
        Television: Omnidirectional TV Set
        Wave Propagation
        Wow: The Last Wow
        Field of Omnidirectional Nothingness
        Shpericity
        Experience in the Round
        Linear vs. Omnidirectional
        Wave Pattern of a Stone Dropped in Liquid

Omnidivergent:

    See Three: Number Function of Three in a Four-axial
        System, 24 Jan'76

RBF DEFINITIONS

Omnidynamic:

"The vector equilibrium produces conservation of
omnidynamic Universe despite many entropic local energy
dissipations of star tetrahedra."

- Cite RBF dictation, Washington, DC, 7 Oct. '71 incorporated
in Synergetics Text at 'Antitetrahedron,' Sec. 638.02.

ANTITETRAHEDRON - SEC. 638.02

---

Omnidynamic:                                              (1)

See Conservation of Omnidynamic Universe

---

Omnidynamic:                                              (2)

See Air Space, May'65
    Future of Synergetics, 19 Apr'66
    Star Tetrahedron & VE, 9 Nov'73

---

Omniecology:

See Trespassing: Not Trespassing (a)

---

Omnieconomic:

See Interaccommodate, 30 Jan'73
    Scheme of Reference, 24 Sep'73
    Energy Event, Mar'71

---

Omniegalitarian:

See Revolution, Jan'72

---

RBF DEFINITIONS

Omniembracing:

"Gravity is circumferentially omniembracing and is never
partial, but is always whole."

"it is the sum of all the no-points embracing all the points;
and it compounds at the surface-embracing second-power rate
of the linear proximity gains. All the ▬▬▬ no-points
(novents) are always embracing all the points."

- Citation and context at Integrity of Universe, 23 Sep'73

---

RBF DEFINITIONS

Omni-embracing:

"Gravity is omni-embracing and is not focusable."

- Cite Synergetics draft, Sec. 270, August 1971

- Citation at Gravity, Aug'71

RBF DEFINITIONS

Omniembracing vs. Permeating:

"Joseph Needham's 'above and below' and his 'higher and lower' are linear.

"'Out' expressly is the containing and the contained: in synergetics, the omniembracing and the permeating."

- Citation & context at Synergetic Hierarchy, 5 May'74

Omniequiangularity:

See Trisection of an Angle, 22 Nov'73
Model of Toothpicks & Semi-dried Peas, (1)

Omniembracing Squeeze:

See Inward Explosion, 8 Apr'75

Omni-equi-divisible:

See XYZ Quadrant at Center of Octahedron, 14 May'75

Omniembracing:                                    (1)

See Gravity
Linear vs. Omniembracing
Love
Omniembracing vs. Permeating
Truth

Omniequilateral:

See Normal to Universe, 10 Sep'74
Model of Toothpicks & Semi-dried Peas, (1)

Omniembracing:                                    (2)

See Ecology, 16 Feb'73
Generalization, 8 Mar'73
Gravity, Aug'71*
Integrity of Universe, 23 Sep'73*
Prime Structural Systems (1)
Principle, 5 Jun'73
Truth & Love, 16 Feb'73
Spherical Quadrant Phases, 9 Jul'75

Omniequi-economic:

See Hierarchy of Constellar Configurations, 1959

RBF DEFINITIONS

Omniequilibrium:                                              (1)

"I seek a word to express most succinctly the complexedly
pulsative, inside-outing, integrative-disintegrative, counter-
vailing behaviors of the vector equilibrium. 'Librium'
represents the degrees of freedom.  Universe is omnilibrious
because it accommodates all the every-time-recurrent,
12-alternatively-optional degrees of equieconomical freedoms.
Omniequilibrious means all the foregoing.

"The sphere is a convex vector equilibrium, and the spaces
between closest-packed uniradius spheres are the concave
vector equilibria or, in their contractive form, the concave
octahedra.  In going contractively from vector equilibrium to
equi-vector-edged tetrahedron ..., we go from a volumetric
20-ness to a volumetric oneness, a twentyfold contraction.
In the vector-equilibrium jitterbug, the axis does not rotate,
but the equator does.  On the other hand, if you hold the
equator and rotate the axis, the system contracts.  Twisting
one end of the axis to rotate it terminates the jitterbug's
20-volume to 4-volume octahedral state contraction, whereafter
the contraction momentum throws a torque in the system with
a leverage force of 20 to 1.  It contracts until it becomes a"

- Cite SYNERGETICS text at Secs. 1030.10 & .11, 27 Dec'73

---

RBF DEFINITIONS

Omniequilibrium:                                              (2)

"volume of one as a quadrivalent tetrahedron, that is, with
the four edges of the tetrahedron congruent.  Precessionally
aided by other galaxies' mass-attractive tensional forces
acting upon them to accelerate their axial, twist-and-torque-
imposed contractions, this torque momentum may account for
the way stars contract into dwarfs and pulsars, or for the
way that galaxies pulsate or contract into the incredibly
vast and dense, paradoxically named 'black holes.'"

- Cite SYNERGETICS text at Sec. 1030.11, 27 Dec'73
  (RBF galley rewrite)

---

Omniequilibrious:  Omniequilibrium:                          (1)

    See Centers of Equilibrious Symmetry
        Omnilibrium

---

Omniequilibrious:  Omniequilibrium:                          (2)

    See Basic Triangle:  Basic Equilibrium 48 LCD Triangle,
        16 Dec'73

---

Omni-equi-optimum:

    See Tensegrity:  Icosahedron Tensegrity, Dec'61

---

Omniexpanding:                                               (1)

    See Expanding Physical Universe

---

Omniexpanding:  Omniexpansive:                               (2)

    See Entropy, (p.90) May'72
        Gravity, (2)
        Universal Integrity: Second-power Congruence of
            Gravitational & Radiational Constants, 9 Jan'74

---

Omniexperienceable:

    See Integer, 15 Oct'72

Synergetics Dictionary

Omniexplicable:

See Skinner, B.F.

Omnifreedom:

See Powering: Fourth & Fifth Dimensions, 18 Nov'72

Omnifavorable:

See Artifacts, (1)

Omnifrequency:

See Individuality & Degrees of Freedom, (1)

RBF DEFINITIONS

Omnifinite:

"Universe is finite because it is the aggregate of omnifinite local experiences. All experiences begin and end. Physics has found no continuums; instead it has found only discrete omniseparate, finite quanta.

"Meaningful segments of scenario Universe are finitely furnished with omnifinite experiences."

- Cite RBF rewrite of Finite Furniture, 1960, done at Sarasota, Fla., 11 Feb'71

Omnifunction:

See Generalized Principle, (4)

Omnifinite:

See Twenty-foot Earth Globe & 200-foot Celestial Sphere, (11)

Omnigeared:

See Irreversibility, 4 May'57

RBF DEFINITIONS

Omnigeometric:

"... A tethered ball on a long string is free to describe
any omnigeometric forms of circles, spheres, or giraffes,
but it cannot get away from the Universe."

- Cite SYNERGETICS draft at Sec. 401.02, 27 May'72

Omni-humanity:

See Cosmic Accounting, 20 Sep'76

Omnigram: Omnigramming:

See Kinetic Omnigramming

Omni-idealized:

See Frame of Reference, 4 Oct'72

RBF DEFINITIONS

Omnihalo:

"The considered relevancy within the zone of lucidity consists
of one tetrahedron or more. For each 'considered tetrahedron,'
there are three complementary always and only co-occurring
parametric tetrahedra. We discover that our omnihalo epistemological accounting consists entirely of rational tetrahedral
quantation."

- Cite SYNERGETICS text at Sec. 535.07; RBF rewrite of
"Omnidirectional Halo," p.153, Nov'71

Omni-inbound:

See Point: Inbound Point, 23 Sep'73

Omnihalo:

See Halo Concept

Omniinclusive:

See Love, May'72; Oct'72
Truth & Love, 16 Feb'73

Omninexorable:

See Artifacts, (1)

Omniintegrity:

See Design, 13 Mar'73
Whole System, 28 May'72

RBF DEFINITIONS

Omni-innate:

"I have powerful reasons for assuming that genius is
omni-innate. Our first child was born at the time of
World War I [and so on, into the Alexandra Theme] . . . "

- Cite Address to Am. Assn. of Museums, p. 1. 2 Jun'71
- Citation at Genius, 2 Jun'71

RBF DEFINITIONS

Omni-Intellectual:

See God, May '72

Omniintegrating: Omniintegration:

See Ecology Sequence (G)
Life Alters Environment & Environment Alters Life,
16 Aug'70
Science: Comprehensive Integration of the Sciences,
4 Apr'73
Precession & Degrees of Freedom, (1)
Unsettling vs. Settlements, 20 Sep'76

Omniinteraccelerating:

See XYZ Coordinate System, (A)

RBF DEFINITIONS

Omni-Integrity:

"But within the mystery
Lies the region
Of humanly discovered phenomena
Whose whole region
Is progressively disclosing
An omni-integrity of orderliness,
Of interactive and interaccommodative
Generalized principles."

- Cite INTUITION, pp.39-40 May '72

RBF DEFINITIONS

Omni-interaccommodation:

"And the why-for and how-come
Of omni-interaccommodation
Of all the known family
Of weightless, eternal, generalized principles--
Thus far discovered
By scientific observation
To be metaphysically governing
In elegant mathematical order
All Scenario Universe's
Interrelationships, transformations and transactions,
Without one principle contradicting another--
Are all and together
Absolute mystery."

- Cite INTUITION, p.42 May '72

RBF DEFINITIONS

### Omni-interaccommodative:

"... The complex code of eternal metaphysical principles

is _omni-interaccommodative_.  That is it has no intercontra-

diction."

- Cite Dreyfuss Preface, "DECEASE OF MEANING," 28 Apr '71, pp 4-5.

---

### Omniinteractions:  Omniinteracting:

See Halo Concept, Jun'71

---

### Omniinteraccommodation:  Omniinteraccommodative:

See Eternal Principles, 22 Nov'73
    Generalized Principle, (3)
    Regularity, 2 Nov'72
    Synegretic Integral, May'72
    Topological Aspects:  Inventory Of, 9 Feb'73
    Design, 8 Sep'75
    Words & Coping, 7 Nov'75

---

### Omniinteraltering:

See Acceleration:  Angular & Linear, 1960

---

RBF DEFINITIONS

### Omni-interacting:

"The Universe is the minimum as well as the maximum
closed system of omni-interacting, precessionally
transforming, complementary transactions of synergetic
regeneration. . . ."

- Cite OMNIDIRECTIONAL HALO, p. 135. 1960

---

### Omni-inter-between:

See Gravity, 11 Feb'76

---

RBF DEFINITIONS

### Omni-interactive:

". . . The orderly complex of _omni-interactive_,

pure, weightless and apparently eternal principles. . . "

- Cite Doxiadis, p. 310. 20 Jun'66

---

### Omniintercomplementation:

See Export-import Centers, 20 May'75

Omniintercoordinating:

See Ecology Sequence, (F)

Omniintermeshed:

See Gear Train: Locking & Blocking, 18 Nov'72

Omniinterdependence:

See Young World, (1); 4 Jul'72

Omniinterorderliness:

See Ninety-two Elements: Periodic Regularities Of, 4 Jan'70

Omniintereffective:

See Precession, 13 Nov'69

Omniinterpulsative:

See Scenario Universe, Jan'72

Omniinterfering:

See Geosocial Revolution, (3)

Omniinterrelationships:

See Crystallization, 28 Oct'64
God as Verb of Optimum Understanding, (1)

Omniinterrelevant:

See Conceptual Systems, 27 May'75

Omniintertransformative:

See Synergetics, 26 May'72
Universal Integrity:  Principle Of, 23 Sep'73

Omniinterresonated:

See Seven Axes of Symmetry, 13 May'73
Precession & Degrees of Freedom, (2)

Omniintertriangulated:

See Comprehension, 16 Feb'73
Curvature:  Compound, 25 Jan'73
Stable & Unstable Systems, 2 Nov'73; 23 Jan'72
Universal Integrity:  VE & Icosa, (2)
Structural System, 9 Nov'73
Model of Toothpicks & Semi-dried Peas, (1)

RBF DEFINITIONS

Omni-intertangency:

"Systems are individually conceptual polyhedronal integrities.
Human awareness's concession of 'space' acknowledges a nonconceptually-defined experience.  The omniorderly integrity of
omnidirectionally and infinitely extensible, fundamentally
coordinating, closest packing of uniradius spheres and their
ever coordinately uniform radial expandibility accommodates
seemingly remote spherical nucleations which expand radially
into omni-intertangency.  Omni-intertangency evidences
closest sphere packing and its inherent isotropic vector
matrix, which clearly and finitely defines the omnirational
volumetric ratios of the only concave octahedra and concave
vector equilibria discretely domaining all the in-betweeness
of closest-packed-sphere interspace.  The closest-packed-
sphere interspace had been inscrutable a priori to the limit
phase of omni-intertangencies; which limit phase is, was, and
always will be, omnipotential of experimental verification
of orderly integrity of omni-intercomplementarity of the
space-time, special-case, local conceptualizing and the
momentarily unconsidered seeming nothingness of all otherness."

- Cite SYNERGETICS draft at Sec. 1006.13, 17 Feb'73

Omniinvisible:

See Life, 5 Jun'75

Omniintertransformable:  Omniintertransformabilities:

See Horseshit, 9 Feb'73
Vector Equilibrium as Starting Point, 8 Apr'75
Model of Nonbeing, 11 Sep'75

Omnikinetic:

See Rearrange the Scenery, (p.92) May'72

Omniknowing:

See Metaphysical Intellect, May'72

Omnimanifest:

See Radiation-gravitation Sequence, (1)

RBF DEFINITIONS

Omnilibrium:

"I want a word to express the integrative-disintegrative balance of the vector equilibrium. 'Librium' represents the degrees of freedom. Omnilibrious: Universe is omnilibrious because it accommodates all the degrees of freedom. Omnilibrious means we do not have to use degrees of freedom any more.

"The sphere is the convex vector equilibrium and the spaces between are the concave vector equilibrium or, in its contractive form, the octahedron.

"We go from a 20-ness to a fourness: a fivefold contraction. . . . as pulsars, stars go to dwarfs. It's a five-power acceleration. . . In the jitterbug the axis does not rotate, but the equator does. On the other hand, if you hold the equator and contract the system, you force the axis to twist; it throws a torque in it at a 20-to-1 leverage. It contracts until it becomes the tetrahedron. This is the way galaxies interpulsate. The nebula plunge through zero and become negative, invisible, the black hole."

- Cite RBF to EJA, 3200 Idaho, DC, 19 Feb '72

RBF DEFINITIONS

Omnimedium Transport Sequence: (1)

"There are two kinds of flying:
　　　　(a) soaring-- like a gull
　　　　(b) running on water-- like a duck. You've seen a duck taking off the water or landing: it's like a hammerthrower or a pole vaulter: jet stilting.

"Fruits and seeds are also streamlined, not just birds. Seeds are tubes designed to withstand the frost, to work down into the Earth, and also to come up at the right time....

"A naked man jumps his own height in the high jump. With a pole vault he can jump about three times his own height, even though he is weighted down by the pole, by running he can build up momentum into the situation. If he could grab another pole each time he could keep up the momentum and vaulting indefinitely.

"A duck keeps falling but builds it up into more altitude. Like a plane launched from a carrier, the first thing it does is to nose down for increased speed. Jet stilts. A duck has two jet stilits; it then builds up the lift like a blimp flier.

- Cite RBF at Penn Bell videotaping, Philadelphia, 29 Jan'75

Omniliterate:

See Revolution, Jan'72

RBF DEFINITIONS

Omnimedium Transport Sequence: (2)

"All this suggests that we could build an omnimedium vehicle without wings; therefore it could be much lighter and be propelled by twin-angled jet stilts. Omnimedium twin-jet orientable stilts. It could have a turbine jet effect with liquid oxygen for jet propulsion and with wheels. The stilts would converge just above your head. Like stilt walking: when you move the stilt forward it becomes the third compression member which is always initiatable. You'd be hanging from the vectors which converge above your head. A tetrahedron.

"There was not enough capital available for a proper design solution to the housing shortage; nor was there enough capital for the development of a full omnimedium transport system. I saw that the first artifact could suggest only one phase of a full omnimedium transport system. The Dymaxion car was not designed as just a new type of automobile; it was designed to test the ground-taxi-ing quality of an omnimedium transport system. The most dangerous condition of flying is when you make contact with the Earth. The fairing and streamlining has to be superb. It was difficult to control the Dymaxion car with wind on the highway and you had to learn how to manage it."

- Cite RBF at Penn Bell videotaping, Philadelphia, 29 Jan'75

Omnilocal:

See Heres & Theres, 4 Jun'72
　　　History, 27 Dec'73
　　　Rain, 11 Feb'76

RBF DEFINITIONS

Omnimedium Transport Sequence: (3)

"I did not design an automobile; I was not putting a car into production. I was merely designing a prototype omnimedium vehicle. The propulsion was up forward and the steering was in the rear-- for ruddering: that's the way nature does it-- with front traction and rear steering.

"Take a wheelbarrow. You push it and a bad bump will hit you in the stomach. But if you pull a wheelbarrow it will not skid.... The front-steered car, due to kingpins, can only turn at about 34 degrees, without a rudder post. But with a rudder post you can turn at 90 degrees. And the center of gravity was so low that you could not turn it over; it was like a gun carriage. At 15 m.p.h. the inboard wheel could turn on a one-foot radius.

"It could carry eleven passengers. It was 19 feet long. But it tended to head into cross winds. So very fine controls were needed. So we had all custom hardware and shivs. The tires would tend to distort.

"One of the oldest creatures known to man is the horseshoe crab. It is designed to go across streams. It is shaped in"

- Cite RBF at Penn Bell videotaping, Philadelphia, 29 Jan'75

# Synergetics Dictionary

RBF DEFINITIONS

Omnimedium Transport Sequence:                                    (4)

a 120-degree crescent with single-tail focus, thus able to
use its secondary tail to go across currents. So I made the
second Dymaxion with its rear wheel on an extensible boom
that retracts when the car slows down. It went 122 m.p.h.
I just wanted to see whether the principles were right. It
had a beautiful faird underbelly. And the car could waltz:
it really could waltz.

"I worked with Starling Burgess. He understood that the
navy is world and the army is local. At one stage we had
what Burgess called the 'flying bedstead': he thought it
could work at low altitude, just above water, with JATO and
ram-jets. The ideal would be to put humans in harness with
jet stilts."

- Cite RBF at Penn Bell videotaping, Philadelphia, 29 Jan'75

---

Omnimobilization:

See Desovereignization Sequence, 15 May'75

---

RBF DEFINITIONS

Omnimedium Transport:

"In the 1930's I first used the term omnimedium transport to
describe an automotive system adopted to land, seam, and air."

- Cite RBF to EJA & BO'R, 3200 Idaho, 18 Feb'72

---

RBF DEFINITIONS

Omnimotions:

"Precession is uniquely dependent
Upon the entirely unexplained,
Ergo mystically occurring,
Omnimotions of Universe
Successfully hypothesized by Einstein
In contradistinction
To Newton's assumed
A priori cosmic norm of 'at rest.'"

- Cite INTUITION, pp.30-31 May '72

---

Omnimedium Transport:                                            (1)

See Dymaxion Car

---

Omnimotion:

See Fourth Dimension, 12 Jul'62
    Motion Apprehension, 1968
    Powering: Fourth & Fifth Dimensions, 18 Nov'72

---

Omnimedium:  Omnimedium Transport:                               (2)

See Humans as Machines, (2)

---

Omniorderly:

See Design, 22 May'73
    Ecology Sequence, (A)
    Scheme of Reference, 26 Sep'73
    Succes as Norm of Today & Tomorrow, May'72

RBF DEFINITIONS

Omni-orientation:

"Omni-orientation of focal points of structure is at most
symmetrical equivalence of interdistancing."

- Citation and context at Radome Sequence (1), 29 Dec'58

TEXT CITATIONS

Omnipersistent:

Synergetics text at Sec. 206

---

Omniorientation:  Omnioriented:

See Halo Concept, Nov'71
Radome Sequence, (1)*

Omni-phase-bond-integration:

See Tetrahedron: Hierarchy of Pulsating Tetrahedral
Arrays, 16 Dec'73

---

RBF DEFINITIONS

Omnipermeative:

"Electromagnetic wave phenomena are . . omnidirectional

and omnipermeative."

- Cite NO MORE SECOND HAND GOD, p. 89. 9 Apr'40

Omniplanetary:

See Economic Accounting System, (D)

---

Omnipermeative:

See Generalization, 8 Mar'72
God, (p.176) May'72
Principle, 5 Jun'73

Omnipotence:                                    (1)

See Omniscience Transcendental of Omnipotence

Omnipotence:  Omnipotential:                          (2)

    See A Priori Intellect, (1)
       Limit Case: Closet-packed Symmetry, 17 Feb'73

Omnipresent:

    See Gravity, 23 Sep'73; 12 May'75

Omnipotential-energy Phase:

    See Tensegrity, 20 Oct'72

Omniproximities:

    See Invention, (a)

Omnipowerful:

    See Metaphysical Intellect, May'72

RBF DEFINITIONS

Omnipulsative Asymmetry:

"The difference between the physical and the metaphysical is
the omnipulsative asymmetry of all the physical oscillation in
respect to the equilibrium."

- Citation & context at Metaphysical & Physical, 28 Feb'71

- Cite RBF dictation to EJA for SYNERGETICS draft Sec. 205.3,
  Oct'71

Omniprecessional:

    See Structure, 29 Dec'58

Omnipulsative:

    See Seven Axes of Symmetry, 13 May'73

Omnipotence:  Omnipotential:

Omnipresent:

RBF DEFINITIONS

Omniradial:

"Omniradial is a special case of omnidiametric. It is very
discrete. It permits only one direction: inwardly OR
outwardly. Omnidiametric permits two directions: inwardly
AND outwardly."

- Cite RBF to EJA, 3200 Idaho NW, 23 Sep'73

---

Omniradiant:

See Gravity, (2)
Jitterbug, 4 Oct'72

---

RBF DEFINITIONS

Omniradially:

"Tension is omniradially conversive and is both electromagnetically and gravitationally tensive because eternally and
integrally comprehensive."

- Cite Synergetics Draft, at Sec. 640.70, Dec. '71.

---

Omniradiational:

See Isotropic Vector Matrix, 13 Nov'69

---

Omniradial:                                    (1)

See Omnidiametric

---

RBF DEFINITIONS

Omnirandomness:

See Crystallization, 28 Oct'64

---

Omniradial:                                    (2)

See Focus - Beamable - Wirable, 1 Apr'72

---

RBF DEFINITIONS

Omnirational Control Matrix:

"The great-circle subdivisioning of the 48 basic equilibrious
LCD triangles of the vector equilibrium may be representation-
ally draw within the 120 basic disequilibrium LCD triangles
of the icosahedron, thus defining all the aberrations-- and
their magnitudes-- exisiting between the equilibrious and
disequilibrious states, and providing an omnirational control
matrix for all topological, trigonometric, physical, and
chemical accounting."

- Cite RBF marginalis at p.483 incorprorated in SYNERGETICS,
2nd. Ed. at Sec. 901.19, 12 May'75

Omnirational Control Matrix:

See Coordinate System
    Grid
    Matrix
    Spherical Grid
    Information Control System

Omnirationality:                                    (2)

          Generalization & Special Case, 23 Jan'77
See Isotropic Vector Matrix, 30 Nov'72
    Oscillation, 21 Dec'71
    Powering: Fourth Dimension, 18 Nov'72
    Powering: Sixth Powering, 26 Nov'72
    Synergetics, 1959
    XYZ Quadrant at Centerof Octahedron, 14 May'75

RBF DEFINITIONS

Omnirationality:

"While nature oscillates and palpitates asymmetrically in respect
to the frame of the omnirational vector equilibrium, the plus
and minus magnitudes of asymmetry are rational fractions of the
omnirationality of the equilibrious state..."

- Citation & context at Vector Equilibrium, 21 Dec'71

Omniregenerative:

See Fail-safe, 5 Jun'73
    God, (p.176) May'72
    Isotropic Vector Matrix, 9 Mar'73
    Export-import Centers, 20 May'75

RBF DEFINITIONS

Omnirationality:

". . . The proton group and the neutron group account
rationally for all physical structures.

"Chemistry's Omnirationality.  When I first sought to
find the comprehensive coordinate system employed by
nature's omnirational associating and disassociating--
always joining in whole low order numbers, as forinstance,
$H_2O$, and never $H_3O$-- persuaded me that nature's comprehensive
coordination must be omnirational despite geometry's
transcendental irrational number and other 'pure' non-
experimentally demonstrable incommensurable inter-integer
relationships."

- Cite NASA Speech, pp. 64. Jun '66

CLOSEST PACKING OF SPHERES - SEC. 410.01

Omniresonant:

See Life is a Sumtotal of Mistakes, (2)

Omnirationality:                                    (1)

See Bubbles in the Wake of a Ship
    Nature Has No Separate Departments
    Low Order Prime Numbers
    Rational Whole Numbers
    Synergetic Hierarchy
    Unity:  Principle Of

Omnisameness:

See Isotropic Vector Matrix, Jun'66

RBF DEFINITIONS

Omniscience:

"What I mean by omniscience

Is synergetically transcendental

Even to Einstein."

- Cite RBF to EJA
  Sarasota, Florida
  7 February 1971

---

RBF DEFINITIONS

Omniscience:

"Omniscience is evidently of comprehensively transcendental
alacrity to the speed of light whose relatively slow
articulations in Universe are readily anticipated by
intellectually initiated and disciplined computation of
mind."

- For citation and context see ▬▬▬▬ Intellection, 1960

---

RBF DEFINITIONS

Omniscience Transcendent of Omnipotence

"There is a question-asking possibility that metaphysical
omniscience may be transcendental in its velocity to that
of omnipotence, i.e., the definitive physical speed of
energy as radiation."

- Cite OMNIDIRECTIONAL HALO, p. 163, as rewritten by RBF in
  Washington DC, 21 Dec. 1971.
- Citation at Metaphysical and Physical, 21 Dec'71

---

RBF DEFINITIONS

Omniscience Transcendent of Omnipotence:

"There is a question-asking-possibility that omniscience
may be transcendental in velocity to the definitive
physical speed of energy omnipotence."

* Citation & context at Future of Synergetics, 1960
- Cite Omnidirectional Halo, p. 163, 1960

---

RBF DEFINITIONS

Omniscience Transcendent of Omnipotence:

"The synergetic anticipatory capabilities of intellect...
imply the possibility of a velocity transcendence of
omniscient functioning over omnipotence functioning,
which could mean an intellectually regenerated evolutionary
extension of Universe in generalized synergetical integrity."

- Citation and context at Anticipatory, 1960

---

Omniscience Transcendent of Omnipotence:                    (1)

See Metaphysical Transcendent of Physical

---

Omniscience Transcendent of Omnipotence:                    (2)

See Anticipatory, 1960*
    Energy, 28 Apr'48
    Future of Synergetics, 1960*
    Intellect: Equation Of, 28 Apr'48
    Metaphysical & Physical, 21 Dec'71*

---

Omniscience vs. Ego:

See Local vs. Comprehensive (2)

Omniscience:                                              (1)

    See Ego:  Separating Ego out of Omniscience
        Omniknowing
        Competence:  A Knowing Competence Greater than
          That of Humans

---

Omnistructured:

    See Model of Toothpicks & Semi-dried Peas, (1)

---

Omniscience:                                              (2)

    See A Priori Intellect, (1)
        Intellections, 1960
        Local vs. Comprehensive, (1)(2)

---

Omnisubconscious:

    See Invisible Architecture, (E)

---

~~RHF DEFINITIONS~~

Omnisimilar:

    See Spherical Octahedron, Aug'72

---

Omnisuccess:

    See Design Revolution, 7 Nov'67; 6 Mar'74
        Economic Accounting System, 18 Feb'71
        Industrialization, (p.95) May'72

---

Omnispecialized:

    See Pollution, Oct'70

---

Omnisurface:                                              (1)

    See Embracement

Omnisurface:                                    (2)

    See Radiation-gravitation: Harmonics, 3 Jan'75

---

Omnisymmetrically Generated:

    See Isotropic Vector Matrix, 30 Nov'72

---

RBF DEFINITIONS

    Omnisurround:

    ". . . of such sizes that the crocodile is large enough to
omnisurround or swallow the 20-foot miniature Earth globe. . . "

    - Citation and context at Twenty-Foot Earth Globe and 200-Foot
        Celestial Sphere (4)

---

Omnisymmetrical:                                (1)

    See Prime Structural Systems

---

RBF DEFINITIONS

    Omnisymmetrical:

    "Poles are symmetrical to each other, but not

omnisymmetrical like the icosahedron and tetrahedron."

    - Cite RBF to EJA, 3200 Idaho, Wash DC, 17 Feb '72

---

Omnisymmetrical: Omnisymmetry:                  (2)

    See Asymmetry, 31 May'71*
        Atom, 3 Nov'73
        Isotropic Vector Matrix, 16 Nov'72
        Life, 31 May'71
        System Totality, 7 Mar'73
        Tetrahedron, 7 Mar'73
        Vector Equilibrium, 3 Nov'73

---

RBF DEFINITIONS

    Omnisymmetrical:

    "Symmetrical means having no local asymmetries.
Omnisymmetrical permits local asymmetries. Universe
is omnisymmetrical.  A three-bladed propeller is
dynamically symmetrical (three pear-shaped blades at
120° to each other inscribed in an equilateral triangle).
The propeller blade is locally asymmetrical."

    - Cite RBF to EJA, Blackstone Hotel, Chicago, 31 May 1971.
    - Citation & context at Asymmetry, 31 May'71

---

RBF DEFINITIONS

    Omnisynergetic:

    "This omnirational, omnidirectional comprehensive
coordinate system of Universe is omnisynergetic."

    "This coordinate system is ever regenerative in respect
to the nuclear centers all of which are rationally
accounted for by synergetics."

    - Cite SYNERGETICS draft at Sec. 1004.11, 30 Jan'73

Omnisynergetic:                                              (1)

See Synergy of Synergies:

---

Omnitetrahedral:

See Viral Steerability, 1960

---

Omnisynergetic:                                              (2)

See Principle, 5 Jun'73

---

RBF DEFINITIONS

Omnitopology:

"The conceptual-system geometries of omnitopology are defined
only by the system withinness and withoutness differentiating
a plurality of loci occurring approximately midway between the
most intimate proximity moments of the respectively
convergent-divergent wavilinear vectors, orbits, and spin
equators of the system."

- Citation and context at Interference: You Really Can't Get
  There from Here, 19 Dec'73

---

Omnisystem:

See Prime Nuclear Structural Systems, 27 Dec'74

---

RBF DEFINITIONS

Omnitopology:

"Omnitopology differs from Euler's superficial topology in
that it extends its concerns to the topological domains of
non-nuclear closest-packed spherical arrays and with the
domains of the non-nuclear-containing polyhedra thus formed.
Omnitopology is concerned, for instance, with the individually
unself-identifying concave octahedra and concave vector
equilibria volumetric space domains betweeningly defined within
the closest-packed sphere complexes; as well as with the
individually self-identifying convex octahedra and convex
vector equilibria, which latter are spontaneously singled out
by the observer's optical comprehendibility as the finite
integrities and entities of the locally and individual-
spherically-closed systems dividing all the Universe into all
the macrocosmic outsideness and all the microcosmic insideness
of the observably closed, finite, local systems-- in contradistinction to the undefinability of the omnidirectional
space nothingness frequently confronting the observer."

- Cite SYNERGETICS draft at Sec. 1006.11, 17 Feb'73

---

RBF DEFINITIONS

Omnitensional:

"Universe is omnitensional integrity."

- Cite Synergetics Draft (Dec '71) at Sec. 650.07.
  Sec. 700.04, 14 Oct'72

---

RBF DEFINITIONS

Omnitopology:

"In contradistinction to, and in complementation of, Eulerian
topology, omnitopology deals with the generalized equatabilities
of a priori generalized omnidirectional domains of vectorially
articulated linear interrelationships, their vertexial interference loci, and consequent uniquely differentiated areal and
volumetric domains, angles, frequencies, symmetries, asymmetries, polarizations, structural-pattern integrities, associative interbondabilities, intertransformabilities, and transforma-
tive-system limits, simplexes, complexes, nucleations, export-
abilities, and omniinteraccommodations."

- Synergetics text at Sec. 1007.15, 9 Feb'73

RBF DEFINITIONS

Omnitopology:

"In omnitopology the domains of volumes are the minimum
volumes topologically enclosable by the fewest points."

- Cite Synergetics draft, Sec. ~~880.2, August 1971~~. 1011.03, Apr '72

---

RBF DEFINITIONS

Omnitopological Domains:

"Topological domains are clearly defined in terms of the
systems involved having unique centrally angled insideness
and surface-angle-defined outsideness."

- Citation at Central Angles & Surface Angles, 20 Dec'71

---

RBF DEFINITIONS

Omnitopology:

"Omnitopology differs from Euler's superficial topology in
that it extends its concerns to the topological domains of
of non-nuclear closest packed spherical arrays and with the
domains of the non-nuclear containing polyhedra thus formed.
Omnitopology is concerned, for instance, with the concave
octahedra and concave vector equilibria volumetric spaces
defined within the closest-packed sphere complexes."

- Cite SYNERGETICS draft at Sec. 1011.01, Apr '72

---

TEXT CITATIONS

Omnitopological Domains:

Synergetics ; Sec. 1006.20

---

RBF DEFINITIONS

Omnitopology:

"Omnitopology differs from Euler's superficial topology,
omnitopology being nuclear."

- Cite RBF to EJA, Fairfield, Conn.,  Chez Wolf.
  18 June 1971.

---

Omnitopology:                                                    (1)

See Nucleated Systems
   Topology:  Synergetic & Eulerian

---

RBF DEFINITIONS

Omnitopological Domains:

"Omnitopological domains are defined in terms of the system's
unique central-angle-defined insideness and its unique
surface-angle-defined outsideness."

- Cite SYNERGETICS, 2nd. Ed., at Sec. 1074.21, 27 Dec'74

---

Omnitopology:                                                    (2)

See Prime Enclosure, 17 Feb'73

Omnitransforming: Omnitransformative:

See Universe, spring'71; 1971
Phase & Interphase, 9 Feb'76

---

RBF DEFINITIONS

Omnitriangulation:

"If you find all the connections between all the points,
the system is omnitriangulated. A spherical polyhedron is
a high-frequency geodesic polyhedron."

- Cite Synergetics draft, Sec. S11.4, August 1971
- Citation & context at Geodesic Sphere, (2), Aug'71

---

RBF DEFINITIONS

Omnitriangulation:

"Omnitriangulation is the most intimate interchording. The
ends of the chords emerge outside the sphere because the
centers of the chords are closer to the center of the sphere."

- Cite RBF at Penn Bell videotaping session Philadelphia, PA.,
20 Jan'75

---

RBF DEFINITIONS

Omnitriangulation:

"It will be discovered . . . that all the polygons formed
by the interacting vectors consist entirely of equilateral
triangles and squares-- the latter occurring as the cross-
sections of the octahedra and the triangles as the external
facets of both the tetrahedra and octahedra."

- Cite NEHRU SPEECH, p. 24, 13 Nov '69

ISOTROPIC VECTOR MATRIX - SEC 420.06

---

RBF DEFINITIONS

Omnitriangulation:

"By structure, we mean a self-stabilizing pattern. The triangle
is the only self-stabilizing polygon.

"By structure, we mean omnitriangulated. The triangle is the
only structure. Unless it is self-regeneratively stabilized,
it is not a structure.

"Everything that you have ever recognized in Universe as a
pattern is re-cognited as the same pattern you have seen
before. Because only the triangle persists as a constant
pattern, any recognized patterns are inherently recognizable
only by virtue of their triangularly structured pattern
integrities. Recognition is as dependent on triangulation as
is original cognition. Only triangularly structured patterns
are regenerative patterns. Triangular structuring is a
pattern integrity itself. This is what we mean by structure."

- Cite SYNERGETICS text at Secs. 610.01-.02-.03; 3 Oct'72

---

RBF DEFINITIONS

OmniTriangulation:

"The sphere is complex unity and the triangle simplex unity.
Here and here alone lie the principles governing finite
solution of all structural and general systems theory
problems. Local isolations of infinite open-ended, plane
and linear edged (seemingly 'flat' and infinite) segments
of what are, in reality, vast spherical systems-- when taken
out of context-- are hopelessly special-cased, indeterminate
situations.

"Unfortunately engineering has committed itself in the past
exclusively to these locally infinite and inherently
indeterminate systems and have had to rely essentially on
the test proven, local behaviors of small systems such as
columns, beams, levers, et. al., opinionatedly fortified
with 'safely guesstimated' complex predictions. Not until
we have universal finite, omnitriangulated, nonredundant,
structural system comprehension can we enjoy the advantage
of powerful physical generalizations concisely describing
all structural behaviors."

- Cite RBF Ltr. to Shoji Sadao, 15 Feb. '66, p. 5.
- Citation and context at Spherical Barrel: Sphere As Complex
Unity, etc. 15 Feb'66

---

RBF DEFINITIONS

Omnitriangulation:

"We start with tetrahedron, octahedron, cube; and the cube
has been triangulated because cubes would not stand up by
themselves. So I make it structural. And then we get
into vector equilibrium and it has to be triangulated. All
I am doing is deliberately omnitriangulating. We have a
square face and we simply put one ▓▓▓▓▓▓ diagonal in.
We take the square face of the cube and put a diagonal in and
▓▓▓
that is all you have to do so that it has structural
stability."

- Cite OREGON Lecture #7, 11 July '62, p. 274

---

RBF DEFINITIONS

Omnitriangulation:

"The largest volume, least event, omnitriangular system
is the icosahedron and its multiple subtriangulated
geodesic patterning . . . what I call geodesic structuring."

- Cite RBD Ltr. to Dr. Urmston, 8 Oct. '64, p. 2.

Omnitriangularly Oriented Evolution:                    (1)

    See Jitterbug

---

Omniuniform:

    See Isotropic Vector Matrix, 16 Nov'72

---

Omnitriangularly Oriented Evolution:                   (2)

    See Quanta Loss by Congruence, (2)

---

TEXT CITATIONS

Omni-unique:

    See Synergetics Draft, Feb '72 at Sec. 952.71

---

Omnitriangulation:                                     (1)

    See Intertriangulated
        Minimum Omnitriangulated Differentiator
        Omniintertriangulated
        Omniselftriangulating
        Prime Structural Systems
        Surface Triangle Structures
        Triangulate: Triangulation

---

Omniuniversal:

    See Relationship Analysis, (1)
        Spherical Interstices, 18 Nov'72

---

Omnitriangulation: Omnitriangulated:                   (2)

    See Four Color Theorem, 23 Sep'73
        Frequency, 15 Oct'72
        Radome Sequence, (1)
        Twelve Universal Degrees of Freedom, Feb'72
        Radial Depth, 20 Dec'74
        Geodesic Sphere, (2)*
        Stable & Unstable Structures, 7 Jun'72
        Vector Equilibrium, 8 Sep'77

---

Omnivalidity:

    See Earning a Living, Dec'72

Omnivisible:

    See Old Man River Project, 20 Sep'76

Omniwholeness:

    See Quantum Wave Phenomena Sequence, (1)

Omnivariability:

    See Change, 9 Nov'72
        Vector Equilibrium, 16 Oct'72

Omnizerophase:

    See Zerophase, 23 Dec'68
        Truth, 22 Jun'75

Omniwave:

    See Vector Equilibrium, 30 Oct'73

RBF DEFINITIONS

    One:

    "Here we may be identifying the cosmic bridge between the
equilibrious prime number one of metaphysics and the
disequilibrious prime number one of realizable physical
reality."

    - Cite RBF rewrite of SYNERGETICS galley at Sec. 954.51, 20 Dec'73

Omniwavilinear:

    See Frame of Reference, 27 Feb'72
        Nucleus, (1)

RBF DEFINITIONS

    One:

    "One is subfrequency."

    - Citation and context at Prime, 17 Feb'73

RBF DEFINITIONS

One:

Unity is plural and at minimum two.  There is a prime one,
but it is half of unity."

- Cite RBF to EJA, Beverly Hotel, New York, 26 Jan '72

---

RBF DEFINITIONS

One:

"In structural systems, the tetrahedron uniquely
articulates the prime number 1, and is therefore logically
to be identified as the most economic quantation unit in
universal energy accounting."

- Cite MARKS, p. 48, 1960

- Citation at Tetrahedron, 1960

---

RBF DEFINITIONS

One:

"The concept one as unity is only available in respect to
one-half of twoness."

- Citation and context at Experience, Feb'50

---

RBF DEFINITIONS

Oneness:

"Tetrahedra have a fundamental prime number: oneness."

- Cite Carbondale Draft
Return to Modelability, p. V.7

- Cite NASA Speech, p.73, Jun'66

---

RBF DEFINITIONS

Oneness:

"Twoness and oneness can't make a system.  They don't have
insideness and outsideness at all."

- Cite Oregon Lecture #7, p. 248.  11 Jul'62

---

RBF DEFINITIONS

One-dimensional Polarity:

"Two individual unresolvable somethings identify a line:
one dimensionality, which has inherent polarity of the two
line-defining somethings."

- Cite SYNERGETICS, 2nd. Ed. At Sec. 1013.13, 11 Sep'75

---

One = None:

See Initial Frequency, 6 Nov'72
Nine = None = Zero, 3 Mar'73

---

One as a Prime:                              (1)

See Prime One

One as a Prime:                                               (2)


See One, 20 Dec'73
    Unity Is Plural, 26 Jan'72
    Prime Number, 16 Feb'78

One-Town World:

Nine Chains to the Moon, p.49ff - 1938

One as Not a Prime:

See Trigonometric Limit: First 14 Primes, 14 Jan'74

One-town World:                                               (1)

See Earth Shrunk to One-town Dimension
    Global Village
    One-world
    World-around

RBF DEFINITIONS

One-Town World:

"... The inexorable development of a one-town world and its
progressively crossbreeding world citizenship lying around the
spherical bottom of the sky ocean.▇▇▇ Modern technology has
terminated the fundamental isolation of any part of the Spaceship Earth's surface from another part. It is effectively
integrating humanity as its individuals live ever more dynamically
around our Spaceship Earth's spherical deck."

- Citation and context at Millay, Edna St. Vincent (3), 1968

One-town World:                                               (2)

See Ekistics, ▇▇▇▇ 11 Nov'75
    World Man, 6 Jul'62

One-town World of 1927:

See Ekistics, 11 Nov'75

TEXT CITATIONS

One as Unity:

Synergetics : Sec. 502.03, (2nd. Ed.)

One as Unity:

    See One, Feb'50
       Sphere of Unit Vector Radius, 20 Nov'75

One World Management:     (2)

    See Electronic Referendum, 9 Jan'75

One Way vs. Round Trip:     (1)

    See Linear vs. Orbital
       Radial vs. Orbital

One vs. Zero:

    See Novent, 23 Sep'73

One Way vs. Round Trip:     (2)

    See Circuitry: Thermionic & Political Analogy, 23 Jan'72
       Decentralization & Centralization, 1 Apr'49
       Most Economical, 15 Jun'74
       Scrap Sorting & Mongering (2)(3)
       Decentralize vs. Centralize, 1 Apr'49

One: Oneness:     (1)

    See Approximately One
       Plus One
       Prime One
       Tetrahedron: One Tetrahedron
       Unity
       Universe: Toward Oneness
       Frequency $\neq$ One
       One vs. Zero
       Plus-and-minus One
       Twelve-around-One
       No One
       Six - Five = One
       Frequency as One

One-world Management:     (1)

    See City Management Concept of World Government
       Making the World Work

One: Oneness:     (2)

    See Building Blocks (1)(2)
       Disparate, 22 Mar'73
       Experience, Feb'50*
       Intereffects, 25 Sep'73
       Prime, 17 Feb'73*
       Tetrahedron, 1960*
       Zero Volume Tetrahedron, 10 Dec'75
       Human Beings & Complex Universe, (9)

Onerousness of Ownership:

    See Ownership

Opaque:  Opacity:         (1)

    See Omnidirectional Shutterable Sieve
        Occulting

Only & Inescapable:

    See Reality: Structurings as the Only & Inescapable
        Reality

Opaque:  Opacity:         (2)

    See Light, 29 Dec'58
        Walls, 29 Jan'75
        Human Beings & Complex Universe, (9)

Only the Whole Big System Works:

    See Big System, 5 Jun'73

Open Circuit:

    See Equiinterval, 17 Feb'73
        Rememberable Numbers, 14 Jan'74

Only:

    See Always & Only
        Only & Inescapable

RBF DEFINITIONS

Openings:

"Our definition of an opening is that it is surrounded, that is framed, by trajectories. Every trajectory in a system will have to have at least two crossings. These are always as viewed, because the lines could be at different levels from other points of observation."

- Cite RBF to EJA, Somerset Club, Boston, 22 April 1971

NOVENT- SEC. 524.31/ 514.03

RBF DEFINITIONS

Openings:

"There are no surfaces. Therefore there are no areas.
So Euler's topological aspects have to be altered to
read: "lines" = trajectories; "vertexes" = crossings; and
"areas" = openings, i.e., where there are no trajectories
or crossings. This relates to systems."

- Cite RBF to EJA, Somerset Club, Boston, 22 April 1971

NOVENT- SEC. 524.31)

---

Opening:

See Area
    Face
    Noncrossing
    Crossings, Openings & Trajectories

---

RBF DEFINITIONS

Open Systems:

"The arbitrary open parameters of infinite systems can never
be guaranteed to be adequate statements of all possible
variables."

- Citation and context at General Systems Theory, 8 Nov'73

---

Open Systems:                                    (1)

See Closed Systems
    Closed Systems & Open Systems
    Infinite Systems
    Pollution:  Infinite Room to Pollute

---

Open Systems:                                    (2)

See General Systems Theory, 8 Nov'73
    XYZ Coordinate System, Jun'66

---

RBF DEFINITIONS

Open Triangular Spirals:

"Triangular Spiral Events Form Polyhedra:  Open triangular
spirals may be combined to make a variety of different figures.
Note that the tetrahedron and icosahedron require both left-
and right-handed (positive and negative) spirals in equal
numbers, whereas the other polyhedra require spirals of only
one-handedness.  (See Sec. 452, Great Circle Railroad Tracks
of Energy.)  If the tetrahedron is considered to be one
quantum, then the triangular spiral equals one-half quantum.
It follows from this that the octahedron and cube are each two
quanta, the icosahedron five quanta, the ████████████
two-frequency spherical geodesic is 15 Quanta."

- Cite SYNERGETICS text at Sec. █613.01; Nov'71

---

Open Triangular Spirals:

See Basic Evenet
    Three-vector Teams
    Z Cobras

---

Open:  Openings:                                 (1)

See Area
    Face
    Plane
    Areas = Openings
    Crossings, Openings & Trajectories
    No Open Endings
    Window

Open: Openings: (2)

See Triangle, 5 Jul'62; Nov'71
Angle, 7 Nov'75
Human Beings & Complex Universe, (1)

RBF DEFINITIONS

Operational:

"The Greeks defined a triangle as an area bound by a closed
line of three edges and three angles. A triangle drawn on the
Earth's surface is actually a spherical triangle described by
three great-circle arcs. It is evident that the arcs divide
the surface of the sphere into two areas each of which is bound
by a closed line consisting of three edges and three angles, ergo
dividing the total area of the sphere into two complementary
triangles. The area apparently 'outside' one triangle is seen
to be 'inside' the other. Because every spherical surface has
two aspects-- convex if viewed from outside, concave if viewed
from within-- each of these triangles is, in itself, two
triangles. Thus one triangle becomes four when the total complex
is understood. 'Drawing' or 'scribing' is an operational term.
It is impossible to draw without an object upon which to draw.
The drawing may be by depositing on, or by carving away, that is,
by creating a trajectory or tracery of the operational event.
All the objects upon which drawing may be operationally
accomplished are structural systems having insideness and outsideness. The drawn upon object may be symmetrical or asymmetrical, a piece of paper or a blackboard system having insideness
and outsideness."

- Cite RBF holograph revised caption for Synergetics Illustration,
#18 (EJA Master Set), typed up 3 Jan'72. (Secs. 811, 812 + 813.)

Operant Psychology: (1)

See Behavioral Science
Behavioral Scientists
Conditioning
Psychology
Behavior & Environment

RBF DEFINITIONS

Operational:

"We cannot produce constructively and operationally,
a real experience-augmenting operational system, with
less than four points, i.e., a fourth point not in
the plane of the first three points. It takes three
points to define a plane. The fourth point not in
the plane of the first three produces a tetrahedron having
insideness and outsideness corresponding with the reality
of operational experience."

- Cite SYNERGETICS draft "Antitetrahedron," 7 Oct. '71.
p. 1. (dictated to EJA.)

Operant Psychology: (2)

See Design Science, 2 Jun'71
Human Tolerance Limits, (B)(D)

RBF DEFINITIONS

Operational:

"We got to that big definition of Universe and we discovered
that it was the only way we could state it and be faithful
to our rule of this game, which is what Bridgman called
operational, that is, we must state whatever we have to
state in terms of our personal experience. Some of the
philosophers of a century ago were calling itpragmatism.
At any rate they were stating what we know about our life
in terms of a description of the events themselves, the
most faithful description of the events themselves that
precipitated any thought in any way we could think about it.
Faithfulness of the description of our own experiences, so
we were not interested in what somebody said they thought
was significant."

- Cite Oregon Lecture #8, p. 276. 12 Jul'62

Operating Manual for Spaceship Earth:

See Spaceship Earth, (c)

RBF DEFINITIONS

Operational:

"Percival Bridgman at Harvard gave a name to Einstein's

strategy of consideration which he called 'operational.'

Bridgman said Einstein became purely operational because

he thought only in terms of experience."

- Cite OREGON Lecture #2 - p. 72, 2 Jul'62

RBF DEFINITIONS

Operational Construction:

"Our operational construction method employs the constant radius and identifies every point on the circumference and every point on the internal radii. This is in contra-distinction to analytical geometry in which the identification is only in terms of the XYZ coordinates and the perpendiculars to them. Analytic geometry disregards circumferential construction, ergo is unable to provide for the direct identifications of angular accelerations."

"Mathematics," Wash. DC, 7 Oct. '71.
- Cite RBF dicaationto EJA for SYNERGETICS, "Operational

---

RBF DEFINITIONS

Operational Mathematics:

"Operationally speaking we always deal only in systems and all systems are characterized projectionally by spherical triangles which control all our experiential transformations."

- Citation at Spherical Triangle, 1971
- Cite SYNERGETICS, "Operational Mathematics, One Spherical Triangle Considered as Four."

---

Operational Field:                                      (1)

        See Unified Operational Field

---

RBF DEFINITIONS

Operational Mathematics:

        See Skinning
             Foldability

---

Operational Field: Operational Evolvement Field:        (2)

        See Field of Cosmic Formabilities, 28 Jan'73
             Synergetics Constant, (A)
             Trisection of an Angle, 22 Nov'73

---

Operational - Physically Realized:

        See Structure, 27 Dec'74

---

RBF DEFINITIONS

Operational Geometry:

""Operational Geometry invalidates all bias."

- Cite SYNERGETICS, "Operational Mathematics, One Spherical Triangle Considered as Four."

---

RBF DEFINITIONS

Operational Procedure:

".... We found out the disparity ourselves by examining the limit-case conditions, which can only be discovered by physical experience. This method of discovery is called operational procedure."

* Citation and context at Human Sense Ranging and Information Gathering (2), 22 Nov'73

Operational Procedure:                                    (1)

    See Rules of Operational Procedure

---

Operations Research:  Operational Research:               (2)

    See Synergetics vs. Model (D)
    General Systems Theory, ■ (B)

---

Operational Procedure:                                    (2)

    See Universe (1)

---

RBF DₑFINITIONS

    Operational Science:
    The "always and only coexisting functions
    of experience and experiments embrace
    the fundamental parameters
    of operational science."

    * Cite SYNERGETICS Draft 'Structures' Mar '71

    - Citation & context at Axis of Conceptual Observation, 25 Mar'71

---

Operational Realizations:

    See Prime Number Inherency & Constant Relative
      Abundance, 27 Dec'74

---

Operational Science:

    See Environmental Inventory, 28 Apr'77

---

Operations Research:  Operational Research:               (1)

    See Bridgman
      General Systems Theory
      Operational

---

Operational:  Operative:                                  (1)

    See Operational = Physically Realized
      Potential vs. Operative
      Trisection of an Angle
      Interoperativeness
      Rules of Operational Procedure

Operational: Operative: (2)

See Analytical Geometry, 7 Oct'71
Drawing, 1971
Franklin, Ben, 22 Jan'73
Human Sense Ranging & Information Gathering, (2)
Mother: Infant Nursing at Mother's Breast, 18 Nov'72
Spherical Triangle Sequence, (a)(e)
Vectorial Geometry Field, 22 Nov'73
Axis of Conceptual Observation, 25 Mar'71*
Proofs, 7 Oct'75

---

Opposite: Opposition: (1)

See Alternate: Alternative
Complementary
Dynamic Opposition
Reversibility
Face Congruence with Opposite Vertex
No Opposites
Action-reaction: Equal & Opposite
Enantiodromia

---

Opinion: (1)

See Public Opinion Polls

---

Opposite: (2)

See Energy, 16 Sep'67
Positive & Negative, 4 May'57
Zero Weight, 1968*
Triangle, Nov'71

---

Opinion: (2)

See General Systems Theory, 4 Jan'70
Excluded Answer Resources, Oct'66

---

RBF DEFINITIONS

Optical:

"Optical means we're using disorderly radiation to identify the positioning of the stars. . ."

- Citation and context at Radiation Sequence (1), Jun-Jul'69

---

RBF DEFINITIONS

Opposite:

"Every fundamental component of Universe has its opposite."

- Citation and context at Zero Weight, 1968

---

RBF DEFINITIONS

Optical Motion Spectrum: (1)

"There are a myriad of economic trends and other vital evolutionary events taking place today which are invisible to humanity only because they are too fast or too slow for man to apprehend and to comprehend them. We will be able to accelerate or decelerate such evolutionary events by electronic controls as played visibly as played on our fottball-field-sized playing surface.

"Humanity has a very limited optical spectrum, wherefore man can see today only one-millionth of the total physical 'reality' as the latter is evidenced by the full range of the electromagnetic spectrum. Man used to think of reality as everything that he could sense with his eyes, ears, nose, taste, and touch. We have learned only since about 1930-- when the first technical chart of the great electromagnetic spectrum was published-- that man has sensorial tunability and is sensorially aware of only one millionth of physical reality. The little rainbow color band of human 'seeing' is less than one-millionth of the stretched-out reality of the invisible colors of all the 92 regenerative chemical elements of associative energy or of the various radiations"

- Cite SENATE HEARINGS, p.6, 4 Mar'69

RBF DEFINITIONS

Optical Motion Spectrum:                                    (2)

"of energy in its disassociative phase.

"In addition to the electromagnetic frequencies spectrum we
have also a motion spectrum. The sense of motion is produced
by an overlapping continuity of afterimages of a plurality of
optically tunable separate and sequentially occurring electromagnetic frequency events just as music is produced for the
hearing by a metrically momentumed sequence of both separate
and resonantly overlapped sound frequency notes. Motion is
visual music made possible by the spontaneous retention in the
brain of a series of separate still pictures frames of our
separate sense experiences scanned and reviewed in the brain
at a vastly accelerated sequence rate. Our brain discovers
that each successive electromagnetic picture is just a little
different from the ones ■■■■ before and our dawning awareness
of that increasing difference constitutes our motion sense."

"The overall range of our human motion spectrum is even more
limited in respect to the full range of cosmic motions than is
our optical frequency spectrum tunability in respect to the
total electromagnetic spectrum. We can't see the atoms in"

- Cite SENATE HEARINGS, p.6, 4 Mar'69

Optical Rainbow Range:                                     (1)

        See Color Spectrum
            Electromagnetic Spectrum
            Sensorial Spectrum
            Tunability

RBF DEFINITIONS

Optical Motion Spectrum:                                    (3)

"motion; we can't see the stars move, though their motions are
thousandsfold faster than our fastest rockets; we can't see the
trees grow; we can't see the hands of the clock move. Most
important of all we cannot see the abstract weightless thoughts
in the minds of other men. When we survey the total inventory
of motions and informations which we can sense, we find it to
be very limited. The significance of all the foregoing is
appreciated when we realize that it is only by such phenomena
as can be seen to be moving or changing by the public that are
politically recognized and heeded. That is why public opinion
and vote sampling has come into ever more reliable use.

"Our computerized world game is designed to accelerate the too
slow and to decelerate the too fast of all the known vital
trendings and thereby to bring them dramatically within
popular consideration and our world game's solution. The game
will show clearly how the trends will affect everybody's lives
everywhere around Earth and how they could be taken advantage
of in ways favorable to all humanity."

- Cite SENATE HEARINGS, p.6, 4 Mar'69

Optical Rainbow Range:                                     (2)

        See Conceptual Tuning, 24 May'72
            Manifest: Two, 1973
            Sweepout: Spherical, (1)(2)

Optical Motion Spectrum:                                    (1)

        See Invisible Motion
            Motion Apprehension

Optical Tuning & Scanning:

        See Brain's TV Studio; (1); 6 Jun'69

Optical Motion Spectrum:                                    (2)

        See Lags (1)(2)
            Visual Symphony (2)

Optical: Optics:                                           (1)

        See Rainbow Optical Rainbow Range
            Seeing
            Sight
            Vision: Visual
            Range Finding

Optical: Optics:                                              (2)

    See Energetic Words, 1 Jul'62
      Senses, 9 Apr'40
      Radiation Sequence (1)*
      Sweepout: Spherical Sweepout (1)(2)

---

RBF DEFINITIONS

Optimism: I Am Not an Optimist:

"People think that I am an optimist, but all that I am
doing is simply to point out that humans do have options.
You don't have to know anything to be negative; but you
have to know really quite a lot in order to be positive."

- Cite RBF to Ben Forgey, Wash Star, Jefferson Hotel, Wash. DC:
 26 Apr'77

---

RBF DEFINITIONS

Optimism: I Am Not an Optimist:

"I often find myself being called an optimist. I am anything
but an optimist. An optimist is as unbalanced as a pessimist.
The point is, I'm able to give you some knowledge you didn't
have before. You have an option. You can make it. You better
do it. Thank you."

             Forum
- RBF concluding remarks to Harvard Law School, 10 Dec'73

---

RBF DEFINITIONS

Optimism: I Am Not an Optimist:

"I say I'm not an optimist at all. Now the fact that I'm
the first person to know by technical and resource information
that it's possible for humanity to be a success is quite
different from wishing or dreaming that humanity could be
successful. Because I can show people it's feasible for
humans to be successful, they acquire new hope, which they
had lost. They then feel optimistic and say I am an optimist.
I could tell them many reasons why humanity may not succeed
despite its potential."

- Cite RBF quoted in HOUSE & GARDEN Interview by Beverly
 Russel, p. 202, May '72

---

Optimism: I Am Not an Optimist:

    See Stillbirth of Humanity, 10 Dec'73
      Options, 13 May'77

---

Optimism:                                                    (1)

    See Reverse Optimism
      Survival Sequence: Love
      Options ≠ Optimism

---

Optimism:                                                    (2)

    See Children as Only Pure Scientists, (B)
      News & Evolution, (2)

---

RBF DEFINITIONS

Optimum: Confluence of Optimum Factors:

"Tensegrity is a confluence of optimum factors."

- Cite RBF to HUD Engineers, Washington, DC, 26 Jan '72
- Citation at Tensegrity, 26 Jan'72

Optimum Limit:

See Sphere, 2 Mar'68

---

RBF DEFINITIONS

Options:

"I don't try to promote my ideas, but rather to make clear the options to let human beings have the tools around when it comes to an emergency, which this clearly is.... I'm not an optimist at all. What I do know--that many people don't-- is that we have the options to make it. Whether we will or not, I really don't know. But my hope that we'll make it lies with the young world."

- Cite RBF to Susan Watter in W (women's Wear Daily); 13 May'77

---

Optimum:                                    (1)

See Determinability: Optimum Degree Of
    God as Verb of Optimum Understaning
    Omni-equi-optimum

---

RBF DEFINITIONS

Options:

"...Truth is ever approaching a catalogue of alternate transformative options of ever more inclusive and refining degrees."

- Citation and context at Truth, 10 Nov'72

---

Optimum:                                    (2)

See Limit Structural Transformative Tendencies, Nov'52
    Prime Number Inherency & CRA: Principle Of, 1959
    Tensegrity, 26 Jan'72*

---

RBF DEFINITIONS

Option:

"Women and their clothes are like poets. They anticipate. All options are open."

- Cite RBF quoted in Queen, May '70

---

RBF DEFINITIONS

Optional:

". . . There is a vast plurality of alternate and optional
patterns of realizability of the change. By adequate
thinking the individual can discover many of the optional
patterns of controlability of evolutionary change. Because
of the vast range of frequencies, magnitudes and angular
directions the number of options is astronomical."

- Cite Museums Keynote Address Denver, p.3. 2 Jun'71

---

Options ≠ Optimism:

See Womb of Permitted Ignorance, (2)

# Synergetics Dictionary

Options:  Optional:                                                    (1)


      See Alternate:  Alternative
           Catalog of Alternate Transformative Options
           Degrees of Freedom
           Electable
           Nature Has So Many Options
           Multioptioned
           Twelve Alternative Options of Action


Oranges:                                                               (2)

      See Model vs. Photograph, 12 May'77


Options:                                                               (2)


      See Economic Accounting System, Sep'72
           Optimism:  I Am Not an Optimist, 10 Dec'73; 26 Apr'77
           Prospect for Humanity, 2 Feb'75
           Stillbirth of Humanity, 10 Dec'73
           Trespassing:  Not Trespassing, (a)-(c)
           Truth, 10 Nov'72*
           Vectorial Orientation, Mar'71
           World Game, (1); Jun-Jul'69
           Children as Only Pure Scientists, (B)
           Womb of Permitted Ignorance, (2)
           Man as a Function of Universe, 30 Apr'78
           Will, (1)(2)


RBF DEFINITIONS

   Orbit:

   "Orbits mean tensive restraints.  A composite of all the
   other pulls..."


   - Citation & context at Ellipse, 20 Jan'75


Oranges:

"...Oranges are icosahedrally based..."


RBF DEFINITIONS

   Orbit:

   "What the physicists have failed to elucidate to themselves
   is that linear acceleration is also orbital but constitutes
   release from co-orbiting (or critical proximity orbiting)
   into the generalized orbiting of all Universe."


   - Cite SYNERGETICS draft at Sec. 1009.66, 14 Feb'73


   - Citation & context at Twelve Pentagons, Aug'71


Oranges:                                                               (1)


      See Stacking of Oranges


RBF DEFINITIONS

   Orbiting:

   "...We are not going to survive unless we become spherically
   integrated and go into cosmically normal, individual orbiting,
   which is always inherently considerate of the rest of the
   Universe.  Knowledge is orbital...."


   - Citation and context at Ecology Sequence (G), 5 Jun'73

RBF DEFINITIONS

Orbiting:

"Ninety-nine point nine-nine percent of the bodies in motion in physical Universe are operating orbitally; therefore normally...."

- Citation at Normal, 6 Mar'73

---

RBF DEFINITIONS

Orbiting:

"Critical proximity occurs

where there is a 90° angular transition

from falling back in at 180°

which is precession."

(This is RBF's explanation of precisely what happens at the moment that an earth satellite goes into orbit.)

- Cite RBF to EJA
    Beverly Hotel, New York
    28 Feb 1971

---

RBF DEFINITIONS

Orbiting:

"As the Sun's pull on the Earth produces orbiting, orbiting electrons produce directional field pulls."

- Citation and context at Mass Attraction, 6 Mar'73

---

RBF DEFINITIONS

Orbiting:

"And the transition from being an entity

to being a plurality of entities

is precession

which is a peeling off into orbit

rather than falling back

into the original entity.

- Cite RBF to EJA
    Beverly Hotel, New York
    28 Feb 1971

---

RBF DEFINITIONS

Orbiting:                                                          (1)

"Unlike ninety-nine point nine nine nine
Percent of all humans,
Goddard, carefully heeding the laws
Of both mass attraction and precession,
Realized that an object,
Rocket-propelled or accelerated,
Into a different velocity--
        And into a different direction
        To that of the Earth's
        Speed and course around the Sun--
Would have ots gravitational pull
Toward the Earth
Reduced fourfold
Every time it doubled
Its distance away from the Earth;
Only a hundred miles out
Form our Earth's surface
The attraction would be
So diminished
That it would permit the Moon's pull
To become significant,
At which distance"

- Cite INTUITION, p.32 May '72

---

RBF DEFINITIONS

Orbiting:

"Each local system has its own orbiting, and its own frequencies, and so forth . . ."

- Citation and context at Relative Asymmetry Sequence (1), JUn'69

---

RBF DEFINITIONS

Orbiting:                                                          (2)

"The rocketed object
Would lose its tendency
To fall abck into the Earth,
And now affected dominantly
By the integrated mass attractions
Of all other celestial bodies,
Would go into orbit
Around our Earth.

"And to understand
How little is that
One-hundred-mile distance
Out from Earth's surface
At which orbiting
Replaces the tendency
To fall back into the Earth,
We note that
The thickness of a matchstick
Out from the surface
Of a twelve-inch diametered
Household 'World Globe'
Is the distance at which
Our first rocketed objects
Do go into orbit."

- Cite INTUITION,pp.32-33, May '72

---

RBF DEFINITIONS

Orbit = Circuit:

"The reality is always orbital.  Orbit = circuit.  All critical paths orbit the Sun.  No path could possibly be linear.  The Universe never reverts to the smaller and simpler circuits."

- Cite RBF to EJA, 3200 Idaho, Wash., DC, 10 Sep'74

Orbital Closure:

    See Events & Novents, 10 Sep'74

---

Orbital Escape from Critical Proximity: (1)

"Human mind, while discovering generalized principles, eternally persisted in special-case experience sequences, but has gradually developed the capability to employ those principles and then self into such acceleration as to escape the fall-back-in proclivity and to escape the general ecological fall-in program of invisible interorbiting regeneration.

"As each human being discovers self and others and employs more principles ■■■ more and more consciously to the advantage of others, the more effectively does the individual retain the integrity of his own unique orbiting in Universe, local though it may seem aboard our planet. His unique orbiting brings him into a vast variety of critical-proximity fall-ins. Man has progressively acquired enough knowledge to raise his vision from the horizontal to the vertical, to stay first atop the watery ocean and next atop the airocean heights, and most recently to orbit beyond the biosphere with ever greater independence, with ever greater competence, and with ever greater familiarity with the reliability of the generalized principles."

    - Cite SYNERGETICS text at Secs. 1009.70 & .71; RBF galley rewrite of 29 Dec'73

---

Orbits Are Elliptical:

"All the experimentally harvested information says that the 'field' must now be recognized as a complex of never-straight lines, which, at their simplest, always will be very great circular orbits. And the orbits are all elliptical due to the fact that unity is plural and at minimum two. There will always be at least one ■■■ other critical proximity aberration with both of its diametric alterations of orbit."

    - Citation and context at Field, 14 Feb'73

---

Orbital Escape from Critical Proximity: (2)

"Little individuals in orbit around little berry patches, fruit trees, nut piles, and fishing holes are instinctively programmed to pick up rocks and pile up walls around the patches, orchards, and gathering places. Some men floating on the waters and blown by the wind were challenged to respond to the accelerating frequence of stress and high-energy impacts, and they went into vastly longer orbital voyages. Others went into lesser and slower orbits on camels and horses, or even slower orbits on their own legs. The effect of human beings on other human beings is always precessional. All of us orbit around one another in ever greater ■■■■■■■■ acceleration, finally going into greater orbits. The critical-proximity fall-in and its 99.9999 percent designed-in programming becomes no longer in critical-proximity evidence, while all the time the apprehending and comprehending of the generalized principles elucidates their eternal integrity in contrast to the complex inscrutability of the local critical-proximity aberrations permitted and effected in pure principle whenever the frictional effect on the two stones lying before us overcomes their tendency to fall into one another-- with ■■■■ naught else in Universe but two stones-- which statement"

    - Cite SYNERGETICS text at Sec. 1009.72; RBF galley rewrite of 29 Dec'73

---

Orbits Are Elliptical: (1)

    See Aberration
        Eccentric: Eccentricity
        Otherness Restraints & Elliptical Orbits

---

Orbital Escape from Critical Proximity: (3)

"in itself discloses our proclivity for forgetting all the billions of atoms involved in the two stones, and their great electron orbits around their nuclei; guaranteeing the omniacceleration, yet synergetically and totally cohered by the mass-interattractiveness, which is always more effective (because of its finite closures) than any of the centrifugal disintegrative effects of the acceleration. All the inter-aberrations imposed on all the orbits bring about all the wave-frequency phenomena of our Universe. The unique wave frequencies of the unique 92 chemical elements are unique to the local critical-proximity event frequency of the elemental event patternings locally and precessionally regenerated. Finally, we must recall that what man has been calling 'linear' is simply big orbit arc seemingly attained by escaping at 90 degrees from local orbit. There are only two kinds of acceleration, greater and lesser, with the greater being like the lesser, with the lesser being like the radius of the nucleus of an atom in respect to the diameter of its electron shell."

    - Cite SYNERGETICS text at Sec. 1009.72; RBF galley rewrite of 29 Dec'73

---

Orbits Are Elliptical: (2)

    See Field, 14 Feb'73*

---

Orbital Escape from Critical Proximity: (4)

"Humanity at this present moment is breaking the critical-proxmity barrier that has programmed him to operate almost entirely as a part of the ecological organisms growing within the planet Earth's biosphere. His visit to Moon is only symptomatic of his total, local, social breakout from a land-possessing, fearful barnacle into a world-around-swimming salmon. Some have reached deep-water fish state, some have become world-around migrating birds, and some have gone out beyond the biosphere. Long ago man's mind went into orbit to understand a little about the stars. And little man on little Earth has now accumulated in the light emanating from all the stars a cosmic inventory of the relative abundance of each of the 92 regenerative chemical elments present in our thus-far-discovered billion galaxies of approximately a hundred billion stars each, omnidirectionally observed around us at a radius of 11 billion light years. Man can always go into infinitely great, eternal orbit. Mind always has and always will."

    - Cite SYNERGETICS text at Sec. 1009.73; RBF galley rewrite of 29 Dec'73

Orbital Escape from Critical Proximity:

See Critical Proximity Threshold
    Fall-in Proclivity
    In-ness Proclivity

Orbital Feedback Circuitry vs. Critical Path:

See Local vs. Comprehensive
    Local Radius vs. Wide Arcs
    Linear vs. Orbital
    Radial vs. Orbital

RBF DEFINITIONS

Orbital Feedbacks:

"Conventional 'critical path' conceptioning is 'linear' and
self-underinformative. Only orbital feedbacks are valid.
Orbital, critical feedback circuits are pulsative, tidal,
importing and exporting. Critical path elements are not
overlapping linear modules in a plane. Each step survives
after completion; like a building, they are regenerative
feedbacks, circuits."

- Cite RBF to EJA, 3200 Idaho, Wash. DC, 10 Sep'74

SECS. 1130.21 + 1130.22

Orbital Interlinking:

See Ninety-degreeness, 5 Jun'73

RBF DEFINITIONS

Orbital Feedback Circuitry vs. Critical Path:

"Orbital feedback circuits are pulsative, tidal, importing
and exporting.

"Each circuit is a year. Years are not linear.

"Critical path conceptioning is 'linear' and self-misinfor-
mative."

- Cite RBF holograph, Wash. DC: 9 Sep'74

Orbiting Magnitudes:                                      (1)

See Astro & Nucleic Interpositioning
    Atom as Solar System
    Chords & Arcs
    Physics as Internal Affairs of the Atom
    Rules of Interval
    Relative Activity Diameters of Stars & Electrons
    Human Sense Ranging & Information Gathering
    Sweepout
    Local Radius vs. Wide Arc
    Nucleus & Nebular: Nucleus & Galaxies
    Orbital Feedback Circuitry vs. Critical Path

TEXT CITATIONS

Orbital Feedback Circuitry vs. Critical Path:

s535.20 - 19 Nov'74

1009.56

s1130.20 - 15 Jan'74

1032.23

RBF holograph, Santa Barbara 12 Feb'73

TEXT CITATIONS

Orbiting Magnitudes:

Synergetics, Sec. 1009.20, 1009.30, 1051.51

RBF DEFINITIONS

Orbiting Magnitudes:                 (2)

    See Compound: Difference Between Atoms & Compounds,
       27 Dec'73
      Acceleration, 15 Feb'73
      Radiation: Speed Of (C)(D)
      Event, 8 Mar'73
      Field, 14 Feb'73
      Constellar, 3 Oct'72
      Pneumatic Structures, 10 Jul'62
      Eternal Designing Capability Sequence (1)
      Subconscious, 14 Feb'72
      Tunability, Mar'66
      Gravity: Circumferential Leverage, (2)
      Orbital Escape from Critical Proximity, (2)(3)

---

Orbit: Orbiting:                  (3)

    See Orbits are Elliptical
      Orbital Feedbacks
      Orbitally Interlinking
      Orbiting Magnitudes
      Orbital Closure
      Orbital Phase
      Orbital Escape from Critical Proximity
      Orbital Feedback Circuitry vs. Critical Path

---

Orbital Phase:                 (1)

    See Umbilical Cord, 4 Mar'73

---

Orchestra: Orchestration:

    See Symphony

---

Orbit: Orbiting:                  (1)

    See Birth: When You are Born You Go into Orbit
      Circle
      Co-orbiting
      Co-orbiting of Earth & Moon Around Sun
      Critical Proximity Co-orbiting
      Ellipse
      Linear vs. Orbital
      Motion: Six Positive & Negative Motions
      Multiorbital
      Radial vs. Orbital
      Spinning & Orbiting
      Unwrap the Orbitals
      Interorbiting
      Otherness Restraints & Elliptical Orbits
      Local Orbit

---

RBF DEFINITIONS

Order:

"There is no true 'noise' or 'static.' There are only as yet
undifferentiated and uncomprehended frequency and magnitude
orders. Chaos and ignorance are both conditions of the brain's
█████████ only-sense-harvested and stored information, as yet
unenlightenedly reviewed and comprehendingly processed by the
order-seeking and -finding mind."

    - Cite SYNERGETICS text at Sec. 532.13; RBF galley rewrite
      7 Nov'73

---

Orbit: Orbiting:                 (2)

      Acceleration of Change (1)
    See Cone, 22 Sep'73
      Critical Proximity, 15 Feb'73; 10 Feb'73
      Ecology, 15 Feb'73
      Ecology Sequence (G)*
      Field, 14 Feb'73*
      Einstein: General Theory & Special Theory, 4 Mar'73
      Dancing, 6 Jul'62
      Gravity (b)
      Line, 7 Nov'72
      Mass Attraction, 6 Mar'73*
      Normal, 6 Mar'73*; 22 Jan'73
      Precession, 24 Sep'73
      Relative Asymmetry Sequence (1)*
      Radiation: Speed Of (D)
      Unity is Plural, 14 Feb'73*
      In, Out & Around Experiences, (1)
      Four Intergeared Mobility Freedoms, 2 Nov'73

---

RBF DEFINITIONS

Order:

"Science has been cogently defined by others as the
attempt to set in order the facts of experience. When science
discovers order subjectively it is pure science. When the
order discovered by science is objectively employed it is
called applied science. The facts of experience are always
special cases. The order sought for and sometimes found by
science is always eternally generalized; that is, it holds
true in every special case. The scientific generalizations
are always mathematically statable as equations with one term
on one side of the equation and a plurality of at least two
terms on the other side of the equation."

    - Cite RBF Ltr. to Karan Singh (draft) incorporated in
      SYNERGETICS at Sec. 161, 13 Mar'73

RBF DEFINITIONS

Order:

"I am not a creator. I am a swimmer and a dismisser of
irrelevancies. Everything we need to work with is already
around us, although most of it is initially confusing. To
find order in what we experience we must first inventory the
total experiences, then temporarily set aside all irrelevancies. I do not invent my thoughts. I merely separate out
some local patterns from a confusing whole. . . . Flight was
the discovery of the lift-- not the push."

/ For full text see Robt. W. Marks citation, 1960. 7

- Cite RBF quoted by William Kuhns in "The Post-Industrial
  Prophets: Interpretations of Technology," Harper- Colophon,
  p.222, 1971

---

RBF DEFINITIONS

Order:

". . . Nature proceeds from the obviously orderly and
symmetrical to the nonobviously, but always orderly
transformation phases known as asymmetries which, having
gone through their maximum or peak positive phase
asymmetry . . . always return transformatively thereafter
through an orderly progression of decreasing asymmetry
to the fleeting passing through the condition of obvious
symmetry or equilibrium popularly recognized as 'order.'"

- Cite Synergetics Draft, "Symmetry," Sec 532.02, July 1971.

---

RBF DEFINITIONS

Order:

"What the scientists have always found by physical
experiment was an a priori orderliness of 'nature' or
'universe' always operating at an elegance level which
made the discovering scientists' own working hypotheses
seem so crude by comparison to the discovered reality
as to seem relatively disorderly."

- Cite Synergetics Draft, "Symmetry," Sec 532.01, July 1971.

---

RBF DEFINITIONS

Order:

"All the biologicals are antientropic. A baby couldn't
grow to be entropic; the child would shrink, getting
smaller and smaller. But a child get's bigger, so it's
antientropic. And it's absolutely order-- the most
beautiful pair of two eyes doing whatever. Everything
about it is antientropic. And everything about a human
being that makes you sit where you're sitting in a quiet
way is because we're seeking to understand and put in
order. Understanding is finding order."

- Citation and context at World Game (7), RBF to World Game
  at NY Studio School, from Saturn tape #327, p.13, Jun-Jul'69

---

RBF DEFINITIONS

Order:

"We become more aware of this uniqueness of organizing principle
in the Universe, in science. The long held myth that science
wrests order out of chaos is fast disappearing in due ratio to
the extent that all great scientists have found the Universe to
exhibit an a priori orderliness. All the various specialties
are discovering that their variously remote studies which
seemingly 'ordered' local aspects of nature are converging
within progressively simpler and more comprehensive patterns.
The 'ordering' is coming together. When we refer to the
computer and automation taking over we refer really to man's
externalization of his internal and organic functions into a
total organic system which we call industrialization. This
metabolic regenerating automated organism is going to be able
to support life in an extraordinary way. The machines will
increasingly assume various specialized functions. Man who was
born spontaneously comprehensive but was focused by survival
needs into specialization is now to be brought back to comprehensivity."

- Citation and context at Population Sequence (5), Feb'67

---

RBF DEFINITIONS

Order:

"Order is achieved through-- positive and negative--
Magnitude and frequency controlled alteration
Of the successive steering angles."
We move by zig-zagging control
From one phase of physical universe evolution to another."

- Cite HOW LITTLE, p. 71.
- Also cite AAUW Journal, May '65.

---

RBF DEFINITIONS

Order:

"As man becomes less of a subconscious function in the
universe,, which he has been, and consciously employs his
faculty to differentiate experiences and to reassociate them
in preferred ways, he will become more and more effective.
By becoming more conscious and developing more and more
orderliness, he simply discovers more facets of the universe.
Neither he nor the universe are getting more complex. As
he learns more, man is becoming more orderly, more understanding, and more understandable."

(The question was: "Do you believe the world is
getting more complex?")

- Cite AAUW JOURNAL, May 1965, P. 176

---

RBF DEFINITIONS

Order:

"Order is achieved through positive and negative,
magnitude and frequency-controlled alteration of the
successive steering angle. We move by zigzagging control
from one phase of physical Universe evolution to another."

- Cite AAUW JOURNAL, May 1965, P. 176

- Citation and context at Ruddering: Rudder Concept, May'65

RBF DEFINITIONS

Order:

The "extraordinary world of weightless, invisible waves is governed by mathematical laws and not by the opinions of men. The magnificent orderliness of that ever individually and uniquely patterning weightless wave universe is not of man's contriving. The infinite variety of evolutionary complexities, inherent to the orderliness of complementary principles operative in the universe, is of unending synergetic uniqueness."

- Cite MEXICO, p. 102, 10 Oct'63

---

RBF DEFINITIONS

Order & Disorder:

"...There is a great deal of difference
Between absolute disorder, i.e., chaos,
And the only one-sidedly considered,
Relative asymmetry, whose pulsative balancing
At a later time with other systems was not awaited
By the too hasty and biased observer.
On the contrary, I am convinced
By comprehensively considered experience
That a total integrity of order prevails..."

- Cite BRAIN & MIND, p.91 May '72

---

RBF DEFINITIONS

Order:

"The actual fact is that each scientist penetrating into his own area, when he has made a discovery, has always discovered orderliness. Orderliness was a priori. There was no beginning of orderliness. He went from a rather rough disorderly hypothesis and had enough conviction to set up an apparatus to make an experiment and after the experiments were made he found orderliness. Now they are beginning to discover that gradually they are all coming into the same room, and all the orderliness is permeated, so the orderliness is all interrelated. They are suddenly coming into a comprehensive coordinate system employed by nature, which apparently, as far as any scientist could possibly tell you, if you were to talk comprehensively, has always been operative. There is no beginning about it."

- Cite Oregon Lecture #4, p. 128. 6 Jul'62

---

RBF DEFINITIONS

Order & Disorder:

"The seeming disorder of physical entropy is only superficial and explains why metaphysical thought can always find the orderliness which engulfs disorderliness. Disorderliness is nonthinking."

- Citation & context at Relationship Analysis (1)(2), Jun'66
- Cite NASA Speech, p.95, Jun'66

---

RBF DEFINITIONS

Order:

"I am not a creator. I am a swimmer and a dismisser of irrelevancies. Everything we need to work with is around us, although most of it is initially confusing. To find order in what we experience we must first inventory the total experiences, then temporarily set aside all irrelevancies. I do not invent my thoughts. I merely separate out some local patterns from a confusing whole. The act is a dismissal of pressures. Flight was the discovery of the lift-- not the push."

- Cit Robt. W. Marks DYMAXION WORLD OF RBF, p.63, 1960

---

RBF DEFINITIONS

Order & Disorder:

"Men of the Einstein Age are discovering the universal orderliness of constant, comprehensive transformation, utterly transcendental in the exquisite and magnificent orderliness of its wavelength and frequency when compared to the crude disorderly, conscious thinking and articulation of mere humans."

- Citation & context at New York City (12); 1964

---

RBF DEFINITIONS

"Order & Disorder:

"Order is obviously the complementary, but not mirror-image, of disorder."

- Citation and context at Syntropy & Entropy, 5 May'74

---

RBF DEFINITIONS

Order & Disorder:

"We don't have any idea of the relative depth of the heavens. The fact that the heavens seem to be a sort of array which we are familiar with is extremely deceiving. Where those stars really are we don't hardly know at all. They seem to be rather disorderly in the sky. They may be in fabulously orderly array if we were able to get better kinds of reports. When we begin to get into the macrocosm this same kind of feeling about this disorderly chaos obtained for a long time. Men's minds have been confused and therefore they have thought of the Universe as confused. Not being a nonsimultaneously conceptual affair gets the human mind into a lot of troubles. At any rate, man thought of the universe as chaotic. . . .

"We find that the portion of the Universe that is still chaos is rapidly diminishing. As fast as we get a telescope or microscope, the orderliness is discovered and it begins to be fairly much in evidence that the Universe was at all times orderly. The only idea of disorderliness was in the human mind. We are dealing in a finite Universe of extraordinary order and which was always orderly and the only thing which has ever been disorderly is in man's mind."

- Cite OREGON Lecture #3 - pp. 104-105, 5 Jul'62

Order & Disorder: (1)

See Symmetry & Asymmetry
Syntropy & Entropy
Wow:  The Last Wow
Expanding Physical Universe vs. Contracting Metaphysical
    Universe
Information vs. Entropy
Meshing & Nonmeshing

---

RBF DEFINITIONS

▆▆▆▆▆  Orderliness Operative in Nature: (1)

"... All of these specialists, we get more and more of them
in there, and even though each one is getting finer and finer,
each of them are shoulder to shoulder representing a larger
and larger angle and they begin to overlap.  I spoke of them
all discovering themselves rally in the same Universe and they
were not in separate departments of nature.  They began then
to have to divide up the work, and every one of them had made
an important discovery, recognizing that in his line he had
discovered a greater orderliness operative in nature than he
had supposed was there; and then they are finding an integrity
of all those informations.

"... In the immediate decade ahead you are going to hear more
and more from the world of science, stating that it is clearly
discovering a comprehensive operational integrity, a very
complex plurality of clearly differentiable principles, such
as tension and compression that are complementary and utterly
reliable in their total interactions and the whole thing is
clearly not something that has come out of the ooze at all
but the pure principles were generalizable and of no weight
at all.  The principles were always there and the generalizable
had nothing to do with the special case.  The generalized was

Cite Oregon Lecture #5, pp.162-163, 9 Jul'62

---

Order & Disorder: (2)

See Baseball, 11 Feb'73
Extraterrestrial Humans, 23 Aug'70
Games, 13 Dec'73
Pendulum Model vs. Scenario Model, 23 Dec'68
Relationship Analysis, (1)(2)*
Syntropy & Entropy, 5 May'74*
Vector Equilibrium, (I)
Wow, (2)
Macro-micro, 1964
New York City, (12)*

---

RBF DEFINITIONS

▆▆▆▆▆  Orderliness Operative in Nature: (2)

"always present in the special case, but it had nothing to do
with the avoirdupois, for it is not weighable.  Mathematics
weighs nothing and this is mathematics.  It is a mathematical
correspondence."

- Cite Oregon Lecture #5, pp. 162-163, 9 Jul'62

---

Order Finds Itself: (1)

See Entropy as Lack of Information
    Information Field

---

Order Underlying Randomness: (1)

See Connections and Relatedness
    Number:  Tetrahedral Number
    Relationship Analysis

---

RBF DEFINITIONS

Order Finds Itself: (2)

See Chaos, Jun'66

---

Order Underlying Randomness: (2)

See Relationships, 15 Oct'64

Order: (1)

See Absolute Order
Antientropic Ordering Principles
Chaos: Myth that Scientists Wrest Order from Chaos
Disorder
Eternal Orderliness
Generalization: Law of Contractively Orderly
Generalizations
Local Order
Omniorderly: Omniinterorderliness
Order & Disorder
Primordial
Progressive Order: Law Of
Manifest
Rearrange Elemental Order
Sorting
Nature's Subvisible Order

RBF DEFINITIONS

Organic:

"Organic means regenerative system integrity."

- Citation and context at Unit, 26 May'72

Order: (2A)

Ecology, 5 Jul'62
See Generalization Sequence (1)
Instrumentation, 1963
Intellect, 6 Jul'62
Life, 22 Apr'68
Man's Conscious Participation in Evolution, May'65
Mind, Dec'72
Number: Tetrahedral Number, May'65
Omnidirectional, 27 Feb'72
Population Sequence (5)*
Proton & Neutron, 22 Jul'71
Ruddering: Rudder Concept, May'65*
Seed, Dec'72
World Game (7)*

Synergetics, 20 Jan'75; 17 Oct'77
Large Pattern, 22 Jan'75
Truth, Jan'72
Invisible Operation of Thousands of Radio
Programs, (a)
Syntropy & Time, 14 May'75
Nucleus, 13 Nov'75

RBF DEFINITIONS

Organic:

"... There is original integral and metabolic regeneration
which we call organic."

- Cite THIS IS YOUR GRAND STRATEGY, 4 Feb '68, p . 32.

Order: (2B)

See Mutual Survival Principles, (3)

RBF DEFINITIONS

Organic Chemistry:

"It could be that organic chemistries do not require
nuclei."

- Cite SYNERGETICS Draft at Sec. 415.20, 22 Jun'72

Ordinates:

See Coordinates: Coordinate System
Subordinate & Superordinate

RBF DEFINITIONS

Organic Chemistry:

"The cube relates to chemistry, the external affairs
of the atom/ Organic chemistry begins with the cube: carbon.
The tetrahedron, octahedron and icosahedron relate to
physics, the internal affairs of the atom."

- Cite RBF to EJA, Blackstone Hotel, Chicago, 31 May 1971.

- Citation an Physics: Difference Between Physics and Chemistry,
31 May'71

# Synergetics Dictionary

RBF DEFINITIONS

RBF DEFINITIONS

Organic Chemistry:

"Apparently, all the chemical compounding in the organic

chemistry relates to the polarized system."

- Cite Oregon Lecture #7, p. 235. 11 Jul'62

---

RBF DEFINITIONS

Organic & Inorganic:

"The scientist as specialist in isolation of phenomenon from phenomena has now come-- by progressive reduction of the superficially remote behavior complexities of the organic and inorganic worlds-- to discover simplified common component behavior phases of each world respectively. Here the energetic interactions of the resultant structures are uniform. Here the man-controlled original inorganic growth is in all ways congruent with the animate, organic 'de-grown' by man, or separated out toward primary functions of the original totality: Universe."

- Cite TOTAL THINKING, (I&I), p.226, May'49

---

Organic Chemistry:                                    (1)

See Hex:  Chemical Hex
          Inorganic Chemistry
          Organic & Inorganic Chemistry
          van't Hoff

---

RBF DEFINITIONS

                    Organic & Inorganic Chemistry:

"What Linus Pauling found for the inorganic chemistry

. . . van't Hoff found for the organic chemistry."

- For citation and context see Tetrahedroning, 10 Jul '62

---

Organic Chemistry:                                    (2)

See Universal Joint:  Tetrahedron, 9 Nov'73

---

Organic & Inorganic:                                  (1)

See Animate & Inanimate

---

RBF DEFINITIONS

Organic & Inorganic:

"Organic chemistry and inorganic chemistry are both tetrahedrally coordinate. This relates to the thinking process where the fundamental configuration came out a tetrahedron. Nature's formulations here are a very, very high frequency thing. Nature makes viruses in split seconds. Whatever she does has very high frequency. We come to the tetrahedron as the first spontaneous aggregate of the experiences. We discover that nature is using tetrahedron in her fundamental formulation of the organic and inorganic chemistry. All structures are tetrahedrally based and we find our thoughts resolving themselves spontaneously into the tetrahedron as it comes the the generalization of the special cases which are the physics or the chemistry."

- Cite SYNERGETICS draft at Sec. 620.08, Nov'71

---

Organic & Inorganic:                                  (2)

See Tetrahedron, 2 Jul'62
    Tetrahedroning, 10 Jul'62
    Social Problems:  Tetrahedral Coordination Of,
    4 May'57

RBF DEFINITIONS

Organic Model:  Biological World as Model for Society:

"We have to look on our society
As we look on the biological world in general
Recognizing, for instance,
The extraordinary contributions
Of the fungi, the manures, the worms, et.al.--
In the chemical reprocessing
And fertility upgrading of the Earth.
We must learn to think
Of the functions of the trees' roots
As being of equal importance
To the leaves' functions.
We tend to applaud
Only the flower and the fruit
Just as we applaud only the football player
Who makes the touchdown
And not the lineman
Who opened the way."

- Cite HOW LITTLE, p. 69.  Oct. '66

- Cite AAUW JOURNAL, p. 174, May '65

---

RBF DEFINITIONS

Organics and the Nucleus:

"It could be that organics doesn't require the nucleus...
that you and I are the nucleus.  The first nuclear cube comes
in at 14."

- Cite RBF to EJA, 3200 Idaho, Wash. DC (1st draft), 28 May'72

---

Organic Model:

See Epigenetic Landscape
    Metabolic Flow
    Social Sciences:  Analogue to Physical Sciences

---

Organic Tunability:

See Space as Nontuned Angle & Frequency Information,
    22 Feb'77

---

RBF DEFINITIONS

Organics and the Nucleus:

"It could be that organics doesn't require the nucleus;
that whatever the mysterious, weightless phenomenon regenerative
life may be, may be the nucleus of all biological species
including you and me.  The first closest-packed, omnitriangulated, ergo structurally stabilized, cube has 14 spheres,
but without a nucleus.  This could be carbon.  And carbon is
the initially closest-packed, omnisymmetrical, polyhedral
fourteenness to present a surface of triangular nest availability
for mounting hydrogen structurally to produce all organic
matter."

- Cite RBF to EJA, 3200 Idaho, Wash. DC (3rd draft), 28 May'72
    incorporated in SYNERGETICS at Sec. 415.21

---

RBF DEFINITIONS

Organism:

"Clearly all organisms consist physically and in entirety
of inherently inanimate atoms."

- Cite RBF correction in margin of "Chronicle" sequence, p.14,
    SYNERGETICS, in EJA car enroute Charlottesville-Wash, 3 Jun'72

---

RBF DEFINITIONS

Organics and the Nucleus:

"It could be that organics doesn't require the nucleus;
that whatever the mysterious weightless phenomenon regenerative
life may be, may be the nucleus of all biological species
including you and me.  The first closest-packed, omnitriangulated, ergo structurally stabilized, cube has 14 spheres,
but without a nucleus.  This could be carbon.  And carbon has
the polyhedral nest availability for mounting hydrogen of all
organic matter."

- Cite RBF to EJA, 3200 Idaho, Wash. DC (2nd draft), 28 May'72

---

RBF DEFINITIONS

Organisms:

"What is inanimate is clearly the whole physical world.
But what is animate they lost track of altogether.  The
organics are information processing devices.  The
creatures and the trees adjust to information.  But life
is none of these things.  The organism gets information
for life, but it is not life.  Man has confused the
telephones with the people talking on the telephones."

- Cite RBF to EJA, 3200 Idaho, DC, 12 Feb '72

RBF DEFINITIONS

Organism:

"The Universe is
The min-max, self-regenerative organism. . . . . "

"Human organisms are Universe's
Most complex local technologies. . . . "

"Organisms are machines,
Life is not the organism-machine.
The organic residues progressively disassociate
And reassociate chemically.
Only the physical reassociations
Are organic machines
Which are inherently temporary
Evolutionary formulations."

- Cite Dreyfus Preface, "Decease of Meaning,"
28 April 1971, pp, 1, 2, and 3.

---

Organism ≠ Life:                                    (1)

See Life is Not Physical
Metabolic Flow ≠ Man

---

Organism ≠ Life:                                    (2)

See Information, 12 Feb'72
Life is Not Physical, 20 Feb'77
Human Beings, 22 Jun'77
Womb of Permitted Ignorance, (1)(2)

---

Organism:                                           (1)

See Animate & Inanimate
Life
Organism ≠ Life
Community as Unit Mechanical Organism
Human Organism

---

Organic: Organics: Organism:                        (2)

See Compoundings of Systems, 10 May'76
House as Terminal of Community Mechanism,
20 Sep'76
Industrialization, (A); Feb'72; Jun'66
Intuition: Hot Line Of, Jan'72
Minimum Awareness, (1)
Physics: Difference Between Physics & Chemistry,
31 May'71*
Regenerativity, 17 Jan'75
Space as Nontuned Angle & Frequency Information,
22 Feb'77
Turtle Hex-pent, 12 May'75
Unit, 26 May'72*
Vector Equilibrium: Polarization, (1)(2)
Environment, 29 Mar'77
Subconscious, 20 Feb'77
Human Beings at the Center, (1)(2)

---

Organic: Organics: Organism:                        (3)

See Organic
Organic Chemistry
Organic & Inorganic
Organic Model: Biological World as Model for Society
Organics & the Nucleus
Organic Tunability
Organism ≠ Life

---

Organizing Principle:

See Order, Feb'67

---

Organization: Organizational Structure:            (1)

See Self-organizing Principle
Social Organization
Social Problems: Tetrahedral Coordination Of
Will of Organizations
No Organization

# Synergetics Dictionary

Organization:  Organizational Structure:                    (2)

        See Wealth, 20 Sep'76

RBF DEFINITIONS

    Originality:

    "It is found in cybernetics that original questions,

    asked either by humans or computers, are always produced

    by unexpected interferences."

        - Citation at Interference, May'65

        - Cite AAUW JOURNAL, May 1965, p. 176.

---

Oriental Feeling About Death:

        See Death, 1970

Origin:  Original Event:                                    (1)

            See Beginning
                Life's Original Event
                Question:  Original Question

---

Orientability:  Orientation:

        See Four-dimensional Reality
            Multidimensional Accommodation
            Observation:  Observing
            Time-angle-size Aspects
            Vectorial Orientation
            Axis of Conceptual Observation
            Omnitriangularly Oriented
            No Up & Down
            In, Out & Around
            System Center of Observation

RBF DEFINITIONS

    Original Sin:

    "The concept of Original Sin is completely invalid.  It is

    a denial of regenerativity.  It derives from failure to

    appreciate the aberration of lags, the differential rate

    of recalls."

        - Cite RBF to EJA, 3200 Idaho, Wash DC, 29 May'72

---

RBF DEFINITIONS

    Originality:

    "An 'original' or 'prime' event is conceptual. . .

    originality being inherently complex integrals."

            (For later context see Energy Event, May'71)

        - Cite RBF marginalis, Synergetics Draft at Sec. 511.01 (Nov)
          done at Boston in April 1971.

Original Sin:                                              (1)

        See Perfection:  Utter Perfection Unattainable by Humans
            Physical:  Corruptibility Of
            Residual Error
            Truth as Progressive Diminution of Original Error
            Residual Ignorance

Original Sin:                                                    (2)

See Local vs. Comprehensive (1)(2)

---

RBF DEFINITIONS

Oscillation:

"So what we call life is oscillation between varying degrees
of asymmetry, or lags in conceptioning, which bring about
what seems to be the temporal."

- Cite RBF to EJA, Beverly Hotel, NYC, 13 Mar'71
- Citation & context at Life, 13 Mar'71

---

Origin:  Original Event:  Originality:                           (2)

See Isotropic Vector Matrix, 30 Nov'72
    Spherics, 30 Nov'72
    Interference, May'65*
    Genius: Children Are Born Geniuses, 8 Apr'75

---

RBF DEFINITIONS

Oscillation & Pulsation:

" . . . The difference between the physical and the

metaphysical ♠ is the omnipulsative asymmetry of all the

physical oscillation in respect to the equilibrium. . . "

- Cite RBF dictation to EJA for SYNERGETICS, Sec. 205.3, Oct. '71.

- Citation at Omnipulsative Asymmetry, Oct'71

---

RBF DEFINITIONS

Oscillation:

"While nature oscillates and palpitates asymmetrically
in respect to the frame of omnirational vector
equilibrium, the plus and minus magnitudes of asymmetry
are rational fractions of the omnirationality of the
equilibrious state, ergo, omnirationally commensurable
and modelable to the sixth power, which order of powering
embraces all experimentally disclosed physical behavior."

- Citation & context at Vector Equilibrium, 21 Dec'71

- Cite RBF to EJA, 3200 Idaho Ave, Washington DC, 21 Dec. '71.

---

RBF DEFINITIONS

Oscillation & Pulsation:

"Physics finds only waves. Some are of exquisitely

high frequency, but inherently discontinuous because

consisting of separate event packages. They are

oscillating to and from negative Universe, that is to

say, in pulsation."

- Cite RBF to EJA, Somerset Club, Boston, 22 April 1971

- Citation & context at Wave, 22 Apr'71

---

RBF DEFINITIONS

Oscillation:

". . . the disappearance, or the isolating aspect, of our
Universe . . . is always present. It oscillates with what
you call the tetrahedra as unit measure. . . "

- Citation and context at ▮▮▮▮▮ Invisible Tetrahedron,
  1 May'71

---

RBF DEFINITIONS

Oscillation & Pulsation:

". . . Temporality is time and the relative asymmetries

of oscillation are realizable only in time-- in the time

required for pulsative frequency cycling. . . "

- Cite RBF dictation for SYNERGETICS, Beverly Hotel, New York.,
  28 Feb. '71.  See Sec. 205.5 of Oct. '71.
- Citation & context at Time, 28 Feb'71

Oscillation & Pulsation:                                    (1)

    See Inward & Outward Twoness
       Triangular-cammed Model

Osculation:

    See Posterioral Osculations
       Kissing

Oscillation & Pulsation:                                    (2)

    See Calculus, Jul'71
       Omnipulsative Asymmetry, Oct'71*
       Time, 28 Feb'71*
       Wave, 22 Apr'71*
       Inward & Outward Twoness, Aug'71
       Vector Equilibrium Field, 20 Dec'73
       Nonstate, 11 Sep'75

Osmosis: Osmotical:

    See Ecology Sequence, (1); (a)

Oscillation:                                                (1)

    See Boltzmann Sequence
       Discontinuity
       Energetic Functions
       Meshing
       Nuclear & Nebular Zonal Waves
       Observing vs. Articulation
       Pulsation
       Radial-circumferential
       Vector Equilibrium: Field of Energy
       Wave-angle Oscillating Extremes
       Wow: The Last Wow
       Pulse: Pulsive: Pulsivity
       Interoscillate

RBF DEFINITIONS

    Other:

      "Humanity can only survive by complete regard for all of
      humanity.  Humans are beginning to learn, 'No other, no me.'"

    - Citation and context at Ecology Sequence (G), 5 Jun'73

Oscillation:                                                (2)

    See Calculus, Jul'71
       Cosmic Discontinuity & Local Continuity, 15 Jan'74
       Invisible Tetrahedron, 1 May'71*
       Inward & Outward Twoness, Aug'71
       Omnipulsative Asymmetry, Oct'71*
       Plastic Flowers, Oct'70
       Reciprocity (3), May'49
       Time, 28 Feb'71*
       Transformation, 10 Oct'50
       Syte, 31 May'71
       Vector Equilibrium, 21 Dec'71*
       Twoness, 23 May'72
       Prime Dichotomy (1)(2)
       Metaphysical & Physical Tetrahedral Quanta,
         25 Mar'71
       Finite Minus De-finite, Nov'71
       Six Motion Freedoms & Degrees of Freedom, (5)(6)
       Energetic Functions, 8 Aug'77

RBF DEFINITIONS

    Other:

      "There will always be at least one other."

    - Citation and context at Field, 14 Feb'73

RBF DEFINITIONS

Other:

"Unity relates to realizable experience which is
omnidirectional. Ergo, there is not just one 'other.'
There are always at least 12 'others.'  Ergo, vector
equilibrium, which is subfrequency."

- Cite RBF to EJA, Bear Island, 25 August 1971.

RBF DEFINITIONS

Otherness:

"Without otherness there is no consciousness and no direction.
If there were only one entity-- say it is a sphere called 'me'--
there would be no Universe: no otherness: no awareness:
no consciousness: no direction.  Once another entity, let's
say a sphere, is sighted, there is awareness and direction.
There is no way to tell how far away the other sphere may
be, nor what its size may be. Size sense comes with
comparative experience."

- Cite SYNERGETICS draft At Sec. 411.03, 28 May'72

RBF DEFINITIONS

Other:

". . . Twoness is the beginning and essence of
consciousness, with which human awareness begins:
consciousness of the other, the other experience,
the other being, the child's mother. . . . Early
humanity's concept of the minimum increment of
time was the second, because time and awareness
begin with the second experience after the other.
. . . Life and the universe that goes with it
begins with two spheres: you and me. . . and you are
always prior to me."

- Cite RBF marginalia on Synergetics draft, Sec. 223.31 - 19 Jun '71.

RBF DEFINITIONS

Otherness:

"Universe is a scenario of events,
The regenerative interactions
Of all otherness and me."

- Cite A Definition of Evolution, p. 1. 15 Sep'71

RBF DEFINITIONS

Otherness:

"Only the tetrahedron can accommodate the otherness which
is the aberration, otherness being essential to awareness
and awareness being the minimum statement of the experience
life."

- Citation & context at Tetrahedron as Primitively Central To
Life, 3 Mar'77

RBF DEFINITIONS

Otherness:

"Consciousness means an awareness of otherness."

- Cite SYNERGETICS, "Universe," Sec. 302. 1971
- Citation at Consciousness, 1971

RBF DEFINITIONS

Otherness:

"Neither Euclid nor Euler credited the surface on which
they were scribing.  They failed to identify the surface
with the otherness."

- Cite RBF to EJA, 3200 Idaho, Wash., DC; 8 Feb'76

RBF DEFINITIONS

Otherness:

"Communicated means informing self or others."

- Cite SYNERGETICS, "Universe," Sec. 302. 1971
- Citation at Communication, 1971

RBF DEFINITIONS

Otherness:.

"The a priori otherness of comparative awareness inherently requires time."

- Cite RBF marginalia on Synergetics draft, Sec. 223.31- 19 Jun '71.

---

Otherness: At Least Twelve Others:

See Self & Otherness, 19 Nov'74
Initial Frequency, 6 Nov'72
Other, 25 Aug'71
Six Degrees of Freedom, Dec'71

---

RBF DEFINITIONS

▆▆▆▆▆ Otherness:

"Life is the difference between temporality and eternity. . . . Instantaneity would eliminate otherness, time, and self-and-other-awareness. Instantaneity and eternal are both timeless: they are the same."

- Cite RBF to EJA
  Beverly Hotel, New York
  13 March 1971

- Citation & context at Life, 13 Mar'71

---

TEXT CITATIONS

Otherness: At Least Twelve Others:

Synergetics : Sec. 502.25

537.12

---

RBF DEFINITIONS

Other: At Least One Other:

"... Unity is plural and at minimum two. There will always be at least one other critical proximity aberration..."

- Citation and context at Orbits Are Elliptical, 14 Feb'73

---

RBF DEFINITIONS

Otherness Point:

"Because of discontinuity, the otherness points and subpoints may be anywhere. We start always with any point-- event points being as yet noncomprehended; ergo, initially only as an apprehended otherness entity. Synergetics, as a strategy of converting apprehension to discrete comprehension, always proceeds vectorially."

- Cite SYNERGETICS draft at Sec. 540.07, 24 Sep'73

---

Otherness: At Least One Other:

See Unity Is Plural, 14 Feb'73
Outside, 26 Jan'73
Aberration, 19 Dec'73

---

RBF DEFINITIONS

Otherness Restraints & Elliptical Orbits:                                    (1)

"Angular acceleration is the local accumulation of momentum; angular deceleration is the local depletion of momentum.

"Release from angular acceleration appears to be linear acceleration but the linearity is only theoretical. Linear acceleration is the release from the restraint of the nearest accelerator over to the angularly accelerative or decelerative restraint of the integrated vectorial resultant of all the neighborly dominant forever-otherness restraints in Universe. Linear acceleration never occurs because there is never innocence of otherness.

"The hammer thrower releases his 'hammer's' ball-and-rod assembly from his extended arm's-end grasp seemingly to allow the hammer to take a linear trajectory, but Earth's gravitational pull immediately takes over and converts the quasi-straight trajectory into an elliptical arc of greater orbiting radius than before, but an arc of ever-decreasing radius as the Earth's gravity takes over and the hammer thrower's steel ball seemingly comes to rest on the Earth's surface which is, however, in reality to travel around the Earth's axis in"

- Cite SYNERGETICS, 2nd. Ed. at Secs. 826.11-.13, 20 May'75

RBF DEFINITIONS

Otherness Restraints & Elliptical Orbits:                     (2)

"synchronized consonance with the other together-huddled atoms
of the Earth's surface which, if near the Earth's equator
would be at a circular velocity of approximately 1000 miles an
hour and, if near the Earth's poles, of only inches an hour
aroudn the Earth's axis; but as yet traveling at 60,000 miles
an hour around the Sun at a radial restraint of approximately
92 million miles, with the galaxies of the Universe's other
nonsimultaneously generated restraints of all the othernesses'
overlappingly effective dominance variations, as produced by
degrees of neighboring energy concentrations and dispersions.
It is the pulsation of such concentrations and dispersions that
brings about the elliptical orbitings.

"This is fundamental complementarity as intuited in Einstein's
curved space prior to the scientific establishment of generalized complementarity, which we may now also speak of as the
'generalized otherness' of Universe. This is why there can
only be curved space.

"Isaac Newton's first law of motion, 'A body persists in a
state of rest or in a straight line except as affected by
other forces,' should now be restated to say, 'Any one"

- Cite SYNERGETICS, 2nd. Ed. at Secs. 826.13-.15, 20 May'75

---

RBF DEFINITIONS

Otherness Restraints & Elliptical Orbits:                     (3)

"considered body persists in any one elliptical orbit until
that orbit is altered to another elliptical orbit by the
ceaselessly varying interpositionings and integrated restraint
effects imposed upon the considered body by the generalized
cosmic otherness.' A body is always responding orbitally
to a varying plurality of otherness forces."

- Cite SYNERGETICS, 2nd. Ed. at Sec. 826.15, 20 May'75

---

RBF DEFINITIONS

Otherness We Call 'Space':

"The closest-packed symmetry of uniradius spheres is the
mathematical limit case which inadvertently 'captures' all the
previously unidentifiable otherness of Universe whose inscrutability we call 'space.'"

- Citation & context at Limit Case:  Closest Packed Symmetry As
Limit Case, 17 Feb'73

---

RBF DEFINITIONS

Other Side of the Universe:

"The other side of the Universe is not like the other side
of a river, but an inside-outing."

- Citation & context at Inside-outing, 17 Jun'75

---

Other Side of the Universe:

See Annihilation
    Rubber Glove

---

Other:  Otherness:                                   (1A)

See Awareness
    Balls Coming Together
    Consideration for Others
    Dichotomy
    Eternity:  Equation Of
    Madonna Theme
    No Otherness ✚ No Awareness
    No Other, No Me
    Observer & Otherness
    Prime Otherness
    Pulsatively Precessed by the Otherness
    Self
    Selfishness
    Self & Otherness
    Shape Awareness
    Swallow the Otherness
    Previous Otherness
    No Innocence of Otherness
    Forever-otherness

---

Other:  Otherness:                                   (1B)

See Future Otherness
    Past Otherness
    Present Otherness
    Integral Otherness
    Secondness = Otherness
    Macro-micro Otherness
    Plural Otherness
    Single Otherness

---

Other:  Otherness:                                   (2A)

See Communication, 1971*
    Conceptualize, 17 Feb'73
    Consciousness, 1971*
    Ecology Sequence, (G)*
    Field, 14 Feb'73*
    Geometry of Thinking, 16 Dec'73
    Eternity, 27 May'72
    Isotropic Vector Matrix, 6 Nov'72
    Life, 13 Mar'71*
    Limit Case:  Closest Packed Symmetry, 17 Feb'73
    Love, May'72; 15 Oct'72
    Mother, 17 Oct'72
    Motion, 27 May'72
    Nature Permits It Sequence, (3)
    Orbits Are Elliptical, 14 Feb'73*
    Pull, 22 Jun'72
    Sensorial Identification of Reality, (1)
    Somethingness, 16 Nov'72
    We-Me Awareness, 31 May'74
    Prospects for Humanity, 1 Feb'75
    Womb, 20 Feb'73

Other: Otherness: (2B)

See Visibility & Invisibility of Systems, ████ (1)
    Individuality & Degrees of Freedom, (2)
    Pronouns: I = We = Us, (1)
    Irrelevancies: Dismissal Of, 8 Feb'76
    Children as Only Pure Scientists, (2)
    Tetrahedrons Primitively Central to Life,
      3 Mar'77*
    Environment, 28 Apr'77
    Sensings & Eventings, 28 Apr'77
    Energetic Functions, 8 Aug'77

---

RBF DEFINITIONS

Out:

"There is only omnidirectional nonconceptional 'out'
and the specifically directioned conceptual 'in.'. . .

"'In' is always a direction. 'Out' is not a direction."

- Citation & context at In & Out, May'71

- Cite SYNERGETICS draft - "Conceptuality: Space" - May, 1971

---

RBF DEFINITIONS

Out:

"Out is directionless and timeless."

- Cite RBF to EJA, Beverly Hotel, New York, 19 June 1971.

- Citation and context at Directionless, 19 Jun'71

---

RBF DEFINITIONS

Out:

"All the word 'out' means is that you are not
inside a system. 'Out' is not a direction."

- Cite RBF to EJA, Beverly Hotel, New York, 24 April 1971

---

RBF DEFINITIONS

Out:

"Out is nondirectional because it is anydirectional."

- Cite SYNERGETICS draft at Sec.524.05; RBF rewrite of 19 Jun'71

---

RBF DEFINITIONS

Out:

"We . . . realize conceptually the finite, yet non-
sensorial, out-ness which can be converted into sensorial
in-ness by the inside-outing process."

- Cite NEHRU SPEECH, p. 12. 13 Nov'69

---

RBF DEFINITIONS

Out:

"You are always in Universe. You cannot get out of
Universe. You can only get out of systems."

- Cite tape transcript RBF to EJA and BO'R, Chicago, 1 June 1971.

---

RBF DEFINITIONS

"Out" as the Containing & the Contained:

"Joseph Needham's 'above and below' and his 'higher and lower'
are linear.

"'Out' expressly is the containing and the contained: in
synergetics, the omniembracing and the permeating."

- Citation & context at Synergetic Hierarchy, 5 May'74

Out:                                                    (1)

       See Anydirectional
         In & Out
         In, Out & Around
         Point:  Outbound Point
         Outside

---

Outbreeding:

       See Inbreeding, Jun'66

---

Out:                                                    (2)

       See Directionless, 19 Jun'71*

---

Outdividual:

       See Events & Nonevents, 16 Dec'73

---

Outbound Packaging of Human Food Waste:                 (1)

       See Resouces:  Fresh vs. Waste
         Valuable Chemistry

---

Outdoors:

       See Indoors vs. Outdoors

---

Outbound Packaging of Human Food Waste:                 (2)

       See Dymaxion Artifacts, (1)
         Wichita House, (2)
         Scrap Sorting & Mongering, (3)(4)

---

RBF DEFINITIONS

Outlaw:

"Three-quarters of the spherical Earth's surface is water and
men's dry-land-made laws were unenforceable upon the seas.
Those whose lives were lived on the sea lived outside any man-
made laws and were inherently 'outlaws,' not because they
flouted other men's laws, but because they lived and operated
where only the physical laws of Universe were enforced.  And
those laws of nature were often formidably harsh.  The sailormen
had to take the initiative moment upon moment, and with keenest
logic, else they perished.  But the sailormen of Penobscot Bay
addresses as 'Darling' or 'Dear' all young people both of its
own family or of the stranger's family.  He didn't learn to do
so from Hollywood's people.  The 'Darling' custom antedates
Hollywood by at least several centuries.  The custom developed,
we may guess, from the coastal-fisherman's throttling to
idling speed his otherwise powerful and incisive capabilities.
Getting angry at hurricanes won't save you.  'Easy does it,'
they say."

- Cite BEAR ISLAND STORY, galley p.17, 1968

# Synergetics Dictionary

The Outlaw Area:

". . . Since the last ice age three-quarters of the Earth
has been water, and of the one-quarter that is land very
little has been lived on. Ninety-nine percent of humanity
has lived on only about five per cent of the Earth-- a few
little dry spots. Now, the law has always been applicable
only to this five per cent of the Earth, and anyone who
went outside of it-- the tiny minority who went to sea,
for example-- immediately found himself outside the law.
And the whole development of technology has been in the
outlaw area, where you're dealing with the toughness of
nature. I find this fascinating and utterly true. All
improvement has to be made in the outlaw area. You can't
reform man, and you can't improve his situation where he
is. But when you've made things so good out there in
the outlaw area that they can't help being recognized,
then gradually they get drawn in and assimilated. . . .

"A good example of what I mean is going on right now in the
space program . . . where there's no atmosphere and no water
and no sewer lines and no berries to eat, for the first
time in history you have to look out for man. Inadvertently,
man is trying for the first time to learn how to make man a
success. It's inadvertent, but it's being done."

- Cite Calvin Tomkins, New Yorker, p.78, 8 Jan'66

---

Outlaw: Outlaw Area:                                    (1)

See Enterprise
    Frontier: Living on the Frontier
    Pirates: Great Pirates
    Laws of Nature vs. Laws of Man

---

Outlaw:                                                 (2)

See Up & Down Sequence, (4)

---

Outline:

See Windowing the Nothingness, 25 Mar'76

---

Out-lining:

"Out-lining = perimetering: empty-picturing the divergent
outwardness, i.e. somethinging the nothingness: How to see
or identify nothing.

"In-lining = in-sighting: conceptualizing in the direction
of multiexperience trends convergence."

- Cite RBF holograph for EJA; Windsor Castle, Berks; 22 Mar'76

---

Outreach:                                               (1)

See Sweepout

---

Outreach:                                               (2)

See Middle, Feb'73

---

Outset:

See Dymaxion Outset
    Eternal Outset
    Beginnings
    Start: Starters

RBF DEFINITIONS

Outside:

"It might be argued that inside and outside are the same,
but not so. While there are an infinity of insides in
Experience Universe there is only one <u>outside</u> comprehensive
to all insides. So they are not the same..."

- Citation and context at <u>Spherical Triangle Sequence</u> (ii), 26 Jan
'73

RBF DEFINITIONS

Outside-Out:

"Now, what we call thinkable is always <u>outside-out</u>.
What we call space is just exactly as real, but it
is inside-out. There is no such thing as right and
left!"

- ~~Cite Tape transcript RBF to BO'R, Carbondale Dome, 1 May 1971.~~
- Citation at ▆▆▆▆ 1 May'71
        <u>Parity</u>

RBF DEFINITIONS

Outside: <u>What's Outside Outside?</u>:

"I'm sure you have often said to yourself: I wonder what's
outside "<u>outside</u>." That question assumes a static, instant,
sculptural, single-frame concept of Universe, which
sculptural, static array has an '<u>outside</u>.' But you cannot
have an <u>outside</u> to a scenario."

- Cite Museums Keynote Address Denver, p. 10. 2 Jun'71

Outside-out vs. Inside-out:

    See Convex & Concave: Law Of, 27 May'72
       Outside-out, 1 May'71

Outside: <u>What's Outside Outside?</u>:     (1)

    See Sight: No Man Has Ever Seen Outside of Himself
       Imaginary Universe vs. This Universe
       Not Out of This World
       Shapeless: Universe Does Not Have a Shape

Outside:     (1)

    See Convex & Concave
       Insideness & Outsideness
       Rubber Glove
       Shape:
       Sight: No Man Has Ever Seen Outside of Himself
       Spherical Wave
       Shell Growth Rate

Outside: <u>What's Outside Outside?</u>:     (2)

    See Sculpture as Single Frame, 22 Jul'71
       Shapeless: Universe Does Not Have a Shape, 1965
       Measurement, (p.65) 1969
       Out, 1 Jun'71
       Scenario, 24 Apr'67

Outside:     (2)

    See Civil War, (2)
       Parity, 1 May'71*
       Spherical Triangle Sequence, (ii)*

Outward Limit of Nuclear Phenomena:

See Vector Equilibrium: Three-frequency VE, 18 Oct'72

Ovational Gearing:

See Energetic Functions, 1954

Outward:

See Inward & Outward

RBF DEFINITIONS

Overlapping:

"Nouns can be at the same time, but verbs cannot. Events can never be omnicongruently simultaneous, which would mean having all the component-four events' beginnings and endings always simultaneous. Events occur. Occur is a time word. The overlappingness of scenario Universe makes events appear simultaneous when they are not. Events are only overlappingly co-occurrent but never omnisimultaneous."

- Cite SYNERGETICS, 2nd. Ed. at Sec. 530.12, 30 May'75

Oval:

See North Face Domes, 20 Sep'76

RBF DEFINITIONS

Overlapping:

". . . That overlapping quality that gives you a continuity of life despite individual births and deaths."

- Cite RBF in Barry Farrell Playboy Interview, 1972 - Draft. p.17.

Ovaries:

See Female, 20 Apr'72

RBF DEFINITIONS

Overlapping:

"Overlapping because every event has duration and their initiating and terminating are most often of different duration."

- Cite RBF marginalia
  Universe draft
  28 Feb '71

* Cite also SYNERGETICS, "Universe," Sec. 302. Oct. '71.

RBF DEFINITIONS

Overlapping:

"We discover our way by overlapping interrelatednesses."

- Citation & context at Thinking (b), 5 Jul'62

---

Overlays:                                                        (2)

See Synergetics, 1959

---

Overlapping:                                                      (1)

See Interweaving
    Partially Overlapping
    Scenario
    Tapestry
    Young & Elders

---

RBF DEFINITIONS

Overload the System:

". . . The system knew what to do and has been 'overloaded'
or 'starved' by ignorance.  Learn how not to overload or
starve.  Let trace elements be available.  Don't meddle."

- Citation and context at Triangular Topology Integrity, 15 May'72

---

Overlapping:                                                      (2)

See Building, 10 Sep'74
    Death, 22 Jul'71
    Ecology Sequence, (A)
    Human Beings, 1972
    Intuition Sequence, (1)
    Music, 4 Mar'69
    Scenario, May'72
    Thinking, (b)*; 1960
    World Game:  Grand Strategy, 2 Jun'74
    Duality of Universe, May'49
    Otherness Restraints & Elliptical Orbits, (2)
    Alloys, 30 May'75
    Nonsimultaneity, 30 May'75
    Thirty Minimum Topological Characteristics, (1)
    Minimum Awareness, (1)
    Starting with Universe, 31 May'75
    Tunability, 24 Apr'76

---

Overpopulation:

See Population Explosion

---

Overlays:                                                        (1)

See Cumulative Patterning Overlays

---

RBF DEFINITIONS

Overproduction:

Q.        Isn't overproduction an inevitable outcome of
          increasing industrialization?

RBF:      "I talk about disassociating industrialization from
          money-making.  Money-makers hoard and prohibit release
          of good information.  It would only be overproduction
          if stupidity was operating."

- Cite RBF videotaping session Philadelphia, Pa., 1 Feb'75

Oversight: (1)

See Science Opened the Wrong Door

Overspecialization of Biological Species: (1)

See Bird's Nest as a Tool
Extinction
Human Beings at the Center

Oversight: (2)

See Abstraction, 22 Apr'71

Overspecialization of Biological Species: (2)

See Divide & Conquer Sequence (1)
Generalized Principle (4)

RBF DEFINITIONS

Overspecialization of Biological Species and Nations:
"At the December 1962 annual meeting of the American
Association for the Advancement of Science a research
paper was read which showed that biological species and
nations which have become extinct did so because of their
becoming overspecialized."

- For citation and context see Computers As Specialists,
13 Aug '64

Overspecialization of the Sciences:
See Club of Rome: Limits to Growth, (C)

TEXT CITATIONS

Overspecialization of Biological Species:
Generalized Principles, p.3, 28 Jan'69
Trend No. 9, The Prospect for Humanity, WDSD Doc. 3, p. 69, Aug'64

Overspecialization:

See Degenius, 26 Sep'68
Pollution, 12 Jun'69
Nonsimultaneity, 7 Nov'73

Ownership: (1)

See Mine: That's Mine
    Private Property
    Obsolete: Inventory of Obsolete Concepts
    Service Industry
    Cosmic vs. Terrestrial Accounting
    Haveness
    Property: You Can't Take it With You
    Land Exploitation
    Deed: (Proprty Deed)
    Mobile Rentability vs. Immobile Purchasing

Oxygen: (2)

See Biosphere, (1)(2)
    Air, 22 Jan'75
    Human Tolerance Limits, (1)-(4)

Ownership: (2)

See Resources, 4 Jul'72
    Design Science (B)
    Telephone (1)(2)

Oxford University:

See Divide & Conquer Sequence, (4)(5)

Oxygen: (1)

See Circuit: Hydrogen & Oxygen as a Circuit
    Air

**P**

RBF DEFINITIONS

Package:

"'Package' is a thing word and I don't think things; I think verbs. I keep housecleaning my language-- but, there, 'house' is a bad word too. In my spontaneous reflexes I often use reflex thing words. I apologize."

- Cite RBF videotaping in Philadelphia, PA., 1 Feb'75

RBF DEFINITIONS

Package:

"... Angular accelerations are in finite package impelments which are chordal (not Arcs)..."

- Citation and context at Hexagon, Nov'71

RBF DEFINITIONS

Package:

"We package our foods coming inbound: Why don't we package them going outbound? It's just exactly as easy. When nature takes so much trouble to separate liquids and solids it is preposterous to put them together again."

- Citation & context at Wichita House, (1)(2), 31 Jan'75

RBF DEFINITIONS

Packaged Concept:

"... Experience is often a packaged concept. Such packages consist of complexedly interrelated and not as-yet differentially analyzed phenomena which, as initially unit cognitions, are potentially re-experienciable."

- Citation and context at Brain and Rose, 3 Jun'72

RBF DEFINITIONS

Package:

"Radiation is always packaged... All the quanta are local-system, center-of-event activity, focal points-- fractionations of the whole point: what are minimally, ergo most economically packaged, and expanded outwardly and omnidiametrically as three-central-angle-defined tetrahedra."

* Citation and context at Integrity of Universe, 23 Sep'73

Packaged Word:

See Conceptuality, 1965
Earth, 1965
Equanimity Model, 26 May'72
Point, 19 Feb'72; 1 Apr'72
Spherical Triangle Sequence, (c)

RBF DEFINITIONS

Package:

"In the quantum and wave phenomena we deal with individual packages. We do not have continuous surfaces. In synergetics we find the familiar practice of second powering displaying a congruence with the points, or little separate energy packages of the shell arrays. Electromagnetic frequencies of systems are sometimes complex, but they always exist in complementation of gravitational forces and together provide prime rational integer characteristics in all physical systems. Little energy actions, little separate stars: this is what we mean by quantum. Synergetics provides geometrical conceptuality in respect to energy quanta."

[31]

- Cite SYNERGETICS draft at Sec. 964.12, 17 Nov'72

RBF DEFINITIONS

Packaged:

"Each experience begins and ends; ergo is finite. Because our apprehending is packaged, both physically and metaphysically, into time increments of alternate awakeness and asleepness as well as into separate finite conceptions such as the discrete energy quanta and the atomic nucleus components of the fundamental physical discontinuity, all experiences are finite."

- Citation & context at Universe (p.62), 1969

RBF DEFINITIONS

Packaged:

"It is the nature of all of our experiences that they begin
and end. They are packaged. For instance, we see in 60
separate picture frames per second, as in a moving-picture
continuity. Each frame is a finite increment. Our brain's
afterimage lag is so powerful that it gives a sense of
absolute eccentricity [ sic ] to our only-subconsciously
packaged seeing. We wake up and go to sleep."

- ~~Cite NASA Speech, p.33, Jun'66~~
- Citation and context at Finite, Jun'66

---

Paddle:

See Precession, (II)

---

Package:                                                (1)

See Container
    Discontinuity
    Discrete
    Energy Package
    Finite Package
    Photon
    Quantum
    Vector Equilibrium Package
    Periodic Experience
    Terminal
    Outbound Packaging

---

Pain:

See Good & Evil Sequence, (2)
    Human Beings & Complex Universe, (1)

---

Package:   Packaged:                                    (2)

See Centers of Energy Rebirth, 16 Nov'72
    Finite, Jun'66*
    Hexagon, Nov'71*
    In, 1 Jun'71
    Integrity of Universe, 23 Sep'73*
    Metaphysics, 2 Jul'62
    Point: Outbound Point, 23 Sep'73
    Polyhedron, 20 Feb'73
    Powering (B)
    Rose, 3 Jun'72*
    Thinkability: Thinkable System Takeout, 16 Jun'72
    Thinking (2)
    Universe (p.62) 1969
    Dwelling Service Industry (B)(D)
    Scenario, 1 Feb'75
    Wichita House, (1)(2)*
    Dome House Grand Strategy: 1927-1977, (2)
    Human Beings & Complex Universe, (1)

---

**PAIRED CONCEPTS: CHECKLIST**                          (A)

See Aesthetics & Intuition*
    Annihilation & Conservation*
    Annihilation & Synergy
    Antipriorities & Priorities*
    Apprehending & Comprehending
    Articulated & Unarticulated
    Articulating & Observing*
    Aesthetics & Integrity
    Angle & Frequency
    Action & Thought*
    Artifact & Grand Strategy
    Always & Only
    Away & Ago

*Indexed under other formulation

---

Packet:

See Autonomous Living Technology Packet

---

Paired Concepts:   Checklist:                           (B)

See Boast & Fear
    Bias: Fear & Political Bias*
    Bonding & Degrees of Freedom*
    Black Holes & Synergetics
    Behavior & Environment

* Indexed under other formulation

Paired Concepts: Checklist:                                    (C)

    See Circuit & Noncircuit
        Comprehending & Apprehending*
        Connections & Relatedness
        Critical Proximity & Orbital Escape*
        Conservation & Annihilation
        Complementary & Reciprocal
        Consciousness & Time*
        Climate & Intellect
        Cosmic Discontinuity & Local Continuity
        Convergence & Nonconvergence
        Cold & Vacuum
        Cognition & Time*
        Coming Apart & Holding Together
        Conceptuality & Space
        Congruence & Incongruence
        Complex Universe & Human Beings*

* Indexed under other formulation

---

Paired Concepts: Checklist:                                    (G)

        See Geometry & Number
            Gravity & Frequency*
            Growth & Decay
            Grand Strategy & Artifact*
            Generalists & Specialists

* Indexed under other formulation

---

Paired Concepts: Checklist:                                    (D)

    See Discovery & Loss
        Domain & Quantum
        Discontinuity & Energy Flow*
        Degrees of Freedom & Bonding
        Decay & Growth*

*Cited under other formulation

---

Paired Concepts:                                               (H)

        See Human Mind & Physical Evolution
            Holding Together & Coming Apart
            Human Beings & Hard Machinery
            Human Beings & Complex Universe

---

Paired Concepts: Checklist:                                    (E)

    See Energy & Number
        Escape: Orbital Escape & Critical Proximity*
        Experiences & Principles
        Energy & Information
        Energy & Intellect
        Energy & Time
        Elliptical Orbits & Otherness Restraints*
        Energy Flow & Discontinuity
        Embracement & Nucleus*
        Energy & Volume
        Energy & Thought*
        Eventings & Sensings*
        Environment & Behavior*
        Everywhere & Everywhen

* Indexed under other formulation

---

Paired Concepts: Checklist:                                    (I)

        See Information & Energy*
            Intellect & Energy*
            Intellect & Climate*
            Intuition & Aesthetics
            Intellect & Physical Universe*
            Integrity & Aesthetics*
            Islanded Radiation & Tensional Constancy
            Incongruence & Congruence*
            Inescapable & Only*

* Indexed under other formulation

---

Paired Concepts: Checklist:                                    (F)

    See Fear & Longing
        Fear & Political Bias
        Figures & Words
        Fear & Boast*
        Frequency & Mass*
        Frequency & Angle*
        Frequency & Gravity
        Frequency & Magnitude
        Frequency & Wave

* Indexed under other formulation

---

Paired Concepts: Checklist:                                    (K)

        See Know-how, Export Of & Transnational Capitalism*

* Indexed under other formulation

Paired Concepts:  Checklist:                                    (L)

    See Longing & Fear*
        Loss & Discovery*
        Local Continuity & Cosmic Discontinuity*
        Love & Truth*
        Line & Nonline

* Indexed under other formulation

---

Paired Concepts:  Checklist:                                    (P)

    See Proximity & Remoteness
        Proximity:  Orbital Escape & Critical Proximity*
        Political Bias & Fear*
        Principles & Experience*
        Priorities & Antipriorities
        Physical Evolution & Human Mind*
        Physical Universe & Intellect*
        Principle & Resource*

* Indexed under other formulation

---

Paired Concepts:  Checklist:                                    (M)

    See Mechanics & Structure*
        Mass & Frequency
        Magnitude & Frequency*

* Indexed under other formulation

---

Paired Concepts:  Checklist:                                    (Q)

    See Quantum & Domain*

* Indexed under other formulation

---

Paired Concepts:  Checklist:                                    (N)

    See Noncircuit & Circuit*
        Nonself & Self*
        Number & Energy*
        Now & Self*
        Nontruth & Truth
        Nonconvergence & Divergence*
        Number & Geometry*
        Nonline & Line*
        Nucleus & Embracement

* Indexed under other formulation

---

Paired Concepts:  Checklist:                                    (R)

    See Remoteness & Proximity*
        Relatedness & Connections*
        Reciprocal & Complementary*
        Review & View*
        Rate & Terminal
        Reinvestable Time & Survival Needs
        Resource & Principle

* Indexed under other formulation

---

Paired Concepts:  Checklist:                                    (O)

    See Orbital Escape & Critical Proximity
        Otherness Restraints & Elliptical Orbits
        Otherness & Self*
        Observing & Articulating
        Only & Always*
        Only and Inescapable

* Indexed under other formulation

---

Paired Concepts:  Checklist:                                    (S)

    See Self & Nonself
        Synergy & Annihilation*
        Self & Unity*
        Structure & Mechanics
        Syntropy & Time
        Self & Otherness
        Self-now
        Surface-volume*
        System & Zero*
        Spheres & Vertexes
        Structural Performance & Size
        Space & Conceptuality*
        Survival Needs & Reinvestible Time*
        Space Nothingness & Time Somethingness
        Synergetics & Black Holes*
        Sensings & Eventings
        Sleeping & Thinking
        Specialists & Generalists*

* Indexed under other formulation

Paired Concepts:  Checklist:                                                    (T)


        See Time & Energy
            Time & Consciousness
            Time & Syntropy*
            Truth & Love
            Truth & Nontruth
            Time & Cognition
            Terminal & Rate*
            Thought & Action
            Thought & Energy
            Tensional Constancy & Islanded Radiation*
            Transnational Capitalism & Export of Know-how
            Time Somethingness & Space Nothingness*
            Tuning-in & Tuning-out
            Thinking & Sleeping*


* Indexed under other formulation

---

Paired Concepts:  Checklist:                                                    (Z)


        See Zero & System

---

Paired Concepts:  Checklist:                                                    (U)


        See Unity & Self
            Unarticulated & Articulated*
            Unstructurings & Restructurings


* Indexed under other formulation

---

FILE INDICATORS

Paired Concepts:  Checklist:                                                    (1)

        See Complementarities:  Always & Only Coexisiting
            Dichotomy:  Dichotomizing
            Equals:  Checklist
            Inventory of Push-pulling Alternations
            Nonequals:  Checklist
            Versus:  Checklist

---

Paired Concepts:  Checklist:                                                    (V)


        See Volume-surface
            Vacuum & Cold*
            View & Review
            Vertexes & Spheres*
            Volume & Energy*


* Indexed under other formulation

---

Paired Concepts:                                                                (2)


        See Complementarity, 12 Sep'71

---

Paired Concepts:  Checklist:                                                    (W)


        See Words & Figures*
            Wave & Frequency*


* Indexed under other formulation

---

Paired Congruency:                                                              (1)


        See Reciprocal Involvement
            Sleeping in the Same Bed

Paired Congruency:                                    (2)


        See Congruence, 25 Aug'71

---

RBF DEFINITIONS

Palpitate:

"... Nature oscillates and palpitates asymmetrically
in respect to the frame of the omnirational vector
equilibrium, the plus and minus magnitudes of asymmetry
are rational fractions of the omnirationality of the
equilibrious state. . ."


- Citation & context at Vector Equilibrium, 21 Dec'71
- Cite RBF to EJA, 3200 Idaho, Washington DC, 21 Dec. '71.

---

Pair: Pairing:                                        (1)


        See Cofunctions
            Coupled: Coupling
            Covariables: Covariation
            Paired Concepts: Checklist
            Prime Numbers: Pairing Of
            Swimmers: Two Swimmers
            Twins
            Two Kinds of Twoness
            Quantum: Event-paired Quanta

---

Palpitate:                                            (1)


        See Oscillation
            Oscillation & Pulsation
            Pulse: Pulsive: Pulsivity

---

Pair: Pairing:                                        (2)

        See Generalized Dichotomy: Grand Srtategy, (1)

---

Palpitate: Palpitation:                               (2)


        See Now, 14 Feb'72
            Physical Reality, 1 May'71
            Vector Equilibrium, 21 Dec'71*; 1 May'71
            Modules: A & B Quanta Modules, 20 Dec'73

---

Palm:


        See Pine Tree & Palm Tree Belts

---

TEXT CITATIONS

Pandora's Box of Invisibility:


        (See Transcript of RBF address to MXC,
        Dubuque, IA, 15 Dec. '71, p. 17.)

Panic:                                                    (1)


        See Official Panic
            Fire in a Theater

---

Parable:

"Playboy: 'But since you mentioned Adam and Eve a moment
ago, let's take the Garden of Eden as a parable and ask if
the element of man's will mightn't make him a stranger to
this universal perfection. Couldn't the Scenario Universe
be a tragedy as far as human affairs are concerned?"

"Fuller: 'In the first place I don't take anything as a
parable. I'm interested in stories if I can understand them,
but I don't use fiction as the basis of doing any strong
thinking, especially when it comes to such matters as
'man's will.' I think we'd better not assume that what
we've been told about the Garden of Eden has any validity
whatsoever. I don't think there was a Garden of Eden, and
I don't think there was an Adam and Eve, and I don't think
Eve was born out of Adam's rib. So I can't accept the
parable.'"

- Cite RBF in Barry Farrell PLAYBOY Interview, February 1972,
  Above passage was in BF transcript, but omitted from final
  passage as it appears on p. 66. of magazine.

---

Panic:                                                    (2)


        See Human Tolerance Limits, (2)

---

Parable:

        See Christian Legend & Philosophy
            Goldilocks and the Three Bears
            Myth
            Naga Theme
            Legend

---

Paper:  Sheet of Paper:                                   (1)


        See Child Tearing Paper
            Newspaper
            Foldability
            Mark Your Paper

---

Parabola:  Paraboloid:

        See Hyperbolic Paraboloid

---

Paper:  Sheet of Paper:                                   (2)


        See Curvature: Simple, (1)
            Drawing, 1971
            Squatters, (1)

---

Paradox:                                                  (1)


        See Computer: Paradox of the Computer
            Zeno's Paradox

Paradox: (2)

See Artist: Histrionics (1)

RBF DEFINITIONS

Parallelism:

"Parallelism is uniquely characterizing the three
dimensional system."

- Cite Carbondale Draft
        Nature's Coordination IV,30
- Cite Oregon Lecture, #7, p. 245. 11 Jul'62

RBF DEFINITIONS

Parallax:

"When the relative circle size in respect to the observer is
of macro-differential magnitudes, such as that of the circumference of the galactic system in respect to each planet
observer, then the central-angle magnitude of the subtended
macrocosmic arc becomes undetectable and the astronomer and
navigator assume parallelism-- parallax-- to have set in, which
produces a constant factor of error which must be incorporated
in mathematical formulation of system descriptions.  In quantum
accounting and analysis of energy events and transformative
transactions, this parallelism separates one quantum tetrahedron
from its three surrounding tetrahedra."

- Cite SYNERGETICS draft at Sec. 539.10, 23 Sep'73

RBF DEFINITIONS

Parallel: Quasi-Parallel Lines:

The bow tie symbol "is currently more fitting as an equation
symbol than the old equation mark because we know that
parallel lines, or conditions, are impossible.  Moreover,
quasi-parallel lines, never coming in contact, are
procreatively sterile."

"The "=" is, then, inaccurate as a sign to link integrators
and product."

- Cite NINE CHAINS, p. 42 , 1938
- Citation & context at Teleology:  Bow Tie Symbol, 1938

RBF DEFINITIONS

Parallel:

"There can be no nucleus with parallels."

- Cite RBF holograph at SYNERGETICS 2, Sec. 100.000; 28 Mar'77

Parallel: Quasi-parallel Lines:

See Teleology:  Bow Tie Symbol, 1938*

RBF DEFINITIONS

Parallel:

"Parallel and antiparallel are precession."

- Cite RBF marginalia dated 5 Sept 1965 in "The Scientific
  Endeavor," (1093) - page 12.
- Citation at Precession, 5 Sep'65

Parallel: (1)

See Antiparallel
    Inflection
    Interparallel
    Nonparallel
    Parallax
    Convergent vs. Parallel Perception
    Series vs. Parallel Circuitry
    XYZ Coordinate System

Parallel: (2)

See Curvature: Simple, (1)(2)
Equation Symbol, 9 May'60
Terminals, 4 Feb'68
Dimensionality, 30 Mar'75
Means, 22 Jun'75
Minimum Limit Case, 12 May'75
Nature in a Corner, 6 Nov'75
Verse vs. Prose, 11 Dec'75
Nuclear Pattern of Growth & Decay, 8 Dec'75
Dynamic Equilibrium, 24 Apr'76
Module: A Quanta Module: Introduction Of,
22 Feb'77

Parallelogram of Forces:

See Force Lines: Omnidirectional Lines of Force

Parallelogram: (1)

See Deliberately Nonstraight Line

Parallelogram: (2)

See Prime Vector, (2)(3)

RBF DEFINITIONS

Parameters:

". . . The variables outside the system may affect
the system from outside. In varying degrees specific
levels of sub-classes of these 'background' or outside
variables are identified as parameters. This background
'inside and outside' concept is a two dimensional or flat-
projection concept."

- Cite OMNIDIRECTIONAL HALO, p. 153 , 1960

RBF DEFINITIONS

Parameters:

"Our omnioriented Halo concept converts the papameter
consideration to conceptual four dimensionality and discloses
a set of parameters inside as well as outside the zone of
lucidly considered ■■■ system■ stars. And the parameters
are at minimum fourfold: (1) the convex twilight zone of
inward relevancy, (2) the concave twilight zone of outward
relevancy, (3) the stark nonconceptual irrelevancy inward,
and (4) the stark nonconceptual irrelevancy outward. Parameter (1) is a tetrahedron. Parameter (2) is a tetrahedron.
Parameter (3) plus parameter (4) comprise an invisible
tetrahedron."

- Cite OMNIDIRECTIONAL HALO, p. 153, 1960

- Citation & context at Halo Concept, 1960

Parameters: Parametric:

See General Systems Theory, 18 Dec'74; ■■ (B)
Halo Concept, 1960*; Nov'71
Variables: Theory Of, 1960; Nov'71
Design Science: Grand Strategy, 31 Jan'75
Omnihalo, Nov'71

Parapsychology:

See No Magic Universe, 8 Apr'75

# Synergetics Dictionary

RBF DEFINITIONS

Parents:

"Sometimes parents say 'don't' because they want to protect the child from getting into trouble. At other times, when they fail to say 'no,' the child gets into trouble. The child, frustrated, stops exploring."

- Cite RBF in AAUW Journal, p. 174, May '65

---

Parent: (1)

See Children
Education
Mother
Television: Third Parent

---

Parent: (2)

See Environment, 22 Jul'71
Fresh, 3 Oct'71

---

RBF DEFINITIONS

Parity:

"That is the way our Universe is. There are the visibles and the invisibles of the inside-outing nonsimultaneity. What we call thinkable is always outside-out. What we call space is just exactly as real, but is inside out. There is no such thing as right and left."

- Cite SYNERGETICS text at Sec. 507.02, Nov'71

---

RBF DEFINITIONS

Parity:

"Now, what we call thinkable is always outside-out. What we call space is just exactly as real, but it is inside-out. There is no such thing as right and left!"

- Cite Rbf to BO'R. Carbondale Dome, 1 May 1971.

CONCEPTUALITY PARITY- SEC 507.02

---

RBF DEFINITIONS

Parity:

"Positive (right) and Negative (left) make
one tetrahedron;
therefore no parity.
1 + 1 = 4.

- Cite P. PEARCE, Inventory of Concepts, June 1967

CONCEPTUALITY- PARITY- SEC 507.04

---

RBF DEFINITIONS

Parity:

"We cannot build Universe with just the rightness or leftness 'blocks' exclusively of one another."

- Citation and context at Monological, Jun'66

---

RBF DEFINITIONS

Parity:

". . . Physics long-held law of conservation of parity held the obverse and reverse to be identical, ergo, redundant."

- Cite OMNIDIRECTIONAL HALO, 1960, Pp. 153-156.

RBF DEFINITIONS

Parity: ▓▓▓▓▓▓▓▓▓▓▓▓▓

"Comprehensive system turbining: the whole system turbines
positively or the whole system turbines negatively.  There
are no polar or opposite hemisphere differences of these
systems.  There are no 'rights' or 'lefts' in Universe."

- Cite SYNERGETICS ILLUSTRATION, #92, caption. 1967

---

Partial Generalization:

See Vector, 26 May'72

---

RBF DEFINITIONS

▓▓▓▓ Parity & Disparity:

"Disparity is a complementary of parity."

- Cite RBF to EJA, Beverly Hotel, New York, 19 June 1971.

CONCEPTUALITY— PARITY— SEC. 507.05)

---

RBF DEFINITIONS

Partiality:

"... A vector is a partial generalization being either
metaphysically theoretical or physically realized, and
in either sense an abstraction of a special case..."

- Citation and context at Vector, 26 May'72

---

RBF DEFINITIONS

Parity & Disparity:

"The complementary of parity is disparity and not a reflective
image."

- Cite RBF reqrite of SYNERGETICS galley at Sec. 507.06, 6 Nov'73

---

RBF DEFINITIONS

Partiality:

Q:  Is partiality a complementary of totality?

A:  Synergy says partiality is inherently a complementary,
    which means it is not witnessable in the part, per se.
    The part does not say it, but they are always intercom-
    plementarities.  You have to have the other parts in
    order for them to be complemented by.

- Cite RBF answer dictated to EJA, Kennedy airport, NY,
  1 Apr '72

---

Parity:

See Complementarity
    Complementor
    Disparity
    Left & Right
    Negative
    Mirror Image
    Non-mirror Image
    Parity & Disparity
    Proton & Neutron
    Rubber Glove

---

RBF DEFINITIONS

Partiality:

"Compression is inherently partial.  Tension is inherently
total."

- Citation at Tension & Compression, Dec'71

- Cite Synergetics Draft at Sec. 640.70, Dec. '71.

RBF DEFINITIONS

Partiality:

"Conceptuality is systematic but always partial."

- ~~Cite RBF at Students International Meditation Seminar -~~
  ~~U. Mass., Amherst, 22 July 1971.~~

- Citation at Conceptuality, 22 Jul'71

---

Partiality:                                               (1)

See Cosmic Partiality
    Part: Parts: Partial: Particulars
    Totality

---

Partiality:                                               (2)

See Conceptuality, 22 Jul'71*
    Experience, 12 Sep'71
    Tension & Compression, Dec'71*
    Vector, 26 May'72*

---

RBF DEFINITIONS

Partially Overlapping:

"The complex of event sequences are most often characterized
by overlappings. A man is born, grows up, has children and
grandchildren. His life overlaps that of his grandfather and
father and that of his children and grandchildren. But his
grandfather's life did not overlap his childrens' nor his
grandchildrens' lives. Hence, partially overlapping."

                    - Cite RBF marginalia
                      Universe draft - 28 Feb 1971

FOOTNOTE - SEC. 302.00

---

Partially Overlapping:

        See Newton vs. Einstein (2)
            Scenario, 1 Feb'75

---

RBF DEFINITIONS

Particle:

"The primitive is quite different from the fundamental
particles game of the high-energy research physicists."

                    - Citation & context at Primitive, 19 Feb'76

---

RBF DEFINITIONS

Particle:

    "A unique energy patterning-- erroneously referred

to in archaic terms as a particle."

                    ~~Cite NEHRU SPEECH, P. 12, 13 Nov'69~~

                    - Citation & context at Annihilation, 13 Nov'69

CONCEPTUALITY - SEC. 507.05

---

RBF DEFINITIONS

Particle:                                                 (1)

"One of the most interesting things about the modern
chemistry and physics is that men have discovered that
there are no things, there are no small particles. The
physicist deliberately misleads society by using the
words 'solid state' and things like that and by still
using the word particle. .. he may say that of course,
he doesn't mean anything by it, but he just doesn't know
what else to call it.. He is so busy with his work that
he doesn't want to bother with semantics so he calls it a
particle. There is some kind of local preoccupation here
and we just call it particle. We identify it as special
local behavior. It is a special local behavior but it is
pure principle, such as the wave concept. It has no weight
whatsoever. . .

"We well then get in to what we call the nucleus, the
positive particles if you want to call them that. But it has
since been discovered that every one of them has an anti-
particle. All the negative particles have negative weight
and so you have neutrons, positrons, and so on: you have
positives, and negatives and neutrals. The sum total of

                    - Cite Oregon Lecture #4, p.123, 6 Jul'62

RBF DEFINITIONS

### Particle: (2)

"all the positive weights and all the negative weights is
zero. You are dealing in pure principle. This is the actual
fact. And it is weightless. There is no smallest thing.
There are very minute energy events in pure pattern, but they
are pure pattern-- just as the knot was not a rope but a pure
regenerative principle. The wave was not the water or the
milk or the kerosene. The quantum in wave mechanics is
simply the way we deal with these pure principles in an
absolutely weightless manner."

- Cite Oregon Lecture #4, pp.122-123, 6 Jul'62

---

RBF DEFINITIONS

### Particles:

"There are no ponderable, smallest, hard-core,
'thing' particles."

Cite SECOND HAND GOD, p.36
9 Apr'40

---

### Particle: Particular: (1)

See ▮▮▮▮▮▮▮▮▮▮▮
    Wave vs. Particle
    Whole to Particular
    Corpuscle: Corpuscular
    Rules of No Actual Particulate Solids
    Strange Particles
    No Building Blocks
    Quarks

---

### Particle: Particular: (2)

See Energy Event, 13 Mar'73
    Minimum Set, 18 Nov'72
    Modelability, (a)
    Invisibility of Macro- and Micro- Resolutions, (2)
    Primitive, 19 Feb'76*
    Proofs, 3 May'77
    Bubble Bursting, 20 Jan'78

---

RBF DEFINITIONS

### Particularity:

"Quantum implies particularity."

- For citation and context see Module,1 Jun '71

---

RBF DEFINITIONS

### Particulate Model:

"Because of indeterminism, discontinuity, the exclusive
tenuous ▬ nature of integrity, means that no hard
particulate models may ever be fashioned by man."

- Citation at Tenuous, 10 Feb'73

---

### Particulate: Particulate Model:

See Quantum, 17 Feb'73

---

RBF DEFINITIONS

### Particulate:

"The tetrahedron can be considered as a whole system or as
a constituent of systems in particular. It is the particulate."

- Citation at Tetrahedron, 7 Mar'73

Parting the Strands:                                (1)


      See Grass:  Putting Aside the Grasses
         Swimmer:  I Am a Swimmer

---

RBF DEFINITIONS

    Parts:

    "Functions occur only as parts of systems."

    - Citation and context at Functions, 26 May'72

---

Parting the Strands:                                (2)


     See Self-experience. 1938

---

RBF DEFINITIONS

    Parts:

    "... The more symmetrical, the less the number of parts types."

    - Citation and context at Simplicity, 1954-59

---

RBF DEFINITIONS

    Part:

    "The Ancient Greeks initiated problem solving
    By recourse to cosmology and cosmogony,
    By proceeding from the whole to the part
    Lest they miss
    The exquisite relevance
    Of each little part or event."

    - Citation at Wholes & Parts, May'72
    - Cite INTUITION, p.174, May '72

---

RBF DEFINITIONS

    Parts:

    "It is a derivative corollary of synergy that there are no
    parts, for parts always turn out to be subsystems of pattern.
    There is only pattern, there is only wholeness to begin and
    cease: the environment and content of all experience or
    experiment.

    "It is a corollary of synergy that behaviors of subdivisions
    are of plural and alternate sets permitted and required of
    the larger pattern; and that there are always sets of
    complementary consequence ◼ in respect to any of the
    selectable alternate permissible sets.  Plurality of
    permitted freedoms within the whole is manyfold.

    "Effectiveness of synergetics is relative to comprehensiveness
    of initiation, its sub-behaviors being determinable to
    degrees of refinement permitting event prognostication
    within circumscribed limits of high fidelity attunement."

    - Cite RBF draft Ltr. to Jim (Fitzgibboh ?), Raleigh, NC, 1954-59,
       ◼ p.4a.

---

RBF DEFINITIONS

    Part:

    "And in fact

    No property of one part

    Considered only by itself

    Predicts the existence of another part--"

    - Cite INDTION, p.27, May '72

---

RBF DEFINITIONS

    Parts:

    "So-called fabricated parts of synergetic general assemblies,
    it should be remembered, are in themselves a complex of
    systems of overall morphation classification and function
    integrations; in turn comprised of multibillions of molecules,
    combining in themselves a plurality of unique atomic nuclear
    systems and their respective subsystem activities, each of
    which responds to its cues in the ever present larger
    synergetic patterns of local alloys or within the far larger
    synergetics of isotopal decay by transformation cycles."

    - Cite RBF draft Ltr. to Jim (Fitzgibbon?) Raleigh, NC, 1954-59
       p.14

Parts: Each Part in View of the Others:                    (1)

See Self-consideration

---

Parts: Each Part in View of the Others:                    (2)

See Design, 9 Dec'73

---

Parts: Self-parts-replacing:

See Industrial Complex, 13 Mar'73

---

Part: Parts: Partial: Particulars:                    (1A) ▬

See Between
No Building Blocks
Energetics
No Absolute Division into Parts
Partiality
Particle
Particularity
Modules
Starting with Parts
Toenail
Wave vs. Particle
Prediction
Nonsystem Parts
Key-keyhole
Wholes & Parts
Highway is Part of the Automobile
Mine is Part of the Mole
Nest is Part of the Bird
Tools are Part of Human Beings
Teleology = Reuniting of Parts

---

Part: Parts: Partial: Particulars:                    (1B)

See Component
Increment
Cosmic Parts: Cosmic Partiality
Human Parts Replacement

---

Part: Parts: Partial:                    (2A) ▬

See Child, 16 Jun'72
Conditioning, 14 Feb'72
Design, 9 Dec'73; 13 Dec'73; 4 Aug'74
Education (2)
Energetics & Synergetics, 10 Jan'74
Epistemology of Quantum Mechanics, 16 Dec'73
Functions, 26 May'72*
Gestalt, 1960
Instant Universe (1)
Local Change, May'49
Mechanical Mind, 22 Jul'71
Simplicity, 1954*
Spaceship Earth (c)
Science (2)
Specialization, 28 Apr'71
Whole System, 28 May'72; 16 Jun'72
Synergetics vs. Model, 28 Apr'74; (A)
Dome: Rationale For (I)(II)
Conceptuality, 16 Aug'70
Thinkability, 16 Aug'70
Time-size, 30 Oct'72

---

Part: Parts: Partial: Particulars:                    (2B)

See Definable. 1959
Plumbing, (1)(2)
Weapons Technology, (2)
Boeing 747 Sequence, 22 Jun'75
Understanding, 30 Sep'76
Generalization & Special Case, 23 Jan'77
Event, 23 Jan'77
Finite Event Scenario, (2)

---

Partitions:

See Privacy, 22 Apr'61

RBF DEFINITIONS

Pass: "And It Came to Pass":

"I used 'pass-age' all the time in Shelter Magazine. It means the same thing as 'and it came to pass,' which means it came to pass, but not to stay."

- Cite RBF to EJA & Bob Kahn in Phila. office, 22 Jun'75

---

Pass: "And It Came to Pass":

See Frame of Reference, 4 Oct'72

---

RBF DEFINITIONS

Pass: "And It Came to Pass":

"...'And it came to pass' is something like an event. It has a 'before' and an 'after'..."

- Cite RBF to Hugh Kenner, NY City, 29 Jun'72

---

Pass:

See Twist-pass

---

RBF DEFINITIONS

Pass: "And It Came to Pass":

"Bill Whitehead had never realized that 'And it came to pass' means 'It came to go by,' that is something we could use as a chart or guidepost."

- Cite RBF to EJA by telephone from Phila., 1 Apr'73

---

Passion:

See Intellection, Oct'66
Technocracy, 1938

---

TEXT CITATIONS

Pass: "And It Came To Pass":

Synergetics text at Sec. 464.08

---

RBF DEFINITIONS

Passive Resistance:

"Passive resistance will not amplify the production of

life support."

- Cite WORLD-AROUND PROBLEMS THAT HAVE TO BE SOLVED BY BLOODLESS DESIGN SCIENCE REVOLUTION, 29 Jun'72

Passive:

See Active & Passive

Past Otherness:

See No-time-and-away-ago, 28 May'75
Tetratuning, 30 May'75
Environment, (A)

Passport:                                          (1)

See World Passports

Past:                                              (1)

See Historical Event Cognition
History
Yesterday
Swivel-moored the the Tonnage of our Past

Passports:                                         (2)

See World Pattern vs. Local Pattern, 29 Jan'75
Desovereignization Sequence, (3)

Past:

See Death, 1970
Life, 1 Jun'71*
Now, 25 Apr'71

RBF DEFINITIONS

Past:

"Life is the Now event with its reaction Past and

resultant Future."

RBF DEFINITIONS

Patent:

"A basic patent must be statable in one line.  That's the
mark of an original invention."

- Citation at Life, 1 Jun'71
- Cite RBF Marginalia, SYNERGETICS Draft (Conceptuality, Life),
  1 June 1971

- Cite RBF to EJA, 3200 Idaho, Wash,DC, 16 Dec'73

RBF DEFINITIONS

**Patent:**

"Patent law and precedence requires specific choices of technical ways and means for each patent claim. A number of claims can be filed covering alternate realizations of the same invention. Overall legal costs per patent are so high that usually but few of the alternate realizations are covered, the most economical under the contemporary economical conditions being hopefully selected by the inventor. . . ."

- Citation and context at Inventability Sequence (2), 9 Jul'73

---

**Patent:**                                                                (1)

See Inventability Sequence
    Invention

---

RBF DEFINITIONS

**Patent:**

"It is interesting that the Russians go along with the old patent idea. You can't apply for one; the government simply awards it at the point when it comes into use. And if the invention is so good that it gets adopted within 12 months, they award a patent and a patent in Russia gives the individual the right to go into any establishment and look things over and see what he might do; it gives him the right to ride wherever he wants on the transportation system; it is really a more effective thing than what we have here. He gets a fundamental advantage and an actual payment.

"It's interesting that the idea of giving inventors some advantage persisted from the olf feudal monarchies through democracy and into communism.

"A patent in the United States is just a license to sue. There have been over 300 licenses of geodesic domes and over 50 have been to big, major corporations. Every time their patent attorneys would come to mine, saying of course we'd like to get around your patent but it's too well written, so we have to come to you.... You absolutely have to have a world patent; a U.S. patent is useless."

- Cite RBF to Barry Farrell; Bear Island; Tape #8, Side A, transcript p.5; 22 Aug '70

---

**Patent:**                                                                (2)

See Einstein, 23 May'72; (A)
    Philosophers, 22 Aug'70
    Cosmic vs. Terrestrial Accounting, (2)
    Large Patterns, (1)
    Dymaxion Airocean World Map, (5)(6); (1)

---

RBF DEFINITIONS

**Patent:**

"In general, it can be said that patents are never granted for covering fundamental principles of nature. You cannot patent any unique geometry. I have a great many patents and none of them are ▮▮▮▮▮▮▮▮▮▮▮ granted in the terms of the specific mechanical, structural, and chemical technology employed to realize an interaction of a plurality of principles.

"It is also necessary that there be a fundamental surprise quality in an invention. Though patents can be secured from the patent office, they hold up in court when this fundamentally unique and illusive quality of surprise is undeniably present....

"I am saying these many things to you not with the idea of discouraging you as an inventor but to save you money in your patent work. I have always found it a great help to have powerful patent searches made. They often disclose earlier invention in areas where I had thought myself to be the inventor. I never let an earlier invention discourage me, but I do not want to kid myself into thinking I am an inventor when I am not."

- Cite RBF Ltr. to Steve Baer, 19 Apr'66

---

**Path:**

See Critical Path
    Parting the Strands
    Trail
    Trajectory

---

RBF DEFINITIONS

**Patent**

"The patent examiner's actions of one-third of a century call for subdivision because there is no comprehensive dynamic class of functioning environment valve.

"This is the case for simplicity in legal action where the simplest rather than the most complicated documents are most effective and most costly. The criterion for a basic patent is one of approximately one sentence, or one line in length-- ergo, most far-reaching and of highest value, and resultant to the largest experience, and greatest breadth and penetration of thought and therefore resultant to greatest experience-- which is basic cost, ergo, most costly; but because of its end result being mistaken by the many for the just naturally obvious simplicity and therefore of negligible cost."

(Slightly edited)

- Cite RBF holograph in cardboard file folder of Synergetic Notes, circa 1955

---

RBF DEFINITIONS

**Pathology: Preventive vs. Curative:**                                     (1)

"Nobody seemed to know where the housing traditions and the diseases they bred came from and why they were going on. I could not seem to be able to maintain health conditions as I wanted them in the kind of rentals I could afford, and I blamed it very much on housing. The more I saw of the housing world the more it seemed to me that about this great ignorance much could be done if we could think of our whole economics in the terms of preventive pathology instead of curative pathology. In our curative pathology we wait until somebody is very sick, and if they are lucky they might be able to get the right drugs from the research institute. I am talking of the picture of 1927.

"This present war has, however, seen an enormous advance in these curative matters. One of our boys here today had an infection in his nose which started in his eye the day before yesterday. They rushed him to the hospital and they gave him penicillin. He is all right now. It might have been a fatal case a few years ago, since the infection would have gone right up into his brain. It is just wonderful; but that has happened now in 1946. War releases an enormous amount of technology, and that is at least one benefit showing up."

- Cite DESIGNING A NEW INDUSTRY, (RBF Reader, pp.153,154) 1946

RBF DEFINITIONS

Pathology: <u>Preventive vs. Curative</u>:         (2)

"But that came as a remedial form of pathology.

"If we were really to attempt preventive pathology, we would
question how these things got started and, it seemed to me in
1927, we would learn to measure and to adopt the enormous
amount of data being sent down by technologists everywhere
relative to measurements of man's Universe and man himself
and the forces seeking to destroy him and we would try to
build in advance a form of environment control for man that
would be both occupationally, in the manufacture of this
environment control, and equally, in its end use, prvent
much of the present inroads of physical and mental and moral
diseases into good health and well-being and general happiness."

      - Cite DESIGNING A NEW INDUSTRY, (RBF Reader, p. 154), 1946

---

Pathology: <u>Preventive vs. Curative</u>:         (1)

      See Mend vs. Cure

---

Pathology: <u>Preventive vs. Curative</u>:         (2)

      See Economics, 1946

---

<u>Patron</u>: <u>Patronage</u>:

      See Artist-scientist, May'60
         Invisible Architecture, (A)(B)(D)

---

RBF DEFINITIONS

<u>Pattern</u>:

"...And what would be necessary ▮▮▮▮ was really to
find out what were the great comprehensive <u>patterns</u>
operating in Universe."

      - Cite RBF quoted by Cam Smith in RBF to CHILDREN OF EARTH, Dec'72

---

RBF DEFINITIONS

<u>Pattern</u>:

"It is a tendency for patterns either to repeat themselves
locally or for their parts to separate out to join singly or
severally with other patterns to form new constellations. All
the forces operative in Universe result in a complex progression of most comfortable--i.e., least effort, rearrangings in
which the macro-medio-micro star events stand dynamically
together here and there as locally regenerative patterns.
Spontaneously regenerative local constellations are cosmic,
since they appear to be interoriented with angular constancy."

      - Cite SYNERGETICS text at Sec. 601.01; 3 Oct'72

---

RBF DEFINITIONS

<u>Pattern</u>:

"The Euler formula should be revised in arrangement of

expression. You must have lines; you have to have two

lines to have a crossing, which is a point (fixed). And

you have to have three lines in order to have an area--

these being the basic constituents of a <u>pattern</u>."

      - Cite RBF to BO'R, 3200 Idaho, DC, 20 Feb '72

---

RBF DEFINITIONS

<u>Pattern</u>:

"Relationships are local to pattern. Patterns are

comprehensive to relationships."

      (Incorporated in SYNERGETICS text at Sec. 505.03)

      - Cite RBF to EJA, 3200 Idaho, Washington DC., 20 Dec. '71.

RBF DEFINITIONS

Pattern:

"One of the things we have to make clear for society is the dilemma of the Max-Planck-descended scientists, the way they do their problems, you can have either a wave or a particle, but not both simultaneously. Heisenberg has the same fault. They make the error of having a wave as a continuity, as a picture-- not as a pulsating frequency. A planar reflex causes them to think of a continuous wave."

- Cite RBF to EJA, Somerset Club, Boston, 22 April 1971

CONCEPTUALITY PATTERN - SEC 505.40

---

RBF DEFINITIONS

Pattern:

"When we speak of patterns we speak of generalized patterns of conceptuality gleaned from a plurality of special case pattern experiences which have been experimentally proven to be without exception, always existent in every special case within the required class of experiences."

- Cite NASA Speech, p. 100, Jun'66

CONCEPTUALITY - PATTERN - SEC. 505.01

---

RBF DEFINITIONS

Patterns:

". . . All patterns, for instance, numbers or phonetic letters, consist of physical ingredients and physical experience recalls. The physical ingredients consist inherently of event-paired quanta and the latter's six-vectored, positive and negative, actions, reactions and resultants. . . "

- Citation and context at Number, Jun'66
- Cite NASA Speech, p. 58, Jun'66

CONCEPTUALITY - PATTERN - SEC. 505.12

---

RBF DEFINITIONS

Patterns:

"Euler showed that all conceptual experiences which we can pattern, or form, are composed exclusively of the three patterning elements: lines, vertexes, and areas. They are all that are necessary to analyze and inventory all parts of, as well as all whole, patterns. And Euler disclosed also three algebraic formulae characterizing the constant relative abundance relationships of these three fundamental topological elements in all patterns."

- Cite CARBONDALE DRAFT IV,41

- NASA Speech, pp. 58-59, Jun'66

CONCEPTUALITY PATTERN SEC 505.11

---

RBF DEFINITIONS

Pattern:

"Kepes at M.I.T. made a beautiful demonstration [of the scientist's and artists need to articulate]. He took hundreds of eight by ten black and white photographs of modern paintings and shuffled them thoroughly with photographs taken by scientists through microscopes or telescopes of all manner of natural phenomena: sound waves, chromosomes, and such. The only way you can classify photographs with nothing recognizable in them is by your own spontaneous pattern classifications. Group the mealy, the blotchy, the striped, and so forth. The pattern groups of photographs were put on display. The artists' work and the scientists' were indistinguishable. Checking the data, it was found that the artist frequently conceived of a pattern in his imagination before the scientist found it in nature. Science began to take a new view of artists."

- Cite RBF to AAUW panel; AAUW Journal, p.174, May'65

PATTERN - SEC 505.07

---

RBF DEFINITIONS

Pattern:

"I see things sometimes in terms of vectors, sometimes in terms of the faces, and sometimes in terms of the vertexes which would be spheres. These are the three main aspects of all pattern as known by Euler. Euler found these incontrovertible minimum aspects of pattern."

- Cite Carbondale Draft Nature's Coordination, p. VI.31
- Cite Oregon Lecture #7, p. 245. 11 Jul'62

CONCEPTUALITY - PATTERN SEC. 505.11

---

RBF DEFINITIONS

Patterns:

"It is very interesting to consider . . a total inventory of the relative abundance of different patterns remembering that the patterns are reciprocal."

- Cite ORGEON Lecture #5 - p. 167, 9 Jul'62

CONCEPTUALITY - PATTERN - SEC. 505.05

---

RBF DEFINITIONS

Pattern:

"Pattern has emerged first from our preoccupation with getting rid of the irrelevancies and out of it has emerged a minimum constellation, a minimum consideration and it is a four-star affair. It is tetrahedral."

- Citation & context at Irrelevancies: Dismissal Of, 2 Jul'62

---

RBF DEFINITIONS

Pattern:

"The integration of all possibilities of the complementary alternates, though confinable, inherently defies exact identity because the minimum is pattern and not isolated integer.

"All pattern has inherent plurality of viewable aspects, which are the reciprocals of pluralities of permissible view-points, for instance, from within or from without, a system.

"All treatable pattern is a subdivision of Universe, and disposes, in its first generalization, of the macrocosmi and microcosmic irrelevancies."

- Citation and context at Residual Error, 1954

---

RBF DEFINITIONS

Pattern Cognition Feedback:

"Fundamental wisdom
Can readily identify any and all
Special case aspects within
The generalized whole
When listening
Sensitively to one's intuitions
By which alone
The generalized sub-subconscious integration
Of pattern cognition feedbacks
Are articulated."

- Cite HOW LITTLE I KNOW, p.62 Oct '66

---

RBF DEFINITIONS

Pattern:

"There is only pattern, there is only wholeness to begin and cease: the environment and content of all experience or experiment."

- Citation and context at Parts, 1954-59

---

RBF DEFINITIONS

Pattern Cognizance:

It is a discovery of synergetics that "the addition of angle and frequency to Euler's inventory of crossings, areas, and lines is the absolute characteristic of all pattern cognizance."

(Synergetics: 251.02)

- ~~Cite RBF marginalia at SYNERGETICS Draft Sec. 251.19 20 Dec. '71~~

- Citation at Synergetics, 20 Dec'71

---

RBF DEFINITIONS

Pattern:

"Abstraction has no pattern."

- ~~Cite RBF marginalia in "Mathematics in Action," by O.G. Sutton. 1955~~
- Citation at Abstraction, 1955

---

RBF DEFINITIONS

Pattern Conservation:

"Structures are constellar pattern conservations. These definitions hold true all the way from whole Universe to lesser and local pattern differentiations all the way into the atom and its nuclear subassemblies. Each of the families of chemical elements, as well as their most complex agglomerations as superstar Galaxies, are alike cosmic structures. It is clear from the results of modern scientific experiments that structures are not things. Structures are event constellations."

- Cite SYNERGETICS text at Sec. 601.02; 3 Oct'72

---

Pattern Analysis:

See Geometry, 14 Nov'73

---

RBF DEFINITIONS

Pattern Conservation:

"Regenerative means local pattern conservation of energy events.

"Structures are pattern conservations."

- Cite RBF to EJA
Beverly Hotel, New York
15 March 1971

Pattern Conservation:                                    (1)


        See Local Pattern Conservation
            Pattern Integrity


Patterns of Experience:


        See Angular Sinus Takeout, Dec'61


Pattern Conservation:                                    (2)


        See Energetic-synergetic Geometry, Jul'59
            Nonmirror-image, 22 May'73
            Regenerative, 15 Mar'71
            Synergetic Accounting Advantages:  Hierarchy Of, (2)
            Structure, 15 Mar'71


                                                          (1)
Patterns of Experience Return Upon Themselves in All Directions:


        See Nature Always Comes Back on Itself
            Returning Upon Itself:  Systems Return Upon Themselves


RBF DEFINITIONS

    Pattern Evolvement:

    "Unique pattern evmolvement constitutes elementality.

    What is unique about each of the 92 self-regenerative

    chemical elements is their nonrepetitive pattern

    evolvement  which terminates with the third layer of 92."


                                                          (2)
Patterns of Experience Returning Upon Themselves in All Directions:


        See Comprehension, Dec'61


    - Gite RBF insert Synergetics draft, Sec 416.4, Bear Island,
                              25 August 1971.

    - Citation at Elementality, 25 Aug'71


    Pattern Evolvement:


        See Elementality, 25 Aug'71*
            Rectilinear Frame, 24 Sep'73
            Scheme of Reference, 24 Sep'73
            Vector Equilibrium Frame, 3 Nov'73


RBF DEFINITIONS

    Pattern Generalization:                               (1)

    "Out of multi-overlaid experience patternings there sometimes
    emerges an awareness of what we may call a coincidence pattern--
    a localized thickening of points.  These emergent patterns of
    frequency congruences and concentrations display a unique
    configuration-██████ -integrity which has up to now been so
    dilute in any one experience as to be only invisibly common to
    many differentiated or special experiences, e.g., a pack of
    one hundred 4-inch by 5-inch file cards each riddled with
    hundreds of different sized ████ small holes.  Each card appears
    to be chaotically patterned with holes.  However, when the cards
    are stacked with edges aligned three holes in each card are
    vertically aligned; all others are obscured by blank spaces on
    one card or another.  A triangular pattern relationship of the
    light coming through three tubes in the stack of cards is now
    lucidly conceptual.  To such persistently emergent, uniquely
    mutual, coincidence-patterning relationships as the same tri-
    angle array of holes in each and every card we may apply the
    term 'pattern generalization' as used in a mathematical sense,
    in contradistinction to the word 'generalization' as used in
    the literary sense.  The latter often means a too-ambitious
    subject range which consequently permits only superficial con-
    siderations of any specific case ███ data."

    - Cite INTRODUCTION TO OMNIDIRECTIONAL HALO, pp.118-119, 1959

RBF DEFINITIONS

### Pattern Generalization: (2)

"When the uniquely emergent generalized patternings become
describable by us in mentally regenerative conceptual terms,
as completely divorced from any one of the specific sensorial
conditions of any of the special experiences out of which they
emerged, yet apparently, as seen in retrospect, to have been
persistent in every special case, then we may tentatively
assume such unique mutual pattern content to be a generalized
conceptual principle, as for instance the conception of tension
as opposed to compression, independent of textures, smells,
colors, sound, or size, of any one tension-dominated experience."

- Cite INTRODUCTION TO OMNIDIRECTIONAL HALO, p.119, 1959

---

### Pattern Generalization:

See Conceptuality, 24 Apr'71

---

### Pattern vs. Integer:

See Minimum, 1954

---

RBF DEFINITIONS

### Pattern Integrity:

"A pattern integrity operates independently of the local
environment in which we find it. Take a piece of rope. A
wave. Its presence is communicated by its interference,
apprehended by our tuning capability."

"We have step-up, step-down transformations. The wave you
can tune tells you of the wave you cannot tune by apprehension
lags."

- Cite RBF at Penn Bell videotaping session, Philadelphia,
22 Jan'75

---

RBF DEFINITIONS

### Pattern Integrity:

"Pattern integrity is conceptual relationship independent
of size."

- Citation and context at Structure, 16 Dec'73

---

RBF DEFINITIONS

### Pattern Integrity:

"When we speak of pattern integrities, we refer to generalized
patterns of ██████████ conceptuality gleaned from a
plurality of special-case pattern experiences that have been
proven experimentally to be existent always, without exception,
in every special case within the required class of experiences."

- Cite SYNERGETICS text at Sec. 505.01; RBF galley rewrite of
6 Nov'73

---

RBF DEFINITIONS

### Pattern Integrity:

"We have topology as a pattern integrity."

- ~~Cite RBF to HiH, 3200 Idaho, DC, 17 Feb '72~~
- Citation at Topology, 17 Feb'72

---

RBF DEFINITIONS

### Pattern Integrity:

"Each of the chemical elements are pattern integrities

formed by their self-knotting, inwardly precessing,

periodically synchronized self-interferences."

- Cite RBF insert Synergetics draft at Sec. 416.4. Bear Island.
25 August 1971.

ALSO - CONCEPTUALITY PATTERN SEC. 505.20)

RBF DEFINITIONS

### Pattern Integrity:

"Comprehensive universe is amorphous and only locally finite
as it transformingly differentiates into serially conceptual
pattern integrities, some much larger than humanly apprehendible,
some much smaller than humanly apprehendible, ever occurring
in nonsimultaneous sets of human observings, time-cancelling,
harmonically integrative synchronizations are supra or sub
human sensibility and longevity experiencability whose
periodicities are therefore so preponderantly unexpected as
to induce human reactions of o'erwhelming disorder, so that
. . . suddenly around comes the comet again for the first
known time in humanly recorded experience, periodically
closing the gap and periodically pulsing through eternally
normal zero."

- Cite RBF amplification to EJA on citation re Comet in
Oregon Lecture #5, p. 158. Now in SYNERGETICS draft Sec.
614, 'Tension and Compression.'                    1971

---

RBF DEFINITIONS

### Pattern Integrity:

"Man is a complex of patterns or processes. We speak of

our circulatory system, our respiratory system, our

digestive system, and so it goes. Man is not weight.

He isn't the vegetables he eats, for example, because

he'll eat seven tons of vegetables in his life. He is

the result of his own pattern integrity."

- Cite I SEEM TO BE A VERB, Bantam, 1970
- Citation at Man as Pattern Integrity, 1970

---

RBF DEFINITIONS

### Pattern Integrity:

"... Man is not alone the physical machine he appears to be.
He is not merely the food he consumes, the water he drinks,
or the air he breathes. His physical processing is only an
automated aspect of a total human experience which transcends
the physical. As a knot in a series of spliced ropes of manila,
cotton, nylon, etc., may be progressively slipped through all
the material changes of thickness and texture along the length
yet remain in identifiable pattern configuration, so man is
an abstract pattern integrity which is sustained through all
the physical changes and processing."

- Citation and context at Population Sequence (4), Feb'67

---

RBF DEFINITIONS

### Pattern Integrity:

"Triangular structuring is pattern integrity itself."

- Cite NASA Speech, p. 54. Jun'66

---

RBF DEFINITIONS                                          (1)

### Pattern Integrity:

"No sharp cleavage is found
That identifies the boundary between life and nonlife,
Between the heretofore so-called 'animate' and 'inanimate.'

"Viruses,
The smallest organized structures
Exhibiting 'life,'
May be classified either
As inanimate or animate,
As crystalline or 'cellular' forms.
This is the level also at which
The DNA/RNA genetic code is essentially
A structural pattern integrity.
Such pattern integrities
Are strictly accountable
Only as mathematical principles.
Pattern integrities are found
At all levels of structural organization in Universe.
The DNA/RNA is a specialized case
Of the generalized principle of pattern integrity
Found throughout life and nonlife."

- Cite HOW LITTLE I KNOW, pp. 71-72, Oct'66

---

RBF DEFINITIONS                                          (2)

### Pattern Integrity:

"All pattern integrity design
Is controlled by
Angle and frequency modulation.
The biological corpus
Is not stictly 'animate' at any point.
Given that the 'ordering'
Of the corpus design
Is accomplished through such codings as DNA/RNA,
Which are essentially angle and frequency modulation.
Then we may go on to suggest
That 'life,' as we customarily define it,
Could be effected at a distance.
Precession is the effect
Of one moving system
Upon another.
Precession always produces
Angular changes of movements
Of the affected bodies,
And at angles other than 180 degrees;
That is, the results are never
Continuance in a straight line.
Ergo, all bodies of Universe"

- Cite HOW LITTLE I KNOW, pp. 72-73, Oct'66

---

RBF DEFINITIONS                                          (3)

### Pattern Integrity:

"Are affecting the other bodies
In varying degrees,
And all the intergravitational effects
Are precessional angular modulations
And all the interradiation effects
are frequency modulations.

"The gravitational and radiation effects
Could modulate the DNA/RNA
Angle and frequency instructions
At astronomical remoteness--
Life could be 'sent on.'

"Within the order of evolution as usually drawn
Life 'occurred' as a series
Of fortuitous probabilities in the primeval sea.
It could have been sent or 'radiated' there.
That is, the prime code
Or angle and frequency modulated signal
Could have been transmitted
From a remote stellar location.
It seems more likely
(In view of the continuous rediscovery of man"

- Cite HOW LITTLE I KNOW, pp. 73-74, Oct'66

---

RBF DEFINITIONS                                          (4)

### Pattern Integrity:

"As a fully organized being
Back to ever more remote periods)
That the inanimate structural pattern integrity,
Which we call human being,
Was a frequency modulation code message
Beamed at Earth from remote location.
Man as prime organizing
'Principle' construct
Was radiated here from the stars--
Not as primal cell,
But as a fully articulated high order being,
Possibly as the synergetic totality
Of all the gravitation
And radiation effects
Of all the stars
In our galaxy,
And from all the adjacent galaxies
With some weak effects
And some strong effects,
And from all time.
And pattern itself being weightless,
The life integrities are apparently
Inherently immortal."

- Cite HOW LITTLE I KNOW, pp.74-75, Oct'66

RBF DEFINITIONS

Pattern Integrity: (5)

"You and I
Are essentially functions
Of Universe.
We are exquisite antientropy.

"I'll be seeing you!
Forever."

- Cite HOW LITTLE I KNOW, p.75, Oct'66

---

RBF DEFINITIONS

▬▬▬▬ Pattern Integrity:

"A pattern has an integrity independent of the medium
by virtue of which you have received the information
that it exists-- the step-up, step-down transformation
medium."

- Cite Oregon Lecture #5, p. 171. 9 Jul'62
- Citation and context at Tunability, 9 Jul'62
CONCEPTUALITY PATTERN - SEC 505.20

---

RBF DEFINITIONS

Pattern Integrity:

"Into the molecular rope
A complex slip knot has been 'tied'
Which complex knot
Is both internally and externally
In the exact pattern
Of the complex pattern integrity--
Me--
Which has been slipped
Along the rope
By time.

"And as the knot passed,
The rope behind it
Disintegrated and
Its atoms dispersed
And deployed into
Other biosphere function patternings."

- Cite HOW LITTLE, p. 21. Oct'66

---

RBF DEFINITIONS

Pattern Integrity:

"Every individual is a pattern integrity and it is an
evolutionary pattern integrity; it is not a static
pattern integrity."

- Cite Oregon Lecture #5, p. 171. 9 Jul'62

CONCEPTUALITY - PATTERN - SEC 505.20

---

RBF DEFINITIONS

Pattern Integrity:

"When I gave you the slip knot on the rope and we moved
it along-- now it was nylon, now it was manila and now
it was cotton-- we agreed that it really wasn't any of these.
They were just again colors and tactile experiences which
reported something to us as a pattern. They were what I call
a pattern integrity. I am saying to you that each of the
chemical elements are pattern integrities, the forms of local
self-interferences." (IN)

- Cite OREGON Lecture #5 - p. 164 , 9 Jul'62

---

RBF DEFINITIONS

Pattern Integrity: (A)

"No longer do I want to talk about the chemical elements as
things but as pattern integrities. Each one of them is a
unique pattern integrity... in a sense a form of knots. So we
get where there are chemical compounds and the knots tend to
be interlinkable and they will catch on one another. This one
is holding together, all right, but this ball of twine and
this ball of twine, suddenly one weaves into the other every
so often and associates...

"One of the interesting things I have found to consider about
humanity, whereas each one of us weighs in at an average of
seven pounds-- there is a pattern integrity that is very extraordinary, because no sooner is a child born than people say,
'That is Aunt Mary,' and so forth. There are certain strange
pattern characteristics that suddenly reappear. And it is not
just that there are species, that they are human-- I don't
think people tend to do this too much, but they do, even in
hybrids of plants-- to bring out the red and the white, split
petal, or whatever it may be. At any rate, we say 'There is
Aunt Mary,' and probably when it only weighed one ounce it
still had Aunt Mary in there."

- Cite Oregon Lecture #5, p.165, 9 Jul'62
FIRST IP - CONCEPTUALITY - PATTERN - SEC. 505.21)

---

RBF DEFINITIONS

Pattern Integrity:

"My working theory is that man is an a priori pattern
integrity of really very great importance."

- Cite Oregon Lecture #5 - p. 173, 9 Jul'62

---

RBF DEFINITIONS

Pattern Integrity: (B)

"There is some pattern integrity that came in in a family--
absolutely discontinuous, because Aunt Mary had absolutely
nothing to do with this wedding. She was just Aunt Mary, and
there is some Aunt Mary in this child, all right. I call that
pattern integrity quite independent of the relative size--
whether it is the one ounce size, or the seven pound size, or
the 70 pound size-- because later on it gets to be 70 pounds--
then it gets to be 170, and then it had better watch its
Metracal. There is a pattern integrity which is something
independent of weight; and each human being is an extraordinary
complex of these pattern integrities."

- Cite Oregon Lecture #5, p.166, 9 Jul'62

RBF DEFINITIONS

Pattern Integrity:

" . . . Waves are essences neither of milk nor water nor gasoline; the waves are distinct and measurable pattern integrities in their own right. The invariant relationships which govern pattern integrities in nature " are "'pure principle.'"

- Cite MARKS, p. 20 , 1960

CONCEPTUALITY - PATTERN - SEC 505.32)

---

Pattern Integrity:  Equation Of:

See Equation:  Philosophical Equations

---

RBF DEFINITIONS

Pattern Integrity:  Atomic Knots:

"Each of the chemical elements is a unique complex pattern of energy event interrelatednesses which interact inter-interferingly to continually relocalize the involved quantity of energy.  These self-interference patterns of atomic element components are in many ways similar to the family of knots that are tied with rope by sailors to produce various local behaviors, all of which, however, result in further contraction of the knot as the two ends of the rope immediately outside the knot are pulled away from one another by forces external to the knot-- and thus all the attractive forces of Universe operating upon the atoms may result precessionally in keeping the atomic knots pulled together."

- Cite RBF rewrite of SYNERGETICS galley at Sec. 505.21, 6 Nov'73

---

Pattern Integrity - Phenomenon Without Name:

See Conversation Sequence, (1)

---

Pattern Integrity:  Atomic Knots:

See Tensegrity Model of Self-interference of Energy

---

Pattern Integrity:                                        (1)

See Eternal Pattern Integrity
    Intellectual Pattern Integrity
    Knot
    Man as Pattern Integrity
    Metabolic Flow
    Pattern Conservation
    Topological Aspects:  Inventory Of
    Viral Steerability
    Pattern Integrity - Phenomenon Without Name
    You & I as Pattern Integrities
    Wave Pattern of a Stone Dropped in Liquid
    Scan-transmission of Pattern Integrities

---

RBF DEFINITIONS

Pattern Integrity:  Equation of Pattern Integrity:

"... All the biologicals are continually multiplying
Their orderly, cellular, molecular, and atomic, structurings
Which metabolic conservation functioning completes
The comprehensive pattern integrity equation
Governing orderly cosmic energy export-import balancing."

- Citation and context at Manifest: Three, 1973

---

Pattern Integrity:                                        (2)

See Conversation Sequence, (1)*
    Heres & Theres, 4 Jun'72
    Man:  Interstellar Transmission of Man, May'72
    Medium, 9 Jul'62
    Necklace, (2)
    Population Sequence, (4)*
    Regenerative Design:  Law Of, (2)
    Structure, 25 Feb'69; 16 Dec'73*; Nov'71; 9 Nov'73
    System, 4 Jun'72
    Triangle, (2)
    Tunability, 9 Jul'62
    Topology, 17 Feb'72*
    Twenty Questions, (4)
    Domain & Quantum, (1)
    Omnitriangulation, 3 Oct'72
    Vector Equilibrium Involvement Domain, 10 Dec'75
    Geodesic Domes, 24 Jan'58
    Stock Market, 1964
    Electromagnetic Transmission of Human Organisms, 4 Jun'77
    Human Beings, 22 Jun'77

RBF DEFINITIONS

▆▆▆▆▆▆ Patterning of Patternings:

"/ In a/ comprehensive view of nature the physical
world / is seen as_/ a patterning of patternings . . .
whose constituent functions are fields of force, each of
which compenetrates and influences other localized fields
of force.

"/ A pattern_/ is a macro-micro-oscillocosm."

                                MARKS
                    - Cite ~~MORRIS~~, P. 8. 1960

CONCEPTUALITY- PATTERN - SECS- 505.04 + 505.05

---

Pattern Sense:

See Blind Date with Principle, Jan'55

---

RBF DEFINITIONS

Pattern Processing Machines:

"The computers, both large and small, are pattern processing
machines of which the human brain is the prototype. As
with the human brain all pattern processing consists of
two main classes: differentiation and integration, i.e.,
specialization vs. generalization."

- Citation and context at Computer, 10 Oct '63

---

RBF DEFINITIONS

Pattern Stabilizing:

"A triangle is a pattern stabilizing complex of energy
events."

- Cite RBF in Corcoran Gallery Address, Washington DC,
  23 Feb '72

---

Pattern-seeking Function:

See Metaphysical, Jun'66

---

RBF DEFINITIONS

Pattern Stability:

"A necklace has no pattern stability."

- Cite RBF to H.U.D. Engineers, 26 Jan '72 at Washington

---

RBF DEFINITIONS

Pattern Sense:

"I resolved to apply the rest of my life to converting
my pattern sense, through teleological principle into
design and prototyping developments governing the
pertinent, but as yet unattended, essential industrial
network functions.."

- Citation and context at Fuller, R.B.: Crisis of 1927, 14 Apr'70

---

Pattern Stability: Pattern Stabilization:

See Structure, 16 Dec'73; 27 Dec'74
    Object, 9 Nov'73
    Restraints, 8 Aug'77

RBF DEFINITIONS

**Pattern Strip Aggregate Wrapabilit␣ies:**

"Thus we learn sum-totally how a ribbon (band) wave, a waveband, can self-interfere periodically to produce in-shuntingly all the three prime structures of Universe and a complex isotropic vector matrix of successively shuttle-woven tetrahedra and octahedra. It also illustrates how energy may be wave-shuntingly self-knotted or self-interfered with (see Sec. 506), and their energies impounded in local, high-frequency systems which we misidentify as only-seemingly-static matter."

- Cite RBF rewrite of SYNERGETICS galley at Sec. 930.26, 19 Dec'73

---

**Pattern Strip Aggregate Wrapabilities:**

See Tetrahelix:  Continuous Pattern Strip
    Waveband
    Tetrascroll

---

RBF DEFINITIONS

**Pattern Uniqueness:**

"Euler said, 'We are dealing in pattern. Mathematics is pattern and there are irreducible aspects of pattern. That is the patterns do represent some kind of events. There are the lines: a line is a unique kind of a pattern. If I have two lines, where the two lines cross is distinctly different from where the lines don't cross.' He called this the vertex, the convergence. He said this is absolute pattern uniqueness."

- Cite Oregon Lecture #7, p. 245. 11 Jul'62

CONCEPTUALITY - PATTERN - SEC 505.10   VERTEXES - 523.01

---

**Pattern Uniqueness:**                                    (1)

See Unique Pattern

---

**Pattern Uniqueness:**                                    (2)

See Synergetics, 1959
    Synergist, 1954
    Vertex, Jun'66

---

**Pattern:  Patternings:**                                 (1A)

See Awareness Patterns
    Circumference Patterns
    Complementary Pattern
    Continuous Pattern Strip
    Cumulative Patterning Overlays
    Ecological Pattern
    Evolutionary Pattern
    Evolvement:  Pattern of Evolvement
    Flux Pattern
    Fountain Pattern
    Happening Patterns
    Hierarchy of Patterns
    Holding Pattern
    Interpatterning
    Interrelationship Patterns
    Largest Pattern
    Local Pattern
    Local Holding Pattern

---

**Pattern:  Patternings:**                                 (1B)

See Local Patterning Aspects
    Memory Album of Patternings
    Metaphysical Wave Pattern
    Minimum Pattern Minimum = Pattern
    Minimum Characteristics of All Patterns in Universe
    Minimum Set of Patterns
    Number Pattern
    Omnidirectional Pattern
    Pattern Strip Aggregate Wrapabilities
    Precessionally Shunted Pattern Relay
    Pulse Pattern
    Set of Patterns
    Shunting:  Relative Motion Patterns
    Structural Pattern
    Subpattern
    Strip:  Continuous Pattern Strip
    Tetrahelix:  Continuous Pattern Strip
    Process Relationships

---

**Pattern:  Patternings:**                                 (1C)

See Tools as Part of the Pattern Man
    Triangulation Pattern Strip
    Unique Pattern
    Equations = Pattern
    Mathematics = Pattern
    World Pattern vs. Local Pattern
    Nuclear Pattern

Pattern: (2A)

See Abstraction, Oct'59; 1955*
Alphabet, Jun'66
Brain's TV Studio, 1960
Comprehensive, Feb'72
Discovery, 11 Jul'62
Energy, 1960
Hair, 9 Jul'62
Intellections, 1960
Irrelevancies: Dismissal Of, 2 Jul'62*
Metaphysical & Physical, 2 Jun'74
Monkey Wrench, 9 Jul'62
Mathematics, 1965
Nature, Dec'72
Number, 1954; Jun'66*
Parts, 1954*
Principle, 12 Jun'56
Intertransformability Systems, 28 Apr'77

---

TEXT CITATIONS

Pauli, Wolfgang:

s201.22

---

Pattern: (2B)

See Rafts: Early World Drifting on Rafts, 11 Jul'62
Recognize, 22 Jul'71
Residual Error, 1954*
Scientific Generalization, 28 Jan'69
Solid State, 13 Jan'73
Structure, 21 Dec'71
Structure Sequence (1)(2)
Synergist, 1954
Triangle, 25 Feb'69
Weather, Feb'73
Wave, 6 Nov'73

---

Pauli: Pauli's Exclusion Principle:

See Brouwer's Theorem, 1960*
Coincidental Articulation Sequence, (1)-(4)
Synergetic Hierarchy, (1)

---

Pattern: (3)

See Pattern Analysis
Pattern Cognition Feedback
Pattern Cognizance
Pattern Conservation
Pattern Evolvement
Patterns of Experience
Patterns of Experiencing Returning Upon Themselves
Pattern-seeking Function
Pattern Generalization
Pattern Integrity
Pattern Integrity: Equation Of
Pattern Processing Machines
Pattern Sense
Pattern Stabilizing: Pattern Stability
Patterning of Patternings
Pattern Strip
Pattern Uniqueness
Pattern vs. Integer

---

RBF DEFINITIONS

Pauling, Linus:

"Since all vectors are divisible by two Linus Pauling was right that you can close pack spheres with two spheres tangent connected."

- Cite RBF to EJA, 3200 Idaho, Wash., DC, 7 Oct'71

---

RBF DEFINITIONS

Pauli's Exclusion Principle:

"Pauli's exclusion principle verifies that each of the stirred points in Brouwer's theorem and the point which did not move have their inherently separate counterpart points, which discloses bot the neutral axis formed by the two points that do not move, and the obverse and reverse set of moving points."

- Citation & context at Brouwer's Theorem, 1960

---

RBF DEFINITIONS

Linus Pauling:

"Dr. Linus Pauling has found and twice published his spheroid clusters designed to accommodate this magic number series in a logical system. Without powerful synergetic tools we find him in the vicinity of the answer; but we now identify these numbers in an absolute synergetic hierarchy which must transcend any derogatory suggestion of pure coincidence, alone, for the coincidence reoccurs with mathematical regularity, symmetry and structural logic which identifies it elegantly as the model for the magic numbers."

- Cite NASA Speech, pages 104-105. Jun'66
MAGIC NUMBERS SEC 482.02 [995.34]

RBF DEFINITIONS

Pauling, Linus:

"After X-ray diffraction in 1932, Linus Pauling who received
the Nobel Prize for his pioneering exploration of chemical
structuring, began to discover that metals were also / see
van't Hoff, 1965_/ tetrahedrally coordinated and interlinked,
not point-to-point but through one another as chains are
linked with dynamically coordinate or coincident gravitational
centers. If we think of six-edged chain links (remembering
that the tetrahedron is a six-edged pyramidal frame) we can
envision the manner in which we may link tetrahedra in six
different directions. That multidirectional connectibility
explains the way in which metals are linked together."

ª Cite Conceptuality of Fundamental Structures (Kepes), p.72-76,
1965

---

Pauling, Linus: (1)

See Magic Numbers
Van't Hoff: Combining van't Hoff & Pauling

---

RBF DEFINITIONS

Pauling: Linus Pauling:

"When you get to the reconstructs from x-ray diffraction,
Linus Pauling began to discover that all the metals were
tetrahedrally organized, but instead of being vertex to
vertex they were center of gravity to center of gravity.
. . . An alloy could be stronger where you had congruent
centers of gravity-- that was a characteristic of metals .
In fact, becausethe tetrahedon has six edges you could
chain or link it in six ways to six others and they would
not be vertex to vertex but edge to edge as linkage. So
the metals were tetrahedronally organized too and Linus
Pauling went on examining metal after metal. He has never
found a metal yet which is not tetrahedrally organized."

- Cite Oregon Lecture #2, pp.74-75, 2 Jul'62

---

Pauling: Linus: (2)

See Chemical Bonds, Jun'66
Closest Packing of Spheres, 7 Oct'71
Inorganic Chemistry, 10 Jul'62
Synergetic Hierarchy, (1)
Teaching, 2 Apr'71
Tetrahedral Coordination of Nature,1965
Viral Steerability: Tetrahelix, 1960

---

RBF DEFINITIONS

Linus Pauling:

". . . Pauling's x ray diffraction analyses show
omnitetrahedral configuration interlinkages of
gravitational centers of compounded atoms in all
metals analyzed. . . "

- Cite Omnidirectional Halo, p. 161. 1960

---

RBF DEFINITIONS

Peace:

"When you use the word peace too many people think of
political reforms, where there's a political struggle and
you try to persuade and that doesn't do any good because
people can't live on persuasion. They've got to eat.
And so I'm interested in how you actually employ those
principles. So I began playing my World Peace Game, in
which I then said I won't use the word peace any more,
because man has no meaning for the word. There never has
been anything ..... peace. What has been called peace
is what pleased the last victor."

- Cite RBF in Watts Tape, p.64, 19 Oct'71

---

TEXT CITATIONS

Linus Pauling:

See NASA Speech, p. 57. + p. 104.

Oregon Lecture #2, pp.73-74 - 2 Jul'62

Omnidirectional Halo, pp.151,161, 1960

931.62                              a201.22

995.34

---

RBF DEFINITIONS

Peace:

"...The prolonged and far more sanguinary private and
nonspectacular chapters of strife under the guise of 'peace.'"

- Citation and context at War, 1947

Peas:

    See Model of Toothpicks & Semi-dried Peas

Pebble:                                    (2)

    See Aggregate, 20 Dec'71

---

Peashooter:

    See Hammerthrow, 6 Jul'62

Peel: Peeling:

    See Precessional Peel-off
        Skinning
        Unpeel

---

RBF DEFINITIONS

    Pebble:

    "A little pebble is a rolling way to make more

    dust and sand."

    - Cite RBF in tape for Wildlife Magazine, 3200 Idaho,
      Wash DC, 30 May'72

RBF DEFINITIONS

    Pellet:

    "Pellet.  That must mean it's been impelled.  I'd never
    thought about that."

    - Cite RBF to EJA, 3 Mar'73

---

Pebble:                                    (1)

    See Rock
        Roundness
        Stone
        Wave Pattern of a Stone Dropped in Liquid

RBF DEFINITIONS

    Penance: Penitent:

    "The Brahmins are pure contemplation... They keep going
    through ablutions and penance when there's nothing to be
    penitent about."

    - Citation & context at Hesse, Herman, 28 Apr'71

RBF DEFINITIONS

## Pencil:

"Rationalization alone, however, is not sufficient. It is not
an end in itself. It must be carried through to an objective
state and materialize into a completely depersonalized instru-
ment-- a pencil. (Who knows who made the first pencil?
Certainly not 'Eberhard Faber' or 'Venus'.) The pencil not
only facilitates communication between men, by making thought
specific and objective, but also enables men cooperatively to
plan and realize the building of a house, oxygen tent, flatiron,
or an x-ray cabinet by virtue of the pencil's availability.
The inventor-- alive or dead-- is extraneous and unimportant;
it is the pencil that carries over. Abstract thought dies with
the thinker, but the mechanism was building for a long time
before the moment of recognized in-vention."

- Citation and context at Rationalization Sequence (4), 1938

## Pencil:

See Design, 1938
    Rationalization Sequence, (4)*
    Teleology, (2)

## Penditure:                                                    (1)

See Expendable
    Indispensable

## Penditure:                                                    (2)

See Twoness, (p.143) 1960

RBF DEFINITIONS

## Pendulum Model vs. Scenario Model:

"The Pendulum Model of Newton's Universe in which the swings
        decrease and the pendulum ultimately comes
            to 'Up and Down Rest'
                        vs.
the inherently endless Scenario Model of Einstein's Universe

in which truth is ever approaching evolutionary and constantly
intertransforming, precessionally behaving, process of a complex
of omniaccommodative, intercomplementary, transactional events
involving in its inward-outward, three-way aroundness, catalogue
of alternate transformative options of ever more inclusive and
refining degrees-- in ever closer proximity to perfect equilibrium of all transformative forces, but never attaining such
equilibrium of 'absolute' truth in which the avoidance of such
omnizerophase condition involves not only a constant metaphysical
apprehending, comprehending, sorting, contracting, and compacting
(by universal mind) of physical entropy's everywhere and every-
while increasing disorder and expansiveness (a disorder which
attains and passes through maximum asymmetry as the metaphysical
passes through, but fails to remain at, the zero of equilibrious
truth), wherefore metaphysical might continually improve the
scenario by conceptual discoveries of new generalized principles."

- Cite PENDULUM MODEL vs. SCENARIO MODEL, (typescript), 23 Dec'68

## Penetration:  Penetrating:                                    (1)

See Compenetration:  Compenetrate

## Penetration:  Penetrating:                                    (2)

See Building, 28 Jan'75

## Peninsula:

See Male & Female, 12 Jan'74

Penis:

See Male & Female, 12 Jan'74; 1 Feb'75

Pentagon: (1)

See Hex-pent
    Tensegrity: Twelve Pentagons
    Twelve Pentagons

Penitence:

See Hesse: Herman, 28 Apr'71

Pentagon: (2)

See Domain of a Point, May'72
    Domains of Polyhedra, 7 Nov'73
    Necklace, (A)

Pensive:

See Expensive - Nonthinking, 24 Jan'76

People's Language:

See English, 28 Jan'75

Pentagonal Polarity:

See Tensegrity Masts: Pentagonal Polarity

RBF DEFINITIONS

Perception:

"The physical aberration is always in our perceptioning but it is not the reality."

- Citation & context at Principle, 6 Apr'75

RBF DEFINITIONS

Perception:

"Our vision is limited to the tiny red, orange, yellow,
green, blue, violet bands of frequency tunabilities representing far less than one-thousandth of one percent of the great
electromagnetic spectrum of the thus far discovered vast range
of the Physical Universe realities. Our afterimage overlapping
which results in our sense of motion, is even more limited in
its perceptual range.

"We cannot see the hands of the clock move. We cannot see life
growing. We cannot see either the stars or the atomic components
move, though they move at fantastic speeds. We can only see the
ultra-slow motions of the clouds, locally running waters, human
beings and other creatures, and their parts.

"No wonder that little man, who within his average lifetime
has seen only about one-millionth of the surface of his planet,
and has lived but a split-second of the astronomical ages, does
not see and cope simultaneously with the larger evolutionary
patternings and life aboard the planet Earth. Only through
memory plus thought-- greatly aided by instruments-- does man
discover the ultra- and infra-motion effects."

- Cite WHAT QUALITY ENVIRONMENT?, 24 Apr'67

---

Perception: Perceptivity:                                    (1)

See Apprehension
    Invisible Motion
    Convergent vs. Parallel Perception
    Frequency Islands of Perception

---

RBF DEFINITIONS

Perception:

"It is the nature of all our experiences that they

begin and end. They are packaged. For instance, we see

in 60 separate picture frames per second as in a moving

picture continuity. Each frame is a finite increment. Our

brain's after image lag is so powerful that (it) gives a

sense of absolute eccentricity' to our only subconsciously

packaged seeing. We wake up and go to sleep.

- Cite NASA Speech, p. 32, Jun'66

- Citation and context at Finite, Jun'66

---

Perception: Perceptivity:                                    (2)

See Principle, 6 Apr'75*
    Invisibility of Macro- and Micro- Resolutions, (1)(2)
    Children as Only Pure Scientists, (1)(2)

---

RBF DEFINITIONS

Perceptual Peephole as Fraction of Reality:

"How did the Universe come into being with its complete
integrity, its comprehensively interaccommodative, omnidifferentiated rates and methods of transforming? Such
questions remain ever more importantly unanswered and seemingly
unanswerable. Yet, all of our present customs, ways of
thinking, and means of communication have been developed under
the misapprehension that only the minuscule, millionth part
of the physical Universe, which the peepholes of our
perceptual senses reveal, comprises the whole of reality.
Because humanity has deliberately fractionated the formal
study of residual reality into ever more minute specializations,
which continually know more and more about less and less, the
residual preoccupations have lost sight completely of any of
the comprehensive and infinitely inspirational mystery of
totality. First pragmatism, then utter despiritization,
have resulted. It is not God who died. It was sophisticated
man who died, choked to death by the ever-tightening noose
of specialization-- 'enlightened selfishness.'"

- Cite ARCHITECTURE AS ULTRA INVISIBLE REALITY, p. 151, Dec. '69

---

RBF DEFINITIONS

Perfect:

"Nature abhors an equilibrium as much as she abhors

a perfect vacuum or a perfect anything."

- For citation and context see Equilibrium, Jun '66

---

Perceptual Peephole:

See Common Sense: Perceptual Peephole

---

RBF DEFINITIONS

Perfect:

"Perfect, though impossible of demonstration, is nonetheless
the criterion of selection. Perfect is not only a direction
but a time direction, perfection being never in 'reality'
attainable. There is herein to be discerned the meaning of
"Never, Never Land." Children dream truly."

- Cite NINE CHAINS TO THE MOON, p.19, 1938

RBF DEFINITIONS

Perfection:

"As a result of the gamut of relative recall time-lags, the physical is always the imperfect experience, but tantalizingly always ratio-equated with the innate eternal sense of perfection."

- Cite RBF rewrite of SYNERGETICS galley at Sec. 443.04, 4 Nov'73

Perfect Man:

See Immaculate Conception, 25 Jan'72

RBF DEFINITIONS

Perfection:

"Intellect... is an infinite refinement in proximation to perfection, which perfection is the zero-inflection... phase through which... the transformations oscillatingly pass..."

- Citation and context at Intellect, 16 Aug '50

RBF DEFINITIONS

Perfect Prototype:

"The vector equilibrium... an invisibly perfect prototype in pure principle."

- Citation & context at Understanding, 4 Oct'72

Perfect = Direction:

See Perfect, 1938

Perfect = Zero:

See Aberrating, 23 Jun'75

Perfect & Imperfect:

See Immaculate Conception, 25 Jan'72

Perfect: Perfection:                                          (1)

See Exact: Exactitude
    Ideal
    Perfect & Imperfect
    Potential
    Perfect = Zero

Perfect: Perfection:                                    (2)

    See Equilibrium, Jun'66
       Eternal Principles, 22 Nov'73
       Frame of Reference, 4 Oct'72
       God, May'72
       Immaculate Conception, 25 Jan'72
       Intellect, 16 Aug'50*

---

Performance Per Pound:                                  (1)

    See Copper
       Design Science
       Displacement of Ships & Buildings
       Ephemeralization
       Metals: Recirculation of Metals
       More With Less
       Weapons Technology

---

RBF DEFINITIONS

Performance: Equation Of:

"When finally solving from the inside out the teleologic
perspective will be universal and the equation of performance
will be:

    Degree of satisfaction encompassment =

        Degree of factor inclusion."

- Citation & context at Teleology, 1938

---

Performance Per Pound:                                  (2)

       Acceleration of Change (2)
    See Aesthetics, Dec'67
       Artifacts (1)(2)*
       Automobile, Feb'72
       Curvature: Compound, 12 Mar'74
       Design Science (B)
       Dome, 9 Jul'73
       Dymaxion, 1967
       Industrialization (1)
       Prestressed Concrete Sequence (3)
       Sovereignty: Elimination Of, 29 Jun'72
       World Game (II)
       Transnationalism vs. Colonialism, (1)
       Bauhaus School: Remoteness Of, 24 Jan'58
       Dymaxion Artifacts, (2)
       Club of Rome: Limits to Growth, (B)(C)
       Form Cannot Follow Function, 20 Sep'76

---

Performance: Equation Of:

    See Equation: Philosophical Equations

---

Performance:

    See Invisible Performance

---

RBF DEFINITIONS

Performance Per Pound:

"Inasmuch as nature's omni-inexorable transformings consist
of a plurality of equieconomical, alternatively employable,
disassociating and associating, principles-- these, together
with the complex of electromagnetic and mechanical principles
can be electively employed by humans to greatly advantage
humanity by producing ever higher performance with ever less
investment of resources as pounds of material, ergs of energy,
and hours of time, per each function designedly satisfied."

- Citation & context at Artifacts (1)(2), 30 Apr'74

---

Perfume:

    See Communications Hierarchy, (2)

## TEXT CITATIONS

### Perimeters:

Synergetics : Fig. 412.01, note.

Sec. 465.42 (2nd. Ed.)

---

### Perimeter:

See Macro-micro, 12 Nov'75
Out-lining, 22 Mar'76

---

### Periodic-continuity:                                    (1)

See Continuity-finiteness
Scenario

---

### Periodic-Continuity:                                    (2)

See Thought, May'49

---

## RBF DEFINITIONS

### Periodic Experience:                                    (1)

"Mathematical concepts of group phenomena may be acquired in principle by the willingness (subjectively initiated) of the individual to be governed by the integrity of progressive conceptioning principle-- the objective synchronizations are implicit and unavoidable competence and comprehensive, realizable design will result. Let us ▮▮▮ pursue further the conceptioning in specifics of group principle.

"It is not difficult to understand that the trends to synchronization by harmonic interval of one collection of events can seemingly and sumtotally create an aspect of such superficial incongruity in respect to the sumtotal collected harmonic events of other phases of functional disposition, of the differentiable Universe, as to predispose us to assume that there might never be synchronization of one major collection with another. We obviously incline to this predisposition by virtue of the persistence of the familiar in our own environmental close-up-- thought, which causes the dynamic interpenetrations to appear as a static, rather than as a periodic-continuity environment reality.

- Cite TOTAL THINKING, I & I, pp.237-238, May'49

---

## RBF DEFINITIONS

### Periodic Experience:                                    (2)

"Misapprehension of our own dynamic significance becomes in environmental close-ups a bundle of persistent periodicities developing into a spontaneous anticipation of repetition of harmonic intervals and their familiar synchronization.

"So marked is our proclivity for such anticipation that we set ourselves as though we were alarm clocks to waken at specific blocks of intervals of familiar periodicities of experience. We relate our own heartbeat to minutes of hours of days, and our meals-- or chemical fueling-- to the days of the postman's coming and going, and even to periodicities such as invented Father's Days and other soon-familiar invented conventions, of the persistent, complex periodic continuities of our days into years. The invented periodicities may become only monotonous.

"Life in retrospect, however, may be informatively discovered to have been comprised of a progressive series of interruptions and penetrations of the successively latest a priori environment continuities-- by unfamiliar frequencies or biodynamic groups of frequencies, always occurring as unfamiliar to the ignorantly accepted trend to mono-tony."

- Cite TOTAL THINKING, I&I, p.238, May'49

---

## RBF DEFINITIONS

### Periodic Experience:                                    (3)

"The new event always comes as an harmonic interruption of frequencies, or an interference with the increasing inventory of already assimilated synchronizations (up to the latest instant), which have only become obvious by virtue of the spontaneous synchronization of the sum total of acquired experiences and progressively integrated interruptions.

"It is necessary that the comprehensive realizer ascertain in principle how the mathematical proportioning of experience is persuasive to the erroneous concept that the sum total bundle of already-experienced frequencies constitutes so unified, or well synchronized an experience whole as to have seemingly always been 'known.' The comprehensive realizer will discover that his adequacy as rearranger of local Universe, in principle, will, if competently effected, be acquired by men as an obvious accretion, and that the more competent his realizing-rearrangements of design, the less grateful the beneficiaries, which will be precisely the objective of the comprehensive realizer.

"A known personality, that is, a life-- with which the comprehensive realizer is concerned-- is a unique bundle of "

- Cite TOTAL THINKING, I&I, pp.238-239, May'49

---

## RBF DEFINITIONS

### Periodic Experience:                                    (4)

"accumulated experience to which the new experience must always be dissynchronous, but only at the moment of original interference, else the new interaction of the greater complex of truth would not have been recognizable and acquirable as new experience and tactical advantage.

"The greatest overall misapprehension regarding the complex-continuities is that which assigns a static or 'at rest' analysis to the sum total sensation of individual experience and consequently to the sum total of all individuals' experience. Against the inertia of a seemingly static whole, each new harmonic incorporation of life therefore seemingly impinges as a dynamic perversity. This is why we frequently remark, 'Man tends to back up into his future.'

"In addition to the simple arithmetical, algebraic, and geometrical progressions of the first, second, and third degrees of acceleration, mathematics discloses other series, and superseries, of superficially unpredictable mathematical frequencies because they are composed of complementary and reciprocal numbers whose products alone, though never occurring"

- Cite TOTAL THINKING, I&I, p.239, May'49

RBF DEFINITIONS

### Periodic Experience: (5)

"simultaneously or in whole, are compositely congruent with complex progressions. But these complex components occur in discontinuous series, and are inherently self-inexplicable. The complementary functions must therefore impinge upon consciousness only as meaningless. As immediately contemplated upon first experience, they of necessity, alone, constitute seemingly absolute perversity of interference. Synergy-- ▓▓▓▓ wholistic behavior unpredicted by parts.

"It is, therefore, the unpredictable degree of the super- and the supersuper- 'n' degrees of complex association of energy frequencies which seem most preposterous. We cannot view the great confluences of separately and remotely significant events forwardly resultant to now. Synergy is inherently surprising.

"When, however, these complexities are viewed in reverse, from the advantage of even the most mathematically supersuper-interference, the whole regains the acceptable sublimity of aspect, such as a fleet of little ocean racers 100 miles off Bermuda struggling with the waves of interference of the Atlantic turning the perversely interfering winds to advantage by virtue"

- Cite TOTAL THINKING, I&I, pp.239-240, May'49

---

RBF DEFINITIONS

### Periodic Experience: (6)

"of the relative inertia of the relative waves of water, eventually to pass Bermuda, as the whole picture is observed from the airplane and its infinitude of subcomplexities.

"Though both are designed with the same family of principles called 'factors of ships,' the comprehensive realizer can see that the superficial difference between the collections of frequencies which makes the Bermuda cruising boat seemingly different from the airplane-- or indeed, man from elephant-- may be in principle the same difference as understandably exists between an early Wright airplane and the latest supersonic airplane, or, yet, between an early Chinese hot air balloon and a late helicopter.

"The only difference between the Wright and the supersonic planes is the sum total of recurrent synchronized cyclic events known as the 'succession of design models'-- evolved in complex out of the physical experience with each trial balance of the designed complex effected by ▓▓▓▓ man, and as let loose after static-load-test-within-limited-controlled-conditions of variables, into the dynamic-load-tests within the unknown, uncontrolled, comprehensive and a priori design"

- Cite TOTAL THINKING, (I&I), p.240, May'49

---

RBF DEFINITIONS

### Periodic Experience: (7)

"complex of the residual uncharted variables of Universe. The uncharted residual function of Universe balances the special-set function of derived functions-- called from out of the total principles of energetic Universe by the designer as a newly realized mutation of species evolution accomplished by synergetic extension.

"Though having no one common component part identification, the difference between the 1904 Wright Brothers' biplane and the 1963 superjet, supersonic, stratosphere monoplane is only a group difference of a minor complex of almost 60 packed years of experience with the same body of experience called airship; which, in turn, only specialized in a few of the greater body of principles called ship; which specialized in a few of the greater body of principles called Earth; which specialized in a few of the greater body of principles called motion; which specialized in a few of the greater body of principles called energy, which specialized as an original function for the comprehensive Universe. The first derived coordinates of Universe would seem to be functions of energy variant▓ in respect to intellect.

- Cite TOTAL THINKING, I&I, pp.240-241, May'49

---

RBF DEFINITIONS

### Periodic Experience: (8)

"We can see that the concept of original separation of Universe into two inherent functions-- and the further subdivision and expansion of one function into a unique plurality of subsets of functions-- and subsequent acceleration of specialized experience with new design events of any one unique subset's evolution, as contrasted against another, can only accelerate superficial differences between any degrees of subsets.

"It is obvious that if the frequency of cyclic events differs in one geographical environment from another, the life within one environment may be accelerated to increasing degrees of experience over the life within another and, therefore, to sets of superficial difference of existence and trend. It can then be seen that what we might designate as natural education-- by induced self-discipline advantage-- represents an accelerated testing of objective-subjective experience, and that acceleration is natural and that natural education may potentially evaporate the inadequacy predilections of original vanity and superstitions and that the original springs of action may become obsolete as the realizations of intellect and the hitherto preoccupations with seeming frustration and self-destruction may be supplanted, through the self-disciplining"

- Cite TOTAL THINKING, (I&I), p.241, May'49

---

RBF DEFINITIONS

### Periodic Experience: (9)

"of the comprehensive designer to orderings of integrity of Universe.

"Where, geographically speaking, of a priori unique environment continuities, the inherent periodicity of the occurrence of interference is at a relatively low frequency, then the rate of dissipation of ignorance is proportionally low, and vice versa.

"The relatively lowest inherent periodicity of interference of forceful variables-- of experience in the dynamic environment (geography)-- occurs in the dry land near sea level in the region of the equator. The periodic frequency of interference by physical variables increases outwardly from the Earth's center into the colder climates of mountain and toward the Earth poles. The periodicity and magnitude of forceful interferences increase even more upon the seas, and yet more as man penetrates outwardly from the unique energy fixations of Earth into the cosmos of major categories of general dynamic principles.

"Sum totally on Earth the residual vanities and superstitions of the ego bulk up most obviously in the warm and mild climates,"
- Cite TOTAL THINKING, (I&I), pp.24-242, May'49

---

RBF DEFINITIONS

### Periodic Experience: (10)

"originally most favorable to the naked, ignorant man, and are most rapidly dispersed and replaced with intellectual ordering in the environments of highest frequency of unprecedented intensities of interference, penetrated now by man at will by virtue of his contriving of realizations in complex principles.

"Each of the sumtotal variety of biological forms represents in simple principle the complex bundling of unique internal experience continuities, and the latter's individual accumulations of external periodic experience, within the greater bundle of persistently unique environmental sequences-- of variable geographic frequency bundle limitations. Humans have abstract 'tree rings' of experience.

"The circling bands of cross-sectioned tree or the scalloped terraces of the shellfish are convergently secreted structures (interference of higher order) of cyclic bundling of experiences. Wave embodiments of cyclic experience appear everywhere in the accredited morphology of nature's omnidirectional, convergent-divergent, synchronous-dissynchronous, infinite plurality of pulsating controls of interactive events in principle."

- Cite TOTAL THINKING, (I&I), p.242, May'49

---

RBF DEFINITIONS

### Periodic Experience: (11)

The cyclic wave accretions-- unique to parents and parent's parent-- make overlapping internal impressions of the periodic and cyclic interferences-structuring-by-accretion, prearranging thereby internal angles of the original turbining tendency of unfoldment, upon the gestating seed of periodic secretion of outside-in then inside-out pulsation-inversion which we call regenerative birth. This is, of course, a union of the infinite inwardness with the infinite outwardness to fulfill the comprehensive duality principle of uni-verse. Human egos are multiconcentric frequency 'halo' systems.

"As with the complex of synchronized convergent principles called airplane, compounded of the succession of flight experiences with a succession of 'improved' designs in-corpor-ating all previous experience in action-reaction juxtapositions (called structure and mechanics), a trend to further inclusion and refinement of accelerating acceleration of improvement is inherent, but always improvement is relative to the whole of already-secreted true experiences, whether as yet detected or not by the redesign-cycle mutators.

""A new design's 'sport' or subspecies may long be latent, a helicopter development postponed by preoccupation with the"

* Cite TOTAL THINKING, (I&I), pp.242-243, May'49

---

RBF DEFINITIONS

### Periodic Experience: (12)

"initial concept of 'airship.' The relative, realized-complex trend accelerates itself in compounding degrees, whereby, eventually, the probability of numbers of immediately detected forward mutations to be refiningly anticipated exceeds in number the sum total of the previously secreted, or experienced, impressions, innately preoccupying the species division.

"A historical shift is now occurring in the scientific view-point, induced by this shift in balance of ▓▓▓ preponderant numbers of effective impressions, pre-and-post-natal, upon behavior probabilities of the various species to be affected preponderantly by the relative number of post-natal, periodic, and cyclic accelerations.

"Hazy awareness of the significance of this historically pivotal event is at the core of hastily taken political positions seeking to establish monopolistic validity of comprehensive viewpoint (where mono-logical explanation of the biologically functioning derivatives of Universe may never be tolera-▓▓▓ble). Both sides are right about their specially selected cases; neither may increase their understanding by arbitrary limitations of experience and conception regarding the next"

- Cite TOTAL THINKING, (I&I), p.243, May'49

# Synergetics Dictionary

RBF DEFINITIONS

Periodic Experience:                                        (13)

"appropriate trial balance of potentials of the apprehended,
and therefore anticipated, periodic inclusions of the
subjective-objective 'beating to windward' of the periodically
shifting advantages of Universe.  The comprehensive realizers
of all time have always realized the implicit truth of these
relationships of Uni-verse.  Bias precludes synergetic
advantage."

- Cite TOTAL THINKING, (I&I), p.243, May'49

---

RBF DEFINITIONS

Periodic Table:  Harmonics of 18:

"The prime number 17 accommodates all the positive-negative,
quanta-wave primes up to ■ and including the number 18, which
in turn accommodates the two nines of the invisible twoness
of all systems.  It is to be noted that the harmonics of the
periodic table of the elements add up to 92:

```
 2
 8 ⎫
 8 ⎬──→ 18
18
18
18 ⎫
18 ⎬──── 36
 2 ⎭
──
92
```

There are five sets of 18, though the 36 is not always so
recognized.  Conventional analysis of the periodic table omits
from its quanta accounting the always occurring invisible
additive twoness of the poles of axial rotation of all systems."

- Cite SYNERGETICS, 2nd. Ed. at Sec. 1238.43, 22 May'75

---

RBF DEFINITIONS

Periodic Table:

"Because people thought the nucleus was one, they missed

for so long the significance of the atomic weights in the

Periodic Table."

- Citation and context at Zero Frequency, 29 May'72

---

Periodic Table:                                        (1)

See Eightness:  Begeted Eightness
    Elementality
    Ninety-two Elements

---

RBF DEFINITIONS

Periodic Table and Closest Packing:

In closest packing of spheres "the third layer of 92
spheres contain eight new potential nuclei which however
do not become active nuclei until each has three more
layers surrounding it-- three layers being unique to
each nucleus.  This tells us that the nuclear group with
92 spheres in its outer or third layer is the limit of
unique, closest-packed assemblage of unit wavelength
and frequency, nuclear symmetry systems.  This is
impressive for the system's three layers of 12, 42, 92
add to 146 which is the number of neutrons in uranium,
which has the highest nucleon population of all the
self-regenerative chemical elements-- and whose 146
neutrons plus the 92, unengaged mass attracting protons
of the outer layer adds 92 to 146 giving the predominant
uranium 238 from whose outer layer the excess two of
each layer-- which functions as a neutral axis of spin--
can be disengaged, which leaves the chain reacting,
uranium 236."

- Cite NEHRU SPEECH, p. 25, 13 Nov'69

---

Periodic Table:                                        (2)

See Number: 64, 22 Jan'73
    Pythagoras, (2)
    Rhombic Dodecahedron, 25 Feb'72

---

Periodic Table & Closest Packing:

See Mite as Model for Quark, 3 May'77

---

RBF DEFINITIONS

Periodicity:

"Because the physical is time, the relative endurances of
all special-case ■■■■■■■ physical experiences are
proportional to the synchronous periodicity of associability
of the complex principles involved."

- Citation and context at Metaphysical Experience, 13 Mar'73

Periodicity: (1)

See Comet
    Harmonics: Harmonic Intervals
    Ninety-two Elements: Periodic Regularities Of
    Relative Abundance
    Tidal
    Invented Periodicities
    Input Periodicities
    Decimal & Duodecimal
    Octave
    Local Periodicity

---

Periphery: Peripheral: (2)

See Projective Transformation, (4)

---

Periodicity: (2)

See Antientropy (1)
    Design Covariables: Principle Of, 1959
    Ignorance (2)
    Intellect, 16 Aug'50
    Metaphysical Experience, 13 Mar'73*
    Personality, May'49
    Physical, 13 Mar'73
    Individuality & Degrees of Freedom, (1)(2)
    Boeing 747 Sequence, 22 Jun'75
    Regenerativity, 17 Jan'75

---

Perishable:

See Mind, 24 Feb'72

---

RBF DEFINITIONS

Peripheral:

". . . Identifications of physical reality have been and
as yet are only awkwardly characterized because of the
inherent rationality of the peripheral hypotenuse aspects
of systems in respect to their radial XYZ interrelationships."

- Citation and context at XYZ Coordinate System, Sec. 825.33, Sep'72 (1), [32]

---

Permanence ≠ Normal:

See New York, 1970; 13 Mar'75

---

Periphery: Peripheral: (1)

See Embracement
    Surround

---

RBF DEFINITIONS

Permanent Symbolic Communication Devices:

"Architects designed temples, cathedrals, and other
buildings as permanent symbolic communication devices."

- Citation and context at ████████ Invisible Architecture,
(B), Aug'72

Permanent Symbolic Communications Devices:

    See Religious Edifices

---

Permeate:  Permeative:  Permeability:    (1)

    See Omniembracing vs. Permeating
        Omnipermeative
        Permeative Topology

---

Permanent Wave Architecture:

    See New York City, (1)

---

Permeate:  Permeative:  Permeability:    (2)

    See Carrier Wave, 9 Mar'73
        Octave Wave, 5 Mar'73
        Synergetic Hierarchy, 5 May'74
        Tetrahedral Dynamics, (3)
        Time, 2 Jul'62
        Truth, (1005.52) 29 Dec'73
        Universe, 4 May'57
        Vector Equilibrium, 16 Oct'72

---

Permanence:

    See Change is Normal

---

Permit:  Permitted:    (1)

    See Degrees of Freedom
        Hammering Sheet Metal
        Nature Permits it Sequence
        Realization
        Womb of Permitted Ignorance
        Event Freedoms
        Reciprocals of Permissible Viewpoints
        Copermitting

---

Permeative Topology:

    See Dymaxion Airocean World, undated

---

Permit:  Permitted:    (2)

    See Artificial, Jan'59: 22 Apr'61
        Awareness, 10 Feb'73
        Free Will, 20 Dec'73
        Invisible, 16 Dec'73
        Rules of Universe, 9 Dec'73
        Tetrahedron:  Coordinate Symmetry, Nov'71
        Twoness, 1960
        Happening, 22 Apr'71
        Isotropic Vector Matrix, Oct'71
        Conceptuality, 28 Feb'71
        Restraints, Dec'71

Permutations:                                             (1)

See Interpermutations

---

Perpendicular:  Perpendicularity:                         (1)

See Interperpendicular
    Internuclear Vector Modulus
    Line Between Two Sphere Centers
    Unique Perpendicularity
    XYZ Coordinate System
    Nonperpendicular

---

Permutations:                                             (2)

See Limit, Oct'71
    Octahedron: Nuclear Asymmetric Octa, 1 Apr'73
    Prime Number, Oct'71
    Resonance, 18 Jun'71

---

Perpendicular:  Perpendicularity:                         (2)

See Calculus, (1)
    Omnidirectional Typewriter, (1)(2)
    Projective Transformation, (6)
    Sixty Degreeness, 17 Nov'72
    Dimensionality, 30 Mar'75
    Nature in a Corner, 6 Nov'75
    Module: A Quanta Module:  Introduction Of,
        22 Feb'77
    Precession of Two Sets of 10 Closest-packed
        Spheres, (1)(2)

---

RBF DEFINITIONS

Perpendicularity:

"Perpendicularity (90-degreeness) uniquely characterizes
the limit of three dimensionality."

- Citation and context at Sixty-degreeness, 17 Nov'72

---

RBF DEFINITIONS

Perpetual Motion Machine:

"Our universe is the only and the minimum perpetual motion
machine.  It is self-regenerative."

- Cite RBF address to Am. Assn. of Museums, Denver, 2 June 1971
- Citation & Context at Self-regenerative, 2 Jun'71

---

RBF DEFINITIONS

Perpendicular:

"The minute you know you are on a sphere or spheroid,
you know that none of the perpendiculars are parallel
to one another,"

- Cite RBF to SIMS Seminar, U. Mass, Amherst, 22 July 1971.

---

RBF DEFINITIONS

Perpetual Motion Machine:

"The Universe is a perpetual motion machine because its
energy is never lost.  So the minimum number of transformations
is Universe.  It is the minimum and only perpetual motion
machine, and perpetual conservation requires this metaphysical
functioning of order and collection inherent to man."

- Citation and context at Intellect:  Equation of Intellect,
    (2)(3), 1970

RBF DEFINITIONS

Perpetual Motion Machine:

"The physical Universe is a machine-- in fact,
Universe is the minimum and only perpetual motion
machine."

- ~~Cite MUSIC OF THE NEW LIFE, U & O, p. 13.   10 Dec'64~~
- Citation & context at Universe, 10 Dec'64

---

Perpetual Motion Machine:                                    (1)

        See Closed System:  Conservation of Energy
            Eternal vs. Finite
            Self-regenerative

---

Perpetual Motion Machine:                                    (2)

            Absolute Velocity, 30 Oct'73
        See Intellect:  Equation Of, (2)(3)*
            Reciprocal, 9 Jul'62
            Regenerative, 1960; 28 Apr'71
            Self-regenerative, 2 Jun'71*
            Sphere, 26 Jan'73; (1)(2)
            Universe, 1960; 10 Dec'64*; 9 Jul'62
            Minimum Sphere, Aug'71

---

Persistence:  Persistent:

        See Matter, 19 Jun'71
            Hierarchy of Constellar Configurations, 1959
            Mobility, 4 May'57
            Atom, 8 Sep'75

---

RBF DEFINITIONS

Personality:

"The interaction of the unique patterns of... inherited genes
and experiences...make personalities..."

- Citation & context at Individuality, 9 Jan'75

---

RBF DEFINITIONS

Personality:

"A known personality, that is, a life-- with which the
comprehensive realizer is concerned-- is a unique bundle of
accumulated experience to which the new experience must
always be dissynchronous, but only at the moment of original
interference, else the new interaction of the greater complex
of truth would not have been recognizable and acquirable as
new experience and tactical advantage."

- Citation & context at Periodic Experience, (3)(4), May'49

---

RBF DEFINITIONS

Personality:

"Continuity of conscious life becomes personality and
is a product of complex periodic interactions known as
cycles, or periodic recurrences of a higher frequency
order."

- Citation & context at Charting Alternating Experiences
  of Man & Nature (1), May'49
- ~~Cite TOTAL THINKING, I&I, p.227, May'49~~

---

Personality:                                    (1)

        See Dual Personality
            Identity
            Individuality
            Multiple Personality
            Self
            Split Personality

RBF DEFINITIONS

Personality:                                             (2)

    See Charting Alternating Experiences in Man & Nature,
       (4)(5)*
      Individuality, 9 Jan'75*
      Periodic Experience, (3)(4)*

---

Persuasion:                                              (2)

    See Peace, 19 Oct'71*
      Religion, May'65

---

Perspective:

    See Central Perspective
      Intellectual Perspective
      Teleologic Perspective
      Time Perspective
      Universal Perspective

---

Perturb: Perturbation:

    See Interperturbation

---

RBF DEFINITIONS

Persuasion:

"People can't live on persuasion.  They've got to eat."

  - Citation and context at Peace, 19 Oct'71

---

Perversity:

    See Future:  Man Backs into His Future, May'49
      Progressions, May'49

---

Persuasion:                                              (1)

    See Education:  Knowing Where the Bridges Are
      Fuller, R.B:  Decision to Be a Doer, Not a Persuader

---

Pessimism:

    See River:  You Might as Well Jump in the River

Petal: Tetrahedron as Three-Petaled Flower Bud:

"Convergence is involuting; divergence is evoluting.

"Each vertex of the tetrahedron precesses its opposite
face. Like the flower petal. The action is pear-shaped
as the pattern of the vertexes opening up. Like the
plus-four and the minus-four of the Indigs, which really
should not be illustrated in a plane: the model is
tetrahedronal as in the tetrahelix.

"The tetrahedron is regenerative-- quite different from
two hemispheres."

- Cite RBF to EJA, Pepper Tree Inn, Santa Barbara, 11 Feb'73

---

Petal: Tetrahedron as Three-petaled Flower Bud:          (1)

See Leaf: Unfolding Leaves

---

Petal: Tetrahedron as Three-petaled Flower Bud:          (2)

See Comprehension, 16 Feb'73; 10 Jan'74
Geometrical Function of Nine, (3)-(6)

---

Pets:

"In Florida one of the porpoises at Marineland picked
me as a pet. People pick dogs as pets. Porpoises pick
people as pets."

- RBF to videotaping audience (between takes), Penn Bell
Studios, Philadelphia, PA., 31 Jan'75

---

Petrocolonialism:

See Transnationalism vs. Colonialism, (5)

---

Petroleum: It Costs a Billion Dollars to Make a Gallon of
Petroleum:

See Cosmic Accounting Sequence, (2)(3)
Cosmic vs. Terrestrial Accounting, (2)
Energy Capital Sequence, (2)(3)

---

Petro-pap-pipelines:

See World Pattern vs. Local Pattern, 29 Jan'75

---

Petroleum:                                               (1)

See Fossil Fuels
Petrocolonialism

Petroleum:                                                          (2)

     See Energy Slave, (3)
       No Energy Crisis, (A)-(C)

---

Phantom Captain:

     See Beautiful, 1938
       False Property Illusion, (1)(2)
       Industrial Man, 1938
       Reflection Sequence: Applew, (2)(3)
       Teleology, (2)(3)

---

RBF DEFINITIONS

    Phantom Captain:

Q. Do you foresee the day when the phantom captains
inhabit vessels of their own design?

A. "The phantom captains can and do inhabit only vessels
of their own design-- there are no other designs than
that of the great cosmic intellect's designing."

- Cite RBF Ltr. to James Coley, Sep'73

---

Pharaoh:

     See Ecology Sequence, (H)
       Pink Stuff, May'70
       Pyramid Technology, Dec'71
       Buddha: Christ: Mohamed, (1)

---

RBF DEFINITIONS

    Phantom Captain:

"An illuminating rationalization indicates that captains--
being phantom, abstract, infinite, and bound to other captains
by a bond of understanding as proven by their recognition of
each other's signals and the meaning thereof by reference to
a common direction (toward 'perfect')-- are not only all
related, but are one and the same captain. Mathematically,
since characteristics of unity exist, they cannot be nonidentical."

- Cite NINE CHAINS TO THE MOON, p.22, 1938

---

Phase: Coming Into Phase:

     See Continuous Man, 1971
       Individual Economic Initiative, 19 Feb'73

---

RBF DEFINITION

    Phantom Captain:

"Common to all such 'human' mechanisms- and without which they
are imbecile contraptions-- is their guidance by a phantom
captain.

"This phantom captain has neither weight nor sensorial
tangibility, as has often been scientifically proven by careful
weighing operations at the moment of the abandonment of the
ship by the phantom captain, i.e., at the instant of 'death.'

He may be likened to the variant of polarity dominance in our
bipolar electric world which, when balanced and unit, vanishes
as abstract unity 1 or 0. With the phantom captain's departure,
the mechanism becomes inoperative and very quickly disintegrates
into basic chemical elements. . . ."

- Cite NINE CHAINS TO THE MOON, p.19, 1938

---

RBF DEFINITIONS

    Phase & Interphase:

"Phase and Interphase of Cosmic System Transformations:
Phases are symmetric and interphases are asymmetric. The
interphases are only locally asymmetric but always
omnitransformatively symmetric."

- Cite RBF rewrite of 8 Feb'76 citation: 9 Feb'76

RBF DEFINITIONS

Phase & Interphase:

"Phases are symmetric and interphases are asymmetric.
The phases are locally and physically asymmetric but
sumtotally symmetric."

- Cite RBF to EJA, 3200 Idaho, Wash. DC.; 8 Feb'76

Phase:                                                      (1A)

   See Behavioral Phases
      Coming Apart Phase
      Coming Towardness:  Coming Together Phase
      Conservation Phase
      Contracted Phase
      Convex Individualizable Phase
      Contracting Metaphysical Universe
      Denucleated Phase
      Equilibrious-balance Phase
      Equimagnitude Phases
      Expanding Physical Universe
      Gestational Phase
      Gibbs:  Phase Rule
      Holding Together Phase
      Inside-out Phase
      Inventory of Proclivities, Phases & Disciplines
      Limit Phase
      Neutral Phase
      Nothingness Phase

Phase:                                                      (1B)

   See Omni-phase-bond Integration
      Omnipotential-energy Phase
      Orbital Phase
      Proclivity
      Push-pull:  Push Phase vs. Pull Phase
      Spherical Quadrant Phase
      Symmetric Phase
      Tetrahedral Octave Phase Model
      Three-phase Vectors
      Vector-equilibrium Phase
      Zerophase
      Split-phase
      Interphase
      Liquid-crystal-vapor-incandescent-phases

Phase:                                                      (2)

   See Atomic Triangulated Substructuring:  Hierarchy Of,
      19 Dec'73
      Congruence, 25 Jan'72
      Inflection, ▮▮▮▮ 1950
      Synergetics, 26 May'72
      Time, 1970
      Transformation, undated
      Universe as Energy & Information, 11 Nov'74
      Metaphysical & Physical Tetrahedral Quanta,
      25 Mar'71
      Dwelling Service Industry, (2)

Ph.D's as Deluxe Quality Technicians or Mechanics:

   See Specialists, May'65

Phenomenology:

   See Vector Equilibrium, Summer'71

Phenomena:  Phenomenon:

   See "Named" Phenomena
      Pattern Integrity = Phenomenon Without Name

RBF DEFINITIONS

Philosophers:

"Some of the best thinkers I know are patent attorneys, many
of them quite impressive philosophers, really trying to think
about what Universe is trying to do: What are the true
equities, difficult questions; and there's a great deal of
study going on now in the patent world about enormous changes
and reforms.  I wouldn't be surprised if that would be an
area where world man forms his own new rules."

- Cite RBF to Barry Farrell; Bear Island; Tape #8, Side B;
  transcript p.7; 22 Aug'70

RBF DEFINITIONS

Philosophy:

"I don't want any credit for having such wisdom as the
ancient philosophers. I was just lucky enough to have been
so busy as a mechanic, never to have learned about them.

"When I enmtered Harvard I had all A's in mathematics and
I took some more advanced math, and so I was able to catch on
to the whole idea of geometric proofs. But I had the good
luck to be insulated from all philosophy and such formal
knowledge. They didn't tell you anything about Plato at
Milton Academy. The nearest we got was the Platonic solids
in solid geometry.

"I knew Shakespeare, and the Fairie Queen, and Thackeray,
and all about the kings in history: who beheaded who and
who put someone in a tower. I had the battle stuff okay.
....And ████████████████████ all I knew about the Greeks
was what my mother had taught me about the Spartan boy
who brought the fox in to eat all his guts."

- Cite RBF to EJA, 3200 Idaho, Wash, DC: 11 Aug'76
  Incorporated in COSMIC FISHING; MS p. 11 - 2.

RBF DEFINITIONS

Philosophy:

"You can't better the world by simply talking to it.
Philosophy to be effective must be mechanically applied."

- Cite RBF to EJA, Wichita, Kansas; 1946

RBF DEFINITIONS

Philosophy:

"Philosophy gains validity by the practical application of
its general principles."

- Cite RBF quoted by Alden Hatch in "RBF: At Home in the Universe,"
  p. 184. Tape transcript probably. 6 Jun'74

RBF DEFINITIONS

Philosophy:

"But you can't better the world by simply talking of or
to it. Philosophy, to be effective, must be mechanically
applied."

- Cite 4-D, Timelock, Chapter 5, 21 May'28

RBF DEFINITIONS

Philosophy:

"The artists are philosophers in cry."

- Citation & context at Artist, 6 Jul'62

Philosophy:                                                      (1)

See Boolean Algebra
    Christian Legend & Philosophy
    Containing & Contained
    Epistemology
    Ethical Physics
    Fuller, R.B: His Neo-Platonism
    Geometry of Thinking
    Logic
    No Thing-in-itself
    Psychological Geometry
    Reductio ad Absurdum
    Teleology
    Thinkability
    Thinking
    Determinism
    Causality
    Equation: Philosophical Equations

RBF DEFINITIONS

Philosophy:

"Technology represents philosophy resolved to the most
cogent argument."

- Citation & context at Technology, 1947

Philosophy: Philosophers:                                        (2)

See Civilization, May'70
    Force, 1946
    Inhibit, 9 Apr'40
    Marx, Karl: Epitaph, undated
    Self-discipline, May'72
    Synergetics, Oct'71
    Technology, 1947*
    Tension, 4 Oct'72
    Theory, 22 Jul'71
    Author, Dec'72
    Epistemology, 28 May'75
    Fear & Longing, 1938
    Communications Hierarchy, (2)

Phobia of Imprisonment:

   See Immobility, 4 May'57

Phonetics:  Phonetic Letters:                                    (2)

   See Phoenician, 28 Jan'75
      Communications Hierarchy, (2)

RBF DEFINITIONS

   Phoenician:

   "Phoenician = phonetic.  The Phoenicians invented the
   alphabet for trade."

   - Cite RBF at Penn Bell videotaping, Philadelphia, 28 Jan'75

Photoelectric:

   See Light Cells

RBF DEFINITIONS

   Phoenician Phonetic Sequence:

   "Poon -- red -- pundit -- thinker -- Phoenician -- Venetian --
   Punic Wars -- punt -- boat..."

   - Cite RBF videotaping Penn Bell Studios, Phila., PA 23 Jan'75

Photography:                                                      (1)

   See Camera
      Macrophotography
      Microphotography
      Model vs. Photograph

Phonetics:  Phonetic Letters:                                    (1)

   See Letters of the Alphabet
      Navy Phonetic Sequence
      Phoenician Phonetic Sequence

Photography:                                                      (2)

   See Eye-beamed Thoughts, (II)(III)

RBF DEFINITIONS

Photon:

"Max Planck's photons of light are separately packaged at
the radiation source and travel in a group-coordinated
flight formation spherical surface pattern which is ever
expanding outwardly as they gradually separate from one
another.  Every photon always travels radially away from
the common origin.  This group-developed pattern produces
a sum-totally expanding spherical wave-surface determined
by the plurality of outwardly traveling photons, although
any single photon travels linearly outwardly in only one
radial direction.  This total energy effort is exactly
expressed in terms of the exponential second-power, or areal
'squaring,' rate of surface growth of the overall spherical
wave; i.e., as the second power of the energy effort expended
in lifting one gram in each second of time a distance of
one 'vertical' centimeter radially outward from the origin
center."

- Cite SYNERGETICS draft at Sec. 223.72, 26 Sep'73

---

Photon:  Tetrahedron Edge as Unit Radius:                    (1)

See Constant Volume of A & B Quanta Modules
    Radial Line as Tetra Edge
    Tetra Edge
    Unit Radius

---

RBF DEFINITIONS

Photon:

"The minimum increment of all radiation, the photon . . ."

"... Max Planck's photon of light. . . expands outwardly as
a spherical wave surface in all directions-- instead of
travelling linearly outwardly in only one ████████ radial
direction..."

- Citation and context at Planck's Constant (C), 15 May'73

---

Photon:  Tetrahedron Edge as Unit Radius:                    (2)

See T Quanta Module, (1)

---

Photon-quantum:

See Spherical Field, 9 Jan'74

---

Photon:                                                       (1)

See Photon-quantum

---

RBF DEFINITIONS

Photon:  Tetrahedron Edge as Unit Radius:

"...We identify the minimum tetrahedron photon as that
with radius = c, which is the speed of light: the tetrahedron
edge of the photon becomes unit radius = frequency limit."

- Cite RBF clarification of garble at galley marginalis,
  SYNERGETICS Sec. 1106.23, by telephone from La Jolla,
  to Wash, DC, 17 Jan'74.

- Citation & context at Unit Radius, 17 Jan'74

---

Photon:                                                       (2)

See Finite Furniture, 7 Nov'73
    Gravity, (2)
    Planck's Constant, (A)-(C)*
    Nonsimultaneity, 7 Nov'73

Photo-satellite:

See Satellite: Telescopes Mounted on Around-Earth,
Fixedly-hovering, Photo-satellites

RBF DEFINITIONS

RBF DEFINITIONS

Photosynthesis:

"Thus Sun energy as heat is impounded into the atmosphere
to produce weather changes. Thus also are the waters refract-
ionally heated by the Sun's radiation. Thus by a series of
relay stages is energy impounded aboard our spaceship Earth
to regenerate life by the photosynthesis of the vegetation,
which is a beautiful process whereby the random energy receipts
are transformed chemically into beautiful orderly molecules,
which are beautiful structures. Here you see the turnaround
from ▮▮▮▮ disorder to order-- from entropy to antientropy.
All the biologicals are converting chaos to beatiful order.
All biology is antientropic."

— Cite Antientropy (2), Oct'69

RBF DEFINITIONS

Photosynthesis:

"Photosynthesis is meaningful communication whereby metaphysical rules the physical (like the Federal Reserve Bank) by
issuing or withdrawing complex coding-identified 'quanta'
currency from the overall, cosmic, transforming and transaction system's accounting."

— Citation & context at Radiation as Information-carrier,
9 Jun'75

Photosynthesis:                                                 (1)

See Biosphere
    Ecology Sequence
    Metabolic Flow
    Radiation Sequence
    Electromagnetic-photosynthetic Programming
    Octahedron as Photosynthesis Model

RBF DEFINITIONS

Photosynthesis:                                                 (1)

"The Sun's radiant energy
Is the prime regenerating source
For all biological life on our planet.
Even while sunburning their skins
Humans and all other mammals
Are unable to take in enough radiant energy
Through their skins
To keep themselves alive.
To circumvent mammals attempting futilely ▮▮▮ so to do
Nature has invented
The green vegetation on the dry lands,
And the algae in the waters around the Earth's surface.
The vegetation and the algae
Impound the Sun's radiation by photosynthesis
Converting the radiation
Into orderly molecules,
Which provide celestial life's prime energy intake.
The vegetation and algae
Provide metabolic sustenance
Of all manner of creatures,
Some of which can in turn.
Nourish humans.

— Cite BRAIN & MIND, Pp. 109-110 May '72

Photosynthesis:                                                 (2)

See Antientropy, (A)(B); (2)*
    Boltzmann Sequence, (5)
    Cosmic vs. Terrestrial Accounting, (2)
    Cosmic Accounting Sequence, (2)
    Design, (2)
    Isotropic Vector Matrix Field, 15 Feb'73
    Manifest: Six; 1973
    Precession, (a)(b); (II)
    Roots, May'72
    Syntropy & Entropy, 31 May'74
    Wind Power Sequence, (2)(3); (A)
    Radiation as Information-carrier, 9 Jun'75

RBF DEFINITIONS

Photosynthesis:                                                 (2)

"Urged by subconsciously initiated desire,
Or genetically programmed
To experience thirst, appetite and breathing,
Biological species are motivated
To 'feed' in the solid, liquid and gaseous
Chemical constituents necessary
To produce the ongoing biological molecules
Whose energies are convertible
Into action and growth."

— Cite BRAIN & MIND, p.110 May '72

RBF DEFINTIONS

Physical:

"The physical is always special case; that's why we spell
Universe with a capital U."

— Cite RBF to EJA & Roger Stoller, 3200 Idaho, Wash, DC; 12 Nov'75

GENERALIZATION + SPECIAL CASE     SEC 262.08

RBF DEFINITIONS

Physical:

"The physicist's first definition of physical is that it is an experience which is extracorporeally, remotely, instrumentally apprehendible."

- Citation & context at Metaphysical & Physical, 27 Dec'74

---

RBF DEFINITIONS

Physical:

"... The physical energy Universe's inexorably expanding momentary disorders..."

_ Cite INTUITION, p.60 May '72

---

RBF DEFINITIONS

Physical:

"The physical is always experienceable and special case."

- Citation and context at Limit-Limitless, 4 Nov'73

---

RBF DEFINITIONS

Physical:

"Waves are not metaphysical.  Waves are physical."

- Citation at Wave, 19 Dec'71

---

RBF DEFINITIONS

Physical:

"P = Physical:  All the physical is energy."

- Cite SYNERGETICS draft at Sec. 1056.20 (item #32), 13 May'73

---

RBF DEFINITIONS

Physical:

"Definition of Intellect:  The metaphysical measures the physical, but not the reverse, i.e., local irreversibility."

-Cite RBF to EJA, Somerset Club, Boston, 22 April 1971

- Citation at Intellect:  Equation of Intellect, 22 Apr'71

---

RBF DEFINITIONS

Physical:

"Because the physical is time, the relative endurances of all special-case physical experiences are proportional to the synchronous periodicity of associability of the complex principles involved."

- Citation & context at Metaphysical Experience, 13 Mar'73

---

RBF DEFINITIONS

Physical:

"Without weight you do not exist physically-- nor without a specific temperature. . . "

- Citation & context at Temperature of the Human Body, 21 Dec'71
- Cite RBF to EJA, 3200 Idaho, Washington DC, 21 Dec. '71.

RBF DEFINITIONS

Physical:

"The physical alone accelerates and is fast. It is really only the destructive things or negative things that accelerate."

- Citation & context at Eternal Slowdown, circa 1970

---

RBF DEFINITIONS

Physical:

"The concept of life
Is unique to the mind.
Brain apprehands
Only the physical.
Brain does not differentiate life and death."

- Cite GENERALIZED PRINCIPLES, p.7, 28 Jan'69

---

RBF DEFINITIONS

Physical:

"The physical is subdivisible
Into two different phenomena
Energy associative as matter-- substance
And energy disassociative as radiation,
Both of which behavioral phenomena
May be transformed into one another."

- Cite RBF Draft BRAIN & MIND, pencil, 1970

---

RBF DEFINITIONS

Physical:

". . . All patterns, for instance, numbers or phonetic letters, consist of physical ingredients or physical experience recalls. The physical ingredients consist inherently of event-paired quanta, and the latter's six-vectored, positive and negative, actions, reactions and resultants. . . "

- Cite NASA Speech, p. 58, Jun'66

- Citation at Pattern, Jun'66

---

RBF DEFINTIONS

Physical:

"The physical is inherently entropic; it gives off energy in ever more disorderly ways."

- Cite NEHRU, p. 39
13 Nov'69

---

RBF DEFINITIONS

Physical:

"The proton group and the neutron group account rationally for all physical structures."

- Cite NASA Speech, p. 64, June '66

- Citation at Proton & Neutron, Jun'66

---

RBF DEFINITIONS

Physical:

"The physical is always special case."

- Citation and context at Generalization Sequence (1), Jun-Jul'69

---

RBF DEFINITIONS

Physical:

"My definition of Universe inherently includes all the ponderable, i.e., weighable, instrumentally detectable, associative and disassociative, material and radiational energy behaviors of the physical subdivision of Universe."

- Cite DOXIADIS, p. 310, 20 Jun'66

RBF DEFINITIONS

Physical:

"Electromagnetic frequencies of systems are sometimes
complex but always constitute the prime rational integer
characteristic of physical systems."

- ~~Cite NASA Speech, p. 91, Jun'66~~

- Citation at Frequency, (p.91) Jun'66

---

Physical Case:

See Vector Equilibrium, Oct'75
Vector Equilibrium Involvement Domain, 10 Dec'75

---

RBF DEFINITIONS

Physical:
                STRUCTURAL            ARE
"All ~~physical~~ phenomena ~~is~~ accounted in the terms of
tetrahedron, octahedron, vector equilibrium and
icosahedron."

        (RBF noted 30 May'72 that "Wavilinear is
        physical but not structural, since it is not
        accounted for by tetrahedron, octahedron,
        vector equilibrium, and icosahedron." -- EJA note.)

- Cite Oregon Lecture #5, p. 179, 9 Jul '62

---

Physical Discontinuity:

See Interference:  You Really Can't Get There From Here,
19 Dec'73

---

RBF DEFINITIONS

Physical:

"It is the nature of physical universe always to operate
in the most economical ways.  Sometimes there are a
plurality of equally economicals and nature might operate
in any one of these equally economicals.  This does not
put nature into a groove.  There is not just a one most
economical way but there are an alternate number of equally
economicals-- and nature will always take one of that set."

        - Cite OREGON LECTURE #2 - p. 70, 2 Jul '62

---

TEXT CITATIONS

Physical Education:

Hyper, World Mag., 10 Apr'73

---

RBF DEFINITIONS

Physical:

"The physical portion of Universe is energetic
and finite."

    - Cite INTRO. to OMNIDERECTIONAL HALO, p. 124, 1959

---

Physical Evolution:

See Cosmogony
Scenario Universe:  Physical Evolution Scenario

Physical Experience Recalls:

See Pattern, Jun'66

Physical Ingredients:

See Pattern, Jun'66

RBF DEFINITIONS

Physical is Always the Imperfect:

"The whole of Universe is a consequence of our not seeing instantly. As a result of the recall lags the physical is always imperfect."

- Citation at Recall Lags, 26 May'72

Physical Law:                                        (1)

See Laws of Nature vs. Laws of Man

RBF DEFINITIONS

Physical Is Always The Imperfect:

"We discover . . . that the physical is always the imperfect, special-case, after-imaged lagging realization of the ideal generalization, which can be realized, or momentized, or experimentally identified, time-ized and measured, only by such limited, ergo imperfect approximation, all of which latter is implicit in Heisenberg's operationally imposed indeterminism."

- For citation and context see Metaphysical, 14 Feb '72

Physical Law:                                        (2)

See Navy:  Theory Of, 22 Dec'74

Physical is Always the Imperfect:

See Recall Lags, 26 May'72*
    Metaphysical, 14 Feb'72*
    Perfection, 4 Nov'73

RBF DEFINITIONS

Physical Life:

"Physical Life is always a special case."

- Citation and context at Generalized Principle (A), 22 May'73

Physical to Metaphysical - Brain to Mind:

    See Triangle, (1)

---

RBF DEFINITIONS

Physical Reality:

"It is a condition that nature apparently does not permit in our life, but what we call physical reality is always a positive and negative pulsating aberration of the whole-- a multifrequency-accommodating, vector equilibrium aberratability whole."

- Cite RBF rewrite of SYNERGETICS galley at Sec. 441.23, 4 Nov'73

---

Physical to Metaphysical:      (1)

    See Cosmic Discontinuity & Local Continuity
        Idea Trending
        Progressions

---

RBF DEFINITIONS

Physical Reality:

"The vector equilibrium and the isotropic vector matrix are the equilibrium or the central set of conditions through which physical reality palpitates. It never stops at the center. . ."

- For citation and context see Vector Equilibrium, 1 May '71

---

Physical to Metaphysical:      (2)

    See Cosmic Accounting, 2 Jun'74
        Process Relationships, 28 Jan'69

---

RBF DEFINITIONS

Physical Reality:

"It is a condition that nature apparently does not permit in our ▓▓▓▓▓ life, but what we call reality is always a positive and negative set of the whole."

- Citation & context at Vector Equilibrium: Zero Tetrahedron, (3), 11 Jul'62

---

RBF DEFINITIONS

Physical Reality:

"Very clearly, vector equilibrium is a zerosize tetrahedron. We have already had tetrahedron as an indestructible phenomenon independent of size. And then we have it getting into its own true zero vector equilibrium. It is a condition that apparently nature does not permit in our life, but what we call physical reality is always a positive and negative pulsating aberration of the whole-- a multifrequency-accommodating, vector equilibrium aberratability whole."

- Cite SYNERGETICS text at Sec. 441.23 as rewritten by RBF on galley, 4 Nov'73

---

Physical Reality:      (1)

    See Potential vs. Physically Realized

Physical Reality: Physical Realization: (2)

See Awareness, 10 Feb'73
Mathematics, undated
No Generalized Boat, 22 Jan'75
Vector, 27 May'72
Vector Equilibrium, 1 May'71*
Vector Equilibrium: Zero Tetrahedron, (3)*
Universe, 11 Dec'75
Regular = Uniangular, 11 Dec'75

RBF DEFINITIONS

Physical Synergy:

"The universal mass interattractions called gravity
Of galaxies, star systems and atoms
All manifest physical synergy."

- Cite EVOLUTIONARY 1972-1975 ABOARD SPACE VEHICLE EARTH,
Jan. '72, p. 6.

Physical Ingredient Recalls:

See Alphabet, Jun'66

Physical Tetrahedron vs. Conceptual Tetrahedron:

See Instantaneity - Eternity

RBF DEFINITIONS

Physical Sciences:

"But physical science lacked the experience which might have
persuaded it to hypothesize what all Universe it. Physical
science therefore restricted its comprehensive accounting
strategy to the special case of definitive isolations within
the physical portion of Universe. This left the remainder of
all experiences, no matter how earnestly and meticulously
reconsidered, outside the definitive portion of comprehended
experiences of Universe, i.e., the physicist said that all
that is not physically encompassed as $E = Mc^2$ is metaphysical."

- Cite INTRODUCTION TO OMNIDIRECTIONAL HALO, p.124, 1959

RBF DEFINITIONS

Physical Universe:

"The whole of physical Universe experience is a consequence
of our not seeing instantly, which introduces time. As a result
of the recall lags the physical is always imperfect."

& context
- Citation at Time, 26 May'72

Physical vs. Structural:

See Physical, 9 Jul'62
Wavilinear, 30 May'72

RBF DEFINITIONS

Physical Universe:

"Minimum Effort is one of the chief characteristics of

our physical Universe."

- Cite RBF to EJA, 3200 Idaho, Washington DC, 21 Dec. '71.

RBF DEFINITIONS

Physical Universe:

"Physics has found the whole physical Universe to be
uniquely differentiated and locally defined as 'waves.'"

- Cite RBF Marginalia, at SYNERGETICS, Sec. 522.04, Nov. '71.

Physical Universe: (2)

See Comprehensive Universe, (1)*
    Dimension, 1 Apr'49*
    Energy, Jun'66
    Frequency, 1970
    Radiation, 18 Mar'65
    Relativity, May'72; Jun'66
    Time, 26 May'72*
    Wave, Nov'71
    Zero, 13 Nov'69
    A Priori Four-dimensional Reality, (1)
    Conservation of Energy, 18 Mar'65
    Poetry, 13 Nov'69
    Left & Right, 7 Nov'75
    Infinite, 15 Oct'72
    Multiplication by Division, 20 Jan'77

RBF DEFINITIONS

Physical Universe:

"The physical universe as we have seen it is
entirely charcterized by entropy-- an ever increasing
randomness, an ever increasing diffusion as all the
different and non-simultaneous transformations and
reorientations occur."

- Cite NASA Speech, p. 87, Jun'66

- Citation and context at Comprehensive Universe (1), Jun'66

Physical Vectors:

See Powering: Sixth Powering, 26 Nov'72

RBF DEFINITIONS

Physical Universe:

"[Synergetics originates] in the assumption that dimension
must be physical. It follows that, inasmuch as physical
Universe is entirely energetic, all dimension must be energetic.
Vectors and tensors constitute all elementary dimension."

- Citation at Dimension, 1 Apr'49

Physical: (1A)

See Body: Bodies
    Field: IVM Field of Thought or Physical Articulation
    Life Cells
    Life is Not Physical
    Metaphysical & Physical
    Mortal
    Omnidirectional: Physical Existence Environment
        Surrounds
    Physical vs. Structural
    Real
    Realization
    Scenario Universe: Physical Evolution Scenario
    Sense Phrases
    Energy & Information
    Metabolic Flow
    Atoms vs. Radiation
    Matter
    Matter vs. Radiation
    Know-how Accounting vs. Physical Accounting
    Human Mind & Physical Evolution

Physical Universe: (1)

See Equanimity Model
    Eternal Universe & Physical Universe
    Intellect in Physical Universe
    Expanding Physical Universe
    Perpetual Motion Machine
    Energy: Energetic

Physical: (1B)

See Frequency = Experienced Physical Energy
    Constant vs. Physical
    Ninety-two Elements

Physical: (2A)

Adam & Eve, 2 Jun'74
See Awareness, 10 Feb'73
Angular Topology: Principle Of, 14 Dec'66
Communication, 13 Mar'73
Electromagnetic Spectrum, Aug'64
Eternal Slowdown, 1970*
Generalization, 13 Mar'73*
Generalization Sequence (1)*
Intellect: Equation of Intellect, 2 Apr'71*
Imperfect, 26 May'72
Limit-limitless, 4 Nov'73*
Organism, 3 Jun'72
Metaphysical Experience, 13 Mar'73*
Frequency, (p.91) Jun'66*
Life, 7 Apr'75
Modelability, 12 May'75
Energy Event, Mar'71
Multiplication by Division, 20 Jan'77

RBF DEFINITIONS

Physics:

"Physics is concerned only with the most economical."

- Cite RBF lecture
Town Hall, New York
12 March 1971

- Citation at Most Economical, 12 Mar'71

---

Physical: (2B)

See Pattern, Jun'66*
Proton & Neutron, Jun'66*
Periodicity, 13 Mar'73
Principle, Jun'69
Real, 20 Apr'72
Reality, 22 Apr'71
Size, 21 Mar'73
Specialization, 28 Apr'71
Structure, 29 Dec'58; 1965
War, 1971
Wave, 19 Dec'71*
Temperature of the Human Body, 21 Dec'71*
Seven Minimum Topological Aspects, 12 Feb'76
Womb of Permitted Ignorance, (1)(2)

RBF DEFINITIONS

Physics:

"All the time phenomena of physicists are linear."

- Citation & context at Time, 8 Mar'71

---

Physical: (3)

Physical Case
See Physical Discontinuity
Physical Education
Physical Experience Recalls
Physical Is Always the Imperfect
Physical Ingredients
Physical Life
Physical to Metaphysical
Physical Reality
Physical Ingredient Recalls
Physical Sciences
Physical vs. Structural
Physical Synergy
Physical Universe
Physical Vectors
Physical Law
Physical Tetrahedron vs. Conceptual Tetrahedron
Physical Evolution

RBF DEFINITIONS

Physics:

"Ernest Mach . . said that 'Physics is experience arranged in the most economical order.' To define the special case of science known as physics Mach added only the two words 'most economical' to Eddington's definition of generalized science. Mach made this qualification because physicists have found that nature always behaves most economically."

- Cite NASA Speech, pp 36,37, Jun'66

- Citation & context at Environmental Events Hierarchy, (5)(6), Jun'66

---

RBF DEFINITIONS

Physics:

"That's what physics is: the energy investment of Universe on a wave-quantum basis."

- Cite RBF remarks at Design Science Institute press conference, N.Y. 28 Jun'72

---

RBF DEFINITIONS

Physics & Chemistry: Difference Between:

"The vector equilibrium is the... zero-inflection, nonmoment of intertransformabilities where anything can happen and must happen single-atomically within and multiatomically without."

- Citation & context at Vector Equilibrium as Starting Point, 8 Apr'75

RBF DEFINITIONS
        & Chemistry:
    Physics:  Difference Between ███████████████:

"In the atoms we are always dealing in equiradius spheres.
Chemical compounds may, and ███████████ often do, consist
of atomic spheres with a variety of radial dimensions.
Since each chemical element's atoms are characterized by
unique frequencies, and unique frequencies impose unique
radial symmetries, this variety of radial dimensionality
constitutes one prime difference between nuclear physics
and chemistry."

- Cite RBF rewrite of SYNERGETICS, Sec. 415.23 (5 July'72)
  per marginalis, Beverly Hotel, NY, 22 Jun'72.

---

RBF DEFINITIONS
        & Chemistry:
    Physics:  Difference Between ███████████:

"The cube relates to chemistry, the external affairs of
the atom.  Organic chemistry begins with the cube:
carbon.  The tetrahedron, octahedron, and icosahedron
relate to physics, the ████████ affairs of the atom."
                            internal

- Cite RBF to EJA, Blackstone Hotel, Chicago, 31 May'71

---

RBF DEFINITIONS
        & Chemistry:
    ███████ Physics:  Difference Between ████████████████:

"In the atoms we are always dealing in equiradius spheres.

Chemical compounds may, and often do, consist of atomic

spheres in a variety of radial dimensions.  This is the

difference between nuclear physics and chemistry."

_ Cite SYNERGETICS draft at Sec. 415.23, 8 Jun'72

---

RBF DEFINITIONS
        & Chemistry:
    Physics:  Difference Between ██████████:

"All the phenomena larger and more complex than vector
equilibria do relate to the chemical compounds and anything
smaller than vector equilibrium relates to the single atoms
and the single atoms do get into the symmetries whereas the
chemical compounds get into a polarized system."

- Cite Oregon Lecture #7, p.235, 11 Jul'62

- Citation and context at Vector Equilibrium, ii Jul'62

VE AS ZERO MODEL   SEC 132.03| 440.03|

---

RBF DEFINITIONS

    Physics & Chemistry:  Difference Between:

"In the atoms we are always dealing with equiradius
spheres.  Chemical compounds have multiradius spheres.
This is the difference between nuclear physics and
chemistry."

- Cite RBF to EJA, 3200 Idaho, Wash DC, 28 May'72

---

RBF DEFINITIONS
        & Chemistry:
    Physics:  Difference Between ██████████:

"The physicist deals with the internal affairs █ and
the chemist with the external affairs of the atom."

- Cite NO MORE SECOND HAND GOD, p.32, 9 Apr'40

---

RBF DEFINITIONS
        & Chemistry:
    Physics:  Difference ██████████████:

"All the internal or nuclear affairs of the atom occur
internally to the vector equilibrium and all the external
or chemical associations occur externally to the vector
equilibrium."

- Cite NASA Speech, pp. 63-84, Jun'66
- Citation and context at Vector Equilibrium (I), Jun'66

---

    Physics & Chemistry:  Difference Between:                    (1)

        See Atoms & Compounds:  Difference Between
            Ninety-two Elements

Physics & Chemistry: Difference Between: (2)

See Organic & Inorganic, Nov'71
Vector Equilibrium, (I)*; 11 Jul'62*

---

Physics: (2)

See Energetic Words, 1 Jul'62
Environmental Events Hierarchy, Jun'66*
Invention, 27 Dec'73
MIT Sequence, (2)
Most Economical, 9 Jul'62; 12 Mar'71*
Time, 8 Mar'71
Topology, 11 Dec'75
Structure, 23 Jan'76
Experiential Mathematics, 15 Oct'76

---

RBF DEFINITIONS

Physics as Internal Affairs of the Atom:

"The tetrahedron, octahedron, and icosahedron relate to physics, the internal affairs of the atom."

- Citation and context at Physics: Difference Between Physics and Chemistry, 31 May'71

---

RBF DEFINITIONS

Pi:

"The neat five value of the nuclear sphere eliminates the necessity of employing pi in synergetics coordinate systems, though it discloses where and why pi coexists, but only as a terminal vestige."

- Citation and context at Cul de Sac, 30 Dec'73

---

Physics as Internal Affairs of the Atom:

See Atom as Solar System

---

RBF DEFINITIONS

Pi: ($\pi$):

"Circle = polygon
"Sphere = polyhedron

"That's what makes calculus and trigonometry seem so difficult. And pi doesn't come in because the arc is just not there. The radian is beyond the limits of experienciable demonstrability."

- Cite RBF to EJA, 3200 Idaho Nw, (Cf. Sec. ~~1005.63~~ draft),8 Feb'73

---

Physics: (1)

See Ethical Physics
Fields
Quantum Mechanics
Relativity
Strange Particles
Conceptual Physics
Quarks

---

RBF DEFINITIONS

Pi: ($\pi$):

"The irrational radian and pi ($\pi$) are not used by nature because angular accelerations are in finite package impelóments which are chordal (not arcs) and produce hexagons because the average of all angular stabilizations from all triangular interactions average at 60 degrees-- ergo radii and 60-degree chords are equal and identical; ergo six 60-degree chords equal one frequency cycle; ergo one unit of quantum."

- ~~Cite RBF undated holograph done in November 1971, probably in New Delhi, India~~
Incorporated in SYNERGETICS at Sec. 423.10, 11 Oct'72
- Citation at Hexagon, Nov'71

RBF DEFINITIONS

Pi: ($\pi$):

"The transcendentally irrational 'constant' pi ($\pi$) is
irrelevant to spherical geodesic polyhedral array calculations
because minimum sphere is a tetrahedron."

- Citation & context at Minimum Sphere, Aug'71

---

RBF QUOTATION

Piaget: Jean: Child's Spontaneous Geometry: (1)

"Study of the child's discovery of spatial relationships--
what may be called the child's spontaneous geometry-- is no
less rewarding than the investigation of his number concepts.
A child's order of development in geometry seems to reverse
the order of historical discovery. Scientific geometry began
with the Euclidean system (concerned with figures, angles,
and so on), developed in the 17th century to the so-called
projective geometry (dealing with problems of perspective),
and finally came in the 19th century to topology (describing
spatial relationships in a general qualitative way-- for
intance, the distinction between open and closed structures,
interiority and exteriority, proximity and separation).
A child begins with the last: his first geometrical discoveries
are topological. At the age of three he readily distinguishes
between open and closed figures: if you ask him to copy a
square or a triangle, he draws a closed circle; he draws a
cross with two separate lines. If you show him a drawing of
a large circle with a small circle inside, he is quite
capable of reproducing this relationship, and he can
also draw a small circle outside or attached to the edge of
the large one. All this he can do before he can draw a"

- Cite Jean Piaget: HOW CHILDREN FORM MATHEMATICAL CONCEPTS,
    "Scientific American," p. 75, Nov'53. Above quote marked by RBF.

---

RBF DEFINTIONS

Pi: ($\pi$):

"Pi ($\pi$) is irrelevant in Synergetics because the sphere
is not experimentally demonstrable and tetrahedron is
the minimum sphere. Compound curvature starts with the
tetetrahedron. Pi drops out because chords are more
economical than arcs. . . ."

~~-Cite RBF to EJA, Blackstone Hotel, Chicago, 31 March 1971-~~

- Citation and context at Sphere, 31 May'71

---

RBF QUOTATION

Piaget: Jean: Child's Spontaneous Geometry: (2)

"rectangle or express the Euclidean characteristics (number
of sides, angles, etc.) of a figure. Not until a considerable
time after he has mastered topological relationships does he
begin to develop his notions of Euclidean and projective
geometry. Then he builds these simultaneously."

- Cite HOW CHILDREN FORM MATHEMATICAL CONCEPTS, by Jean Piaget,
    "Scientific American," p.75, Nov'53. Above passage marked
                                                        by RBF.

---

Pi: ($\pi$): (1)

See Bubbles in the Wake of a Ship Sequence
    Circle: Synergetics Formula for Triangular Area
        of a Circle
    Irrational Constants
    Sphere: Synergetics Formula for Area & Volume
        of a Sphere

---

RBF DEFINITIONS

Piano Top:

"I am enthusiastic over humanity's extraordinary and
sometimes very timely ingenuities. If you are in a shipwreck
and all the boats are gone, a piano top buoyant enough to
keep you afloat that comes along makes a fortuitous life
preserver. But this is not to say that the best way to
design a life preserver is in the form of a piano top. I
think that we are clinging to a great many piano tops in
accepting yesterday's fortuitous contrivings as constituting
the only means for solving a given problem. Our brains
deal exclusively with special-case experiences. Only our
minds are able to discover the generalized principles
operating without exception in each and every special-case
experience case which if detected and mastered will give
knowledgeable advantage in all instances."

- Cite opening paragraph, Chapter One of OPERATING MANUAL
    FOR SPACESHIP EARTH, 1969

---

Pi: ($\pi$): (2)

See Chords, 22 Jul'71; 31 May'71
    Cul de Sac, 30 Dec'73*
    Disparity, 1960
    Hexagon, Nov'71*
    Spherical Interstices, 18 Nov'72
    Starting with Parts: The Nonradial Line, 29 Dec'73
    Universal Integrity: Principle Of, 21 Dec'71
    Vector Equilibrium: Spheres & Spaces (1)
    Vector Equilibrium: Zerophase, 1 May'71
    Geodesic Sphere, (1)

---

Piano:

See Neutral, 1 Feb'75
    Standardization, 13 May'30

RBF DEFINITIONS

Picasso Duo-face Painting:

"This 2½ positive superimposed upon the 2½ negative, 120-LCD
picture is somewhat like a Picasso duo-face painting with
half a front view superimposed upon half a side view..."

- Citation and context at Basic Triangle:  Basic Equilibrium
  48 LCD Triangle, 17 Dec'73

---

Picture Puzzle:

See Puzzle

---

RBF DEFINITIONS

Picasso Duo-face Painting:                                          (1)

See Split Personality
    Profile:  There is No Half-Profile

---

Picture:                                                            (1)

See Children's Picture of the Sun & the Moon
    Conceptual Geometry
    Picasso Duo-face Painting
    Time Entered the Picture through Poetry

---

RBF DEFINITIONS

Picasso Duo-face Painting:                                          (2)

See Basic Triangle:  Basic Equilibrium 48 LCD Triangle,
    17 Dec'73

---

Picture:                                                            (2)

See Brain, 30 Nov'72
    Frame, 15 Dec'73
    Reflection Sequence:  Apple (2)*
    Topology:  Synergetic & Eulerian (2)
    Polyhedron, 1 Jan'75
    Simplest Knot, 1 Jan'75
    Invisibility of Macro- and Micro- Resolutions, (1)

---

RBF DEFINITIONS

Picture:

"...Light absorption and reflection are mechanical considerations
because neither life nor mind activity is involved until the
essence of the picture has been articulated in the 'brain' and
has been automatically referred to the memory filing department
(the system of which is even more complicated than the worldwide Bertillon system of finger-print identification) for
comparison with all of the apple experiences of the 'see-er."

- Citation and context at Reflection Sequence:  Apple (2), 1938

---

Piezo- : Piezo-crystals: Piezo-electricity:

See Quantum Mechanics:  Minimum Geometrical Fourness,(1)

Synergetics Dictionary

Pigment:  Pigmentation:

    See Skin Pigmentation

RBF DEFINITIONS

Pink Stuff:

"The Pharaoh said to the doctor,

'Doctor, give me that pink stuff.'

The doctor said, 'Pharaoh, I think

The pink stuff is the wrong stuff.'

The Pharaoh said, 'Give me the

Pink stuff!'

The doctor did.

They put the living doctor

Into the tomb with the dead Pharaoh."

- Cite I SEEK TO BE A VERB, Queen, May '70 (Not in Bantam edition)

Pin:  Head of a Pin:

    See Invisible Circuitry, (1)

Pipe:                                                      (1)

    See Closest Packing of Rods
    Monopolizable over Pipe or Wire
    Petro-pap-pipelines

Pine Tree & Palm Tree Belts:

    See Ecology Sequence, (E)

Pipe:  Pipes:                                             (2)
    See New York City (8)

Pine Tree:

    See Hierarchies, 16 Jun'72

RBF DEFINITIONS

Pirates:  Great Pirates:

Q.     "Are there still great pirates?... Can I become one?"

RBF:    "The top ones were called sovereigns and the lesser
ones were called pirates, and the even lesser ones hi-jackers.
The British Empire began as a subterfuge for Queen Elizabeth I
to go into private enterpise with the East India Company... The
American flag was actually derived from that of the East India
Company.... The German cartels were owned partly by the allies
and they played both sides.  The East India people switbhed over
and backed the new American colonies.

"There are no great pirates left.  It's all lawyers now, and
lawyer-capitalism.  It's all now corporate: the safest and
surest way to make the most money."

- Cite RBF to World Game Workshop'77; Phila., PA: 22 Jun'77

288

RBF DEFINITIONS

Pirates:  Great Pirates:                                    (1)

"Penobscot, Blue Hill, and Frenchman's Bay were up to World
War I the summer residence country of what Bucky Fuller speaks
of as history's 'Great Pirates.'  These were the men who ran
the world as a consequence of their commanding the oceans of
the Earth-- for the oceans of the Earth governed three-quarters
of our planet.  Because the laws invented and adopted by dry-
land-dwelling people cannot be enforced either logically or
practically over the ever moving ocean waters beyond their
political entity's shores, the ocean seas are inherently outside the man-made laws.  Only the physical laws of raw nature
govern the seas.

"The high seas sailormen were inherently 'outlaws'-- therefore
pirates.  When one high seas crew seized another ship, she was
called a prize into which they entered-- ergo, enterprize.
Because the greatest pirates were, literally speaking, 'privately
enterprising outlaws,' Bucky used the contracted form of this
term, which is simply 'pirate', to identify them.  The great
pirates were inherently world people because they were masters
of the World Ocean.  Land people are local people and think locally.  Ocean people are world people and think world."

- Cite BEAR ISLAND STORY, galley pp.25-26, 1968

RBF DEFINITIONS

Pirates:  Great Pirates:                                    (2)

"The headquarters of the 'Greatest Pirates' were the British
Isles because the British Isles represented the unsinkable
flagships commanding the majority of the best harbors of Europe
where lived the richest customers for their world trade.  The
greatest pirates manned their ships with men from their
shipyard's country.  Because the most conveniently recruited
or 'Shanghaied' their sailors from the British Isles waterfront
saloons, their operation came to be called the 'British
Empire' though such an empire was never the democratic ambition
of the British Isles people.  World-around sea battling narrowed
the field of contenders for world supremacy.  Finally there was
established amongst the greatest pirates the top or IN pirates.
The IN pirates called themselves 'sovereign' and called all the
OUT pirates 'outlaws.'

"When the North American ███████ colonists broke away from the
greatest IN pirates in 1775, those British Isles-based great
pirates came to America where, finding it impossible to
dominate or conquer the colonists politically, they conquered
their business world through financing acumen and control of
the corporation shares."

- Cite BEAR ISLAND STORY, galley p.26, 1968

RBF DEFINITIONS

Pirates:  Great Pirates:                                    (3)

"When World War I was declared in August 1914, the British
Ambassador to the United States, Sir Arthur Spring-Rice was in
residence at Isleboro in Penobscot Bay.  That's where the
great IN pirates were making their war defense plans.  World
War I was waged by the greatest OUT pirates against the great
IN pirates.  With its mighty new armored steel ships replete
with modern mechanics, World War I was the first comprehensive
world-around industrial technology and science war in history.
It was waged around the whole planet Earth between the great IN
and great OUT world pirates.

"World War I and its post-war decade saw the end of the world
ruled by either the top IN or OUT great pirates.  In World War
I the great pirates lost their world mastery forever because
the fundamental controls of the new world of industry, technolgy,
and science went from wire to wireless communication, from
tracked to trackless transport, and from visible to the invisible structural strengths of atomic element alloying.  Con-
comitantly the controling factors of science and technology
founded industry went entirely out of human sight into the vast
ranges of the nonsensorially tunable electromagnetic spectrum.
The great pirates who ruled with their senses were helplessly and"

- Cite BEAR ISLAND STORY, galley p.26, 1968

RBF DEFINITIONS

Pirates:  Great Pirates:                                    (4)

"hopelessly blind.  Also in 1929 a one-ton airplane in flight
launched a torpedo which sank a 20-ton battle cruiser and this
shifted mastery of the economic and social affairs of Spaceship
Earth from a sea to an air dominance strategy.

"Not long before the stock market crash of 1929 when the great
pirates lost their world power by silent default, J.P. Morgan's
great steam yacht, the 'Corsair' went on a reef entering Gilkey's
harbor on Isleboro.  No Morgan yacht had ever before touched a
rock.  The captain claimed the reef was uncharted.  The 'Corsair'
was floated safely off on the next tide.  No one ever knew what
happened to that captain.  This event however was full of
mystical foreboding of the great stock market crash that took
place two months later.  The great pirates went on the rocks
forever.

"The great pirates were great!  They did run the world and they
ran it with magnificent selfishness and brilliant foresight--
that is within the limits of their comprehension of the supreme
scheme of physical laws of Universe.  Their thinking was however
too limited.  It was based on the seemingly scientific 1810
finding of Thomas Malthus, Professor of Political Economics of"

- Cite BEAR ISLAND STORY, galley p.27, 1968

RBF DEFINITIONS

Pirates:  Great Pirates:                                    (5)

"their East India Company.  Malthus discovered that the world
people were multiplying themselves much more rapidly than they
could produce goods with which to support themselves.  His calculations showed an arithmetical progression in the rate of gain
of the vital supplies and a geometrical progression in human
reproduction.  Darwin's 'Evolution' and his explanation of it as
being caused by 'survival only of the fittest' was formulated
25 years after Malthus and successful survival of only a minor
fraction of humanity-- by the shrewdest, toughest, swiftest,
most foresighted, and hardest hitting-- seemed to be as scientific fact.  To their thinking, any altruism was fatal.

"This was the basic conception upon which the great pirates
and all the sovereignties which they established were operated.
Neither they nor the rest of the world society ever foresaw an
era of technology which would continually do much more with ever
less resource investments per each function until, as today,
suddenly, all unexpected by the world's economists, businessmen, and politicians of all ideological persuasions, a 1/4-ton
communications satellite outperforms the transoceanic message-
carrying capability of 150,000tons of copper cables."

- Cite BEAR ISLAND STORY, galley p.27, 1968

Pirates:  Great Pirates Are Dead:

See Meek Have Inherited the Earth, 10 Oct'63
    Pirates:  Great Pirates, 22 Jun'77

TEXT CITATIONS

Pirates:  Great Pirates:

Mexico '63, p.7, 10 Oct '63

Pirates:  Great Pirates:                                    (1)

See Divide & Conquer Sequence
    Eggs:  You Just Lay Eggs
    Enterprise
    King's Sign
    Leaders:  Leadership
    ███████   Invisible Masters
    Money
    Outlaw
    Realm
    Rule

Pirates:  Great Pirates:                                      (2)

        See Artist, Jun'66
            ▬▬▬▬▬
            Education (B); Jun'66
            Lever (b)
            Country, 12 Aug'70

---

RBF DEFINITIONS

Planar Reflex:

"One of the things we have to make clear for society
is the dilemma of the Max-Planck-descended scientists,
the way they do their problems, you can have either a
wave or a particle, but not both simultaneously.
Heisenberg has the same fault.  They make the error of
having a wave as a continuity, as a picture-- not as a
pulsating frequency.  A planar reflex causes them to
think of continuous waves."

- Citation at Wave vs. Particle, 22 Apr'71
- Cite RBF to EJA, Somerset Club, Boston, 22 April 1971

---

RBF DEFINITIONS

Plagiarism:

"What is often mistermed as plagiarism is more precisely
'talent.'  Plagiarism is an ethical offshoot label of the
false property illusion..."

- Citation and context at Talent (2), 1938

---

Planar:

        See Plane:  Planar

---

Plagiarism:

        See Coincidental Articulation
            Idea Stealing
            Intellectual Kleptomaniac

---

RBF DEFINITIONS

Planck's Constant:                                          (A)

"Whereas:  All the volumes of all the equi-edged regular polyhedra are irrational numbers when expressed in the terms of the
volume of a cube = 1;

Whereas:  The volume of the cube and the volumes of the other
regular polyhedra, taken singly or in simple groups, are
entirely rational;

Whereas:  Planck's constant was evaluated in terms of the cube
as volumetric unity;

Whereas:  Synergetics finds the tetrahedron, whose volume is
one-third that of the cube, to be the prime structural system
of Universe;

Whereas:  Structuring stability is accomplished by triangularly
balanced energy investments;

Whereas:  Cubes are structurally unstable;

Whereas:  The radial arrangement of unit tetrahedral volumes"

- Cite SYNERGETICS draft at Sec. 223.71, 15 May'73

---

Planarity of Civil & Agrarian Law:                          (2)  ▬

        See Grid:  Crisscross, Right-angle Grid
            Local Squareness, 9 Jul'62
            Air Space, May'65

---

RBF DEFINITIONS

Planck's Constant:                                          (B)

"around an absolute radiation center (the vector equilibrium)
constitutes a prime radiational-gravitational proclivity model
with a volume of 20 where the cube is 3 and the tetrahedron 1;

"It becomes evident that:  In order to convert the value of the
photon, which occurs as a whole rational energy entity, to
conformity with the ill-chosen cube, Planck's constant emerged
empirically, and to reconvert it to conformity with synergetics
the 6.6-ness is cancelled out:

$$6.6 = \frac{20}{3} = \frac{\text{volume of vector equilibrium}}{\text{volume of cube}}.$$

"Planck's constant: Symbol = h.  h = 6.6 -- multiplied by
$10^{-27}$ grams by square centimeters per each second of time.
h is the invariable number found empirically by Planck by
which each of the experimentally discovered minimum increment
of all radiation, the photon, must be multiplied to equate
the photon's energy value as rated by human's energy-rating
technique, which is predicated on the effort expended in lifting"

- Cite SYNERGETICS draft at Secs. 223.71 +.72, 15 May'73

RBF DEFINITIONS

### Planck's Constant: (C)

"weights vertically against gravity given distances in given times. Thus automotive horsepower or electromagnetic kilowatts per hour are rated.

"In the case of Max Planck's photon of light, which expands outwardly as a spherical wave surface in all directions-- instead of travelling linearly outwardly in only one radial direction-- the energy effort involved is expressed in terms of the exponential second power, or areal 'squaring' rate of surface growth of the spherical wave; i.e., as the second power of the energy effort expended in order to lift, in each second of time, a distance of one 'vertical' centimeter radially away from the Earth's center, one gram of weight, i.e., the weight of one cubic centimeter of water whose temperature is $4^0$ centigrade. The invariable number which accomplishes this rating is $h$ = 6.6 multiplied by $10^{-27}$; whereas the gravitational constant = 6.6+ multiplied by $10^{-8}$ grams per second 'squared.'"

- Cite SYNERGETICS draft at Secs 223.72 + .73, 15 May'73

---

RBF DEFINITIONS

### Planck's Constant:

"Planck's constant corrects for the error of science's

predicating its comprehensive coordinate mensurating

system upon the cubic centimeter of water at a specific

temperature as the volume-weight geometrical coordinating

factor, whose centimeter of edge-length-height on the

XYZ three-dimensional system became the distance of anti-

gravitational work to be accomplished in one second of

time as constituting the most logical system for integrating

the energy information science was acquiring instrumentally

from the vast invisible ranges of physical reality."

- Cite RBF entry of 22 July 1971 as re-written by him
in Washington, 7 October 1971.

---

RBF DEFINITIONS

### Planck's Constant:

"Planck's constant corrects the cubic centimeter. It accommodates a number which relates what man is doing to electromagnetic theory."

- Cite RBF to SIMS Seminar, U.Mass, Amherst, 22 Jul'71

---

RBF DEFINITIONS

### Planck's Constant:

"Now Planck's Constant was simply how you forced what

you find out about energy into calculatability and

manipulatability mathematically in respect to rectilinear

analytic geometry. That's plotting things only on the

XYZ coordinates. Always having to go round corners. . . "

- Cite RBF tape transcript to BO'R, Carbondale Dome, 1 May 1971.
Page 43.

---

RBF DEFINITIONS

### Planck's Constant:

"Planck's constant is purely an accommodative number. Put together. The central angles of the octahedron are the 90-degree coordinate system; the coordinates are there, but that's not what nature uses. There's no denying man's way of accounting for things-- which is absolutely awkward. With the synergetics conversion constant I'm discovering how you can take the same fundamental data and really make it come out right."

- Tape #6A, Side A, transcript p.3; RBF to Barry Farrel, Bear Island, 16 Aug'70

---

RBF DEFINITIONS

### Planck's Constant: (1)

"In synergetic geometry the vector equilibrium's mass value of 20 shows why nature requires that the cube's volumetric value of three be multiplied by Planck's empirically discovered, but heretofore scientifically inexplicable, constant 6.665--? to correct for the mistaken assumption by both mathematics and physics that the cube's volume was nature's logical volume of one-- instead of its actual volume of three, in nature's most economical system of both physical and metaphysical accounting. The physicist finds that nature is always most economical. Planck's empirical constant of correction was also required to remedy the mistaken assumption by physics that the cube of one centimeter to the edge, filled with water at four degrees centigrade (as the unity of the XYZ, 90-degree-corrdinate, gram," temperature "second system) was also suitable as the basic unit of energy for computing radiational propagation. The 6.6 radiational constant correction, of the mistakenly assumed suitability of the cube and its conversion therby to the value of the vector equilibrium's base 20 also required the further $10^{--}$ reduction in size to reduce the gram of water's reference size to a photon's energy magnitude."

- Cite NEHRU SPEECH, pp. 27-28. 13 Nov'69

---

RBF DEFINITIONS

### Planck's Constant: (2)

"The closest packed sphere layers of the vector equilibrium account for the non-solid proton-quantation of the wave's outer layer value of frequency (or velocity) to the second power as required by Einstein's $c^2$ of his equation $E = Mc^2$ and eliminates the necessity to consider the second power as characterizing continuous surfaces of systems.

"The vector equilibrium's surface sphere growth rate of the second power also accommodates Newton's discovery of gravitation's mass attraction as being governed by the second power of the relative proximities of the masses, expressed in terms of their respective radii (or modular frequency.) The gravitational constant also requires the 6.66+ 1 correction of its gram-cube base to conform the vector equilibrium and requires a $10^{-8}$ reduction of size to conform to the electron volt magnitude of energy."

IT TO

- Cit NEHRU SPEECH, p. 28. 13 Nov'69

---

RBF DEFINITIONS

### Planck's Constant: (3)

"The many mildly differing values arrived at empirically for both Planck's constant and for the gravitational constant seem to indicate that the radiational constant is just a little less than 6.666 and thatthe gravitational constant is ▪▪▪▪ complementarily just a little bit greater then 6.666

- Cite NEHRU SPEECH, p. 28 , 13 Nov'69

RBF QUOTATION

Planck:

"If one wishes to obtain a definite answer from nature one must attack the question from a more general and less self-ish point of view."

- Cite RBF undated holograph quoting Max Planck: SURVEY OF PHYSICS, PUL. London & N.Y.

---

RBF DEFINITIONS

Plane:

"A plane is a tetrahedron of macro base and micro altitude.... Planes... are real, conceptual, experienceable visually and mentally..."

- Citation & context at Point, 20 Dec'73

---

TEXT CITATIONS

Planck's Constant:

-- Barry Farrell & RBF Tapes; Tape 6A, Side B, pp.13-15; Bear Island, 16 Aug'70

-- Synergetics: Sec. 223.70ff, 26 Sep'73

511.04

204.01

223.71-223.91

240.65

511.04

1024.25

---

RBF DEFINITIONS

Plane:

"A planar system is the first stage of comprehension..."

- Citation and context at Comprehension, 16 Feb'73

---

Planck's Constant:     .

See Whole System: Synergetics Principle Of,(1)
    Photon, 26 Sep'73
    Attic Window, 20 Jan'75
    Quantum: Event-paired Quanta, 1971
    Synergetics Constant, 10 Dec'75

---

RBF DEFINITIONS

Plane:

"All lines are curvilinear and ultimately close back on themselves, ergo short line increments are always segments of weak geodesic loopings. In the same way a plane is always just a local facet aspect of a system. Planes do not exist independent of systems. The nonsynergetic consideration and articulated employment of points, lines, and planes exclusive of system identities induces unconsidered, inexorably complex developments of covariant functions of always integrated generalized system laws. The unconsidered complex of omnidirectional event developments of an almost exclusively 'specializing,' self-considerate society occasions the continuous generation of unwanted problems at ever greater scale in twentieth century world affairs. A linear preoccupied strategical play scenario in Monte Carlo and Wall Street may win money while vitiating the wealth accounting system and deferring the realization and general distribution of synergetically augmented commonwealth."

- Cite RBF re-write ▪▪▪▪▪▪▪▪▪▪▪ of Plane, 17 Feb '72 : 19 Feb'72

---

Planck, Max:

See Light: Speed Of, 1 May'71
    Conceptual Mathematics, (2)

---

RBF DEFINITIONS

Plane:

"A plane is just a facet of a system."

- Cite RBF to EJA + BU'R, 3200 Idaho, DC, 17 Feb '72

RBF DEFINITIONS

Plane:

"Theoretically, a flat surface is infinitely extensible laterally, i.e. in ▓▓▓▓▓▓ all diametric planar directions. As a laterally unbounded, or infinitely open, extensibility the theoretical flat plane is only partially definable. That which is definable of the plane forbids its returning upon itself."

Cite NEHRU SPEECH, P. 12, 13 Nov'69

RBF DEFINITIONS

Planes:

"There are, of course, no planes. It is experimentally demonstrable that an apparent plane is a 'surface' area of some structural system.

"There are no experimentally demonstrable continuums.

"All that has been found is discontinuity as in star constellations or atomic nuclear arrays. Areas are discontinuous, by constructional definition. Areas, as system 'faces' are inherently empty of actions or events, and therefore are not 'surfaces.'"

- Cite NASA Speech, p. 60, Jun'66

NOVENT - SEC 524.20)

RBF DEFINITIONS

Plane:

"Planes described supposedly by three points have, in experimental fact, four points, with two very close together, ergo, all planes are warped."

- Cite RBF marginalis at old Chap. 2, "Synergy," I.5, 18 Mar'69

RBF DEFINITIONS

Plane:

Since "lines cannot go through the same point,

then there cannot be a plane: so planes are eliminated."

- Cite Ledgemont, p. 13, 15 Oct'64

RBF DEFINITIONS

Plane:

"If there are six equilateral triangles around a vertex we cannot define a three-dimensional structural system, only a plane."

- Cite SYNERGETICS ILLUSTRATIONS - # 7 1967

RBF DEFINITIONS

Plane:

"A 'plane' is a tetrahedron of negligible altitude and significant base dimensionality. . .

"There are no impervious surface continuums.

- Cite COLLIER'S, p. 115, Oct'59

RBF DEFINITIONS

Plane:

"I can't get six triangles around a vertex because their corners would add up to 360°. A 360° intersection of triangles is 'flat.' They form a theoretically and experimentally nonexistent, non-experimentally demonstrable plane which would go to 'infinity,' and could not therefore subdivide the universe, by a local conceptual system."

- Cite NASA Speech, p. 61, Jul'66

Plane as Facet:

See Polyhedron, 1 Jan'75
Plane, 19 Feb'72

Plane: (1)

See Area
    Geometry: Plane Geometry
    Planar: Planarity
    Surface
    Tools of Geometry
    Facet
    Eternal Plane
    No Planes
    Tuck in a Plane
    Sphere Tangent with a Plane

---

Plane: Planar: (2)

See Comprehension, 16 Feb'73*
    Fourth Dimension, 29 Nov'72
    Meaningless, Oct'66
    Probability (1)

    Point, 20 Dec'73*
    Systematic Realization, 20 Dec'74
    Systems & Nonsystems, 26 May'72
    Bubbles, 7 Nov'73
    Threeness, 27 May'72
    No Opposites, 12 Nov'75
    Polygon, 14 Oct'76
    Four-dimensional Reality, 30 Apr'77

---

Planetarium:

See Children as Planetarium Audiences

---

RBF DEFINITIONS

Planetary Democracy: (1)

Q: (Sen. Clark): "Do you feel any form of world government
is in order or that we are moving toward
that? Or that there is any possibility that
the American people, after years of plowing
the field, are ready to accept any concept
like that?"

A: (RBF): "I have been asking myself the question you ask me
for a very long time. I am a student of large patterns
and am trying to see what evolution does to some of
these things. I ▆▆▆▆ think that human beings do not
often realize how powerful, knowledgeable, and
competent is universal evolution.

"X-ray cinema makes visible organization of a chicken-- the
gradual assembly from its embryo, all taking place inside the
egg, much of which process seems chaotic and discretely uncontrolled. Humans do not see the logical interrelatedness
of big evolutionary development. All the technical happenings
which were unpredicted in my youth seem only in retrospect to
have been obviously sequitur to their immediate predecessor"

- Cite RBF in committee transcript, US Senate, 15 May'75

---

RBF DEFINITIONS

Planetary Democracy: (2)

"developments. Humans tend to think that Universe is waiting
upon them to make the evolutionary decisions. I do not. That
is why I have tried to stress the fact with you today that--
when considered before they occurred-- all the technological
events in my life were thought to be absolutely impossible.
Therefore, they were not the consequence of society deliberately
undertaking to bring them about. Individual inventors, often
called 'crackpots,' brought them into realization. It was
completely unexpected.

"When I was five years of age no one realized that we would
develop any of the 20th Century technology. Anyone who even
suggested humans reaching safely to and returning from the
Moon were called lunatics and in jeopardy of being incarcerated
in a lunatic asylum.

"As an infinitely small detail in designing terrestrial ecology
Nature designed the honey bees with their chromosomic drive to
go after honey in order to have them inadvertently cross-
pollinate the vegetation; so too, by a million other chromosomically programmed behaviors, nature arranged to grow and"

- Cite RBF in committee transcript, US Senate, 15 May'75

---

RBF DEFINITIONS

Planetary Democracy: (3)

"sustain humans on our planet. Also, 99-percent-programmed
humans usually have been doing a lot of the right things for
the wrong reasons. What we think of as side effects are usually
evolution's main events. The time has come when we must
participate directly in the mainstream of Universe, instead of
only accidentally, while playing lethally-biased, exclusive-
survival games instead of the all-inclusive main show.

"When our forebears evolved the system of democratic represen-
tation of the United States all the first representatives were
well and favorably known to their neighbors. Everybody knew
them. Their term of office was predicated on the realization
that they would have to go to the central meeting place in
Philadelphia by foot or by horse over footpaths, Indian trails,
or very small highways, stopping overnight at inns and talking
with everybody along the way. And while in Philadelphia-- or
later in Washington-- three or four important letters might
come from Europe during the whole year you were there. Everybody at the capital knew what the letters said. They all*
talked about the letters with one another. Then all of the
representatives started back homeward talking to the people"

- Cite RBF in committee transcript, US Senate, 15 May'75

---

RBF DEFINITIONS

Planetary Democracy: (4)

"along the way, at the inns and homes. They would tell everybody at home about the four letters from Europe this year and
what everybody in Philadelphia (or later in Washington) thought
about the situation, and what the people along the way think,
and would then say to their home people, 'How do you feel about
it and what do you want me to do about it?' They were told;
and then they walked or rode on these, often many-days travel
to the capitol. We had what scientists call a one-to-one
correspondence between stimulation and response.

"With the unexpected development of the telegraph 30 years
later news short-circuited the represntatives' direct communications system and reached people in minutes instead of in
months; and the people had no way to respond to the stimulation.
Since that time radio and television broadcasting have added
to the telegraph-fed newspapers in producing a constant barrage
adding to hundreds of thousands of stimulations before any
political response could be manifest by the citizenry.

"Democracy worked well with the initial one-to-one correspondence. Today, democracy is not working. It is not the fault"

- Cite RBF in committee transcript, US Senate, 15 May'75

---

RBF DEFINITIONS

Planetary Democracy: (5)

"of the concept of democracy. Democracy is unable to express
itself. That is why samplings of political viewpoints have
developed. The Congress conducts as many inquiries as possible
to discover in advance of elections what their constituents
are thinking. Particularly amongst the young there is a feeling
of absolute futility. The system is not working.

"Over a great many years I have been following the technology
of electromagnetic communications to find out if it did not
contain its own answer to how one-to-one correspondence might
be regained. In 1940 I was science and technology consultant
to 'Fortune' magazine. After checking with the telephone system
engineers and finding it technically feasible, and not disrup-
tive of all other regular services.. I proposed daily voting
by telephone on all prominent questions before Congress. That
was back in 1940 and I published my proposal in my book, 'No More
Secondhand God.'

"Since World War II studies have been scientifically conducted
disclosing the electromagnetic energy output of human brains.
The work has been scientifically conducted in veterans' hospitals
with electrodes fastened to the heads of volunteers. Then, "

- Cite RBF in committee transcript, US Senate, 15 May'75

RBF DEFINITIONS

Planetary Democracy:                                    (6)

"using recording oscillographs, unique patterns were discovered
to be identified with certain dreams.  Most recently experiments
have disclosed an electromagnetic field surrounding the whole
body of a human, which field discloses a positive or a negative
attitude of response to various stimuli-- very much as does the
polygraph or lie detector through direct contact.

"With the sensors now mounted in satellites orbiting our planet,
broadcasting to us, there is present in this room right now
one electromagnetic program amongst several million, which, if
tuned in by the right radio set, can tell us where every beef
cattle on Earth is located.  As a consequence, we may soon have
the capability to directly sense how each and every human feels
about each and every common human problem of the moment as
each such problem and its alternative solutions are separately
broadcast.  This might well develop within the critical 10
years of which I have been speaking.

"Senator Percy, you have asked me what kind of world government
may develop.  It may well be akin to the city management concept,
where the management has to do whatever the satellite-sensor-"
harvested and computer analysis says that the world majority"

- Cite RBF in committee transcript, US Senate, 15 May'75

---

RBF DEFINITIONS

Planet Earth:

"This planet is a low pressure area for gathering the Universe
together again.  And I can see man arriving here as part of that
function.  So we're a gathering point; and every time a
gathering point■ gets to the place where it needs the mental
capability of man on board, man arrives...."

- Citation & context at Man:  Interstellar Transmission of Man,
  14 Aug'70

---

RBF DEFINITIONS

Planetary Democracy:                                    (7)

"thinks ought to be done.  Undoubtedly the world majority would
make many mistakes, but as the mistake becomes evident the
majority of humans will think that this alternative will work
better; and because they think so, it will be satellite
sensed and the computer will instruct management to immediately
alter the course.

"This is the way all mechanical steering mechanisms of airplanes or ships of the sea work.  The servomechanisms responding to sensed error in first one direction and then the other,
successively correcting the steering-- first this way, then
that way-- averaging an accomplished course halfway between.
The variations get finer and finer, trending toward but never
attaining, 'absolute straightness.'  This is the essence of
cybernetics.  This way humans reached the Moon.  It is the
essence of all life growth.  Development of such satellite-
harvested, electromagnetic-field sensing of how world democracy
feels about any proposed solution of any given problem is close
at hand or has already been technically prototyped.  An incorruptible, true, direct planetary democracy with all of humanity
franchised and always voting, may well render all of humanity
sustainable, successful.  So those are my thoughts, sir."

- Cite RBF in committee transcript, US Senate, 15 May'75

---

Planet Earth:


    See Earth
        Spaceship Earth

---

Planetary Democracy:


    See Electronic Referendum
        World-around Communication Transcends Politics
        World Democracy

---

Planetary Inventory:


    See Time-energy Economics, 15 Jun'74
        Interrelatedness vs. Names, (1)

---

RBF DEFINITIONS

███████████  Planet Earth:

Q:    (Allegheny Airlines lost baggage agent tracing lost
       RBF suitcases sent to Pittsburgh by mistake.)

      "What is your permanent addrss?"

A: (RBF) "Address!  That isn't the right question.  Young man,
       I live on Planet Earth!... Man was born with legs,
       not roots!"

- Cite RBF, red-faced and banging the counter with his fists,
  Washington National Airport, with EJA, 12 Feb'72

---

TEXT CITATION

Planets: Prediction of Unknown Planets:

Synergetics,  Sec. 115, Sept'71

Planets: Prediction of Unknown Planets:

See Whole System: Principle Of, (1)

RBF DEFINITIONS

Planilinear:

"The statisticians think almost exclusively in lines or planes; they are what I call planilinear."

- Citation and context at Probability Model of Three Cars on a Highway (2), 26 Sep'73

---

Planets: Probable Myriads of Consciously Operated Planets: (1)

See Extraterrestrial Humans

RBF DEFINITIONS

Planilinear:

"Probability is purely mathematics: just points on curves. But they are thought of as linear. Or planar. What I call planilinear."

- Cite RBF to EJA, 3200 Idaho, DC, 17 Feb '72

---

Planets: Probably Myriads of Consciously Operated Planets: (2)

See Metaphysical: Supremacy Of, May'72

Plasmics:

See Compound, 13 Mar'73

---

Planets: Planetary:

See Coherence, 10 Feb'73
    Curvature: Compound, 22 Sep'71
    Economic Accounting System: Human Life-hour
        Production, (1)
    Sphere, 1971
    Synergetic Strategy of Commensing with Totality,
        28 May'72
    Earth, 17 May'77

RBF DEFINITIONS

Plastic:

"There is an unfortunate tendency to abhorency of the plastic. Our fingernails are plastic. Our eyes are plastic...."

- Citation & context at Reproducible, 30 May'72

RBF DEFINITIONS

### Plastics:

"There's really a whole new generation of chemistry coming through again. We're getting new skins and tubes that go three and four times as far. The first skins only lasted two years; now they last six. So with all these inventive kids, and the new chemistries, and the aerospace industry which has been depending on the war and is going to have to find new capabilities after they stop the nonsense... these things are really going to come along. There's a whole new era coming through-- with new skins and new foldabilities. You'll be able to fold your dome up in a little package and just explode it into something really big."

- Cite transcript of RBF tape to Barry Farrell, Tape #1, p.3; Bear Island, 10 Aug'70

### Plastic Tube of Universe:

See Metaphysical Gas, 27 Dec'73

---

### Plastic Call-girl Angels:

See Dwelling Service Industry, (6)

### Plastic: (1)

See Artificial

---

### Plastic Flowers:

See Dwelling Service Industry, (6)

### Plastic: (2)

See Reproducible, 30 May'72
    Alcohol, 1946
    Wood Technology, (4)
    New York City, (4)
    Hex-pent Sphere: Transformation into Geodesic
      Spiral Tube, (1)(2)

---

### Plastic Replica of a Cotswold Cottage:

See Dwelling Service Industry, (1)

RBF DEFINITIONS

### Platonic Solids:

"The Platonic solids do not stand in a vacuum of Universe. They are in Universe and if you change that thing you change the rest of Universe. Nothing can change locally without changing everything else."

- Cite Oregon Lecture # 8, p. 285. 12 Jul'62
- Citation & context at Restraints, 12 Jul'62

Plato's Solids:  Platonic Geometries:

See Size (A)
    Transformation, 12 Jul'62
    Prime Structural Systems (2)
    Restraints, 12 Jul'62*
    Vectors & Tensors, 19 Oct'72
    Dodecahedron, 1 Feb'75
    Subvisible Discontinuity, 19 Oct'72
    Philosophy, 11 Aug'76

Pleased or Displeased:  We Are Not Here to Be:          (1)

See Amused:  We Are Not Here to Be

Plato:
    See Philosophy, 11 Aug'76

Pleased or Displeased:  We Are Not Here to Be:          (2)

See Humane City, (10

Play Acting:

See Population Sequence, (6)
    Pretending, 8 Apr'75

Plenitudes:

See Acceleration of Change, 1938

Playbacks:

See Feedback
    Recall Playbacks

Plumbers:
    See Labor Unions

RBF DEFINITIONS

Plumbing: (1)

"My self-disciplining strategy of never losing the large-pattern comprehensivity doesn't mean that you have to disregard the particulars. For instance, when I was designing my stamped-out bathroom, doing the research for it, I discovered that there was one man in Toledo, Ohio, who designed all the toilet bowls in the U.S. His problem was largely one of manufacture, where the crude ceramics employed did not permit any fine tolerances.

"Scientists are simply not looking at plumbing. There is a feeling that pure scientists shouldn't stoop to that sort of nonsense. Nature spends a lot of time separating materials out into solids and liquid-- as you know if you've ever done any mining or refining. We should always pay close attention when nature does this kind of thing. If we employed stainless steel instead of ceramics we could have very fine tolerances and we wouldn't have to waste seven gallons just to flush one pint of waste.

"The point is that you can be a generalist and still plunge into the particular. I've done such plunges for one month at a time or for six months at a time, such as the time I was doing my

- Cite RBF at Penn Bell studios, Philadelphia, Pa., 25 Jan'75

---

Plumbing: (1)

See Autonomous Living Technology Packet
    Bathroom as Symbolism & Association
    Excrement: Excremental Functions
    Toilet
    Sewers: Sewage Systems
    Outbound Packaging of Human Food Waste

---

RBF DEFINITIONS

Plumbing: (2)

cartography. But you always can come back from the artifact to the grand strategy."

- Cite RBF at Penn Bell studios videotaping, Philadelphia, PA., 25 Jan'75

---

Plumbing: (2)

See Buildings as Machines (2)
    Livingry Science, 1 Apr'49
    Junkyard, 1971*
    Buildings: Multiple Occupancy, 30 Apr'74
    Romance, 30 Jan'75
    Desovereignization Sequence, (1)
    Building Business, (4)
    Doing What Needs to Be Done, (1)(2)
    Back Pack, 20 Sep'76
    Dome House Grand Strategy: 1927-1977, (1)-(3)
    Invented Jobs, 20 Sep'76

---

RBF DEFINITIONS

Plumbing:

". . . Science has hooked up the everyday plumbing to the cosmic reservoir."

- Citation and context at Junkyard, 1971

---

RBF DEFINITIONS

Pluralistic:

"We cannot have disorder

Because Universe is not monological;

It is pluralistic and complementary..."

- Citation and context at Universe, pp.156-157 May '72

---

RBF DEFINITIONS

Plumbing:

"Many scientists live in houses-- they look at the plumbing, often find that the plumbing isn't working, twiddle the knob, and send for the plumber. You know as architects that you do not design the plumbing which you buy. You design the superficial use and arrangement of fixtures which are designed by non-architects and manufactured by commerce for you. You are free only to choose the coloring of the bathroom tiles and the coloring of the fixtures. But what goes on back of the bathroom tile is not part of the architectural design. Even if you studied 'plumbing' and detailed the pipe layouts, your design would not be followed or even looked at. The layout would be as dictated by the plumbers' scientifically illiterate craft code and frequent whimsy.

"The fact is that the plumbing system and the sewer system and the aqueduct system have not been importantly changed for 4,500 years. Only one improvement in the system was made, 100 years ago, in England. That was the development of the roof vented plumbing stack and water seal in plumbing fixtures to keep the sewer gases from entering the house."

- Cite MEXICO '63, p. 10, 10 Oct '63

---

RBF DEFINITIONS

Plurality:

"Plurality of systems is a plurality of micros, but only one macro."

"Each of a plurality of systems forces all other systems into lesser proportions of totality.

"Likewise, Universe is inherently infinite and systems are inherently finite."

- Cite RBF holograph in synergetics notes, 5 Mar'55

Plural Otherness:

    See Environment, (A)

---

Plural: Plurality:        (1)

    See Singular & Plural
        Understanding Must Be Plural
        Unity is Plural

---

RBF DEFINITIONS

    Plural Unity:

    "...There are only two fundamental kinds of observable
transformational changes, i.e., angular, or subunity
alterations, and linear or plural unity (frequency modulated)
accelerations."

    - Citation and context at Acceleration: Angle and Linear
      Acceleration, 1960

---

Plural: Plurality:        (2)

    See Awareness, 10 Feb'73
        Differentiation, 27 May'72
        Experience, 1971
        Is, 24 Apr'72
        Second, May'72
        Universe, 26 May'72
        Whole System, 16 Jun'72
        Geometry of Vectors, 15 Jun'74
        Isotropic Vector Matrix, (p.j2) undated
        Polarity, 11 Sep'75

---

Plural Unity:        (1)

    See Unity as Plural

---

RBF DEFINITIONS

    █████ Plus and Minus:

    "Physics hasn't really associated radiation with (+) and

    gravitation with (-), but that's what they are."

    - Cite RBF to EJA, 3200 Idaho, Washington DC, 25 Jan '72.

---

Plural Unity:        (2)

    See Cosmic Discontinuity & Local Continuity, 15 Jan'74
        Interawareness, 9 Jul'75
        Multiplication by Division, 20 Jan'77

---

RBF DEFINITIONS

    Plus and Minus:

    "The average of all plus (+) and minus (-) weights of
Universe is zero weight. The normal is eternal."

    - Citation at Normal, 25 Apr'71

Plus-and-minus One Equilibrium:                                    (1)


     See Zero Frequency

---

Plus & Minus:                                                      (2)


    See Algebra, Oct'66
       Coupler (2); 27 Jan'75
       Death, 13 Mar'71
       Normal, 25 Apr'71*
       Polar Points, 7 Nov'73
       Powering: Sixth Powering, 26 Nov'72
       Twinkle Angle, 19 Dec'73
       Vector Equilibrium, 21 Dec'71
       Polarization, 10 Nov'74
       Conception-birth, 27 Dec'74
       Superstition, May'49
       XYZ Quadrant at Center of Octahedron, 14 May'75

---

Plus-and-minus One Equilibrium:                                    (2)


    See Vector Equilibrium, 23 Oct'72

---

RBF DEFINITIONS

    Plus One:

    "So it is really never infinite because you are not looking
    at one part. It is never just Plus One; it is always plus
    the rest of the Universe when you separate that One out.
    You can separate unity up further and further. You can
    multiply the subdivisions of unity."




                Infinity & Finity,
   - Citation and context at ▮▮▮▮▮▮ (1)(2), 9 Jul'62

---

Plus-minus Polarity:


    See Number: Even Number, 26 Sep'73
       Vector Equilibrium (2)
       Polarization, 10 Nov'74

---

Plus Two:                                                          (1)


    See Additive Twoness
       Coring
       Two:Twoness
       Polar Points
       Vertexial Unities

---

Plus & Minus:                                                      (1)


    See Asymmetry: Plus & Minus Magnitudes
       Positive & Negative
       Split Personality

---

Plus Two:                                                          (2)


    See Euler, (2)
       Theta, 11 Mar'69
       Topology: Synergetic & Eulerian, (2)
       Torus, 11 Jul'62
       Thinking, (II)
       Ten, 22 Jun'75
       Modules: A & B Quanta Modules, 20 Dec'73

Plus:                                                    (1)


See Positive ≠ Negative

---

RBF DEFINITIONS

Pneumatic Bag:

"We assume that pneumatic bags are not permitted as

solutions of the problem as they prohibit omnidirectional

penetrations and provide no local resistance against

high ▇▇▇▇▇ impact."

- Cite Pennsylvania Triangle, Nov. '52, p. 11.

---

Plus:                                                    (2)


See Circuitry:  Thermionic & Political Analogy,
23 Jan'72

---

RBF DEFINITIONS

Pneumatic-hydraulic Structures:

"Hydraulics and aerodynamics and pneumatics-- Nature is using
them in making trees and everything else, but we're just
beginning to use them in buildings.  This is the reason great
trees can go through hurricanes.  Nature uses the crystals
only for tension; all the compression she uses hydraulics for.
In between the molecules of liquids of the tree are the gases,
so the branches sway-- five tons, ten tons-- waving in the
wind.  And it's doing so because the hydraulics holds its shape
under pressure in compression, with the very high tensile
strength of the fibers, and the pneumatics there, taking all
that shock.

"No man has built any buildings like that yet.  That's the truth.
That's the way nature does it.  That's the way she designs you.
You're a beautiful piece of design, and what a contrast you are
to a stone fortress!  Can you imagine architects saying I am
unaesthetic because I didn't want to work with stone?  Yes,
Italy is beautiful: every stone laid by a prisoner.  The reason
you don't have stone buildings now is that a man has to earn a
wage.  If you pay him so he can live decently you can't afford to
lay stone."

- Cite RBF to Barry Farrell; Bear Island; Tape #8, Side A,
transcript p.2; 22 Aug'70

---

RBF DEFINITIONS

Pneumatics:

Synergetics has discovered "the identification of

tensegrity with pneumatics and hydraulics-- it's load

distribution, that's the point."

- Cite RBF to EJA re  SYNERGETICS, Sec. 251.19, 20 Dec. '71.

BALLOON - SEC. 656.30

---

Pneumatic-hydraulic:


See Intuition Sequence (2)
Spectrum, 15 Oct'72
Tensegrity, 10 Nov'73
Human Beings & Hard Machinery, 20 Apr'72
Tensegrity Model of Self-interference of Energy,
25 Mar'75
Humans as Machines, (1)

---

RBF DEFINITIONS

Pneumatics:

"When I use the six-strut tetra tensegrity with

tensegrity octa in triple bond I get an omnidirectional

symmetry tensegrity which is compressible and expandible

as are gasses."

(N.B. Caption supplied by RBF on Holograph)

- Cite undated RBF holograph on paper of Onchiota Conference
Center, Sterling Forest/ Tuxedo, New York.

TENSEGRITY  650.11

---

RBF DEFINITIONS

Pneumatic Structures:

"A fleet of ships maneuvering under power needs more room than
do the ships of the same fleet when docked side by side.  The
higher the speed of the individual ships, the greater the sea
room required.  This means that the enclosed and pressurised
molecules in pneumatic structural systems are accelerated in
outward-bound paths by the addition of more molecules by the
pump and, without additional room, each must move faster to
get out of the way of the others."

- Cite SYNERGETICS draft at Sec. 703.04, 25 Sep'72

RBF DEFINITIONS

Pneumatic Structures:                                                    (1)

"I have considered a great deal about footballs and balls
and pneumatics from being a little kid. And I saw that as
I pumped up my basketball or football, it went from supine
. . . flat, into this beautiful firm condition. But this
is because the molecules of gas were trying to get out of
the system. And they got hot because they were in such
action. The kinetics of gas are something easy for the
brain to understand and feel.. . . the action of those
individual molecules of gas. I saw all the molecules of
gas were trying to get out of the system-- that gives it
the high pressure-- and they were stretching it outwardly
and so, therefore, the skin is designed to go the other way,
holding it inwardly so that the skin is finite and comes
back upon itself. And it represents a tensional force with
the arrows bound inwardly, balancing all the molecules,
bouncing, hitting it, caroming around every action having
its reaction. So I began to see that it would be possible
that geodesics could be similar to what could be called
discontinuous compression/continuous tension, where every
molecule has to have one it pushes from, like two swimmers
in the middle of a tank."

- Cite RBF Interview by Hans Meyer, Dome Book II. p. 90. Dec'70

BALLOON     SEC. 656.03 + 656.10

---

RBF DEFINITIONS

Pneumatic Structures:                                                    (2)

"When you are swimming you dive from one end of the tank--
gives you a little acceleration into the tank, when you get
to the end, you can put your feet up and double your body
up and so forth and shove off from the tank, and if two
swimmers could meet in the middle of the tank and double
their bodies up like that and put the soles of their feet
together and thrust and go in opposite directions, I saw
that the molecules that are in motion... and every action has
its reaction... there has to be some reaction set, so each
molecule which is caroming around, circularly hitting
glancing blows and then making a chord, then another
glancing blow, had to have one it shoved off from. Each one
would have to be balanced, so a balanced pair... all the
forces are caroming around... each one will represent one
of the ████████ chords, the compression chords, which
the two ends pressing outwardly glancing blows against the
tension skin, which are trying to pull inwardly and they
are pulling outwardly. So there's a net arrow outwardly in
the middle of the chord against the net of arrows pointing
inwardly. So... I saw this represents what the gases are
doing and you could make discontinuous compression/continuous
tension geodesic structures in this way. So all this came

- Cite RBF Interview by Hans Meyer, Domebook, II, p. 90. Deec'70

BALLOON - SECS. 656.10+11

---

RBF DEFINITIONS

Pneumatic Structures:                                                    (3)

"in as a fundamental feeling that in dealing with geodesics
in contradistinction to compressional arches where men had
made lesser rings of stone and bricks and so forth, like
Santa Sophia, fitting them beautifully and very mathematically,
one to the other, so they wouldn't fall in, and taking and
putting chain around the bottom of the dome to take care of
the thrust of the enormous weights of the buildings, they
could build a dome that would not thrust outwardly at the
base and allow it to collapse.... I saw that in tension ██
there is no limit-- you can make as big a pneumatic bag as
you want . . . I saw that in the comprehensive geodesically
omnitriangulated tensegrity structure I would be able to go
to unlimited spans, because your only limitation is tension.
I've found that there is no inherent limit to cross section
due to length. We get to where there is no cross section
visible at all, as in the pull between the Earth and the
Moon. . . The beautiful intuitive feelings have been there
right from the beginning. Always I could really feel the
apple in those terms of hydraulics and doing the same tricks."

- Cite RBF Interview by Hans Mayer, Domebook II, p. 90. Dec'70

BALLOON - SEC. 656.30

---

RBF DEFINITIONS

Pneumatic Structures:

"Pneumatic structures are tensegrity structures . . . all
structures are tensegrity structures from the solar system
tom the atom."

- Cite OREGON Lecture #6, p. 197, 10 Jul'62

TENSEGRITY - SEC. 650.04

---

RBF DEFINITIONS

Pneumatic Structures:

"Tensegrity structures are pure pneumatic structures
and pneumatic structures do what they do at the
subvisible range."

- Cite OREGON Lecture #5 - p. 189, 9 Jul'62

TENSEGRITY   SEC. 650.10

---

Pneumatics:   Pneumatic Bag:                                             (1)

        See Balloon
            Hydraulics
            Human Beings & Hard Machinery
            Pneumatic-Hydraulic
            Prestressed Concrete Sequence
            Tensegrity Sphere
            Invisible Pneumatics
            Geodesic Spinnaker

---

Pneumatics:   Pneumatic Bag:                                             (2)

        See Sphericity of Whole Systems, 26 Sep'73
            Three-way Great Circling:  Three-way Grid, 17 Feb'72

---

TEXT CITATIONS

Pocket Calculator:

See RBF Introduction to Schlossberg & Brockman:
        "Pocket Calculator Game Book, 2 Sep'75

RBF DEFINITIONS

Poe, Edgar Allen:

"I'm sorry to say Edgar Allen Poe drank, quite heavily....
No, I'm not sorry about anything."

- Cite RBF at Penn Bell videotaping, Philadelphia, 30 Jan'75

---

RBF DEFINITIONS

Poetry:

"Ralph Waldo Emerson defined poetry as 'saying the
most important things in the simplest way.' By that
definition Einstein became and will probably remain
history's greatest poet-- for who could say so much so
simply as did Einstein when he described physical universe
as $E = mc^2$."

- Cite NEHRU, p. 78, 13 Nov'69
(The Leonardo Type)

---

Poe, Edgar Allan:

See Artist, 24 Jan'72
Artist: Histrionics, (1)

---

RBF DEFINITIONS

Poetry:

"If you say it is poetry that is because engineering
is poetry. Take out for yourself some engineering and
science textbooks and break the words up into phrases
in similar manner and prove it for yourself. Then try
some non-engineering prose and it probably won't work.
I would not be surprised if some day it were proven a
law that the better the science the better the poetry."

- Cite Foreword to No More Second Hand God, p.3, 1962 1962
(Incorrect attribution)

---

RBF DEFINITIONS

Poet:

"The word poet in this professorship of poetry /i.e., the
Charles Eliot Norton Professorship of Poetry at Harvard_7
is a very general term for a person who puts things
together in an era of great specialization wherein most
people are differentiating or 'taking things apart.'
Demonstrated capability in the integration of ideas is
the general qualification for this professorship."

- Cite EDUCATION AUTOMATION, p. 3, ▬ 22 Apr'61

---

**POETS**

"Poets tend to say things a little earlier than the others
regarding the significance of what it is that we are experiencing."

- Cite RBF in Milton Eisenhower Lecture, Johns Hopkins,
Baltimore, 3 Oct'73

---

RBF DEFINITIONS

Poetry:

Q. "Is there any type of poetry, or any poet you can't
stand?"

A. "No, I have nothing negative to say about petry, except
to tell you that rhyme is not poetry."

- Cite RBF in tape interview with Mike Bandler for BOOK
WEEK, 3200 Idaho, Wash, DC, 29 May'72

---

RBF DEFINITIONS

Poets:

"Poets have been history's consistently competent
anticipators of forward evolutionary transformations."

- Cite Dreyfuss Preface, "Decease of Meaning."
28 April 1971, p. 14

RBF DEFINITIONS

Poets:

"The young life realizes that the older life is holding
to the familiar, in opposition to evolution. This is an
interesting point to identify the prescience of the poet.
What man tends to call a poet is one whose sensitivity
has not been ████████ so damaged, where the thoughts flow
almost subconsciously, where all the tastebuds of sound
have been undamaged and the communication capability is
very, very high. Their full vision is unimpaired. Time
and again the poet will say what the nonpoet will not
dare to say. He is afraid to hear his own voice-- the
poet's not. The poet's not afraid because he's not
thinking in terms of his own voice. It's irrepressible;
and so time and again poets have said very extraordinary
things long before the rest of society recognized the
significance of what they were saying."

- Cite RBF in Preface for Francis Warner, p. 5, ████ circa 1970

---

FILE INDICATORS

Poets Cited in this File:

See Aiken, Conrad
    Emerson, Ralph Waldo
    Kipling, Rudyard
    Morley, Christopher
    Millay, Edna St. Vincent
    Fowler, Gene
    Eliot, T.S.
    Pound, Ezra
    Joyce, James
    Tennyson, Alfred Lord
    Frost, Robert
    Poe, Edgar Allen

---

RBF DEFINITIONS

Poets:

"Women and their clothes are like poets. They anticipate.

All options are open."

- Cite RBF quoted in Queen, May '70
- Citation at Option, May'70

---

Poetry: Poets:                                    (1)

See Artist-explorer
    Artist-scientist
    Concrete Poetry
    Economist-poet
    Einstein as Poet
    Ford, Henry as Poet
    Time Entered the Picture through Poetry
    Prose: Prosaic
    Verse vs. Prose

---

RBF DEFINITIONS

Poets:

"...Poets are the earliest to foresee and express almost all
of the important concept changes in the evolution of humanity's
development around the surface of the spherical Spaceship
Earth."

- Citation and context at Millay, Edna St. Vincent (3), 1968

---

Poetry: Poets:                                    (2)

See Generalization Sequence, (2)
    Millay, Edna St. Vincent, (3)*
    Nature Permits It Sequence, (2)
    Option, May'70*
    Slang, 28 Apr'71
    Culture, 1 Feb'75
    Words, May'44
    News & Evolution, (1)
    Custom: Lest One Good Custom Corrupt the World, (A)

---

Poets Anticipate Discoveries of Science:

See Artist, May'65
    Heisenberg-Eliot-Pound Sequence, 28 Jan'69
    Time, 1938

---

RBF DEFINITIONS

Points:

"Points are point-to-able microscale systems which at
minimum consist of one tetrahedron which is always potentially
amplifiable independently of size to conceptual inspectability."

- Cite RBF holograph for EJA; Windsor Castle, Berks; 22 Mar'76

RBF DEFINITIONS

Point:

"A point is always a microsystem or a plurality of microsystems, ergo at minimum one tetrahedron."

- Citation & context at Microsystems, 22 Mar'76

RBF DEFINITIONS

Point:

"Reality is a priori Universe. What we speak of geometrically as having been vaguely identified in early experience as 'specks' or dots or points has no reality. A point in synergetics is a tetrahedron in its vector-equilibrium, zero-volume state, but too small for visible recognition of its conformation. A line is a tetrahedron of macro altitude and micro base. A plane is a tetrahedron of macro base and micro altitude. Points are real, conceptual, experienceable visually and mentally, as are lines and planes."

- Citation & context at A Priori Four-dimensional Reality, (2) 20 Dec'73

RBF DEFINITIONS

Point:

"Points are subdifferentiable systems; i.e., microsystems of event points too far apart to resolve."

- Citation & context at Minimum Awareness Model, (1), 9 Jun'75

RBF DEFINITIONS

Point:

"In omnitopology, a vertex (point) is the only-approximate, amorphous, omnidirectional region occurring mid-spatially between the most intimate proximity attained between two almost-but-never-quite, yet critically intertransformatively, interfering vectors."

- Citation and context at Interference: You Really Can't Get There From Here, 19 Dec'73

RBF DEFINITIONS

Point:

"Points are unresolvable, untunable somethingnesses occurring in the twilight zone between visible and supravisible experience."

- Citation & context at Somethingness & Nothingness, 9 Jun'75

RBF DEFINITIONS

Point:

"It takes four to define insideness and outsideness. It is called a point only because you cannot resolve it....

"When concentrically and convergently resolved, the 'point' proves to be the 'center'-- the zero moment of transition from going inwardly and going outwardly....

"Physical points are energy-event aggregations.... A 'point' often means 'locus of inflection' when we go beyond the threshold of critical proximity and the inness proclivity prevails..."

- Cite RBF rewrite of SYNERGETICS galley at Secs. 519.03 + 519.10, 6 Nov'73

RBF DEFINITIONS

Point:

"A point is a somethingness."

- Citation & context at Somethingness & Nothingness, 9 Jun'75

RBF DEFINITIONS

Point:

"Every 'point' (event embryo) may articulate any of its four event vector sets, each consisting of six positive and six negative vectors, but only one set may be operative at any one time; its alternate sets are momentarily only potential."

- Cite RBF galley correction to SYNERGETICS at Sec. 240.28, 28 Oct'73

RBF DEFINITIONS

Point:

"What we speak of as a point is always eight tetrahedra converged to no size at all. The eight tetrahedra have been brought to zero size and are abstracted from time and special case. They are generalized. Though the empty vector equilibrium model is now sizeless, we as yet have the planes converging to intercept centrally ▮▮▮▮ indicating the locus of their vanishment. The locus of vanishment is the nearest to what we mean by a point. The point is the macro-micro switchabout between convergence and divergence."

[33]

- Cite SYNERGETICS draft at Sec. 1012.34; 20 Feb '73

RBF DEFINITIONS

Point:

"Points are complex but nondifferentially resolvable by superficial inspection. A star is something you cannot resolve. We call it a point, playing Euler's game of crossings. One star does not have an insideness and an outsideness. It is a point because you cannot resolve it.

"Two remotely crossing trajectories have no insideness nor outsideness but do produce optically observable crossings or fixes which are positionally alterable in respect to a plurality of observation points."

[63]

- Cite RBF rewrite of Synergetics Sec. 519.10 (Jul'71) done 1 Apr'72 (At Kennedy Airport)

RBF DEFINITIONS

Point:

"Any point or locus inherently lacks insideness."

- Citation and context at Prime Enclosure, 17 Feb'73

RBF DEFINITIONS

Point:

"A point's definitively unresolved event relationships inherently embrace potential definitions of a complex of local events. When resolved, the point is the microcosmic turning around between going inwardly and going outwardly."

- Cite RBF rewrite of SYNERGETICS Dec '71 draft Secs. 519.11 & 519.12, Kennedy Airport, 1 Apr '72.

POINT - SEC. 519.03

RBF DEFINITIONS

Point:

"Any point can tune in any other point in Universe. All that is necessary is that they both employ the same frequency, the same resonance, the same system, center to center."

- Cite SYNERGETICS Draft at Sec 960.08, 16 Nov'72

RBF DEFINITIONS

Point:

"Without insideness there is no outsideness, and without both there is no point, ergo points are inherently nondemonstrable and the phenomena accommodated by the package-word 'point' will always prove to be a focal center of differentiating events.

"A point constitutes conceptual genesis which may be realized in time.

"Any conceptual event in Universe must have insideness and outsideness. This is a fundamental self-organizing principle."

- Cite RBF to EJA, 3200 Idaho, DC (19 Feb'72) rewritten by RBF Kennedy Airport, 1 Apr'72

POINT SEC. 519.02

RBF DEFINITIONS

Point:

"A point is not a relationship. . ."

- Citation and context at Line, 7 Nov'72

RBF DEFINITIONS

Point:

"Without insideness there is no outsideness, and without both there is no point. Ergo, points are inherently nondemonstrable and the phenomena accommodated by the packaged word 'point' will always prove to be a focal center of differentiating events. A point constitutes conceptual genesis which may be realized in time."

- Cite RBF to EJA, 3200 Idaho, DC, 19 Feb '72; as rewritten by RBF, Kennedy Airport, 1 Apr '72.

POINT. SEC 519.02

RBF DEFINITIONS

Point:

"What we really mean by a point is an unresolved definition of an activity. A point by itself does not enclose. There are no indivisible points.

"A point's definitively unresolved event relationships inherently embrace potential definition of a complex of local events.

"When resolved, the point is the microcosmic turning around between going inwardly and going outwardly."

- Cite RBF rewrite of Synergetics draft at Secs. 519.11+12 (Dec'71) done at Kennedy Airport, 1 Apr'72

---

RBF DEFINITIONS

Point:

"A point by itself does not enclose."

- Cite Synergetics draft, Sec. 880.2, August 1971.

POINTS - SEC.519.01

---

RBF DEFINITIONS

Point:

"Without insideness there is no outsidenss, and without both there is no point. Any conceptual event in Universe must have insideness and outsideness. This is a fundamental self-organizing principle."

- Cite RBF to EJA, 3200 Idaho, Wash DC, 19 Feb'72

---

RBF DEFINITIONS

Point:

"Points are complex but nondifferentially resolvable to superficial inspection. A star is something you cannot resolve. We call it a point, playing Euler's game of crossings. One star does not have an insideness and an outsideness. It is a point because you cannot resolve it.

- Cite SYNERGETICS draft at Sec. 519.to, [03] Jul'71

---

RBF DEFINITIONS

Point:

"In a vector equilibrium the points are only in equilibrium when they get to be the icosahedron. . . Points are always tetrahedra-- whether it's a neuron, or whatever. . . A point is a minimum tetrahedron just as a tetrahedron is a minimum sphere. Without insideness there is no outsideness, and without both there is no point. Any conceptual event in Universe must have insideness and outsideness. This is a fundamentally self-organizing principle."

(EJA NOTE: The above is superseded by RBF rewriting of 1 Apr '72.)

- Cite RBF to EJA, 3200 Idaho, DC, 19 Feb 1972

---

RBF DEFINITIONS

Point:

"Points are energy event aggregations; when they converge beyond the critical fall-in proximity threshold, they orbit co-ordinatedly, as loose pebbles on our Earth orbit the Sun in unison and chips ride around on men's shoulders. A point, then, is when we go beyond the threshold of critical proximity and the inness proclivity prevails, in contradistinction to the differentiable other fallen-in aggregates orbiting precessionally in only mass-attractively cohered remoteness outwardly beyond the critical proximity threshold. Points are complex but nondifferentiably resolvable to superficial inspection."

- Cite RBF to EJA, Beverly Hotel, New York, 19 June 1971.

POINT - SEC. 519.01 +02 + .10

---

RBF DEFINITIONS

Point:

"A point is an as-yet-undifferentiated focal star embracing a complex of local events.

"The point is the microscopic turning around between going inwardly and going outwardly.

"What we really mean by a point is an unresolved definition of an activity. A point by itself does not enclose. There are no indivisible points."

- Cite SYNERGETICS draft at Secs. 519.11+12, Dec'71

---

RBF DEFINITIONS

Point:

"A point on a sphere is never an infinitesimal tangency with a plane."

- Citation at Tangency, 31 May'71

- Cite RBF to EJA, Blackstone Hotel, Chicago, 31 May 1971.

POINTS SEC. 519.21

RBF DEFINITIONS

Point:

"The domains of vertexes are spheres.  This is all
the symmetries around the exquisite point."

- Cite RBF tape Blackstone, Hotel, Chicago, 31 May 1971
p. 37.

POINTS - SEC. 519.221

---

RBF DEFINITIONS

Point:

"What we really mean by point then is an unresolved
identification of an activity."

- Cite Oregon Lecture #8, p. 284. 12 Jul'62

POINTS - SEC. 519.01

---

RBF DEFINITIONS

Point:

"The point is the microcosmic turning around between going
inwardly and going outwardly."

- Cite RBF to EJA, Blackstone Hotel, Chicago, 31 May 1971.

POINTS, SEC 519.03

---

RBF DEFINITIONS

Point:

"There are no indivisible points."

- Cite SYNERGETICS Corollaries, Sec. 240.  Oct'59

POINTS - SEC. 519.01

---

RBF DEFINITIONS

Point:

"A star is something you can't resolve.
We call it a point,
playing Euler's game of crossings.
One star doesn't have and outsideness and an insideness.
It is a point because you can't resolve it."

- Cite RBF to EJA
Carbondale
2 April 1971

POINTS - SEC. 519.03

---

RBF DEFINITIONS

Point:

"For every point in universe there are six uniquely and
exclusively operative vectors."
"Each vector is reversible having its negative alternative.
"Every point may export all or any of its six positive or
six negative vectors by importing like numbers.
"Each point in universe could be said to have twelve unique
and exclusive vectors, but one set of six is operative
and its alternate reverse effect set is only potential."

- Cite COLLIER's, p. 113. Oct'59
- Citation & context at Vector, Oct'59

POINTS - SEC. 519.30

---

RBF DEFINITIONS

Point:

If light or any other experiential phenomenon . . .
were instantaneous it would be less than a point."

- Cite RBF SYNERGETICS Draft Mar '71

POINTS - SEC. 519.20

---

RBF DEFINITIONS

Point:

"A point is an as-yet undifferentiated focal star
embracing a complex of local events."

- Cite Collier's, p. 113, Oct'59

POINTS. SEC 519.

RBF DEFINITIONS

Point:

"A 'point' is a tetrahedron of negligible altitude and
base dimension."

- Cite SYNERGETICS corollaries, Sec. 240. Oct'59

---

Points, Areas & Lines:                                                (2)

See Euler, (1); 1969
    Minimum Awareness Model, (1)
    Domains of Polyhedra, 7 Nov'73

---

RBF DEFINITIONS

Point:

"There is no pointal center of gravity."

- Citation and context at Gravitational System Zone, 14 Jan'55

---

RBF DEFINITIONS

Point-to-able Something:

"A point-to-able something may be much too small to be optically
resolved into its constituent polyhedral characteristics, yet
be unitarily differentiated as a black speck aginst a white
background. Because a speck existed yet defied their discern-
ment of any feature, mathematicians of the premicroscope era
mistakenly assumed a speck to be self-evidently unitary,
indivisible, and geometrically employable as a nondimensional
'point.'"

- Cite SYNERGETICS 2 draft at Sec. 100.032; 30 Apr'77

---

RBF DEFINITIONS

Point:

"A point is a tetrahedron of combined zerophase of
both altitude and base."

- Cite PENNSYLVANIA TRIANGLE, p. 10 , Nov'52

---

Pointable:  Point-to-able:

See In & Out:  Go In to Go Out, 16 Dec'73
    Vector, 16 Dec'73
    Primitive Dimensionality, 1 Mar'76
    Tetrahedron as Microsystem, 12 May'77
    In, Out & Around, 17 May'77

---

Points, Areas & Lines:                                                (1)

See Constant Relative Abundance
    Events, Novents & Event Interrelatabilities
    Fixes, Discontinuities & Continuities
    Crossings, Opening & Trajectories
    Vertexes, Faces & ▮▮▮ Edges
    Joints, Windows & Struts

---

Point Growth Rate:  External:

See Powering:  Second Powering

TEXT CITATIONS

Point: Humans First Conception of a Point:

Sec. 262.02 (2nd. Ed.)

    264.03    "

    265.03    "

---

RBF DEFINITIONS

Point: Outbound Point:     (2)

"Ergo; Radiation finite: tension infinite. Therefore, Universe is infinitely cohesive and limitedly chaotic."

- Cite RBF holograph, 6 Mar'48

---

RBF DEFINITIONS

Point: Inbound Point:

"The omni-inbound gravity works collectively toward the invisibility of the central zero-size point."

- Cite SYNERGETICS Draft at Sec. 541.05, 23 Sep'73

---

RBF DEFINITIONS

Point: Outbound Point:

"Inbound point diminishes or contracts to straight line: therefore, shortest distance B to A.

"Outbound point must expand to direction of cone or tetra: therefore, radiation tends to take angle, and therefore, longest distance A to B.

"Therefore, gravity swifter than radiation; therefore, Universe collects its masses in ever tighter concentrations."

- Cite RBF holograph, circa 1948

---

RBF DEFINITIONS

Point: Outbound Point:

"The outbound, tetrahedrally-packaged, fractional point works toward and reaches the inherent visibility phases of radiation."

- Cite SYNERGETICS draft at Sec. 541.05, 23 Sep'73

---

Point Population:

    See Powering: Second Powering, 28 Oct'73
        Powering: Third Powering, 28 Oct'73

---

RBF DEFINITIONS

Point: Outbound Point:     (1)

"Trigem (trimetric) system of airways--

Is just like a plane on the ground with three-point support.

"The four-point landing of a plane is ridiculous, as, in fact, is the automobile for which we have had to build plane (carpet) highways... Individual spring was to loose fourth wheel.

"Three dimensions invoked four-square scaffolding of civilization, which os o.k. at diminutive scale like a needle floating on water... as relative tension supports the otherwise untenable transgression of principle.

"Inbound point concentrates infinitely as point and foges (sic) an infinite tensile cohesiveness.

"Outbound point expands to fourth dimension: therefore is point annihilations and fissions at limits."
- Cite RBF holograph, 6 May'48

---

RBF DEFINITIONS

Point of No Return:

". . . Humanity
Is approaching a crisis
In which its residual ignorance, shortsightedness
And circumstance-biased viewpoints
May dominate,
Thus carrying humanity
Beyond the 'point of no return'--
Enveloping his exclusively Sun-regenerated
Planetary home
In chain-reactive pollutionings
And utter disorder."

- Cite INTUITION, pp.60-61 May '72

TEXT CITATIONS

Point - Eight Tetrahedra:

s1053.810

---

Point: points                                                              (b)

<u>519</u>: (Main text)

535.11 geodesic array

537.11 six vectors for every point

541.09 tetra: points & no-points

541.10 novents embrace points

707.02 points, planes, and lines are systemic

713.06 subvisible aggregates

713.07 convergence & twist

825.27 triangulation and trigonometric fix

960.08 any point can tune in any other point

966.12 specks an dots are unreal; points are conceptual

985.20 spheric experience of three or more vectors converging

985.21 points define systems

---

Point - Eight Tetrahedra:


See Point, 20 Feb'73
    Nonpolar Points, 29 Nov'72
    Tetrahedron:  Nine Schematic Aspects, 30 Aug'75
    Vector Equilibrium: Zerophase, 30 Aug'75
    Hedra, 10 Apr'75


Sec. 1012.33

---

Point: points (c)                                                          (c)

1009,11 vertex between converging vectors

1011.10 four points for prime enclosure

1011.11 no interior point in a domain

1012.33 point = eight tetra: zerosize: generalized

---

Point vs. Zone:


See Gravitational System Zone, 14 Jan'55

---

Point:                                                                    (1A)

    See Brouwer's Theorem
        Congruence with the Points
        Cosmic Limit Point
        Crossing
        Disturbance Initiating Point
        Domain of a Point
        Ineffable Point
        Intertangency Points
        Kissing Point: K
        Localized Thickening of Points
        Nonpolar Points
        No Points
        Otherness Point
        Polar Points
        Spherical Point System
        Subpoint
        Surface Points
        Vector Center Fix
        Zero Point
        Lines Cannot Go Through the Same Point at the Same Time

---

Point: points                                                              (a)

223.40 external, superficial points of a system

223.65 points defining modular subdivisions (length, area, vol.)

224.07 sphere; center & surface

240.05 tetra of negligible altitude & base

240.09 undifferentiated focal star complex

240.10 undivisible

240.11 complex unities

240.12 six vectors for every point

240.28 embryo articulates as six vectors

445.05 VE as domain of a point

510.01 star event: fix

510.05 star event: focus

515.011 points defining modular subdivisions (length, area, vol.)

---

Point:                                                                    (1B)


    See Conceptual Genesis
        Event Embryo
        Locus Fix
        Starting Point
        Limit Point
        Event-points
        Interpointal
        Vertexial Topology
        Vector Equilibrium as Starting Point
        Interconnection of Any Two Points
        Interconnection of Any Four Points
        Reachable Point
        Whyte, L.L: Point System
        Somethingness
        Benday Screen

Point:      (2A) ■

See Aggregate, 20 Dec'71
    A Priori Four-dimensional Reality, (2)*
    Constant Relative Abundance, 29 Nov'72
    Coupler, 5 Apr'73
    Crystallography, 17 Aug'70
    Domain, 22 Jun'72
    Gravitational System Zone, 14 Jan'55
    Interference: You Really Can't Get There from Here,
      19 Dec'73*
    Line, 7 Nov'72*
    Meaningless, Oct'66
    Needle, 10 Feb'73
    Powering: Second Powering, 5 Apr'73
    Prime Enclosure, 17 Feb'73*
    Start, 29 Dec'58
    Surface, 17 Feb'72
    Tangency, 31 May'71*
    Two, (2)
    Vector, Oct'59
    Vector Equilibrium, (1); Feb'48

---

TEXT CITATIONS

Poisson Effect:

Oregon Lecture #3, p. 152, 6 Jul'62

Synergetics - Secs. 1005.30-32

---

Point:      (2B)

See Systematic Realization, 20 Dec'74
    Minimum Limit Case, 9 Jun'75
    Somethingness & Nothingness, 9 Jun'75*
    Minimum Awareness Model, (1)*
    Proofs, 7 Oct'75
    Invisibility of Macro- and Micro- Resolutions, (2)
    Primitive Dimensionality, 1 Mar'76
    Microsystems, 22 Mar'76*
    Six Motion Freedoms & Degrees of Freedom, (1)-(3)

---

Poisson: Poisson Effect:

See Electric Motor, 25 Jan'72
    Tidal, (pp.129-130) May'72

---

Point:      (3)

See Pointable: Point-to-able
    Points, Areas & Lines
    Point Growth Rate
    Point: Inbound Point
    Point of No Return
    Point: Outbound Point
    Point Population
    Point vs. Zone
    Point = Eight Tetrahedra
    Point-to-able Something

---

RBF DEFINITIONS

Polarity:

"All systems are polarized.... There is an inherent polarity
in all observation: that is the additive twoness."

- Citation & context at Nonpolarized, 12 Nov'75

---

RBF DEFINITIONS

Poisson Effect:

"These vectorial resultants of forces articulated in
planes perpendicular to the axis of the applied force vector,
with concomitant right-angle transformation of compression
into tension, and vice versa, are altogether known as the
Poisson Effect (as named for their human discoverer and not
for a fish-like behavior). We now know that this impre-
cisely recognized reciprocal effect is a precisely operative
physical system phenomenon known as precession."

- Cite "Tensegrity," PORTFOLIO AND ART NEWS, p. 119, Dec. '61

---

RBF DEFINITIONS

Polarity:

"Polarity is inherent in the plurality of the con of congruence."

- Citation & context at Two-dimensional Polarity, 11 Sep'75

RBF DEFINITIONS

Polarity:

"Absolutely straight lines or an absolutely flat plane would, theoretically, continue outwardly to infinity. . . The difference between infinity and finity is governed by the taking out of angular sinuses, like pieces of pie, out of surface areas around a point in an absolute plane. This is the way lampshades and skirts are made. Joining the sinused fan-ends together makes a cone; if two cones are made and their open end, ergo infinitely trending, edges are brought together, a finite system results. It has two polar points and an equator. These are inherent and primary characteristics of all systems."

- Citation at Angular Sinus Takeout, Dec'61

- ~~Q~~ ~~EONGLED DRAWT~~

- Cite ~~TENSEGRITY (Portfolio: Art News Annual), pp. 119-120, Dec'61~~

SYSTEM - SEC 400.10

RBF DEFINITIONS

Polarization:

"Here we have a positive and a negative event in opposition to one another as a polarized system. Up to now I have been giving you symmetrical systems, not polarized. There is nothing at all polarized about tetrahedron or icosahedron, but now when we ■ oppose these two there is a north pole and a south pole in equatorial aspect."

(Comment on SLIDE 3:4 - 1)

- Cite OREGON Lecture #5 - pp. 179-180, 9 Jul'62

RBF DEFINITIONS

Polarity:

"Because of a hemisphere's polar symmetry to its opposite polar hemisphere the total inventory of great circle grid triangles in the comprehensive world grid is always even in number. . . "

- Cite Undated Sheet: The DYMAXION AIROCEAN WORLD FULLER PROJECTIVE-TRANSFORMATION

Polar Coupling:

See Associability, 21 Mar'73

RBF DEFINITIONS

Polarization:

"The precessional processing of plus-minus polarization is" a synergetic proclivity.

- Citation & context at Synergetic Proclivity, 10 Nov'74

Polar Focus:

See Focus - Beamable - Wirable, 1 Apr'72

RBF DEFINITIONS

Polarization:

"There are in closest packing, we find, always alternate spaces that are not being used so that triangular groups can be rotated into one position or 60 degrees to an alternate nestable place. . . In other words you take the vector equilibrium, rotate it 60 degrees to the next nestable position and suddenly it is polarized.

- ~~Cite Oregon Lecture #7, pp. 234-235, 11 Jul'62~~
- Cite Sixty Degreeness, 11 Jul'62

Polar Azimuthal Projection:

See Projective Transformation, (II)

Poles of Inward-outward Consideration:

See Macro-Micro, 12 Nov'75

RBF DEFINITIONS

Polarized Precession:

"Polarized precession is special case."

- Citation and context at General Case, 16 Feb'73

RBF DEFINITIONS

Polar Points:

"Polar points are two dimensional: plus and minus, opposites."

- Cite RBF rewrite of SYNERGETICS galley at Sec. 527.21,
7 Nov'73

Polarized Precession:

See Polarization, 10 Nov'74
Heaven & Hell, 31 May'71

RBF DEFINITIONS

Polar Points:

"Polar points are two dimensional: North-South."

- Cite SYNERGETICS draft at Sec. 527.21, 29 Nov'72

RBF DEFINITIONS

Polar Symmetry:

"Poles are symmetrical to each other, but not
omnisymmetrical like the icosahedron and tetrahedron."

- Cite RBF to EJA, 3200 Idaho, Wash Dc, 17 Feb '72

Polar Points:

See Vertexial Unities
Plus Two
Neutral Axis

Polar Symmetry:

See Projective Transformation, (8)
Tetrahedron: Polarization Of, 13 Nov'75

Polarized System:

    See Physics: Difference Between Physics & Chemistry,
        11 Jul'62

---

RBF DEFINITIONS

Polar Vertexes:

"Every event has its coexistant system's topological
characteristics.  Initially to be considered are the two
polar axis points of every event observer's axis of view,
i.e., the viewer's 'up and down,' eye to foot, vertical
axis of right and left footprints.  In our analysis of our
spontaneous conceptioning controls we extract these two
polar points and there remains a constant relative of two
areas and three edges of every event fix.  In respect to
our spontaneously adopted axis of view, me or we, can
describe ▓▓▓▓▓▓▓▓▓▓ the shape of anything in
Universe exclusively in terms of angle and frequency."
- Cite RBF re-write 19 Feb '72, of same caption 17 Feb.

---

Polar Torque:

    See Jitterbug, 1 Dec'65

---

RBF DEFINITIONS

Polar Vertexes:

"Every event has two points.  Every event has two polar
points derived from the axis of reference.  We need to
extract these two polar points and there will be a
remaining constant relative abundance of two areas and
three edges.  We take an axis of observation-- Me--
and we can describe anything else in Universe in terms
of angle and frequency."

- Cite RBF to EJA + BO'R, 3200 Idaho, DC, 17 Feb '72

---

RBF DEFINITIONS

Polar Vertexes:

"For every point in Universe except two there are always
and only six intertriangulating connective lines because
every action has its reaction, every event vector line has
its diametrically always coexistant exposed PUSH ▓▓▓ and pull
forces, ergo every visible line has its coexistant counterpart, ergo in addition to the ▓▓▓ visible six, there are
six invisible lines (or twelve universally unique degrees
of freedom of alternately optional articulatabilities.)"

- Cite RBF re-write 19 Feb '72 at 3200 Idaho, DC, of
    undated 1971 holograph, same citation.

---

Polar Vertexes:          (1)

    See Additive Twoness

---

RBF DEFINITIONS

Polar Vertexes:

"For every point in Universe except two there are always and
only six intertriangulating connective lines."

- Cite RBF undated holograph (1971)

---

Polar Vertexes:          (2)

    See Two, 25 May'72

RBF DEFINITIONS

Poles:

"At any instant of time any two of the evenly coupled vertexes of a system function as poles of the axis of inherent rotatability."

- Cite SYNERGETICS, "Corollaries," Sec. 240.63. 1971

---

RBF DEFINITIONS

Pole Vaulter:

"Repetition is inherent to frequency and wave phenomena in writing and expression as in music and sports, where rhythm is fundamental and expression is the essence. Whether it is a kid jumping over a ditch or a pole-vaulter seeking a new world record, he cannot do it all in no-time-at-all nor all the first time. It is part of the grand strategy that the pole-vaulter has to run over the same cinder path hundreds and hundreds of times before comprehendingly omni-coordinating his degrees of freedom and rising to that additional quarter of an inch for a record. And no one ever gets tired watching him."

- Cite SYNERGETICS, 2nd. Ed., front matter, Author's Note on Rationale for Repetition in This Work, p.xxii; 2 Jul'75

---

Polar: Polarity: Pole: Polarization:                    (1)

See Additive Twoness
    Axis entries
    Electromagnetic
    Fountain Pattern
    Magnetic Field
    Nonpolar
    Omnidirectionality v.s. Polarization
    Precession: Polarized Precession
    Plus-minus Polarity
    Tetrahedron: Polarity Of
    Vector Equilibrium: Polarization Of
    Minimum Polar Triangle
    Coring
    Toration
    Topological Aspects: Inventory Of
    Synergetic Proclivity
    Positive & Negative: Four Kinds
    Eternal Pole
    One-dimensional Polarity
    Two-dimensional Polarity
    Pentagonal Polarity

---

TEXT CITATIONS

Pole Vaulter:

Total Thinking, I&I, p.228, May'49

---

Polar: Polarity: Pole: Polarization:                    (2)

                Four Intergeared Mobility Freedoms, 2 Nov'73
See Angular Sinus Takeout, Dec'61*
    Brouwer's Theorem, 10 Nov'73
    Colloidal Chemistry, 1938
    Compound, 3 Nov'73
    Great Circle, 10 Nov'73
    Number: Even Number, 26 Sep'73
    Sixty Degreeness, 11 Jul'62*
    System, 8 Jan'55; 1954
    Twoness, 23 May'72
    Vector Equilibrium, 11 Jul'62
    Organic Chemistry, 11 Jul'62
    Prime Numbers: Pairing Of, 17 Jan'74
    Synergetic Proclivity, 10 Nov'74*
    Positive & Negative: Four Kinds, 10 Nov'74
    Heaven & Hell, 31 May'71
    Fear & Longing, 1938
    Two-dimensional Polarity, 11 Sep'75*
    Nonpolarized, 12 Nov'75*
    Hex-pent Sphere Transformation into Geodesic
        Spiral Tube, (1)
    Tensegrity Masts: Pentagonal Polarity, 27 Dec'76

---

RBF DEFINITIONS

Pole Vault: Pole Vaulter:

See Charting Alternating Experiences,(4)
    Jet Stilts, 29 Jan'75
    Omnimedium Transport Sequence, (1)
    Repetition, 8 Mar'75

---

Polar: Polarity: Pole: Polarization:                    (3)

See Polar Coupling
    Polar Focus
    Polar Azimuthal Projection
    Polarized Precession
    Polar Symmetry
    Polarized System
    Polar Torque
    Polar Vertexes

---

RBF DEFINITIONS

Politicans:

"Politicians are merchants of woe. They get elected because of what's bothering people now."

- Cite RBF to EJA at Kennedy Center in Washington after National Town Meeting of the Air, 10 Sep'75

# Synergetics Dictionary

RBF DEFINITIONS

Politicians:

(In response to newspaper account: "McGovern Wonders Why
the Public is so Apathetic about the Watergate?")

"Society has always assumed that politics is crooked.  So
if you just get experts to say this is so, why nobody is
surprised.  They just find it a little more sophisticated
crookedness.  Where the McGoverns and the Humphreys-- and
even Adlai to some extent-- go wrong is when they try to
appear as pure saints when they are politicians too.  You
couldn't be a politician and not have some important
compromise in your background.  You may not have done
anything personally wrong.  But you may have temporized.
You may have put up with.  You may have kept quiet.  You
may have looked the other way..."

- Cite RBF to EJA, 3200 Idaho, Wash DC, 20 Oct'72

RBF DEFINITIONS

Politicians:

"Politicians are going to confess the obvious-- that no
human beings can keep in mind all the special interests of
all people and all the whereabouts and unique behaviors of
all the resources of Earth.  No human beings can persuade
other people to behave in unfamiliar,untried ways, but the
computer can integrate and disclose the critical information
and be completely convincing... As the world game is played
progressively it will disclose a myriad of politically
untried, unprecedented yet effective ways of solving hitherto
unsurmountable problems.  These will become big news items of
the world's press and international wire services.  As man
gets into more critical proximity to a full-scale World War
Three, the people of the world will begin to say in
increasing numbers, 'Now that we can see a way in which this
and that can be done, we must obviously adopt the policies
inidicated by the World Game.'  Popular pressures will
gradually force world politics to yield to these mutually
beneficial world game programs.

"Our greatest problem is the educational problem of getting
man to realize in time what his programs are, and what the
most effective priorities may be for saving them."

+ Whole Earth
- Cite RBF quoted by Gene Youngblood in LA. Free Press, Cat. Mar+70

RBF DEFINITIONS

Politicians:

"The number of scientists today who really know the world
could work is something less than one percent.  Society
doesn't know the world could work.  Politicians haven't the
slightest idea it could work.  They really don't.  They're
the most earnest people, and I think we as human beings are
putting a horrible load on politicians, who can't really
solve the problems.  Their lives are really quite horrible
lives.  And we're blaming them, and it really is just that
they don't have the capabilities.  So we're at fault in asking
them to solve the problems.  I'm perfectly confident that no
politician can ever yield to the other politician on the other
side; he'd be a traitor and he's de immediately dispplaced,
because the other politician is waiting to displace him that
way.  So I do know that every politician can yield to the
computer."

- Cite RBF to World Game at NY studio School, 12 Jun-31 Jul'69,
  Saturn Film transcript, Sound 1, Reel, 1, pp.108-109.

RBF DEFINITIONS

Politician:

"The politician is someone who deals in man's problems of
adjustment.  To ask a politician to lead us is to ask the
tail of a dog to lead the dog."

- CiteDESIGNERS AND THE POLITICIANS, I&I, p.305, 1962

RBF DEFINITIONS

Politicians & Defense Budgets:

"Because of the rocketing costs of TV time and other public
relations organizations, politicians have become electable
only by the money power either of unions or of business
management; and since World War II's close, it has been left
to the politicians to keep the mass-production economy
going and growing--a task which politicians of all sides
found could be best accomplished through $50-100-billion-a-
year 'defense' budgets, and having their military (or their
satellite governments' military) establishments continually
buy ever-advancing power, range, and accuracy of their
armaments' hitting-power in anticipation of the always
politically logical assumption of the 'next' vastly more
sophisticated war."

- Citation & context at Building Industry, (4); 20 Sep'76

Politicians & Defense Budgets:

See Houses & Infrastructure, 20 Sep'76

RBF DEFINITIONS

Politics:

"All politics are not only obsolete but lethal."

- Citation and context at War, 13 Dec'73

RBF DEFINITIONS

Politics:

"Politics is always on one side of how you deal with fundamental inadequacy."

- Cite RBF address to Yale Political Union, New Haven, 9 Dec'73;
  as rewritten by him at 3200 Idaho, 13 Dec'73

318

RBF DEFINITIONS

Politics:

"Politics is always on the side of how you deal with fundamental inadequacy."

- Cite RBF address to Yale Political Union, New Haven, 9 Dec'73

---

RBF DEFINITIONS

Politics:

"We find that generally speaking the geographically larger the physical task to be done, the duller the conceptual brain is brought to bear upon the technically realized applications. Finally we get to international affairs and you know what is happening today. The most highly polished of the dullest class, scientifically and intellectually speaking, may wear their striped pants very beautifully and be charming fellows but they have not produced any mutually acceptable, constructive world peace generating ideas. They traffic successfully only in people's troubles and emergency compromises."

- Cite RBF quoted by Hal Aigner in ROLLING STONE, 10 June, 1971

---

RBF DEFINITIONS

Politics:

"My hopes then are not founded on acts of political wisdom or adoption of altruistic conventions. They are predicated exclusively on an informed and experienced competence adequate to the task of physically accomplishing fundamental cosmic success of humanity. Appropriate political actions must be sequitur to actual capability. Political actions without knowledge of how to attain universal success are inherently wishful and even specious, ergo doomed to failure, or to only momentary advantage gains of an exclusive nature."

- Citation and context at Design Science (3), 29 Jun'73

---

RBF DEFINITIONS

Politics:

"I'm confident that Politics is losing its credit with the world, while people are growing continually more confident in the kind of results they can get out of computers."

- Cite Transcript of RBF tape to Barry Farrell, Tape #2; Side A, p.4; Bear Island, 11 Aug'70

---

RBF DEFINITIONS

Politics:

"Unless you have the technical solution, politics can't do anything."

- Citation & context at Office Buildings: Conversion to Apartments, 28 Jun'72

---

RBF DEFINITIONS

Politics:

"Politics are only appropriate to an economy of scarcity. Within the scarcity context politics play tricks short-of-war by which the successful politicians' side monopolozes the limited survival supply. Death by want-- i.e., by metabolic inadequancies is much slower than by the sword or gun and causes much more anguish and pain than that of the swift hero's death. Death by want imposed on many by the successful politicians' warfaring only with laws and police guns obscures the identity of their executioner from both the politicians and the slow-dying victim. Only if there is an inherent major life support inadequancy aboard our planet and even in the Universe, politics and politicians are valid functions of Universe. If there is a fundamental adequacy of life support aboard our planet which is as-yet popularly unrealized, politicians can go on playing their trincks in seemingly good conscience. But the politicians' self-deceptive scarcity game playing and the ultimately lethal consequences for many humans inherent in the politicians' one-sided victories tend to prolong and obscure from social consideration the now dawning scientific awareness of the technical feasibility of universal economic success for all."

- Cite RBF Ltr. to Prime Minister Indira Gandhi, 4 Jan '70, p. 5.

---

RBF DEFINITIONS

Politics: ███████████████

"Playboy: Is there a single statement you can make that expresses the spirit of your philosophy?"

"RBF: I always try to point one thing out-- if we do more with less, resources are adequate to take care of everybody. All political systems are founded on the premise that the opposite is true. We've been assuming all along that failure was certain, that our Universe was running down and it was strictly you-or-me, kill-or-be-killed as long as it lasted. But now in our century we've discovered that man can be a success on his planet, and that is the greatest change that has come over our thinking."

- Cite Barry Farrell Playboy Interview, 1972 - Draft, p. 1.

---

RBF DEFINITIONS

Politics:

". . . All politicians can and will yield enthusiastically to the computers . . . in bringing all of humanity in for a happy landing."

- Citation & context at Leaders Can Yield to the Computer, 1969

- Cite Operating Manual for Spaceship Earth, 1969

RBF DEFINITIONS

Politics:                                              (1)

"We need not be against politicians to realize that their local
preoccupations are futile. They have good convictions and are
individually moved as human beings by what they regard as a
responsibility to 'their' side or 'our' side. But every
political ideology and all extant political systems assume
that there is not enough to go around: it is either you or me;
there can't be enough for both. So we eventually assume war;
and that is the cause of the weapons race.

"The reasoning was once correct. When there is enough available
a healthy human will eat three pounds of dry food a day, drink
six pounds of water, and breathe 54 pounds of air: or six pounds
net of oxygen. For most of the history of man on Earth there
has not been enough of that dry food and humanity has fought
about this, time and again. Many times there has not been
enough water; and humanity has fought over this. There has been
no time when there has not been enough air. Humanity has so
much air available that no one has even thought of putting
meters on air and trying to make money out of it. But there
are times, for example in a great theater fire, when humanity,
completely unused to competing for air, finds itself suffocating
and goes mad."

– Cite YEAR 2000, AD, Feb'67

---

RBF DEFINITIONS

Politics:                                              (2)

"It seems perfectly clear that when there is enough to go
around, man will not fight any more than he now fights for air.
When man is successful in doing so much more with so much less
that he can take care of everybody at a higher standard, then
there will be no fundamental cause for war.

"In the years ahead, as man does become successful, the root
cause of war will be eliminated. Scientists assure us over and
over again that this is feasible. There can be enough energy
and organized capability for all men to enjoy the whole Earth.

"This is the most important prediction I can make: in 10 years
from now we will have changed so completely that no one will
say that you have to demonstrate your right to live, that you
have to earn a living. Within 10 years it will be normal for
man to be successful-- just as through all history it has been
the norm for more than 99 percent to be economic and physical
failures.

"Politics will become obsolete."

– Cite YEAR 2000, AD, Feb'67

---

RBF DEFINITIONS

Politics:

"Science paces technology, technology paces industry,

industry paces economics, and economics paces politics.

Quite clearly, then, political leaders are at the tail

end of affairs. And for man to ask change of political

leaders is like asking the cow's tail to redesign to cow."

– Cite RBF quoted by Michael S. Gruen, Harvard Crimson story
on Charles Eliot Norton lectures, January 1962.

---

RBF DEFINITIONS

Politics:

"The unfamiliar complex of the new wealth accounting
requirements of the evoluting human experiences emerges
as an aggregate of unique and popularly discerned
everyday 'news' problems. In turn the popularly discerned
inventory of problems altogether provides the raw materials
to be processed by the machinery of politics. It is
the purpose of politics to digest the problems and to
provide adequate accounting and readjustments to the
unexpected and often disconcerting changes in the patterns
of technical advantage realizations. Politics must thus
implement life's continually increasing sweepout and
penetration of Universe with a continually changing set
of operational rules and accounting conventions."

– Cite NO MORE SECONDHAND GOD, Preface, pp. ix, x. 9 May'62
– Citation and context at Science-Technology-Industry-Economics-
Politics Sequence (2)(3), 9 May'62

---

RBF DEFINITIONS

Politics:

"An outmoded activity. . . . A naive attempt to

achieve through games of words what must ultimately

be derived from technology."

– Cite MARKS, P. 10, 1960

---

RBF DEFINITIONS

Politics:

"Politics can only redeal the inadequate cards. . . "

– Cite I&I, THE COMPREHENSIVE MAN, p. 81. Jan'59

---

RBF DEFINITIONS

Politics:

"At present all the world's industrial, or surfaced,
processed and reprocessed, ▓▓▓▓▓▓▓▓▓ funtional
tonnage is in the service of one-quarter of the world's
population. . . All the politicians can do regarding the
problem is to take a fraction of that inadequate ratio
of supply from one group and apply it to another without
changing the overall ratio. . . All that money can do is
shower paper bills of digits on the conflagration. . . "

– Cite RBF quoted by Elaine de Kooning in Art News, Sept. '52

---

RBF DEFINITIONS

Politics:

"No politician can yield to another politician but
all politicians can-- and eventually will-- yield to
the complex problem solutions of the computer."

– Cite NEWSWEEK, "Architecture, The Present Scene," p. 10
– Citation & Context at Leaders Can Yield to the Computer, undated

RBF DEFINITIONS

### Politics:

". . .Political force . . . is one of the survivals of
feudalistic patronage systems, embodying self
indulgence of the few. Industry is replacing political
control. Unscrupulousness in politics thrives on the
unenlightenment and unindividualism of mobs. So called
'mob psychology' is only group motivation through animal
instinct, selfconsciously denying itself of its
individual reasoning power. . ."

- Cite 4-D, Chapter 5, May 1928

---

RBF DEFINITIONS

### Political Mandates: Inventory Of:

"...Little humans on tiny planet Earth each becoming Mr. Big
with a suddenly mistaken sense of power over environmental
transformations-- participation in which permitted him to feel
himself as a manager of inventories of logistical multiplicities
which, at the most ignorant level, manifests itself as
politically assured mandates and political-world gambling =
gamboling = ideological warfare = national sovereignties =
morally rationalizing public = body politic = individual nations
as United Nations."

- Citation & context at Nature's Subvisible Order (2), 27 Dec'73

---

RBF DEFINITIONS

### Politics: Accessory After the Fact:

"Politics are an accessory after the fact."

- Cite RBF to steak crowd at
  LBJ Grille, Carbondale, Ill.
  1 April 1971

---

RBF DEFINITIONS

### Politics & Property:

"The young people recognize the integrity of the Queen--
in contrast to the corruptibility of all the big politicos.

"There were no radical or hostile demonstrations anywhere
over the 4th of July...although, in a new phase of the
psycho-guerrilla warfare, the young are developing their
own antibodies to political exploitation."

"The young are frustrated by the obsolescence of our politics
and our economics, but they are all now coming to realize
that nothing worthwhile is for sale!"

- Cite RBF in response to direct query from Anthony Crosland,
  UK Foreign Secretary, re US youth's interest in the
  royal visit; at a small reception given by the Queen and
  Prince Philip aboard the Royal Yacht Britannia, Philadelphia, PA., 6 Jul'76.

---

RBF DEFINITIONS

### Politics: Accessory After the Fact:

"Politics exists and will always exist-- but it must always be
an accessory after the fact... an accessory after the fact of
whatever the circumstances may be. So if you change the
environment, the circumstances change and politics will have to
have new problems. Politics can't really begin until you have
a plow at hand, or a pick-axe at hand. They can't create that;
and once you do have tools at hand, then you use them. And
that becomes part of the circumstances. I'm not saying there
isn't going to be political action, but it must be an accessory
after the fact. So I can see that we can get the political mood,
the mood of man, to simply demand that their political parties
on both sides merely yield in a direction that neither of them
ever thought of before. The one will not be yielding to the
other man's policy at all. He'll be yielding to the computer.
And I find that anybody can yield to the computers. He can't
lose face by yielding to a machine."

- Cite transcript of RBF tape to Barry Farrell, Tape #3, Side A,
  p.10; Bear Island, 12 Aug'70

---

RBF DEFINITIONS

### Political Revolution:

"It is impossible for us under the present comprehensive
design pattern of world industrialization to make the Earth's
total metals serve 100 percent of humanity exclusively
through political revolutions or peaceful reforms and
rearrangements of the way of administering the economic
accounting of the commercial and social affairs of man.
All we can do politically with the fundamental resource
inadequacy is to take from one group and give to another.
Competitive enterprise assumes exclusive success."

- Cite MEXICO '63, p.2, 10 Oct '63

---

RBF DEFINITIONS

### Politics: Accessory After the Fact:

"Political reform is only and always accessory after the
fact."

- Citation and context at Problem: Statement of the Problem,
  1954-59

---

RBF DEFINITIONS

### Politics vs. World Game:

Bill Wolf: "Is there an evolutionary or gradual path from the
present to the goals of World Game, or is there a
sharp discontinuity?"

RBF: "I say politics is an exclusive system at this point
and World Game is an inclusive system. Whatever it is,
and to the extent that the exclusive system is running
itself out, and it equals out to simply the inverse of
what's out. So it simply melts into one another at
some point."

- Cite Tape #3, p. 13; RBF to W. Wolf, Phila., PA, 15 Jun'74

Politicians: Politics:                                    (1A)

See Bias on One Side of the Line
    Circuitry:  Thermionic and Political Analogy
    Conservatism
    Democracy
    Leaders
    Leaders Can Yield to the Computer
    Leaders:  Take Away the Leaders
    Freeways
    Nation
    Narcotics as Political Strategy
    Peace
    Revolution
    Socialism
    Sovereignty
    Science-Technology-Industry-Economics-Politics
      Sequence
    Survival Recourse:  Last Chance Adoption of
      Unheeded Principles
    Technocracy
    Social Organization

---

Poll: Polling:

See Electronic Voting

---

Politicians: Politics:                                    (1B)

See United States:  One of the Most Difficult Sovereignties
      To Break Up
    War
    War:  Official War & Unofficial War
    World Game:  Men Landing on Moon
    Nonpolitical
    Politics vs. World Game
    Social Economics
    Apolitical
    World-around Communication Transcends Politics
    Ideology
    Ideologies Become Supranational
    Merchants of Woe
    Global Political Revolution

---

Pollen: Pollination:                                      (1)

See Bee:  Honey-seeking Bee
    Inadvertence:  Inadvertent

---

Politics: Politicians:                                    (2 A-N)

See Air Delivery & Submarine Cities, (3)
    Automobile, 5 May'72

    Building Industry, (11)(12)

    Communications, 1967
    Culture, 27 Jan'77

    Doing What Needs to be Done, (1)(2)
    Design Science, (3)*

    Ego, 9 Nov'75
    Electrical Network, 12 Jun'69
    Fuller, R.B:  On Drinking Liquor, 22 Jun'77
    Individual Economic Initiative, 2 Jun'71; 13 Jul'74
    Inhibit, 9 Apr'40
    Invented Jobs, 20 Sep'76

    Laissez-faire Process, 10 Oct'63

    Meek Have Inherited the Earth, 10 Oct'63

    No Energy Crisis, (A)-(C)

---

Pollen: Pollination:                                      (2)

See Male & Female, 1 Feb'75
    New York City (12)

---

Politics: Politicians:                                    (2 O-Z)

See Obsolescence, Apr'72
    Office Buildings, 28 Jan'72*

    Population Explosion, (1)
    Private Enterprise, 9 May'57
    Problem:  Statement Of, 1954

    Soleri, Paolo, 8 Feb'76
    Structure, 8 Sep'75
    Sweepout, 9 May'62

---

RBF DEFINITIONS

Pollution:

"Man talks carelessly and ignorantly of such words as... (the
popular, modern) pollution... where nothing but absolute order
is subvisibly maintained by Universe and her transformation
arrangements unfamiliar to man.  Universe does not have any
pollution.  All the chemistries of Universe are always essential
to the integrity of eternal transformation..."

- Citation & context at Nature's Subvisible Order (1), 27 Dec'73

RBF DEFINITIONS

Pollution:

"I'm perfectly confident that the way we are going to get around pollution and so forth is by developing much better tools for handling energy. You make /a tool_/ and you have it available. If it does work it makes things obsolete that have been inadequate... Desperate people say 'I'm not going to pollute.' But oil is coming out of the refinery down there and people are using the automobile. People can't design their own autombbiles. They can't design refineries as a body politic. Somebody has to take the trouble to discover how you refine and how you don't pollute. This can be done."

- Quoted by Rasa Gustaitis, WHOLLY ROUND, p.153 (Holt, Rinehart & Winston, NY) 1973 - Feb'73

---

RBF DEFINITIONS

Pollution:

"All the chemistries of Universe are essential to Universe. Nature has no pollution."

- Cite RBF at Catholic University Address, Washington DC, 24 Feb '72

---

RBF DEFINITIONS

Pollution:

"Pollution is a natural resource that we are failing to harvest."

(Slightly adapted.)

- Cite article on RBF by Barry Farrel, LIFE, 26 Feb '71

---

RBF DEFINITIONS

Pollution:

"Collect it in the nozzle-- not in the spray!"

- RBF to EJA, 1970

---

RBF DEFINITIONS

Pollution:

"Ignorant humans aboard Space Vehicle Earth are now screaming, "Pollution!" There is no such phenomenon. What they call pollution is extraordinarily valuable chemistry essential to Universe and essential to man on Earth. What is happening is that the egocentricity of omnispecialized man makes him ignorant of the value with which his processing is confronting him. The yellow-brown content of fume and smog is mostly sulfur. The amount of sulfur going out of the smokestacks around the world each year is exactly the same as the amount of sulfur being taken from the Earth each year to keep the world ecology going. It would be far less expensive to catch that sulfur while concentrated in the stack, and to distribute it to the original users, than to do the original mining and to get it out of human lungs, etcetera, when all the costs to society over a deteriorating 25 years are taken into account. But humanity insists on holding to this year's profits, crops, and elections. World society is lethally shortsighted."

- Cite RBF Intrdduction to Gene= Youngblood's EXPANDED CINEMA, 1970. p. 21.

---

RBF DEFINITIONS

Pollution:

"When people use the word pollution it simply means that they have some chemistry they aren't familiar with. . . There is powerful evidence as you study the total Universe and the total relative abundancies that there is an extraordinary continuous interplay of those chemistries, and so it's simply a matter of man getting much too overspecialized and not realizing that what you have here, is exactly what's needed there."

- Cite RBF to World Game at NY Studio School, 12 Jun-31 Jul'69, Saturn Film transcript, Sound 2, Part 3, p.75.

---

RBF DEFINITIONS

Pollution:

"For the strange carelessness of urban society in polluting and corrupting the beauty of the environment is an inherited precedent set by big corporation factories belching smoke into the sky and vomiting chemical residues into the waters. Finding one's self born within the ugly city streets with no fundamental outlet for the innate energies and explorational initiatives, breeds early contempt for the environment and for those who perpetuate its inadequacies. Because humanity has been born without asking so to be, and must frequently grow within environments which disregard their developing needs, most of society tends to cast aside its refuse in unmeditated disdain for the economic masters who seem exclusively preoccupied with making quick profits out of men's desperately vital needs."

- Cite BEAR ISLAND STORY, galley p.32, 1968

---

RBF DEFINITIONS

Pollution Control:                                                    (1)

"I was told by the chief engineer of Combustion Engineering that the apparatus for precipitating all of the fumes, particularly the sulfur which makes the public utilities the worst urban sky polluters, was in complete mechanical solution. I asked what the additional cost per kilowatt hour would be if the apparatus were installed. The answer was 25 percent additional.

"On speaking to the Edison Electric utility managers I pointed this out and was told by them that the chief customers were industries and that the industries only buy from them because the public utilities can provide power at only a fraction less than it would cost the companies to produce their own. Therefore, if they did add the 25 percent, the public would gladly pay but their prime customers would forsake them; ergo, they could not do so.

"The sulfur coming out of all the world's chimneys annually exactly equals what we are taking out of the Earth annually to supply industry's rubber making and other such needs. Vast amounts of energy, knowledge, and skill are expended in the progressive stages of separating out and refining metals from"

- Cite RBF Ltr. to Marshall McLuhan, 2 Sep'74

RBF DEFINITIONS

Pollution Cotrol:                                                        (2)

"their original random ore matrix. This process of separating
out that which the processor desires inadvertently produces
a left-over concentrate of chemical substances unwanted by
the producer, which are now or soon may be essential constituents
of other humanity serving industries. Therefore the unwanted
or so-called waste products are highly valuable concentrates--
before diffusion ot of the stacks or nozzles.

"Nature has no exclusively polluting substances. All physical
substances consist of complexes of some of the 92 regenerative
chemical elements all of which are essentials at different
frequencies of time and in different magnitudes to the success
of eternally regenerative Universe. Pollution is a word invented
by and manifesting human ignorance.

"Many metallic elements may be combined to produce special
behavior alloys which other elements serve as catalyzers, and
so forth, while altogether accommodating all of Universe's
intertransformative capabilities with only a few of which humanity
is as yet familiar and many of which may be essential to
humanity's future survival and service functions."

- Cite RBF Ltr. to Marshall McLuhan, 2 Sep'74

---

RBF DEFINITIONS

Pollution Control:                                                       (3)

"When any one of our various competitively producing industrial
companies are told that they must stop polluting the atmosphere
or waters, they say that the added cost would prevent them from
competing in their respective industries; ergo pollution abate-
ment would mean bankruptcy for them; ergo no compliances. The
atmospheric airs drift and the waters flow interconnectedly around
our planet. They and all resources are essential to all
humanity and the Universe of which humans are just such a
function.

"Clearly the problem won't be solved until central governments
make complete precipitation mandatory and rebate the costs
thereof from the annual taxes of the industries while forcing
the utilities to turn over to the central government all the
valuable chemical elements recovered. The governments would
find their stockpiles worth many times what they seemingly
were losing in tax rebates. The saving to governments in medicare
and general pollution-caused deteriorations would be profound.
The computers would soon inform the government that they were
saving so much money that they could almost completely eliminate
taxes. They would be converting commonwealth to sorted-out
metals that would continually recirculate and with each 22-year"

- Cite RBF Ltr. to Marshall McLuhan, 2 Sep'74

---

RBF DEFINITIONS

Pollution Control:                                                       (4)

"average recirculation would employ the interim harvest of
improved know-how to produce the manyfold performance increase
per pound of the previous recirculation. As for instance, each
melted down Cadillac today can produce two superior-to-Cadillac
Japanese vehicles. I am not promoting automobiles, just
clarifying the point."

- Cite RBF Ltr. to Marshall McLuhan, 2 Sep'74

---

RBF DEFINITIONS

Pollution: Infinite Room to Pollute:

"If the Earth was flat-- out to infinity-- there'd be
infinite room to pollute. You just get rid of it. It goes
to infinity. That's been the practical idea up to now. And
if it went to infinity there'd be an infinite amount of
resources to replace the resources we've exhausted. That's
been our experience in the past. Let's be practical. Let's
get down to Earth! That's the way it is. . . . And then look
at the extraordinary editorial in yesterday's N.Y. Times
quoting Maurice Stans, the Secretary of Commerce, saying let's
go slow on environmental controls: if it gets in the way of
making money, we can't afford it. I think it is a most ghastly
demonstration of the magnitude to which humans are really
entrapped by shortsightedness and selfishness. Now I don't
think ill of any of my fellow men. Each one has his own
evolutionary pattern, but I am intent, wherever I can, to free
my fellow men of the entrapment in ignorance and shortsightedness. . ."

- Cite RBF at SIMS, U. Mass., Amherst, 22 July '71,
    Talk 13, pp. 20-21

---

RBF DEFINITIONS

Pollution: Infinite Room to Pollute:

"If there is an infinite system, then there are an infinite
number of resources to be exploited. You can be just as
careless and stupid as you want, since there are an infinite
number of resources out there and we'll never run out. And
there's an infinite amount of space in which you can get
rid of all your filth as you waste all those resources. But
in a closed system you can't do that-- and that's the kind
of system we're in. We have anything but an infinite number
of resources! We have just enough to make the experiment."

- Cite APPROACHING THE BENIGN ENVIRONMENT, pp. 77-78, 1970

---

RBF DEFINITIONS

Pollution: Infinite Room to Pollute:

"Thinking of Universe only as an infinitely extensive
plane, humanity felt itself logically justified in throwing
away its refuse outside the boundaries of its particular
domain-- there was infinity into which all pollution would
be ultimately dissipated into infinite innocuousness. It
meant nothing to dump a teacup into an infinite ocean. If
there is an infinitely extended world, then we may assume
that when we exhaust the present familiar resources, we
will, as in the past, keep on finding new and better
alternate resources, ad infinitum-- so why should we worry
and be fussy. Never mind about tomorrow. Never mind about
the other fellow. The more ruthlessly selfish one is, the
better off is one and all his dependents."

"So the difference between closed system surfaces and a
closed Universe in respect to the utterly open, infinite
flat slab world concept with which man has been ignorantly
rationalizing all past experience, is the 'similar difference'
between humanity's extinction or its continuation upon this
beautifully equipped and provisioned, closed system, space
vehicle Earth. It is clearly to be utopia or oblivion-- and
no half measures. We must begin today to expose our youth and
ourselves to the fundamental self-discipline conceptioning  13Nov'69
which is the only real educational process." - NEHRUSPEECH,pp.22-23

---

'Pollution' as an Invented Word:


                    See Pollution Control (2)

---

RBF DEFINITIONS

Pollution: News as Most Polluted Resource:

"Probably our most polluted resource is that of the

tactical information to which humanity spontaneously

reflexes,"

- Citation at Information: Tactical Information, 13 Nov'69

~~- Cite NEHRU SPEECH, p. , 37, 13 Nov'69~~

Pollution: News as Most Polluted Resource:

See News, 25 Jul'72
    Tactical Information, 13 Nov'69*

---

RBF DEFINITIONS

Polygon:

"...The 'gon' stands for sides, as in 'polygon,' a planar affair."

- Citation & context at Synergism vs. Energism, 14 Oct'76

---

Pollution: Pollution Control:                                    (1)

See Conservation
    Desalinization
    Excrement: Excremental Functions
    Feeding Lots
    Junkyards
    Metals: Recirculation Of
    Methane Gas Engine
    No Energy Crisis
    Resources: Fresh vs. Waste
    Scrap Sorting & Mongering
    Wind Power
    Ecology
    Only the Whole Big System Works

---

RBF DEFINITIONS

Polygon:

"A polygon's perimeter . . . returns upon itself

as viewed from either pole of the axis of the perimeter."

- Cite NASA Speech, p. 42
    Jun'66

---

Pollution: Pollution Control:                                    (2)

See Afford, (1)-(3)
    Corporation, 28 Apr'71; (2)(3)
    Nature's Subvisible Order (1)*
    Point of No Return, May'72
    Spherical Triangle (4)
    Sulfur, 12 Jun'69
    Syntropy, 7 Feb'71
    Young World, (1)(2); 4 Jul'72
    No Energy Crisis, (B)

---

Polygon:                                                         (1)

See Minimum Polygon
    No Twogon
    Circle = Polygon

---

Polyconic Projection:

See Projective Transformation, (II)

---

Polygon:                                                         (2)

See Structure, Nov'71
    Domains of Polyhedra, 7 Nov'73
    Object, 9 Nov'73
    Triclinic, 31 Aug'76

Polygraph:

See Planetary Democracy, (6)

---

RBF DEFINITIONS

Polyhedron:

"The word polyhedron has to go because itm says 'many-sided'
which implies a continuum. We don't even have the faces.
Faces become spaces. They become intervals. They become
nothing. The Einsteinian finite Universe is predicated on
the absolute finiteness of the local energy event packages."

- Cite SYNERGETICS at Sec. 1023.12, 20 Feb'73

---

RBF DEFINITIONS

Polyhedra:

"Polyhedra consist only of polyhedra. Polyhedra are
always pro tem. constellations of polyhedra. Polyhedra
are defined only by polyhedra--and only by a minimum of
four polyhedra.

"All systems are polyhedra: all polyhedra are systems.

"The observed or tuned-in polyhedra whose plurality of
corners, faces, and edges and frequency of subdivisioning
are ████████ tunably discernible to the tuning-in station
(the observer) consist of corners which are infra-
threshold-tunable polyhedra and whose faces or openings
are ultra-threshold-tunables."

Cite RBF to EJA and RBF rewrite; 3200 Idaho, Wash, DC; 18 Jul'76,
incorporated in SYNERGETICS, 2nd. Ed. at Sec. 400.55-400.57.

---

RBF DEFINITIONS

Polyhedral Understanding:

"...Great circles, unlike spiral lines, always return upon
themselves in the most economical manner. All the system's
paths must be topologically and circularly interrelated for
conceptually definitive, locally transformable, polyhedral
understanding to be attained in our spontaneous-- ergo, most
economical-- geodesically structured thoughts."

- Citation & context at Geodesic, 1969

---

RBF DEFINITIONS

Polyhedral Systems:

"All the interrelationships of system foci are conceptually
representable by vectors. A system is a closed configuration
of vectors. It is a pattern of forces constituting a
geometrical integrity which returns upon itself in a plurality
of directions. Polyhedral systems display a plurality of
polygonal perimeters all of which eventually return upon
themselves. Systems have an electable plurality of view-
induced polarities. The polygons of polyhedra peregrinate
systematically and sometimes wavilinearly around three or
more noncongruent axes."

- Cite SYNERGETICS draft at Sec. 400.09, RBF rewrite, 25/2 May'72

---

Polyhedron: Polyhedra: (1)

See Conceptuality as Polyhedral
    Equi-edged Polyhedra
    Interpolyhedral
    Nuclear & Nonnuclear Polyhedra
    Prime Hierarchy of Symmetric Polyhedra
    Regular Polyhedra
    Rollability of Polyhedra
    System Enclosure
    Cheese Polyhedra
    Clear Space Polyhedra
    Sphere = Polyhedron
    String-connected Polyhedra
    Domains of Polyhedra
    Minimum Polyhedron
    Cosmic Hierarchy
    Triacontrahedron as Limit Regular Polyhedron
    Euler's Uncored Polyhedral Formula

---

RBF DEFINITIONS

Polyhedron:

"But operationally speaking a plane exists ████████ only as
a facet of a polyhedral system. Because I am experiential I
must say that a line is a consequence of energy: an event,
a tracery upon what system? A polyhedron is a system separated
out of Universe. Systems have an inside and an outside. A
picture in a frame has also the sides and the back of the
frame which is in the form of an asymmetrical polyhedron."

- Cite SYNERGETICS, 2nd. Ed. at Sec. 1007.25, 1 Jan'75

---

Polyhedron: Polyhedra: (2)

See Halo Concept, 22 Feb'72
    Superficial, 6 Mar'73
    Topology: Synergetic & Eulerian, 2 Jun'74
    Centers of Energy Rebirth, 16 Nov'72
    Open Triangular Spirals, Nov'71
    Quantum Mechanics: Minimum Geometrical Fourness,(1)
    Triclinic, 31 Aug'76
    Hex-pent Structure of Purines, 15 Dec'76
    Genralization & Special Case, 23 Jan'77

---

Polynesians:

    See Binary, 1970

---

RBF DEFINITIONS

Population of Cities:

Q. - (William Raspberry): "Mr. Fuller, should we put a gate up
        in the city and keep the people out after it reaches
        a certain size, or not? Should we limit the size of
        our cities? Should we limit the population of our
        cities?"

A. - (RBF): "We shouldn't limit anything. That's what human
beings are all about... to delimit their capabilities, to give
them a chance to really function. We're probably here to find
out how it's supposed to function. So I do not expect anything
positive from negative beginnings."

- Cite RBF to "Town Meeting of the Air," Wash., DC; 10 Sep'75

---

Ponderable:                         (1)

    See Imponderable
        Weighable

---

RBF DEFINITIONS

Population Density:

"All the cities of the world occupy less than one percent

of the Earth's surface."

- Cite I SEEM TO BE A VERB, Queen, May '70 (Not in Bantam version)

---

Ponderable:                         (2)

    See Metaphysics, Jun'66
        Universe, (B); Oct'66; 13 Nov'69

---

RBF DEFINITIONS

Population Density: Manhattan Cocktail Party:

"All the people in the world today could be housed in

the buildings of Manhattan with each person having as

much room as at a cocktail party."

- Cite I SEEM TO BE A VERB, Queen, May '70 (Not in Banatm edition)

---

RBF DEFINITIONS

Population:

"I find that as industrialization increases, the population
decreases. With industrialization, the life expectancy
increases. When that happens, families don't have to be
large. In the last five years the absolute number of
babies has been less each year. The big bulge everyone's
worried about occurred because all the people that used to
die have not been dying, particularly at birth. This bulge
is working up to a time when there will be a great,great many
people who are very old. But the number coming in at the
bottom is lessening very rapidly."

- Cite RBF to William Marlin, Architectural Forum, Feb'72

---

RBF DEFINITIONS

Population Density: Manhattan Jet Dispersal:

"Here is how New York is going to solve its transportation
problem. First you'll have to do away with the automobile
altogether. It is a matter of geometries. You take a point
and then a line. That's what a highway is, a line between
two points. Well, you have areas which are much vaster than
lines, and you have all the volume above the areas, which is
space. If you take all the 30 million people of the New York
metropolitan area and give them little harnesses with jets
and have them put on the proper clothes, and if you send them
up in the air to a reasonable altitude, say 10,000 feet, where
they wouldn't need any additional oxygen, all simultaneously,
people would be so far apart they couldn't see each other.
That would solve your traffic jams!"

- Cite RBF quoted in New York magazine, p.27, 30 Mar'70

Population Density: Manhattan Cocktail Party:

      See New York City, 1938; (8)
         Population Explosion, (1)(2); 1959

---

Population Density:

      See Community
         Privacy
         Proxemics
         Proximity ≠ Neighborliness

---

RBF DEFINITIONS

Population Explosion:

"The population explosion is a myth. As we industrialize, down goes the annual birth rate. If we survive, by 1985, the whole world will be industrialized, and, as with the United States, and as with all Europe and Russia and Japan today, the birth rate will be dwindling, and the bulge in population will be recognized as accounted for exclusively by those who are living longer.

"When world realization of its unlimited wealth has been established there as yet will be room for the whole of humanity to stand indoors in greater New York City, with more room for each human than at an average cocktail party.

"We will oscillate progressively between social concentrations in cultural centers and in multideployment in greater areas of our Spaceship Earth's as yet very ample accommodations. The same humans will increasingly converge for metaphysical intercourse and deploy for physical experiences."

- Cite OPERATING MANUAL FOR SPACESHIP EARTH, pp.131-132, 1959

---

RBF DEFINITIONS

Population Explosion:

"There has been a great debate about the so-called

population explosion in recent years. . . The cause of

the bulge in census population is, of course, that more

people are living longer. But the underlying reality of

the population problem, if there is a problem, is that as

we industrialize the rate of births decrease. . . Clearly,

as man industrializes and improves the probability of

human survival, whatever the drives or controls of nature

are, she does not have to have anywhere as many birth

'starts.' This is one of the fundamental points about

industrialization. . . which will be world wide by 1985."

    - Cite THE YEAR 2000, San Jose State College, 1966
        Column 4.

---

RBF DEFINITIONS

Population Explosion: (1)

"Desirable time investment alternatives inherently decrease overall baby-making time. That explains 'the rich getting richer and the poor getting children.' Prime designing commands the fundamental solution of the overpopulation threat. As with all the fundamental problems of man on Earth fundamental solutions are not to be had by political reforms of either the peacetime prohibitory law enforcement variety, or of the never convincing wartime annihilation variety. Fundamental solutions are not for sale. Mass subscriptions to support professional do-gooders are futile.

"Fortunately population explosion is only the momentary social hysteria's cocktail conversation game. Real population crisis is fundamentally remote. There is room enough indoors in New York City for the whole 1963 world's population to enter, with room enough inside for all hands to dance the twist in average nightclub proximity. There is ample room in the New York streets for one-half the world's population to amble about in, leaving enough room inside buildings for the other half to lie down and sleep. This would be a good moment to call for all scientists, engineers, tool makers, machine fitters, mechanics, and aircraft pilots present, all of whom"

- Cite PRIME DESIGN, I&I, p.248, May'60/63

---

RBF DEFINITIONS

Population Explosion: (2)

"amount to less than one per cent of humanity, and to send them out from New York City all around the world to get total automation of world production and services going. After this the world's population could start enjoying the whole Earth as students, archaeologists, playwriters, players, poets, artists, dancers, skin divers, tourists, etc. There would be no further muscle and reflex jobs to be done and no need to earn a living, for the living would be generated as effortlessly as apples grow on trees."

- Cite PRIME DESIGN, I&I, pp.248-249, May'60/63

---

TEXT CITATIONS

Population Explosion:

"Thinking Out Loud (1): Disproving the Population Explosion," World Mag. 3 Jul'73

"Playboy, Ltrs. to Editor, Feb'72 pp. 50-51, (Discussion of RBF Views.)

---

RBF DEFINITIONS

Population Sequence: (1)

"There are many prognostications about immediate technology... It is all Buck Rogers and it will happen. But, such speculation is a waste of time, it is more important to consider what will happen to our relationship one with another.

"In its broadest aspect this area must be considered under 'population.' There has been a great debate about the so-called population explosion in recent years. This has been occasioned in part by the fact that we have only recently had accurate census in many countries. Even in Europe population figures only go back a short time.

"In the USA, though there was an increase in the post-war birth rate between 1947 and 1954, since then it has declined. This trend is also evident in all the industrialized countries, including Russia. During the last 12 years then the birth rate has been declining in the industrialized countries, yet the main problem is thought to be population increase. The cause of the bulge in census population of these countries, is of course, that more people are living longer. But the underlying reality of the population problem, if there is a problem, is that as we industrialize, the rate of births decreases. We may see this most clearly in, for example, the US, where the"

- Cite THE YEAR 2000, reprinted in AD, Feb'67

RBF DEFINITIONS

## Population Sequence: (2)

"the early settlers had an average of 13 children per family and survival rate was very poor. We may then plot the decrease in number of children per family against improvement in technological services, public health, indoor water supply, bathrooms, refrigeration, general improvement in life expectancy, and so on. Clearly as man industrializes and improves the probability of human survival, whatever the drives or controls of nature are, she does not have to have anywhere as many birth 'starts.' This is one of the fundamental points about industrialization.

"We should also consider the rate at which countries become industrialized. England took 200 years to get industrialization going and up to the present level. The US 'took off' from England's vantage point and did it in 100 years. Russia came in and accomplished in 50 what had taken the USA 100 years, because it was able to start at a more advantageous point. We find the new countries come in where others left off, not where they started. Japan did not start flying with the Wright Brothers bi-planes, but with the 'Zero' and 'Spitfire' types; China has never flown anything but jets. China came into the world of industrialization after the transistors, computers, and atomic fission were available-- so she will come to indus"

- Cite THE YEAR 2000, reprinted in AD, Feb'67

RBF DEFINITIONS

## Population Sequence: (3)

"trial parity with the west in about five years. India will probably be even faster. The acceleration of capabilities coming to bear on India and Africa are of the very highest. As far as one can see, industrialization will be worldwide by 1985.

"By this date, as the world industrial process is completing, and birth rates reducing, every individual human being will still have about ten acres of dry land and approximately 20 acres of ocean averaging half a mile deep. In terms of a family of five that would be 50 acres of land and 100 acres of ocean-- 150 acres per family. The amount of food supply would be ample.

"We may glimpse in such patterning certain total behaviors in Universe that we know little about. We noted, for instance, that as survival rate and life sustaining capability increased fewer birth starts were required. This may be related to our developing capacities in interchanging our physical parts, of producing mechanical organs, of having progressively fewer human organisms to replenish. The drive in humanity to reproduce as prodigally as possible decreases considerably. This may be reflected in social behaviors-- when all the girls"

- Cite THE YEAR 2000, reprinted in AD, Feb'67

RBF DEFINITIONS

## Population Sequence: (4)

"begin to look like boys and boys and girls wear the same clothes. This may be part of a discouraging process in the idea of producing more babies.

"We shall have to stop looking askance on trends in relation to sex merely as a reproductive capability, i.e., that it is normal to make babies. Society will have to change in its assessment of what the proclivities of humanity may be. Our viewpoints on homosexuality, for example, may have to be reconsidered and more wisely adjusted.

"Central to such readjustment will be the concept that man is not alone the physical machine he appears to be. He is not merely the food he consumes, the water he drinks, or the air he breathes. His physical processing is only an automated aspect of a total human experience which transcends the physical. As a knot in a series of spliced ropes of manila, cotton, nylon, etc., may be progressively slipped through all the material changes of thickness and texture along the length yet remain an identifiable pattern configuration, so man is an abstract pattern integrity which is sustained through all the physical changes and processing."

- Cite THE YEAR 2000, reprinted in AD, Feb'67

RBF DEFINITIONS

## Population Sequence: (5)

"We become more aware of this uniqueness of organizing principle in the Universe, in science. The long-held myth that science wrests order out of chaos is fast disappearing in due ratio to the extent that all great scientists have found the Universe to exhibit an a priori orderliness. All the various specialties are discovering that their variously remote studies which seemingly 'ordered' local aspects of nature are converging within progressively simpler and more comprehensive patterns. The 'ordering' is coming together. When we refer to the computer and automation's taking over we refer really to man's externalization of his internal and organic functions into a total organic system which we call industrialization. This metabolic regenerating automated organism is going to be able to support life in an extraordinary way. The machines will increasingly assume various specialized functions. Man who was born spontaneously comprehensive but was focused by survival needs into specialization is now to be brought back to comprehensivity.

"As enormous numbers of men are freed for more education and research and as they become more and more comprehensive in their dealings with nature, there will be engendered a total"

- Cite THE YEAR 2000, reprinted in AD, Feb'67

RBF DEFINITIONS

## Population Sequence: (6)

"philosophic awareness of the significance of the whole human experience. There will be a rediscovery of what Einstein described in 1930, in an article on the 'cosmic religious sense'-- the intellectual integrity of the Universe and an orderliness that was manifestly a priori to man.

"We are going to have an increasing number of human beings as scientists and philosophers thinking about the total significance of human experience and realizing that there is an intellect far greater and far more powerful than that of man-- and anticipatory of the whole trend of his development. An era of extraordinary integrity might ensue.

"This would be for me, the most important and exciting aspect of all the trend curves-- that in A.D. 2000, to a marked extent, the integrity of humanity will be of an unbelievably high order. What one human being says to another regarding what he thinks or what he has observed, will be reliable. There will be play-acting still, but it will very clearly be play-acting. In looking forward to the year 2000 it is not the 'Buck Rogers' details which are important but whether the world will be a good place for our children and grandchildren. In the past,"

- Cite THE YEAR 2000, reprinted in AD, Feb'67

RBF DEFINITIONS

## Population Sequence: (7)

"man had to do many things shortsightedly and we have wasted a great deal of our natural heritage. We have squandered the fossil fuels which represented an extraordinary 'savings' or energy capability account stored up in the Earth. The great change now will be in a new type of accounting when we begin to draw more consciously on the fabulous 'income' energies of Sun, water, wind, and tidal powers-- which, if not used, will not be 'saved' or impounded on the Earth. We will adopt new accountancy standards for all wealth. To account for our success in terms of gold and various traditional banking practices is irrelevant. Real wealth is organized capability. One of its major characteristics is that it is irreversible. No matter how much wealth you have, you cannot change one iota of yesterday. Wealth can only be used now and in the future. What we really mean by wealth is how many days forward we have energy available and organized for work to keep the machines running, to keep the foods growing, the refrigeration, transportation, and so on. The basis for our new accounting system will be 'How many forward days of organized capability do we have available to serve how many men'. We will be able to make the working assumption that it is normal not only for man to be successful but also normal for him to move as freely as he wishes without interfering with any other man. Our overall"

- Cite THE YEAR 2000 reprinted in AD, Feb'67

RBF DEFINITIONS

## Population Sequence: (8)

"accounting assumption will be based on whatever amount of organized energy capability is required so as to make it possible for any man to travel around and enjoy the whole Earth, and be completely supported in doing so. There will be no such thing as deficit accounting. You cannot live on deficit accounting. You cannot eat deficitly or drink water deficitly. What is to eat is there-- as the water is there.

"All such negative accounting procedures went along with the need for exploiting others in the 'you or me' phase of man's past struggle for basic survival.

"Much of the most exciting and important part about tomorrow is not the technology or the automation at all, but that man is going to come into entirely new relationships with his fellow men. He will retain much more in his everyday relations of what we term the naivete and idealism of the child. This will be completely justified and not exploited or exploitable in any way. I think then that the way to see what tomorrow is going to look like is just to look at our children."

- Cite THE YEAR 2000 reprinted in AD, Feb'67

RBF DEFINITIONS

## Population: Stabilization Of:

"Japan was the first country in the world to actually stabilize its population. China is going in for birth control in a major way if they industrialize, and they industrialize at a very rapid rate. The only place where we're making an enormous amount of babies is in the nonindustrial countries where the probability of survival is very poor: just as clearly identified as it can be. . . "

- Cite RBF to World Game at NY Studio School, 12 Jun-31 Jul'69, from Saturn film transcript, Sound 1, Take 1, p. 9.

Population: Center of World Population:

See Three-way Weaving vs. Two-way Crisscross, 13 Mar'75

Porcupine: Runover Porcupine:

See Cartography: Conventional Projections, (1)
Twenty-foot Earth Globe & 200-foot Celestial
Sphere, (9)

Population: Population Stabilization:                    (1)

See Acres per Individual Human Being
Homosexuality
Procreation
Womb Population

Porpoise Sounds:

See Universal Language, 28 Apr'71

Population: Population Stabilization:                    (2)

See Artifacts, 28 Apr'74
Lags (1)
India, 12 May'75

Porpoise:

See Pet, 31 Jan'75
Pure Principle, 6 Jul'62
Surfing: Surfboarding, 5 Jul'62

Population:                                              (3)

See Population of Cities
Population Density
Population Density: Manhattan Cocktail Party
Population Density: Manhattan Jet Dispersal
Population Explosion
Population: Stabilization Of
Population: Center of World Population

Ports:

See Seaports

RBF DEFINITIONS

Positional Differentials:

"Positional differentials in Universe derive only from the sixness of the 12 degrees of freedom."

- Citation & context at Twelve Universal Degrees of Freedom, 1 Feb'75

---

Positive Matter:                                                    (2)

See Antientropy, 10 Oct'63

---

Position:                                                          (1)

See Celestial Position Integrity
    Interpositioning
    Self-positionability
    Fix

---

RBF DEFINITIONS

Positive and Negative:

"...What we call physical reality is always a positive and negative pulsating aberration of the whole..."

- Citation and context at Physical Reality, 11 Jul'62

---

Position:                                                          (2)

See Individuality & Degrees of Freedom, (2)

---

RBF DEFINITIONS

Positive and Negative:

". . . Everything that we know as reality has to be either a positive or negative condition."

- Cite Carbondale Draft
       Nature's Coordination p. VI.43
       Oregon Lecture # 7, p. 235.
       11 Jul'62
- Citation at Reality, 11 Jul'62. (Incorporated in SYNERGETICS at Sec. 441.23)

---

Positive Matter:                                                  (1)

See Matter & Antimatter
    Negative Matter

---

RBF DEFINITIONS

Positive and Negative:

"Positive and negative cancel as the principle zero."

- Citation and context at Principle, May'49

RBF DEFINITIONS

### Positive and Negative:

"...'Right' and 'left' should be replaced by the nonequal and opposite words 'positive' and 'negative'..."

- Citation and context at <u>Left & Right,</u> ▮▮▮▮▮▮▮▮▮▮▮ 4 May'57

### Positive & Negative:     (1)

       **Active & Passive**
See Annihilation
    Complementarity
    Energetic Functions
    Interwave Behavior of Number
    Mite:  Positive & Negative Functions
    Motion:  Six Positive & Negative Motions
    Nonmirror Image
    Oscillation
    Parity & Disparity
    Polar & Hemispherical Positive-negativeness
    Pulsation
    Reciprocity
    Structural Functions
    Tensegrity:  Miniature Masts:  Positive & Negative
    Plus & Minus
    Outside-out vs. Inside-out
    Basic Event
    Symmetry:  Positive or Negative

---

RBF DEFINITIONS

### Positive & Negative:  Four Kinds:

"There are four kinds of positive and negative:

    (1) the eternal, equilibrium-disturbing plurality of differentially unique, only-positively-and-negatively-balanced aberratings;

    (2) the north and south poles;

    (3) the concave and convex; and

    (4) the inside (microcosm) and outside (macrocosm) always cosmically complementing the local system's inside-concave and outside-convex limits."

- Citation & context at <u>Two Kinds of Twoness</u>, (A), 10 Nov'74

### Positive & Negative:     (2A)

See Aberration, 22 Nov'73
    Algebra, Oct'66
    Antientropy, 10 Oct'63
    Atomic Computer Complex, (2)
    Axis of Spin: Tetrahedron, 7 Oct'71

---

### Positive & Negative Set of the Whole:

    See Physical Reality, 11 Jul'62

### Positve & Negative:     (2C)

    See Considerable Set, 1959
    Crystallography, 17 Aug'70

---

### Positive ≠ Negative:

    See Positive & Negative, 4 May'57

### Positive & Negative:     (2D)

    See Dynamic Symmetry, 31 May'71

Positive & Negative: (2E)

    See Energy, 16 Sep'67
       Energy Event, 9 Jul'62
       Equilibrium, 25 Feb'69
       Eternity, (2)

Positive & Negative: (2L)

    See Left & Right, 4 May'57

Positive & Negative: (2F)

    See Frequency:  Half Frequency, 29 Nov'72

Positive & Negative: (2M)

    See Mite & Coupler, 13 May'73
       Mites & Quarks as Basic Notes, (1)-(3)

Positive & Negative: (2G)

    See Game of Cosmic History, 27 Dec'73

Positive & Negative: (2N)

    See Nature, Jun'66; 13 Nov'69
       News & Evolution, (1)(3)(4)

Positive & Negative: (2I)

    See Information Transmitting & Nontransmitting Model,
       27 May'75
       Invisible ≠ Negative, 28 May'75
       Intertransforming, Jun'66

Positive & Negative: (2O)

    See Odd Ball, 27 Sep'72
       Optimism:  I Am Not an Optimist, 26 Apr'77

Positive & Negative:                                          (2P)

    See Particle, (1)(2)
       Physical Reality, 11 Jul'62*
       Planetary Democracy, (6)
       Population of Cities, 10 Sep'75
       Plastic Flowers, Oct'70
       Powering: Fifth Dimension, 29 Nov'72
       Prime Dichotomy, (1)(2)
       Prime Structural Systems, 11 Jul'62; 3 Nov'75
       Principle, May'49*


Positive & Negative:                                          (2T)

    See Tetrahedron: Nine Schematic Aspects, 30 Aug'75
       Tetrahedral Dynamics, (2)
       Tetrahelix, 10 Sep'74
       Tidal, 9 Nov'73
       Triangle, (A); (a); Nov'71; Jun'71
       Twoness, 23 May'72; 1967


Positive & Negative:                                          (2Q)

    See Quantum: Event-paired Quanta, Jun'66
       Quanta Loss by Congruence, (1)


Positive & Negative:                                     (2 UVWXYZ)

    See Vector Equilibrium, (I)

      X Configuration with One Ball at the Center,
       (1)(2)

      Zero, 9 Apr'40; May'49


Positive & Negative:                                          (2R)

    See Reality, 11 Jul'62*; Jun'66
       Reflection Sequence: Applew, (1)(2)
       Ruddering, May'65


Positive:                                                     (1)

    See Low Pressure vs. Positive


Positive & Negative:                                          (2S)

    See Seeability, 31 May'71
       Scenario vs. Absolute Symmetry, 11 Dec'75
       Star Event & Degrees of Freedom, 12 May'75
       Stability, 18 Mar'69
       Syte, 31 May'71
       Six Motion Freedoms & Degrees of Freedom, (1)(4)(5)


Positive:                                                     (2)

    See Navy Sequence (7)
       Optimism: I Am Not an Optimist, 26 Apr'77

RBF DEFINITIONS

Positron:

See Electron & Positron

---

Possible Into Probable:

See Life, 16 Aug'50

---

RBF DEFINITIONS

Possession:

"Galen Handy's quote, 'since truth is universal, truth cannot
be possessed, only the untruth can be possessed;' to which I
append that all possession must be founded on delusions, lies,
or self-deceptions."

- Cite RBF Ltr. to N. Kaiser, p.1; 10 Jun'74

---

Possibility:

See Question-asking Possibility

---

RBF DEFINITIONS

Possession:

"Possession is becoming progressively burdensome and
wasteful and therefore obsolete."

- Cite Operating Manual for Spaceship Earth. 1969

---

RBF DEFINITIONS

Posterioral Osculations:

"'Soldiering,' pretentious hustling, officiousness, abstract
posterioral osculations are amplifications of the momentum
of the subconsciously sustained fallacial notion of a
necessity of evidenced quasi-justification of existence."

- Citation and context at Industrial Hypocrisy, May'32

---

Possession:

See Mine: That's Mine
Ownership
Private Property
Thing: Thingness

---

Post-uraniums:

See Ninety-two Elements: Chart of Rate of Acquisition
Superatomics

RBF DEFINITIONS

Potential:

"Life is fully potential and the entirely sublimated human organism coordinates omnisubconsciously."

- Cite ▓▓▓▓▓▓ Invisible Architecture: (E), Aug'72

---

RBF DEFINITIONS

Potential:

"The mathematical patterning and intertransformability of nature's geometrical structurings are the only reality of Universe. The infinitely regenerative dynamism, always potential in the fundamental relationship of the principles, in itself constitutes the intellectually tunable and ever inescapable reality."

- Citation at Reality: Structurings as the Only Inescapable Reality, 1963
- Cite I&I, DOMES, p. 147. Date undetermined

---

RBF DEFINITIONS

Potential:

"...We have the theoretically perfect man as he goes through the vector equilibrium, he no longer needs the physical. Everyone is 3.702 short of his potential."

*- Citation & context at Immaculate Conception, 25 Jan'72

---

Potential vs. Active:

See Industrial Principle, 1 Jun'49
Precession, 8 Dec'72

---

RBF DEFINITIONS

Potential:

"Potential lines are metaphysically straight, all physically realized relationships are geodesic and curved trajectories."

- Cite SYNERGETICS Corollaries, Sec. 240. 1972
- Citation at Metaphysical & Physical, 1971

---

Potential vs. Manifest:

See Universal Integrity: Manifest Ratios & Potential Ratios, 1 Apr'72

---

RBF DEFINTTIONS

Potential:

"Universe is a nonsimultaneously potential vector equilibrium."

- Cite SYNERGETICS Corollaries, Sec. 240. 1972

---

Potential vs. Operationally Effective:

See Mite & Coupler, 13 May'73

---

RBF DEFINITIONS

Potential vs. Operative:

See Vector, Oct'59
Vector Equilibrium, 2 Nov'73

Potential vs. Radiant:

See Cube: Diagonal of Cube as Wave Propagation Model,
22 Jun'72

Potential vs. Physically Realized:

See Line, Oct'59
Theoretical, 26 May'72

Potential Ratios of Volume to Quanta Values:

See Universal Integrity: Manifest Ratios & Potential
Ratios, 1 Apr'72

RBF DEFINITIONS

Potential vs. Primitive:

"The potential activation of tetravolume quantation in
the geometric hierarchy is still subfrequency but accounts
for the doubling of volumetric space.

"The potential activation of tetravolume accounting is
plural; it provides for nucleation. Primitive tetravolume
accounting is singular and subnuclear."

- Cite RBF to EJA, 3200 Idaho, Wash. DC; 12 May'77
  (Incorporated in SYNERGETICS 2 draft at Sec. 1033.181.)

Potential vs. Realized:

See Angle & Frequency Design Control, Jul'71
Metaphysical & Physical, 1971
Nucleus, 12 Jul'62
Vector, 26 May'72
Wavilinear, 28 Oct'73

Potential vs. Primitive:

See Vector Equilibrium: Potential & Primitive
Tetravolumes

RBF DEFINITIONS

Potential Sphere:

"All spheres are potential spheres."

- Citation & context at Six Motion Freedoms & Degrees of
  Freedom, 8 Aug'77

Potential: (1)

See Copotentials
    Embryo
    Full Potential
    Interpotential
    Perfection
    Relevant System Potential
    Superficial Potential
    Latent
    Behavior Potential

---

RBF DEFINITIONS

Pound: Ezra Pound: (1885-    )

"Before Heisenberg's 'indeterminism,' T.S. Eliot said
'the act of considering history alters history.' Ezra
Pound anticipated them both when he remarked much earlier
that 'the act of thinking alters thought.'"

- Cite The Generalized Laws of Design, p. 1. 22 Apr'68

---

Potential: (2)

    Cosmic Hierarchy, 23 Jan'77
See Eternal Instantaneity, 22 Jun'72
    Fix, 6 Nov'73
    Fuller, R.B: On Creativity, 23 May'72
    God, 26 May'72
    Ideals, 14 Feb'72
    Immaculate Conception, 25 Jan'72
    Invisible Architecture, (E)*
    Metaphysical & Physical, 1971
    Powering: Third Powering, 15 Oct'72
    Reality: Structurings as the Only & Inescapable
      Reality, 1963*
    Sixty Degreeness, 8 Dec'72
    Synergetic Strategy of Commencing with Totality,
      28 May'72
    Tension & Compression, 1944
    Theoretical, 26 May'72
    Tongue: Bite Your Tongue, Aug'72
    Vector, 14 Oct'72
    Vector Equilibrium, Oct'59; 1971; 23 Oct'72
    Vector Equilibrium: Zero Model, 31 May'71
    Individual Life as One Way Universe Could Have Turned
      Out, 5 Jun'75

---

Pound, Ezra:

See Heisenberg-Eliot-Pound Sequence

---

Potential: (3)

See Potential vs. Active
    Potential vs. Manifest
    Potential vs. Operationally Effective
    Potential vs. Operative
    Potential vs. Radiant
    Potential Ratio of Volume-to-Quantum Values
    Potential vs. Realized
    Potential vs. Primitive
    Potential Sphere

---

RBF DEFINITIONS

Poverty:

"And humanity's enlightenment is delayed
Because the Earth planet is so large,
And man is so infinitely tiny
And so myopically preoccupied with personally avoiding
The erroneously assumed inevitability of poverty for the many,
Which has slavishly and fearfully conditioned his reflexes."

- Cite BRAIN & MIND, p.94 May '72

---

RBF DEFINITIONS

Pound: Ezra Pound:

"Heisenberg said that observation alters the phenomenon
observed. T.S. Eliot said that studying history alters
history. Ezra Pound said that thinking in general alters
what is thought about. Pound's formulation is the most
general, and I think it's the earliest."

- Cite Hugh Kenner, "The Rope and the Knot," Kentucky
  Review, Autumn 1968, who attributes this quote to R.B.F.

---

Poverty: Slow Slum Death: (1)

See War: Official & Unofficial
    War: Slow Death by Slums vs. War as Quick Death

Poverty: <u>Slow Slum Death</u>:                                    (2)


See Design Science, (2)
    Resource Inadequacy, May'72

---

RBF DEFINITIONS

<u>Powering</u>:

"In the topology of synergetics powering is identifiable
only with the uni-angular vectorial convergences."

Citation and context at <u>Convergence</u>, 16 Nov'72

---

Poverty: <u>Poor</u>:


See Success, 10 Sep'75
    News & Evolution, 15 Mar'77
    Enough to Go Around, (1)(2)

---

RBF DEFINITIONS

<u>Powering</u>:

"Number powers refer to the number of times any given
number is multiplied by itself. While empty set numbers
may be theorized as multipliable by themselves, so long
as there is time to do so, all experimental demonstrability
of science is inherently time limited. Time is the only
dimension. It is expressable as frequency."

- Cite Synergetics Draft at Sec. 960.03, 16 Nov'72

---

<u>Power Factoring</u>:

See Six Motion Freedoms & Degrees of Freedom, 11 Aug'77

---

RBF DEFINITIONS

<u>Powering</u>:

"Powering means the multiplication of a number by itself."

- Cite SYNERGETICS draft at Sec. 960.02, 16 Nov'72

---

<u>Power Generation</u>:


See Electromagnetic Generating
    Wind Power Sequence
    Inanimate Energy Power

---

RBF DEFINITIONS

<u>Powering</u>:

"Powering is numbers self-multiplying."

- Cite RBF to EJA, 3200 Idaho, 28 Oct'72

RBF DEFINITIONS

Powering:

"Powering means the development of dimensions that require
the introduction of constant angular interception of a
constant angle system of planes by a plane not already
in the system."

- Cite RBF re-write of Oregon Lecture #4, p. 131 on 12/13
Sep '71, in SYNERGETICS draft 770.01, Jan. '72.

---

RBF DEFINITIONS

Powering:

"Nature needs only triangles to identify arithmetical
powering for self-multiplication of numbers. Therefore,
'triangling' is twice as efficient as 'squaring.'"

- Cite Carbondale Draft
Return to Modelability, p. V.9
- Cite NASA Speech, p.75, Jun'66

---

RBF DEFINITIONS

Powering:

"In the topology of synergetics powering is identifiable
only with uni-angular vectorial convergences. The number
of superficial vertex convergeneces of the system are
identified with second powering, and not with anything we
call 'areas,' that is, not with the surfaces nor with any
experimentally nondemonstrable continuums."

- Cite Nasa Speech, p. 90 as rewritten 12/13 Sep '71,
by RBF in SYNEREGTICS Draft at Sec. 770.02, Jan '72.

---

RBF DEFINITIONS                                                        (A)

Powering:

Re Equation 10 $F^2 + 2$:

"That is a very interesting kind of mathematics for you to
think about for certain reasons. To start off, you have second
power. This second power is a number characterizing layers
or surfaces. What we use for surface is a shell-- in a sense it
becomes the 'surface' or a package in the system. I get a
bigger package and I can tell what the number is by using the
second power. We have been very used to using second power for
the surface of a cube or any other thing. We say the linear
measure is first power; this is the radius or edge of the cube
and the surface is the second power, and the volume is the
third power. Second power has been connected uniquely with
surface area and it is still the surface or the shell. But
what it is showing is very interesting: there is no continuous
shell, there are actually only points. They are little
spheres. You can have this very high frequency and we would
be counting the points in the shell, and not the surface as a
whole, so we find second power representing points in the
system and not surface. . . What we really discover in physics
is that there are no such things as solids, and there are no
such things as surfaces, because what we simply meant was a
solid surface.

POWERING - SEC 774.05  - Cite Oregon Lecture #7, p.239, 11 jul'62

---

RBF DEFINITIONS

Powering:

"IN a radiational (eccentric) or gravitational (concentric)
wave system:

Second powering is identified with the point population of
the circumferential arrays of any given radius stated in
terms of frequency of modular subdivisions of the circumferential array radially-read system's concentricity
layering;

Third powering is identified with the total point population
of all the successive ▓▓▓▓ wave layers of the system;

Fourth powering is identified with the interpointal domain
volumes; and

Fifth and Sixth powerings are identified ▓▓▓ as products
of multiplication by frequency doublings and treblings, etc."

- Cite SYNERGETICS Draft, Corollaries - May 1971 (▓▓▓▓)
See Secs. 240.44 and "Modelability, Powering," Secs.
772.3, 773.1, 774.1, and 775.1.

---

RBF DEFINITIONS                                                        (B)

Powering:

"We have been used to the idea of the second power for
plotting the solid surface. In the quantum and wave
phenomena, they have been dealing in individual packages
that do all of their accounting. They don't have continuous
surface at all. Suddenly we find here then a congruence of
the phenomena we have been very familiar with, the second
power, and we understand it now to mean the shell and you can
identify the second power with points or little separate
packages and not as a continuous solid surface. You could
relate it to little energy actions, little separate stars,
and you are coming out all right. This is what you really
mean by quantum. Now you have actually conceptuality in
respect to the quantum."

- Cite Oregon Lecture #7, pp.239-240, 11 Jul'62

---

RBF DEFINITIONS                          �▓▓▓▓▓▓▓▓▓

Powering:

"'Powering' . . . in this topology is identifiable
only with the vertexes and not with something we
call 'area,' that is, not with a surface or an experimentally non-demonstrable continuum."

(Adapted.)

(I deleted "second" before
"powering.")

- Cite NASA Speech, p. 90, Jun'66

PRINCIPLES 223.54 + POWERING 770.02

---

RBF DEFINITIONS                                                        (1)

Powering:

"Science had thought that it was impossible to be conceptual
because it had felt that fourth dimensionality which had been
showing up time and again as an arithmetical behavior of the
physics, could not be accommodated by the XYZ coordinate
system and it can be accommodated by synergetics. Why can it
be? Because the vector equilibrium has a volume of 20. You
can get eight cubes around one point, and so the third power
of two, which is eight, has used up all the space, but using the
tetrahedra I can get a volume of 20 around one point as I do in
the vector equilibrium. Twenty is two to the fourth power
plus two to the second power and it makes it quite possible to
make models of fourth powering by using tetrahedroning. In fact
we find vector equilibrium is unity because its edge module is
one, as is the cube the module of one. It is when it is one,
when it is unity, that its volume is 20. When its edge module
is two, it is two to the third power times 20 which is 160 and
the volume is 160 where the edge module is two. It will
accommodate very high powering, the sixth powering, and s o
forth. It makes possible the actual modelling of the multi-
powers that have characterized some of the physics and some
of the chemistry which have not been modellable before and
had only been treatable mathematically-- and calculatable but

- Cite Orgeon Lecture #6, p.233, 10 Jul'62

RBF DEFINITIONS

Powering: (2)

"not modellable. Now that they are modellable again, we find
that modellability goes with using the right coordinate system
and therefore conceptuality and modelability has returned and
is valid so that we will probably have an entirely new kind of
day dawning for man because it is going to mean that it is
possible for the scientist really to talk to the kindergarten
children and these are very simple increments. We are not
having any numbers that are not easy to handle in the very
earliest phases, so the coordinating capability of the child
is going to be able to accommodate the nuclear physics and
that is a very new kind of day."

- Cite Oregon Lecture #6, p.233, 10 Jul'62

---

RBF DEFINITIONS

Powering:

"Powering, the development of dimensions that require

a unique perpendicularity to a plane not already in

the system."

- Cite Oregon Lecture #4, p. 131.6July 1962.

POWERING SEC. 770.01

---

RBF DEFINITIONS:

Powering: (Synergetics' Six Dimensional Reference Frames.)

". . . I identify second powering with the point population
of any one radiant (eccentric) or gravitational (concentric)
wave systems circumferential arrays of any given radius
stated in terms of frequency of modular subdivisions of the
circumferential arrays radially-read systems' concentricity
layering; third powering with the total point population
of all the successive wave layers of the system; fourth
powering with the interpointal domain volumes; fifth
and sixth powering as products of multiplication by
frequency doublings and treblings,etc.. The Doppler
effect or wave reception frequency-modulation caused by
motions of the observer and the observed are concentric
wave system fourth and fifth power accelerations."

- Cite INTRODUCTION TO OMNIDIRECTION HALO, P. 126, 127
1959

POWERING - SECS - IN 770

---

RBF DEFINITIONS

Powering. (Synergetics' Six Dimensional Reference Frames.)

"All local events of universe may be calculatively
anticipated by inaugurating calculation with a local vector
equilibrium frame and identifying the distrubance
initiating point, direction, and energy of introduced
action.
"/Synergetics'/ six positive and six negative dimensional
reference frames are reinitiated and regenerated in respect
to specific local developments and interrelationships of
universe.
"Arithmetical one dimensionality is identified geometrically
with linear, pointal frequency.
"Arithmetical two dimensionality is identified geometrically
with areal pointal frequency.
"Arithmetical six dimensionality is identified geometrically
with vectorial system modular frequency relationship.
"Arithmetical size dimensionality is identified geometrically
with relative frequency modulation."

- Cite COLLIER'S, P. 114, Oct'59

---

RBF DEFINITIONS

Powering: Zero Power:

"Zero power is the fix. It can be just an angle, which is
subcyclic. It is a fix. No module."

- Cite RBF to EJA, 3200 Idaho, DC, 14 Oct'72; as rewritten by
RBF, 15 Oct'72

---

RBF DEFINITIONS

Powering: Zero Power:

"Zero power is the point. It can be just an angle, which is
subcyclic. It is a fix. No module."

- Cite RBF to EJA, 3200 Idaho, DC, 14 Oct'72

---

RBF DEFINITIONS

Powering: One Dimension:

"We say the linear measure is the first power, that is,
the radius of the sphere or the edge of the cube. First
powering expresses only one vector, i.e. one-twelfth of
relevant system potential."

- Powering, Jan'71 as rewritten by RBF 15 Oct'72

---

RBF DEFINITIONS

Powering: One Dimension:

"We say the linear measure is the first power, that is, the
radius of the sphere or the edge of the cube."

- Cite SYNERGETICS text at Sec. 773.02, Jan'71

RBF DEFINITIONS

Powering: One Dimension:

"We say the linear measure is the first power, that is, the radius of the sphere or the edge of the cube.

"First powering expresses only one vector, i.e., 1/12th of relevant system potential."

- Cite SYNERGETICS draft at Sec. 773.02, Jan'71 as expanded by RBF, 3200 Idaho, 14 Oct'72

RBF DEFINITIONS

Powering: Second Powering:

"Second powering relates to points and not to surfaces."

- Citation and context at Fuller, R.B.: Meeting With Fernandez-Moran (2), 5 Apr'73

RBF DEFINITIONS

Powering: First Power:

"First power is linear. A time-size module."

- Cite RBF to EJA, 3200 Idaho, 14 Oct'72

RBF DEFINITIONS

Powering: Second Powering:

"In synergetics we find the familiar practice of second powering displaying a congruence with the points, or little separate energy packages of the shell arrays."

- Citation and context at Package, 17 Nov'72

RBF DEFINITIONS

First and Third Power Concentric Shell Growth Rates:

"The discovery of the formula for the rational whole number expression of the tetrahedral volume of both the spherical and interstitial spaces of the first and third power concentric shell growth rates of nuclear closest packed vector equilibria."

- Cite SYNERGETICS draft at Sec. 251.47, 15 Oct'72

RBF DEFINITIONS

Powering: Second Powering:

"The number of superficial radiantly regenerated vertex convergences of the system are identified with second powering, and not with anything we call 'areas,' that is, not with surfaces nor with any experimentally demonstrable continuums."

- Citation and context at Convergence, 16 Nov'72

RBF DEFINITIONS

Powering: Second Powering:

"Synergetical second-powering is identified with the point population of the progressively embracing, closest-packed point arrays at any given radius stated in terms of frequency of modular subdivisions of the circumferential array's radially-read concentricity layering."

- Citation and context at Dimensionality (1), 28 Oct'73

RBF DEFINITIONS

Powering: Second Powering:

"Second powering is areal: superficial area modularly outlined. Second powering expresses only superficial potential."

- Cite Powering: Second Powering, 14 Oct'72 as rewritten by RBF 15 Oct'72

RBF DEFINITIONS

Powering: Second Powering:

"Second powering is areal: superficial area modularly outlined."

- Cite RBF to EJA, 3200 Idaho, DC, 14 Oct'72

---

RBF DEFINITIONS

Powering: Second Powering: (2)

"surfaces and solids of the systems, neither of which have been experienced by experimental science. On the other hand electromagnetic frequencies of systems are sometimes complex but always constitute the prime rational integer characteristics of physical systems."

- Cite NASA Speech, pp.90-91, Jun'66

SYNERGETICS - SECS - 774.04- 774.06

---

RBF DEFINITIONS

Powering: Second Powering:

"The synergetic discovery of the identification of the surface points of the system with second powering accommodates quantum mechanics' discrete energy packaging of photons and elucidates Einstein's equation, $E = Mc^2$, where the omnidirectional velocity of radiation to the second power-- $c^2$-- identifies the rate of the rational order growth of the discrete energy quantation. This also explains synergetics' discovery of t he point-rate external growth of systems. It also elucidates and identifies the second power factoring of Newton's gravitational law."

- Cite RBF to EJA, 21 Dec. '71, Washington DC, incorporated in SYNERGETICS AT, Sec, 251.25.

---

RBF DEFINITIONS

Powering: Second Powering:

"The word second power gives you something to do now with radials and surfaces."

- Cite Oregon Lecture #7, p. 241. 11 Jul'62

---

RBF DEFINITIONS

Powering: Second Powering:

"The mathematical regularity identifies the second power of the linear dimensions of the system with the number of non-polar crossings of the comprehensive three-way great circle gridding, in contradistinction to the previous mathematical identification of second powering exclusively with surface areas."

- Cite RBF to EJA, 21 Dec. '71, Washing on DC, incorporated in SYNERGETICS Draft at Sec. 251.24.

---

Powering: Second Powering: (1)

See Linear Becoms the Second-power Rate of Growth
Universal Integrity: Second-power Congruence of
    Gravitational & Radiational Constants
Vertexial Topology

---

RBF DEFINITIONS

Powering: Second Powering: (1)

"'Second powering' in this topology is identifiable only with the vertexes and not with something we call 'area,' i.e., not with a surface or an experimentally nondemostrable continuum.

"There are no topologically indicated or implied surfaces or solids. Because the vertexes are the external points-- the higher the frequency of the system, the more dense the number of external points. We discover then that 'second powering' does not refer to 'squaring' or to surface amplification but to the number of the system's external vertexes in which equating the second power and the radial or circumferential modular subdivisions of the system multiplied by the prime number one if a tetrahedral system; by the prime number two if an octahedral system; the prime number three if a triangulated cubical system; and the prime number five if an icosahedral system; each multiplied by two and added to by two will accurately predict the number of superficial points of the system. This fact eliminates our dilemma of having to think of the second and third powers of systems as referring exclusively to continuum

- Cite NASA Speech, pp.90-91, Jun'66

SYNERGETICS - SECS 223.54 + 529 09

---

Powering: Second Powering: Two Dimensions: (2)

See Convergence, 16 Nov'72*
    Dimensionality, (1)*
    Gravity: Circumferential Leverage, (3)
    Isotropic Vector Matrix, 16 Nov'72
    Mass, 16 Nov'72
    Package, 17 Nov'72*
    Polar Points, 29 Nov'72
    Variables: Theory Of, 1960
    Vertexial Topology, Aug'71
    Ten, 22 Jun'75
    T Module, 31 Jul'77

RBF DEFINITIONS

Powering:     (Second and Third Powering.)

"Second powering = point aggregate quanta = area.

"Third powering = volumetric quanta = volume."

- Cite P. PEARCE, Inmvetory of Concepts, June 1967

POWERING - SEC. 774.02+

---

Powering:  Third Powering:                                    (1)

See Third-power Rate of Variation Model

---

RBF DEFINITIONS

Powering:  Third Powering:

"Synergetical third-powering is identified with cumulative total point population of all the successive wave layer embracements of the system."

- Citation and context at Dimensionality (1), 28 Oct'73

---

Powering:  Third Powering:                                    (2)

See Dimensionality, (1)
    Gravity: Circumferential Leverage, (4)
    Nothingness, 16 Nov'72
    Perpendicularity, 17 Nov'72
    Powering: Sixth Powering, 20 Dec'73
    Somethingness, 16 Nov'72
    Synergetic Constant, (1)(2)

---

RBF DEFINITIONS

Powering:  Third Powering:

"Third power is volume modularly and areally embraced. Third powers express full potentials."

- Cite Powering: Third Powering, 14 Oct'72 as rewritten by RBF 15 Oct'72

---

RBF DEFINITIONS

Powering: (Three and Four Dimensions:)

". . . The four dimensionality works in convergences and divergences. Parallelism is uniquely characterizing the three dimensional system."

OREGON LECTURE #7, p. 245
- Cite Carbondale Draft
  Nature's coordination - VI.30
  11 Jul'62

POWERING - SEC 776.03

---

RBF DEFINITIONS

Powering:  Third Powering:

"Third power is volume modularly and areally embraced."

- Cite RBF to EJA, 3200 Idaho, Wash DC, 14 Oct'72

---

Powering:  Three & Four Dimensions:

See Hole in the Victrola Disc, 24 Jan'75

RBF DEFINITIONS

Powering: _Fourth Dimension_:

"While nature oscillates and palpitates asymmetrically in respect to the frame of the omnirational vector equilibrium, the plus and minus magnitudes of asymmetry are rational fractions of the omnirationality of the equilibrious state, ergo omnirationally commensurable and modelable to the _fourth power_ volumetrically, _which order of powering_ _embraces all experimentally disclosed physical volumetric_ _behavior._

"The volume of the vector equilibrium = 20 F$^3$. When frequency = 20, we have 20 x 20 x 20 x 20; Vol. = 20$^4$."

- Cite same caption, 21 Dec'71 to which RBF added "volumetrically" on 26 Nov'72
- SYNERGETICS Sec. 966.11, 18 Nov'72, modified accordingly

---

RBF DEFINITIONS

Powering: _Fourth-Powering_:

"Synergetical fourth-powering is identified with the interpointal domain volumes."

- Citation and context at _Dimensionality_ (1), 28 Oct'73

---

RBF DEFINITIONS

Powering: Fourth ████████ Dimension:

"It was the failure of the exclusively three-dimensional XYZ coordination that gave rise to the concept that fourth dimensionality is experimentally undemonstrable, ergo its arithmetical manifestation even in physics must be a mysterious, because nonconceivable, state which might be spoken of casually as the "time dimension.""

- Cite SYNERGETICS draft at Sec. 966.06, 18 Nov'72

---

RBF DEFINITIONS

Powering: _Fourth Powering_:

"Fourth powering would be always the nuclear propagative as described in convergence and divergence. Fourth power would thus be the energy content: the energy involvement as mass and frequency, vectorially expressed. Radiation vs. gravity are fourth power behaviors. Fourth power expresses behaviors."

- Cite _Powering_: _Fourth Powering_, 14 Oct'72 as rewritten by RBF 15 Oct'72

---

RBF DEFINITIONS

Powering: _Fourth Dimension_:

"While nature oscillates and palpitates asymmetrically in respect to the frame of omnirational vector equilibrium, the plus and minus magnitudes of asymmetry are rational fractions of the omnirationality of the equilibrious state, ergo omnirationally commensurable to the _fourth power_, ~volumetrically. which order of powering embraces all experimentally disclosed physical behavior. The volume of the vector equilibrium = 20 F$^3$. When frequency = 20 we have 20 x 20 x 20 x 20; Vol. = 20$^4$."

- (For later context see _A Priori Four-dimensional Reality_, (1) 20 Dec'73.)

- Originally derived from RBF statement to EJA at 3200 Idaho, 21 Dec'71. Above text is altered and expanded version incorporated in SYNERGETICS draft at Sec. 966.11, 18 Nov'72

MODELABILITY SEC. 966.16

---

RBF DEFINITIONS

Powering: _Fourth Powering_:

"Fourth powering would be always the nuclear propagative as described in convergence and divergence. Fourth power would thus be the energy content: the energy involvement as mass and frequency, vectorially expressed."

- Cite RBF to EJA, 3200 Idaho, Wash. DC, 14 Oct'72

---

RBF DEFINITIONS

Powering: _Fourth Powering_:

"Fourth powering identifies the nuclear propagation rates inherent in the radiation vs. gravity, convergent and divergent interoscillatory wave propagations which pulsate through the omnidirectional aerophase of the vector equilibrium. Fourth powering identifies the magnitude of energy involvement as either particulate mass or wave frequency, vectorially expressed."

- Cite RBF rewrite of _Powering_: _Fourth Powering_, 15 Oct'72 incorporated in SYNERGETICS, 2nd. Ed. at Sec. 966.13, RBF reqrite as of 9 Sep'75

---

Powering: _Fourth Powering_:                    (1)

See Fourth Dimension

Powering: _Fourth Powering_:       (2)

   See Loss: Discovery Through Loss, 14 Dec'73
      Nonpolar Points, 29 Nov'72
      Dimensionality (1)*
      Synergetic Surprise, 9 Apr'71
      Words, 15 Jun'74
      Gravity: Circumferential Leverage, (4)
      Modelability, (b)(c)

---

Powering: _Fourth & Fifth Dimensions_:

   See Imaginary Number, Jun'66
      Sixty Degree Modulatability, 19 Nov'72
      Synergetics, 20 Jun'66
      Vector Equilibrium: Field of Energy, (C)(D)
      Multidimensional Accommodation, 11 Dec'75

---

RBF DEFINITIONS

Powering: _Fourth and Fifth Dimensions_:

"In an omnimotional Universe it is possible to join or lock together two previously independently moving parts of the system without immobilizing the remainder of the system, because four dimensionality allows local fixities without in any way locking or blocking the rest of the system's omnimotioning of intertransforming. This independence of local formulation corresponds exactly with life experiences in Universe. This omnifreedom is calculatively accommodated by synergetics' fourth and fifth power transformabilities."

- Cite SYNERGETICS draft at Sec. 966.07, 18 Nov'72

---

RBF DEFINITIONS

Powering: _Fourth_, _Fifth_, and _Sixth Dimensions_:

"Synergetics discloses the rational fourth, fifth, and sixth powering modelability of nature's coordinate transformings as referenced to the 60-degree, equiangular, isotropic vector matrix."

- Citation at _Fourth Dimension_, 21 Dec'71

---

RBF DEFINITIONS

Powering: _Fourth and Fifth Dimensions_:

"When we begin to integrate our arithmetical identities, as for instance $\underline{n}^2$ or $\underline{n}^3$, with a 60-degree coordination system, we find important coincidence with the topological inventories of systems, particularly with the isotropic vector matrix which makes possible _fourth-_ and _fifth-power_ modeling."

- Cite SYNERGETICS draft, Sec. 423.04, 9 Jun'72

---

RBF DEFINITIONS

Powering: _Fourth_, _Fifth_, and _Sixth Dimensions_:

"The awkward irrationalities were the consequence of man's attempts to measure the omnidynamically transforming fourth, fifth, and sixth dimensional Universe with a static, three-dimensional system."

- Citation and context at _Future of Synergetics_, 19 Apr'66

---

RBF DEFINITIONS

Powering: _Fourth and Fifth Dimensions_:

"We find that the volume of the two-frequency cube equals eight, which is two to the third power, expressed as $2^3$, whereas the volume of the two-frequency vector equilibrium equals 160, which is two to the fifth power multiplied by five, expressed as $5 \cdot 2^5$. In 60-degree vector equilibrium accounting when the edge module reads two, and we have an energy quantity of _two to the fifth power times five_, we understand why the previous nonmodelabity of _fourth_ and _fifth_ dimensions occasioned the century ago discard by science of the generalized modelability which now returns with energy-vectored tetrahedroning."

- Cite NASA Speech, pp. 81-82. Jun'66

---

RBF DEFINITIONS

Powering: _Fifth Dimension_:

"We know that the sphere points on the outershell of the vector equilibrium and the icosahedron, between which states the pulsative propagation of electromagnetic waves oscillates between the icosahedron and the vector equilibrium, but the number of points remains the same: $10 F^2 + 2$."

[51]

- Cite SYNERGETICS draft at Sec. 527.52, 29 Nov'72

RBF DEFINITIONS

Powering: <u>Fifth Dimension</u>:

"Five-dimensionality is realized by the pulsation of the positive-negative VE -- Icosa -- VE -- as 2.5 -- five."

- Cite SYNERGETICS draft at Sec. 527.54, 29 Nov'72

---

RBF DEFINITIONS

Powering: <u>Fifth & Eighth Powering</u>:

"The vector equilibrium at initial frequency (frequency$^2$) manifests the fifth powering of nature's energy behaviors. Frequency begins at two. The vector equilibrium of frequency$^2$ has a ▆▆▆▆▆ prefrequency, inherent tetravolume of 160 (5 x 2$^5$ = 160) and a quanta-module volume of 120 x 24 = 1 x 3 x 5 x 2$^8$ nuclear-centered system as the integrated product of the first four prime numbers; 1, 2, 3, 5. Whereas a cube at the same frequency accommodates only eight cubes around a nonnucleated center."

(Sec. 1006.33) (2nd. Ed.)

-Cite SYNERGETICS, 2nd. Ed., at Sec. 1006.33; 25 Jan'76

---

Powering: <u>Fourth</u>, <u>Fifth</u> & <u>Sixth Dimensions</u>:

See Fourth Dimension, 21 Dec'71*
Future of Synergetics, 19 Apr'66*
Six Motion Freedoms & Degrees of Freedom, (B)
Synergetics, Dec'61
Synergetics Constant, (A)

---

RBF DEFINITIONS

Powering: <u>Fifth & Eighth Powering</u>:

"The vector equilibrium at initial frequency (frequency$^2$) manifests the fifth powering of nature's energy behaviors Frequency begins at two.. The vector equilibrium of frequency$^2$ has a tetravolume of 160 modules (5 x 2$^5$ = 160) and a quanta-module volume of 120 x 24 = 3 x 5 x 2$^8$. Whereas the cube at the same frequency$^2$ accommodates only 8 cubes around a nonnucleated center."

- Cite RBF to EJA + RBF holograph, Wash., DC; 11 Dec'75

---

RBF DEFINITIONS

Powering: <u>Fourth Dimension and Sixth Dimension</u>:

". .. Whereas we can only get eight cubes around a point. . . 90 degreeness uses up all the space around a point. When I am dealing in 60 degreeness, when I am using tetrahedron as unity, we can get the whole volume of 20 tetrahedra around one point. The tetrahedron is unity. Then we are getting 20 around a point insteda of eight around a point. Eight is the third power of two. When I have a stack of cubes coming together around a point, the edge count is two cubes. Unity is two there. There is just one set of radii from the center of gravity in the system and you can only have a total volume of eight which is the third power of two. If I have a volume of 20 around a point, then two to the fourth power is 16, plus two to the second power. I can then accommodate two to the fourth power plus two to the second power around a point. It is very easy to make models of the fourth dimensioaalities. We discover that when we do that-- this is what we call the vector equilibrium-- the edge count is ▆▆▆ one. When the edge count is one we have a vector equilibrium, not two as in the cubes. The volume is 20. You start with unity as 20. . . And we find that we are able to accommodate sixth powering."

- Cite Oregon Lecture #4, pp. 137-138. 6 Jul'62

---

RBF DEFINITIONS

Powering: <u>Sixth Dimension</u>:

"Sixth-powering is all the perpendiculars to the 12 faces of the rhombic dodecahedron."

- Cite RBF rewrite of SYNERGETICS galley at Sec. 621.05, 9 Nov'73

---

RBF DEFINITIONS

Powering: <u>Fifth- and Sixth-Powerings</u>:

"Synergetical fifth- and sixth-powerings are identified as products of multiplication by frequency doublings and treblings, and are geometrically identifiable."

- Citation and context at <u>Dimensionality</u> (1)(2), 28 Oct'73

---

RBF DEFINITIONS

Powering: <u>Sixth Dimension</u>:

"Synergetical six-dimensionality is identified geometrically with vectorial system modular frequency relationship."

- Citation and context at <u>Dimensionality</u> (2), 28 Oct'73

RBF DEFINITIONS

    Powering:  Sixth Dimension:

"Linear, as manifest in the tetrahedron, the simplest
structural system of Universe, is six dimensional, providing
for the six degrees of universal freedom and the operational
six-wave (sexave) phenomenon of number."

    - Cite SYNERGETICS draft at Sec. 527.41, 29 Nov'72

---

RBF DEFINITIONS

    Powering:  Sixth Powering:

"Sixth powering is all the perpendiculars to the rhombic
dodecahedron which is all the internal truncations of the
tetrahedron."

    - Cite RBF to EJA, Bear Island, 25 August 1971.

TETRAHEDRON - SEC 621.05

---

RBF DEFINITIONS

    Powering:  Six Dimensions:

"Synergetics posits six positive and six negative dimensional
reference frames corresponding to the 12 universal degrees
of freedom unique to each point in Universe.  The six
dimensional reference frames are reinitiated and regenerated
in respect to specific local developments and interrelationships of Universe."

        (N.B. On 30 Oct'72 RBF wrote in margin of this
        passage at Sec. 972.01 Synerggtics draft:
        "Sonny: drop out this paragraph.  The six edges
        of the tetrahedron lie in three planes." )

    - Cite COLLIER Ltr, p. 113, Oct'59
    - Incorporated in SYNERGETICS drfat at Sec 770.05, Aug'71
      later re-edited as Sec. 972.01, Jan'72.

---

    Powering:  Sixth Powering:  Sixth Dimension:

      See Chess: A Priori Intellect Invents a Game Called
        "Life", (2)
      Vector Equilibrium, 21 Dec'71; 19 Nov'74

---

RBF DEFINITIONS

    Powering:  Sixth Powering:

"Since the original point was a tetrahedron and already,
a priori volumetric, the third powering is in fact
sixth powering: $N^3 \times N^3 = N^6$."

    - Cite RBF rewrite of SYNERGETICS galley at Sec. 965.01, 20 Dec'73

---

RBF DEFINITIONS

    Powering:  Seventh Powering:  Seventh Dimension:

"Like the octahedron, the vector equilibrium also has eight
triangular facets; while also explosively extroverting the
octahedron's three square central planes, in two ways, to each
of its six square external facets, thus providing seven unique
planes, i.e., seven-dimensionality."

    - Cite SYNERGETICS text at Sec. 1011.23; rewrite of 26 Dec'73

---

RBF DEFINITIONS

    Powering:  Sixth Powering:

"While nature oscillates and palpitates asymmetrically in
respect to the frame of the omnirational vector equilibrium,
the plus and minus magnitudes of asymmetry are rational
fractions of the omnirationality of the equilibrious state,
ergo omnirationally commensurable and modelable to the
sixth power vectorially, which order of powering
embraces all experimentally disclosed physical vectorial
behavior."

    - Cite Vector Equilibrium, 21 Dec'71

    - Cite same caption, 21 Dec'71 to which RBF added "vectorially"
      on 26 Nov'72

MODELABILITY
966.18

---

    Powering:  Powers:                    (1)

      See Dimensional Growth
          Dimensional Supremacy
          Equatability of Volumes & Powers
          Fourth Dimension
          Limit of Powering
          Sixty-degree Modulatability
          Triangling
          Volumes = Powers
          Scheherazade Numbers:  Declining Powers Of
          Multirepowerings
          Point Growth Rate

Powering:  Powers:                                          (2)

     See Convergence, 16 Nov'72*
        Perpendicularity, 17 Nov'72
        Pythagoras, 18 Jun'71
        Time-size, 20 Dec'73

---

Pragmatism:                                                 (1)

     See Operational
        Specializations of Residual Physical Reality

---

Power Structure:  Symbols Of:

     See Child Sequence, (3)
        Interrelatedness vs. Names, (1)

---

Pragmatism:                                                 (2)

     See Intuition, 1971

---

Power Transmission:                                         (1)

     See High Voltage Power Transmission
        World Power Grid

---

Practical:  Practice:

     See Earth:  Let's Get Down to Earth
        Reduction to Practice

---

Power Transmission:                                         (2)

     See Communications Theory, Oct'66
        Invention Sequence, (2)

---

Prayer:  Praying:

     See Christ, 7 Oct'71

RBF DEFINITIONS

Precess:

"Compression members precess to bend."

- Citation and context at Rope, 6 Mar'73

---

RBF DEFINITIONS

Precession:

"Nature uses rectilinear patterns only precessionally; and precession brings about orbits and not straight lines."

- Citation and context at Rectilinear Frame, 24 Sep'73

---

RBF DEFINITIONS

Precess:

"Precess means for two or more bodiesm to move in an interrelationship pattern of other than 180 degrees."

- Cite KEPES
  Caption Figure 7e, Page 84, 1965

PRECESSION, SEC. 533.01

---

RBF DEFINITIONS

Precession:

"Precession and mass-attractive gravity convert centrifugal into orbital motion."

- Citation and context at Radiation-Gravitation Sequence (2)(3), 5 Jun'73

---

RBF DEFINITIONS

Precession:                                                    (I)

"Precession is the intereffect of individually operating cosmic systems upon one another. Since the Universe is an aggregate of individually operative systems all of the intersystem effects of Universe are precessional and the 180-degree imposed forces usually result in redirectional resultants of 90 degrees.

"Gravity's 180-degree circumferential omniembracement effect results in a 90-degree inwardly effected pressure which gains rapidly in intensity as the initially sixfold leverage advantages of the circumferentially tensed embracement gains exponentially in locally induced pressure as the radial distance outwardly from the sphere's center is decreased.

"The Sun's direct 180-degreeness interattraction pull upon Earth begets precessionally the latter's 90-degreeness orbiting around the Sun. And the Earth's circumferential orbiting direction begets the Earth's own 90-degreeness of axial rotation. The Sun's radiational 180-degree impingements upon Earth's waters begets 90-degree circumferential cloud travel, which in turn begets 90-degree radially inward precipitation."

- Cite SYNERGETICS, 2nd. Ed. at Sec. 533.08 + .09, 19 Nov'74

---

RBF DEFINITIONS

Precession:                                                    (a)

"Precession is the effect of discrete motion systems on other discrete motion systems. Since all the Universe consists of differential motion subsystems all of the intersystem effects of Universe are precessional and the 180-degree directional efforts of systems always impose 90-degree directional resultants in the motions of all other systems.

"Gravity's 180-degree circumferential tension, as omniembracement effect, begets 90-degree effects; as for instance, the Sun's direct 180-degreeness begets 90-degreeness of orbiting; and the orbitings' directional 180-degreeness begets the 90-degreeness of axial rotation.

"The Sun's radiational 180-degree impingements upon the Earth's waters beget 90-degree evaporation and circumferential cloud traveling, which, in turn, beget 90-degree rain precipitation. Precessional 180-degree efforts beget 90-degree effects such as the photosynthesis of agriculture around the land and photosynthesis of algae around the waters of Earth, regenerating as food."

- Cite RBF holograph, New Delhi, 8 Dec'72 as rewritten by
  RBF, 13 May'73

PRECESSION - 533.07

---

RBF DEFINITIONS

Precession:                                                    (II)

"Precessional 180-degree efforts beget 90-degree effects such as the Sun's radiation impoundment on Earth by the photosynthesis of agriculture (around the land) and photosynthesis of algae (around the waters of Earth), which regeneration occurs as precessionally impounded life-sustaining foods. The 180-degree Sun radiation effect precesses Earth's atmosphere in 90-degree circumferential direction as wind power, which wind power in turn precesses the windmills into 90-degree rotating.

"All the metaphysical generalizations of physical principles produce physical indirect acceleration effects which are precessional.

"Leverage, Sun power, wind power, tidal power, paddles, oars, windlasses, fire, metallurgy, cooking, slings, gears, electromagnetic generators, and metabolics are all 180-degree effort that result in 90-degree precessional intereffects."

- Cite SYNERGETICS, 2nd. Ed. at Secs. 533.10 +.11+.12, 19 Nov'74

---

RBF DEFINITIONS

Precession:                                                    (b)

"The 180-degree Sun effort precesses 90-degrees as wind power, which wind power in turn precesses 90-degrees the windmills and sailing ships. All the metaphysical generalizations of physical principles disclose direct acceleration (which is synergetic), or indirect acceleration (which is precessional). Leverage, Sun Power, wind power, tidal power, paddles, oars, windlasses, fire, metallurgy, cooking, slings, gears, electromagnetic generators, and metabolics in general are all 180-degree efforts that go into 90-degree precessional intereffects."

- Cite RBF holograph, New Delhi, 8 Dec'72; as rewritten by RBF, 13 May'73.

RBF DEFINITIONS

Precession:

"It could be that in always-and-only-coexisting
action-reaction

$180^\circ$-ness begets $90^\circ$-ness )
)
and ) ergo (active)
)
$90^\circ$-ness begets $180^\circ$-ness )

and

$60^\circ$-ness is neutral ) ergo (potential)"

- Cite RBF holograph, New Delhi, 8 Dec'72

PRECESSION — SEC. 533.11)

---

RBF DEFINITIONS

Precession:

"Precession is the behavioral interrelationship

Of remote and differently velocitied,--

Differently directioned,

And independently moving bodies

Upon one another's

Separate motions

And motion inter patternings."

- Cite INTUITION ~~Draft Dec 70, p. 7a~~
p.30, May '72

---

RBF DEFINITIONS

Precession:

"Precession is synergetic to mass attraction."

- Citation and context at Hierarchies, 16 Jun'72

---

RBF DEFINITIONS

Precession:

"Mass attraction is to precession

As a single note is to music.

Precession is angularly accelerating

Regeneratively progressive

Mass attraction."

- Cite INTUITION ~~Draft Dec 70, p. 7a~~
p.30, May '72

---

RBF DEFINITIONS

Precession:                                      (A)

"Precession is a second-degree synergy
Because it is not predicted by mass attraction
Considered only by itself.
Mass attraction
Is experienced intimately by Earthians
As gravity's pulling
Inward toward Earth's center
Any and all objects
Within critical proximity
To Earth's surface,
And moving through space
At approximately the same speed
And in the same direction
As those of planet Earth.

"Not until we learn by observation
That the mass attraction
Of any two, noncritically proximate
Bodies in motion
Imposes a motional direction
At ninety degrees
To their interattraction axis,"

- Cite INTUITION, p.31 May '72

---

RBF DEFINITIONS

Precession:

"Precesssion is the effect of any moving system upon any other
moving system and the closer the proximity the more powerful
the effect. Mass attraction is inherent in precession. Mass
attraction is to precession as a single note is to music. We
do not pay much attention to precession because we think only
of our own integral motions instead of the Universe, though we
are precessing the Universe every time we take a step."

- Cite SYNERGETICS draft at Sec. 533.02, Nov'71

---

RBF DEFINITIONS

Precession:                                      (B)

"Do we learn of this second surprise behavior
Of two or more bodies.
They no longer 'fall-in,'
One to the other.

"Thus is the Moon
Precessed into elliptical orbit about the Earth
As the Earth and Moon, together,
Are precessed into elliptical orbit around the Sun,
Yielding only in a ninety-degree direction
To the Sun's massive pull--
Being beyond
The critical proximity distances
For falling into one another."

- Cite INTUITION,pp.31-32 May '72

---

RBF DEFINITIONS

Precession:

"And the transition from being an entity to being a plurality
of entities is precession, which is a peeling off into orbit
rather than falling back in to the original entity. This
explains entropy intimately."

- Citation & context at Entropy, 28 Feb'71

RBF DEFINITIONS

Precession:

"Critical proximity occurs

where there is a 90° angular transition

from falling back in at 180°

which is precession."

- ~~Cite RBF to SJA~~
~~Beverly Hotel, New York~~
~~28 Feb 1971~~

- Citation at <u>Critical Proximity</u>, 28 Feb '71

---

RBF DEFINITIONS

Precession:

"The effects of one moving system upon another moving system.

Precession is describable in vectorial terms: i.e., of physically-realized, design, expressed differentially as relative angle, velocity and mass (size) modification's in respect to an axis.

The precessional result of all <u>events</u> are always three-fold, embracing (1) <u>action</u>, (2) <u>reaction</u>, and (3) <u>resultant</u>. None of these interprecessional event components occur at 180° to any other components. A system must have a minimum of four vertexes in order to have an omni-directional insideness and outsideness and six is the minimum minimum number of vectorial edges uniquely connecting the four vertexes of the minimum system. The six vectorial edged are comprised of two energy event's inherent three-vector componentation of action, reaction, and resultant."

- Cite "Word Meanings," EKISTICS, Vol. 28, No 167
Oct'69

1ST SENTENCE - PRECESSION - SEC. 533.02 + 533.06

---

RBF DEFINITIONS

Precession:

"<u>Precession</u> is the behavioral interrelationship
Of remote and differently velocitied,
Differently directioned,
And independently moving bodies
Upon one another's
Separate motions
And motion inter-patternings.

Mass attraction is to <u>precession</u>
As a single note is to music.
<u>Precession</u> is angularly accelerating,
Regeneratively progressive
Mass attraction.

The elliptic orbiting
Of the sun's planets
As well as the solar system's motion
Relative to the other star groups
Of the galactic nebula
Are all and only accounted for
By <u>precession</u>."

PRECESSION - SEC. 533.11 + 533.15    - Cite INTUITION, Draft Feb '71, p. 19

---

RBF DEFINITIONS

Precession:

"Prcession is the effect of one moving system upon another.

"Precession always produces
Angular changes of the movements
Of the affected bodies
And at angles other then 180 degrees,
That is, the results are never
Continuance in a straight line.
Ergo all bodies of Universe
Are affecting the other bodies
In varying degrees,
And all the intergravitational effects
Are precessional angular modulations
And all the interradiation effects
Are frequency modulations."

- Cite HOW LITTLE I KNOW, p.73, Oct'66

PRECESSION - SEC. 533.03    533.07

---

RBF DEFINITIONS

Precession:

"Because precession imposes angles other than 180° upon all interactions of all moving systems of the Universe there are no straight lines demonstrated in Nature. The fundamental wave behavior of all nature is a consequence of the omnintereffective precession."

- Citation & context at <u>Social Science</u>: <u>Analogue to Physical Science</u>, (1), 13 Nov'69

---

RBF DEFINITIONS

Precession:

"Reactions and resultants are always precessional."

- Citation & context at <u>Action-reaction-resultant</u>, Jun'66

---

RBF DEFINITIONS

Precession:

"<u>Precession</u> is the effect of any body in motion upon any other body in motion and the closer the proximity the more powerful the effect, and since all known bodies of macro-micro Universe are always in motion all the inter-effects of all bodies are always precessional and those effects always result in the production of an angular change of course in the affected bodies-- thus, for instance, does the Sun's pull on the Earth induce its orbiting in a course around the Sun at 90 degrees to the gravitational pull; that is, the effect on the other body is always produced as an angular re-direction other than a 180 degrees direction towards or away from one another. . . .

"Mass attraction is also involved in precession, which is another of the important, but popularly unknown, generalized principles. Precession allows a spinning top to lean over sideways without tipping further. Precesssion makes the gyro-compass hold its true north orientation without magnets and despite the ship's changes in course."

1ST SENTENCE - PRECESSION - SEC. 533.02    Cite NEHRU SPEECH, P. 35, 13 Nov'69

---

RBF DEFINITIONS

Precession:

"Parallel and antiparallel <u>are</u> precession."

- Cite RBF marginalis date! 5 Sept. 1965 in "The Scientific Endeavor," (1963) - page 12

RBF DEFINITIONS

Precession:

". . . We don't pay much attention to precession because we think only of our own integral motions instead of the universe, though we are precessing the universe every time we take a step. Precessional effects are always angular and always something other than 180 degrees; they are very likely to be 90 or 60 degrees. . . Precessions are regenerative."

- Cite LEDGEMONT, pp. 46, 47 , 15 Oct'64

PRECESSION — SEC. 535.02

---

RBF DEFINITIONS

Precession:

"There are five motions we are all familiar with: spin, orbit, turn inside out, expand and torque.

"There is a sixth motion which very few people are familiar with called precession."

- Cite OREGON Lecture #4 - p. 143, 6 Jul'62

- Citation and context at Motion: Six Positive and Negative Motions, 6 Jul'62

---

RBF DEFINITIONS

Precession:

The energy event action itself "is inherently precessional because it is against gravity. It is a linear acceleration and an angular acceleration simultaneously as functions with a prominent resultant and a prominent reaction. Because we have now learned that these are going to be at angles of other than 180° and this three-fold affair is obviously not going to occur in a plane. Therefore, we are not surprised to find our event. . . make the tetrahedron."

- Citation & context at Energy Event, 9 Jul'62
- Cite Oregon Lecture #5, p. 175, 9 Jul'62

---

RBF DEFINITIONS

Precession:

"When the stone drops in the water it impinges on the atoms and everything is in motion, and immediately there is a resultant at 90°. The resultant is the wave and the 90 degreeness begets another 90 degreeness and this 90 degreeness begets another 90 degreeness and so on until you have a series of 90 degreenesses. . .

"Precesssion is regenerative and that is why you have the wave. It is very simple to see why there is a wave. Pure precession."

- Cite Oregon Lecture #4, p. 152, 6 Jul'62

- Citation and context at Wave Pattern of a Stone Dropped In Liquid, 6 Jul'62

PRECESSION SEC 533.04

---

RBF DEFINITIONS

Precession:

"The effects of all components of universe in motion upon any other component in motion is precession and inasmuch as all the component patterns of universe seem to be motion patterns, in whatever degree they do affect one another, they are interaffecting one another precessionally and they are bringing about angular resultants other than the 180 degreenesses."

- Cite OREGON Lecture #5 - p. 164, 9 Jul'62

PRECESSION - SEC 533.01

---

RBF DEFINITIONS                                                                                      (1)

Precession:

"Precession plays the major role in my re-statement of the first law of motions, which says, 'The entire regenerative hierarchy of major, intermediate, and minor constellations of component-patterns-within-component-patterns of Universe are continual processes of synchronous, yet independent and unique, transformative patternings. That is, all components of Universe are in continually accommodative, associative-disassociative motion reciprocity, and all the moving components of Universe continuously affect all the other moving components-- in varying degrees, ranging between high and low tide reciprocities of critically intense to critically negligible. All of these intereffects of all these motional components upon one another are precessional, and precession always produces transformative resultants in vectorial patterns which always articulate angular accelerations in directions other than the 'straight' lines of directions between the inter-effective components.'

"This is to say that the effects of all local motion systems in the Universe are always precessional, and that none of the resultants of any forces operative between them are

- Cite "Tensegrity," PORTFOLIO AND ART NEWS, p.119, Dec '61

---

RBF DEFINITIONS

Precession:

"There are no straight lines. Nobody has ever thrown a straight ball. Everything is always moving in the direction of least resistance. That is one thing about the relation of all the forces. A body in motion affecting another body in motion . . . the effect is always precession. When the top is in motion and you in motion touch it, then the result is precession. Now inasmuch as the whole Universe is in motion, all the parts affecting each other are always precessing each other. Precession is the most predominant. You might say the first law of motion is precession. You could say that the first law of motion, if it had been properly written, was that all the Universe is continually in motion and all the other affecting it in various degreees: the effect is always precession."

- Cite Oregon Lecture #4, p. 151. 6 Jul'62

---

RBF DEFINITIONS                                                                                      (2)

Precession:

"ever straight line patterns. Individual lines of vectorial trajectory interactions never go through the same points. They diverge periodically to innocuity of inter-effectiveness, or they periodically converge to critical proximities. Their local interferences, through critical proximity, produce reflections, refractions, and regenerative-shunting patterns."

- Cite "Tensegrity," PORTFOLIO ART NEWS, p. 119, Dec. '61

RBF DEFINITIONS

Precession:

"Universe is the minimum as well as the maximum closed system of omni-interacting, precessionally transforming, complementary transactions of synergetic regeneration. . . ."

- Cite OMNIDIRECTIONAL HALO, p.135. 1960

---

RBF DEFINITIONS

Precession:

"...The effect of all the local systems of events upon any and all other systems of local events is precessional."

- Citation and context at Newton's First Law of Motion: RBF Restatement Of, 4 May'57

---

RBF DEFINITIONS

Precession:

"Synergetic geometry precession explains radial-circumferential acceleration transformations."

- Citation and context at Gravitational System Zone, 14 Jan'55

---

RBF DEFINITIONS

Precession & Degrees of Freedom:                              (1)

"Despite the angularly modified resultant complexities of omnidirectionally operative precessional forces upon ever varyingly interpositioned cosmic bodies, Universe may be manifesting to us that there is always and only operative an omniintegrated cosmic coordination of cosmic independents' actions and reactions wherein, with radial broadcasting of energy there is an exponentially increasing diffusion as well as disturbance-diminishing resultant energy effectiveness producing widely varying angular aberrations of the precession, wherein nonetheless there is always an initial individual-to-individual operative attractiveness whereby

          180-degreeness begets 90-degreeness

                         and

          90-degreeness begets 180-degreeness

all of whose angularly aberrated complexity of resultant directional effects always pulsate in respect to a neutral or static 60-degreeness which (only staticly) imposes an everywhere-else 60-degreeness of resultants which in turn induces the coexistence of the isotropic vector matrix."

- Cite SYNERGETICS, 2nd. Ed. at Sec.533.21, 19 Nov'74

---

RBF DEFINITIONS

Precession & Degrees of Freedom:                              (2)

"The 56 axes of cosmic symmetry (see Sec. 1042.05) interprecess successively to regenerate the centripetal-centrifugal inwardness, outwardness, and aroundnesses of other inwardnesses, outwardnesses, and aroundnesses as the omnipulsative cycling and omniinter-resonated eternally regenerative Universe, always accommodated by the six positive and six negative alternately and maximally equieconomical degrees of freedom characterizing each and every event cycle of each and every unique frequency-quantum magnitude of the electromagnetic spectrum range."

- Cite SYNERGETICS, 2nd. Ed. at Sec. 533.22, 19 Nov'74

---

Precessional Intertransformability:

        See Acceleration:  Angular & Linear, 11 Feb'73

---

Precessional Peel-off:

        See Doing What Needs to be Done, 26 Jan'75

---

TEXT CITATIONS

Precession of Side Effects & Primary Effects:

Synergetics, 2nd. Ed. draft Sec. 325.10ff

Precession of Side Effects & Primary Effects:

See Good & Badding Kind of Idea

---

Precession: Analogy of Precession & Social Behavior:

See Social Sciences: Analogyue to Physical Sciences, (1)

---

Precession of Octa Edge-vector:

See Octahedron as Photosynthesis Model, 11 Dec'75

---

RBF DEFINITIONS

Precession of Two Sets of 10 Closest-packed Spheres:          (1)

"I'm sure a number of you have been with me at previous
lectures and you may have seen these ∠ two sets of 10
closest-packed spheres--see sec. 260.50 _∫, but the majority
of you, I am sure, still have not been with me all this
time. I know that four years ago I was asked to speak
at a congress of mathematics teachers in Oregon and there
were 2000 mathematicians there and I asked them if any of
them were familiar with the se objects. And they said 'No.'
And I said would any of them be willing to come up on the
stage with me and put them together in a way that we would
all agree is the way. There is a the way.

"So one of them came up and he looked them over, and he saw
these two quadrangles and he tried matching those... then he
saw two triangles and he tried matching those... then he saw
these--what we call trapezoids--and he tried matching those.
So then he tried to put them together like that, and that
didn't seem to be too impressive either. Then he tried what
we might call like a raft ahd that wasn't too good either.
So he started all over again and I saw he wasn't getting anywhere, so I said I'm going to have to show you how to do it."

- Cite RBF talk at Am. Museum of Natural History, NYC,
    EJA transcript, pp.8-9; 1 May'77

---

RBF DEFINITIONS

Precessionally Shunted Pattern Relay:

"Resistance... in synergetics is called the precessionally
shunted pattern relay."

- Citation and context at Tunability, 1960

---

RBF DEFINITIONS

Precession of Two Sets of 10 Closest-packed Spheres:          (2)

"One reason that this is not self-evident is that because,
in all the great motions employed by Universe, there are six
fundamental kinds of motion and five of them very familar:
spinning, orbiting, turning inside-out, expanding, and
torquing.... These are very well-known fundamental behaviors
of nature. But there's a sixth one called precession. And
you say: I don't remember... I've heard of it. I've heard of
the word precession, but that's about the most people can do....

"Precession is one of the most important things to understand--
and its the mistaken 180-degreeness that finds humanity
missing a lot. At any rate, I'm going to precess these (two
sets of 10 closest-packed spheres) now at 90 degrees. OK?
And I'm going to now put them together and obviously they are
now not going to fit! (Applause.) And the reason you didn't
see that--and the thing about it is--that you all went to
school being taught the XYZ coordinates of parallels and
perpendiculars.... And you try to bring in together perpendicularly. But Universe is not operating that way. Universe
is operating in radiational-divergence and gravitational-
convergence. Divergent and convergent: that's the way
Universe operates. This is nothing like the XYZ coordinates"

- Cite RBF talk at Am. Museum of Natural History, NYC,
    EJA transcript, pp. 9-10, 1 May'77

---

RBF DEFINITIONS

Precession: Analogy of Precession and Social Behavior:

"Mass attraction and ████████ precession
Provide the first scientific means
Of elucidating social behavior.
When humans affect one another
Metaphysically,
The least thoughtful
Goes into local system orbit
Around the most thoughtful.
When humans tense one another
Physically,
The least strong
Falls into the other,
'Falls' in love.
When they repel one another physically
The least strong is rocketed
Into remote system orbit."

- Cite INTUITION, pp.33-34, May '72

---

RBF DEFINITIONS

Precession of Two Sets of 10 Closest-packed Spheres:          (3)

"and all that--they have nothing to do with the way the
Universe works. Things in parallel never get resolved.
Convergent things get beautifully resolved, they get exactly
... they get nature int a corner... that's why you couldn't
have a nucleus in a perpendicular parallel system. You
can only have nuclei when you have convergence. And's that's
why I say how far out our schooling really is."

- Cite RBF talk at Am. Museum of Natural History, NYC,
    EJA transcript, pp.9-10; 1 May'77

TEXT CITATIONS

Precession of Two Sets of 10 Closest-Packed Spheres:

Synergetics : Sec. 260.50 (2nd. Ed.)

527.08

---

Precession of Tetra Edges:

See Interconnection of Any Two Lines in Universe

---

TEXT CITATIONS

Precession of Two Sets of 60 Closest-packed Spheres:

417:  417.01-417.04

(Fig. 417.01)

s527.08

---

RBF DEFINITIONS

█████████  Precessional Thinking:

The "central and surface angle understandings are fundamental to precessional thinking which deals locally with the falling-inward critical proximities outwardly of which gravity suddenly induces precession at 90 degrees to the earlier falling-inward proclivity."

- Cite Synergetics draft, Sec. 860., August 1971.

---

Precession - Tension:

See Interaffecting, 9 Jul'62

---

Precessed Triangle:

See Yin-yang, 28 Jan'75

---

RBF DEFINITIONS

Precession of Tetra Edges:

"There are six edges of a tetrahedron, and each edge precesses the opposite edge toward a 90-degrees-maximum of attitudinal difference of orientation. Any two discrete opposite edges can be represented by two aluminum tubes, X and Y, which can move longitudinally anywhere along there respective axes while the volume of the irregular tetrahedra remains constant. They may shuttle along on these lines and produce all kinds of asymmetrical tetrahedra, whose volumes will always remain unit by virtue of their developed tetrahedra's constant base areas and identical altitudes. The two tubes' four ends produce the other four interconnecting edges of the tetrahedron, which vary as required without altering the constantly uniform volume."

- Cite SYNERGETICS text at Sec. 923.10, Apr'72

---

Precession:                                          (1A █

         Angular Precession
See      Chemical Bonds
         Energetic Functions
         Intereffects
         Interprecess
         Knight's Move in Chess
         Motion:  Six Positive & Negative Motions
         Mass Attraction
         Omnimotions
         Orbiting
         Omniprecessional
         Petal:  Tetrahedron as Three-petaled Flower Bud
         Polarized Precession
         Poisson Effect
         Shunting:  Relative Motion Patterns
         Critical Proximity
         Primary vs. Side Effects
         Sideways
         Synergy vs. Precession
         Reprecession

Precession: (1B)

See Precession = Tension
    Metaphysical Precession
    Complementaries Precess
    Reciprocal Self-precessors
    Regenerative Intersupport
    Modulation vs. Precession
    Gyrocompass:  Gyroscope
    Regenerative Precession
    Quantum Model
    Wave Pattern of a Stone Dropped in Water

Precession: (3)

See Precession & Degrees of Freedom
    Precessional Intertransformability
    Precessional Peel-off
    Precession of Side Effects & Primary Effects
    Precessionally Shunted Pattern Relay
    Precession:  Analogy of Precession & Social Behavior
    Precession = Tension
    Precession of Tetra Edges
    Precessional Thinking
    Precessed Triangle
    Precession of Two Sets of 10 Closest-Packed Spheres
    Precession of Two Sets of 60 Closest-Packed Spheres
    Precession of Octa Edge-vector

Precession: (2A)

        Breakwater, 15 Jun'74
See Bonding Hierarchies, 19 Dec'73
    Chemical Bonds, May'72
    Compression, 19 Jun'71
    Design Covariables:  Principle Of, 1959
    Energy Event, 9 Jul'62*
    Entropy, 28 Feb'71*
    Gravitational Zone System, 14 Jan'55*
    Hierarchies, 16 Jun'72*
    Mass Attraction, 6 Mar'73
    Multiorbital, 1960
    Newton's First Law of Motion:  RBF Restatement Of,
        4 May'57*
    Pull, 25 Sep'73
    Radiation-Gravitation, Oct'66; (2)(3)*
    Rectilinear Frame, 24 Sep'73*
    Side Effects, 9 Dec'73
    Supersynergeticall, May'72
    Synergetics, pj3, undated
    Step, Nov'71
    Eccentricity, 7 Feb'71

Prediction:  Socio-economic vs. Engineering:

    See Structural Sequence, (C)

Precession: (2B)

    See Tetrahedral Dynamics (1)(2)
        Tetrahedron, 10 Dec'73; 1 Feb'75
        Twelve-inch Steel World Globe (B)
        Transformations, 10 Oct'50
        Vector Equilibrium:  Spheres & Spaces (1)
        Wave, 13 Nov'69
        Wave Pattern of a Stone Dropped in Liquid, 6 Jul'62*
        Action-reaction-resultant, Jun'66*; May'71
        Tidal, 15 Oct'64
        Truth & Love, 16 Feb'73
        Polarization, 10 Nov'74
        Scratched Surface, 27 Jan'75
        Prism, 31 May'71
        Gravity, 6 Apr'75
        Inward Explosion, 8 Apr'75
        In, Out & Around Experiences, (1)(2)
        Invisible Quantum as Tetrahelix Gap Closer, 23 May'75
        Octahedron as Conservation & Annihilation Model,
            23 Jun'75
        Yin, yang, (2)

Predictability:  Prediction: (1)

    See Prognostication
        Synergetic Advantage:  Principle Of
        Synergetic Hierarchies
        Synergy:  Degrees Of
        Synergy of Synergies
        Unpredictable:  Unpredicted
        Viral Steerability
        Sequence
        Unpredicted:  Sequence of Unpredicted Events
        Planets:  Prediction of Unknown Planets
        Forecasting Capability

Precession: (2C)

    See Geometrical Function of Nine, (1)
        Octahedron as Photosynthesis Model,(B)(C)
        Social Sciences:  Analogy to Physical Sciences, (1)*
        Six Motion Freedoms & Degrees of Freedom, (5)(6)

Predictability:  Prediction: (2)

    See Ignorance (2)
        Jet Engine (1)
        Science, p.7, 1947
        Synergetic Accounting Advantages:  Hierarchy Of (3)
        Hierarchy of Patterns, 1954
        Nature Permits It Sequence (3)
        Synergetic Integral, 1960
        Education, 1 Jul'62
        Vertexial Topology, Aug'71
        Modelability, (b)
        Modulations, 17 Jun'75
        Structural Sequence, (C)

# Synergetics Dictionary

RBF DEFINITIONS

Pre-experienceable:

See Primitive Regeneration, 27 Dec'74


Prefix:

See Deprefixing


Prefabricated Credos:

See Fuller, R.B: Crisis of 1927, 14 Apr'70
Robin Hood Sequence (1)


Prefrequency:                                              (1)

See Presize
Subfrequency
Prime


Prefabrication:

See Prestressed Concrete Sequence, (2)


Prefrequency:                                              (2)

See Conceptuality Independent of Size & Time, 2 Jun'74
Prime, 20 Dec'74
Primitive Regeneration, 27 Dec'74
Fourth Dimension, 19 Feb'76
Powering: Fifth & Eighth Powering, 11 Dec'75;
25 Jan'76
Generalization & Special Case, 23 Jan'77
Six Motion Freedoms & Degrees of Freedom, (B)


RBF DEFINITIONS

Preferred Directions of Least Resistance:

See Fuller, R.B: What I Am Trying To Do, 8 Jan'66


Pregnant Mother: Communication with Child She is Bearing:

See Tactile Sense, 6 Jun'69
Tactile Sequence, (1)

Pregnancy:  Pregnant:

See Unique Frequencies, 18 Aug'70

Pre-Scenario:

See Dynamic vs. Static, 12 Nov'75

RBF DEFINITIONS

Prehending:

"Prehending is pure tension; it's like gravity."

- Cite RBF to EJA, 3200 Idaho, Wash, DC, 19 Dec'74

Prescience:

See Poets, 1970

Prehending:

See Intuition, 26 Dec'74

Present Otherness:

See No-time-and-away-ago, 28 May'75
Tetratuning, 30 May'75
Environment, (A)

Prehierarchical:

See Prime, 20 Dec'74

Present:                                    (1)

See Omnipresent
Now

Present: (2)

See Minimum of Four Tetrahedra, 22 Feb'77

RBF DEFINITIONS

Pressive; ▆▆▆▆▆

See Compression, 1 Apr'49

President of the U.S:

See Error: Pullout from Error, 17 Jul'73
The One: Watergate, 13 May'73
United States: Most Difficult Sovereignty to Break Up, (2)

RBF DEFINITIONS

Pressure:

"Velocity gives ▆▆ us what we call pressure or heat;
it can be read either way."

- Cite OREGON Lecture #5, p. 187, 9 Jul'62

- Citation at Velocity, 9 Jul'62

Presize: (1)

See Conceptuality Independent of Size
Prefrequency
Subsize
Sizeless

Pressure = Heat:

See Balloon (C)

Sec. 763.02

Pre-special Case:

See Primitive Regeneration, 27 Dec'74

Pressure: (1)

See Interattraction ≠ Pressure
Compression

Pressure:                                                    (2)


        See Gravity: Circumferential Leverage, (3)

---

**RBF DEFINITIONS**

Prestressed Concrete Sequence:                               (3)

"This principle of tensional blueprints-- prestressed
concrete is an example-- is manifesting itself as the
direction which building will take. In order to make the
resources of the Earth adequate to the needs of all
people, we must increase the performance per pound of
those resources in a very big way, thus giving man
environmental controls. This must be done to accommodate
all the new shifting patterns of man around the face of
the Earth. We will have to employ nature's much more
economical grand logistical strategies. Emulating nature,
man must distribute mathematical information as basic
pattern, which does not weigh anything at all. The highly
technical components of very fine high-tension steels and
aluminums and fine alloys can then be centrally processed
and distributed. Those will be used primarily for
tensional functions, and will be rigidified by the local
compressional pneumatics and hydraulics.... This is the most
comprehensive statement that I could make regarding the
most recent discovery of nature's forever permitted
structural strategies."

- Cite CONCEPTUALITY OF FUNDAMENTAL STRUCTURES, Ed. Kepes.,
    1965. P. 88.

---

Press:


        See Stretch-press

---

Prestressed Concrete:


        See Colloidal Chemistry
              Hydraulics

---

**RBF DEFINITIONS**

Prestressed Concrete Sequence:                               (1)

"I began to initiate such a 'regenerative tree' [See Trees]
strategy in experimental undertakings in structures about a
third of a century ago. I gave myself the task of exploring
the practicality of assembling the components of buildings
under the most preferred conditions of technology and science,
in order to achieve a very high degree of efficiency. This
collection of components had to be capable of economical air
transport to any part of the Earth. I saw that the essentils
were local hydraulics and pneumatics and generalized tensional
packages-- broadly speaking. Familiar examples of this are
all kinds of pneumatic structures, from inflatable toy sea
horses and life rafts to dirigibles. Beyond these, there are
very complex structures. For examples, I have made geodesic
domes-- omnitriangulated spheres-- with pneumatic components.
Geodesic tensegrity spheres are highly magnified, pneumatic
principle structures."


- Cite CONCEPTUALITY OF FUNDAMENTAL STRUCTURES, Ed. Kepes,
    1965, p. 86.

---

Pretence Bio-organism:


        See Corporation, (2)

---

**RBF DEFINITIONS**

Prestressed Concrete Sequence:                               (2)

"The hydraulics possibilities include the local cements,
water, air, gravel, sand, and rocks. The economic theory
behind prestressed concrete is based on prefabrication and
shipping only the small bulk of steel as a tensional sinew
system, and applying the local water, sand, gravel, and cement
as the building bulk. The particles which make up cement are
sifted sand and gravel, which, though they look rough, pack
averagedly as spheres would pack-- in 60-degree angular
packing. Few people think of cement that way, but if it is
shaken down, agitated well, and lubricated together with a
colloid, it will automatically avail itself of nature's
tetrahedral structuring in closest packing pattern."



- Cite CONCEPTUALITY OF FUNDAMENTAL STRUCTURES, Ed. Kepes,
    1965, p. 86.

---

**RBF DEFINITIONS**

Pretending:

"There's nothing wrong with pretending; in fact we have to
pretend. Pretending is just the same thing as our image-
ination. We have to formulate something like 'going down
town' before we can actually go down town. Even Christopher
Robin with Alice. It's really not a matter of pretence
but more of a trial balance. It's not a pretence: you might
just not have had time to do it yet.

"You write the play; Then you act the play. You have to write
it first. It's like the lag between the navigating and the
conceptioning. You can't just go... except off the deep end,
and even a child knows better than that!"


                (N.B: Above comments in response to EJA showing RBF
                a quote from Wittgenstein (Philosophic Investigations:
                II, xi - 229e : "A child has much to learn before it
                can pretend.")

    - Cite RBF to EJA, 3200 Idaho, Wash., DC, 8 Apr'75

Pretending = Image-ination:

See Pretending, 8 Apr'75

Previous Otherness:

See Awareness, 24 Apr'72

Pretime:                                                    (1)

See Prefrequency
    Timeless

Pride:                                                      (1)

See Selfishness
    Sheath of Pride
    Ego
    Self-deception
    Vanity

Pretime:                                                    (2)

See Conceptuality Independent of Size & Time, 2 Jun'74
    Synergetics vs. Model (B)-(D)

Pride:                                                      (2)

See Genius:  Children Are Born Geniuses,(1)
    Life is a Sumtotal of Mistakes, (1)
    Mistake, 7 Nov'75
    Crowd-reflexing, 7 Nov'75

Prevent: Preventive:

See Pathology:  Preventive vs. Curative

Priestly, Joseph: (1733-1804)

See Lavoisier, 1 Oct'71

Primacy: (1)

See Prime Number
Primitive

---

RBF DEFINITIONS

Primary vs. Side Effects:

"Nature arranges for the side effects-- at 180° to become the major thrusts. We tend to think of the chromosomic 180° 'drive' programming as the primary effect, but it's not.

"Only mind can discover mind: that's what society is doing right now. The brain is the honey-bee, honey-money reflex."

- Cite RBF to Yale Students, New Haven, 10 Dec'73
  (See also, RBF Holographs)

---

Primacy: (2)

See Trigonometric Limit: First 14 Primes, 14 Jan'74

---

Primary vs. Side Effects: (1)

See Precession of Side Effects & Primary Effects
Evolution by Inadvertence

---

Primary Faculties:

See Intellect & Quickness

---

Primary vs. Side Effects: (2)

See Ecology Sequence, (F)(G)
Proton & Neutron, (B)
Two Kinds of Twoness, (B)
Ecology, 3 Apr'75
Planetary Democracy, (3)

---

RBF DEFINITIONS

Primary vs. Side Effects:

"We don't pay enough attention to the side effects. The primary effects are really very,very tiny. What we have is the intercomplementation of the primary effects with the side effects, in which the side effects-- due to precession-- become the really important operation."

- Cite RBF to Yale students, New Haven, 9 Dec'73

---

RBF DEFINITIONS

Primary Structure:

"Whenever cutting or joining is introduced, complex structures occur. That is, the hole may be filled with a primary structure and therefore all the structural events of the surrounding ring are second-layer structural emergences of the primary structure."

- Citation and context at Moebius Strip, 10 Jan'50

Primary Structure:

    See Icosahedron: Inside-outing of Icosahedron,
        10 Jan'50

---

RBF DEFINITIONS

Prime:

"Prime means sizeless, timeless, subfrequency."

    - Cite RBF typescript shown to EJA, Wash. DC., 18 Dec'74

---

Primary Systems:

    See Equations: Primary Systems

---

RBF DEFINITIONS

Prime:

"Prime means the first possible realization. It does not
have frequency. It is subfrequency. One is subfrequency.
Interval and differentiation are introduced with two.
Frequency begins with three-- with triangle, which is the
minimum cyclic enclosed circuitry."

                                        1011.30
    - Cite SYNERGETICS draft At Sec. ~~1011.31~~, 17 Feb'73

---

TEXT CITATIONS

Primary Systems:

    Synergetics text: Sec. 223.20, et.seq., Feb'72

---

RBF DEFINITIONS

Prime:

"Prime means the first layer. It does not have frequency.

It is subfrequency. One is subfrequency. Frequency

begins with two. Frequency and size are the same
phenomena. Subfrequency prime tetra, octa and icosa

consist of one vertex and an edge module of one."

    ~~- Cite RBF to EJA, Bear Island 22 August 1971, Synergetics~~
                             ~~draft Sept. '71, Sec. 882.1~~
    - Citation at Subfrequency, 23 Aug'71

---

RBF DEFINITIONS

Prime:

"Prime means sizeless, timeless, subfrequency. Prime is
prehierarchical. Prime is prefrequency. Prime is generalized,
a metaphysical experience, not special case."

    - Cite SYNERGETICS, 2nd. Ed. at Sec. 1071.10, 20 Dec'74

---

RBF DEFINITIONS

Prime Awareness:

"Sphere is prime awareness."

    - Citation and context at Vector Equilibrium, 18 Nov'72

Prime Conceptuality:                                      (1)

    See Conceptuality Independent of Size & Time
      A Priori

---

Prime Design:

    See Artist-scientist, May'60

---

Prime Conceptuality:                                      (2)

    See Domain & Quantum, (2)
      Unity as Plural, 1960

---

RBF DEFINITIONS

Prime Dichotomy:                                          (1)

"In the prime dichotomy of Universe into a thinkable
tetrahedronal zone between unconsiderable irrelevancies,
which in turn requires a secondary zonal separation into
macro-micro momentarily unthinkable cosmoses, it becomes
evident that the tetrahedronal zone itself introduces a
tertiary dichotomy into the two inherent twilight zones of
almost ▓considerable bigness and almost considerable
littleness, respectively.

"We find a fourth stage dichotomy of Universe when we
consider that the big and little twilights each respectively
are again also comprised of two tetrahedra as minimal
requirement, one as the concave inward tetrahedron and the
other as the convex outward tetrahedron.

"We next, fifthly, discover that the positive-negative (convex-concave) tetrahedra constitute only the minimum functional
dichotomy of finite Universe resulting in a minimum portion
of the Universe disposed in the microcosm and a maximum
portion of the Universe assigned to the macrocosm.  An
approximately spherical polyhedral zonal dichotomy of finite"

    - Cite OMNIDIRECTIONAL HALO, pp.140-141, 1960

---

Prime Convergence:

    See Vertex, 11 Oct'71

---

RBF DEFINITIONS

Prime Dichotomy:                                          (2)

"Universe by a spherical array of considered relevancies
provides the minimum portion of sum totally finite Universe
assigned to the macrocosm and the maximum relative portion
of finite Universe assignable to the microcosm..."

""The alternate relative proportions of finite Universe's
micro-macro magnitude limits of definitive dichotomy as
tetrahedronal minimum or spherical maximum introduce an
inherently alternative propensity of universal finite
accountability whose alternative eccentric-concentric
reciprocity of omnidifferential-lag-rate compensations
inherently propagate and regenerate preferably considered
universal evolution accomplished by omnidirectionally
expansive-contractive, wave propagating oscillations."

    - Cite OMNIDIRECTIONAL HALO, pp.143-144, 1960

---

RBF DEFINITIONS

Prime Definition:

"Whenever I can I always try to make a comprehensive prime
definition then break it into the main parts. . ."

    - Citation and context at Environment (1), 19 Feb'73

---

RBF DEFINITIONS

Prime Domain:

"A vector equilibrium is not a prime domain or a prime volume,
because it has a nucleus and consists of a plurality of definitive volumetric domains.  The vector equilibrium is inherently
subdivisible as defined by most economical triangulation of all
its 12 vertexes into eight tetrahedra and 12 quarter-octahedra,
constituting 20 identically volumed, minimum prime domains."

    - Citation & context at Vector Equilibrium, 26 Dec'73

RBF DEFINITIONS

### Prime Domains:

"While generalizably conceptual the prime structural systems and their prime domains, linear, areal, and volumetric, are inherently subfrequency, ergo independent of time and size."

- Citation and context at Subfrequency, 17 Feb'73

RBF DEFINITIONS

### Prime Epistemology:

"Prime epistemology is generalized thinkability. Epistemology discovers intuition."

- Citation & context at Prime Thinkability, 26 Dec'74

### Prime Domains:

See Prime Volumes
Spheric Domain

### Prime Generation:

See Seven Axes of Symmetry: Prime Generation Of

RBF DEFINITIONS

### Prime Enclosure:

"Omnitopology describes prime volumes. Prime volume domains are described by Euler's minimum set of visually unique topological aspects of polyhedral systems. Systems divide all Universe into all of the Universe occurring outside the system, all of the Universe occurring inside the system, and the remainder of the Universe constituting the system itself. Any point or locus inherently lacks insideness. Two event points cannot provide enclosure. Two points have betweeness but not insideness. Three points cannot enclose. Three points describe a volumeless plane. Three points have betweeness but no insideness. A three-point array plus a fourth point which is not in the plane described by the first three points constitutes prime enclosure. It requires a minimum of four points to definitively differentiate cosmic insideness and outsideness, i.e., to differentiate macrocosm from microcosm, and both of them from here and now."

- Cite SYNERGETICS draft at Sec. 1011.11, 17 Feb'73

RBF DEFINITIONS

### Prime Hierarchy of Symmetric Polyhedra:

"It was our synergetics' discovery and strategy of taking the two poles out of Euler's formula that permitted disclosure of the omnirational constant relative abundance of the V's, F's, and E's, and the disclosure of the initial additive twoness and multiplicative twoness whereby the unique prime number relationships of the prime hierarchy of omnisymmetric polyhedra occurred, showing Tetra = 1; octa = 2; cube = 3; VE or Icosa = 5."

- Citation & context at Constant Relative Abundance, 29 Nov'72

RBF DEFINITIONS

### Prime Enclosure:

". . . Two points do not constitute enclosure. A point by itself does not enclose. Three points do not constitute enclosure. Three points constitute a plane. A three-point array plus a fourth point not in the plane of the first three points do constitute prime enclosure. Four points minimum have insideness and outsideness."

- Cite Synergetics draft, Sec. 8002, August 1971, 30 JAN'73

### Prime Hierarchy of Symmetric Polyhedra:

See Equations: Primary Systems

Prime Interrelationships:

See Understanding, May'67

Prime Nucleated System:

See Vector Equilibrium, 2 Nov'73

Prime Invention:

See Dome, 9 Jul'73

RBF DEFINITIONS

Prime Nucleus:

"The isotropic vector matrix equilibrium multiplies omnidirectionally with increasing frequency of concentric vector-
equilibrium-conformed, closest-packed uniradius sphere shells,
conceptually disclosing the cosmically prime unique sequence
of developed interrelationships and behaviors immediately
surrounding a prime nucleus."

- Citation and context at Atomic Computer Complex (2), 13 May'73

Prime Minimum System:

See Mites as Prime Minimum System

Prime Nucleus:

See Energy Event, May'71

RBF DEFINITIONS

Prime Nuclear Structural Systems:

"All prime nuclear structural systems have one-- and only one--
(unity two) interior vertex.

"Nuclear structural systems consist internally entirely of
tetrahedra which have only one common interior vertex:
omniconvertex.

"In nuclear structural system each of the surface system's
external triangles constitutes the single exterior facet of an
omnisystem-occupying set of inter-triple-bonded tetrahedra, each
of whose single interior-to-system vertexes are congruent with
one another at the convergent nuclear center of the system.

"In all nonredundant prime nuclear structural systems the
congruently interior-vertexed, omnisystem-occupying tetrahedra
of all prime structural systems may all be interiorly truncated
by introducing special case frequency, which provides chordal
as well as radial modular subdivisioning of the isotropic-
vector-matrix intertriangulation of each radial, frequency-
embracing wave layer, always accomplished while sustaining the
structural rigidity of the system."

- Cite SYNERGETICS, 2nd. Ed., at Secs. 1074.10-.13, 27 Dec'74

RBF DEFINITIONS

Prime Number:

"...There really is a number one, and there is a number two.
The prime numbers are unique behaviors.... Prime numbers
are unique to what I call primitive experience and minimum
experience."

- Citation & context at Human Beings & Complex Universe, (7),
16 Feb'78

RBF DEFINITIONS

Prime Number:

"Man accommodated the primes one, two, three and five
in the decimal and the duodecimal system. But he left
out seven. After seven the next two primes are eleven
and thirteen: man calls these very bad luck. In playing
dice seven and eleven are crapping and thirteen is awful."

- Cite SYNERGETICS, "Numerology," p. 16 Oct. '71.

---

RBF DEFINITIONS

Prime Number:

"Electromagnetic frequencies of systems are sometimes
complex but always constitute the prime rational integer
characteristic of physical systems."

- Cite NASA Speech, p. 91, Jun'66

- Citation at Frequency, Jun'66

---

RBF DEFINITIONS

Prime Number:

"We have some absolutely beautiful rememberable numbers
which are all primes. I have discovered that all the
primes until 31 would form the positives and the negatives
of all the phenomena we can possibly group in the
permutations of the elements. The number of these
permutations is a rememberable number. Every so often
out of absolute chaos of millions and billions of numbers
there suddenly comes a rememberable number which shows the
beautiful balance at work in nature."

- Cite SYNERGETICS, "Numerology," pp. 17-18, Oct. '71.

---

Prime Numbers Factorial:                                    (1)

See Scheherazade Numbers:
    Scheherazade Numbers:  Declining Powers Of

---

RBF DEFINITIONS

Prime Number:

"A prime number cannot be produced by the interaction
Of any other numbers--
It is only divisible by itself and one.

- Cite NUMEROLOGY Draft, p. 32 - April 1971

---

Prime Numbers Factorial:                                    (2)

See Triacontrahedron:  Great Circles Of, 27 Apr'77

---

RBF DEFINITIONS

Prime Number:

"A prime number is a basic event. Every event has
three parts."

- Cite RBF to EJA
    Beverly Hotel, New York
    7 March 1971

- Citation ay Basic Event, 7 Mar'71

---

RBF DEFINITIONS

Prime Number: First 15 Primes:

"But so long as the comprehensive cyclic dividend fails to
contain prime numbers which may occur in the data to be
coped with, irrational numbers will build up or erode the
processing numbers to produce irrational, ergo unnatural,
results. We must therefore realize that the tables of the
trigonometric functions include the first 15 primes 1, 2,
3, 5, 7, 11, 13, 17, 19, 23, 29, 31, 41, 43."

- Cite RBF addition to SYNERGETICS galley at Sec. 1230.11,
    Santa Monica, CA, 14 Jan'74

RBF DEFINITIONS

Prime Numbers:  Pairing Of:

"The pairing of prime numbers has something to do with the poles.". . . It has to do with the 14 poles of the seven axes of symmetry."

- Cite RBF to EJA by telephone from LaJolla to Wash, DC, 17 Jan'74

---

TEXT CITATION

Prime Numbers:  Pairing Of:

Synergetics draft at Sec. 1239.20, galley

---

RBF DEFINITIONS

Prime Number Inherency & Constant Relative Abundance:

"Structural systems are always special case operational realizations in which there is a constant relative abundance of all the topological and system characteristics with the only variable being a quantity multiplier consisting of one of the first four prime numbers-- 1, 2, 3, and 5-- or an intermultiplied plurality of the same first four prime numbers."

- Cite SYNERGETICS, 2nd. Ed. at Sec. 1072.10, 27 Dec'74

---

RBF DEFINITIONS

Prime Number Inherency of Structural Systems:  Principle Of:

"What I have discovered is that: the number of vertexes of every omnitriangulated symmetrical structural system is always rationally accountable as 2 (polar vertexes of the neutral axis of spin) plus the product of 2 multiplied by one of the first four primes (1, 2, 3, or 5) times frequency to the second power; and the number of triangular faces will always be two times, and the number of edges three times the number of nonpolar vertexes.

"This is the principle of prime number inherency and constant relative abundance of the topological characteristics of structural systems."

- Cite RBF Ltr. to Dr. Robt. W. Horne, p.2, 14 Feb'66; as rewritten by RBF Feb'72

---

RBF DEFINITIONS

Prime Number Inherency of Structural Systems: Principle of:

"Omnitriangulated symmeteric systems are ployhedra whose vertexes derive from the external set of the closest packing of spheres and are rationally accountable in terms of the first four prime numbers (N), that is 1 or 2, or 3, or 5.

Equation:  $X = 2N(F^2) + 2$

where: $X$ = number of crossings, vertexes, or spheres in the outer layer or shell of any symmetrical system

$N$ = one of the first four primes numbers: 1, 2, 3, or 5

$F$ = edge frequency, i.e., the number of outer layer edge modules.

- Cite SYNERGETICS Draft, March 1971 (Rev)

---

RBF DEFINITIONS

Prime Number Inherency of Structural Systems:  Principle Of:

"What I have discovered is that: the number of vertexes of every omnitriangulated symmetrical system is always 2 (polar vertexes of the neutral axis of spin) plus the product of 2 multiplied by one of the first four primes (1, 2, 3, 04 5) times frequency to the second power; and the number of triangular faces will always be two timess, and the number of edges three times the number of nonpolar vertexes."

- Cite RBF Ltr. to Dr. Robt. W. Horne, 14 Feb'66, p.2.

---

RBF DEFINITIONS

Prime Number Inherency and Constant Relative Abundance of Structural Systems:  Principle Of:

"The precessionally regenerative concentricity of structure is antientropic and evelutes toward optimally economic local compressibility and symmetry.

/ This principle of_7 "omni-optimally-economic, omnitriangulated point system, symmetry relationships and relative abundance of frequency-modulated multiplicative subdivision of unitary local systems; i.e., M (mass) means: All the Universe's self-interfering complexes having ▨▨▨ concentrically self-precessing, local-focal-holding patterns resulting in locally regenerative constellar associabilities as positive-outside-in structures. C² (radiation) means: All the Universe's nonself-interfering complexes having eccentrically interprecessing, omnidirectionally diffusing patterns resulting in comprehensively degenerative negative limits of dissociabilities as negative (inside-out) de-structures."

- Cite INTRODUCTION TO OMNIDIRECTIONAL HALO, p.126, 1959

---

RBF DEFINITIONS

Prime Number Inherency & Constant Relative Abundance:  Table:

"The table of synergetics hierarchy (223.64) makes it possible for us to dispense with the areas and lines of Euler's topological accounting and provide a definitive description of all omnitirangulated polyhedral systems exclusively in terms of points and prime numbers."

- Cite RBF to EJA, 3200 Idaho, Wash., DC., 28 May'75

TEXT CITATIONS

<u>Prime Number Inherency and Constant Relative Abundance of the</u>
<u>Topology of Symmetrical Structural Systems</u>:  <u>Principle Of</u>:

Synergetics, Sec. 223

---

TEXT CITATIONS

<u>Prime Number Consequences of Spin-halving of Tetrahedron's</u>
<u>Volumetric Domain Unity</u>:

Table s1033.192

---

<u>Prime Number Inherency & Constant Relative Abundance of</u>          (1)
<u>The Topology of Symmetrical Structural Systems</u>:  <u>Principle Of</u>:

See Vertexial Topology
    Shell Growth Rate
    Equation:  Omnidirectional Closest Packing Of
        Spheres

---

<u>Prime Number</u>:                                                    (1)

    See Low Order Prime Numbers
        One as a Prime
        One as Not a Prime
        Primacy
        Primitive
        Scheherazade Numbers
        SSRCD
        Trigonometric Limit

---

<u>Prime Number Inherency & Constant Relative Abundance of</u>          (2)
<u>The Topology of Symmetrical Structural Systems</u>:  <u>Principle Of</u>:

See Ten, 22 Jun'75
    Vector Equilibrium:  Unarticulated VE, 2 Nov'73

---

<u>Prime Number</u>:                                                    (2)

    See Basic Event, 7 Mar'71*
        Cube, (1)
        Disparate, 22 Mar'73
        Frequency, Jun'66*
        Modulo 10, 26 Sep'73
        Octant, 20 Jul'73
        XYZ Quadrant at Center of Octahedron, 14 May'75
        Human Beings & Complex Universe, (7)&

---

<u>Prime Numbers</u>:  <u>First Four Primes</u>:

    See Quantum Mechanics:  Minimum Geometrical Fourness,
        (4)
        Triacontrahedron:  Great Circles Of, 27 Apr'77

---

RBF DEFINITIONS

<u>Prime One</u>:

"Unity is plural and at minimum two.  There is a <u>prime one</u>,
but it is one-half of unity."

- Citation at <u>Unity Is Plural</u>, 26 Jan'72

---

Prime One:

    See One as a Prime

---

Prime Otherness:              (2)

    See Intereffects, 25 Sep'73
        Environment, (A)

---

RBF DEFINITIONS

Prime Otherness:

"Prime otherness demands identification of the other's--
initially nebulous-- entity integrity, which entity and
subentities' integrities first attain cognizable self-inter-
patterning stabilization, ergo, discrete considerability,
only at the tetrahedron stage of generalizable entity
interrelationships. Resolvability and constituent
enumerability, and systematic interrelationship cognition
of entity regeneration presence, can be discovered only
operationally. (See Secs. 411, 411.10, 411.20, and 411.30.)
After the four-ball structural interpatterning stability
occurs, and a fifth ball comes along and, pulled by mass
attraction, rolls into a three-ball nest, and there are
now two tetrahedra bonded face-to-face."

- Cite SYNERGETICS draft at Sec. 540.06, 24 Sep'73

---

RBF DEFINITIONS

Prime Rational Integer Characteristics:

"The frequencies of systems modify their prime rational
integer characteristics."

- Cite SYNERGETICS Draft at Sec 223.41, Feb '72

---

RBF DEFINITIONS

Prime Otherness:

"Prime otherness was first hypothetically discovered in the
early 1920's and was identified by the term 'fundamental
complementarity.'

"Prime otherness has been experimentally evidenced in 1956 when
the Nobel prize was given for the proof that the complementaries
were inherently dissimilar, non-mirror-imaged systems. For
instance, proton and neutron always and only coexist; they are
interchangeable but have different masses and other dissimilar
characteristics.

"The limit case of prime otherness is that of the point and
the no-points; the events and the novents. Numerically, one
vs.zero. Because it is the limit case it is prime. Zero is
prime otherness."

- Cite RBF to EJA, 3200 Idaho, Wash DC, 23 Sep'73

---

RBF DEFINITIONS

Prime Rational Integers:

"Other characteristics of systems: Prime rational integer
characteristics: Electromagnetic frequencies of systems are
sometimes complex but always exist in complementation of
gravitational forces to constitute the prime rational integer
characteristics of physical systems.

"Systems may be symmetrical or asymmetrical.

"Systems are domains of volumes. Systems can have nuclei,
and prime volumes cannot."

- Cite SYNERGETICS text at Secs. 400.50-.51-.52; partly from
NASA Speech, p.91; last rewrite, 28 May'72

---

Prime Otherness:

    See Plural Otherness
        Past Otherness
        Present Otherness
        Single Otherness
        Future Otherness

---

RBF DEFINITIONS

Prime Rational Integer Characteristics:

"Electromagnetic Frequencies of systems are sometimes complex
but always constitute the prime rational integer characteristic
of physical systems."

- Cite SYNERGETICS text at Sec. 515.32; from NASA Speech (p.91),
Jun'66

## Prime Rational Integer Characteristics: (1)

See Rational Whole Numbers
Single Integer Differentials
Geometry & Number

## Prime Rational Integer Characteristics: (2)

See Frequency, 17 Nov'72
Physical, Jun'66

RBF DEFINITIONS

## Prime State:

"The systems as described in Colums 1 through 9 are in the prime state of conceptuality independent of size: metaphysical. Size is physical and is manifest by frequency of length, area, volume, and time. Size is manifest in the four variables of relative length, area, volume, and time; these are all four expressible in terms of frequency. Frequency is operationally realized modular subdivision of the system enclosure."

- Cite SYNERGETICS Table of topogical hierarchies, Sec. 223.65 21 Mar'73

RBF DEFINITIONS

## Prime Structural Systems:

"There are three types of omnitriangular, symmetrical structural systems. We can have three triangles around each vertex; a tetrahedron. Or we can have four triangles around each vertex; the octahedron. Finally we can have five triangles around each vertex; the icosahedron.

"The tetrahedron, octahedron, and icosahedron are made up, respectively, of one, two, and five pairs of positively and negatively functioning open triangles.

"We cannot have six symmetrical or equiangular triangles around each vertex because the angles add up to 360 degrees-- thus forming an infinite edgeless plane. The system with six equiangular triangles 'flat out' around each vertex never comes back upon itself. It can have no withinness or with- outness. It cannot be constructed with pairs of positively and negatively functioning open triangles. In order to have a system, it must return upon itself in all directions."

- Cite SYNERGETICS text at Secs. 610.21-.22-.23; second printing; 3 Nov'75

RBF DEFINITIONS

## Prime Structural Systems: (1)

"The domain of the tetrahedron is the tetrahedron as defined by four spheres in a tetrahedronal, omni-embracing, closest- packed tangency network. The domain of an octahedron is an octahedron as defined by six spheres closest packed octa- hedronally. The domain of an icosahedron is an icosahedron as defined by 12 spheres closest packed without a nucleus. All of the three foregoing non-nuclear-containing domains of the tetrahedron, octahedron, and icosahedron are defined by superficially omnitriangulated closest packing of the four spheres, six spheres, and 12 spheres, respectively, which we have defined elsewhere as omnitriangulated systems or as prime structural systems. There are no other symmetrical non-nuclear-containing domains of closest-packed volume- embracing agglomerations.

"While other total closest-packed-sphere enbracements, or agglomerations, may be symmetrical or superficially asymmetrical in the form of crocodiles, alligators, pears, or billiard balls, they constitute complex associations of prime structural systems. Only the tetrahedral, octahedral, and icosa- hedral domains are basic structural systems without nuclei."

- Cite RBF marginalia at Synergetics draft "Omnitopology," July '71
See Sections 1010.10+11+12, Apr. '72

RBF DEFINITIONS

## Prime Structural Systems: (2)

"All the Platonic polyhedra and many other more complex multidimensional symmetries of sphere groupings can occur. Non of them can occur as a consequence of closest packed spheres having no nucleus."

- Cite RBF marginalia at Synergetics draft "Omnitopology," July '71
See Sections 1010.10+11+12, Apr '72

RBF DEFINITIONS

## Prime Structural Systems:

"The tetrahedron, octahedron and icosahedron are prime structural systems: there are no other symmetrical non-nuclear domains in closest packed agglomerations. . . . Their domains are defined by superficial omni- triangulation of 4, 6 and 12. The domain of a tetrahedron is a tetrahedron. The domain of an octahedron is six spheres closest packed octahedronally. The domain of an icosahedron is an icosahedron and is defined by the closest packing of twelve spheres without a nucleus."

- Cite RBF to EJA, Fairfield, Conn., Chez Wolf.
18 June 1971.

RBF DEFINITIONS

## Prime Structural Systems:

"Only the tetrahedron, octahedron and icosahedron are prime structural systems which can be arrived at in structural stability without a nucleus. All the Platonic "solids" and many more complex regular polyhedra are stable structural systems, but they all have a nucleus."

- Cite RBF to EJA, Fairfield, Conn., Chez Wolf.
18 June 1971.

RBF DEFINITIONS

_____ Prime Structural Systems:

"there are only three possible cases of fundamental

omni-symmetrical, omni-triangulated, least effort structural

systems in nature: the tetrahedron with three triangles at

each vertex, the octahedron with four triangles at each

vertex, and the icosahedron with five triangles at each

vertex."

Cite SYNERGETICS ILLUSTRATIONS - # 7, 1967

---

RBF DEFINITIONS

Prime Structure and Prime System:

"Exploring experimentally, synergetics finds the tetrahedron, whose volume is one-third that of the cube, to be the prime structural system of Universe: prime structure because stabilized exclusively by triangles that are experimentally demonstrable as being the only self-stabilizing polygons; and prime system because accomplishing the subdivision of all Universe into an interior microcosm and an external microcosm; and doing so structurally with only the minimum four vertexes topologically defining the insideness and outsideness."

- Cite SYNERGETICS draft at Sec 223.73, 26 Sep'73

---

RBF DEFINITIONS

Prime Structural Systems:                    (A)

"A structure divides Universe into two main parts-- al the Universe that is inside and all the rest of the Universe which is outside of the structural system. We find that there are only three types of fundamental omnitriangulary, symmetrical structural systems. We can have three triangles around each vertex of a symmetrical structure; this makes a regular tetrahedron. Or we can have four triangles around each vertex; this makes the regular octahedron. Finally we can have five triangles around each vertex which makes the icosahedron. The tetrahedron, octahedron, and icosahedron, are made up respectively of one, two, and five pairs of positively and negatively functioning open triangles. We cannot have six symmetrical or equilateral triangles around each vertex because the angles add up to 360°-- thus forming an infinite edgeless plane. The structural system with six equilaterals around each vertex never comes back upon itself. It can have no withinness and withoutness. It cannot be constructed with pairs of positive-negative function open triangles. In order to have a structural system it must return upon itself in all directions. If the system's openings are all triangulated it is structured with minimum effort."

- Cite Mexico '63, p. 27. 10 Oct'63

---

RBF DEFINITIONS

_____ Prime Structural Systems:

"Of the three fundamental structures (tetrahedron,

octahedron, and icosahedron) the tetrahedron contains the

least volume with the most surface and is therefore the

strongest structure per unit of volume."

- Cite MEXICO 63, p.28
                                        10 Oct'63

* - Citation at Tetrahedron, 10 Oct'63

---

RBF DEFINITIONS

Prime Structural Systems:                    (B)

"There are only three possible omnisymmetrical, omni-triangulated least effort structural systems in nature. They are the tetrahedron, octahedron, and icosahedron. When their edges are all equal in length, the volumes of these three structure are respectively: one; four and 18.51."

(Last word substituted.)

- Cite Mexico '63, p. 27. 10 Oct'63

---

RBF DEFINITIONS

Prime Structural Systems:

"Light (as typical wave frequency group) obstruction is greatest where structural components converge (grid photostats show this as stars at convergent points). A multi-axial or dynamical system cannot have only two triangles around one vertex. It can have three, four, or five equilateral triangles, but cannot have six or more equilateral triangles in a finite system."

(Above extract is in the context of a discussion of radomes)

- Cite typescript "Definitions by RBF," 29 Dec'58
  Context at Radome Sequence (1)

---

RBF DEFINITIONS

Prime Structural Systems:

"We find there are only three possible omnitriangulated systems that subdivide Universe. There are the three faces around one vertex which is the tetrahedron; the four faces around one vertex which is the octahedron; and the five faces around one vertex which is the icosahedron.

"You can't have six because it would be flat and would not come back on itself to close the system. It would be neither concave nor convex. We have the positive and negative condition of these three things. Remember that you cannot have a polygon of less than three sides. So the triangle is minimum polygon; it is the only polygon that is inherently stable. We have learned that the triangle stabilizes itself with minimum effort, so we learn that triangulated systems are the systems of the least effort. If they are equilateral triangles then all the system is of equal effort in all directions... so that there are only three possible cases: tetrahedron, octahedron, and icosahedron."

· Cite Oregon Lecture #7, p.249, 11 Jul'62

---

TEXT CITATIONS

Prime Structural Systems:

Synergetics - Sec. 1011.30 "Prime Tetra, Octa and Icosa."

Synergetics - Sec. 724 "Three and Only Basic Structures"

Synergetics - Sec. 610.20 "Omnitriangular Symmetry: Three Prime
                                Structural Systems"
Synergetics - Sec. 532.40 "Three Basic Omnisymmetrical Systems"

Synergetics - Sec. 612.00 "Subtriangulation: Icosahedron"

Synergetics - Sec. 1010.20 "Nonnuclear Prime Structural Systems."

Synergetics - Sec. 1031.10 "Dynamic Symmetry. (Esp. 1031.13)

Synergetics - Sec. 611.00

Synergetics - Sec. 905.13

| | |
|---|---|
| 223.73 | s251.19 |
| 982.02-982.06 | s937.14 |
| 1222.20 | s1074.10-1074.13 |

# Synergetics Dictionary

Prime Structural Systems:                                    (1)

      See Icosahedron
          Octahedron
          Tetrahedron

          Primary Structure
          Prime Volumes
          Tensegrity:  Basic Tensegrity Structures:  Three
             and Only
          Prime Minimum System
          Domains of Tetra, Octa & Icosa
          Tetra, Oct & Icosa

---

Prime Thinkability:

"Systematic Character of Prime Thinkability."

- Cite section caption in SYNERGETICS, 2nd. Ed., at Sec. 1071.00,
20 Dec'74

---

Prime Structural Systems:                                    (2)

      See Cycle, 10 Feb'73; 1955
          Least Effort, 1967
          PatternStrip Aggregate Wrapabilities, 19 Dec'73
          Radome Sequence (1)*
          Sphere, 25 Feb'74
          Planck's Constant (A)
          Tetrahedron, 5 Mar'73; 10 Oct'63*
          Z Cobras, 6 Nov'73
          Subfrequency, 17 Feb'73; 23 Aug'71
          Physics:  Difference Between Physics & Chemistry,
             31 May'71
          Frequency, Jun'66
          Dyanamic Symmetry, (2)
          Octahedron Model of Doubleness of Unity, (1)(2)
          Quantum Sequence, (2)(5)
          Stable & Unstable Structures, & Jun'72
          Icosahedron: Subtriangulation, 9 Nov'73

---

Prime Vector:                                                (1)

"All structural accounting of nature is accomplished with
rational quantities of tetrahedra.  The XYZ coordinates may
be employed to describe the arrangements, but only in awkward
irrationality because the edge of the cube is inherently
irrational in respect to the cube's facial diagonal.  The
hypotenuses actually function only as the edges of the positive
and negative tetrahedra which alone permit the cube to exist
as a structure.  The hypotenuses connect the sphere centers at
the cube corners; they function concurrently and simultaneously as the natural structuring of the tetrahedra edges in
the omnidirectional isotropic vector matrix; as either
hypotenuse or tetra edge they are prime vectors."

"Of the eight corners of the cube only four coincide with the
sphere centers of closest-packed, unit-radius spheres; therefore
only the cube's facial diagonals can interconnect closest
packed spheres.  One closed set of six cube face diagonals
can only interconnect four sphere centers corners of the prime
tetrahedron which alone provides the structural stability of
the cube, whose eight-cornered, structural stability completeness
requires the saturation of the alternate set of six diagonals"

- Cite SYNERGETICS, 2nd. Ed., at Secs. 540.11 +.12, 19 Nov'74

---

Prime System:                                                (1)

      See Minimum System
          Primary Systems
          Prime Nucleated System

---

Prime Vector:                                                (2)

"in each of the cube's six faces, which alternate set of six
diagonals intertriangulates the other four sphere centers of
the cube's eight corners.  The cube diagonals and the edges of
the tetrahedra structuring the cube are two aspects of the same
phenomenon.  The tetra-edge, cube-face diagonals connecting the
two sets of four corners each of the cube's total of eight
corners are the prime vectors of the vector equilibrium and the
isotropic vector matrix.

"The second power of the length of the prime vector that
constitutes the diagonal of the cube's face equals the sum of
the second powers of any two edges of the cube.  Because these
two edges converge at the cube's corner to form one standing
wave which may be multifrequenced to apparently coincide with
the cube's facial diagonal, we discover that this relationship
is what we are talking about in the deliberately nonstraight
line.  It is the same mathematical relationship demonstrated
in the ancients' proof of the Pythagorean theorem, wherein the
square of the hypotenuse is proven to be equal to the sum of the
squares of the triangle's two legs.  Thus the deliberately
nonstraight line displays an evolutionary transformation from"
coincidence with the two sides of the paralellogram to "

- Cite SYNERGETICS, 2nd. Ed. at Secs. 540.12 +.13, 19 Nov'74

---

Prime Thinkability:

"Prime thinkability is inherently systemic.  Prime epistemology
is generalized thinkability.  Epistemology discovers intuition."

- Cite SYNERGETICS, 2nd. Ed., at Sec. 1071.26, 26 Dec'74

---

Prime Vector:                                                (3)

"coincidence with the seemingly straight, wavilinear diagonal
of the parallelogram.

"Prime vector may be considered variously as

        -- the axis of intertangency (Secs. 521.21 & 537.22);
        -- the control line of nature (Sec. 982.21);
        -- the deliberately nonstraight line (Sec. 522);
        -- the diagonal of the cube (Sec. 463);
        -- half vectors (Sec. 537.21);
        -- the hypotenuse (Sec. 825.26);
        -- the internuclear vector modulus (Sec. 240.40);
        -- the line between two sphere centers (Sec. 537.21);
        -- linear meneration unity (Sec. 982.51);
        -- the radial line (Sec. 537.21);
        -- the tetra edge (Sec. 982.51); or
        -- unit radius (Sec. 1106.23).

- Cite SYNERGETICS, 2nd. Ed. at Secs. 540.13 +.14, 19 Nov'74

RBF DEFINITIONS

### Prime Vector:

"Of the eight corners of the cube only four are sphere centers; therefore only cube diagonals can connect spheres.

"The diagonals of the cube which connect sphere centers coincide with the tetra edges of the two tetrahedra that structure the cube. They are two aspects of the same thing.

"The tetra edge connecting the two cube corners that are sphere centers is the prime vector-- just another aspect of the radial line connecting any two tangent sphere centers.

"This is what I am talking about in the Deliberately Nonstraight Line. It is what the ancients were talking about in the Pythagorean Theorem: the square of the hypotenuse equals the sum of the squares of the two legs."

- Cite RBF to EJA by telephone from Pacific Palisades, CA, 20 Jul'74

---

### Prime Vector:     (1)

See Axis of Intertangency
    Control Line of Nature
    Cube: Diagonal Of
    Deliberately Nonstraight Line
    Hypotenuse
    Internuclear Vector Modulus
    Line of Interrelationship
    Line Between Two Sphere Centers
    Mensural Unity
    Pythagorean Theorem
    Radial Line as Tetra Edge
    Synergetics Constant
    Tetra Edge
    Vector: Half Vectors
    Vector: One-second Vector Length
    Radial Unity
    Unit: Unity
    Unit Radius: Unit Vector Radius

---

### Prime Vector:     (2)

See T Quanta Module, (1)

---

RBF DEFINITIONS

### Prime Vertexes:

"The 25 great circles of the vector Equilibrium all go through the prime vertexes."

- Citation & context at Seven Axes of Symmetry, 16 Aug'70

---

RBF DEFINITIONS

### Prime Volumes:

"A prime volume has unique domains but does not have a nucleus.

"A prime volume is different from a generalized regenerative system. Generalized regenerative systems have nuclei; generalized prime volumes do not.

"There are only three prime volumes: tetrahedron, octahedron, and icosahedron. Prime volumes are characterized exclusively by external structural stability."

(Sec. 1010.01-.03)

- Cite SYNERGETICS text at Sec.s 1010.01-.02-.03; 17 Feb'73

---

RBF DEFINITIONS

### Prime Volumes:

"A prime volume is different from a system. Systems have nuclei and prime volumes do not. There are only three prime volumes: tetrahedron, octahedron, and icosahedron. Prime volumes are characterized exclusively by external structural stability."

1010.02 - APR'72

- Cite SYNERGETICS text, at Sec. 880.1, Jun '71

---

RBF DEFINITIONS

###     Prime Volumes:

"A prime volume is different from a system. Systems can have nuclei and prime volumes cannot. There are only three prime volumes: tetrahedron, octahedron and icosahedron. They have to have exclusively external structural stability to be prime volumes."

Cit Synergetics draft, Sec. 880.1, August 1971.

---

RBF DEFINITIONS

###     Prime Volumes:

"Systems can have nuclei and prime volumes cannot. There are only three prime volumes."

[EJA comment: Tetrahedron, Octahedron and Icosahedron.]

- Cite RBF to EJA, Fairfield, Conn., Chez Wolf. 18 June 1971.

SYSTEM - 460.53

RBF DEFINITIONS

Prime Volumes:

"Systems can have nuclei and prime volumes cannot.

There are only three prime volumes."

- Cite RBF to EJA, Fairfield, Conn., Chez Wolf, 18 Jun '71

PRIME VOLUMES — SEC. 1010.02)

---

Prime Volumes: (1)

See Prime Enclosure
Spheric Domain
Tensegrity: Basic Tensegrity Structures: Three &
Only
Three & Only Structural Systems in Nature
System vs. Prime Volume

---

Prime Volumes: (2)

See Prime Domain, 26 Dec'73
Domain & Quantum, (1)(2)
Prime Rational Integers, 28 May'72

---

Prime: (1)

See Between: Vector Equilibrium as Prime Between-ness
Model
Conceivable Entity = Prime
Limit
Primacy
Primitive
Vector Equilibrium as Prime Nucleated System
Tetrahedron as Prime Nonnucleated Structural System

---

Prime: (2)

See Complex, 17 Feb'73
Originality, Apr'71
Subfrequency, 23 Aug'71*
Vector Equilibrium, 15 May'73
System, 27 May'72
Basic Nestable Configurations: Hierarchy Of, 29 May'72

---

Prime: (3A)

See Prime Awareness
Prime Conceptuality
Prime Contractors
Prime Convergence
Prime Definition
Prime Design
Prime Dichotomy
Prime Domain
Prime Enclosure
Prime Hierarchy of Symmetric Polyhedra
Prime Interrelationships
Prime Invention
Prime Nucleated System
Prime Nucleus
Prime Number Inherancy of Structural Systems:
Principle Of
Prime Number
Prime Numbers: Pairing Of
Prime Numbers: First Four Primes

---

Prime: (3B)

See Prime One
Prime Otherness
Prime Rational Integer Characteristics
Prime State
Prime Structural Systems
Prime System
Prime Vector
Prime Volumes
Prime Vertex
Prime Epistemology
Prime Thinkability
Prime Generation
Prime Minimum System

---

RBF DEFINITIONS

Primitive:

"Primitive is what you conceptualize sizelessly without words. Primitive has nothing to do with Russian or English or any special case language. My original 4-D, convergent-divergent, vector equilibrium conceptualizing of 1927-28

was primitive ⋈ Bow Tie: the symbol of intertrans-

formative equivalence as well as of complementarity:

convergence ⋈ divergence

⋈ Also the symbol of syntropy-entropy

and of wave and octave

-4, -3, -2, -1,

+1, +2, +3, +4"

- Cite RBF rewrite of 19 Jul'76; incorporated in Synergetics, 2nd. Ed. at Sec. 1033.453

RBF DEFINITIONS

Primitive:

"Primitive is what you say without words. . . it has nothing to do with Russian or English. Like the triangular grid in "4-D." Frequency: Hex: In, out and around."

- Cite RBF to EJA, 3200 Idaho, Wash, DC; 18 Jul'76

RBF DEFINITIONS

Primitive Dimensionality:

"Primitive dimensionality is systemic. You could not point to something that is less than a system. The points are the ins. What is non-point-to-able is simply the untuned. This primitive way of looking at things affords prime intertransformable magnitude independent of size."

- Cite RBF to EJA, by telephone from Jim Fitzgibbon's in St. Louis; 1 Mar'76

RBF DEFINITIONS

Primitive:

"We may use the word 'primitive' to describe the initial self-starting condition of divergence.... Thus the primitive is quite different from the 'fundamental particles' game of the high-energy research physicists."

- Citation & context at Starting with Divergence, 19 Feb'76

Primitive Experience:

See Prime Number, 16 Feb'78

RBF DEFINITIONS

Primitive:

"Primitive is principle and not a special case. (virgin soil = primitive.) Virginity is an aspect of primitive. There can't be any ▓▓▓▓▓ special case vrgins; viriginity is prefrequency."

- Cite RBF to EJA, 3200 Idaho, 18 Dec'74

Primitive Fourness:                                    (1)

See Fourfold Twoness
    Minimum of Four Tetrahedra
    Minimum Tetrahedron
    Tetrahedral Minimum

RBF DEFINITIONS

Primitive:

"Primitive means a priori, rather than prime."

- Cite RBF to EJA, Waldorf Astoria, 10 Jan'74

Primitive Fourness:                                    (2)

See Number: Cosmically Absolute Numbers, 5 Mar'73
    System, 26 Dec'74
    Cosmic Hierarchy, 23 Jan'77

Primitive vs. Frequency:

See Synergetics: Evolution Of, 14 Oct'76

Primitive Inventory:

See Quanta Loss by Congruence, (3)

Primitive Hierarchy: (1)

See Cosmic Hierarchy
    Geometric Hierarchy

RBF DEFINITIONS

Primitive Regeneration:

"Prime = primitive. Primitive is generalized principle and
not a special case. Virgin = primitive. 'Virgin soil' =
special case. Virgin female human = special case, only
because of the 'human' case realization. Virginity is a
generalized aspect of primitive. There can be no special
case generalized virgins. Virginity is not only prefrequency,
it is pretime, pre-special-case, and pre-experienceable dimension."

- Cite SYNERGETICS, 2nd. Ed., at Sec. 1076.10, 27 Dec'74

Primitive Geometric Conceptuality:

See Tetrahedron as Conceptual Model, 28 Jan'73

Primitive Regeneration:

See Conceptual Genesis
    Life's Original Event

Primitive Hierarchy: (2)

See Quanta Loss by Congruence, (2)
    Six Motion Freedoms & Degrees of Freedom, 11 Aug'77;
    (A)(B)
    Synergetics, 17 Oct'77

Primitive: (1)

See Conceptuality Independent of Size
    Conceptuality Independent of Size & Time
    Initial: Initiating
    Prefrequency
    Primacy
    Prime
    Prime Number
    Tetrahedron as Primitively Central to Life
    Virgin = Primitive
    Potential vs. Primitive

Primitive: (2)

See Octave Wave, 5 Mar'73
    Models, 9 Jan'74
    Tetrahedron, 5 Mar'73
    Time, (1)
    Universal Integrity: Second-power Congruence of
       Gravitational & Radiational Constants, 9 Jan'74
    System, 26 Dec'74
    Starting with Divergence, 19 Feb'76
    Tunability, 24 Apr'76
    Minimum of Four Tetrahedra, 22 Feb'77
    Cosmic Hierarchy, 23 Jan'77
    Generalization & Special Case, 23 Jan'77
    Energetic Functions, 8 Aug'77

---

RBF DEFINITIONS

Primordial Soup:

"All the scientific talk of probabilities is asinine.
Ther is no probability about mass attraction.  They all
want primordial soup, out of which improbable selection
would begin.  But the LAWS were always there."

- Cite RBF to KJT, Royal Scots Grill, N.Y. 14 Sept. 1971.
- Citation at Probability, 14 Sep'71

---

Primitive: (3)

See Primitive Fourness
    Primitive Geometric Conceptuality
    Primitve Dimensionality
    Primitive Regeneration
    Primitive vs. Frequency
    Primitive Hierarchy
    Primitive Inventory
    Primitive Experience

---

Primordial: (1)

See Chaos
    Life's Original Event
    Orderliness Operative in Nature

---

RBF DEFINITIONS

Primordial:

"One physicist remarked recently,
'I am tiring of the nonsense legend
Which finds one end of Universe closed,
By a required beginning event
And the other end open to infinity.'
The concept of primordial--
Meaning before the days of order--
Which imply an a priori,
Absolute disorder, chaos, a beginning
('The primordial ooze-gooze explosion')
Is now scientifically invalidated, passe."

- Cite BRAIN AND MIND, p.156 May '72

---

Primordial: (2)

See Probability, 14 Sep'71*

---

RBF DEFINITIONS

Primordial:

"The idea of anything primordial could not exist.
There could not be anything prior to order.  Man is
disorderly only in his ignorance."

- Cite RBF to SIMS Seminar, U. Mass., Amherst, 22 July 1971.

---

RBF DEFINITIONS

Principle:

"Principles can be realized independent of size."

- Citation & context at Proofs, 7 Oct'75

RBF DEFINITIONS

Principle:

"The principles are the only reality. They are so absolute
that you can taste them. The physical aberration is always
in our perceptioning but it is not the reality."

- Cite RBF to EJA and BO'R, 3200 Idaho, Wash., D.C., 6 Apr'75

RBF DEFINITIONS

Principle:

"All principles are omniembracing, omnipermeative,
omnisynergetic."

- Citation and context at Ecology Sequence (F), 5 Jun'73

RBF DEFINITIONS

Principles:

Q:     How did you come to know what you know?

RBF:   I intuited principles. I don't know whether I
       discovered principles, as such, or not. You should
       say: How did we happen? and I don't know."

- Cite RBF videotaping session Philadelphia, Pa. 1 Feb'75

RBF DEFINITIONS

Principle:

"The principle is more of a reality than the qualities they
produce. The teacher knew that Euclid's planes and lines
didn't exist."

- - Cite RBF to EJA, 3200 Idaho, DC, 22 Feb'72

RBF DEFINITIONS

Principle:                                                    (1)

"I've worked very hard on my audiences to make sure that they
understand that it's only the human mind that is able to
discover those eternal principles that are operative,
governing the eternal regeneration of the Universe. Humans
are here for functioning in a special capability of reference
to the eternal laws. When you have something as complex in
design as the Boeing 747 you have to have all those instruments
up forward and every once in a while the instruments tell the
pilot that they're non functiong-- or they're not saying anything.
It tells the pilot he's got to take over now himself, not to
rely any more on automatic and only by direct access to the
principles of the Universe can he possibly save his ship.

"The Universe must be a problem of design of eternal regeneration,
a design that makes the Boeing 747 look like a toothpick in
simplicity compared to the complexity of eternally regenerative
Universe. There must be some local things that go on as there
would be in the Boeing 747, where you find out where the stresses
are, or where the heat is: something you've got to attend to.
You need a local monitor on some part of the Universe... and that's
what we're here for.

- Cite tape transcript RBF to W. Wolf, Gloucester, Mass., p.13,
  2 Jun'74

RBF DEFINITIONS

Principle:

"Principles governing all the atomic behaviors that associate
triangularly and tetrahedrally with the 12 degrees of freedom
all are eternal design evolution, such as must include the
complex of potential, symmetrical and asymmetrical limited,
pulsative regeneration, all of which are ideally conceivable,
as is experimentally manifest in synergetics and in my
explorations of the idealistic ramifications."

(Rewritten as Nucleated Systems, 15 Feb'72.)

- Cite RBF marginalis in Eccles' "Facing Reality," p.3,
  3200 Idaho, Wash DC, 14 Feb'72

RBF DEFINITIONS

Principle:                                                    (2)

"The one thing common to all lives everywhere-- regardless
of differences in size, or ethnics-- the one thing common is
that we're here with this beautiful mind with access to
principles to solve problems by principles not by force.
We're born as force; we're born as physical. But mind is our
great function here. Our relationship to Universe is
completely abstract.

"We find then humanity is still in a bind with all the politics,
all the big business, all the organization, all for the power
structure... who's got the biggest gun? And I say, if we're
going to stay here it's so we can actually graduate in our
function. This is a priori."

- Cite tape transcript, RBF to W. Wolf, Gloucester. Mass., p.13,
  2 Jun'74

RBF DEFINITIONS

Principle:

"There can't be a principle that has a 'beginning' and an
'ending.' We cannot suggest that an abstraction could have
a beginning and an end. The words 'beginning' and 'end' have
to do with the physical."

- Citation and context at Generalization Sequence (3), Jun-Jul'69

RBF DEFINITIONS

Principle:

"Principles do not begin and end.  Experiences do."

- Cite RBF to Hugh Kenner, Santa Barbara, Dec'67

---

RBF DEFINITIONS

Principle:

"...In comprehensive Universe, dimension drops out and conceptual principle remains.  Physical interferences of our sensibilities are alike true and real, or realizable, only in principle.  Positive and negative cancel as the principle zero."

- Citation and context at Reciprocity (3), May'49

---

RBF DEFINITIONS

Principle:

"...The pure principles were generalizable and of no weight at all.  The principles were always there and the generalizable had nothing to do with the special case.  The generalizable was always present in the special case, but it had nothing to do with the avoidupois, for it is not weighable.  Mathematics weighs nothing and this is mathematics.  It is a mathematical correspondence."

- Citation and context at Orderliness Operative in Nature, (1)(2), 9 Jul'62

---

Principle vs. Aberration:

See Man as a Function of Universe, 21 Jan'75

---

RBF DEFINTIONS

Principle:

"By the word principle I mean those generally describable behaviors of local frequency and angle patternings subsidiary to obviously more comprehensive and universally integrative patternings; despite that the local patternings wavelengths are infra or ultra to our sensorial tunabilities, wherefore these infra and ultra sensorial wave frequency and angle complexes are apprehendible and comprehendible only through relayed step-up or step-down transformations of the pattern as a generalizably recognizable pattern behavior as it consistently displaces locally cooperating frequency patternings of lesser or greater wavelengths, e.g., . . . the outwardly moving wave in water is a pattern comprehensivity by a plurality of reported patternings of local displacements of locally operative pattern relaying as water molecules of waves go in and out from the center of the Earth."

- RBF holograph, 12 Jun'56

---

Principles:  Hierarchy Of:

See Generalization of Generalizations
Synergy of Synergies

---

RBF DEFINITIONS

Principle:

"... Magnitude vanishes; only principles endure.

The fantastic, being of purely superficial magnitude, vanishes in the face of principle."

- Cite TOTAL THINKING, I&I, p.226, May'49

---

Principle:                                          (1A)

See Aggregates of Principles
    Antientropic Ordering Principles
    Blind Date with Principle
    Equatability of Generalized Principles
    Generalized Principle
    Industrial Principle
    Interference of Principles
    Inventory of Principles
    Inventory of Characteristics of Principles
    Lag Rates of Principles
    Objective Employment of Principles
    Organizing Principle
    Pure Principle
    Reciprocal Involvement of Experiences & Principles
    Reciprocal Patterning of Principles
    Reality as Structural Interaction of Principles
    Resource vs. Principle
    Self-organizing Principle

Principle:                                                      (1B)

    See Synergetics Principles
       Undiscovered Principles
       Schematic of the Principles
       Interaoperativeness
       Omniinteraccommodative
       Fantasy vs. Principle
       Experiences & Principles
       ~~Last Chance Adoption of Unheeded Principles~~
       Individual & Group Principle
       Bundle of Principles
       Mutual Survival Principles

Priority:  Priorities:                                          (1)

    See Antipriorities

Principle:                                                      (2)

    See Anticipatory, 3 Nov'64
       Antientropy, 20 Jun'66
       Artifacts (1)(2)
       Ecology Sequence (F)*
       Generalization Sequence (3)*
       Orderliness Operative in Nature, 9 Jul'62*
       Reciprocity (3)*
       Word, May'49
       Chess: A Priori Intellect Invents a Game Called
         "Life" (1)(2)
       Adam & Eve, 2 Jun'74
       Fantastic, May'49
       Airplane, May'49
       Prrofs, 7 Oct'75*

Priority:  Priorities:                                          (2)

    See Ship, (3)

Printing:  Printing Press:                                      (1)

    See Benday Screen

RBF DEFINITIONS

    Prism:

    "A prism can twist to becoming two tetrahedra by
    precessing until the legs cross in the middle.  Interconnect
    the corners and you have the octahedron."

    - Cite RBF to EJA, Blackstone Hotel,  Chicago, 31 May 1971

Printing Press:  Printing:                                      (2)

    See Rolls, 20 Apr'72
       Publishing, 30 Jan'75
       Resolvability Limits, 30 Apr'77

Prison:                                                         (1)

    See Inventions that Decrease the Degrees of Freedom

Prison:                                    (2)

    See Teleology, 20 Jun'66


Privacy vs. Community:                     (2)

    See Dome, 3 Jan'71
        Old Man River Project, 20 Sep'76


Pristine: Pristinity:

    See Intuition of the Child, (4)
        Nuclear Uniqueness, 18 Feb'73


Privacy:                                   (1)

    See Community
        Proxemics
        Hearable You
        Touchable You
        Smellable You


RBF DEFINITIONS

Privacy:

"Get yourself the tools and ways of enclosing enormous amounts
of space, and make it possible for large numbers of human beings
to come together under more preferred conditions than have ever
before come together.  Then give them large clear spaces so
that their privacy results from having sufficient distance
between people or groups of people.  Get over the idea of
partitions.  Partitions are like socialism.  They came out of
living and working in fortresses where there wasn't enough room
to go around, so they put up partitions-- really making cells.
Partitions simply say you shall not pass.  That's all they do.
They are improvised to make that which is fundamentally inadequate work 'after a fashion.'

"There are four kinds of privacy: if I can't touch you, we're
tactilely private; if I can't smell you, we're olfactorily
private; if I can't hear you, we're aurally private; and if I
can't see you, we're visually private.  Just a little space
will take care of the first three.  For the fourth-- since we
can see a great distance-- all we need are delicate occulting
membranes, possibly rose bushes or soap bubbles or smoke screens."

    - Cite EDUCATION AUTOMATION, pp.83-84, 22 Apr'61


Privacy:                                   (2)

    See Walls, 29 Jan'75


Privacy vs. Community:                     (1)

    See Introversion vs. Extraversion
        Proximity ≠ Neighborliness
        Proximity & Remoteness


RBF DEFINITIONS

Private Enterprise:

"Auto     = ½ Motoring
 Highway  = ½  "   "

"During the last twenty years while automobile companies
produced and sold $220 billion worth of autos the government
spent $200 billion on roads.

"'Private enterprise' is a dependent function.  It is
subsidized self deceit."

    - Cite RBF Holograph, Delos Conference, 1971.

RBF DEFINITIONS

### Private Enterprise:

"This is a powerful trend. Private enterprise is taking the initiative entirely away from politics. Politics lingers in the twilight of geographical islands. Enterprise operates transcendentally to such limits. Major enterprise is inherently bound by Universe alone..."

- Citation and context at <u>World Corporations</u>, 9 May'57

---

RBF DEFINITIONS

### Private Property:

"Private ownership is going to go, not by political revolution, but because it becomes obsolete, onerous. Our young people are going to want to live around the world, and it just isn't possible to carry 'all that stuff' with them. So we will take all of the beautiful things out of the museums, rebuild Babylon, rebuild Egypt, and spend a week in Egypt living the way the people lived. We will call our dwelling rental service, tell them what we want, and it will be ready for us when we arrive."

- Cite THE FUTURE OF THE FAMILY, undated, p. 8

---

### Private Enterprise:

See Capitalism
    Corporation
    Enterprise
    Free Enterprise

---

### Private Property:

See Capitalism
    False Property Illusion
    Obsolete: Inventory of Obsolete Concepts
    Possession
    Mine: That's Mine
    Property
    Real Estate Development
    Tollgate: Private Tollgate
    Yesterday's Private Castle Mentality

---

RBF DEFINITIONS

### Private Property:

"Property Rights will stop because they are simply

nonexistent!"

- Cite RBF to SIMS Seminar, U. Mass., Amherst, 22 July 1971.

---

### Prize:

See Enterprise, 1968

---

RBF DEFINITIONS

### Private Property:

"Look for the obsolescence of Acquisitions and Possessions. Ownership will become progressively onerous, because it imposes undesirable local restraints and frustrates realization of world citizenship which is progressively accommodated by the service industries' ever higher performing rentable facilities."

- Cite Dreyfuss Preface, "Decease of Meaning."
    28 April 1971, p. 15

---

RBF DEFINITIONS

### Probability:

"Probability is mathematically proven and useful but, as its name states, it is far from incisive prediction. It is a tool but a weak tool. If you want to cross the Atlantic to a given port, probability per se won't you there. It can only say that your chances of getting there are such and such a bet-- as ███████████ '48 to 1'. Probability says any easterly direction is more favorable than a westerly, but a westerly could probably get you there. But probability would not tell you anything useful about the rocks or continents that might intervene. 'There will probably be rocks and continents in your way.' Probability could not get you to a given port. Navigation can do so. Navigation is discrete and is a powerful tool."

- Cite RBF Ltr. to James Coney, Sep'73

# Synergetics Dictionary

RBF DEFINITIONS

Probability: (1)

"Nature's probability is not linear nor planar, but the mathematical models with which it is treated today are almost exclusively linear. Real Universe probability accomodates the omnidirectional interaccommodative transformating transactions of universal events which humanity identifies superficially as environment. Probability articulates locally in Universe in response to the organically integral generalized omnidirectional in, out, inside-out, outside-in, and around events of the self system as well as with the self system's extra-organic travel and externally imposed processing around and amongst the inwardly and outwardly contiguous forces of the considered system as imposed ███ by both its synchronously and ██████████ contiguously critically near macrocosmic and microcosmic neighbors.

"Real Universe's probability laws of spherically propagative whole systems' developments are intimately conditioned by the three-way great-circle grids inherently embracing and defining the nonredundant structuring of all systems as formingly generated by critical proximity interferences of the system's components' behaviors and their dynamical self-"

- Cite SYNERGETICS draft at Secs. 538.01 + 02, 26 May'72

RBF DEFINITIONS

Probability:

"Probability is not linear nor planar, but it is following the laws of sphericity of whole systems. It ties up with the three-way grid and with the constant relative abundance of points, areas and lines as disclosed by synergetics."

- Cite RBF to EJA + BO'R, 3200 Idaho, DC, 17 Feb '72
  (For expanded context see Three-Way Great Circling: Three-Way Grid, 17 Feb '72.)

RBF DEFINTTIONS

Probability: (2)

"triangulations into unique system structuring symmetries whose configurations are characterized by the relative abundance patterning laws of topological crossing points, areas, and lines of any considered system as generally disclosed by the closed system hierarchy of synergetics.

"Synergetics, by relating energy and topology to the tetrahedron, and to systems, as defined by its synergetic hierarchy, replaces randomness with a rational hierarchy of omni-intertransformative phase identifications and quantized rates of relative intertransformations."

- Cite SYNERGETICS draft at Secs. 538.02 + 03, 26 May '72

RBF DEFINITIONS

Probability:

"Probability doesn't know anything about shapes. It's just number, purely mathematical."

- Cite RBF to EJA and BO'R, 3200 Idaho, Wash DC, 17 Feb'72

RBF DEFINITIONS

Probability:

"Nature's probability is not linear nor planar as it is almost exclusively employed today. Probability accommodates the omnidirectional conditions of the universal environment of events and articulates, in response the the generalized omnidirectional in, out, and around-the-self system, and of the self-system around and amongst the inwardly and outwardly contiguous forces imposed upon the considered system by both its macrocosmic and microcosmic neighbors.

"Probability's laws of spherically propagative whole systems' developments are intimately conditioned by the three-way great-circle grids inherently embracing and defining all systems as formingly generated by critical proximity interferences of the system's components' behaviors and their dynamical self-triangulations into unique system structuring symmetries whose configurations are characterized by the relative abundance patterning laws of topological crossing points, areas, and lines of any considered system as generally disclosed by the closed system hierarchy of synergetics."

- Cite RBF 20 Feb re-write of 17 Feb citation, 20 Feb'72

PROBABILITY— SEC. 538.01 + 02

RBF DEFINITIONS

Probability:

"Probability is purely mathematics: just points on curves. But they are though of as linear. Or planar. What I call planilinear. Gibbs, in his phase rule ties up the probability with chemistry. His phase rule and topology are the same. But still all the different chemistries and topologies seem to be random. But synergetics, by relating energy and topology to the tetrahedron, and to systems as defined, and by its synergetic hierarchy, replaces randomness with a rational hierarchy."

- Cite RBF to EJA, 3200 Idaho, DC, 17 Feb '72

LAST SENTENCE—
PROBABILITY— SEC. 538.03

RBF DEFINITIONS

Probability:

"The specialized mathematical probability art and its developed tables is exclusively linear and is exclusively preoccupied with amorphous, planar graphable, and linearly plottable rate of covariant change calculus. Specialized probability disregards reality shapes and considers itself to be concerned with pure number abstractions."

- Cite RBF 19 Feb re-write of Probability, 17 Feb '72

RBF DEFINITIONS

Probability:

"Statistical Probability is a very crude tool-- like using a hammer for a screw driver."

- Cite RBF to EJA, Beverly Hotel, New York 15 Sept. '71.

RBF DEFINITIONS

Probability:

"All the scientific talk of probabilities is asinine.
There is no probability about mass attraction.  They all
want primordial soup, out of which improbable selection
would begin.  But the LAWS were always there."

- Cite RBF to EJA, Royal Scots Grill, N.Y. 14 Sept. 1971.

---

RBF DEFINITIONS

Probability:

"Probability, the strongest tool of statistics
which deals only with parts, at its best is a weak tool.

"Were probability strong it would predict stock-
market behavior with precision and would foretell horse
race results with reliability.  Contrariwise, synergy
and general systems theory are powerful forecasting tools
and have been the backbone of modern physics, astronomy,
and chemistry."

- Cite DOXIADIS, p. 314, 20 Jun'66

---

RBF DEFINITIONS

Probability:

"Probability is anything but comprehensively anticipatory:
if it had any force there would not be a stock market or
a horse race."

- Cite RBF to EJA, Somerset Club, Boston, 22 April 1971

- Citation & context at Happening, 22 Apr'71

SYNERGETICS. SEC. 503

---

RBF DEFINITIONS

Probability:

"It is discovered in principle that probability probing
of physical Universe on a statistical basis is now becoming
of necessity frustrated while, probing in empty conceptual
principle could be instituted and accelerated for further
advancement or fundamental information.  Exploration in
principle is re-rewarding."

- Citation and context at Reciprocity (2) + (3), May'49

---

RBF DEFINITIONS

Probability:

"You don't program 'happen.'

Probability is anything but comprehensive.

And we find that 'happenings' contradict probability.

- Cite RBF to EJA
  Carbondale
  2 April 1971

SYNERGETICS, SEC.503.

---

Probability Laws:

See Probability, (1)

---

RBF DEFINITIONS

Probability:

"Society has been trained to think only statistically and
probability is the most powerful phase of statistics.  But
probability is a weak tool.  If it were strong the stock
exchanges and gambling houses would have to close their doors.
. . . But nature does use synergy."

- Cite RBF marginalia on Old Chap. 2, "Synergy," 18 Mar'69

---

RBF DEFINITIONS

Probability Model of Three Cars On a Highway:                    (1)

"I am tying up the social experience, often observed, in which
three independently and consistently velocitied automobiles
(and only three) come into close proximity on the highway-- often
with no other cars in sight.  Mathematically speaking, three
points-- and only three-- define both a plane and a triangle.
The cars make a triangle; and because it is mathematically
discovered that the total number of points, or areas, or lines
of a system are always even numbers; and that this
divisibility by two accommodates polar-and-hemispherical
positive-negativeness of all systems; because the defining of
one small triangle on the surface of a system always inadvertently defines a large triangle representing the remainder of the
whole system's surface, and this large triangle's corners will
always be more than 180-degrees each; ergo, the triangle is an
'inside-out,' i.e., negative triangle, and to convert it to
positive condition requires halving or otherwise fractionating
each of its three corners by great circle lines running together
somewhere within the great negative triangle;  thus there develops
a minimum of four positive triangles embracing the Earth induced by such three-car convergences."

- Cite SYNERGETICS draft at Sec. 538.11, 26 Sep'73

RBF DEFINITIONS

### Probability Model of Three Cars on a Highway: (2)

"The triangle made by the three cars is a complementarity of the three other spherical triangles on the Earth's surface. The triangle formed by the two cars going one way, and one the other way, gets smaller and smaller and then reverses itself, getting ever larger. There is always a closer proximity between two of the three. This is all governed by topological "pattern integrity." Probability is exclusively abstract mathematics: theoretically calculated points on curves. The statisticians think almost exclusively in lines or planes; they are what I call planilinear. Willard Gibbs in evolving his phase rule was engaged in probability relating to chemistry when he inadvertently and intuitively conceived of his phase rule for explaining the number of energetic freedoms necessary to introduce into a system complexedly constituted of crystals, liquids, and gases, in order to unlock them into a common state of liquidity. His discovered phase rule and topology are the same: they are both synergetic. Despite the synergetic work of such pioneers as Euler and Gibbs, all the different chemistries and topologies still seem to be random. But synergetics, by relating energy and topology to the tetrahedron, and to systems as defined, and by its synergetic hierarchy, replaces"

- Cite SYNERGETICS draft at Sec. 538.12, 26 Sep'73

---

RBF DEFINITIONS

### Probability Model of Three Cars on a Highway: (3)

"randomness with a rational, cosmic, shape-and-structural-system hierarchy. This hierarchy discloses a constant relative abundance of the constituents; i.e., for every nonpolar point there are always two faces and three edges. But systems occur only as defined by four points. Prime structural systems are inherently tetrahedral, as is also the quantum.

"A social experience of three cars: they make a triangle changing from scalene to equilateral to scalene. The triangles are where the cars don't hit. (These are simply the windows.) But you can't draw less than four triangles. The complementarity of the three triangles makes the spherical tetrahedron-- which makes the three-way grid. The little spherical triangle window is visible to human observers in greatest magnitude of human observability and awareness of such three-car triangles at 15 miles distance, which is 15 minutes of the spherical arc of our Earth. Such dynamically defined Earth triangulation is not a static grid because the lines do not go through the same point at the same time; lines-- which are always action trajectories-- never do. All we have is patterning integrity of critical proximities. There is always a nonviolated intervening boundary condition. This is all that nature ever has."

- Cite SYNERGETICS draft at Sec. 538.13, 26 Sep'73

---

RBF DEFINITIONS

### Probability Model of Three Cars on a Highway: (4)

"Nature modulates _probability_ and the degrees of freedom, i.e., frequency and angle, leads to the tensegrity sphere; which leads to the pneumatic bag; all of which are the same kind of reality as the three automobiles. All the cosmic triangling of all variety of angles always averages out to 60 degrees. That is the probability of all closed systems of which the Universe is the amorphous largest case. Probability is not linear or planar, but is always following the laws of sphericity or whole systems. Probability is always dependent on critical proximity, omnidirectional, and only dynamically defined, three-way gridding pattern integrity, and with the concomitant topologically constant relative abundance of points, areas, and lines, all governed in an orderly way by low-order, prime-number, behavioral uniqueness as disclosed by synergetics."

- Cite SYNERGETICS draft at Sec. 538.14, 26 Sep'73

---

RBF DEFINITIONS

### Probability Model of Three Cars on a Highway:
~~Social Highway Experience: Three Autos:~~

"I am tying up the social experience of three cars meeting on the highway. They make a triangle which is a complementarity of the three other spherical triangles on the Earth's surface. The triangles get narrower and narrower and then reverse themselves. There is a proximity between two of the three. We have topology as a pattern integrity. . . Probability is pure mathematics, just points on curves. . . A social experience of three cars. They make a triangle changing from scalene to equilateral to scalene. The triangles are where the cars don't hit. (These are simply the windows.) But, you can't draw less than four triangles. The complementary of the three triangles makes the spherical tetrahedron-- which makes the three-way grid. . . "

- Cite RBF to EJA, 3200 Idaho, DC, 17 Feb '72

---

RBF DEFINITIONS

### Probability Model of Three Cars on a Highway:
~~Social Highway Experience: Three Autos:~~

"In the early days of the auto on a lonely road-- when you saw another car coming-- there was always a third coming into view or already in view. Three cars frequently come to approximately the same highway point at approximately the same time. This is not surprising because when we, having first taken away the two points from the system to accommodate the axis of the observer, and you always have the topologically constant relative abundance of interference crossings, areas, and lines. Edges are lines. The guided car paths are in reality lines, traces, with universal three-foldness of energy event trajectory vectors. Universe keeps sorting its event traces into bundles of three. The social highway experience of three cars is the inexorably present, tri-complementarity relationship of the little local triangle on the Earth's surface complemented by the three other great circle triangles of the terrestrial spherical tetrahedron always inevitably produced in all systems formulations and transformings law. Critical proximity imposes triangulation."

(For preamble to above see immediately preceding statement: Polar Vertexes, cited to 17 Feb '72.)

- Cite RBF 19 Feb re-write of same caption 17 Feb.

---

### Probability Model of Three Cars on a Highway: (1)

See Social Highway Experience: Three Autos
    Spherical Triangle Sequence

---

### Probability Model of Three Cars on a Highway: (2)

See Sphericity of Whole Systems, 26 Sep'73
    Three-way Great Circling: Three-way Grid, 17 Feb'72

---

### Probability: (1)

See Happening
    Navigation vs. Probability
    Possible into Probable
    Randomness
    Nature Modulates Probability
    Discrete vs. Probability

Probability: (2)

See Direction, 1938
Life, 16 Aug'50
Reciprocity (2)(3)*
Three-way Great Circling: Three-way Grid, 17 Feb'72*
Threshold of Life, 6 Jul'62
Omnidirectional Typewriter (1)
Equimagnitude Phases, 19 Dec'73
Synergy, 26 May'72
Means, 22 Jun'75
General Systems Theory, (B)
Modules: A & B Quanta Modules, 20 Dec'73

---

RBF DEFINITIONS

Problem:

"Problems are metaphysical entropy. Humans are here to function syntropically as solvers of problems as guided by mind-discovered cosmic principles."

- Citation and context at <u>Man as Local Problem Solver</u> (1), Dec'72

---

RBF DEFINITIONS

Problem:

"Our problems are almost exclusively metaphysical and can only be coped with by scientific competence and intellectual integrity on the part of the discovering humans."

- Citation & context at <u>Gravity</u> (k), 12 Jun'74

---

RBF DEFINITIONS

Problem:

"Being between: That's what humans always are. That's where the problems start."

- Citation at <u>Between</u>: <u>VE as Prime Between-ness Model</u>, 7 Nov'72

---

RBF DEFINITIONS

Problems:

"Our fundamental proclivity is to keep intercepting problems. Nothing could be more fallacial than the notion that a normal life is one without problems. Even all human games are ways of initiating disorder to be parried by converting the disorder to order."

- Cite RBF address to Yale Political Union, New Haven, 9 Dec'73; as rewritten by RBF at 3200 Idaho, Wash DC, 13 Dec'73

---

RBF DEFINITIONS

Problems:

"Inevitable, important local <u>problems</u> develop in maintaining the comprehensive integrity of the omni-regenerative universal design. I think it probable that humans are designed to . . . be aboard planet Earth as the complex local <u>problem</u> processor. . . Certainly, each of our own lives manifest just such experiencing of 'problems, problems, problems.' I have worked very hard on problems and I find that for every problem I solve I induce twelve more problems or challenges. You can look at problems as unattractive or attractive, but the problem is that we are faced with problems. Nothing can be more descriptive of life than a sequence of problems. We are beautiful problem analyzing, differentiating and sorting faculties. All that goes on in this room between you and me is absolutely weightless. We are sorting out our experiences."

- Cite Museums Keynote Address Denver, pp. 13-14 from transcript as rewritten by RBF. 2 Jun'71

---

RBF DEFINITIONS

Problems:

"Our fundamental proclivity is to keep intercepting problems. Nothing could be more wrong than the notion that a normal life is one without problems."

- Cite RBF address to Yale Political Union, New Haven, 9 Dec'73

---

RBF DEFINITIONS

Problem:

". . . The regeneration of the Universe probably depends on these local monitors of very high capability to solve very complex <u>problems</u>. Certainly our lives manifest just problems, problems, problems. Nothing can be more descriptive of life than problems." But we have a beautiful sorting capability."

- Cite RBF address Am. Assn. of Museums, Denver, 2 June 1971.

# Synergetics Dictionary

RBF DEFINITIONS

Problem Solving:

"... An intellectual integrity of Universe evokes its own theoretical evolvement of a Universe of ever-multiplying problems and pure principles solutions and eternal regeneration of multiplying problem solving."

- Cite RBF marginalia, 20 Dec, '71 at SYNERGETICS Draft, Sec. 529.07

---

RBF DEFINITIONS

Problem:  Statement of the Problem:

"Our problem is really one of information. We're in this condition where we have to get the information out to all humanity, which in the past was content with following a leader. Some time ago I made the discovery that if I can communicate something to somebody else, write it, put it into print, it goes out of me and I can look at it to be sure I'm not kidding myself. And then suddenly you make the discovery that if you state the problem correctly, the problem is solved. I simply happened to get to that realization a little earlier than others due to my comprehensive training and my thoroughness and the inspiration of knowing that if I could communicate these possibilities, humanity really might make it. I've had a deep feeling about this all along, and it's a very critical matter. Without that information that we need, we do risk a runaway of ignorance, and that's where the great peril lies."

- Cite RBF tape transcript for Barry Farrel Playboy Interview, Feb '72. Above passage deleted. See draft p. 61.

---

Problem Solving:                                        (1)

See General Systems Theory
    Local Problem Solver
    Man as a Function in Universe
    Man as Local Problem Solver
    Man as Local Universe Technology
    Starting with Universe
    Mistakes
    Trial and Error
    Synergetic Advantage: Principle Of

---

RBF DEFINITIONS

Problem:  Statement of the Problem:

"Other men's consciously articulated awareness of the problem, its existence, and the sequitor conclusion that inherent in its comprehensive statement that once properly stated it could even then only by teleologically solved through competent design, and not by political reform, for not until the comprehensive-competent-teleologic designer formulates and calculates the total involvement, differentiation and subsequent integration, and initiates the wheel-starting essential tasks do the minimum physical constituents of the 'reform' exist. Ergo, political reform is only and always accessory after the fact. And the concepts of the ultimate products consequent to our synergetically conceived designing, were all alike nonexistent prior to out personally-unique-experience-pattern induced abstract apprehension, and subsequent systematic design conception of them, and our production of their component subsystem items and their testing and assembly."

- RBF draft Ltr. to Jim (Fitzgibbon?), Raleigh, NC, 1954-59

---

Problem Solving:                                        (2)

See Artifacts, 10 Aug'70; 17 Sep'74
    Dreams, 10 Aug'70
    Individual Universes, (2)
    Manifests: Eight, 1973
    Omnidirectional Typewriter, (1)
    Questions: Answering Questions, Sep'73
    Rationalization Sequence, (4)
    Twelve Universal Degrees of Freedom: General
        Systems, (II)
    Geometry, 14 Nov'73
    Part, May'72
    Performance; Equation Of, 1938
    Electronic Referendum, 9 Jan'75
    Humane City, (3)
    Nucleus, 13 Nov'75
    Nature in a Corner, 12 Nov'75
    Dymaxion Artifacts, (2)
    Children as Only Pure Scientists, (A)
    Child, 1 May'77
    Load Distribution, 17 Oct'77

---

Problem:  Statement of the Problem:                     (1)

See Question Asking

---

RBF DEFINITIONS

Problem:  Statement of the Problem:

"It is my philosophy that a properly stated problem is a problem solved. The adequate statement must contain an inventory of all the resources available and all the variable parameters uniquely involved. The solutions are inherent in such adequacy of statement."

- Cite SET "Y", p. 14, Aug'72

---

Problem:  Statement of the Problem:                     (2)

See Dreams, 10 Aug'70
    Formulation, 1963
    Sunclipse, 1968
    General Systems Theory, (2)

RBF DEFINITIONS

Problems: Ten World-Around Problems That Have to Be Solved
By Bloodless Design Science Revolution:

"(1) Education Revolution, The Highest Priority Of All;
(2) Conversion of World Accounting System;
(3) Elimination of Property By Making Ownership Onerous;
(4) World Democracy By Electronic Referendum;
(5) Elimination Of All World Sovereignties;
(6) Theoretical Exploration Through World Game;
(7) Realization Of Design Science Competence;
(8) Recognition of Humanity's Unique Functioning in Universe;
(9) Identification of Mathematical Coordinate System of Universe;
(10) Philosophical Realization That Physical Is Not Life.

- Cite WORLD-AROUND PROBLEMS THAT HAVE TO BE SOLVED BY BLOODLESS
DESIGN SCIENCE REVOLUTION, NY Times, 29 Jun'72

---

TEXT CITATIONS

Problems:

World-Around Problems that Have to be Solved by
Bloodless Design Science Revolution, 29 June 1972

---

Problem: Problems:                                                    (1)

See Finite Solutions
Social Problems:  Tetrahedral Coordination Of

---

Problem: Problems:                                                    (2)

See Between:  VE as Prime Between-ness Model, 7 Nov'72*
Consciousness, 12 Sep'71
Electronic Referendum, 29 Jun'72
Eternal Slowdown (2)
Fuller, R.B:  Crisi of 1927 (a)
Gravity (k)*
Individual Universes, (1)(2)
Mutual Survival Principles, (1)

---

RBF DEFINITIONS

Process Relationships:

"The transition of initial awareness of sensorially experienced
physical forms and process relationships through their
progressively

ephemeral → diaphanous → etheral →

brain-to-mind → physical-to-metaphysical →

idea trending toward and attaining absolutely weightless
conceptual integrity of interangular proportionality...

a triangle."

- Citation & context at Triangle, (1), 28 Jan'69

---

Process Relationships:

See Connections & Relatedness
Relationship Analysis

---

RBF DEFINITIONS

Process vs. Thing:

"Everybody is a process and not a thing."

- Citation at Everybody, 3 Oct'71

---

Process vs. Thing:                                                   (1)

See Behaviorist Word vs. Static Word
Eventing

Process vs. Thing:             (2)

      See Individual Universes, (2)
         Critical Proximity, Jun'71
         Environment, 12 May'77

---

TEXT CITATIONS

    Proclivities: Differentiated vs. Synergetic:

    Synergetics, 2nd. Ed. - Sec. 201.10

---

Process:             (1)

      See Pattern Processing Machines
         Process vs. Thing
         Process Relationships
         Automation of Metabolic & Regenerative Processes
         Urban Processes: Inventory Of
         Metabolic Process

---

Proclivities: Differentiated vs. Synergetic:

      See Absolute Network, 10 Nov'74

---

Process:             (2)

      See Bird's Nest as a Tool, May'67; (A)(C)
         Everybody, 3 Oct'71
         Universe, 1944
         Man as an Invention, 1 Apr'49
         Geometry, 21 Jan'75
         New York, 1970

---

TEXT CITATIONS

    Proclivities, Phases & Disciplines: Inventory Of:

    Synergetics, 2nd. Ed. : Sec. 201.10

---

Proclivities: Basic vs. Secondary:

    See Anger, (1)-(3)
       Human Tolerance Limits, (A)-(D)

---

TEXT CITATIONS

    Proclivities: Inventory Of:

    Synergetics - Sec. 1007.15

    Synergetics - Sec. 905.16

           - Sec. 201.10

Proclivities: Inventory Of: (1)

See Absolute Network
Behavioral Phases
Behavior Potential
Energetic Functions
Motion Freedoms & Degrees of Freedom
Structural Functions

---

Procreation:

"If you think about it, it's probably a very difficult
design problem to get an organism to want to procreate.
Go to the mirror and stick your tongue way out and have
a good look at it. If you didn't have one of those and
a salesman came to your door and said, 'I'd like to sell
you one of these things. You stick it in your mouth and
it does you a lot of good,' I doubt that you'd be very
likely to buy that tongue. If you were to take a look
at your guts, your kidneys, and then had to go to a
supermarket and buy a kit to make a baby, I don't think
you could put it together at all. If each of us could
see all the organic equipment required to regenerate
this extraordinary walking coral reef thatwe really are,
I don't think anybody would procreate.

"So in order to be able to get us to procreate, nature
gave us a beautiful covering which sort of simplifies,
at least, all the frightening colors and coils and such.
We have a simplified skin stretched over us, and nature
has done a whole lot of tricks, trying to make this thing
attractive enough so that procreation will actually occur."

- Cite Barry Farrell PLAYBOY Interview, ███ Transcript, 30 Oct'71

---

Proclivities: Inventory Of: (2)

See Avogadro, Jun'66
Chemical Bonds, May'72
Compound, 13 Mar'73
Cosmic Discontinuity & Local Continuity, 15 Jan'74
Einstein: RBF Draft Letter To, (2)
Epistemology of Quantum Mechanics, 16 Dec'73
Field of Cosmic Formabilities, 28 Jan'73
Functions, 26 May'72
Isotropic Vector Matrix, Jul'61
Planck's Constant, (B)
Radiation, 20 Jun'66
Structure, 16 Dec'73
Vector Equilibrium, (2); Feb'48; 13 Nov'69
Wealth, 28 Jan'75

---

Procreatively Sterile: (1)

See Masturbation

---

Proclivity: Proclivities: (1)

See Computer: Atomic-proclivity Computer
Differentiated Proclivities
Energy Proclivity Model
Fall-in Proclivity
Functions
In-ness Proclivity
Phase
Proclivities: Inventory Of
Proclivities, Phases & Disciplines: Inventory Of
Synergetic Proclivity

---

Procreatively Sterile: (2)

See Abstraction, 24 Feb'72
Parallel: Quasi-parallel Lines, 1938

---

Proclivity: Proclivities: (2)

See Functions, 26 May'72
Valving, 13 May'73
Vector Equilibrium, 15 May'73
Invented Periodicities, May'49
Life & Death, (1)(2)
Man: Interstellar Transmission of Man, (A)
Cube & VE as Wave Propagation Model, 23 Feb'72
Psychiatry, (3)

---

Procreation: (1)

See Adam & Eve
Automation of Metabolic & Regenerative Processes
Baby Button
Life's Original Event
Longing: Fear & Longing
Man: Automated Metabolism of Man
Naked Girl on the Bed
Gestation
Sex
Survival Sequence: Love

Procreation: (2)

See Artifacts, 28 Apr'74
Beautiful, 1938
Divide & Conquer Sequence, (2)
Promote: I Don't Promote, 2 Jun'74
Short Cuts, 9 May'57
Tactile Sequence, (2)(3)
Wealth as "Know-how", (2)
Love, 1 Feb'75
Helpless: Humans Born Helpless, 15 May'75
Mistake, 9 Nov'75

---

RBF DEFINITIONS

Profess: Profession:

"By my own rules I may not profess any special

preoccupation or capability. I am a random element."

- Cite EDUCATION AUTOMATION, p.4 ▇ 22 Apr'61

---

Production: (1)

See Economic Accounting System: Human Life-hour
Production
Nonproduction

---

RBF DEFINITIONS

Profession: Professional:

""... I am neither a neurosurgeon nor a professional

of any discipline. . ."

- Cite BRAIN AND MIND, first verse, ▇ 1970

---

Production: (2)

See Human Events, Feb'71
Irreversible, 6 Nov'73

---

RBF DEFINITIONS

Professors:

"You can forget the Universe and, like the other

professors, you can become completely unnatural masters

and doctors of theoretical myopias."

- Cite NASA Speech, p. 97. Jun'66

---

Profanity:

See Spit-punctuated Monosyllabic Verbalism

---

Professable: Profession: (1)

See Tenure: Academic Tenure
Slave Professions: Slave Disciplines

RBF DEFINITIONS

Professable:  Profession:                          (2)

    See Artist, 1968
        Invention, 9 Feb'64
        Prototype, 13 Mar'73
        World Game, 12 Jun'69
        Word Trends, May'44
        Verb:  I Seem to Be A Verb, 26 Apr'77

---

Profile of Industrial Revolution:

    See Industrial Revolution:  Profile Of

---

RBF DEFINITIONS

    Profile:  There Is No Half-Profile:

    "There is no half-profile of you.  All conceptuality is
systemic; it has to be finitely closed."

    - Citation and context at Conceptuality, 5 Nov'73

---

RBF DEFINITIONS

    Profit:

    "Profit is just taking the input from the many for the
advantage of the few."

    - Citation & context at Industrialization, (A), 22 Jan'75

---

Profile:  There is No Half-profile:                (1)

    See Facial Asymmetry
        Picasso Duo-face Picture
        Split Personality

---

Profit:  Annual Profit & Failure System:

    See Economic Accounting System:  Human Life-hour
        Production, (1)

---

Profile:  There is No Half-profile:                (2)

    See Conceptuality, 5 Nov'73*
        Design, 23 Jan'72

---

RBF DEFINITIONS

    Profit:  Man-Invented Game of Quick Profit:

    "Most of man's technology is of meager endurance being
comprised at the outset of destructive invention, such as
that of weaponry, or for something in support of the quick
profit, man invented game of selfishly manipulative game-
playing and rule inventing for the playing of his only
ignorantly-preoccupying value system."

    - Citation and context at Technology, 13 Mar'73

Profit: "We Stars Have Got to Make a Profit":

    See Afford, 29 Jun'72

---

Profit: Profitability:  (1)

    See Afford
        Capitalism
        Deficit Accounting
        Economic Accounting System
        Expense: Without Any Individual Profiting at the
         Expense of Another
        Feeding Lots
        Money-bee Humans
        Status Quo
        Money: Making sense vs. Making Money

---

Profit: Profitability:  (2)

    See Immorality, 22 Aug'70
        Pollution, 1968
        Industrialization, (A)
        Humane City, (10
        Doing What Needs to Be Done, (1)
        Building Industry, (3)(4)

---

RBF DEFINITIONS

Prognostication About Future of Man:

"I don't think we tend to accredit at all the fact that we might go on to have some other form of living in Universe."

 

- For citation and context see Automation of Metabolic and Regenerative Processes, May '65

---

Prognostications About Future of Man:  (1A)

    See Age of Cybernetics
        Destiny of Humanity
        Evolution: Subconscious Coordinate Functioning
        Extraterrestrial Humans
        Future of Synergetics
        Historical Event Cognition
        New Universe: Disclosure of in Next Decade
        Optimism: Reverse Optimism
        POint of No Return
        Prospect for Humanity
        Stillbirth of Humanity
        Suicide of Humanity
        Survival
        Survival Sequence: Love
        Surprise: The Nonpolitical Surprise Has Already
         Occurred
        Tomorrow
        Womb Population
        Year 2000
        Transnationalism vs. Colonialism

---

Prognostications About Future of Man:  (1B)

    See Humanity's Final Cosmic Exam
        Progress
        Enough to Go Around
        Fuller, R.B: Ecological Predictions of 1927
        Race with Evolution

---

Prognostications About Future Of Man:  (2)

    See Automation of Metabolic & Regenerative Processes,
        May'65*
        Child: A Little Child Shall Lead Them, May'65
        Communications, 1967
        Computer, (B)(C)
        Earning A Living Sequence, (3)
        Economic Accounting System, Sep'72
        Environment, 15 Feb'66
        Gross World Product Sequence, (3)(4)
        Isotropic Vector Matrix, 6 Nov'72
        Naivete, Mar'66
        Newspaper, 16 Oct'72
        Population Sequence, (1)-(8)
        Scrap Sorting & Mongering, (2)
        Spacehip, (2)
        Success, May'70
        Synergetics, 6 Nov'72
        News & Evolution, (3)(4)
        Enough to Go Around, (1)(2)
        Options, 13 May'77
        Womb of Permitted Ignorance, (2)

---

Prognostication:  (1)

    See Prediction
        Synergetic Advantage: Principle Of

Prognostication: (2)

See Parts, 1954

---

Program: Programming: (1)

See Computer Programming
Design Programming
Linear Programming
Critical Proximity Programming
Chromosomic Programming
Electromagnetic-photosynthetic Programming

---

RBF DEFINITIONS

Program:

"You can program in any of the parts, but you cannot
program what's between and not."

- Cite RBF at Students International Meditation Seminar,
U. Mass., Amherst, 22 July '71, p. 1]

- Citation & context at Mechanical Mind, 22 Jul'71

---

Program: Programming: (2)

See Ecology, 29 Dec'73
Ecology Sequence, (C)-(I)
General Systems Theory, (1); (B)
Human Beings & Complex Universe, (4)(5)
Hunger, 16 Feb'73
No Mechanical Mind, 22 Jul'71*
Orbital Escape from Critical Proximity, (1)
Probability, 2 Apr'71*

---

RBF DEFINITIONS

Program:

"You don't program 'happen'.

. . . and we find that 'happenings' contradict probability."

- Cite RBF to EJA
Carbondale
2 April 1971
- Citation at Probability, 2 Apr'71

---

Progress: (1)

See Improve the Scenario
Prospect for Humanity

---

RBF DEFINITIONS

Program:

"You can't program what it is you're looking for--
because they are the connections--
and not the things.
The only thing you can program
is the dismissal of irrelevancies."

- Cite RBF to EJA
Carbondale
2 April 1971

---

Progress: (2)

See Belief, 6 Jul'75

RBF DEFINITIONS

Progressions:

"In addition to the simple arithmetic, algebraic, and geometrical progressions of the first, second, and third degrees of acceleration, mathematics discloses other series, and superseries, of superficially unpredictable mathematical frequencies because they are composed of complementary and reciprocal numbers whose products alone, though never occurring simultaneously or in whole, are compositely congruent with complex progressions.

"But these complex components occur in discontinuous series, and are inherently self-inexplicable. The complementary functions must therefore impinge upon consciousness only as meaningless. As immediately contemplated upon first experience, they of necessity, alone, constitute seemingly absolute perversity of interference. Synergy-- wholistic behavior unpredicted by parts."

- Citation & context at Periodic Experience, (4)(5), May'49

RBF DEFINITIONS

Progressions:

"... All progressions are from material to abstract..."

- Citation and context at 'Ephemeralization,' p.256 '38
  NINE CHAINS TO THE MOON

Progressive Invention of Universe:

See Sensorial Identification of Reality, (2)

Progressive Order: Law Of:

See Conservation of Finite Universe: Principle Of,
20 Jun'66

Progressive Reduction of Residual Error:

See Exactitude, May'72
General Systems Theory, (B)

Progression & Regression:

See Radiation-gravitation: Harmonics, 3 Jan'75

Progressions:                                                    (1)

See Dimensions
    Hierarchies
    Manifests
    Synergy: Degrees Of
    Trends: Trending
    Powering
    Idea Trending
    Physical to Metaphysical
    Truth as Progressive Diminution of Residual Error

Progression: Progressive:                                        (2)

See Life, May'49
    Quantum Mechanics: Grand Strategy, 10 Apr'75
    Tunability: Intra & Ultra, 1954

Prohibitions:

    See Society: Control Of, 1938

---

RBF DEFINITIONS

### Projective Transformation: (III)

"I use three fundamental reference lines instead of two. When only two lines cross, infinity is involved since one or two lines are open-ended and have no finitely contained areas. If three lines overlap one another they make a triangle. Thus, a finite area is inherently contained. I do not have to break open the data transferred from the sphere to the plane by triangles.

"There is, however, what we call spherical excess in the topological transformation of the spherical data to the flat surface. Spherical excess is the only source of distortion. . . Spherical excess refers to the amount by which the sum of the spherical triangle's angles exceed 180°. Spherical excess for a large spherical triangle is very much larger than for a small spherical triangle. For instance, on a spherical tetrahedron each of the angles is 120 degrees, so that the total of the three angles of each of the spherical tetrahedron's four triangles is 360 degrees, 360 degrees minus 180 degrees leaves an excess of 180 degrees. In a spherical octahedron obtained by bisecting the edges of a spherical tetrahedron and interconnecting the three great circles, each of them angles will be 90 degrees, or

    - Cite RBF, Univ. of Rhode Island, 26 Aug. '66, p . 197.

---

RBF DEFINITIONS

### Projective Transformation:

RBF does not like above terminology. Approved designation is "Triangular Geodesics Transformational Projection."

    - Cite RBF to EJA, 200 Locust, Phila., 22 Jan'73

---

RBF DEFINITIONS

### Projective Transformation: (IV)

"a spherical triangle total of 270 degrees, which means an excess of 90 degrees. If the edges are bisected again each of the corners will be 72° 32' with a total of 221°36' so the spherical excess of 221° 36' minus180° is equal to 40° 36' and is being reduced very rapidly. Smaller and smaller spherical triangles give less and less spherical excess. Therefore, I subtriangulate the total of the Earth's surface in the largest number of identical equi-edged small triangles, i.e., the spherical icosahedron, where the spherical excess is a minimal 36°. . . ."

"I have found that if I wanted to take off the total world's data in the largest number of identical triangles and have them symmetrical, the triangles have to be equilaterals. The maximum number of equilateral triangles into which we can subdivide a spherical unity is twenty: a spherical icosahedron." You might ask,"Why can't you have more triangles than twenty?" To explain, I shall first take two triangles and put them together. We see that they hinge and just come to be congruent one to the other."

    - Cite RBF, Univ. of Rhode Island, 26 Aug. '66, p. 197.

---

RBF DEFINITIONS

### Projective Transformation: (I)

"One of the things I've always wanted to be able to do was to see the whole Earth at once with minimum distortion and maximum effectiveness. That brought me to a method of translating spherical data to a flat surface, which was a direct extrapolation of my mathematical investigations. . . Making a world map took me into the high stratosphere of polyhedra. . . If we put information on a sphere, the maximum that can be read is about one-quarter of the sphere. The tangential information cannot be read. Since our real objective is to be able to read all the information of the total sphere, the whole Earth, then possibly a bigger globe would give more data. But if a bigger globe will do, then why not go to the maximum condition and use the Earth itself? Actually, the bigger the globe, the smaller the reader is in relation to it and the greater the reduction in the material that can be read. There are certain optimal distances of readability. . . Rather empirically, a 12- to 16-inch globe held at arm's length is about the best that can be read from a sphere per se."

    - Cite RBF, Univ. of Rhode Island, 26 Aug, '66, pp. 195-196.

---

RBF DEFINITIONS

### Projective Transformation: (V)

"A two triangle system has neither insideness nor outsideness. I want to make a system which subdivides Universe into all the Universe inside the system and all the Universe outside the system. Now, I can take three triangles and I can put them together around one vertex and make the tetrahedron. A round each vertex there are always" a mnimum of "three triangles. I can insert a fourth triangle around each vertex and get the octahedron. I can next put a fifth triangle around each vertex and get the icosahedron. In this closed system there are 12 vertexes with five equilateral triangles around each vertex." In a system "the largest number of triangles you can possibly have around a vertex is five. I can take that into the planar condition or the spherical, and in the spherical each of the corners will be 72°. Now that I find that I can get the total Earth's surface on to the icosahedron, the edges of the icosahedron's spherical triangles will all be 63° 26'. If possible, one of the things I want is to take the 12 vertexes of the icosahedron and manipulate them in such a way in relation to the sphere of the Earth that the vertexes always fall in the oceans."

    - Cite RBF, Univ. of Rhode Island, 26 Aug. '66, p. 197.

---

RBF DEFINITIONS

### Projective Transformation: (II)

"How can I get a total surface to give me the best information? In traditional methods of projection such as Mercator, polyconic, or polar-azimuthal, there is only one point, or line, or pair of lines where there is a true reading: that special line along which the conically or cylindrically curved paper is in actual contact with the sphere. From the line of true contact, accuracy diminishes outwardly in projection. The errors increase very rapidly, particularly in the Mercator projection in which the sphere is split open from the great circle of the equator and spread flat so that two points in the middle of Russia are split to the map's ends and seem to be 25,000 miles apart.
"I have found then, that instead of trying to use infinitely severed lines with two polar azimuthal projected hemispheres breaking the whole Earth into two separate circular planes, or the polyconic projection with the northern and southern hemispheres projected as fan-shaped planes with their curved edges tangent to one another at only one point, it is possible to avoid introducing infinity within the projected system."

    - RBF, Univ. of Rhode Island, 26 Aug. '66. p. 196.

---

RBF DEFINITIONS

### Projective Transformation: (VI)

"Going from the spherical to the planar condition with fige 60° anglesaround each vertex means that there are going to be sines opening up to 60°. I would like to have the sine opening in the ocean and not on the land because one of the most unsatisfactory things about looking at the Earth's data on classical map projections is that the continents themselves are always being distorted in an unfair way. The other fellow's continent is always being broken up instead of our own.

"Taking all the Earth's data from the spherical icosahedron to the planar icosahe ron permits the corners of the large equilateral triangles to be reduced from 72° to 60° so that there remains only a 20° spherical excess. By using an equilateral triangle that is symmetrical with each of the corners having equal subsidence, the amount of contraction becomes invisible and concentric uniform boundary scale is held for the entire length of the triangle edge, and there is no change in this when going from the spherical to the planar condition. .

    - Cite RBF, Univ. of Rhode Island, 26 Aug. '66, pp. 197-198.

RBF DEFINITIONS

Projective Transformation: (VII)

"There is local contraction within each small triangle of the three-way grid and that contraction is symmetrical. In all the other familiar methods of map projection, projection errors are dismissed outwardly from the point or line of reference and thereby greatly increased. Compare a circle of radius one with w circle of radius two; because the area of a circle of radius two is approximately four times the area of a circle of radius one, when the dimensional variables of a projected surface are outwardly distributed, the proportion of total map area that is in relatively greatest distortion exceeds by the ratio of three to one the relatively least distorted areas. In my system, the spherical surface subsides inwardly by symmetrical contraction and the proportion of the map which is in relatively greatest dimensional distortion is less by a ratio of one to three than its relatively undistorted area. In my map the error is sent inwardly and is at maximum at the center of each small spherical triangle of the three-way grid system.' Every triangle is contracted symmetrically at the same rate."

- Cite RBF, Univ. of Rhode Island, 26 Aug. '66. p. 198.

RBF DEFINITIONS

Projective Transformation: (VIII)

"Cutting out around the edge of the map in the planar condition and bringing the parts back together makes an icosahedron. If the edges of the triangle are six inches, the folded system is the same as a 12-inch diameter globe. Of course, if you make an icosahedron, you will find it faceted into 12 equilateral triangles. If, however, the faceted icosahedron is compared to a 12-inch globe, the efficiencies of conveying information are equal between the two map systems."

- Cite RBF, Univ. of Rhode Island, 26 Aug. '66., p. 198.

RBF DEFINITIONS

Projective Transformation: (1)

"Since 1917 Mr. Fuller has been evolving his Airocean World Map and new projection method. . . Due to its inherent advantages in respect to astronomical observation, aerial mosaicing, and comprehensive world triangulation by great circle grid the projection comprises a world-around Airocean strip map of approximately invisible dimensional distortion. . . . The Dymaxion Airocean World Map and its projective transformation strategy was glimpse-conceived in 1917, but required over a third of a century of development of" synergetics "to bring it to its present condition. . . the projection is contained entirely within a plurality of great-circle bounded triangles-- or quadrangles-- of constant, uniform modular subdivision whose identical length edges. . . permit their hinging into flat mosaic-tiled continuities at the planar phase of the transformation and thereby permit a variety of hinged-open complete flat world mosaics."

- Cite Undated sheet THE DYMAXION AIROCEAN WORLD FULLER PROJECTIVE-TRANSFORMATION.

RBF DEFINITIONS

Projective Transformation: (2)

"To provide a continuous one-surface world map-- while peeling off the sections of the globe-- the transformation must be such that the pieces have straight and matching edges when peeled off and flattened out. Unlike any of its cartographic predecessors which present the whole shperical world surface data within a unit flat surface map, the Fuller projection maintains a uniformly modulated and constant length great circle boundary scale in closed-- 360 degree-- equilateral periphery controls."

- Cite Undated sheet: THE DYMAXION AIROCEAN WORLD FULLER PROJECTIVE-TRANSFORMATION

RBF DEFINITIONS

Projective Transformation: (3)

"The Fuller Projection operates in a series of transformattion stages. It first subdivides the total world surface into a plurality of great circle bound polygonal zones. Next it transfers the data from the sphere's surface in separate mosaic 'tiles' corresponding to each of the great circle bound polygonal zones of step one. While migrating as a zonal mosaic tile, each tile (independently) transforms internally from compound curvature to flat surface by methods shown" in the projective transformation model. Each tile transforms entirely within the respective polygonally closed uniform symmetrical containers, allowing none of the data to spill outwardly in perverse distortion.

"When all the tiles have tranformed independently from spherical to planar, their straight polygonal edges-- unaltered in length during the transformed in transit migration-- permit re-association in a variety of continuous data mosaics.

"The Fuller projection has the relationship to all other known projection methods that a mechanically fillable and sealable set of flasks bear to hair combs, hair pins, fish bones, and star spurs, as instruments of liquid transfer."

- Cite Undated sheet: Dymaxion Airocean World Fuller Projective-

RBF DEFINITIONS

Projective Transformation: (4)

"The Fuller Projection not only contains its surface data increments within uniform and linearly unaltered closed great circle arc polygonal peripheries-- all the way from its spherical to its planar positions-- but also uniquely concentrates all of its spherical angle excess. It concentrates the excess into 360 degree symmetry within equilateral polygons. This means that the compound curvature subsides by symmetrical internal concentric contraction into a flattened condition entirely within its neither elongating nor shortening peripheral integrity. The internal subsidence of the Fuller Projection is in contrast to all predecessor projective methods for showing the whole world within one unitary surface. All the predecessors disperse spherical excess by outward 'fanning', i.e., by stretching out to flattened condition."

- Cite Undated Sheet: DYMAXION AIROCEAN WORLD FULLER PROJECTIVE-TRANSFORMATION

RBF DEFINITIONS

Projective Transformation: (5)

The projective transformation "transfers the spherical data to the planar by employing only great circle coordinates, while all other projections employ a progressively complex admixture of great circle and lesser circle coordinates."

In the projective transformation "from spherical to planar condition the radii of the sphere of reference which penetrate perpendicularly each spherical surface coordinate point of the comprehensive great circle grid, separate from one another at their respective internal ends-- and each and all remain constantly perpendicualr to the transforming, internally shrinking surfaces throughout the transformation, and their original uniform lengths also continue as 'constant' throughout the transformation."

- Cite Undated Sheet: DYMAXION AIROCEAN WORLD FULLER PROJECTIVE-TRANSFORMATION

RBF DEFINITIONS

Projective Transformation: (6)

"Becuase of the constant perpendicularity of the Fuller Projection's radii to the transforming surface, the Fuller Projection greatly simplifies celestial calculations. All astronomical phenomena always occur in outward perpendicularity-- zenith-- to the Fuller Projection's internal spherical coordinates. On transformation to planar grids the astronomical data always remains in identical perpendicular zenith to the corresponding coordinate positions in the planar phase of the Fuller Transformation.

"Because of this property the Fuller Transformation would be more suitable than any other projection for a comprehensive planar mosaic of a total covering-set of world-around aerial photographs. Aerial photographs are always taken from zenith positions and at a constant altitude, or radius distance from the Earth's spherical ▪▪▪▪▪▪ surface."

- Cite Undtaed Sheet: DYMAXION AIROCEAN WORLD FULLER PROJECTIVE-TRANSFORMATION

RBF DEFINITIONS

Projective Transformation:                                    (7)

The projective transformation "consists of great circle
bounded triangles of any angular magnitude which can
transform the comprehensive geographical data of the world
from the spherical to the planar by employment of either
the spherical tetrahedron, spherical cube, spherical
octahedron, or spherical vector equilibrium and its
alternate, the icosahedron, or any development of these. . .
It is a discovery of synergetics that there are no other
spherical triangular grid bases."

- Cite Undated Sheet: DYMAXION AIROCEAN WORLD FULLER
  PROJECTIVE-TRANSFORMATION

---

RBF DEFINITIONS

Projective Transformation:                                    (8)

"It is a matter of Dymaxion cartographic strategy that:
the greater number of great circle polygonal zones
employed in the transformation, the less the spherical
excess to be subsidingly concentrated within each zone
surface, and therefore the less the residual distortion
distibuted to each of the planar mosaic aspects of the
whole world's reassembled surface when arrayed in one
continuous flat 'skin.'"

The projective transformation "represents the only method
by which the whole world data can be transferred from the
spherical to the planar within an all great circle grid
triangularly, quadrangularly, multipolygonally or all two
or three together."

"Because of a hemisphere's polar symmetry to its opposite
polar hemisphere the total inventory of great circle
grid triangles in the comprehensive world grid is always
even in number, therefore adjacent triangles may always be
associated in total or partial quadrangular pattern-phases
without increase in vertex count."

- Cite Undated Sheet: THE DYMAXION AIROCEAN WORLD FULLER
  PROJECTIVE-TRANSFORMATION

---

RBF DEFINITIONS

Projective Transformation:  Raleigh Edition:                  (2)

"The map may be cut around its periphery and bent on its
main triangular edges and the exterior edges brought
together-- closing all exterior sinuses-- thus making a
continuous or finite surface and constituting a planar
facted icosahedron transformed from the psherical
icosahedron.  When the surface is thus closed-- proving
itself to be a finite continuity-- and the resulting
icosahedron is compared to a globe of the world, the
relative shapes and area sizes will be found to be entirely
faithful to the spherical globe's relative sizes and shapes."

- Cite Undated Sheet: THE DYMAXION AIROCEAN WORLD FULLER
  PROJECTIVE-TRANSFORMATION

---

RBF DEFINITIONS

Projective Transformation:  Raleigh Edition:                  (1)

The projective transformation employed "in the Raleigh
Edition of the Dymaxion Airocean World is that of the
spherical icosahedron , chosen because the latter has the
largest number of identical and symmetrical spherical
triangles, and therefore the least 'spherical excess' of
all the possible symmetrical triangular great circle bound
mathematical cases.  The spherical icosahedron was also
chosen because its controlling arc boundary of 63 degrees 26
minutes 05.816... seconds was just adequate to the
triangular spanning of the maximum continetal aspects
encountered in the unpeeling of the Earth's data-- within
20 symmetrical great-circle bound control triangles--
spanning those continents in such a manner that all 12
vertexes of the spherical icosahedron grid lay in the
open waters.  As a result this peeled strip map contains
all the world's continental contours. . . with no dis-
pleasing distortions of the shapes."

- Cite Undated Sheet: THE DYMAXION AIROCEAN WORLD FULLER
  PROJECTIVE-TRANSFORMATION

---

RBF DEFINITIONS

Projective Transformation: (Dymaxion Airocean World Map:)

"The projection system of the Dymaxion Airocean World Map

divides the sphere into 20 equilateral spherical triangles

which are then flattened to form the icosahedron. These

20 triangles are each projected into a flat plane. . .

This method results in a map having less visible distortion

than any previously known map projection syste. . . To

flatten the globe it is simply necessary to 'unfold' the

icosahedron."

- Cite Synergetics Illustration, #119, caption. 1967

---

RBF DEFINITIONS

Projective Transformation Model:                             (I)

"I am going to give you a mental model of what I did in
developing my method of projection.  This is really a
'topological transformation' rather than a 'projection'
since it isn't a shadowgram.  I am going to take a thin
tempered steel band and I am going to mark it with sub-
modules, with increments like an engineer's scale.  If I
bend the band, the modules will all stay in their same
original uniform lengths.  In a bent condition, or in a
flat condition the modules will all read the same.  Now I am
going to punch holes vertically throygh both the end module
marks of the band and I'm going to take two more such bands
each marked with the same modules and I am going to overlap
their hole-punched ends, and I'm going to put a round rod
through the holes.  The rods going through each of the
corners of the steel band edged triangles make little
swivels.  The rods go through the bands vertically and
perpendicular to the plane of the triangle formed by the
steel bands.  If I take hold of the bottom ends of two such
rods that go through the holes at the end of one of the steel
bands and pull them towards each other, I make the steel band
bend.  Now I take hold of the bottom ends of all three
perpendicular steel rods and pull them towards one another."

- Cite RBF, Univ. of Rhode Island, 26 Aug. '66, p. 197.

---

RBF DEFINITIONS

Projective Transformation Model:                            (II)

"This will make each one of the steel bands bend.  As each
one of these bent or arched bands also rotates away from
the others, each of the corner angles will be openming up
and the three swivel end bands form a spherical triangle."

"In my projection I've used great circles for the edges of
the spherical triangles and marked them with a uniform
boundary scale.  A set of fundamental perpendiculars to the
great circles, as the radii of the sphere, come at even modules
onto the great circles.  I have interconnected these edge
modules           of the spherical triangles with the three-
way grid.  With this three-way grid I could do as I did above
with the tempered steel bands and produce a three-way grid of
small spherical triangles within the large spherical
triangles of the icosahedron.  I can put a grommet where each
of these steel bands cross and run a rod through perpendicularly which would represent the radius of the Earth going
into the center.  Imagine the triangle in a flat or planar
condition, with a great many of these bristle-like rods
going perpendicular to the surface of the triangle and then
pulling them all togebher at their free ends.  The triangles
of the three-way grid all form spherical triangles."

- Cite RBF, Univ. of Rhode Island, 26 Aug. '66, p. 197.

---

RBF DEFINITIONS

Projective Transformation Model:                           (III)

"We find that these rods remain perpendicular to the surface
of the triangle throughout all of their transformations.  It
doesn't matter whether the triangle is flat or is spherical
or how it is spherical or what the corner angles are.  Each
one of these rods will be perpendicular to its spherical
triangle at its vertex of attachment just as the radii of the
Earth are to the great circles.  This means that when we take
the geometric data of the stars, any star that is in its
zenith over the Earth at any given moment will remain in my
map in this vertical position over that point on the Earth
whether my map is in a planar condition or a spherical
condition."

- Cite RBF, Univ. of Rhode Island, 26 Aug. '66, p. 197.

RBF DEFINITIONS

### Projective Transformation Model:

"The" projective "Transformation is contained entirely within
a plurality of great-circle bounded triangles-- or quadrangles--
of constant uniform modular subdivision whose identical length
edges-- shown as steel bands in the illustrations. . .
--permit their hinging into flat mosaic-tiled continuities
at the planar phase of the transformation and thereby permit
a variety of hinged-open complete flat world mosaics."

- Cite Undated sheet: THE DYMAXION AIROCEAN WORLD FULLER
  PROJECTIVE-TRANSFORMATION.

---

RBF DEFINITIONS

### Projective Transformation Model:

The projective transformation model demonstrates how the
"zonal mosaic tiles migrate, how each tile independently
transforms internally from compound curvature to flat
surface."

- Cite Undated sheet: THE DYMAXION AIROCEAN WORLD FULLER
  PROJECTIVE-TRANSFORMATION.

---

### Projective Transformation:

See Constant Zenith Projection*
Transformational Projection*
Internal Control of Distortion

(** Preferred terminology)

---

### Project:

Deproject

---

RBF DEFINITIONS

### Promote:  Promotion:

"If you promote you cannot invent."

- Cite RBF to EJA & Michael Denneny, Nicholas Restaurant,
  N.Y. City; 7 Oct'76

---

RBF DEFINITIONS

### Promote:  I Don't Promote:

"There is a gestation rate and that's why I don't promote.
You can't make babies by Madison Avenue. Nature has to have
its due course: the chemical process, so much pressure, and
so much heat. You can't overdo it or you'll boil the egg.
You'll have a hard-boiled egg.

- Cite tape transcript, p.19; RBF to W. Wolf, Gloucester, Mass.,
  2 Jun'74

---

RBF DEFINITIONS

### Promote:  ▓▓▓▓▓▓  I Don't Promote:

"... The Design Science Institute will keep his
books and writings available and will promote such
ideas as his geodesic dome." (Press Release, DSI,
29 Jun'72)

RBF wrote marginal instructions to EJA as follows:

"Sonny: it is one of my own strictest disciplines
NOT to promote! The Design Science Institute will
also avoid all promotion and is committed as am I
to giving forth only when asked by others so to do.
Please try to have this sentence deleted from your
release. Thanks. B. Fuller, Oct. 6, 1972.

- Cite RBF marginalis as above, 6 Oct'72

---

### Promote:  I Don't Promote:                    (1)

See Anonymity
Fuller, R.B: His Decision He Must Not be a Persuader,
But a Doer
Fuller, R.B: Lecture Invitations
New Forms vs. Reforms

Promote:  I Don't Promote:                          (2)

        See Religion, May'65
           Robin Hood Sequence (2)
           World-around Communication Transcends Politics,
             (2)(3)
           Evolutionary Checks & Balances, 26 Aug'75
           Options; 13 May'77

---

Pronouns:  Checklist:                                (2)

        See Vector Equilibrium, Oct'75

---

RBF DEFINITIONS

Pronouns:  I = We = Us:                              (1)

"The pronoun 'I' is simply the observing system's oversimplified I-dentification as with the only-threshold-tunable but
directionally-identifiable noise, or point-to-able, as-yet-
undifferentiable 'pointal' somethingness.

"The experience life being most minimally described as awareness,
and awareness being dependent on system otherness, unity is
at minimum two: 'I' means 'We.'  I is only the system symbol of
the observer side of the awareness equation.

"You (We) become so preoccupied with interrelationship
principles as to become unconscious and unaware of any special
case aspects of both the observer and originally observed
correspondent as to momentarily lose all consciousness of
their mutual environment.

"You (I) (We) become one with the environment.  You and I and
the lamppost.  I am a system; you are a system.  Systems embrace
systems.  'System' is interchangeable with and could replace
the you-and-I I-dentities.  We are both subtunable systems of
a greater system of systems.  Me-Us is a system.  I-We are a"

- Cite RBF holograph, 3200 Idaho, Wash., DC; 10 Dec'75

---

RBF DEFINITIONS

Proofs:

"Proofs must proceed from the minimum whole system to
Universe and the differentiation-out of Universe of the
special case conceptual system.  Proofs must start from
the minimum something which is the minimum structural
system.  All geometrical and numerical values derive from
fractionation of the whole."

- Cite SYNERGETICS 2 draft at Sec. 1052.361; RBF rewrite
  8 Aug'77

---

RBF DEFINITIONS

Pronouns:  I = We = Us:                              (2)

"a system.  The system insideness may be hungry; the system's
external environment may be cold.

"The systemic inside-outness-defining considerability, its
fourness, and its sixfold interrelationships which provide the
awareness of relevance and irrelevance, is always a priori--is
always there in every mo-ment."

- Cite RBF Holographm 3200 Idaho, Wash., DC; 10 Dec'75

---

RBF DEFINITIONS

Proofs:

"Proofs must proceed from the whole to the particular,
starting from the minimum something.  All geometrical and
numerical values derive from fractionation of the whole."

- Citation & context at Mite as Model for Quark, 3 May'77

---

## PRONOUNS: CHECKLIST                              (1)

      See He-even
        Matrix of You & I
        We-me
        Complex It
        Self
        Subjective & Objective
        Individual & Group Principle
        Objective Intellect
        Transcendental
        It
        You & Me

---

RBF DEFINITIONS

Proofs:

"...The thing about proofs is that I am really operational
and for me the test is: if the airplane flies.  If it does
fly, then that's operational.  But the mathematicians... you
read about them in Courant and Robbins... they have a
different kind of criteria.  Even though they know that a
certain situation always produces predictable results every
time, it's not necessarily proven.... The way they might
have points on a surface but don't credit the fact that the
points are also on the other side of the surface.  But you
know the way I start out with one point, then two points,
then three points, and the insideness and outsideness with
four points.... That shows that principles can be realized
independent of size."

- Cite RBF to EJA, by telephone from Phila. Office; 7 Oct'75

RBF DEFINITIONS

Proofs: ▪▪▪▪▪▪▪▪▪▪▪▪▪▪

". . . Any individual has only limited knowledge of what
the total Universe frontiering may be. The list embraces
what I know to be my own discoveries and I have no knowledge
of others having made those discoveries prior to my own.
I am claiming nothing. Proofs may have been made by myself
and will be made by myself. Proofs have been made by others
and will be made by others. Proofs are satisfying. But many
mathematical theorems are of great advantage to humanity over
a long period of time before their final mathematical proofs
are discovered. The whys and wherefores of what is rated as
mathematical proof have been evolved by mathematicians; they
are formal and esoteric affirmations from one specialist
to another."

- Cite RBF to EJA, Washington DC, 20 Dec. '71 incorporated
  in SYNERGETICS, at Sec. 250.69.
  [61]

Proof: Proofs:                                    (1)

See Circumstance-proved
    Knowns Harvested From All the Unknowns
    Experimental Demonstrability

Proof: Proofs:                                    (2)

See Science: Left Hand & Right Hand, May'65
    Synergetic Strategy of Commencing with Totality,
       28 May'72
    Geometry, 14 Nov'73
    Systematic Realization, 20 Dec'74
    Minimum Limit Case, 9 Jun'75
    Philosophy, 11 Aug'76
    Fourth-dimensional Synergetics Mathematics, 14 Dec'76
    Multiplication by Division, 20 Jan'77
    Mite as Model for Quark ,3 May'77

RBF DEFINITIONS

Propaganda:

"All the Western world's free-enterprise-controlled media's
propaganda is designed to rationalize selfishness--this is
its function in a world where there is supposed to be lethal
inadequacy of life support which therefore assumes a survival-
only-of-the-fittest raison d'etre."

- Cite RBF to White House Fellows, Watergate Hotel, Wash. DC;
  28 Mar'77; as rewritten by RBF 29 Mar'77

Propaganda:                                       (1)

See Psychological Warfare

Propaganda:                                       (2)

See Design Revolution, 7 Nov'67
    Law, May'65
    Superstition, circa 1955
    Democracy, 10 Sep'75
    New York City, (6)

Propagative Transformation of the Vector Equilibrium:

See Jitterbug

Propagation: Propagative:                         (1)

See Electromagnetic Wave Propagation
    Energetic Functions
    Feedback
    Propagative Transformation of the Vector Equilibrium
    Spherical Propagations
    Quantum Propagation
    Wave Propagation Inward-outward Tendency
    Wave Propagation Model
    Wave System Propagations
    Nuclear Propagation Rate

# Synergetics Dictionary

Propagation: Propagative: (2)

See Frequency, 22 Jun'72
   Isotropic Vector Matrix, 30 Nov'72
   Life, May'49
   Observing vs. Articulating, Mar'71
   Radiation, May'72
   Spheric Domains, 6 Nov'72
   Vector Equilibrium, 30 Oct'73
   Zerophase, (1)
   Male & Female, 1 Feb'75
   Abstraction, 24 Feb'72
   Convergence & Divergence, 6 Jun'75
   Synergetics, 11 Oct'73
   Metaphysical & Physical Tetrahedral Quanta,
     25 Mar'71
   Energetic Functions, 8 Aug'77

---

RBF DEFINITIONS

Property:

"The Elimination of Property By Making Ownership Onerous: The elimination of property by making ownership onerous is to be accomplished by making man a world citizen, each to enjoy all the treasures of the whole Earth. He can't any more 'take it with him' around the world than he could 'take it with him' in yesterday's concept of 'into the next world.' He 'can't take it with him' and enjoy the new world of Universe citizenship, and its natural emancipation from slavery chained to ponderous thingness."

- Cite WORLD-AROUND PROBLEMS THAT HAVE TO BE SOLVED BY BLOODLESS DESIGN SCIENCE REVOLUTION, 29 June 1972

---

RBF DEFINITIONS

Propeller:

"Let me take one propeller blade by itself. I am going to split it longitudinally and get an S curve, one in which the rates are changing and no power in the curve is the same. So it is asymmetrical by itself: it is repeated six times: positive, negative, positive, negative. . . and the six blades come round in dynamic symmetry. The energy forces involved are in beautiful absolute balance. We have energetic balance."

- Cite SYNERGETICS text at Sec. 532.23; Dec'71

---

Property: You Can't Take it With You:

See Transnational Capitalism & Export of Know-how, (1)

---

Propeller: (1)

See Diesel Ship at Sea
   Dynamic Symmetry

---

Property: (1)

See False Property Illusion
   Obsolete: Inventory of Obsolete Concepts
   Ownership
   Private Property
   Thing: Thingness
   Politics & Proprty

---

Propeller: (2)

See Ecology Sequence, (G)
   Wave, 11 Jul'62
   Wind Power Sequence, (2)

---

Property: (2)

See ▮▮▮ Literacy, 18 Aug'70
   Real, 20 Apr'72
   Cosmic vs. Terrestrial Accounting, (4)
   Invention, (a)
   Dome Over Manhattan, 26 Apr'77

Proportion: Proportionality:

    See Interangular Proportionality
        Interproportional

Prospects for Humanity:

Q.      What are your dreams for the future of society?

RBF:      "No society: no Me.  I am the product of two, to
start off with.  No otherness: no me.  No otherness: no
awareness.  The individual is here for problem-solving.  We
will become much more concerned by Universe than by society.
Earning a living is really the mischievous nonsense.

"People will be living in the Macro and the micro.  You can
put all the things back in the museum and live 3,000 years ago.
You can go backwards or forwards in time.  We will have fellowships just to think, and fishing is a better place to think
than a schoolhouse."

RBF to videotaping session Philadelphia, Pa., 1 Feb'75

---

Prose:                                                    (1)

    See Ventilated Prose
        Verse vs. Prose

Prospect for Humanity:

    See Meek Have Inherited the Earth, (1)(2)
        Walls vs. Airspace Technology, (2)
        Success, 10 Sep'75

---

Prose:  Prosaic:                                          (2)

    See Threshold of Life, 6 Jul'62

Prospero-proletarian Predilection:

    See Computer Asks an Original Question, (3)

---

Prospect for Humanity:

"Russians, Arabs, Israelis-- wherever you look-- there is a
popular resentment of the political.  People are ready....
Businessmen are not bad, they're just caught in playing the
wrong game.... Integrity: it's up to each of us in the little
things each of us do... if we don't pick up the paper to clean
up our own mess.  Humanity is at the final exam.  Humanity is
not marking the papers.... We are prone to think that the
Universe is here to please us and the stars are just so much
decoration.... And there are so many false jobs that do not
produce life support.  My predictions?... I know the options,
but I don't know whether we're going to make it or not."

- Cite RBF at videotaping session Philadelphia, PA., 2 Feb'75

Protein Shells:

    See Tensegrity Masts:  Pentagonal Polarity, 27 Dec'76

RBF DEFINITIONS

Proton and Neutron: (1)

"I will give another example
Of always and only co-occurring phenomena.
Physicists today observe
That the proton and neutron
Always and only co-occur.
While they are not 'mirror' images of one another
And have different weights,
They are transformable
One into the other,
And are thus complexedly complementary,
As are isosceles and scalene triangles.
None of the angles and edges of either need be the same
To produce triangles of equal area.
And the sums of the three angles of each
Will always be one hundred and eighty degrees.

"The mathematical balancing or complementation
Of the proton and neutron are analogously balanced,
Each one having two small energy teammates.
The proton has its electron and its antineutrino,
And the neutron has its positron and its neutrino.
And each of these little three-member teams"

- Cite BRAIN & MIND, p.134 May '72

RBF DEFINITIONS

Proton and Neutron: (A)

"The astrophysicists say that no matter how far things come
apart, they never come further apart fundamentally than
proton and neutron which always and only coexist. While
one is convertible into the other, the masses are not the
same. The conversion of one into the other is only by
virtue of each having two side energy effects. In other
words the proton and the neutron have its two side energy
effects. These are like the resultant and the
reaction. And in relation to complementarity. . . The Nobel
Prize being given 16 years ago to two young men who
discovered that the complementarity was not in mirror-image,
as it had been assumed up to that time. We had been
assuming that all you had to do was to multiply the Universe
by two. For some years it was discovered and demonstrated
scientifically, physically, that the complementarity was
not the mirror-image.

"I'd like to give you a way you can understand how the proton
and neutron, which do not have the same mass, yet are interchangeable one with the other, are always known to coexist
and are complementary to one another: how could they then do
this and not be mirror-image?"

- Cite RBF at SIMS, U. Mass, Amherst, 22 July '71, pp 20-21

RBF DEFINITIONS

Proton and Neutron: (2)

"Constitute what the physicist calls half-spin or a half-quantum.
They complement one another
And altogether comprise one unit of quantum.
We have now discovered experientially
An always and only coexisting tension and compression;
An always and only coexisting concave and convex;
And an always and only coexisting proton and neutron."

- Cite BRAIN & MIND, pp.134-135 May '72

RBF DEFINITIONS

Proton and Neutron: (B)

"For instance, you could have an isosceles triangle. And
you could have a scalene triangle where all three edges are
different. So the scalene and isosceles triangle quite
clearly are different triangles. Yet the sums of the
angles on the scalene and the isosceles are all 180°. And
you could have the sums of the lengths of the edges of the
scalene and the sums of the lengths of the edges of the
isosceles also the same, which is exactly what we do have
in the proton's and neutron's side energy effects, where we
have the proton with its electron and its antineutrino; and
neutron with its positron and its neutrino. Each of these
teams is called one-half quantum; or one-half spin in the
physics."

- Cite RBF at SIMS, U.Mass, Amherst, 22 July '71, p. 21

RBF DEFINITIONS

Proton and Neutron:

"The physicist finds
That the proton and neutron
Not only always and only co-occur,
And are interchangeably transformable,
But also could not occur independently
Any more than a triangle could occur
With only two points. . .

"We are founded on
The orderly base
Of the proton-neutron tripartite teams
Of six unique energy integrity vectors."

Citation and context at Universe, pp.156-157 May '72

RBF DEFINITIONS

Proton and Neutron:

"I'm simply giving you complementarity. We find that
nature, with proton and neutron always and only coexisting,
by virtue of which the astrophysicist of today has to say
that there never could have been anything primordial, that
is, something before order-- that there was original chaos
and disorder, out of which, surprisingly, order developed.
I would say very surprisingly, because it is fundamental to
antientropy that order inherently increases, disorder
inherently decreases, and it would be completely counter
probability that out of inherent disorder there would
develope a beautiful human being or a lily. . . So the
astrophysicist discovers that we must always have had
proton and neutron, always and only coexisting: that we
must always had order. Man was disorderly in his
ignorance. We find that fundamental complementarity. . .
to have to have two to explain and complement one another,
is not an illogical matter."

- Cite RBF at Sims, U. Mass., Amherst, 22 July '71,
Talk 12, p. 27

RBF DEFINITIONS

Proton and Neutron:

"When you isolate the neutron you are isolating the
concave. When you isolate the proton you are isolating
the convex."

- Citation at Convex and Concave
- Cite RBF to EJA, 3200 Idahi, Wash DC, 29 May '72

RBF DEFINITIONS

Proton & Neutron:

"...A basic orderliness of Universe is provided by the always
coexisting proton and neutron which, though complexedly
intertransformable, are not mirror images of one another, nor
are of equal mass or weight."

- Citation and context at Chaos, 13 Nov'69

RBF DEFINITIONS

Proton and Neutron:

"Of all the essential, harmonic, wave-frequency associable phenomena none is more compatible with all other phenomena than are the <u>proton-neutron teams</u> of physical energy. At the next higher level of complexity no phenomena is more univers- ally associable than is the hydrogen atom. No physical complex is more prolifically reproduced in Universe than is the hydrogen atom. But the proton-neutron teams and the hydrogen atoms are individually invisible to the naked eye and are aesthetically appreciated only by the scientists who deal with the invisible ranges of the great electromagnetic spectrum 'reality.' As the essential complexes first become visibly discernible as snowflakes, minuscule flower blossoms, crystals, or any other of the myriads of minutiae, they are spontaneously acclaimed by man as aesthetically pleasing. This aesthetic pleasure includes not only all other ▮▮▮▮▮ visible phenomena ranging from small to large, from starfish to celestial star, but also ranging in biochemical, structural, mechanical, and electromagnetic complexity from the simplest algae and radiolaria to the elephant, the giant redwood, and the human being. The spontaneous aesthetic satiffaction does not stop here but goes on to include the products of these living complexes, which in turn includes humanity's invented tools."'

- Cite GENERALIZED LAWS OF DESIGN, p.3, 22 Apr'68

RBF DEFINITIONS

Proton and Neutron:

"The proton group and the neutron group account

rationally for all physical structures."

- Cite NASA Speech, p. 64, Jun '66

Proton & Neutron:                                                    (1)

See Dog Pulling on a Belt
    Nucleon
    Quantum
    Universal Integrity: VE & Icosa

Proton & Neutron:                                                    (2)

See Chaos, 13 Nov'69*
    Convex & Concave, 29 May'72*
    Coupler (2)
    Equilibrium, 25 Feb'69
    Icosahedron as Local Shunting Circuit, 22 Jun'72
    Integrity, 24 Jan'72
    Modules: A & B Quanta Modules, Apr'72
    Quantum: Event-paired Quanta, Jul'66
    Universe, May'72*
    Vector: Threeness of the Vector (1)(2)
    Crystallography, 17 Aug'70
    Human Beings & Complex Universe, (2)(3)

Protoplasm:

See Spectrum, 15 Oct'72
    Viral Steerability: Angle-frequency Design
        Control, 22 Jul'71
    Animate & Inanimate, 11 Dec'75

RBF DEFINITIONS

Prototype:

"Just as in art, science, and poetry the most lasting is proven to be the most profoundly understanding and yet most simply articulated, so too may the word prototype in the mass reproducible undertakings of humanity in the most recent decades and most recent century and most recent millenium of humans' known presence on Earth, only be given in retrospect to those one amongst thousands of inventions which are in fact so timely and simply appropriate and adequate as to induce mass reproduction and can thus warrant the only-retrospective identity of prototype. Just as myriads profess to be artists, poets, or scientists, yet history fails to confirm their claim, so too the word prototype is prematurely claimed for enterprise initiating designs which fail to be reproduced."

- Cite RBF draft Ltr. to Karan Singh; above omitted from
   passage incorporated in SYNERGETICS, Sec.260, 13 Mar'73.

TEXT CITATIONS

Prototype:

Nine Chains to the Moon, p. 38ff, 1938

Letter to Karan Singh - 1973

Prototype:                                                          (1)

See Aesthetics of Uniformity
    Development
    Fuller, R.B: What I Am Trying To Do
    Perfect Prototype
    Reduction to Practice
    Regenerative Design: Law Of
    Reproducibleness: Law Of
    Research & Development

Prototype:                                                    (2)

See Dwelling Service Industry, (2): (A)
    Frame of Reference, 4 Oct'72
    Omnimedium Transport Sequence, (3)
    Reproducible, 30 May'72
    Dome House Grand Strategy: 1927-1977, (1)
    Building Industry, (3)

RBF DEFINITIONS

Proximity & Remoteness:

"Whereas none of the geodesic lines of Universe touch one
another, the lines approach one another, passing successively
through regions of most critical proximity, and diverge from
one another, passing successively through regions of most
innocuous remoteness."

                            - Citation at Geodesic Lines, Oct'59

---

Proxemics:                                                    (1)

See Population Density: Manhattan Cocktail Party
    Privacy

RBF DEFINITIONS

        ████████ Proximity & Remoteness:

    "Where all the local vectors are approximately equal,
we have a potentially isotropic local vector equilibrium,
but the operative vector complex has the inherent qualities
of proximity and remoteness in respect to any locally
initiated ██████████ action ergo a complex of relative
velocities of realization lags."

            ███████████████

                            - Cite COLLIER'S, p. 113 , Oct'59

SEC. 425.01 + 240.37

---

Proxemics:

See Community, (2)

Proximity & Remoteness:                                       (1)

See Convergence & Divergence
    Cosmic & Local
    Privacy vs. Community
    Unsettling vs. Settlements
    World Pattern vs. Local Pattern

---

Proximity ≠ Neighborliness:

See Community, (2)

Proximity & Remoteness:                                       (2)

See Covariation, 14 May'73
    Energy, 6 May'48
    Geodesic Lines, Oct'59*
    Local Vector Equilibrium, 2 Nov'73
    Triangular-cammed, In-out-and-around Jitterbug
        Model, 11 Dec'75
    Old Man River Project, 20 Sep'76

## Proximity: (1)

See Critical Proximity
Fall-in, Shunt-out Proximities
Interproximity
Proximity & Remoteness
Venus Proximity

## Proximity: (2)

See Tensegrity Sphere: Six Pentagonals (1)(2)

RBF DEFINITIONS

## Psychedelic:

"I can really understand psychedelic experiences where we depress our definitive resolution capabilities which leaves the phenomenon color uncontestedly supreme."

- Cite Museums Keynote Address Denver, p. 4. 2 Jun'71

RBF DEFINITIONS

## Psychiatry: (1)

"I have your questions here. You asked me first my general impressions, ideas, and experiences in psychiatry. I haven't any personal experience with psychiatry; that is, I have never been to a psychiatrist. I have known a number of psychiatrists, however, and I have talked to them. . . I have gone back to 50 years ago here in Chicago when a friend of mine was a student of Jung. . . and I have had conversations with people for many years and I have had a number of students at the university who have been going to psychiatrists. And I have always really questioned whether those students who were going to psychiatrists really needed to go to psychiatrists--almost all of them were students of wealthy families and were having troubles with their families and maybe that was the thing to do. I had a tendency to feel that these students depended too much on the psychiatrist. They were just making another parent and continuiung with whatever the problems were and they were just not trying to figure things out on their own.

"I have been told by my friends--and particularly by my friend of 50 years ago, Dr. Douglas _____ the man who was a studentof Jung. . . he said that I had self-analyzed"

- Cite transcript p.1 of RBF tape with Dr. Michael Bruwer, Ritz Carlton, Chicago; 20 Feb'77

RBF DEFINITIONS

## Psychiatry: (2)

"myself and by the age of 32 I had changed my whole life pattern. . . and at that time I reviewed very truthfully my relationships with my family--particularly my mother--in such a way that I would be able to be very fair to her and to bring out whatever the truth really was. And this is a very important part of doing my own thinking . Whether I did or did not follow the practice of psychoanalysis according to the various theories, I did have some kind of an experience all right--enough to have had an experience that made me think about other human beings and their problems. . . and I certainly think that I got myself into that much of a cul de sac in life that I had to start very fresh and do my own thinking.

"I had been brought up in an era that was no longer operative, where the older people were utterly convinced that the younger people's thinking was completely unreliable. . . that it was something that did not firm up until they were 30 or so. And all the younger people were continually being told by the ▓▓▓▓▓▓ older people: 'Never mind what you think! Listen, we're trying to teach you.' And we were taught to get over our sensitivity and to give up all the things that seemed"

- Cite transcript (pp. 1 & 2) of RBF tape with Dr. Michael Bruwer, Ritz Carlton, Chicago; 20 Feb'77

RBF DEFINITIONS

## Psychiatry: (3)

"to be our fundamental faculties and proclivities. . . . And there was a game. . . there was something called life, and that's the way life really is. . . really a game. And, knowing that my father died when I was very young, and my mother--I knew how much she loved me, that she sent me to the kind of school where she thought I would get something excellent in the way of education, but I was continually being told: 'Never mind what you think!" . . . So I simply made up my mind to try to give up and pay no attention to what I think . . . . to give up all my sensitivites and put on an act, and I actually got to be very good at it.

"I confused my realities. When I was running and high-jumping, and so forth, I was really very true to whatever I am there. I was very true to myself in a ship at sea and I did very well in the Navy, but the naval officer was a game in itself. We had to be an officer. . . and I did very well in the Navy, did very well as a mechanic--because I didn't have to make any money aboard ship. . . I didn't have another game to be superimposed on it."

- Cite Transcript (p.2) of RBF tape with Dr. Michael Bruwer, Ritz Carlton, Chicago; 20 Feb'77

RBF DEFINITIONS

## Psychiatry: (4)

"When I got out of the Navy and had to come into the building world, I found that I was interested in putting up good buildings; and I was not interested in making money. I never had the slightest feeling for making money. I was really tremendously surprised and ▓▓▓▓▓▓▓ actually felt very badly about why people wanted to play games for money with me--and this spoiled the whole thing. The money idea was obnoxious to me really fundamentally. I tried very hard to play the game and I was no good at it. I was in this cul de sac. I had made a mess of it.

"A lot of people thought I was very bright with high initiative and all, and they bet on me and so they lost all their money. I was in a real mess. And I had either there to do away with myself, because I had a new child, and this was not just our first child, but a second child. Our first child died before her fourth birthday--and after a five-year hiatus here was this new life entrusted to us--that my wife and I were to have in Chicago. . . our families were in the East far away when we had this new child."

- Cite transcript (pp. 2 & 3) of RBF tape with Dr. Michael Bruwer, Ritz Carlton, Chicago; 20 Feb'77

RBF DEFINITIONS

## Psychiatry: (5)

"And so I really had to. . . saying I'm not going to pay any attention to the game. . . and had to actually do my own thinking.

"So I tried to understahd again how and what human beings are, and how we happen to be in our Universe, and above all learn how to use all the faculties and senses we are given as part of our regular design--a fundamentally important design. That is really all I have to say about my general impressions and experiences with psychiatry--and my relationships to psychiatry--and I have now lived 50 years with this new way of employing my faculties."

- Cite transcript (p.5) of RBF tape with Dr. Michael Bruwer, Ritz Carlton, Chicago; 20 Feb'77

Psychiatry: Psychoanalysis:                                    (1)

    See Schizophrenia

---

Psychology:                                                    (1)

    See Behavioral Science
        Mob Psychology
        Operant Psychology
        Reflexes
        Deja Vu
        Human Tolerance Limits
        Motive: Motivation
        Determinism
        Inferiority Complex
        Conditioned Reflex
        Mentality
        Fortress Mentality
        Mind
        Yesterday's Private Castle Mentality
        Behavior & Environment
        Feeling Good
        Mental Health

---

Psychiatry: Psychoanalysis:                                    (2)

    See Dwelling Service Industry, (6)
        Responsibility, Dec'69
        Self-discipline, May'72
        Anger, (1)-(3)
        Fuller, R.B: Moratorium on Speech, (1)-(3)
        Six Motion Freedoms & Degrees of Freedom, (5)(6)

---

Psychology: Psychologists:                                     (2)

    See Consciousness, 14 Feb'72
        Metaphysics, Jun'66
        Synergetics, 15 Jul'73*
        Design Science, 22 Apr'67
        Anger, (1)-(3)

---

Psycho-guerilla Warfare:                                       (1)

    See Narcotics as a Political Strategy

---

# PSYCHOLOGICAL GEOMETRY                                       (1A)

    See Awareness
        Balls Coming Together
        Conceptuality as Polyhedral
        Ethical Physics
        Ego
        Geometry of Thinking
        Identity
        Individuality
        Individual: Theory of the Individual
        Interference as a Social Model
        I
        Loss: Discovery Through Loss
        Matrix of You & I
        Otherness
        Me
        Middle
        Observer & Observed
        Me the Observer
        Madonna Theme
        Individual Universes

---

Psycho-guerilla Warfare:                                       (2)

    See China (A)
        Womb Population, (3)
        Politics & Property, 6 Jul'76

---

Psychological Geometry:                                        (1B)

    See Precession: Analogy of Precession and Social Behavior
        Personality
        Prime Otherness
        Self
        Subjective & Objective
        Social Problems: Tetrahedral Coordination Of
        Self-now
        Self & Otherness
        Swallow the Otherness
        Tetrahedral Dynamics
        Thinking: Analogy of Sphere Layers
        We-Me Awareness
        Unselfishness
        You
        You & Me
        You or Me
        Daddy
        Teleology
        Me Ball
        Pronouns: I = We = Us

Psychological Geometry: (1C)

    You & I as Pattern Integrities
    Pronouns
    Complex It
    Individual & Group Principle
    Split Personality
    Metaphysical & Physical

RBF DEFINITIONS

Psychology:

"No consciousness: no psychologist."

- Cite RBF marginalia at Eccles, 'Facing Reality, '
  p. 3., 14 Feb '72

Psychological Geometry: (2)

    See Individual, Jun'66
       Environment: A Priori Environment, May'72
       Remember, 20 Feb'72
       Evolution, 22 Apr'71
       Free Will, 20 Dec'73
       In, Out & Around, 17 May'77

Public Lands:

    See Squatters, (2)

Psychological Warfare:

    See Narcotics as Political Strategy
       Mob Psychology
       Propaganda

Public Opinion Polls: (1)

    See Electronic Voting

RBF DEFINITIONS

Psychology:

". . . I find I don't use the word 'psychological'."

Public Opinion Polls: (2)

    See World Game, 4 Mar'69

# Citation and context at Synergetics, 15 Jul'73

RBF DEFINITIONS

Psychology:

RBF DEFINITIONS

Public Relations:

"You need public relations because the new dome you are building is on a technological frontier but not out of this world."

- Cite RBF at Penn Bell videotaping, Philadelphia, 28 Jan'75

---

Publishing:                                                    (1)

See Books
    Idea Stealing
    Energetic-synergetic Geometry:  Original Publication
        In 1944
    Fuller, R.B:  On Galley Proofs
    Fuller, R.B:  Unpublished Mathematical Discoveries
    Writing

---

Public Relations:

    See Corporation, (2)
        Robin Hood Sequence, (2)
        Politicians & Defense Budgets, 20 Sep'76

---

Publishing:                                                    (2)

    See Anonymity, 19 Dec'71
        Boole, 1970
        Problem:  Statement Of, Feb'72
        Question Answering, Sep'73

---

RBF DEFINITIONS

Publishing:

"The printing machine belongs to humanity.  There is something mysterious in the system of how things get into print-- and once they do then you no longer have the same responsibility."

- Cite RBF at Penn Bell videotaping, Philadelphia, 30 Jan'75

---

Puerto Ricans Moving into New York:

    See City as Center of Abstract Intercourse (2)

---

RBF DEFINITIONS

Publish:

"Finally after about five years I published this list [of environmental hazards] in an engineering magazine and once it was published it got out of me. I have found that it is good to get things published and forget about them."

- Cite OREGON Lecture #2 - p. 64, 2 Jul'62

---

Pugh, Anthony:

    See Four-triangular Circuits Tensegrity, 6 Apr'77

RBF DEFINITIONS

Pull:

"Precession is the pull."

- Citation and context at Intereffects, 25 Sep'73

Pullout:

See Error: Pullout from Error

RBF DEFINITIONS

Pull:

"A chord has pull: we would probably not think about the connections unless there was some pull between them. The function of the chords is to relate. The event is the vertex. The reaction is the chord, the pulling away."

- Citation and context at Chord, 20 Feb'73

Pull:                                                          (1)

See Airplane Flight as Lift
    Bottom: Pulling the Bottom Up
    Directional Field Pulls
    Low Pressure vs. Positives
    Push-pull
    Push-pull: Push Wave & Pull Wave
    Wind Sucking Sequence
    Dog Pulling on a Belt

RBF DEFINITIONS

Pull:

"The beginning of awareness of intellect is otherness, the mass attraction of another with a pull which relates it to all our system."

- Citation and context at Eternal Instantaneity, 22 Jun'72

Pull:                                                          (2)

See Chord, 20 Feb'73*
    Eternal Instantaneity, 22 Jun'72*
    Intereffects, 25 Sep'73*
    Rate, 9 Nov'72
    Rowing Needles (1)(2)
    Orbit, 20 Jan'75
    Weather as Exchange of Highs & Lows, (1)
    Wind Stress & Houses, (7)
    Integrity, 2 Nov'73
    Gravity, 11 Feb'76

RBF DEFINITIONS

Pull:

"In all our experiences there are relatively few principles that are operative in nature; as for instance we had the first instance when we tried to pull something as a child. We tried to pull paper apart, pull books apart, and then we began to try to pull sheets apart and we tried pulling things apart. Then we get onto a boat and someone says "Hold on to that rope," and you find you are pulling very hard. They say pull this way and then that way-- one is called a sheet and one a halyard and so forth. You have this experience on a special boat and are very excited and for many years you will always think about the "Primrose" and your fun sailing the 'Primrose' on this special day. You gradually get onto other boats and you find there are the same kind of things to be pulled. And you find there is a general kind of thing to be pulled in contrdistinction to things that are pushed. This is what we call a generalization. We are beginning to discover patterns that persist, principles that are operative independent of whether the rope was white, or dirty, or yellow, whether it was plastic or whatever it was, you still pulled it."

- Cite Oregon Lecture #2, p. 55. 2 Jul'62

Pulmotor:

See Scenery: Rearrange the Scenery, (2)

Pulsars: (1)

See Black Hole
    Omnilibrium

---

RBF DEFINITIONS

Pulsation:

"One of the things we have to make clear for society
is the dilemma of the Max-Planck-descended scientists,
the way they do their problems, you can have either a
wave or a particle, but not both simultaneously.
Heisenberg has the same fault. They make the error of
having a wave as a continuity, as a picture-- not as a
pulsating frequency. A planar reflex causes them to
think of continuous waves."

- Cite RBF to EJA, Somerset Club, Boston, 22 April 1971
- Citation at Wave vs. Particle, 22 Apr'71

---

Pulsar: (2)

See Omniequilibrium, (2)

---

RBF DEFINITIONS

Pulsation: ████████████

"What appears to be congruence will require pulsation,
synchronized pulsation of two separate entities."

- Cite RBF to EJA, 3200 Idaho, Washington DC, 25 Jan '72
- Citation & context at Congruence, 25 Jan'72

---

RBF DEFINITIONS

Pulsation:

"The inward-outward expandibility is the basis of convergence-
divergence and radiation-gravitation pulsation-- which seems
furthest from man's awareness. This is what science has
discovered: a world of waves in which waves are interpenetrated
by waves in frequency modulation. There is a systemic
interrelationship of basic fourness always accompanied by a
sixness of alternatives or freedoms."

- Cite RBF to EJA, 3200 Idaho, incorporated in SYNERGETICS
  draft at Sec. 411.36; 9 Nov'72
           [35]

---

Pulsating Controls:

See Cyclic Bundling of Experiences, May'49

---

RBF DEFINITIONS

Pulsation:

"Pulsation, the vector equilibrium is the nearest thing we
will ever know to ███ eternity and God: the zerophase of
conceptual integrity inherent in the positive and negative
asymmetries which propagate the problems of the
consciousness. . . ."

- Citation & context at Experience, 12 Sep'71
- Cite RBF to EJA, Beverly Hotel, 12 Sept. 1971

---

Pulsation: Pulsativeness: (1)

See Asymmetric Pulsation
    Discontinuity
    Feedback: Self-accelerating Feedback
    Interpulsativeness
    Inward & Outwardness
    Nuclear & Nebular Zonal Waves
    Omnipulsative: Omniinterpulsative
    Oscillation & Pulsation
    Resonance
    Wave System Propagations
    Wow
    Pulse Pattern
    Pulse: Pulsive: Pulsivity
    In, Out & Around Experiences
    Expanding & Contracting

---

---

RBF DEFINITIONS

Pulse Pattern:

". . . Talking about edges of the three frequency vector equilibrium where there are 92 balls on the surface. Now there would be then a frequency of ■ three, but there are four balls to an edge going point-to-point, with three spaces in between them. An edge of four balls could either belong to the adjacent square ot it could belong to the triangle. It can't belong to them exclusively: it is like our bonding ..... where we get common edges. When I began to take the sequence of the ■ wave pattern I found them running through the indigs of always eight of the zero nine. I found some of them are characterized by not only that one that 's plus one, plus two, plus three, plus four, minus, plus four, plus three--- what am I saying? Minus one, minus two, minus three, minus four, plus four, plus three, plus two, plus one."

- Cite RBF to EJA. Tape transcript. Chez Wolf. 18 June 1971. pp. 36-37.

---

RBF DEFINITIONS

Pulse Pattern:

"The great circles of the vector equilibrium. . . There is

one that goes through six vertexes: it has the most possible connections. Six great circles are only going through two vertexes. . . So you've got a very even amount of minus one, minus one, plus two. This is a sequence that occurs time and again. Which is, I have a ball . . and this is no, no, yes, yes, no, no-- this is nestability of the ball in the center. It is the same as that yes, no, no, yes or yes, no, no, or minus one, minus one, plus two. It is that kind of a sequence. . . Then it goes on again yes, yes, no, yesy, yes, no. Or it goes always yes, yes, yes, yes, yes. Or yes, yes, no, yes, yes, no. Or it goes yes, no, yes, no, yes, no. Or it goes yes, yes, yes, yes. There are three ways it can behave. . . . You hemispheres are the opposite of the same so it goes yes, yes, no or no, no, yes. . . Or it could go yes, no, yes, no , yes, no. Or it goes yes, yes, yes. These are all the combinations you can get. . . "

- Cite tape transcript RBF to EJA and BO'R, Chicago, Blackstone Hotel, 1 June 1971. pp. 14-15.

---

RBF DEFINITIONS

Pulse Pattern:

"Beginningless and endless Scenario Universe

With its vast frequency ranges

Of omni-interpulsative

Yes-no, give-and-take

Radial expansions and circumferential contractions.

p Citation at Scenario Universe, Jan'72
- Cite EVOLUTIONARY 1972-1975 ABOARD SPCE VEHICLE EARTH, Jan '72.

---

RBF DEFINITIONS

Pulse Pattern:

"But the six is really the beautiful connector on the vector equilibrium side and it is the one that goes through all the six vertexes. It has the most possible connections. ■■■■

". . . It's a kind of double pulsation. . . It's only going to send energy when it's going through a vertex. So it does this twice in a cycle. Its energy increments between the two going: yes, yes, no; yes, yes, no: so they add up to a pulse. It goes yes, yes, no; boom, no, no; boom, no, no. "

- Cite tape transcript RBF to DK and BO'R, 2 May 1971, pp. 8-9.

---

RBF DEFINITIONS

Pulse Pattern:

"How brilliant and conceptually advanced
Were the Phoenicians' high seas predecessors,
The Polynesians,
For the latter had long centuries earlier
Discovered the binary system of mathematics
Whose 'congruence in modulo two'
Provided unambiguous,
Yes - no; go - no go
Cybernetic controls
Of the electronic circuitry
For the modern computer
As it had for milleniums earlier
Functioned most efficiently
In storing and retrieving
All the special-case data
In the brains of the Polynesians
By their chanted programming
And their persistent retention
Of the specific but no longer comprehended
Sound pattern words and sequences
Taught by their successive
Go - no go, male-female pairs of ancestors."

- Cite Numerology draft August 1971, p.22.

---

RBF DEFINITIONS

Pulse Pattern:

". . . Those have the extraordinary quality of going through a pumping business...54°44'; 55° 44'; 70° 32'. . . . I use 60° as normal instead of 90°, so 54° 44' is 6° 16'; 5° and 16'. There's 10° and 32'. This is plus two and this is minus one, minus one, plus two, if 5° 16' is unity. . .

"54° 44' and it leaves you 5° 16'; two time 5° 16' is 10° 32', so it's Minus One Minus One, Plus Two, Minus One, Minus One, Plus Two,. . . As it revolves these are where 60° is again our vector equilibrium so you've got the very even amount of Minus One, Minus One, Plus Two. This is a sequence which occurs time and again. . . I have a ball nest in the center. This is no, no, yes; or yes, no, no. . . Then it goes again: yes, yes, no; yes, yes, no, always. This is a basic nuclear arrangement. So you want t o get a telegraph system that is going to flash with nuclei and it's going to go yes, yes, no; yes, yes, no. That's what you're getting on the six great circles."

- Cite tape transcript RBF to DK and BO'R - 2 May, pp. 6-7. '71

RBF DEFINITIONS

Pulse Pattern:

"It is fascinating to learn that, with the development
of the computer, nature uses a Yes-No or binary system.
This is the basis of waves.  Consequently the polynesians
have been using the most advanced techniques during the
period that we have presumed them to be inferior because
they only counted to two."

- Cite NAGA TO THE INVISIBLE SEA, p. 6, 1970

---

RBF DEFINITIONS

Pulse Pattern:

"We come into some very interesting conditions of the
tetrahedron where we find that a strip of paper, remember
remember that we are exploring ways in which nature with
a given frequency will do certain things.  Remember also
precession.  We find resultant of forces are not at 180°
and therefore there is a tendency to go off angularly.
Therefore a zig-zag like this of identical length members
becomes a very fundamental precessional consequence of a
high frequency event. . . . A continuous strip like this
when folded down, down, up, down, down, up, down, down, up,
would fold back on itself and form the tetrahedron and
octahedron. . . . and the octet truss and fill all space."

- Cite Oregon Lecture #8, p. 300, 12 Jul'62

---

RBF DEFINITIONS

Pulse Pattern:

"In the sixth frequency there is a ball again.  So if you
go on layer after layer you will find that it reads:
nucleus, no nucleus, no nucleus, nucleus, no nucleus, no
nucleus, nucleus, no nucleus, no nucleus.  In other words
it is yes, no, no, yes, no, no.  It is a very different
kind of pattern from yes, no, yes, no . . . or yes, yes, yes,
or no, no, no. . . . When I folded the piece of paper into
a strip and said it was precessing, I said: hill, hill,
valley, hill, valley.  It is this kind of one.  That is, a
nucleus set of events could give you a yes, yes, no which
would be the same as hill, hill, valley-- so it was a
permitted kind of folding in a nuclear set of fundamental
prime set of interactions."

Cite Oregon Lecture #8, p.305, 12 Jul'62

---

Pulse Pattern:                                    (1)

See Binary
    Bits:  Bitting
    Diesel Ship at Sea
    Dot-dash-dot-dash
    Go-no-go
    Yes-no-no
    Yes-no-yes-no
    Now-you-see-it-now-you-don't

---

Pulse Pattern:                                    (2)

See Awareness, Feb'50
    Foldability of Great Circles:  Spherical Vector
        Equilibrium, 11 Oct'62
    Integer, 15 Oct'72
    Nucleus, 18 Feb'73
    Scenario Universe, Jan'72*

---

Pulsivity of Realizations:

See Vector Equilibrium, 30 Oct'73

---

Pulse:  Pulsive:  Pulsivity:                      (1)

See Heartbeat
    Pulsation:  Pulsativeness
    Oscillation
    Oscillation & Pulsation
    Palpitate
    Pulse Pattern
    Pulsation

---

Pulse:  Pulsive:  Pulsivity:                      (2)

See Experience, 12 Sep'71*
    Life, May'49
    Regenerative Design:  Law Of, (2)
    Sphere, 31 May'71
    Time, 6 Mar'73; 27 Dec'73
    Universal Integrity:  Principle Of, Dec'72
    Vector Equilibrium, 30 Oct'73
    Weather, Feb'73
    Critical Proximity, May'71
    Frequency Islands of Perception, 13 Nov'75
    Time is Only Now, 19 Jul'76
    Orbital Feedback Circuitry vs. Critical Path,
        9 Sep'74

Pumping Model:

    See Jitterbug

Punishment:

    See Design Revolution:  Pulling the Bottom Up, (8)(9)
    Human Tolerance Limits, (1): (B)

---

Pump:  Pumpable:        (1)

    See Angle:  Pumping Fraction Factors
    Hydraulics
    Pulsation:  Pulsative

Purchasing:

    See Mobile Rentability vs. Immobile Purchasing

---

Pump:  Pumpable:        (2)

    See Trees, (3)

'Pure' as an Invented Word:

    See Line:  Imaginary Straight Line, 22 Apr'71

---

Punched Cards:

    See File Cards with Triangular Array of Holes

RBF DEFINITIONS

Pure Principle:

"What I am saying is that we have only eternity and integrity.
Unity is plural in pure principle.  The awareness we speak of
as life is inherently immortal and equi-eternal."

- Citation & context at Awareness, 10 Feb'73

- Cite SYNERGETICS draft at Sec. 1009.38, 10 Feb'73

RBF DEFINITIONS

Pure Principle:

"There is nothing that the tough man can get hold of.
That is really what happened during World War I and
society paid no attention to it.  We went off the invisible
and it had been discovered by the people who deal with the
invisible that there are no hard core things.  If you say
that the thing goes off with an awful bang, it is just
like I said to you that the water in a wave isn't going
from here to there.  Yet it is possible for the porpoise
to go from here to there surfboarding along with gravity
pulling him down forwardly in angles, but the water isn't
going from here to there. (There is some top water that gets
blown slowly from east to west, but I'm not talking about
that.)  The ▓▓▓▓▓ is moving at a very great velocity,
and there is no wave of water going there.  It is moving in
pure principle so it is possible for us to realize that
what we call physically pure principle of that bang, because
that porpoise can bang up on the beach pretty hard. What he
is dealing in is weightless."

- Cite Oregon Lecture #4, pp. 123-124.  6 Jul'62

Pure:                                                          (1)

See Inventions vs. Pure Science Events
    Science:  Pure & Applied Science

Pure Principle:                                               (1)

See Generalized Principle
    Perfect Prototype
    Principle

Pure:                                                         (2)

See Communication & Culture, 1 Feb'75
    Male & Female, 21 Jan'75

Pure Principle:                                              (2)

See Absolute Integrity, 4 Nov'73
    Awareness, 10 Feb'73*
    Epistemology of Quantum Mechanics, 16 Dec'73
    Event, 29 May'72
    Particle (2)
    Radiolaria (1)(2)
    Surfing: Surfboarding, 5 Jul'62
    Tetrahedron, 20 Feb'73
    Understanding, 4 Oct'72
    Womb of Permitted Ignorance, 13 Dec'73
    Wave Pattern of a Stone Dropped in Liquid, (1)
    Invisible Tetrahedron, (1)(2)
    Atom, 8 Sep'75
    Cyclic Experience, 1961
    Geodesic Domes, 24 Jan'58

Purge:  Purging:

See Self-purging

Pure Science Events:

See Inventions vs. Pure Science Events

Purines:

See Hex-pent Structure of Purines

Purpose:

    See Ends
        Design
        Meaning
        Teleology

---

Push vs. Attraction:              (2)

    See Hammering Sheet Metal, (2)

---

Purposeless:

    See Culture, 11 Aug'76

---

Push Button & Dial Systems:      (2)

    See Industrial Principle, 1 Jun'49

---

RBF DEFINITIONS

Push:

"...I had kept pushing things, trying them out. And it always seemed to come to a dead end..."

- Citation and context at Fuller, R.B.: Crisis of 1927 (A) Feb'72

---

RBF DEFINITIONS

Pushive:

"Radiation is pushive, ergo tends to increase in curvature.... The pushive tends to arcs of ever lesser radius (microwaves are the very essence of this)..."

- Citation and context at Curvature, 23 Sep'73

---

Push vs. Attraction:              (1)

    See Tensive vs. Pushive

---

RBF DEFINITIONS

Pushive:

"Explosions are pushive and evolute and involute as do rubber toruses."

- Cite RBF caption for Synergetics Illustration #67. Beverly Hotel, New York, 24 April 1971.

- Citation at Explosions, 24 Apr'71

Pushive:

See Tensive vs. Pushive

---

RBF DEFINITIONS

Push-Pull:

"My philosophy also takes heed of the approximately unlimited ratio of length to girth of tensional controls which always tend to _pull true_, versus the very limited length to girth ratio of _pushing_ devices which, when pushed, tend to bend and break."

- Citation and context at _Ruddering Sequence_ (5), 1963

---

RBF DEFINITIONS

Push-pull:

⌐In reviewing with EJA Athena V. Lord's manuscript of PILOT FOR SPACESHIP EARTH, RBF came across a description of conventional stone structures held together by compression . . . "where the top stones are pushing down on the ones beneath._⌐

RBF: "Nothing could be more ███████ erroneous. How could a top stone push? What would it have to push against? . . . . What happens is that gravity pulls the top stone--and all the others--against each other."

- Cite RBF to EJA, 3200 Idaho, Wash, DC.; 28 Mar'77

---

Push-pull Limits:

See Ignorance, (1)

---

RBF DEFINITIONS

Push-Pull:

"The shift between spheres and spaces is accomplished precessionally. You introduce just one energy action-- _push_ or _pull_-- into the field and its inertia provides the reaction to your push or pull; and the resultant propagates the sphere-to-space, space-to-sphere, transformation whose comprehensive synergetic effect in turn propagates an omnidirectional wave. Dropping a stone in the water discloses a planar pattern of precessional wave regeneration. The curves are seen generating and regenerating and are not instantaneous."

- Cite SYNERGETICS draft at Sec. 1032.21, 22 Feb'73
  [20]

---

RBF DEFINITIONS

Push-pull Members:

"Minimum structural stability requires six struts, each of which is a push-pull member. Push-pull structural members embody in one superficially solid system both the axial-linear tension and compression functions.

"Tensegrity differentiates out these axial-linears into separately cofunctioning compression vectors and tension tensors. As in many instances of synergetic behavior, these differentiations are sometimes subtle. For instance, there is a subtle difference between Eulerian topology, which is polyhedrally superficial, and synergetic topology, which is nuclear and identifies spheres with vertexes, solids with faces, and struts with edges. The subtlety lies in the topological differentiation of the relative abundance of these three fundamental aspects whereby people do not look at the four closest-packed spheres forming a tetrahedron in the same way that they look at a seemingly solid stone tetrahedron, particularly when they do not accredit Earth with providing three of the struts invisibly cohering the base ends of the camera tripod."

(Sec. 722)

- Cite SYNERGETICS text at Sec.s 722.01 & 722.02; 28 Oct'72

---

RBF DEFINITIONS

███████ Push-Pull:

"The twelve degrees of freedom are also then identified

as the _push-pull_ directions of the tetrahedron's six edges."

- Cite RBF ltr. to Prof. Theodore Caplow, 18 Feb. '66.

- Citation & context at _Twelve Universal Degrees of Freedom_, 18 Feb'66

---

Push-pull Members:

See Structure, 22 Jul'71

---

Push-pull: Push Phase vs. Pull Phase:

See Visible Light vs. Electricity, 1946

Push-pull: Push & Pull: (2)

See Necklace (1)(2)
Polar Vertexes, 19 Feb'72
Ruddering Sequence (5)*
String, 14 Feb'74
Tensegrity, 20 Oct'72
Tensegrity Sphere, 19 Dec'73
Tetrahedron, 18 Feb'66
Vector Equilibrium, 13 Nov'69; (I)
Structure, 22 Jul'71
Building, 10 Sep'74
Hammering Sheet Metal, (2)
Male & Female, 1 Feb'75
Economics, 1 Feb'75
Omnimedium Transport Sequence, (3)
Invisible ≠ Negative, 28 May'75
Wind Stress & Houses, (10)(11)
Basic Event, Dec'71
Triangle, Nov'71
Window, 22 Nov'77

Push-pull Stabilization:

See Tensegrity Geodesic Grid: Three-way Grid, 10 Oct'63

Push: (1)

See Pushive
Push-pull

RBF DEFINITIONS

Push-Pull: Push Wave & Pull Wave:

"The push wave is high frequency.

The pull wave is low frequency.

The vector equilibrium consists not of curved lines but

of wave lines."

- Cite RBF to EJA, Bear Island, 25 August '71.

Push: (2)

See Curvature, 23 Sep'73
Explosions, 24 Apr'71
Flight, 1971
Evolution, 22 Jun'75

Push-pull: (1)

See Energetic Functions
Inventory of Push-pull Alternations
Intereffects
Oscillation
Structural Functions
Tidal
Push vs. Attraction
Tension & Compression

RBF DEFINITIONS

Puzzle of Washington Crossing the Delaware: (1)

"I am holistic and I really don't want to be limited. It's
like a bunch of picture puzzles that we used to have with a
picture on the box of what you were making. But let's just
suppose we had no picture on the box, and we had ten puzzles
in different transparent plastic bags, and we mixed them all
up each of the puzzles with the other. puzzles. I think we
could, you and I, sort of intuit which kinds of pieces must
be with one puzzle and which kinds of pieces with another and
eventually we could at least get them all in the right bags
again so they could be worked out.

"That's what it's been like here working these days. Like we
had a picture puzzle of George Washington Crossing the Delaware.
We'd have one little piece that looked like some ice and we'd
have another little piece that looked like George's hat. And
we're really just throwing in the tiles and that's what I'm
doing giving a lecture, when the kids are all following it
and you really can go very fast while you're talking about
George Washington's hat and then you're talking about the ice
around the boat. All that you really have to say and all that
you have time for in the lecture is just to say HAT or just to"

- Citation and context at Cosmic Fish Sequence (4), 16 Oct'72

RBF DEFINITIONS

Puzzle of Washington Crossing the Delaware:                    (2)

"say ICE, like that. And everybody follows and we're really
throwing in the tiles and we have the picture of George
Washington Crossing the Delaware."

- Citation and context at Cosmic Fish Sequence (4), 16 Oct'72

---

Pyramid = Half-octahedron:

See Pyramid, 17 Oct'72
    Dimpling Effect, (B)

---

Puzzle of Washington Crossing the Delaware:

See Generalizations Reduced to One Word
    Idea Increments

---

RBF DEFINITIONS

Pyramid Technology:

"With starvation-provoked universal thieving they had to
build a strong pyramid to guard the Pharaoh's after-life
equipment. This required the invention of scaffolding
technology in the present life. When successive Pharaohs
passed into heaven the scaffolding technology accumulated
on Earth. With a mounting technology the nobles also
acquired protective entry into the after-life. As generations
of Pharaohs and nobles went from this world into heaven, this
world's technology multiplied. Inevitably the citizens or
middle class exploited the burgeoning technology to gain
entry into heaven with the Pharaohs and the nobles.
Inaugurating the Greco-Roman period of history with knowledge
and technology multiplying swiftly, the Moses, Buddhas,
Christs, and Mohammeds proclaimed the feasibility of safe
entry into heaven of everybody. This ushered in 1500 years
of building cathedrals, temples, synagogues, mosques and
their graveyards to secure everyone's after-life."

- Cite RBF dictation to BO'R, Chicago, Dec. '71 to be inserted
  at galleys of Barry Farrell PLAYBOY Interview.

---

RBF DEFINITIONS

Pyramid:

"An Egyptian pyramid is a half-octahedron. The other
half is hidden in the ground."

- Cite RBF in address to Dag Hammerskjold College, Columbia,
  Md., 17 Oct'72.

---

Pyramid Technology:  Pyramids:

See Inertia, 20 Apr'72
    Buddha:  Christ:  Mohamed, (1)

---

TEXT CITATIONS

Pyramid of Generalizations:

Synergetics, 2nd. Ed. draft Secs. 325.20 - .25

---

Pyramid:  Great Pyramid at Gizeh:

See Octahedron:  Eighth-octahedra, (1)

Pyramid Mystery Cults:

    See Octahedron: Eighth-octahedra, (4)

Pythagoras:                          (1)

"We come then to Greece and the earliest of the going from just geometry into numbers and arithmetic and we get to our friend Pythagoras. Pythagoras was a very unknown kind of a character, he's quite a mystical one; he's almost like one of the prophets. The Pythagoreans kept things secret. Pythagoras taught us many things about the second powers of numbers. He was the first to discover the arithmetical second powering and third powering. All the integration of the arithmetic with the geometry comes from Pythagoras.

"And we have Pythagoras... having experimentally tried twanging a string, what you might call a stringed instrument and finding that when it had a flat at half the length of the prime string it brought about a change in notes which we today would call on the $\angle$ ? $\sqcup$ scale, exactly one octave. This is a Pythagorean discovery; and a man who was terribly interested in fundamental rates of change of number, by various operations of the numbers, one with the other, and all the powerings.

"We have him also then thirding the end of the string and discovering that this took the tone what we call 'down,'"

- Cite tape transcript, RBF to EJA, Chez Wolf, 18 Jun'71

---

Pyramid:                          (1)

    See Octahedron: Half Octahedron
        Tetrahedron: Quarter Tetrahedron

Pythagoras:                          (2)

"either down or up, what we call a fifth, and what we then have is the keys of the sharps or the flats, these are the fifths up and down, the sharps being a fifth up and the flat being a fifth down; five notes in the scale-- so that we have very interesting prime numbers halving the number two and the thirding bringing about fifths. This would certainly indicate quite clearly a fundamental in our relationship between wave frequencies and number behaviors of octaves. And inasmuch as I'm talking about physics and the waves of the periodic table... its unique frequencies would interact... and what the permutations would be mathematically and I found this highly suggestive that the octave with its characteristically flat resonance really governing the interactions of frequencies. The resonances are the key to much of modern physical exploration. And I think that the very fact that the Pythagoreans were particularly secret is of importance."

- Cite RBF to EJA, tape transcript, Chez Wolf, 18 Jun'71

---

Pyramid:                          (2)

    See Cube: Diagonal Of, 10 Jul'62
        Harmonics, (1)-(4)
        Octahedron as Photosynthesis Model,(B)(C)
        Octahedron: Eighth-octahedra, (1)(4)

Pythagoras:  Pythagorean Theorem:       (1)

    See Control Line of Nature
        Hypotenuse
        Cube: Diagonal of Cube as Control Length
        Tensed String

---

Pyramidines:

    See Hex-pent Structure of Purines, 15 Dec'76

Pythagoras:  Pythagorean Theorem:       (2)

    Cube: Diagonal of Cube as Wave Propagation Model,
          22 Jun'72
        Prime Vector, 20 Jul'74; (2)
        Radiation-gravitation: Harmonics, 3 Jan'75
        Harmonics, (1)
        Mites & Quarks as Basic Notes, (2)

Quadrangle: Quadrangular:

See Triangular Accounting vs. Quadrangular Accounting

Qualitative:

See Quantitative vs. Qualitative

Quadrant:

See Spherical Quadrant Phases
XYZ Quadrant at Center of Octahedron

RBF DEFINITIONS

Quantize:

"The A and B modules quantize our total experience."

* Cite RBF in Synergetics draft 740.1, 14 Sept. 1971.
Re-editing of Oregon Lecture #8, p. 285.

Quadrivalent:                                    (1)

See Omnicongruence.
Self-congruence Packing
Chemical Bonds: Quadruple Bond

Quantized Models:

See Synergetics vs. Model (D)

Quadrivalent:                                    (2)

See Octahedron, 10 Dec'75
Quanta Loss by Congruence, (1)(2)
Four Intergeared Mobility Freedoms, 2 Nov'73

Quantitative vs. Qualitative:

See Synergetic vs. Model (A)

Quantitative: Quantation: Quantized: (1)

See Conceptual vs. Quantitative
    Accounting
    Measurement
    Tetravolume

---

Quantitative: Quantation: Quantized: (2)

See Information, 1967
    Synergetic Hierarchy, 13 Nov'69
    Unit, 1960
    Energy Involvement of 92 Elements, (2)
    Critical Proximity, May'71
    Epistemological Accounting, Nov'71
    Modules: A & B Quanta Modules, 20 Dec'73
    Energetic Information, 20 Dec'74
    Potential vs. Primitive, 12 May'77

---

RBF DEFINITIONS

Quantum Sequence: (1)

"Omnitriangulation —→ strutural system —→ one unit of quantum —→ Lavoisier thought of the nothingness (air) under the bell jar as a plurality of somethingnesses (elements). Under these circumstances you did not have to wait long for the inevitable development of the steam engine.

"Then, invisible electromagnetics —→ no models. Black body radiation involves fourth-power rates of change. Therefore, they said, nature is not using models; she is just using mathematics. The scientists were flying blind on instruments; they said there was no point in trying to look out of the windows; there is nothing to see.

"Design science employs the method of accounting employed by nature.... Suppose you need six hours to solve your problem. The XYZ coordinates only provide a four-hour clock, a positive-negative, positive-negative, 90-degree clock: perpendicularity gives you only four hours. But since you need six hours you have to resort to mathematics in which you can borrow from yesterday's or from tomorrow's clock.... But with the 60-degree hexagon you have an integral six-hour clock."

- Cite RBF to World Game Workshop, Rainey Auditorium, U. Penn., 23 Jun'75

---

RBF DEFINITIONS

Quantum Sequence: (2)

"Scientists deal only in linear acceleration reduced to 90-degree grids. They have no model for angular acceleration. The circumferntial and chordal measurements are always in terms of irrational hypotenuses. In the XYZ coordinate system the parallels never converge and the cube has no inherent nucleus: eight cubes around a common center. But the symmetrical expansion of radiation is a divergent phenomenon. Thus we see how man entered the world of nature through the attic window.

"Design science and our very way of thinking deals in terms of limit cases. We have the tetrahedron with three triangles around each vertex; the octahedron with four triangles around each vertex; and the icosahedron with five triangles around each vertex. The limit cases of a system are three (tetra) and five (icosa). A perpendicular bisector of each of the icosahedron's 20 triangles (from each of the three edges) describe 60 right triangles; actually 120 similar triangles. But in their spherical conformation the 120 spherical right triangles are not identical. There are 60 positive and 60 negative because of the convexity and concavity of spherical projection. The Babylonians were very close but they were unable to get their"

- Cite RBF to World Game Workshop, Rainey Aud. U. Penn., 23 June'75

---

RBF DEFINITIONS

Quantum Sequence: (3)

"geometry and their clock working together.

"Even the centimeter-gram-second (C.G.S.) system had not temperature in their accounting except as a superscript. C.G.$_t$.S - for temperature.... The human proclivity for 'building blocks' enhanced their proclivity for cubes and cubic accounting. The stacking of regular tetrahedra leave $7^\circ$ 20' gaps which seemed to inhibit their allspace-filling function.

"So I saw that the vector is a specific angular direction in respect to an axis of observation. The vector is beautiful and unique because its discrete length is a product of mass and velocity. All the qualities of physical reality are present: the mass is in the discrete length and the time is in the velocity. Vectors do not go to infinity. Here is the basis for a generalized Avogadro system as it occurred to me 60 years ago.

"The crystals may be probably unique to our planet; they might be incandescent at a different distance from the Sun.... So the peas and toothpicks of kindergarten gave me the first model for closest packing."

- Cite RBF to World Game Workshop. Rainey Auditorium, U. Penn., 23 Jun'75

---

RBF DEFINITIONS

Quantum Sequence: (4)

"You can get 20 tetrahedra around one point omnidirectionally. .... Frequency does not begin until you have modular subdivision. String polyhedra are like the necklace models. The cube, strung through vertexial connections, will not stand up. Only the tetra hedra, octahedm and icosahedron will stand up as string-connected polyhedra with string joints.

"Octahedron: The XYZ quadrant at the center of the octahedron complements the tetrahedron. We may disconnect alternate triangles of the surface of the octahedron and pull eight of them out for the eight-octahedra to make a cube on the octa faces. Thus 1 tetra = ½ octa (i.e. 4 x the eight eighth-octahedra on the corners.) Ergo, cube = 3.

"Two spheres in Universe —→ mass attraction —→ vector equilibrium —→ nuclear assembly. Nuclear assembly starts with an inherent volume of 20, which is the minimum model of nucleation.

"How much do I know? How do I know anything? Our firsthand knowledge of minimum limits is better than all the physics in the textbooks. "

* Cite RBF to World Game Workshop. Rainey Auditorium, U. Penn., 23 Jun'75

---

RBF DEFINITIONS

Quantum Sequence: (5)

"Then we have the total topological inventory of 30 minimum components. Plus two additional components in the poles of the axis of spinnability: 32.... and the ultimate 33rd is the rest of Universe.

"Octahedron: So we have the octahedron in the middle. (Between the tetra and icosa.) It is also the second power of the only even prime number: $2^2 = 4$. The octahedron is the most common form of energy associated as matter. We may consider the octahedron as a water-filled tube, pulling on a water-filled tube. The pulling will make it bulge in the middle. As we pull the gravitational embracement causes a precessional rearrangement of the vector edge whereby one tetrahedron drops out. One quantum has dropped out but, topologically, it is still an octahedron:

        $6V + 8F = 12 + 2$ (Three face-bonded tetra) or

(octahedron) $6V + 8F = 12 + 2$, topologically there is no difference. This is the quantum leap, the quantum jump. With interference it precesses from matter to radiation; and then back again into matter. This is the lever that will bring science into further consideration of synergetics."

- Cite RBF to World Game Workshop, Rainey Auditorium, U. Penn., 23 Jun'75

---

RBF DEFINITIONS

Quantum:

"Quantum as prime-structural-system volume is eternally generalized, ergo transcends any particulate, special-case, physical-energy quantation. Generalized quanta are finitely independent because their prime volumetric-domain-defining lines do not intertouch."

- Citation & context at Domain & Quantum, 17 Feb'73

RBF DEFINITIONS

Quantum:

"Happenability has the vector equilibrium as its minimum
model, ergo the Universe, experience, can't be one quantum."

- ~~Cite RBF to EJA, Bear Island, 25 August 1971.~~
- Citation and context at Happenability, 25 Aug'71

---

RBF DEFINITIONS

Quantum ▧:

"The tetrahedron is a vectorial model of one
quantum of energy."

- Cite NEHRU SPEECH, p. 14, 13 Nov'69

---

RBF DEFINITIONS

Quantum:

"One quantum . . turns out to be also the minimum
structural system of Universe."

- Cite RBF at SIMS, U. Mass, Amherst, 22 July '71, p.22

---

RBF DEFINITIONS

Quantum ▧:

"One quantum = one tetrahedron

"One-half quantum = One-half tetrahedron = One triangle =
= One event."

- Cite P. Pearce Inventory of Concepts, June 1967

---

RBF DEFINITIONS

Quantum ▧:

"At the end of a piece of rope we make a metaphysical
disconnect and a new set of observations are inaugurated,
each consisting of finite quanta integral ingredients
such as the time quality of all finite-energy quanta."

- ~~Cite RBF marginalia of Infinity entry from HOW LITTLE,
Confirmed and expanded Beverly Hotel, N.Y., 19 June 1971.~~
- Citation at Metaphysical Disconnect, 19 Jun'71

---

RBF DEFINITIONS

Quantum ▧:

"An association of positive and negative half quantum
units identifies the tetrahedron as one quantum unit."

(See Illustration #4.)

* Cite SYNERGETICS ILLUSTRATION, caption #4.
1967

---

RBF DEFINITIONS

Quantum:

"Quantum implies particularity."

- For citation and context see Module, 1 Jun '71

---

RBF DEFINITIONS

Quantum ▧:

"The right and left helixes formed of two triangles'
respective sets of three edges each constitute the
vectorial modelling in conceptual array of the positive
and negative "half spins" or "half Quanta" corresponding
respectively to the proton set and the neutron set
consisting of neutron and /positron ? / and neutrino
on the left hand and the proton, electron, and antineutrino on
the right hand. Together these six make one quantum unit,-
which is identified as the tetrahedron."

- Cite DOXIADIS, pp. 312, 313, 20 Jun'66

RBF DEFINITIONS

Quantum ▆▆▆:

"... The number of all the lines, which is to say
the number of all the vectors in the universe, is always
a number which is divisible by six. There are no exceptions.
Now these six vectors are the six edges of the tetrahedron,
which is the basic quantum unit, and consist as we have
seen of two sets of three vectors each, each of which sets
of three comprises one event, each event consisting always of
action, reaction, and resultant."

- Cite ~~CARBONDALE DRAFT IV.17~~
NASA Speech, p. 63. Jun'66

---

RBF DEFINITIONS

Quantum: Event-paired Quanta:

"As vectors, the proton and neutron-- being energy events--
both have reaction and resultant vectors which, due to precession,
are never 180° angular diversions of the actions. Each set of
three vectors looks like a Z. Both the proton's vector group,
with its electron and antineutrino, and the neutron's group,
with its positron and neutrino, are each called one-half Planck's
constant; or one-half spin; or one-half of an energy quantum.

"When we bring together these two sets of three vectors each,
they integrate as six vectors and make one unit of quantum and
coincidentally also make one tetrahedron (of six vector edges).
The eterahedron is veritably the conceptual unit of one energy
quantum."

- Cite NEHRU SPEECH, p.23, 13 Nov'69

---

RBF DEFINITIONS

Quantum ▆▆▆:

"The tetrahedron with three positive edges and three

negative edges consists of two half quanta. These add to

exactly one quantum unit. The tetrahedral quantum unit

constitutes the basic structural system of universe. It

is transformable, but ▆▆▆ ITS topological ▆▆▆ and quantum

identity persists in whole units throughout all experi-

ments with physical universe. It is the only polyhedron

that can be turned inside-out and vice versa by one

energy event."

- ~~Cite NASA Speech, p. 56, Jun'66~~

- Citation ▆▆▆▆▆ at Tetrahedron, Jun'66

---

RBF DEFINITIONS

~~Proton Group and Neutron Group~~ Quantum: Event-Paired Quanta.

"The discovery ▆ that a structural system  may be

described as the sum of its surface angles /in increments of7

720° . . . bears out. . . that the tetrahedron is the basic

quantum unit. It also demonstrates the fundamental

~~twoness~~ twoness of ₔ THE energy quantum's proton-neutron. It also provides

the experimental basis of the Theory of Functions in which

a function can only and always coexist with another function

as demonstrated ▆▆ experimentally in all systems as the

inside-outside, convex-concave, tension-compression couples.

All the foregoing brings us to ▆recognition of why the proton

group and neutron group account rationally for al physical

~~Cite Carbondale IV.18~~ structures."
~ Cite NASA Speech, pp. 63-64. Jul'66

---

Quantum Accounting:

See Parallax, 23 Sep'73

---

RBF DEFINITIONS

Quantum: Event-paired Quanta:

". . . All patterns, for instance, numbers or phonetic

letters, consist of physical ingredients and physical

experience recalls. The physical ingredients consist

inherently of event-paired quanta and the latter's six-

vectored, positive and negative, actions, reactions and

resultants . . . "

- Citation & context at Number, Jun'66

- ~~Citation at Pattern, Jun'66~~

- ~~Cite NASA Speech, p.58, Jun'66~~

---

RBF DEFINITIONS

Quantum: Event-Paired Quanta:

"The six edges of the tetrahedron consist of two sets
of three vectors each corresponding to the three-vector
teams of the proton and neutron, respectively, each of
which three-vector teams are identified by nuclear
physics as
          one-half quantum, or
          one-half Planck's constant, or
          one-half spin,
with always and onlu co-occurring proton and neutron's
combined two sets of three-vector teams together
constituting one unit of quantum of energy, which in turn
is vectorially identifiable as one tetrahedron, which in
turn is identifiable as the mnimum structural system of
Universe."

- Cite SYNERGETICS, "Corollaries," Sec. 240.65. 1971

---

Quantum: Event-paired Quanta:                                    (1)

See Action
    Action-reaction-resultant
    Happening Patterns
    Minimum System:  Minimum Structural System
    Proton & Neutron
    Reaction
    Resultant
    Three-vector Teams
    Z Cobras

Quantum: Event-paired Quanta: (2)

See Cube: Diagonal Of, (1)

---

Quantum Jump: Quantum Leap: (1)

See Octahedron as Conservation & Annihilation Model

---

Quantum Hierarchy:

See Topological & Quantum Hierarchies

---

Quantum Jump: Quantum Leap: (2)

See Basic Triangle: Basic Equilibrium 48 LCD Triangle,
    16 Dec'73
Octahedron as Annihilation Model, 30 Dec'73
Octahedron as Conservation & Annihilation Model,
    23 Jun'75
Geometrical Function of Nine, (6)

---

RBF DEFINITIONS

Quantum Jump:

"The doubling of the vectors is where the quantum comes
in: Nothing is lost!

"It all occurs between the Duo-Tet Cube of 3 (tetra = $1\frac{1}{2}$
and space = $1\frac{1}{2}$) and the biggest nucleated cube of 24. The
six edges of the quantum loss can appear in the VE to
stabilize it as an icosa. The quantum reappears as edges
rather than volume...."

    - Citation & context at Quantum Mechanics: Minimum Geometrical
    Fourness, (3); 26 Aug'76

---

RBF DEFINITIONS

Quanta Loss by Congruence: (1)

"Euler's Uncored Polyhedra Formula:    $V + F = E + 2$

    Vector Equilibrium        $12 + 14 = 24 + 2$

    Octahedron               $6 + 8 = 12 + 2$

    Tetrahedron             $4 + 4 = 6 + 2$

"Though the tetrahedron superficially seems to have only
six vector edges, it has in fact 24. The tetrahedron is
quadrivalent, meaning that four positive and four negative
tetrahedra are congruent."

    - Cite RBF/JRMarquette poster "Deceptiveness of Topology,"
    Phila, PA; circa 15 Dec'76
    (Incorporated in SYNERGETICS 2 draft at Sec. 1033.51, 6 May'77

---

TEXT CITATIONS

Quantum Jump: Quantum Leap:

Goldylocks, p.D1, 27 May'75

▆▆▆▆▆▆▆▆▆▆

539.09

905.51                          $\underline{s1013,60:-}$
982.71                           1013.64

982.73

985.07

1032.11

---

RBF DEFINITIONS

Quanta Loss By Congruence: (2)

"In exploring the intertransformability of the primitive
hierarchy of structuring-as-you-go, omnitriangularly
oriented evolution and the interbonding of its evolving
structural components, we soon discover that the universal
interjointing of systems and their foldability permit the
angularly hinged convergence into congruence of vectors,
faces, and vertices, (see VE Jitterbug) each of whose
multicongruences appear only as one edge, or one vertex, or
one face aspects, wherefore topological accounting as
presently practiced accounts each of these multicongruent
topological aspects as consisting of only one of such aspects.

"Only synergetics accounts for all the congruent (doubled,
tripled, fourfolded) topological aspects' presences by always
accounting for the initial inventory of the comprehensive
rhombic dodecahedron's tetravolumed 48-ness and the vector
equilibrium's inherent tetravolume 20-ness, together with
their respective initial or primitive inventories of vertices,
faces, and edge lines, which are always present in all stages
of the 48 ➔ 1 convergence transformation, though often
imperceptibly so."

    - Cite RBF/JRMarquette poster "Deceptiveness of Topology,"
    Phila, PA; circa 15 Dec'76 See SYNERGETICS 2 at 1033.52+.53

RBF DEFINITIONS

Quanta Loss by Congruence:                                              (3)

"With recognition of the foregoing topological deceptiveness
and always keeping account of the primitive total inventory
of such aspects, we find it possible to conceptually demonstrate
and prove not only the validity of Boltzman's concepts, but
of all quantum phenomena, and thereby to conceptually inter-
link synergetics' mathematical accounting with the operational
data of physics and chemistry and their complex associabilities
manifest as geology, biology, et al."

- Cite RBF/JRMarquette poster "Deceptiveness of Topology,"
  Phila, PA; circa 15 Dec'76
- Incorporated in SYNERGETICS 2 draft at Sec. 1033.54

---

RBF DEFINITIONS

Quantum Mechanics:  Grand Strategy:

"The grand strategy of quantum mechanics may be described
as progressive, numerically rational fractionating of the
limit of total energy involved in eternally regenerative
Universe."

- Cite SYNERGETICS, 2nd. Ed., at Sec. 937.11, 10 Apr'75

---

RBF DEFINITIONS

Quantum:  Paired-event Quanta:

"The recallable ingredients of experience consist inherently
of paired-event quanta of six-vectored, positive and negative,
actions, reactions, and resultants."

⌐N.B.:  RBF corrections to SYNERGETICS galley
at Sec. 505.12 suggest his preference for above
term as replacement for Event-paired Quanta. ⌐

- Citation and context at Happening Patterns, 6 Nov'73

---

RBF DEFINITIONS

Quantum Mechanics:  Grand Strategy:

"... Fractionating the whole: that is quantum strategy.
Everything should be neutral until muted."

- Citation & context at Harmonics, (1), 1 Feb'75

---

RBF DEFINITIONS

Quantum Mechanics:

"I saw that the whole complex of everyday reality which

compounded to constitute the 'environment' continuity

was altogether identifiable as pure quantum mechanics.

It could therefore be treated with rigorously as a design

science."

- ~~Cite NASA Speech, p. 36.~~ Jun'66
- Citation & context at Environmental Events Hierarchy (4), Jun'66

---

RBF DEFINITIONS

Quantum Mechanics:  Grand Strategy:

"The quantum mechanics of Universe reveals that the big
ones are the least frequent.  This is the hierarchy of
environmental events.  Tornadoes vs. Mosquitoes.  There
is an hourglass pattern.  And there are specific designing
criteria.  I wouldn't know how to make a house nova-proof.
I don't have to try.  This is quantum mechanics."

- Cite RBF at Penn Bell videotaping, Philadelphia, 30 Jan'75

---

RBF DEFINITIONS

Quantum Mechanics:

"As a consequence of discovering that the 'environment'

could be effectively analyzed by quantum mechanics, it

then became clear that what men had been designating as

'typhoons' or 'dew' fell into a table of abstract numbers

elegantly arrangeable in an order of energy magnitudes."

- ~~Cite NASA Speech, p. 36.~~ Jun'66
- Citation & context at Environmental Events Hierarchy (5), Jun'66

---

RBF DEFINITIONS

Quantum Mechanics:  Grand Strategy:

"Dealing always in terms of a finite Universe or totality

of behavior, we are able to work from the generalized whole

to the particular or special-case manifestation of the

generalized accounting.  This is the basis of the grand

philosophical strategy of quantum mechanics."

UNIVERSE - SEC. 305.627
- Cite NASA Speech, pp. 29-30.  Jun'66

RBF DEFINITIONS

Quantum Mechanics:  Grand Strategy:

"My working assumption that unity was plaural and at minimum
two actually changed the grand strategy in quantum wave mechanics."

- Citation & context at Unity Is Plural, 6 Jul'62

---

Quantum Mechanics:  Grand Strategy:

      See Harmonics, (1)*
         Unity Is Plural, 6 Jul'62*
         Considerable Set, 1959
         Generalization & Special Case, Nov'71

---

RBF DEFINITIONS

Quantum Mechanics:  Minimum Geometrical Fourness:                    (1)

"You can take stones and break them into smaller stones
and they will always remain polyhedra--no matter how small.
It is like piezo-crystals. You can break down stones →
into crystals → into atoms → into minimum set. There
is the inevitable minimum set = crystal = tetra.
Electromagnetics--like ultrasonics--has a minimum geometrical fourness: What is a chord? What is a quark? well,
there are a minimum of four frequencies. The crystals are
four-dimensional. Time → spectrum."

- Cite RBF to EJA, from Deer Isle, Sunset, ME; 26 Aug'76

---

RBF DEFINITIONS

Quantum Mechanics:  Minimum Geometrical Fourness:                    (2)

"The cosmic hierarchy shows that the rhombic dodecahedron,
rather then the vector equilibrium, is the largest in the
hierarchy and is also allspace-filling. The successive
polyhedra result from further closest packing in which
every closest packed sphere has its passive complement.
The spheres transform into spaces and the spaces into
spheres (as shown in Sec. 1032.)
"This explains why the physicists did notunderstand Boltzmann's law and how they didn't employ the powerful tool
of Euler's topology. They would not have seen the connection with Euler's constant relative abundance without my"

- Cite RBF to EJA, telephone from Sunset,ME; 26 Aug'76

---

RBF DEFINITIONS

Quantum Mechanics:  Minimum Geometrical Fourness:                    (3)

"extraction of the polar twoness and without synergetics'
analysis which demonstrates the doubling of the vectors.
The doubling of the vectors is where the quantum comes in:
Nothing is lost!
"It all occurs between the Duo-Tet Cube of 3 (tetra = 1½
and space = 1½ ) and the biggest nucleated cube of 24.
The six edges of the quantum loss can appear in the VE to
stabilize it as an icosa. The quantum reappers as edges
rather than volume. The hierarchy is topological. Even
the rhombic dodecahedron has to be omnitriangulated to
become stabilized. Each of its diamond faces has to be"

- Cite RBF to EJA, by telephone from Sunset, ME: 26 Aug'76

---

RBF DEFINITIONS

Quantum Mechanics:  Minimum Geometrical Fourness:                    (4)

connected (along the short fold) . . . and you will find
that it takes two quanta to do that.
"The 1, 2, 3, and 5 sequence : these are the three-event
vectors that also show up in the vector model of the
magic numbers (Sec. 995.)"

- Cite RBF to EJA, by telephone from Sunset, ME; 26 Aug'76

---

Quantum Mechanics:  Minimum Geometrical Fourness:

      See Polyhedra, 18 Jul'76
        Tetrahedron as Microsystem, 12 May'77

---

Quantum Mechanics:                                                   (1)

      See Epistemology of Quantum Mechanics
        Quantum & Wave
        Half Spin
        Chain Reaction
        Quark
        Superatomics
        Transuranium Elements
        Electron

# Synergetics Dictionary

Quantum Mechanics:                                              (2)

See Considerable Set, 1959
    Environmental Events Hierarchy (4)*; (5)*
    Minimum Set, 18 Nov'72
    Multiplication By Division, 24 Sep'73; 20 Jan'77
    Octantation, May'73
    Spin, Dec'71
    Subfrequency (1)
    Synergetics,(p.101) Jun'66
    Unity is Plural, 6 Jun'62
    Wholes & Parts, 10 Dec'73
    Nine, 16 May'75
    Tetrahedron:  Nine Schematic Aspects, 30 Aug'75
    Environment, 29 Mar'77
    Human Beings & Complex Universe, (4)

Quantum Values:                                                (2)

See Universal Integrity:  Manifest Ratios & Potential
    Ratios, 1 Apr'72

Quantum Propagation:

See Frequency, 22 Jun'72

RBF DEFINITIONS

Quantum Wave Phenomena Sequence:                               (1)

"We say that Universe is design and that design is governed
exclusively by frequency and angular modulations, wherefore
the 'angle' and 'frequency' must be discretely equatable with
quantum mechanics which deals always synergetically with the
totality of Universe's finite energy.

"The relative acutenesses and the relative obtusenesses of the
angle and frequency modulating must relate discretely to the
relative mass experienciabilities of Universe.

"Quantum wave phenomena's omni-wholeness of required a priori
accountability and persistent consideration is always systematically conceivable as a sphere and may be geodesically
fractioned into great-circle-plane subsets for circular plane
geometry considerability.  Quantum waves always complete their
cycles (circles).  The circle can be divided into any number
of arc increments as with the teeth of a circular gear-- many
little teeth or a few big teeth.  In quantum wave phenomena we
may have a few big, or many small, differentiated events, but
they will always add to the same whole."

- Cite SYNERGETICS draft at Secs. 539.01-.03, 23 Sep'73

Quantum Theory:

See Neutral Axis, 1 Jan'75
    Uncertainty Principle, May'67

RBF DEFINITIONS

Quantum Wave Phenomena Sequence:                               (2)

"The rate of angular change in a big wave is very much slower
than the rate of angular change in a small wave, even though
they look superficially to be the same forms-- as do two circles
of different size appear to be the same form.  The difference
in the wave that is big and the wave that is small, is always
in relation to the dimensioning of the observer's own integral
system and determines the discrete difference, (i.e., the
'relativity') of the wave angle.

"What is 'the most economical relationship' or 'leap' between
the last occurred event and the next occurring event?  It is
the chord (identifiable only by central angle) and the rate
of the central-angle reorientation-aiming most economically
toward that event, which is the angular (momentum) █████
energy change involved in the angular and frequency modulation
of all design of all pattern integrity of Universe."

- Cite SYNERGETICS draft at Secs. 539.04 + .05, 23 Sep'73

Quanta Values:                                                 (1)

See Energy Quanta Values

Quantum & Wave:

See Divide & Conquer Sequence, (1)
    Environment Controls, (1)
    Environment Events Hierarchy, 1954
    Physics, 28 Jun'72
    Periodic Table:  Harmonics of 18, 22 May'75
    Synergetics, Nov'71
    Environment, 29 Mar'77

Quantum: (1)

A Quanta Module
B Quanta Module
T Quanta Module
See Control Quantum
Discontinuity
Energy Quanta
Package
Proton & Neutron
Relative Quanta Ratios
Structural Quanta
Teleologic Quanta Series
Vector: Threeness of the Vector
Wave Quantum
Wave Quantum & Indig Bow Ties
Wave vs. Particle
Z Cobras
Volumetric Quantum
Photon-quantum
Domain & Quantum
Invisible Quantum
Metaphysical & Physical Tetrahedral Quanta
Fourth Quantum
Basic Event
Structural Quanta vs. Volumetric Quanta

TEXT CITATIONS

Quark:

(For RBF discussion of quark in synergetics see Ltr. to Dr. Robt. W. Horne, pp. 3 - 6, 14 Feb '66.)
Sec. 260.12 (2nd. Ed.)

s260.12

s1052.32

s1052.343

s1052.357

Quantum: (2)

See Angular Topology: Principle Of, 14 Feb'66
Finite, 14 Feb'66
Finite Furniture, 11 Feb'71
Gravity (2)
Happenability, 25 Aug'71*
Isotropic Vector Matrix, 13 Nov'69
Metaphysical Disconnect, 19 Jun'71*
Minimum Set, 18 Nov'73
Neutral Angle, 16 Dec'73
Omnifinite, 11 Feb'71
Pi, Nov'71
Powering (B)
Module, 1 Jun'71
Seven Axes of Symmetry, 13 May'73
Tetrahedron, 20 Jun'66; (2); 5 Mar'73; Jun'66*
Universe, 25 Aug'71
System & Structure, 16 Aug'70
VE & Icosa, 10 Apr'75
Invisible Tetrahedron, (1)

Quark: (1)

See Mite as Model for the Quark
Half Spin
Quantum Mechanics
Mites & Quarks as Basic Notes
Strange Particles

Quantum: (3)

See Quantum Accounting
Quantum: Event-paired Quanta
Quantum Hierarchies
Quantum Jump
Quantum: Paired-event Quanta
Quantum Mechanics
Quantum Mechanics: Grand Strategy
Quantum Propagation
Quantum Theory
Quantum Values
Quantum & Wave Mechanics
Quantum Wave
Quantum Wave Phenomena Sequence
Quanta Loss by Congruence

Quark: (2)

See Angular Topology: Principle Of, 14 Feb'66
Invisibility of Macro- and Macro- Resolutions, (2)
Microsystems, 22 Mar'76
Quantum Mechanics: Minimum Geometrical Fourness, (1)
Tetrahedron as Microsystem, 12 May'77

RBF DEFINITIONS

Quarks:

Q.     "The high-energy particle physicists have their devices ever seeking the final smallest particle. Will the quarks become quarklets? Are the quarks a by-product of the devices used to seek them, or are they a priori?"

RBF:     "Yesterday I gave you the A and B Quanta Modules... and a tensed string as a system with mathematical properties. Thus the Mites identify with quarks.

"Being tetrahedra, it is no trouble to halve the mites into lower and lower altitude scalene tetrahedra... the infinite spinnability of the quarter tetrahedra. There is no limit; but they may arrive at incredibly small volume.... These may well show up as quarklets."

- Cite RBF to World Game Workshop'77; Phila., PA; 22 Jun'77

RBF DEFINITIONS

Quarry: Quarrying:

". . . By progressively eliminating the degrees of absurdity and working back to the not too absurd . . . he is liable to be able at least to learn the quarry, where his quarry is in a small area. What we call quarrying is objective. These are hunting terms."

- Cite tape transcript RBF to EJA and BO'R, Chicago, 1 June 1971.

- Citation and context at Reductio ad Absurdum, 1 Jun'71

Quarry: Quarrying: (1)

See Boole
    Irrelevancies: Dismissal Of
    Reductio ad Absurdum
    Twenty Questions

---

Quarry: Quarrying: (2)

See Reductio ad Absurdum, 1 Jun'71* ; Nov'71

---

Quarterback:

See Ignorance as Quarterback

---

Quarterback: We Applaud the Quarterback and Not the Lineman: (2)

See America, 22 Jul'71
    Organic Model, Oct'66

---

Queen Mary: (Steamship):

See Continuous Man, (1)
    Industry, 1963
    Ruddering Sequence, (2)
    Tools: Craft & Industrial, 1970; 5 May'67
    Trim Tab, Feb'72
    Dome over Manhattan, 28 Jan'75
    Geoscope, 29 Jan'75
    North-south Mobility of World Man, (1)

---

RBF DEFINITIONS

Questions: Answering Questions:

Q. Do you wish to continue this communications mode?

A. "I do not wish anything. I am grateful for 'what happens.'
I am committed to problem solving by positive competent
participation in the inexorable physical evolution's transformative stratagems. I am 78. My mail is prodigious. I cannot
answer each letter. Therefore, I write books of answers to
most pressing questions. Have published 12 books. If you read
them all you would not have had to ask the questions that you
did for most of them are answered as best I know how in those
books. Please do not think that I consider myself an authority.
I have been asking myself questions for my whole lifetime and,
a half-century ago, challenged myself to find my own answers
by experiemnt or in the books instead of asking live questions
of others. This did not preclude listening to others when they
spoke voluntarily to me. I decided to commit my answers to
paper so that I could check myself at a later date; in order
by trial and error to learn how to think more adequately and
incisively. I am glad that you have written to me and above
all that you as a young human are interested in such important
questions-- at least to me they are important."

- Cite RBF Ltr. replying to one from James Coley, Sep'73

---

Question Answering:

See Self-querying

---

RBF DEFINITIONS

Question Asking:

"Many years ago I developed a system of question asking in
which I ruled that I must always answer the questions from
experience. My answers must not be based on hearsays, beliefs,
axioms, or seeming self-evidence."

- Citation and context at Science, Jun'66

RBF DEFINITIONS

▨▨▨▨▨▨ Question-asking Possibility:

"There is a question-asking possibility that metaphysical omniscience may be transcendental in its velocity to that of omnipotence, i.e., the definitive physical speed of energy as radiation."

- Cite OMNIDIRECTIONAL HALO, p. 163, as rewritten by RBF in Washington DC, 21 Dec. 1971.
* Citation at Metaphysical and Physical, 21 Dec'71

---

RBF DEFINITIONS

▨▨▨▨▨▨ Question-asking Possibility:

"There is a question-asking-possibility that omniscience may be transcendental in velocity to the definitive physical speed of energy omnipotence."

- Cite Omnidirectional Halo. p. 163. 1960
- Citation at Omniscience Transcendent of Omnipotence, 1960

---

Question Asking:                                                      (1)

        See Problem:  Statement of the Problem
                      Self-querying
                      Why For? & How Come?

---

Question Asking:                                                      (2)

        See Computer, 1960
            Conscious & Subconscious, Jun'66
            Experience, Jun'66
            Formulations, 1963
            Metaphysical & Physical, 21 Dec'71*
            Omniscience Transcendent of Omnipotence, 1960*
            Science, Jun'66*

---

Question:  Largest Askable & Answerable Question:

        See Universe, (A); Oct'66

---

Question:  Most Comprehensive:

        See Universe, (1)

---

RBF DEFINITIONS

Question:   Original Question:

". . . Here then is an original question: born through occurrence of unexpected interference in experimental interpatternings. ▨▨▨ Original questions of computers or humans probably are, always, products of unexpected interferences. . . "

- Citation and context at Computer (D), 10 Dec'64

---

RBF DEFINITIONS

Question:  Original Question:

"The scientist-philosophers of computer integration say that because the asking of original questions is a consequence of interferences, and because interferences are products of time sequences, it follows that original questions are both functions and products of time.  There must be a great number of moves and a vast number of computer components before enough time can elapse to develop new types of secondary or tertiary interferences, which in turn may from time to time provoke original questions."

- Citation and context at Computer Asks an Original Question (4) (5), 29 Aug'64

Question: Original Question:                                    (1)


                See Computer Asks an Original Question
                        Starting with Universe

---

Question:                                                      (1)


                See Answer: Answerable
                    Answer: Unit Answer
                    Forty Questions
                    Self-querying
                    Strategic Questions: Inventory Of
                    Twenty Questions
                    Light Side vs. Serious Side of any Question
                    Unanswerable
                    Why: The Unanswerable Why
                    Forgotten Questions

---

Question: Original Question:                                    (2)


                See Computer (D)*
                    Cybernetics, May'65
                    Interference, May'65

---

Question: Questions:                                            (2)


                See Children as Only Pure Scientists, (1)(2)
                    Experience, Oct'66
                    Sculpture as Single Frame, 22 Jul'71
                    Survival, 1938
                    Thinking, 6 Nov'73
                    Wealth as Know-how, (1)

---

RBF DEFINITIONS

    Question Period:

    "Q.  Mr. Fuller, will you be available for a question
            period after the lecture?

    "A.  Sure we can have a question period.  Each young
            person after the lecture can ask himself his own
            good questions and come up with his own answers."


    - Cite RBF on Telephone to Dr. Edwin Elkin, Wash. DC, 16 Oct'72

---

Question:                                                      (3)


                See Question Asking
                    Question: Answering Questions
                    Question-asking Possibility
                    Question: Largest Askable & Largest Answerable
                    Question: Most Comprehensive
                    Question: Original Question
                    Question Period
                    Question: Each Next Good Question
                    Question: Old Question
                    Question: The Question is Survival

---

Question: Each Next Good Question:


                See Future of Synergetics, 1960

---

RBF DEFINITIONS

    Quick and the Dead: Song Of:

    "Song of the Dead
    and the Quick--
    Newton was a noun
    And Einstein is a verb.
    Einstein's norm makes Newton's norm,
    INSTANT UNIVERSE,
    Absurd."


    - Cite HOW LITLLE I KNOW, p.34, Oct'66

Quick & the Dead:                                    (1)

     See Animate & Inanimate


Quick:  Quickness:                                   (2)

     See Locomotion:  Radius of Man's Locomtion, 1 Apr'49


Quick & the Dead:                                    (2)

     See All-acceleration Universe (2)
        Instant Universe, vs. All-motion Universe, 22 Apr'61
        New York City (10)


Quick Death:

     See Death:  Slow Death by Slums vs. War as Quick Death


Quick:  Quickness:                                   (1)

     See Intellect & Quickness
        Reflex

**R**

RBF DEFINITIONS

Race:

"There is no race other than the human race.

"Those who look superficially different
Are the consequence only
Of milleniums of isolation, attrition inbreeding
And inbreeding of the survival types
Under unique environmental conditions.

"If, in fact, there were different races
No political contriving
Could close the psychological gap.

"But in fact
There is only one race."

- Cite EVOLUTIONARY 1972-1975 SPACE VEHICLE Earth,
  Jan. '72, p.14

---

RBF DEFINITIONS

Race:                                                            (4)

"was not genetic, but the consequence of undernourishment:
i.e., the non-chemically-interbalanced and chemically deficient
diet during gestation or the first year of post-wombland
life, which resulted from the meat-eating nobility's monopoly
of the animal flesh resources and the animals' multi-herb
diet."

- Cite Fragment on RACE, 7 Aug'70

---

RBF DEFINITIONS

Race:                                                            (1)

"University stir-ups, also greatly heightened by the cold-
war-stimulated awareness of a century of nonfulfilment of
the U.S.A. war for the emancipation of Blacks, and the
economic and cultural bans which prolong the racist discrimi-
nations against nonwhites... with Blacks skillfully persuaded
into activism...

"I well remember the sense of exultant camaraderie which I
experienced in 1907 when entering 'Upper School' at Milton
Academy. I discovered that the big boys were derisively
displeased with the headmaster and, in learning that he was
to resign, went into a townwide riot of joy. How I whooped
and danced and ran with the others, knowing absolutely nothing
of the merits or demerits of the case against the maligned
and dishonored 'Head.' This gives me insights into the mass
actions of today's students.

"The latter have much more cause for fundamental skepticism,
scorn, displeasure, and action against the establishment in
general because their elders are asleep at the switch of
history's express trains, and because the so-called educational
system is failing to give them powerful insights about what"

- Cite Fragment on RACE, 7 Aug'70

---

Race with Evolution:

    See Synergetics, 21 Jun'71

---

RBF DEFINITIONS

Race:                                                            (2)

"they need to know and do regarding their elders' dereliction.

"There is no social class distinction, no genetic difference:
only history-long brain damaging by undernourishment between
conception and one-year old. There is no race differentiation,
only a bleach-out of hibernating skin-covered, sub-freezing
dwelling zones: Swarthy pink; Sailor mew; Crossbreed-- and go
into the north to remain as Eskimos. Finns and Scandinavian
blondes-- milleniums of tribally inbred long arctic night
hibernaters. Man, born naked prior to invention of clothes,
stayed in temperate zones where his nakedness was tolerable;
but going from Polynesia westward across the Indian Ocean into
arid Africa, he became greatly blackened on his topsides, but
his hands and feet bottoms and fingernail-shielded skin stayed
'white man's' pale pink. White's are bleached out colored
people who are the normal people. The undernourished cereal-
roots- nuts- and bread-eating poor, constituting 99.9 percent
of history-long humanity, thought to be not only illiterate,
but incapable of becoming literate, due to an assumed innate
'dumbness' of the masses. Nobility was assumed, by self and
commoners, to be a kind of god-contrived, different genetic
breed; ergo it was required that the king's sons, daughters,"

- Cite Fragment on RACE, 7 Aug'70

---

Race:

    See Crossbreeding World Man
        No Race: No Class
        World Man
        Nation
        Ethnic

---

RBF DEFINITIONS

Race:                                                            (3)

"nephews, and nieces marry only sons and daughters of royal
or noble stock, whether they be friend or foe.

"Karl Marx assumed the scientific validity of both Malthus
and Darwin with their combined 'fundamental inadequacy of
popular life support' and 'survival only of the fittest.'
He assumed that the working masses were the fittest because,
though dumb, they instinctively understood how to cultivate
agriculture, husband animals, and work the craft tools.
Wherefore the great pirates, the nobility, and the bourgeoisie
who serviced the nobility, were parasites and must perish.
Marx also assumed that the genetic difference between the
nobility and the masses was valid; ergo his fundamental
class warfare inherent in the economic inadequacy to support
both. He also assumed the necessity of downgrading standards
in order to stretch support systems to serve all; and he
assumed minority-party rule by dogmatic adherence to nonindivid-
ualistic code, and annihilation of the treacherous 'other class.'

"For only the last ten years of human history, since 1960,
have we known beyond scientific doubt that the 'mass dumbness'

- Cite Fragment on RACE, 7 Aug'70

---

Racing:

    See Sailboats, Aug'72

Radar Reflector:

See Octahedron: Eighth-octahedra, (2)-(4)

---

RBF DEFINITIONS

Radial-Circumferential:

"We have demonstrated circumferential complementarity, and circumferential twoness of systems such as the Northern and Southern Hemisphers of our Earth. There is also inward and outward complementarity, inward and outward twoness. As a consequence there are also circumferential oscillations and inward and outward pulsations."

- Cite SYNERGETICS draft at Sec. 1051.01, Apr'72 [10]

---

Radar: Radarscope:

See Twenty-foot Earth Globe & 200-foot Celestial Sphere, (1)
Lasso, 1946
Octahedron: Eighth-octahedra, (2)-(4)

---

RBF DEFINITIONS

Radial-Circumferential:

Expansion is radial and contraction is circumferential.

(Adapted)

- Citation at Expansion & Contraction, Jan'72

- Cite EVOLUTIONARY 1972-1975 ABOARD SPACE VEHICLE EARTH, Jan. '72, p. 3.

---

RBF BEFINITIONS

Radial:

"The time dimension being the radial dimension..."

- Citation & context at Dimension, 16 Nov'72

---

RBF DEFINITIONS

Radial-Circumferential:

"We have demonstrated circumferential complementarity, the circumferential twoness of systems such as the Northern and Southern Hemispheres of our Earth. There is also inward and outward complementarity, inward and outward twoness. As a consequence there are also circumferential oscillations and inward and outward pulsations."

- Cite Synergetics, Draft, Sec. 824, August 1971.

---

RBF DEFINITIONS

Radial-circumferential:

"Complementarity of Circumferential Oscillations and Inward and Outward Pulsations: We have demonstrated circumferential complementarity, the circumferential twoness of systems such as the northern and southern hemispheres of our Earth. There is also concave inward and convex outward complementarity, inward and outward twoness. As a consequence, there are also circumferential skew oscillations and inward and outward pulsations."

- Cite RBF rewrite of SYNERGETICS galley at Sec. 1051.10, 9 Jan'74

---

RBF DEFINITIONS

Radial-circumferential:

". . . Circumferential micro- or macro- being finite, and radial being infinite."

- Citation and context at Macro-Micro, 1955

Radial-circumferential Accelerations:


See Gravitational System Zone, 14 Jan'55

---

Radial-Circumferential Modularity:

"The linear measurements represent the radial going-away
accelerations or resultants of earlier or more remote
events as well as of secondary restraints. The rigid
rectlinear angularity of the 90° central angle XYZ mensuration
instituted by the Greeks made impossible any unit language
of direct circumferential or peripheral coordination between
angular and linear phenomena. As a consequence, only the
radial and linear measurements have been available to physics.
For this reason physics has been unable to make simultaneous
identification of both wave and particle aspects of energy
events."

- Cite SYNERGETICS at Sec. 826.04, Sept'72

---

RBF DEFINITIONS

Radial-Circumferential Coordination:

"The coordinate systems of synergetics are omnidirectionally
▌▌▌▌▌▌ regenerative by both lines and planes parallel
to the original converging set. The omnidirectional
regeneration of synergetic coordination may always be
expressed in always balanced equivalence terms either of
radial or circumferential frequency increments."

[50]
- Cite SYNERGETICS draft at Sec. 962.51, 17 Nov'72

---

RBF DEFINITIONS

Radial-Circumferential Modular Growth:

In Synergetics there is a total "correspondence of radial
wave modular growth with circumferential modular
frequency growth of the totally involved vectorial
geometry." This means that "angular and linear
accelerations are identical."

- Cite Ltr. to Prof. Von Hochstetter, p.4 and footnote,
28 Oct'64

---

Radial-circumferential Coordination:

See Analytical Geometry, 7 Oct'71
Life & Death, 26 Jan'76

---

Radial-circumferential Modular Growth:                    (1)


See Frequency Modulation
Modular Subdivision

---

RBF DEFINITIONS

Radial-Circumferential Modularity:

"Had the Greeks originally employed a universal model of
x-dimensional reality as their first tool upon and within
which they could further inscribe and measure with their
divider, scriber, and straightedge, they would have been
able to arrive at unity of circumferential as well as
radial modularity. This would have been very convenient
to modern physics because all the accelerations of all the
constantly transforming physical events of Universe are
distinguished by two fundamentally different forms of
acceleration, the angular and linear accelerations."

- Cite SYNERGETICS at Sec. 826.01, Sept'72

---

Radial-circumferential Modular Growth:                    (2)


See Frequency, Jun'71

Radial-circumferential:                                      (1)


      See Boundary Layer
          Circumferential Finite vs. Radial Infinite
          In, Out & Around
          Inward & Outwardness
          Nuclear & Nebular Zonal Waves
          Radial & Orbital
          Spherical Barrel: Radial Compression vs.
              Circumferential Tension
          Spherical Field
          Inwardness vs. Omnidirectional
          Frequency & Wave

---

RBF DEFINITIONS

   Radial Depth:

   "Operationally omnitriangulated polyhedra may only be
   realized systematically, i.e., with special case dimensionality
   or special case radial depth of insideness. Dimensionality =
   radial depth = frequency. Radial depth is expressed in
   frequency of omnidirectional wave propagations per unit of time."


      - Cite SYNERGETICS, 2nd. Ed., at Sec. 1071.23, 20 Dec'74

---

Radial-circumferential:                                      (2A)


      See Acceleration: Angular & Linear, 18 Oct'64
          Cosmic Discintinuity & Local Continuity, 15 Jan'74
          Electric Motor, 25 Jan'72
          Expansion & Contraction, Jan'72*
          Fourth Dimension, 1965
          Frequency, 15 Oct'72
          Gears: Spherical Gears, May'72
          Gravity, 18 Oct'72
          Integrity of Universe, 23 Sep'73; 30 Oct'73
          Jitterbug, 11 Oct'71
          Macro-micro, 1955*
          Powering: Second Powering, 28 Oct'73
          Scenario Universe, Jan'72
          Shunting: Relative Motion Patterns, 1955
          Sixty Degreeness, 1965; 18 Jun'71
          Synergetics, 14 May'73; 14 Jan'55

---

Radial Depth:                                                (1)


          See Dimensionality = Radial Depth = Frequency

---

Radial-circumferential:                                      (2B)


      See Tension & Compression, 1944
          Vector Equilibrium, 4 Nov'73
          Zoneness: System Zoneness, 8 Jan'55
          Peripheral, Sep'72
          Vertexial Topology, Aug'71
          Evaginating, 22 Jun'75
          Gravity: Speed Of, 21 Oct'72

---

Radial Depth:                                                (2)


          See Structure, 26 Dec'74

---

Radial Compression vs. Circumferential Tension:


      See Spherical Barrel: Radial Compression vs.
          Circumferential Tension

---

RBF DEFINITIONS

   Radial Line:

   "The particular line of geometrical reference humans picked
   happened not to be the line of most interattractive integrity.
   It was neither the radial line of radiation nor the radial line
   of gravity of spherical Earth...."


      - Citation & context at Starting With Parts: The Nonradial Line,
          29 Dec'73

RBF DEFINITIONS

Radial Line as Tetra Edge:

"We Identify the minimum tetrahedron as that with radius = c...
the tetrahedron edge of the photon becomes unit radius."

- Citation & context at Photon: Tetrahedron Edge as Unit Radius,
17 Jan'74

Radial Reach: (1)

See Sweepout
Reachability Range

Radial Line as Tetra Edge: (1)

See Line Between Two Sphere Centers
Prime Vector
Photon: Tetrahedron Edge as Unit Radius

Radial Reach: (2)

See Central Angle, 23 Sep'73

Radial vs. Orbital: (1)

See Linear vs. Orbital
Radial-circumferential
Embracing vs. Linear
One Way vs. Round Trip
Local vs. Comprehensive
Local Radius vs. Wide Arcs
Orbital Feedback Circuitry vs. Critical Path

Radial Set: (1)

See Vector Equilibrium, (I)

Radial vs. Orbital: (2)

See Frequency, 11 Mar'69
Umbilical Cord, 4 Mar'73
Einstein: Special Theory & General Theory, 4 Mar'73

RBF DEFINITIONS

Radial Symmetries:

"... Each chemical element's atoms are characterized by
unique frequencies, and unique frequencies impose unique
radial symmetries, this variety of radial dimensionality
constitutes one prime diffrence between nuclear physics
and chemistry."

- Citation and context at Physics: Difference Between Physics
And Chemistry, 22 Jun'72

Radial Symmetries:  Radially Symmetric:

See Mites Make All Regular Polyhedra, 27 May'72
Physics & Chemistry:  Difference Between, 22 Jun'72*

Radial Waves:                                                        (1)

See Nuclear & Nebular Zonal Waves

Radial Unity:                                                        (1)

See Prime Vector
Unit Radius:  Unit Vector Radius

Radial Waves:                                                        (2)

See Gears, (p.89) May'72

Radial Unity:                                                        (2)

See Rhombic Dodecahedron, 13 Apr'77

Radial:                                                              (1)

See Nonradial
Omniradial
Radial-circumferential
Radius
Rain as Radial
Omnidirectional:  Physical Existence Environment
Surrounds
Zenith Constancy of Radial Coordination

Radial Wave Modular Growth:

See Vector Equilibrium:  Field of Energy, (C)(D)
Einstein Equation:  E = Mc$^2$, 1959

Radial:                                                              (2)

See Dimension, 16 Nov'72*
Einstein:  General Theory & Special Theory, 4 Mar'73
Hexagonal Vector Patter, 8 May'72
Omnidirectional, 1954
Omniintertangency, 17 Feb'73
Sweepout, May'72

Radial:                                                    (3)

    See Radial-circumferential
       Radial-circumferential Accelerations
       Radial-circumferential Coordination
       Radial-circumferential Modularity
       Radial-circumferential Modular Growth
       Radial Line
       Radial Line as Tetra Edge
       Radial & Orbital
       Radial Reach
       Radial Set
       Radial Symmetries
       Radial Waves
       Radial Unity

---

Radiant:                                                   (1)

    See Omniradiant
       Potential vs. Radiant
       Latent vs. Radiant
       Convergent vs. Radiant

---

Radian:

    See Pi, 8 Feb'73
       Hexagon, Nov'71

---

Radiant:                                                   (2)

    See Convergence, 16 Nov'72
       Earth, Jun'66
       Geodesic Dome, 12 Mar'74
       Frequency, 22 Jun'72
       Hexagonal Vector Pattern, 8 May'72
       Isotropic Vector Matrix, 30 Nov'72
       Radiation-gravitation, 12 Jun'74
       Spherical Interstices, 18 Nov'72
       Halo, 1938
       Nucleus, 13 Nov'75

---

Radiantly Alternate Vertexes:

    See Isotropic Vector Matrix, 30 Nov'72
       Rhombic Dodecahedron, 30 Nov'72

---

RBF DEFINITIONS

Radiation:

"Radiation is special case, systematically centered, and discontinuously islanded....

"Electromagnetic radiation is distributive and entropic; its frequency magnitudes represent multiplication by division."

   - Citation & context at Radiation-gravitation, 11 Feb'76

---

RBF DEFINITIONS

Radiant Valvability of IVM-defined Wavelength:

"We can resonate the vector equilibrium in many ways. An isotropic vector matrix may be both radiantly generated and regenerated from any vector-centered fix origin in Universe such that any one of its vertexes will be congruent with any other radiantly reachable center fix in Universe; i.e., it can communicate with any other noninterfered-with point in Universe. The combined reachability range is determined by the omnidirectional velocity of all radiation, $c^2$ within the available investable time."

[40]
   - Cite SYNERGETICS draft at Sec. 426.††, 30 Nov'72

---

RBF DEFINITIONS

Radiation:

"The symmetrical expansion of radiation is a divergent phenomenon."

   - Citation & context at Quantum Sequence, (2), 23 Jun'75

RBF DEFINITIONS

### Radiation:

"Radiation distributes energy systems outwardly in omnidiametric directions. Radiation fractionates whole systems into
multidiametrically dispatched separate packages of the whole.
The packaging of spherical unity is accomplished by radii-
defined, central-angle partitioning of the spherical whole
into a plurality of frequency-determined, simplest, central
divisioning, thus producing a plurality of three-sided
cornucopias formed inherently at minimum limit of volumetric
accommodation by any three immediately adjacent central angles
of any sphere of any omnitriangulated polyhedron. The threefold
central-angle vertex surroundment constitutes the inner vertex
definition of a radially amplified tetrahedral pack of energy;
while the three inner faces of the package are defined by the
interior radial planes (there is a great-circle plane common
to any two radii) of the sphere of omnidiametric distribution;
and the fourth, or outermost, face is the spherical triangle
surface of the tetrahedron which always occurs at the radial
distance outwardly traveled from the original source at the
speed of radiation, symbolized as lower-case $c$."

- Cite SYNERGETICS draft at Sec. 541.01, 23 Sep'73

RBF DEFINITIONS

### Radiation:

"It is also characteristic of these waves
And of all radiation
That when the wave propagation
Is beamingly aimed
Perpendicularly outward from Earth's surface
They experience little or no interferences,
Once outside our atmo-, strato, and ionospheres,
Other then by collision with meteorites
And other celestially traveling objects.

"There seems to be no impedance
And no inherent limitation to the distance
Which such electromagnetic wave signals can go
Once outside the Earth mantles.
As far as we know,
The waves can go on forever in Universe--
Unless they hit some object,
And when they hit an object they lose some energy
Then bounce away
And keep going
In a new direction."

- Cite BRAIN & MIND, pp.158-159 May '72

RBF DEFINITIONS

### Radiation:

"Radiation is pushive, ergo tends to increase in curvature....
Radiation tends to increase in its overall curvature
(as in the 'bent space' of Einstein). The pushive tends to
arcs of ever lesser radius (microwaves are the very essence
of this)..."

- Citation and context at Curvature, 23 Sep'73

RBF DEFINITIONS

### Radiation:

"The star tetrahedron's entropy may be the basis of
irreversible radiation. . .

~~- Cite SYNERGETICS Draft "Antitetrahedron," 8 Oct. '71, p. 8.~~
- Citation & context at Star Tetrahedron, 8 Oct'71

RBF DEFINITIONS

### Radiation:

"Euler deals with the physical Universe as radiation, or
it 'coming apart' phase."

- Cite SYNERGETICS draft at Sec. 1054.12, 6 Mar'73

RBF DEFINITIONS

### Radiation:

"Radiation is physical, entropic, incoherent,
propelling, disassociative, pushing."

- Cite DOXIADIS, p. 310, 20 Jun'66

RBF DEFINITIONS

### Radiation:

"When adequate acceleration
Is imparted to micro aggregations
Of atoms
Sufficient for them to escape
The critical limits
Of both mass attraction
And precession intereffects
Then radiation
At 186,000 m.p.s.
Of the separate energy quanta
Ensues
Which phenomena we speak of as fission
Or fusion
And the generalized behavioral law
Governing fission or fusion
And radiation in general — DELETED IN FINAL DRAFT
Is that cited by Einstein
Of E = mc²."

*RBF SAYS THESE TWO LINES SHOULD BE RESTORED*

- Cite INTUITION ~~Draft Feb '71, p. 24~~
  pp.37-38 May '72

RBF DEFINITIONS

### Radiation:

"Wave magnitude and frequency are experimentally
interlocked as co-functions and both are experimentally
gear locked with energy quanta."

- Citation at Frequency, Jun'66

~~- Cite NASA Speech, p. 100, Jun'~~

RBF DEFINITIONS

Radiation:

"... $c^2$ (radiation) means; All the Universe's nonselfinterfering complexes having eccentrically interprecessing, omnidirectionally diffusing patterns resulting in comprehensively degenerative negative limits of dissociabilities as negative (inside-out) de-structures."

- Cite INTRO. to OMNIDIREGTIONAL HALO, p.126, 1959

RBF DEFINITIONS

Radiational Constant:

"... The gravitational constant... is always... more powerful in syntropically cohering the Universe than is the radiational constant of 6.6666665 in entropically disintegrating the Universe by explosion."

- Citation and context at Universal Integrity:  Principle Of,
8 May '72

RBF DEFINITIONS

Radiation:

"Radiation is generalized compression..."

- Citation and context at Generalization:  Second Degree, 1959

Radiational Constant:                                    (1)

See Gravitational Constant
Newton vs. Einstein
Universal Integrity:  Principle Of
Congruence of Gravitational & Radiational Constants

RBF DEFINITIONS

Radiation Sequence:                                      (1)

"And we've got no help at all from the stars because they're all areas where the Universe is increasingly disorderly, giving off enormous amounts of radiation in strange kinds of Sun rays, and so forth-- great Sun spots, which we begin to find have some regularity.  But you and I didn't know that regularity before because, in a sense, it was so infrequent-- whatever it might be.  We didn't have observation to know there were Sun spots up to yesterday.

"Then all the physical is the visible, astronomical world where we use the optical telescope to give us the information. Optical means we're using that disorderly radiation to identify the positioning of the stars. . . So, looking around for some phase of Universe where energies are contracting and becoming increasingly orderly, we find the only example that we really know much about is our own Earth.  We do know that in the last International Geophysical Year that we're collecting somewhere around 100 tons of stardust daily. And we're finding our radiation from all the stars, the cosmic radiation-- and primarily from the Sun-- is not just bouncing off our Earth at all, but being impounded as energy. The radiation to start off with is in the Van Allen belts."

- Cite RBF to World Game, Jun-Jul'69

Radiational Constant:                                    (2)

See Icosahedron as Electron Model, 7 Mar'73

RBF DEFINITIONS

Radiation Sequence:                                      (2)

"Then the atmosphere bends that radiation very readily so that it gives us the red-yellow-orange-green-blue-violet colors themselves.  Then when the radiation gets to the water-- three-quarters of the Earth being covered with water-- you see how much it is bent simply by putting a pole into the water and looking at the bending of it. . . There's bending, bending, bending until finally the radiation is so bent it gets now impounded horizontally into the surface of the water around our Earth, and we get these horizontal moving streams such as the Gulf Stream, the great warmth.  We have then the enormous impounding of the energy of the Sun in just the heating of the atmosphere, bringing about all our storms, the various low pressures and high pressures depending the heating is being impounded by large moisture concentrations or low.

"And so this enormous energy is being collected here, and this radiation then is atomizing the ocean, and then it gets dropped back again, pulled back by gravity as rain.  And we find then vegetation operating; vegetation on the dry land and algae in the sea, impounding the energy of the Sun by photo-synthesis."

- Cite Rbf to World Game, Jun-Jul'69

RBF DEFINITIONS

Radiation vs. Crystal Model:

"... In addition to its heat-transmitting properties, the radiation is also a yes-no, frequency programmed, information carrier-- which precessionally transforms the three tetrahedral quanta of radiation into the four-quanta octahedral crystals in the atomic formation of the hydrocarbon molecules."

- Citation & context at Radiation as Information-carrier,
9 Jun'75

Radiation vs. Crystal Model:

    See Information Transmitting & Nontransmitting Model

---

RBF DEFINITIONS

Radiation-Gravitation:

"Electromagnetic radiant energy is entropic; gravitational energy is syntropic."

- Citation & context at Gravity (d), 12 Jun'74

---

Radiation as Entropy:

    See Instant Universe, (1)(2)
    Celestial Radiation Accumulators, 28 Apr'77

---

RBF DEFINITIONS

        Radiation-Gravitation:

"Radiation is disintegrative; gravity is integrative."

- Cite SYNERGETICS draft at Sec. 541.05, 23 Sep'73

---

RBF DEFINITIONS

Radiation-gravitation:

"Radiation is special case, systematically centered, and discontinuously islanded.  Gravity is continuous tension omni-inter-between all systems.  Because gravitational intertensional intensivity varies as the second power of the arithmetical interdistancing variations, whose unique variations are locally periodic, it manifests periodic intensities of tidal pulls, but the overall tensional integrity is constant independent of local intensity variabilities.

"Electromagnetic radiation is distributive and entropic; its frequency magnitudes represent multiplication by division.  Gravity is nondivisive and syntropic; its conservation is accomplished by holistic embracement of variable intensities.  Gravity is integral.  Holistic gravity has no frequency."

- Citation & context at Islanded Radiation & Tensional Constancy, 11 Feb'76

---

RBF DEFINITIONS

        Radiation-Gravitation:

"Radiation has shadow while gravitation does not."

- Citation and context at Fuller, R.B.:  Meeting with Fernandez-Moran (2), 5 Apr'73

---

RBF DEFINITIONS

Radiation-gravitation:

"All bodies of Universe interaffect all other bodies in varying degrees; and all the intergravitational effects are precessionally angular modulations and all the interradiation effects are frequency modulations."

(For earlier version of above see Precession, Oct'66)

- Cite SYNERGETICS 2nd. Ed. draft at Sec. 533.07, 15 Nov'74

---

RBF DEFINITIONS

        Radiation-Gravitation:

"The generalizations are of the mind and are omniembracing and omnipermeative.  Like the rays of the Sun radiations are radii and are focusable.  Gravity cannot be focused; it is circumferentially embracing.  Radiation has shadows; gravity has none.  Radiation produces the phenomenon known to Einstein as the bending of space, the gravitational field."

[97]

- Cite SYNERGETICS draft at Sec. 1009.98, 8 Mar'73

RBF DEFINITIONS

######## Radiation-Gravitation:

"Physics hasn't really associated radiation with (+)
and gravitation with (-), but that's what they are."

- Cite RBF to EJA, 3200 Idaho, Washington DC, 25 Jan '72
- Citation and Plus and Minus, 25 Jan'72

---

RBF DEFINITIONS

######## Radiation-Gravitation:

". . . l give you then a tetrahedron which has an
external and an internal: a terminal condition . . .
You get to the outside and you turn yourself inside out,
and come the other way. This is why radiation then does
not go off into a higher velocity. Radiation gets to a
maximum and then turns itself inwardly again-- it becomes
gravity. Then gravity comes to its maximum concentration
and turns itself and goes outwardly-- becomes radiation."

- Cite RBF Tape to EJA + BO'R, Blackstone, Chicago,
  31 May 1971. Pp. 17-18.
- Citation and context at Zero, 31 May'71

---

RBF DEFINITIONS

######## Radiation-Gravitation:

"Gravity is circumferential. All the superficial surface
angles are the gravity. Central Angles are the radiation."

* Cite RBF to EAJ, 3200 Idaho, Washington DC, 21 Dec. '71.

---

RBF DEFINITIONS

######## Radiation-Gravitation:

"Radiation can be focused;
explosions can be linear.
Gravity cannot be focused;
it is circumferential contraction."

- Cite RBF to EJA
  Sarasota, Florida
  7 February 1971

---

RBF DEFINITIONS

######## Radiation-Gravitation:

"The differences between the central angles and surface
angles' functionings are identifiable with radiational
and gravitational functionings. Radiation identifies
with central angles. Radiation is outwardly focusable."

- Citation & context at Gravity, Aug'71
- Cite Synergetics draft, Sec. 870, August 1971.

---

RBF DEFINITIONS

######## Radiation-Gravitation:

". . . All bodies of Universe are affecting the other
bodies in varying # degrees and all the intergravitational
effects are precessional angular modulations, and all
the interradiation effects are frequency modulations."

- Cite HOW LITTLE I KNOW, p. 73. Oct'66
- Citation & context at Precession, Oct'66

---

RBF DEFINITIONS

######## Radiation-Gravitation:

"The coming apart phase of critical proximity is
radiation. The coming together and holding together
phase is emphasized in our ken as gravity."

- Cite RBF insert to SYNERGETICS (Conceptuality, Critical
  Proximity), Chicago, 1 June 1971

---

RBF DEFINITIONS

######## Radiation-Gravitation:

"... Gravity is swifter than radiation, therefore, Universe
collects its masses in ever tighter concentrations."

- Citation and context at Point: Outbound Point, circa 1948

RBF DEFINITIONS

## Radiation-Gravitation Sequence: (1)

"The complementarity of the great regenerative pattern is geometrically omnimanifest as gravity and radiation. The radiation radiates in rays, or lines, of spherical, energy-source radii. These may be cross-sectionally conceptualized as the radially packed staves of a wooden barrel that try to escape outwardly from the barrel's center. Gravity, however, like the steel bands encircling the barrel's girth, operates embracingly. The individual barrel stays, like the radii, try to go out, to disintegrate; but the finitely closed, circumferential gravity hoops operate integratively, embracingly. The 92-million miles distant Sun's rays impinge approximately in parallel on only one hemisphere of the Earth at a time, while gravity embraces our entire planet, all cosmic systems from all around being equally effective, for instance, on the shadow hemisphere of Earth. Gravity has no shadow. Gravity is uninterferable; radiation is interferable. Gravity is omnidirectional, mass interattraction, which, as Newton discovered, is directly interproportional relative to the respective mass involved, and varies as the second power relative to the interproximities of the respective bodies considered: Halving the distance between any two will fourfold their interaction."

- Cite "No Title," (Part II), WORLD Mag., p.39, 5 Jun'73

RBF DEFINITIONS

## Radiation-Gravitation Sequence: (2)

"All the Universe is in motion, and all the effect of bodies in motion on other bodies in motion are what we call 'precessional.' Precession and mass-attractive gravity convert centrifugal into orbital motion. And precession always affects the motion of other bodies in directions other than 180 degrees, not toward or away from one another but at approximately 90 degrees to the line between the most powerfully interprecessing of the bodies. Holding a string in your hand, which, like mass attraction, is fastened to a weighty object on the other end, you precess this object into orbit around you by axial rotation of your body. Thus the precessional effect of the axially rotating Earth on the Moon is to make the lesser mass go into orbit around the greater.

"Mass attraction and precession cooperate synergetically to affect all of the Universe: 99.9999 percent of all entities of the Universe are in orbit around some other spinning entity, macro- or micro- cosmic in scale. And once in a while some of the entities accelerate so congruently close to one another that their inter-mass-attraction renders the precessional effect negligible, and the lesser body falls into the greater."

- Cite "No Title," (Part II), WORLD Mag., p.39, 5 Jun'73

RBF DEFINITIONS

## Radiation-Gravitation Sequence: (3)

"You and I are going around the Sun at 60,000 mph. So too is the Earth. We are so close to our Earth that gravity makes us 'fall in' in orbiting company. Little children find gravity forever pulling them in toward the Earth's center; although they know nothing about gravity they feel it pulling them to the floor. All of the Earth's biological organisms respond so powerfully in a linear manner to the gravitational effect that it is much like the organisms being linearly programmed to a specialized behavioral program. Thus we fail to realize that gravity really works as circumferential embracement. We find everything operating at 90 degrees tangent while humanity fools itself into thinking that it accelerated the object in a 180-degree direction. Because of this, humanity has come to think illogically in 180-degree, straight-line, ways. The fact is that entities are always traveling away at 90 degrees from the direction at which we are aiming.

"All the cosmic generalized principles are omniembracing-always-true. Truth, like gravity, is nonlinear; it is omniembracing. And of all the creatures on our planet, only humans have demonstrated the ability to discover such truth."

- Cite "No Title," (Part II), WORLD Mag., p.39, 5 Jun'73

RBF DEFINITIONS

## Radiation-gravitation: Angular Functions:

"The differences between the central angles' and surface angles' functionings are identifiable with radiational and gravitational functionings. Radiation identifies with central angles. Radiation is outwardly divergent. Gravity identifies with the three surface angles' convergent closure into the surface triangle's finite perimeter. Gravity is omniembracing and is not focusable. Gravity is Universe-conservingly effective in its circumferential coherence."

- Cite RBF rewrite of SYNERGETICS galley at Sec. 1051.40, 9 Jan'74

RBF DEFINITIONS

## Radiation-gravitation: Harmonics:

"The second-power rate of interattractiveness gain occurring with each halving of the intervening distance of two heavenly bodies recalls Pythagoras's whole, rational number, harmonic octave integrity progression (or regression) occurring with each halving of the length of the tensed cord (with thirding resulting in sharping or flatting key progressions); wherefore gravitational-radiational second-power, spherical surface rate of gain in respect to radial linear rate of identification of omnidirectionally propagated sound waves at a gain of the second power of the linear. This gravitational omnisurface-embracement mathematics apprehending coincides with harmonic resonances:

|  | Arithmetical rate of symmetrical system's radius |  |
|---|---|---|
| E = Mass | linear radial shortening with system contraction | Newton's gravitation |
| E = Mass | linear radial lengthening with system expansion | Einstein's radiation |

- Cite SYNERGETICS, 2nd. Ed. at Sec. 1052.68, 3 Jan'75

RBF DEFINITIONS

## Radiation-Gravitation Model:

"The radial arrangement of unit tetrahedral volumes around an absolute radiation center (the vector equilibrium) constitutes a prime radiation-gravitational energy proclivity model with a containment value of 20 tetrahedra (where cube is 3 and tetrahedron 1)."

- Cite SYNERGETICS TEXT AT SEC. 223.73, 26 Sep'73

## Radiation Gravitation Model: (1)

See Octahedron as Photosynthesis Model
Jitterbug Model

## Radiation-gravitation Model: (2)

See Jitterbug, 11 Oct'71
Vector Equilibrium, 15 May'73

Radiational ≠ Gravitational:

    See Radiation-gravitation, circa 1948
      Boltzmann Sequence, (3)
      Universal Integrity: Principle Of, 8 May'72; 24 Mar'71;
       13 Nov'69

Radiation-gravitation:               (2C)

    See Structure, Nov'71
      Synergetic Hierarchies, (C)
      Synergetics, 14 May'73
      Syntropy & Time, 14 May'75

      Two Kinds of Twoness, (B)

      Vector Equilibrium, 3 Jan'75

Radiation-gravitation:               (1)

    See Eccentric-concentric
      Energetic Functions
      Intereffects
      Radial-circumferential
      Universal Integrity
      Electromagnetic Membrane
      **Coming Apart & Holding Together**
      Balance of Universe

Radiation-gravitation:               (3)

    See Radiation-gravitation: Angular Functions
      Radiation-gravitation Model

Radiation-gravitation:               (2A)

    See Bow Ties, 6 Oct'72
      Building Industry, (11)

      Coherence, 11 Feb'73
      Convergence & Divergence, 6 Jun'75; 1 May'77
      Cosmic Limit Point, 3 Nov'73
      Cosmic Vacuum Cleaner, 16 May'75

      Dimensionality, (1)

      Fourth-dimensional Synergetics Mathematics, 14 Dec'76

      Gravity, (d)*; 6 Apr'75
      Gravity: Speed Of, 21 Oct'72
      Growthability, 6 Mar'73

      Interference, 5 Jun'73
      Interrelationship Twoness, 27 Dec'74
      Islanded Radiation & Tensional Constancy, 11 Feb'76*
      Isotropic Vector Matrix, 16 Nov'72

RBF DEFINITIONS

Radiation as Information-carrier:

"What has not been understood thus far by human scientists
regarding the transmittal of energy from the Sun to support
biological life on planet Earth as accomplished through the
photosynthesis of Sun radiation to produce hydrocarbon molecules
by terrestrial vegetation and algae, is that in addition to its
heat-transmitting properties, the radiation is also a yes-no,
frequency-programmed, information carrier-- which precessionally
transforms the three tetrahedral quanta of radiation into the
four-quanta octahedral crystals in the atomic formation of the
hydrocarbon molecules. Photosynthesis is meaningful communication whereby metaphysical rules the physical (Like the Federal
Reserve Bank) by issuing or withdrawing complex coding-identified 'quanta' currency from the overall, cosmic, transforming
and transaction system's accounting."

    - Citation & context at Man: Interstellar tRansmission of Man,
      (B)(C), 9 Jun'75

Radiation-gravitation:               (2B)

    See Limit Point, 9 Jun'72
      Love, 23 Oct'77

      Metaphysical & Physical, 19 May'75

      Nuclear Pattern of Growth & Decay, 8 Dec'75
      Nucleus, 13 Nov'75

      Octahedron as Photosynthesis Model, (A)-(E); 11 Dec'75

      Plus & Minus, 25 Jan'72*
      Point: Outbound Point, 1948*
      Powering: Fourth Powering, 15 Oct'72; 9 Sep'75
      Precession, (a)(b); Oct'66*
      Pulsation, 9 Nov'72

      Rain, 11 Feb'76

      Series vs. Parallel Circuitry, 11 Dec'75
      Star Tetrahedron, 8 Oct'71
      Structural Sequence, (B)
      Star Tetrahedron & Vector Equilibrium, 9 Nov'73

Radiation as Information-carrier:

    See Electromagnetically Transmittable Logistics
      Cosmic Transmission
      Transmission

Radiational Mensurability:

　　　See Vector Equilibrium, (2)

---

RBF DEFINITIONS

Radiation:  Speed Of:

"The speed of light, at the limit case, becomes the time.
The speed of radiation is the limit case, but it is the
initial limit.  It always comes back to itself."

　　　- Cite RBF to EJA, Beverly Hotel, NY, 22 Jun'72

---

Radiation:  Minimum Increment Of:                               (1)

　　　See Photon

---

RBF DEFINITIONS

Radiation:  Speed Of:

"The speeds of all the known different phases of measured
radiation are apparently identical despite vast differences
in wavelength and frequency.  Einstein's adoption of
electromagnetic radiation expansion-- omnidirectionally in
vacuo-- as normal speed suggests a top speed of omnidirectional
entropic disorder increase accommodation at which radiant
speed reaches its highest velocity.  This highest velocity
is reached when the last of the eternally regenerative Universe
cyclic frequencies of multi-billions of years have been
accommodated, all of which complex of nonsimultaneous
transforming multivarietied frequency synchronizations is
complementarily balanced to equate as zero by the sum totality
of locally converging orderly and synchronously concentrating
energy phases of scenario Universe's eternally pulsative,
and only sum totally synchronous, disintegrative, divergent,
omnidirectionally exporting and only sum totally
synchronous, integrative, convergent and discretely
directional individual importings."

- Cite RBF in response to a request to repeat his
　"brief sentence" on the sphere as a meeting of
　convergences.  See SYNERGETICS, "Scenario Universe,"
　Sec. 325., and "Tension and Compresssion," Sec. 614.08. ▄
　Oct'71

---

Radiation:  Minimum Increment of Radiation:                     (2)

　　　See Unit Radius, 17 Jan'74

---

RBF DEFINITIONS

Radiation:  Speed Of:

"The speed of light had been measured linearly
in a tube-- this is the speed of light in any one
direction from its source.
But radiation is called radiation
because it goes in all directions from its source
unless reflectively beamed.
When we double the linear dimensions of any object--
the surface of the symmetrically amplified system
grows as the second power of the linear.
Science had to choose the lower-case letter c
to represent the speed of the radiation linearly,
to arrive at the rate at which it grew in an
omnidirectional spherical way-- the rate at which the
surface of the omnidirectional radius increases as
the second power of the radius-- or linear speed: $c^2$."

　　　　　　　- Cite RBF to EJA, Sarasota, Florida,
　　　　　　　　7 Feb '71

---

RBF DEFINITIONS

Radiation:  Speed Of:

"Wavelength times frequency is the speed of all radiation.
If the frequency of the vector equilibrium is four, its
vector-radius, or basic wavelength = 186,000/4 miles
reachable within one second = 46,500 reach-miles.  Electromagnetically speaking the unarticulated vector equilibrium's
vector length is always 186, 282.396 miles."

　　　(For later version & context of above,
　　　see Vector Equilibrium: Unarticulated VE,
　　　2 Nov'73)

　　　　　　[44]
　_ Cite SYNERGETICS draft at Sec. 426.45, 30 Nov'72

---

RBF DEFINITIONS

Radiation:  Speed Of:                                           (A)

"There are no instant lines--
Reaching instantly to eternity;
For the concepts
Of instantaneity, simultaneity, and eternity
Were anulled by the discovery
That light and all radiation
Have an approximately discrete speed
Of seven hundred million miles an hour,
Which, of course, is too fast for man's
Perceptive detection,
But accounts lucidly
For humanity's assuming erroneously
That his sight experience
Is instantaneous.
Prior to the Michelson-Morley experiments--
Throughout all past history--
On every clear night
Man could seemingly witness for himself
The 'instantly eternal' stars.

"However, with the measurement of light's
And of other"

- Cite GENERALIZED PRINCIPLES, p.5, 28 Jan'69

RBF DEFINITIONS

Radiation:   SpeedOf:                                    (B)

"Electromagnetic radiations' speed
We learned that it took
Eight minutes for light
To reach us from the Sun
And two and one-half years
From the next nearest star,
And an astronomical variety of other
Greater and different time lags
For light to reach us
From each of the other
Myriads of stars.

"These time lags were far different
From instantaneous and simultaneous.
And experiments made evident
That such light sources
Are always exhausting
(Their) ~~these~~ local energy concentrations,
Wherefore they cannot be eternal.

"Prior to that measurment
The illusion of instantaneity
Induced false concepts
    - Cite GENERALIZED PRINCIPLES, p.5, 28 Jan'69

---

Radiation:   Speed Of:                                   (1)

See Absolute Velocity
    Light:  Speed Of
    Radiant Valavability
    Relativity:  Special Theory
    Spherical Wave Terminal Limit Velocity
    Shunting:  Relative Motion Patterns
    Top Speed:  Top Velocity

---

RBF DEFINITIONS

Radiation:   Speed Of:                                   (C)

"Which man formalized into statements
And labeled as axioms
Holding them to be self-evident and a priori,
Ergo fundamental, characteristics of nature
Reduced to their respective simplest degrees.

"Typical of such
Axiomatic illusions
Were the concepts
Of solids, continuums, at rest,
Surfaces, and straight lines
That reach instantly to infinity;
All of which concepts are contradicted
By experimental physics
Which has found only
Discontinuity and
Nonsimultaneity
As, for instance, is witnessible
In the discontinuity of the stars
In the Milky Way,
And is instrumentally discoverable
In the remoteness of electrons"

    - Cite GENERALIZED PRINCIPLES, pp.5-6, 28 Jan'69

---

Radiation:   Speed Of:                                   (2)

See Central Angle, 23 Sep'73
    Conscious World, 1938
    Engineering, 13 Nov'69
    Intellect, 27 May'72
    Light, 22 Nov'73
    Limit Reach, 17 Jan'74
    Nuclear Sphere, 16 Dec'73
    Omnidirectional, 1965
    Time, 30 Nov'72; 22 Jun'72
    Unit Magnitude, 13 May'73
    Visual Symphony (1)(2)
    New York City (10)
    Eyes, 1964

---

RBF DEFINITIONS

Radiation:   Speed Of:                                   (D)

"From their nuclear protons
Which remoteness is equal
To the star spacing
In relation to their respective
Relative activity diameters.

"We have learned experimentally
That lines are always energy events
And because of their ever variant
Complex of other energy events
Of the total environment
There are always a myriad
Of precessionally steering ██████ effects
Which result in curvilinear
Orbits, rotations, pulsations,
Implosions, explosions, and torations.

"Lines are finitely developed events.
And their durations
Are always relative
To some cyclic experience in time.

"Size and time are synonymous."
    - Cite GENERALIZED PRINCIPLES, p.6, 28 Jan'69

---

Radiation:                                               (1)

                 T Quanta Module
                 Einstein Equation:  $E = Mc^2$
See Biosphere
    Black Body
    Broadcast
    Center of Radiation
    Exporting
    Impoundment
    Interradiation
    Intellect vs. Radiation
    Matter vs. Radiation
    Omniradiational
    Photon
    Photosynthesis
    Radiation-gravitation
    Ecology Sequence
    Energy-as-radiation
    Concentration vs. Radiation
    Visible Light vs. Electricity
    Electromagnetic-photosynthetic Programming
    Coming Apart Phase
    Islanded Radiation
    Celestial Radiation Accumulators

---

RBF DEFINITIONS

Radiation:   Speed Of:

". . . $C^2$ /radiation/ equals all the eccentrically
disassociative individual patternings of all energy
(C being the radial or linear speed of radiant energy,
which is approximately 186,000 mps)."

          Cite INTRODUCTION TO OMNIDIRECTIONAL HALO, P.124, 1959

---

Radiation:                                               (2)

See Chemical Phenomenon, May'72
    Colloidal Chemistry, 1938
    Curvature: 23 Sep'73*
    Energy, 1960; Apr'68; Jun'66; 18 Mar'65
    Frequency, Jun'66
    Generalization:  Second Degree, 1959*
    Package, 23 Sep'73
    Point:  Outbound Point, circa 1948; 23 Sep'73
    Star; Dec'72
    Star Tetrahedron, 8 Oct'71*
    Stardust, (2)
    Tetrahedron, 23 Sep'73
    Wind Power Sequence (4); (C)
    Quantum Sequence, (2)*
    Visual, 22 Feb'77

---

Radiation:                                      (3)

        See Radiational Constant
           Radiation as Entropy
           Radiation-gravitation
           Radiation-gravitation Model
           Radiational Mensurability
           Radiation:  Minimum Increment of Radiation
           Radiation:  Speed Of
           Radiation as Information-carrier
           Radiation vs. Crystal Model

---

Radio Set is Not the Music:                     (2)

        See Invisible Architecture, (C)

---

Radical:

        See Assumptions, 1946

---

RBF DEFINITIONS

    Radio Tuning Crystal:

    "The first radio tuning crystal must have been a rhombic
dodecahedron."

    - Citation and context at Rhombic Dodecahedron, 30 Nov'72

---

Radio Ham Language:

        See World-around Language, (1)

---

Radio:  Radio Waves:                            (1)

        See Ball at the Center
           Broadcast
           Invisible Operation of Thousands of Radio Programs

           Tunability

---

Radio Set is Not the Music:                     (1)

        See Telephone is Not the Information

---

Radio:  Radio Waves:                            (2)

        See All-acceleration Universe, 20 Jun'66
           Ball at the Center, 9 Mar'73
           Visual Symphony, (1)
           Seeing vs. Hearing, 22 Jan'75
           Individuality & Degrees of Freedom, (3)
           Lasso, 1946

Radioactivity:                                                    (1)

    See Stars: Implosive Forces Of
       Superatomics
       Strange Particles

---

Radiolaria:

    See Invention, 3 Oct'72; Dec'61

---

Radioactivity:                                                    (2)

    See Now, 14 Feb'72

---

Radionics:

    See Universal Vertex Center Model, 29 Apr'43

---

RBF DEFINITIONS

    Radiolaria:                                            (1)

"The micro animal structures, the radiolaria, if you study
them, will always show that they are based on either the
tetrahedron, the octahedron, or the icosahedron. This
picture (R-4-1) was drawn by English scientists almost a
century ago as they looked through a microscope at these
micro-sea structures.

"Today I have given you some fundamental structural principles
and subsequently shown you their use by nature. I didn't,
however, start by studying thses structures of nature seeking
to understand their logic. The picture of the radiaria has
been available for 100 years, but I didn't happen to see it
until after I had produced the geodesic structures from the
mathematical sequence of developments which I reviewed with
you earlier. In other words I did not copy nature's
structural patterns. I did not make arbitrary arrangements
for superficial reasons. What really interests me therTore
in all these recent geodesic tensegrity findings in nature
is that they apparently confirm that I have found the
coordinate mathematical system employed in nature's structuring.
I began to explore structure and develop it in pure mathematical principle out of which the patterns emerged in pure"

    - Cite MEXICO '63, pp. 58-59, 10 Oct '63

SYNERGETICS- SEC 203.09|

---

RBF DEFINITIONS

    Radius:

"It is very easy to be greatly misled when you see two

spheres in tangency. There is only one line between the

two. This is where you see that unity is two because

the line breaks itself into radii of the two spheres."

    - Cite RBF tape Blackstone Hotel, Chicago, 31 May 1971, p.37.

    - Citation and context at Tangency, 31 May'71

---

RBF DEFINITIONS

    Radiolaria:                                            (2)

"principle. I then realized those developed structural
principles as physical forms, and in due course applied
them to practical tasks. The reappearance of these
structures as recent scientists' findings at various levels
of inquiry are pure coincidence-- but excitingly validating
coincidence."

    - Cite MEXICO '63, p. 59, 10 Oct '63

SYNERGETICS- SEC. 203.09|

---

RBF DEFINITIONS

    Radius:

"As a chord turns into an arc the radius contracts."

    - For citation and context see Vector Equilibrium: Spheres
      and Spaces, 31 May '71

RBF DEFINITIONS

### Radius:

"Omniconvergent

is the opposite of radius."

~~- Cite RBF to EJA~~
~~Sarasota, Florida~~
~~7 February 1971~~

- Citation at Omniconvergent, 7 Feb'71

---

### Radius: (2)

    See Frequency, 11 Jul'62*
        Geometry of Vectors, Aug'71
        Omniconvergent, 7 Feb'71*
        Powering: One Dimension, 15 Oct'72
        Radiation, 8 Mar'73
        Rotate, 6 May'48
        Tangency, 31 May'71*
        Tension & Compression, Jun'67*
        Vector Equilibrium: Spheres & Spaces, 31 May'71*

---

RBF DEFINITIONS

### ▬▬ Radius:

"Tension tends towards arcs of increasing radius;
compression tends towards arcs of decreasing radius."

~~- Cite P. PEARCE, Inventory of Concepts, June 1967~~

- Citation at Tension & Compression, Jun'67

---

RBF DEFINITIONS

### Radome Sequence: (A)

"This is one of the geodesic radomes tested for the Arctic. They
are made out of polyester fiberglass and the diamond-shaped, pan-
edged pieces are made with bolt holes in their adjacent flanges.
All the mathematics must be done very accurately to permit these
pieces to be interchangeably bolted together. We hold our
spherical trigonometry calculations to an accuracy of 1/1000 of
a second of circular arc. The geodesic radome structures go up
in an average of 14 hours each in the Arctic.

"Our Air Force Radomes were installed in the Arctic mostly by
Eskimos and others who had never seen them before. The mass
production technology made assembly possible at an average rate
of 14 hours each. One of these radomes was lent by the U.S.
Air Force to the Museum of Modern Art in New York City for an
exhibition of my work in 1959-1960. It took regular building
trades skilled labor one month to assemble the dome in New York
City.

"American labor fought a great and worthy battle to win the
working man's share of the synergetic productivity of industry.
Labor's battle proved doubly worthwhile because it inadvertently
brought about mass consumption. Without mass consumption you
cannot maintain mass production. You cannot have the mass"
- Cite RBF photo caption, Fig. 177, dome photos, about 1960.

---

RBF DEFINITIONS

### Radius:

In closest packing of sphere "we discover that the number
of balls in any one layer, we could call it frequency or
radius, because we have found that they are the same words."

- Citation at Frequency, 11 Jul'62
- ~~Cite OREGON Lecture #7, p. 239, 11 Jul'62~~

---

RBF DEFINITIONS

### Radome Sequence: (B)

"production of industrialization without an original investment
of vast capital effort of work and that original capital came
first and long ago from serfdom or outright slavery. In order to
bring industrialization to benefit comprehensively emancipated
man, you must have mass purchasing power, which in due course
will underwrite automation, which in turn will eventually
produce so much wealth as to be able to free man's time for
further education and research to increase the wealth long
generated by unimpeded automation. American labor will not yield
that unimpeded until it is clearly demonstrated that all men
will prosper directly by doing so. American labor did bring
about the vast purchasing power in industry, but in so doing it
established all kinds of rules which inadvertently protected the
obsolete inefficiencies of building.

"When the kind of structure which goes up in the Arctic in 14
hours takes a month in New York City, clearly there has been an
inordinate shunting of social wealth in a direction in which
legitimate value was not added to the product. This is an
indirect, illogical, and therefore indefensible way of distribu-
ting wealth for it hides the new advantages and therefore retards
the growth of those advantages as wealth generators of the"
- Cite RBF photo caption, Fig. 177, dome photos, about 1960.

---

### Radius: (1)

    See Edge vs. Radius
        Frequency = Radius
        Line Between Two Sphere Centers
        Local Radius
        Omniradial
        Radial
        Unit Radius

---

RBF DEFINITIONS

### Radome Sequence: (C)

"commonwealth. We must be very careful in judging the new,
high production technology structural experiments so as not to
have our fundamental tactical information distorted by ill
conceived labor tactics. We have very real social problems which
must be solved by realistic acceptance of the facts rather than
deferred from realistic consideration of the inherent new wealth-
generating advantages by hiding the new technical advantage
under the wing of individually conceived palliatives which are
operated by old rules that do not permit the real advantages to
be recognized by the labor movement's management. We are going
to have to bring industrial mass purchasing ability to all of
humanity. But first we are going to have to get labor rates
evened up all around the world in order to have every man's raw
time worth as much as any other man's time when translated into
purchasing power per kilowatts or pounds of specific metal goods.
Next we are going to let automation take over after we find ways
to pay everyone dividends from its wealth making to keep up
purchasing power at a maximum and thereby to regenerate the
industrial evolution advance."

- Cite RBF photo caption, Fig. 177, dome photos, about 1960.

RBF DEFINITIONS

Radome Sequence: (1)

"A radome unit provides means for automatically excluding the weather. It must admit the widest electronic wave frequency spectrum. It requires greatest strength with minimum structure and minimum site assembly operations.

"Omnitriangulation is implicit for structural stability. Omni-orientation of focal points of structure is at most symmetrical equivalance of interdistancing.

"Light (as a typical wave frequency group) obstruction is greatest where structural components converge (grid photostats show this as stars at convergent points). A multi-axial or dynamical system cannot have only two triangles around one vertex. It can have three, four, or five equilateral triangles, but cannot have six or more equilateral triangles in a finite system.

"Touch = <u>tex</u> of ver-tex, i.e., converging toward touchability, meaning a frequency-complex clustering whose frequencies interfere, or tune in, with the frequency array of the molecular complex of the atoms altogether constituting the Galaxy of"

- Cite typescript "Definitions by RBF," Pp.1A,2a,1, 29 Dec'58

RBF DEFINITIONS

Radome Sequence: (2)

"frequencies of our life cell tissues or Milky Way nebulae of locally regenerative frequency, locally recurrent through self-interference patterning.

"Mass is a word of inherently synergetic connotation. It is a behaviorist word popularly mistaken and used as a static word. Mass recognizes an inherent plurality of unique consequences resultant upon any infra- or ultra-sensorial recognizable, i.e., timable, collection of regenerative systems of precessionally self-associative energy-vector events. All the atoms and stars, as well as all the macro-remote astronomical cluster nebulas and remote micro-molecules, are such unique synergetically regenerative, infra-ultra-sensorial, unique multi-atomic mass clusters.

"A system is a man-thinkable, tune-in-able constellation of generalized experience event cluster foci. Energy-cluster foci are starts, or topological <u>ver-texes</u>, which are only the as-yet-nonanalyzed group phenomenon whose energetic point centers of event clustering locals are as yet too remote for the present observer's position. . . Systems are star inter-relationship considerations which logically continue to return upon themselves due to the related preoccupying importance of
- Cite typescript "Definitions by RBF," p.1, 29 Dec'58

RBF DEFINITIONS

Radome Sequence: (3)

"locally dominate event frequency proximities which altogether function as a fundamental, i.e., simplest or most unique, geometrical set which inherently subdivides the total Universe. The cell-time-man-experienced events fall into two main and clearly distinguishable classes:
(1) All those relatively too large or macrocosmic events of Universe which must clearly occur outside the presently thought-considered tunable range capabilities and are therefore outside the timable system set; and
(2) All those relatively too small, negligible, microcosmic clan which occur inherently within and infra to the tunable frequency and relative size ranging of the considered set.

"We may define structure as a local and finite system of energy events of physical Universe consisting of a patterning of interaimed or intervectorially frequency-synchronized, associ-ative and disassociative interferences omniprecessionally resulting as a pattern-regenerative constellation of system-inward-angled vectors, in dynamically symmetrical, precessional constellar equilibrium."

- Cite Typescript "Definitions of RBF," p.2, 29 Dec'58

RBF DEFINITIONS

Radome Sequence: (4)

"The energy proximity economy of ideal structuring as vectorially interaimed and synchronized energy, ergo energy-balanced interference patterns, comprise system complexes whose discrete angle and frequency modulations are, in turn, tunably controllable by man to provide a local energy-environment controll means for interference. Shunting of the known, relatively-important-to-man patterning and random local event program and angle patterning of Universe into orderly, man-preferred, locally regenerative program and angle patterns: this is local energetic environment controlling by anticipatory design science.

"Energy events of structure is a local and finite system of regenerative Universe consisting of a constellar patterning of interaimed and frequency synchronized, associative and dis-associative interferences resulting as a net set of inwardly angled, precessionally interaligned, vectorial resultants. Resultants of ▮▮▮▮▮▮ vectorial interaimed events must be to provide a local control of discrete frequency and angle modulation to control local energy-- to be known as local energetic environment controls, i.e. <u>radomes</u>.

- Cite typescript "Definitions of RBF," Pp.2-3, 29 Dec'58

RBF DEFINITIONS

Radome Sequence: (5)

"Radomes provide means for automatically excluding weather and including local warmth and dryness. They should admit the widest possible spectrum of electronic wave frequencies. ▮▮▮

"Omnitriangulation is implicit in the requirement for greatest strength with minimum structure. Omni-orientation of focal points of structure is at the most symmetrical equivalence of interdistancing. The strucrure's vectorial components converge at the vertexes, i.e. points, of the system. The triangular relationship of all points of any system show a constant relative abundance in which, of the total number of points, two are recognized as the poles of the system.

"The principle of constant relative abundance of topological features of all omnitriangulated systems, provides:

N - 2 = number of nonpolar vertexes;

(N - 2)2 = number of triangular faces

N - 2 = number of diamond faces        tensional vectors

(N - 2)3 = number of edges, i.e., compressional or
- Cite typescript "Definitions of RBF," Pp.2A,3, 29 Dec'58

RBF DEFINITIONS

Radome Sequence: (6)

"Whereas compressional functions of structures are inherently the most dense and obstructive of electric wave trapping, convergence should be kept at a minimum with the vector edges leaving the maximum number of wholes. Triangles are minimum holes. We can however have triangular ▮▮▮▮▮▮ interconnected hex-pent holes. The frequency of triangular relationships of approximately symmetrical point systems may be elected over a wide range. Therefore we choose a layout of triangles which will provide maximum weather exclusion and nondeterioration of structures and optim installability. This calls for low frequency tensile integrity and islanded compression with booms which are optimum to site handling gear, in respect to which pneumatic lozenges can be omni-interconnected and applied into a unitary double skin.

.   .   .   .   .   .

"Whenever or wherever compressional functions (or vectors) of structures are inherently most dense and compoundingly self-impending (sic) at second power, or relative proximities in respect to local electromagnetic wave frequency, the geodesic"

- Cite typescript "Definitions of RBF," Pp, 2A,3A,3, + 4, 29 Dec'68

RBF DEFINITIONS

Radome Sequence: (7)

"frequency design traffic should keep compressional compo-nentation and its interconvergence at minimum, i.e., in edge or vector function leaving a maximum pattern of holes (I.e. hex-pent triangular faces). . . . "

- Cite typescript "Definitions of RBF," p.4, 29 Dec'58

Radome:

See Dome entries
DEW Line Radomes

RBF DEFINITIONS

Raft:

"The raft is tangent to the sphere at midpoint. The early
navigators all knew this. They saw the islands disappearing
over the horizon in the distance and they were all very
conscious of a spherical world."

- Cite RBF to EJA, Michael Denneny & Arthur Morey, at Belmont
  Stakes restaurant breakfast, NYC, 3 Apr'75

---

Rafts: Early World Drifting on Rafts:

See Death, 1970
    Orbital Escape from Critical Proximity, (2)

---

RBF DEFINITIONS

Raft:

"The origins of the raft are simple: take a man standing
on the bank of a river. He falls in but he doesn't know
how to swim. If he grabs a stone he will sink but if he
hold on to a large enough piece of wood it will support
him. Next we take a man climbing on to a floating log.
He notices that it rolls so he tumbles back into the water.
But if it has a big enough branch or a smaller branch that
falls across another log, he will be able to stand up.
This is a basic raft. If this raft consists of two logs
separated by a distance like an outrigger, the resistance
is much less if the wind is blowing on the sides.
Therefore it will move in that course since everything
goes in the direction of least resistance."

- Cite NAGA TO THE INVISIBLE SEA, p. 12. 1970

---

Raft:                                                    (1)

    See Basic Raft

---

RBF DEFINITIONS

Rafts: Early World Drifting on Rafts:                    (1)

"If you were part of the very early world that drifted
on rafts, with currents and with the winds, you just rarely
came back to anything that you were familiar with. The
patterns were very, very large and you just kept sweeping on,
and you could say goodbye to those people and you never ever
saw them again. Because you were saying goodbye to people
and never seeing them again, the phenomena really of life
and death-- you are alive and they are alive, but you never
see them again-- so life and death to those people did not
have the distinction that it had later on. If you never
came to anything that you recognized, you would not then
recognize any really fundamental pattern. Furthermore,
there were some patterns of stars in the sky, but you
didn't get the same orientation of them ever again, so you
don't tend to recognize that pattern. If you were, however,
some of the early people who went offshore and accomplished
some of the sailing with the beginning of the ability to
navigate to windward, when sailing ships first developed the
ability to work to windward, you could retrace your steps,
and if you did retrace your steps, you would then begin to
get the same star patterns that you had before. You
wouldn't have any islands or anything around you, but one
thing that would be familiar is that you would get the same

---

Raft: Rafts:                                             (2)

    See Four-dimensional Reality, 30 Apr'77

---

RBF DEFINITIONS

Rafts: Early World Drifting on Rafts:                    (2)

"stars around you. And anyone who does any amount of sailing
knows how very familiar those stars become in the different
aspects."

- Cite Oregon Lecture #7, pp.251-252, 11 Jul'62

---

RBF DEFINITIONS

Railroad Tracks: Great Circle Energy Tracks on the Surface
Of A Sphere:

"The vector equilibrium railroad tracks are trans-world--
like being in an airplane; you can go anywhere. But the
icosahedron is stuck locally with no way to get to another
continent. The vector equilibrium is how you go from one
sphere to another, from Earth to Mars."

- Citation and context at Icosahedron As Local Shunting
  Circuit, 22 Jun'72

RBF DEFINITIONS (A)

Railroad Tracks:  Great Circle Energy Tracks on the Surface
                  Of A Sphere:

"Now I have found that nature insists on doing things most
economically.  We find that energy insists on following the
convex surface.  It has to follow the great circles.  We
find the 25 great circles of symmetry of the VE have a very
interesting characteristic: every one of them goes through
the 12 vertexes.  The 12 vertexes are made out of spheres in
closest packing, packed 12-around-one.  These are the points
of tangency of spheres in closest packing.  We have here 25
railroad tracks by which energy can go from here to there
anywhere in the Universe in the shortest possible way and it
is the only way it will go.  Thses are the only possible
transfers from here to there.  So then if you want to go from
here to there in the Universe, you have to follow these
surfaces and you have to go through these contact points.
So these 25 great circles represent a very special set of
events because some of them, for instance the four great
circles go through six vertexes; three great circles only go
through four vertexes, etc.; they have different opportunities
to peel off.  They require different frequencies.  I think"

    - Cite RBF to Verner Smythe, NYC, Reel 2, pp.8-9, 25 Feb' 69

---

RBF DEFINITIONS (B)

Railroad Tracks:  Great Circle Energy Tracks on the Surface
                  Of a Sphere:

"if you follow different great circles and their frequencies,
incidentally, every one of the chemical elements has been
identified by four different frequencies which absolutely
leads to that chemical element.

"This has all the symmetries there are.

"Now the same sphere could become the icosahedron. . . It has
the only great circles we have which don't go through the
transfer points.  Then they are not in agreement any more.
When they get into an icosahedron you can shut off the energy
supply and any waves would start going through the system and
vector equilibrium would go through it."

    - Cite RBF to Verner Smythe, NYC, Reel 2, p.9, 25 Feb'69

---

RBF DEFINITIONS (1)

Railroad Tracks:  Great Circle Energy Tracks on the Surface
                  of a Sphere:

"The shortest distance between points on the surface of a
sphere are the great circles.  They are called the geodesic
lines and inasmuch as there is no such thing as a straight
line and we are working in some kinds of developing surfaces,
the great circles are called geodesic lines.  We are now
getting into the axes of spin which are inherent in any
system.  We found that systems could be joined up /See Rubber
Tires_/ and they develop axial aspects, but they don't
frustrate the rest of the Universe.

"Now we are very interested in the kinds of great circles
which are developed by the various spins because they must
have some kind of important relationship.  We saw that if
we had twelve spheres in what we call closest packing--
if you wanted to go the shortest distance between points on
the surface of spheres-- supposing you were an electric
charge, an electron.  We make great copper spheres, the
old Van de Graaff generators and so forth, you could build
up enormous charges of electricity on the surface of this
sphere."

    - Cite Oregon Lecture #7, p. 266. 11 Jul'62

---

RBF DEFINITIONS (2)

Railroad Tracks:  Great Circle Energy Tracks on the Surface
                  of a Sphere:

"The charges never try to go on the concave side of this
sphere.  They always stay on the convex side.  You run into
this kind of behavior just in trying the electroplate
phenomenon.  You will find that you cannot plate the concave
side.  You automatically electroplate the convex side.  The
convex side goes into higher tension which means that it is
actually thinner and therefore less resistant and therefore
the energy tries to follow the convex surfaces.  Supposing
you were the kind of energy that always follows the convex
kind of surfaces and yet, being energy, you always have to
do it the shortest way.  You want to go from sphere to sphere
on the surface of the sphere so you would have to take the
great circles at the points where the spheres touch one another
and therefore you would take the great circles of them.
Therfore those 25 great circles are very important because
they are all the possible great circles that carry all the
traffic between the twelve points-- they are all the possible
geodesic railroads.  With that kind of energy which always
has to follow surfaces, these are the railroad tracks that
you would have to follow. . . "

    - Cite Oregon Lecture #7, pp. 266-267. 11 Jul'62

SYSTEM-SEC. 452.03

---

RBF DEFINITIONS

Railroad Tracks:  Great Circle Energy Tracks on the Surface
                  of a Sphere:  Convex and Concave:

"Dr Einstein pointed out that you could be the little man in
the Universe who always went from sphere to sphere and
through the points of tangency.  You lived inside the
concave surface of a sphere and you could get to the point
of tangency in the next sphere, and the next sphere,
concavely, and you could go right through the Universe that
way.  Or you could be the little man who lived on the
outside of the sphere, and always lived convexly, and you
came to the same point of tangency and you went on.  This
is one way of looking at Universe and the sphere is another
way of looking at Universe.  This is typical of not being
fooled by just looking at the spheres-- or just looking
at the little triangle locally on the surface of your big
sphere where you had your big triangle.  This is beginning
to give us ways of seeing the complementarity at all times."

    - Cite Oregon Lecture #7, p. 258. 11 Jul'62

SYSTEM-SEC 452.02

---

RBF DEFINITIONS

Railroad Tracks:  Great Circle Energy Tracks on the Surface
                  of a Sphere: Foldability:

"This may be pure accident but I could say something to
you now categorically that is really very fascinating,
that is, I found that you could fold and make all the 25
and 31 great circles.  There are no other circles though
that I know how to fold and make any other kind of great
circle patterns on spheres.  They and they alone seem to
be foldable into these conditions.  This seems to be a very
strange kind of control because if they did they all relate,
they are the ways of the grand central station and all the
shortest, most economical railroad tracks between all the
points in Universe-- flying either concave or convex."

    - Cite Oregon Lecture #7, p. 271. 11 Jul'62

---

RBF DEFINITIONS

Railroad Tracks:  Triangular Systems of Energy Networks.

"In any network high energy charges refuse to take the
long way round to their opposite pole.  They tend to push
through, the separating space, striving to 'short.'  Thus
energy will automatically triangulate via a diagonal of
a square, or via the triangulating diagonals of any other
polygon to which the force is applied.  Triangular systems
represent the shortest, most economical energy networks. . .
The triangle is the basic unit of energy configurations,
whether occurring as free energy or as structure."

    - Cite R.W. MARKS, p. 43. 1960

SYSTEM- SEC. 452.04

---

Railroad Tracks:  Great Circle Energy Tracks on the Surface:

                  of a Sphere:                                    (1)


            See Foldability of Great Circles
                Frequency: Alternate Wavelength Frequency
                Grand Central Station of Universe
                Holding Circuit
                Kissing Point: K:
                Tensegrity: Vertexial Connections
                Vector Equilibrium: Great Circles Of

Railroad Tracks: Great Circle Energy Tracks on the Surface
of a Sphere: (2)

See Allspace Filling: Octa & VE, 1967
Gravitational Constant (1)(2)
Omnidirectional Typewriter (2)-(4)

RBF DEFINITIONS

Rain:

"Earth's biospheric inventory of water is radially
dispersed outwardly by vaporization and omnilocally
condensed as inwardly 'falling' drops of rain, which are
gravitationally and convergently collected as ocean."

- Citation & context at Islanded Radiation & Tensional
Constancy, 11 Feb'76

Railroads: Railroad Tracks: (1)

See Airplanes vs. Railroads

Rain as Radial:

See Cosmic vs. Terrestrial Accounting, (3)
Ecology, 16 Feb'73
Precession, (I)
Rain, 11 Feb'76

Railroads: Railroad Tracks: (2)

See Dymaxion Airocean World,(I)
Convergent vs. Parallel Perception, 13 Nov'75

Rain:

See Ecological Pattern, 19 Sep'64
Ecology Sequence, (a)
Radiation Sequence, (2)
Trespassing, (1)
Water, May'65
Wind Power Sequence, (5)
Islanded Radiation & Tensional Constancy, 11 Feb'76*

Railway Trains: Loosely Coupled:

See Diesel Ship at Sea, May'72

Rainbow:

See Optical Rainbow Range

RBF DEFINITIONS

Raison d'Etre:

"The illogically developed stigma*
Which misinforms millions today
Is being swiftly eradicated
As its championship raison d'etre
Is manifest in world athletics."

⎡*of race⎤

- Cite EVOLUTIONARY 1972-1975 ABOARD SPACE VEHICLE EARTH,
  Jan '72, p. 15

---

RBF DEFINITIONS

Raison d'Etre:                                                      (1)

---

RBF DEFINITIONS

Raison d'Etre:

"Environment is the whole raison d'etre of man's

existence. . . This is why I became preoccupied with

environment: how do we protect the infant, being born

a genius, from being de-geniused by his environment."

- Cite RBF to Students International Meditation Seminar,
  U.Mass., Amherst, 22 July 1971.

- Citation at Environment, 22 Jul'71

---

Raison d'Etre:                                                      (2)

See DNA, 31 May'71
    Environment, 22 Jul'71*
    More With Less:  Sea Technology, (4)
    Building Industry, (12)
    Propaganda, 29 Mar'77

---

Raison d'Etre of Boast & Fear:

See Superstition, May'49
    Ignorance, (1)(2)

---

RBF DEFINITIONS

Ramify:

"Unlike Siddhartha . . I decided to ramify the ramifiable."

- Cite RBF to EJA, Governor House Motel, Bethesda, 28 April 1971
  after reading Herman Hesse's "Siddhartha" the night before,
  given him by Mary  Cohen.

---

Raison d'Etre of Going Awayness:

See Repulsion, 7 Feb'71

---

Ramify the Idealistic:

See Now, 14 Feb'72

---

RBF DEFINITIONS

Ramify:                                                              (1)

See Multiramifications

Random Element:                                                      (1)

See Inadvertence - Random Element

Ramify:                                                              (2)

See Capabilities, 20 Apr'72
    Thinking, (3)
    Dymaxion Airocean World Map,(5)

Random Element:                                                      (2)

See Inadvertence, 1938
    Man as a Function of Universe, (B)
    Profess:  Profession, 22 Apr'61
    Stardust, May'65
    Wow:  The Last Wow, 22 Apr'71

Random Element:  Law of Increase of The:                            (1)

See Entropy
    Expanding Physical Universe
    Thermodynamics:  Second Law Of

RBF DEFINITIONS

Randomness:

"All stars radiate energy in a random manner.  Randomness
begets increasing disorder which is self-expansive."

- Citation and context at Boltzmann Sequence (5), Dec'72

Random Element:  Law of Increase of The:                            (2)

See Antientropy, 10 Oct'63
    Man as a Function of Universe, (B)
    Sorting, May'65
    Stardust, May'65

RBF DEFINITIONS

Randomness:

"Randomness of lines automatically works back to a

set of interactions and a set of proximities which begin

to triangulate themselves. . . . The most comfortable

condition of triangles is equilateral so there will be a

tendency for them to try to become equilateral. . . .

This effect goes on in depth and in to the tetrahedra or

ocaahedra."

- Cite Carbondale Draft
  Nature's Coordination, p. VI.1

- Cite Ledgmont Lab, p.20, 15 Oct'64

RBF DEFINITIONS

Randomness:

"Entropy is not random; it is always one negative
tetrahedron."

- Cite OMNIDIRECTIONAL HALO, p. 157, 1960

- Citation at Entropy, 1960

---

Random: Randomness:                                    (1)

See Brouwer, L.E.J:
Coincidental Articulation Sequence
Intercept the Random Event
Omnirandomness
Order Underlying Randomness:  Principle Of
Probability
Rearrange Random Receipts
Entropy ≠ Randomness
Happen: Happening: Happenstance

---

Random: Randomness:                                    (2)

See Boltzmann Sequence (5)*
Entropy, 1960*
Nebula, 29 Oct'72
Space Technology (7)
Triangle, 8 Oct'64
Biological Life, (1)
Thinking, 6 Nov'73
Light on Scratched Metal, 9 Nov'73

---

RBF DEFINITIONS

Range Finder:

"Dual personality... provides two viewpoints... equivalent to
the eyes of a range finder, an instrument which mechanically
widens the distance between the two human eyes..."

- Citation and context at Genius, 1938

---

RBF DEFINITIONS

Range Finder:  Range Finding:

See Convergent vs. Parallel Perception, 13 Nov'75

---

RBF DEFINITIONS

Rate:

"Rate occurs only when there is terminal. Rate is a modulation
between terminals. With termination, a system's integrity is
brought about by the individually covarying magnitudes and the
omnidirectional experience pulls on the system."

- Cite SYNERGETICS text at Sec. 411.37; galley rewrite, 2 Nov'73

---

RBF DEFINITIONS

Rate:

"You don't get rate until there is terminal. Rate is a
modulation between terminals. With termination of a
system's integrity is brought about by the individually
covarying magnitudes and the omnidirectional experience
pulls on the system.

- Cite RBF to EJA, 3200 Idaho, incorporated in SYNERGETICS
draft At Sec. 411.38, 9 Nov'72
[37]

---

RBF DEFINITIONS

Rate:

"...Rate being the inseparable relationship of time and space."

- Citation and context at Conscious World, 1938

RBF DEFINITIONS

Rate:

"Speed is a unit of rate which is an integrated ratio of
both time and space and no greater rate of speed than that
provided by its cause, which is pure energy, latent or
radiant, is attainable."

- Citation & context at Einstein Equation: Telegram to Nogucmhi,
  1938

---

Rate & Terminal

See Terminal Rate

---

Rates & Magnitudes:                                              (1)

See Fast & Slow
    Big & Little
    Universal Integrity:  Second-power Congruence of
        Gravitational & Radiational Constants
    Frequency & Magnitude
    Slower & Closer vs. Faster & Far Apart

---

Rate:                                                            (1)

See Degree of Freedom Rate
    Expansion-contraction System Accumulating Rates
    Frequency
    Lag Rates
    Melting:  Rate Of
    Rates & Magnitudes
    Tetrahedron:  Dissimilar Rate of Change Accomodation
    Terminal Rate
    Omnidifferentiated Rates
    Third-power Rate of Variation Model
    Nuclear Propagation Rate
    Recall Rates
    Point Growth Rate
    Shell Growth Rate

---

Rates & Magnitudes:                                              (2)

See Integration, 29 Aug'64
    Shunt, Jun'66
    Tetrahedron:  Coordinate Symmetry, 15 Oct'64
    Time, 23 May'72
    Time-energy Economics, 15 Jun'74
    Pollution Control (2)
    Gravity:  Circumferential Leverage, (4)
    Historical Event Cognition, 2 Mar'68
    Vector Equilibrium, 3 Jan'75
    Periodic Experience, (9)
    Intellect:  Equation Of, (A)(B)
    Hyperbolic Paraboloid, 14 May'75
    Structural Sequence, (B)
    Frequency Islands of Perception, 13 Nov'75
    Flywheels, 11 Dec'75
    Gestation Rate, 1 Mar'77

---

Rate:                                                            (2)

See Change, 9 Nov'72
    Comprehensive, 1960
    Conscious World, 1938*
    Future of Synergetics, 22 Apr'68
    Good & Evil Sequence, (1)
    Pythagoras, (1)
    Subset, 1960
    Synergetics, 26 May'72
    Tidal, May'72
    Calculus, Mar'71
    Individuality & Degrees of Freedom, (1)
    Life, 25 Mar'71
    Machines vs. Structures, 13 Nov'75

---

Rate & Terminal:

See Rate, 2 Nov'73

---

**RATIOS: CHECKLIST**
                                                                 (1)

See Volume-energy Ratios
    Volume-number Ratios
    Volume-quanta Ratios
    Volume-surface Ratios
    Volume-weight Ratios
    Twentyness in Mass Ratio of Electron & Proton
    Universal Integrity:  Vector Equilibrium & Icosahedron
    Vector Equilibrium:  Ratio of Volume to Quantum
    Gravitational Constant
    Quantum Values:  Potential Ratio of Volume to
        Realized Quantum Values
    Universal Integrity:  Manifest Ratios & Potential
        Ratios
    Slenderness Ratio
    Length-to-girth Ratio
    Coordinate Abundance Ratios
    Surface-mass Ratios

Ratios: Ratio-ing: (2)

See Cartilage vs. Bone, Dec'61
Efficiency, 22 Jan'75
Greater Intellect, (2)
Inverse, 11 Jul'62
Trigonometry: Spherical Trigonometry, (1);
11 Jul'62

Rational Fractions: (1)

See Modules: A & B Quanta Modules

Rational Action in a Rational World:

See Dymaxion, 1967

Rational Fractions: (2)

See Vector Equilibrium Field, 20 Dec'73

Rationality by Complementation:

See Icosahedron & Vector-edged Cube

Rational - Relational:

See Reason, Aug'73

Rational Concentricity:

See Unified Operational Field, 30 Dec'73

Rationalization of Selfishness:

See Propaganda, 29 Mar'77
News & Evolution, (3)
Technology: Enchantment vs. Disenchantment, (3)(4)

RBF DEFINITIONS

██████████ Rational Whole Numbers:

"Rational values . . . can be expressed as a ratio of a whole number. . . . Nowhere in" Synergetics "is it necessary to introduce irrational numbers such as pi, (3.14159..+)."

* Cite MARKS, pp 47-48, 1960

---

Rationality:                                               (2)

See Cosmic Accounting, 20 Dec'73
    Dymaxion, 1967; 1960
    Oscillation, 21 Dec'71
    Powering:  Second Powering, 21 Dec'71
    Vector Equilibrium, (1)(2)
    Triacontrahedron, 3 May'77
    Min-max Limits, 8 Aug'77

---

Rational Whole Numbers:                                    (1)

See Low Order Prime Numbers
    Asymmetry:  Plus & Minus Magnitudes as Rational
        Fractions
    Prime Rational Integer Characteristics
    Single Integer Differentials

---

RBF DEFINITIONS

Rationalization Sequence :                                 (1)

"Upon the premise that the sumtotal human desire to survive is dominant over the sumtotal ████ of the impulse to destroy, this book is designed.  It does not seek to provide a formula to attainment.  To do so would develop dogma and nullify the process of individual rationalization that is utterly essential for growth.

"Rationalization is an act similar to walking through a half-frozen, marshy, unexplored country to mark out a trail that others may eventually follow.  It involves not only the familiar one-two progression of shifting the weight and balance from one foot to the other, but an unknown quantity progression of selective testing to avoid treacherous ground before putting full weight upon the forward foot.

"Rationalization is a time-word to replace 'thinking,' which is an ancient, mystically evolved word tentatively signifying an attempt to force the power of god into one's self.  Rationalization connotes a constant, selective balancing of relative values, gained from experience, for the purpose of harmonious, inclusive recomposition and subsequent extension.

- Cite NINE CHAINS TO THE MOON, p. ix, 1938

---

Rational Whole Numbers:                                    (2)

See Simplex, 1965
    Vector Equilibrium (1)
    Twelve Universal Degrees of Freedom, Dec'61
    Energy Has Shape, 24 Sep'73
    Absolute Network, 10 Nov'74
    Omnihalo, Nov'71
    Module:  A Quanta Module:  Introduction Of,
        22 Feb'77
    Multiplication by Division, 20 Jan'77
    Mites & Quarks as Basic Notes, (1)-(3)
    Trigonometry, 26 Sep'77

---

RBF DEFINITIONS

Rationalization Sequence:                                  (2)

"It is central to my philosphy that everything in the Universe is constantly in motion, atomically if not ████████ visibly, and that opposing forces throughout this kinetic picture are always in neat balance; furthermore, that everything invariably moves in the direction of least resistance.

"The history of man's creative effort is the story of his struggle to control 'direction' by the elimination of known resistances.

"To the degree that the direction of least resistance is controlled by vacuumizing the advance and de-vacuumizing the wake, the course of society can be progressively better charted and eventually determinable with a high degree of certainty.

"The creative control, or streamlining, of society by the scientific-minded (the right-makes-mightest) is in direct contrast to attempts by scheming matter-over-mindists (the might-makes-rightist) to control society by increasing, instead of lessening, resistance to natural flows through such devices as laws, tariffs, prohibitions, armaments, and the cultivation of popular fear.

- Cite NINE CHAINS TO THE MOON, p.x, 1938

---

Rationality:  Rational:                                    (1)

See Omnirationality
    Prime Rational Integer Characteristics
    Reason
    Nuclear Geometrical Limit of Rational Differentiation

---

RBF DEFINITIONS

Rationalization Sequence:                                  (3)

"By controlling direction it becomes possible , scientifically, to increase the probability that specific events will 'happen.'

"Preparation of the material herein set forth dates from the very beginning of my experience.  Up to a point in that experience I lived by the common code of loyalty and good fellowship with all of its convincing and romantic 'tradition.'  Then, through my own particular quota of important slaps in the face, it became apparent that in 'tradition' lies fallacy, and that to be guided in conduct and thought by blind adherence to tenets of tradition is, as said in slang, bravely to 'stick the neck out.'  I realized that experience is the vital factor, and that, since one can think and feel consciously only in terms of experience, one can be hurt only in terms of experience.  When one is hurt, then somewhere in the linkage of his experience can be discovered the parting of the strands that led to the hurt.  Therefore it follows that strict adherence to rationalization, within the limits of self-experience, will provide corrections to performance obviating not only for one's self, but for others, the pitfalls that occasion self-hurt.  By cultivating the ability to rationalize in the absolute, one acquires the power of so ordering experience that truths are"

- Cite NINE CHAINS TO THE MOON, p.x, 1938

RBF DEFINITIONS

Rationalization Sequence: (4)

"clarified and susceptibility to self-hurt is diminished to the point of negligibility. Through rationalizations anyone may evolve solutions for any situations that may arise, and by the attainment of this ability through experience one obtains his license to be of service to mankind.

"Rationalization alone, however, is not sufficient. It is not an end in itself. It must be carried through to an objective state and materialize into a completely depersonalized instrument-- a 'pencil.' (Who knows who made the first pencil? Certainly not Eberhard Faber or 'Venus.') The pencil not only facilitates communication between men, by making thought specific and objective, but also enables men cooperatively, to plan and realize the building of a house, oxygen tent, flat iron, or an x-ray cabinet by virtue of the pencil's availability. The inventor, alive or dead, is extraneous and unimportant; it is the 'pencil' that carries over. Abstract thought dies with the thinker, but the mechanism was building for a long time before the moment of recognized in-vention.

"The substance of this book develops my conviction of these truths. In a final chapter I have recorded certain thought-"

- Cite NINE CHAINS TO THE MOON, pp.x-xi, 1938

RBF DEFINITIONS

Rationalization Sequence: (5)

"processes and results of abstract intuitive thinking which would be obscure without reading the preceding sections. The reason for exposing myself to possible suspicion of 'mysticism' is to show how important it is to transcribe the faint thought messages coming into our personal cosmos at the time of occurrence-- sketchy and puzzling though they may be-- b'ecause time, if well served, will turn them into monkey-wrenches and gas torches.

"The title 'Nine Chains to the Moon' was chosen to encourage and stimulate the broadest attitude toward thought. Simultaneously, it emphasizes the littleness of our Universe from the mind viewpoint. A statistical cartoon whould show that if, in imagination, all of the people of the world were to stand upon one another's shoulders, they would make nine complete chains between the Earth and the Moon. If it is not so far to the Moon, then it is not so far to the limits-- whatever, whenever, or wherever they may be.

"Limits are what we have feared. So much has been done to make us conscious of our infinite physical smallness that the time has come to dare to include the complete Universe in our"

- Cite NINE CHAINS TO THE MOON, p.xi, 1938

RBF DEFINITIONS

Rationalization Sequence: (6)

"rationalizing. It is no longer practical to gaze at the surfaces of 'named' phenomena within the range of vision of the smoking car of the 5.15 with no deeper analysis of their portent than is ▓▓▓▓▓▓▓▓▓ derivable from a superficial exchange of complexed opinion-notions with fellow-commuters.

"After all,' Jeans said, 'it is man who asked the question.' The question is survival, and the answer, which is unit, lies in the progressive sumtotaling of man's evolving knowledge. Individual survival is identifiable with the whole-- as extension or extinction. There is no good country doctor on Mars to revive those who, through mental inertia, are streamlining into extinction."

- Cite NINE CHAINS TO THE MOON, p.xi, 1938

Rationalization:

See Political Mandates: Inventory Of, 27 Dec'73
Selfishness, 20 Sep'76

RBF DEFINITIONS

Razor:

"... The blade of a razor is a randomly dumped breakwater of spherical rubble."

- Cite SYNERGETICS draft at Sec. 1009.41, 10 Beb'73

Reachable Point:

See Vector Equilibrium: Unarticulated VE, 2 Nov'73

Reach-miles:

See Radiation: Speed Of, 30 Nov'72
Vector Equilibrium: Unarticulated Ve, 2 Nov'73

Reach: Reachability Range: (1)

See Limit Reach
Radial Reach
Radiant Valvability of IVM-defined Wavelength
Sweepout

Reach:  Reachable:                                    (2)


       See Isotropic Vector Matrix, 30 Nov'72
          Point, 16 Nov'72
          Time, 30 Nov'72

---

RBF DEFINITIONS

   Reading:

   "We don't know how we retrieve information from our brain.
The conscious part does some triggering; it acts as a valve;
it can be a brake or it can be an accelerator.  But the
conscious part is less than one-millionth of the retrieval
process.  The rest is subconscious.  There is an automatic
process.  When we can't remember a name the brain doesn't
forget we asked the question, although maybe we have forgotten.
But the lags are variable, and therefore the feedbacks are
not orderly.  The only conscious part is the holding back of
irrelevancies.  And this is true of reading, too."

      - Cite RBF in tape interview with Mike Bandler, Wash. Post,
        "Portrait of a Man Reading," 3200 Idaho, Wash DC, 29 May'72

---

RBF DEFINITIONS

   Reaction:

   "While the human's actions are antientropic, his reactions

   are entropic, ergo unpredictable."


   - Citation and context at Individuality, May'65

   - Cite RBF in AAUW Journal, ████ p. 176, May '65.

---

RBF DEFINITIONS

   Reading:                                            (1)

   Q.  "Mr. Fuller, you're quite a traveler.  Where do you find
      the time and the places to read?"

   A.  "Obviously airplanes and airports are great places, as
are hotel rooms very late at night.  I'm convinced you can't
put out if you don't put in.  In other words, thinking does
come from experience.  Reading increases the number of
experiences from which you may gradually adduce generalized
principles.  I am now fairly aware of what my conscious part
is in this very complex system called thinking.  That conscious
part, which is only one-millionth of the picture, can do
some triggering, can be a brake or an accelerator, a valve
that can shut off or turn off a process.
    "We experience different rates of retrieval of information.
Even in my vocabulary and in my reading, there are lags, and
when people talk about speed reading, it's really just a means
of diminishing the lag.  I'm not interested in speedreading,
but rather in content and understanding.  But I find the
subconscious is very powerful.
    "During 1938-1940 I was consultant in science and tech-
nology to the editor of Fortune magazine, and my function
was to emphasize the science foundations of great industry.

   - Cite Michael Bandler Interview, BOOK WEEK, 11 Jun'72

---

Reaction:                                              (1)


      See Action
         Action-reaction-resultant
         Resultant
         Z Cobras

---

RBF DEFINITIONS

   Reading:                                            (2)

   "I read 'Patent Gazette,' and I could literally spin the
pages, and when my eyes saw something I wasn't familiar with
they would stop me.  They recognized absolutely everything
I wasn't familiar with.  So when I read today I don't have
to process the material.  I know my subconscious will stop
me when I'm not familiar with something.  Everybody has that
capacity, but not ██████████ everyone uses it."


   - Cite "Books and Buckminster Fuller," Interview by Michael J.
     Bandler, BOOK WEEK, 11 Jun'72

---

Reaction:                                              (2)


      See Sixty Degreeness, 8 Dec'72

---

RBF DEFINITIONS

   Reading:  Escapist Reading:

   Q:  "What do you do in the way of what might be called
      escapist reading?"

   A:  "I have nothing to escape.  I'm really so fascinated
      with life."


   - Cite query from Mike Bandler, Wash. Post, "Portrait of a Man
     Reading," to RBF in tape interview, 3200 Idaho, 29 May'72

RBF DEFINITIONS

Reading Out Loud:

"We read all of Dickens out loud. In reading out loud your
eye really goes several lines ahead and you can anticipate
the meaning and inflections. Out loud reading went right on
through the time of World War I, but it went out just like
that when popular radio came in."

- Cite RBF in tape interview with Mike Bandler, Wash. Post.,
"Portrait of a Man Reading," 3200 Idaho, Wash DC, 29 May'72

---

Real:                                                    (2)

See Principle, May'49
Vector, 27 May'72*

---

Reader:  Reading:

See Child Sequence, (3)
Fuller, R.B: Books Read in His Youth, 1971
Semantics, 20 Feb'73

---

RBF DEFINITIONS

Real Estate:

"Big money has left all the sovereignly locked-in, local-
property-game players holding the unmovable bags of real
estate...."

- Citation & context at Transnational Capitalism & Export
Of Know-how, (1); 20 Sep'76

---

RBF DEFINITIONS

Real:

"... Vectors being the product of physical energy

constituents, are 'real,' having velocity multiplied

by mass operating in a specific direction; velocity

being a product of time and size modules; and mass being

a volume-weight relationship."

- Citation at Vectors, 27 May'72
- Cite SYNERGETICS draft, Sec. 410.05, RBF rewrite 27/2 May'72

---

RBF DEFINITIONS

Real Estate Development:

"We find that generally speaking the geographically larger

the physical task to be done, the duller the conceptual brain

is brought to bear upon the technically realized applications."

- Cite RBF quoted by Hal Aigner, in Rolling Stone, 10 June 1971
- Citation and context at Politics, 10 Jun'71

---

Real:                                                    (1)

See Ideal vs. Real
Realm: Real: Royal
Real Models of Reality
Real Universe

---

Real Estate:  Real Estate Development:              (1)

See Building Business
Realm: Real: Royal
Whitehead's Dilemma
Land Exploitation
Deed: (Property Deed)
Miniature Castle Building

Real Estate: Real Estate Development:                    (2)

    See New York City (12)
        Transnational Capitalism & Export of Know-how, (1)ᵂ
        Houses & Infrastructure, 20 Sep'76

---

RBF DEFINITIONS

Reality:

"Nature modulates probability and the degrees of freedom,
i.e., frequency and angle, leads to the tensegrity sphere;
which leads to the pneumatic bag; all of which are the same
kind of reality as the three automobiles."

  _ Citation and context at Sphericity of Whole Systems, 26 Sep'73

---

TEXT CITATIONS

Realistic:

Synergetics draft at Sec. 1001.14, 16 Feb'73

---

RBF DEFINITIONS

Reality:

". . . What we call reality is always a positive or

negative set of the whole. "

        (This is in the context of a description of
        zero vector equilibrium.)

- Citation & context at Vector Equilibrium: Zero Tetrahedron (3),
                                         11 Jul'62
         - Cite Carbondale Draft
             Nature's Coordination, p. VI.45
  - Cite Oregon Lecture #7, p. 236. 11 Jul '62
    Incorporated in SYNERGETICS draft at Sec. 441.23, 9 Jun'72
  - See RBF rewrite on galley at Sec. 441.23, cited at Physical
    Reality, 4 Nov'73

---

RBF DEFINITIONS

Reality:

"The reality is always orbital."

  - Citation & context at Orbit - Circuit, 10 Sep'74

---

RBF DEFINITIONS

Reality:

"What the mathematicians have been calling abstraction
is reality.  When they are inadequate in their abstraction
then they are irrelevant to reality.  The mathematicians
feel they can do anything they want with their abstraction
because they don't relate it to reality.  And, of course,
they can really do anything they want with their abstractions
but, like masturbation, it is irrelevant to the propagation
of life.

"The only reality is the abstraction of the principles, the
eternal generalized principles. . . Most people talk of
reality as what are just the after-image effects-- the
realization lags, which register superficially and are
asymmetric and off center. (The principles themselves have
different lag rates and different interferences.)  When we
get to reality it's absolutely eternal.

"The inherent inaccuracy is what people call the reality.
Man's way of apprehending is always slow: ergo the superficial and erroneous impressions of solids and things, which
can actually be explained only in principle."

  - Cite RBF to EJA, 3200 Idaho, Wash. DC, 24 Feb '72
  - Citation at Abstraction, 24 Feb'72

---

RBF DEFINITIONS

Reality:

"Reality is always indeterminate."

  - Cite RBF to EJA, 3200 Idaho, Wash. DC, 5 May'74

---

RBF DEFINITIONS

Reality:

"The principle is more of a reality than the qualities

they produce."

  - Cite RBF to EJA, 3200 Idaho, DC, 22 Feb '72
  - Citation and context at Principle, 22 Feb'72

RBF DEFINITIONS

Reality:

"...There is no straight line; only the wave coincides with reality."

- Citation & context at Now, 14 Feb'72

---

RBF DEFINITIONS

███████  ████████████  Reality:

"All of the weightless metaphysical thoughts concerning reality are mentally understandable independently of any special-case physical sense experience. All such weightless thoughts can be imaginatively described by one person either to himself or to another person by weightless conceptions. Such weightless thinking-- independent of physical sensing-- plus our scientific discovery of the great infra- and ultra-to-human-sense-ranging of physical energy's electromagnetic spectrum regularities altogether combine to both establish and confirm that less than one-millionth of reality is now directly apprehensible by the human senses."

- Cite ARCHITECTURE AS ULTRA INVISIBLE REALITY, p. 150, Dec. '69

---

RBF DEFINITIONS

Reality:

"The nonsimultaneity and dissimilarity
Of the complementary interpatternings
Produce what we sense to be reality,
Otherwise they would cancel one another
And there would be no sensoriality."

- Citation at Senses, 1971

---

RBF DEFINITIONS

Reality:

"The wellspring of reality is the family of weightless generalized principles."

- Cite NEHRU SPEECH, p.41, 13 Nov'69

---

RBF DEFINITIONS

Reality:

". . . Not until we have size, not until we have energetic experienceability, i.e., not until we have reality, do ███ we have structural stabilization of the nuclear 12 ⌐balls of the vector equilibrium ⌐."

- Cite RBF to EJA, Bear Island, 23 August 1971.

- Citation & context at Vector Equilibrium, 23 Aug'71

---

RBF DEFINITIONS

Reality:

"Every chemical element has its unique frequencies. That became the way that you know, this is what you mean by that, mathematically and scientifically this is the element, this is the reality. Copper is real, and copper was those frequencies. . . "

- Cite RBF Address THE HABITABLE CITY, 14 Oct '69.
UNIQUE FREQUENCIES - SEC. 418.12 REJECTED BY RBF, 11 Nov '74

---

RBF DEFINITIONS

Reality:

"Conceptuality is metaphysical and weightless.

"Reality is physical."

- Cite RBF to EJA, Somerset Club, Boston, 22 April 1971

- Citation & context at Conceptuality & Reality, 22 Apr'71

---

RBF DEFINITIONS

Reality:

"...Everything we know as reality has to be either a positive or negative condition."

- Citation and context at Nature, Jun'66

RBF DEFINITIONS

Reality:

"Pure science events represent openings of windows
through the wall of ignorance and fiction, to reveal
the only reality-- the behavior of the naked Universe
that always was, is, and will be. True it is that the
first glimpses may be hazy and imperfect, but the behavior
itself is absolute and progressively clarified. . . ."

- Citation and context at Science, p.13, 1947

TEXT CITATIONS

Reality = Inexactitude

s543.05

---

RBF DEFINITIONS

Reality: Fuller's Reality vs. Popular Reality:

"I really very clearly differentiate today what I call
reality and what most people call reality. Their reality
is that you have got to make money and you have got to pay
your bills. I consider that really a game. So it is part
of my reality that man is hooked with a game, which makes
it very inconvenient for me where they are not dealing with
reality. The game includes social standings, reputation...
that there is a place called Chicago... because in my reality
there are probably no names."

- Citation & context at Interrelatedness vs. Names, (1);
  20 Feb'77

RBF DEFINITIONS

Reality as Structural Interaction of Principles:

"The relative abundances of reciprocally patterning
principles everywhere constitute the so far discovered
inventory of minimally complex, ergo fundamentally differentiable
structurally regenerative universal governance. The complex
of interactively accommodating principles and their relative
abundance accommodation are reality-- the only reality. What
man, in his sensorially preoccupied misapprehending, has termed
'abstract,' in contradistinction to sensorial, as well as
that which man has designated as metaphysical in contradistinction to physical, are altogether one reality. The fact
of meagerness of the experience-generated knowledge of
man in respect to the omniregenerative structure of reality
and the observational facts taken in the twilight zones
between the meager known and the as-yet -unexperienced, in
no way alters the unitary integrity of the utter interaccomo-
dation of complex structural interaction of the principles
as so far sum totally inventoried by the faithfully reported
experiences of man."

- Cite I&I, DOMES, p. 147. 1963

---

Reality: Fuller's Reality vs. Popular Reality:

   See Earning a Living

Reality as Structural Interaction of Principles:

   See Universe (p.131) 1960
       Airplane, May'49
       Periodic Experience, (7)

---

RBF DEFINITIONS

Reality vs. Generalization:

"There are a lot of different realities. That is the
difference between reality and generalization. There is
only one generalization."

- Citation & context at Individuality & Degrees of Freedom, (3)
  17 Jun'75

RBF DEFINITIONS

Reality: Structurings as the Only and Inescapable Reality:

"The mathematical patterning and intertransformability

of nature's geometrical structurings are the only reality

of Universe. The infinitely regenerative dynamism, always

potential in the fundamental relationship of the principles,

in itself constitutes the intellectually tunable and ever

inescapable reality."

- Cite I&I, DOMES, p. 147. 1963

Reality & Unreality:

See Dynamic Equilibrium, 24 Apr'76

Reality:                                                                    (2B)

See Vector Equilibrium, 23 Aug'71*; 1 May'71
    Vector Equilibrium:  Zero Tetrahedron (3)*
    Velocity, 12 Jul'62
    Senses, 1971*
    Orbit = Circuit, 10 Sep'74*
    Principle, 6 Apr'75
    Thought, May'49
    In, Out & Around, Nov'71
    Multidimensional Accommodation, 11 Dec'75
    Life & Death, 26 Jan'76
    Me, 18 Dec'76
    Life is Not Physical, 20 Feb'77
    Conceptual Limits, 22 Jun'77

Reality:                                                                    (1A)

See Common Sense Reality
    Conceptuality & Reality
    Cosmetry
    Earth:  Let's Get Dow to Earth
    Game of Reality
    Geometry of Reality
    Ideal vs. Real
    Invisible Reality
    Local Reality
    Mind as Reality
    Minimum Reality
    Nonreality
    Official Reality
    Perceptual Peephole
    Physical Reality
    Residual Reality
    A Priori Four-dimensional Reality
    Mind-over-matter Reality
    Temporality = Tempo-reality = Time-reality

Reality:                                                                    (3)

See Reality:  Fuller's Reality vs. Popular Reality
    Reality vs. Generalization
    Reality as Structural Interaction of Principles
    Reality:  Structurings as the Only & Inescapable
        Reality
    Reality & Unreality

Reality:                                                                    (1B)

See Sensorial Identification of Reality
    Spherical Reality
    Superficial Reality
    Wellspring of Reality
    Vectors Are Real
    Four-dimensional Reality
    Momentary Reality

RBF DEFINITIONS

Realizable:

"Physical interferences of our sensibilities are alike
true and real, or realizable, only in principle."

- Citation and context at Principle, May'49

Reality:                                                                    (2A)

See Abstraction, 24 Feb'72*
    Apprehending, 22 Nov'73
    Benday Screen, 28 Oct'72
    Conceptuality & Reality, 22 Apr'71*
    Dream, 1968
    God, May'68
    Invisible Colors, 4 Mar'69
    Imaginary Universe vs. This Universe, 22 Feb'72
    Magic, 18 Nov'72
    Mother:  Infant Nursing at Mother's Breasts, 18 Nov'72
    Nature, Jun'66
    One, 20 Dec'73
    Now, 14 Feb'72*
    Positive & Negative, 11 Jul'62
    Principle, 22 Feb'72*
    Quantum Mechanics, Jun'66
    Responsibility, 14 Oct'69
    Science, 1947*
    Sphericity of Whole Systems, 26 Sep'73*

RBF DEFINITIONS

Realization:

"...All physical realizations are always disequilibrious."

- Citation and context at Basic Triangle:  Basic Disequilibrium
    120 LCD Triangle, 20 Dec'73

RBF DEFINITIONS

Realization:

"A vector is a partial generalization being either
metaphysically theoretical or physically realized, and
in either sense, an abstraction of a special case. . . "

- Citation and context at Vector, 26 May'72

---

RBF DEFINITIONS

Realization:

"The new reliable understanding of meaning. . .
requires the revision not only of semantics but also of
their complex aspect as thought habits employed to
describe experience with accuracy, such as . . .
the substitution of the word 'realization' for the very
inaccurate use of the verb 'to create.' Man creates
naught. If he comprehends in principle, he rearranges
locally in Universe by realization of the interactions
of principles."

- Cite TOTAL THINKING, I&I, P.234, May'49

- Citation & context at Meaning, May'49

---

RBF DEFINITIONS

Realization:

"Realizations are always imperfect."

- Citation and context at Physical Is Always the Imperfect, 14 Feb
                                                                '72
- Cite RBF marginalia at Eccles, 'Facing Reality,' p. 1.,
   14 Feb. '72

---

RBF DEFINITIONS

Realization Lag:

"Where all the local vectors are approximately equal
we have a potentially local isotropic vector equilibrium,
but the operative vector complex has the inherent qualities
of both proximity and remoteness in respect to any
locally initiated action, ergo, a complex of relative
velocities of realization lags."

- Citation at Proximity, Oct'59

( Cite SYNERGETICS, Corollaries, Sec. 240. 1971 )

---

RBF DEFINITIONS

Realization:

"Potential lines are metaphysically straight,
all physically realized relationships are
geodesic and curved trajectories."

- Cite SYNERGETICS Corollaries, Sec. 240. 1970
- Citation at Metaphysical & Physical, 1971

---

Realization Lags:

See Abstraction, 24 Feb'72
    Local Vector Equilibrium, 2 Nov'73
    Metaphysical, 14 Feb'72
    Proximity, Oct'59*
    Time, 23 May'72

---

RBF DEFINITIONS

Realization:

"Realization is objective integrity."

- Cite I&I, PRIME DESIGN, p. 245. May'60

---

Realization: Realizable:                                        (1)

See After-image
    Conceptual Genesis
    Creativity
    Cyclic Realization
    Discovery
    Potential vs. Realized
    Pulsivity of Realizations
    Regenerative Design: Law Of
    Quantum Values
    Self-realization
    Time-somethingness
    Systematic Realization
    Operational Realizations
    Comprehensive Realizer
    Operational = Physically Realized
    Temporary Realizations

Realization: Realizable: (2A)

See Basic Triangle: Basic Disequilibrium 120 LCD
      Triangle, 20 Dec'73*
    Conceptuality & Reality, Jun'66
    Experience, 1960
    Four, 26 Jan'73
    Frame of Reference, 4 Oct'72
    Interference, May'49
    Isotropic Vector Matrix, 6 Mar'73
    Isotropic-vector-matrix Field, 20 Dec'73
    Meaning, May'49*
    Metaphysical & Physical, 1971*
    Physical Is Always the Imperfect, 14 Feb'72*
    Principle, May'49*; 7 Oct'75
    Space Nothingness & Time Somethingness, 28 Dec'73
    Timeless, 1 Apr'72
    Time-sizing, 30 Nov'72
    Vector, 26 May'72*
    Wavilinear, 28 Oct'73
    Radial Depth, 20 Feb'74

---

Realms vs. Surface:

    See Black Holes & Synergetics, 1 Mar'77

---

Realization: Realizable: (2B)

    See Special Case, 27 Dec'74
    Scenario vs. Absolute Symmetry, 11 Dec'75
    Children as Only Pure Scientists, 28 Apr'77

---

ETYMOLOGICAL DICTIONARY (WEEKLEY)

Realm:

OF reame, reeme, L. regimen, later becoming realm, reiaume
(royaume under influence of real, royal. Mod. form, later
influencing pronunc., is due to influence of ME real, royal,
usual early forms being reame, reme.

---

RBF DEFINITIONS

Realm: Real: Royal:

"All of us really carry on much on a really safe basis,
going back again to people with swords and farming the land.
We go back to somebody with weapons more powerful than
other people saying, 'I claim this and don't anybody say No.'
If nobody said 'No' then you called your officers to write
the deeds... We have our deedings going back to whoever is
the sovereign of that land. The word real in Spanish is
the word royal or our word real-- coming from is it valid
to the king... Our real estate going back to royalty's
estate. Valid to the king-- comes back to the deeds of the
king. Then we have man monopolizing the physical. Fanatas-
tic laws we have protecting the land and almost no laws
protecting man's ideas, the metaphysical. We protect the
physical. It is the underlying financing of the building
in terms of the land. This land exploitation is very
dominant in the building world, making the equities of land
more and more, not thinking at all about the fundamentals
of how do you really serve man."

                    (Edited and slightly
                        rearranged.)

- Cite Transcript Univ. of Alaska Address, p.2, 20 Apr '72

---

ETMOLOGICAL DICTIONARY (WEEKLEY)

Real:

Adj. F. réel, Late L., realis, from res, thing.
As trade description perh. influenced by ME real, rial (royal),
stock epithet for superior merchandise.

---

RBF DEFINITIONS

Realm: Real: Royal:

"The great pirates came into the various lands and picked
the strongest man in each to be their local head man. He
became their general manager of the local realm (realm =
real-m). Real (pronounced re-al) means royal in Spanish.
Roi means king (French). Roy means grand ruler (India).
All are derived from Ra or Re: Thu sun gods of India,
China, Mesopotamia, and Egypt. From this comes 'the real
thing,' realization, and reality, i.e., the commonly recognized experience-- ergo, real estate which was certified
under royal deeds issued by the original sovereign claimant
of the land. There is an official reality which is
sometimes unnatural."

- Cite ENVIRONMENT AND CHANGE, Ed. W.R. Ewald, P. 350.
    Above passage omitted from OPERATING MANUAL FOR SPACE*
    SHIP EARTH text at P. 28. 1968

---

Realm: Real: Royal:

    See Religion: Related to 'Reglio ' or Rule

Real Models of Reality: (1)

See Grand Central Station of Universe
    Local Vector Equilibrium
    Railroad Tracks:  Great Circle Energy Tracks on
    The Surface of a Sphere

RBF DEFINITIONS

Real World:

"The real world is a special case."

- RBF confirmed his authorship of above bumber sticker by
  leaping out of EJA car on 34th Street in Georgetworn en
  route to a State Dept. Meeting.  RBF chatted with woman driver
  of DC license # 160-585; she also attributed statement to
  RBF; 12 May'75

---

Real Models of Reality: (2)

See Graphable, 27 May'72

RBF DEFINITIONS

Rearrange Elemental Order:

"Energy is the capability or the capacity to rearrange
elemental order."

- Citation & context at Energy, 1967

---

Real Universe: (1)

See Real World

RBF DEFINITIONS

Rearranging the Environment:

"I'm experienced in going from original conceptions, i.e.
inventions-- ergo, unknown to others-- to altering the
environment in a complex of ways which are omni-considerate
of all side effects on the altered environment.  I am
accustomed to starting from primitive conditions, where as
far as one can see no other man has explored.  I have
learned how to rearrange the environment in such a way that
it does various things for our society that we could not
do before, such as building a dam which in turn produces a
pond..."

- Cite RBF Introduction to Victor Papanek's "Design for the
  Real World," 9 Apr'71

---

Real Universe: (2)

See Graphable, 27 May'72
    Probability, (1)

Rearrange the Environment:

See Success, May'72
    Wealth, 8 Dec'75

Rearranging the Furniture:

See Furniture

---

Rearrange Random Receipts in Molecular Chains:

See Antientropy, (A)(B)
Earth, Jun'66

---

RBF DEFINITIONS

Rearrange the Landscape:

"It is only the metaphysical that can rearrange the physical
landscape to human advantage..."

- Cite Nehru Speech, pp.46-47, 13 Nov'69

---

RBF DEFINITIONS

Rearrange the Scenery:

"To date, we have gained vast inventories
Of trial-and-error experience
From all of which information we have developed
A family of generalized scientific principles
Which are weightless pattern concepts.
Being weightless they are metaphysical.
From the metaphysics
We have in turn designed
Rearrangements of the physical behavior constituents
Of our omnikinetic environment scenery.
We have rearranged the scenery
In the pattern of world-around occurring power-driven tool networks
All of which teleologic process
Has produced an ever-increasing survival advantage for humanity."

- Cite BRAIN & MIND, p.92 May '72

---

Rearrange Locally:                                        (1)

See Comprehension = Rearrange Locally

---

RBF DEFINITIONS

Rearrange the Scenery:                                    (1)

"I'd like to answer one more sort of challenge we had a
little earlier, and that is that I've learned not only this
grand strategy of not trying to reform the individual; to
assume that the individual can concentrate entirely on rearranging the scenery in permitted ways to make it more
favorable for life-- to demonstrate its capabilities.  I have
also learned that where you see things that need to be done--
you can see the scenery can be rearranged.  Your experience
tells you that scenery can be rearranged to a higher advantage
for man. . . And there's nobody to tell you to do it. . . You
will try to do something about it, to rearrange it, and then
he says, 'What have you done?' And then you explain what you've
done and how it works, and then he says 'Well, that's very
interesting,' but then goes right on about his regular
business.  Then I find that there's always an emergency, when
you have to have something waiting there.  So my whole
strategy is-- and I've been able to live now on the frontier
without anybody guaranteeing me anything, or telling me what
to do-- taking the economic initiative and trying to find out
what nature needs to be done."

- Cite RBF to World Game at NY Studio School 12 Jun-31 Jul'69,
  Saturn Film transcript, Sound 2, Part 3, pp. 68-69.

---

Rearrange Locally:                                        (2)

See Hammering Sheet Metal, (1)
Realization, May'49

---

RBF DEFINITIONS

Rearrange the Scenery:                                    (2)

"When you can't go any further with one thing, then you look
over to another one that needs attending to, and you keep
shifting from one to the other.  So, at any rate, I've learned
how to survive there.  One of the things I do is never try to
persuade anybody.  I don't try to sell anything.  You see what
needs to be done and you do it.  And you wait until a man
says 'What is that?' and then you tell him what it is.  For
instance, I've learned that there's no use going around with
pulmotors door-to-door like a Fuller Brush man and say 'I'd
like to sell pulmotors.'  But all of a sudden there's some
suffocation and you have to have a pulmotor in a hurry, and
then it's lucky you did it.  So I find that society has its
emergencies. . . So you have what I call emergence by emergency.
And that's what is really going on at this table with the
individuals really beginning to find out how you do do it.
That's the thing, not talking about it theoretically, but just
really looking at what can be done-- and more than just
getting the figures.  This then leads to design: What are the
things that need designing?"

- Cite RBF to World Game at NY Studio School, 12 Jun-31 Jul'69,
  Saturn film transcript, Sound 2, Part 3, pp. 69-71

Rearrange the Scenery:                                    (1)

    See Environment: Altering the Environment
        Furniture entries
        Individual Economic Initiative
        Reform of Environment Rather than Reform of Man

---

RBF DEFINITIONS

    Reason:

    "Reason ≠ Cause. (See Introduction to "Nine Chains to

    the Moon".)*

    "Rational = Relational."

            ⌜*N.B. - Passage from Introduction to NINE CHAINS

            TO THE MOON cited in this file as Rationalization

            Sequence (1)-(6). ⌟

    - Cite RBF marginalia at Foundations of Physics, Vol. 1, No.4,
      1971, pp.362-363. D. Bohm: "Quantum Theory as an Indication
      of a New Order in Physics."

---

Rearrange the Scenery: Rearrange the Landscape:          (2)

    See Biosphere Inventory, 15 Nov'74
        Copper, (1); (A)
        Leonardo Type, 13 Nov'69
        Man as a Function of Universe, Jun'69
        Comprehensive Realizer, May'49

---

Reason ≠ Cause:

    See Reason, Aug'73

---

Rearrange: Rearrangements:                                (2)

    See Hammering Sheet Metal, (1)
        Invention, 27 Dec'73
        Pattern, 3 Oct'72
        Windows of Nothingness, (2)

---

Reason: Reasonable: Reasoning:

    See Faculty: Conceptual & Reasoning Faculties
        Knowing vs. Reasoning

---

Rearrange:                                                (3)

    See Rearrange Elemental Order
        Rearrange the Environment
        Rearranging the Environmental Furniture
        Rearrange the Furniture
        Rearrange the Landscape
        Rearrange Locally
        Rearrange Random Receipts
        Rearrange the Scenery

---

Rebirth:                                                  (1)

    See Centers of Energy Rebirth
        Eternal Rebirth System

Rebirth:                                    (2)

    See Eternal Slowdown, (2)
        Isotropic Vector Matrix, 16 Nov'72
        Time-size, 20 Dec'73

Recall Playbacks:

    See Brain's TV Studio, (2)

Rebonding:

    See Unbonding-rebonding

RBF DEFINITIONS

Recall Set:

"Brains differentially correlate the succession of special
case informations communicated to the brain by the plurality
of senses.  The brain distinguishes the new, first-time-event,
special case experiences only by their comparison with the
set of all its recalled prior cognitions."

    - Cite SYNERGETICS 2 draft at Sec. 100.015; 28 Apr'77

RBF DEFINITIONS

    Recall Lags:

"The whole of Universe is a consequence of our not seeing

instantly.  As a result of the recall lags the physical is

always imperfect."

    - Cite RBF to EJA, 3200 Idaho, Wash DC, 26 May'72
        (Citation and context at Equanimity Model, 26 May'72)

Recall Set:

    See Set, 5 Jul'62

RBF DEFINITIONS

Recall Momentum:

"Again reviewing for recall momentum..."

    - Cite RBF marginalis on SYNERGETICS galley at Sec. 954.55,
        28 Dec'73

Recall:  Recall Lags:                          (1)

        See Afterimage
            Double Take
            Experience Recalls
            Physical Experience Recalls
            Memory Call-ups

Recall: Recall Lags:                                    (2)

   See Brain, 5 Jun'75
      Equanimity Model, 26 May'72*
      Frequency Islands of Perception, 13 Nov'75
      Happening Patterns, 6 Nov'73
      Life, 25 Mar'71
      Metaphysical & Physical Tetrahedral Quanta,
        25 Mar'71
      Pattern, Jun'66
      Thinking, (A)(B); 22 Oct'72; 7 Nov'73
      Thought, 31 May'71
      Unitary Conceptuality, 22 Oct'72

---

RBF DEFINITIONS

Reciprocal:

"It is very interesting to consider . . . a total
inventory of the relative abundance of different
patterns remembering that the patterns are reciprocal."

- Cite OREGON Lecture #5 - p. 167, 9 Jul'62

- Citation at Pattern, 9 Jul'62

---

Recall: Recall Lags:                                    (3)

   See Recall Lags
      Recall Momentum
      Recall Playbacks
      Recall Set

---

RBF DEFINITIONS

Reciprocal:

"Since universe is the minimum perpetual motion machine,
there is a minimum set of patterns that is a consequence
of this set of patterns reacting with that set of
patterns."

- Cite OREGON University Lecture #5 - p. 167, 9 Jul'62

- Citation and context at Minimum Set, 9 Jul'62

---

RBF DEFINITIONS

Recede:

"The external crossing points of the system continually
recede."

- Cite RBF 16 Feb citation Surface as re-written 17 Feb '72 (Q.V.)

---

Reciprocal Involvement:                                (1)

   See Paired Congruency
      Sleeping in the Same Bed

---

Recentering:

   See Structure, 3 Oct'72

---

Reciprocal Involvement of Experiences & Principles:

   See Simplicity, 1954

Reciprocals of Permissible Viewpoints:

See Pattern, 1954-59

Reciprocating Torus Model:

See Rubber Tires, 24 Jan'75

Reciprocal Self-precessors:

See Omnidirectional, 1954
Zoneness: System Zoneness, 8 Jan'55

RBF DEFINITIONS

Reciprocity:                                          (1)

"But as we come to explore for the fundamental principles
of interpotentials and interactions called atoms, we find
that , despite the astronomical number of aspects and events,
only a few principles of behavior pervade the whole of
Universe as, for instance, 92 tendencies to self-impoundment
of energy; a fundamental inwardness and outwardness relative
only to the 'system' center of observation; the corollary
principles of inherent first tendencies to inward-outward
pulsations and to precession, and the principles of inside-
outing-- convergence-divergence, spin and counterspin,
torque and countertorque tension and pressure, the biological
reciprocals of Universe (and diaphragming).

"Relativity leads us toward fundamental classification of
our experience and observation, in the terms of a few
hierarchies of dynamic interactions and principle transformations of an all-energy, continuous-discontinuous, synchronous-
dissynchronous Universe tensionally cohered, precessional
of local compressive spherical energetic collections-- as
(Suns) stars or planets or moons or asteroids or meteorites;
and the progression of within-ward sub-sets of events of
interactions at planet crust, ▪▪▪ etc., and inward to "

- Cite TOTAL THINKING, I&I, pp.235-236, May'49

Reciprocating Engine:

See Cosmic Accounting Sequence, (4)

RBF DEFINITIONS

Reciprocity:                                          (2)

"the 92 common principles of atomic convergence of energy in
principle, and the pervasive sets of dynamic associations
by contraction, expansion, spin, orbit, torque, push, and
pull, and precession. This all brings us by progressive
collections of thoughts into a fundamental twoness of
dynamic reciprocities which, internally paired, ultimately
become one with outwardly paired principles of reciprocity.

"The becoming one of both the finity inward with the finity
outward indicates a sensibility of experience preoccupying
man as a superficial reality which only occurs at middling
dimensions of Universe and appears schematically as a
magnetic field. Its flux patterns, like two tangent balls,
include every size of particle, as their hour-glass-like
tangentially ▪▪▪▪▪▪ linked inwardness, displays both
inwardly and outwardly mingled sets of fountain and reverse
fountain flows-- concurrently at both ends-- and through the
middle. Periodically, the whole double-bulbed dynamic flux
contracts axially, as the two bulbs of dynamic flow merge
progressively, and then merge completely, and again separate
axially. It is obvious that inasmuch as the whole system
was always in flow, that the new bulbs of flux are of necessity"

- Cite TOTAL THINKING, I&I, p.236, May'49

Reciprocating Sub-sets:

See Relativity, May'49

RBF DEFINITIONS'

Reciprocity:                                          (3)

"new and are therefore only identifiable in principle with
the previous comprehensive duality of shapes. The system
has inherent yet empty twoness.

"The reality is real-- or realized-- in principle only, by
events of relative interaction transpiring only in principle.
The whole of the above pulsive-waveful-dynamic-duality is
schematic, and is in principle clarifing only, for, though
it progressively groups all-energy Universe into an oscillating
binary system, it must be understood that ▪▪▪▪▪▪ the
whole scheme cancels out by virtue of a super paradox which
finds that the infinity inward and the infinity outward of
an infinite plurality of centers must be identical, and one
with the infinity inward, of an infinite plurality of centers,
and that: in comprehensive Universe, dimension drops out
and conceptual principle remains. Physical interferences
of our sensibilities are alike true and real, or realizable,
only in principle. Positive and negative cancel as the
principle zero.

"It is discovered in principle that probability probing of
physical Universe on a statistical basis is now becoming of"

- Cite TOTAL THINKING, I&I, PP.236-237, May'49

RBF DEFINITIONS

Reciprocity:                                                    (4)

"necessity frustrated while, probing in empty conceptual
principle could be instituted and accelerated for further
advancement or fundamental information.  Exploration in
principle is re-rewarding.

"It is necessary that the comprehensive designer explore in
principle for verification of this significance of relativity,
whereby it is discovered that in the consciously realizable
comprehensive binary, truth may not be dealt with as isolated,
but only as relative relationships of interaction governing
in principles the interactions of specially nonsimultaneous
sets of dynamic principles.  The comprehensive realizer thus
will come, with acceleration, to competence in rearranging
forwardly anticipated events, measured in principle, and
forwardly projected, in associated principles of reciprocal
interaction and juxtaposition to the anticipated energetic
magnitudes of variable stresses and flows.  These interactions
are known as structures and mechanics.

"Thus it is discerned how the comprehensive realizer of
relativity may become competent as an integrator of the
until-then- threatening chaotic dissipation of common"

- Cite TOTAL THINKING, I&I, p. 237, May'49

---

Reciprocal:  Reciprocate:  Reciprocity:                        (3)

            See Reciprocal Involvement of Experiences & Principles
                Reciprocals of Permissible Viewpoints
                Reciprocal Self-precessors
                Reciprocating Engine
                Reciprocating Subsets
                Reciprocity

---

RBF DEFINITIONS

Reciprocity:                                                    (5)

"advantage of men in Universe brought about by runaway,
diametric preoccupations of specializations.  The comprehensive realizer becomes a synergist."

- Cite TOTAL THINKING, I&I, p.236, May'49

---

Recirculation:

            See Ecological Balance
                Metals:  Recirculation Of
                Roundtrip
                Scrap Sorting & Mongering
                Recycling

---

Reciprocate:  Reciprocity:  Reciprocal:                        (1)

            See Axes of Corotation
                Design Reciprocity
                Energetic Functions
                Gear Train:  Locking & Blocking
                Motion Reciprocity
                Reality as Structural Interaction of Principles
                Structural Functions
                Twoness of Dynamic Reciprocities
                Complementary & Reciprocal
                Alternate:  Alternative
                Mutual:  Mutuality
                Bicycle Wheel Model

---

RBF DEFINITIONS

Recognition:

"Everything that you have ever recognized in Universe as a
pattern is re-cognited as the same pattern you have seen
before.  Because only the triangle persists as a constant
pattern, any recognized patterns are inherently recognizable
only by virtue of their triangularly structured pattern
integrities.  Recognition is as dependent on triangulation as
is original cognition...."

- Citation & context at Omnitriangulation; 3 Oct'72

---

Reciprocal:  Reciprocate:  Reciprocity:                        (2)

            See Automation, 4 Mar'69
                Intellect, 16 Aug'50
                Minimum Set, 9 Jul'62*
                Pattern, 1954; 9 Jul'62*
                Prime Dichotomy (2)
                Simplicity, 1954
                Spaceship, 26 Sep'68
                Technology, 12 May'39
                Tidal, Dec'61
                Hierarchy of Patterns, 1954
                Zoneness:  System Zoneness, 8 Jan'55
                Simplicity, 1954
                Ninety-two Eelements, 15 Jun'74
                Jitterbug, 1 Dec'65
                Synergetics Constant, 10 Dec'75
                Fourth Dimension:  VE as Fourth-dimension Model,
                  22 Jun'77

---

RBF DEFINITIONS

Recognition:

"We have an expression, something we say very often, 'I

recognize that.'  Recognition means that you have seen

that pattern before.  You have probably seen its several

time before you say, 'I recognize it.'  Recognizability

of pattern would depend upon the stability of the pattern;

it would have to have some fundamental shape.  Only a

triangle has any reliability of pattern.  So I say ▬▬▬▬

everything and anything that you and I ever say 'I

recognize,' must go back to a triangle.  Only triangle is

structure."

- Cite RBF Address at National Conference for Philosophy
  of Creativity at SIU, Carbondale, Ill., 16 Oct. '69. - p. 64.

RBF DEFINITIONS

Recognition:

"Everything that you have ever recognized in the
Universe as a pattern is re-cognited as the same pattern
you have seen before. Because only the triangle persists
as a constant pattern any recognized patterns must be
recognizable only by virtue of being a triangle or a
complex of triangles. This is the only possible basis
of recognition."

- Cite NASA Speech, p. 54. Jun'66

---

Recognition: Recognizable: (2)

See Experience, 1971
Mass, 29 Dec'58
Thinkable You (1)
Triangle, 25 Feb'69
Understanding, 1960
Minimum Awareness, (1)
Identity, 2 Jul'75
Local System, Jun'66
Omnitriangulation, 3 Oct'72

---

Recognition Lags:

See Mind, 24 Feb'72
Tunability, 24 Apr'76

---

Recollect: Recollections:

See Design Covariables: Principle Of, 1959
Words, 2 Jul'62
Conceptual Systems, 27 May'75

---

RBF DEFINITIONS

Recognizability:

"Everything you say you recognize, means that you
recognize a pattern. The recognizability of the
pattern must go back to some triangles."

- Cite RBF at SIMS Seminar, U. Mass., Amherst, 22 July '71,
Transcript p. 18

---

Reconsider: Reconsideration:

See Metaphysical & Physical Tetrahedral Quanta,
25 Mar'71
Thought, 31 May'71
Conscious & Subconscious, 1960
In, Out & Around, Nov'71
Nonsimultaneity, 7 Nov'73

---

Recognition: Recognizable: (1)

See Pattern Cognition: Pattern Cognizance
Unrecognized
Cognition vs. Recognition

---

Record: Off the Record:

See Fuller, R.B: His Modus Operandi, 15 Jun'74

# Synergetics Dictionary

Recourse:

See Survival Recourse

Rectilinear:   Rectilinear Grid Systems:                                      (2)

See Air Space, May'65
     Frame of Reference, 27 Feb'72
     General Systems Theory, 8 Nov'73
     Nucleus, (1)
     Spherical Triangle:  Equator as Square, (3)
     Twelve Universal Degrees of Freedom:  General
         Systems, (III)

Rectification:

See Social Adjustment, Feb'72

RBF DEFINITIONS

Recyclings:

"... The integrity of Scenario Universe's

Never exactly identical recyclings."

- Citation and context at Metaphysical, p.152 May '72

RBF DEFINITIONS

Rectilinear Frame:

"A vectorial evolvement in no way conforms to a rigid
rectilinear frame of the XYZ coordinate analysis which
arbitrarily shuns most economical directness and time
realizations-- by virtue of which calculus is able only
awkwardly to define positions rectilinearly, moving only
as the chessman's knight.  Nature uses rectilinear patterns
only precessionally; and precession brings about orbits
and not straight lines."

- Cite SYNERGETICS draft at Sec. 540.09, 24 Sep'73

Recycling:                                                                 (1)

See Junkyard
     Metabolic Flow
     Recirculation
     Spiral

Rectilinear Grid Systems:  Rectilinear:                          (1)

See Grid:  Crisscross, Right-angle Grid in Civil &
         Agrarian Law
     Local Squareness
     Ninety Degreeness
     Two-way Rectilinear Grid
     XYZ Coordinate System
     Right Angle
     Square
     Two-way Crisscross

Recycling:                                                                 (2)

See Time, circa 1970

Redemonstrable:

See Children as Only Pure Scientists, 28 Ape'77

Redesign Cycle:

See Energy & Intellect, May'49
Improvement, May'49
Periodic Experience, (6)

RBF DEFINITIONS

Reductio ad Absurdum:

"The deliberately nonstraight line of synergetics employs the mathematicians' own invention for dealing with great dilemmas: the strategy of reductio ad absurdum. Having moments of great frustration, the mathematician learned to forsake looking for local logic; he learned to go in the opposite direction and deliberately to choose the most absurd. And then, by progressively eliminating the degrees of absurdity, he could work back to the not too absurd. In hunting terms, we call this quarrying his objective. Thus he is able at least to learn where his quarry is within a small area."

- Cite SYNERGETICS text at Sec. 522.03; Nov'71

RBF DEFINITIONS

Reductio ad Absurdum:

"Having demonstrated to the mathematician that his imaginary straight line gets worse and worse-- every time he gives me an example, I am going to employ the mathematician's own strategy of dealing with the great dilemmas as invented by Boole-- the reductio ad absurdum. Where I now a Deliberately Non-Straight Line / q.v. /.

"The mathematician having moments of great frustrations learned to forsake looking for local logic by going in the opposite direction and choosing the most absurd, and then progressively eliminating the degrees of absurdity and working back to the not too absurd. And he is liable to be able at least to learn the quarry, where his quarry is a small area. What we call quarrying is objective. These are hunting terms."

- Cite Tape transcript RBF to EJA and BO'R, Chicago, 1 June 1971.

RBF DEFINITIONS

Reductio ad Absurdum:

"When scientists and mathematicians fail to find positive clues leading towards solution of their problems, they sometimes reverse their frontal strategies and employ reductio ad absurdum, which by a process of eliminating all the impossibles and improbables, leaves a residue of least absurd, ergo most plausible solutions, which may be reduced, by physically testing to unequivocable answers."

- Cite RBF foreword to Samuel Rosenberg's "The Come As You Are Masquerade Party," 1970

Reductio ad Absurdum:                                                (1)

See Boole
    Absurd
    Boolean Algebra
    Twenty Questions

Reduction By Bits:

See Bits: Bitting

RBF DEFINITIONS

Reduction of Myriadness to Unity:                                    (1)

See Fractionating the Whole

Reduction of Myriadness to Unity: (2)

See Metaphysical & Physica;, Jun'66

---

Reduction to Practice: (1)

See Development
 Science-Technology-Industry-Economics-Politics
  Sequence
 Prototype
 Artifact

---

RBF DEFINITIONS

Reduction to Practice:

"There is no use talking about bright ideas. Everyone has bright ideas. But there is no use talking about the artifact until we reduce it to practice, until we see whether nature permits it, whether society permits it-- including worldwide distribution."

- Cite RBF at Penn Bell videotaping, Philadelphia, 29 Jan'75

---

Reduction to Practice: (2)

See Dome: Rationale for the Big Dome (A)
 Generalized Principle, 5 Jul'62
 Intuition of the Child (3)
 Inventability Sequence (2)
 Invention Sequence (B)(C)
 Omnidirectional: Physical Existence Environment
  Surrounds (2)
 Philosophy, 21 May'28; 1946
 Surfing: Surfboarding, 5 Jul'62
 ▮▮▮▮▮▮▮▮▮▮
 Trim Tab, 22 Jul'71*
 Design Science (A)
 Navy Sequence (2)
 Artifacts, 17 Sep'74
 Icosahedron: Subtriangulation, (2)

---

RBF DEFINITIONS

Reduction to Practice:

"Back in 1932 then, thinking that I would commit myself to only alterations of the environment-- not to 'multidisciplines' and so forth. I must never then 'talk about' anything. Whatever ideas I have I must find out how to translate them into some effect on the environment, in principle, and I must not talk about them until I have reduced them into practice and have discovered advantage for man. And I've really been able to prove to myself-- I find that bright ideas are so profuse-- but they don't get reduced to practice, you don't really know what the interactions are with the times and other environmental events. . . . So I would never talk about it until I have reduced it to practice: something physical. And somebody would say: What is that? And then I'd have the responsibility of telling them what it was. But I mustn't even ask them to look at it. I've really held very tightly to these disciplines, because I was interested in what the individual could do on behalf of his fellow man. . . even in a very few years."

- Cite RBF lecture at Wistar Inst, U. of Penn. EJA transcript pp 8-9, 19 Feb'73

---

Redundant Excess:

See Norm: Tetrahedron as Norm, 15 May'72

---

RBF DEFINITIONS

Reduction to Practice:

"A trim tab is a physical environmental control device in a Universe where change, motion, and evolution are inexorable.... You must not just have a theoretical idea but reduce it to practice. That is my strategy."

- Citation at Trim Tab, 22 Jul'71

---

RBF DEFINITIONS

Redundancy:

"Edges and vertexes do not come together as the same number system. You can describe the world both ways and not be redundant. The world as seen by a child and the world as seen by an old man could not be redundant descriptions."

- Cite RBF to EJA, 25 August 1971, Bear Island.

- Citation at Description, 25 Aug'71

RBF DEFINITIONS

Redundancy:

"... Redundancy being a temporal consequence of brain lagged dullness of comprehension and ignorance."

- Citation and context at Differentiation, 27 May'72

RBF DEFINITIONS

Redundancy:

"Redundancy cannot be determined by energetic observation of behaviors of single struts, (beams or columns) or any chain-linkage of same which are less than six in number, or less than tetrahedron."

- Citation & context at Strut, 1950's
  - Cite RBF undated holograph on M.I.T. memo pad. (1950's)

RBF DEFINITIONS

Redundancy: Reduction Of:

"In the Greek temple each column carries its share of the stone on top of it. Figuring the ultimate compressive weight of the stone as 50,000 psi-- which equals 25 tons-- the result is that each column can carry 1000 tons when it only has to carry 25 tons. The rest of the column is unnecesary except for stability. We can make it a cone or a tripod, like a camera tripod.

"We find the only thing holding up the Greek column was a tetrahedron.... The thorns and buds of trees are tetrahedra: concentric cones-- the wing roots of the limbs. Goethe spoke of trees as waves.

"Only the tetrahedron can become visible and invisible. This is life: life is male & female, visible and invisible, but immortal.

"Hydraulics, mechanics, and the wave connection cofunction as the bio-connection: bio-logic. (A nice name.)"

- Cite composite of RBF holographs drawn for EJA at Somerset Club, Boston, 22 Apr'71

Redundancy: Redundant:  (1)

See Necklace
    Nonredundance
    Safety Factor

Redundancy: Redundant:  (2)

See Antipathy, 15 May'72
    Cube, (1)
    Description, 25 Aug'71*
    Differentiation, 27 May'72*
    Knot: Square Knot, 20 Oct'72
    Strut, 1950's*
    Tensegrity: Unlimited Frequency of Geodesic
       Tensegrities, (9)
    Triangular Topology Integrity, 15 May'72
    Minimum System: Minimum Structural System, Nov'71

Reef:

See Coral Reef

Reel:

See Fish: Playing the Fish on a Reel

Reel of Tape Recorder:  (1)

See Hole in the Victrola Disc

Reel of Tape Recorder:                    (2)

See Axis of Spin, (1)(2)


Reference:                                (2)

See Size, 22 Jun'72


Re-exterior:                              (1)

See Obverse


Referendum:

See Electronic Referendum


Re-exterior:                              (2)

See Brouwer's Theorem, 1 Jan'75


Refinement:  Refining:

See Relativity, May'49
    Truth, 10 Nov'72


Reference:                                (1)

See Axis of Reference
    Cyclic Reference
    Frame of Reference
    Scheme of Reference
    Sphere of Reference


RBF DEFINITIONS

Reflection:

". . . It is possible

To conserve energies by reflection

As well as to reach

Great distance by beaming. . ."

- Citation & context at Eye-beamed Thoughts (I), May'72

- Cite BRAIN & MIND, p.163 May '72

RBF DEFINITIONS

Reflection Sequence: __Apple__:                              (1)

"__I see an apple__.

"The light of the Sun is reflected from the surface of an apple, after the occurrence of the spectroscopic action of light segregation through the medium of crystals on the surface of the apple.

"Not all of the energy ray tones are reflected, however. Those that are useful to the apple are absorbed by it, while the remainder, i.e., the non-useful, or nondigestible, or, more specifically, non-chemically combinable ray tones are reflected from the surface of the apple through the air to and through the lens of the human eye, where they are analyzed by the retina and telephotographed to the brain of the beholder.

"Incidentally the light that the apple gives off is a negative, that is, the opposite of the light complementary to the growth phenomenon 'apple.' It is not one of the chemical apple's actual constituents. This is something like the phenomenon of the camera film negative except that the latter is more honest than the eye's for the eye reverses light and shadow instead of properly appraising them as does the camera. In printing,"

- Cite NINE CHAINS TO THE MOON, pp.42-43, 1938

---

RBF DEFINITIONS

Reflection Sequence: __Apple__:                              (2)

"the black and white of the film have to be reversed in order to represent the illusion of the apple as the eye sees it. Many apples are probably blue, having taken blue from the spectrum, but the eye, taking up the rejected red, 'sees' the apple as red.

"Whether or not the eye sees a negative or a positive of the apple, light absorption and reflection are mechanical considerations because neither life nor mind activity is involved until the essence of the __picture__ has been articulated in the 'brain' and has been automatically referred to the memory filing department (the system of which is even more complicated than the worldwide Bertillon system of finger-print identification) for comparison with all of the apple experiences of the 'see-er.' The new picture of 'apple' is laid out on the table for comparison with the whole reference file by the executive officer 'brain,' who never sees the phantom captain although under his permanent orders to lay out the file in the captain's outer study. Then 'brain' retires through the front door, closes it behind him, and the phantom captain enters from his inner sanctum to peruse the exhibit.

- Cite NINE CHAINS TO THE MOON, p.43, 1938

---

RBF DEFINITIONS

Reflection Sequence: __Apple__:                              (3)

"If interested at all-- generally he is not-- the captain considers the progression of apple phenomena, as indicated by the pictures in the file, and decides that the latest addition is a better or worse apple, i.e., it is an apple that would, or would not, be useful as fuel for his ship, in the cleansing process of his machinery, or as bait. Having decided 'yes' or 'no,' he leaves a message for 'brain' beside the exposed file and retires."

- Cite NINE CHAINS TO THE MOON, pp.43-44, 1938

---

__Reflecting Lake Waters__:

See Invisible Pneumatics, 27 Dec'73

---

__Reflection__:                                              (1)

See Beamable: Beaming
    Bounce Patterns of Energy
    Focal: Focus
    Interference
    Light on Scratched Metal
    Radar Reflector

---

__Reflection__:                                              (2)

See Broadcast, May'72
    Eye-beamed Thoughts, (I)*
    Interference, (2)
    Radiation, (pp.158-9) May'72
    Sight, 1 Apr'49
    Vertexial Spheres, 8 Apr'75
    Cloud Chamber, Nov'71
    Octahedron: Eight-octahedra, (3)(4)
    Visual, 22 Feb'77

---

RBF DEFINITIONS

__Reflexes__:

"In 1927 when I was starting to re-educate myself, trying to unlearn all the things that I'd been taught to be so, that I had proven not to be so, I tried to get my __reflexes__ disconnected from the false reactions or the unfavorable and the hard reactions and try to become sensitive again."

- Cite Museums Keynote Address Denver, p. 6. 2 Jun'71

---

RBF DEFINITIONS

__Reflexes__:

" . . . The designing capability . . .of human organisms . . . to offset the gamut of non-thinking conditioned reflexes of all biological systems."

- Cite Museums Keynote Address, p. 14. 2 Jun'71

RBF DEFINITIONS

Reflexes:

"Probably our most polluted resource is that of the
tactical information to which humanity spontaneously
reflexes."

- Citation at Information: Tactical Information, 13 Nov'69

- Cite NEHRU SPEECH, p. ■ .37, 13 Nov'69

---

RBF DEFINITIONS

Reform of Environment Rather than Reform of Man:

"I developed a fundamental philosophic concept in 1927
which was that it is posssible, instead of trying to reform
man, to reform the physical patterns-- to reform the
environment in such a way as to make the physical environment patterning more favorable to the new life being born
into it. It seemed possible that the new human generation,
born into the streamlined environment, might quickly react
by re-employing the newly designed advantages, and in so
doing might establish a new level of integrity of human
response to environmental stimuli whereby society might
come to act in creative spontaneity to continually convert
the highest knowledge born of the cumulative experience of
man toward the direct enhancement of the life processes,
instead of, as at present, leaving the prime social
initiative for the weaponry exploiters who derive their
mandate only from the negative fears born of ignorance,
and the congealing inertia of that ignorant fear."

- Cite MEXICO '63, p.18, 10 Oct '63

---

Reflex: Reflexes:                                               (1)

    See Automatics
        Bias on One Side of the Line
        Common Sense: Official News
        Conditioning
        Conditioned Reflexes
        Decondition My Subconscious Reflexing
        Feedback
        Ignorance
        Knowledge as Reflexes
        Mine: That's Mine
        Nonthinking
        Muscle & Reflex Jobs
        Planar Reflex
        Sensorial Reflex
        Structure vs. Reflexes
        Quickness
        Habit Reflexes
        Mind vs. Reflex
        Crowd-reflexing
        Proclivities: Basic vs. Secondary

---

Reform of Environment Rather than Reform of Man:         +1)

    See Blind Date with Principle
        Design Revolution
        Design Science
        Fuller, R.B: Crisis of 1927
        Fuller, R.B: His Decision that he Must not be a
            Persuader but a Doer
        Fuller, R.B: What I Am Trying To Do
        Individual Economic Initiative
        Inventions as Lifeways of Human Behaviors
        Leonardo Type
        Rearrange the Scenery

---

Reflex: Reflexes:                                              (2)

    See Antithinking, 2 Jun'71
        Awareness, Feb'50
        Computer, (B)
        Ecology Sequence, (H)(I)
        Environment Events Hierarchy, (2)
        Fighting, 7 Nov'67
        Gross World Product Sequence, (1)
        Information: Tactical Information, 13 Nov'69*
        Intuition, 22 Jun'72
        Fuller, R.B: Crisi of 1927,(2)
        Life Is Not Physical, 13 Jul'74
        Mind, 26 Nov'72
        Poverty, May'72
        Spaceship, (D)
        Space Technology, (2)
        Survival Sequence: Love, (1)
        Telepathy, 29 Jun'72
        War: Official & Unofficial, (1)
        Semantics, 20 Feb'73
        Death, 29 Mar'77

---

Reform of Environment Rather than Reform of Man:         (2)

    See Artifacts (1)(2); 17 Sep'74
        Bridge, 13 Nov'69
        Design Science, (1); 29 Jun'73; (A)
        Environment, May'65
        Trim Tab, 8 Jan'66
        Fuller, R.B: I am Apolitical, 15 May'75

---

RBF DEFINITIONS

Reform of Environment Rather than Reform of Man:

"My discipline is to reform the environment in ways favorable
to the success of all humanity with confidence that propitious
environmental circumstances induce spontaneously pro-social
behaviors."

- Citation and context at Design Science (1), 29 Jun'73

---

Reform: Reformers:

    See Trim Tab Sequence, (1)
        Political Revolution, 10 Oct'63
        Success, 10 Sep'75

---

Refraction: (1)

See Interference
Manifest: Two
Color Spectrum: Red, Orange, Yellow, Green,
Blue, Violet

---

Regeneration:

"The Universe is
The min-max, self-regenerative organism.
The regeneration is
A nonsimultaneous sequence
Of only partially overlapping
Physical transformation events--
Occurring in a vast range
Of ever-and-anon, synchronizing,
Pulsative frequencies
With associative concentrations
Here and there
Nonsimultaneously accommodating
Disassociative dispersals
In other heres and theres--
Like the 'high' and 'low' interalternations
Of the forever changing atmosphere's weather.'"

- Cite Dreyfus Preface, "Decease of Meaning."
28 April 1971, pp. 1 - 2.

- Citation & context at Universe, 28 Apr'71

---

Refraction: Refractive: (2)

See Boltzmann Sequence, (5)
Interference, (2)
Radiation Sequence, (2)
Sweepout: Spherical Sweepout, (1)
Van Allen Belt, May'72
Bendings, 23 Jun'75
Wind Stress & Houses, (9)(10)
Cloud Chamber, Nov'71
Halo Concept, Jun'71

---

Regeneration:

"Universe is the minimum as well as the maximum closed
system of omni-interacting, precessionally transforming,
complementary transactions of synergetic regeneration. . ."

- Citation & context at Universe, 1960
- Cite UNIDIRECTIONAL HALO, p. 135, 1960

---

Refrigeration:

See More With Less: Sea Technology, (3)(4)
Human Unsettlement, (2)

---

Regenerative:

The isotropic vector matrix "coordinate system is
ever regenerative in respect to the nuclear centers
all of which are rationally accounted for by synergetics."

- Citation and context at Omnisynergetic, 30 Jan'73

---

Regeneration:

"The significance of Einstein's electromagnetic radiation's
top speed unfettered in vacuo is that there is a cosmic limit
accommodation point of complete regeneration by which Universe
is the only and minimum perpetually self-regenerative system."

- Citation at Absolute Velocity, 30 Oct'73

---

Regenerative:

"Regenerative means local energy-pattern conservation."

- Cite SYNERGETICS text at Sec. 600.04, 3 Oct'72

RBF DEFINITIONS

Regenerative:

"Regenerative means local energy pattern conservation.

"Regenerative means local conservation of energy events interpatterning.

"Structures are pattern conservations."

- Cite RBF to EJA, Beverly Hotel, NYC, 15 Mar'71

STRUCTURE - 600.04 + 601.02

---

RBF DEFINITIONS

Regenerative:

"I use the term regenerative because in an all-motion universe (which Einstein posited and the physicists in due course found to be true), all the patterns of the universe are continually but non-simultaneously affecting all the other patterns of Universe in varying degrees and are continually reduplicating themselves in unique local configurations.

"These patterns may be described as constellar because their component events stand dynamically together like star groupings, and any event patterings which become locally regenerative are constellar patterns. It is a tendency for patterns either to repeat themselves locally or for their parts to separate-out to join severally or singly with other patterns or to form new constellations."

~~- Cite KEPES, p. 66, 1965~~
- Citation and context at Structure Sequence (1)(2), 1965

---

RBF DEFINITIONS

Regenerative:

"Universe... a closed system of complementary patterns that is regenerative, that is, adequate to itself...."

- Citation and context at Chess: Game of Universe, 9 Jul'62

---

RBF DEFINITIONS

Regenerative:

"Regenerative means multiorbital, cyclic, precessionally concentric.

"Regenerative means the ability to display one form, then another, in a gamut of phases; each phase, however, like a tree ring, or a wave generated by a stone thrown into water, has its own orbit; and the various orbits progress outward or inward in concentric circles or shells.

"A seed is regenerative. A crystal is regenerative. Energy itself is an ever-regenerative patterning entity. Its forms are protean. It can appear as the breath of a hawk or coign of a cliff. It can cloak itself as radiation, as mass, as design, and as the wellspring of work. And since by fundamental law, energy can neither be created nor destroyed, its fate in the cosmic scheme is to meander through eternity in persistent, regenerative bliss."

-Cite MARKS, P. 8, 1960

---

RBF DEFINITIONS

Regenerative:

"If the spheres* are close packed" to form a vector equilibrium, "and the center sphere is removed or compressed, the remaining spheres close in to form a 20-sided 'solid,' the icosahedron. From this it follows that a vector equilibrium can be translated into an icosahedron and vice versa. They are close relatives. Each has twelve vertexes and the same number of surface-defining spheres. And each is a model of symmetrical regularities. Each, in fact, has a place in a family of relationships which is capable of cycling through a sequence of phases, hence . . . regenerative."

- Cite MARKS, p. 41, 1960

---

Regenerative Birth:

See Duality of Universe, May'49

---

RBF DEFINITIONS

Regenerative Design: Law Of: (1)

"The prime eternal law governing design science as thus-far accrued to that of the cosmic law of generalized design science exploration, is realizability and relative magnitude of reproducibility which might be called the law of regenerative design: which is, that the relative physical time magnitude of reproducibility is proportional to the order of magnitude of generalizability. Because the higher the order of generalization the more embracing and simple its statement, only the highest orders can embracingly satisfy the plurality of low-order interaccommodation conditions.

"There are several corollaries to the prime law of regenerative design durability and amplitude of reproducibility. Corollary A is: The simpler, the more enduringly reproducible. Corollary B: The special-case realizations of a given design complex correlate as: the more symmetrical, the more reproducible. Corollary C: There being limit cases of optimum symmetry and simplicity, there are simplicities of conceptual realization. The most enduringly reproducible design entities of Universe are those occurring at the min-max limits of simplicity and symmetry."

- Cite RBF draft Ltr. to Karan Singh incorporated in SYNERGETICS at Secs. 166-7, 13 Mar'73

---

RBF DEFINITIONS

Regenerative Design: Law Of: (2)

"Corollary D: There being unique minimum-maximum system limits governing the transformation of conceptual entities in Universe which differentiate the conceptually unique entities of Universe into those exceptions occurring exclusively outside the system considered and all of the Universe inside of the conceptual entity, together with the structural pattern integrity system separating the inside from the outside, there being a minimum limited set of structural and operating principles eternally producing and reproducing recognizable pattern integrity. And there are likewise a minimum set of principles which interact to transform already orderly patterns into other structured patterns, and there being minimum constituent patterns which involved the complex intertransformings and structural formings of symmetrical orders and various magnitudes of asymmetrical deviations tolerated by the principles complexedly involved. There are scientifically discoverable nuclear aggregates of primary design integrity as well as complex symmetrical reassociabilities of the nuclear primary integrities and deliberately employable relationships of nuclear simplexes which designedly impose asymmetrical-symmetrical pulsative periodicities."

- Cite RBF draft Ltr. to Karan Singh incorporated in SYNERGETICS text at Sec. 168, 13 Mar'73

RBF DEFINITIONS

Regenerative Design: Law Of: (3)

"Corollary E: The more symmetrical and simple and nuclear, the more frequently employable; ergo more frequently occurring in eternally regenerative Universe transformative problem solutions.

"Corollary F: The smaller and simpler, more symmetrical, frequently-occurring in Universe and the larger and more complex, less-frequently originally occurring, and periodically re-occurring: for example, the hydrogen limit minimum simplex constituting not only nine-tenths of physical Universe but most frequently and most omnipresent in Universe; with asymmetrical terrestrial battleships (fortunately) least-frequently and compatibly recurrent throughout the as-yet known cosmos, being found only on one minor planet in one typical galaxy of one hundred billion stars amongst already-discovered billion galaxies, there having been only a few score of such manmade battleships recurrent in the split-second history of humans on infinitesimally minor Earth."

- Cite RBF draft Ltr. to Karan Singh incorporated in Synergetics text at Secs. 169, 170, 13 Mar'73

Regenerative Design: Law Of: (1)

See Reproducibleness: Law Of

Regenerative Design: Law Of: (2)

See Design, 1938

Regenerative Economic Sustenance:

See Money: Making Sense vs. Making Money, 22 Jun'77

RBF DEFINITIONS

Regenerative Intersupport: Equation Of:

"Precession + ecology = regenerative intersupport."

- Cite RBF to State Dept. Senior Seminar, Rosslyn, Va., 22 Dec'74

Regenerative Intersupport: Equation Of:

See Equation: Philosophical Equations

Regenerative Organics:

See Gonads, 22 Sep'71

Regenerative Precession:

See Spiralinearity, Nov'71

Regenerative Stimulations:

    See Discovery, 20 Dec'71

---

Regenerativity:    (2)

    See Concentricity, 1959
        Ecology, 16 Feb'73
        Petal: Tetrahedron as Three-petaled Flower Bud,
          11 Feb'73

---

Regenerative System Integrity:

    See Organic, 26 May'72

---

Regeneration: Regenerative:    (2A)

    See Absolute Velocity, 30 Oct'73*
        Chess: Game of Universe, 9 Jul'62*
        Cosmic Accounting Sequence, (1)
        God, 26 May'72
        Infinite, 15 Oct'72
        Intertransformation, 22 Jul'71
        Isotropic Vector Matrix, 30 Nov'72
        Metaphysical & Physical, 2 Jun'74
        Monkey Wrench, 30 Oct'73
        Nuclear & Nebular Zonal Waves, 1955
        Octet Truss, 1955
        Omnisynergetic, 30 Jan'73*
        Principle, (1)
        Push=pull, 22 Feb'73
        Spaceship, 26 Sep'68
        Star, Dec'72
        Structure Sequence, (1)(2)*
        Tactile Sequence, (2)
        Universe, 28 Apr'71*; 1960*
        Wow: The Last Wow, 22 Apr'71

---

RBF DEFINITIONS

    Regenerativity:

    "The regeneration may be that of a complete new baby
or the local regeneration of cells in an ongoing organism.
Rebirth is continual. The overall growth and refinement
of information and comprehension by continuous humanity
transcends the separate generations of life and steadies
toward eternal unalterability; the special case physical
experiences and the identification of their significance in
the overall scheme of eternal cosmic regenerativity ever
accelerate as the information bits multiply exponentially;
wherefore the overall rate of gain of metaphysical comprehension of the physical behavior in general accelerates
exponentially in respect to such arithmetical periodicities
as that of the celestial cycles of the solar system."

    (s1052.67)

    - Cite RBF rewrite of SYNERGETICS, 2nd. Ed. at Sec. 1052.67;
      17 Jan'75

---

Regeneration: Regenerative:    (2B)

    See Technology, 20 Jan'75
        Quantum Mechanics: Grand Strategy, 10 Apr'75
        Constellar, May'71
        Aesthetics of Uniformity, (1)
        Cosmic & Local, 3 Oct'75
        Object, 9 Nov'73
        Great Circles, May'44
        Self-discipline, 28 Mar'77
        Electron, 12 May'77
        Identity, 16 Feb'78

---

Regeneration: Rgenerative:    (1)

    See Automation of Metabolic & Regenerative Processes
        Biologicals
        Center of System Regeneration
        Epigenetic Landscape
        Integrity Coherence
        Local Regeneration
        Metabolic Regeneration
        Minimum Regenerative Set
        Ninety-two Elements
        Rganic Model
        Origin
        Primitive Regeneration
        Procreation
        Rebirth
        Self-regenerative
        Cosmic Regeneration
        Nuclear = Regenerative
        Eternally Regenerative
        Infinite = Eternally Regenerative
        Syntropy

---

Regeneration: Regenerative:    (3)

    See Regenerative Design: Law Of
        Regenerativity
        Regenerative Organics
        Regenerative Stimulations
        Regenerative System Integrity
        Regenerative Intersupport: Equation Of
        Regenerative Birth
        Regenerative Precession
        Regenerative Economic Sustenance

RBF DEFINITIONS

### Regenerativity:

"I've been looking for the word to take the place of creativity and it's _regenerativity_ . . . it suggests not the creation of something new but simply the reorganization of something that was always there."

- Cite RBF to EJA, 3200 Idaho, DC, 14 Feb '72

---

RBF DEFINITIONS

### Regularity:

"Regularity is eternal. But the regularities are eternally omni-interaccommodative, permitting approximately limitless freedoms of selectable alternative developments involving a vast plurality of time-dimensioned frequency involvements."

- Cite SYNERGETICS draft at Sec. 780.33, 2 Nov'72

---

### Regenerativity: (1)

See Creativity
Feedback
Rebirth

---

### Regular Polyhedra: (1)

See Mites Make All Regular Polyhedra

---

RBF DEFINITIONS

### Regenius:

"Man shows synergetic regenius inferior to nature's regeneration."

- Citation & context at Charting Alternating Experiences of Man & Nature (1), May'49

---

### Regular Polyhedra: (2)

See Planck's Constant, (A)
Subvisible Discontinuity, 19 Oct'72

---

### Regression:

See Progression & Regression

---

RBF DEFINITIONS

### Regular Tetrahedron:

"The four obtuse central angles of convergence of the four perpendiculars of the regular tetrahedron pass convergently through the center of the ▓▓▓▓▓ tetrahedral volume at 109° 28'."

- Cite SYNERGETICS draft at Sec. 966.22, 29 Nov'72

RBF DEFINITIONS

Regular = Uniangular:

"The regular--regular means absolutely uniangular--tetrahedron
is absolute and generalized, and thus never physically
realized."

(Sec. 532.18, 2nd. Ed.)

-Citation & context at Crystallography, 11 Dec'75

Reintegrative:

See Heres & Theres, 4 Jun'72

---

Regularity:                                              (1)

See Harmonic: Harmony
    Ninety-two Elements: Periodic Regularities Of
    Reproducible

RBF DEFINITIONS

Reinvestable Time and Survival Needs:

"The most incredible thing is that in the areas where all
the people are there is no power or food. . . You need food
so everything comes back to electrical power.

These figures on the Dymaxion Airocean World Map projection
". . . Each of the people have their hands raised and they
have a number of fingers on each hand indicating how much of
their time is reinvestable and how much they have to devote
to survival needs. The people in this area have no time:
their hands are in their fists. In the areas in the United
States they have all their fingers up: they have their whole
life to reinvest in the way they want to reinvest it. . .
So it begins all of a sudden . . . just thinking about
mobile areas and politics, you begin to see a whole Earth at
once and how man is doing on whole Earth."

- Cite RBF to World Game at NY Studio School, 12 Jun-31 Jul'69,
  from Saturn Film transcript, Sound 1, Take 1, pp.24-26.

---

Regular: Regularity:                                     (2)

See Conceptions, Dec'69
    Cryogenics, 28 Oct'72
    Einstein: Cosmic Religious Sense, (2)
    Environment Controls, (1)
    Solid State, 13 May'73
    Eyes, 1964

Reinvestable Time & Survival Needs:

See Electable: Elective
    Lifetime: Personal Lifetime Experience for
    Elective Experience

---

Reinforced Concrete:

See Prestressed Concrete

RBF DEFINITIONS

Relationships:

"I am not sure that there are relationships; maybe

there are only interrelationships."

- Cite RBF to EJA, 3200 Idaho, Wash, DC; 24 Apr'76

RBF DEFINITIONS

Relationship:

"A point is not a relationship.  A line is the simplest
relationship. . ."

- Citation and context at Line, 7 Nov'72

---

RBF DEFINITIONS

Relationship:

"Abstractions may be stated in pure principle of
relationship."

- Cite SYNERGETICS, "Corollaries," Sec. 240.58. 1971

- Citation & context at Abstraction, 1971

---

RBF DEFINITIONS

Relationship:

"Relationships are local to pattern.  Patterns are
comprehensive to relationships."

- Cite RBF to EJA, 3200 Idaho Ave., NW, Wash, DC, 20 Dec. '71.

- Citation at Pattern, 20 Dec'71

---

RBF DEFINITIONS

Relationships:

"I have two events and they have one relationship.  I have
three events and they have three relationships.. . Four
events and we have six relationships.  And five events, we
have ten relationships.  Six, it will be fifteen relationships.
So the numbers of relationships are not the same as the
numbers of events at all.  They are a different progression.
. . . Of course these events can be in any kind of an array
and need not be simultaneous, yet they will have their
relationships. . .

"You will find that the relationships are triangular. . .
look at the stars . . . You will find that every one of the
sets of relationships will always be triangulatable.  There
is no case where they are not."

- Cite LEDGEMONT LAB. Lecture, 15 Oct. '64, pp 14, 15

---

RBF DEFINITIONS

Relationships:

"We have relationships-- but not space."

* Citation and context at Space, Nov'71

---

RBF DEFINITIONS

Relationships:

"In a nonsimultaneous Universe all the relationships are
geodesic."

- Cite Oregon Lecture #3, p. 112. 5 Jul'62

---

RBF DEFINITIONS

Relationships:

"We have time relationships but not static space relationsips."

- Citation & context at Space, May'71

---

RBF DEFINITIONS

Relationships:

"Generalized systematic conceptuality's omnidirectional relationships are only angularly configured
and are independent of size or dimension."

- Cite OMNIDIDRECTIONAL HALO, p. 135, 1960

RBF DEFINITIONS

Relationships:

"Relationships which have definite integrity and
independence of size are conceptual principles of abstract
thought independent of physical realization."

- Cite OMNIDIRECTIONAL HALO, p. 146, 1960

RBF DEFINITIONS

Relationship Analysis:                                                    (2)

"interconnect the experiences and to find the generalized
patterns and orderly principles underlying all our randomly
encountered experiences."

- Cite Nasa Speech, p.95, Jun'66

RBF DEFINITIONS

Relationships:

"The whole of Universe is the minimum consideration
and the relationship of its regenerative subsystem
functionings are alone elementary."

- Citation and context at University, 15 Apr '55

Relationship Analysis:

See Connections and Relatedness
    Order Underlying Randomness
    Number: Tetrahedral Number
    Process Relationships

RBF DEFINITIONS

Relationship:

"There are no empty sets but only generalized group or
system synergetical relationship characteristics."

- Cite RBF Synergetics notes, Feb'50

Relation:   Relationship:   Relatedness:                                 (1)

See Absolute Relationship
    Arelational
    Behavioral Relationships
    Connections & Relatedness
    Envelopmental relationship
    Epistemological Stepping Stones
    Nonrelationship
    Order Underlying Randomness
    Number: Tetrahedral Number
    Process Relationships
    Omniinterrelationships
    Rational = Relational
    Interrelationships

RBF DEFINITIONS

Relationship Analysis:                                                    (1)

"We look at the stars and they look very random scattered
throughout the sky. I will tell you then that the numbers of
relationships between all the stars is always $\frac{N^2 - N}{2}$ and

this chart tells you quite clearly and simply that I am mathematically justified in doing so. This will give you a
personal sense of the power of the infinitely tiny human's
mind in the presence of that vast array of stars whose distances
and occurrences can only be identified in terms of millions and
billions and higher numbers of years and miles away.

"This relationship analysis discloses the omniuniversal orderliness that scientific man finds to be always underlying all
superficial randomness of experience. This tells us that the
seeming disorder of physical entropy is only superficial and
explains why metaphysical thought can always find the orderliness
that engulfs the disorderliness. Disorderliness is nonthinking.
Brain, which stores the memories of all specialcase experiences,
does not find the relationship any more than a library in
itself can find or does find the interrelationships of the data
that it houses. Only mind, the great metaphysical, pattern-
seeking function, has demonstrated to us the capability to"

- Cite Nasa Speech, pp.94-95, Jun'66

Relation:   Relatedness:   Relationship:                                 (2)

See Abstraction, 1971*
    Constants, 26 Sep'73
    Line, 7 Nov'72*; 9 Jun'75
    Pattern, 20 Dec'71*
    Potential, 1963*
    Reason, Aug'73*
    Space, Nov'71*
    Thinkable You, (1)
    Time & Space, May'71*
    University, 15 Apr'55*
    Twoness, 27 May'72
    Threeness, 27 May'72
    Human Beings & Complex Universe, (1)

RBF DEFINITIONS

<u>Relative Abundance</u>:

"I began to play a game of looking at relative total
abundances of various patterns in various systems and
looking at a daisy and looking at a tortoise
and looking at a waste basket, I find that the relative
abundance of the fundamental patterns called chemical
elements vary quite greatly.  I sort of began to play a
game of relative abundance because this is a nice 100 per
cent game and that is the kind of game that the physicist
learned to do so ably as a synergetic capability because
he was always dealing in 100 per cent.  Remember that when he
had an unknown percentage showing in an experiment, that
is what gave him his clue to meson or whatever it might be.
I found it very interesting to look at the total pattern
man. ▬▬▬▬▬

- Cite OREGON Lecture #5 - p. 168, 9 Jul'62

---

<u>Relative Abundance</u>:                                      (1)

See Constant Relative Abundance
    Euler
    Man:  Relative Abundance of Chemical Elements In
      Man & Universe

---

<u>Relative Abundance</u>:                                      (2)

See Gravity:  Circumferential Leverage, (3)
    Reality as Structural Interaction of Principles, 1963
    Sweepout:  Spherical Sweepout, (2)

---

<u>Relative Activity Diameters of Stars & Electrons</u>:        (1)

See Atom as Solar System
    Astro & Nucleic Interpositioning
    Invisibility of Macro- and Micro- Resolutions
    Nuclear & Nebular:  Nucleus & Galaxies

---

<u>Relative Activity Diameters of Stars & Electrons</u>:        (2)

See Gravity:  Circumferential Leverage, (2)
    Radiation:  Speed Of, (C)(D)

---

<u>Relative Activity Diameters</u>:

See Orbiting Magnitudes

---

RBF DEFINITIONS

<u>Relative Asymmetry Sequence</u>:                             (1)

"Observing that there is a fundamental complementarity, and
that the complementations are rarely mirror images of one
another, we find that the physical Universe is always
locally entropic-- that is, it is always giving off energy
in one way or another.  Because each local system has its
own orbiting, and its own frequencies and so forth, the ways
in which they give them off are not synchronized with the
others.  Therefore, as they're given off, they're relatively
disorderly. . . . And actually calculably disorderly; they're
not infinitely disorderly at all.  They're not something we
might call chaos.  It may look disorderly to you as you look
at the turbulence of a waterfall, and the water's going down
there, But I've become very fascinated with the fact that
I'm beginning now to understand what the different turbulences are.  I can begin to see what the vortex is and all
the interprecessional effects.

"It's no longer looking quite as disorderly to me as it used
to look.  Our word 'disorder' is a relative matter: it gets
to be <u>relatively asymmetrical</u>.  Relative to the symmetry of
equilibrium it gets to be relatively asymmetrical, and I
find that it goes to a maximum asymmetry and then comes back"

- Cite RBF to World Game, Jun-Jul'69

---

RBF DEFINITIONS

<u>Relative Asymmetry Sequence</u>:                             (2)

"to symmetry again.

"I think this is why we might have something we call
octaves in music.  There are sort of octaves in our
thinking.  We think octavely. . . We say the atom has its
nuclear arrangement, has its own synergetics, which is how
they associate to form molecules and the molecules associate
to form cells and how the cells associate to form living
organisms, and so forth."

- Cite RBF to World Game at New York Studio School, 12 Jun-
  31 Jul'69, from Saturn Film transcript, #327, pp.3-4.

Relative Asymmetry: (1)

See Asymmetric Pulsation

---

Relative: (2)

See Avogadro: Generalized Avogadro System, 1959
Description, Jun'66
Epigenetic Landscape, May'49
Functions, 26 May'72
Synergetics, undated
Unique Frequencies, 9 Jul'62

---

Relative Asymmetry: (2)

See Entropy, Jan'72

---

RBF DEFINITIONS

Relativity:

"Lines are relativity. A line is the first order of
relativity: the basic sixness of minimum system and
cosmically constant sixness of relationship identifies
lines as the relativity in the formula $\frac{N^2 - N}{2}$."

- Citation and context at Line, 7 Nov'72

---

Relative Volumetric Frequency & Interval:

See Mass, 12 May'77

---

RBF DEFINITIONS

Relativity:

"Size is where relativity becomes generated. The eternality
of synergetics is conceptually experienciable independent of
the successive experiences of relativity of time and size."

- Citation and context at Size, 22 Jun'72

---

Relative: (1)

See Constant Relative Abundance
Relative Abundance
Shunting: Relative Motion Patterns

---

RBF DEFINITIONS

Relativity:

"I have a railroad train going west through the desert and
a man leans out the window and drops a flaming apple. He
sees it go East. He has a sextant and a stopwatch with him
and measures the angle and the amount of time, and so forth.
But he sees that he himself is standing still. He is like
all of the people standing on the surface of the Earth not
realizing that the Earth is going around the Sun at 60,000
miles per hour. And so for him the apple seems to go in an
easterly direction.

"Another man standing at a great distance simply sees the
apple descend toward the Earth.

"Then a man standing very much to the north sees the apple
go west-- with the motion of the train.

"All these different observers then come out with different
results concerning the same experiment."

- Cite RBF to BO'R, Kent, Ohio, 23 May'72

RBF DEFINITIONS

Relativity:

"Is is always special case relativity."

- Citation and context at Is, 24 Apr'72

---

RBF DEFINITIONS

Relativity:

"The theory of functions holds for Universe itself. Universe consists at minimum of both the metaphysical and the physical. The fundamental twoness of physical Universe was embraced in Einstein's one word, 'relativity,' and in a more specific and experimental way in the physicists' concept of complementarity."

- Cite Carbondale Draft
  Return to Modelability, p. V.3

- Cite NASA Speech, p.68, Jun'66

---

RBF DEFINITIONS

Relativity:

"We cannot have relativity
Without at least two phenomena to be differentially related.
There is also the word complementarity.
We cannot have one phenomenon complemented
By less than one other phenomenon.
The words complementarity and relativity
Do not identify identical physical phenomena.
We need to discover
Whether there exists a generalized concept
Which embraces both phenomena,
And we find that the ponderable physical energy Universe
That is, physical Universe,
In contradistinction to the Universe's
Weightless, metaphysical aspects,
Does embrace both complementarity and relativity."

- Cite BRAIN & MIND, p.135 May '72

---

RBF DEFINITIONS

Relativity:

"Time can be expressed only ███████ as

'relativity' in the terms of relative frequency of reoccur-

rence of any constantly recycling behavior of any chosen

sub-system of universe."

- Cite NASA Speech, p. 19, Jun'66

- Citation at Time, Jun'66

---

RBF DEFINITIONS

Relativity:

"Time, relativity and consciousness

Are always and only coexistent functions

Of an a priori Universe. . . "

- Citation and context at Consciousness, p. 12, May '72

---

RBF DEFINITIONS

Relativity:

"Science states that the entire physical universe

is energy.  $E = mc^2$."

- Cite HOW TO MAINTAIN MAN AS A SUCCESS, p. 228 , Mar'65

---

RBF DEFINITIONS

Relativity:

". . . What Einstein realized has not as yet been

comprehended in any important way except that of developing

the atomic bomb. . . "

"Einstein intuited from scientific observations, such

as that of the Brownian Movement in water, and black body

radiation. that the physical universe is always transform-

ing complexedly. Massively twisted, the geology of our

Spaceship Earth's crust makes clear how severe have been

the great transformings of its history."

- UNESCO TIFLIS 1968, p. 9

---

RBF DEFINITIONS

Relativity:

"Relativity leads us toward fundamental classification of
our experience and observation, in terms of a few hierarchies
of dynamic interactions and principle transformations of
an all-energy, continuous-discontinuous, synchronous-
dissynchronous Universe tensionally cohered, precessional
of local compressive spherical energetic collections--
as (Suns) stars or planets or moons or asteroids or meteorites;
and the progression of within-ward sub-sets of events of
interactions at planet crust, etc., and inward to the
92 common principles of atomic convergence of energy in
principle, and the pervasive sets of dynamic associations
by contraction, expansion, spin, orbit, torque, push, and
pull, and precession. This all brings us by progressive
collections of thoughts into a fundamental twoness of
dynamic reciprocities which, internally paired, ultimately
become ██ one with outwardly paired principles of reciprocity."

- Citation and context at Reciprocity (1) + (2), May'49

RBF DEFINITIONS

Relativity:

"The concept of relativity involves high frequency of re-established awareness, and progressively integrating con-sideration ▆▆▆▆▆▆▆ of the respective, and also integrated, dynamic complexities of the moving and trans-forming frame of reference and of the integrated dynamic complexities of the observed, as well as of the series of integrated sub-dynamic complexities, in respect to each of the major categories of the relatively moving frames of reference of the observer and the observed. It also involves constant reference of all the reciprocating sub-sets of the comprehensive totality of nonsimultaneous Universe, from which naught may be lost."

- Citation and context at Dynamic Frame of Reference (5), May'49

RBF DEFINITIONS

Relativity: Special Theory of Relativity:

"The Special Theory of Relativity states that (1) the laws of physical phenomena are the same for all inertial systems, and (2) the velocity of light in any given inertial system is independent of the velocity of that system."

- Cite RBF Glossary of terms bound with "The Live Book Squad," 1967. (Reconfirmed by RBF, 3200 Idaho, Wash DC, 15 Jul'73.)

RBF DEFINITIONS

Relativity:

"Relativity treats with concepts in principle; therefore, it can be treated in words as well as in mathematical phrasing. Relativity is inherently convergent, though convergent toward a plurality of centers of abstract truths. Degrees of accuracy are only degrees of refinement, and magnitude in no way affects the fundamental reliability, which refers, as directional or angular sense, toward centralized truths. Truth is a relationship."

- Cite TOTAL THINKING, I&I, p.233, May'49
- Citation & context at Words, May'49

Relativity: (1)

See Dynamic Frame of Reference
    Einstein
    Generalization: Fourth Degree
    Generalizations Reduced to One Word
    Synergy: Metaphysical Synergy
    Stars as Live Shows Billions of Years Ago

RBF DEFINITIONS

Relativity:

"The invisible structure was $E = mc^2$."

- Cite PREVIEWS, I&I, p. 211, 1 Apr'49

Relativity: (2)

See Complementarity, Jun'66
    Consciousness, May'72*
    Dynamic Frame of Reference, (5)*
    Is, 24 Apr'72*
    Line, 7 Nov'72*
    Reciprocity, (1)(2)*
    Size, 22 Jun'72*
    Tetrahedral Dynamics, (1)
    Time, 23 May'72; May'72; Jun'66*
    Words, May'49*
    Time-angle-size Aspects, 30 Apr'77
    Mass, 12 May'77

Relativity: Marriage of Social & Natural Law:

See Air Space, May'65

Relax: Relaxed:

See Hexagon, 30 Dec'73

Relay:  Relaying:                                    (1)


        See Noninterference Relaying
            Precessionally Shunted Pattern Relay
            Social-industrial Relay
            Substitutional Relaying
            Telemation:  Satellite-relayed
            Interference-noninterference Relaying
            Valvability

---

RBF DEFINITIONS

    Relevant:   Lucidly Relevant Set:

        ". . . All irrelevancies fall into two main categories
    or 'bits.'  One set embraces all the events which are
    irrelevant because they are too large in magnitude and too
    delayed in rate of reoccurrence to have any effect on the
    set of relationships we are considering.  The other set of
    irrelevancies embraces all the events ▆▆ that are too small
    and too frequent to be differentiably resolved at the
    wave length we are tuned in at . . in any discernible way
    to alter the interrelationship values of the set of
    experience relationships we are considering.  Having dis-
    missed the two classes of irrelevances there remains the
    lucidly relevant 'set to be studied."


                                    - Cite NASA Speech, p. 40, Jun'66


    CONSIDERABLE SET — SEC 509.03

---

Relay:  Relaying:                                    (2)


        See Ecological Pattern, 19 Sep'64
            Eye-beamed Thoughts, (I)
            Manifest:  Two:  1963
            Dynamic vs. Static, 12 Nov'75

---

RBF DEFINITIONS

    Relevant.  Lucidly Relevant Set:

        "Thinking is a momentary dismissal of irrelevancies.

    . . . There is a twilight zone of tantalizingly almost

    relevants.  There are two such twilight zones-- the macro

    and the micro-- tantalizingly almost relevants.  Between

    them there is always a set of extraordinarily lucid items

    of ▆▆▆▆▆▆ relevance."


                                    - Cite SUMMARY VISION 65, p. 138, Oct'65
                    - Citation at Thinking, Oct'65

---

RBF DEFINTTIONS

    Relevance:

    "Relevance is systematic; a relatedness; something going on
    around the intertriangulation of the six vectors.  (What is
    the structure involved?)"


    - Cite RBF to EJA, Beverly Hotel, NY, 22 Jun'72

---

RBF DEFINITIONS

    Relevant:  Lucidly Relevant Set:

        "Thinking consists . . of a self-disciplined deferment

    of conscious consideration of any incoming information

    traffic other than that which is lucidly relevant to the

    experience intuited quest for comprehension of the signif-

    icance of the emergent pattern under immediate priority of

    consideration."


            - Cite OMNIDIRECTIONAL HALO, p. 136, 1960

    CONSIDERABLE SET — SEC 509.04

---

Relevant:  Almost Relevant:


        See Twilight Zone

---

Relevant System Potential:


        See Vector as 1/12th of Relevant System Potential

# Synergetics Dictionary

<u>Relevant</u>: <u>Relevance</u>: <u>Relevant Set</u>: <u>Lucidly Relevant</u>:    (1)

See Corelevant
    Bits: Bitting
    Irrelevancies: Dismissal Of
    Irrelevancy
    Stark
    Thought = Relevant Set
    Omniinterrelevant
    Exterior Relevants
    Interior Relevants
    Star Events
    Zone of Lucidity
    Interrelevant

---

<u>Relevant</u>: <u>Relevance</u>: <u>Relevant Set</u>: <u>Lucidly Relevant</u>:    (2)

See Part, May'72
    Powering: One Dimension, 15 Oct'72
    Stark, 29 May'72
    Thinking, Oct'65*
    Repetition, (1)
    Halo Concept, Nov'71
    Omnihalo, Nov'71
    Pronouns: I = We = Us, (2)
    Human Beings, 22 Jun'77

---

<u>Reliable</u>: <u>Eternal Reliability</u>:

See A Priori Mystery, 22 Jul'71
    Integrity, 25 Jan'72
    Inherent, 3 Oct'72

---

RBF DEFINITIONS

<u>Religion</u>:

"I do not want to inaugurate another religion and persuade people to believe in a set of rules. I am convinced that the Almight does not need anybody to promote God."

    - Citation & context at <u>God</u>, May'65

---

RBF DEFINITIONS

<u>Religion</u>:    (1)

"...Another young lady came to me and said was I going to talk some more about these religious ideas. I really had talked a whole lot about it to you but... I had never really used the word <u>religion</u>. I knew what she was talking about because she spoke about some kind of faith, some confidence in an integrity and a meaning in our experience of life... The word really is 'religio.' They had come out of a set of rules of dogma, interpretations at second-, third, and fourth-handings, sometimes very remote, a thousandfold secondariness of experiences of others and thought which have occurred spontaneously to original explorers.

"I myself am quite confident that the more we know about who specifically inspired religions-- Christ, Mohamed, Buddha, and Confucius-- these may be generalized characters, but there was one or several men who at various times in history tended to have the kinds of experiences that are accounted for word by word, mouth by mouth, word of mouth. These experiences are experiences of individuals who have extreme confidence in the integrity of the invention man and the invention Universe, who in every instance find this integrity to have great power, to be a priori to human intellect."

    - Cite Oregon Lecture #5, p. 160, 9 Jul'62

---

RBF DEFINITIONS

<u>Religion</u>:    (2)

"None of them ever account experiencing a god in the image of man. That is one thing that Einstein was talking about in his nonanthropomorphic concept of the scientists. At any rate, they are people who experience an a priori integrity, a comprehensive anticipatory intellectual integrity greater than that of man. And they have enormous confidence in it, great faith in it, and try to help others to understand the success that they have experienced through their confidence in that integrity. At any rate, apparently these people have had such success as to have excited people by various patterns of experiences that have occurred. There are many then who in their day were excited, really very blindly and superstitiously, into subscribing to what was going on. This man was a man of powrs without their trying to understand what those powers were. When they die then there were those who do better than others and they tend to become the authorities; and while they are alive they then are asked to make various recordings of what they think had been said and what the rules were. Gradually this gets thinner and thinner and we have official custodians of the information and interpretations and that is the way our religions have developed."

    - Cite Orgeon Lecture #5, p.161, 9 Jul'62

---

RBF DEFINITIONS

<u>Religion</u>:

"As these individual explorers of the sciences went off into their laboratory and went down with their blinders on, men of enormous integrity, they said they never found anytthing in that particular area that seemed to confirm any of the given <u>religions</u>. Therefore, atheism began to develop, not as something you profess-- but there was sort of a double life. These men tended to honor their forebears, honor the literature, honor the humanism, and they would say probably the trouble is that I am such a narrow person from being in such a narrow field, that I just don't understand your other things. But there is nothing that I am doing experimentally here that seems to tell me that what the people have said about how the Universe was put together and the way it works, particularly from a religious ▆▆▆▆ ▆▆▆▆ viewpoint, that really seems to be valid. I think these people over here are dear muddleheaded people, but I am just going to have to leave them alone for my own professional part. So what has been thought of as an atheism is really just an evasion. It wasn't a declaration of againstness, and was not something against religion, but there seemed to be nothing to take its place."

    - Cite Oregon Lecture #4, p. 130. 6 Jul'62

---

RBF DEFINITIONS

<u>Religious Edifices</u>:

"... The enormous credit and physical investment of local undertakings in the most transcendental class as mystical insurance for eternal equanimity as built into the great <u>religious edifices</u> by the local communities, as representing the most generalized problem treatment and infinite range planning known to man's history."

    - Citation and context at <u>Ships</u> (1), 1954-59

Religious Edifices:

    See Permanent Symbolic Communications Devices

---

TEXT CITATIONS

Religion:

Oregon Lecture #5 - pp. 160-163 - 9 Jul'62

203.10                                         s531.05

1056.20 (24)

---

Religion as Make-believe:

    See Synergetics, Apr'72

---

Religion: Religions:            (1)

    See Catholic Church
        Christian Legend & Philosophy
        Einstein: Cosmic Religious Sense
        Faith
        God
        Belief

---

RBF DEFINITIONS

Religion: Related to 'Reglio' or Rule:

"I personally interpret the word religion as being related to 'reglio' or rule. You begin with the assumption that everyone is very ignorant, and somebody much wiser comes along and says, "Darling, you're not old enough to understand. I do understand however, and I want you to beleive every word I say." And you say, "All right, father, I know you love me and wouldn't mislead me or cause me harm, So I believe you. There you have an exchange that I'd call religious. It is built on subscription to dogma. You're told what to believe and you learn how to repeat it."

Feb'72
- Cite RBF in Barry Farrel Playboy Interview Transcript, Pp. 19-20

---

Religion: Religious:            (2)

    See A Priori Mystery, May'72
        Child Sequence, (1)
        Modelability, (3)
        Synergetics, 19 Jun'71
        Thinking, (1)
        Iceland, 7 Oct'75
        Word Trends, May'44
        Belief, 20 Feb'77
        Greater Intellect, (2)

---

ETYMOLOGICAL DICTIONARY (WEEKLEY)

Religion:

F., L. religio-n, from religens, careful, opposite of negligens, and prob. cogn. with diligens.

---

RBF DEFINITIONS

Remember:

"To be remembered, it must first be membered, to be membered it must be structured, to be structured it must be triangulated."

- Cite RBF to BO'R, 3200 Idaho, DC, 20 Feb '72

Remembersble Entity:

See Member, 9 Nov'73
Dodecahedron, 23 Feb'72

Remembersble Number:                                    (2)

See Prime Number, Oct'71

Remembering Names:

See Subconscious, Jun'66

RBF DEFINITIONS

Remembered:

"Experiences remembered by none are, in effect, nonexistent--
may never have occurred."

- Citation and context at Experience, 1968

RBF DEFINITIONS

Remembersble Numbers:

"When nature gives us a number we can remember, she is
putting us on notice that the cosmic communications
circuits are open: you are connected through to many
sublime truths!"

- Cite RBF addition to Synergetics Galley at Sec. 1234.02,
  Santa Monica, CA, 14 Jan'74

Remember:                                                (1)

See Memory
    Pattern Cognizance
    Trail Making & Trail Remembering
    Furniture of Remembered Experiences
    Unremembered = Nonexistent

Remembersble Number:                                     (1)

See SSRCD
    Scheherazade Number

Remember:  Remembering:                                  (2)

See Model, 22 Jan'75
    Universe, May'72
    Minimum Awareness, (1)
    Environment, (B)

Remergent Synchronization:

    See Hot Line of Intuition, 15 Aug'72

---

Remote: Remoteness:     (1)

    See Maximum Remoteness
       Proximity & Remoteness
       Remote = Intellectual
       Cosmic & Local

---

RBF DEFINITIONS

    Remote:

    "The remote aspect of a spiral is a wave because there are
no planes."

    - Citation & context at Spiralinearity, Nov'71

---

Remote: Remoteness:     (2)

    See Energy, 6 May'48
       Physical, 27 Dec'74
       Spiralinearity, Nov'71*
       Structure, 15 Oct'64

---

RBF DEFINITIONS

    Remote = Intellectual:

    "The more remote the function the more intellectual the
perspective we have on it and the greater the speed with which
we accelerate its adaptability into our economic life."

    - Citation & context at Intellectual Perspective, 1 Jul'62

---

Renting: Rental:     (1)

    See Mobile Rentability vs. Immobile Purchasing
       Service Industry

---

Remote = Intellectual:

    See Largest Pattern

---

Rent: Rental:     (2)

    See Service Industry, 15 May'73
       Mobile Homes, (1)(2)
       Dome House Grand Strategy: 1927-1977, (3)
       Building Industry, (8)
       Energy Environment-harvesting Machines, 27 Jan'77

Reoccur:  Reoccurrence:                                    (1)

    See Cycle:  If You Wait Long Enough the Cycles All Reoccur

---

Re-origin:  Re-originatable:

    See Origin
        Regenerative

---

Reoccur:  Reoccurrence:                                    (2)

    See Entropy, 16 May'72

---

Repelling Fields:

    See Domains of Actions, 9 Jul'62; 21 Dec'71
    Black Holes & Synergetics, 1 Mar'77

---

Reorganize:

    See Rearrange

---

RBF DEFINITIONS

Repetition:

"In a recent study of the use of repetition in literature,
Bruce F. Kawin observes that 'Events whose repetition is not
extraordinary do not seem worth recording, in fact, hardly
seem worth noticing.' This statement is very close to what
has been the strategy of my life. This is what it means to
dare to be naive. The preoccupied search for the extraordinary
pattern cannot fail to obscure the larger and more obvious
ordinary patterns-- so obvious that they always seemed to be
missed."

    - Cite SYNERGETICS, 2nd. Ed. front matter, Author's Note on
      Rationale for Repetition in This Work, p.xxi, 2 Jul'75

---

Reorientation:

    See Tools of Reorientation

---

RBF DEFINITIONS

Repetition:

"Le Corbusier told the whole story on the first page. And
then he told it again in a few pages. And then he told it
again in the whole book. And that's the only way people can
really understand it. You have to keep retelling it. This
is the way Le Corbusier did it in his book called
      ... and everyone loved it that way.

"This gives me another metaphor.... It is all part of the
grand strategy. You know how a pole vaulter can't do it all
the first time. He has to run over the same cinder path
hundreds and hundreds of times before he gets to his new
record. And that's the way we should tell it in the book."

    - Cite RBF to EJA, by telephone from Philadelphia, 8 Mar'75

RBF DEFINITIONS

Repetition: (1)

"It is the writer's experience that new degrees of comprehension are always and only consequent to ever-renewed review of the spontaneously rearranged inventory of significant factors. This awareness of the processes leading to new degrees of comprehension spontaneously motivates the writer to describe over and over again what-- to the careless listener or reader-- might seem to be tireless repetition, but to the successful explorer is known to be essential mustering of operational strategies from which alone new thrusts of comprehension can be successfully accomplished.

"To the careless reader seeking only entertainment the repetition will bring about swift disconnect. To those experienced with the writer and motivated by personal experience with mental discoveries-- co-experiencing comprehensive breakthroughs with the writer-- are not dismayed by the seeming necessity to start all over again inventorying the now seemingly lucidly relevant.

"Universe factors intuitively integrating to attain new perspective and effectively demonstrated logic of new degrees of comprehension-- that's the point! I have not forgotten that"

- SYNERGETICS front papers; RBF to EJA, Wash. DC, 30 Oct'72

---

Repetition: Repetitive: (1)

See Reproducibleness
   Standardization
   Nonidentically Repetitive
   Pole Vaulter

---

RBF DEFINITIONS

Repetition: (2)

"I have talked about these things before. It is part of the personal discipline, no matter how formidable the re-inventorying may seem, to commit myself to that task when inspired by intuitive glimpses of important new relationships-- inspired overpoweringly because of the realized human potential of successful escape from ignorance."

- Cite SYNERGETICS front papers, "Author's note on Rationale for Repetition in this Work," p. xxi, from notes of RBF to EJA, 3200 Idaho, Wash., DC, 30 Oct'72

---

Repetition: Repetitive: (2)

See Interval, 6 May'48
   Reproducible, 30 May'72
   Generalized Principle, (1)
   Scenario, 2 Jun'71
   Harmonic Interval, May'49
   Identity, 2 Jul'75
   Metaphor, 2 Jul'75
   Aesthetics of Uniformity, (1)

---

RBF DEFINITIONS

Repetition:

"Of course it can be abused, like cast iron souvenir statues of G.I.'s. where the motive and integrity is so low the effect is cloying. But repetition has a very high function."

- Citation & context at Reproducible, 30 May'72

---

Reprecession: (1)

See Regenerative Precession

---

RBF DEFINITIONS

Repetitive:

"Metaphor is repetetive. Wave function and frequency are inherently repetitive. Sight, the awareness of all the electromagnetic-spectrum reality, is identified only by its unique frequencies of reliable repetition. Identity results only from a family of uniquely repetitive frequencies."

- Cite RBF to EJA and RBF marginalia in Bruce F. Kawin, "Telling It Again and Again," p.5; 28 May'75

---

Reprecession: (2)

See Two Kinds of Twoness, (B)

RBF DEFINITIONS

Reproducible:

"The more symmetrical: the more reproducible.  The more
asymmetrical, the less it fits Universe.  The most successful
design in Universe is the hydrogen atom.  The more adequate
the prototype, the better it fits Universe.. . . .
There is an unfortunate tendency to abhorency of the plastic.
Our fingernails are plastic.  Our eyes are plastic.  Of
course it can be abused, like cast iron souvenir statues of
G.I.'s, where the motive and integrity is so low the effect
is cloying.  But repetition has a very high function."

- Cite RBF to Bill Whitehead, 3200 Idaho, Wash DC, 30 May'72

Reproducible:  Reproducibility:

See Aesthetics of Uniformity
    Mass Production
    Prototype
    Regenerative Design;  Law Of
    Simplicity
    Standardization

RBF DEFINITIONS

Reproducible:

"...The Sun energy impounding functions of the billions
times billions of blades of grass around its spherical
surface are essential to the regeneration of life aboard
Spaceship Earth, ergo Whitman's 'Blades of Grass' are
almost infinitely reproducible."

- Cite GENERALIZED LAWS OF DESIGN, pp.2-3, 22 Apr '68

Reproduction:                                    (1)

See Procreation
    Sex
    Survival Sequence:  Love
    Tactile Sequence
    Aesthetics of Reproduction

RBF DEFINITIONS

Reproducible:

"It seems to be a law of nature that the more fundamentally
simple and biologically propitious an evolutionary growth may
be, the more aesthetically satisfying and lastingly acceptable
is its multireproduction, e.g., roses, stars, and blades of
grass."

- Cite ARCHITECTURE: THE PRESENT SCENE, Newsweeek, 1968

Reproduction:                                    (2)

See Reproducible, 1968
    Aesthetics of Uniformity, (1)

Reproducibleness:  Law Of:

See Harmonic, 22 Apr'68

Repro-shelter Industry:

See Industrial Hypocrisy, May'32

RBF DEFINITIONS

Repulsion:

When humans "repel one another physically

The least strong is rocketed

Into remote system orbit."

- * Citation and context at Precession: Analogy of Precession and Social Behavior, May'72

---

Repulsion: (2)

See Domains of Actions, 9 Jul'62*
    Geometry of Vectors, Aug'71
    Gravity (1)*
    Precession: Analogy of Precession & Social Behavior, May'72*
    Structure, Nov'71

---

RBF DEFINITIONS

Repulsion:

"Repulsion, or the raison d'etre of going awayness..."

- Citation and context at Gravity (1), 7 Feb'71

---

Require: Requirements:

See Need: Necessity
    Universal Requirements of a Dwelling Advantage

---

RBF DEFINITIONS

Repulsion:

In the kinetics of gas under pressure "there are critical proximities tensionally and critical proximities compressionally, that is, there are repellings. . . as we would find out in electromagnetics so there are domains of actions. . . "

- Cite OREGON Lecture #5 - p. 186, 9 Jul'62

- Citation & context at Domains of Actions, 9 Jul'62

---

RBF DEFINITIONS

Re-rewarding:

"Exploration in principle is re-rewarding."

- Citation and context at Probability, May'49

---

Repulsion: (1)

See Repel: Repelling

---

RBF DEFINITIONS

Research: (1)

"We must break a barrier in the kind of thinking we've been doing about the word 'research.' You have to have search before you can have research. The word research came into use in industry and business during the '20's. They started going over the things they were throwing away. They began to apply new technologies. So you searched once and exploited your findings; then you researched what you'd done and exploited it again. It was very spottily done between 1900 and World War I; research really begins in 1929. Today it covers all kinds of things. When we talk about research in a university, that's new too. The research professor is something very new. You had large corporations paying for a chair in the chemistry department and it was really a racket because what it meant was that you had a large number of people, graduate students working for you for nothing. You had a research professor giving your company very special benefits. The ulterior motives are frequently visible.

"A researcher is always someone who goes over things again. He is a technician staying in one area to see what he can find. Research is very different from pure science exploration and invention. Research can just be processing and refining without"

- RBF to Barry Farrell; Bear Island, Tape #7, Side A, Transcript p.4, 18 Aug'70

RBF DEFINITIONS

Research:                                                    (2)

"initiating anything.  I don't expect people to initiate very
much, very often.  The whole technique is to find what are the
first things first in Universe."

- RBF to Barry Farrell; Bear Island, Tape #7, Side A; transcipt
  p.4, 18 Aug'70

---

Research:                                                    (1)

See Fuller, R.B:  Personal Resaerch File Colors
    Search vs. Research

---

Research & Development:                                      (1)

See Fellowships:  Life Fellowships in Research &
    Development
    Prototype
    Buggy Industry Could Never Invent Automobile
    Adoption of the New Only as Last Resort
    Dome House Grand Strategy

---

Research:                                                    (2)

See Labor:  American Labor, 1960

---

Research & Development:                                      (2)

See Ephemeralization, 1 Jun'49
    Invention Sequence (A)-(D); (b)
    Everybody's Business, (1)

---

Reserve:  Reserves:

See Complementarity Reserves

---

Research Fellowships:

See Fellowships:  Life Fellowships in R & D

---

Reservoir:                                                   (1)

See Cosmic Reservoir

Reservoir:                                                    (2)

See Shunt, Jun'66

Residual Ignorance:

See Understanding, 1 Apr'49

RBF DEFINITIONS

Residual Error:

"There will always be residual error to surprise man.
The integration of all possibilities of the complementary
alternates, though confinable, inherently defies exact
identity because the minimum is pattern and not isolated
integer.  All pattern has inherent plurality of viewable
aspects, which are the reciprocals of pluralities of
permissible viewpoints, for instance, from within or from
without a system.  All treatable pattern is a subdivision
of Universe, and disposes, in its first generalization,
of the macrocosmic and microcosmic irrelevancies.  Ergo,
thought identification and communication to self or others
must tune in a zoned system, with inherent center-of-zone,
equilibrium 'sphere,' and therefore possessed of inherent
wave propagative inward-outward tendency between the
unstable variable limits, or infra-ultra twilights
confining the clearly tunable mean interior-exterior
zone limits occurring between the ultra-tunable macro-
cosmos and the intra-tunable microcosmos."

- Cite RBF draft Ltr. to Jim (Fitzgibbon?), Raleigh, NC, 1954-59

Residual Reality:

See Specialization, Dec'69

Residual Error:

See Observing & Articulating, 4 Aug'75
    Cybernetics, 7 Nov'75

Residual:

See Truth as Progressive Diminution of Residual Error

RBF DEFINITIONS

Residual Ignorance of Temporality:

"Only residual ignorance of temporality dulls the growing
comprehension and allows fear to corrupt the child's innately
absolute trust in love."

- Citation and context at Death, 11 Sep'73

Residual:                                                    (2)

See Exactitude, May'72
    Historical, 1971

Residual:

    See Residual Error
        Residual Ignorance of Temporality
        Residual Reality

---

RBF DEFINITIONS

Resolution:

"Things in parallel never get resolved. Convergent things get beautifully resolved; they get exactly... they get nature into a corner."

- Citation & context at Convergence & Divergence, 1 May'77

---

Resilience:

    See Bend:  Bending
        Rigidity vs. Resilience

---

RBF DEFINITIONS

Resolution:

"...The resolution is not linear nor planar; it is omnidirectional; it is hierarchical in ascending or descending hierarchies."

- Citation & context at Minimum Limit Case, 12 May'75

---

Resistance:                                      (1)

    See Least Resistance
        Passive Resistance
        Precessionally Shunted Pattern Relay

---

RBF DEFINITIONS

        Resolution:

"Vectors are not abstractions: they are resolutions."

- Citation at Vector, 21 Dec'71
- Cite RBF to EJA, 3200 Idaho, Washington DC, 21 Dec. '71.

---

Resistance:                                      (2)

    See Tunability, 1960

---

RBF DEFINITIONS

        Resolution:

"Points are complex but nondifferentiably resolvable to superficial inspection."

- Cite RBF to EJA, Beverly Hotel, New York, 19 June 1971.

- Citation & context at Point, 19 Jun'71

RBF DEFINITIONS

■■■■■■ Resolution:

"A star is something you cannot resolve. We call it a
point, playing Euler's game of crossings. One star
does not have an outsideness and an insideness. It is
a point because you cannot resolve it."

- Cite RBF to EJA, Carbondale, 2 April 1971.

- Citation & context at Point, 2 Apr'71

---

Resolution:   Resolvable:                                    (2)

See Female Leg, Aug'64
    Point, 6 Nov'73; 19 Jun'71*; 2 Apr'71*
    Prime Otherness, 24 Sep'73
    Tetrahedron as Conceptual Model, Nov'71
    Vector, 21 Dec'71*
    Clusters, 7 Nov'73
    Minimum Limit Case, 12 May'75*
    Convergence & Divergence, 1 May'77*
    Six Motion Freedoms & Degrees of Freedom, (1)(2)

---

RBF DEFINITIONS

Resolution:

". . . Think about some of the limits of thinking of
what we call resolution. Just look at this ruler . . .
it is divided into centimeters and it is down to tenths
of centimeters. . . Or if you take an engineers' rule
and get down to hundredths of an inch a good eye can
see and resolve the black from the white, but beyond that
you stop operating and you see gray. These are
frequencies. From now on we really get into the phenomena
of frequency-- and then you see pink and yellow. I want
you to realize you are seeing something to do with
frequencies, where you do not have resolution of separation
and this is not at all mysterious. We realize how very
limited we are, and then when we begin to see things
superficially-- they are tactile-- we don't realize how
much confusion we are having on an extraordinary set of
frequencies."

- Cite Oregon Lecture #3, pp. ■■-100. 5 Jul'62

---

RBF DEFINITIONS

Resonance:

"... Lines are always curvilinearly realized because
of universal resonance, spinning, and orbiting."

- Citation and context at Line, 7 Nov'72

---

RBF DEFINITIONS

Resolvability Limits:

"The visual limits of 'now-you-see-it-now-you-don't,'
yes-no-yes-no, something-nothing-something-nothing, dot-dash-
dot-dash are relative size-scale discernabilities spoken of
technically as resolution. These resolvability limits of
the human eye may be pictured as follows:

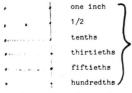

| | |
|---|---|
| • ┃ | one inch |
| •   • ┃ | 1/2 |
| •········ ┃ | tenths |
| •····· • | thirtieths |
| • ···· • | fiftieths |
| •   ┃ | hundredths |

} The Engineers' Scale

"The finest 'smooth' surface, intercolor-crossblending,
continuum photogravure printing is accomplished with a benday
screen which employs 200 unique color dots per each square
inch of printed surface."
- Cite SYNERGETICS 2 draft at Sec. 100.031; 30 Apr'77

---

RBF DEFINITIONS

Resonance:

"I'm talking about physics and the waves of the periodic
table... its unique frequencies would interact... and
what the permutations would be mathematically-- And I found
this highly suggestive that the octave with its characteristically flat resonance really governing the interactions of
frequencies. The resonances are the key to much of modern
physical exploration."

- Citation and context at Pythagoras (2), 18 Jun'71

---

Resolution:  Resolvability:                                  (1)

See Benday Screen
    Differentiation
    Point
    Tunability
    Abstraction vs. Resolution
    Unresolvable
    Frequency Islands of Perception
    Invisibility of Macro- and Micro Resolution
    Conceptual Genesis

---

RBF DEFINITIONS

Resonance Field:

"...Employing as a resonance field all the intertransforming
spheres and between-sphere spaces; and employing the myriadly
selectable, noninterfering frequencies of such propagatable
intertransformation resonance..."

- Citation and context at Atomic Computer Complex (8), 13 May'73

Resonance: Resonatability:                                    (1)


        See Feedback
            Omniinterresonated
            Oscillation
            Pulsation
            Synchro-resonance
            Tidal
            Zone of Neutral Resonance
            Omniresonant
            Heard & Unheard Resonances
            Wavelength, Frequency & Resonance
            Harmonic:  Harmony
            Tensed String
            Chords & Notes

---

RBF DEFINITIONS

    Resources:

    "... Spaceship Earth's prime resources belong to everybody."




        - Citation and context at Young World (1), 4 Jul'72

---

Resonance:  Resonatability:                                    (2)


        See Integer, 15 Oct'72
            Isotropic Vector Matrix, 16 Nov'72; 30 Nov'72
            Line, 7 Nov'72*
            Music, 4 Mar'69
            Observing vs. Articulating, Mar'71
            Octave, 18 Jun'71
            Point, 16 Nov'72
            Pythagoras, (2)*
            Synergetics Calculation, 30 Oct'72
            Time-size, 20 Dec'73
            Tunability, 19 Oct'72; 16 Nov'72
            Radiation-gravitation:  Harmonics, 3 Jan'75
            Womb of Permitted Ignorance, 13 Dec'73
            Metaphysical & Physical Tetrahedral Quanta,
                25 Mar'71
            Energy Involvement of 92 Elements, (1)
            Metaphysical & Physical, 13 Nov'75
            Aural, 22 Feb'77
            Olfactoral, 22 Feb'77
            Mites & Quarks as Basic Notes, (3)

---

Resource Effectiveness:


        See Industrial Man, 10 Oct'63
            Revolution by Inadvertence, 10 Oct'63

---

RBF DEFINITIONS

    Resources:

    "If there's so little of it, it must be used in a broad sense.
    I must never have helium in a retail pub; it must be in the tools
    that serve the tools....

    "I want to really do something, but I don't want to sell boron
    on the street-corner to use for toothpicks.  I want to see
    that everything is used where it's meant to be used."




    1st. Para - Cite Scrap Sorting & Mongering (3), 15 Jun'74

    2nd. Para - Cite Tape transcript, p.4; RBF to W. Wolf, 2 Jun'74

---

Resources:  Fresh vs. Waste:                                  (1)

        See Outbound Packaging of Human Food Waste

---

RBF DEFINITIONS

    Resources:

    "...All the 'cream rich' initial discoveries of original
    resource geography lodes become exhausted..."




        - Citation and context at Womb of Permitted Ignorance, 13 Dec'73,

---

Resources:  Fresh vs. Waste:                                  (2)

        See Biological Life, (2)

---

RBF DEFINITIONS

Resource Inadequacy:

"I also realize intuitively
That the elimination
Of the condition of resource inadequacy
And thereby the elimination of human want
May probably eliminate war
-- Or quick death--
Which is always consequent to the overlong protraction
Of the slow and more anguished poverty's
Slow dying
As brought about by lethal ignorance
In respect to the design revolution potentials
As society takes its only known recourse
In political actions..."

- Cite INTUITION, pp.63-64 May '72

---

Resource Inadequacy: (1)

See Inadequacy of Life Support
Scarcity: Not Enough to Go Around

---

Resource Inadequacy: (2)

See Political Revolution, 10 Oct'63
Selfishness, 22 Jun'75

---

Resource Integration:

See Leaders: Take Away the Leaders, 4 Jul'72

---

Resource Inventorying: (1)

See Satellite: World Satellite Sensing

---

Resource Inventorying: (2)

See Biosphere, (1)
Problem: Statement Of, Aug'72

---

RBF DEFINITIONS

Resource & Principle:

"Inventions are extemporaneous. They represent trial
balances of resource and principle drawn off in the light of
shifting needs."

- Citation & context at Inventions, 1947

---

Resource: Resources: (1)

See Pollution Control
Wilderness Resources

Resource: Resources:                                    (2)

    See Biological Life, (1)
        Biosphere, (1)(2)
        Leaders: Take Away the Leaders, 4 Jul'72
        Miniature Earth, 28 Apr'74
        Wealth, 1947 ; 20 Sep'76
        Womb of Permitted Ignorance, 13 Dec'73*
        World Game: Grand Strategy, 2 Jun'74
        Young World, 4 Jul'72*
        Intellect, 21 Jun'77

---

RBF DEFINITIONS

Responsibility:

"We are all equally responsible not only for the big
complementary surface areas which we develop on systems by
our every act. . . We are inherently responsible for the
transformation of Universe, inwardly, outwardly, and all
around every system which we alter."

- Citation and context at Spherical Triangle (4), 13 Nov'69

---

Resource: Resources:                                    (3)

    See Resource Effectiveness
        Resource Inadequacy
        Resource Integration
        Resource Inventorying
        Resource & Principle

---

RBF DEFINITIONS

Responsibility:

""... Up to the nineteenth century, or the beginning of the
twentieth century, what we could smell, see, hear, and
touch was what he meant by reality. I think to many in our
society today that is still what you mean by reality. Freud
and Mesmer shook society's concept of this kind of reality,
because man up to this time had been saying, because that is
reality, every human being knows just what he is doing. If
he is of sound mind, when he is awake, then he knows just
what he is doing. Therefore, he must be entirely responsible
for his every act. So as we developed laws, we made man
utterly responsible for his every act. But Freud and Mesmer,
through their hypnotism, were able to disclose behaviors of
human beings for which the human being was not responsible
at all. So this shook the idea of the courts, and we have
had to have psychiatrists and others come in to bring you a
reconsideration of the responsibilities of human beings.
Now, what has really not been paid attention to in our
society, again because we are all so specialized, is that
there is almost no tendency to look at the whole and to really
understand the whole."

- Cite RBF Address, THE HABITABLE CITY, 14 Oct. '69.

---

RBF DEFINITIONS

Responsible:

"We have to take the responsibility of being responsible.
So far we have not been very responsible. You don't say
to a new child, 'You'd better go back in there, you're
not very responsible...' They're just using words-- foxes
and daisies... I say: What might I do that made it logical
for man not to do these things? That's what I'm caring
about. That's what design science is."

- Citation and context at Spaceship (C), Feb'73

---

Responsibility:                                          (1)

    See Man's Conscious Participation in Evolution
        Doing What Needs to Be Done
        Everybody's Business

---

RBF DEFINITIONS

Responsibility:

"Our history of social customs indicates that until very
recently, when Freud offered evidence to the contrary, man
thought of his awake self as being utterly conscious. The
laws held people absolutely responsible for all their awake
acts. Reality was what could be seen, smelled, touched,
tasted, and heard. There was no popular awareness of sub-
or ultra-visible reality. There were beliefs of invisible
gods or demons playing tricks on the humans."

- Cite ARCHITECTURE AS ULTRA INVISIBLE REALITY, p. 149, Dec. '69

---

Responsibility:                                          (2)

    See Design Scientist, 30 Jan'75
        Publishing, 30 Jan'75
        Success, 10 Sep'75

RBF DEFINITIONS

Rest:  At Rest:

"The words 'at rest,' artificial, and failure are all
meaningless."

- Citation and context at Meaningless, Oct'66

---

Rest:  At Rest:                                                    (1)

See Immobility
    Instant Universe
    Newton's Cosmic Norm of "At Rest"
    No Change
    No Speed
    Static

---

Rest:  At Rest:                                                    (2)

See Norm of Einstein as Absolute Speed, Jun'56
    Radiation: Speed Of, (C)
    Future:  Man Backs into His Future, May'49
    Dynamic Equilibrium, 24 Apr'76

---

Restlessness:

    See Energetic Functions, 8 Aug'77

---

RBF DEFINITIONS

Rest of the Universe:

"The complementarity of the octahedron with the vector
equilibrium permits us to get down to the local and not
be afraid of missing the rest of the Universe, because we
know the fundamental complementations of macro tetra and
micro tetra.  We were always looking at the XYZ quadrant--
focusing on the quadrant at the center of the octahedron,
rather than on the functioning of the covariations."

- Citation and context at Trigonometric Limit, 22 Jun'72
- Cite SYNERGETICS draft At Sec. 1238.23, 3 Feb'73

---

RBF DEFINITIONS

Rest of the Universe:

". . . You and I are matched by the rest of the Universe.
There is an invisible hole-- a matrix of you and I sitting in
the Universe.  So it really isn't annihilated, but it is
nonlocally identifiable. . . "

- Citation and context at Invisible Hole, 16 Jun'72

---

RBF DEFINITIONS

Rest of the Universe:

"The Platonic Solids do not stand in a vacuum of Universe.
They are in Universe and if you change that thing you change
the rest of Universe.  Nothing can change locally without
changing everything else."

- Citation at Platonic Solids, 12 Jul'62

---

Rest of Universe Other than Earth:

    See Spherical Triangle Sequence, (iii)

Rest of Universe: (1)

See Local Change
        Motion Freedom from Rest of Universe
        Nonconceptuality

---

RBF DEFINITIONS

Restraints:

"Nothing stands in a vacuum of Universe. Nothing can change
locally without changing everything else. We have to look
for conditions where there is permitted transformability and
where there is some really great unanimity of degrees of
freedom. We see that certain kinds of patterns accrue from
certain numbers of restraints. You could see how planar
things could happen as a consequence of two restraints and how
linear things could happen as a consequence of three
restraints. (See Sec. 401, Twelve Vectors of Restraint Define
minimum System.) We see, then, that we are in a Universe
where there is a certain limited number of permitted freedoms.
Synergetics discovers that whatever is rigidly related to
anything else discloses 12 restraints. There are a minimum
of 12 restraints in developing anything we might call a
rigidly related set of events."

- Cite SYNERGETICS text at Sec. 537.01; RBF modified and
  deleted much of text on galley, 7 Nov'73, but EJA
  reinstated text to conform to manuscript of Dec'71.

---

Rest of Universe: (2A)

See Allspace Filling: Octahedron & Ve, 22 Jun'72
        Eternity: Equation Of, 27 May'72
        Event, 1968
        Invisible Hole, 16 Jun'72
        Local Entity, 1960
        Nonmirror Image, 13 Jun'74
        Orbiting, 5 Jun'73
        Key-keyhole Sequence, (1)(2)
        Platonic Solids, 12 Jul'62*
        Plus One, 9 Jul'62
        Rubber Tires, (4)
        Sphere, (1)
        Tetrahedron: Coordinate Symmetry, 10 Jul'62
        Thinkable System Takeout, (2)
        Thinking, (1)
        Trigonometric Limit, 22 Jun'72*

---

RBF DEFINITIONS

Restraints: (1)

"I've got a way of checking degrees of freedom. I said
there is myself and the universe, and I see a hole in the
stars. I try to shoot out through the stars. I go like
the Pleiades; the stars get closer and closer together. I seem
to be very far. All the stars in the rest of the universe
are in one huddle, and I am over here. . ."

"I can't get away from the universe: one tension restraint.
I can do as a tetherball; you hit it and make any kind of a
spherical form that you want. . . I give myslef now two
restraints, I only had one restraint, now I have two
restraints, not as if I were a ball in the middle of a
music string. I can still move but I can only move in a
plane. I give myself a third restraint: I am in a drumhead;
I can still move, but only in a line. Then I give myself a
fourth restraint and first I am pulling the drumhead in
one direction and I seem to be immobilized. . . . I found
that even though semi-immobilized, you could put a monkey-
wrench on it and it would contort. . .

"I had to get each one of the four restraints; they had to
be three-folded and come in tangentially, making a total of 12.
There would be six positive and six negative, corresponding

SYSTEM  SEC  408.1 +2+3  - Cite Ledgemont Lab. Lecture, p.52, 15 Oct'64

---

Rest of Universe: (2B)

See Universal Joint: Tetrahedron, 9 Nov'73
        Minimum Sphere, Aug'71
        Quantum Sequence, (5)
        Time is Only Now, 19 Jul'76
        In, Out & Around, 17 May'77
        Human Beings & Complex Universe, (4)

---

RBF DEFINITIONS

Restraints: (2)

"to the six edges of the tetrahedron, negative and positive...
They keep showing up in these models.

"You are trying to make a wire wheel. How many spokes does it
take? You have to have three out this way and three out that
way to keep the hub from shimmying. You have to take care of
the rotation and the torque-- that way and this way-- we had
six... multiply each of these ▓▓▓▓▓ by two... comes 12.
You cannot have a wire wheel with less than 12 spokes."

- Cite Ledgemont Lab. lecture, p.53, 15 Oct'64

---

RBF DEFINITIONS

Restraints:

"Six restraints are essential to structure and pattern
stability."

- Cite RBF marginalia to SYNERGETICS 2 draft at Sec. 400.664;
  8 Aug'77

---

RBF DEFINITIONS

Restraints:
"The Platonic Solids do not stand
Nothing "Stands in a vacuum of Universe. Nothing can change
locally without changing everything else. We have to look
for conditions where there is permitted transformability
and where there is some really great unanimity and I have
been looking for degrees of freedom-- ways in which this
could happen, the kinds of patterns that accrue to one
restraint, two restraints and so forth. You could see how
linear things could happen as the consequence of three
restraints and how planar things could happen as the
consequence of two restraints and so forth. We then get
into a Universe of a certain number of permitted freedoms
and I have discovered that nothing was-- you might say--
rigidly related to anything else unless there were twelve
restraints so there was a minimum of twelve restraints to
develop anything we might call rigidly related set of events."

- Cite Oregon Lecture #8, p. 285. 12 Jul'62

12 DEGREES OF FREEDOM - SEC. 537.01

RBF DEFINITIONS

Restraints:

"Here are those degrees of freedom that I spoke about and illustrated where we have the single ball able to move to all kinds of patterns, but when there are two restraints they can only move in a plane, when there are three restraints they can only move in a line, and with four restraints it stays fixed, but it can rotate locally."

- Cite OREGON Lecture #6, p. 208, 10 Jul'62

---

Restructurings:

See Unstructurings & Restructurings

---

Restraint Focus:

See Aberration, 19 Dec'73

---

RBF DEFINITIONS

Resultant:

"The resultant was not recognized until it was realized that light had a speed."

- Cite RBF at Penn Bell videotaping session, Philadelphia. PA., 20 Jan'75

---

Restraints:                                                    (1)

See Degrees of Freedom
    Inventions which Decrease the Degrees of Freedom
    Mast in the Earth
    Me Ball
    Otherness Restraints
    Vectors ≠ Restraints

---

RBF DEFINITIONS

Resultant:

"Now, up to the speed of light measurement, engineers spoke of every action as having a reaction and it was thought by the engineers-- because the public didn't understand-- that every action had a reaction. Little man is so small, and Earth is so big, he doesn't realize that when he steps this way, he's pushing the Earth the other way. But you can feel it in an automobile when it accelerates rapidly, shoving the pebbles in the opposite direction. Now with the speed of light measurements, we discover while the speed of light is very great, say 700 million miles an hour. . . While, That's very fast, it is very slow in contrast to no time at all. And the engineers have not updated their thinking since the speed of light. They hadn't realized the speed of light had anything to do with their action and reaction. But because there is now no instantaneity, no simultaneity, there is always some energy lag, and time is involved here. Therefore every action not only has a reaction but it has its resultant, and the resultant and the reaction are not the same. So we now realize that every energy event is characterized not only by a reaction but also by a resultant."

- Cite RBF at SIMS, U.Mass, Amherst 22 July '71, pp 19-20

---

Restraints:                                                    (2)

See Lifetime:  Personal Lifetime Experience for
    Elective Investment, 31 May'74
    Ellipse, 20 Jan'75

---

Resultant as Disturbance Diminishing:

See Precession & Degrees of Freedom, (1)

Resultant: (1)

See Action
   Action-reaction-resultant
   Interference
   Reaction
   Z Cobras
   Integrated Vectorial Resultant
   Vectorial Model of Interference

---

Returning Upon Itself: Systems
Return Upon Themselves:

"To be able to return upon itself is a chracteristic of
all systems. A plane would go on to infinity, so to form
a system you would have to take an angle out."

- Cite RBF at Students International Meditation Seminar,
   U. Mass., Amherst, 22 July '71, p. 10

SYSTEM- SEC. 400.08

---

Resultant: (2)

See In, Out & Around, Nov'71

---

Returning Upon Itself: Systems Return Upon Themselves: (1)

See Closed System
   Embracement
   Finite
   Geometrical Integrity
   Nature Always Comes Back on Itself
   Patterns of Experience Return Upon Themselves
      in All Directions
   Wave Returns Upon Itself

---

RBF DEFINITIONS

Retirement:

"Retirement was invented by the insurance companies.
There are 9,000 Ph.D.'s in physics today and only 2,000
of them have jobs."

- Cite RBF at Penn Bell videotaping, Philadelphia, 28 Jan'75

---

Returning Upon Itself: Systems Return Upon Themselves: (2A)

See Closed System, 26 May'72
   Comprehension, Dec'61
   Congruence, 25 Jan'72
   Considerable Set, 1959
   Finite, 13 Nov'69
   Gears, 7 Nov'73
   Geometrical Integrity, 25 May'72
   Infinity & Finity, Jun'66
   Interference, 15 Oct'64
   Motion, 4 Feb'68
   Omnidirectional, 23 Sep'73
   Polygon, Jun'66
   Prime Structural Systems, 11 Jul'62 ; 3 Nov'73
   Radiation: Speed Of, 22 Jun'72
   Simultaneous, 5 Jul'62
   System, (1)(2)
   Thinkability, 1 May'71
   Triangle, 5 Jul'62

---

Retirement: Retiring:

See Squatters, (1)(2)
   Building Industry, (2)

---

Returning Upon Itself: Systems Return Upon Themselves: (2B)

See Vector, 25 May'72
   Vectors Are Real, 23 May'72
   Vertexes, Faces & Lines, 1 Jan'75
   Plane, 19 Feb'72; 13 Nov'69
   General Systems Theory, (A)

Return to Modelability:                                    (1)

      See Modelability
         Science: Gap Between Science & the Humanities

---

Reverse Atomics:                                          (1)

      See Electrostatic Generating

---

Return to Modelability:                                    (2)

      See Artist, 6 Jul'62
         Powering, (1)(2)
         Synergetics, Dec'72; 30 Dec'73
         Xyz Coordinate System, 1965

---

Reverse Atomics:                                          (2)

      See Lightning & Atoms, 28 Apr'74

---

Reverify: Reverifiable:

      See Unknown: All the Unknown, 13 May'73

---

Reverse Fountain Flow:

      See Wind Stress & Houses, (9)

---

RBF DEFINITIONS

      ▬▬▬ Reverse Atomics:

"Maybe we ought to try to capture lightning in electrostatic
generators underground: build up charges of lightning and then
release it later.

"We might really reverse our atomics: instead of learning how
to release atomic energy we could learn how to make the atoms
and how to employ the exponential increase of their gravitational
energy as their components are allowed to self-assemble themselves."

- Cite tape transcript, DSI Project; RBF to W. Wolf, pp.10-11,
  28 Apr'74; as rewritten by RBF at 3200 Idaho, 10 Sep'74

---

RBF DEFINITIONS

      ▬▬▬ Reverse Optimism:

"Optimism is usually thought of as constituting a mildly
unwarranted hopefulness in respect to the future. But there
is a reverse projection of optimism in the nostalgia-
generated myths that recall only the rare and sublime moments
of yesterday. Forgetting the negative, reverse optimism
overemphasizes, thus deliberately shuts its eyes to reality,
and is therefore unable to see the values immediately present.

"I am convinced that we are swiftly emerging from the abysmal
conformities of yesterday's illiterate, spit-punctuated
profanity and monosyllabic verbalism, in which rags, filth,
diseased bodies, prevalent stenches, devastating superstition,
and local bias reigned supreme."

         (Compare with Conformity, 10 Oct'63 - EJA)

- Cite THE PROSPECT FOR HUMANITY, WDSB Doc. 3, p.74, Aug'64

RBF DEFINITIONS

Reversibility:

". . . The syntropic vector equilibrium's reversibility--
inwardly-outwardly-- is the basis for the gravitationally
maintained integrity of Universe."

- Citation at Star Tetrahedron, 8 Oct'71

- Cite SYNERGETICS draft "Antitetrahedron," 8 Oct. '71, p. 8.

---

Review:

See View & Review

---

RBF DEFINITIONS

Reversibility:

"Each vector is reversible having its negative alternate."

-Cite SYNERGETICS Corollaries, Sec. 240. 1970

- Citation & context at Vector, Oct'59

---

RBF DEFINITIONS

Revolution:

"The revolution is not being effected by pulling the top
down. It is being effected by pulling the bottom up. It is
being effected by doing more with ever less in such a manner
as to take care of all without taking away the functional
capabilities and fundamental advantages of any. The surprise--
constantly doing vastly more with ever fewer physical
resources per function-- is our legacy from the millenia-long
armaments struggle to do more with less in a world where a
pea-size transistor now does more than an army of yesterday
and a fistful of atomic fuel takes a large ship around the
Earth."

- Cite THE PROSPECT FOR HUMANITY, WDSD Doc. 3, p. 65, Aug'64

---

Reversibility: (1)

        See Inward & Outwardness
            Irreversibility
            Obverse & Reverse
            Opposite: Opposition
            Moving Picture Run Backwards
            Negative
            Future: Man Back Into His Future
            Mirror Reversal
            Darwin: Evolution May Be Going the Other Way
            Enantiodromia

---

Revolution: Design Science Revolution vs. Global
                      Political Revolution:

        See Montreal Expo'67 Dome, (B)

---

Reversibility: Reverse: (2)

        See Energy, 16 Sep'67
            Star Tetrahedron, 8 Oct'71*
            Star Tetrahedron & VE, 9 Nov'73
            Vector, Oct'59*
            Vector Equilibrium, (I); 8 Oct'71
            Implosion- explosion, Jun'66
            Octahedron as Conservation & Annihilation Model,
              23 May'75
            Error, 30 May'75

---

RBF DEFINITIONS

Revolution: Hard Revolution + Soft Revolution: (1)

"The exponentially accelerating rate
of a new world order realization
is irreversibly emergent
through chain reaction emergencies
transpiring as a primarily invisible
soft revolution
As omni humanity's critical thoughts
break out as news events,
with the break-outs too swiftly shifting
their geography
and too frequently multiplying and altering
their run-off routes
to develop any local power clotures
and consequent burst-out bores
of sufficient local magnitude
to detonate full scale hard world revolution,
yet so far out-performing hard revolutions
in omni egalitarian social advancement--
by elevating the bottom
instead of depressing the top--
Thereby arriving at a world's socio-economic ocean
which levels spherically
to contain any magnitude of local energy outbursts
as storms or volcanoes

RBF DEFINITIONS

Revolution:  Soft Revolution + Hard Revolution:     (2)

"Whose violence is swiftly dissipated
by circumferential hydraulic wave displacements.
The brimming ocean wave of commonwealth
is bound radially by gravity
in spherical mantle unity.
Thereafter, the ocean will pulse
only in world tidal integrity
as an omniliterate, closed sphere system democracy
consciously, spontaneously, instantly
rearticulating its responses
to world around electro-telepathetic info-waves.

- Cite EVOLUTIONARY 1972-1975 ABOARD SPACE VEHICLE EARTH, Jan. '72.

---

Revolution:     (1)

See Communications Revolution
    Design Revolution
    Education Revolution
    Geosecial Revolution
    Political Revolution

---

RBF DEFINITIONS

Revolution By Inadvertence:

"Each nation has been looking out for itself and each man
within the nations has been looking out for himself and his
family!  Therefore the surprising and continual increase in
the proportion of world humanity being served at ever higher
industrial standards . . . cannot be attributed in any way
to any consciously organized effort of humanity to make the
resources go further.  It is in no way attributable to
chariAtble gifts.

"Forced to look elsewhere for an explanation, we find that
the increase in the world's numbers who are prospering has
been brought about entirely by indirection and inadvertence
as the consequence of man's earlier heavy and prime subsidy
of weapons race evolution."

- Cit MEXICO '63, p.8, 10 Oct '63

---

Revolution:     (2)

See Birth, 22 Dec'74
    News & Evolution, (3)

---

Revolution by Inadvertence:     (1)

See Evolution by Inadvertence

---

Rewarding:

See Re-rewarding
    Operant Psychology

---

Revolution by Inadvertence:     (2)

See Economic Accounting System:  Human Life-hour
    Production, (2)
    Geosocial Revolution, (1)
    Ignorance, (1)(2)

---

Re-wow:

See Wow:  The Last Wow

RBF DEFINITIONS

Rhombic Dodecahedron:

"The total space is 24--with the vector equilibrium's
Eighth Octahedra extraverted to form the rhombic dodecahedron.

"For every space there is always an alternate space: this
is where we get the 48-nesss of the rhombic dodecahedron as
the domain of a sphere.

$$2\tfrac{1}{2} \times 8 = 20$$

$$6 \times 8 = 48$$

(Incorporated in SYNERGETICS 2 draft at Sec. 1033.184)

- Cite RBF to EJA, 3200 Idaho, Wash. DC: 12 May'77

---

RBF DEFINITIONS

Rhombic Dodecahedron:

"The rhombic dodecahedron is the most faceted, identical
faceted (diamond) polyhedron and accounts, congruently and
symmetrically, for all the isotropic-vector-matrix vertexes
in closest packed spheres and their 'tween' spaces.  Each
rhombic dodecahedron's diamond face is at the long-axis center
of each coupler (Vol. = 1) asymmetrical octahedron, with each
of the rhombic dodecahedra sharing it 12 omni-adjacent
spherics..."

- Citation and context at Coupler (1)(2), 22 Mar'73

---

RBF DEFINITIONS

Rhombic Dodecahedron:

"The rhombic dodecahedron is the domain of omni-closest-
packed spheres; the middle of its diamond face is the
control point for the sphere's radius, the unity vector."

※ Citation & context at Triacontrahedron as Limit Regular
Polyhedron, 13 Apr'77

---

RBF DEFINITIONS

Rhombic Dodecahedron:

"The fact that the rhombic dodecahedron can have its 144
modules oriented as either introvert-extrovert, or as
three-way circumferential, provides its valvability between
broadcasting-transceiving and noninterference relaying.
The first radio tuning crystal must have been a rhombic
dodecahedron."

- Cite SYNERGETICS draft at Sec. 426.43 [42], 30 Nov'72

---

RBF DEFINITIONS

Rhombic Dodecahedron:

"The rhombic dodecahedron, like the cube, fills allspace.
It has a volume of six.  It is the epitome of the behavior
of closest packing.  The rhombic dodecahedron is the domain
of a sphere = spheric."

- Citation & context at Vectorial & Vertexial Geometry, (20,
27 Jan'75

---

RBF DEFINITIONS

Rhombic Dodecahedron:

"The rhombic dodecahedron symmetrically fill allspace in
symmetric consort with the isotropic vector matrix.  Each
rhombic dodecahedron defines exactly the unique and omnisimilar domain of every radiantly alternate vertex of the
isotropic vector matrix as well as the unique and omnisimilar
domains of ▆▆▆ each and every interior-exterior vertex of any
aggregate of closest packed, uniradius spheres whose respective
centers will always be congruent with every radiantly alternate
vertex of the isotropic vector matrix, with the corresponding
set of alternate vertexes always occurring at all the intertangency points of the closest packed spheres."

= Cite SYNERGETICS draft at Sec. 426.21 [20], 30 Nov'72

---

RBF DEFINITIONS

Rhombic Dodecahedron:

"The rhombic dodecahedron contains the most volume with the
least surface of all the allspace-filling geometrical forms,
ergo, rhombic dodecahedra are the most economical allspace
subdividers of Universe.  The rhombic dodecahedra fill and
symmetrically subdivide allspace most economically, while
simultaneously, symmetrically, and exactly defining the respective domains of each sphere as well as the spaces between
the spheres, the respective shares of the inter-closest-
packed-sphere interstitial space."

- Cite RBF rewrite of SYNERGETICS galley at Sec. 426.21,
2 Nov'73

---

RBF DEFINITIONS

Rhombic Dodecahedron:

"The rhombic dodecahedron six is entirely outside, but
twelvefoldedly tangential to, the initial sphere..."

- Citation and context at Constant Relative Abundance, 29 Nov'72

RBF DEFINITIONS

### Rhombic Dodecahedron:

"The rhombic dodecahedron can be put together with MITE's and so it is all-space filling.

"The symmetrical arrays of the rhombic dodecahedron may explain the chemical compoundings of periodic atomics."

- Cite RBF to EJA, 3200 Idaho, DC, 25 Feb '72

---

RBF DEFINITIONS

### Rhombic Dodecahedron:

"I employ . . . the icosahedron and the rhombic dodecahedron in almost all the geometrical forms where one or another provides unique economic advantage. I use the rhombic dodecahedron as the hub of my octahedron-tetrahedron truss-- the octet truss. Its twelve facets represent the planes perpendicular to the six fundamental degrees of freedom."

- Cite RBF Ltr. to Steve Baer, 19 Apr'66

ISOTROPIC VECTOR MATRIX - SEC. 426.04

---

RBF DEFINITIONS

### Rhombic Dodecahedron:

"Nature always starts over again with the isotropic vector matrix. Energy is not lost; just not available.

"At the heart of the vector equilibrium is the ball in the center of the rhombic dodecahedron at the core-- the one sphere all by itself. You put 12 rhombic dodecahedra around one central rhombic dodecahedron and you get the vector equilibrium.

"This is why synergetics can investigate nuclear symmetries: it all comes out absolutely discretely. And it does have both the A and B Quanta Modules in it. Look at the picture /MARKS, p. 167, Pl. L.8._/ which shows the one-half of the rhombic dodecahedron. Of all the polyhedra nothing really falls into a group so easily as the rhombic dodecahedron, the most common polyhedron in nature."

- Cite RBF to EJA, 3200 Idaho, Wash., DC, 24 Feb. '72

---

RBF DEFINITIONS

### Rhombic-Dodecahedron:

"The rhombic-Dodecahedron" has a volume of "six." The rhombic-Dodecahedron is an all space filler like the cube. . . . This is one of the most common naturally occuring crystals."

- Cite Carbondale Draft
  Nature's Coordination, p. VI.20

- Cite Oregon # , p.224, 11 Jul'62

---

RBF DEFINITIONS

### Rhombic Dodecahedron:

"The rhombic dodecahedron is fundamentally associative."

- Cite RBF to EJA, 3200 Idaho, Washington DC, 24 Jan '72

---

RBF DEFINITIONS

### Rhombic Dodecahedron #1:   United Sphere:

"In the rhombic dodecahedron #1 there is one sphere integrated at the center. The A and B Quanta Modules as viewed at the peak from above are arrayed around a united sphere. It represents the proton model."

▪ A's
▪ B's

- Cite RBF to EJA, 3200 Idaho, Wash. DC, 24 Feb '72 + 22 Feb holograph.

---

RBF DEFINITIONS

### Rhombic Dodecahedron:

"Sixth powering is all the perpendiculars to the rhombic dodecahedron which is all the internal truncations of the tetrahedron."

- Cite RBF to EJA, Bear Island, 25 August 1971.

- Citation at Powering: Sixth Powering, 25 Aug'71

---

RBF DEFINITIONS

### Rhombic Dodecahedron #2:  Fractionated Sphere:

"In the rhombic dodecahedron #2 there are a large variety of asymmetrical interior aggregations. There is one sphere disintegrated into six symmetrically deployed parts. The A and B Quanta Modules as viewed at the peak from above are arrayed around a fractionated sphere. It represents the neutron model."

▪ A's
▪ B's

- Cite RBF to EJA, 3200 Idaho, Wash, DC, 24 Feb '72
  + RBF Holograph of 22 Feb '72.

Rhombic Dodecahedron:                                          (1)

See Dodecahedron
    Spheric
    Spheric Domain
    Vector Equilibrium Involvement Domain
    Minimum Limit Case:  Hexagon & Rhombic Dodecahedron


Rhythm:                                                        (1)

See Pulse Pattern


Rhombic Dodecahedron:                                          (2)

See A & B quanta Modules, 10 Jul'62
    Constant Relative Abundance, 29 Nov'72*
    Coupler, 5 Apr'73; 20 Dec'73; (1)(2)*
    Isotropic Vector Matrix, Feb'72
    Octet Truss, 1959
    Powering:  Sixth Dimension, 9 Nov'73
    Powering:  Sixth Powering, 25 Aug'71*
    Vectorial & Vertexial Geometry, (2)*
    Mite:  Positive & Negative Functions, (1)(2)
    Domains of Interferences, 7 Nov'73
    Domain of a Point, 7 Nov'73
    Stable & Unstable Structures, 7 Jun'72
    Vector Equilibrium Involvement Domain, 11 Dec'75
    Quantum Mechanics: Minimum Geometrical Fourness,
      (2)-(4)
    Triclinic, 31 Aug'76
    Triacontrahedron as Limit Regular Polyhedron,
      13 Apr'77 *
    Quanta Loss by Congruence, (2)
    Triacontrahedron, 13 May'77
    Vector Equilibrium:  Potential & Primitive Tetravolumes,
      12 May'77


Rhythm:                                                        (2)

See Montessori System, 1928
    Pole Vaulter, 2 Jul'75
    Ghana Dome:  Self-chilling Machine, (1)


Rhombic:                                                       (1)

See Antirhombic


Ribbon:

See Pattern Strip
    Wrapability
    Tetrascroll


Rhombic:                                                       (2)

See Tensegrity:  Unlimited Frequency of Geodesic
    Tensegrities, (2)


Rich Man Drowning in Shipwreck:

See Wealth, (A)(B)
    Wealth as "Know-how", (1)

# Synergetics Dictionary

Richter Transformation:

    See Octahedron as Conservation & Annihilation Model, (4)
        Octahedron as Photosynthesis Model,(D)

---

RBF DEFINITIONS

Right:

"Now, what we call thinkable is always outside-out.
What we call space is just exactly as real, but it is
inside-out. There is no such thing as right and left!"

- Cite Tape transcript RBF to BO'R, Carbondale Dome, 1 May 1971.
- Citation at Parity, 1 May'71

---

Richter: Don:

    See Curvature: Compound, Aug'72
        Triacon, 22 Jun'72

---

RBF DEFINITIONS

Right Angle:

"The Greeks knew a right angle, but they never called it
90 degrees."

- RBF on telephone to EJA from Philadelphia, 25 Nov'73

---

TEXT CITATIONS

Riemann, G.F.R:

Robt. W. Mors, p. 44 : 1960

Synergetics : Sec. 522.22

---

Right Angle:                                                    (1)

    See Ninety Degreeness
        Rectilinear
        Roads Turn at Right Angles
        No Right Angles in Nature

---

Riemann, George Friedrich Bernhard: (1826-1866)

    See Spherical Triangle Sequence, (V)
        Geodesics, (1)(2)

---

Right Angle:                                                    (2)

    See Tidal, 15 Oct'64
        Model of Toothpicks & Semi-dried Peas, (1)

Right to Live:  Proving Your Right to Live:                    (1)


See Earning A Living

---

Right-over-Might:                                             (2)


See Continuous Man (5)
    Design Revolution, 6 Mar'74
    Ephemeralization, 1938
    Rationalization Sequence (2)(3)
    Society:  Control Of, 1938
    Superstition of Social Superiority, 1946

---

Right to Live:  Proving your Right to Live:                   (2)


See Fuller, R.B:  Crisis of 1927, 26 Sep'68
    Superstition of Social Superiority, 1946

---

Right:


See Doing Right things for Wrong Reasons
    Left & Right

---

RBF DEFINITIONS

'Right Makes Might' Dominance:

"Great historical leaders have always hoped that we may be
trending from 'might makes right' to 'right makes might'
dominance, which means from a rooted, programed creature,
a 'specialist'-- just going after its own honey and stinging
others who interfere with its program-- to an ecologically
cognizant, spontaneously synergetic, omni-integration of
cosmic functioning. . . ."


- Citation and context at Ecology Sequence (G), 5 Jun'73

---

RBF DEFINITIONS

Rigid:

"Rigid means 'sized'-- arbitrarily sized.  'Rigid' is always
special case."


- Citation and context at Scheme of Reference, 24 Sep'73

---

Right-over-Might:                                             (1)


See Individual Rights
    Lincoln
    Metabilical Cord
    Might Makes Right
    Mind-over-Matter
    Mind-over-Muscle
    Metaphysical Transcendent of the Physical

---

RBF DEFINITIONS

Rigidity:

D. Bohm, Foundations of Physics, Vol. 1, No.4, 1971, p.369:

"The new order and measure introduced in relativity theory
implies new notions of structure, in which the idea of a
rigid body can no longer play a key role."

RBF Comment:

"Generalization of tetrahedra utterly independent of rigidity."


- Cite RBF marginalia at QUANTUM THEORY AS INDICATION OF NEW
ORDER IN PHYSICS, p.369, done Aug'73

RBF DEFINITIONS

Rigidity:

"This [thirty strut tensegrity dome] is made out of
steel turnbuckles and could be tightened into a very tight
structure. As you tighten it up it ▬ simply means that
the frequencies increase, it gets higher and higher pitched,
and finally gets to a point where you don't seem to have
any audible tone at all and you call it rigid. In other
words then, what we call the rigid structures are not
because they are redundant in nature, the atoms, but
because they are at a non-aurally tunable frequency."

- Cite OREGON Lecture #5 - p. 181 , 9 Jul'62

---

Rigid: Rigidity: (2)

See Chemical Bonds, May'72
    Rectilinear Frame, 24 Sep'73
    Scheme of Reference, 24 Sep'73*
    Triangle, 8 Oct'64; 1960
    Prime Nuclear Structural Systems, 27 Dec'74
    Chemical Bonds: Triple Bond, 19 Dec'73
    Light on Scratched Metal, 9 Nov'73

---

RBF DEFINITIONS

Rigidity vs. Resilience:

"Rigid structural systems consist of whole or truncated
interior tetrahedra. If the truncated tetrahedra are shoal
enough and if the frequency of the system is high enough, the
surface's structural triangles' edge legs may permit resilient
bending which will allow an exterior vertex to dimple inwardly
of the structural system."

- Cite SYNERGETICS, 2nd. Ed. at Sec. 1071.24, 20 Dec'74

---

RBF DEFINITIONS

Ring:

"Rings are lines . . . which are all inherently curved
and must eventually meet or rejoin their ends."

- Citation, context, and sketch at Two (2), 10 Jan'50

---

Rigid = Sized:

See Scheme of Reference, 24 Sep'73

---

Ring:

See Moebius Strip, 10 Jan'50
    Two, (2)*

---

Rigid: Rigidity: (1)

See Crystal: Crystalline
    Inflexibility
    Rigidity vs. Resilience
    Rigid = Sized

---

RBF DEFINITIONS

River: You Might as Well Jump in the River:

"... People who like to be prosaic and like to make man
feel so small can say everything is just going to turn out to
be inanimate chemistry and you are all the consequence of
probabilities and you might as well jump in the river."

- Citation and context at Threshold of Life, 6 Jul'62

River: (1)

See Boats at Anchor Retard the River's Flow
Bridge
River: You Might as Well Jump in the River

---

Roads: Roadway Systems: (2)

See Tools: Craft & Industrial, (2)

---

River: (2)

See Lever (II)
Naga, (3)

---

Robertson, Donald, W:

See Invention Sequence, (A)-(D)

---

Roads Turn at Right Angles:

See Local Squareness, 9 Jul'62

---

RBF DEFINITIONS

Robin Hood Sequence: (1)

"The chronofile persuaded me ten years after its inception to
start my life as nearly new as is humanly possible to do. It
persuaded me to dedicate my life to others instead of myself.
Not on an altruistic basis but because the chronofile for the
first 32 years of my life clearly demonstrated that I was
positively effective in producing wealth only when I was
dedicated to others. Further chronofile observations then
showed me that the larger the number for whom I worked the
more positively effective I became.

"Thus it became obvious through the chronofile that if I worked
for all of humanity I would be optimally effective. Setting out
to start life all over again, I did not try to make myself a
new, or a different, man, another man. I sought only to allow
myself to articulate my own innate motivational integrity
instead of trying to accommodate everyone else's prefabricated
credos, educational theories, romances, and mores that had
occurred in my first life.

"One basic tenet of my new volition was that whatever was to
be accomplished for anyone must never be at the cost of another.
Robin Hood was a story my father read aloud to me when I was"

- Tape transcript #6, Side A, p.17; RBF to Barry Farrell;
Bear Island, 16 Aug'70

---

Roads: Roadway Systems: (1)

See Automobile as Only Half the Invention
Freeways
Highways

---

RBF DEFINITIONS

Robin Hood Sequence: (2)

"very young, not long before my father died. Robin Hood became
my most influential early years' mythical hero. This meant that
in my first life I had improvised methods in general to effect
swift moral and romantic justice for those whom I'd found in
trouble or danger. Foolishly self-confident in my first life,
I had often rushed thoughtlessly to assume responsibilities
beyond my physical and legal means. This rashness led me into
complex dilemmas, for in an attempt to keep my assumptions of
responsibility legal, I inadvertently borrowed from my unwitting
family dragging them into preposterous financial sacrifices

"In inaugurating my new life I took away Robin Hood's long bow
and staff and gave him only scientific textbooks, microscopes,
calculating machines, transits in industrialization and a
network of tooling in general: I made him substitute new and
inanimate forms for animate reform. I did not allow Robin any
further public relations professionals or managers or agents to
promote or sell him. It seemed obvious that if the new tools
that the new Robin Hood did develop could provide valid man
advantage increases, they would inevitably be adopted by
society in general as the inexorable emergencies which dictate
the proper rate of regenerative gestation of evolution took place."

- Tape transcript, 6A, Side A, pp.17-18; RBF to Barry Farrell;
Bear Island, 16 Aug'70

Robin Hood Sequence:

      See Consideration for Others
         Golden Rule

Rock:  Rocks:                           (2)

      See Artifact, 26 Jan'75
         Weather, Feb'73

RBF DEFINITIONS

Rock:

"I begin to look at all these rocks, and it doesn't look like anything.  Then I begin to pick them up, and I pick up any rock, and I find it has a beautiful face here, and them another beautiful face, another beautiful face... These are not carelessley done.  You begin to study these rocks a little more, and you find face, face, face, face.  Their corners have been knocked off...but all of these rocks were once tetrahedrons."

- Cite RBF to Cam Smith in RBF TO CHILDREN OF EARTH, Dec'72

Rockabye Baby:

      See Fear, 1938

Rocks Don't Love:

      See Youth, Truth & Love, 1 Apr'73
         Fuller, R.B: On Christopher Morley, 22 Jun'77

Rockefeller, David:

      See Cosmic Accounting, 2 Jun'74

Rock:  Rocks:                           (1)

      See Pebble
         Roundness
         Stone
         Gibraltar: Rock Of
         Scenario of the Child

Rocketable Logistics:

      See Airspace Technology, 20 Sep'76

Rockets: Steerable Rockets:                     (1)

    See Tracer Bullet Sequence

---

Rods:

    See Closest Pcking of Rods

---

Rockets: Steerable Rockets:                     (2)

    See Locality, May'71
    Measurement, Jun'66

---

Rogers, Will:

    See Funambulist, 1938

---

Rockets: Rocketry:                              (1)

    See Four Nosimultaneous Rocket Bursts

---

RBF DEFINITIONS

Rollability of Polyhedra:

"The more evenly faceted and the more uniform the radii of the respective polygonal members of the hierarchy of symmetrical polyhedra, the more closely they approach rollable sphericity. The four-facet tetrahedron, the six-faceted cube, and the eight-faceted octahedron are not very rollable, but the 12-faceted, one-sphere-containing rhombic dodecahedron, the 14-faceted vector equilibrium, and the 14-faceted tetrakaideca-hedron are easily rollable."

- Cite RBF insert at SYNERGETICS galley, Sec. 942.70, 20 Dec'73

---

Rockets: Rocketry:                              (2)

    See Buildings as Machines, (2)
    Twelve-inch Steel World Globe, (A)
    General Systems Theory, (B)

---

RBF DEFINITIONS

Rolls:

"We want to think about production and getting then films and environments under controls, separating from outside to inside. There is no way man develops such high speed production as in rolling devices that produce sheet steel at fantastic rates coming out from those rollers-- and film which can be such barriers. And the other one is paper-making. You make a number of rollers of paper and you have two of them coming together and corrugated ones in between and gluing them together, making the corrugated paper board out of half paper is very good; it has a very high wet tensile strangth-- doesn't bother it at all if it gets wet. But as you have something coming out of rolls, the roll going around, and you have another roll, and there's a printing press. So you can get some newspaper coming out. And so you can ▉▉ print information. . . Any kind of shapes you want, any picture. So I find then you can do any complex kind of work you want and print it right out on your paper-board as it comesout at fantastic high speed, and not only print it, you can put a little groove in it. You press the paper down, and that's the way you want it to fold. And paperboard domes can really be produced at a fantastic rate."

- Cite Univ. of Alaska Address, pp.39-40, 20 Apr '72

RBF DEFINITIONS

Rolls:

"Of all the materials that man can produce fast
the things that come out of rolls are the fastest.
Newsprint is the fastest thing he can produce."

- Cite RBF tape of CHARAS Script
14 March 1971

---

Roll: Rolls:      (1)

See Cleave-roll
    Log: Fireplace Log

---

Roll: Rolls: Rolling:     (2)

See Invention Sequence (B)
    Evaginating, 22 Jun'75
    Tetrascroll, (1)
    Hex-pent Sphere: Transformation into Geodesic
      Spiral Tube, (1)(2)
    Four Intergeared Mobility Freedoms, 2 Nov'73
    Membranes, 21 Jun'77

---

RBF BEFINITIONS

Romance:

"There's nothing you have to do that isn't fascinating.
Whether you're a plumber's helper and have to wipe a joint
or whatever it is."

- Cite RBF at Penn Bell videotaping, Philadelphia, 30 Jan'75

---

Romance of History in the Making:

See New York City, (5)

---

RBF DEFINITIONS

Romantic:

"I find that universe has not lost one iota
of its romance for me. I find living now quite
as satisfactory as ever."

- RBF to EJA in mid fast stride at
corner of 44th and Vanderbilt,
New York City 11 March 1971

---

RBF DEFINITIONS

Romantic:

"Over a very large period of time, I think that the total
data recorded by Charles Fort from around the world may
prove of great scientific worth. Above all this there is
something extremely inspring about Fort's interest in his
Universe. His interest is very romantic. It isn't written
in romantic terms at all, but man is full of dreams-- dreams
of significance. Fort was in love with the world that
jilted him. Fort, and humanity was looking for significance
in experience. Fort is becoming increasingly popular with
the university students who all around the world are looking
for significance. Billions of young people are in love
with a world whose complexity seems to be trying to jilt
them. I don't think their love will be unrequited. Fort's
superb humor and tenderness are communicated with
economically telling skill is rarely equalled."

- Cite RBF, "Charles Fort Introduction," p. 11. Draft 1969

---

Romance: Romantic:

See Fuller, R.B: Crisis of 1927, 14 Apr'70
    Robin Hood Sequence, (1)

# Synergetics Dictionary

RBF DEFINITIONS

Rootless:

"I don't like the word 'rootless'because it shoudn't suggest running away from things. I'm not leaving town. My backyard is just getting bigger."

- Cite RBF to Elizabeth Drew, WETA-TV, Wash. DC, 19 Oct'72

---

RBF DEFINITIONS

Roots:

"Man is born with legs, not roots."

- Citation at Legs, 26 Aug'66

- Cite Edw. C. Higbee introduction, 26 Aug. '66, quotung RBF.

---

RBF DEFINITIONS

Roots:

"Biological life... would be dehydrated were it not osmotically watercooled by its root-connected hydraulic circuitry of Earth waters' atomization for return into the sky-distributed, fresh-water-regenerating biological support system, which rooting frustrates integral procreation of the vegetation..."

- Citation and context at bumblebee, 6 Nov'72

---

Roots vs. Blossoms:

See Good & Evil Sequence (1)

---

RBF DEFINITIONS

Roots:

"At one time people thought of themselves as having roots. Why? Because in order to survive they had to be near the vegetation. And the vegetation had to have roots so it could be water-cooled, and the animals fought the people for it. But now we have the refrigeration which preserves the food, we have the canning and the other processes, and nobody has to be near the roots anymore. They can live anywhere they want. They do have legs and they can go round this world, and the food will be brought to them and none of us has to perish. We can free ourcelves from these other kinds of roots just as simply, merely by recognizing that the necessity no longer exists."

- Cite RBF tape transcript for Barry Farrel Playboy Interview Feb '72. Above passage omitted from final text. See transcript p. 61.

---

RBF DEFINITIONS

Roots:   (In Mathematics)

"In synergetics 'square' roots and 'cube' roots are treated as triangular and tetrahedreal roots. Therefore, we do not lose the radical. The root becomes rational, as $\sqrt{4}$. The fractions will come out rationally with triangular and tetrahedreal roots."

- Cite RBF to EJA, Beverly Hotel, New York, 14 Sept. 1971.

---

RBF DEFINITIONS

Roots:

"As the prime energy impounder,
The vegetation on the land has to have roots
In order to get enough water to cool itself
So that it will not be dehydrated
While it photosynthesizes the radiation energy of the Sun
Into the beatiful molecular structures
That provide the metabolic energy exchange functions
Of terrestrial life support."

- Cite BRAIN & MIND, p.110 May '72

---

Roots:   Rooted:                                              (1)

See Roots vs. Blossoms
    Trees
    Legs:  Man Born with Legs not Roots

Roots: Rooted: (2)

See Bumblebee, 6 Nov'72*
Ecology Sequence, (G); (a)
Lags, (1)
Legs, 26 Aug'66*
Manifests (1)
Organic Model, Oct'66
Sovereignty: Elimination Of, 29 Jun'72
United States: One of the Most Diffcult Sovereignties
    To Break Up, 28 Jun'72
Redundancy: Reduction Of, 22 Apr'71
Human Unsettlement, (4)

---

RBF DEFINITIONS

Rope:

"I started out our brain-mind differentiation
By saying, 'I take a piece of rope.'
I've done this before many audiences,
And no audience has ever said,
'You don't have a piece of rope.'
But the fact is I didn't have a piece of rope.
Nor has anybody ever said,
'Is it nylon, manila or cotton?'
Or, 'What is its diameter?'"

- Cite BRAIN & MIND, p.136 May '72

---

RBF DEFINITIONS

Rope:

"There is much within the critical proximity environment
which demonstrates the normal-- where the disparate mass
relativities are not operating, as, for instance, when a rope
is tensed and reacting at 90° to the direction of the
tensing and thus becomes tauter.  Compression members
precess to bend."

- Citation and context at Normal, 6 Mar'73

---

RBF DEFINITIONS

Rope:

"Each fiber in the rope is randomly spiral.  The larger
braided strands are also spiral together into three final
spiral bundles which, in turn, spiral together as a piece
of rope, clearly the rope is an aggregate non-straight lines
of many varieties of spiraling curvature.  The design final
twisting of the rope, when its ends are spliced together,
will expose a unique number of profile humps.  If the twist
of the rope has 1/16th inch humps per quarter-inch of rope
length, and 64 profile humps per inch, and 768 per foot;
then there will be 768 times 64, or 49,152 humps in its
total peripheral horizon, inside or outside: that 's a
great complex of wavilinear integrations."

- Cite RBF dictation to Alexandra Snyder, Ashoka Hotel, New
  Delhi, India, Dec. '71

---

RBF DEFINITIONS

Rope:

"To present my scientific differentiation
Of brain and mind
I proceed as follows--
First I say:
'I take a piece of rope and tense it.'
As I purposely tense it
I inadvertently make it tauter.
But I was not tensing the rope
For the purpose of making it tauter,
I was only trying to elongate the rope.
Its girth is inadvertently contracting and
The rope is also inadvertently getting harder.

"In contracting and getting harder
The rope is going into radial compression
In a plane at ninety degrees to the axis of
My consciously purposeful tensing... "

- Cite BRAIN & MIND, p.124 May '72

---

RBF DEFINITIONS

Rope:

"Physicists have never discovered any straight lines in
Universe.  They have discovered only waves which are inherently
curvilinear, that is, they are corkscrew or spiral traceries
between covariable events, such as You and Me, with our
relationship identified by a rope stretched between us with
two reels at each end to pay out as we move independently
with varying lags in the rate of the rope's response to other
forces acting upon it than thos of our two independent pulls,
as for instance the effect of wind on the rope; or the Earth's
gravitational heated expansion of the rope; and the lag or
inertia of the rope in changing the rope's shapes given it
progressively by You, Me, the wind, gravity, Sun, and atoms
of which the rope itself is composed, whose behaviors are
very directionally discrete in order to give the rope its
unique recognizability."

- Cite RBF dictation to Alexandra Snyder, Ashoka Hotel, New
  Delhi, Dec. '71.

---

RBF DEFINITIONS

Rope:

"As recounted before,
Saying, 'Let us take a piece of rope...'
To demonstrate the generalized rope concept--
I am drawing on
A multiplicity of special-case rope experiences
As a brain-stored resource of that audience,
Probably amounting to over a hundred experiences each:
With different kinds of pieces of rope,
Ergo-- I am drawing upon a memory resource
Of more than one hundred thousand experiences
With as many different pieces of rope,
When I speak to an audience of one thousand."

- Cite BRAIN & MIND, p.146 May '72

---

RBF DEFINITIONS

Rope:

"I take a piece of rope and I tense this piece of rope as
vigorously as I know how.  And the more I tense it the tauter
it becomes.  When it becomes taut, it means it is contracting
in its girth.  This means that while I am purposely tensing
it in its linear axis, it is going into compression at 90
degrees to my purposeful tensing.  Compression is occurring,
though I am only applying tension.  You understand that?  The
rope is contracting, going into compression, as a consequence
of my pulling it."

- Cite RBF at Students International Meditation Seminar,
  U. Mass., Amherst, 22 July '71, p. 8

RBF DEFINITIONS

Rope:

"Parallel lines can be torqued.  So may the parallel lines
of a cylinder be twisted as we see them in a rope.  A rope
and a cone are both forms of simple curvature."

~~- Cite I&I, p. 217, Preview of Building, 1 Apr'49~~

- Citation at <u>Torque</u>, 1 Apr'49

---

Rope: (2)

See Abstraction, 10 Dec'64
    Civil War, (2)
    Intellect:  Equation Of, (1)
    Normal, 6 Mar'73*
    Pull, 2 Jul'62
    Tension, (1)(2)
    Pattern Integrity, 22 Jan'75
    Tidal, May'72
    Torque, 1 Apr'49
    Hex-pent Sphere:  Transformation into Geodesic
        Spiral Tube, (1)

---

Rope:  <u>Knots vs. Coils</u>:

See Matter vs. Radiation, 7 Nov'73

---

RBF DEFINITIONS

Rose:

"... Packages consist of complexedly interrelated and not
as-yet differentially analyzed phenomena which, as initially
unit cognitions, are potentially re-experienciable. A <u>rose</u>
for instance, grows, has thorns, blossoms, and fragrance,
but often is stored in the brain only under the single
word -- '<u>rose</u>.'

"As Korzybski, the founder of general semantics, pointed
out, the consequence of its single-tagging is that the 'rose'
becomes reflexively considered by man only as a red, white,
or pink device for paying tribute to a beautiful girl, a
thoughtful hostess, or last night's deceased acquaintance.
The tagging if the complex biological process under the
single title '<u>rose</u>' tends to detour human curiosity from
further differentiation of its integral organic operations
as well as consideration of its interecological functionings
aboard our planet.  We don't know what a <u>rose</u> is, nor what
may be its essential and unique cosmic function.  Thus for
long have we inadvertently deferred potential discovery of
the essential roles in Universe which are performed complementarily by many, if not most, of the phenomena we experience..."

- Cite SYNERGETICS draft, Chronicle, pp.3-4, from Nehru Speech,
    as rewritten by RBF 3 Jun'72

---

TEXT CITATIONS

Rope:

Univ. of Alaska Address, p.11ff, 20 Apr '72

Approaching the Benign Environment. p. 82. 1970  (also p.86-cited)

506.01-506.15

522.04-522.09                    s326.22

<u>640.60</u>                          s535.22

644.01                           s936.11

711.01-711.04

1005.30

1054.61

---

RBF DEFINITIONS

Rose:

"Biology, chemistry, and physics can explain some of the
characteristics of the mechanics and processes that constitute
the composite, constantly changing living-machine <u>rose</u>, but
neither Julia nor the scientist could presume to tell little
Tim what a rose <u>is</u>."

- Cite NINE CHAINS TO THE MOON, p.10, 1938

---

Rope: (1)

See Deliberately Nonstraight Line
    Dog Pulling on a Belt
    Funambulist
    Generalizations:  First Degree
    Knot
    Metaphysical Disconnect
    Pattern Integrity
    Waterspout

---

Rose Bushes:

See Privacy, 22 Apr'61

Rose:

See Brain, 3 Jun'72*
Design, (1); 1938
Reproducible, 1968
Aesthetics of Uniformity, (1)

Rotation of Night as a Shadow:

See Sleep, 1963

RBF DEFINITIONS

Rotate:

"One thing we have learned about all systems when isolated
from other systems, is that they have the ability to be
rotated or for things to rotate around them."

- Citation and context at Axis of Spin (1), 11 Mar'69

RBF DEFINITIONS

Rotation of Spheres:

"A single sphere is free to rotate in any direction.

"Two spheres although free to rotate in any direction
must do so cooperatively, assuming no slippage between
the touching spheres.

"Three spheres can only rotate cooperatively about
respective axes which are parallel to the edges of the
equilateral triangle defined by joining the sphere centers,
that is, each sphere rotates toward the center of the triangle.

"Four spheres lock together. No rotation is possible,
making the minimum stable system: the tetrahedron."

(See Illustration #8.)
Cite SYNERGETICS ILLUSTRATIONS caption #8, 1967

RBF DEFINITIONS

Rotate:

"Radii must grow from point to surface. . . .
therefore, spherical irregular tetrahedra
(irretetra), therefore as spheres are interacting and
spinning and energy is both local and remote as radius
expands it, or generates unfolding leaves.... Because
man rotates he has fingers and toes. Maybe hen rotates
around egg with a nuclear gyro."

- Cite RBF holograph, 6 May'48

Rotative Systems:

See Associability, 21 Mar'73

Rotational Aberrating Limit:

See Basic Triangle: Basic Equilibrium 48 LCD Triangle,
17 Dec'73

Rotation: Rotatability:                                    (1)

See Axis of Inherent Rotatability
Co-rotation
Wind Power: Effect of Earth's Rotation
Vertex-vortex Rotations

Rotation: Rotatability: (2)

See Axis of Spin, (1)*
Omnidirectional, 2 Jul'62
Radiation: Speed Of, (D)
Cybernetics, 7 Nov'75

RBF DEFINITIONS

Rowing Needles: (1)

"I'd like to make good rowing available to the average man. He'd soon get tired then of having an outboard motor and just putt-putting from here to there. But the average rowing boat is a very awkward affair, so you can't blame people for staying away from them. But with rowing needles it's easy. Three good pulls, and I'm out of the harbor. The satisfaction is enormous.

"The bows are domed. With a sharp point you've got a plow pushing the water out ahead of you. This does exactly the opposite: the molecules roll off and they roll off in all directions and because they're rolling in all directions they exhaust the cone of entry and it builds up a vacuum.

"Watch a little, tiny guppy in a great tank. He gives a kick of his tail and it builds up low pressure on his nose and it sails right across the tank without any more effort at all. It opens its mouth and builds up that low pressure a little higher and it pulls it right across. I want to really exploit that capability. The bows on atomic submarines are also spherical for the same reasons. As the molecules roll, they take up more"

- Cite transcript of RBF tape to Barry Farrell, Tape #1, pp.5-6; Bear Island, 10 Aug'70

RBF DEFINITIONS

Roundness:

Imagination "means man's communication of what he thinks it is that he thinks his brain is doing with the objects of his experience. His discovery of general conceptual principles characterizing all of his several experiences-- as the rock, having insideness and outsideness, the many pebbles, having their corners knocked off and developing roundness: the thinks there could be pure 'roundness' and thus imagined a perfect sphere."

- ~~Cite RBF to EJA Somerset Club, Boston, 22 April 1971~~

- Citation at Sphere, 22 Apr'71

RBF DEFINITIONS

Rowing Needles: (2)

"and more of their own medium and the vacuum builds up and just pulls you forward. Today, if you want to punch through steel, you don't use a sharp point. This form is it. Atoms are discontinuous and you want to push between them, not obliterate them. You can't obliterate them."

- Cite transcript of RBF tape to Barry Farrell, Tape #1, p.6; Bear Island, 10 Aug'70

Round: Roundness:

See Experience in the Round
Omnidirectional
Pebble
Rock
Sphere
Sphericity
Stone

Rowing:

See Lever, (b)

Round Trip:

See Circuit
One Way vs. Round Trip
Two-way Feedback

Royal:

See Realm: Real: Royal

RBF DEFINITIONS

Rubber Glove:

"Entropic dispersal . . . and syntropic association.
. . . Between the two they work very much like the
rubber glove. There really is an annihilation into
eternity with no time and dimensioning-- these are
only in our temporal relativity."

- Citation and context at Eternity (1), 23 May'72

RBF DEFINITIONS

Rubber Glove Sequence:

"So we find that complementarity is even more complex; that
there had to be not only the keyhole, but that the keyhole
had to be in something. The keyhole that was in something
had to be related to the rest of the Universe. So then
we had a rubber glove which was stripped off this hand,
which we called the left hand, fairly ignorantly, and now
it fits the other hand. So where has the other one gone?
Then I strip it off here and there goes the other hand.

"Quite clearly, both were there all the time, but only one
of them could we detect. So there is not only the glove,
which could have a keyhole, and we could put the key in
that, but it would have to be in something of the rest of
the Universe as well as the system we can see by. There's
always a conceptual system, and there's the rest of the
Universe which is nonconceptual because it's a scenario
Universe and not a single frame Universe."

- Cite RBF to world game  at NY Studio School, 12 Jun-31 Jul'69,
  Saturn Film transcript #327, pp.2-3.

RBF DEFINITIONS

Rubber Glove:

"The glove is seeability, experiencability-- we go
through the invisible. The annihilation is the invisible
and the timeless.

"There is no geometry of space-- only of local aggregates
of principles, of special cases.

"The lag is the whole of life. It is lag and aberration."

- Cite RBF to BO'R, Kent, Ohio, 23 May'72

Rubber Glove:                                           (1)

See Annihilation
    Key-keyhole Sequence
    Novent
    Parity
    Other Side of the Universe

RBF DEFINITIONS

Rubber Glove:

"If you have a rubber glove on your left hand and strip

it off, it now fits your right hand. There's only one

rubber glove. The left hand has been annihilated. That's

the way our Universe is. There are the visibles and the

invisibles of the inside-outing nonsimultaneity."

- Cite Museums Keynote Address Denver, p. 10.  2 Jun'71

CONCEPTUALITY- PARITY- SEC 507.01

Rubber Glove;  ■                                        (2)

See Equilibrium, 25 Feb'69
    Eternity, (1)*
    Invisible Hole, 16 Jun'72
    Irreversibility, 4 May'57
    Superatomics Sequence, (1)-(5)
    Nuclear Domain & Elementality, (1)(2)
    Human Beings & Complex Universe, (4)

RBF DEFINITIONS

Rubber Glove:

"The rubber glove stripped inside-outingly from off the
left hand now fits only the right hand. First the left
hand was conceptual and the right hand was nonconceptual.
Then the process of stripping off inside-outingly seemingly
annihilated the left hand and created the right hand--
then vice versa as the next strip off occred. When physics
finds experimentally that a unique energy pattern--
erroneously refered to in archaic terms as a particle--
is annihilated, that annihilation is only of the rubber
glove kind. The positive becomes the negative and the
positive only seems to have been annihilated. We begin
to realize conceptually the finite, yet nonsensorial outness which can be converted into sensorial in-ness by
the inside-outing process. Ergo, Novent is the finite
but nonsensorial continuum."

*(marginalia: CONTINUUM INTEGRITY)*
*(marginalia: INSIDE-OUTING)*

*BUT ONLY AT THE EXPENSE OF LOSING AFTERIMAGE
OF THE PREVIOUS SENSE -EXPERIENCED
CONCEPTUAL FIXATION*

CONCEPTUALITY
PARITY
SEC.507,

*INSERTS FROM R.B.F.
MARGINALIA ON SYNERGETICS DRAFT*

- Cite NEHRU SPEECH, p .12. 13 Nov'69

RBF DEFINITIONS

Rubber Tires:

"Miniature rubber automobile tires may be substituted for
the triangles of the vector equilibrium to provide a model
of reciprocating toruses. The eight wheels should be
independently journaled but touching one another with
sufficient friction so that when you move any one of them
all of the eight will rotate reciprocally. We can also
consider each rubber tire as a torus and we can see how they
can involute and evolute at the same time the wheels are
reciprocatingly rotating. This provide a model of what
turbulence really is."

- Cite RBF at Penn Bell studios videotaping marathon, Philadelphia, PA., 24 Jan'75

RBF DEFINITIONS

Rubber Tires: (1)

"You can make this model out of little automobile tires
and you can run them up on the shaft and use tape to act as
a thrust bearing to keep them from coming outwardly. You
brought them in until each of these tires are barely touching
the other tires in three points-- so it really is a triangle.

"Remember how gears work. We have a train of gears where
around any hole there are always four gears, so as this wheel
goes one way the other wheel can go that way very comfortably.
And since there are four we find that the trains reciprocate.
There is no blocking anywhere. All of the holes are four-
sided so it is an even-numbered train of gears. When I
rotate one wheel in this whole system all the other wheels
move very neatly. They are in friction to one another. I can
also hold on to one of the wheels and turn the system
around it. If I do that a very interesting thing happens.
. . . A rubber tire can be mounted like a torus, or can be
rotated outwardly like the big atomic bomb mushroom cloud--
opening in the center and coming in at the bottom. That is
what we call an evoluting or involuting torus. These rubber
tires could do that-- and not only could they rotate around
on each other this way, but it is quite possible to make

- Cite Oregon Lecture, #7, p. 262, 11 Jul'62

---

RBF DEFINITIONS

Rubber Tires: (2)

this wheel in such a way that it has little roller
bearings along its rim and each of these roller bearings
allows the rubber tire to rotate in the rim so that the
tire could be involuting and evoluting. Therefore, if
any one tire started to evolute all the other tires
reciprocate."

- Cite Oregon Lecture #7, pp. 262-263. 11 Jul'62

---

RBF DEFINITIONS

Rubber Tires: (3)

". . . It is quite possible to make an automobile tire and
mount it in such a way that it looks triangular. That is,
it gets to a very small radius on its corners. I can simply
take the same rubber tire and stretch it onto a triangular
frame and also have the same little roller bearings so it
can involute and evolute. . . The triangular tires we pump
from being the vector equilibrium into being the octahedron,
the way we saw it before, in and out again. If I were then
to immobilize one part of it, if I were just holding it with
one finger like this, doing this means that I won't let this
one involute and evolute-- but the rest of the system, due to
the rotation, is contracting to become an octahedron so it
makes all the others reciprocate-- involuting and evoluting
so that I am able to immobilize one axis and the rest of the
system can work comfortably."

- Cite Oregon Lecture #7, p. 264. 11 Jul'62

---

RBF DEFINITIONS

Rubber Tires: (4)

"What we are learning here is something very fascinating and
it means the following: That in an omnimotional Universe
it is possible for me to take two moving systems-- if you
have two systems-- which move four dimensionally, comfortably,
the way you see those four sets of wheels, eight wheels
altogether moving perfectly comfortably, but I can fasten
one vector equilibrium to another by a pair of wheels,
immobilizing one of them and getting one of theses axes--
the axis which is immobilized but on which the rest of the
system can keep right on rolling around. By fastening one
such part of the Universe literally, you don't stop the
rest of the motion of Universe. That is what we are
learning here.

"In all the other kinds of mechanical systems that you will
ever run into on a three-dimensional basis, if anything is
blocked then everything is blocked. In a four-dimensional
system this is not true at all. You are able then to have
one local thing occur. You can have two atoms join one
another perfectly well and the rest of Universe can go right
on in its motion. Nothing is frustrated but they themselves
do certain polarized things in relation to one another, which
begins to explain a lot of the basic joinings."
- Cite Oregon Lecture #7, pp. 264-265. 11 Jul'62

---

Rubber Tires:

See Gear Train

---

RBF DEFINITIONS

Rudder:

"The interesting thing about a rudder is that the ship has
already gone by, all but the stern, and you throw the rudder
over, and what you're really doing is to make a little
longer distance for the water to go round; in other words,
you're putting a low pressure on the other side, and the
low pressure pulls the whole stern over and she takes a new
direction. The same in an airplane-- you have this great big
rudder up there, with a little tiny trim tab on the trailing
edge, and by moving that little trim tab to one side or the
other you throw a low pressure that moves the whole
airplane. The last thing, after the airplane has gone by,
you just move that little tab."

- Cite Calvin Tomkins, The New Yorker, 8 Jan 66, p. 64.

---

RBF DEFINITIONS

Ruddering: Rudder Concept:

"Order is achieved through positive and negative,
magnitude and frequency-controlled alteration of the
successive steering angle. We move by zigzagging control
from one phase of physical universe evolution to another.
The rudder concept of social law is most apt. Norbert
Wiener chose the word 'cybernetics,' derived from the
Greek roots of 'rudder,' because Wiener, Shannon and others
in communication theory were exploring human behaviors and
their brain-controlled 'feedback,' and the like, as a basis
for the design of computers, and it became evident that the
human brain steers man through constant change."

The identical text to the
above appears in blank verse
form in "How Little I Know."
Page 71, 1966.
- Cite AAUW JOURNAL, May 1965, P. 176

---

RBF DEFINITIONS

Ruddering Sequence: (1)

"Within the grand strategy of anticipatory problem solving
to be accomplished exclusively through design transformations
of human ecology's physical environment apparatus, the
design strategems range from powerful to subtle. For
instance, instead of attempting to push the bow of an ocean
liner from one side to the other in order to steer it (as we
do the front ends of automobiles, as well as of social trend
fronts) inasmuch as the great seas also try to push the bows
to one side or the other thus tending to throw the ship out
of control, the naval architect must design in such a way that
the ship's course will not tend to be diverted by heavy seas,
yet will be steerable. To do this he designs a ship's hull
with the hinge or pivot point of the ship occurring
forwardly under the step of the bow. This makes a long
lever arm aft and a very short lever arm forward of the
pivot, and the long lever overpowers the short one as in a
weathervane 'ship.' Thus the naval architect makes the
stern of the ship (rather than the bow) swing to one side or
the other of the course. The course tends to be held
steadily by the bow. The stern tries to follow the ship out
a straight course. The keel then makes the stern follow the"

- Cite NEW FORMS VS. REFORMS, WDSD.#1, p.52, 1963

RBF DEFINITIONS

Ruddering Sequence: (2)

"bow when the ship is in motion.  In order to change course, the stern is deliberately swung to one side or the other. This is done by the rudder at the stern which is so small as to be easily manipulated.  The rudder, by making a small drag angle, creates a partial vacuum on the side of the rudder opposite to that of the direction in which the rudder is moved.  This partial vacuum starts to pull the stern of the boat, which causes a much larger partial vacuum to build up on the stern quarter of the ship on the side toward which the stern swings as the ship moves through the water in this askew attitude.  This vacuum is built up for the same reason that the horizontal askew attitude of a wing foil in motion through the air creates the lifting vacuum on its cambered or top surface.  The reason is that it is a longer distance around the cambered askew side for the parted water to reach, as suddenly displaced by the ship's motion, which makes the longer-way-reach tense the air-interspersed water molecules creating a partial vacuum.  So powerful is this partial vacuum, or negative pressure, chain reaction buildup that it can, for instance, suck-pull the 30-knot speeding hull of the 85,000 ton, Empire State Building-sized Queen Mary into a new angle in respect to the directionally fixed"

- Cite NEW FORMS VS REFORMS, WDSD Doc. #1, p.52, 1963

RBF DEFINITIONS

Ruddering Sequence: (3)

"momentum of her bow-pivot center, which thus hinges the Queen Mary into a new course attitude, which is fixed when the rudder is returned past 'midship' to 'meet her,' or break the vacuum buildup, and then returned to midship position.

This principle of creating vacuums with minimum effort that will self-regenerate to build up large vacuums to govern very large pattern-transforming work is even more dramatically emphasized in the case of the giant jet airliners where, literally, postage-stamp size trim tabs in the trailing edges of the large vertical and horizontal ruddering surfaces are all that are used by the automatic gyro-pilot servomechanisms to keep these 100-ton sky giants hurtling along at 600 miles per hour on accurate multidimensional course despite invisible atmospheric turbulences far greater in size and velocity magnitude than those of the water ocean.

"My philosophy takes primary heed of the fact that all in Universe is in constant transformative complex motion and all transform in patterns of least resistance.  Therefore, philosophically, it became evident that by subtly designed"

- Cite NEW FORM VS. REFORMS, WDSD Doc.#1, p.53, 1963

RBF DEFINITIONS

Ruddering Sequence: (4)

"'trim-tab' size inventions we could, with least physical effort, control the least resistant directions of various fundamental transformings.  This could be done by devices which would so control the angle and frequency occurrences of little vacuums and tension which could cause man's ecological patterning to evolve in preferred patterns. Designs could also detect and discretely vitiate specific subtle vacuums chain-reacting into larger vacuums and thereby holding certain transforming systems on socially deleterious courses.

"How much more powerful is the minuscule ship's rudder when in good order than a squadron of ships trying to move a rudderless ship in a heaving sea by attempting to push the rudderless one with their plunging bows in preferred directions as do tugs maneuver a big ship in still water when the ship is moving too slowly to have steerage way! Also how futile are shouted words of warning and exhortations in such situations!  Only the rudder and the brain that directs the rudder are effective.  No wonder Norbert Wiener included the Greek name for rudder in coining his 'cybernetics' to identify the newly emergent computer's"

- Cite NEW FORMS VS. REFORMS, WDSD Doc #1, p.53, 1963

RBF DEFINITIONS

Ruddering Sequence: (5)

"feedback system science.  No wonder the early Egyptian and Greek shipmasters stood in the stern of their ships facing forwardly alongside the single-oar-steering slave as the crew of backwards-facing slaves tensed at the banks of vacuum fulcrumed oars.  Here is the picture of society straining at its slavishly accepted work, backing up blindly into its future as an, often nearsighted, excursion captain cons the course.

"My philosophy also takes heed of the approximately unlimited ratio of length to girth of tensional controls which always tend to pull true, versus the very limited length-to-girth ratio of pushing devices which, when pushed, tend to bend and break.

"Philosophically it is clear that trim tabs in the trailing edges of trailing devices-- in the tail-end of tail-end events-- at the stern of the ship as the last event and not at the bow as the first event.  The bow is important to keep the ship on a chosen course but the stern rudder puts and holds it on the chosen courses.  The real steering takes place when the non-scientifically informed observer thinks"

- Cite NEW FORMS VS. REFORMS, WDSD Doc. #1, p.53, 1963

RBF DEFINITIONS

Ruddering Sequence: (6)

"everything is all over.  But that final steering has to be done from 'on board,' Just 'having the last word' from way back in the wake of the ship is futile.  Scientists have often said that the most important part of their great discoveries occurred at the outset in the proper formulation of the project's objectives, forgetting that those enlightened formulations were really the afterimage inducements of tail-end events of earlier and seeming failures of experimentation."

- Cite NEW FORMS VS. REFORMS, WDSD Doc. #1, p.53, 1963

Rudder: Ruddering: (1)

See Cybernetics
    Trim Tab
    Servomechanism
    Zigzag: Right-left: Halfway Averaging

Rudder: Ruddering: (2)

See Omnimedium Transport Sequence, (3)
    Feedback, 7 Nov'75

Ruler: (1)

See Straightedge

Ruler: (2)

See Resolution, 5 Jul'62

Rule of Communication: (2)

See Comprehension, Sep'72

# RULES

Rule of Communication:

"At this time I developed a thought which has been very powerful in my theory of communication ever since. I said, 'I don't care if I am not understood as long as I am not misunderstood. For if I am misunderstood the captain of a ship may do the wrong thing with fatal consequences, but if he does not understand me, he queries the message and you give it to him again until he gets it right.' This principle became absolutely fundamental in my life from then on."

- Cite RBF to Alden Hatch in "RBF: At Home in the Universe," p.65. From Hatch's 1972 tape recapitualting RBF formulation of 1918.

Rules of Interval: (1)

See Orbiting Magnitudes
      Vertexial Connections: Rules of Never-quite-touching

RBF DEFINITIONS

Rule of Communication:

"I made up my mind as a Rule of Communication that I wouldn't care if I was not understood -- so long as I was not misunderstood."

- RBF to EJA and assembled company, Carbondale, Illinois 2 April 1971.

See also Intro, to Gene Youngblood

Rules of Interval: (2)

See Coherence, 10 Feb'73

Rule of Communication: (1)

See Misunderstanding, i.e., Being Misunderstood

Rules of Operational Procedure:

See Whole System, 28 May'72

Rules of No Actual Particulate Solids:

    See Coherence, 10 Feb'73

Rules of Universe:

    See Individuality & Degrees of Freedom, (4)
       Fuller, R.B:  On Drinking Liquor, 22 Jun'77

---

Rules of Never-quite-touching:          (1)

    See Vertexial Connections:  Rules of Never-quite-touching

Rule:  Regulation:         (1)

    See Conformity
    Law:  Laws

---

Rules of Never-quite-touching:          (2)

    See Coherence, 10 Feb'73

Rule:  Regulation:         (2)

    See Technology, 13 Mar'73

---

RBF DEFINITIONS

        The Rules of Universe:

"It's not an either/or condition ever-- so much is permitted by the rules of Universe."

Rule:  Regulation:         (3)

    See Rule of Communication
       Rules of Interval
       Rules of No Actual Particulate Solids
       Rules of Never-quite-touching
       Rules of Operational Procedure
       Rules of Universe

- Citation and context at Degrees of Freedom, 9 Dec'73

Rule: Ruler:

See Realm
Religion: Related to "Reglio" or Rule

Runaway of Ignorance:

See Problem: Statement Of, Feb'72

Russia:

See Soviet
USSR

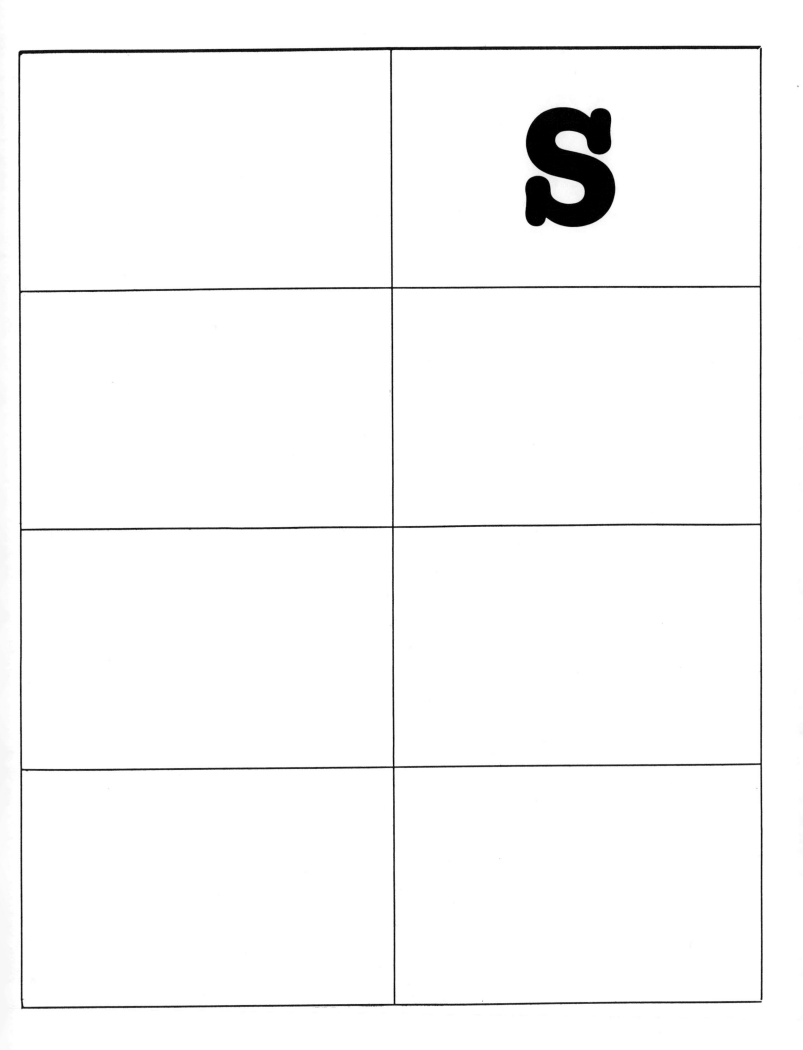

<u>S</u>:

See Structuralism in Language, 1 Feb'75

S Quanta Module:

s100.322

s100.105

sTable 987.121

s987.413

s987.988.00-112

RBF DEFINITIONS

S Quanta Module:

"When the icosahedron is extracted from the octahedron the remaining corners fractionate into 24 S Modules."

- Cite RBF to EJA, by telephone from Philadelphia; 3 Oct'77

RBF DEFINITIONS

S-Curve:

"Our S-curve is a very interesting kind of form. I have two S-curves and one could get in a critical proximity at one end and we would call it a triangle. . .We know triangles can be open-ended, as there has never been a closed triangle; it has always been a spiral"

"The middle positive sector of the S-curve is opposite the middle negative vector, each with its axis rotated at 90° to the other by inter=precession."

- ~~Cite CARBONDALE DRAFT Pp. IV.32 + IV.36~~

- Cite Nasa Speech, pp.53+56, Jun'66

S Quanta Module:

See T Quanta Module

S Curve:                                                     (1)

See Z Cobras

RBF DEFINITIONS

S Quanta Module:

"The A and B Quanta Modules also have their volumetric counterparts in the nonnucleated icosahedron in the form of the S Quanta Modules--each of which is 1/120th tetrahedron of which the triacontrahedron is composed. This makes the S Quanta Modules probable electron complements of the nucleated system-halvings fractionated 459 times, i.e., 4 x 459 = 1836."

- Citation & context at Mites & Quarks as Basic Notes, (1); 4 Jun'77

S Curve:                                                     (2)

See Yin-yang, (2)
     Propeller, Dec'71

S: Six S's:

See Architectural Aesthetics: Six S's

Safety:

See Scaffolding, 20 Apr'72

RBF DEFINITIONS

Safety Factor:

". . . The big geodesic domes thus far erected have been way
overbuilt by many times their logically desirable ███████
███████ two-to-one safety factor.

"While the building business uses safety factors of four, five,
or six-to-one, aircraft-building employs only two-to-one or
even less because it knows what it is doing. The greater the
ignorance in the art, the greater the safety factor that must
be applied. And the greater the safety factor, the greater
the redundancy and the less the freedom of load distribution."

- Cite SYNERGETICS draft at Secs. 703.07 +.08, 25 Sep'72

Sailing with the Wind: Sailing into the Wind:

See Social Sciences: Analogue to Physical Sciences,
(1)(2)

Safety Factor:

See Fail-safe: Fail-safe Advantage

Sailing Ship: Sailboats:                          (1)

See Geodesic Spinnaker
Intuition: RBF Sailing Yacht "Intuition"
Water: Trend toward Living on Water
Boats
Fleet of Sailboats
Beating to Windward

Safety Valve:

See Dome: Rationale For (III)

Sailing Ship: Sailboats:                          (2)

See Pull, 2 Jul'62
Octahedron: Eighth-octahedra, (2)-(4)

Synergetics Dictionary

Saint:

See Engineer-saint

Sand:

See Sixty Degreeness, 1965

Salmon:

See Social Breakout from Barnacle to Salmon

Sandwich:

See Earth as a Sandwich

Salvation vs. Self-discipline:
See Macro-micro, 1964

Sanity:
See Human Beings & Complex Universe, (4)

Sameness:

See Aesthetics of Uniformity, May'28

Santa Sophia:

See Pneumatic Structures, (3)

555

Saran:

See Hex-pent Sphere: Transformation into Geodesic
Spiral Tube, (2)

Satellite:   Telescopes mounted on around-Earth, fixedly-
Hovering photo-satellites:

See Twenty-foot Earth Globe & 200-foot Celestial
Sphere, (1)(2)

Satellite-linked Computers:

See Cosmic Accounting, 20 Sep'76

RBF DEFINITIONS

Satellite:   World Satellite Sensing:

"With omnidirectional complex computerized world satellite
sensing, comprehensive resources inventorying and inter-
routing, the triangular geodesics transformational projection
can alone bring visual comprehending and schematic network
elucidation."

- Citation and context at Twenty-Foot Earth Globe and 200-Foot
Celestial Sphere (11), 25 Jan'73

Satellite Environment Controls:                        (1)

See Floating City
    Space Structures
    Habitable Satellites

Satellites:   Satellite Sensing:                        (1)

See Communications Satellites
    Habitable Satellites
    Space Structures
    Telemation:  Satellite-relayed

Satellite Environment Controls:                        (2)

See Balloon, (2)
    Tensegrity:  Unlimited Frequency of Geodesic
        Tensegritis, (1)

Satellites:   Satellite Sensing:                        (2)

See Sovereignty, (20
    Planetary Democracy, (6)(7)
    Communications Hierarchy, (3)

Satisfaction:                                    (1)


See Performance:  Equation Of

---

RBF DEFINITIONS

Savings:

"During each one-second heartbeat of time humans were making
and 'saving' $1 net.  They were in fact saving memories of
experiences, which ever multiply, from which accumulate
metaphysical know-how that has never been entered into the
ledgers of world-wealth accounting..."

                                        (Adapted)


- Citation and context at Gross World Product Sequence (1),
  13 Mar'73

---

Satisfaction:                                    (2)


See Inventions as Lifeways of Human Behaviors, 1965
    Life, 22 Apr'68
    Performance Per Pound, 30 Apr'74
    Survival, May'65

---

RBF DEFINITIONS

Scaffolding:

"I like to give you components to go out into the field
where no man has to wait for any other man to help him--
where any part ought to be so light that one man has the
other hand free to fasten it into place.  You must do
things in such a way that nobody is going to get hurt.
Make it possible then to work from the ground up.  You make
a structure where you keep climbing on to it and adding
to it-- being absolutely safe in making its own scaffolding."


- Cite Univ. of Alaska Address, p.39, 20 Apr '72

---

(To) Save Time, Tape, & Type:


See Creativity, May'65

---

Scaffold:  Scaffolding:                          (1)


See Cube as Scaffold
    Four-square Scaffold

---

Savings Account:


See Energy Capital
    Energy Savings Account

---

Scaffold:  Scaffolding:                          (2)


See Pyramid Technology, Dec'71

Scale:                                                    (1)

> See Uniform Boundary Scale
> Chords & Notes

Scan-transmission of Pattern Integrities:

> See Electromagnetic Transmission:  Subjective &
>     Conscious
>     Atomic Computer Complex
>     Billboard Model
>     Pattern Processing Machines
>     Man:  Interstellar Transmission of Man
>     Information Control System

Scale:                                                    (2)

> See Invisibility of Macro- and Micro- Resolutions, (1)

Scanning:

> See Electromagnetic Transmission
>     Billboard Model

Scalene:

> See Proton & Neutron, (p.134) May'72
>     Semisymmetry, 15 Oct'72
>     Dynamic Symmetry, (1)(2)

RBF DEFINITIONS

Scarcity:

"We have millions of people who no longer have anything to
do on farms.  We keep plowing it under.  We run only eight
hours on the machinery instead of 24, when it could perfectly
well run 24 hours.  We are doing everything we can to keep
scarcity because the only thing we are familiar with is
scarcity.  I simply say to you that we're in an absolutely
inadequate accounting system, which did relate to yesterday's
agricultural perishability.  The agricultural did automatically
depreciate.  We are now in an entirely new economy where the
wealth consists of energy, the metaphysical and the physical.
. . . They are not on the books of any of the corporations
anywhere."

- Cite RBF at DSI Press Conference, p.9, 28 Jun'72

RBF DEFINITIONS

Scan-transmission of Pattern Integrities:

Q.        "What is the connection between synergetics and
          teleportation?"

RBF:      I know of no connection between such phenomena and
synergetics.  Synergetics is a frame of reference for the
intertransformings--I don't connect it with the metaphysical.
We can identify synergetics with the electromagnetic wave
propagation and that may turn out to have something to do
with the physical...It's a good question.  No, since I don't
use 'good' or 'bad', we'll say an interesting question.

"We can scan.  We have pattern integrities.  The patterns can
be recognized.  You might be scannable like the Broadway
electric light signs--in which each of the closest packed
spheres might be a lightable light.  It might scan your
organisms but I wouldn't expect the physical body to be moved--
just the events."

- Cite RBF in reply to question by Dr. Michael Bruwer at World
  Game Workshop'77; Phila., PA; 22 Jun'77

RBF DEFINITIONS

Scarcity:

"All economics is committed to a fundamental formula of
scarcity-- even to the point where it may be necessary to
invent scarcity."

- Cite RBF to Henry Liberman, NY Times, 22 Jun'72

RBF DEFINITIONS

Scarcity:

"Scarcity, the fundamental thesis of all our statecraft, in invalid."

- Cite RBF at Corcoran Gallery Address, Washington, DC, 23 Feb '72

---

Scarcity:   Not Enough to go Around:                                    (2)

See Design Science, 8 May'71
    Fuller, R.B: Crisis of 1927 (1)
    Nonproduction, 12 Jun'69
    Politics (1)(2)
    World Game (II)*
    Thinking, 10 Dec'73
    Young World (1)(2)
    War, 13 Dec'73
    Lying, 22 Jan'75
    Humane City, (2)(3)
    Doing What Needs to Be Done, (2)
    Selfishness, 20 Sep'76
    Building Industry, (11)(12)
    Culture, 27 Jan'77
    No Energy Crisis, (2)
    Man as a Function of Universe, 30 Apr'78

---

RBF DEFINITIONS

Scarcity:   Not Enough To Go Around:

"It is very logical that man should fight to the death when he thinks that there's not enough to go around.  In a fire, he loses all reason, goes mad, and tramples his fellow men to death as he competes for air.  It is also very logical that man won't fight when he knows there's enough to go around.  It is logical.  It is logical.  It is logical."

- Cite I SEEM TO BE A VERB, Queen, May '70

---

Scarcity:   Economy of Scarcity:

See Economic Accounting System, 29 Jun'72
    Marx, Karl, 7 Aug'70
    Obsolescence, Apr'72
    Political Revolution, 10 Oct'73
    Politics, 4 Jan'70
    World Game, (II)

---

RBF DEFINITIONS

Scarcity:   Not Enough to Go Around:

"We are not educatable fast enough to realize that scientists could bring us enough to go around."

- Citation and context at World Game (II), 25 Feb'69

---

Scarcity as an Invention:

See Economics, 22 Jun'72

---

Scarcity:   Not Enough to go Around:

See Design Revolution:  Pulling the Bottom Up
    Earning a Living
    Inadequacy of Life Support
    Making the World Work
    Resource Inadequacy
    Watergate
    You or Me
    Human Tolerance Limits

---

Scavage:   Scavaging:

See Self-scavenging

RBF DEFINITIONS

Scenario:

Q.    How can an event be a finite energy package?

RBF:    "Say quanta instead of package. Events discontinue. Scenarios stop and go. The continually flowing reality is not end-to-end but a partially overlapping continuity."

- Cite RBF in videotaping session, Philadelphia, Pa., 1 Feb'75

---

RBF DEFINITIONS

Scenario:

"An aggregate of non-simultaneous
And partially overlapping
Ever complexedly transforming experience,
Is an evolutionary sequence
Which is defined as a scenario.

"The totality of experience
Which is scenario Universe
As a serially transformative cognition
Of individually different
And scenically static individual pictures,
Conceptual frames,
Is inherently non-unitarily
Or momentarily conceptual."

- Cite RBF Draft, BRAIN & MIND, pencil
  1970

---

RBF DEFINITIONS

Scenario:

"Yesterdays and now
Are neither simultaneous
Nor mirror-imaged;
But through them run themes
As overlappingly woven threads,
Which though multipliedly individualized
Sum-totally comprise a scenario."

* Cite BRAIN & MIND, p.131 May '72

---

Scenario of the Child:    (1)

See Children as Only Pure Scientists
    Goldilocks

---

RBF DEFINITIONS

Scenario:

"In scenarios you have to have a pretty long sequence

run in order to get any clue at all to what is going on.

You cannot learn what it is all about from a single

picture.  You cannot understand life without much experience."

- Cite Museums Keynote Address Denver, p. 10.2 Jun'71

CITE SYNERGETICS- SCENARIO UNIVERSE  SEC 322.2

---

Scenario of the Child:    (2)

See Six Motion Freedoms & Degrees of Freedom, (1)-(6)

---

RBF DEFINITIONS

Scenario:

"We can clarify the accurate but formidably complex definition of scenario Universe. A moving picture scenario is an aggregate of nonsimultaneous and only partially overlapping events. One single picture-- one 'frame'-- does not tell the story.  The single picture of a caterpillar does not tell or imply the transformation of the creature first into the chrysalis stage and much later into the butterfly phase of its life.

"When people say of Universe, 'I wonder what is outside of outside?' they are trying to conjure a unitary conception and are asking for a single picture of an infinitely transforming nonsimultaneous scenario.  Therefore their question is not only unanswerable but unrealistic and indicates that they have not listened seriously to Einstein and are only disclosing their ignorance of its significance when they boastfully tell you that the speed of light is 186,000 miles per second."

- Cite WHAT QUALITY ENVIRONMENT, 24 Apr'67

SCENARIO UNIVERSE - SEC 322.1

---

Scenario Model:    (1)

See Pendulum Model vs. Scenario Model

Scenario Model:                                                   (2)


        See Truth, 10 Nov'72

---

RBF DEFINITIONS

Scenario Universe:

"Universe is a scenario. Uni-verse is a static takeout. . . what we do when we start with wholes. When we start with wholes we have to deal with the scenario--like the frog the snake was swallowing.

"Time is only now. Time and size and ▇▇▇▇ special case are now, as referenced to the cosmic hierarchy of geometries through which they pulsate and never stop. The rest is shapeless: not tuned in."

        - Cite RBF to EJA, 3200 Idaho, Wash. DC: 18 Jul'76

---

RBF DEFINITIONS

Scenario Principle:

"I have found a general law of total synergetical structuring which we may call the scenario principle. This law discloses that 'Universe' of total man experience may not be simultaneously recollected and reconsidered but may be subdivided into a plurality of locally tunable event foci or 'points' of which a minimum of four positive and four negative points are required as a 'considerable set'; that is, as a first finite subdivision of finite Universe."

        - Cite INTRODUCTION TO OMNIDIRECTIONAL HALO, p.125, 1959;
          the above passage described the general law as "The Law
          of Structure," the same title given to a second law on
          the same page. To anticipate SYNERGETICS the caption
          was changed to "Scenario Principle" in the 1971 Doubleday
          edition of NO MORE SECONDHAND GOD with approval of RBF.--EJA.

SYNERCETICS - SEC. 228.01

---

RBF DEFINITIONS

Scenario Universe:

"We are dealing with the Universe and the difference between conceptual thought (see Systems) and nonunitarliy conceptual Universe (see Scenario Universe). We cannot make a model of the latter but we can show it as a scenario of conceptual frames."

(s1007.21)

        - Cite RBF rewrite of SYNERGETICS, 2nd. Ed. at Sec. 1007.21;
          18 Sep'74

---

RBF DEFINITIONS

Scenario vs. Absolute Symmetry:

"Symmetry is systemic. Symmetry has nothing to do with the scenario series; it has nothing to do with local, special case realizations. You can find balances in series--positive and negative energies--but absolute symmetry is characteristic only of generalized systems."

(Sec. 532.17)

- Citation & context at Symmetry & Asymmetry, 11 Dec'75

---

RBF DEFINITIONS

Scenario Universe:

"... The integrity of Scenario Universe's

Never exactly identical recyclings."

        _ Citation and Context at Metaphysical, p.152 May '72

---

RBF DEFINITIONS

Scenario Universe:

"Universe is a scenario. Scenario Universe is the finite but nonunitarily conceptual aggregate of only partially overlapping and communicated experiences of humanity.

"Uni-verse is a momentarily glimpsed, special case, systemic episode takeout.

"When we start synergetically with wholes we have to deal with the scenario within which we discover episodes--like the frog the snake is swallowing.

"Time is only now. Time and size are always special case asymmetric episodes of now whose systemic aberrations are referenced to the cosmic hierarchy of primitive and symmetrical geometries through which they pulsate actively and passively but at which they never stop. The rest of Scenario Universe is shapeless: untuned-in."

        - Cite RBF rewrite of 19 Jul'76; incorporated in SYNERGETICS,
          2nd. Ed. at Sec. 321.04 and 321.05.

---

RBF DEFINITIONS

Scenario Universe:

"Einstein started Holistically
With the concept of Scenario Universe
As an aggregate
Of nonsimultaneous,
Complexedly frequencied,
And only partially overlapping
Ever and everywhere
Methodically intertransforming events
Which conceptioning
Is superbly illustrated by an evening
Of overlappingly frequenced fireworks."

        - Cite INTUITION, p.48 May '72

          - Citation & context at Fireworks (1), May'72

RBF DEFINITIONS

Scenario Universe:

"The definition of Universe as a Scenario of nonsimultaneous and only partially overlapping events, all the physical components of which are ever transforming, and all the generalized metaphysical discoveries of which ever clarify more economically as eternally changeless."

- Citation at Metaphysical & Physical, 26 Jan'72
- Cite RBF marginalia, 26 Jan '72, incorporated in SYNERGETICS draft at Sec. 251.17, Feb '72.

---

RBF DEFINITIONS

Scenario Universe:

"Einstein's adoption as normal speed, the adoption of electromagnetic radiation expansion-- omnidirectionally in vacuo-- because the speeds of all the known different phases of measured radiation are apparently identical, despite vast differences in wavelength and frequencies, suggests a top speed of omnidirectional entropic disorder increase accommodation at which radiant speed reaches highest velocity when the last of the eternally regenerative universe cyclic frequencies of multi-billions of years have been accommodated, all of which complex of nonsimultaneous transforming multivarietied frequency synchronizations is complementarily balanced to equate as zero by the sum-totality of locally converging orderly and synchronously concentrating energy phases of scenario universe's eternally pulsative and only sum-totally synchronous, disintegrative, divergent, omnidirectionally exporting and only sum-totally synchronous integrative, convergent and discretely directional individual importings."

- Cite RBF to EJA in response to a request to repeat his 'brief sentence' on the sphere as a meeting of convergences. See SYNERGETICS draft, 'Tension and Compression,' Sec. 614.08.
  1971

SYNERGETICS - SCENARIO UNIVERSE - SEC 325

---

RBF DEFINITIONS

Scenario Universe:

". . . the cosmically eternal totality
Of interminable Scenario Universe."

- Citation & context at Entropy, Jan'72
- Cite EVOLUTIONARY 1972-1975 ABOARD SPACE VEHICLE EARTH, Jan '72, p. 7.

---

RBF DEFINITIONS

Scenario Universe:

"The Heisenberg indeterminism implies eternity to be persistent within the physical and metaphysical ever-evolving continuity-finiteness of scenario Universe, in which the myriads of nonsimultaneously shaken kaleidoscopes are never either simultaneous or identically repetitious."

- Citation and context at Measurement (1), Dec '69

---

RBF DEFINITIONS

Scenario Universe:

"Beginningless and endless scenario Universe
With its vast frequency ranges
Of omni-interpulsative
Yes-no, give-and-take
Radial expansions and circumferential contractions."

- Cite EVOLUTIONARY 1972-1975 ABOARD SPACE VEHICLE EARTH, Jan. '72.

---

RBF DEFINITIONS

Scenario Universe:

"In the endless, but finite and never exactly repeating (Heisenberged) 'film strip' scenario of Evolutionary Universe after the film strip has been projected it goes through a 'molten' phase and congeals again to receive the ever latest self-intertransforming patterning just before being again projected. The rate of change and numbers of special case self-retransformings of physical evolution tend ever to accelerate, differentiate and multiply; while the rate of change and numbers of self-remodifyings of generalized law conceptionings of metaphysical evolution tend ever to decelerate, simplify, consolidate and ultimately unify."

- Cite Generalized Laws of Design, p. 2. 22 Apr'68
- Citation at Metaphysical, 22 Apr'68

SYNERGETICS - SCENARIO UNIVERSE    SEC. 323

---

RBF DEFINITIONS

Scenario Universe:

"The Universe can only be thought of competently in terms of a great unending but finite scenario whose as-yet unfilled film strip is constantly self-regenerating."

- Cite Museums Keynote Address Denver, p. 10. 2 Jun'71

SYNERGETICS - SCENARIO UNIVERSE - SEC. 322.1

---

Scenario Universe vs. Big Bang Theory:

See Black Holes & Synergetics, 1 Mar'77

RBF DEFINITIONS

Scenario Universe: Physical Evolution Scenario:

(Mind enables humans to discover and employ
generalized principles brought from Eternal Universe...)

"Brought into

Time and energy synchronized consciousness

Of the physical evolution scenario. . . "

- Citation and context at ▬▬▬▬▬ Brain & Mind (3), Feb'72

---

Scenario:                                                         (1)

See Afterimage
    Allspace Filling = Scenario
    Brain's TV Studio
    Continuity-finiteness
    Finite Eevent Scenario
    Improve the Scenario
    Moving Picture Continuity
    Overlapping
    Model vs. Scenario
    Periodic-continuity
    Pre-Scenario
    System vs. Scenario
    Visual Symphony

---

RBF DEFINITIONS

Scenario Universe:                                              (1)

        See Afterimage
            Brain's TV Studio
            Continuous Man
            Nonunitarily Conceptual
            Moving Pictures
            Conservation of Scenario Universe
            Universe as a Kaleidoscope
            Serial Universe
            Overlapping

---

Scenario:                                                         (2)

        See Packaged, Jun'66
            We-Me Awareness, 31 May'74
            World Game: Grand Strategy, 2 Jun'74
            Tetrascroll, (1)

---

Scenario Universe:                                          (2A)■

        See Allspace Filling, 2 Nov'72
            A Priori Intellect, (1)
            Communication, Oct'70
            Conceptuality, 1965; 22 Oct'72
            Education, May'72
            Einstein, 23 May'72
            Entropy, Jan'72*
            Fireworks, (1)*
            Future of Synergetics, 23 Dec'68
            Key-Keyhole Sequence, (2)
            Measurement, (1)
            Metaphysical, May'72*; 22 Apr'68*
            Metaphysical & Physical, 26 Jan'72*
            Motion, 4 Mar'69
            Omniinteraccommodation, May'72
            Spherical Field, Aug'73
            Invisible Tetrahedron, 13 Nov'69
            Time-sizing, 13 Nov'■ '72
            Two Kinds of Twoness, (B)
            Vacuum, 19 Feb'72

---

Scenery: Rearrange the Scenery:

        See Rearrange

---

Scenario Universe:                                            (2B)

        See Spheres & Spaces, 14 May'75
            Words & Coping, 7 Nov'75
            Space, 9 Feb'76
            Tunability, 24 Apr'76
            Human Beings & Complex Universe, (4)(5)

---

Scenery:

        See Finite Event Scenario, 23 Jan'77

RBF DEFINITIONS

### Scheherazade Number:

"I think the Arabian priest-mathematicians and their Indian ocean navigator ancestors knew that the binomial effect of 1001 upon the first four prime numbers 1,2,3, and 5, did indeed provide comprehensive quotient accommodation of all the permutative possibilities of all the possible 'story-telling-taling-tallying,' or computational systems of the octave system of integers.... Suffice it to say that the functions of the Grand Vizier to the ruler was that of the mathematical wizard, the wiz of wisdom; and the wiz-ards kept their mathematical navigational ability to go to faraway strange places and to bring back strange miracle objects, was here involved."

[230.50]

- Cite SYNERGETICS draft at Sec. 1210.05, 18 Jul'72

---

RBF DEFINITIONS

### Scheherazade Number:

"It is probable that this fifth power comprehensive quotient number can also accommodate all the interpermutations of all atomic structuring (stable integration) or destructuring (unstable disintegration)."

- Cite SYNERGETICS text at Sec. 1210.02, 18 Jul'72

---

RBF DEFINITIONS

### Scheherazade Number:

"The Scheherazade Number is the product of three prime numbers: 7 x 11 x 13 = 1001.

"1001 x 1001 = 1002001."  It is palindromic.

- Cite RBF to EJA, Beverly Hotel, NYC, 22 Jun'72

---

RBF DEFINITIONS

### Scheherazade Number:  Geometrical Manifestations:

Ten-illion Nonillion   - Manifest in the spherical Octahedron.

Eight-illion Septillion   - Manifest in the vector equilibrium

---

RBF DEFINITIONS

### Scheherazade Numbers:  Declining Powers Of:

"The reoccurrence of the prime number two is very frequent. The number of operational occasions in which we need the prime number 43 is very less frequent than the occasions in which the prime numbers 2, 3, 5, 7, and 11 occur. This Scheherazade Number provides an abundance of repowerings of the lesser prime numbers characterizing the topological and vectorial aspects of synergetics' hierarchy of prime systems and their seven prime unique symmetrical aspects (see Sec. 1040) adequate to take care of all the topological and trigonometric computations and permutations governing all the associations and disassociations of the atoms."

"We find that we can get along without multirepowerings after the second repowering of the prime number 17. The prime number 17 is all that is needed to accommodate both the positive and negative octave systems and their additional zero-nineness. You have to have the zero-nine to accommodate the noninterfered passage between octave waves by waves of the same frequency."

- Cite SYNERGETICS, 2nd. Ed. at Secs. 1238.41-.42, 22 May'75

---

RBF DEFINITIONS

### Scheherazade Numbers:  Declining Powers Of:

"My intuition about the declining powers of the primes factorial is that they reflect the way the patterns appear in nature. From my early hand and pencil calculations it is clear that you have to use the prime number five and the prime number three more often in your calculations than you use the higher number primes. And you use the three more than you would the five. Hence 3 to the 8th power and 5 to the 5th power to work out all the possible nuances within the 45-degree limit. This might be the pattern of reducing from Universe in a binary way.

"The higher powers for the first primes are to accommodate the very large numbers of calculations necessary to come up really sharp!  You have tetra = 1; and octa = 2; and 5 is both the vector equilibrium and the icosahedron. This relates to the rate at which the outer shells accumulate: the prime number times two plus two. By providing enough moves for each of the low number primes you should be able to work it out by bitting with sharp results. Such a discrete method would be more elegant than a probability approach."

- Cite RBF to EJA by telephone from Miami, 17 Mar'75

---

RBF DEFINITIONS

### Scheherazade Numbers:  Declining Powers Of:

Q: (EJA)   In the factorial primes of the Scheherazade Numbers why do you have high, but declining, powers in the first primes and no powers in the higher primes at the end of the series?

RBF:   "Well the reoccurrence of the number two is very frequent. We have to provide a lot of powers for 3, 5, and 7 to take care of all the computations and permutations. But the number of times you need 43 is very low compared to the number of times you need the number 11. The powering really stops at 17, which is all you need to accommodate the octave system from 0 through 9. You have the zero to accommodate the waves. But 17 gives you all the primes up to 18 which accommodates the two nines."

[1234.41 + .42]

- Incorporated in SYNERGETICS, 2nd. Edition draft at Sec. 1232.30, Cite RBF to EJA in videotaping session, Philadelphia, PA, 1 Feb'75

---

RBF DEFINITIONS

### Scheherazade Numbers:  Declining Powers Of:

$1^{nth}$, $2^{12th}$, $3^{8th}$, $5^{5th}$, $7^{4th}$, $11^{3rd}$, $13^{3rd}$, $17^{2d}$.

This descending order of powers embraces the first eight primes (seven positive and seven negative primes.) These represent the spaces between the spheres.

"These powers have to do with the number nucleations required to accommodate $17^2$. Seventeen is the outer shell. There are seven different magnitudes of powers involved.

"$45^o$ is the limit."

(Above relates to Ten-illion SSRCD-- which did not survive in SYNERGETICS :  It is 48,521,045,268,603,838,698,691,521,290,000)

- Cite RBF to EJA, Beverly Hotel, NY, 22 June'72

Scheherazade Numbers:

See SSRCD

---

RBF DEFINITIONS

Scheme of Reference:

"I do not like the word frame. What we are talking about is
the multi-optioned omni-orderly scheme of behavioral reference;
simply the most economic pattern of evolvement. Pattern of
evolvement has many, many equieconomical intertransformability
options. There are many transformation patterns, but tetrahedron is the absolute minimum limit case of structural system
interself-stabilizing. A tetrahedron is an omnitriangulated,
four-entity, six-vector interrelationship with system-defining
insideness and outsideness independent of size; it is not a
rigid frame and can be any size. 'Rigid' means 'sized'--
arbitrarily sized. 'Rigid' is always special case. Synergetics
is sizeless generalization."

- Cite SYNERGETICS draft at Sec. 540.04, 24 Sep'73

---

Scheme of Behavioral Reference:

See Scheme of Reference, 24 Sep'73; 26 Sep'73

---

RBF DEFINITIONS

Scheme of Reference:

"Synergetics is not a frame at all but a pattern of most
omnieconomic (ergo, spontaneous) interaccommodation of all
observed self-and-otherness interexperiencing (ergo, geodesic--
geodesic being the most economical interrelationships of a
plurality of events)."

- Cite SYNERGETICS draft at Sec. 540.05, 24 Sep'73

---

RBF DEFINITIONS

Schematic of the Principles:

"Conceptual systems like that of the vector equilibrium are
subsize and pretime and yet provide a schematic of the constant
interrelationship of all the principles involved which may be
treated mathematically as topology."

_ Citation & context at Synergetic vs. Model (D), 10 Sep'74

---

Scheme of Reference: Schemata: Scheme:

See Field
Frame of Reference
Frame of Reference: Six Schemata

---

RBF DEFINITIONS

Scheme of Reference:

"'Multioptioned, omniorderly scheme of behavioral reference.'

That's what we should say instead of 'frame of reference.'"

- Cite RBF to EJA, 3200 Idaho, DC, 26 Sep'73

---

Schizophrenia:

See Equilibrium & Disequilibrium, (1)(2)

Scholarships:

    See Fellowships

RBF DEFINITIONS

Schoolroom:

"The least favorable environment for study is the schoolroom and closely-packed desk prisons. The real schoolhouse is in the home and outdoors."

- Cite I SEEM TO BE A VERB, Bantam, 1970

---

School: Schoolroom:    (1)

    See Education
        Kindergarten
        Teaching

Schoolroom:

    See Study, May'70

---

School: Schoolroom:    (2)

    See Fuller, R,B: Moratorium on Speech, (1)

School:    (1)

    See Architectural Schools
        Education
        Learning
        University

---

Schools: Shoals:

    See Cosmic Fish, 8 Feb'73

School: Schooling:    (2)

    See Self-education, 1974
        Convergence & Divergence, 1 May'77

RBF DEFINITIONS

Science:

"Science begins with the awareness of the absolute mystery

of Universe."

- Cite RBF in Barry Farrell Playboy Interview, 1972 - Draft. p. 21.

---

RBF DEFINITIONS

Science:

"Science is metaphysical.

"My definition of universe embraces both the physical
and the metaphysical, the latter being all the weightless
experiences of thought which include all the mathematics
and the organization of the data regarding all physical
experiments, science, both first and last, being metaphysical.

- Cite DOXIADIS, P. 309, 20 Jun'66

---

RBF DEFINITIONS

Science:

"Science identifies as subjective and objective, respectively,
the inadvertently experienced stimulations of life, on the
one hand, and the deliberately initiated and experimentally
instituted responses to the subjective stimulations..."

- Citation and context at Subjective and Objective, 14 Sep'71

---

RBF DEFINITIONS

Science:

"Many years ago I developed a system of question
asking in which I ruled that I must always answer the
questions from experience. My answers must not be based
on hearsays, beliefs, axioms, or seeming self-evidence.

"It has been part of my experience that there are
others who, while experiencing what I was experiencing,
were able to describe what we mutually were experiencing
equally, well, or better than I could. Therefore, my
experience taught me that I could trust the reporting of
some others as reliable data to be included in my
'answering' resources. For instance, I could include the
experimentally derived data of scientists."

- Cite NASA Speech, p. 31 , Jun'66

---

RBF DEFINITIONS

Science:

"Experience is the raw material of science."

- Cite RBF Lecture
Town Hall, New York
12 March 1971

- Citation at Experience, 12 Mar'71

---

RBF DEFINITIONS

Science:

"Science has always been a complex of independent and

subjective economic slave disciplines, primarily concerned

with the harvesting of information, rather than with the

practical application of that information."

- Citation and context at Space Technology (6) , 10 Oct'63

---

RBF DEFINITIONS

Science:

"Everything that constitutes science
Is unteachable.
And we recall that
Eddington said: 'Science
Is the earnest attempt
Of individual initiative
To set in order
The facts of experience.'
Scientific routines for specialized technicians
And scientific formulas for their reference
Alone are teachable."

- Cite HOW LITTLE I KNOW, Oct. '66, p. 65

---

RBF DEFINITIONS

Science:                                                    (1)

"The function of science is to prospect for total
society by taking the universe apart, that is, resolve it
into primary factors and elements by progressive isolation
and subsequently to obtain precise measurements of the
behavior characteristics of the isolated events or components.

"For example, science isolated the phenomenon fire
from extraneous factors, and by isolating the constituent
events and the product of events discovered that fire is
not in itself an element but an accelerated combining
process of a newly recognized primary element, that is,
oxygen, combining with carbohydrates in ever-constant
arithmetical proportion. Thus the isolation of the fire
caused the subsequent isolation, recognition and naming
of the new elements oxygen and hydrogen, and provided
behavior measurements of the latter, by which man could
predict events of combustion in such a way as to make
combustion an accurate tool of technical advantage.

- Cite DESIGN FOR SURVIVAL, I&I, pp.188-189, Jan'49

RBF DEFINITIONS

Science:                                                      (2)

"As water and vapor are $H_2O$ events, the comprehensive event
was a precise mathematical process. This was the beginning of
purposefully produced steam as a tool. The steam engine was a
victory of chemical science, not of mechanics as we have
popularly supposed. However the functions of science ended
with the separating out of the newly discovered elements from
the universal matrix and with the measurement of the unique
behavior characteristics of the respective elements (it being
the unique behavior that constitutes elementality). It is readily
seen that the present invocation of science to put together
again the world it has taken apart, is futile inprinciple.
Summarizing, it is the essential function of science to take
the Universe apart and measure the parts and sort them into
usable categories. The functioning of science is exclusive."

- Cite DESIGN FOR SURVIVAL, I&I, pp.188-189, Jan'49

---

RBF DEFINITIONS

Science:    Cause of Science for Man:

"Science really hasn't done anything about looking out

for man. Science has found out how to make great explosives

and great guns calibrated with little control instruments

so any ignoramus could learn to fire it and hit pretty well

in a couple of days experience. But science didn't have to do
                            /until the space age/
anything about the man/because the air was waiting there to

be breathed and water was pretty handy. . . going out into

space for the first time you have to really know what a

man needs."

- Cite RBF taping CHARAS Script
14 March 1971

---

RBF DEFINITIONS

Science:

"Unlike inventions,
pure science events are absolute and irrevocable.

Pure science events represent openings of windows
through the walls of ignorance and fiction,
to reveal the only reality: ■
the behavior of the naked ● universe that always was, is, and will be
True it is that the first glimpses may be hazy and imperfect,
but the behavior itself is absolute and is progressively clarified.
Therefore, this comprehensive curve
of the chronological rate of acquisition of knowledge
concerning the pure science absolutes
separated out from all other events of history
may be inspected as the basic means of prediction
of inherent technical and social events--
immediate or somewhat distant."

- Cite Part II of Earth, Inc.
Fuller Research Foundation
Yellow paper draft, p. 7
1947

---

RBF DEFINITIONS

Science:    The Cause of Science for Man:

"I figure that when the environment is scientifically

conceived and rendered, that the human occupants can then

divest themselves of the necessity of onerous and puritanic

hardship of conduct and yet accomplish successful and happy

living in naturally engendered sanity."

(N.B.  Christopher Morley's phrase for the Dymaxion

philosophy was "Pleading the cause of Science for Man.)

- Cite extract from RBF writings submitted by EJA
■ to Morley -- Wichita, Kansas 1946

---

RBF DEFINITIONS

Science:

"Science works equally well
under private or public subsidy . . . "
while "industry is the pure product
of free enterprise, imagination and personal risk
of the individual or small groups of individuals."

- Cite Part II, Earth. Inc.
Fuller Research Foundation
Yellow typescript, p. 8 1947

- Citation at Industrialization, 1947

---

RBF DEFINITIONS

Science:    Comprehensive Integration of the Sciences:

". . . The vastly increasing genetic knowledge and the
omni-integration at the virology level of cross discipline
teams of physicists, geneticists, chemists, biologists,
mathematicians, each and any one of whom may broaden the
scope of his interests to include all or some of the others'
logic."

- Cite HYPER, World Mag., 4 Apr'73

---

RBF DEFINITIONS

Science:

"Science has hooked up the everyday economic plumbing
to the cosmic reservoir . . .

"Science continually does more with less
each time it obsoletes and scraps old inventions."

- Cite Part II., Earth, Inc.
Fuller Research Foundation
Yellow typescript, p. 10, 1947

---

RBF DEFINITIONS

Science:    Comprehensive Integration of the Sciences:

"Many scientists of Darwin's time felt there were many parts
and aspects of the Universe which had nothing to do
scientifically with other parts of the Universe. In contrast
to that century-ago viewpoint, the overlap of the once
separate sciences now is so great that, for instance, both
chemists and physicists are now primarily concerned with
atoms. World War II witnessed the introduction of hyphens
between the scientific categories-- bio-chemistry, for
example. Now the trend to comprehensive integration is
far advanced. . .

""The trend to specialization is being abruptly reversed.
We are coming to a comprehensive reintegration of our
knowledge. That is why suddenly the most advanced scientists
are becoming comprehensivists. This will overnight make
obsolete 90 percent of the overspecialized professional
teachers."

- Cite RBF in AAUW Journal, p. 175, May '65

RBF DEFINITIONS

### Science:  Comprehensive Integration of the Sciences:

"Scientists, having developed double names for their over-lapping work (biochemistry, biophysics, etc.), are now finding their total field interconnected and unitary.  This is a general trend of science.  And so many scientists are now being educated that it may be forecasted ▓ that within the next half century, not only all science but much of what educated society will have come naturally through its own explorations and experiences to discover the comprehensive order of the Universe."

- Citation and context at Einstein: Cosmic Religious Sense, (3), 19 Sep'64

---

### Science:  Comprehensive Integration of the Sciences:      (1)

See Hyphenated Sciences

---

### Science:  Comprehensive Integration of the Sciences:      (2)

See Twenty Questions, (2)

---

### Science:  "Foreign-hieroglyphicking" Science:

See Tetrahedral Coordination of Nature, 1965

---

RBF DEFINITIONS

### Science:  Gap Between Science and the Humanities:      (1)

"There is excitement in the air as we undertake this last phase of a fifty-year search for the re-bridging of the gap between Science and the Humanities-- created when science, abandoning fundamental conceptual modeling, started a century ago to 'fly' exclusively 'on instruments.'  We have, I am confident, the new conceptual bridge between the sciences and the humanities.  Because the instrument- and mathematical-symbol-conditioned world of science has great momentum and competence in 'blind flight,' it is not going to take quickly to our new tools-- so you are the bridge builder from me to the rest of science.

"I would like you to say what I say-- in my explorer's half-century-developed, experimentally formulated language-- to the scientists, in their language.  Our terms often coincide but are ambiguous and, at times, contradictory. I think you can easily smooth out the differences.

"I am confident that I can talk lucidly to the public and particularly to the young world.  I know that you and I can talk lucidly to one another.  I am therefore confident that"

- Cite RBF Ltr. to Dr. Arthur Loeb, 6 Jan'67

---

RBF DEFINITIONS

### Science:  Gap Between Science and the Humanities:      (2)

"we have not only discovered the comprehensive, omnirational, omni-intertransforming coordinate system most economically employed by physical energy Universe, but also that we have developed a communications relay system of high integrity with which most effectively to speed the realization by society of the advanatges accruing to the rewedding of the Sciences and Humanities which, Lord Snow agreed with me, is accomplishable by our Synergetics and its omniconceptualⱡty."

- Cite RBF Ltr. to Dr. Arthur Loeb, 6 Jan'67

---

RBF DEFINITIONS

### Science:  Gap Between Science & the Humanities:

"With the return to valid, rationally computable conceptuality of nature's dynamic formulating, there returns to literary man the ability to re-establish the communication integrity of science and world society.  The rate of re-establishment of conceptual comprehension of scientific frontiering and its technical, ergo economic, ergo practical significance, will be painfully slow to those who now have discovered nature's sublimely rational comprehensibility.  It may take a whole new generation but that is an historically short period for so vital a recovery from world society's present intellectual comprehension tail-spinning."

- Cite KEPES, p. 81. 1965

---

RBF DEFINITIONS

### Science:  Gap Between Science and the Humanities:      (A)

"... There has been the thought of nonconceptuality in the area you explored and it seemed to be just purely mathematical. It didn't seem to be easy to communicate between science and the general public and the literary man has been the man who was supposed to explain what is going on to the public. He is the fellow who communicates but he couldn't understand. The scientist said: you can't follow, and that in a sense, is what Snow is writing about-- about the real chasms that have grown up between the scientist and the people. He speaks about it in the terms of the literary man because he is a literary man and there is nothing he can explain to people of what is going on in science. I will make a prediction to you that in this next half century you will see a development of comprehension of science by everybody.  Science is comprehending in the terms of conceptuality...

"In the period we speak of as the gay nineties, about that era of time, the physics was moving ahead rapidly and we are coming out of the time of Clerk Maxwell and Hertz and the development of the electromagnetic wave, the phenomenon electricity is beginning to come along, and this is the beginning of the era of dynamos, and so forth.  Principles are being"

- Cite Oregon Lecture #4, pp.130-131, 6 Jul'62

RBF DEFINITIONS

Science: Gap Between Science and the Humanities: (B)

"discovered that are operative in the electricty. There is electrical engineering. In the mathematics, the the coordinate system of XYZ coordinates we had identified what we call powering, the development of dimensions that required a unique perpendicularity to a plane not already in the system.

"We had the first dimension all right, and the second and third dimension. But we couldn't seem to find any fourth dimension. The trouble was that in the gay nineties fourth power relationships were beginning to show up in the physics and in relation to electromagnetic phenomena. But you couldn't make a model of it. What the mathematicians found yoy could do was fairly nifty because in dealing with 90-degreeness you just think about your XYZ coordinates; you think about your 90-degree angle and you have lines going out so many units from the centers. In XYZ coordinates, they were also called the quadrants; 90-degrees four times, you might call it a clock with four hours.

"One of the things the mathematicians found you could do to accommodate the seeming phenomena that was going on in electro-magnetics where physical Universe seemd to be using the fourth power-- you could handle the fourth power simply by borrowing"

- Cite Oregon Lecture #4, p.131, 6 Jul'62

RBF DEFINITIONS

Science: Gap Between Science and the Humanities: (C)

"a little from the clock. You could go around the clock and borrow a little from tomorrow or you could go backwards on the clock and borrow a little from yesterday. It is kind of like going to the bank and you accommodate it on a time payment affair. This is called imaginary number, complex number, where the square root of minus one is going into yesterday one quadrant. They found they could accommodate the fourth power mathematically but they couldn't make a model of it.

"In the nineties, then, it began to happen thatthe scientists said: We are sorry. We have had models up to now, and you asked me to explain what we are doing in science, and there was a model but suddenly models seemed to be invalid. Mathematics could carry on so you gave un models. That is what happened in the nineties. Not everybody knew this right away. This was not such a big fashionable thing. There were no decrees along these lines but it gradually became known that the scientists were carrying on with purely with mathematical notation and were getting along very well and they could handle invisible phenom-ena. They simply said: all this stuff that's invisible here is also nonconceptual. There are no models."

- Cite Oregon Lecture #4, pp.131-132, 6 Jul'62

RBF DEFINITIONS

Science: Gap Between Science and the Humanities: (D)

"This irritated a great many other human beings, as for instance, artists who are philosophers in cry. They may not have had very much mathematics, but they are human beings-- who possibly may not have done very well in school-- but they really are full of a sense of importance of the Universe. And there were many principles to be discovered so they could persist. The artist said: I could deal in abstracts, and so they felt they could deal in principles. So we have the leaving to the nonrepresentational art. That is a move that comes along with the invalidity of models in science. It is something we call abstraction. It really wasn't very abstract; many times it was a principle. An artist really did learn it was a principle and there would be inversions of equations and things like that. They were intuitive that conceptuality was there all the time. They had felt that there was something inadequate in the matheamtics, that's all... I've found time and again that artists have very powerful intuitions. They hadn't quite learned their way around well enough in the languages of the various sciences, but I am sure they have been intuiting that therrre was conceptual validity so they insisted on trying to make conceptual arrangements."

- Cite Orgeon Lecture #4, pp.131,132, 6 Jul'62

Science: Gap Between Science & the Humanities:

See Blind Man's Bluff
Generalizations: Mathematical vs. Literary
Return to Modelability
Snow, C.P.
Technology: Enchantment vs. Disenchantment
Instruments: Science Blind-flying "On Instruments"

Science: Gap Between Science & the Humanities: (2)

See Algebra, 28 Oct'64
Artist, Sep'71
Conceptuality, 1965
Fourth Dimension: Borrowing from Tomorrow's
Clock, 22 Jul'71
Joyce, James, 1965
Modelability, Jun'66
Synergetics, Dec'72; (B)
Wealth, (E)
XYZ Coordinate System, 6 Jul'62
Synergetics, 7 Apr'75

RBF DEFINITIONS

Science: The Great Design:

"Contact with the great design: this is the most mysterious of all experiences we know. I find the design of a regenerative Universe must inherently have very complex problems, local problems. And I think that the human has been given access to the great eternal mind in order to be able to cope with the extremely difficult local problems of the regeneration of the Universe. It becomes a very thrilling realization of our responsibility. . .

"Science, at its beginnings, starts with a priori, absolute mystery, within which there loom these beautiful behavior patterns of the physical Universe where the reliabilities are eternal."

- Cite RBF at SIMS Conference, U. Mass., Amherst, 22 July '71
As quoted in Symposium publication, Ed. by Mylo Housen

Science: The Great Design:

See A Priori Great Design
Eternal Designing Capability

RBF DEFINITIONS

Science Opened the Wrong Door:

"Now we suddenly find elegant field modelability and conceptuality returning. We have learned that all local systems are conceptual. Because science had a fixation on the 'square,' the 'cube,' and the 90-degree angle as the exclusive forms of unity, most of its constants are irrational. This is only because they entered nature's structural system by the wrong portal. If we use the cube as volumetric unity, the tetrahedron and octahedron have irrational volume numbers."

- Cite RBF re-write of SYNERGETICS galley at Ser. 990.05, 30 Dec'73
- Citation & context at Synergetics, 30 Dec'73

Science Opened the Wrong Door: (1)

See Oversight
    Starting with Parts:  The Nonradial Line
    Attic Window
    Earth Fault:  Society is Living in a Sort of Earth
      Fault

---

Science:  History Of: (2)

See Modelability, (3)(4)
    Teaching, 2 Apr'71

---

Science Opened the Wrong Door: (2)

See Flatland, 1 Oct'71
    Synergetics, 30 Dec'73*
    XYZ Coordinate System, (p.96) Jun'66
    Quantum Sequence, (2)
    Fourth-dimensional Synergetics Mathematics, 14 Dec'76

---

RBF DEFINITIONS

Science:  Left Hand and Right Hand Sciences:

"To adopt themselves to change has now been pronounced in
Washington as 'creativity.'  Philip Morrison, Cornell's
head of the department of nuclear physics, talks about what
he calls 'left hand' and 'right hand' sciences.  Right hand
science deals in all the proven scientific formulas and
experiments.  Left hand science deals in the unknown and
unproven, and the intellect, intuition, and imagination
required in man to make it known.

"The great scientists were great because they dealt
successfully with the unknown: They were left-behind
scientists.  Morrison says that we have been extending only
the right-hand science, making it bigger and sharper.  How
could Congress justify appropriation of billions for dreams?
For the billions went only for the swiftly obsoleting bigger,
faster, and more incisive modifications of yesterday's
certainties."

- Cite RBF transcribed in AAUW Journal, p. 173, May '65

---

RBF DEFINITIONS

Science:  History of Science:

"This explains why
The history of science
Is a history of
Unpredicted discoveries
And will continue
So to be."

- Cite INTUITION, p.39 May '72

---

RBF DEFINITIONS

Science:  Pure & Applied:

"My chart of the isolation of the isolation of the 92
chemical elements shows" that innovation and discovery
require aesthetically motivated curiosity, "in re scientific
breakthroughs which always slow down in war and accelerate
in nonwartime."

- Cite RBF marginals at Cyril Stanley Smith Article, NY Times,
  24 Aug'75; done by RBF, Wash. DC, 8 Sep'75

---

Science:  History Of: (1)

See Babylonian Mathematics
    Navigators:  Early Navigators

---

RBF DEFINITIONS

Science:  Pure and Applied Science:

"When science discovers order subjectively it is pure
science.  When the order discovered by science is objectively
employed it is called applied science."

- Citation and context at Order, 13 Mar'73

RBF DEFINITIONS

### Science: Pure & Applied:

"Pure science seeks to find mathematical order permeating
the subjectively acquired data; and applied science employs
objectively the mathematical orders discovered in formulating
them into special design uses.

"Both the pure science analysis of the subjectively acquired
data and the applied science employment of the relationships
involves mathematically patterned identification of the
pertinent special-case use data in respect to a universally
coordinate dimensioning system and a transformational frame
of reference."

- Cite RBF holograph (edited), Beverly Hotel, NYC 14 Sep'71

---

Science: Pure & Applied:                                    (2)

See Metaphysical & Physical, 1967
    Universe as Energy & Information, 11 Nov'74
    Communications Hierarchy, (3)

---

RBF DEFINITIONS

### Science: Pure and Applied Science:

"Applied science is physical.  Theoretical science is
metaphysical."

- Cite Peter Pearce checklist for RBF foreword, 1967
- Citation & context at Metaphysical & Physical, May'67

---

RBF DEFINITIONS

### Science-Technology-Economics-Politics Sequence:

"The rate at which man found chemical elements seems

to be the key controlling the development of the

application of science to technology, and, following

from this, the application and effect of that technology

on economics and, utlimately, the effect of the new

technology on society itself."

- Cite THE YEAR 2000, San Jose State College, Mar'66

---

RBF DEFINITIONS

### Science: Pure & Applied Science:

"Pure science does not prosper in time of war--
which is contrary to all popular notions.  Scientists
are made to apply science in wartime, rather than to
look for fundamental information."

- Cite THE YEAR 2000, San Jose State College, Mar'66

---

RBF DEFINITIONS

### Science-Technology-Industry-Economics-Politics Sequence:    (1)

"My philosophy... requires the attempt to solve problems by
inanimate invention of comprehensive anticipatory design
science, rather than yielding to the easier behavior of problem
discovery and the exhortation of others to solve these problems.
Ideas come readily to all.  Translation of ideas into theoretically effective physical design takes considerable self-
disciplining to be effective.  Reduction of such theoretically
effective designs into physically operating structural and
mechanical advantages requires even greater self-disciplining.
Reduction of the physical mechanical advantage into timely and
spontaneous inhibitability by our contemporarily evolving
society requires patience as well as self-discipline.

"These coordinate self-disciplines are inherent in the
inventory of faculties with which we are endowed and are potential of realizations in the inventory of reported experiences
that we have inherited from all men before us.  The individual
intellect disciplinedly paces the human individual.

"The individual disciplinedly paces science.

"Science disciplinedly paces technology by opening up both"

- Cite Intro. to NO MORE SECONDHAND GOD, p.ix, 9 May'62

---

Science: Pure & Applied:                                    (1)

See Know-how & Know-what

---

RBF DEFINITIONS

### Science-Technology- Industry-Economics-Politics Sequence:    (2)

"Widened and refined limits of technical-advantage generating
knowledge.

"Technology paces industry by progressively increasing the
range and velocity inventory of technical capabilities.

"Industry in turn paces economics by continually altering and
accelerating the total complex of environment controling
capabilities of man.

"Economics in turn paces the everyday evolution acceleration
of man's affairs.  The everyday patterning evolution in turn
poses progressively accelerating problems regarding the
understanding of the new relative significance of our extraordinarily changing and improving degrees of relative advantage
in respect to controlling our physical survival and harmonic
satisfaction.  Happily realized augmentation of forward
capability is all that we mean by wealth.

"The unfamiliar complex of the new wealth accounting requirements of the evolving human experiences emerges as an aggregate
of unique and popularly discerned everyday 'news' problems."

- Cite. Intro. to NO MORE SECONDHAND GOD, pp. ix-x, 9 May'62

RBF DEFINITIONS

Science-Technology-Industry-Economics-Politics Sequence:     (3)

"In turn the popularly discerned inventory of problems
altogether provides the raw material to be processed by the
machinery of politics.  It is the purpose of politics to
digest the problems and to provide adequate accounting and
readjustments to the unexpected and often disconcerting changes
in the patterns of technical advantage realizations.  Politics
must thus implement life's continually increasing sweepout
and penetration of Universe with a continually changing set
of operational rules and accounting conventions."

- Cite Intro. to NO MORE SECONDHAND GOD, p.x, 9 May'62

---

EJA COMMENT

Science-Technology-Industry-Economics-Politics Sequence:

The total sequence involved is approximately as follows:

Man's participation in evolution (individual intellect)
        paces design pattern strategies for survival;

Ideas pace physical design;

Self-disciplining paces structural and mechanical advantage;

Intellect paces the individual;

The individual paces science;

Science paces technology

Technology paces industry;

Industry paces economics;

Economics paces wealth; wealth paces politics; politics paces

  accounting readjustments for increasing sweepout of Universe.

---

Science-Technology-Industry-Economics- Politics Sequence:     (1)

    See Making the World Work

---

Science-Technology-Industry-Economics-Politics Sequence:     (2)

    See Industrial Lag, 5 Jul'62
      Politics, Jan'62; May'28
      Technology, 1960
      Mutual Survival Principles, (3)

---

RBF DEFINITIONS

Science as a Tool:

"... Science and technology are only manipulative tools
like inanimate and cut-offable hands which may be turned
to structuring or de-structuring.  How it is to be
employed is not a function of the tool but of human
choice.  The crisis is one of the loving and longing
impulse to understand and be understood which results as
informed comprehension.  It is the will to structure versus
ignorant yielding to fear impulsed reflexive conditioning
resultant to being born utterly helpless.  Infellectual
information accumulating processing is necessary and
anticipatory faculties to be only slowly discovered as
exclusively able to overcome the ignorantly feared
frustrating experiences of the past.  Science must be seen
as a tool of fundamental advantage for all, which Universe
requires that man understand and use exclusively for the
positive advantage of all humanity, or humanity itself
will be discarded by Universe as a viable evolutionary
agent."

- Cite SYNERGETICS at Sec.826.05, Sept'72

---

Science:     (1)

    See Applied Science
      Exact Sciences
      Experimental Demonstrability
      Hyphenated Sciences
      Inexact Sciences
      Invention vs. Pure Science Events
      Operational Science
      Physical Science
      Science-Technology-Industry-Economics-Politics-
        Sequence
      Social Sciences
      Source of All Scientific Knowledge
      Hierarchy of Patterns
      Generalizations: Mathematical vs. Literary
      Instruments: Science Blind-flying "On Instruments"
      Overspecialization of the Sciences, ■
      Children as Only Pure Scientists

---

Science:     (2)

    See Mathematics, undated
      Ninety-two Elements:  Chart of Rate of Acquisition (2)
      Experience, 12 Mar'71*
      Industrialization, 1947*
      Subjective & Objective, 14 Sep'71*
      Space Technology (6)*
      Tenure, 28 Jun'72
      XYZ Coordinate System (A)
      Unknown:  All the Unknown, 13 May'73
      Nonthing, 11 Sep'75
      Closed System, 10 Nov'75
      Metaphysical & Physical, 22 Jun'77

---

Science:  Scientific:     (3)

    See Science:  Cause of Science for Man
      Sciences:  Comprehensive Integration Of
      Science:  "Foreigh-hieroglyphicking" Science
      Science:  Gap Between Science & the Humanities
      Science:  The Great Design
      Science Opened the Wrong Door
      Science:  History Of
      Sciences:  Left Hand & Right Hand
      Science:  Pure & Applied
      Science-Technology-Economics-Politics Sequence
      Science as a Tool
      Scientific Events Appearing in Fun & Play
      Scientific Generalization
      Scientific Laws
      Scientific Words

573

Scientific Events Appearing in Fun & Play:

See Funambulist, 1938

RBF DEFINITIONS

Scientist:

"The pure scientist is just like an egg-laying hen.

Take the egg away-- and no matter. That's just it."

- Cite RBF to EJA
  Beverly Hotel, New York
  14 March 1971

RBF DEFINITIONS

Scientific Generalization:

"The scientific generalizations are always mathematically
statable as equations with one term on one side of the
equation and a plurality of at least two terms on the
other side of the equation."

- Citation and context at Order, 13 Mar'73

RBF DEFINITIONS

Scientists:

"Scientists differ from people who just make lists by

trying to set them in order."

- Cite OREGON Lecture #2 - p. 69 " 2 Jul'62

Scientific Laws:

See Synergetics Principles

RBF DEFINITIONS FILE INDICATORS

Scientists: Scientists Cited in RBF Works:

| | |
|---|---|
| Avogadro. | Percival Bridgeman |
| Democritus | Frankland, Edward |
| Euler | van't Hoff, Jacobus Henricus |
| Euclid | Pauling, Linus |
| Newton | Grebe, Dr. John |
| Copernicus | Hilbert, David |
| Kepler | Poisson |
| Heisenberg | Brouwer, L.E.J. |
| Einstein | Eccles, J.C. |
| Pythagoras | Pauli |
| Eddington | Jeans |
| Waddington | Planck |
| Darwin | Aston |
| Galileo | Lavoisier |
| Dalton | Bernouilli |
| Boole | Dirac |
| Mach | Smith, Cyril Stanley |
| Teller, Edward | |

Scientific Words:

See Energetic Words

Scientists:                                                  (1)

See Artist-scientists
Chaos: Myth that Scientists Wrest Order from Chaos
Leonardo Type
Eggs: You Just Lay Eggs

**RBF DEFINITIONS**

**Scrap Sorting & Mongering:** (1)

"We are going to have to keep track of the 92 regenerative chemical elements but not just as elements because we have them in literally thousands of millions of compounds and different complex structures as they are used in various industrial processes. We won't be using the elements by themselves; we'll be using the various compounds. I am interested in the concentrates. And I see buildings as high and low grade. I see my 92 chemical elements rarely in the pure condition; in a more complex way they are in practical dissociability for further realignment.

"When we talk about all the aluminum or the bauxite some is below grade in the mines and some is already in use and recirculating. There are really two classes. There is a recirculating group. When they're pulling a building down there's part of the steel that's no longer in the building holding it together, but it may not have been put on the market yet as scrap. But it's what they call high melting scrap and should go right into the furnace; it will command a much bigger price than the small stuff."

- Tape transcript #4, pp.8-9, RBF to W. Wolf; Phila. PA., 15 Jun'74

---

**RBF DEFINITIONS**

**Scrap Sorting & Mongering:** (2)

"Scrap sorting is going to be one of the great sciences now. It is one of the typical social changes from the linear patterns of the honey-bee to the precessional circulatory patterns. To man's old way of thinking he was going to build this building and it's going to stay there forever. All the architects are that way. It was like a one-way street. But nature found that the metal didn't get destroyed and so it resulted in the monger.

"The monger was sort of a low-grade character because everybody thought the materials had deteriorated, that the iron was all rusting and that everything would really rust and go away. But the monger was sitting in there and society found that things were not getting eaten up. Now the mongers are getting all their dung and really turning it into something. There's a scandal now in Philadelphia about their sewage and waste removal because some of these guys are beginning to turn some of this tonnage into money. They had been throwing out the dung but now they are beginning to process it and they find that it really pays them.

"One of the big changes around here is when the monger is no longer a low calling. But the mongers tend to sit on it and"

- Tape transcript #4, pp.9-10; RBF to W.Wolf, Phila. PA., 15 Jun'74

---

**RBF DEFINITIONS**

**Scrap Sorting & Mongering:** (3)

wait for a good market. That keeps enormous powerful heaps of junk in sight. We don't have to have those unsightly places. This is where the government should start to take over the function of recirculation. That's what society is not doing; it's not taking care of any of its recirculation. Everybody is trying to disconnect and make their money. So one of the big functions of government is going to be changing the scrap sorting from a one-way street into the circulatory system. I don't think anything could be more visible from the World Game point of view.

"I am going to account for everything. There are going to be some priorities. Because there are a number of these materials that are so relatively scarce thay have to be of absolutely high priority. If there is so little of it it must be used in a broad sense. I must never have helium in a retail pub; it must be in the tools that serve the tools.

"Incidentally, I see tools having a hierarchy just like our own guts: things that are glandular, there are energy secretions, there are pumping stations, and so forth. Purifying things like the lungs and livers are all big recirculatory systems:

- Tape transcript #4, pp.10-11; RBF to W.Wolf; Phila. PA, 15 Jun'74

---

**RBF DEFINITIONS**

**Scrap Sorting & Mongering:** (4)

"Nature takes great pains to separate the liquid from the solid matter. When nature takes the great trouble to separate things like that it's a very expensive matter. But then we, as people, put them right back together again. It's incredible. Nature has its little dogs pissing on the tree groups that need the water and crapping over there for the fertilizer."

- Tape transcript #4, p.11; RBF to W.Wolf, Phila., PA, 15 Jun'74

Scrap Sorting & Mongering:

    See Metals:  Recirculation of Metals
        Junkyard
        Pollution Control

Screen:

    See Benday Screen
        Membrane
        Walls

Scratch-chorded:

    See Light on Scratched Metal, 9 Nov'73

RBF DEFINITIONS

Screwing:

"People who listen to me say, 'Here's a man who's selling screwdrivers... they don't realize how mysterious screwing is."

- Citation and context at Fuller, R.B.:  RBF Modus Operandi, Feb'73

RBF DEFINITIONS

Scratched Surface:

"You look at any scratched surface and you will always see circles.  Where there is light present there are lines that get lit up since they are precessional to the direction of the light.  This gives you the sunburst effect in a hubcap or fender."

- Citation & context at Vectorial & Vertexial Geometry, (2), 27 Jan'75

Scribing:                (1)

    See Drawing
        Spherical Reality Scribing
        Scissors Held in Fixed Opening
        Tools of Geometry
        Severance-tracing

Scratched: Scratched Surface:

    See Light on Scratched Metal

Scribing:                (2)

    See Otherness, 8 Feb'76

Scroll:

See Tetrascroll

---

Sculpture:  Sculptor:                                (1)

See Sculptor vs. Engineer

---

Scrutability:  Magnitude Of:

See Twenty-foot Earth Globe & 200-foot Celestial Sphere,
(2)

---

Sculpture:  Sculptor:                                (2)

See Design, 23 Jan'72
    Fuller, R.B:  His Writing Style, 22 Jan'75 ; 26 Apr'77
    News & Evolution, (2)

---

RBF DEFINITIONS

███████  Sculpture as Single Frame:

"I'd then like to point out that if you say I wonder what's
outside outside, you're asking a single frame picture.  You
have a sculpture in mind.  The Universe is a sculpture.
These are where the stars are in sculptural array.  So that
question is a single frame. . . and we realize that no
single frame gives the meaning."

- Cite RBF to SIMS, U.Mass., Amherst, 22 July '71, p. 27

---

RBF DEFINITIONS

Sea:

"In 1961... three jet airplanes in one year outperformed the
Queen Mary and the steamship United States at a very much
less cost; and suddenly the sea became obsolete as a way in
which human beings would get from here to there."

- Citation & context at North-south Mobility of World Man, (1),
10 Sep'75

---

Sculptor vs. Engineer:

See Soleri, Paolo, 10 Sep'75

---

RBF DEFINITIONS

Sea:  The Sea:

"The sea's curvature enabled her to keep her secrets."

- Cite RBF videotaping, Penn Bell Studios, Phila., PA, 23 Jan'75

RBF DEFINITIONS

### Sea: The Sea:

"Playboy: It seems a very melodramatic kind of evolution
that would have man verge so close to extinction before
discovering his function. Do you think that risking extinction
may be part of the process of discovery?

"RBF: He's done it all the time. He kept going to <u>sea</u>,
kept going after those fish, and his boat was inadequate and
he was lost. Of all the people who have gone to sea
historically, I imagine that very few returned. There was
such loss in the beginning. But out of it man began gradually
to learn his engineering, to learn how to anticipate the
enormous stresses, the constant peril. And he began to
develop beautiful fibers, better ropes, better sails,
I think our breakthroughs always come to the people who were
risking themselves very close to the brink."

- Cite RBF in Barry Farrell Playboy Interview, 1972 - Draft. p. 15.

---

RBF DEFINITIONS

### Sea: The Sea:

"Laws are not extendable over the surface of the water.

The sea offered secrecy because its curvature meant

that you only had to get 14 miles away to be out of sight.

. . . to disappear over the horizon and then reappear. . .

only the navigators could do it."

- Cite RBF to EJA, Fairfield, Conn., Chez Wolf.
  18 Jun '71

---

### Sea Gulls:

See Feeding a Flock of Sea Gulls

---

### Seaports:

See Unsettling vs. Settlements, 20 Sep'76

---

RBF DEFINITIONS

### Sea Power:

"The British Isles were used as unsinkable flagships.... Sea
power was determined in the first few seconds of contact:
after the first or second salvo you knew who was going to
run the world for the next 25 years.

"Blitzkrieg was just sea warfare brought up onto the land.

"There is no such thing as a secondhand navy."

- Cite RBF videotaping, Penn Bell Studios, Phila., PA, 23 Jan'75

---

### Searchlight:

See Octahedron: Eighth-octahedra, (3)(4)

---

RBF DEFINITIONS

### Sea Technology:

"You get at least twice as much experience at sea because
you're at work 24 hours a day. On the sea it's a flood all
the time and you have to stay on top of it."

- Cite RBF at Penn Bell videotaping session, Philadelphia,
  23 Jan'75

---

### Sea Technology Conversion to Land Technology:

See Dymaxion Airocean World, (I)
    Tank, 23 Jan'75
    Electric Lights, 15 Oct'64
    Wealth, (C)
    Bicycle Wheel, 29 Jan'75
    Sea Power, 23 Jan'75

Sea Technology:                 (1)

     See Battleship
        Displacement of Ships and Buildings
        Electric Lights
        More With Less: Sea Technology
        Navigation
        Navy Sequence
        Refrigerator
        Sea Technology Conversion to Land Technology
        Weapons Technology
        Air Delivery & Submarine Cities

---

RBF DEFINITIONS
vs.
Search  Research:

"In the early 1930s, in my Saturday Review and three-hours-
for-lunch-club days, I introduced a deprefixing logue and
logue dialogue. Chris Morley, Bill Benet, Don Marquis and
others were intrigued with its revealed, vealed trigues which
are tri- or triangular involvements.

"You had to search before you could research. Search pioneers:
research is routine exploitation.

"You must view before you can review, overview a powerful world
geoview... copyrightable, trademarkable, markably remarkable."

- Cite RBF holograph initiating "Eccles Piece" on Barclay Hotel,
  Phila, writing paper, 14 Feb'72

---

Sea Technology:                 (2)

     See Civil War, (2)
        Engineering, 9 Dec'73
        Size, (A)(B)
        Dome House Grand Strategy: 1927-1977, (2)
        Human Unsettlement, (2)(3)

---

RBF DEFINITIONS

Second:

"Minimal consciousness evokes time,
As a nonsimultaneous sequence of experiences.
Consciousness dawns
With the second experience.
This is why consciousness
Identified the basic increment of time
As being a second.

Not until the second experience
Did time and consciousness
Combine as human life.

Time, relativity and consciousness
Are always and only coexistent functions
Of an a priori Universe,
Which, beginning with the twoness of secondness,
Is inherently plural."

- Cite INTUITION, p. 12, May '72

---

Sea:                 (1)

     See Ocean
        S.O.S.
        Waterocean
        Naga
        Swim: Dynamic Sea Where Man Must Swim

---

RBF DEFINITIONS

Second:

"...Consciousness
Identified the basic increment of time
As being a second.
Not until the second experience
Did time, consciousness--
Which is human life--
Begin.
Time, relativity and consciousness
Are always and only coexistent functions
Of an a priori universe
Which beginning with the twoness of secondness
Is inherently plural."

"As a nonsimultaneous sequence of experiences,
Consciousness begins at minimum
As a second experience.
This is why ...."

- Cite INTUITION, Draft Feb '71, p. 1-2.

---

Sea:                 (2)

     See Male & Female, 12 Jan'74
        North-south Mobility of World Man, (1)*

---

RBF DEFINITIONS

Second:

"Early humanity's concept of the minimum increment

of time was the second, because time and awareness

begin with the second experience after the other."

- Cite RBF marginalia on Synergetics draft, See 223.31- 19 Jun '71.

- Citation & context at Time, 19 Jun'71

RBF DEFINITIONS

Secondhand:

"I... had had mechanical training and was very much impressed
with the wonderful equipment that was put at the disposal of
the Navy.  It was a world in which there was no such thing as
a secondhand battleship.  You cannot win a war on secondhand
equipment; we have had this well demonstrated recently.  It
was equally impressive to me later when I left the Navy and
went into the building world and discovered how unscientific and
secondhand most of the approach to housing was-- how people
really drifted from one old house to another, and the few new
houses that were built were without any benefit of engineering."

- DESIGNING A NEW INDUSTRY, (RBF Reader, p.149), 1946

---

RBF DEFINITIONS

████████████ Secondhand Gadgetry:

"We find ourselves continually advancing in domestic technology,

but only as the second-hand gadgetry, by-producted by the

cast-off segments of the weapons industry."

- For sitation and context see Weapons Technology, 10 Oct '63

---

Secondhand Gadgetry:

See Electric Lights, 15 Oct'64

---

Secondhand God:

See Religion, (1)

---

Secondhand:                                                    (1)

See No Secondhand Battleship
No Secondhand God

---

Secondhand:  Second Hand:                                      (2)

See Copper, 9 Dec'73
Lags, (1)
Sea Power, 23 Jan'75

---

Second Hand:

See Lags (1)

---

Second Layer:

See Icosahedron:  Inside-outing Of, 10 Jan'50
Primary Structure, 10 Jan'50

Secondness = Otherness:

See Somethingness & Nothingness, 7 Oct'75

Secrecy of the Artist:

See Artist, May'65, Jun'66, 2 Jun'71

---

Second Power:  Second Dimension:

See Powering: Second Powering
Two-dimensionality

RBF DEFINITIONS

Secrecy:  Secrecy of Mathematical Knowledge:

"I am quite confident that the early navigators knew a
great deal about the Earth and that they were doing just
what navigators and others were doing in my day in the
Navy when the Navy instructions were when I was Commanding
Officer, that if anybody was about to take my ship the
first thing I would do would be to go to the rail and take
all the leaded books, anything of importance was covered
in lead, and throw them overboard. Men had been hiding
their secrets in the sea for great ages, so I felt that many
people carrying on their navigation could remember some
of the principles in their head but much of the important
record could get lost."

- Cite Oregon Lecture #7, p. 251. 11 Jul'62

---

Second:                                         (1)

See Intuition:  Second Intuition
Vector:  One-second Vector Length

RBF DEFINITIONS                                 (1)

Secrecy:  Secrecy of Mathematical Knowledge:  Navigation:

"I said to myself, I think that the first mathematics
which related to a plurality of stars, and where you are,
the first triangulation, occurred in relation to the
navigators. I think then that the people who sailed into
the windward, who started going into the prevailing winds
westward, became the first inventors of the navigation.
You cannot invent navigation unless you have something that
you became familiar with. I think then that the people who
invented the navigation invented the first really important
kinds of mathematics dealing in triangulation, in major
patterns. And so I think that mathematics and navigation
developed in a very high way on the sea, and later on came
up onto the land. But people who knew their way about the
sea knew how to get to very important resources, and there
were great premiums paid for what they could bring in a
very secret kind of a mind-- and they began to guard their
secret of navigation very carefully. I think that the
great mathematical secrets were really very progressively
hidden. When the navigators were going westward out of
the Straits Settlements areas, and so forth, and finally
negotiated across westward of the Indian Ocean to the
eastern shores of Africa and the southern shores of

---

Second:                                         (2)

See Awareness, 24 Apr'72
Heartbeat, 13 Mar'73
Time, 19 Jun'71*
Time-sizing, 30 Nov'72

RBF DEFINITIONS                                 (2)

Secrecy:  Secrecy of Mathematical Knowledge:  Navigation:  (Cont.)

Mesopotamia. And they began to memorialize their
navigational capabilities upon the land. They go up on the
land and using the same kind of navigational capabilities
they navigate across the land to get to the Mediterranean.
Then they go northward down the Nile and they come to the
Mediterranean. And there they build the same kind of boats
built out of the patterns they can carry in their head.
And they go on with what we call this lateen sailing in the
Indian Ocean and it gets into the Mediterranean. We find,
then, this navigating moving westward, and the men who
became the great ████████ priests are the men who are monopolizing this very secret information which makes it possible
to do this very powerful wealth making through trade which
is controlled through navigation. You can take a lot of
sailors to sea with you but they don't know where they have
been-- just in a lot of water. So it is very easy to keep
your secret. So these navigators began to make pyramids
and other forms. You will find them in India and we find
in Babylon, the beginnings of our very impotant kind of
mathematics: of the 60-degree angles, of the 360 degree
concept, of the 60-minute seconds, and so forth. The first
real handling of time and angles-- which are the very

RBF DEFINITIONS (3)

Secrecy: Secrecy of Mathematical Knowledge: Navigation: (Cont.)

essence of the navigation. I think that these secrets were
deliberately hidden by the priests and kept from the people,
even possibly from the kings.

"At any rate the priests of the Roman Catholic Church began
to tell me that this is a hierarchy of Heavenly Host . . .
we have all kinds of legends mixed up here, but I think that
this is one way that the priesthood found a way of carrying
very important mathematical information."

- Cite Oregon Lecture #7, pp. 252-253. 11 Jul'62

---

Secrets: Secretion:

See Cyclic Bundling of Experiences, May'49
Duality of Universe, May'49

---

Secrecy of Mathematical Knowledge: (1)

See Vizier: Grand Vizier
Wizard

---

RBF DEFINITIONS

Sectionless Tensioning: (1)

See Length-to-Girth Ratio
Co-orbiting of Earth & Moon Around Sun

---

Secrecy of Mathematical Knowledge: (2)

See Malthus, 23 Feb'72
More with Less: Sea Technology, (1)(2)
Pythagoras, 18 Jun'71
Sea, 18 Jun'71
Yin-yang, (2)

---

RBF DEFINITIONS

Sectionless Tensioning: (2)

See Chemical Bonds (2)
Coherence, 9 Jul'62

---

Secrecy:

See Chronofile, (1)
Dymaxion House, 13 Jul'74
Navy Sequence, (3)-(6)
Sea, 18 Jun'71; 23 Jan'75
Ship, (3)
Spaceship Earth, (c)
Understanding, 1 Apr'49

---

RBF DEFINITIONS

Seeability:

"Our seeability is so inherently local that we never see
anything but the asymmetries."

- Cite RBF to EJA, Blackstone Hotel, Chicago, 31 May 1971

- Citation and context at Asymmetry, 31 May'71

RBF DEFINITIONS

Seeability:

"That's what I've been gibing you all the time, with the
positive and the negative: I've been giving you the visible
and the invisible. That's exactly what we've been accounting.
So you can only see the locally asymmetrical. You can't
see the total. . . . You'll never see anything but the
asymmetrical, because we are so local. Our seeability is
inherently local."

- Cite tape transcript RBF to EJA and BO'R, Chicago, 31 May '71.

---

See: Seeability:          (1)

See Seeing
   Sight
   Unseeable: Unseeability
   Visibility: Vision: Visual

---

See: Seeability:          (2)

See Asymmetry, 31 May'71*
   Rubber Glove, 23 May'72
   Symmetry & Asymmetry, Dec'71

---

RBF DEFINITIONS

Seed:

"...The vegetation impounds the Sun radiation by exquisitely
orderly photosynthesis and produces beautiful orderly molecular
structures, thus converting very random, cloud-interrupted
radiation into orderly molecular growths as little seeds,
transforming into trees, lambs, and a myriad of other highly
regular organic species."

- Citation and context at Boltzmann Sequence (5), Dec'72

---

RBF DEFINITIONS

Seed:

"Nature is always shipping tension by seeds. The
compression comes in locally."

- Cite RBF to EJA, 3200 Idaho, 30 Oct'72

---

RBF DEFINITIONS

Seed:          (1)

"Nature makes many potential 'starts.'
As for instance
All the vegetation which impounds the Sun's energy
Must be regenerated and multiplied.
But it cannot have its progeny
Within its immediate vicinity,
As the trees shadow
Would prevent its young
From impounding the Sun's radiant energy.

"Wherefore all the trees
Launch their seeds
Into the air or upon the waters
To drift to chance landings,
Where the seeds may be favorably nourished
And grow.
The chances of such auspicious landing
Are so unfavorable
That Nature must send
Billions times billions of seeds away
From the parent vegeation,
Which, though potential of complete success,"

- Cite BRAIN & MIND, pp.153-154 May '72

---

RBF DEFINITIONS

Seed:          (2)

"May never germinate and prosper.
The airs and waters
Of the planet Earth
Are filled with the aimlessly migrating seeds."

- Cite BRAIN & MIND, p.154 May '72

---

RBF DEFINITIONS

Seed:

"We find that in the seed nature provides a blueprint
pattern tightly folded up in a triangular tension grid."

- Cite CONCEPTUALITY OF FUNDAMENTAL STRUCTURES, Ed. Kepes,
1965, p. 85.

# Synergetics Dictionary

Seeds: (1)

    See Ecology Sequence
        Tensile Blueprints
        Gestating Seed
        Nature Ships Tension

Seeing the Whole World at Once: (1)

    See World Looks at Itself

Seeds: Seed: (2)

    See Boltzmann Sequence (5)*
        Trees (c)
        Fire (A)
        Regenerative, 1960
        Shadow, 1970
        Male & Female, 1 Feb'75

Seeing the Whole World at Once: (2)

    See Dymaxion Airocean World Map, (1)

RBF DEFINITIONS

Seeing:

"...Man has sensorial tunability and is sensorially aware of only one-millionth of physical reality. The little rainbow color band of human 'seeing' is less than one-millionth of the stretched-out reality of the invisible colors of all the 92 regenerative chemical elements of associative energy or of the various radiations."

    - Citation and context at Optical Motion Spectrum (1), 4 Mar'69

Seeing: (1)

    See Optical
        Seeability
        Seeing vs. Hearing
        Sight
        Vision

RBF DEFINITIONS

Seeing vs. Hearing:

"Seeing is universal vs. hearing which is ethnic, like languages. Hearing is 700 m.p.h. and seeing is 700 million m.p.h. Television is a million times greater than radio."

    - Cite RBF at Penn Bell videotaping session, Philadelphia, 22 Jan'75

Seeing: (2)

    See Moving Picture Continuity, Jun'66
        Perception, Jun'66
        Picture, 1938

Segment of Inclusion: Segment of Conclusion:

See Teleology: Bow Tie Symbol, 1938

RBF DEFINITIONS

Self:

"To each human environment is everything that isn't me.
And Universe is 'everything that isn't me' and me--
environment and me."

- Cite RBF to EJA
  Beverly Hotel, New York
  15 March 1971

- Citation at Environment, 15 Mar'71

---

Selectable: Selective: (1)

See Electable
    Elective
    Options
    Size-selective
    Tunability

RBF DEFINITIONS

Self:

"And self which is entirely metaphysical
Is not the metaphysically observable
Biological organism
With which it is intimate
Any more than is the telephone
The self of those who communicate
With one another
By means of the telephone's observable
Frequency differentiating capability
As it relays its tunable patterning
To the physical nervous system's tuning
To be arrayed for consideration
By the metaphysical self, the mind."

- Cite RBF Draft BRAIN & MIND, pencil, 1971

---

Selectable: Selective: (2)

See Resonance Field, 13 May'73
    Spherics, 30 Nov'72
    Modulations, 17 Jun'75

Self-annihilation:

See Economists, Jun'66
    Television: Third Parent, May'65

---

RBF DEFINITIONS

Self:

"Self is not a priori evident."

Self-awareness:

See Complementary, May'72

- Context and citation at Synergetic Strategy of Commensing
  With Totality, 28 May'72

Self-balancing:

See Humans as Machines, (1)

---

RBF DEFINITIONS

Self-communicate:

"Communication will probably be accomplished by thinking alone, ergo more swiftly and realistically than by sound and words."

- Citation & context at Individuality, 9 Jan'75

---

Self-bounding System:

See Tetrahedron as Conceptual Model, 28 Jan'73

---

RBF DEFINITIONS

Self-Communicate:

N.Y. Times, 15 May'72, H.M. Schmeck, Jr. "Immunology: A Code Spelling Life or Death": "The populations of cells communicate with one another and trigger into activity any of several kinds of immune response."

R.B.F. Marginalia: "Only number can self-communicate as structural or destructural associabilities. ⊙—⊙ "

- Cite RBF Marginalia presumably 15 May'72

---

Self-chilling:

See Ghana Dome: Self-chilling Machine

---

Self-communicate:                    (1)

See Communication to Self or Others

---

RBF DEFINITIONS

Self-communicate:

EJA:   "How can you communicate without culture? How can you have language without culture?"

RBF:   "You don't need language to communicate with self. It can be nonverbal; that's the point. We may not know the name for a 'circle' but we would recognize it absolutely every time.

       "Children self-communicate putting blocks in slots with no words about it at all."

- Cite RBF to EJA, 3200 Idaho, Wash. DC., 8 Apr'75

---

Self-communicate:                    (2)

See Zoned System: Zone Limits, 1954
     Individuality, 9 Jan'75*

RBF DEFINITIONS

### Self-Congruence Packing:

"The openmost condition or single bonding corresponds in
flexibility or mutability with the behavior of gases. The
medium packed condition or double bonded hinged arrangement
corresponds to the behaviors of liquid aggregates. The closest
packing triple bonded fixed-end arrangement corresponds with
rigid structural molecular compounds; the closest packing
concept which was developed in respect to spherical aggregates
only with their concave octa and vector equilibrium spaces
between spheres, overlooks a much closer packed condition of
energy structures, which however had been comprehended in
organic chemistry, that of quadrivalence and four-fold
bonding which corresponds to outright congruence of the
octahedra or tetrahedra with themselves. When carbon transforms
from its soft, pressed cake, carbon-black, powder, or
charcoal arrangement to its diamond arrangement it converts
from triple bonding or so-called closest arrangement to
quadrivalence. We might call this self-congruence packing, as
a single tetrahedron arrangement in contradistinction to
closest packing as a neighboring group arrangement of spheres."

- Cite RBF Ltr. to Prof. Von Hochstetter, 28 Oct '64, p. 2.

### Self-congruence Packing:

See Self-packability
    Clear Space Polyhedra
    Multiple Self-congruence

### Self-congruence:                                    (1)

See Multiple Self-congruence
    Self-packability

### Self-congrunce: Self-congruent:                      (2)

See Octahedron, 10 Dec'75

### Self-consciousness:

See Life, (pp.8-9) Jan'72

### Self-considerate Society:

See Austranesia, 10 Aug'75

RBF DEFINITIONS

### Self-consideration:                                  (1)

See Tetrahedron Discovers Itself and the Universe
    Universe Considers Itself
    World Looks at Itself
    Parts: Each Part in View of the Others
    Self-considerate Society

### Self-consideration:                                  (2)

See Plane, 19 Feb'72

RBF DEFINITIONS

██████████ Self-Debiasing:

"First your members can develop an effective anticipation
of the things that are to happen.  Though it is impossible
to anticipate the precise set of transitional events, you
can be in the vicinity of important event occurrences.
Your most important task is to help your members become
comprehensive by intellectual conviction and self-debiasing,
not as an ignorant yielding, but as a progressively informed
displacement of invalid assumptions and dogma by discovery
of the valid data.  In this development the young will lead
the old in swiftly increasing degree."

- Cite RBF in AAUW Journal, Pp. 177-8, May '65

---

**Self-definition:**

SEE MIT Sequence, (1)

---

RBF DEFINITIONS

Self-Deception:

"The degree of self deception is proportional to the width

of the angle of disagreement."

- Cite RBF in "The Listener" transcript by John Donat, 26 Sep'68

---

**Self-development:**

See Man as a Function of Universe, (2)

---

Self-deception:                                    (1)

See Omission vs. Admission

---

**Self-dichotomizing:**

See Star Tetrahedron & VE, 9 Nov'73

---

**Self-deception:**                                (2)

See Possession, 10 Jun'74
    Life is a Sumtotal of Mistakes, (1)
    Mistake, 7 Nov'75
    Sin, 7 Nov'75
    Crowd-reflexing, 7 Nov'75

---

RBF DEFINITIONS

**Self-discipline:**

Q.     "Which of the disciplines do you think are the most
critical for our current problems?"

RBF:   "The only important one of all the disciplines is
self-discipline.  At the front of one of my books I have
said 'Dare to be naive.'  That is what we must all dare to
be--to make our own choices from all the shams around us.

"Each of us must dare to go along with the truth as experience
teaches us and as our own intellect realizes its significance
only in relation to the welfare of all humans around their
local Universe functioning as information apprehenders and
articulaters in relation to the integrity of eternal regeneration."

- Cite RBF to White House Fellow Anspacher; Watergate Hotel,
  Wash, DC: 28 Mar'77

RBF DEFINITIONS

Self-Discipline:

"Today I see many engaging in yoga. I am sympathetic with
what they're trying to do, but I don't think you have to
be coached by yoga or anything else to learn self-discipline.
You've got to discover yourself. I don't think you can get
it from somebody else. I don't think you can get it by
having somebody else psychoanlayze you. I see many of my
students who go to psychoanalysts getting in more and more
trouble rather than getting out of it. And the ones who
don't go in for being psychoanlayzed I see learning to
understand themselves and consciously disciplining themsleves.
Self-discipline is the key-- and we've all got it if we want
to use it. . . . At the time I was going through this self-
discipline process I evolved a philosophy which assumed that
most problems of humanity can be solved."

- Cite RBF quoted in HOUSE & GARDEN Interview by Beverly
  Russel, p. 199, May '72

RBF DEFINITIONS

Self-Discipline:

"The fundamental self-discipline conceptioning . . . is

the only real educational process."

- Cite NEHRU SPEECH, p. 22, 13 Nov '69

RBF DEFINITIONS

Self-Discipline:

"Systematic conceptioning and recollected conceptioning,

both universal and local, which progressively traces,

relates, and compares nonsimultaneously observable

locally functioning entities, is self-disciplined."

- ~~Cite OMNIDIRECTIONAL HALO, p. 135, 1960~~

- Citation at Conceptioning, 1960

Self-discipline:                                    (1)

See Salvation vs. Self-discipline

Self-discipline:  Self-disciplining:               (2)

See Conceptioning, 1960*
    General Systems Theory, Jun'66
    Periodic Experience, (8)
    Plumbing, (1)(2)
    Thinking, 1960; (A)(B)
    World Game, Jun'66
    God, 7 Nov'75
    Anger, (1)-(3)

Self-discovery:                                    (1)

See Tetrahedron Discovers Itself
    Universe Considers Itself

Self-discovery:                                    (2)

See Synergetic Strategy of Commencing with Totality,
    28 May'72

Self-divisioning:

See Triacontrahedron, 31 Jul'77

RBF DEFINITIONS

Self-education:

"The highest priority of education should be to accommodate
humanity's innate, chromosomically programmed, intellectual
appetite for comprehending the interrelationships between all
the events of which their senses progressively inform them.
Our schools have failed to adequately satisfy those appetites.
They have failed to inspire because inspiration springs from
realization of the interrelated significances....

"Alternative education provides opportunities for the spontaneous learner to apprehend the whole picture and thus to
become a comprehensivist. This is what young people instinctively desire....

"One of the most important events of the education revolution
now under way is the discovery that each of us is born comprehensively competent and spontaneously coordinate, quite capable
of treating large quantities of data and families of variables
from the start. A child spontaneously integrates total information. It craves to understand and be understood.... For half
a century I have explored self-educating ways for making the
world work for everyone. It is exciting to witness groups of
dedicated young people... peeling of and investing their time
in alternative routes... which hold high promise for them."
- Cite RBF Introduction to Guide to Alternative Colleges, 1974

Self-education:                                              (1)

   See Self-teaching

Self-education:                                              (2)

   See Education, 20 Jan'75
      Conceptual Mathematics, (2)
      Learning, 18 Jul'76

Self-embracement:

   See Vectc. Equilibrium, 22 Jun'72

Self-entrapment:

   See Word Trends, May'44

RBF DEFINITIONS

Self-Evident:

"Self is not a priori evident."

- Citation and context at Synergetic Strategy of Commencing
With Totality, 28 May'72

Self-evident:

   See Axiomatic
      Obvious

Self-expansive:

   See Randomness, Dec'72

RBF DEFINITIONS

Self-experience:

"So the strategy I was employing, and the tiny little capital you and I have, which is just our experience. Self-experience. Beautiful equipment. . . . And how it can ▓ really be turned to the powerful advantage of the many."

- Citation and context at Individual Economic Initiative, 19 Feb'73

---

Self-halving:

See Triacontrahedron, 31 Jul'77

---

RBF DEFINITIONS

Self-experience:

"...Experience is the vital factor... since one can think and feel consciously only in terms of experience, one can be hurt only in terms of experience. When one is hurt, then somewhere in the linkage of his experience can be discovered the parting of the strands that led to the hurt. Therefore it follows that strict adherence to rationalization, within the limits of self-experience, will provide corrections to performance obviating not only for one's self, but for others, the pitfalls that occasion self-hurt...."

- Citation and context at Rationalization Sequence (3), 1938

---

Self's Honey-seeking Preoccupation:

See Bee, 9 Nov'72

---

RBF DEFINITIONS

Self-experience:

See Time Vector, 24 Sep'73

---

Self-hurt:

See Self-experience, 1938

---

Self-expression:

See Architecture, May'70

---

Self-inexplicable:

See Progressions, May'49

Self-inside-outable:  Self-inside-outing:

    See Octahedron Model of Doubleness of Unity, (1)(2)
       Octave Wave, 5 Mar'73

---

Self-interstabilizing:

    See Prime Otherness, 24 Sep'73
       Tetrahedron, Aug'72; 24 Sep'73

---

Self-interdeterioration:

    See Tensegrity:  Miniature Masts:  Positive & Negative,
       Dec'61

---

Self-invertable:

    See Octave Wave, 5 Mar'73

---

Self-interference:             (1)

    See Non-self-interference
       Pattern Integrity:  Atomic Knots
       Tensegrity Model of Self-interference of Energy

---

RBF DEFINITIONS

    Self-ish:

    "If one wishes to obtain a definite answer from Nature

    one must attack the question from a more general and

    less self-ish point of view."

    - Cite RBF holograph, undated, in Max Planck's "Survey
       of Physics," London & NY.

---

Self-interference:  Self-interfering:      (2)

    See Design Covariables:  Principle Of, 1959
       Mass, 1959
       Matter vs. Radiation, 7 Nov'73
       Ninety-two Elements, 25 Aug'71
       Pattern Integrity, 25 Aug'71
       Pattern Strip Aggregate Wrapabilities, 19 Dec'73
       Tetrahedral Dynamics, (2)
       Touch, 29 Dec'58
       Unique Frequencies, 9 Jul'62
       Structure, 3 Oct'72
       Object, 9 Nov'73
       Einstein Equation: $E = Mc^2$, 1959

---

RBF DEFINITIONS

Selfishness:

"...Vastly wealthy interests... were continuing to do what
money had done in the past: i.e., to rationalize selfishness.
Assuming the political concept of fundamental inadequacy
of life-support for all the humans around our planet,
selfishness had been able to say, 'I have those for whom I'm
responsible and because there is not enough life-support
for all, I am obliged to do various things that are utterly
and completely selfish.'"

"I felt that the Club of Rome's pronouncement of the 'Limits
to Growth' represented history's last attempt on the part
of organized capitalists' selfishness to justify to the
world public why their wealth should be unable to do anything
about the third world."

    - Citation & context at Club of Rome:  Limits to Growth, (A); (B),
       20 Sep'76

RBF DEFINITIONS

<u>Selfishness</u>:

"My greatest discovery-- besides my mathematics-- is in ■
sociology: the realization that selfishness can no longer
be rationalized.  The fears of resource inadequacy are no
longer valid.  Probably only several hundred thousand
people know this.  Nothing could be more critical than the
fact that the individual is now unbuttoned from his selfishness."

- Cite RBF to EJA in Pagano's Rest., Phila. PA., 22 Jun'75

---

<u>Selfishness</u>:                                                      (2)

See Antisynergetic, Jan'72
    Club of Rome:  Limits to Growth, (A)(B)*
    Economics, 16 Feb'73
    Inflation, Sep'73
    Invisible Architecture, (F)
    Obvious, Jan'72
    Pirates:  Great Pirates, (4)

---

RBF DEFINITIONS

<u>Selfishness</u>:

"Selfishness is a drive so that we'll be sure to regenerate.
It has nothing to do with morals."

- Citation and context at <u>Economics</u>, 16 Feb'73

---

RBF DEFINITIONS

<u>Selfist</u>:

". . . all the short-sighted, expedient 'things' applauded
by the most powerfully advantaged <u>selfists</u>, so swiftly
consigning man to extinction as 'unfit' for survival. . ."

- Citation and context at <u>Up and Down Sequence</u> (2), 13 Nov'69

---

RBF DEFINITIONS

<u>Selfishness</u>:

"Selfishness (self-preoccupation pursued until self loses
its way and self-generates fear and spontaneous random
surging, i.e., panic, the plural of which is mob outburst
in unpremeditated wave synchronizations of the individually
random components.]"

- Cite NO MORE SECONDHAND GOD, "Universal Requirements of
  a Dwelling Advantage." p. 49. (Anchor.) 1960

---

<u>Self-knotting</u>:

See Ninety-two Elements, 9 Apr'40
    Pattern Integrity, 25 Aug'71

---

<u>Selfishness</u>:                                                      (1)

See Anonymity
    Enlightened Selfishness
    Idea Stealing
    Monofocus Upon Self
    Pollution:  Infinite Room to Pollute
    Unselfishness
    Rationalization of Selfishness

---

<u>Self</u>:  <u>I Would Like to Be Myself</u>:

See Identity, May'70

RBF DEFINITIONS

■■■■ Self & Nonself:

"Self is metaphysical and

All that self observes is physical

Which is not to say

That the environment

Which is also all the non-self

Is all physical

For all the non-observable experiences
Of abstract cognition,
Which consider and re-consider
The observable experiences,--
Are metaphysical."

                    - Cite RBF Draft, BRAIN & MIND, pencil
                         1971

---

Self-Now:

    See Now Hourglass:  Cross Section of Teleological Bow Tie

---

RBF DEFINITIONS

Self-Now:

"...Genius has the ability to fix events by the convergent
angle of two or more sight lines, not only in time (or space)
past, but also, in time (or space) ahead, from the central
perspective of self-now.  Resultantly it becomes possible for
genius first to analyze teleologically such 'fixed' phenomena,
and then to objectify them in a precise time-energy composition.
Genius's dual or multiple personalities may be said to be
representative of a breadth of viewpoint, more-than-average,
highly worldly, and having an exquisite sense of Timeliness."

    _ Citation and context at Genius, 1938

---

Self-organizing Principle:

    See Conceptuality, 19 Feb'72

---

RBF DEFINITIONS

Self-Now:

"Macro-exquisite speed-of-light self-interfering radiation
     patterns energetic self-tying into concentric
              knots of relative mass in a mathematically
                idealized variety of symmetrical-
                       asymmetrical atomic
                          assemblages whose
                             local micro-
                               orbiting
                               induces

                           N O W

                         which
                      multilpies by
                  progressive subdividung into
               micrscopically ever greater speeds of
            transformation through insectine phase magni-
         tudes dividing into the micro-organisms phase, and
      then dividing progressively into molecular and atomic phases;
   then phasing into radioactivity at 586,000 m.p.s, expanding once
more to micro-eternity of no-time.

    - Cite RBF holograph, 3200 Idaho, Wash DC, Mar'72

---

RBF DEFINITIONS

Self & Otherness:

"Awareness = the otherness saying 'See Me' to the observer.
Awareness = the observer saying to self, 'I see the otherness.'
Otherness induces awareness of self.  Awareness is always
otherness inductive.  The total complex of otherness is the
environment.

    - Cite SYNERGETICS 2 draft at Sec. 100.011; 28 Apr'77

---

RBF DEFINITIONS

Self-Now:

"The macro-microcosm of minimum frequency of omnidirectional interference
restraint exquisite speed of light 700 million m.p.h.  self-interfering
radiation patterns energetic self-tying into concentric knots of
relative mass in a mathematically idealized variety of symmetric-
al-asymmetrical atomic assemblages whose local subvisibly
resolvable micro-orbiting induces the superficially
deceptive motionless thingness of
             mini-micro-microcosm
                    of
                  NOW
                 which
         progressive experience-won
       knowledge multiplies by progressive■
      intellectually contrived instrumentally implemented
    exploratory subdividing into microscopically ever greater
   speeds of transformation through insectine phase magnitudes
 dividing into the micro-organisms phase, and then dividing progressively into ■■■■ molecular and atomic phases; then passing into
radioactivity at 700 million m.p.h. expanding once more into macro's
700 million at least macroseem . . .

       - Cite RBF Holograph, 3200 Idaho, Wash DC, Mar'72

---

RBF DEFINITIONS

Self & Otherness:

"Experience is inherently omnidirectional; ergo there are
always a minimum of twelve 'others' in respect to the nuclear
observing self."

    - Citation & context at Experience, 19 Nov'74

RBF DEFINITIONS

### Self and Otherness:

"Only through relationships with otherness can self learn of principles; only by discovery of the relationships existing between self and othernesses does inspiration to employ principles objectively occur. There is nothing in self per se, or in otherness per se, that predicts the interrelatedness behaviors and their successively unique characteristics. Only from realization of the significance of otherness can it be learned further that only by earnest commitment of self to otherness does self become inadvertently advantaged to effect even greater commitment to others, while on the other hand all self-seeking induces only ever greater self-loss."

(behaviorally)

- Cite RBF galley correction to SYNERGETICS at Sec. 411.12, 2 Nov'73

---

RBF DEFINITIONS

### Self & Otherness: Four Minimal Aspects:

"If you use the 'area' of Euler it doesn't work. You have to convert the area to nothingness to arrive at the four minimum aspects of self and otherness."

- Cite RBF to EJA, Paganmo Restaurant, U. Penn, 22 Jun'75

---

RBF DEFINITIONS

### Self & Otherness: Four Minimal Aspects:

"Life, minimally described is 'awareness,' which is inherently plural for at minimum it consists of the individual system which becomes aware and the first minimum 'otherness' of which it is aware, the otherness being integrally or separately internal or external to the observing system's 14 integral topologically componented subsystem: $4V + 4A + 6L$.

"Together the observer and the observed constitute two points differentiated against an area of nothingness with an inherent line of 'awareness'-interrelationship running between these two points. Euler's generalized formula, which he named topology, says that the number of points plus the number of areas will always equal the number of lines plus the number two, which, Goldy finds to be at minimum $2P + 1A = 1L + 2$, which minimum set of awareness aspects of life adds to four:i.e., (a) the observer; (b) the observed; (c) the line of interrelationship; and (d) the nothingness area against which the somethingness is observed.

"There are no experimentally demonstrable absolute maximum limits. Only the minimum limit is demonstrably absolute. The minimum limit experienceable is always a 'system-- even when it looks like a point."

- Cite GOLDYLOCKS Ms. p.A3, 9 Jun'75

---

### Self & Otherness: Four Minimal Aspects:

See Minimum Awareness Model
Minimum Four Awareness Aspects of Life
Tetrahedron as Primitively Central to Life

---

RBF DEFINITIONS

### Self-and-otherness Interbehaving:

"The octet truss is the evolutionary patterning... of the ever-recurrent 12 alternative options of action, all 12 of which are equally the most economical ways of self-and-otherness interbehaving-- all of which interbehavings we speak of as Universe."

- Citation and context at Octet Truss, 24 Sep'74

---

### Self & Otherness:                                                   (1)

See Communication to Self & Others
Observer & Observed
Otherness: At Least One Other
Otherness: At Least Twelve Others
Minimum Awareness
Awareness
Tetrahedron Discovers Itself
Integral Otherness
Tetrasystem
Individual & Group Principle

---

### Self & Otherness:                                                   (2)

See Experience, 1971; 19 Nov'74*
Scheme of Reference, 24 Sep'73
Initial Frequency, 6 Nov'72
Orbital Escape from Critical Proximity, (1)
Love, 3 Apr'75
Background Nothingness, 2 Jun'75
Me, 26 Jan'72
Thirty Minimum Aspects of a System,(B)
Timeless, Dec'71
Modules: A & B Quanta Modules, 20 Dec'73
Awareness, 28 Apr'77
Freedom, Jan'77
Human Beings & Complex Universe, (3)

---

### Self-packability:

See Self-congruence Packing
Clear Space Polyhedra

Self-perpetuating:

See Inside, 26 Jan'73

Self-querying: Self-questioning:                    (1)

See Questions: Answering Questions
Question Asking

Self-polarization: Self-polarizing:

See Three-way Great-circling: Three-way Grid, 15 Feb'66

Self-querying: Self-questioning:                    (2)

See Synergetics, 1959
Universe, 1959

Self-positionability:

See Star Tetra & VE, 9 Nov'73

Self-realizing: Self-realization:

See Synergetic Strategy of Commencing with Totality,
28 May'72
Bridge, 13 Nov'69

Self-purging:

See Hunger: Stones Do Not Have Hunger, 20 May'75

Self-reassociation:

See Carbon, Jun'72

Self-rebuilding Telephones:

You & I as Pattern Integrities, 22 Jan'75

---

Self-regeneration: Self-regenerative:

See Irreversibility, Feb'71
Ruddering Sequence, (3)
Success, 1972
Omnitriangulation, 3 Oct'72
Nuclear Domain & Elementality, (1)

---

RBF DEFINITIONS

Self-Regenerative:

"The significance of Einstein's radiational top speed
is that there is a point of complete regeneration
by which our Universe is the only and minimum perpetually
self-regenerative system. It is a self-regenerative
Universe of fantastic complexities and design of great
integrity in which the sum total of running through the
total film takes hundreds of billions of years before
it accomplishes its remotest re-wow."

- Cite Museums Keynote Address Denver, p. 13. 2 Jun'71

---

Self-scavenging:

See Hunger: Stones Do Not Have Hunger, 20 May'75

---

RBF DEFINITIONS

Self-Regenerative:

"Our universe is the only, and the minimum, perpetual
motion machine. It is self-regenerative."

- Cite RBF address Am. Assn of Museums, Denver, 2 June 1971.

---

RBF DEFINITIONS

Self-seeking:

"Self-seeking brings a potential loss which engenders first
caution, then fear: fear of change, change being inexorable.
Fear increases and freezes. Self-seeking always eventuates in
self-destruction through inability to adapt."

- Cite RBF to EJA, 3200 Idaho, 7 Nov'72; incorporated in
  SYNERGETICS draft at Sec. 411.24. Rewrite as of 8 Nov'72
  411.23

---

Self Regeneration: Self-regenerative:          (1)

See Closed System
Ninety-two Elements
Perpetual Motion Machine

---

RBF DEFINITIONS

Self-Seeking:

"Self-seeking brings a potential loss which engenders
first caution, then fear: fear of change, change being
inexorable. Self-seeking always eventuates in self-
destruction through inability to adapt."

- Cite RBF to EJA, 3200 Idaho, 7 Nov'72 incorporated at SYNERGETICS
  draft at Sec. 411.24, 8 Nov'72
  23

Self-seeking:

    See Loss: Discovery Through Loss

---

Self Starter: (2)

    See Biosphere, (3)
    Brain's TV Studio, 1960
    Energy Capital, (2)
    Intellect: Equation Of, Dec'48
    Social-industrial Relay, 1 Apr'49
    Nonstate, 11 Sep'75

---

Self-stabilization: (1)

    See Inter-self-stabilizing
    Self-interstabilizing
    Structural Self-stabilization

---

Self-structuring:

    See Icosahedron as Electron Model, 7 Mar'73
    Universal Integrity: Ve & Icosa, (1)
    Mites & Quarks as Basic Notes, (1)(2)

---

Self-stabilization: (2)

    See Structure, 21 Dec'71; Nov'71; 8 Feb'71; 13 Nov'69; Mar'71
    Necklace, (A)-(C)
    Triangle, 9 Nov'73
    Stable & Unstable Structures, 7 Jun'72
    Omnitriangulation, 3 Oct'72

---

Self System:

    See Extraorganic Travel, 26 May'72
    Probability, 20 Feb'72

---

Self Starter: (1)

    See Main Engines of Universe
    Group Starters

---

Self-teaching: (1)

    See Self-education

Self-teaching:                     (2)

    See Learning, (1)(2)
        Dymaxion Artifacts, (1)(2)

---

Self:                          (1A)

    See Bumblebee
        Comprehensive: Self-debiasing
        De-selfed
        Dualism of Self
        Ego
        Feedback: Self-accelerating Feedback
        History's Human Self-education
        I
        Identity
        Individual
        Loss: Discovery Through Loss
        Most Economical Way of Behaving Relative to Unity and
          Self
        Ninety-two Tendencies of Self-impoundment of Energy
        Nonself
        Matrix of You & I
        Me, the Observer
        Me
        Other
        Outsideness of Self

---

Self-tightening: 

    See Knot, 7 Nov'73

---

Self:                          (1B)

    See Personality
        Sybchro-resonance
        Returning Upon Self
        Starting with Self
        Unselfishness
        Monofocus Upon Self
        Reciprocal Self-precessors
        Unity & Self
        Universe Considers Itself
        World Looks at Itself

---

Self-triangulating:               (1)

    See Inter-self-triangulating

---

Self:                          (2)

    See Annihilation, 22 Jun'75
        Apprehension Lags, 11 Sep'75
        Communication, 13 May'73
        Environment, 15 Mar'71*
        Kissing, 1 May'77
        Octet Truss, 24 Sep'73
        Synergetic Strategy of Commencing with Totality,
          28 May'72*
        Thinking, 1938
        Whole System, 28 May'72
        Human Beings & Complex Universe, (3)

---

Self-triangulating: Self-triangulation:     (2)

    See Probability, (1)(2)

---

Self:                          (3A)

    See Self Annihilation
        Self Awareness
        Self-bounding System
        Self-communicate
        Self-congruence Packing
        Self Consciousness
        Self-consdierate Society
        Self Condideration
        Self Debiasing
        Self Deception
        Self Definition
        Self Development
        Self-dichotomizing
        Self Discipline
        Self-discovery Process
        Self Embracement
        Self-evident
        Self-expansive
        Self Experience
        Self-balancing

Self:                                                    (3B)

      See Self Expression
          Self's Honey-seeking Preoccupation
          Self Hurt
          Self-inside-outable
          Self-interdeterioration
          Self Interference
          Self-interstabilizing
          Self-invertable
          Self-ish
          Selfishness
          Selfist
          Self-knotting
          Self:  I Would Like to be Myself
          Self & Nonself
          Self-Now
          Self-organizing Principle
          Self & Otherness
          Self-perpetuating
          Self-polarizing

Semantics:                                               (1)

      See Communication
          Definitions
          Koryzbski
          Meaning
          Verbs
          World-around Language

Self:                                                    (3C)

      See Self-positionability
          Self Precessors
          Self Querying
          Self Realization
          Self-realizing Planet
          Self Reassociation
          Self-regenerative
          Self Seeking
          Self Stabilization
          Self Starter
          Self Structuring
          Self Ssytem
          Self Teaching
          Self-triangulating
          Self-education
          Self is not A Priori
          Self-chilling
          Self-divisioning
          Self-halving

Semantics:                                               (2)

      See Babbling, 18 Mar'72
          Realization, May'49
          Sphere, 20 Feb'73*
          Me, 26 Jan'72; 28 Oct'73

Selling:  Selling Anything:

      See Obsolescence, Apr'72
          Mobile Rentabilyt vs. Immobile Purchasing, 20 Sep'76

Semiautonomous Dwelling Facilities:

      See House, 1971
          Inventability Sequence, (1)

RBF DEFINITIONS

Semantics:

"If you get too semantically incisive the reader loses
all connections with anything he has ever read before.  That
might not be a great loss.  But I like to assume that the
reader can cope with his reflexes and make connections
between the old words and the new and better words..."

- Citation and context at Sphere, 20 Feb'73

TEXT CITATIONS

Semihelix:

Synergetics text at Sec. 623.11

Semimetaphorical:

See Verity, 29 Dec'73

---

RBF DEFINITIONS

Senses:

"The nonsimultaneity and dissimilarity
Of the complementary interpatternings
Produce what we sense to be reality,
Otherwise they would cancel one another
And there would be no sensoriality."

- Cite BRAIN & MIND draft, p.13, 1971

---

RBF DEFINITIONS

Semisymmetry:

"Semisymmetry means that out of the six edges of a
tetrahedron there are two pairs of symmetries.

"An isosceles is semisymmetric."

Symmetry         =   equiangle
Semisymmetric    =   isosceles
Asymmetric       =   scalene

"People want to be either symmetric or asymmetric.  They love
bias, but the don't like isosceles, the fence-straddler.
Real love is isosceles: inclusive but not exlusive.  What
people seem to mean by love is they want the other to join
them: scalene.  The real love includes the other; it is
omni-inclusive, semisymmetric, isosceles."

- Cite RBF to EJA, 3200 Idaho, Wash DC, 15 Oct'72

---

RBF DEFINITIONS

Senses:

"The senses have to do with the brain.  The senses, per se,
are nothing.  Just the brain.  And it's what began the
real metaphysical you-and-I, feel about what the brain is
saying. . . You take the senses away, then there is no
consciousness.  Consciousness comes from experience."

- Cite WATTS TAPE, p. 14, 19 Oct '70

---

RBF DEFINITIONS

Senses:                                                    (1)

"The range of the first three senses are so close together,
and sight is so different, that we may best rank them as
#1, touch, being a primary set; with both #2, olfactoral
coupled with #3, aural, as a secondary set; and #4 sight, as
a tertiary set:  wherefore in effect, touch is the yesterday
set; while the olfactoral and aural (what you are smelling,
eating, saying, and hearing) are the now set; while sight
(what only may be next) is the future set.  (We can seem to
see, but we have not yet come to it.)  Whereas reality is
eternally now, human apprehending demonstrates a large
assortment of lags in rates of cognitions whose myriadly
multivaried frequencies of myriadly multivaried, positive-
negative, omnidirectional aberrations, in multivaried
degrees, produce such elusively off-center effects as
possibly to result in an illusionary awareness of an approximately unlimited number of individually different awareness
patterns, all of whose relative imperfections induce the
illusion of a reality in which 'life' is terminal, because
physically imperfect; as contrasted to mind's discovery of
an omni-interaccommodative complex of a variety of different
a priori, cosmic, and eternal principles, which can only be"
- Cite RBF addition to SYNERGETICS galley at Sec. 801.12,
      22 Nov'73                                          [13]

---

RBFDEFINITIONS

Senses:

     ". . . Fractional information is furnished only

by those wave frequencies which are directly apprehendable

exclusively within man's very limited

sensorial spectrum frequency bands--

tactile, olfactoral, aural and optical--

and these sensorial frequencies in turn occur

only as minuscule trace zones

and only at the middle ranges

of the now partially explored, obviously vast

and inferentially extensible

electromagnetic frequency spectrum."
                              - Cite NO MORE SECOND HAND GOD, pp 86,87
                                        9 Apr'40

---

RBF DEFINITIONS

Senses:                                                    (2)

"intellectually discovered, have no weight, and apparently
manifest a perfect, abstract, eternal design, the metaphysical
utterly transcendent of the physical."

- Cite RBF addition to SYNERGETICS galley at Sec. 801.12,
      22 Nov'73                                          [13]

---

Sense Disconnection:

See Dollar Bills: $200 Billion One-dollar Bills
            Circling Around Earth, (2)

RBF DEFINITIONS

Sensibility:

"Physical interferences of our sensibilities are alike true and real, or realisable, only in principle."

- Citation and context at Principle, May'49

Sensibility:

See Naivete, 1 Feb'75

RBF DEFINITIONS

Sensings & Eventings:

"The child's awareness of otherness phenomena can be apprehended only through its nerve-circuited sense systems and through instrumentally-augmented, macro-micro, sense-system extensions-- such as eyeglasses. Sight requires light, however, and light derives only from radiation of celestial entropy, where Sunlight is starlight and fossil fuels and fire-producing wood logs are celestial radiation accumulators, ergo all the sensings are imposed by cosmic environment eventings."

- Cite SYNERGETICS 2 draft at Sec. 100.014; 28 Apr'77

RBF DEFINITIONS

Sensing, Storing & Intuiting Device:

"The metaphysical mind employs these organically regenerative, subjectively interacting, sensing, storing, and intuitive devices, as well as all the organism's unique, objectively articulate faculties to harvest critically relevant information."

- Citation & context at Life, 9 Jun'75

Sensing, Storing & Intuiting Devices:

See Humans as Machines

RBF DEFINITIONS

Sensitivity of the Artist-scientists:

"Scientists and artists haven't too many valves closed. . . . They are children with a great deal of experience. Education can ruin real sensitivity to the Universe."

- Cite RBF quoted by Noel FRackman in his review of the Tetrascroll show, ARTS Magazine, Apr'77

Sensitivity of Childhood:

See Doing What Needs to Be Done, 17 Dec'74
Child as Laboratory, (1)

Sensitive: Sensitivity:                                      (1)

See Artist: Histrionics
    Intuition & Aesthetics
    Intuition: Second Intuition
    Valve of Sensitivity

Sensitive: Sensitivity: (2)

See Artist: Histrionics (1)
Average Man (1)(2)
Intuition Sequence (6); 15 Jun'74
Reflexes, 2 Jun'71
Earning a Living, 2 Jun'71
Thinking, 10 Sep'75
Psychiatry, (2)(5)
Anger, (1)

---

RBF DEFINITIONS

Sensoriality:

"Sensoriality is a corporeally external phenomena--
reportingly relayed inwardly to the brain and therein
imaginatively scanned by the mind which conceptualized
independently in generalized formulations such as the
conception of a nuclear grouping around a nucleus, quite
independently of size."

- Citation & context at Brain & Mind, 13 Nov'69
- Cite NEHRU SPEECH, p. 12, 13 Nov'69

---

RBF DEFINITIONS

Sensorial Identification of Reality: (1)

"From physics we learn that every fundamental behavior of Universe
Always and only coexists with a nonmirror-imaged complementary.
The nonsimultaneity and dissimilarity
Of the complementary interpatterning pulsations
Integrate to produce
The complex of events
We sensorially identify as reality.
Without the pulsative asymmetries and asynchronous lags
The complementations would cancel out one another
And centralize equilibriously,
And there would be no sensoriality,
Ergo, no self-awareness, no life;
For we have also learned from physics
That all the positive and negative weights
Of the fundamental components of matter
Balance out exactly as zero.
Life may well be a dream,
A comedy and tragedy
Of errors of conceptioning
Inherent in the dualistic
Imaginary assumption
Of a self differentiated
From all the complex otherness
- Cite BRAIN & MIND, pp.96-97 May '72

---

RBF DEFINITIONS

Sensoriality:

"Size and intensity are sensorial comparing functions of
the special case experiences by brain and not by mind.
Mind is concerned only with principles that hold true
independently of size yet govern the relative size
relationships."

- Cite NEHRU SPEECH, p. 12, 13Nov'69
- Citation at Brain and Mind, 13 Nov'69

---

RBF DEFINITIONS

Sensorial Identification of Reality: (2)

"Of reasonably conceivable Universe
For it must be remembered
That no human has ever seen directly
Outside himself.
What we call seeing
Is the interpretive imagining in the brain
Of the significance and meaning
Of the nervous system reports
Of an assumed outsideness of self,
All of which organic design conception
May be that of a great intellect
Which is inventing Universe progressively
Evolving mathematically elegant
Integral equations
For each conceivable challenge
Including the invention
You and me.
But you and I cannot escape
And are given extraordinary faculties
Which we are supposed to use.
So here we go again
From right where we are Now."

- Cite BRAIN & MIND, p.97 May '72

---

RBF DEFINITIONS

Sensoriality:

"The word 'form' implies direct sensoriality. The
word 'conformity' likewise implies direct sensoriality--
it means dealing only with forms."

- Cite MEXICO, p. 101, 10 Oct'63
- Citation at Form, 10 Oct'63

---

RBF DEFINITIONS

Sensoriality:

"The omni-interactions impinge on your nervous system
in all mannner of frequencies-- some so high as to
appear 'solid' things, some so slow as seeming to be
'absolute voids.'"

- Cite SYNERGETICS DRAFT - "Conceptuality: Doppler Effect."
RBF marginalia - 26 April 1971

- Citation at Halo Concept, 25 Apr'71

---

RBF DEFINITIONS

Sensorial Model:

"Experience is always sensorial and so I can always get a
sensorial base or model."

- Citation & context at Experience, 28 Apr'74

RBF DEFINITIONS

Sensorial Reflex:

"Humanity's intellect and sensorial reflexes are completely
uncoordinated.  We see clouds floating by, birds flying and
people moving, but we can't see plants or humans growing.
We can't see the economic charts realistically: Humanity gets
out of the way only when it sees the motion..."

"Like parrots, we learn to recite numbers without any sensorial
appreciation of their significance.  We have yielded so
completely to specialization that we disregard the comprehensive significance of information."

- Citation and context at ███████ Invisible Motion, 13 Mar'73

---

Sensorial & Nonsensorial:

See Inside-outing, 13 Nov'69

---

RBF DEFINITIONS

Sensorial Spectrum:

"Apprehension means information furnished by those wave

frequencies tune-in-able within man's limited sensorial

spectrum."

- Cite SYNERGETICS, "Universe," Sec. 302, 1971
- Citation at Apprehension, 1971

---

Sense:  Sensoriality:                                        (1A)

See Architectural Aesthetics:  Six S's
    Abstract vs. Sensorial
    Angular Sense
    Aural
    Common Sense
    Common Sense:  Perceptual Peephole
    Directional Sense
    Electromagnetic Spectrum
    Extrasensoriality
    Human Sense Ranging & Information Gathering
    Local Information-sensing Devices
    Olfactoral Sense
    Optical Tuning & Scanning
    Hearing
    Pattern Sense
    Sensorial & Nonsensorial
    Smellable
    Spherical Sensation
    Seeing:  Seeability
    Satellite:  World Satellite Sensing

---

Sensorial-frequency-spectrum Inventory:

See Individual Universes, 28 Oct'73

---

Sense:  Sensoriality:                                        (1B)

See Sweepout
    Sight:  No Man has ever Seen Outside of Himself
    Inventory of Sensations
    Tunability
    Form = Sensoriality
    Taste
    Integral Functions of Man
    Non-sensoriality:  Infra & Supra
    Tactile
    Visual

---

Sensorial Spectrum:

See Invisible Reality, May'72
    Twelve Universal Degrees of Freedom:  General
        Systems, (11)(III)

---

Sense:  Sensoriality:                                        (2)

See Apprehension, 1971*
    Brain & Mind, 13 Nov'69*
    Disconnect, 13 Nov'69
    Form, 10 Oct'63*
    Halo Concept, 25 Apr'71*
    Invisible Motion, 13 Mar'73*
    Experience, 28 Apr'74*
    Communications Hierarchy, (4)
    Dynamic vs. Static, 12 Nov'75

Sense:  Sensoriality:                                    (3)

        See Sense Dosconnection
            Sensibility
            Sensitive:  Sensitivity
            Sensorial Identification of Reality
            Sensorial Model
            Sensorial Reflex
            Sensorial Spectrum
            Sensorial & Nonsensorial
            Sensing, Storing & Intuiting Device
            Sensings & Eventings

Sense Phrases:                                            (D)

        See Democratically Coagulating
            Distortion Massaged to the Center

**SENSE PHRASES**                                        (A)

        See Attraction Link-up
            Angularly Hinged Convergence

Sense Phrases:                                            (F)

        See Fibrous Crystalline Units
            Fit:  Pressured or Tensed Fit
            Force-fluids

Sense Phrases:                                            (B)

        See Bounce-impel

Sense Phrases:                                            (G)

        See Girth-tensed Bonds
            Glimpse-discover
            Gear-locked

Sense Phrases:                                            (C)

        See Cleave-roll
            Coalescing Adherence
            Corkscrew Spiral Traceries
            Contact Coincidence
            Critical Convergence & Flying Huddle
            Critical Proximity Co-orbiting
            Corner-converge

Sense Phrases:                                            (H)

        See Holding Patterns of Energy

<u>Sense Phrases:</u>                                      (I)

    See Impact Extrusion
        Invisible Trampoline
        Instrumental Hook-up
        Interface Couplings
        Indrinking
        Internestability
        Intergeared Mobility Freedoms


<u>Sense Phrases:</u>                                      (P)

    See Pattern Strip Aggregate Wrapabilities
        Precessional Peel-off
        Pumping Fraction Factors
        Push-pull Members
        Perimeter Tangent


<u>Sense Phrases:</u>                                      (J)

    See Jet Stilts:  Jet-stilting


<u>Sense Phrases:</u>                                      (R)

    See Reach-miles


<u>Sense Phrases:</u>                                      (K)

    See Kiss:  Locked Kiss


<u>Sense Phrases:</u>                                      (S)

    See Scratch-chorded
        Severance-tracing
        Shuttle-woven
        Smell-discover
        Spin-halving
        Stretch-press
        Swivel-moored
        Self-scavenging


<u>Sense Phrases:</u>                                      (O)

    See Omniembracing Squeeze
        Ovational Gearing
        Off-molded Offspring
        Omnitriangularly Oriented Evolution


<u>Sense Phrases:</u>                                      (T)

    See Tastebuds of Sound
        Tangential Avoidance
        Thrust-throw
        Touch-feel
        Tepee:  Half-spin Tepee Twist
        Twist-sprung
        Twist-pass
        Torque Momentum
        Tendril Curve

Sense Phrases: (U)

See Unpeel the Gravitationals
Unwrap the Orbitals
Unbandage the Sphere

Separate: Separating Out: (2)

See Halfway-round-the-Worlding (1)
Plus One, 9 Jul'62
Stability, 18 Mar'69
Polyhedron, 1 Jan'75
Life, 16 Aug'50
Plumbing, (1)
Boeing 747 Sequence, 22 Jun'75
Synergy, Nov'71
Human Beings & Complex Universe, (12)

Sense Phrases: (V)

See Vacuum-fulcrumed Oars
Vectorial Near-miss
Vertex-vortex Rotations
Variable Strands Braiding
Visual Symphony

**SEQUENCES: METAPHORS** (A)

See Animate & Inanimate Sequence
Agricultural Accounting System
Air is Socialized
Airocean World Map
Airplanes: Far Apart in the Sky
Airplanes: Four Airplanes in the Sky
Airplanes Stacked Up For Landing
Airplane Flight As Lift
Airplane Stalled Airplane
Action-reaction-resultant
Aesthetics of Uniformity
Atomic Computer Complex
Autonomous Living Technology Packet
Average Human Being
Acres Per Individual Human Being
Advantage: Enjoyment of All Earth Without One
Individual Being Advantaged at Expense of Another
Atoms: All the Experiences with All the Atoms
Adoption of the New Only as Last Resort

Sense Phrases: (W)

See Wedge-spread (Sec. 981.07)
Wrapability

FILE INDICATORS

Sequences: Metaphors: (B)

See Berry Picking
Bird's Nest as a Tool
Brain's TV Studio
Boats at Anchor Retard the River's Flow
Blind Man's Buff
Boltzmann Sequence
Brouwer's Theorem
Brownian Movement
Bubbles in the Wake of a Ship Sequence
Brain's Alarm Clocks
Bullet: Synchronization of Bullets through
Airplane Propeller Blades
Building Blocks
Buddha: Christ: Mohamed
Bottom: Pulling the Bottom Up
Brain as Library
Boeing 747 Sequence
Buggy Industry Could Never Invent Automobile

Separating Out: Separate: (1)

See Ego: Separating Ego out of Omniscience
Time: Separating Time out of the System
Liquid vs. Solid
Differentiation: Differentiable
Dome House: Separation of Mechanical Service
Core & Structural Shell
Membranes

FILE INDICATORS

Sequences: Metaphors: (C)

See Child As Laboratory
Child: A Little Child Shall Lead Them
Child Pushes Spoon Off Edge of Table
Children's Pictures of the Sun and the Moon
Chain Stronger than its Weakest Link
Chaos: Myth That Scientists Wrest Order From Chaos
Collision: Ships Colliding on the Globe
Cul de Sac: Inuitively Inadvertent
Child Sequence
Coincidental Articulation Sequence
Closest Packing of Spheres Sequence
Cosmic Fish Sequence
Conversation Sequence
Cosmic Accounting Sequence
Charts: We Need Only Rotate Our Charts 90 Degrees
Computer Asks an Original Question
Continuous Man
Copper Sequence
Critical Convergence & Flying Huddle
Children as Only Pure Scientists

FILE INDICATORS

Sequences: Metaphors: (C)'

See Crossbreeding World Man
Custom: Lest One Good Custom Corrupt the World
Coin Toss in the Air
Common Sense: Perceptual Peephole
Communications Revolution
Communication to Self and Others
Comet: Around Comes the Comet Again
Chick Breaking Out of the Egg
City Management Concept of World Government
Community as Unit Mechanical Organism

FILE INDICATORS

Sequences: Metaphors: (E)'

See Epistemological Stepping Stones
Eternal Designing Capability
Expense: Without Any Individual Profiting at the
    Expense of Another
Eye-beamed Thoughts
Education Automation
Eggs: You Just Lay Eggs
Earth Model as Bundle of Nutcrackers
Electronic Referendum: Electronic Voting
Earth: Let's Get Down to Earth
Everybody's Business
Energy Involvement of 92 Chemical Elements
Enough to Go Around
Emergence by Emergency
Electromagnetic Transmission of Human Organisms
Energy-harvesting Dwelling-machine Devices
Exempt: We Are Not Exempt from Universe
Everyone in on the Information

FILE INDICATORS

Sequences: Metaphors: (D)1

See Divide & Conquer Sequence
Diesel Ship at Sea
Dollar Bills: $200 Billion One-dollar Bills
    Circling Around Earth
Death: Weighing of People as they Die
Dog Pulling on a Belt
Darwin: Evolution May Be Going the Other Way
Dead Center of Universe
Death: Slow Death by Slums
Death: Weighing People as they Die
Decreasing Confusion: Law Of
Deficit Accounting
Deliberately Nonstraight Line
Departments: Nature Has No Separate Departments
Design Science Revolution
Diminishing Chaos: Law Of
Dismissal of Irrelevancies
Dominoes: Tumbling a Set of Dominoes
Dwelling Service Industry
Dymaxion Airocean World Map

FILE INDICATORS

Sequences: Metaphors: (F)

See Fisherman Theme
Fossil Fuel Sequence
False Property Illusion
File Cards With Triangular Array of Holes
Fountain Pattern
Form Cannot Follow Function
Fail-safe Advantage
Failure as Norm of Yesteryears
Fault: Society is Living in a Sort of Earth Fault
Feedback by Eye
Fellowships: Life Fellowships in Research &
    Development
File: RBF Research File Colors
Finger: Cut Your Finger
Finite Furniture
Fire in a Theater
Fish: Playing the Fish on a Reel
Flight: Fixed Formation Flight
Floating City

FILE INDICIATORS

Sequences: Metaphors: (D2)

See Desovereignization Sequence
Doing Right Things for Wrong Reasons
Deceptiveness of Topology
Doorknobs as Disease Carriers

FILE INDICATORS

Sequences: Metaphors: (F)'

See Fluid Geography
Flying Huddle
Foldability of Great Circles
Force Lines: Omnidirectional Lines of Force
Force: Don't Oppose Forces; Use Them
Football Player Metaphors
Frontier: Living on the Frontier
Form Cannot Follow Function

FILE INDICATORS:

Sequences: Metaphors: (E)

See Economic Accounting System
Energy Slave
Education Revolution
Earning A Living Sequence
Energy Income Sequence
Ecology Sequence
Eternal Designing Capability Sequence
Eternal Slowdown
Eternal Wellspring
Energy Capital Sequence
Earth: Let's Get Down to Earth
East-is-East Theme
East-to-West Trend
Eddington's Proof of Irreversibility
Education: Knowing Where the Bridges Are
Electric Lights in Battleship
Energy Has Shape
Environment: Altering the Environment
Environmental Events Hierarchy
Epigenetic Landscape

FILE INDICATORS

Sequences: Metaphors: (G)

See Geosocial Revolution
Gross World Product Sequence
Generalizations: Mathematical vs. Literary
Generalization Sequence: Degrees Of
Good: If All the Good People were Clever
Game of Life
Game of Universe
Generators: Tumbling a Set of Dominoes to the
    Generating Station
Geophysical Year: IGY
Ghostly Greek Geometry
Grass: Putting Aside the Grasses
Group Womb
Guinea Pig
Genius: Children Are Born Geniuses

FILE INDICATORS

Sequences: Metaphors: (H)

See Hierarchies
How Little I Know
Heartbeats & Illions Sequence
Heisenberg-Eliot-Pound Sequence
Halo Concept
Hammer Thrower
House as Terminal of Community Mechanism
Human Beings at the Center
Humanity's Final Cosmic Exam

---

FILE INDICATORS:

Sequences: Metaphors: (K)

See Knight's Move in Chess
Key-Keyhole Sequence
Kindergarten Level of Comprehension
Knot Sequence
Kepler Alone with the Stars
Kleptomaniac: Intellectual Kleptomaniac
Know-how
Knowing More and More about Less and Less

---

FILE INDICATORS

Sequences: Metaphors: (I)

See Individual Economic Initiative
Inventability Sequence
Invention Sequence
Immunology Series
Intuition of the Child
Impossible: Only the Impossible Happens
In & Out: Go In to Go Out
Individual Economic Initiative
Individual Life as One Way Universe Could Have
Turned Out
Individual Universes
Industrial Lag
Industrial Man
Industrial Revolution: Profile Of
Industrialization: Successive Halving and Time of
National Industrialization
Infinity: Letting Infinity into the System
Instant Universe
Intellect: Equation Of
Intellectual Kleptomaniac
Intellect: Speed Of

---

FILE INDICATORS

Sequences: Metaphors: (L1)

See Leaders: Take Away the Leaders
Lever Sequence
Leaders Can Yield to the Computer
Lever: Fallen Tree as a Lever
Lag Rates
Land Technology
Law: Crisscross, Right-angle Grid in Civil &
Agrarian Law
Life is not Physical
Lifetime: Personal Lifetime Experience for
Elective Investment
Life's Temporary Vehicles
Light Side vs. Serious Side
Local Holding Patterns
Locked Kiss
Longing: Fear & Longing
Loss: Discovery Through Loss
Legs: Man Born with Legs Not Roots
Life is a Sumtotal of Mistakes
Live Show Reaching Us Took Place Billions Of
Years Ago

---

FILE INDICATORS

Sequences: Metaphors: (I)'

See Interference as a Social Model
Interference: Two Lines Cannot Go Through the Same
Point at the Same Time
Intuition: Hot Line Of Intuition
Intuition: Second Intuition
Inventability Sequence
Inventories
Invisible Aesthetics
Invisible Architecture
Invisibility: Trends To
Irrelevancies: Dismissal Of
Irreversibility: Principle Of
Isotropic Vector Matrix
Industrial Accounting vs. Agricultural
Internal Control of Distortion
Improve: You Can't Improve on the Middle

---

FILE INDICATORS

Sequences: Metaphors: (L2)

See Light on Scratched Metal
Learning: You Can't Learn Less

---

FILE INDICATORS

Sequences: Metaphors: (J)

See Jitterbug
Jump in the River
Jump: Man Jumping From a Boat

---

FILE INDICATORS

Sequences: Metaphors: (M)

See Madonna Theme
Might Makes Right
Man as a Function of Universe
MIT Sequence
Meek Have Inherited the Earth
Macro→ Micro: Synergetic Advantage
Magic Numbers: Isotopal Magic Numbers
Main Engines of Universe
Making the World Work
Mammalian-vegetation Interchange of Gases
Man as a Function of Universe
Man: Automated Metabolism of Man
Man as Halfway in Range of Size of All Creatures
Man: Interstellar Transmission of Man
Man as an Invention
Man as Local Problem Solver
Man as Local Universe Technology
Man: Relative Abundance of Chemical Elements in
Man and Universe
Man as One Way Universe Might Have Come Out
Manifest: One through Eight

FILE INDICATORS

Sequences:   Metaphors:                                              (M)'

See Mars:  No Country Doctor on Mars
    Mast in the Earth
    Matchstick Thickness at which Objects go into Orbit
    Matter Over Mindist
    Meaning:  Decease of Meaning
    Mechanical Extensions of Man
    Mental Moutfuls
    Metabolic Flow
    Metals:  Recirculation of Metals
    Metaphysical Disconnect
    Mind-over-Mattering
    Mind Over Muscle
    Mines Above the Earth
    Miniature Earth
    Minimum Knot
    Mini Earth
    Mole:  Industrial Man as Universal Mole
    Money Metaphors
    More With Less
    Morley Christopher:  The Greatest Poem Ever Known

FILE INDICATORS

Sequences:   Metaphors:                                              (O)

See Objective Design
    Obnoxico
    Obsolete:  Inventory of Obsolete Concepts
    Octave Limits of Variation
    Odd Ball
    Official Reality
    Official War
    Old Life Informing the New
    Old Man's River's Project
    Old Words
    Omnidirectional Closest Packing of Spheres
    Omnidirectional Halo
    Omniscience Transcendent of Omnipotence
    One-Town World
    Onerousness of Ownership
    Operating Manual for Spaceship Earth
    Optimism:  I Am Not an Optimist
    Options:  Discovering What the Options Are
    Orderliness Operative in Nature
    Organic Model:  Biological World as Model for Society
    Outlaw Area

FILE INDICATORS

Sequences:   Metaphors:                                              (M)''

See Motion Freedom from Rest of Universe
    Muchness of the Unfamiliar
    Multiplication Only by Division
    Myself:  I Would Like to be Myself
    Musical Chairs
    Mark Your Paper:  Nobody to Mark Your Paper
    Mutual Survival Principles
    Motion Economics
    Marine Life Analogy of Humans
    Mobile Rentability vs. Immobile Purchasing
    Mite as Model for Quark
    Money:  Making Sense vs. Making Money
    Model of Toothpicks & Semi-dried Peas

FILE INDICATORS

Sequences:   Metaphors:                                              (O)'

See Overspecialization of Biological Species & Nations
    Outside:  What's Outside Outside?
    Outbound Packaging of Human Food Waste
    Office Buildings:  Conversion to Apartments
    Only the Whole Big System Works

FILE INDICATORS

Sequences:   Metaphors:                                              (N) 1

See Nature Has No Separate Departments
    Naga Theme
    Narcotics as a Political Strategy
    Nature Always Comes Back on Itself
    Nature Has So Many Options
    Nature:  What Nature Needs to be Done
    Navigational Ability to go to Faraway Strange Places
        And Bring Back Strange Miracle Objects
    Navigators:  Early Navigators
    Necklace
    New Life
    Newton's Cosmic Norm of "At Rest"
    Nine Chains to the Moon
    Nucleus = Nine = Nothing
    Ninety-two Elements:  Chart of Rate of Acquisition
    Norm of Einstein as Absolute Speed
    Now Hourglass:  Cross Section of Teleological
        Bow Tie
    Nuclear Computer Design
    Number:  Tetrahedral Number

FILE INDICATORS

Sequences:   Metaphors:                                              (P)

See Piano Top
    Population Sequence
    Probability Model of Three Cars on a Highway
    Prestressed Concrete Sequence
    Packaged Concept
    Pass:  And It Came to Pass
    Panic:  Official Panic
    Parallelogram of Forces
    Partially Overlapping
    Parting the Strands
    Parts:  Fallacy of 'Basic Building Parts'
    ~~Pathology:  Preventive Pathology of Specialty Pathology~~
    Pattern Conservation
    Pattern Integrity:  Equation Of
    Pattern Processing Machines
    Peashooter
    Pendulum Model vs. Scenario Model
    Perceptual Peephole as Fraction of Reality
    Performance Per Pound
    Permanent Symbolic Communication Devices

FILE INDICATORS

Sequences:   Metaphors:                                              (N2)

See Nature Trying To Make Man a Success
    Nature Permits it Sequence
    Nature's Subvisible Order
    Navy Sequence
    Nozzle:  Harvesting Pollution at the Nozzle
    Nature is Neither Good nor Bad
    North-south Mobility of World Man
    Nature in a Corner
    Nature's Technology vs. Humans' Technology

FILE INDICATORS

Sequences:   Metaphors:                                              (P)'

See Permeative Topology
    Permitted Ignorance
    Perpetual Motion Machine
    Petal:  Tetrahedron as Three-petaled Flower Bud
    Petroleum:  It Costs a Billion Dollars to Make
        A Gallon
    Phantom Captain
    Pharaoh:  Only the Pharaoh Was Informed
    Phobia of Imprisonment
    Physical Is Always the Imperfect
    Physical Ingredient Recalls
    Physics:  Difference Between Physics & Chemistry
    Physics as Internal Affairs of the Atom
    Piaget:  Child's Spontaneous Geometry
    Picasso Duo-face Painting
    Pine-tree and Palm-tree Belts
    Pirates:  Great Pirates
    Planarity of Civil & Agrarian Law
    Plastic Call-girl Angels
    Plastic Flowers

FILE INDICATORS

Sequences: Metaphors: (P)''

See Plural Unity
Pneumatic Structures
Poets Anticipate Science
Point: Inbound & Outbound Point
Pole Vaulter
Pollen-delivering Inadvertencies
Pollution: Infinite Room to Pollute
Pollution: News as Most Polluted Resource
Polyhedral Understanding
Population Density: Manhattan Cocktail Party
Population Sequence
Poverty: Slow Slum Death
Precession: Analogy of Precession & Social Behavior
Problem: Statement of the Problem
Process vs. Thing
Proclivities: Inventory Of
Profile: There Is No Half-profile
Profile of the Industrial Revolution
Profit: Annual Profit and Failure System
Profit: "We Stars Have Got to Make a Profit!"
Prognostications About Future of Man

FILE INDICATORS

Sequences: Metaphors: (R)'

See Raison d'Etre of Boast & Fear
Ramify the Idealistic
Reachability Range
Reader Can Cope with his Reflexes
Real Estate Development
Realm: Real: Royal
Rectilinear Grid Systems
Reductio ad Absurdum
Reduction by Bits
Reduction to Practice
Reel of Tape Recorder
Reflex: Conditioned Reflex of Bias
Reform of Environment Rather then Reform of Man
Regenerative Design: Law Of
Reinvestable Time & Survival Needs
Relevant: Lucidly Relevant Set
Religion Related to 'Reglio' or 'Rule'
Rememberable Number
Research Fellowships

FILE INDICATORS

Sequences: Metaphors: (P)'''

See Projective Transformation
Prospect for Humanity
Prototype Sequence
Pulse Pattern
Punched Cards
Push Button & Dial Systems
Push-pull Members
Puzzle of Washington Crossing the Delaware
Pyramid Technology
Politics: Accessory After the Fact
Promote: I Don't Promote
Planetary Democracy
Pathology: Preventive vs. Curative
Property: You Can't Take it with You

FILE INDICATORS

Sequences: Metaphors: (R)''

Regenerative Economic Sustenance
See Resource Inadequacy
Resource Inventorying
Returning Upon Itself: Systems Returning Upon
Themselves
Return to Modelability
Revolution: Hard Revolution & Soft Revolution
Revolution by Inadvertence
Right to Live: Proving Your Right to Live
Right-Makes-Might Dominance
Rocks Don't Love
Rockabye Baby
Rockets: Steerable Rockets
Rope: I Take a Piece of Rope
Rotation of Night as a Shadow
Rule of Communication
Rules of Operational Procedure
Reel: Playing the Fish on a Reel
Robin Hood Sequence
Romance of History in the Making

Rain as Radial

FILE INDICATORS

Sequences: Metaphors: (Q)

See Quantam Wave Phenomena Sequence
Quantum Mechanics: Grand Strategy
Quarrying
Quest-asking Possibility
Question: Original Question
Quick Death
Quanta Loss by Congruence
Quantum Mechanics: Minimum Geometrical
Fourness

FILE INDICATORS

Sequences: Metaphors: (R-4)

See Race with Evolution

FILE INDICATORS

Sequences: Metaphors: (R)

See Radome Sequence
Ruddering Sequence
Railroad Tracks: Great-circle Energy Tracks on
the Surface of a Sphere
Rearrange the Scenery
Radiation-Gravitation Sequence
Rationalization Sequence
Reflection Sequence: Apple
Rich Man Drowning in Shipwreck
Rest of the Universe
Relative Asymmetry Sequence
Radiation Sequence
Rubber Glove Sequence
Radio Programs: Invisible Operation of Thousands
Of Radio Programs
Rafts: Early World Drifting on Rafts
Railway Trains: Loosely Coupled
Rainbow: Optical Rainbow Range

FILE INDICATORS

Sequences: Metaphors: (S)

See Science Opened the Wrong Door
Science: Gap Between Science and the Humanities
Social Highway Experience: Three Autos
Structure Sequence
Science-Technology-Industry-Economics-Politics
Sequence
Spaceship Earth Sequence
Superatomics Sequence
Spinach
Spherical Triangle Sequence
Survival Sequence: Love
Synergey Sequence: Two Massive Spheres
Sailing with the Wind: Sailing into the Wind
Satellite: World Satellite Sensing
Scaffolding Technology
Scarcity: Not Enough to go Around
Scenario Universe: Physical Evolution Scenario
Scenery: Rearrange the Scenery
Scheherazade Number
Science Opened the Wrong Door

FILE INDICATORS

Sequences: Metaphors: (S)'

See Scissors Held in Fixed Opening
    Sea Technology Conversion to Land Technology
    Secrecy of Mathematical Knowledge
    Self-discovery Process
    Selfinside-outable
    Self: I Would Like to be Myself
    Self-Now
    Shapeless: Universe Does Not Have a Shape
    Ships: A Fleet of Ships Needs More Room at Sea
    Sight: No Man Has Ever Seen Outside of Himself
    Skin Pigmentation
    Sky-island City
    Slow: The Slower We Get, the More Crowded
    Snake Swallows its Own Tail
    Snow, C.P: Gap Between Science & Humanities
    Social Sciences: Analogue to Physical Sciences
    Solid State
    Sovereignty: Elimination Of
    Spheres & Spaces
    Space Technology

FILE INDICATORS

Sequences: Metaphors: (T)'

See Three-petaled Flower Bud
    Thinking Out Loud
    Three and Only Structural Systems
    Threshold of Life
    Tiger's Skin
    Time Is Not the Fourth Dimension
    Tissue Cells of Animal Flesh
    Toenail in No Way Predicts Humans
    Tollgate: Private Tollgate the Society has to
        Go Through
    Tomorrow's Clock: Borrowing From Tomorrow's Clock
    Tong: Biting Your Tongue
    Tongue: Stick Out Your Tongue
    Tools: Craft Tools & Industrial Tools
    Trail Making & Trail Remembering
    Transformational Projection
    Travel in a Human Lifetime
    Trees Sequence
    Trespassing: Not Trespassing
    Technology & Culture

FILE INDICATORS

Sequences: Metaphors: (S)''

See Specialist Born with One Eye and a Microscope
    Spherical Barrel
    Scheherazade Number
    Stars: Invisible Motion Of
    Starting with Universe
    Starved by Ignorance
    Statement of the Problem
    Sticks: Falling Sticks
    Stone Falling and it's Going to Hit You on the Head
    Subconscious Coordinate Functioning
    Success as Norm
    Sugar on the Table
    Suicide of Humanity
    Sun is Not Saying Earth Hasn't Paid its Bill
    Superatomics Sequence
    Surprise: The Nonpolitical Surprise Has Already
        Occurred
    Surprise: Utter Surprise to be Born
    Survival Sequence: Love
    Swallow the Otherness
    Sweepout
    Synergy of Synergies

FILE INDICATORS

Sequences: Metaphors: (T)''

See Tracer Bullet Sequence
    Trial & Error
    Trim Tab
    Trinity: Equation of Trinity
    Truth: Thinking About Truth Alters Truth
    Tuck in the Universe
    Tunability
    Tolerance Sequence
    Twelve-inch Steel World Globe
    Twenty-foot Earth Globe and 200-foot Celestial Sphere
    Twilight Zone
    Twenty Questions
    Twinkle Angle
    Two Balls Coming Together
    Transnationalism vs. Colonialism
    Time is an Invention
    Time is Only Now
    Transnational Capitalism & Export of Know-how
    Tetrahedron as Primitively Central to Life
    Technology: Enchantment vs. Disenchantment
    Toothpicks & Semi-dried Peas

FILE INDICATORS

Sequences: Metaphors: (S)'''

See Service Industry
    Service: Serve
    Superstition of Social Superiority
    Stacking of Oranges & Cannon Balls
    Stars as Live Shows Billions of Years Ago

FILE INDICATORS

Sequences: Metaphors: (U1)

See Up & Down Sequence
    Universe as Verb
    Universe as Invention
    Universe Citizenship
    Universe as Energy & Information
    Universe as Kaleidoscope
    Universe as Perpetual Motion Machine
    Universal Vertex Center Model
    Ultimate Computer
    Ultra Micro Computer (UMC)
    Umbilical Cord
    Uncertainty Principle
    Uncorked Bottle
    Understanding is Exquisitely Total
    Understanding: Urge to Understand & to be Understood
    Undimensional Night
    Undiscovered Principles
    Unemployment as Freedom to Think
    Unfolded Nothingness
    Uni-angular Vectorial Convergence

FILE INDICATORS

Sequences: Metaphors: (T)

See Tactical Information
    Tactile Sequence
    Take Away the Leaders
    Task: The Larger the Task the Duller the Brain
        Brought to Bear
    Tastebuds of Sound
    Teleological Schedule of Universal Design
        Requirements
    Television: Third Parent
    Temperature of the Human Body
    Tennis Ball Hits the Big Earth
    Tensile Strength of Chrome-nickle-steel
    Tension & Compression
    Tenure: Academic Tenure
    Tether Ball
    Tetrahedral Tuck in the Universe
    Tetrahedron: Three Triangles: 2 + 1 = 4
    Tetrahedron: Two Triangles: 2 + 1 = $
    Thinkable System Takeout
    Thinkable You

FILE INDICATORS

Sequences: Metaphors: (U2)

See Unified Operational Field
    Uniform Boundary Scale
    Unique Perpendicularity
    Uniquely Variant Integral
    Unique Way of Playing the Game
    Unitary Communication Tools
    Unitary Conceptuality of Allspace Filling
    United States is Not a Nation
    United States: One of the Most Difficult
        Sovereignties to Break Up
    Units of Environment Control
    Unity: Complex & Simplex
    Unity Is Plural
    Unity As Two
    Universal Integrity
    Universal Language
    Universal Maelstrom
    Universal Requirements of a Dwelling Advantage
    Universal Research Fellowships
    Universe Citizenship

FILE INDICATORS

Sequences:  Metaphors:                                    (U3)


        See Universe Considers Itself
            Unpredicted:  Sequence of Unpredicted Events
            Unspoken Communication
            Unzipping Angle:  Tetrahelix
            Utopia or Oblivion

---

FILE INDICATORS

Sequences:  Metaphors:                                    (W)


        See Wind Sucking Sequence
            World Game Sequence
            Wave Pattern of a Stone Dropped in Liquid
            Wire to Wireless
            Wind Power Sequence
            Weapons Technology Sequence
            War:  Official War & Unofficial War
            Wellspring of Reality
            World-around Communications Transcends Politics
            Wind Always Blows within 100 Miles
            Wind Power:  Effect of Earth's Rotation
            Wind Power Feeding into Electric Utility Grid

---

FILE INDICATORS

Sequences:  Metaphors:                                    (XYZ)


        See XYZ Coordinate System

            Youth, Truth & Love
            You Do Not Belong to You
            Yesterday's Private Castle Mentality

---

TEXT CITATIONS

    Sequence:  Sequential:

    Sec. 1032.21

---

Sequence:  Sequential:                                     (1)


        See Scenario
            Overlapping
            Intervariable Sequences
            Trend:  Trending

---

Sequence:  Sequential:                                     (2)


        See Awareness, 24 Apr'72
            Life-time-space Phenomena, 22 Feb'73
            Line, 6 Nov'73
            Energy & Intellect, May'49

---

Serf:  Serfdom:  Serf Complex:                             (1)


        See Industrial Hypocrisy
            Slave

---

Serf:  Serfdom:  Serf Complex:                             (2)


        See Labor:  American Labor, 1960

Serial Communication:

See Communication, Oct'70

Series:  Superseries:

See Progressions, May'49
  Scenario vs. Absolute Symmetry, 11 Dec'75

RBF DEFINITIONS

Serial Universe:

"The term 'serial Universe' was first employed by the British scientist James Dunn.  It approaches my concept of Scenario Universe."

- Cite RBF videotaping session Philadelphia, Pa., 20 Jan'75

Serious:

See Light Side vs. Serious

RBF DEFINITIONS

Series vs. Parallel Circuitry:

"The difference between gravitation and radiation is analogous to the difference between parallel wiring and series wiring in electricity.  Series wiring is like the lights on a christmas tree in which circuitry if one light goes out the whole system goes out.  In parallel wiring when one light goes out the other lights remain operative.  This is a demonstration of integration and disintegration.  Series wiring is a disintegrative system, an open system.  Parallel wiring is an integrative system, a closed system.  It is not the "parallelism' that matters but the fact that the circuit is closed.  The word parallel came into use only because of the diagram first used to demonstrate the principle as well as the fact that the closed circuit wire is conveniently doubled back upon itself and bound into one 'lead' for house-wiring purposes.  The fact that the vectors are parallel is only a convenience of the construction industry.  The same length vectors--ergo the same energy magnitude involvement--used correctly, can provide either function.  Here we have the convergent integrations and divergent disintegration language of synergetics in the language of electricity."

- Cite SYNERGETICS, 2nd. Ed. at Sec. 527.09; RBF rewrite 11 Dec'75

RBF DEFINITIONS

Service Industry:

"Great corporations have not as yet ventured into this field because wind energy has not seemed to be monopolizable over a pipe or wire.  However, enterprise can be rewarded, in greater magnitude than ever before, by producing and renting world-around wind-harnessing apparatus-- as they already do in the computer, telephone, car rental, and hotelling service industries."

- Citation and context at Wind Power Sequence (6), 15 May'73

Series vs. Parallel Circuitry:

See Closed Systems & Open Systems
  Shunting

RBF DEFINITIONS

Service Industry:

"We can have an integrator calculating, designing and automatically manufacturing and putting together a geodesic dome in a giant jig, after which an automated 'sky tug' helicopter will carry the dome away to install it and prepare it for human occupancy, thus providing a telephone-system type of inventing, developing, installing, maintaining, relocating, and continually self-improving service industry, able to provide telephone-ordered 'instant housing,'  Such a computer-controlled housing and livingry service industry is even now feasible at one percent of the weight, time, and energy involvement per unit of volume and living equipment found in conventional high-standard suburbia or Park Avenue skyscraper technology."

- Cite THE PROSPECTS FOR HUMANITY, Sat. Review, 29 Aug'64

Service Industry:                                          (1)

        See Automation of World Production and Services
            Dwelling Service Industry
            Dymaxion House
            Fuller, R.B: What I Am Trying To Do
            Telephone
            More You Use it the More it Improves
            Mobile Rentability vs. Immobile Purchasing

---

Service: Serve:

        See Feedback Servomechanisms
            Fellow Man
            Man: How Do You Really Serve Man
            No License to Be of Service
            Mechanical Service Core

---

Service Industry:                                          (2)

        See Private Property, 28 Apr'71
            Wind Power Sequence, (a)(b); (6)*
            Design Science: (B)
            Cosmic vs. Terrestrial Accounting, (4)
            Disarmament, (1)(2)

---

RBF DEFINITIONS

Servomechanism:

"Servomechanisms responding to sensed error in first one
direction and then the other, successively correcting the
steering-- first this way, then that way-- averaging an
accomplished course halfway between. The variations get
finer and finer, trending toward but never attaining,
'absolute straightness.' This is the essence of cybernetics.
This way humans reached the Moon. It is the essence of all
life growth...."

        - Citation & context at Planetary Democracy, (7), 15 May'75

---

Service vs. Instrument:

        See Telephone, 26 Jan'75
            Distribution, 25 Jan'75

---

Servomechanism:                                            (1)

        See Feedback Servomechanism
            Ruddering

---

Service Terminal Installation:

        See Dome House Grand Strategy: 1927-1977, (2)

---

Servomechanism:                                            (2)

        See Sovereignty, (2)
            Planetary Democracy, (7)*
            Life is a Sumtotal of Mistakes, (1)(2)
            Feedback, 7 Nov'75

RBF DEFINITIONS

Set:

"Even the development of sets derives from experience
because mathematics is generalization-- and generalization
itself is sequitur to experience... The mathematicians
talk of 'pure imaginary numbers' on the false assumption
that mathematics could be a priori to experience."

- ~~Cite RBF to EJA, Beverly Hotel, NYC, 13 March '71~~

- Citation at Mathematics, 13 Mar'71

---

Set of Patterns:

See Conversation Sequence, (2)
Minimum Set, 9 Jul'62

---

RBF DEFINITIONS

Set:

"All we do is deal in . . .images. We traffic in the
memory sets, the TV sets, the recall sets and certain
incoming sets."

- ~~Cite Oregon Lecture #3, p. 98, 5 Jul '62~~

- Citation & context at Imagination, 5 Jul'62

---

Set:                                                    (1A)

See Central Set
    Circumferential Set
    Closed Set
    Comprehensive Set
    Conceptual Set
    Consuderable Set
    Considered Set
    Empty Set
    Future Set
    Filled Set
    Local Set
    Loose Set
    Minimum Set
    Minimum Regenerative Set
    Net Set
    Nonsimultaneous Set
    Now Set
    Nuclear Set
    Number:  Abstract Number Set Concepts

---

RBF DEFINITIONS

Set:

"Neither the set of all-experiences nor the set of
all-the-words which describe them nor the set of all the
generalized conceptual principles harvested from the
total of experiences are either instantly or simultaneously
reviewable."

- ~~Cite OMNIDIRECTIONAL HALO, pp 131, 132, 1960~~

- Citation at Nonsimultaneity, 1960

---

Set:                                                    (1B)

See Radial Set
    Recall Set
    Relevant:  Lucidly Relevant Set
    Positive or Negative Set of the Whole
    Subset
    Thinkable Set
    Variables:  General Theory Of
    Challenging Set
    Tunable Set:  Tuned-in Set
    Intertransformability System Sets

---

Set of Feelings:

See Conversation Sequence, (2)

---

Set:                                                    (2)

See Experience, Oct'71
    Imagination, 5 Jul'62*
    Mathematics, 13 Mar'71*
    Nonsimultaneity, 1960*
    Parts, 1954
    System, 25 May'72
    Star Events, 1960
    Etymology, Aug'71
    In, Out & Around, Nov'71

Settlements:

See Ekistics
Human Unsettlement
Unsettling vs. Settlements
Squatters
Community

---

RBF DEFINITIONS

Seven Axes of Symmetry:

"There are 25 great circles on the vector equilibrium. On the icosahedron there are 31. These are all the symmetries; there are no other points or aspects of symmetry that you could develop either on the vector equilibrium or the icosahedron (electron) side. The 25 great circles of the vector equilibrium all go through the prime vertexes."

- Tape transcript Tape 6A, Side A, p.6; RBF To Barry Farrel, Bear Island, 16 Aug'70

---

RBF DEFINITIONS

Seven Axes of Symmetry:

"The 56 axes of cosmic symmetry (See Sec. 1042.05) interprecess successively to regenerate the centripetal-centrifugal inwardnesses, outwardnesses, and aroundnesses of other inwardnesses, outwardnesses and aroundnesses as the omnipulsative cycling and omniinterresonated eternally regenerative Universe, always accommodated by the six positive and six negative alternately and maximally equi-economical degrees of freedom characterizing each and every event cycle of each and every unique frequency-quantum magnitude of the electromagnetic spectrum range."

(For later context see Precession & Degrees of Freedom, 19 Nov'74.)
- Cite RBF holograph, New Delhi, 8 Dec'72 as rewritten by RBF 13 May'73

PRECESSION SEC 533.12|

---

RBF DEFINITIONS

Seven Axes of Symmetry:

"I made many other subdivisions of octahedra and so forth and found the components always coming apart, as long as there is any cutting on the axes of symmetry, any of the ways in which nature could chop herself up with various extensions of planes, and they always come apart in whole rational numbers."

- Cite Oregon Lecture #6, p. 228. 10 Jul '62

SEVEN AXES OF SYMMETRY SEC. 1042.01|

---

RBF DEFINTTIONS

Seven Axes of Symmetry:

"These are the seven axes of symmetry of crystallography. They describe the only great circles foldable into bow ties.

Axes of Symmetry:

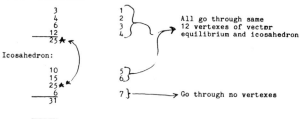

Vector Equilibrium:

| 3 |
| 4 |
| 6 |
| 12 |
| 25 ★ |

Icosahedron:

| 10 |
| 15 |
| 25 ★ |
| 6 |
| 31 |

1
2
3
4 }  All go through same 12 vertexes of vector equilibrium and icosahedron

5
6 }

7 }  → Go through no vertexes

56

- Cite RBF to EJA, Bear Island, 25 August 1971.
SEVEN AXES OF SYMMETRY - SEC. 1042.04|

---

RBF DEFINITIONS

Seven Axes of Symmetry:  Prime Generation Of:

"The prime generation of the seven axes of symmetry derives from the truncation of the tetrahedron:

4  original faces
4  triangular truncated vertexes
6  truncated edges
14  new faces of truncated tetrahedron,

whose axes generate the seven axes of symmetry."

- Cite RBF at Penn Bell studios videotaping, Philadelphia, PA., 24 Jan'75. Incorporated in SYNERGETICS, 2nd. Ed. at Sec. 1041.11

---

RBF DEFINITIONS

Seven Axes of Symmetry:

"Note that the seven axes of symmetry do not include the equator nor any single great circle."

- Cite RBF to EJA, Bear Island, 25 August 1971.

SEVEN AXES OF SYMMETRY - SEC. 1042.05|

---

RBF DEFINITIONS

Seven Axes of Symmetry.  Superficial Axes:

"There are only three superficial axes of symmetry of crystallography. They are:

Spin of vertex )
Spin of mid-edge )  = three superfical axes
Spin of center of area )
(that is, c.g. of mid-faces) )

"These are all the superficial surface angles which are the gravity. The central angles are the radiation."

- Cite RBF to EJA, 3200 Idaho, Washington DC, 21 Dec. '71.

SEVEN AXES OF SYMMETRY - SECS. 1041.01 + 02|

Seven Axes of Symmetry:                                    (1)

    See Bow Ties
        Foldability of Great Circles
        Great-circle Spinnable Symmetries: Hierarchy Of
        Fourteen Axes of Truncated Tetrahedron

---

RBF DEFINITIONS

Seven Minimum Topological Aspects:

"Euler + Synergetics: The first three topological aspects
of all minimum systems--vertexes, faces, and edges--were
employed by Euler in his formula V + F = E + 2. Since
synergetics geometry embraces nuclear and angular topology
it adds four more minimum aspects to Euler's inventory of
three:

        vertexes
        faces        — EULER
        edges

        angles
        insidensess & outsideness
        convexity & concavity   — SYNERGETICS
        axis of spin

- Cite SYNERGETICS 2 draft at Sec. 1044.01; 8 Feb'76

---

Seven Axes of Symmetry:                                    (2)

    See Omnidirectional Typewriter (3)
        Prime Numbers: Pairing Of, 17 Jan'74
        Trigonometric Limit: First 14 Primes, 14 Jan'74
        Scheherazade Numbers: Declining Powers Of, 22 May'75

---

Seven:                                                     (1)

    See Powering: Seventh Powering: Seventh Dimension

---

RBF DEFINITIONS

Seven Fundamental Symmetries:

"I will give you the design of the crystallogicals.

We find seven fundamental symmetries" and they relate

to the "seven great circles that are foldable."

- Cite RBF tape transcript, Chicago, Blackstone Hotel,
        1 June 1971 - pp. 8-9.

SEVEN AXES OF SYMMETRY     SEC. 1042.04

---

Seven:                                                     (2)

    See Prime Number, 16 Oct'71
        Vector Equilibrium: Eight-pointed Star System,
        16 Dec'73
        Vectorial & Vertexial Geometry, (3)

---

RBF DEFINITIONS

Seven Minimum Topological Aspects:

"The subsequent definition of four additional topological
aspects to Euler's three aspects of vertexes, faces, and
edges, synergetics adding (1) angles, (2) irrelevant
untuned insideness and outsideness, (3) convexity and
concavity, and (4) axis of spin, for a total of seven
topological aspects (see Sec. 1044); and recognizing the
addition of frequency as being always physically manifest
in every special case."

- Cite SYNERGETICS,(2nd. Ed.) at Sec. 251.021; 12 Feb'76

---

Seventeen:

    See Limit, 15 Oct'71
        Scheherazade Numbers: Decling Powers Of,
        22 May'75; 22 Jun'72
        Periodic Table: Harmonics of 18, 22 May'75

Severance-tracing:

See Yin-yang, (1)(2)

---

Sex:

". . . As . . . surprising as is the spontaneous synergetic urge of males and females to cohabit and thereby accidentally to start the synergetic formulation of another human being."

- Cite Dreyfuss Preface, "Decease of Meaning"
  28 April 1971, p. 8

---

Sewers: Sewage Systems:                                    (1)

See Excrement: Excremental Functions
    Plumbing
    Toilet
    Outbound Packaging of Human Food Waste

---

Sex:

"As survival rate and life sustaining capability increase, fewer births are 'required.' This may be related to our developing capacities in interchanging our physical parts, of producing mechanical organs, of having progressively fewer human organisms to replenish. The drive in humanity to reproduce as prodigally as possible decreases considerably. This may be reflected in social behaviors-- when all the girls begin to look like boys and boys and girls wear the same clothes. This may be part of a discouraging process in the idea of producing more babies.

"We shall have to stop looking askance on trends in relation to sex merely as a reproductive capability, i.e., that it is normal to make babies. Society will have to change in its assessment of what the proclivities of humanity may be. Our viewpoints on homosexuality, for example, may have to be reconsidered and more wisely adjusted."

- Cite THE YEAR 2000, San Jose State College, Mar'66

---

Sewers: Sewage Systems:                                    (2)

See Architecture, 26 Sep'68; 2 Jul'62
    Building Industry, (7)
    Houses & Infrastructure, 20 Sep'76
    Scrap Sorting & Mongering, (2)

---

Sex:                                                        (1)

See Gonads
    Homosexuality
    Male & Female
    Man: Automated Metabolism of Man
    Masturbation
    Penis
    Procreation
    Naked Girl on the Bed
    Survival Sequence: Love
    Virgin
    Kissing
    Love

---

Sex:

"The metaphysical is what is very suddenly coming into prominence. These kids just really take sex. . . and how different it is now than when evolution had to reproduce itself and they had to think of their bodies as just this great baby-making machine home. Well, all that's becoming extinct and the kids don't act that way anymore and the metaphysical is emerging terribly fast."

- Citation and context at Cosmic Fish Sequence (2), 16 Oct'72

---

Sex:                                                        (2)

See Cosmic Fish Sequence, (2)*
    Emotion, May'65
    Fuller, R.B: Moratorium on Speech, (1)(2)
    Human Beings & Complex Universe, (9)-(11)

---

Sexave:

See Sixwave (Sexave)

Shadow:                                                                (2)

See Gravity, 23 Sep'73
    Radiation-gravitation, 8 Mar'73*
    Universal Integrity, 7 Nov'73
    Weather, Feb'73
    Wind Power Sequence (3)
    Omnidirectional:  Physical Existence Environment
        Surrounds, (1)

RBF DEFINITIONS

Shadow:

"Vegetation has to regenerate its young, but it can't have
its young if there is a shadow.  The young plants would not
be able to get any of the necessary radiation.  Therefore,
most vegetation launches its new life in little seeds on the
winds and on the waters.  The possibility of these seeds
landing in just the places where they will prosper is poor,
and nature makes many starts-- enough to make sure that the
species survives."

- Cite RBF in Franklin Lecture, Auburn, Ala., p.88, 1970

Shadowless:

See Gravity, 23 Sep'73

RBF DEFINITIONS

Shadow:

"Radiation has shadows; gravity has none."

Shakespeare:

See Man as a Function of Universe, 22 Jul'71
    World Game, (3); Jun'69

Radiation-Gravitation,
- Citation and context at ████████ 8 Mar'73

Shadow:                                                                (1)

See Me & My Shadow
    Rotation of Night as Shadow
    Shadowless
    Wind Power:  Effect of Earth's Rotation

RBF DEFINITIONS

Shape:

"Euler has the visual inventory.  Aural sensing has no shape.
Our visual sense verifies our tactile sense of shape.
Smelling and sound have no shape.  Smelling has less shape
than sound.  Sound has a little shape in reflecting bouncings
of electromagnetic wave phenomena.  Visually, when we don't
see something, we call it space...."

- Citation & context at Silence, 30 Sep'76

RBF DEFINITIONS

Shape:

"Every time you enter eternity everything called shape
is cancelled. . . The episodes have shape, but the
shape is always mildly asymmetrical and continually
transforming. There is ▬ conceptual shape in the ideal,
i.e., the ideal tetrahedron, but no size, no time."

- Citation and context at Eternity (1)(2), 23 May'72

---

RBF DEFINITIONS

Shape:

"Shape is exclusively angular.

Shape is independent of size.

. . .

Shape being independent of size is abstractable."

- Cite COLLIER'S, p. 115, Oct'59

---

RBF DEFINITIONS

Shape:

"Generalized shape conceptioning is independent of size.

A triangle is a triangle independent of size.

- Cite OMNIDIRECTIONAL HALO, p. 119, Oct'60

---

RBF DEFINITIONS

Shape Awareness:

"You can have no awareness ▬▬▬▬ sense of shape with
just one otherness or two othernesses. Shape awareness
commences only with three othernesses where the relationship
of three as a triangle has finite closure. Shape is what
you see areally and until there is closure there is no
area of otherness."

- Cite SYNERGETICS draft at Sec. 1023.18, 20 Feb'73

---

RBF DEFINITIONS

Shape:

"Abstractions are conceptually shapable!"

- Cite SYNERGETICS "Corollaries," Sec. 240.59, Oct'59
- Citation & context at Abstraction, Oct'59

---

Shape of Things:

See Frame of Reference, 4 Oct'72

---

RBF DEFINITIONS

Shape:

"Different shapes, ergo different abstractions, are

nonsimultaneous; but all shapes are de-finite components

of integral though nonsimultaneous, ergo shapeless,

Universe."

- Cite SYNERGETICS "Corollaries," Sec. 240.60, Oct'59
- Citation & Context at Conceptuality, 1971

---

Shape:                                                  (1)

See Duality of Shapes
    Energy Has Shape
    Shapeless
    Thought Has Shape
    Graph: Graphable

Shape:                                                                    (2)

    See Wind Stress & Houses;(2)(3)
        Silence, 30 Sep'76*

---

Shapeless:  Universe Does Not Have a Shape:                               (2)

    See Sculpture as Single Frame, 22 Jul'71
        Universe, May'71; 1965

---

RBF DEFINITIONS

Shapeless:  Universe Does Not Have a Shape:

"Because of the fundamental nonsimultaneity of universal
structuring, a single, simultaneous, static model of Universe
is inherently both nonexistent and conceptually impossible
as well as unnecessary.  Ergo, Universe does not have a shape.
Do not waste your time as man has been doing for ages, trying
to think of a unit shape 'outside of which there must be
something,' or 'within which, at center, there must be a
smaller something.'"

- Cite SYNERGETICS draft at Sec. 307.04, Oct'71

---

Shapeless:

    See Amorphous
        Formless
        Nonform

---

RBF DEFINITIONS

    Shapeless:  Universe Does Not Have a Shape

    "Because of the fundamental non-simultaneity of
universal structuring, a single, simultaneous, static
model of universe is inherently both 'nonexistent,'
and 'conceptually impossible,' as well as, 'unnecessary.'
Ergo, universe does not have a shape.  Do not waste
your time, as man has been doing for ages, trying to
think of a unit shape 'outside of which there must
be something,' or 'within which, at center, there must
be a smaller something.'"

        Cite KEPES
        Caption Fig. 1, p. 66 , 1965

---

Shapeless:                                                                (2)

    See Eternity, (1)
        Ideal, 23 May'72
        Integral, 1971
        Transcendental, 6 Jul'62
        Probability, 17 Feb'72
        Silence, 30 Sep'76
        Time is Only Now, 19 Jul'76

---

Shapeless:  Universe Does Not Have a Shape:                               (1)

    See Outside:  What's Outside Outside?
        Sight:  No Man Has Ever Seen Outside of Himself

---

Sharp:  Sharps:

    See Flats & Sharps

Sheath of Pride:

See How Little I Know, 1 Feb'75

---

RBF DEFINITIONS

Shell Growth Rate:

"The icosahedron can only show one shell growth layer.
The vector equilibrium can show all shell growth layers
omnidirectionally."

- Cite RBF tp EJA, 3200 Idaho, Wash. DC: 23 Oct'77

---

Sheet Metal:

See Hammering Sheet Metal

---

Shell Growth Rate:     (1)

See ▬▬▬▬▬▬▬
    Spherical Wave
    Vector Equilibrium: Odd or Even Shell Growth
    Concentric Layering

---

Shell Arrays:

See Powering: Second Powering, 17 Nov'72

---

Shell Growth Rate:     (2)

See Einstein, 1959
    Multiplication By Division, 4 Nov'73
    Prime Nucleus, 13 May'73
    Regenerative, 1960
    Spherical Interstices, 18 Nov'72
    Three-dimensional, 28 Oct'73
    Scheherazade Numbers: Declining Powers Of, ▬▬▬▬
        17 Mar'75
    Ten, 22 Jun'75
    Photon, 26 Sep'73
    Surface Strength of Structures, Mar'72
    Nuclear Domain & Elementality, (1)(2)

---

Shell Generating Frequency:

See Shell Growth Rate

---

RBF DEFINITIONS

Shell Ratio:

Egg shells have a shell ratio of 85 to 1. Geodesic radomes

have a shell ratio of as much as 200 to 1."

- Cite RBF to HUD Engineers, Washington, DC, 26 Jan '72

---

Shell: (1)

See Icosahedron: Circumferential Closest Packing
Boundary Layer
Vessel
**Turtle Dome**
Structural Shell
Protein Shell

Shelter: (1)

See Antipriorities
Dwelling: Dwelling Service Industry
House: Housing
Repro-shelter
Environment Controls
Dwelling Machines

Shell: (2)

See Powering, (B)
Wichita House, (1)
Cyclic Bundling of Experiences, May'49
Icosahedron: Subtriangulation, (2)

Shelter: (2)

See Squatters, (1)(2)
Ecology, Dec'72

RBF DEFINITIONS

Shelter:

"The Anglo-Saxon origin of <u>shelter</u> would be: <u>shell</u> -- scyld (shield) + <u>ter</u>-- trum (firm): that which covers or shields from exposure or danger; a place of safety, refuge, or retreat."

- Cite NINE CHAINS TO THE MOON, p.33, 1938

Shelter Magazine: Publication in 1930's:

See Ecology, Dec'72

RBF DEFINITIONS

Shelter:

"Shelter is by far the greatest single item among man's requirements in point of physical volume, weight, cost, and longevity of tenure. Yet it is among the last to receive his scientific attention."

- Cite NINE CHAINS TO THE MOON, pp.15-16, 1938

RBF DEFINITIONS

Ship:

"A ship of the sea is not a ship because it is built of wood, for ships can be built of steel or aluminum or polyester fiberglass or pig skin or bark. And ships are inherently a complex of associative principles, and subsets of which are each in turn independent of any local resource limitation. For example, ships' fastenings may be of rivets, nails, screws, or bolts; of bronze, steel, or monel-- or welds. It is true, of course, that ships of special component chemistry may outperform others of less appropriate chemistry, but this is by obvious subsynergetic evolutionary improvement, and not by surprise."

- Cite RBF draft Ltr. to Jim (Fitzgibbon?), Raleigh, NC, 1954-59

RBF DEFINITIONS

Ship: (1)

"Throughout the documented milleniums of man's evolutionary
technologies and their progressively integrated inventories,
recognized environmentally as successive eras, there has been
one fundamental category of technical, strategic, and
economic undertakings which, of inherent necessity, transcended
the going local traditions of opinion-governed expediency in
treatment of physical problems and expenditures of local
wealth and credit for those local ends; that is, if we
except the enormous credit and physical investment of local
undertakings in the most transcendental class as mystical
insurance for eternal equanimity as built into the great
religious edifices by the local communities, as representing
the most generalized problem treatment and infinite range
planning known to man's history.  If instead, we confine
our selves to discovering what has been the longest-range and
most generalized case of the economic communities investment
in equipment-- simplex and complex-- designed for the
improved satisfaction of living needs,  we will discover
that ships and watercraft building in the vast majority of
historic communities, who of necessity lived near water bodies,
undoubtedly represents the most generalized problem treatment"

- Cite RBF draft Ltr. to Jim (Fitzgibbon?), Raleigh, NC, 1954-59

---

Ship's Bow Waves:

See Dihedral Angles of Tetra & Octa, 16 Dec'73

---

RBF DEFINITIONS

Ship: (2)

"and longest range, time and geography wise, pattern
planning.  Why?  Simply because a ship had to be designed to
meet far more than the pattern indicated by the physical
experience within the local environment of harbored
confines; indeed, the more resources to be fetched for the
complementation of the locally-occurring resources for
integration into comprehensive capital goods wealth and
higher productivity, the more extremes of climate and weather
hazards, the more days and miles of possible hazards needed
to be anticipated with approximate safety factors.  Ships had
to be designed for the generalized case of all oceans and
all tasks.  To accomplish all-ocean, all-task efficacy, men
learned through bitter, mortal, dramatic experience that they
must invest all the best of their commonwealth resources of
time and physical goods inventory and cumulative science
and craft know-how into the building and management of their
long-range,wealth-integrating ships.

"No arts nor knowledge of design and pattern failed to
place in the undertaking.  Because of the myriad conflicts
of ambition of competitively lesser plan leaders and their
easy expediency and shortsighted gain in recourse to piracy,"

- Cite RBF draft Ltr. to Jim (Fitzgibbon?), Raleigh, NC, 1954-59

---

Ships: Fleet of Ships Needs More Room at Sea than in Harbor: (1)

See Airplanes:  Far Apart in the Sky but Slowed Down
                   When Close Together on Land
     Fleet of Sailboats
     Slow:  The Slowe We Get the More Crowded

---

RBF DEFINITIONS

Ship: (3)

"those whose foresight and comprehensiveness and throughness
of realized competence effected the actualities of history,
are found to have recognized in their major strategies that
secrecy and closed-mouthedness in respect to the great
ventures proved most effective insurance towards the day
when 'our ship comes in.'

"For this very reason the most effective strategies of men
have been temporarily lost to history and historical accounting has been made in a myriad of secondary and almost
irrelevant legend manufacture.  As new day tools allow us
to go to oceans bottom, and above all allow us greater
perspective of time and distance, we have been able to
reintegrate into informative pattern the outstanding historical fact that the whole concept of shipbuilding out of all
the best resources to accomplish the highest limits of
schedule performance, represents not only the essence of the
meaning of 'priority' in access to the most effective
commonwealth means, but over and above this identity to
discern also that synergetic effectiveness was the very
essence of the word 'wealth' itself."

- Cite RBF draft Ltr. to Jim (Fitzgibbon?), Raleigh, NC, 1954-59

---

Ships: Fleet of Ships Needs More Room at Sea than in Harbor: (2)

See Airspace Technology Environment Controls, (2)
    Pneumatic Structures, 25 Sep'72

---

RBF DEFINITIONS

Ship: (4)

"For it was the products of complex pattern integration
which made the great ships do what the wood logs and the iron
ore and the fibrous plants could not and would not do of
themselves.  The broader the integration, the higher the
synergetic effectiveness, and the more unexpected, and therefore invisibly harvestable individually managed wealth: i.e.,
the accrued new greater ability to initiate even greater
synergetic effects in respect to unprecedented pattern
articulation by those who could see the larger patterns
while the eyes of the many were fascinated and gratified by
the component aspects."

- Cite RBF draft Ltr. to Jim (Fitzgibbon?), Raleigh, NC, 1954-59

---

Shipwreck:

See Collision:  Ships Colliding on the Globe
    Piano Top
    Rich Man Drowning in Shipwreck

TEXT CITATION

Ships:

Mexico '63, p. 4, 10 Oct '63

RBF DEFINITIONS

Short Cut:

"I do not allow myself what's called the luxury of
a short cut.  People say 'Why don't you cut it short?'
Because I've got to take you from an experience to
the thing.  There's no use talking about it unless you
feel it yourself."

- Cite RBF quoted in ROLLING STONE, 10 June 1971.

---

Ships:                                                         (1)

See Battleship
    Boats at Anchor Retard the River's Flow
    Bubbles in the Wake of a Ship Sequence
    Collision:  Ships Colliding on the Globe
    Diesel Ship at Sea
    Displacements of Ships & Buildings
    Generalized Boat
    Navy Sequence
    Ruddering Sequence
    Sailboats
    Sailing Ship
    Sailing Ship Effect
    Sea Technology
    Oil Tankers:  Size Of
    History from the Sailor's & Shipbuilder's
      Viewpoint
    Factors of Ships
    City as a Ship
    House as a Ship
    Spaceship

RBF DEFINITIONS

Short Cuts:

"There are no short cuts in the way of making babies:
you can't accelerate fundamental processes.  Nature is
always operating at most efficient and economical
time:energy rates of transformations."

- Cite CULTIVATE THE POSITIVE, 9 May'57

---

Ships:                                                         (2)

See Air Delivery & Submarine Cities (1)-(3)
    Lever (b)
    Size (A)(B)
    Trails & Wakes, 8 Apr'75
    Walls vs. Airspace Technology, (1)
    New York City, 31 Jul'75
    Cybernetics, 7 Nov'75

Short:  Shortest:                                             (1)

See Most Economical vs. Shortest

---

Shoals:

See Schools:  Shoals

Short:  Short Cut:                                            (2)

See Triangle, 1960

Shrink: Shrinking:

See Earth Shrunk to One-town Dimension

---

RBF DEFINITIONS

Shunting: Relative Motion Patterns: (1)

"Synergetics discloses that the apparently different velocities, or rates of acceleration, of which the physicist speaks do not truly exist. The seemingly different velocities are a plurality of angularly precessed-- or shunted-- energy action systems regeneratively operated in respect to other systems.

"Velocity is always 186,000 miles per second. All other relative motion patterns are the result of remotely observed, angularly precessed, 186,000 m.p.s. energy-action shunting.

"Angularly precessed shunting may divert omnidirectional energy into focused (angularly shunted) actions and reactions, of either radial or circumferential patternings, or both.

"Frequency modulation is accomplished through precession-shunted circuit synchronizations. 'Valving' is angular shunting. Competent design is predicated upon frequency modulation by application of the precessional shunting principle."
- Cite Synergetics Notes, p.9, 1955. Incorporated at SYNERGETICS, Sec.647, 1 Oct'72

---

RBF DEFINITIONS

Shunt:

"Shunt is an angular change."

- Cite RBF Lecture
  Town Hall, New York
  12 March 1971

---

RBF DEFINITIONS

Shunting: Relative Motion Patterns: (2)

One shunt:

(loop)

E.G., From here to there, synergetically, seems relatively to an observer as 10 m.p.h.

- Cite Synergetics Notes, p.9 et. seq., 1955. Incorporated at SYNERGETICS SEC. 647, 1 Oct'72

---

RBF DEFINITIONS

Shunt:

"Modifications in relative magnitude of the system's import and export programming and their rates of reoccurrence is accomplished by component events of the system which interfere with and thus intercept and shunt (or valve) the import event receipts into holding patterns. From the holding pattern or reservoir the events may be valved into the system's component event patterning for use at preferred rates and magnitudes in extending or altering the regenerative integrity of the system. Scientific design controls these frequency and magnitude events ■ by (valving), i.e. angle and frequency modulation."
- Cite NASA Speech, p. 42 , Jun'66

---

RBF DEFINITIONS

■■■ Shunting and Re-Shunting:

"The compressively interprecessional cooperative and accommodative functionings of all structural systems are locally persistent constellations of resultant force-vectors, which are always angularly shunted, and regeneratively re-shunted, inwards of the system's tangential lines, i.e., at resultant angles less than 180 degrees in respect to the direction of origin of the generative force."

- Cit TENSEGRITY, Art News Annual, p. 120. Dec'61

---

RBF DEFINITIONS

Shunting:

"The icosahedron's function in Universe may be to throw the switch of cosmic energy into a local shunting circuit. In the icosahedron energy gets itself locked up even more by the six great circles-- which may explain why electrons are borrowable and independent of the proton-neutron group."

- Cite RBF rewrite of SYNERGETICS galley at Sec. 458.11, 5 Nov'73

---

Shunt: Shunting: (1)

See Icosahedron as Local Shunting Circuit
    Holding Patterns
    Precessionally Shunted Pattern Relay
    Valving: Valvability
    Fall-in, Shunt-out
    Focus = Angular Shunting

Shunt:  Shunting:                                         (2A)

    See Boats at Anchor Retard the River's Flow, 1960
        Copper (A)
        Continuous Man (4)
        Design Covariables:  Principle Of, 1959
        Environment Controls (1)
        Manifest:  One, 1973
        Motion, 27 May'72
        Mass Production, May'72
        Ninety-two Elements, 9 Apr'40
        Pattern Strip Aggregate Wrapabilities, 19 Dec'73
        Radome Sequence (4); (B)
        Spherical Octahedron, Aug'72
        Solid State, 13 May'73
        Tensegrity, 20 Oct'72
        Tensegrity Sphere:  Six Pentagonals (1)(2)
        Trespassing (1)(2)
        Water, May'65
        Wave Pattern of a Stone Dropped in Liquid, 6 Jul'62
        Omnidirectional Typewriter (4)

Shuttle:  Shuttling:  Shuttle-woven:                      (2)

    See Jitterbug, 4 Oct'72
        Pattern Strip Aggrgeate Wrapabilities, 19 Dec'73
        Star Tetrahedron, 8 Oct'71
        Two, (2)

Shunting:                                                 (2B)

    See Tensegrity Model of Self-interference of Energy,
        25 Mar'75
        Vector Equilibrium:  Field of Energy, (A)
        Environment, 29 Mar'77

Side Effects:                                             (1)

    See Primary vs. Side Effects
        No Sides

Shutter:

    See Omnidirectional Shutterable Sieve

Side:  Side Effects:                                      (2)

    See Children as Only Pure Scientists, (A)

Shuttle:  Shuttling:  Shuttle-woven:                      (1)

    See Intershuttling

Sideways:

    See Inadvertent = Sideways
        Oblique = Sideways

Side:

See Moon: Other Side of the Moon
Other Side of the Universe

---

RBF DEFINITIONS

Sight:

"Before the speed of light was measured, sight

seemed . . . to be instantaneous. . . But neither light

nor any other phenomenon is instantaneous."

- Cite NASA Speech, p.52, **Jun'66**

---

RBF DEFINITIONS

Sieve:

"A sieve is an angular valve."

- Cite RBF at Penn Bell videotaping, Philadelphia, 30 Jan'75

---

RBG DEFINITIONS

Sight:

"Man **sees** only by omni-directional images illuminated
within the experience-inventoried brain after images
regeneratively fed-back by the energy of momentary
sensorial scannings. It is significant that he gets
direct or nondelayed visual report only from the actively
radiant energetic centers of light, notably the stars.
All other visual reports wait upon indirect routing
by their superficial reflection from passive structures
of energetic impasse, the planetary mass phenomena."

- Cite PREVIEWS, I&I, p. 203,1 **Apr'49**

---

Sieve:

See Omnidirectional Shutterable Sieve
Dwelling Sieve

---

RBF DEFINITIONS

▬▬▬ Sight: No Man Has Ever Seen Outside of Himself:

"... It must be remembered
That no human has ever seen directly
Outside himself.
What we call seeing
Is the interpretive imagining in the brain
Of the significance and meaning
Of the nervous system reports
Of an assumed outsideness of self,
All of which organic design conception
May be that of a great intellect
Which is inventing Universe progressively
Evolving mathematically elegant
Integral equations
For each conceivable challenge
Including the invention
You and me."

- Citation and context at SENSORIAL IDENTIFICATION of Reality,
(2), May '72

---

RBF DEFINITIONS

Sight:

". . . We **see** in 60 separate picture frames per second

as in a moving picture continuity. Each frame is a finite

increment. Our brain's after image lag is so powerful that

(it) gives a sense of absolute 'excentricity' to our only

subconsciously packaged seeing."

- Citation at Eccentricity, Jun'66
- Cite NASA Speech, p. 32, Jun'66

---

RBF DEFINITIONS

Sight: No Man Has Ever Seen Outside of Himself:

"No man has ever seen outside of himself. He always

sees in his brain."

- Cite Letter to Dr. R. Urmston, 8 Oct '64, p. 2

RBF DEFINITIONS

Sight: No Man Has Ever Seen Outside of Himself:

"No man has ever 'seen' outside himself."

▬▬▬▬▬▬▬▬▬▬▬▬▬▬

- Citation and context at Brain's TV Studio, 1960

---

Sight: No Man Has Ever Seen Outside of Himself:            (1)

See Brain's TV Studio

---

Sight: No Man Has Ever Seen Outside of Himself:            (2)

See Slides: Use of Slides in Lecturing, 6 Jul'62
    You & I as Pattern Integrities, 22 Jan'75

---

Sight:                                                      (1)

See Invisible Motion
    Optical Motion Spectrum
    Optical Tuning & Scanning
    Perception
    Seeability
    Seeing

---

Sight:                                                      (2)

See Recall Lag, 26 May'72
    Senses, (1)
    Television, 5 Jul'62
    Twelve Universal Degrees of Freedom:  General
        Systems, (II)
    Repetitive, 28 May'75
    Celestial Radiation Accumulators, 28 Apr'77

---

Signal:

See Information Signal

---

Signature of God:

See Triangle as Signature of God

---

Significance:

See Mutual Survival Principles, (2)

RBF DEFINITIONS

Silence:

"Silence is the untuned.  Silence takes the electromagnetic place of space.  Space is a sort of tactile error. . . the frozen thing.

"With awareness and consciousness you already are thinking; but the point is that you didn't start out with the notion of doing some thinking; it wasn't your fault that you started to be conscious of something.

"Euler has the visual inventory.  Aural sensing has no shape. Our visual sense verifies our tactile sense of shape.  Smelling and sound have no shape.  Smelling has less shape than sound.  Sound has a little shape in reflecting bouncings of electromagnetic wave phenomena.  Visually, when we don't see something, we call it space.  But hearing is like smelling, when it is not tuned-in, it is silent.  I've been saying tuned-out, but what I've meant all along is silence."

- Cite RBF to EJA; 3200 Idaho, Wash.DC; 30 Sep'76

---

RBF DEFINITIONS

Silence:

"Space nothingness is the untuned.  I now call it silence."

- Cite RBF to EJA; 3200 Idaho, Wash.DC; 29 Sep'76

---

Silence:

See Absolute Silence
     Nothingness = Silence
     Fuller, R.B: Moratorium on Speech

---

Similar & Dissimilar:

See Triangling (1)(2)

---

RBF DEFINITIONS

Simple:

"Corollary A is: The simpler, the more enduringly reproducible."

- Citation and context at Regenerative Design:  Law Of (1), 13 Mar'75

---

Simplest Case:

See Modelability, (a)

---

RBF DEFINITIONS

Simplest Knot:

"Look at any picture, point your finger at any part of the picture, and ask yourself: Which aspect is that, and that, and that?  That's an area; or it's a line; or it's a crossing (a fix, a point).  Crossings are loci.  You may say, 'That is too big to be a point;' if so, you make an area by drawing a line around it.  Here is the simplest knot drawn on the surface of a sphere:

"This identifies topology and knots at the simplest limit case."

- Cite SYNERGETICS, 2nd. Ed. at Sec. 1007.24; 1 Jan'75

---

(1)

Simplest Something:

See Minimum Something
    Tetrahedron

Simplest Something:

See Tetrahedron, 26 Apr'77

---

Simplicity:

"It seems to be a law of nature that the more
fundamentally simple and biologically propitious an
evolutionary growth may be-- the more aesthetically
satisfying and lastingly acceptable is its multireproduction, e.g., roses, stars, and blades of grass."

- Cite Newsweek, "Architecture, The Present Scene, 1968
- Citation at Reproducible, 1968

---

RBF DEFINITIONS

Simplex:

"Chemistry seemed to laugh at our coordinate awakwardness
as nature contrived all of our physical 'matter' entirely
out of rational, whole integer simplexes."

- Citation and context at Calulus (2) + (3), 1965

---

RBF DEFINITIONS

Simplicity:

"The law seems to be that the more universal, the more
symmetrical (see the helicopter versus the bomber); and the
more symmetrical, the less the number of parts types. This
is to say that the greater the superficial simplicity, and
therefore the more adaptive the tool, the greater the required
investment in anticipating teleology in the processing of
proportionately larger blocks of self- and historically-
relayed knowledge concerning ▮▮▮▮▮ experiences,
principles, and their reciprocal involvements."

- Cite RBF draft Ltr. to Jim (Fitzgibbon?), Raleigh, NC, 1954-59

---

Simplex:                                                    (1)

    See Complex & Simplex
        Limit Minimum Simplex
        Nuclear Simplex
        Toplogical Aspects:  Inventory Of

---

RBF DEFINITIONS

Simplification:

"We may hypothesize that as information increases
exponentially-- explodes-- conceptuality implodes,
becoming increasingly more simplified."

- CITE WDS DECADE, Document 6, 'Man and the Biosphere,' p. 52, 1967
- Citation at Conceptuality, 1967

---

Simplex:                                                    (2)

    See Calculus, (2)(3)*
        Regenerative Design:  Law Of, (2)

---

Simple:  Simplicity:  Simplification:                       (1)

                See Circle as Simplest
                    Complex & Simplex
                    Primary Structure
                    Curvature:  Simple
                    Aesthetics of Uniformity
                    Reproducible
                    Most Economical = Simplest

Simple: Simplicity: Simplification:                    (2)

> See Environment Events Hierarchy, 1954
>    Calculus (2)(3)*
>    Conceptuality, 1967*
>    Patent, 1955
>    Reproducible, 1968*
>    Regenerative Design: Law Of (1)*
>    Scenario Universe, 22 Apr'68
>    Synergetics, undated
>    Tetrahedron, Nov'71
>    Structural System, Nov'71
>    Mutual Survival Principles, (4)
>    Awareness, 28 Apr'77

---

Simultaneity:                                          (2)

> See Dimension, 29 Nov'72*
>    Interaccommodative, 13 Mar'73
>    Meaningless, Oct'66
>    Tension, 5 Jul'62*
>    Visual Symphony (2)

---

RBF DEFINITIONS

Simultaneous:

"All dimensions are simultaneously considerable."

- Citation at Dimension, 29 Nov'72

---

RBF DEFINITIONS

Sin:

"I'm the only man I know who can sin. I find everybody else really too innocent. They don't really know what they're doing. I find that people who seem to be the most offensive are fantastic innocents. They really couldn't know what they're doing because they'd be mortified at the idea of doing something so unbecoming. But I've really had enough experience, such a fantastic amount, that I really know what it is to sin. And that would be to cheat on the great accounting system of Universe, trying to take something out and hang on to it.

"I could very easily transgress. I could rest and sleep and make all kinds of money. The opportunities keep coming in all the time. But I have no desire to sin, I assure you. The point is: I know how. There are many things I did in my life that wouldbe sinful if I did them today. I still feel I'm entitled to make experiments, but once I find out-- do it again? No. That's sinful."

- Cite RBF in Barry Farrel Playboy Interview, (FEB) 1972 - Draft. p. 40.

---

RBF DEFINITIONS

■■■■ Simultaneous:

"The big jobs are done in tension and the small jobs in compression. We find that the tensions, because they are always curved, never can get straight and there is no meaning to the word straight in Universe. Therefore the tension members spiraling around must always come back into themselves. They are inherently self-closing; maybe not within simultaneous experiences-- obviously not in simultaneous experiences-- but around comes Halley's Comet. Every 70 years around she comes again. It is not a simultaneous experience at all. Several life times may be involved, and some of them may be coming around much more slowly, but there is an integrity of the tensions as around they come again. We find an idea about some kind of closed circuit."

- Citation at Tension, 5 Jul'62

- See Oregon Lecture #3, pp. 111-112, 5 Jul'62

---

Sin:                                                   (1)

> See Good & Evil
>    Immorality

---

Simultaneity:                                          (1)

> See Children's Pictures of the Sun and the Moon
>    Instantaneity
>    Juggler
>    Overlapping
>    Nonsimultaneous
>    Radiation: Speed Of
>    Static
>    Synchronous
>    Unitary Conceptuality

---

RBF DEFINITIONS

Sin: Angle of Error:

"The courage to adhere to the truth as we learn it involves, then, the courage to face oneself with the clear admission of all the mistakes we have made. Mistakes are sins only when not self-admitted. Etymologically, sin means omission where admission should have occurred. An angle is a sinus, an opening, a break in a circle, a break in the integrity of the whole human individual. Trigonometrically, the sine of an angle is the ratio of the length of the chord facing the central angle considered, as ratioed to the length of the radius of the circle whose center is also the apex of the angle, or sinus, considered. The angle is the angle of error of viewpoint of the individual whose circular integrity has been violated. The relative size of the chord opposite that angle of error as proportioned to the radius (taken as unity 1) of the circle of experienced knowledge of the individual; and being the sine of the angle considered, it is also the relative magnitude of the individual's sin. (Drawing attached.)"

- Cite RBF Ltr. to Bro. Jos. Chuala, p.3; 7 Nov'75

Sin:  Angle of Error:

The sine of X = $\frac{a}{b}$

- Cite RBF Ltr. to Bro. Jos. Chuala, attachment; 7 Nov'75

---

Single Atomic vs. Multiatomic:                               (1)

See Atoms & Compounds:  Difference Between

---

Sin:                                          (2)

See Emotion, May'65

---

Single Atomic vs. Multiatomic:                          (2)

See Physics & Chemistry:  Difference Between, 8 Apr'75
Model of Nonbeing, 11 Sep'75

---

Singing Early in the Morning:

See Superstition, 1938

---

Single Frame:                                          (1)

See Frame

---

Single Bonding:

See Chemical Bonds

---

Single Frame:                                          (2)

See Machines vs. Structures, 13 Nov'75
New York City, (7)

RBF DEFINITIONS

### Single Integer Differentials:     (1)

"In synergetics we find the difference of one whole integer
frequently manifest in our geometrical interrelationship explorations.  Beyond the one additional proton and one additional
electron characterizing the hierarchy of the already-discovered
family of 92 regenerative chemical elements and their short-
lived transuranium manifestability by high-energy physics
experiments, we find time and again a single integer to be
associated with the positive-negative energetic pulsations in
Universe.

"Because the energetic-synergetic relationships are usually
generalized relationships independent of size, these single
rational integer differentials are frequently found to charac-
terize the limit magnitudes of asymmetric deviations from the
zerophase vector equilibrium.

"The minor aberrations of otherwise elegantly matching phenomena
of nature, such as the micro-weight aberrations of the 92
regenerative chemical elements in respect to their atomic
numbers, was not explained until isotopes and their neutrons were
discovered a few decades ago.  Such discoveries numerically
elucidate the whole-integer rationalization of the unique"

- Cite SYNERGETICS, 2nd. Ed. at Secs. 310.11 and .12, 10 Nov'74

RBF DEFINITIONS

Singular & Plural:

"Compressions are plural.  Tension is singular."

- Cite Synergetics Draft at Sec. 640.70, Dec. '71.
- Citation at Tension & Compression, Dec'71

RBF DEFINITIONS

### Single Integer Differentials:     (2)

"isotopal system's structural-proclivity agglomeratings."

- Cite SYNERGETICS, 2nd. Ed. at Sec. 310.12, 10 Nov'74

Singular & Plural:

See Love & Hate, Oct'71
    Tension & Compression, Dec'71 *
    Synergetics, 11 Oct'73
    Potential vs. Primitive, 12 May'77
    Environment, (A)

### Single Integer Differentials:

See Odd Ball
    Rational Whole Numbers

Sink:  Sinking:

See No Sinking:  Man Cannot Sink

### Single Otherness:

See Environment, (A)

Sinus:     (1)

See Angular Sinus Takeout

Sinus:                                    (2)

   See Angle, 7 Nov'75

---

RBF DEFINITIONS

   Six:

     "The number of edges are always divisible by <u>six</u>
in a structural system."

     - Cite P. PEARCE, Inventory of Concepts, June 1967

---

RBF DEFINITIONS

   <u>Six</u>:

   "There are six vectors or none."

    - Cite SYNERGETICS Corollaries, Sec. 240, by RBF 11 Oct. '71,
      Haverford, Penna.

---

RBF DEFINITIONS

   <u>Six</u>:

   "The number of all the lines-- which is to say the number of
all the vectors-- in Universe, is always a number which is
divisible by <u>six</u>.  There are no exceptions.  Now these <u>six</u> edges
are the <u>six</u> edges of the tetrahedron..."

    - Citation & context at <u>Quantum</u>, Jun'66

---

RBF DEFINITIONS

   <u>Six</u>:

   "Six unique vectors constitute a tetrahedral event."

   - Citation at <u>Event</u>, 11 Oct'71

   - Cite SYNERGETICS Corollaries, Sec. 240., by RBF, 11 Oct.
    '71, Haverford, Penna.

---

RBF DEFINITIONS

   Six:

     "The minimum set, affording macro-micro separation
of universe is a set of four local event foci.  These
four stars have an inherent <u>sixness</u> of relationships.
This four-foci, six-relationship set is definable as the
████████ tetrahedron."

       (Adapted.)

     - Cite OMNIDIRECTIONAL HALO, p. 140, 1960

   - Citation at <u>Tetrahedron</u>, 1960

---

RBF DEFINITIONS

   <u>Six</u>:

   "You have <u>six</u> vectors or none for every energy event."

   - Cite RBF to EJA, Washington, DC, 7 Oct. '71.

---

RBF DEFINITIONS

   <u>Six</u>:

   "It is a synergetic characteristic of minimum structural
systems (tetra) that the system is not stable until the
last strut is introduced.  Redundancy cannot be determined
by energetic observation of behaviors of single struts
(beams or columns) or any chain-linkage of same which are
less than <u>six</u> in number, or less than tetrahedron."

    - Cite RBF undated holograph on MIT memo pad. (1950's)

   - Citation at <u>Strut</u>, 1950's

RBF DEFINITIONS

Sixness:

"There is a systematic interrelationship of basic fourness always accompanied by a sixness of alternatives or freedoms."

- Citation and context at Pulsation, 9 Nov'72

---

RBF DEFINITIONS

Six Degrees of Freedom:

"The rhombic dodecahedron . . . its twelve facets represent the planes perpendicular to the six fundamental degrees of freedom."

- Citation and context at Rhombic Dodecahedron, 19 Apr'66

---

RBF DEFINITIONS

Six Degrees of Freedom:

"Experiments show that there are six positive and six negative degrees of fundamental transformation freedoms, which provide 12 alternate ways in which nature can behave most economically upon each and every energy-event occurrence. Ergo, there is not just one 'other'; there are always at least 12 'others.'"

- Cite SYNERGETICS text at Sec. 537.12; Dec'71

---

RBF DEFINITIONS

Six Degrees of Freedom:

"The number of vectors (structural or force lines) cohering each and every subsystem of Universe is always a number subdivisible by six, i.e., consisting of one positive and one negative event, each of three vectors, which add up to six. This holds true topologically in all abstract patterning in Universe as well as in fundamental physics. The six vectors represent the fundamental six, and only six, degrees of freedom in Universe."

- Cite RBF Ltr. to Prof. Theodore Caplow, 18 Feb. '66.

---

RBF DEFINITIONS

Six Degrees of Freedom:

"The connection between the six degrees of freedom and omnidirectionality is, of course, the vector equilibrium, which combines the threeness of the cube in relation to 20 as unity = VE."

- Citation & context at Vector Equilibrium, 25 Aug'71

EXPERIENCE - SEC. 502.25

---

Six Degrees of Freedom:                                    (1)

See Cosmic Event
    Degrees of Freedom
    Frame of Reference:  Six Schemata
    Powering:  Sixth Dimension
    Twelve Universal Degrees of Freedom

---

RBF DEFINITIONS

Six Degrees of Freedom:

"Experiments show that there are six positive and six negative degrees of fundamental transformation freedoms, which provide twelve alternate ways in which nature can behave most economically upon each and every energy event occurrence."

- Citation & context at Environment Events Hierarchy (6), Jun'66

- Cite NASA Speech, p. 37, Jun'66

ENERGY EVENT - SEC. 511.03

---

Six Degrees of Freedom:                                    (2)

See Artifacts (1)
    Closed System, 21 Oct'65
    Coherence, 18 Feb'71; 11 Feb'73
    Conceptuality, 1 Apr'72
    Dimensional Reference Frame, 1972
    Energy Unit, 17 Jan'74
    Environment Events Hierarchy, (6)*
    Point, 28 Oct'63; Oct'59
    Polar Vertexes, 19 Feb'72
    Pulsation, 9 Nov'72
    Rhombic Dodecahedron, 19 Apr'66*
    Synergetics, 1 Apr'72; 20 Jun'66
    Vector Equilibrium, 25 Aug'71*
    Cosmic Hierarchy, 23 Jan'77
    Technology:  Enchantment vs. Disenchantment, (1)
    Will, (1)

RBF DEFINITIONS

## Six - Five - One:

"The difference of <u>one</u> between the spheric domain of the rhombic dodecahedron's <u>six</u> and the nuclear sphere's <u>five</u>--or between the tetra volume of the octahedron and the three-tetra sections of the tetrahelix--these are the <u>prime wave pulsation propagating quanta phenomena</u> that account for local aberrations, twinkle angles, and unzipping angles manifest elsewhere and frequently in this book."

- Cite SYNERGETICS text at Sec. 985.08; RBF rewrite, Beverly Hotel, NYC; 8 Jan'74

---

RBF DEFINITIONS

## Six Motion Freedoms & Degrees of Freedom:

"You are right that what we are talking about here--in the articulation of the primitive hierarchy--is more than what we usually mean by dimensionality.

"In addition to dimension, what we are talking about is the interaction of the degrees of freedom, the six positive and negative motions--as well as the power factoring... the identification and quantation of the full behavior potential of energetic structurings."

(NB: RBF had said that we are probably dealing with up to the <u>24th-dimension</u>, when EJA objected to using dimension in this way. - eja.)

- Cite RBF to EJA, in presentation by Chris Kittrick and Rob Grip in back room at 3500 Market St.; Phila. PA; 11 Aug'77

---

## Six - Five - One:

See Octahedron as Annihilation Model, 30 Dec'73
   Volumetric Hierarchy, (2)
   Nuclear Cube, 23 Feb'76
   Spherical Interstices, 9 Jul'76

---

RBF DEFINITIONS

## Six Motion Freedoms & Degrees of Freedom: (1)

"There are the six positive and negative exercises of the motion freedoms, but the freedoms themselves come from the fact that the minimum system in the Universe consists of six vectors: the tetrahedron. The tetrahedron has a minimum of six edges. I want you to try to think about a minimum something. A something, a substance, has an insideness and an outsideness.

"You cannot have a surface without the other surface. We teach kids that in two dimensionality there is only one surface, but we're always kidding them--we do that on a piece of paper or on a blackboard when they both have more than one side: therefore we have extracted a plane very improperly.

"And we talk about a point which is dimensionless. A line was ▭▭▭▭▭ one-dimensional; a plane was two-dimensional; and a cube is three-dimensional. I say we don't have dimensionality less than four dimensionality. If we have something it is four-dimensional. It is only recently that we have had a microscope. If we took an engineer's scale we get down to 1/50th of an inch--you can really pick that off with the naked eye. You get down to 100th, you get a glass."

- Cite transcript p.14, RBF interview with Dr. Michael Bruwer, 20 Feb'77

---

RBF DEFINITIONS

## Six Motion Freedoms & Degrees of Freedom: (A)

EJA:  "Rob Grip is worried that your new sphere is .499 and not a clean 5. Also, you are talking about three-dimensionality for the first time. I don't understand. You used to say that 'Time is not the fourth dimension.'?

RBF:  "I say .499 because that is the closest that Heisenberg is going to let us come.

"And the sphere emerges from the primitive hierarchy when it begins to spin. Spinning is just one of the degrees of motion freedom. Spinning and orbiting give you the sphere-- at the point where frequency comes into time-size.

"I have done a new piece for you on dimensionality in answer to your very good questions about the relationships between the six motion freedoms and the six degrees of freedom. And I have discovered that just as there are in reality 12 degrees of freedom, so there are in reality 12 motion freedoms.

"All spheres are potential spheres. The sphere that the mathematicians have been dealing with in the primitive"

- RBF to EJA by telephone from Pacific Palisades, CA; 8 Aug'77

---

RBF DEFINITIONS

## Six Motion Freedoms & Degrees of Freedom: (2)

"You get down to 1/200th of an inch and you can't see it at all. Long before people had microscopes there was a black speck against a white background: it was too small, it was under the dimensions that you and I can differentiate. You have a speck of 200th of an inch; you can see it as a speck but you couldn't resolve anything about it as a polyhedron. This is where man invented the idea of a point. You could point to it, but it was subdimensional--he said.

"I started to see how we could make the mistake of points, and lines, and planes as something that you put together and find that you make reality. I started with my reality, and then if there's a point to it, well, there's something there; and if I put a really powerful magnifying glass to it I'm going to find there is a crystal. It is a polyhedron and it has an insideness and an outsideness. Anything that is substantial has an insideness and an outsideness. Any substance has something that stands below it: sub-stance, withinness.

"I am going to take the minimum something. I take a rock and I get a child to hit the rock; you keep hitting it and"

- Cite transcript p.15, RBF taped interview with Dr. Michael Bruwer, Ritz Carlton Hotel, Chicago; 20 Feb'77

---

RBF DEFINITIONS

## Six Motion Freedoms & Degrees of Freedom: (B)

"hierarchy is only three-dimensional because it is timeless and sizeless and prefrequency. Where you begin with insideness and outsideness is three-dimensional. But when the somethingness enters--when you go beyond primitive conceptuality, then you have to go beyond the primitive three-dimensionality. It was only that static three-dimensionality that the mathematicians used to talk about in their coordinate system.

"But with frequency you have time-size and you come to fourth-, fifth-, and sixth-dimensionality. It is true that I say 'Time is not the fourth dimension,' that's why I say 'time-size'."

- Cite RBF to EJA by telephone from Pacific Palisades, CA; 8 Aug'77

---

RBF DEFINITIONS

## Six Motion Freedoms & Degrees of Freedom: (3)

"you finally get to a something. You can't get to something less than four corners. It may be kind of flat and look like a flat triangle but it has really an altitude and you find that the minimum is four corners and six edges and four faces. You cannot get a rock with less than three faces around a corner. If it looks flat, it is just so many faces.

"The tetrahedron is fourfold symmetry: four minimum absolute faces. A cube has only three. The minimum something has four faces of symmetry, four vertexes of symmetry. Now that is then the minimum something, degrees of freedom. I cannot have something less than four corners and I cannot have a face of less than three edges so that the minimum something has six edges altogether. Any one face has three edges so these six edges are vectors in that structure and they really are the defining set of events and with every turn to play in Universe we always get six moves so the minimum something is a minimum play.

- Cite transcript p. 15, RBF taped interview with Dr. Michael Bruwer, Ritz Carlton Hotel, Chicago; 20 Feb'77

RBF DEFINITIONS

Six Motion Freedoms & Degrees of Freedom:                    (4)

"You always get six edges. They can be at all kinds of
angles so that's where the degrees of freedom are. We find
in topology that all somethings have vertexes, faces, and
adges, but the numbers of the edges in Universe is evenly
divisible by six. These are the six degrees of freedom and
they can be positive or negative and they are always there.
They are not on a plane; they are omnidirectional.

"The six motion freedoms are complex consequences of the
six degrees of freedom. If you want to get an instrument held
in position, it takes six restraints. If I have just five
restraints, then the tetrahedron will change shape. Shape
requires six restraints. Six restraints are what give
structure.

"A minimum system is a tetrahedron; a minimum structure has
six restraints, so anything that holds its shape has a
minimum of six restraints so that the system itself can
spin or the system itself can orbit. The system itself
can inside out. There are systems behaviors and the six
degrees of freedom are internal to it."

- Cite transcript p.16 RBF taped interview with Dr. Michael
  Bruwer, Ritz Carlton Hotel, Chicaog; 20 Feb'77

RBF DEFINITIONS

Six Motion Freedoms & Degrees of Freedom:                    (5)

"So there are six internals and six externals. The six
system motions... will be part of the larger system in order
to have them stop: they will be frozen in part of the larger
system, they are going to have to lose one of those freedoms.
... we come to the six positive and the six negatives and
there really are always 12 and they alternate equi-economically.

"If he doesn't have these six degrees of internal restraints,
he's going to be very unstable internally.... You see if he
doesn't want to get on with the system, he spins by himself...
Oscillating is ambivalence:approaching and avoiding,...
Inside-outing I saw as being deceptive, putting the wrong
surface on themselves on the other way: giving up this game
person and being a real person--when he really believes in
the game so it is almost an unnatural thing....

"Precession I see as an effort I make to manipulate you, to
cause you to move... because it is really at 90 degrees...
you are looking this way... very inadvertent.

"I am saying that society doesn't realize that the most"

- Cite transcript p.17, RBF taped interview with Dr, Michael
  Bruwer, Ritz Carlton Hotel, Chicago; 20 Feb'77

RBF DEFINITIONS

Six Motion Freedoms & Degrees of Freedom:                    (6)

"powerful social behavior is precessional... where my effect
is inadvertent. If you are a strong psychiatrist and your
patient thinks well of you, he orbits around you literally.
All society is going in orbit in various realms...literally,
the weak ones around the strong ones.

"We get such a static picture of people standing with one
another in a house... we don't think of this. The mother will
be in orbit about somebody else and the children will be in
orbit about her.

"...Torquing is a squeeze, all right. You go through the
wringer, as they say. That's torquing.

"...while oscillation is expansion and contraction: like we
eat our food and then we get rid of it. So our friendship
proceeds. We see so much of each other and then we stop,
much as I am going to do with you. I would like to give you
so much and let you have something and then you can study
that and then come back for more. That's oscillating to me.
You put on food and expend it--put on metaphysical fuel and
expend it."

- Cite transcript p. 18, RBF taped interview with Dr. Michael
  Bruwer, Ritz Carlton Hotel, Chicago; 20 Feb'77

Six Motion Freedoms & Degrees of Freedom:                    (1)

        See Absolute Network
            Behavioral Phases
            Behavior Potential
            Proclivities: Inventory Of
            Motions: Six Positive & Negative
            Energetic Functions
            Structural Functions

Six Motion Freedoms:                    (1)

        See Basic Motions
            Motions: Six Positive & Negative

Six Motion Freedoms:                    (2)

        See Equilibrium & Disequilibrium, (1)

RBF DEFINITIONS

Six-Ridge Tetrahedral Globe:                    (1)

"As we take a close-up view of our little Spaceship Earth we
see that the three-quarters of it which is covered with water
has a greatest depth of about six miles, which is about the
same as the six-mile altitude of its greatest dry land mountain
peaks. We find that these ten-mile maximum variations of the
spherical Spaceship Earth's 8,000-mile diameter are comparatively
negligible. If we are looking at a 12-inch diameter globe, the
distance between the outermost mountain peak and the innermost
ocean depth is only 1/50th of an inch, which visually is an
almost undetectable amount. As we look at a 12-inch globe, the
thickness of the ink with which an ocean is depicted is deeper
in proportion to the globe than in the real ▮▮▮▮▮▮▮▮
Earth globe's ocean depth in respect to its diameter.

"Three major mountain ridges of the Spaceship Earth converge in
the Antarctic continent. From the South Pole one runs northwardly in the high continental plateau of Africa, and thence
into Europe culminating as the Alps. A second ridge runs
northwardly under water and emerges as Australia Malaysia, and
later as Indo-China. A third ridge consists of South America's
Andes which runs northward through Central America to terminate"

- Cite BEAR ISLAND STORY, galley p.6, 1968

RBF DEFINITIONS

Six-Ridge Tetrahedral Globe:                    (2)

"in North America's Mexican mountains.

"In the northern hemisphere, the northern ends of these three
southern-hemisphere-emanating ridges are interconnected by
fourth, fifth, and sixth ridges, respectively. The fourth
consists of the Alps, Asia Minor's highlands and islands, and
the Himalayas. This fourth ridge runs between Europe and
Indo-China and interconnects the northern terminals of ridges
one and two. The fifth ridge consists of the China-Kamchatka
mountains, and the Aleutian and North America's Rockies, which
joins the northern end of ridge two with the northern end of
ridge three in Mexico. The sixth ridge runs from Mexico and
the terminals of ridges three and five via El Paso, Texas, and
is thereafter momentarily broken through by the Mississippi;
it continues as the Ozarks and the Appalachians and reaches
northeastward as a chain via Newfoundland, Labrador, Greenland,
Iceland, British Isles, Scandinavia, and Urals to final
juncture with ridges one and four at the Alps.

"These six main ridges have for long been seen by physical
geologists and geographers to constitute the now distorted--
sunken here and risen there-- six edges of a spherical tetrahedron."

- Cite BEAR ISLAND STORY, galley p.7, 1968

RBF DEFINITIONS

Six-Ridge Tetrahedral Globe:                                  (3)

"The spherical tetrahedron's four spherical triangle areas are
roughly to be identified as: (1) the Indian Ocean and its
abutting countries; (2) the Pacific Ocean; (3) the Atlantic
Ocean (including Europe); and (4) the northern portion of
North America (U.S.A., Canada), the Arctic Russia and China. . . .

"The spherical tetrahedron's twisted ridges tell the evolutionary
history of Spaceship Earth's contractual shrinkings and yieldings
to primary force events of complex universal energy transactions.
The Earth sphere's shrinking and ridge twisting is like that of
cooked green peas."

- Cite BEAR ISLAND STORY, galley p.7, 1968

---

RBF DEFINITIONS

Six-Wave (Sexave) Phenomenon of Number:

"...Six dimensional" provides " for the six-wave
(sexave) phenomenon of number."

- Citation and context at Powering:  Sixth Dimension, 29 Nov'72

---

Six S's:

        See Architectural Aesthetics:  Six S8s

---

Sixness:                                                      (1)

        See Frame of Reference:  Six Schemata
            Hexagonal Vector Pattern
            Interrelationships:  Fourness & Sixness
            Minimum Six
            Powering:  Sixth Dimension
            Powering:  Sixth Powering
            Tensegrity:  Stability Requires Six Struts
            Foldability:  Six Cases of Foldability of Great
              Circles
            Interrelationship Twoness
            Basic Event
            Motions:  Six Positive & Negative

---

Sixthing of the Circle:

        See Foldability:  Six Cases of Foldability of Great
            Circles; 22 Nov'73

---

Six:  Sixness:                                               (2A)

        See Coherence, 11 Feb'73; 18 Feb'71
            Dimensional Reference Frame, 1972
            Energy Event, 7 Oct'71
            Event, 11 Oct'71*
            Geometry of Thinking, 16 Dec'73
            Insideness & Outsideness, 11 Oct'71
            Integer, 15 Oct'72
            Line, 7 Nov'72
            Minimum System, 26 May'72
            Minimum Set, 18 Nov'72
            Norm:  Tetrahedron as Norm, 15 May'72
            Pulsation, 9 Nov'72*
            Quantum, Jun'66*
            Relevance, 22 Jun'72
            Rhombic Dodecahedron, 29 Nov'72; 27 Jan'75
            Strut, 1950s*
            Structure, 16 Dec'73
            Tetrahedron, 1960*; (1)(2); 1965
            Universal Joint:  Tetrahedron, 9 Nov'73
            Pauling, Linus, 1965

---

Six-vector Teams:

        See Proton & Neutron
            Quantum:  Event-paired Quanta

---

Six:  Sixness:                                               (2B)

        See Vectors Are Real, 23 May'72
            Positional Differentials, 1 Feb'75
            Interference, (517.10) Nov'71
            Structural Quanta, 9 Nov'73
            Restraints, 8 Aug'77

Sixteen: Sixteen-ness:

See Spherical Triangle Sequence, (iii)

---

RBF DEFINITIONS

Sixty Degreeness:

"The metaphysically permitted frame of reference for all
the asymmetrical physical experience of humanity is
characterized by the 60-degree coordination with which
synergetics explores nature's behaviors-- metaphysical
or physical."

- Cite RBF dictation for SYNERGETICS, Beverly Hotel, New York,
  28 Feb.'71. See Sec. 205.4 of Oct.'71.
- Citation at Frame of Reference, Oct'71

---

RBF DEFINITIONS

Sixty Degreeness:

"Sixty degrees is the vector equilibrium neutral angle relative
to which life-in-time aberrates."

- Citation & context at Neutral Angle, 16 Dec'73

---

RBF DEFINITIONS

Sixty Degreeness:

With regard to Z-cobra open triangular spiral which make
up the tetrahedron: "Note the approximately 60 degree
angularly precessional reactions or resultants."

- Cite RBF Marginalis on Synergetics Illustration #2,
  7 Oct. 1971, Washington, DC.

TETRAHEDRON-622.02

---

RBF DEFINITIONS

Sixty Degreeness:

"All the cosmic triangling of all varieties of angles
always averages out to 60 degrees."

- Citation and context at Sphericity of Whole Systems, 26 Sep'73

---

RBF DEFINITIONS

Sixty Degreeness:

"Among the Phoenicians and the Polynesians . . the
sixty degreeness was known to them and it was the king's
capability. The common people on the island were kept
in just by having ninety degreees with which they were
not able to do any important kind of mathematics at all.
But what you could do with sixty degreeness was very
powerful. So the sixty degreenes is part of the
coordinate system that I am talking about. When we begin
to integrate our arithmetic on a sixty degree basis, then
we begin to find some coinciding with the topological
interactions of systems, particularly the vector equilibrium."

- Cite Tape transcript RBF to EJA, Chez Wolf, 18 June 1971.  P. 36

---

RBF DEFINITIONS

Sixty Degreeness:

"Energetic geometry discloses the rational fourth, fifth,
and sixth powering modelability of nature's coordinate
transformings as referenced to the 60° equiangular
isotropic vector equilibrium."

- Cite RBF to EJA, 3200 Idaho, Washington DC, 21 Dec'71.
- Citation at Fourth Dimension, 21 Dec'71

---

RBF DEFINITIONS

Sixty Degreeness:

"If we accept 60 degreeness we find that instead of getting
only four right triangles around a point in a plane, or eight
cubes around a point in space, we get six 60-degree angles
about the point in the plane, and 20 tetrahedra around one
point in space. Furthermore the circumferential modular
frequency of planar or omnidirectional patterning will always
be in one-to-one correspondence with the radial frequencies
of modular subdividing. When we do this, we find we have made
a model of the spontaneously coordinate structure which
nature actually uses / the vector equilibrium /."

- Cite Conceptuality of Fundamental Structures (Kepes), p.72,1965

RBF DEFINITIONS

Sixty Degreeness:

"... The particles which make up cement are sifted sand and gravel, which, though they look rough, pack averagely as spheres would pack-- in 60-degree angular packing. Few people think of cement that way, but if it is shaken down, agitated well, and lubricated together with a colloid, it will automatically avail itself of nature's tetrahedral structuring in 'closest packing' pattern."

- Cite CONCEPTUALITY OF FUNDAMENTAL STRUCTURES, Ed. Kepes 1965, p. 86.

---

Sixty Degree Modulatability:

See Vector Equilibrium: Field of Energy, (C)(D)

---

RBF DEFINITIONS

Sixty Degreeness:

"There are in closest packing, we find, always alternate spaces that are not being used so that triangular groups can be rotated into one position or 60 degrees to an alternate nestable place. . . . In other words you take the vector equilibrium, rottate it 60 degrees to the next nestable position and suddenly it is polarized."

- Citation & context at Vector Equilibrium: Polarization, (1) 11 Jul'62
- Cite Oregon Lecture #7, pp. 234-235, 11 Jul'62

---

RBF DEFINITIONS

Sixty Degreeness: vs Ninety Degreeness:

"It could be that in always only coexistant action-reaction

$180^{o}$-ness begets $90^{o}$-ness )
　　　　　　and　　　　　　) ergo (active)
$90^{o}$-ness begets $180^{o}$-ness )

and $60^{o}$-ness is neutral, ergo (potential)

- ▬▬▬▬▬▬▬▬▬▬▬▬▬▬
- Citation at Precession, 8 Dec'72

---

RBF DEFINITIONS

Sixty Degreeness:

". . . Whereas we can only get eight cubes around a point . . . 90 degreeness uses up all the space around a point. When I am dealing in 60 degreeness, when I am using tetrahedron as unity, we can get the whole volume of 20 tetrahedra around one point. The tetrahedron is unity. We are getting 20 around a point instead of eight. . . . If I have a volume of 20 around a pointm then two to the fourth power is 16 plus two to the second power. . . It is very easy to make models of the fourth dimensionalities."

- Cite Oregon Lecture #4, pp. 137-138. 6 Jul'62

---

RBF DEFINITIONS

Sixty Degreeness: vs. Ninety Degreeness:

"Perpendicularity (90-degreeness) uniquely characterizes the limit of three-dimensionality. Equiangularity (60-degreeness) uniquely characterizes the limits of four-dimensional systems."

- Cite SYNERGETICS draft at Sec. 965.04, 17 Nov'72

---

RBF DEFINITIONS

Sixty Degree Modulatability:

(While) "... The cubes always and only co-occur in the eternal cosmic vector field and are symmetrically oriented within the field, none of the cubes' edge lines are ever congruent or rationally equatable with the most economical energetic vector formulating which is always rational of low number or simplicity as manifest in chemistry. Wherefore humanity's adoption of the cube's edges as its dimensional coordinate frame of scientific event reference gave him need to employ a family of irrational constants with which to translate their findings into their unrecognized isotropic vector matrix relationships where all nature's events are most economically and rationally intercoordinated with omni-sixty-degree, one-, two-, three-, four-, and five-dimensional omnirational frequency modulatability."

- Cite SYNERGETICS draft at Sec. 982.13, 19 Nov'72

---

RBF DEFINITIONS

Sixty Degreeness: vs. Ninety Degreeness:

". . . What shows up as so very important in all our synergetics is the sixty degree coordination whether it is circumferential or radial, giving a sixty degreeness. You have a fundamental coordination that way that you cannot get in a ninety-degreeness where the hypotenuses of the nintey degree angles will not be congruent and logically integratable with the radii."

- Cite tape transcript RBF to EJA, Chez Wolf, 18 June 1971. p. 35.
60-DEGREE COORDINATION - SEC. 432.02

RBF DEFINITIONS

Sixty Degrees: vs. Ninety Degreeness:

"I use 60 degrees as normal instead of 90 degrees."

- Citation at Normal, 2 May'71

---

Sixty Degreeness:                                                          (1)

See Babylonian Mathematics
    Cosmic Neutral
    Closest Packing of Spheres
    Equiangularity
    Hexagon
    Octet Truss
    Spherical Octahedron
    Tetrahelix:  Continuous Pattern Strip
    Vector Equilibrium:  Field of Energy
    Sixty Degreeness vs. Ninety Degreeness

---

RBFDEFINITIONS

Sixty Degreeness: vs. Ninety Degreeness:

"I am quite confident that I have discovered the coordinate system employed by nature and it uses 60 degrees instead of 90 degrees.  Also the lines don't go through a point but they are 60-degreee convergences even though the lines don't ever get together. They get in critical proximities-- and there are the domains of the convergences-- and so forth, even though they are open as you get to the non-closed convergences."

- Cite Oregon Lecture #4, p, 133.  6 Jul '62

---

Sixty Degreeness:                                                          (2)

See Aberration Limit, 22 Jun'72
    Fourth Dimension, 21 Dec'71*
    Frame of Reference, 21 Dec'71*
    Dihedral Angles of Tetra & Octa, 16 Dec'73
    Energy & Number, Oct'71
    Frequency, 2 Nov'73
    Nestable, 11 Jul'62
    Neutal Angle, 16 Dec'73*
    Normal to Universe, 10 Sep'74*
    Pi, Nov'71
    Precession, 8 Dec'72*
    Sphericity of Whole Systems, 26 Sep'73*
    Synergetics, 14 May'73
    Tetrahedron:  Coordinate Symmetry, (A)
    Three-way Great Circling:  Three-way Grid, 17 Feb'72
    Universe, 26 Sep'73
    Vector Equilibrium:  Polarization, (1)*
    Vector Equilibrium, 26 Aug'75
    Zero Volume Tetrahedron, 10 Dec'75
    Dymaxion Airocean World Map, (a),(c), (g)-(i)
    Gravity:  Speed Of, 21 Oct'72
    Triacontrahedron, 31 Jul'77

---

Sixty Degreeness vs. Ninety Degreeness:

See Precession & Degrees of Freedom, (1)*
    Vector Equilibrium:  Field of Energy, (A)-(D)
    Normal, 2 May'71*
    Spherical Octahedrom, 29 Nov'72
    Domains of Convergences, 7 Nov'73
    Model of Toothpicks & Semi-dried Peas, (1)(2)

---

RBF DEFINITIONS

Size:

"Size is special case."

- Context and citation at Shape:  Energy Has Shape, 25 Sep'73

---

RBF DEFINITIONS

Sixty Degrees as Norm:

"I use 60 degrees as normal instead of 90 degrees."

- Citation at Sixty Degrees, 2 May'71

---

RBF DEFINITIONS

Size:

"Size is physical and is manifest by frequency of length, area, volume and time.  Size is manifest in the four variables of relative length, area, volume, and time; these are all four expressible in terms of frequency."

- Citation and context at Prime State, 21 Mar'73

RBF DEFINITIONS

Size:

"Size is always special-case experience."

- Citation and context at Equiangularity, 25 Sep'72

RBF DEFINITIONS

Size:

"Every event has size."

- Cite SYNERGETICS Corollaries, Sec 240., by RBF 11 Oct.'71, Haverford, Penna.

RBF DEFINITIONS

Size:

"The relative size of the vector equilibrium begins with the initial omnidimensional geometrical configuration of reference. Vector equilibria, as with the tetrahedra or other polyhedra, are conceptually valid vector equilibria or tetrahedra, independent of size. Size is where relativity becomes generated. The eternality of synergetics is conceptually experienceable independent of the successive experiences of relativity of time and size."

- Cite RBF rewrite at SYNERGETICS Sec. 445.[04], 22 Jun'72

RBF DEFINITIONS

Size:

"Vectors are size.

No vectors = No size.
No size = No vectors."

- Cite SYNERGETICS Corlollaries, Sec. 240. By RBF 11 Oct. 1971, Haverford, Penna.

RBF DEFINITIONS

Size:

"Size sense comes with comparative experience."

- Citation and context at Otherness, 28 May'72

RBF DEFINITIONS

Size:

"Frequency and Size are the same phenomena."

- Cite RBF to EJA, Bear Island, 23 August 1971, Synergetics Sept. '71 draft, Sec. 882.1.

SIZE - SEC. 528.03

RBF DEFINITIONS

Size:

"... velocity being a product of time and size modules; and mass being a volume-weight relationship..."

- Citation and context at Time, 27/2 May'72

RBF DEFINITIONS

Size:

"Size alone can come to zero-- not conceptuality. We have a sizeless nucleus for the jitterbug pumping model."

. . . The point is the micrososmic turning around between going inwardly and going outwardly."

- Cite RBF to EJA, Blackstone Hotel, Chicago, 31 May 1971

SIZE - SEC. 52802

RBF DEFINITIONS

Size:

"There are three different aspects of size: linear, aerial and volumetric and each one has a different velocity." In coordinate symmetry "as they move in toward the opposite vertex, all these velocities come to zero at the same time. But because of the 60-degreeness, the six edges and the four faces and the symmetry were never being altered, they were not variables. The only variable was size. So size and size alone can come to zero. The conceptuality of these aspects never changes."

- Cite RBF tape, Blackstone Hotel, Chicago, 31 May 1971, Pp. 25 and 26.

- Citation and context at Coordinate Symmetry, 31 May'71

SIZE - SEC 528.02

---

RBF DEFINITIONS

Size:

"Size and intensity are sensorial comparing functions of the special case experiences by brain and not by mind. Mind is concerned only with principles that hold true independently of size yet govern the relative size relationships."

- Cite NEHRU SPEECH, P.12. 13 Nov'69

＊ Citation & context at Brain & Mind, 13 Nov'69

SIZE - SEC 528.06

---

RBF DEFINITIONS

Size:

"The word locally means locally in time and space. By space we mean size-- a function of time."

- Cite RBF to EJA, Somerset Club, Boston, 22 April 1971

- Citation at Local, 22 Apr'71

---

RBF DEFINITIONS

Size:                                                              (A)

"Concept of an experience's relationship to other experiences, defined in term of cyclic repetition of any one experimental demonstrable self-terminating or single-cycle experience. (A triangle, a tetrahedron, or a sphere, etc., is a triangle, a teterahedron, or a sphere independent of size. An angle is an angle independent of the length of its edges. All of Plato's solids may have the same length edges because their differences are entirely angular. An angle is inherently a subdivision of a single cycle. Therefore an angle is sub-size.)

"Size begins with one specific cycle's completion. Angles are conceptual independently of size. Size is linear. As linear size of an object is doubled, surface is fourfolded and volume is eightfolded-- ergo areas increase at a velocity of the second power and volumes at a velocity of the third power-- ergo size variation relationships are deceptive and not superficially predictable by any one experience. As we double the length of a ship its surface is fourfolded. Inasmuch as the power to drive a ship through the sea and air at a given speed is directly proportional to its surface, when we double its linear

SIZE - SEC. 528.04   - Cite WORD MEANINGS, "Ekistics," Vol #28, Oct'69

---

RBF DEFINITIONS

Size:                                                              (1)

"We can say an angle is an angle independent of the length of its edges. Likewise, a triangle is a triangle independent of its size. By Size we do not refer to the angle, but to the length of the edges, or magnitude of the faces or volumes, described by the linear boundaries. How long the edges are can be determined experimentally only in the terms of the repetitive multiples of some given pattern experience. The given experience module has a fundamental time consideration. All experience of size refers to the duration of the pattern-describing events. And the observer's time sense refers to any of his own afterimage consideration of one of his integral recycling organs.

"A basic time cycle is a circle or a loop back.

"Therefore an angle is subcyclic, for it is only part of a circle.

"Angles, being cyclic, are subsize, for size begins with one cycle."

- Cite RBF holograph with old Synergetics draft, circa 1970

---

RBF DEFINITIONS

Size:                                                              (B)

"size, we fourfold its rate of expenditure of energy but we eightfold its payload capacity. A ship's size is popularly thought of in terms of her length. Therefore it comes as a surprise that a man with a ship twice the length of another's can make eight times as much profit. That is why shipowners and sailors talk to one another in terms of tonnages, which is based on volumetric displacement of water by weight."

- Cite WORD MEANINGS, "Ekistics," Vol. #28, Oct'69

---

RBF DEFINITIONS

Size:                                                              (2)

"When man refers to dimension he refers to the size aspects of his experiences as related to other experiences.

"That he had found the linear coordinates of an XYZ-rectilinear interrelationship useful in analyzing omnidimensional pattern experiences does not pre-empt the arithmetical evaluation of alternatives in dimensioning our experiences.

"In book (SYNERGETICS) I must eliminate the words three-dimensional as meaningful, and always use omnidirectional observation of multi-dimensional characteristics, with angle and frequency of cyclic reference as the only requirements."

- Cite RBF holograph with old Synergetics Draft, circa 1970

---

RBF DEFINITIONS

Size:

"Size and time are synonymous."

- Cite GENERALIZED PRINCIPLES, p. 6 - 28 Jan '69.

SIZE - SEC. 528.03

RBF DEFINITIONS

Size:

"Size is a measure of relative magnitude of separate
linear, areal, volumetric, weight and other energetic
experiences."

"Conceptuality operates independent of size."

- Cite NASA Speech, p. 99, Jun'66

SIZE - SEC. 528.01 + 528.02

---

RBF DEFINITIONS

Size:

"Shape is independent of size."

- Cite SYNERGETICS, "Corollaries," Sec. 240.56.  Oct'59
- Citation & context at Shape, Oct'59

---

RBF DEFINITIONS

Size:

"Size is simply three different things:  linear,
areal, and volumetric rates of change."

"So you have three rates of change in the phenomenon
called size."

- Cite OREGON Lecture #6 - pp. 210, 209 respectively
10 Jul
'62

- Cite Carbondale Draft,
NATURE'S COORDINATION - VI.7

SIZE - SEC. 528.02

---

RBF DEFINITIONS

Size:

"Arithmetical size dimensionality is identified
geometrically with relative frequency modulation."

- Cite COLLIER'S, p. 114, Oct'59

---

RBF DEFINITIONS

Size:

"The phenomenon size consists of frequency modulated
linear, that is, vectorial, dimension."

- Cite OMNIDIDRECTIONAL HALO, p. 144, 1960

---

RBF DEFINITIONS

Size:

". . . Size is not a generalized conceptual principle.
Whether referring to the size of an object in respect to
other objects or the sizes of any one object's subdivision,
size emerges exclusively as a frequency concept uniquely
differentiating out each 'specialized case.'"

N.B. BRACKETED PHRASE DELETED FROM SYNERGETICS DRAFT AT
SEC. 528.01 - BY RBF - OCT. 1971

- Cite INTRO. to OMNIDIRECTIONAL HALO, p. 119, 1959

SIZE - SEC. 528.01

---

RBF DEFINITIONS

Size:

"The relative size of a triangle is a secondary observer-
induced consideration and depends upon the frequency
modulated edge increments of the triangle as ratioed to
some other physical experience entity."

- Cite OMNIDIRECTIONAL HALO, p. 144, 1960

---

RBF DEFINITIONS

Size:

"Generalized shape conceptioning is independent
of size.  A triangle is a triangle independent
of size."

- Cite Intro, to OMNIDIRECTIONAL HALO, p. 119, 1959

RBF DEFINITIONS

### Size Dimensionality:

"Synergetical size dimensionality is identified geometrically
with relative frequency modulation."

- Citation and context at <u>Dimensionality</u> (2), 28 Oct'73

---

### Size:                                                                    (2)

See Acceleration:  Angular & Linear (1)(2)
    Brain & Mind, 13 Nov'69*;
    Coordinate Symmetry, 31 May'71*
    Equiangularity, 25 Sep'72*
    Frequency, 16 Feb'73
    Local, 22 Apr'71*
    Otherness, 28 May'72*
    Prime State, 21 Mar'73*
    Reality, 23 Aug'71
    Rigid, 24 Sep'73
    Shape: Energy Has Shape, 25 Sep'73*
    Shape, Oct'59*
    Time, 27 May'72
    Synergetics vs. Model (A)
    Structure, 27 Dec'74
    Infinity = Frequency, 19 Feb'76

---

RBF DEFINITIONS

### Size Dimensionality:

"Arithmetical <u>size dimensionality</u> is identified geometrically

with relative frequency modulation."

- Cite COLLIER's and SYNERGETICS "Corollaries," Sec. 240.46
  and "Modelability, Poering," Sec. 777.

---

RBF DEFINITIONS

### Sizeless:

"The vector equilibrium is absolutely dead center of

Universe and will never be seen by man in any physical

experience-- yet it is the frame of reference.  And it

is not in rotation and it is <u>sizeless</u> and timeless."

- ~~Cite tape transcript RBF to BO'R, Carbondale Dome, 1 May 1971
  P. 39.~~
- Citation at <u>Vector Equilibrium</u>, 1 May'71

---

RBF DEFINITIONS

### Size-selective:

"Isotropic vector matrixes . . . are inadvertently, i.e.,
subjectively activated by the <u>size-selective</u> metaphysical
consideration initiatives, or . . . objectively and
physically articulated in consciously tuned electromagnetic
transmission..."

- Citation and context at <u>Isotropic Vector Matrix</u>, 30 Nov'72

---

### Sizeless:                                                                (1)

See Conceptuality Independent of Size
    No-size Conceptual Model
    Zerosize
    Prime
    Subfrequency
    Zerophase

---

### Size:                                                                    (1)

See Independence of Size
    Magnitude
    Presize
    Sizeless
    Subfrequency
    Subsize
    Time-size
    Zerosize
    Oil Tankers:  Size Of
    Rigid = Sized
    Structural Performance & Size
    Time-angle-size Aspects

---

### Sizeless:                                                                (2)

See Conceptual Tuning, 24 May'72
    Frequency, 2 Nov'73
    Mind As Reality, 27 Mar'73
    Multiplication By Division, 4 Nov'73
    Omnidirectional, 1960
    Point, 20 Feb'73
    Synergetics, 24 Sep'73
    Tepee:  Half-spin Tepee Twist, 20 Feb'73
    Tetrahedron, 24 Sep'73
    Timeless, 1 Apr'72
    Vacuum, 17 Feb'72
    Vector Equilibrium, 1 May'71*
    Prime, 18 Dec'74
    Tensegrity Vector Equilibrium, 28 Jan'75
    Model vs. Form, 8 Apr'75
    Life, 5 Jun'75
    Nuclear Cube, 11 Dec'75; 23 Feb'76
    Six Motion Freedoms & Degrees of Freedom, (B)

Skew: Skew-aberrated:

See Radial-circumferential, 9 Jan'74
Dynamic Symmetry, (3)

Skiing: Skier:                                                    (2)

See Design Science: Education For, 1 Feb'75

RBF DEFINITIONS

Skiing:

"That's all skiing is-- the angular valving of gravity."

- Cite RBF to Mary-Averett Seelye, Trapier Theater, St. Albans
  School, 20 Oct'72

RBF DEFINITIONS

Skinner: B.F.:

"I know and like Skinner. He is sincere and committed to his
theories. I observe that he does not differentiate between
brain and mind. (See my book 'Intuition.') Assuming only
brain, chromosomes, DNA-RNA, and that life is entirely physical,
it is logical for him to see everything as mechanistically
behavioral and omniexplicable by humans because he excludes
from consideration an a priori, eternally inexhaustible,
mysterious integrity governing Universe; only a few of those
reliably guiding principles have thus far been discovered by
humans."

- Cite RBF Ltr. to James Coley, Sep'73

RBF DEFINITIONS

Skiing:

"...A ski compresses the snow into a grooved track of icy
slidability."

- Citation & context at Airplane Flight as Lift, 4 Oct'72

Skin It, Milk It, or Eat It:

See Female, 17 Oct'72; May'65
Male & Female, 19 Dec'71

Skiing: Skier:                                                    (1)

See Surfing: Surfboarding

RBF DEFINITIONS

Skinning:

"When you transfer the projected data from the surface of a
sphere to a plane, you have to break open the spherical skin
in order to 'peel' it. There will be various angular cuts in
the periphery of the skin when it is laid out flat, just as
you take the skin off an animal. The openings along the
edges are called sinuses. The sinuses on my map occur in
the water. None of the cuts go into the land. Therefore, I
am able to take all of the data off the Earth globe and make
it accurately available in the flat."

- Cite RBF to Wm. Marlin, Architectural Forum, p.71, Feb'72

RBF DEFINITIONS

Skinning:

"As in skinning an animal, a fruit, or a vegetable to
provide a flat skin stretch-out, the development of a flat
map of the complete world involve's arbitrary piercing of
the world ball's surface map-skin, thereby making one or
more holes or gashes from which ▅▅ to start the stretching-
out and peeling-off process of the skin until it is liftable
from off its ball center. After the data has been further
stretched it may be laid out as one or more flat map sections.
If the skinning is accomplished in separate peelings and
those sections have curved peripheries they may be tangentially
only as 'gears' or 'fans', which destroys the chance of
forming a continuous one-surface comprehensive world map.

"To provide a continuous one-surface world map-- while
peeling off the sections of the globe-- the transformation
must be such that the pieces have straight and matching
edges when peeled off and flattened out."

- Cite Undated Sheet: "THE DYMAXION AIROCEAN WORLD FULLER
      PROJECTIVE-TRANSFORMATION

---

Skin Pigmentation:

See Race, (1)-(4)

---

RBF DEFINITIONS

Skinning:   Tiger's Skin:

"Typical of all the finitely conceptual objects or systems,
the tiger's skin can be pierced and slotted open. Thereafter, by enlarging the slotted hole by gashes in various
directions, the skin can be peeled off all in one piece.
It can be made to lay out flat by making a lunar-gash from
the skin's edge into any remaining domical area of the
skin. The slitting of a paper cone from its circular edge
to its apex allows the paper to be layed out ▅▅ as a flat
'fan,' intruded by an angualr sinus. . . The surface contour
of every object or system-- be it a complex creature such
as crocodile, or a simple cube or a dodecahedron can thus
be 'skinned' and laid out in the flat."

- Cite NEHRU SPEECH, p. 13. 13 ,Nov'69

SYSTEM - SEC. 401.4

---

Skin:   Skins:                                                      (1)

See Membrane
    Sieve
    Walls

---

Skinning:

See Angular Sinus Takeout, Dec'61
    Thinkable System Takeout (1)

---

Skins:   Skin:                                                     (2)

See Plastics, 10 Aug'70
    Good & Evil Sequence (1)
    Octahedron as Photosynthesis Model, 11 Dec'75
    Montreal Expo'67 Dome, (A)
    North Face Domes, 20 Sep'76
    Human Beings & Complex Universe, (9)(10)

---

RBF DEFINITIONS

Skin Pigmentation:

"At the heart                  "As the Sun's radiation
Of the heart                   Is phtosynthesized
Of the Applewhite              Into regeneration
Heart                          Of biologically accommodated
Are ever                       Intelligent life
The black seeds                Around planet Earth
Whose skins                    By unique differentiations
Like the Skin                  Of total electromagnetic
Of its stem                    Spectrum
Are its skin kin               Into most locally effective
To the barks                   Pigmentations."
Of the appletrees
Ad infinitum,

- Cite RBF Valentine to the Applewhites, "with dearest love
   for them from Uncle Bucky," 14 Feb '72, 3200 Idaho, Wash.,
   D.C., U.S.A., Earth.

---

Skirt:   Skirts:

See Angular Sinus Takeout, Dec'61

Skybreak Bubble:

See Dome: Montreal Expo '67 Dome Sequence, (4)

Sky Harbor:

See Heaven, 13 Nov'69

Sky Ocean:

See Airocean

Skyscraper:                                                    (1)

See Horizontal Skyscraper
Crystalline Asparagus

Sky Dwelling:  Sky-island City:                    (1)

See Floating City
Habitable Satellite
Space Structures
Skybreak Bubble

Skyscrapers:                                                  (2)

See Buildings as Machines, 13 Nov'69
New York City, 13 Mar'75; (1)-(12)
Invented Jobs, 20 Sep'76

Sky Dwelling:  Sky-island City:                    (2)

See Dwelling Service Industry (5)
Inventability Sequence (1)

Sky Tug Helicopter:

See Air Delivery & Submarine Cities (3)
Service Industry, 29 Aug'64

Sky:                                                          (1)

    See Air
       Biosphere
       Heaven: Heavens

---

Slaps in the Face:

    See Rationalization Sequence, (3)

---

Sky:                                                          (2)

    See Order & Disorder, 5 Jul'62
       Visual Symphony (2)

---

Slave-eliminating Machine:

    See Invention Sequence, (2)

---

RBF DEFINITIONS

Slang:

"Slang is the human drive to say more with less.  Slang
gains its users by its poetical economy."

  - Cite Dreyfuss Preface, "Decease of Meaning."
    28 April 1971, p. 20

---

Slave Mentality:

    See Life Is Not Physical, 29 Jun'72

---

Slang:

    See Fresh, 3 Oct'71

---

Slave Profession: Slave Discipline:

    See Architecture, Nov'66
       Science, 10 Oct'63

Slave: Slavedom:                                               (1)


     See Academic Tenure
        Divide & Conquer
        Energy Slave
        Industrial Hypocrisy
        Serf:  Serfdom:  Serf Complex

---

RBF DEFINITIONS

Sleep:

"Though one-third of our time is pre-allotted to the discontinu-
ance of consciousness as sleep, the rotation of night as a
shadow around the Earth results in a rotating wave of shadow
sleepers, while two-thirds of all mankind are at all times
continuously awake."


    - Citation & context at Continuous Man (2), 1963

---

Slave: Slavedom:                                               (2)


     See Comprehensiveness, 3 Nov'64
        Energy Slave (1)
        Labor:  American Labor, 1960
        Specialization, 1970

---

Sleeping Bag:

     See Back Pack, 20 Sep'76
        North Face Domes, 20 Sep'76

---

RBF DEFINITIONS

Sleep:

"Sleep is the great normalizer.  The brain can only do its
subconscious sorting when we are asleep.  It accommodates
the asymmetries and restores the symmetrical."


    (Above observation was a propos Arthur Clarke's
    contention that sleep is an intolerable waste
    of time.)


    - Cite RBF to EJA, Pepper Tree Inn, Santa Barbara, 11 Feb'73

---

Sleeping in the Same Bed:                                      (1)


     See Paired Congruency
        Reciprocal Involvement

---

RBF DEFINITIONS

Sleep:

"I've finally learned to accept the fact that apparently
nature intends us to get to a point where we're supposed to
sleep.  For years I managed to get by on just two or three
hours, letting myself sleep a half-hour ever four, or six
or whatever it was.  It worked fine, but it was a terrible
inconvenience for my wife and she made me stop it.  You can
theorize about what sleep is, but it seems to me that each
day we just get more and more asymmetrical until we have to
sleep to get back into symmetry again.  So I know I have
to sleep and I know that if I use the reserve energies I'll
have to take time to fill those reserve tanks.  They're in
an inconvenient position and they have small nozzles, and it
takes longer to fill them.  But the point of all this is that
I'm so convinced of what's happening that I don't have any
personal option at all.  So just being tired is not enough
reason to take it easy.  I know that I get to the point where
I'm so fuzzy-,imded that I'll mess things up more than help
them, and then sleep is something I don't consider sinful."

    - Cite RBF in Barry Fowler Playboy Interview, 1972 - Draft. p. 39.

---

Sleeping in the Same Bed After the Other Guy Has Gotten Out Of It:

                                        (2)

     See Congruence, 25 Jan'72

RBF DEFINITIONS

Sleeping & Thinking: (1)

Q.          "Do you practice meditation?  Is there a kind
            of Dymaxion sleep?"

RBF:     "I have never practiced it and I have never used
either of those terms.  I try to comprehend what my faculties
may be.  I can go to sleep in 30 seconds.  Animals can go to
sleep and still spring instantly into action.  I thought this
might be a good way to make the most of your time and energy,
as a runner has a second wind--drawing on his reserve tanks.
But it takes much more time and piping to replenish the
reserve tanks.

"So I decided to try and see if I could sleep at a higher
frequency than the daily and nightly periods of the earning-
a-living game.  So I slept whenever I felt like it.  You
cannot put out unless you are putting in.  After two years
I found that I was sleeping only a half-hour every six hours,
or getting only a total of two hours sleep a day and all the
while I was incredibly healthy.

"That may be something like the idea of meditation... we have
all these messages coming in... I like to focus on some"

- Cite RBF to World Game Workshop; Phila., PA; 22 Jun'77

---

RBF DEFINITIONS

Sleeping & Thinking: (2)

"familiar object such as a boat I particularly like... and
in 30 seconds I am asleep: that's the most I do in the way
of meditation.

"But I do a great deal of thinking, trying to put events
together and sort out the significance of my experiences.
By employing word tools we are able to compound the experiences
of total humanity.  I found a lot of nonsense coming out of
my mouth.  So I let my wife do the talking for me for all
our everyday needs as I was resolved to say nothing until I
was sure what its effect would be on other human beings...
So I just kept at work... paying no attention to others."

- Cite RBF to World Game Workshop; Phila. PA; 22 Jun'77

---

Sleep: (1)

        See Awakening
        Dream
        Subconscious Sorting
        Awakeness & Asleepness
        Waking Up

---

Sleep: Sleeping: (2)

        See All-acceleration Universe (1)
        Conscious & Subconscious, Jun'66
        Continuous Man (2)*
        Metaphysics, 2 Jul'62
        Packaged, Jun'66
        We-me Awareness, 31 May'74
        Invented Jobs, 20 Sep'76
        Equilibrium & Disequilibrium, (1)(2)
        Human Beings & Complex Universe, (15)

---

RBF DEFINITIONS

Slenderness Ratio:

"The Greek architects found experientially
That when a stone column's heaight
Exceeds eighteen diameters of its girth
It tends to fail by buckling.
The length to diameter ratio
Of compressional columns
Is called its slenderness ratio.
Steel columns are more stable
Than stone columns.
Steel columns are structurally usable
With slenderness ratios as high as thirty-to-one.
But such columns are called long columns.
A short column is one whose slenderness ratio
Is far below that of the Greek column.
Short columns tend to fail by crushing
Rather than by buckling.
A twelve-to-one slenderness ratio
Provides a short column.

- Cite BRAIN & MIND, p.127, May'72

---

Slenderness Ratio: (1)

        See Cigar Shape
        Length-to-girth Ratio

---

Slenderness Ratio: (2)

        See Sphere, 2 Mar'68
        Tension, 15 Oct'64

---

RBF DEFINITIONS

Slides: Use of Slides in Lectures:

"A lot of people tease me about how I start to give a lecture
and have someone get out the projector and then we never get
around to using the slides.  I am so convinced though that
what I have been saying to you-- about the fact that men do
not see outside themselves, they only see in here-- that I
am quite sure you have the best illustrating capability in
sight.  If I put it on the wall here it tends to make you
lazy and short circuits.  Not until I am quite confident that
you are constructing in here, in your head, do I feel
confident that it is all right to expose you to the slides."

- Cite Oregon Lecture #4, p. 140. 6 Jul'62

RBF DEFINITIONS

▬▬▬▬ Slides: Graphics vs. Words:

"I hope that I have been successful in communicating this to you conceptually without recourse to pictures. No man has ever seen outside of himself. He always sees in his brain. I think it is as easy to stimulate the brain conceptioning by words as it is by graphics. I often find in lectures that I don't have to show the slides which I had been prepared to do because I found that people had conjured up in their own brains from my words the very picture which I had intended to show but had gone on spontaneously to describe in advance. It is my intuitive surmise that the pictures thus conjured up are more powerfully planted in the other man's brain than those resulting from the beams of light bounced off a photograph back to the human eye lenses, retina and nerve connections and after to be scanned and IMAGE-ed (imagined) in the brain."

- Cite Letter to Dr. R. Urmston, 8 Oct '64, p. 2

---

Slides: Graphics vs. Words:

See Model, 22 Jan'75

---

RBF DEFINITIONS

Slides:

See Lecturing

---

RBF DEFINITIONS

Slingshot:

See Charting Alternating Experiences (4)

---

Slings:

See Precession, (II)

---

Slipper:

See Flying Slippers

---

RBF DEFINITIONS

▬▬▬▬ Slow:

"Very,very slow changes humans identify as inanimate.

Slow changes of pattern they call animate and natural."

- Cite RBF Introduction to Gene Youngblood's EXPANDED CINEMA, p.25, Oct'70
- Citation at Animate & Inanimate, Oct'70

---

RBF DEFINITIONS

Slower & Closer vs. Faster & Far Apart:

"A little body moving at sufficient velocity could have the same effect upon another body with which it interferes as could a big body moving at a slower rate."

- Citation & context at Interference (2), Jun'66

Slower & Closer vs. Faster & Far Apart:                      (1)

    See Energy Magnitudes:  Order Of
    Fast & Slow
    Frequency:  High & Low
    Local Radius vs. Wide Arc
    Rates & Magnitudes
    Slow:  The Slower We Get the More Crowded
      We Get

---

Slowdown:                                                    (1)

    See Eternal Slowdown

---

Slower & Closer vs Faster & Far Apart:                       (2)

    See Environmental Events Hierarchy (4)(5)
    Domains of Actions, 9 Jul'62
    Freeways, Mar'66
    Gestation Rate, 1 Mar'77

---

Slowdown:                                                    (2)

    See Now, 14 Feb'72

---

Slow:  The Slower We Get the More Crowded We Get:            (1)

    See Airplanes:  Far Apart in the Sky but Slowed Down
      When Close Together on the Land
    Ships:  A Fleet of Ships Needs More Room at Sea
      Than When Docked Side by Side
    Population Density:  Manhattan Jet Dispersal

---

Slow Slum Death:

    See Death:  Slow Death by Slums vs. War as Quick
      Death
    Death by Want

---

Slow:  The Slower We Get the More Crowded We Get:            (2)

    See Balloon (C)
    Freeways, Mar'66
    Pneumatic Structures, 25 Sep'72

---

Slow:  Slowness:                                             (1)

    See Change
    Fast & Slow
    Speed
    Velocity
    Lag:  Lag Rates

Slow: Slowness:                                    (2)

    See Eternal & Temporal, 4 Sep'77


Smash-up:                                          (1)

    See Explosion


Slums:                                             (1)

    See Death: Slow Death by Slums


Smash-up:                                          (2)

    See Interference, (2); Nov'71


Slums:                                             (2)

    See Building Industry, (2)
        Buildings: Multiple Occupancy, 30 Apr'74
        Conformity, 10 Oct'63
        Empty, May'70
        Invented Jobs, 20 Sep'76
        Office Buildings, 28 Jun'72
        Reverse Optimism, Aug'64
        Weapons Technology, (2)


Smellable You:

    See Hearable You, 22 Nov'73


Small:

    See Big & Little
        Element: Smallest Chemical Element
        Little
        Nuclear-smallest
        Tetrahedron as Smallest System


Smell-discover:

    See Transistor, 22 Jun'74

Smell: (1)

See Olfactoral Sense
Odor: Odors

Smythe: Verner: RBF Patent Attorney:

See Billboard Model

Smell: (2)

See Fail-safe, 17 Oct'72
Harmonics, (1)(2)
Wind Stress & Houses, (9)
Silence, 30 Sep'76

Snake Swallowing Frog:

See Scenario Universe, 19 Jul'76

Smith, Cyril Stanley:

See Fuller, R.B: Meeting with Fernandez-Moran, (1)
Gravity, (e)-(k)

Snake Swallows its Own Tail:

See Interference, Feb'72

Smoke Screens:

See Privacy, 22 Apr'61

Snake: Snakes:

See Children as Only Pure Scientists, (A)

Snowflake:

See Design, (1)


Soap Bubbles:

See Bubbles


RBF DEFINITIONS

Snow Mound:

"A child, when playing in sticky snow, may make a big
mound of snow and hollow it out with his hands or a
shovel to make a cave.  Then, looking at the hollowed
mound from outside, he may discover that he has made a
rough dome.  He might then conclude that whatever makes
that structure stand up and span space is not dependent
on what was at the center because the snow has been
removed from the center.  Whatever makes it stand up has
to do with the circumferential interaction of the snow
crystals and their molecules and the latter's atoms.  He
may find out by experiment that he could put not only one
hole, but many holes through the snow dome shell and it
continues to stand up.  It becomes apparent that it would
be possible to take a pneumatic balloon, pair the molecules,
and get rid of all the molecules at the center that were
not hitting the balloon-- for it is only the molecules
that hit the balloon at high frequency of successive
bounce-offs that give the balloon its shape."

(For text immediately following see Tensegrity Geodesic Grid)

- Cite SYNERGETICS ILLUSTRATION #96, caption.
  (Same text: Mexico '63, pp. 46-47), 10 Oct'63

BALLOON - SECS, 656.40+41


RBF DEFINITIONS

Social Adjustment:

"You'll find that energies are so distributed in Universe
that the number of times large amounts of energy is available
at any one point to do large things is very much less frequent
than the number of times small amounts are available to do
small things.  The things we're talking about here, the
social adjustments are very big.  They're magnificent, the
most marvelous part of the whole show.  They don't get done
overnight, but they're actually happening so fast that I
can't believe it.  I've seen in my lifetime rectification,
rectification, rectification.  And we really are getting
these, I'm convinced of it."


- Cite RBF tape transcript for Barry Farrel Playboy Interview,
  Feb '72.  Deleted.  See draft p. 64.


RBF DEFINITIONS

Snow Mound:

"In the case of the pneumatic bag . . . what makes the net
take the shape that it does is simply the molecules that
happen to hit it.  The molecules that are not hitting it
have nothing to do with its shape. . .

"When you were a little child, the first time you went out
in a fairly deep snow, or the first time you were allowed
to go out on your own, you tended to make a mound of the
snow.  It was a fascinating thing because you could push
it together and it would take shapes, it had coherence.
I am sure that almost every child with mittens on builds
himself a mound and then starts chipping and working away
at the mound and makes a hole in it and he makes a cave.
He finds that he can get in it and what he discovers
is that the structural integrity has nothing to do with
the snow that used to be at the middle.  It has something
to do with the circumferential set of action of molecules
there that you are accounting for.  So we develop a
strong intuition about this when we are very young.  What
I saw that might be possible was that we might hollow out
the pneumatic network and we could do away with the
molecules that weren't doing the work, if we had the ones
that were doing the work neatly paired."

BALLOON - SECS 656.40+41   - Cite Oregon Lecture #5,   9 Jul'62


Social Breakout from Barnacle to Salmon:                    (1)

See Coral Reef
    Marine Life Analogy of Humans


Snow Mound:

See Balloon


Social Breakout from Barnacle to Salmon:                    (2)

See Orbital Escape from Critical Proximity, (4)

Social Economics:  Majority Control of Social Economics
Man by 1975:


See Economic Accounting System:  Human Life-hour
          Production, (1)
     Dymaxion Artifacts, (1)(2)

---

Social Highway Experience:  Three Autos:

"In the early days of the auto on a lonely road-- when you saw
another car coming-- there was always a third.  Three cars always
come to approximately the same point at approximately the same
time.  This is not surprising because when we take away the two
points for the axis of the observer, you always have the
constant relative abundance with its three edges.  Edges are
lines.  The cars are really lines... They are trajectories.
They are simply averaging out.  Universe tends to keep sorting,
then, this way.

"We are really relating the social highway experience of three
cars to the complementarity of the little triangle on the
Earth's surface with the other three triangles.  Critical
proximity imposes the generalization.  The triangle imposes the
triangle."


- Cite RBF to EJA + BO'R, 3200 Idaho, Wash, DC, 17 Feb'72

---

Social Economics:                                          (1)

     See Design Revolution:  Pulling the Bottom Up
          Standard of Living

---

Social Highway Experience:  Three Autos:                   (1)


     See Probability Model of Three Cars on a Highway
          Spherical Triangle Sequence

---

Social Economics:                                          (2)

     See Disarmament, (1)(2)
          Old Man River Project, 20 Sep'76

---

Social Highway Experience:  Three Autos:                   (2)


     See Sphericity of Whole Systems, 26 Sep'73
          Three-way Great Circling:  Three-way Grid, 17 Feb'72

---

Social Highway Experience:  Three Autos:

"In the early days of the auto on a lonely road-- when you saw
another car coming-- there was always a third coming into view
or already in view.  Three cars frequently come to approximately
the same  highway point at approximately the same time.  This is
not surprising because when, having first taken away the two
points from the system to accommodate the axis of the observer,
we always have the topologically constant relative abundance
of interference crossings, areas, and lines.  Edges are lines.
The car paths are reality lines, traces, with universal three-
foldness of energy-event trajectory vectors.  Universe keeps
sorting its event traces into bundles of three.  The social
highway experience of three cars is the ▮▮▮▮▮▮▮▮▮▮▮▮▮▮▮▮
inexorably present tricomplementarity relationship of the little
local triangle on the Earth's surface complemented by the
three other great-circle triangles of the terrestrial spherical
tetrahedron always produced in all system formation and transforming.  Critical proximities impose three triangulations."

- Cite RBF to EJA, 3200 Idaho, 17 Feb'72 as rewritten by RBF 18 Feb
                                                             '72

---

Social Ignorance:


     See Synergy:  Degrees Of, (6)

RBF DEFINITIONS

Social-industrial Relay:

"Despite intermittent submissiveness to runaway momentums of
residual ignorance, man guards most dearly and secretly his
freedom of thought and initiative.  Therefrom emanates the
social-industrial relay, from self-starters to group starters."

_ Citation & context at Understanding, 1 Apr'49

---

RBF DEFINITIONS

Socialism:

". . . Disarmament is stalled in the U.S. because the country
cannot keep its economy going through the 'irrigations system'
now fed at the top through annual weaponry undertakings without
seeming subscribing to 'socialism.'  In wartime emergencies,
national management of economic activity is exempt from charges
of socialism, but by custom and law such centralized authority
is forbidden in peacetime.  To avoid this embarrassment and
to keep our economy healthy, wartime emergency powers are
extended to meet the threat of the next war.  This extension
is called 'cold war.'  The U.S. knows that the world needs and
wants disarmament and that its socialism-avoiding subterfuge
becomes increasingly evident to the rest of the world and thus
less tenable.  The government and powerful Washington lobbies
of the armaments contractors, supported by the labor unions,
are seeking ways to keep the economic irrigation system fed
from the top while also attaining progressive disarmament."

- Cite THE PROSPECT FOR HUMANITY, Sat. Review, 19 Sep'64

---

RBF DEFINITIONS

Socialism:

"Socialism is just a boring way of speeding up the mess."

- Cite RBF in Corcoran Gallery Address, Washington, DC
  23 Feb '72

---

RBF DEFINITIONS

Socialism:

"Socialism was one of yesterday's ways of dealing with

inadequate wealth.  Socialism is now as obsolete as the

stone hammer.  So also is undeveloped static proprty,

or gold capitalism.  Gold coins wear out; land erodes.

That is why capitalism is obsolete.  Industry and biology

are metabolic; they grow."

- Cite I&I, THE DESIGNERS AND THE POLITICIANS, p. 304. 1962

---

RBF DEFINITIONS

Socialism:

"Socialism means universal austerity."

- Cite RBF to EJA
  Carbondale
  2 April 1971

---

RBF DEFINITIONS

Socialism:

"Socialism-- the theory of austerity for all and the

sharing of the inadequacy with slow approach to certain

untimely demise."

Cite ARCHITECT AS WORLD PLANNER. July'61

---

RBF DEFINITIONS ·

Socialism:

"The word socialism was invented to describe equal sharing

in the inadequacies of agricultural life support, ergo,

austerity for all.  Who wants universal austerity?  The

whole concept of socialism originated from an agricultural

(and only dawning) industrial era which is now finished

and is kept effective by 'lying-in-state' as an ignorance-

sustained conditioned reflex of society."

- Cite YORTY LTR, p. 5, 1 Apr '71

---

Socialism:                                          (1)

See Air is Socialized
    Public Lands
    Technocracy

Socialism: (2)

See Acceleration of Change, 1938
Design Revolution: Pulling the Bottom Up, (7)(8)
Initiative, 10 Aug'70
No Energy Crisis, (B)(C)

---

Social Justice:

See Television: Third Parent, May'65

---

RBF DEFINITIONS

**Social Organization:**

"Now I would ask the question if this isn't of some importance, this matter of fooling ourselves into thinking that we see and feel the modern when it is unfeelable and unseeable. I should think that it wouldhave very great significance. It could have something to do with why it is at the present moment that our technology is so developed that we could feed and make everybody technically more successful than any man has ever been before, and yet we don't have the ability socially to organize ourselves to do anything about it. We seem to be on the road to blowing ourselves up. We have more and more emergencies of higher and higher frequency, so I would say that our social capability is lagging. And I would say that much of our social disabilities has have to do with our being preoccupied with certain myths. What I then intend to do in giving you the subject "Trends to Invisibility," is to really try to examine if I can, the ways in which we have deceived ourselves, and then examing ways in which we might be able to organize ourselves towards informing ourselves more effectively regarding where we are in our Universe and what we might do about it."

- Cite Oregon Lecture #1, pp. 22-23. 1 Jul'62

---

RBF DEFINITIONS

Social Problems: Tetrahedral Coordination Of:

"...The tetrahedron can be extrapolated into life in all its experience phases, thus permitting man's entry into a new era of cosmic awareness."

- Citation and context at Synergetics, 28 Oct'73

---

RBF DEFINITIONS

Social Problems: Tetrahedral Coordination Of:

"I have received your paper on 'Organizational Structure' entitled 'Mechanics of Group Dynamics'. It is splendid. I find it fascinating to observe your extension of my work into your social problems. I have intuited that they should be so extendable because of their fundamental and general nature. Colonel Lane made use of my tetrahedral coordinate system in logistical and maintenance procedures in Marine Corps Aviation. A Catholic priest, high in the councils of Rome, identified my coordinate system with the High Church's interpretation of the Heavenly Host. I myself have applied the tetrahedronal co-ordinating system to the synergy of unique efforts of individuals of the chemical science world who themselves have discovered and verified the tetrahedral coordination of both the organic and inorganic chemical structuring. I was, therefore, aware of the extensibility of the principles but am therefore better prepared to judge and acclaim your efforts as extraordinary and repre-sentative of a major seasonal advance of the regenerative growth of our seeds."

- Cite RBF Ltr. to Lewis E. Lloyd, Dow Chemical economist, Midland, Mich., 4 May'57

---

Social Problems: Tetrahedral Coordination Of: (1)

See Lloyd, Lews E: Dow Chemical Economist
Social Sciences: Analogue to Physical Sciences
Synergetic Accounting Advantages: Hierarchy Of
Tetrahedral Dynamics

---

Social Problems: Tetrahedral Coordination Of: (2)

See Synergetics, 28 Oct'73
Twelve Universal Degrees of Freedom (1)(2)

---

RBF DEFINITIONS

Social Sciences: Analogue to Physical Sciences:

"Our seeability is so inherently local that we never see anything but asymmetries. Sociologists have such trouble because they see (rather than principles) such a high frequency of asymmetries."

- Cite RBF to EJA, Blackstone Hotel, Chicago, 31 May 1971
- Citation & context at Asymmetry, 31 May'71

RBF DEFINITIONS

Social Sciences: Analogue to Physical Sciences:

"It is notable that the hard sciences, even mathematics, have the generalizations. But the social scientists, the behaviorists, have just the exceptions and not the generalizations."

- Citation and context at Economics, 16 Feb'73

---

RBF DEFINITIONS

Social Sciences: Analogue to Physical Sciences: (A)

"I think the social sciences are going to be admitted, in due course, into the rigorously operative ranks of the physical sciences, but only as a consequence of physical science entering the social field. Modern physical science and industrial technology sprang from the discovery of natural law. There are natural laws operative in both individual and collective human behaviors. So far, however, the social scientists have failed to find any of the quantitative values governing the natural laws in human behavior. But the physical scientists, through cybernetics, behavioral science, and electrical probing of the brain, and so on, are finding some of those behavioral laws and their chemical, physical, and mathematical relationships..."

"We can say that reform-intending social laws have been needed when man did not understand adequately the physical laws. The 1895 'It is forbidden to stick your head out of the railroad car window' should not be needed today...."

"I think the social scientist ought to rejoice that he..."

- Cite RBF in AAUW Journal, p.176; May'65

---

RBF DEFINITIONS

Social Sciences: Analogue to Physical Sciences: (1)

"Social relationships must follow the rational energy quantum laws of physics but at a complex level. Social behaviors must follow all the generalized scientific principles such as synergy and precession. Because precession imposes angles other than 180° upon all interactions of all moving systems of Universe there are no straight lines demonstrated in nature. The fundamental wave behavior of all nature is a consequence of the omni-intereffective precession. Most of our social undertakings try to analyze subjectively and to persuade objectively individuals to move in 180° or straight-line paths. Such attempts are inherently futile. When society recognizes realistically that everything moves in an angular wave patterning, society will be able to accommodate its behavior in a more realistic and satisfactory manner. Democracy's right-left pulsations are imposed by nature's wave behavior. When society comprehends the omnirational isotropic vector matrix 60-degree angle coordinate system it may then be able to emulate the behavior of sailing ship masters and will learn how to beat, which means angling first left and then right 45° off the course leading directly into the wind, in order to

- Cite NEHRU SPEECH, p.31, 13 Nov'69

---

RBF DEFINITIONS

Social Sciences: Analogue to Physical Sciences: (B)

"has been unable to find absolute social formulas. We might say to the social scientists, 'It is just as scientific to discover that there is no formula as it is to discover a formula.'

"It was more difficult, socially and scientifically, to discover zero than to discover one or two."

*
- Cite AAUW JOURNAL, p.176, May'65

---

Social Sciences: Analogue to Physical Sciences: (2)

"accomplish distances in the direction from which the wind moves. Society finds it easy to sail with the wind but has demonstrated a lesser capability in negotiating windward passages. To sail with the wind is to yield to evolutionary forces. To sail into the wind is to master forces."

(Edited.)

- Cite NEHRU SPEECH, pp. 31-32. 13 Nov'69

---

RBF DEFINITIONS

Social Sciences: Analogue to Physical Sciences:

"... By my definition of Universe all that was relegated to metaphysical nebulosity is now embraced by finite Universe along with the physically energetic, wherefore all the hitherto 'inexact sciences' may become rigorously defined, enjoying equatable treatability at optimum degree of determinability."

- Cite INTRODUCTION TO OMNIDIRECTIONAL HALO, pp.124-5, 1959

---

RBF DEFINITIONS

Social Sciences: Analogue to Physical Sciences:

"Though our social sciences have been earnestly seeking generalized principles which might give them the insights and design virtuosity enjoyed by physics, chemistry, et. al., they have until now had no important success. The reason we have introduced the general systems' vectorial geometry today is because it provides the connection between social and physical science. It opens the doors to powerful planning."

- Cite Nehru Speech, pp. 29-30. 13 Nov'69

---

RBF DEFINITIONS

Social Sciences: Analogue to Physical Sciences:

"... Most socio-economic phenomena defy the exact treatments effective and necessary in chemistry, physics, astrophysics, etc., our case is different for it grew out of mathematical treatment ..."

- Cite Ltr. to Jim Fitzgibbon (?), Raleigh NC, p.j3, undated

# Synergetics Dictionary

<u>Social Sciences</u>: <u>Analogue to Physical Sciences</u>:

-- For a discussion of triads and triangular structure in social
organization and fundamental physics see correspondence
between Prof. Theodore Caplow, Dept. of Sociology, Columbia,
24 Jan'66 and RBF reply of 18 Feb'66.

<u>Social Sciences</u>: <u>Analogue to Physical Sciences</u>:  (1)

See Closed-sphere-system Democracy
    Circuitry: Thermionic & Political Analogy
    Exponential Model vs. Limits to Growth
    Grid: Crisscross Right-angle Grid in Civil &
        Agrarian Law
    Individual: Theory Of
    Interference as a Social Model
    Metaphysical & Physical
    Organic World: Biological World as Model For
        Society
    Organization
    Precession: Analogy of Precession & Social
        Behavior
    Relativity: Marriage of Social & Natural Law
    Synergetic Hierarchy
    Social Problems: Tetrahedral Coordination Of
    Prediction: Socio-economic vs. Engineering
    Laws of Nature vs. Laws of Man

<u>Social Sciences</u>: <u>Analogue to Physical Sciences</u>:  (2)

See Acceleration of Change, 1938
    Air Space, May'65
    Asymmetry, 31 May'71*
    Democracy, 13 Nov'69
    Economics, 16 Feb'73*
    Energy, 28 Apr'48
    Intellect: Equation Of, 28 Apr'48
    Least Resistance, 1938
    Local Squareness, 9 Jul'62
    Marx, Karl, 6 Jul'62
    Public Opinion Polls, 4 Jan'70
    Ruddering Sequence (1)(4)(5)
    Synergetic Hierarchy, 31 May'71
    Design Science & World Game (A)-(C)
    Scrap Sorting & Mongering (2)
    Navy Sequence (2)
    Structural Sequence, (C)

RBF DEFINITIONS

<u>Society</u>: <u>Control Of</u>:

"The creative control, or streamlining, of society by the
scientific-minded (the right-makes-mightist) is in direct
contrast to attempts by scheming matter-over-mindists (the
might-makes-rightist) to control society by increasing,
instead of lessening, resistance to natural flows through
such devices as laws, tariffs, prohibitions, armaments, and
the cultivation of popular fear."

"By controlling direction it becomes possible, scientifically,
to increase the probability that specific events will 'happen.'"

- Citation and context at <u>Rationalization Sequence</u> (2 (3), 1938

<u>Society</u>: <u>Control Of</u>:

See Least Resistance, 1938

<u>Society Does Not Understand Nature</u>:

See Synergy, 4 Mar'69

RBF DEFINITIONS

<u>Sociology</u>:

"Sociology permits such fantastical asymmetrical extremes
that we're looking at special casees instead of principles.
. . . Such a high frequency of asymmetry. . .And not knowing
this, they don't realize that communism induces capitalism."

- Cite tape transcript of RBF to EJA and BO'R, Chicago, 31 May '71.
- Citation and context at <u>Communism</u>, 31 May'71

<u>Social</u>: <u>Society</u>: <u>Sociology</u>:  (1)

See Earth Fault: Society is Living in a Sort Of Earth
        Fault
    Fuller, R.B: As Harbinger of Society
    Metabolics
    Metabilical Cord
    Organic Model: Biological World as a Model For
        Society
    Precession: Analogy of Precession & Social
        Behavior
    Self-considerate Society
    Superstition of Social Superiority
    Design Revolution: Pulling the Bottom Up
    Standard of Living
    Behavior & Environment
    Conditioning

Social: Society: Sociology: (2)

See Average Human Being, 1 Apr'73
    Culture, 27 Jan'77
    Dome Over Manhattan, 26 Apr'77
    Ego, 9 Nov'75
    Fear, Feb'72
    Franklin, Ben, 22 Jan'73
    Selfishness, 22 Jun'75
    Symmetry & Asymmetry, Dec'71
    Truth, 1967
    Unselfishness, ▆▆▆▆▆ Jan'72

Solar Panel Water Heating:

    See Now House, (4)

Social: Society: Sociology: (3)

See Social Adjustment
    Social Economics
    Social Highway Experience:  Three Autos
    Social Ignorance
    Social-industrial Relay
    Social Justice
    Socialism
    Social Organization
    Social Problems:  Tetrahedral Coordination Of
    Social Sciences:  Analogue to Physical Sciences
    Society:  Control Of
    Society Does Not Understand Nature
    Sociology

Solar Power: (1)

See Income Energy
    Wind Power
    Sun Energy
    Wind Power = Sun Power

Soft Revolution:

    See Revolutions:  Soft & Hard

Solar Power: (2)

    See Precession (b)

RBF DEFINITIONS

Soil:

    See Topsoil

RBF DEFINITIONS

Solar System Model:

"The model of the solar system itself
is a flattened polyhedron."

- Cite RBF to EJA, Beverly Hotel, New York, 18 June 1971.

Solar: Solar System: (1)

See Atom as Solar System
Sun: Sunlight

---

Solids:

"Solids... are themselves only wave complexes."

- Citation and context at Noninterfering Zero Points, 9 Mar'73

---

Solar: Solar System: (2)

See Black Hole (1)
Regenerativity, 17: Jan'75

---

Solids:

"The superficially deceptive microaggregates
Which defied differentiating resolution,
Into their myriads of separate parts,
By the instrumentally unaided
Human sight."

- Cite INTUITION, p.40 May '72

---

Soleri: Paolo:

"Soleri is the example of the sculptor as politician.
A bunch of people living together in the desert may be
very attractive but what's that got to do with architecture?
He is just a politician.  I am not interested."

- RBF to Lady architect Hay-Adams brunch, Wash Dc; 8 Feb'76

---

Solids:

"Solids are high tide aspects of faces."

- Cite RBF to EJA, Blackstone Hotel, Chicago, 31 May 1971

- Citation and context at Tidal, 31 May'71

---

Soleri, Paolo:

"I know Paolo Soleri very well and think very well of him
as a human being.  I find him very inspiring to  many other
human beings in his humane viewpoints.

"I think of him more as a sculptor than as an engineer, so I'm
very sympathetic with his hope to serve humanity by what he
gives you as an idea.  But I do not think that is probably the
way it is going to go.  I think everything we produce will be
produced more mobilely and with much more flexible kinds of
relationships for humanity.  All humanity is now prone to
become world beings so we're going to have to accommodate the
comings and going in very new places."

/For follow-on entry se East-west Mobility Of
World Man, (1)(2)_7

- Cite RBF to "Town Meeting of the Air," Wash,, DC; 10 Sep'75

---

Solids:

"The omniinteractions impinge on your nervous system in all
manner of frequencies-- some so high as to appear 'solid'
things, some  so slow as ██ seeming to be 'absolute voids.'"

- Citation At Halo Concept, 25 Apr'71

RBF DEFINITIONS

Solid State:

"Science evolved the name 'solid state' physics when, immediately after World War II, the partial conductors and partial
resistors-- later termed 'transistors'-- were discovered. The
phenomena were called 'solid state' because without human
devising of the electronic circuitry, certain small metallic
substances accidentally disclosed electromagnetic pattern-holding,
shunting, route-switching, and frequency-valving regularities,
assumedly produced by the invisible-to-humans, atomic complexes
constituting those substances. Further experiment disclosed
unique electromagnetic circuitry characteristics of various
substances without any conceptual model of the 'subvisible
apparatus.' Ergo, the whole development of the use of these
invisible behaviors was conducted as an intelligently resource-
ful trial-and-error strategy in exploiting invisible and
uncharted-by-humans natural behavior within the commonsensic-
ally 'solid' substances. The addition of the word ▊▊▊▊▊▊
▊▊▊▊▊▊▊▊▊ 'state' to the word 'solid' implied regularities
in an otherwise assumedly random conglomerate. What I have
discovered goes incisively and conceptually deeper than the
blindfolded assumptions and strategies of solid state physics--
whose transistors' solid state regularities seemingly defied
discrete conceptuality and scientific generalization and kinetic
                                            omnigramming."
- Citation and context at Atomic Computer Complex (4)(5), 13 May'73

Solid State:                                        (1)

See Transistor

---

RBF DEFINITIONS

Solid State:

"We have physics of the 'solid state,' a very late phase of
physics very improperly called 'solid.' Even in the 'solid'
state the voids between the atoms are as voids of interstellar
space. The nucleus itself is as empty as space itself. But
the concept that you could make everything solid was a most
comfortable kind of concept."

- Cite SYNERGETICS draft at Sec. 525.03, Nov'71

Solid State:                                        (2)

See Atomic Computer Complex, (4)(5)*
    Particle, (1)

---

RBF DEFINITIONS

▊▊▊ Solid State:

"Take the simple word solid. We have physics of the
'solid state,' a very late phase of physics, very
improperly called. 'solid,' Even in the 'solid' state
the voids between atoms are as the voids of space, and
the nucleus itself is as empty as space itself. But the
concept that you make everything solid was a most
comfortable kind of concept."

- Cite MERGERS & ACQUISITIONS
       Vol. 1, No. 1., p . 44, 1965

SOLIDS: MATTER — SEC. 525.03

Solids:                                             (1)

See Entity
    Liquid vs. Solid
    Matter
    Particle
    Rules of No Actual Particulate "Solids"
    Tensegrity:  Miniature Tensegrity Masts
    Bodies:  Solid Bodies
    Liquid Solid
    No Solids

---

RBF DEFINITIONS

Solid State:

"One of the words we use a great deal is solid. Infact,
in quite modern physics in relation to defense and so forth,
we have solid state physics. It is a very strange phrase
for the physicists to use because they have discovered that
there is nothing solid. I don't know why they insist on
using the words, but it seems to be good for bureacracy to
have a solid state, and so you can handle it academically
that way, but let's not get fooled becausewe haven't found
anything solid. . . "

- Cite Oregon Lecture #3, p. 109. 5 Jul'62

Solids:                                             (2)

See Halo Concept, 25 Apr'71* ; Jun'71
    Invisible Circuitry, (2)
    Meaningless, Oct'66
    Noninterfering Zero Points, 9 Mar'73*
    Powering, 11 Jul'62
    Radiation:  Speed Of, (C)
    Structure Sequence, (3); 15 Oct'64
    Synergetics, (p.j3) undated

Solving:  Solution:


See Finite Solutions
    Problem Solving
    Problem:  Statement of the Problem

---

RBF DEFINITIONS

Somethingness & Nothingness:

"All the characteristics of a system are absolute because each
of its components is the minimum limit case of its respective
conceptual category, for all conceptuality, as the great
mathematician Euler discovered and proved, consists at minimum
of points, areas, and lines.  Goldy further clarifies and
simplifies Euler by saying that an area is a nothingness; a
plurality of areas are framingly separated views of nothingness.
A point is a somethingness.  A line is a relationship between
two somethingnesses.

"An enlarged seemingly single somethingness may prove to consist
of a plurality of somethingnesses between which the defined
interrelationship lines fence off the nothingness into a
plurality of separately viewable nothingnesses.  Points are
unresolvable, untunable somethingnesses  occurring in the
twilight zone between visible and supravisible experience."


    - Cite GOLDYLOCKS Ms. p.A3, 9 Jun'75

---

Somersaults:

    See Intertransformability Systems, 28 Apr'77

---

RBF DEFINITIONS

Somethingness & Nothingness:

"There is a fourfold twoness: one of the exterior, cosmic
finite ('nothingness') tetrahedron, i.e., the macrocosm outwardly complementing all ('something') systems and the interior
microcosmic tetrahedron of nothingness complementing all
conceptually thinkable and cosmically isolatable 'something'
systems."


    - Citation & context at Two Kinds of Twoness, (A)(B), 10 Nov'74

---

RBF DEFINITIONS

Something:

"We'll have to cut out this word something.  I'd like

some day to do something about this word 'something.'

Some. Thing."



    - Cite RBF to EJA, Somerset Club, Boston, 22 April 1971

---

RBF DEFINITIONS

Somethingness & Nothingness:

"The third power accounts both the untuned nothingness
and the finitely tuned somethingness."


    - Citation and context at Nothingness, 16 Nov'72

---

RBF DEFINITIONS

Somethingness & Nothingness:

"These young scientists... said I had the answer to the
age-old problem of how you start your accounting... of whether
you start with two, or one, or zero.... I gave them awareness
and otherness, identifying the secondness with otherness....
The topology of the windows of nothingness.  Somethingness
is the same tunability of systems.  Nothingness is ultra or
infra, an untunability between the crests of waves of other
systems, where there is no tuning at all."



    - Cite RBF to EJA, by telephone from Phila. office; 7 Oct'75

---

RBF DEFINITIONS

Somethingness & Nothingness:

"In synergetics the total mass somethingness to be
acceleratingly expended is 10 $F^2$, with always a bonus 2 :
Me and the Otherness.  In synergetics the total nothingness
and somethingness involved in both inbound and outbound
field is 20 $F^3$.  (Nothing = 10.  Something = 10.  Both = 20.)
The multiplicative twoness of me and the otherness.
$F^3$ = Unexpected nothingness $F^1$ + Expected somethingness $F^2$ = $F^3$."



    - Cite SYNERGETICS draft at Sec. 960.13, 16 Nov'72

Something-nothing-something-nothing:                    (1)

See Binary
    Conceptuality & Nonconceptuality
    Now-you-see-it-now-you-don't
    Pulse Pattern

Something: Somethingness:                    (1)

See Somethingness & Nothingness
    Time-somethingness
    Thing: Things
    Nothingness = Untuned Somethingness
    Simplest Something
    Point-to-able Something
    Minimum Something

Something-nothing-something-nothing:                    (2)

    See Resolvability Limits, 30 Apr'77

Simplest Something:                    (2)

    See Tetrahedron, 26 Apr'77

Somethingness & Nothingness:                    (1)

    See Space Nothingness & Time Somethingness
        Unstructurings & Restructurings
        Cosmic Discontinuity & Local Continuity
        Interference & Noninterference
        Visible & Invisible

Something: Somethingness:                    (2)

    See Bunch, 5 Mar'73
        Jitterbug, 4 Oct'72
        Lot, 5 Mar'73
        Tetrahedron, 20 Feb'73
        Triangle, 20 Apr'72
        Two Kinds of Twoness, (G)
        Thinking, 23 Feb'72
        One-dimensional Polarity, 11 Sep'75
        Two-dimensional Polarity, 11 Sep'75
        Minimum Tetrahedron, 22 Feb'77

Somethingness & Nothingness:                    (2)

    See Cosmic Discontinuity & Local Continuity, 15 Jan'74
        Fourfold Twoness, 10 Nov'74
        Minimum of Four Tetrahedra, 22 Feb'77
        Nonthing, 11 Sep'75
        Out-lining, 22 Mar'76
        Quantum Sequence, (1)
        Self & Otherness: Four Minimal Aspects, 9 Jun'75
        Two Kinds of Twoness, (A)(B)*
        Windows of Nothingness, (1)
        Nature in a Corner, 20 Jun'77

Son of God:

    See Man as Son of God
        Trinity: Equation Of

Sonics:

    See Ultrasonics

RBF DEFINITIONS

    S.O.S.:

    "There's no S.O.S. on land-- only at sea!"

    - Cite RBF to EJA, 1970

---

RBF DEFINITIONS

    Sorting:

    "Men sort, classify, and order in direct opposition to entropy-- which is the law of the increase of the random element-- increase of disorder. Men sort and classify internally and subconsciously as well as externally and consciously, driven by intellectual curiosity and brain. All 92 chemical elements can be inhibited into complementary and orderly interfunctioning in the integral organic process of man. Man seems to be the most comprehensive antientropy function of Universe."

    - Cite RBF in AAUW Journal, p. 175, May '65

Soul:

    See Life is Not Physical, (1)(2)

---

Sorting: (1)

    See Angular Sorting
        Antientropy
        Problem
        Irrelevancies: Dismissal Of
        Parting the Strands
        Scrap Sorting & Mongering
        Subconscious Sorting
        Brain-sorting
        Tuning-in & Tuning-out

Sound Name:

    See Universal Language, 21 Sep'74

---

Sorting: (2)

    See Biological Life (1)
        Boltzmann Sequence (1)
        Cosmic Fish, 8 Feb'73
        Ecology Sequence (B)
        Comprehensive Universe (2)
        Frequency, 1970
        Man:: Interstellar Transmission of Man, May'72
        Metaphysical & Physical, Jun'66; 1970
        Monitor, Feb'73
        Problem, 2 Jun'71
        Stardust, May'65
        Communications Hierarchy, (3)
        Children as only Pure Scientists, (1); 22 Apr'77

Sound: Speed Of:

    See Cosmic Structuring, (1)

Sound: Sound Waves: (1)

See Aural
    Babbling
    Hear
    Music
    Tastebuds of Sound

Source:

See Cosmic Source
    Mysterious Source

---

Sound: Sound Waves: (2)

See Music, 4 Mar'69
    Radiation-gravitation: Harmonics, 3 Jan'75
    Harmonics, (1)
    Wind Stress & Houses, (9)|10)
    Limit Speed, 11 Sep'75

RBF DEFINITIONS

Sovereignty: (1)

Q. (Sen. Percy): "What do you mean, sovereignty is dead?"

A. (RBF): "I am a student of large patterns. And as I look around I try to see what evolution is trying to do. We sometimes forget how important is the role of Universe. I have just been telling you that all the things that came in since I was born, automobiles, jet planes and the Queen Mary, radio, satellite communications, they were all unexpected, they were all surprises, and none of them were the result of conscious and deliberate development.

"I do not look on it policywise. I see it as a worldwide biospheric pattern of honey bees and chromosomes.

"The continental congress in Philadelphia has been so movingly described this morning, how people designed a democratic and marvelously representative government. But the congressman went back home on foot or horse. The city of Washington got one or two letters from Europe a month; and everyone knew what was said and went home and talked about it. Democracy flourished in a one-to-one correspondence of stimulation and response. With the advent of telegraph we lost all this;"

- Cite RBF at Senate Foreign Affairs Subcommitte on UN,
    Washington, DC, 15 May'75        (EJA live notes)

---

Sound Word: (1)

See Names
    Sound Name

RBF DEFINITIONS

Sovereignty: (2)

"The effect of telegraphy on the news was mostly one-way, despatches from the field; by and large they provided no response. Democracy works on one-to-one correspondence, but now our communications are not working that way. In 1940 I explored the technology of communications, how if everyone voted daily would it affect the frequency of telephone use. Now we wonder if there might not be some electromagnetic patterns from the brain with all of humanity manifesting some ▬▬ kind of high-frequency electromagnetic, yes-or-no-field. If the satellite sensors are mapping our beef cattle, might they not also have a capability of picking up how humanity feels about a question. It's all going to be completely different from the ways of the past. You mentioned world government. There could be a sort of city management concept taking its orders from a consensus of humanity. Of course the majority might often be wrong, but with such instant communication errors would be recognized soon enough to correct them. Measuring what humanity is really thinking.

"Servomechanisms work this way. All this is technically looming into view."

- Cite RBF at Senate Foreign Affairs Subcommitte Hearing on
    US role in UN, Senate Office Bldg., Wash. DC, 15 May'75
    (EJA live notes)

---

Sound Word: (2)

See God, May'72
    Democritus, 6 Jun'69
    Names, 20 Jan'75
    Thinktionary, 27 May'75
    Fuller, R.B: Moratorium on Speech, (1)

RBF DEFINITIONS

Sovereignty:

"Sovereign nations and states are examples of now obsolete

but seemingly natural phenomena which were in fact concepts

arbitrarily invented by the pirates."

- Cite NASA Speech, p. 22. Jun'66

RBF DEFINITIONS

Sovereignty: Elimination Of:

"Elimination of All World Sovereignties: All the customs
barriers disappear as man goes from guarding the local roots
of his originally exclusive agrarian metabolics life support
into a world-around imperishable metals-sustaining impoundment of cosmic energy, and eternally regenerative energy,
labeled industrialization in the world economy.

"The high performance necessary to sustaining all life can
only be realized by free access to all sources everywhere."

- Cite WORLD-AROUND PROBLEMS THAT HAVE TO BE SOLVED BLOODLESSLY
  BY DESIGN SCIENCE REVOLUTION, NY Times, 29 Jun'72

---

Sovereignty: Elimination Of:                                (1)

     See Leaders:  Take Away the Leaders
         Transnational
         United States:  One of the Most Difficult Soverignties
            To Break Up
         World Man
         Desovereignization Sequence
         Planetary Democracy
         Ideologies Become Supranational
         Spaceship Earth
         Homogenizing of Nations
         Competition:  Elimination Of

---

Sovereignty: Elimination Of:                                (2)

     See Individual Economic Initiative, 13 Jul'74
         Economic Accounting System:  Human Life-hour
            Production, (1)
         Culture, 27 Jan'77

---

Sovereignty: Sovereign States:                              (1)

     See Countries
         Geographical Identity
         Nation
         Political Mandates:  Inventory Of
         Realm

---

Sovereignty: Sovereign States:                              (2)

     See Cosmic vs. Terrestrial Accounting, (1)
         Dollar Bills:  $200 Billion One-dollar Bills
            Circling Around Earth, (3)
         Linear Programming, 5 Jun'73
         Pirates:  Great Pirates, (2)
         Spaceship Earth, 21 Jan'77
         United Nations, 29 Mar'77

---

Soviet Academy of Sciences:

     See Fuller, R.B:  A Propos Ben Franklin, (1)

---

Soviet: ▬▬▬ Soviet Union:                                   (1)

     See Amtorg Engineers
         USSR

---

Soviet: Soviet Union:                                       (2)

     See Intuition Sequence (4)
         Literacy, 18 Aug'70
         Patent, 22 Aug'70

RBF DEFINITIONS

Space:

"Silence is the untuned. Silence takes the electromagnetic place of space. Space is a sort of tactile error. . . the frozen thing."

- Citation & context at Silence, 30 Sep'76

RBF DEFINITIONS

Space:

"The space is a priori mystery that the space vehicle goes in."

- Citation and context at Spaceship (E), Feb'73

RBF DEFINITIONS

Space:

"I've finally arrived at the definition of space that I've been looking for all along. I've said space is the untuned nothingness, but the point is that space is simply whatever is untuned electromagnetically!"

- Cite RBF to EJA, on RBF's debarking from supersonic 'Concorde' flight from Paris, at Dulles Airprort, 2 Jul'76

RBF DEFINITIONS

Space:

"The multiply furnished but thought-integrated complex called space by humans occurs only as a consequence of the imaginatively recallable consideration of an insideness-and-outsideness-defining array of contiguously occurring and consciously experienced time-energy events."

- Cite SYNERGETICS text at Sec. 780.10, 20 Oct'72

RBF DEFINITIONS

Space:

"Space is finite as a complementary remainder of a finite system takeout from finite Scenario Universe."

- Cite RBF rewrite of SYNERGETICS, 2nd. Ed. at Sec. 526.13, 3200 Idaho, Wash., DC; 9 Feb'76

RBF DEFINITIONS

Space:

"I don't start with space. I start with nothing."

- Citation & context at Vacuum, 19 Feb'72

RBF DEFINITIONS

Space:

"Human awareness's concession of 'space' acknowledges a nonconceptually-defined experience."

- Citation and context at Omni-intertangency, 17 Feb'73

RBF DEFINITIONS

Space:

"There is no shape of space. There is only omnidirectional nonconceptual 'out' and the specifically directioned conceptual 'ins.' Space has no identifiable meaning.

"'In' is individually unique as a direction toward the center of any one system-- but 'out' is common to them all.

"The atmosphere's molecules over any place on Earth's surface are forever shifting position. The air over the Hamalayas is enveloping California a week later. The stars now overhead are underfoot twelve hours later. The stars themselves are swiftly moving in respect to one another. Many of them have not been where you see them for millions of years; many burnt out long ago. The sun's light takes eight minutes to reach us. We have relationships-- but not space."

- Cite SYNERGETICS draft, ▊▊▊▊ at Sec. 526ff, Nov'71

RBF DEFINITIONS

Space:

"Critical proximity accounts for the whole universe as we observe it, the collections of things and matter and noncontiguous space intervals."

- ~~Cite RBF insert to SYNERGETICS (Conceptuality, Critical Proximity), Chicago, 1 June 1971~~

- Citation at Critical Proximity, Jun'71

RBF DEFINITIONS

Space:

"The word locally means locally in time and space. By space we mean size-- a function of time."

- ~~Cite RBF to EJA,~~ Somerset Club, ~~Boston,~~ 22 April 1971

- Citation at Local, 22 Apr'71

RBFDEFINITIONS

Space:

"Space is the absence of events. Space is the absence of energy events, physically. Space is the absence of events, metaphysically."

- Cite SYNERGETICS Draft - "Conceptuality: Space" - May, 1971

SEC. 526.03)

RBF DEFINITIONS

Space:

"Alan Watts: But I mean there is a common assumption-- it is ordinary common sense-- that space is nothing at all.

Fuller: That's novent. I call it no-event. I don't like the word space anymore because it implies something. We have only frequencies. We have events and no-events. We have the unique energy packages."

Watts: But any sort of solid energy package seems to me inconceivable without a special ground.

Fuller: It doesn't bother me at all about the no-event.

Watts: Well, how can you talk of curved space, the properties of space?

Fuller: But you can't talk of straight space. There are no straight lines. Physicis has found nothing but waves.

- Cite WATTS TAPE, p. 52, 19 Oct'70

RBF DEFINITIONS

Space:

"There is no universal space nor static space in universe. The word 'space' is conceptually meaningless except in reference to intervals between high-frequency events momentarily 'constellar' in specific local systems. There is no shape of universe. There is only omnidirection nonconceptual 'out' and the specifically directioned conceptual 'in.' We have time relationships, but not static space relationships."

- Cite SYNERGETICS Draft - Conceptuality: Space - May 1971

RBF DEFINITIONS

Space:

"In view of their limited range capabilities in respect to the electromagnetic spectrum and the relative rates of transformation which we speak of as motion, it is not surprising that the passengers aboard the skyship Earth make the mistake of talking about, 'Space' which is as meaningless as 'up' and 'down.' There is no static geometry. There are momentarily existant geometrical relationships. There are events and lack-of-events. The electromagnetic spectrum is a manifest of the gamut of unique frequencies of event recurrence. There are no 'solids,' no 'surfaces,' no 'continuums,' no straight lines or planes. We have only events and no-events-- the events being finite and their energies limited. . . .

"We are talking about no event, so let us contract those two words into one word, novent, meaning nothing occurs."

- Cite BEAR ISLAND STORY, galley p.6, 1968

RNF DEFINITIONS

Space:

"The omniinteractions impinge on your nervous system in all manner of frequencies-- some so high as to appear 'solid' things, some so slow as seeming to be 'absolute Voids.'

- Citation at Halo Concept, 25 Apr'71*

RBF DEFINITIONS

Space:

"Space is the absence of energy events."

(Adapted.)

- Cite caption to SYNERGETICS ILLUSTRATION #94 - "Function of a Balloon as a Porous Network." 1967

RBF DEFINITIONS

Space:

". . . There is no static space frame of universe.
The word 'space' is conceptually meaningless and dimensions
may only be expressed in magnitudes of time, energy,
frequency concentrations, and angular modulations. Time
can be expressed only as 'relativity' in the terms of relative
frequency of reoccurence of any constantly recycling
behavior of any chosen sub-system of universe."

- Cite NASA Speech, p. 49, Jun'66
- Cite CARBONDALE DRAFT IV.26

SPACE- SEC. 526.01 + 527.03

---

RBF DEFINITIONS

Space:

"Velocity is the complementarity of time and space.

Time and space are simply functions of velocity.

Velocity is really the reality. You can examine the

time or the space increment, but they are never

independent of one another. They are unified as

velocity."

- Cite Oregon Lecture #8, p. 298, 12 Jul'62

- Citation at Velocity, 12 Jul'62

SPACE - SEC. 526.02

---

RBF DEFINITIONS

Space Capsule:

"The word 'capsule' has hidden from man the fact that

what science is really working on is a little house;

not much room to move around in, no garden of roses

outside, but nonetheless, a little house with a six

billion dollar mortgage."

- For citation and context see Space Technology (2), 10 Oct '63

---

Space Capsule:

See Autonomous Living Technology Packet
Space Technology
Space Travel

---

Space vs. Conceptuality:

See Conceptuality Independent of Size & Time, 5 May'74

---

Space Filling:

See Allspace Filling

---

Space - Nontunability:

See Bubble Bursting, 20 Jan'78
Human Beings & Complex Universe, (4)

---

RBF DEFINITIONS

Space as Nontuned Angle & Frequency Information:

"This moment in the evolutionary advance and psychological
transformation of humanity has been held back by the non-
physically-demonstrable, ergo non-sensorial, conceptionless
mathematical devices and their resultant incomprehensibility
of the findings of science. There are two most prominent
reasons for this incomprehensibility: the first being the
non-physically-demonstrable mathematical tools, the second
being our preoccupation with the sense of static fixed
'space' as so much unoccupied geometry imposed by square,
cubic, perpendicular, and parallel attempts at coordination,
rather than regarding 'space' as being merely systemic angle
and frequency information which is presently nontuned-in
within the physical, sensorial range of tunability of the
electromagnetic equipment with which we personally have been
organically endowed."

- Cite SYNERGETICS 2 draft at Sec. 100.33; 22 Feb'77

RBF DEFINITIONS

Space Nothingness & Time Somethingness:

"The only instantaneity is eternity.

"All temporal (temporary) equilibrium life-time-space phenomena are sequential, complementary, and orderly disequilibrious intertransformations of space-nothingness to time -somethingness, and vice versa. Both space realizations and time realizations are always of orderly asymmetric degrees of discrete magnitudes. The hexagon is an instantaneous, eternal, simultaneous, planar section of equilibrium, wherein all the chords are vectors exactly equal to all the vector radii: six explosively disintegrative, compressively coiled, wavilinear vectors exactly and finitely contained by six chordal, tensively-coil-extended, wavilinear vectors of equal magnitude."

28

- Cite SYNERGETICS text at Sec. 1032.21, ■ Dec'73

RBF DEFINITIONS

▬▬▬▬▬▬▬ Space Nothingness & Time Somethingness:

"The only instantaneity is eternity. All temporal (temporary) equilibrium life-time-space phenomena are sequential, complementary, and orderly transformations of space-nothingness into time-somethingness, and vice versa. Both space realizations and time realizations are always of orderly asymmetric degrees of discrete magnitudes."

- Citation and context at Hexagon, 22 Feb'73

Space Nothingness & Time Somethingness:                    (1)

    See Articulated & Unarticulated
        Cosmic Discontinuity & Local Continuity
        Somethingness & Nothingness
        Tuning-in & Tuning-out
        Interference & Noninterference

Space Nothingness & Time Somethingness:                    (2)

        See Jitterbug, 4 Oct'72
            Hexagon, 22 Feb'73

RBF DEFINITIONS

Space Program:

"We are nothing but a space program. We are so physically negligible as to be approximately space itself."

- Citation and context at Twelve-Inch Steel World Globe (3)(4), 17 Jul'73

Space Program:

        See Outlaw Area, Jun'66

RBF DEFINITIONS

Spaceship Earth:

"Competition among nations holds us back. With 135 countries in the world, we have a spaceship with 135 absolute admirals-- each of whom wants to sink the rest of the ship."

- Cite RBF quoted in Lincoln Star, front page, Lincoln, Nebraska; 21 Jan'77

RBF DEFINITIONS

Spaceship Earth:

"Spaceship Earth: I invented the term at the University of Michigan in 1951."

- Cite RBF at Penn Bell videotaping, Philadelphia, 29 Jan'75

RBF DEFINITIONS

Spaceship Earth:

"Though brilliantly theorized to be so several thousand years earlier, it is only for the last 500 years that we humans have had proven to us by Magellan's circumnavigation that we indeed are dwelling aboard a spherical planet. It is only for five years that, having 'seen ourselves as others see us' from humans-on-the-Moon advantage, that we are beginning to realize that we are ▆▆▆▆▆▆▆▆ indeed living on a once superbly-equipped spherical spaceship and that we are a space program.

"Despite our considerable resource of present-day theoretical knowledge, all humans continue to reflex in the manner to which they have been powerfully conditioned throughout millions of misconceptioning years. As a consequence, even today we all seem to see the Sun rising and sinking, think in terms of 'up' and 'Down', 'wide, wide world', the four corners of the Earth', and our 'air space', which misconceptions have no correspondence with the realities of Universe."

- Cite RBF Address to MENSA International, Chicago, IL, 22 Jun'74

RBF DEFINITIONS

Spaceship Earth:   (A)

But when I question his Spaceship Earth metaphor he becomes annoyed and distressed. "It is a spaceship. That's not an analogy. It's a fact," he says.

"But a spaceship is built by man, all the factors have been designed for a particular known purpose. The earth is an organic thing on which we live," I argue.

"The planet is designed-- superbly designed-- by a greater intellect than that of man," he says. "And it's moving through space."

"But are we passengers or an organic part of it?"

"We've got three billion and a half passengers on board."

"What about the plants, whales, horses-- are they also passengers?"

"A passenger is someone taking passage aboard a vehicle," he says with a sharp edge of impatience. "You are aboard a"

- Cite Rasa Gustaitis, WHOLLY ROUND (HR&W, NY), p.158, Feb'73

RBF DEFINITIONS

Spaceship Earth:   (B)

"vehicle moving at 60,000 miles an hour through the heavens and you're aboard as a passenger. I'm sorry but your objection is invalid.

So decreed Justice Fuller. I tried a different angle having, apparently, failed to make myself understood: "There's an organization just formed in San Francisco called Living Creatures Associates. It's a press agency claiming to represent other species-- whales, garter snakes, foxes-- represent them publicly on their own terms, with a right to exist on this spaceship, then, in the same way as I do. With some rights that conflict, perhaps, with those of men."

"Did the foxes invite them? Did the daisies elect them?... I have no objection to other people's doing what they do but nothing could be more remote from me," says Fuller. "I call this a do-gooder organization, idealistic and so forth. And their effectiveness approximately zero.. I think it is a very nice manifest of ▆▆ consciousness of man. He's beginning to think about things."

"The idea is that.. we must accept the rights of other beings."

- Cite Rasa Gustaitis, WHOLLY ROUND (HR&W, NY), p.159, Feb'73

RBF DEFINITIONS

Spaceship Earth:   (C)

"What happened to those dragons?" he replied. "What happened to the flying creatures of a few million years ago? What happened to their rights? What about the rights of volcanoes when the whole Earth was volcanic? Who took their rights away?"

"But it's a fact that certain birds and animals are dying because of man's actions. Don't we have to take responsibility for that?"

"We have to take the responsibility of being responsible. So far we have not been very responsible. You don't say to a new child, 'You better go back in there, you're not very responsible...' They're just using words-- foxes and daisies. ... I say: What might I do that made it logical for man not to do these things? That's what I'm caring about. That's what design science is...

(See Tree, Feb'73 )

He was shocked that I found fault with his Spaceship Earth analogy.

- Cite Rasa Gustaitis, WHOLLY ROUND (HR&W, NY), p. 160, Feb'73

RBF DEFINITIONS

Spaceship Earth:   (D)

"I invented this phrase, Spaceship Earth, a number of years ago when I was trying to get man to-- trying to help him, personally, particularly young people, to shake themselves loose of preoccupation with the powerfully conditioned reflex that there is something called Earth and something called space, this Heaven and Earth idea. I used to have students say to me 'I wonder what it would be like to be on a spaceship?' And I'd say: 'What does it feel like?'

"The relative size of things.. When you get to the size of our Earth in space, 8,000 miles' diameter-- the Sun's corona when you look at it with filters through a telescope we can actually see it-- in the larger magnification, one of the flames would be about an inch. One inch of flame is often an altitiude of over a hundred times the diameter of our Earth. The size of our Earth would be undetectable in one of those flames.

"The distance to the next nearest star to ur Sun takes light coming 700 million miles and hour four and two-thirds years to get here. So somewhere between that kind of distance we have a tiny invisible spot of 8,000 miles' diameter, our planet,

- Cite ▆▆ Rasa Gustaitis, WHOLLY ROUND, p.161, (HR&W,NY) Feb'73

RBF DEFINITIONS

Spaceship Earth:   (E)

"going around the Sun at 60,000 miles an hour. And the Sun itself, and the galactic system... sum totally we're making something like a million miles an hour right now."

Now usually when someone mentions a multidigit number to me , I blank out. But Fuller has led me into those interstellar spaces. That's Fuller the poet, conveying reality, not describing with words.

"So we couldn't be more of a spaceship and we couldn't be tinier and we couldn't be more beautifully designed... If we were to say that man was God, if that's what you're objecting to, that this design is so much better, then OK. But neverthe-less, I call it a design... The space is a priori mystery that the space vehicle goes in. And you don't think that it's a mysterious thing that he had the capability to get there? It's all part of the same mystery."

"People who listen to me say, 'Here's a man who's selling screwdrivers. . . They don't realize how mysterious screwing is."

- Cite Rasa Gustaitis, WHOLLY ROUND (HR&W, NY), p. 161, Feb'73

RBF DEFINITIONS

Spaceship Earth:   (F)

"...I've been identified only with the physical so far. I went through 25, 30 years of people saying: this the the bathroom man, or the automobile man-- that's all they thought about me. It's only in the last couple of years that they discover I'm a thinker. And I started as a thinker. I didn't start with bathrooms. I started off with God and my charge was to work on the physical. That's where I had the capability; that's why we're here. I accepted this. And to find myself identified, then, with just being a fishing-pole salesman! I find this thing echoed when you say that about my analogy, 'cause I use a very good tool there. I have helped to shock man into realizing he's on board a space vehicle. He's a passenger on it and he's intimately related to it."

- Cite Rasa Gustaitis, WHOLLY ROUND (HR&W, NY), p.162, Feb'73

RBF DEFINITIONS

Spaceship Earth:   (1)

"Your Senate hearing gives me a short but welcome opportunity to talk thus about all that man has learned from his two million years aboard our spaceship Earth, wherefore I wish to point out vigorously to you that we are indeed aboard an 8,000-mile-diameter spherical space vehicle. We were excited during the Christmas days when we first looked at the Earth from the Moon. But I heard our President speaking down to Earthedly' to the astronauts about their going up to the Moon. There is no 'up' or 'down' in Universe. We find so-called practical men saying, 'Never mind that space stuff, let's get down to earth.'

"And we retort 'Where is that? Where is 'down" and what and where is that non-space existing theory avoiding Earth?'

"Despite their ignorant urging of 'Never mind that space stuff, let's get down to earth,' we find that our little 8,000-mile-diameter planet Earth, together with the Moon, is flying formation at 60,000-miles-per-hour around the Sun."

- Cite RBF at Senate Hearings, p. 9, 4 Mar'69

RBF DEFINITIONS

██████ Spaceship Earth: (2)

"Earth is a beautifully designed <u>spaceship</u> equipped and
provisioned to support and regenerate life aboard it for
hundreds of millions of parts, even until the time when
so much energy of Universe has been collected aboard
Earth as to qualify it to become a radiant star, shortly
before which man will have anticipatorially resituated
himself on other planets at nonincineratable distance█
from the Earth nova."

- Cite RBF at Senate Hearings, █ p.9, 4 Mar'69

---

RBF DEFINITIONS

██████ Spaceship Earth:

"I just say to all of you: 'Hullo, astronauts,' You're
all astronauts. I'm sure you're not thinking of yourselves
as astronauts or you wouldn't have the word for somebody else.
But you're all astronauts, you never have been anything else.
You've just got to catch on that you're all astronauts. It's
a very small little ship we've got here; it's superbly
equipped and every part of it is reciprocal; there are no
labels on it which say anything belongs to anybody. Everything
that's there is to regenerate all of life."

- Cite RBF in "The Listener" transcript by John Donat, 26 Sep'68

---

RBF DEFINITIONS

Spaceship Earth: (a)

"Once upon a time and aboard a spaceship there were almost
four billion passengers, each so small and the ship so large
that the passengers wandering about on its spherical deck,
pulled feetward toward its center of gravity, could see only
about one two-millionth of the ship's total deck surface at
any one time. Usually they ███ all told, only a millionth
of it in their entire lifetime. As a consequence they did not
realize that the only locally irregular surface on which they
walked did not stretch away as a plane to infinity and was in
fact a finite or closed spherical surface system.

"That spaceship had been given the name 'Earth' by its
passengers, this name being descriptive of its hard-packed
dust, dirt, and rock-surfaced deck stretching away surrounded
by water seemingly to infinity. So impressed have the passengers been with that stationary, egocentric, two-dimensional
concept that they have for long, and as yet, begin their
children's education with plane geometry-- its surfaces and
lines-- stretching away to infinity. . . .

"Three-quarters of Spaceship Earth's surface is covered with
water and only about half of the dry one-quarter is both"

- Cite BEAR ISLAND STORY, galley pp.2-3, 1968

---

RBF DEFINITIONS

Spaceship Earth: (b)

"habitable and suitable for providing vital support of the
passengers. This meager ten percent of the spaceship's surface
with its vitally hospitable damp surface is divided into many
small fractions scattered so remotely from one another around
the Earth's sphere and with such vast and formidable waters,
mountains, deserts, and ice intervening, that as a result each
of the local groups of inhabitants of the various areas-- for
99 percent of the period of their known presence on Earth--
have been unaware of the other groups' existence or whereabouts
aboard the spaceship.

"Equipped materially to take care of its passengers for millions
of celestial travel years, but needing additional energy to
produce, maintain, and regenerate its complex, interchemically
exchanging, life-support system, it was designed by the conceivor
of the vast, ever and everywhere nonsimultaneously transforming
Universe, that the additional and vital energy ██ constantly
transmitted to the spaceship by the electromagnetic radiations
emanating from enormous, fiery, unmanned, automated mother
spaceships traveling in company with, but at great distances
from, the little Spaceship Earth."

- Cite BEAR ISLAND STORY, galley pp.3, 1968

---

RBF DEFINITIONS

Spaceship Earth: (c)

"And to make things even more challenging and intelligence-
invoking for the passengers, no instruction book on identification of the parts and what they do and how to operate them
came with the spaceship. Because some of the red berries were
healthily sustaining while other red berries were poisonous,
the passengers were forced to learn by trial and error about
the myriad of life-advantaging principles that have been
secretly built into the integral metabolics of Spaceship Earth
and that spaceship's complementary universal environment, which
is ever energetically transforming and evoluting. This was
made possible by the apparently ample tolerance for their many
errors which was included in the design of the ship and the
celestial support system. Though often obvious for millions of
years, most of these vital advantage-giving principles long
have remained unrecognized for what they are and can do; it
would seem to be a part of the designed scheme of Universe
that-- for the nonce, anyway-- nothing is quite so invisible
to Spaceship Earth's passengers as the obvious. . . .

"As all of the Spaceship Earth's passengers see all their
experiences only by image-ination in their brains, we too may
imagine ourselves aboard the little spherical, 8,000-mile

- Cite BEAR ISLAND STORY, galley p.3, 1968

---

RBF DEFINITIONS

Spaceship Earth: (d)

"diameter Spaceship Earth with its then atmospheric, ionic,
and radiation-shielding Van Allen ████ mantles, speeding
integrally at 17 miles per second in a vast elliptical orbit
around our 92-million-miles distant, fully automated energy
supply ship-- the Star Sun-- in the presence of our 10-trillion-
miles further distant, next nearest star.

"These two stars are our Spaceship Earth's nearest prime energy,
life-giving and life-sustaining, regenerating supply ships. As
do also the myriad█ of even further away supply ships, these
two stars 'fly formation' with our Spaceship Earth in the vast
inconceivable ocean of time. The energy supply ships are flown
at a distance sufficient to prevent their heat and radiation
from drying up and incinerating the many forms of life aboard
Spaceship Earth.

"Large though 8,000 miles may seem to the human passengers,
who are only one-thousandth of a mile tall, Spaceship Earth's
diameter as seen from another planet is only a tiny pinpoint
of Sun-reflected light similar in appearance to the Spaceship
Mars or Venus as seen from Spaceship Earth."

- Cite BEAR ISLAND STORY, galley p.4, 1968

---

RBF DEFINITIONS

Spaceship Earth: (e)

"After at least two million years of experience aboard it,
many of the almost four billion amateur astronauts aboard
Spaceship Earth have become theoretically well informed
regarding a few behavioral characteristics of a meager fraction
of the celestial phenomena. But none of them-- excluding
possibly the Russian and U.S.A. professional spacemen [ the
three bears, Goldilocks, and her father_7-- as yet consciously
and realistically sense that their own planet is a spaceship
and see and feel themselves zooming through Universe upon that
spherical ship. . . .

[See Up and Down Sequence (A) - (B) ]

"Because the Spaceship Earth is also spinning equatorially
at 1,000 miles per hour as it orbits the Sun at 60,000 miles
per hour, when we launch a tiny, two- or three-man-carrying,
capsule by rocket from our Earth Spaceship, we must give the
capsule an additional acceleration boost of approximately
16,000 miles per hour in order to break out of Earth's gravitational pull. This means that we on out big mother Spaceship
Earth must give our small space 'launches' a local space speed
of 76,000 mph., or 16,000 mph. faster than Spaceship Earth's"

- Cite BEAR ISLAND STORY, galley pp.4-5, 1968

---

RBF DEFINITIONS

Spaceship Earth: (f)

"Sun-orbiting speed. Aboard Earth we are accustomed to the
idea of big ships carrying small lifeboats; launches, tenders,
and gigs. We must now think of our space-rocketed capsules
as small boats launched outwardly from our bigger spaceship.

"But these speed variations of our spaceship and its launches
become minuscule and negligible in comparison the the speed of
Spaceship Earth as a solar system component as that solar█
system itself orbits within our galactic nebula's even greater
perimeter motion and our galactic nebula's collective motion
in respect to the other nebulae."

- Cite BEAR ISLAND STORY, galley p.5, 1968

BARBARA WARD QUOTATION

Spaceship Earth:

"To my esteemed and beloved friend friend, Buckminster Fuller, who provided much more than the title of this book."

   -- Barbara Ward Jackson

   -- 23 May'66

[N.B. This debt to R.B.F. acknowledged only in

her presentation copy to him. (...and buried in text at p.15.]

- Cite Lady Jackson inscription in RBF presentation copy of her SPACESHIP Earth, Columbia Univ. Press, N.Y. 1966, inscribed 23 May'66

---

Spaceship Earth:       (2)

See Antientropy (A)
  Man as a Function of Universe (B)
  Miniature Earth, 28 Apr'74
  Know-how & Know-what, 11 Nov'74
  Millay, Edna St. Vincent, (3)
  Wealth, 20 Sep'76
  Building Industry, (11)
  United Nations, 29 Mar'77

---

BARBARA WARD QUOTATION

Spaceship Earth:

"In fact, I can think of only one way of expressing the degree to which interdependence and community have become the destiny of modern man. I borrow the comparison from Professor Buckminster Fuller, who, more clearly than most scientists and innovators, has grasped the implications of our revolutionary technology. The most rational way of considering the whole human race today is to see it as the ship's crew of a single spaceship on which all of us, with a remarkable combination of security and vulnerability, are making our pilgrimage through infinity. Our planet is not much more than the capsule within which we have to live as human beings if we are to survive the vast space voyage upon which we have been engaged for hundreds of millenia-- but without yet noticing our condition. This space voyage is totally precarious. We depend upon a little envelope of soil and a rather larger envelope of atmosphere for life itself. And both can be contaminated and destroyed. Think what could happen if somebody were to get mad or drunk in a submarine and run for the controls. If some member of the human race gets dead drunk on board our spaceship, we are all in trouble. This is how we have to think of ourselves. We are a ship's company on a small ship. Rational behavior is the condition of survival."

- Cite Barbara Ward, SPACESHIP EARTH, Columbia Univ. Press, NY, 1966, P.15.

---

Space Structures:       (1)

See Floating City
  Moon Structures
  Habitable Satellite
  Satellite Environment Controls
  Sky Dwelling
  Sky-island City
  Skybreak Bubble

---

RBF DEFINITIONS

Spaceship Earth:

"For at least 2,000,000 years men have been reproducing and multiplying on a little automated spaceship called Earth, in an automated Universe in which the entire process is so successfully predesigned that men did not even know that they were ▓▓▓▓ automated, regenerative passengers on a spaceship and were so naive as to think they had invented their own success as they lived egocentrically on a seemingly static Earth."

⌐N.B. At Hugh Kenner's house in Baltimore, in response to an inquiry from the Baltimore SUN, RBF said that to the best of his recollection this citation was his earliest reference to spaceship Earth in print. -- 3 Oct'73. ⌐

- Cite PROSPECT FOR HUMANITY, Sat. Review, 19 Sep'64

---

Space Structures:       (2)

See Biosphere, (1)-(4)
  Necklace, Nov'71

---

Spaceship Earth:       (1)

See Earth
  Planet Earth
  Competition: Elimination Of
  Sovereignty: Elimination Of

---

RBF DEFINITIONS

Space Technology:       (1)

"In contrast to the home arts let us look at the space rocketry world. At the present moment we have the enormous, major governments subsidized weaponry race into space undertaken by both Russia and the United States. In order to be able to put a man in space-- to stay in space, not to make a few orbits-- in order to have man, in effect, live continuously in outer space for weeks and months and possibly years, we have to solve scientifically the problem of mastering the ecological pattern of the human being and the metabolic pattern of the human being. We have to realize that the energy events that take place metabolically in supporting man ecologically on Earth involve energy transforming functions of trees, worms, water, sunlight, the slowly forming topsoil, et. al. The delicately balanced pressure and heat of energy exchanges and chemical transformings involve very large ecological domains to complete the cycles of a man-supporting environment process on Earth. We are going to have to compress the total ecological domain of man from approximately a one-mile radius process into a ten-foot radius process. We are going to reduce the total volume of energy transformation patterning several millionfold. In order to be able to send that man off into"

- Cite MEXICO '63, p. 11, 10 Oct '63

RBF DEFINITIONS

Space Technology: (2)

"space, we have to scientifically anticipate and effectively service all his processes and psychological reflex requirements. In order to be able to do that we are, in effect, building a little house-- a little space house. We had been using the word 'capsule,' which has hidden from us the fact that what science is really working on is a little house; not much room to move around in, no garden of roses outside, but nonetheless, a little house with a six billion dollar mortgage.

"In this strange battle of man to anticipate offensive-defensive weaponry battles in the cold warring, the battle to attain the moon, or protracted living upon a platform in space, has brought about a race in capital funding initiatives between Russia and the United States specifically in relation to this little house, amounting to six billion dollars. This staggering amount is now approrpriated to hire scientists to go to work to design and produce one little sky house, the first scientific human dwelling in history. It must be capable of sustaining man as a metabolic success anywhere in Universe. It won't be a very charming little house. It won't be 'good architecture' by the tradional a-la-mode"

- Cite MEXICO '63, p.11, 10 Oct '63

RBF DEFINITIONS

Space Technology: (3)

"aesthetics. Above all I want you architects at this Seventh World Congress of the I.U.A. to realize that what the space scientists are working on is in fact the design of a house: that is architecture. The scientists are in your business competing with you in the solution of all the problems that a house for regenerative man involves. It involves every one of the fundamental principles ever discovered by man in Universe. The scientists are attending to the dwelling problems that you have failed to attend to or have left to someone else to solve, as for instance, the plumbers. When the prototype moon dwelling and its space autonomy mechanics are developed, and it has been satisfactorily test orbited for 100 days, and that house has finally taken man successfully to the moon, or to a space platform, there to dwell for months, then we will have history's first scientific semi-autonomous dwelling. In that sky dwelling we will have the energy exchange processes, internal and external to man's ecology, becoming locally regenerative.

"This process and its scientific tooling and instrumentation must become locally regenerative on an extraordinarily satisfactory basis before we shoot man to the moon or in"
- Cite MEXICO '63, pp.11-12, 10 Oct '63

RBF DEFINITIONS

Space Technology: (4)

"to protracted space orbiting. We are not going to pick the finest, healthiest world specimens, the best coordinated human specimens we have, and send them off to space to live in some highly inadequate and swiftly deteriorating condition. All the world will be hooked up by TV to observe the details of man's first home life in the sky. The technology will have to be performed superlatively before we shoot man to the moon or sky platform. This means that the problems will be solved on Earth and not in the sky. The mechanics of solution will be produced here on Earth. The establishment of this capability here on Earth also is going to make possible a very different kind of dwelling technology right here on Earth. We will no longer have to have water pipes and sewer systems. Mankind will suddenly start mass-producing the space house prototype's pipeless, wireless, trackless ability to deploy man around the Earth's surface as well as in space. Man will be able to take position anywhere on the face of the Earth, as an eagle takes firm, safe poise on his beautiful mountain peak vahtage, with many able to readily reach such points by rotoflight and able to survive at such remote spectacular points at very high living standards, comfort, and low cost with swift ability to"

- Cite MEXICO '63, p.12, 10 Oct '63

RBF DEFINITIONS

Space Technology: (5)

"reconvene in cultural centers, etc. . .

"For the first time in the history of man on Earth we are actually applying the highest scientific capability to that extraterrestrial space dwelling, underwritten inadvertently and exclusively by weaponry supremacy ambitions for celestial control of world fire power. This celestial supremacy involves, however, an unprecedented weaponry system requirement: that of making man a successfully semi-autonomous biological intelligence system remote from Earth where he will be unable to survive normally by himself, as detached reconnaissance soldiers have been able to do in all previous history. A surprise event thus entered into the age-old weaponry system evolution, the significance of which has not as yet been publicly nor politically apprehended or comprehended.

"All weaponry up to this moment in history has been designed primarily to kill men with maximum scientific skill. Here we discover the as-yet uncomprehended surprise. Now for the first time in history the space weaponry race has forced the weaponry system directors inadvertently to design a"

- cite MEXICO '63, pp.12-13, 10 Oct '63

RBF DEFINITIONS

Space Technology: (6)

"means of housing and servicing men (or women or both) anywhere in Universe which means under vastly more difficult conditions than on Earth and, because of the superman requirements of the service, at a higher standard of satisfaction of living fundamentals than any men have ever known.

"Tents won't do in airless space. If you spit in space the spit goes into orbit and you retro-orbit. There is no sewer system in space. There is no gravity to pull matter down the drain. There are no water supply lines, no electric wires, no supermarkets. Because of the completely un-Earthly sky dwelling for our celestial fire-power soldiers, science has at last been brought to bear objectively and"

- Cite MEXICO '63, p.13, 10 Oct '63

RBF DEFINTTIONS

Space Technology: (7)

"integratively upon the generalized problem of converting man's combined ecological and metabolic patterning in Universe from a random matrix of happenstance interferences, of unknown miles of overall dimension, into a compacted metabolic coordinate system of high certitude of controllability, ergo a local ecological success under approximately any conditions other than those of falling into the Sun or other stars. The sky house man must be made capable of taking position at will, either by interior or remote control, approximately anywhere in the dynamic intercoordination of physical Universe. Yet, by virtue of entropy, that is of inherent local loss of energy of all local systems in Universe, the sky house may not be perpetually independent and self-regenerative. It is ultimately dependent upon the good will replenishment of that local and remote ecological system by the organized energetic activities of other men acting both as individuals and as vast teams, coordinated under the predominant will of organizations of men on Earth."

- Cite MEXICO '63, pp.13-14, 10 Oct '63

Space Technology: (1)

See Autonomous Living Technology Packet
Fuel Cell
Moon Structures
Moon Trip
Space Capsule
Space Structures
World Game: Men Landing on Moon
Airspace Technology
Walls vs. Airspace Technology

Space Technology: (2)

See Dwelling Service Industry (3)-(6)
General Systems Theory, 4 Jan'70
Science: Cause of Science for Man, 14 Mar'71
Spherical Triangle Sequence (VIII)
Tolerance Sequence, Jun'69
Plastics, 10 Aug'70
Dome: Rationale For (I)

Space-time:

See Time-space

---

Space Travel: (2)

See Atomic Computer Complex (7)
Biosphere (1)-(3)
Disparity, 1960
Icosahedron as Local Shunting Circuit, 22 Jun'72*
Invisible Circuitry (1)(2)
Radiation, May'72
Spaceship (2); (e)(f)
Orbital Escape from Critical Proximity, (1)

---

RBF DEFINITIONS

Space Travel:

"... The icosahedron is stuck locally with no way to get to another continent. The vector equilibrium is how you get from one sphere to another, from Earth to Mars."

- Citation and context at Icosahedron As Local Shunting Circuit, 22 Jun'72

---

Space ≠ Unoccupied Geometry:

See Space as Nontuned Angle & Frequency Information, 22 Feb'77

---

TEXT CITATIONS

Space Travel:

Synergetics draft Secs. 1009.71 - ff, 15 Feb'73

Hyper, World Mag., 4 Apr'73 - p. 38; 1st & 2nd Cols.

780.22-780.28

1009.65

---

TEXT CITATIONS

Space Walking:

Synergetics draft at Secs. 1009.66 - ff. 14 Feb'73

---

Space Travel: (1)

See Astrogator
Cosmic Transmission
Eye-beamed Thoughts
Man: Interstellar Transmission of Man
Man's Universe Penetrations
Travel: Extraorganic Travel
World Game: Men Landing on Moon
Space Capsule
Planets: Probable Myriads of Consciously Operated
Planets
Moon: Humans Reach Moon and Return
Electromagnetic Transmission of Human Organisms
Extraorganic Travel

---

Space: (1)

See Air Space
Allspace Filling
Available Space
Conceptuality & Space
Curved Space: Bent Space
Domain
Field of Omnidirectional Nothingness
Interspace
Interstitial: Interstitial Space
No Geometry of Space
Nothing
Nothingness of Areal & Volumetric Spaces
Novent
Otherness We Call Space
Spheres & Spaces
Static Invalidity of Solid Things vs. Empty Space
Thinkability vs. Space
Time-space
Vacuum
Volume
Void

Space: (2)

See Critical Proximity, Jun'71*
Face, 20 Feb'73
Halo Concept, 25 Apr'71*
Infinite, 15 Oct'72
Local, 22 Apr'71*
Omniintertangency, 17 Feb'73*
Vacuum, 19 Feb'72*
Velocity, 12 Jul'62*
Graphable, 27 May'72
Events & Novents, Nov'71
Silence, 30 Sep'76*
Tuning-in & Tuning-out, 17 May'77

Speaking:

See Speech

Space: (3)

See Space Capsule
Space Filling
Space Nothingness & Time Somethingness
Space Program
Spaceship Earth
Space vs. Conceptuality
Space Structures
Space Technology
Space Travel
Space Walking
Space ≠ Unoccupied Geometry
Space as Nontuned Angle & Frequency Information
Space = Nontunability

RBF DEFINITIONS

Spear:

"Vectors are like spears. I could 'massage' any object
into a spear shape, point and thrust-throw it in a discrete
direction. I intuitively liked those directional vector
'spears.' I felt that they tended at least to embody all
the energetic qualities of represented experiences."

- Cite "Bucky" by Hugh Kenner, p. 105; probably from Snyder
or Farrel, Summer'71

Spar Crystals:

See Iceland Spar Crystals

Spear: (1)

See Javelin
Vector

Sparking & Nonsparking:

See Copper, 15 Aug'70

Spear: (2)

See Geometry of Vectors, 10 Oct'64

RBF DEFINITIONS

Special Case:

Q.         "You look at the world in such a different way. .
. . Why?"

RBF:       "It's just because all people are special.
Everyone is a special case."

- Cite RBF to Sue Liberman at WAMU*FM, taping, Wash, DC: 26 Apr'77

---

RBF DEFINITIONS

Special Case:

"Though special-case experiences exemplify employment of
eternal principles those special cases are all inherently
terminal; that is, in temporary employment of the principles."

- Citation and context at Eternal, 13 Mar'73

---

RBF DEFINITIONS

Special Case:

"Structures are always special case. Structures are operational.
Operational = physically realized. Structures always have unique
size. By definition, a structure is a complex of energy events
interacting to produce a stable pattern.

"An energy event is always special case. Whenever we have the
experienced energy we have special case. The physicist's first
definition of physical is that it is an experience which is
extracorporeally, remotely, instrumentally apprehendible.
Metaphysical are all the experiences that are excluded by the
definition of physical. Metaphysical is always generalized
principle."

- Cite SYNERGETICS, 2nd. Ed., at Secs. 1075.10-.11, 27 Dec'74

---

RBF DEFINITIONS

Special Case:

"The facts of experience are always special case."

- Citation and context at Order, 13 Mar'73

---

RBF DEFINITIONS

Special Case:

"Special case is always realized by its energetic information....
Time incrementation is special case information."

- Citation & context at Energy & Information, 27 Dec'74

---

RBF DEFINITIONS

Special Case:

"Special case always has frequency and size-time."

- Cite SYNERGETICS draft at Sec. 1011.34, 17 Feb'73

---

RBF DEFINITIONS

Special Case:

"The physical is always experiencable and special case."

- Citation and context at Limit-Limitless, 4 Nov'73

---

RBF DEFINITIONS

Special Case:

"Polarized precession is special case. Omnidirectional
precession is generalized."

- Citation and context at General Case, 16 Feb'73

RBF DEFINITIONS

Special Case:

"The special cases seem to go racing by because we are now
having in a brief lifetime experiences which took centuries
to be recognized in the past."

[55]

- Cite SYNERGETICS draft at Sec. 1005.56, 16 Feb'73

---

RBF DEFINITIONS

Special Case:

"A vector is . . . an abstraction of a special case,

as are numbers abstract (empty sets) or special case

(filled sets)."

- Citation and context at Vector, 26 May'72

---

RBF DEFINITIONS

Special Case:

"And all the categories of creatures act individually as
special case... but... they are all interaffecting one
another synergetically..."

- Citation and context at Linear and Spherical Analysis, 16 Feb'73

---

RBF DEFINITIONS

Special Case:

"The human brain apprehends and stores each sense-
reported bit of information regarding each special-
case experience.  Only special-case experiences are
recallable from the memory bank."

- Cite Dreyfuss Preface, "Decease of Meaning."
  28 April 1971, p. 5

CONCEPTUALITY  SPECIAL CASE - SEC. 504.02

---

RBF DEFINITIONS

Special Case:

"All special case events are generated in critical
proximity."

- Citation and context at Critical Proximity, 15 Feb'73

---

RBF DEFINITIONS

Special Case:

"Experience is always special case."

- Cite RBF to EJA
  Carbondale
  2 April 1971

CONCEPTUALITY- SPECIAL CASE- SEC. 504.01

---

RBF DEFINITIONS

Special Case:

"...Ever-multiplying Universe's special-case experiences."

- Citation and context at Cosmic Fish, 8 Feb'73

---

RBF DEFINITIONS

Special Case:

"The physical is always special case."

- Citation and context at Generalization Sequence (1), Jun-Jul'69

RBF DEFINITIONS

Special Case:

"If you try to remember all of the special case experiences of which your life is composed, your brain will be very quickly overloaded in the given category of recall. It is going to ▓ take too long to get this information back and sorted out to use. Instead of trying to deal in all the special cases, deal with exactly the opposite; work towards the great generalizations."

- Citation at Generalization & Special Case, 26 Aug'66
- ~~Cite RBF address to Geographers 1 n Rhode Island, 26 Aug. '66~~

Special Case: (1)

See Abstraction of a Special Case
    Brain
No  Generalized Boat
    General Case
    Generalization & Special Case
    Generalization of the Special Case
    Filled Set
    Time-limited
    Size
    Whole to Particular
    Pre-special-case

RBF DEFINITIONS

Special Case:

"... The generalizable was always present in the special case."

- Citation and context at Principle, 9 Jul'62

Special Case: (2A) ▉

See Black Hole (1)
    Cosmic Fish, 8 Feb'73*
    Creativity (1)*
    Critical Proximity, 15 Feb'73*
    Education Revolution (1)
    Evolution, 1970
    Einstein: General Theory & Special Theory, 4 Mar'73
    Eternal, 13 Mar'73*
    Frequency, 16 Feb'73
    Generalization, 17 Feb'73; 26 May'72
    Generalization Sequence (1)
    Is, 24 Apr'72
    Limit-limitless, 4 Nov'73*
    Local, 23 May'72
    Lever (ii)
    Linear & Spherical Analysis, 16 Feb'73*
    Order, 13 Mar'73
    ~~Physical Is Always Special Case, 14 Feb'72~~
    Principle, 9 Jul'62*
    Physical, 12 Nov'75; 4 Nov'73; Jun'69

RBF DEFINTTIONS

Special Case Event:

"Now there is, in the universe, a vast order. It never lets you down. I throw a coin in the air and it ▉ returns and hits the floor every time. Nature is never at a loss what to do when she takes over after you and I sign off. Nature never vacillates in her decisions. The rolling oceans cover three-fourths of the Earth. Along the beaches, the surf is continually pounding on the shore. No two successive local surf poundings have ever been the same, nor will they ever be the same. They typify the infinitude of individualism of every special-case event in the universe. While there is great music in the pounding of the surf, as the infinite creative integrity of the universe is manifest, I cannot identify man, who hears this music, as the creator. I therefore do not use the word 'creativity' in man's employment of a priori infinite variety."

- Citation and context at Creativity (1), spring'66
    - ~~Cite MERGERS & ACQUISITIONS, Vol 1, No.3~~
      ~~Spring 1966~~        ~~P. 43~~

CONCEPTUALITY - SPECIAL CASE - 504.63

Special Case: (2B)

See Physical Sciences, 1959
    Physical Life, 22 May'73
    Rigid, 24 Sep'73
    Spheric Domains, 6 Nov'72
    Things, 17 Feb'72
    Truth, 16 Feb'73 ; 31 Jan'75
    Vector, 26 May'72*
    Conceptuality Independent of Size & Time, 2 Jun'74
    Radial Depth, 20 Dec'74
    Energy & Information, 27 Dec'74
    Identity, 24 Jan'75
    Spherical Triangle, 23 Jan'75
    Pattern Integrity, 6 Nov'73
    Number, 7 Nov'73
    Real World, 12 May'75
    Verbs, 12 Nov'75
    Metaphysical & Physical, 13 Nov'75
    Universe, 11 Dec'75
    Modules: A & B Quanta Modules, 20 Dec'73

RBF DEFINITIONS

Special-case Experience:

"Weightless, abstract human mind reviews and from time to time discovers mathematically reliable and abstractly statable interrelationships existing between and amongst, but not 'in' or 'of,' any of the special-case experience components of the relationship.

"When a long-term record of testing proves the relationship to persist without exception, it is rated as a scientifically generalized principle. Whenever human mind discovers a generalized principle to exist amongst the special-case experience sets, the discovery event itself becomes a new special-case experience to be stored in the brain bank and recalled when appropriate. Amongst a plurality of brain-stored, newly understood experiences, mind has, from time to time, discovered greater and more significant understandings, which in their turn as discoveries, which are 'experiences,' constitute further very special-case experiences to be stored in the recallable and reconsiderable brain bank's wealth of special-case experiences."

- Cite SYNERGETICS text at Sec. 504.04; galley rewrite, 6 Nov'73

Special Case: (2C)

See Seven Minimum Topological Aspects, 12 Feb'76
    Height, Length & Width, 19 Jul'76
    Trigonometry, 18 Jul'76
    Radiation, 11 Feb'76
    Human Beings & Complex Universe, (1)

RBF DEFINITIONS

**Specialist: Born with One Eye and a Microscope:**

"I find it surprising that society thinks of specialization as logical, necessary, desirable, if not inevitable. I observe that when nature wants to make a specialist she's very good at it, whereas she seems to have designed man to be a very generally adaptable creature-- by far the most adaptable creature we know of. If nature had wanted man to be a specialist, I am sure she would have grown him with one eye and a microscope on it. She has designed no such creatures. I observe that every child demonstrates a comprehensive curiosity. Children are interested in everything and are forever embarrassing their specialized parents by the wholeness of their interests. Children demonstrate right from the beginning that their genes are organized to help them to apprehend, comprehend, coordinate, and employ-- in all directions."

- Cite RBF at Franklin Lecture, Auburn, Ala. 1970

---

**Specialist Born with One Eye & a Microscope:**

See Degenius, 26 Sep'68

---

RBF DEFINITIONS

Specialization:

"Specialization is the divide and conquer of the intellectuals by the muscle men."

- Citation and context at Divide and Conquer Sequence (E) 5 May'72

---

RBF DEFINITIONS

Specialization:

"The omnicommitment
Of the twentieth century's
World-around society
To the synergy invalidated misconception
That specialization
Is desirable and inevitable,
Tends to preclude humanity's
Swift realization
Of its many misconceptionings
And its necessity to substitute therefore
Tactically reliable information.
Specialization is antisynergy."

- Cite INTUITION, p.41, May '72

---

RBF DEFINITIONS

Specialization:

"Extinction is the consequence of overspecialization. Inbreeding concentrates special-capability genes, but only at the expense of losing general adaptability, i.e., the ability of the species to cope with the infrequently occurring large, surprising and hostile events of the environment melange, while prospering-- only temporarily-- during the long intervals of innocuous, high-frequency, low-magnitude, environmental changes."

- Cite Dreyfuss Preface, "Decease of Meaning"
28 April 1971, p. 10

---

RBF DEFINITIONS

Specialization:

"Specialization, being concerned with parts, is

inherently preoccupied with the physical." . . .

"Specialization is antisynergetic."

- Cite Dreyfuss Preface, "Decease of Meaning"
28 April 1971, p. 8.

---

RBF DEFINITIONS

Specialization:

"Part of the scheme of specialization is that

there has to be a head man."

- Cite RBF Lecture
Town Hall, New York
12 March 1971

---

RBF DEFINITIONS

Specialization:

"Specialization is antisynergy."

- Cite INTUITION Draft Feb. '71, p. 30.

RBF DEFINITIONS

Specialization:

"Specialization is only a fancy form of slavery wherein the 'expert' is fooled into accepting his slavery by making him feel that in return he is in a socially, culturally preferred, ergo, highly secure life-long position."

- Cite I SEEM TO BE A VERB, Bantam, 1970

---

RBF DEFINITIONS

Specialization:

"There is a strong awareness that we have been overproducing the army of rigorously disciplined, scientific, game-playing academic specialists who through hard work and suppressed imagination earn their PH.D.'s only to have their specialized ▬▬▬ field become obsolete or bypassed by evolutionary events in five years. Despite their honor grades they prove not to be the Natural Philosopher scientist-artist, but just deluxe quality technicians or mechanics."

- Cite AAUW JOURNAL, May 1965, P. 173

---

RBF DEFINITIONS

Specialization:

"Because humanity has deliberately fractionated the formal study of residual reality into ever more minute specializations, which continually know more and more about less and less, the residual preoccupations have lost sight completely of any of the comprehensive and infinitely inspirational mystery of totality."

- Citation & context at Perceptual Peephole as Fraction of Reality, Dec'69

---

RBF DEFINITIONS                                        (1) ▬

Specialization:

"Whitehead pointed out that the men going into those graduate schools and then going into a very specialized area instead of having a broad focus were getting down to a very narrow focus and within that very narrow focus would become specialists themselves so they would be professors of specialization within specialization. The specialists would then become so linear, instead of comprehensive-- instead of being broadcast, they would be narrowly beamed-- and being very bright ones they would make great speed in their linear acceleration. It would mean that they would speed outwardly through the Universe and would become very bright stars in the firmament, but as stars, very remote from one another.

"He pointed out then that because the specialists had been very carefully picked as individuals of high intellectual capability and, of course, intellectual integrity would be implicit. Their own integrity would make clear to them how little anyone outside their specialization could possibly know about their area of inquiry. They wouldn't feel any pride about it-- it would just be a fact that no one else in the public would tend to know anything about what they were talking about. Because they would
- Cite Oregon Lecture #2, pp.39-40, 2 Jul'62

---

RBF DEFINITIONS

Specialization:

". . . Specialists working within the graduate shool saw saw great possibilities for further specialization within their special subject and . . . their energies then developed a linear acceleration instead of a comprehensive acceleration. They went out like rockets and became remote stars, remote one from the other. . . "

- Cite RBF Rhode Island Address, 26 Aug. '66.

---

RBF DEFINITIONS                                        (2)

Specialization:

"tend to recognize that to be a fact in their own experience, they would also not presume to go into any other specialists' laboratory and assume what the significance was of the work going on there. They would be the first to say: I can't talk about that. So these specialists would tend to talk to each other about football or tennis, and would not have much that they would feel they could converse about."

- Cite Oregon Lecture #2, pp.39-40, 2 Jul'62

---

RBF DEFINITIONS

Specialization:

"Life, as born, is inherently comprehensive in its apprehending, comprehending and coordinating capabilities. Every child is interested in the universe. His questions are universal. Dvelopment of specialization has been either a forced training affair or is a product of inbred talent-- as two musician parents tend to produce musical aptitude chilren.

"Specialization, as a consequence of educational or craft training, was invented by the great pirates. Pirates had to be forever on guard against those ambitious to displace them. They were worried only about the bright ones who might detect the pirates' secret stratagems. Consequently, the pirates deliberately and anticipatroially subdivided and conquered the bright ones as each one came along simply by making them specialists."

- ~~Cite NASA Speech, p. 19, Jun'66~~
- Citation and context at Education (B), Jun'66

---

RBF DEFINITIONS

▬▬▬ Specialization Tollgate:

"...Your specialty: You have to have your little private tollgate that society will have to go through..."

- Citation and context at Intuition of the Child (2), Feb'73

RBF DEFINITIONS

        ▆▆▆▆▆▆ Specialization Tollgate:

"Now, men in our industrial and educational system have become
more and more specialized.  Everyone, wanting economic security,
has seemed to think that as specialist he could command the
tollgate of an expressway to unique and essential information.
He thought: 'A great many people will have to go through my
specialization tollgate and I'll have a special, education-
guaranteed economic security."

- Cite THE PROSPECTS FOR HUMANITY, Sat. Review, 29 Aug'64

---

TEXT CITATIONS

    Specialization:

    Operating Manual for Spaceship Earth, pp.27-28,

    Oregon Lecture #1, pp.26-27, 1 Jul '62

    Wood Design in a Dynamic Technology, p.9

    University of Chicago Address, in toto■■, 5 May'72

---

Specialization: Specialist:         (1)

      See Categoryitis
           Divide & Conquer
           Academic Tenure
           Inbreeding
           More & More About Less & Less
           Nature Has No Separate Departments
           Overspecialization of Biological Species and Nations
           Pirates:  Great Pirates
           Specialization Tollgate
           Whitehead's Dilemma
           Overspecialization of the Sciences
           Generalists & Specialists

---

Specialization: Specialist:         (2)

      See See Computer (A)
           Differentiation, 10 Oct'63; 10 Dec'64
           Diplomats, 5 May'72
           Education (B)*
           Generalized Principle (2)
           Human Beings, 10 Dec'73
           Intuition of the Child (2)*
           Linear Programming, 5 Jun'73
           Materials, 7 Nov'67
           Nation, Oct'70
           Eternal Orderliness, 15 May'72
           Orderliness Operative in Nature (1)(2)
           Perceptual Peephole, Dec'69*
           Real Estate Development, 10 Jun'71
           Sensorial Reflex, 13 Mar'73
           Organic & Inorganic, May'49
           Nonthing, 11 Sep'75

---

Species:

    See Charting Alternating Experiences of Man & Nature, (1)
        Synergy:  Degrees Of, (5)
        Synergy of Synergies, 31 May'71
        Viral Steerability:  Angle-frequency Design
            Control, 22 Jul'71

---

Specific:

    See Lever, (2)
        Line, 7 Nov'72

---

Speck:

    See Invisibility of Macro- and Micro- Resolutions, (1)
        Point-to-able Something, 30 Apr'77

---

RBF DEFINITIONS

    Spectrum:

    "... Unique resonances and frequencies of the electromagnetic,
protoplasmic, pneumatic-hydraulic, and crystallographic
spectrums...."

    - Citation and context at Integer, 15 Oct'72

Spectrum:

 See Color Spectrum
  Electromagnetic Spectrum
  Extrasensoriality
  Invisible Spectrum
  Optical Motion Spectrum
  Sensorial Spectrum
  Sensorial-frequency-spectrum Inventory

---

RBF DEFINITIONS

Speed:

"There is a question-asking-possibility that omniscience may be transcendental in velocity to the definitive physical speed of energy omnipotence."

*cite Omnidirectional Halo. p. 163. 1960
- Citation at Metaphysical & Physical, 21 Dec'71

---

Speculation:

 See Irreversible, 6 Nov'73

---

RBF DEFINITIONS

Speed:

"Speed is a unit of rate which is an integrated ratio of both time and space..."

- Citation & context at Rate, 1938

---

Speech: Speaking:     (1)

 See Lecturing
  Moratorium on Speech
  Vision vs. Speech
  Conversation
  Cliche
  Cussing

---

Speed:     (1)

 See Eternity is Simply the Highest Speed
  Fast & Slow
  Instantaneity
  Intellect: Speed Of
  Light: Speed Of
  No Speed
  Radiation: Speed Of
  Rate
  Sound: Speed Of
  Top Speed
  Velocity
  Terminal Speed
  Limit Speed
  Gravity: Speed Of
  Cosmic Speed

---

Speech: Speaking:     (2)

 See Fresh, 3 Oct'71
  Communication, 21 Jun'77

---

Speed:     (2)

 See Metaphysical & Physical, 21 Dec'71*
  Rate, 1938*

RBF DEFINITIONS

Spending:

"Naught had been spent but thoughtful hours."

- Citation and context at Copper (2), May '72

RBF DEFINITIONS

Spending:                                                    (1)

       See Afford
          Available Time
          Conservation
          Conservatism
          Economic Accounting System
          Wealth

---

RBF DEFINITIONS

Spending:

"Naught gets spent but human time
As cosmically inexhaustible energy
Is tapped exclusively
By intellect-discovered and employed
Cosmic principles
Which to qualify as principles
Must be eternal."

- Cite Muskie Telegram
  N.Y. Times
  27 March 1971

Spending:                                                    (2)

     See Closed System:  Conservation of Energy, 1968*
        Economists, Jun'66
        Unanswerable, 20 Jun'66

---

RBF DEFINITIONS

Spending:

"The only thing that's expendable is what we do

with our time-- all the rest is cumulative."

- Cite RBF to EJA
  O'Hare Airport Chicago
  25 March 1971

Sperry:

     See Gyrocompass
       Gyroscope

---

RBF DEFINITIONS

Spending:

"The Universe is a mammoth perpetual motion process.  We see
then that the part of our wealth which is physical energy is
conserved.  It cannot be exhausted-- cannot be spent, which
means exhausted.  We realize that the wording spending is now
scientifically meaningless; it is obsolete."

- Citation & context at Closed System:  Conservation of Energy,
  1968

RBF DEFINITIONS

Sphere:

"Spinning and orbiting give you the sphere--at the point
where frequency comes into time-size."

- Citation & context at Six Motion Freedoms &Degrees of Freedom,
  (A)(B); 8 Aug'77

RBF DEFINITIONS

Sphere:

"'The sphere is the tetrahedron or octahedron or icosahedron.'
I did write 'There are no others,' but I think it is stronger
just the way it is.  They obviously can be of any frequency."

"The spun frequency of all three = superficial sphericity."

- Cite RBF Ltr. to EJA, 25 Feb'74

---

RBF DEFINITIONS

Sphere:

"If you get too semantically incisive the reader loses all
connections with anything he has ever thought before.  That
might not be a great loss.  But I like to assume that the
reader can cope with his reflexes and make connections
between the old words and the new and better words.  For
example, we have had to clear up what we mean by a sphere.
It is not a surface; it is an aggregate of events in close
proximity.  It isn't just full of holes: it doesn't even
have the connections."

- Cite SYNERGETICS draft at Sec. 1023.11, 20 Feb'73

---

RBF DEFINITIONS

Sphere:

"Physically, spheres are high-frequency event arrays whose
spheric complexity and polyhedral system unity consist structurally
of discontinuously islanded, critical-proximity-event huddles,
compressionally divergent events, only tensionally and omni-
interattractively cohered.  The pattern integrities of all
spheres are high-frequency, traffic-described subdivisioningss
of either tetrahedral, octahedral, or icosahedral angular interference, intertriangulating structures profiling one, many, or
all of their respectuve great-circle orbiting and spinning event
characteristics.  All spheres are high-frequency geodesic
spheres; i.e., triangular-faceted polyhedra, most frequently
icosahedral because the icosasphere isthe structurally most
economical."

- Cite SYNERGETICS text at Sec. 985.22, drafted 30 Dec'73

---

RBF DEFINITIONS

Sphere:

"No sphere large enough for a flat surface to occur is
imaginable.  This is verified by modern physics experimentally
induced abandonment of the Greeks' definition of a sphere
which absolutely divided the Universe into all the Universe
outside and all the Universe inside the sphere with an
absolute surface closure permitting no traffic between the
two and making inside self-perpetuating to infinity complex,
ergo the first locally perpetual motion machine completely
contradicting entropy.  Since physics has found no solids or
impervious continuums or surfaces, and has found only finitely
separate energy quanta, we are compelled operationally to
redefine the spheric experience as an aggregate of events
approximately equidistant in a high-frequency aggregate in
almost all directions from one only approximate event.  Since
nature always interrelates in the most economical manner, and
since great circles are the shortest distances between points
on spheres, and since chords are shorter distances than arcs,
then nature must interrelate the spheric aggregated events by
the chords, and chords always emerge to converge, ergo converge convexly around each spheric system vertex, ergo the
sums of the angles around the vertexes of spheric system never
add to 3600."

- Cite SYNERGETICS text at Sec. 1106.23, [22] 26 Jan'73

---

RBF DEFINITIONS

Sphere:

"The Greeks defined the sphere as a surface outwardly
equidistant in all directions from a point. As defined,
the Greeks' sphere's surface was an absolute continuum,
subdividing all the Universe outside it from all the
Universe inside it; wherefore, the Universe outside could
be dispensed with and the interior eternally conserved."

- Cite RBF galley correction to SYNERGETICS at Sec. 224.07,
  28 Oct'73

---

RBF DEFINITIONS

Sphere:

"... Every system is always losing energy.  But they always
have imports as well as exports.  And physics has found no
solids.  Physics has found no continuums.  So our only way
of defining a spherical experience in modern scientific terms
is an aggregate of events approximately equidistant in
approximately all directions from one approximate event.
That's the nearest we can come.  It is then a Galaxy of very
approximate event points.  There being no continuum, these
energy events have relationships.  And the most economical
relationships between circular or spherically arrayed points
are not the arcs, but the chords.  I've come to discovering
how very powerful all this is as its going on in geodesic
domes which is simply what I'm talking about: an array of
points approximately equidistant from one point and making
all the most economical chordal interrelationships which makes
them always triangulated."

- Cite RBF Tel Aviv Address, p.7, 16 Jun'72

---

RBF DEFINITIONS

Sphere: ·

"...The sphere (i.e., the high-frequency, omnitriangulated,
geodesic, spheroidal polyhfdron) encloses the most volume
with the least surface."

- Citation and context at Tetrahedron, 26 Sep'73

---

RBF DEFINITIONS

Sphere:

"It is not surprising . . . that ball bearings prove to be
the most efficient compression members known to and ever
designedly produced by man.  Nor are we surprised to find
all the planets and stars to be approximately spherical
mass aggregations, as also are the atoms, all of which
spherical islands of the macrocosmic and microcosmic aspects
of scenario universe provide the comprehensive, invisible,
tensional, gravitational, electromagnetic and amorphous
integrity of universe with complementarily balancing
internality of compressionally most effective, locally and
temporarily visible, islanded compressional entities."

- Cite RBF marginalia, SYNERGETICS text, Sec. 614.081, 1971

RBF DEFINITIONS

Sphere:

"The moment you know you are on a sphere or spheroid,
You know that none of the perpendiculars are parallel
to one another."

- Cite RBF to SIMS Seminar, U. Mass., Amherst, 22 July 1971.

---

RBF DEFINITIONS

Sphere:

"Spheres are high tide aspects of vertexes. Solids are
high tide aspects of faces. Spheres in closest packing are
high tide aspects of vertexes."

- Cite RBF to EJA, Blackstone Hotel, Chicago, 31 May 1971

- Citation at Tidal, 31 May '71

---

RBF DEFINITIONS

Spheres:

"Spheres are just very high-frequency geodesics."

- Cite RBF to EJA, Fairfield, Conn., Chez Wolf.
  18 June 1971.

---

RBF DEFINITIONS

Sphere:

"Pi ($\pi$) is irrelevant in synergetics because the sphere
is not experimentally demonstrable and the tetrahedron is
the minimum sphere. Compound curvature starts with the
tetrahedron. Pi drops out because chords are more economical
than arcs. Chords of an omnidirectional system never add
up to $360^\circ$ around a point. They are always geodesics. A
point on a sphere is never an infinitesimal tangency with
a plane."

- Cite RBF to EJA, Blackstone Hotel, Chicago, 31 May 1971

---

RBF DEFINITIONS

Sphere:

"The sphere is an asymmetrical phenomenon. It is an
inward-outward pulsative from the vector equilibrium."

- For citation and context see Vector Equilibrium: Spheres
  and Spaces, 31 May '71

---

RBF DEFINITIONS

Sphere:

"Imagination means man's communication of what he thinks
it is that he thinks his brain is doing with the objects
of his experience. His discovery of general conceptual
principles characterizing all of his several experiences--
as the rock, having insideness and outsideness, the many
pebbles, having their corners knocked off and ▮▮▮
developing roundness: he thinks there could be pure
'roundness' and thus imagined a perfect sphere."

- Cite RBF to EJA, Somerset Club, Boston, 22 April 1971

CONCEPTUALITY SEC. 502.41 b]

---

RBF DEFINITIONS

Sphere:

"A sphere is an asymmetrical phenomenon. It is
an inward-outward pulsative from the vector equilibrium.
The sphere's spaces are interchangeable."

- Cite RBF tape transcript, Blackstone Hotel, Chicago,
  31 May 1971, p. 48.

---

RBF DEFINITIONS

Sphere:

"In further demonstration of the non-mirrored
complementary phenomena, we note that compression columns
become more and more effective as we make them fatter and
fatter going from long, thin cylinders to cigar-shaped
systems. By increasing the compression member's relative
girth and shortening its height still further, we finally
develop a compression structure that is spherical.

"The sphere is compressionally ideal. As a slender column
it had to be loaded carefully on its neutral vertical axis
to avoid eccentric bending. When it is a sphere, however, the
compression loads applied from any direction are automatically
opposed by one of an infinity of neutral axes. The sphere
provides nature's optimum limit in structural opposition to
compressive forces in universe-- ergo, the stars and planets
and atoms are all spherical islands of compression."

- Cite GODDESSES, Sat Review, 2 Mar 68

RBF DEFINITIONS

Sphere:

"A _sphere_ is a plurality of events approximately equidistant in approximately all directions from approximately one event at approximately the same time."

- Cite DEFINITIONS FOR SYNERGETICS BY PETER PEARCE. 1967

---

RBF DEFINITIONS

Sphere:

"The best definition we make of spherical appearing system is 'a constellation of event focii approximately equidistant in approximately all directions from one approximate event at approximately the same time.' By the time we have been able to measure many of the distances others would have changed their positions and conditions."

- Cite NASA Speech, p. 85, Jun'66

---

RBF DEFINITIONS

Sphere:

Topologically speaking, a _sphere_ is a spherical constellation and /sic/ vertexes between which there are always the most economical inter-relationship which consist of chordal distances between the vertexes. These chords form multi-faceted polyhedra and the sums of the angles around all the vertexes of the polyhedral system will always be the number of vertexes times 360 degrees minus 720 degrees."

"When we get into the sphere, I find that relatively few people really think in terms of spherical thinking. Spherical thinking has not been used too much because calculus seems to take its place in many ways, and it is important to realize that in spherical thinking the angles don't add up to 180 degrees."

- Cite NASA Speech, p. 85, Jun'66
- Cite CARBONDALE DRAFT IV.53, IV. 54

---

RBF DEFINITIONS

Sphere:

"The _sphere_ is complex unity and the triangle simplex unity. Here and here alone lie the principles governing finite solution of all structural and general systems theory problems."

- Cite RBF Ltr. to Shoji Sadao, 15 Feb '66, p. 5.
- Citation and context at _Unity: Complex and Simplex Unity,_ 15 Feb'66

---

RBF DEFINITIONS

Sphere: (1)

"The Greeks defined a sphere as 'A surface equidistant in all directions from a point.' As defined there could be no holes in the sphere because if there were any holes the surface would be turning inwardly around the holes rim, and radius would change and the holes would leave areas within them where radius would not be equal in _all_ directions. The Greeks' definition inferred that there is some kind of continuous and impervious continuum which absolutely subdivides all the universe which is outside the sphere forever, from all the universe which is inside the sphere. Were there no holes in the sphere, there could be no _possible_ energy traffic inbound or outbound-- therefore entropy. Entropy-- the second law of thermodynamics showsthat every local energy system in physical universe is always losing or emitting energy. The minimum set of all energy transactions and transformation is physical universe itself. Therefore only universe as an aggregate of non-simultaneous energy event transformings is the only possible perpetual motion system. If we could have a local perpetual motion machine we could throw away the rest of universe. Therefore the sphere, as defined by

- Cite NASA Speech, pp.84-85, Jun'66

---

RBF DEFINITIONS

Sphere:

"The only definition of a sphere now tenable by experimental physics is: 'A plurality of energy event foci approximately equidistant, in approximately all directions, at approximately the same time from the approximate center of progressive measuring actions."

- Cite Ltr. to Dr. Robt. W Horne, 14 Feb '66, p. 4

---

RBF DEFINITIONS

Sphere: (2)

"the Greeks was the first proposed fallaciously perpetual motion machine."

- Cite NASA Speech, p.85, Jun'66

---

RBF DEFINITIONS

Sphere:

"A _sphere_ is a plurality of events approximately equidistant in all directions from one event."

- Cite MUSIC, Caption to Figure 9, p. 65 10 Dec'64

RBF DEFINITIONS

Sphere:

"Now a sphere is defined by the Greeks as a surface equidistant in all directions from a point. No man has ever witnessed an impervious surface so we can't say that any more. The definition by the Greeks of a surface equidistant in all directions means it could have no holes in it because then the radius would change. This would be the first definition of antientropy that you would successfully subdivide an inwardness from an outwardness-- subdivide the Universe in two parts and have no traffic" between them. "But my definition of a sphere-- really like a Hilbert point system-- is a plurality of events approximately equidistant in one direction / sic / from one event. This is a very satisfactory one." It accommodates a "very high frequency of events, but it does change mathematics completely. You will find it affects us."

- Cite LEDGEMENT LAB. Address, p.50, 15 Oct'64

RBF DEFINITIONS

Sphere:

"Aiming of the compressional loading of a short column into the neutral or central-most axis of the column provides the greatest columnar resistance to the compressing because, being the neutral axis, it brings in the most mass coherence to oppose the force. To make a local and symmetrical island of compression from a short column which axial loading has progressively twisted and expanded at girth, into a cigar shape, you have to load it additionally along its neutral axis until the ever-fattening cigar shape squashes into a sphere. In the spherical condition, for the first and only time, any axis of a spherical structure is neutral-- or, ergo, in its most effective resistant-to-compression attitude. It is everywhere at highest compression and tension resisting capability to withstand any forces acting upon it."

- Cite RBF expansion of Ledgemont, p.32. See SYNERGETICS text, 'Tension and Compression- Sphere: An Island of Compression.' Sec. 614.08. 15 Oct'64

RBF DEFINITIONS

Sphere:

". . . As a condition of the sphere for the first time, any axis is ▪ neutral axis, in the spherical condition, it has aptitude in any direction to withdraw the forces on it; it is not surprising that ball bearings become the most effective compression members ever designed by man. I am not surprised to find more or less spherical planets in the heavens tensionally cohered, compression at its most effective."

- Cite LEDGEMONT, p. 32, 15 Oct'64

RBF DEFINITIONS

Sphere:

"A sphere contains the most volume and the least surface and is in the most comfortable condition. These energy patterns are always the most comfortable and the most economical conditions."

- Cite Oregon Lecture #5, pp. 186-187, July '62

RBF DEFINITIONS

Sphere:

"Among geometrical systems a tetrahedron encloses the minimum volume with the most surface and a sphere the most volume with the least surface."

- Cite OMNIDIRECTIONAL HALO, p. 141, 1960

RBF DEFINITIONS

Sphere:

"We can state that the number of vertices of any system (including a 'sphere' which must, geodesically, in universal energy conservation, be a polyhedron of $\underline{n}$ vertices) minus two times $360°$ equals the sum of the angles around all the vertices of the system."

- Cite OMNIDIDRECTIONAL HALO, p. 152, 1960

RBF DEFINITIONS

Sphere:

A sphere is a multiplicity of discrete events, approximately equidistant in all directions from a nuclear center."

- Cite MARKS, P. 138, 1960

RBF DEFINITIONS

Sphere:

"All the points in the surface of a sphere may be interconnected. If most economically interconnected, they will subdivide the surface of the sphere into an omnitriangulated spherical web matrix."

- Cite OMNIDIRECTIONAL HALO, p. 150, 1960

RBF DEFINITIONS

Sphere:

"A sphere is a plurality of events approximately
equidistant in approximately all directions from
one event."

- Cite ITEM "O", p. 4 , May'55

RBF DEFINITIONS

Sphere:

"The sphere is not a minimal system because no completely
enclosed surface exists and therefore no line spherical
integrity. The sphere has a plurality of sides which makes
it a polygon reducible to triangles and hence, tetrahedron.

"The sphere on the other hand encloses or defines more volume
with the least surface than any other geometric figure.

". . . The sphere is an invisibly multifaceted polyhedron--
each facet reducible to trusses and hence to triangles."

- Cite Undated typescript among Synergetics Papers (from RBF)

RBF DEFINITIONS

Sphere:

"The regular six-chord-edged tetranedron encloses
(defines) the minimum volume with the most surface of all
geometric polyhedrons or structural systems; whereas sphere
encloses most volume with least surface and the minimum
sphere-defining structure is the regular six-great-circle-
arc-edged tetrahedron of 109°28' central angles and 120°
surface angles. As there may be no absolute division of
energetic universe into isolated or non-communicable parts,
there is no absolute enclosed surface or absolutely enclosed
volume; therefore, no true or absolutely defined simultaneous surface sphere integrity. Therfore, a sphere is a polyhedron of invisible plurality of trussed facets ('trussed'
because all polygons are reducible to triangles or trusses
and are further irreducible) and trusses are therefore basic
polygons. Infinite polyhedron is infinitely faceted by
basic trusses."

ISOTROPIC VECTOR MATRIX - SEC 420.07) — Cite MCHALE, Plate 36, caption.
(The same language appears earlier in PENNA. TRIANGLE, p.10, Nov,52

Sphere Center:

See Indispensable Center, 19 Feb'72
    Omnitriangulation, 20 Feb'75
    Triacontrahedron, 13 May'77
    T Quanta Module, (10

RBF DEFINITIONS

Sphere:

"No sphere is large enough to be flat."

- Citation and context at Dynamic, 1950

Sphere Integrity:

See No Sphere Integrity

RBF DEFINITIONS

Sphere:

"In a compound curvature sphere of paper all the
surface represents an intertriangulation of great circles,
wherefore each great circle helps the other. Each is a
compression circle enclosed within a tension circle. If
we try to flatten the sphere, its equator cannot move
outwardly to accomodate the down thrust as did the girth
of the paper cylinder. Therefore, no one circle can
lever its compressive interior against polar points, and,
disunited, fail. In the sphere, the pressure at one
point must invoke an infinity of great circles to crush
an infinity of points simultaneously in a progressively
rolling radius as the sphere is gradually pushed inside
out-- but never flattened-- and only rolls the wave
to the equator, which holds. Even in its inside-outness
the sphere maintains its comprehensive interaction of
system, seeking to re-establish its shape. Thus do balls
tend to bounce."

- Cite IDEAS AND INTEGRITIES, p. 219
Preview of Building, Apr'49

Sphere - Polyhedron:

See Pi, 8 Feb'73

Sphere of Reference:

    See Omnidirectional:  Physical Existence Environment
        Surrounds, (3)

---

RBF DEFINITIONS

    Spheres & Spaces:

    "Considering spaces between is one way of looking at
universe and the sphere is another way of looking at
universe.  This is typical of not being fooled by just
looking at spheres or just looking at the little triangle
locally on the surface of the big sphere where we had our
big triangle.  This is beginning to give us ways of seeing
the complementarity at all times."

        - Cite Carbondale Draft
          Nature's Coordination, p. VI.53
    - Cite Oregon #7, p.258, 11 Jul'62

---

RBF DEFINITIONS

    Spheres & Spaces:

    "The sphere-to-space, space-to-sphere intertransformability
is a conceptual generalization holding true independent of
size, which therefore permits us to consider the generalized
allspace-filling complementarity of the convex (sphere) and
concave (space) octahedra with the convex (sphere) and
concave (space) vector equilibria; and also permits us to
indulge our concentrated attention upon local special-case
events without fear of missing further opportunities of
enjoying total synergetically conceptual advantage regarding
nonsimultaneously-considerable scenario Universe."

    - Cite SYNERGETICS, 2nd. Ed. at Sec. 1238.22, 14 May'75

---

Spheres & Spaces:          (1)

    See Mite:  Positive & Negative Functions
        Resonance Field
        Allspace Filling:  Octahedron & VE
        Vector Equilibrium:  Field of Energy
        Vector Equilibrium:  Spheres & Spaces
        Interstitial:  Interstitial Spaces
        Internuclear Voids

---

RBF DEFINITIONS

    Spheres and Spaces:

    "The spheres and spaces are disequilibrious, i.e.,
asymmetrical phases of the vector equilibrium's complex
of both alternate and coincident transformabilities. . .
By virtue of these transformations and their accommodating
volumetric involvement, the spheres and spaces are
interchangeably intertransformative.  For instance, each
one can be either a convex or a concave asymmetry of the
vector equilibrium."

    - Citation and context at Interchangeable Intertransformativeness,
      22 Feb'73

---

Spheres & Spaces:          (2)

    See Interchangeable Intertransformativeness, 22 Feb'73*
        Push-pull, 22 Feb'73
        Sphere, 31 May'71
        Valve, 20 Feb'72
        X Configuration with Ball at the Center (2)
        Trigonometry:  Spherical Trigonometry (3)
        Harmonics, (2)(3)
        Modules:  A & B Quanta Modules, 20 Dec'73
        Vector Equilibrium Involvement Domain, 24 Apr'76
        Quantum Mechanics:  Minimum Geometrical Fourness,
          (2)
        Wave Pattern of a Stone Dropped in Liquid,
          22 Jun'77

---

RBF DEFINITIONS

    Spheres and Spaces:

    "A sphere is a convexly expanded vector equilibrium and
all spaces are concavely contracted vector equilibria and
octahedra at their most disequilibrious pulse moments."

    - Cite RBF to EJA, 3200 Idaho, incorporated at SYNERGETICS
      Sec. 970.17, 14 Oct'72
        .13

---

Spheres Become Spaces and Spaces Become Spheres:

    See Spheres & Spaces

Spheres & Vertexes:

See Push-pull Members, 28 Oct'72

Sec. 722.02

Sphere Tangent with a Plane:

See Calculus, 1960
Infinity & Finity, Jun'66
Raft, 3 Apr'75
Sphere, 31 May'71
Zero Condition, 14 Feb'66
Geodesic Sphere, (1)(2)
Halo Concept, Nov'71

---

RBF DEFINITIONS

Sphere: Synergetics Formula for the Volume of a Sphere:

"Here are a lot of illustrations for 'Synergetics. This one where we have 12 spheres closest packed around one, I did freehand. It shows all the geometries that occur from 12 spheres around one, and how they all appear as rational values. We show in the book (Sec. 982.60) that the value of the sphere itself turns out to be the number five, a whole rational number five, without any pi, where the volume of the tetrahedron is one."

(This is RBF comment on Illustration at 982.62.)

- Cite RBF to HUGH Kenner, Phila. PA, transcript p.11; 9 Jun'75

RBF DEFINITIONS

Sphere of Unit Vector Radius:

"The concentric hierarchy was conceived from the outset and as early as 1934, but I had one value more to establish--which was the volume of the sphere of unit vector radius, which proved out at five."

- Cite RBF marginalia on EJA's "Cosmic Fish" ms. Chap. X, p.8; 20 Nov'75

---

TEXT CITATIONS

Sphere: Synergetics Formula for Area & Volume of a Sphere:

Synergetics:    Sec. 982.60

985.00 - 985.08

RBF DEFINITIONS

Sphere: Volume-surface Ratios:

"The largest number of similar triangles into which the whole surface of a sphere may be divided is 120. The surface triangles of each of these 120 triangles consist of one angle of 90°, one of 60°, and one of 36°. Each of these 120 surface triangles is the fourth face of a similar tetrahedron whose three other faces are internal to the sphere. Each of these 120 tetra has the same volume as have the A or B Quanta Modules. Where the tetra is 1, the sphere's volume is 5. Dividing 120 by 5 = 24 quanta modules per tetra. The division of the sphere of volume 5 by its 120 quanta modules discloses another unit system behavior of the number 24 as well as its appearance in the 24 external vector edges of the vector equilibrium."

- Cite RBF to EJA, 3200 Idaho, Wash., DC; incorporated in SYNERGETICS, 2nd. Ed. at Sec. 1053.36; 11 Dec'75

---

Sphere: Synergetics Formula for the Volume of a Sphere:

See O Module, 29 Sep'76
Triacontrahedron, 13 May'77

RBF DEFINITIONS

Spherics:

"A spheric is any one of the rhombic dodecahedra, the center of each of whose 12 diamond facets is exactly tangent to the surface of each sphere formed equidistantly around each vertex of the isotropic vector matrix."

[31]

- Cite SYNERGETICS at Sec. 426.12, 30 Nov'72

RBF DEFINITIONS

Spherics:

"Because the rhombic dodecahedra fill and symmetrically
subdivide allspace, while simultaneously, symmetrically,
and exactly defining the respective domains of each sphere
as well as the respective shares of the interclosest-packed-
sphere interstitial space, the rhombic dodecahedra are called
'spherics' for their respective volumes are always the
unique closest packed, uniradius spheres' volumetric domains
of reference within the electively generatable and selectively
'sizable' or tunable of all isotropic vector matrixes of all
metaphysical 'considering' as regenratively re-origined by
any thinker anywhere at any time; as well as all the electively
generatable and selectively tunable (sizable) isotropic
vector matrixes of physical electromagnetics, always
re-originatable physically by anyone anywhere in Universe."

[21]
- Cite SYNERGETICS draft at Sec. 426.22, 30 Nov'72

RBF DEFINITIONS

Spheric:

"I like to use 'spheric' because it seems to take in more
than 'spherical.' It would include the 'spheroidal.'
Both a ball and a tomato are 'spheric.'"

* Cite RBF to EJA, 3200 Idaho, 15 Oct'72

RBF DEFINITIONS

Spheric Domains:

"All the well-known Platonic polyhedra, as well as all
the symmetrically referenced crystallographic aberrations
are symmetrically generated in respect to the centers of
the spheric domains of the isotropic vector matrix and its
inherently nucleating radiational and gravitational
behavior accommodating by concentrically regenerative,
omnirational, frequency and quanta coordination of vector
equilibria which may operate propagatively and coheringly
in respect to any special-case event fix in energetically
identifiable Universe."

- Cite SYNERGETICS draft at Sec. 981.20, 6 Nov'72

RBF DEFINITIONS

Spheric Domain:

"Spheric domain is prime volume."

- Citation and context at Vector Equilibrium, 18 Nov'72

Spheric Domain vs. Nuclear Domain:

See Six - Five - One, 8 Jan'74

Spheric Domain:                                        (1)

See Domains
    Prime Domains
    Rhombic Dodecahedron
    Spheric
    Prime Volumes

Spheric Domain:

See Coupler, 20 Dec'73
    Rhombic Dodecahedron, 2 Nov'73
    Domains of Interferences, 7 Nov'73

Spheric Event:

See System Enclosure, (1)

RBF DEFINITIONS

### Spheric Experience:

"The spheric experience is simply an ultra-high frequency of finite event occurrences in respect to the magnitude of the tuning of the observer. (High frequency to the human may be low frequency to the molecule."

- Cite SYNERGETICS draft at Sec. 1023.13, 20 Feb'73

---

RBF DEFINITIONS

### Spherical Barrel:

"This whole spherical barrel system is non-redundant because of the triangular 'three-point' contacts of each of the three interfaces of the truncated cork star octahedra, but would be redundant with the trapezoidal interfaces of simply truncated tetrahedra formed inwardly on each and every geodesic sphere's omnitriangular grid."

- Cite Ltr. to Shoji Sadao, 15 Feb '66, p. 4

---

TEXT CITATIONS

### Spheric Experience:

Synergetics draft at Sec. 985.40, 14 May'73

---

RBF DEFINITIONS

### Spherical Barrel:    Kumasi Dome:                (1)

"In this particular experiment the triangular 'corks,' (i.e., octahedra) were small enough to render this ⟨ .005 aluminum ⟩ foil of structural effectiveness. . . .

"What is unique about this Kumasi dome is that the octa corks had their triangular radial great-circle plane surfaces mathematically guided together only by two control holes in each of their abutting triangular great-circle plane faces . . . to tentatively guide the approach of these surfaces toward one another and thereafter to cohere the whole spherical system in a loose manner. . . . Wire bands described all 31 of the basic great circles of the icosahedron's symmetrical subdividings.. Fifteen of these great circles lie alternately along the edge of the icosa-hedron and then act as vertical bisectors of the next two icosahedronal major triangles. Of the 31, the remaining ten and six great circles interact with the 15 great circles in such a manner that they form approximately uniform tensional triangles overlying a six-frequency truncatable icosahedronal pattern, with the wires crossing over all the vertexes as well as the mid-faces of the system to impinge vertically on the edges opposite each of the verticals."

- Cite Ltr to Shoji Sadao, 15 Feb '66, p.2

---

RBF DEFINITIONS

### Spheric Experience:

See Geodesic Spheric Experience

---

RBF DEFINITIONS

### Spherical Barrel:    Kumasi Dome:                (2)

"Thus it is found that 31 great circles act as the most effective 'spherical barrel' bands (where a 6 - 12 frequency, truncatable, icosahedronal pattern is employed) for each of the wires runs over the external surface centers of each of the octa-cork's triangular faces, thrusting each 'cork' inwardly toward the center of the system in such a manner that the tightening of the bands brings about a universal contraction of the sphere.

"As the tensional great circle bands were contracted pro-gressively at Kumasi, it was found most practical to first tighten the set of six great circles. This left the sphere with a set of 12 dodecahedronal 'mountain' bulges. We next contracted the 15 great circles. This brought the sphere into greater symmetry which was totally effective when the 10 great circles were also tautened.

"Where the great circle wire bindings crossed, they had to be tied together but not tightly, i.e., they were run through rings. They didn't need to be tied tightly together, merely guided."

- Cite Ltr. to Shoji Sadao, 15 Feb '66, p. 3

---

RBF DEFINITIONS

### Spherical:

"Having the form of a sphere; includes bodies having the form of a portion of a sphere; also includes polygonal bodies whose sides are so numerous that they appear to be substantially spherical."

- Cite Patent No. 2,682,235, June 29, 1954
  BUILDING CONSTRUCTION

---

RBF DEFINITIONS

### Spherical Barrel:    Sphere as Complex Unity:    Triangle as Simplex Unity:

"Everything I have said here adds up to the fact that the sphere is 'complex unity' and the triangle 'simplex unity.' Here and here alone lie the principles governing finite solution of all structural and general systems theory problems. Local isolations of infinite open-ended plane and linear edged (seemingly 'flat' and infinite) segments of" what are "in reality vast spherical systems-- when taken out of context-- are hopelessly special-cased indeterminate situations.

"Unfortunately engineering has committed itself in the past exclusively to these locally infinite and inherently indeterminate systems and have had to rely essentially on the test-proven local behaviors of small systems such as columns, beams, levers, et. al., opinionatedly fortified with 'safely guesstimated' complex predictions. Not until we have universal finite omnitriangulated nonredundant structural system comprehension can we enjoy the advantage of powerful physical generalizations concisely describing all structural behaviors."

- Cite Ltr. to Shoji Sadao, 15 Feb '66, p. 5

TENSEGRITY- SEC. 650.72

RBF DEFINITIONS

Spherical Barrel:    Fail-Safe Advantage:

"It should elucidate also the increased fail-safe advantage
accomplished with each increase of frequency of triangular
module subdivisions of the sphere's unitary surface; i.e.,
failure of one triangular cork in an omnitriangulated  spherical
grid leaves a triangular hole which is utterly innocuous.
Failure of one stave in a simple curvature barrel and the
whole thing collapses.

"Failure of two adjacent triangular corks in a spherical
system leaves a diamond-arched opening which is stable and
innocuous; likewise the failure of five or six triangles
leaves a completely arched pent or hex opening which is
circumferentially corked and innocuous.  Failure of one
spherical tension member likewise leaves an only slightly
relaxed, two-way detoured, i.e., diamonded relaying of the
throughway tensional continuity."

Considerable relaxing of the spherical triangulated cork
barrel system by many local tension failures can occur without
freeing the corks to dangerously loosened local rotatability.
The higher the frequency and the deeper the inter-trussing,
the safer this type of spherical structure."

TENSEGRITY-
SEC.
650.68   - Cite Ltr. to Shoji Sadao, 15 Feb '66, p. 5

---

RBF DEFINITIONS
                                    vs.
Spherical Barrel:  Radial Compression ▓▓ Circumferential Tension:

"This letter plus the structural portion of my discourse and
illustrations of my Mexican speech to the U.I.A. (in WDSD Doc.
II.) should make possible the elegant mathematical formulation
of engineering theory governing the radial compression and
circumferential tension behaviors unique and exclusively
accomplished through three-way spherical gridding."

- Cite Ltr. to Shoji Sadai, 15 Feb '66, p. 4

TENSEGRITY - SEC 650.69

---

Spherical Barrel:

    See Cork:  Triangular Corks in Spherical Barrels
       Three-way Great Circling:  Three-way Grid

---

RBF DEFINITIONS

Spherical Comprehension:

"The second stage of ⌐comprehension⌐ is spherical..."

- Citation and context at Comprehension, 16 Feb'73

---

RBF DEFINITIONS

Spherical Excess:                                          (1)

"Spherical excess is the amount of angle by which the

three internal angles of spherical triangles exceed the

constant internal angular sum of 180 degrees-- which

characterizes all planar triangles."

- Cite Undated Sheet: DYMACION AIROCEAN WORLD FULLER
     PROJECTIVE-TRANSFORMATION.

---

RBF DEFINITIONS

Spherical Excess:                                          (2)

"The internal angles of spherical triangles always add to
more than 180 degrees and the larger the spherical triangles
the greater the 'excess.'  Convince yourself of this
infraction of your planar thinking by drawing a meridian of
longitude which is a great circle from the North Pole to
the Earth's equator, which is also a great circle.  Meridians
and the equator always intercept each other at 90 degrees.
Draw a line along the equator a quarter of the way around the
world, which is 90 degrees.  Then draw a line returning by
meridian to the North Pole.  You will have completed a
spherical triangle whose three angles are each 90 degrees and
add to 270 degrees, or 90 degrees 'spherical excess.'"

- Cite Undates Sheet: DYMAXION AIROCEAN WORLD FULLER
     PROJECTIVE-TRANSFORMATION

---

Spherical Excess:                                          (1)

    See Equimagnitude Phases
       Minimum Spherical Excess

---

Spherical Excess:                                          (2)

    See Fifteen, 22 Jun'72
       Module:  A Quanta Module & Basic Triangle, 20 Dec'73
       Neutral Angle, 16 Dec'73
       Projective Transformation, (4); (III)-(VII)
       Projective Transformation:  Raleigh Edition, (1)
       Spherical Icosahedron, 13 Oct'71
       Dymaxion Airocean World Map, (2)
       Vector Equilibrium, 26 Aug'75

RBF DEFINITIONS

Spherical Field:

"Physics' discovery of universally-multifrequenced, periodic-
event-discontinuity outness (in complementation to equally
frequenced, event-occurrence in-ness) is inherent in the always-
experientially-verifiable, wave-duration frequency, photon-
quantum phenomena; wherefore synergetics had to redefine both
volumes and surfaces in terms of dense (high-frequency)
aggregates of only pointally-positionable, energy events'
geometrical formulations, with spherical 'surfaces' being in
operational reality a dense, outermost, single-photon-thick,
'cloud' layer, everywhere approximately equidistant in all
directions from one approximately-locatable event center. For
this reason the second-power exponential rate of area gain is
not to be identified as a continuum, i.e., with a continuous
system, but only with the high-frequency outermost layer
population aggregate of energy-event points. With numbers of
photons and wave frequency per primitive volume, the relative
concentration of given masses are determinable."

- Cite RBF rewrite of SYNERGETICS galley at Sec. 1052.20, 9 Jan'74

---

Spherical Grid:

See Tensegrity Geodesic Grid: Three-way Grid
Omnirational Control Matrix
Great Circle Subdivisions of Spherical Unity

---

RBF DEFINITIONS

Spherical Field:

David Bohm, Foundations of Physics, Vol. 1, No. 4, 1971, p.369:

"...Einstein did in fact very seriously try to obtain such a
description in terms of a unified field theory. He took the
total field of the whole Universe as the primary description.
This field is continuous and indivisible. Particles are then
to be regarded as certain kinds of abstraction from the total
field, corresponding to regions of very intense field (called
singularities)."

RBF Comments:

"$2PF^2 + 2$, where P = prime No and F = frequency."

"... of conceptualities. BF's segment 'scenario' of limited
conceptuality."

- Cite RBF marginalia at QUANTUM THEORY AS AN INDICATION OF
NEW ORDER IN PHYSICS, p.369, done Aug'73

UNIVERSAL INTEGRITY - SEC. 1052.33

---

Sphere = Icosa:

See O Module, 29 Sep'76

---

Spherical Field:

See Circumferential Field
Embracement
Halo Concept
Radial-circumferential
Sphere of Reference
Vector Equilibrium: Field of Energy
Spherical Point System
Unified Operational Field

---

RBF DEFINITIONS

Spherical Icosahedron:

"We can take an icosahedron and put a sphere congruent to
each of the 12 vertexes and if we place a light inside and
project the shadows of the chords out on to the sphere, the
result is a spherical icosahedron. The 20 equilateral
triangles of the planar icosahedron can be symmetrically
subdivided into six small right triangles by perpendicularly
bisecting each angle. The angles of each small triangle
are 90°, 60° and 30° and therefroe each of the sides is
different in length. In the spherical icosahedron, however,
the angles are 90°, 60° and 36° with the last angle 60° more
than the corresponding angle in the planar icosahedron.
This is due to spherical excess."

- Cite SYNERGETICS, "Numerology," p. 13, Oct. '71.

---

Spherical Gears:

See Gears: Spherical Gears

---

RBF DEFINITIONS

Spherical Icosahedron:

"An icosahedron 'exploded' onto the surface of
a sphere; bears the same relation to an icosahedron as a
spherical triangle bears to a plane triangle; the sides of
the faces of the spherical icosahedron are all geodesic
lines."

- Cite Patent No. 2,682,235, June 29, 1954
BUILDING CONSTRUCTION

Spherical Icosahedron: (1)

See Icosahedron
    Projective Transformation:  Raleigh Edition
    Tensegrity Icosahedron

---

RBF DEFINITIONS

Spherical Interstices:

"Synergetics Isotropic Vector Matrix omnisymmetric,
radiantly expansive or contractive growth rate of interstices
which are congruent with closest packed uniradius spheres
or points, are also rational.  There is elegant,
omniuniversal, metaphysical, rational, whole number
equating of both the planar bound polyhedral volumes and
the spheres, which relationships can all be discretely
expressed without use of the irrational number pi, ($\pi$),
3.14159, always required for such mathematical expression
in strictly XYZ coordinate mathematics."

- Cite SYNERGETICS draft at Sec. 970.13, 18 Nov'72

---

Spherical Icosahedron: (2)

See Sphere, 25 Feb'74
    Central Ball:  Central Sphere, 13 Nov'75

---

RBF DEFINITIONS

Spherical Interstices:

"A sphere is a convexly expanded vector equilibrium and
all inter-closest-packed sphere spaces are concavely
contracted vector equilibria or octahedra at their most
disequilibrious pulsative moments."

[13]
- Cite SYNERGETICS draft at Sec. 970.15, 18 Nov'72

---

RBF DEFINITIONS

Spherical Interstices:

"When unit radius spheres are closest packed, they have
a space between them whose volume is exactly tetravolume-1
as ratioed to the spherically occupied tetravolume-5 with
a combined space occupancy of tetravolume-6."

- Cite RBF Ltr. to William Hess; 9 Jul'76
- Incorporated in SYNERGETICS 2 draft at Sec. 1032.101

---

Spherical Interstices:

See Interstitial:  Interstitial Spaces
    Sphers & Spaces

---

RBF DEFINITIONS

Spherical Interstices:

"All of [the jitterbug] stages are rationally concentric
in our unified operational field of 12-around-one closest-
packed spheres that is only conceptual as equilibrious.  We
note also that per each sphere space between closest packed
spheres is a volume of exactly one tetrahedron: 6 - 5 = 1."

- Citation & context at Octahedron as Annihilation Model, 30 Dec'73

---

Spherical Maximum:

See Prime Dichotomy, (2)

RBF DEFINITIONS

Spherical Necessity:

"Gravity has been described as the nostalgia of things to
become spheres. The nostalgia is poetic, but the phenomenon
is really more of a necessity than it is a nostalgia. Spheres
contain the most volume with the least surface: gravity is
circumferential: nature is always most economical. Gravity
is the most effective embracement. Gravity behaves spherically
of necessity because nature is always most economical."

- Cite SYNERGETICS, 2nd. ed. at Sec. 646.21, 30 May'75

---

RBF DEFINITIONS

Spherical Nostalgia:

"Here we have clarification of the Copernican 'nostalgia'
or synergetic proclivity of the circumferentially arrayed
spheres to associate symmetrically around the nucleus sphere
or the nucleus void which, as either configuration--the
vector equilibrium or the icosahedron-- rotates dynamically
producing a spherical surface."

- Citation & context at Gravity (1), 12 Jun'74

---

Spherical Nostalgia:

See Spherical Necessity, 30 May'75

---

Spherical Observation:

See Nucleus (1)
    Omnidirectiona; Physical Existence Environment
      Surrounds
    Vectorial Geometry Field, 22 Nov'73

---

RBF DEFINITIONS

Spherical Octahedron:

"The spherical octahedron's three inside-out symmetrically
unique diameters and the three unique external chords produce
two unique sets of three nonparallel lines each, but with
one set coordinating at 60 degrees and the other set coordinating
at 90 degrees."

- Cite SYNERGETICS draft at Sec. 527.23, 29 Nov'72

---

RBF DEFINITIONS

Spherical Octahedron:

"Each of any three great circles of a sphere not having
common polar crossings must cross each other twice in a
symmetrical manner in which the six crossings must produce
either two similar polar triangles and six similar equatorial
triangles, or must produce eight equilateral and equiangular
triangles all cases of which are spherical octahedra,
regular or irregular."

- Cite SET X, p.10, Aug'72

---

RBF DEFINITIONS

Spherical Octahedron:

"When two force vectors operating in great circle paths inside
a sphere impinge on each other at any happenstance angle, that
angle has no amplitude stability. But when a third force vector
operating in a great circle path crosses the other two spherical
great circles, a great-circle-edged triangle is formed with its
inherent 180° mirror-image triangle. With successive inside
surface caromings and angular intervector impingements, the
dynamic symmetry imposed by a sphere tends to equalize the
angular interrelationship of all those triangle-forming sets
of three great circles which, shunting automatically, tend
averagingly to reproduce spherically closed symmetrical
systems of omnisimilar triangles exactly reproduced in their
opposite hemisphere, quarter-spheres, and octa-spheres. This
means that if there were only three great circles they would
tend swiftly to interstabilize comprehensively as the spherical
octahedron all of whose surface angles and arcs (central angles)
average as 90°."

- Cite SET X, p.12, Aug'72

---

RBF DEFINITIONS

Spherical Octahedron:

"Here we have a spherical octahedron made out of the
three great circles. But you cannot make them by folding
up three great circles. It is impossible to fold it and
have it come out. But you can fold six great circles.
You can bring those six together and they will make
the spherical octahedron, but it is all doubled up. Now
that ought not to surprise you because you remember that
when we took the vector equilibrium and collapsed it, it
became the octahedron and all the vectors were doubled,
so this is fairly logical. This is six great circles but
the first that I could make. I couldn't make it with one,
or two, or three, but I can make it with four. This is
of six."

"This is a very peculiar kind of folding . . . they never
duplicate each other and never double up except in the one
case where the octahedron made out of six are all doubled."

- Cite Oregon Lecture #7, p. 269. + p. 270. 11 Jul'62

Spherical Octahedron:

    See Sphere, 25 Feb'74
       Octahedron: Eighth-octahedra, (1)(4)

RBF DEFINITIONS

Spherical Quadrant Phases:

"There is always a total of eight (four positive, four
negative) unique
          -- interpermutative,
          -- intertransformative,
          -- interequatable,
          -- omniembracing
phases of all cyclically described symmetrical systems
(see Sec. 610.20), within any one octave of which all the
intercovariable ranging complementations of number occur."

- Cite SYNERGETICS, 2nd. Ed. at Sec. 1238.28, 9 Jul'75

Spherical Point System:          (1)

    See Spherical Field

Spherical Quadrant Phases:

    See XYZ Quadrant at Center of Octahedron

Spherical Point System:

    See Basic Raft, Feb'50
      Recede, 17 Feb'72

Spherical Reality Scribing:

    See Vectorial Geometry Field, 22 Nov'73

Spherical Propagation:

    See Probability, (1); 20 Feb'72

Spherical Sensations:

    See Halo Concept, 22 Feb'72

RBF DEFINITIONS

## Spherical Structures:

"Because spherical sensations are produced by polyhedral arrays of interferences identified as points approximately equidistant from a point at the approximate center, and because the mass-attractive or repulsive relationships of all points with all others are most economically shown by chords and not arcs, the spherical array of points is all interconnected triangularly by the family of generalized principles being operative as Universe, which produces very high-frequency, omnitriangulated geodesic structures which are an aggregate of chords leading to all points whose angles always add up to less than 360°."

\* Citation at <u>Halo Concept</u>, 22 Feb'72
- Cite SYNERGETICS draft at Secs. 535.10, 14 Mar'72

---

RBF DEFINITIONS

## Spherical Tetrahedron:

"The least distorted transformational projection of the Dymaxion airocean world map is an icosahedron, but the simplest frame of reference is the spherical tetrahedron which provides the omni-triangulated grid, strip-wrapped tetrahedron. This is how you bring the omnidirectional into a flat projection. This is how the tetrahedron, the basic structural system of Universe, unwraps linearly into an infinity of varying frequencies of angle and frequency modulation. Here we have a conceptual model that you can program..."

- Citation & context at <u>Omnidirectional Typewriter</u> (4)(5), 10 Sep'74

---

RBF DEFINITIONS

## Spherical Tetrahedron:

"When stressed with relative high internal pressure all polyhedra tend to transform toward defining the maximum volume with the minimum surface, i.e., toward the spherical convex-arc edge tetrahedra (the basketball and the baseball are tetra structured)."

- Cite PENNA. TRIANGLE, p. 11 Nov '52

---

## Spherical Tetrahedron:

    See Baseball, 28 Jan'75
        Cosmic Neutral, 16 Dec'73
        Omnidirectional Typewriter, (4)(5); 10 Sep'74
        Sphere, 25 Feb'74
        Spherical Triangle Sequence, (VIII)
        Three-way Great Circling: Three-way Grid, 17 Feb'72
        Yin-yang, (1)
        Domain of a Line, 7 Nov'73

---

RBF DEFINITIONS

## Spherical Thinking:

"When we get into the sphere I find that relatively few people really think in terms of spherical thinking. Spherical thinking has not been used too much because calculus seems to take its place in many ways, and it is important to realize that in spherical thinking the angles don't add up to 180 degrees."

- Citation & context at <u>Sphere</u> (p.86), Jun'66

---

## Spherical Thinking:

    See Sphere, (p.85) Jun'66\*

---

RBF DEFINITIONS

## Spherical Triangle :

"What you and I have been brought up on as a triangle is the most extreme case of the most local aspect of what is inherently a spherical triangle. Even if we imagine it, it is still special case. And when we make it conceptual the brain immediately makes it special case. The brain is designed for special case.

"I say to a child: Draw a triangle. And he says: Where? And I say: Draw a triangle. And he draws it on the ground. The triangle divides the whole Earth into two areas: the complementary very big triangle and the local little triangle. Concave and convex are not the same: ergo, we have inherently four triangles. And the four triangles mean the manifestation of our friend the tetrahedron which is always there for the accountability. There is nothing you can do without the tetrahedron being there.

"A plane triangle is just an extremely limited case of the spherical. If you learn the spherical the plane geometry is included, but not the reverse. It is starting with wholes. Plane trigonometry is an abstract ratio of edges to angles but spherical trigonometry is all ratios of angles to angles, which is much simpler."
- Cite RBF at Bell Lab. videotaping, Phila., PA, 23 Jan'75

---

RBF DEFINITIONS

## Spherical Triangle:

"Operationally speaking we always deal in systems and all systems are characterized projectionally by <u>spherical triangles</u> which control all our experiential transformations."

- Cite SYNERGETICS, "Operational Mathematics, One Spherical Triangle Considered as Four." 1971

RBF DEFINITIONS

**Spherical Triangle:**

". . . Spherical trigonometry is a very different kind of trigonometry from the plane. I want you to get familiar with it because there is no plane flat surface on Earth. So therfore there are no plane triangles and we are always dealing in systems. Systems are characterized by triangles which are spherical triangles. These are the kinds of triangles which control our fundamental transformations."

- Cite OREGON Lecture #6, pp. 205-6, 10 Jul'62

---

RBF DEFINITIONS

**Spherical Triangle Sequence:** (i)

"No surface is conceivable without its inherent sphere as a truly flat Universe reaching outwards laterally in all directions to infinity, though illusionarily accepted as 'obvious' by historical humanity, is contradictory to experience. The surface of any system must return to itself in all directions and is most economically successful in doing so as an approximate true sphere which contains the most volume with the least surface. Nature always seeks the most economical solutions, ergo the sphere is normal to all systems experience and to all experiential, i.e., operational consideration and formulation. The construction of a triangle involves a surface and a curved surface is most economical and experimentally satisfactory. A sphere is a closed surface, a unitary finite surface. Planes are never finite. Once a triangle is construcued on the surface of a sphere-- because a triangle is a boundary line closed upon itself-- the finitely closed boundary lines of the triangle automatically divide the unit surface of the sphere into two separate surface areas. Both are bounded by the same three great circle arcs and their three vertexial links: which is the description of a triangle. Therfore both areas are true triangles, yet with common edge"

- Cite SYNERGETICS text at Sec. 1106.12, 26 Jan'73

---

RBF DEFINITIONS

**Spherical Triangle Sequence:** (ii)

"boundaries. It is impossible to construct one triangle alone. In fact, four triangles are inherent to the oversimplified concept of the construction of 'one' triangle. In addition to the two complementary convex surface triangles appropriate to them and occupying the reverse, or inside, of the spherical surface. Inasmuch as convex and concave are opposites, they cannot be the same. Therefore, a minimum of four triangles is always induced when any one triangle is constructed, and which one is the initiator or inducer of the others is irrelevant. The triangle initiator is an inadvertent but inherent tetrahedron producer; it might be on the inside constructing its triangle on some cosmic sphere, or vice versa.

"It might be argued that inside and outside are the same, but not so. While there are an infinity of insides in Experience Universe there is only one outside comprehensive to all insides. So they are not the same; and the mathematical fact remains that four is the ▬▬▬ minimum of realizable triangles that may be constructed if any are constructed. But that is not all, for it is also experimentally disclosed that not only does the construction of one triangle on the surface of the"

- Cite SYNERGETICS text at Secs. 1106.12+13, 26 Jan'73

---

RBF DEFINITIONS

**Spherical Triangle Sequence:** (iii)

"sphere divide the total surface into two finite areas each of which are bound by three edges and three angles, ergo by two triangles, but these triangles are on the surface of a system whose unity of volume was thereby divided into centrally angled tetrahedra because the shortest lines on sphere surfaces are great circles and great circles are always formed ▬ on the surface of a sphere by planes going through the center of the sphere, which planes of the three-great-circl-arc-edged triangle drawn on the surface automatically divide the whole sphere internally into two spherical tetrahedra-- each of which has its four triangles, ergo inscribing one triangle 'gets you Eight,' like it or not. And each of those eight triangles has its inside and outside, wherefore inscribing one triangle, which is the minimum polygon, like 'Open Sesame,' inadvertently gets you 16 triangles. And that is not all: the sphere on which you scribed is a system and not the whole Universe, and your scribing a triangle on it ▬ to stake out your 'little area on Earth' not only begat 16 terrestrial triangles but also induced the remainder of Universe outside the system and inside the system to manifest their invisible or nonunitarily conceptual 'minimum inventorying' of 'the rest of Universe other than Earth'"

- Cite SYNERGETICS text at Sec. 1106.13, 26 Jan'73

---

RBF DEFINITIONS

**Spherical Triangle Sequence:** (iv)

"each of which micro and macro otherness system integrity has its induced sixteen triangles for a cosmic total of 64."

- Cite SYNERGETICS text at Sec. 1106.13, 26 Jan'73

---

RBF DEFINITIONS

**Spherical Triangle Sequence:** (I)

"I spoke to you earlier today about our teacher at the school giving us some arithmetic and then saying she was going to teach us a little bit about plane geometry. She said, 'Don't worry, it's just plane geometry.' Then she taught us about the triangle as an area bound by closed lines: three edges and three angles. A circle is an area bound by a closed line of equal radius from a point. A square is an area bound by a closed line of four equal edges and four equal angles. Everything we learned about geometry were areas bound by closed lines. And then we learned about logic within those closed lines about that area. Reliability and understandability was all on one side of the line. A very nice small tight package, but it couldn't tell us anything about the other side of the line. Why? Because it is plane geometry and goes to infinity so the other side of the line is undefinable. What do you mean by infinity? It's infinite, therefore it can't be defined. So that we start the children off with this extraordinary prejudice that only on one side of the line is there reliability.

"Your family is very reliable. The next family over there is"

- Cite SIMS Address, U.Mass, Amherst, Talk 13, p.15, 22 Jul'71

---

RBF DEFINITIONS

**Spherical Triangle Sequence:** (II)

"questionable now. As for those foreigners, well, they're awful. They're very unreliable. Now I want you to see how we really build prejudice, how easy it is in terms of the superficial assumption of the reality of this great plane-- that this is a safe place to start children off. Now I want you to realize that when we made that closed line we did it on a blackboard and I did it with a piece of crayon, and this blackboard ends and goes around to the other side. It has another side here /He knocks on it._7 and it has edges▬ on it. It is a system. This blackboard, I can take it off here▬, and I find that it is a system. It has insideness and outsideness and is fairly thick-- about a quarter of an inch. And I'm still inside it. So it is a system even though it's an asymmetrical system. When I take a unit system it has a unit surface. When I draw a closed line on a system which is a unit surface I divide the whole area of that system, the whole surface area, into two areas. There is the rest of the board here that is an area bound by this closed line of three edges and three angles.

"So this is white inside here and all the rest is green."

- Cite SIMS Address, U.Mass., Amherst, Talk 13, p.16, 22 Jul'71

---

RBF DEFINITIONS

**Spherical Triangle Sequence:** (III)

"I'll paint this green all around, a green area which is bound by a closed line of three edges and three angles. You say it doesn't look like a triangle to me. And I say it /the outside green area-- EJA note._7 must be; that's your definition of a triangle, an area bound by a closed line of three edges and three angles. Now the board being asymmetrical makes it more difficult for you for the moment, but I want you to think about our Earth. We had a circle which was an area bound by a closed line with equal radius from a point. Well, taking our Earth, I'm now going to make a closed line on it and it happens to be 90 degrees from each of the poles and you would call it the equator. It's a closed line on the surface and it divides the Earth into a southern hemisphere and a northern hemisphere. You credit both sides of the line. Now I'm going to take you up to 80 degrees north latitude and draw a lesser circle. It divides the surface of the Earth into two areas: a very large souther one and a very small northern. We can just call it the Arctic circle and the rest of the Earth. But you don't negate the rest of the Earth and you do recognize both sides of the line."

- Cite SIMS Address, U.Mass., Amherst, Talk 13, p.17, 22 Jul'71

RBF DEFINITIONS

## Spherical Triangle Sequence: (IV)

"Now instead of drawing a circle on the Earth I'm just simply going to draw a triangle. Now I divide the whole surface of the Earth into two areas, a very large southern and a very small northern and they both are triangles so they're both bound by a closed line with three edges and three angles. And you say, 'Oh Mister, you're wrong, because I see 60 degree corners to that triangle, and this must be 300 degrees' outside the corner "and this must be 300 and this must be 300 and the sum of the angles of triangles are always 180 degrees.' You say can that really be so. And I say yes it is so and let me demonstrate that to you.

"Take, for instance, what we call a great circle. A great circle is a line formed on a sphere by a plane going through the center of the sphere. The equator is such a great circle. The meridians of longitude are just such great circles and they go trhough the center. 80 degrees north latitude is a lesser circle: it does not go through the center of the sphere. Now great circles are the shortest distances between points on the surface of a sphere. If you would like to demonstrate that we'll simply go up to 85 degrees north latitude-- it's really a very small little circle here-- and take the radius"

- Cite SIMS Address, U.Mass., Amherst, Talk 13, p.17, 22 Jul'71

RBF DEFINITIONS

## Spherical Triangle Sequence: (V)

"of it in my dividers and I'll superimpose it on the equator. And, of course, the equator is A and B. And quite clearly it's a much shorter distance between A and B if you stay on the equator than it is to take this detour over 90 degrees, like this, and come back 90 degrees again.

"So great circles are called geodesics. The word geodesic is old but it was revived by both Einstein and the Indian Riemann /sic/, and it means the most economical relationship between events in the Universe, and they are never straight lines. If, for instance, we see two airplanes in flight. They're independent of the surface of the Earth. They are steerable planets if you will. Photographs were taken at night of airplanes fighting during WWII at night with tracer bullets. Both were using machine guns with tracer bullets, and you'll see one of them hit the other and it goes inward to the Earth. You see the tracery is an absolute corkscrew. If you are for instance wanting to faire at a bird, which I hope you don't want to fire at one, but if you did want to fire at a bird you wouldn't hit it if you aim at whwere it is. You'd have to aim at where you think it's going to be. And gravity is going to start affecting it, even though it's a short"

- Cite SIMS Address, U.Mass., Amherst, Talk 13, p.18, 22 Jul'71

RBF DEFINITIONS

## Spherical Triangle Sequence: (VI)

"distance and going through the atmosphere there's always a spin that's brought about by rotation. There is as a result pressure drafts on one side, and there's air in motion-- wind-- and all your traceries are always going to be corkscrew. But they are the most economical relationships and they are geodesics.

"So geodesics are curved lines. And I've given you the most prominent geodesics like the ███████ great circles, the most economical relationships between events on the surface of our Earth. Now, understanding that, you will understand that our spherical trigonometry is always done with great circles. You were brought up with your plane geometry where a straight line is the shortest distance between two points. Now I gave you earlier today the non-straight line. . .

"Here then is our Earth. I'm going to the north pole and I'm going to take a meridian which is a great circle and it's going to impinge on the equator at 90 degrees. So this meridian comes and impinges on it and here's the center of our Earth. It would go like that. And now, having impinged on the equator at 90 degrees, I'm going to leave the meridian and"

- Cite SIMS Address, U.Mass., Amherst, Talk 13, p.19, 22 Jul'71

RBF DEFINITIONS

## Spherical Triangle Sequence: (VII)

"travel on the equator. I'm going to go one-quarter way around the Earth. Then I'm going to take another meridian and ride up to the north pole again. And because I went a quarter way around the Earth, and then I left the equator at 90 degrees, looking down on top of what I've done, I went like this, and therefore the angle at the north pole must also be 90 degrees. So here's a spherical triangle of 90°, 90°, and 90°, adding up to 270° in its corners. These are the triangles we really do deal with in our Universe.

"If we were to bisect the edges of that triangle with great circles, interconnecting them, the angles would be about 73° at each corner. If I bisect them again and interconnect them with much smaller triangles, the corners are around 63°. Then if I get a smaller one here that 60 degrees and some minutes, or maybe 60 degrees and some seconds-- but they never get down to exactly 60° in each corner. That is, it will always be a little more than 180 degrees. So the smaller the triangle, the more you approach the 180-degreeness which you never arrive at. But the amount the triangles at the corners add up to more than 180 degrees we call the spherical excess, which you must always calculate when you're doing"

- Cite SIMS Address, U.Mass., Amherst, Talk 13, p.19, 22 Jul'71

RBF DEFINITIONS

## Spherical Triangle Sequence: (VIII)

"your spherical trigonometry.

"Now if I made another triangle bigger still, in which the 90° corners were 120° angles . . . that's exactly what you get with a spherical tetrahedron. If I put a tetrahedron inside of a sphere with the light I had last night, and have the shadows cast outwardly from the light at the center of the sphere, it would show you this 120 degree interaction at four vertexes. So there would be a triangle where each of the corners would be 120° and it would add up to 360°. Now I'll simply say to you then, that when you draw a triangle on our Earth, even though it's very local-- and you draw a little tiny triangle here locally-- you divide the total surface of the Earth into two areas. And one is a very large triangle with corners of about 300° each, and there are these little local ones of about 60° each if you try to make it equilateral. The boy said, 'But I didn't mean to draw the big triangle.' I said, 'That's just the trouble. We keep drawing these big triangles and don't realize we are.' We've been thinking what's been called realistic. Let's get down to Earth, never mind that space stuff, but when we're all the time just a tiny little speck in space. It's nothing but a space program, which we'd better catch on to pretty quickly."

- Cite SIMS Address, U.Mass., Amherst, Talk 13, p.20, 22 Jul'71

RBF DEFINITIONS

## Spherical Triangle Sequence: (a)

"All this comes because man starts with the idea of over-simplifying. . . what seems to be reality. The Earth at that time seemed to be a plane going to infinity. So you were dealing in a plane. So you start your geometry with plane geometry. You start trigonometry with plane trigono-metry. But in due course you discovered that it wasn't a plane, it was a sphere. A closed system, not an open system. And you found that you were only defining on one side of the line because the other side went on to infinity. So you learned about the triangle, and the circle, and all these areas bound by closed lines. And you learned that all logic and reliability is one one side of a line: the area bound. On the other side of the line-- you couldn't define it because it went to infinity-- therefore it is undefinable. So as geometry is taught to you, and trigonometry is taught to you, you can only deal with one side of the line.

"But if you are operational, the way Einstein is, and say I've got to take into account all the conditions that obtain at the time of the experience, you can say that in drawing a line on a blackboard that the blackboard does not go on to infinity. It comes to its edge and the edge is a slate,"

- Cite RBF tape Transcript, Carbondale Dome, pp.18-20, 1 May'71

RBF DEFINITIONS

## Spherical Triangle Sequence: (b)

"or whatever it is, and you go around, its mild thickness, you go around its back. And whether you like it or not you have divided the surface of the blackboard into two areas. Anything that comes back into itself is a closed system. And all systems, in fact thinkability, does that. What we call thinking is trying to find out how it does return upon itself: What is the outline of that man? What is going on? What is on the other side of the Moon? I have got to get all the sides in order to understand it.

"I think this Moon thing is typical of seeming to be a plane. You didn't have to think about the other side of it. This is typical of yesterday's way of thinking. Things were just a disc. But even if it was a disc you could have another side. As a coin does. Now, once you are operational, you realize that if you take the unit surface of any system, whether it is symmetrical, a nice regular thing like a sphere, or whether it is a blackboard with very thin edges but none-theless it has surfaces and it has backs. It might be a triangular blackboard, a broken piece of slate, but it has this back. And when you then draw any closed line coming back on itself, whether it is a triangle or a circle,"

- Cite RBF Tape Transcript, Carbondale Dome, pp.20-22, 1 May'71

RBF DEFINITIONS

## Spherical Triangle Sequence: (c)

"automatically that closed line divides the total surface of the system into two areas, both of which are bound by that line. And you have only been looking at what is on one side of that line.

"A bathing cap stretches around and you have the opening of the bathing cap where the little snap rests-- stretched around it. Packaged. Now, if it were a sphere you could see it a little better. I am going to draw a closed line on a sphere. It happens to be the equator. It divides the Earth into two areas, you say, the southern and northern hemispheres, and you can be perfectly happy about that. If I go to 85° north latitude and draw a latitude, a lesser circle. I divide the whole Earth into a very large southern and a very small northern. Now I am perfectly clear at this point that dividing surfaces you have to credit both sides. So if I drew a triangle on the Earth locally I divide the whole surface of the Earth into two areas, both of which are bound by my closed line, the three edges and three angles. And the boy said, 'Well, I drew a 60° angle here . . .' and so I learned the sums of the angles of the triangles only "

- Cite RBF Tape Transcript, Carbondale Dome, pp.22-24, 1 May'71

RBF DEFINITIONS

## Spherical Triangle Sequence: (d)

"add up to 180°, so each of the other corners. . . seems to
be 300° so it adds up to 900°. Well you have been taught
the wrong way because the sums of the angles never add up to
180°, because you cannot make an absolutely flat plane.
There is always something a little more. And this is a case
where you really see how much more.

"If you have a very big triangle, for instance, going to the
north pole, taking a meridian to the equator, impinging on
the equator at 90°; go one-quarter of the way back around the
Earth and take a meridian back to the north pole; it leaves
the equator at 90° and comes back where the two come together
and th angle at the top will be 90°. So 90°, 90°, 90° is
270°-- that is the typical spherical triangle. And the sums
of the angles of spherical triangles are approximately never
the same. If I make a smaller triangle just inside of the
one that I just talked about where there is 90°,90°, 90°,
the sums of the angles are going to be a little less. It
approaches, but never gets down to 60°, 60°, 60°. It is always
a little more. So the smaller they are, the more they approach
180°. And so in all our surveying around our Earth, doing
geodesy, we are always dealing with what we call spherical excess,"

- Cite RBF Tape Transcript, Carbondale Dome, pp. 24-26, 1 May'71

RBF DEFINITIONS

## Spherical Triangle Sequence: (e)

"How much more do the angles add up to more than 180°.

"All the great circles are the shortest distance between two
points on spheres. Great circle triangles give simply what
we say. There is a triangle there literally of 300° in each
corner. 300° minus; and (60,60,60) 180° plus.

"If I started you off with reality operationally, like
Einstein, I couldn't ever start you off with a plane, but I
would start you on a sphere. Once you do that you realize
that what we call the edges of a triangle-- or arc-- is
simply the central angle. You are dealing in central angles
and surface angles. You are dealing all in angles and you
have no incompatibility for your fractions. This is where
we should have started all of our arithmetic and all of our
geometry. We should have started with whole systems."

- Cite RBF Tape Transcript, Carbondale Dome, pp.24-27, 1 May'71

RBF DEFINITIONS

## Spherical Triangle: Circle Version: (1)

"If we draw a closed line such as a circle around our Earth
it must divide its total unit surface into two areas as does
the equator divide our Earth into southern and northern
hemispheres. If we draw a lesser sized circle on the Earth
such as the circle of north latitude 70 degrees, it divides
our Earth's total surface into a very large southern area
and a relatively small northern area. If we go outdoors and
draw a circle on the ground it will divide the whole area of
our planet Earth into two areas and one will be very small
and the other very large. If our little circle has an area
of one square foot, the big circle has an area of approximately
five quadrillion square feet, because our eight-thousand mile
diameter Earth has an approximately 200 million-square-mile
surface and each square mile has approximately 25 million
square feet which, multiplied, gives a five followed by
fifteen zeros-- 5,000,000,000,000,000 square feet. This is
written by the scientists as 5 x 10$^{15}$ square feet which,
while compact, tends deliberately to disconnect from our
senses. Scientists have been forced to disconnect from our
senses due to the errors of our senses which we are now able
to rectify. As we reconnect our senses with the reality of
Universe, we begin to regain competent thinking by humans"

- Cite NEHRU SPEECH, p.19, 13 Nov'69 OPERATIONAL MATH SEC. 813

RBF DEFINITIONS

## Spherical Triangle: Square Version: (2)

"and thereby possibly their continuance in Universe as
competently functioning team members-- members of the varsity
or University team of Universe. If, instead of drawing a
little one-square-foot circle on the ground-- which means on
the surface of the spherical Earth-- we were to draw a
square one foot on each side, this would give us the same
size local area as before: one square foot.

"A square as defined by Euclid is 'an area bound by a closed
line of four equal length edges and four equal and identical
angles.' By this definition our little square, one foot to
a side, which we have drawn on the ground is a closed line of
four equal edges and equal angles. But this divides all the
Earth's surface into two areas both of which are equally
bound by four equal length edges and four equal angles. Therefore, we have two squares: one little local one and one
enormous one. And the little one's corners are approximately
90 degrees each, which makes the big square's corners 270
degrees each. While you are not familiar with such thinking,
you are confronted with a physical experiment's results
which have informed you that you have been laboring under
many debilitating illusions."

- Cite NEHRU SPEECH, pp.19-20, 13 Nov'69 OPERATIONAL MATH SEC. 813

RBF DEFINITIONS

## Spherical Triangle: Equator As Square: (3)

"If you make your small square a little bigger and your
bigger one a little smaller by increasing the little one's
edges to one mile each, you will have a local one square
mile-- a customary unit of western United States' ranches--
and the big square will be approximately 24,999,999 square
miles. As you do so, using great circle lines, which are the
shortest distances on a sphere between any two points, to draw
the squares' edges, you will find the small square's corner
angles are increasing and the big one's corners are decreasing.
If you now make your square so that it's area is one-half that
of Earth 25 million square miles, in order to have all your
edges the same and all your angles the same, you will find that
each of your edges is approximately six thousand miles long
and t hat each of the corners of both squares are 180 degrees
each. That is to say that the edges of both squares lie
along the Earth's equator so that the areas of both are
approximately 12,500,000 square miles.

"And so it would go with a triangle, a pentagon, an octagon,
or any other equi-edged, closed line figure which you may draw
on any system's surface. The closed line surface figure will
always and only divide the whole area into two complementary areas."

- Cite NEHRU SPEECH, pp.20-21, 13 Nov'69 OPERATIONAL MATH SECS. 813-814

RBF DEFINITIONS

## Spherical Triangle: (4)

"That each human thus discovering this experimentally
says spontaneously, 'I didn't mean to make the big triangle,'
or 'the big square,' or indeed the big mess of pollution,
in no way alters these truths of Universe. We are all equally
responsible not only for the big complementary surface areas
which we develop on systems by our every act, but also for the
finite, complementary outward tetrahedron automatically
complementing and enclosing each system which we devise. We
are inherently responsible for the complementary transformation of Universe, inwardly, outwardly, and all around every
system which we alter."

- Cite NEHRU SPEECH, pp.20-21, 13 Nov'69

OPERATIONAL MATH SEC. 814

RBF DEFINITIONS

## Spherical Triangle Sequence:

"A triangle drawn on the earth's surface is actually
a spherical triangle bounded by great circle arcs. If the
triangle is drawn large enough, it is evident that the arcs
divide the surface of the sphere into two triangles
enclosed by common edges. The are apparently 'outside'
one triangle is seen to be 'inside' the other. Because
every spherical surface has two aspects-- convex if
viewed from outside; concave if viewed from within--
each of these triangles is, in itself, two triangles.
Thus one triangle becomes four when the total complex is
understood."

- Cite SYNERGETICS ILLUSTRATIONS, caption #18. 1967

RBF DEFINITIONS

## Spherical Triangle Sequence: (A)

"I often ask a young student to draw a triangle and,
when he says, 'Where shall I draw it?' I say, 'Draw it
on the ground.' So he scratches a triangle and I say,
'You have drawn four triangles: When you draw on the
Earth you must recognize that the Earth is a great sphere.
As a sphere it is a closed or finite surface in contrast to
the infinity of the plane. You will agree with me when I
make a closed line around the middle of the Earth (that
is, I delineate the equator) that this will divide the
Earth into two finite and equally valid areas, a northern
and a southern hemisphere. If I made a lesser circle
north of the equator it would still run around and close
back on itself and divide the Earth's surface into two
unequal areas, a smaller northerly and a larger southerly area,
simply because I have divided the total unitary and
finite surface of the sphere into two sub-areas.' So when
a student draws a triangle for me on the unitary, closed
finite surface of our spherical planet, he divides the
total area of our sphere into two sub-areas, one very
large and one very small, both triangular.

"Now we begin the slide projections and as you will discover"

- Cite BEIRUT Address, pp.23-24, May 4-6'67

RBF DEFINITIONS

## Spherical Triangle Sequence:           (B)

"looking at my first picture that your eye does not want to see the bigger triangular area.

"I find this biased concept very important because it plays such a big part in how competently or incompetently we conceive of and think about our environment.

"Those are what we call <u>spherical triangles</u> and you probably are not familiar with spherical triangles because you have been educated to start with planar triangles wherein the sum of the angles . . . is always 180 degrees.

"In a spherical triangle the angles never add up to 180°. To comprehend that fact let us go to the north pole and follow south along a meridian to impinge perpendicularly upon the equator, i.e., at 90°, and go along the equator a quarter of the way around the Earth. Then take a meridian back to the north pole. Taking the northbound meridian we leave the equator at 90° and, since we went a quarter of the way around the Earth, the two meridians followed-- first southbound and then northbound-- will form another 90° angle at the north pole. (Figure 1) Therefore we have"

- Cite BEIRUT Address, p.24, 4-6 May67

---

RBF DEFINITIONS

## Spherical Triangle Sequence:           (C)

"traveled a triangular course with three right angles, which means that this particular spherical triangle's angles do not add up to 180°. In fact, they add up to 270°.

"This is a typical spherical triangle. The spherical triangle's angles add up to a variety of sums other than 180°. The amount that the spherical triangle's angles add up to more than 180° is called the spherical excess. The excess may vary all the way from 720° to 1°.

"Now if we make the triangle bigger (Figure 2), we can go for instance, to the regular spherical tetrahedron each of whose four spherical surface triangles has three corners consisting of 120° each. Its spherical excess is then 360° minus 180°, which is an excess of 180°. If we draw one spherical triangle on the Earth's surface with each of its corners having 120° angles, it will divide the total spherical surface of the Earth into two areas each of which is bound by a closed line of three angles and three edges."

- Cite BEIRUT Address, p.24, 4-6 May'67

---

RBF DEFINITIONS

## Spherical Triangle Sequence:           (D)

"This means then that the bigger of the two spherical triangles which subdivide the total closed surface of the Earth, has three corners of 240° each.

"In this next picture we see two spherical triangles which subdivide the sphere into two equal areas-- two hemispheres (Figure 3). Here each of the corner angles of the two complementarytriangles covering together the whole sphere have 180° at each corner. This shows us that the equator of the Earth is the boundary between two spherical triangles, each with each of its three corners being 180.°

"In this next picture what was originally the little spherical triangle at the top of the spherical-space model has become the big traingle, and what was the big spherical triangle has now become the little one. If you put those four pictures successively into the projector and then reverse the order and accelerate their sequential reappearance, you will begin to see both the triangles all the time and see the otherwise 'invisible' space sphere.

"Now I must explain that because the sphere is concave as"

- Cite BEIRUT Address,p.25, 4-6 May'67

---

RBF DEFINITIONS

## Spherical Triangle Sequence:           (E)

"viewed from the inside and convex as viewed from outside, and that convex and concave are not the same. Therfore, we have both large and small convex and concave spherical triangles always present. And that was my reason for saying to the boy, 'You have drawn four triangles,' when he thought he had drawn only one. You are not used to thinking of great circles in this way, but that is the way nature operates, so you had better get used to it from now on."

FIG. 1

FIG. 2

FIG. 3

- Cite BEIRUT Address, p.25, 4-6 May'67

---

RBF DEFINITIONS

## Spherical Triangle Sequence:           (a')

"I have a hypothetical sphere here now and you are looking at one spherical triangle on the sphere and these are the three radii to it. . . . Whereas in plane geometry, in the regular geometrical triangles of the Greeks, the sums of the angles were always 180 degrees in the inside of a triangle. In a spherical triangle the sum of the angles of the tr iangle are never 180 degrees, so that spherical geometry is a very different kind of geometry from the plane. I want you to get familiar with it because there is no plane flat surface on Earth and so therefore there are no plane triangles and we are dealing always in systems and the systems are characterized by triangles which are spherical triangles and these are the kinds of triangles which control our fundamental transformations."

- Cite OREGON Lecture #6, p. 205-6, 10 Jul'62

---

RBF DEFINITIONS

## Spherical Triangle Sequence:           (b')

". . . This is now a spherical triangle in which the angles are 120 degrees each. . . Now this other spherical triangle has angles of 180 degrees each: what we call a circle turns out to be a spherical triangle. Remember there is a hemisphere up there and one down here; and quite clearly that is the equator. . . . Here we have the spherical triangle of 120 degree angles in the northern hemisphere of the sphere-- which you don't tend to see, simply because you tend to look at the smaller one. There is a tendency of man to look at the smaller one. In fact, I will draw a triangle on the board and one of the problems when i put two triangles together and got four, you remember, was because they turned out to be complementary triangles. I draw a triangle on the board here and you are used to the Greek way of just looking at the area bound by the three sides. In fact, the Greeks defined a triangle as an area bound by three lines turning upon themselves, a closed line of three increments. It happens, howver, that I have dividied the surface of the blackboard into an area on this side of the line and an area on the other side of the line and every time I put in a line it actually divides something. We have a tendency to be extremely biased and only to look at an area on one side of the line."

- Cite OREGON Lecture #6, p. 206, 10 Jul'62

---

RBF DEFINITIONS

## Spherical Triangle Sequence:           (c')

"If I draw a triangle on the Earth . . . and I asked a student to do that . . . and I said all right, I see four triangles. And he said, I see only one. There is the little area, the area he has defined quite clearly. He has divided the surface of the Earth (which was unit before he drew the triangle) into two areas, the areas on either side of the line. The little local triangle and the big spherical triangle goes clear around the Earth. It is a closed area bound by a line of three increments. It was such a big one he didn't see it. And it is very typical of us to miss it. One of the most typical tricks I have found in humanity is to see the little small one and miss the big one and the big one is the one that counts. Then I told him he drew four triangles and he said how did that happen. Well, they are spherical triangles and there is a concave little and a concave big as viewed from inside and there is a convex little and a convex big as viewed from outside. Convex and concave are not the same, so there are inherently four. In fact you will always find there are four there. Four is the minimum; and when we get to any kind of system, there is always four there. You will get used to that fourness and get used to not allowing yourself to become over confined and looking at the little ones."

- Cite OREGON Lecture #6, pp. 206-7, 10 Jul'62

---

RBF DEFINITIONS

## Spherical Triangle Sequence:           (d')

"When we get to the middle /of the sphere/ you are more or less willing to concede both hemispheres, and then you get caught on to the fact that those were 180 degree triangles. . . . What had been the big one is now becoming the little one, and what had been the little one is becoming the big one . . . We get down finally to triangles where the angles are approaching 70 degrees, and they finally get down nearer to sixty degrees and so many minutes. They will never get to 60. Even the most local one will never be 60 degrees. So spherical triangles then do have a great variety of sums of their angles."

- Cite OREGON Lecture #6, p. 207, 10 Jul'62

TEXT CITATIONS

Spherical Triangle on Earth's Surface = Four Triangles:

See:     Ledgmont Lab. Address, pp. 52-55 [MARGINAL]
         Oregon Lecture #3, pp. 87, et. seq.
         Oregon Lecture #6, pp. 205-207
    **   RBF Tape Transcript, Carbondale Dome, 1 May '71,
         pp. 21-27 [CITED]
    *    NEHRU speech, pp. 18-21 [CITED]
    **   Beirut, AUB Address, pp. 19-24 (rough); 24-25 (smooth),
                                                        [CITED]
         SIMS Address at U. Mass, Amherst, 22 July '71,
         pp. 16-18. + 19-20. [CITED]

Synergetics, Sec. 810.00
                505.81 (2nd. Ed.)
                261.02 (2nd. Ed.)

    538.11

    Fig. 812.03

    981.16-981.18        1106.10-1106.25

RBF DEFINITIONS

Spherical Unity:

"Systems are, in effect, spherical gears. Their internal-
external pulsating and rotating teeth consist in reality
ob both circumferential and radial waves of various
frequencies of subdivision of spherical unity."

- Cite RBF draft of BRAIN & MIND, p. 8, 1971

- Citation and context at Gears: Spherical Gears, May'72

---

Spherical Triangle on Earth's Surface = Four Triangles:    (1)

    See Probability Model of Three Cars on a Highway
        Social Highway Experience:  Three Autos
        Triangle:  Minimum of Four Triangles

RBF DEFINITIONS

Spherical Unity:

"The largest number of identical triangles in a sphere
that unity will accommodate is 120: 60 positive and 60
negative.  We can subdivide the surface of a sphere into
120 equilateral triangles by dividing the base of each
of the 20 original triangles which made up the icosahedron,
into six triangles.  Being spherical, they are positive
and negative, consisting of arcs which cannot hinge back.
On is inside, concave and the other is outside, convex.
So 60 positive and 60 negative triangles are the largest
common denominator of unity."

- Cite SYNERGETICS, "Numerology," p. 15, Oct. '71

- Citation at Basic Triangle:  Basic Disequilibrium 120 L CD
  Triangle, 14 Oct'71

---

Spherical Triangle on Earth's Surface = Four Triangles:    (2)

    See Bias on One Side of the Line, May'65
        China, May'65
        Omnidirectional, 1954
        Operational, 3 Jan'72
        System, 10 Jul'62
        Three-way Great Circling:  Three-way Grid,
          17 Feb'72
        Zoneness:  System Zoneness, 8 Jan'55
        Background Nothingness, 2 Jun'75
        Windows of Nothingness, (1)

Spherical Unity:

    See Great Circle Subdivisions of Spherical Unity
        Sphere as Complex Unity

---

Spherical Triangular Lattice:

    See Dymaxion Airocean World Map, (b)

Sphere:  Volume-5 Sphere:

    See Triacontrahedron, 13 May'77

Spherical Wave:                                                    (1)


     See Omnidirectional
        Shell Growth Rates

---

Sphericity of Whole Systems:  Laws Of:


     See Probability, 17 Feb'72; 18 Feb'72

---

Spherical Wave:                                                    (2)


     See Mass, 14 May'73
        Nuclear Sphere, 16 Dec'73
        Photon, 26 Sep'73; 15 May'73
        Tensegrity Sphere, 19 Dec'73

---

Spheroids:


     See Colloidal Chemistry, 1938

---

RBF DEFINITIONS

   Sphericity:

   "Compound curvature, or sphericity, gives you the

   greatest strength with the least material."


   - Citation at Curvature:  Compound, 3 Oct'71
   - Cite RBF to EJA, 3200 Idaho, Washington, 3 Oct. 1971.

---

Sphere:  Spherical:  Sphericity:                            (1A)


     See Ball
        Balls Coming Together
        Bubble
        Celestial Sphere
        Cloud-island Spheres
        Closest Packing of Spheres
        Dome
        Equilibrium Sphere
        Embracement
        Geodesic Sphere
        Globe
        Ghostly Greek Geometry:  Sphere
        Initial Sphere
        Linear & Spherical Analysis
        Line Between Two Sphere Centers
        Maximum:  Spherical Maximum
        Nuclear Sphere
        Rhombic Dodecahedron #2:  Fractionated Sphere
        Synergy Sequence:  Two Massive Spheres

---

RBF DEFINITIONS

   Sphericity of Whole Systems:

   "Nature modulates probability and the degrees of freedom,
   i.e., frequency and angle leads to the tensegrity sphere;
   which leads to the pneumatic bag; all of which are the same
   kind of reality as the three automobiles.  All the cosmic
   triangling of all varieties of angles always averages out
   to 60 degrees.  That is the probability of all closed systems
   of which the Universe is the amorphous largest case.  Probability
   is not linear or planar, but is always following the laws of
   sphericity or whole systems.  Probability is always dependent
   upon critical proximity, omnidirectional, and only dynamically
   defined, three-way gridding pattern integrity..."


   - Citation and context at Probability Model of Three Cars (4)26Sep'73

---

Sphere:  Sphericity:  Spherical:                            (1B)


   See Trigonometry:  Spherical Trigonometry
       Tetrahedron & Sphere Model
       Tensegrity Sphere
       United Sphere
       Spun Frequency = Sphericity
       Vertexial Accounting = Spherical Accounting
       No Sphere Integrity
       Domain of a Sphere
       Hex-pent Sphere
       Potential Sphere

Sphere:  Spherical:                                                  (2)

See Association & Disassociation, 9 Nov'73
    Bow Ties, 6 Oct'72
    Chords, 22 Jul'71
    Dynamic, 1950*
    Focus, 22 Jul'71
    Gravity (d)
    Infinity & Finity, Jun'66
    Integral, 16 Feb'73
    Prime Awareness, 18 Nov'72
    Tetrahedron, 26 Sep'73*
    Tidal, 31 May'71*
    Unity:  Complex & Simplex, 15 Feb'66*
    Zero Condition, 14 Feb'66
    Raft, 3 Apr'75
    Unit, 1938
    Triacontrahedron:  Great Circles Of, 27 Apr'77
    Triacontrahedron, 20 Jun'77
    Six Motion Freedoms & Degrees of Freedom, (A)¶B)

---

Sphericity:                                                         (1)

See Curvature:  Compound
    Halo Concept
    Omnidirectional
    Radial-circumferential
    Rollability of Polyhedra
    Sweepout:  Spherical Sweepout
    Three-way Great Circling:  Three-way Grid
    Experience in the Round

---

Sphere:                                                             (3)

See Sphere Center
    Sphere Integrity:  There Is No
    Sphere of Reference
    Spheres & Spaces
    Sphere Tangent with a Plane
    Sphere:  Synergetics Formula for Area & Volume
        of a Sphere
    Sphere = Polyhedron
    Sphere of Unit Vector Radius
    Spheres & Vertexes
    Sphere = Icosa
    Sphere:  Volume-5 Sphere

---

RBF DEFINITIONS

Sphinx:

"Four planes of the tetrahedron going through the same
point at the same time:  The zero volume tetrahedron:  Also
this is the vector equilibrium:

Tetrahedron as simplest structure in Universe:

"Tetrahedron as four closest-packed spheres:

"Head of the Sphinx is cross section vertically of vector
equilibrium:

- Cite RBF postcard to Peter Jahlin, 28 Sep'73

---

Spherical:                                                         (3A)

See Spherical Barrel
    Spherical Comprehension
    Spherical Excess
    Spherical Field
    Spherical Gears
    Spherical Icosahedron
    Spherical Interstices
    Spherical Nostalgia
    Spherical Observation
    Spherical Octahedron
    Spherical Point System
    Spherical Propagation
    Spherical Reality Scribing
    Spherical Sensations
    Spherical Structures
    Spherical Tetrahedron
    Spherical Thinking
    Spherical Triangle
    Spherical Unity
    Spherical Wave

---

---

Spherical Maximum:                                                 (3B)

See Spherical Maximum
    Spherical Necessity
    Spherical Quadrant Phase

---

Spider's Web as a Tool:

See Bird's Nest as a Tool, 6 May'67
    Mechanics, (2)
    Tools, 1967;

Spider's Web:

See Environment Events Hierarchy (3)
Industrialization, (A)

Spin Equator:

See Critical Proximity, 15 Feb'73
Omnitopology, 19 Dec'73

RBF DEFINITIONS

Spin:

"When other scientists seemed to have language more valid
than my own I accepted their terminology.  But I held to
my own terminology when I found it to be warranted,  and when
other claimants could not be justified.  For example, quantum
mechanics came many years after I did to employ the term
spin.  The physicists assured me that their use of the word
did not involve any phenomena which truly spun.  Spin was
only a convenient word for accounting certain unique energy
behaviors and investments.  My use of the term was to describe
a direct investment of experimentally demonstrable unique
magnitude of rotation, an actually spinning phenomenon.
This was a case when I held to my own terms.  In most recent
years it is beginning to be realized by the physicists as an
actually spinning phenomenon-- as I had demonstrated it as
actually occurring almost half a century ago.  . . In recent
years I found the term spin being adopted by others; sometimes with the same meaning, sometimes with other meanings.
But from the viewpoint of half a century there appears to be
an increasing convergence of scientific explorations,
epistemology, and semantics with my own evolutionary develppment."

- Cite RBF to EJA, 20 Dec. '71 at SYNERGETICS text Sec. 250.04.

Spin-halving:                                          (1)

See Prime Number Consequences of Spin-halving
Dichotmy:  Dichotomising
System-halving

RBF DEFINITIONS

Spinnability:

"Spinnability has to be totally independent of the system's
local surface transformations."

Spin-halving:                                          (2)

See Quarks, 22 Jun'77

- Cite RBF rewrite of 24 Apr'76

RBF DEFINITIONS

Spinnability:

"Spinnability has to be totally independent of the
transformations that it is entertaining."

Spinning & Orbiting:

See Dancing, 6 Jul'62
Gravity (g)
Sphere, 8 Aug'77

- Cite RBF to EJA, 3200 Idaho, Wash. DC; 23 Apr'76

RBF DEFINITIONS

Spin Twoness & Duality Twoness:

"Having identified (a) the constant additive twoness of the
vertexial poles of the axial spinnability operative in all
independent systems, and (b), the multiplicative twoness
characterizing the concavity and convexity congruently
operative in all independent systems, we find the first four
prime numbers-- 1, 2, 3, and 5-- are the only variables
present in the Eulerean topological inventorying of all the
omnitriangularly, nonredundantly stabilized, symmetrical
polyhedra.

"Spin twoness is additive.

"Duality twoness is multiplicative."

- Cite SYNERGETICS, 2nd. Ed. at Sec.s. 1074.31-.32, 27 Dec'74

---

Spin Twoness & Duality Twoness:                                (1)

See Twoness:  Additive & Multiplicative

---

Spin Twoness & Duality Twoness:                                (2)

See Conception-birth, 27 Dec'74

---

Spin Twoness:

See Cosmic Inherency, (2)
    Conception-birth, 27 Dec'74

---

Spin:  Spinning:                                               (1)

See Axis of Spin
    Additive Twoness
    Great-circle Spinnable Symmetries:  Hierarchy Of
    Half Spin
    Motions:  Six Positive & Negative Motions
    Twin-spin
    Rotate
    Spun Frequency

---

Spin:  Spinning:  Spinnability:                                (2)

See Cone, 22 Sep'73
    Euler, 11 Jul'62
    Line, 7 Nov'72
    Omnidirectional, 1960
    Sphere, 25 Feb'74
    Synergetics, 10 Jan'50
    Neutral Axis, 1 Jan'75
    Triacontrahedron:  Great Circles Of, 27 Apr'77
    Four Intergeared Mobility Freedoms, 2 Nov'73

---

RBF DEFINITIONS

Spin:  Spinning:                                               (3)

See Spinnability
    Spin Equator
    Spin-halving
    Spinning & Orbiting
    Spin Twoness & Duality Twoness
    Spin Twoness

---

RBF DEFINITIONS

Spinach:

"Copper taken directly by humans is toxic.  When spinach
grows in the presence of copper as in those great fields in
Northern Michigan (near the copper deposits I got to know
at Phelps Dodge), the spinach takes in the copper in a way
that is structurally and mechanically geared with the
metabolic gears of humans.  Copper is all right and fills
in a deficiency if it fits properly.  Spinach accomplishes
the gearing.  A gear is designed to mesh with other gears.
But one loose gear put into the machinery will strip all
the others.  When it is on the right pinion it meshes with
the other gears and can bridge a gear-train gap.  That's
exactly what happens to copper and spinach.  Henry Schroeder
worked with the trace elements.  He showed that one Chromium
atom is the difference between a diabetic and a nondiabetic.
The word diet makes for great confusion.  It's not undernourishment, it's just getting the right deficiency chemistry
into the brain which may be lacking certain gears."

- Cite RBF to EJA, Pepper Tree Inn, Santa Barbara, 11 Feb'73

RBF DEFINITIONS

Spinach:

"Copper if it is present in the soil where you are growing
spinach-- spinach tends to inhibit the copper as a pattern
and spinach that has inhibited copper also will inhibit
some gold and silver and then the human being can inhibit
the gold, silver and the copper in very small percentages,
but they are literally inhibitable and apparently measurably
to the advantage of the human being.  Copper taken in other
ways than being inhibited first by spinach can poison a
man; it can be lethal.  We find that copper taken in the
right way can be beneficial and in the wrong way makes
trouble.  Remember now that we are dealing not in a thing but
in a pattern. . . "

"Apparently the human being can inhibit all the chemical
elements if they come in at the right sequence, so as part
of spinach, as part of that pattern, then it is tightening
you up [ see Monkey wrench ] in a better way. . .

"Whatever spinach does it does it better if it has copper."

- Cite OREGON Lecture #5 - pp. 166-167/9 July 1962

---

Spinach:                                                    (1)

            See Copper
                Inhibit

---

Spinach:                                                    (2)

            See Heredity, 15 May'72
                Metabolic Flow, (1)

---

Spinnaker:

            See Geodesic Spinnaker

---

RBF DEFINITIONS

Spiral:

"Radiation's waves are non-self-interfering spirals."

- Citation and context at ▓▓▓▓▓▓▓▓ Matter vs. Radiation,
  7 Nov'73

---

RBF DEFINITIONS

Spiral:

"A spiral articulated in a direction perpendicular to

our observation presents an illusory wavilinear planar

profile."

- Cite RBF marginalis, SYNERGETICS Draft (Conceptuality, Time)
  31 May 1971, Chicago.

---

RBF DEFINITIONS

Spiral:

"All the time phenomena of physicists are linear."

"All actions are spirals because they cannot go through

themselves and because there is time.  The remote aspect

of a spiral is a wave because there are no planes."

- Cute RBF to EJA
  Beverly Hotel, New York
  8 March 1971

- Citation at Time, 8 Mar'71

WAVILINEARITY: FIXES - SEC. 520.11

---

RBF DEFINITIONS

Spiral:

"An event trajectory
Cannot 'go through itself.'
A recycling event
Can only produce a spiral,
Which, when viewed axially
Appears misinformedly
To be a circle.
You may say the hands of the clock
Go round and around
In the same circle.
But as they go around
So does the Earth
On which the clock is situated;
And as the Earth spins
So also does it orbit the Sun
Which is moving within the Galactic nebula;
And the nebulae moving in respect
In respect to other nebulae;
And the pattern
Made by the clock's hands in Universe
Which is the minimum reality
Is a very complex pattern."

- Cite GENERALIZED PRINCIPLES, p.8, 28 Jan '69

RBF DEFINITIONS

Spiral:

"A triangle is a spiral and is one energy event."

- Cite SYNERGETICS ILLUSTRATIONS, caption #2.
  1967

---

RBF DEFINITIONS

Spiralinearity:

In tensors and vectors of equal magnitude, the
spiralinearity of the vector is shorter in overall
spatial extent than is the spiralinearity of the tensor.
Compressed lines or rods tend to arcs of diminishing
radius; tensed lines or rods tend to arcs of
increasing radius."

- Cite RBF to EJA
  Blackstone Hotel, Chicago
  25 March 1971

WAVILINEARITY : FIXES — SEC. 520.12

---

RBF DEFINITIONS

Spiral:

" . . . . lines
As curves
Cannot re-enter, or
'Join back into themselves,'
Therefore, the circling line
Can only wrap around
And over its earlier part - -
As the knot making
Sailor says it,
The circle when followed
Around and around
Results in a coil
Which is
An asymmetric spiral,
Which may be followed experimentally
Only as long as intellect follows."

- Cite HOW LITTLE, Pp. 59-60, Oct '66

---

Spiral: Spiralinearity: (1)

See Circle
Coil
Cornucopia
Minimum Spiral
Wavilinearity
Critical Spiral Path
Tetrahelix
Open Triangular Spirals
Helix
Flat Spiral
Geodesic Spiral Tube

---

RBF DEFINITIONS

Spiral:

"Not even a graphed spiral is forever possible because the
errors in a graphed line constantly dislocate the line and
insist upon an ultimate intersecting contact."

- Citation & context at Line, 1938

---

Spiral: Spiralinearity: (2)

See Matter vs. Radiation, 7 Nov'73*
Rope, Dec'71
Time, 8 Mar'71*
Triangle, 7 Oct'71
Triangle as A Priori Two, Feb'72
Tetrahedron: Coordinate Symmetry, Nov'71
Cheese Polyhedra, Nov'71
In, Out & Around Experiences, (2)
Line, 1938*
Critical Proximity, May'71

---

RBF DEFINITIONS

Spiralinearity:

"Regenerative precession imposes wavilinearity on vectors
and tensors. Wavilinearity is spiralinear.

"All actions are spiral because they cannot go through
themselves and because there is time. The remote aspect of
a spiral is a wave because there are no planes.

"As with coil springs, in tensors and vectors of equal magnitude, the spiralinearity of the vector is shorter in overall
spatial extent than is the spiralinearity of the tensor.
Compressed lines or rods tend to arcs of diminishing
radius; tensed lines or rods tends to arcs of increasing
radius."

- Cite SYNERGETICS text at Secs. 520.101,.11,.12; Nov'71

---

Spirit:

See Life is Not Physical, (1)(2)

---

Spit-punctuated Monosyllabic Verbalism:

See Conformity, 10 Oct'63
Reverse Optimism, Aug'64

Split Personality: (2)

See Basic Triangle:  Basic Equilibrium 48 LCD Triangle,
16 Dec'73
Cosmic Discontinuity & Local Continuity, 15 Jan'74*

RBF DEFINITIONS

Spit in Space:

"If you spit in space the spit goes into orbit and you
retro-orbit."

- Citation and context at Space Technology (6)

RBF DEFINITIONS

Spontaneity:

"Compression behaviors are disassociative while tension
behaviors are inherently associative and spontaneously
cohering."

- ~~Cite CONCEPTUALITY OF FUNDAMENTAL STRUCTURES, Ed. Kepes,
1965, p. 85.~~
- Citation at Tension & Compression, 1965

RBF DEFINITIONS

Split Personality:

"...This split personality +2½, -2½; +5, -5; +0, -0..."

- Citation and context at Cosmic Discontinuity & Local
Continuity, 15 Jan'74

Spontaneous Aggregates:

See Tetrahedron as Conceptual Model, Nov'71
Unitary Conceptuality, 22 Oct'72

Split Personality: (1)

See Dichotomy
Picasso Duo-face Painting
Profile:  There is No Half Profile
Half Visible:  Half Invisible

Spontaneous Deputies: (1)

See Coincidental Articulation
Fuller, R,B:  His Associates & Collaborators

Spontaneous Deputies:                                    (2)


See Cosmic Fish Sequence, (1)
    Depression:  Great Depression of 1930's, (2)
    Sublimation, 21 Oct'71

---

RBF DEFINITIONS

Spontaneous Truth of Childhood:

". . . Every child is born with faculties-- with ears,
eyes, nose and mouth and the child says that is what I see.

"You don't have to teach a child to say what it is that he
sees; he tells you spontaneously.

"In other words, truth is spontaneous, and the lying has been
taught to the children by those who are afraid that the
child's truthfulness will get them into trouble.  So the
fact that truth is spontaneous is equally mysterious as the
fact of mass attraction and gravity cohering our
Universe; as is the phenomenon love.  We experience so much of
it we tend to take it very much for granted."

- Cite RBF at SIMS, U. Mass., Amherst, 22 July '71, Talk 12, p. 16.

---

Spontaneous Education of Choice:


See Montessori System, 1928

---

Spontaneity:  Spontaneous:                               (1)


See Lecturing
    Piaget Jean:  Child's Spontaneous Geometry
    Society:  Spontaneity Of
    Teleology:  Spontaneous vs. Emergency
    Thinking Out Loud
    Three-way Great-circling:  Three-way Grid:
        Spontaneity
    Child's Spontaneous Interest in Totality
    Most Economical = Spontaneous

---

Spontaneous Equilibrious Model:


See Vector Equilibrium as Starting Point, (1)

---

Spontaneity:  Spontaneous:                               (2)


See Bridge, 13 Nov'69
    Evolution, May'72
    Life, 22 Apr'68
    Structure, 16 Dec'73
    Scheme of Reference, 24 Sep'73
    Survival, May'65
    Tetrahedron as Conceptual Model, Nov'71
    Unselfishness, Jan'72
    Most Economical, 3 Apr'75
    Symmetry & Asymmetry, 11 Dec'75
    Gravity:  Speed Of, 21 Oct'72
    Children as Only Pure Scientists, (1)

---

Spontaneous Tolerance:


See Truth as Progressive Diminution of Residual
    Error, Oct'66

---

Spontaneity:  Spontaneous:                               (3)


See Spontaneous Aggregates
    Spontaneous Deputies
    Spontaneous Education of Choice
    Spontaneous Tolerance
    Spontaneous Truth of Childhood
    Spontaneous Equilibrious Model

Spool:

    See Omnidirectional Typewriter (1)
      Tetrascroll, (1)

Spring:                (1)

    See Coil
        Hexagonal Vector Pattern
        Spiral

Spoon:

    See Child Pushes Spoon Off Edge of Table

Spring:                (2)

    See Tools:  Craft & Industrial, (2)

Sports:                (1)

    See Competition
        Game
        Hammer Thrower
        Pole Vaulter

Spun Frequency - Sphericity:

    See Sphere, 25 Feb'74

Sports:                (2)

    See Civilization, May'70